STATISTICS

For Engineering and the Sciences

FOURTH EDITION

William Mendenhall
University of Florida

Terry Sincich
University of South Florida

PRENTICE HALL
Upper Saddle River, New Jersey 07458

· ·

Library of Congress Cataloging-in-Publication Data
Mendenhall, William.
    Statistics for engineering and the sciences / William Mendenhall, Terry Sincich.   4th ed.
    Includes index.
    ISBN 0-02-380581-1
    1. Mathematical statistics.   2. Engineering—Statistical methods.
  I. Sincich, Terry. II. Title.
QA276.M429 1994
519.5 dc20   94-41303
                                                       CIP

On the cover is *Zongo* by California artist Joseph Slusky. The work is enamel on steel and measures $30'' \times 23'' \times 22''$. The artist uses the enamel paint on the metal surfaces to create a combination of a painting on a sculpture. This is a process that he has mastered over the years. Slusky's geometric imagery and his intricate surfaces create a continuum of small floating surfaces that seem to be influenced by William T. Wiley or Robert Hudson, and yet Slusky takes his work to a further extreme. Slusky received his B.A. and M.A. from UC Berkeley and has shown in various galleries in Sweden, San Francisco, Los Angeles, and Chicago. He is represented by the John Natsoulas Gallery in Davis, California.

 ©1995 by Prentice-Hall, Inc.
A Simon & Schuster Company
Upper Saddle River, New Jersey 07458

Printed in the United States of America

10 9 8 7

ISBN 0-02-380581-1

Prentice-Hall International (UK) Limited, *London*
Prentice-Hall of Australia Pty. Limited, *Sydney*
Prentice-Hall Canada Inc., *Toronto*
Prentice-Hall Hispanoamericana, S.A., *Mexico*
Prentice-Hall of India Private Limited, *New Delhi*
Prentice-Hall of Japan, Inc., *Tokyo*
Simon & Schuster Asia Pte. Ltd., *Singapore*
Editora Prentice-Hall do Brasil, Ltda., *Rio de Janeiro*

Contents

CHAPTER FOUR

Discrete Random Variables   143

CHAPTER FIVE

Continuous Random Variables   203

CHAPTER SIX

Bivariate Probability Distributions   257

CHAPTER SEVEN

Sampling Distributions   289

CHAPTER EIGHT

Estimation   337

CHAPTER NINE

Tests of Hypotheses   421

CHAPTER TEN

Categorical Data Analysis   495

CHAPTER FOURTEEN

Analysis of Variance for Designed Experiments   789

CHAPTER FIFTEEN

Nonparametric Statistics   919

CHAPTER SIXTEEN

Statistical Process and Quality Control   981

CHAPTER SEVENTEEN

Product and System Reliability   1035

Preface

· ·

The fourth edition of *Statistics for Engineering and the Sciences* is a text for a two-semester introductory course in statistics for students majoring in engineering or any of the physical sciences. Inevitably, once these students graduate and are employed, they will be involved in the analysis of data and will be required to make inferences from their analyses. Consequently, they need to acquire knowledge of the basic concepts of statistical inference and familiarity with some of the statistical methods that they will be required to use in their employment.

Pedagogy

Chapters 1–7 identify the objectives of statistics, explain how we can describe data sets, and present the basic concepts of probability. Chapters 8 and 9 introduce the two methods for making inferences about population parameters: estimation and testing hypotheses. These notions are extended in the remaining chapters to cover other topics that are useful in analyzing engineering and scientific data, including the analysis of categorical data (Chapter 10), regression analysis and model building (Chapters 11–13), the analysis of variance for designed experiments (Chapter 14), nonparametric statistics (Chapter 15), statistical quality control (Chapter 16), and product and system reliability (Chapter 17).

The assumed mathematical background is a two-semester sequence in calculus—that is, the course could be taught to students of average mathematical talent and with a basic understanding of the principles of differential and integral calculus. Presentation requires the ability to perform one-variable differentiation and integration, but examples involving topics from multivariable calculus are designated as optional. Thus, the theoretical concepts are sketched and presented in a one-variable context, but it is easy for the instructor to delve deeper into the theoretical and mathematical aspects of statistics using the optional topics, examples, and exercises.

Features

Specific features of the text are the following:

1. **Blend of theory and applications.** The basic theoretical concepts of mathematical statistics are integrated with a two-semester presentation of statistical methodology. Thus, the instructor has the opportunity to present a course with either of two characteristics—a course stressing basic concepts and applied statistics or a course that, while still tilted toward application, presents a modest introduction to the theory underlying statistical inference.

2. **Computer applications with instructions on how to use the computer.** The instructor and student have the option of using a computer to perform the statistical calculations. Printouts from two popular statistical software packages available at

· ·

most university computing centers, SAS and MINITAB, are fully integrated into the text. Additionally, we provide the SAS and MINITAB commands required to generate the printouts in "Computer Lab" sections at the end of most chapters. These tutorials are designed for the novice user; no prior computer experience is needed. The instructions on how to use SAS and MINITAB for statistical analysis of data apply to both large mainframe computers and personal computers (PCs).

3. **Broad coverage of topics.**   To meet the diverse needs of future engineers and scientists, the text provides coverage of a wide range of data analysis topics. The material on exploratory data analysis (Chapter 2), regression analysis and model building (Chapters 11–13), quality control (Chapter 16), and reliability (Chapter 17) sets the text apart from the typical introductory statistics text. The material often refers to theoretical material covered in earlier chapters, but the presentation is oriented toward applications.

4. **Applied exercises extracted from scientific journals.**   The text contains a large number of applied exercises designed to motivate a student and suggest future uses for the methodology. Most of these exercises require the student to analyze actual data or interpret experimental results extracted from professional journals in the engineering and physical sciences.

5. **Optional theoretical exercises.**   Where appropriate, theoretical exercises are provided to motivate those students who have a stronger desire to understand the mathematical theory that forms an underpinning for the applications. These exercises are labeled "optional" because they require greater mathematical skill for their solution.

6. **Key concepts highlighted.**   Definitions, theorems, formulas, steps to follow in performing a statistical procedure, and warnings (indicating a specific situation where a student might misuse a statistical technique) are boxed and highlighted to enable the student to assimilate easily the most important concepts in a chapter.

7. **Real data sets.**   Explanations of basic statistical concepts and methodology are based on and motivated by the use of real scientific data sets. Four large data sets are provided in the appendices for use as instructional vehicles:

Appendix III.   Length, weight, and DDT measurements for 144 fish of various species captured from the Tennessee River by the U.S. Army Corps of Engineers.

Appendix IV.   The central processing unit (CPU) times of 1,000 computer jobs run by a small statistical consulting firm.

Appendix V.   Percentage iron content for 390 1.5-kilogram specimens of iron ore selected from a 20,000-ton consignment of Canadian ore.

Appendix VI.   Federal Trade Commission rankings of 372 domestic cigarette brands.

These data sets are also available (in ASCII format) on floppy diskette. Consequently, they can be loaded into computer storage and analyzed with SAS, MINITAB, or some other statistical software package. For example, the data sets can be used by the instructor to illustrate the concept of a sampling distribution and the theoretical interpretation of a "95% confidence interval."

8. **Short answers to exercises provided.**   To aid the student in working the exercise sets, short answers (mostly numerical in nature) to all exercises are provided at the end of the text.

Revisions

Although the scope and coverage remain the same, the fourth edition contains several substantial changes, additions, and enhancements:

1. **More computer printouts.**   Throughout the text, we have greatly increased the number of SAS and MINITAB printouts. A printout now accompanies every statistical technique presented, allowing the instructor to emphasize interpretations of the statistical results rather than the calculations required to obtain the results.

2. **Chapter 2: Summary frequency tables.**   A discussion of how to construct and use summary frequency tables has been added to the section on describing qualitative data (Section 2.1).

3. **Chapter 4: Bernoulli distribution.**   A new section (Section 4.5) describing Bernoulli trials and their importance in binomial experiments is included.

4. **Chapter 5: Descriptive methods for assessing normality.**   A new section (Section 5.6) on determining whether a data set is approximately normal has been added to the chapter on continuous probability distributions. In addition to the traditional graphical methods (histogram, stem-and-leaf display), we present the ratio of the interquartile range to the standard deviation as a check on normality. The emphasis on these techniques early in the text makes the student aware of the importance of checking assumptions in later chapters.

5. **Chapter 9: More emphasis on p-values.**   Throughout the test of hypothesis chapter, we present both the rejection region approach and observed significance level (p-value) approach to making decisions. Since a computer printout is provided with nearly each example, it is easy for the instructor to emphasize the p-value approach to hypothesis testing.

6. **Chapter 13: Comprehensive example on model building.**   The key ideas and techniques of the chapter are applied to a practical problem on detecting collusive bidding in road construction (Section 13.11).

7. **Chapter 14: Principles of experimental design.**   Two new sections (Sections 14.4 and 14.5) present an overview of designed experiments and the principles of noise-reducing and volume-increasing designs.

8. **Chapter 14: Regression approach to ANOVA.**   Although we present both the traditional ANOVA approach and the regression approach to analyzing data from designed experiments, our emphasis is on the regression approach. For each design, we give the corresponding regression models and show how to conduct the ANOVA F tests using the models.

9. **Chapter 16: Total quality management (TQM).** A new section on total quality management (Section 16.1) has been added to the chapter on statistical process and quality control.

10. **More exercises with real data.** Many new "real-life" scientific exercises have been added throughout the text. All of these are extracted from news articles, magazines, and professional journals.

Numerous, less obvious changes in details have been made throughout the text in response to suggestions by current users and reviewers of the text.

Supplements

The text is also accompanied by the following supplementary material:

1. **Student's solutions manual** (by Nancy S. Boudreau). The manual contains the full solutions for all the odd-numbered exercises contained in the text. ISBN 0-02-312718-X.

2. **Instructor's solutions manual** (by Mark Dummeldinger). The manual contains the full solutions to all the even-numbered exercises contained in the text. ISBN 0-02-380582-X.

3. **Data sets on diskette.** All four large appendix data sets and numerous smaller data sets (containing 20 or more observations) analyzed in exercises are available (in ASCII format) on a 3½" IBM PC diskette. ISBN 0-02-380583-8.

4. **ASP statistical software diskette.** New to this edition, the text includes (inside the back cover) a 3½" micro disk containing the ASP program, *A Statistical Package for Business, Economics, and the Sciences.* ASP, from DMC Software, Inc., is a user-friendly, totally menu-driven program that contains all of the major statistical applications covered in the text, plus many more. ASP runs on any IBM-compatible PC with at least 512K of memory and two disk drives. With ASP, students with no knowledge of computer programming can create and analyze data sets easily and quickly. The appendix contains start-up procedures and a short tutorial on the use of ASP. Full documentation is provided to adopters of the text.

5. **ASP Tutorial and Student Guide** (by George Blackford). Most students have little trouble learning to use ASP without documentation. Some, however, may want to purchase the *ASP Tutorial and Student Guide.* Bookstores can order the tutorial from DMC Software, Inc., 6169 Pebbleshire Drive, Grand Blanc, MI 48439.

Acknowledgments

We wish to acknowledge several individuals who contributed to the revision of this text. Susan Reiland managed the production of the fourth edition with the same high degree of professionalism she exhibited with the first three editions. Faith Sincich served in several capacities, including word-processing specialist, proofreader, moral supporter, and our toughest critic. Finally, we thank the reviewers of this latest edition, who suggested many of the changes listed above. The names of these reviewers follow:

Carl Bodenschatz (United States Air Force Academy)
Christopher Ennis (Normandale Community College)
Nasrollah Etemadi (University of Illinois-Chicago)
Carol Gattis (University of Arkansas)
Jeffery Maxey (University of Central Florida)
Giovanni Parmigiani (Duke University)
David Powers (Clarkson University)
Shiva Saksena (University of North Carolina-Wilmington)

We again thank the reviewers of previous editions:

George C. Derringer (Battelle Columbus, Ohio, Division)
Danny Dyer (University of Texas-Arlington)
Herberg B. Eisenberg (West Virginia College of Graduate Studies)
Linda Gans (California State Polytechnic University)
K. G. Janardan (Eastern Michigan University)
H. Lennon (Coventry Polytechnic, Coventry, England)
Curtis C. McKnight (University of Oklahoma)
Chand Midha (University of Akron)
Balgobin Nandram (Worcester Polytechnic Institute)
Paul Nelson (Kansas State University)
Carol O'Connor (University of Louisville)
Norbert Oppenheim (City College of New York)
David Robinson (St. Cloud State University)
Dennis Wackerly (University of Florida)
Donald L. Woods (Texas A&M University)

CHAPTER ONE

Introduction

Objective

To identify the role of statistics in the analysis of data from engineering and the sciences

Contents

1.1   Statistics: The Science of Data

According to *The Random House College Dictionary*, statistics is "the science that deals with the collection, classification, analysis, and interpretation of numerical facts or data." In short, **statistics** is the **science of data**.

Definition 1.1

Statistics is the science of data. This involves collecting, classifying, summarizing, organizing, analyzing, and interpreting data.

The science of statistics is commonly applied to two types of problems:

1. Summarizing, describing, and exploring data
2. Using sample data to infer the nature of the data set from which the sample was selected

As an illustration of the descriptive applications of statistics, consider the United States census, which involves the collection of a data set that purports to characterize the socioeconomic characteristics of the approximately 250 million people living in the United States. Managing this enormous mass of data is a problem for the computer scientist, and describing the data utilizes the methods of statistics. Similarly, an engineer uses statistics to describe the data set consisting of the daily emissions of sulfur oxides of an industrial plant recorded for 365 days last year. The branch of statistics devoted to these applications is called **descriptive statistics**.

Definition 1.2

The branch of statistics devoted to the organization, summarization, and description of data sets is called **descriptive statistics**.

Sometimes the phenomenon of interest is characterized by a data set that is either physically unobtainable, or too costly or time-consuming to obtain. In such situations, we sample the data set and use the sample information to infer its nature. To illustrate, suppose the phenomenon of interest is the waiting time for a data-processing job to be completed. You might expect the waiting time to depend on such factors as the size of the job, the computer utilization factor, etc. In fact, if you were to run the same job over and over again on the computer, the waiting times would vary, even for the same computer utilization factor. Thus, the phenomenon "waiting time before job processing" is characterized by a large data set that exists only conceptually (in our minds). To determine the nature of this data set, we *sample* it—i.e., we process the job a number n of times, record the waiting time for each run, and then use this sample of n waiting times to infer the nature of the large conceptual data set of interest. The branch of statistics used to solve this problem is called **inferential statistics**.

In statistical terminology, the data set that we want to describe, the one that characterizes a phenomenon of interest to us, is called a **population**. A **sample** is a subset of data selected from a population. Sometimes the words *population* and *sample* are used to represent the objects upon which the measurements are taken. In a particular situation, the meaning attached to these terms will be clear by the context in which they are used.

Definition 1.3

A **population** is a data set that is the target of our interest.

Definition 1.4

A **sample** is a subset of data selected from a population.

Definition 1.5

The branch of statistics concerned with using sample data to make an inference about a population is called **inferential statistics**.

CASE STUDY 1.1 / Contamination of Fish in the Tennessee River

Chemical and manufacturing plants often discharge toxic waste materials into nearby rivers and streams. These toxicants have a detrimental effect on the plant and animal life inhabiting the river and the river's bank. One type of pollutant, commonly known as DDT, is especially harmful to fish and, indirectly, to people. The Food and Drug Administration sets the limit for DDT content in individual fish at 5 parts per million (ppm). Fish with DDT content exceeding this limit are considered potentially hazardous to people if consumed. A study was undertaken to examine the DDT content of fish inhabiting the Tennessee River (in Alabama) and its tributaries.

The Tennessee River flows in a west–east direction across the northern part of the state of Alabama, through Wheeler Reservoir, a national wildlife refuge. Ecologists fear that contaminated fish migrating from the mouth of the river to the reservoir could endanger other wildlife that prey on the fish. This concern is more than academic. A manufacturing plant was once located along Indian Creek, which enters the Tennessee River 321 miles upstream from the mouth. Although the plant has been inactive for over 10 years, there is evidence that the plant discharged toxic materials into the creek, contaminating all the fish in the immediate area. Have the fish in the Tennessee River and its tributary creeks also been contaminated? And if so, how far upstream have the contaminated fish migrated? To answer these and other questions, members of the U.S. Army Corps of Engineers in the summer of 1980 collected fish specimens at different locations along the Tennessee River and three tributary creeks: Flint Creek (which enters the river 309 miles upstream from the river's mouth), Limestone Creek (310 miles upstream), and Spring Creek (282 miles upstream). Each fish was first weighed (in grams) and measured (length in centimeters), then the fillet of the fish was extracted and the DDT concentration (in parts per million) in the fillet was measured.

Appendix III contains the length, weight, and DDT measurements for a total of 144 fish specimens.* Obviously, not all the fish in the Tennessee River and its tributaries were captured. Consequently, the data are based on a sample collected from the population of all fish inhabiting the Tennessee River. Here, the words *population* and *sample* are used to describe the objects upon which the measurements are taken, i.e., the fish. We could also use the terms to represent data sets. For example, the 144 DDT measurements represent a sample collected from the population consisting of DDT measurements for all fish inhabiting the river.

Notice that the data set also contains information on the location (i.e., where the fish were captured) and species of the fish. Three species of fish were examined: channel catfish, largemouth bass, and smallmouth buffalo. The different symbols for location are interpreted as follows. The first two characters represent the river or creek, and the remaining characters represent the distance (in miles) from the mouth of the river or creek. For example, FCM5 indicates that the fish was captured in Flint Creek (FC), 5 miles upstream from the mouth of the creek (M5). Similarly, TRM380 denotes a fish sample collected from the Tennessee River (TR), 380 miles upstream from the river's mouth (M380). In subsequent chapters, we will use the data in Appendix III to compare the DDT contents of fish at different locations and among the different species, and to determine the relationship (if any) of length and weight to DDT content.

EXERCISES

1.1   Pesticides applied to an extensively grown crop can result in inadvertent ambient air contamination. *Environmental Science & Technology* (Oct. 1993) reported on thion residues of the insecticide chlorpyrifos used on dormant orchards in the San Joaquin Valley, California. Ambient air specimens were collected daily at an orchard site during an intensive period of spraying—a total of 13 days—and the thion level (ng/m^3) was measured each day.
a. Identify the population of interest to the researchers.
b. Identify the sample.

1.2   Research engineers with the University of Kentucky Transportation Research Program have collected data on accidents occurring at intersections in Lexington, Kentucky, over a period of 5 years. One of the goals of the study was to compare the average number of left-turn accidents at locations with and without left-turn-only lanes to develop numerical warrants (or guidelines) for the installation of left-turn lanes.
a. What is the population of interest?
b. What is the sample?
c. How can the sample information be used to attain the researchers' goal?

*Source: U.S. Army Corps of Engineers, Mobile District, Alabama.

1.3   Electrical engineers recognize that high neutral current in computer power systems is a potential problem. To determine the extent of the problem, a survey of the computer power system load currents at 146 U.S. sites was taken (*IEEE Transactions on Industry Applications*, July/Aug. 1990). The survey revealed that less than 10% of the sites had high neutral to full-load current ratios.
a. Identify the population of interest.
b. Identify the sample.
c. Use the sample information to make an inference about the population.

1.4   Researchers have developed a new precooling method for preparing Florida vegetables for market. The system employs an air and water mixture designed to yield effective cooling with a much lower water flow than conventional hydrocooling. To compare the effectiveness of the two systems, 20 batches of green tomatoes were divided into two groups; one group was precooled with the new method, and the other with the conventional method. The water flow (in gallons) required to effectively cool each batch was recorded.
a. Identify the population, the samples, and the type of statistical inference to be made for this problem.
b. How could the sample data be used to compare the cooling effectiveness of the two systems?

1.5   Computer tomography (CT) scanners are highly sensitive, visual computer systems designed to aid a physician's diagnosis by generating radiographlike images of inner organs and physiological functions. Suppose you want to estimate the average *scan time*—that is, the average time required for a CT scanner to project an image. Describe how you could collect the sample data necessary to make the desired inference. What is the population of interest?

1.6   Checking all manufactured items coming off an assembly line for defectives would be a costly and time-consuming procedure. One effective and economical method of checking for defectives involves the selection and examination of a portion of the items by a quality control engineer. The percentage of examined items that are defective is computed and then used to estimate the percentage of all items manufactured on the line that are defective. Identify the population, the sample, and a type of statistical inference to be made for this problem.

1.2   Types of Data

Data can be one of two types, quantitative or qualitative. **Quantitative data** are those that represent the quantity or amount of something, measured on a numerical scale. For example, the power frequency (measured in megahertz) of a semiconductor is a quantitative variable, as is the waiting time (measured in seconds) before a computer job begins processing. In contrast, **qualitative** (or **categorical**) data possess no quantitative interpretation. They can only be classified. The set of n occupations corresponding to a group of n engineering graduates is a qualitative data set. A list of the manufacturers of n minicomputers owned by n small businesses is a set of qualitative data.*

---

*A finer breakdown of data types into nominal, ordinal, interval, and ratio data is possible. **Nominal** data are qualitative data with categories that cannot be meaningfully ordered. **Ordinal** data are also qualitative data, but a distinct ranking of the groups from high to low exists. **Interval** and **ratio** data are two different types of quantitative data. For most statistical applications (and all the methods presented in this introductory text), it is sufficient to classify data as either quantitative or qualitative.

> **Definition I.6**
>
> ....
>
> **Q**uantitative data are those that represent the quantity or amount of something.

> **Definition I.7**
>
> ....
>
> **Q**ualitative data are those that have no quantitative interpretation, i.e., they can only be classified into categories.

EXAMPLE I.1

Refer to the data set in Appendix III (see Case Study 1.1). Classify each of the five variables in the data set (location, species, length, weight, and DDT concentration) as quantitative or qualitative.

Solution

Length (in centimeters), weight (in grams), and DDT concentration (in parts per million) are all measured on a numerical scale; thus, they represent quantitative data. In contrast, location and species cannot be measured on a quantitative scale; they can only be classified (e.g., channel catfish, largemouth bass, and smallmouth buffalo for species). Consequently, data on location and species are qualitative.

The proper statistical tool used to describe and analyze data will depend on the type of data. Consequently, it is important to differentiate between quantitative and qualitative data.

EXERCISES

I.7   Refer to the *IEEE Transactions on Industry Applications* (July/Aug. 1990) survey of computer power system load currents in Exercise 1.3. In addition to the ratio of neutral current to full-load current, the researchers also recorded the type of load (line-to-line or line-to-neutral) and the computer system vendor. Identify the type of data for each variable recorded.

I.8   The *Journal of Performance of Constructed Facilities* (Feb. 1990) reported on the performance dimensions of water distribution networks in the Philadelphia area. For one part of the study, the following data were collected for a sample of water pipe sections. Identify the data as quantitative or qualitative.
   a. Pipe diameter (inches)
   b. Pipe material
   c. Age (year of installation)
   d. Location
   e. Pipe length (feet)

     f. Stability of surrounding soil (unstable, moderately stable, or stable)
     g. Corrosiveness of surrounding soil (corrosive or noncorrosive)
     h. Internal pressure (pounds per square inch)
     i. Percentage of pipe covered with land
     j. Breakage rate (number of times pipe had to be repaired because of breakage)

1.9 "Deep hole" drilling is a family of drilling processes used when the ratio of hole depth to hole diameter exceeds 10. Successful deep hole drilling depends on the satisfactory discharge of the drill chip. An experiment was conducted to investigate the performance of deep hole drilling when chip congestion exists (*Journal of Engineering for Industry*, May 1993). Some important variables in the drilling process are described here. Identify the data type for each variable.
     a. Chip discharge rate (number of chips discarded per minute)
     b. Drilling depth (millimeters)
     c. Oil velocity (millimeters per second)
     d. Type of drilling (single-edge, BTA, or ejector)
     e. Quality of hole surface

1.10 A preliminary study was conducted to obtain information on the background levels of the toxic substance polychlorinated biphenyl (PCB) in soil samples in the United Kingdom (*Chemosphere*, Feb. 1986). For each soil sample taken, the researchers recorded the location (rural or urban) and the PCB level (measured in grams per kilogram of soil). Identify the variables measured as quantitative or qualitative.

1.3 The Role of Statistics

Experimental research in engineering and the sciences involves the use of experimental data—a sample—to infer the nature of some conceptual population that characterizes a phenomenon of interest to the experimenter. This inferential process is an integral part of the scientific method. Inference based on experimental data is first used to develop a theory about some phenomenon. Then the theory is tested against additional sample data.

How does the science of statistics contribute to this process? To answer this question, we must note that inferences based on sample data will almost always be subject to error, because a sample will not provide an exact image of the population. The nature of the information provided by a sample depends on the particular sample chosen, and thus will change from sample to sample. For example, suppose you want to estimate the proportion of all steel alloy failures at U.S. petrochemical plants caused by stress corrosion cracking. You investigate the cause of failure for a sample of 100 steel alloy failures and find that 47 were caused by stress corrosion cracking. Does this mean that exactly 47% of all steel alloy failures at petrochemical plants are caused by stress corrosion cracking? Of course, the answer is "no." Suppose that, unknown to you, the true percentage of steel alloy failures caused by stress corrosion cracking is 44%. One sample of 100 failures might yield 47 that were caused by cracking, whereas another sample of 100 might yield only 42. Thus, an inference based on sampling is always subject to *uncertainty*.

The theory of statistics uses *probability* to measure the uncertainty associated with an inference. It enables us to calculate the probabilities of observing specific samples, under specific assumptions about the population. The statistician then uses these probabilities to evaluate the uncertainties associated with sample inferences.

Thus, the major contribution of statistics is that it enables us to make inferences—estimates of and decisions about population parameters—with a known measure of uncertainty. It enables us to evaluate the *reliability* of inferences based on sample data.

Although we will present some useful methods for exploring and describing data sets (Chapter 2), the major emphasis in this text and in modern statistics is in the area of inferential statistics. The flowchart in Figure 1.1 is provided as an outline of the chapters in this text and as a guide when selecting the statistical method appropriate for your particular analysis.

1.4   Summary

Statistics—the **science of data**—is concerned with two types of problems: (1) summarizing and describing data (**descriptive statistics**), and (2) using **sample** data to make inferences about a large set of data—a **population**—from which the sample has been selected (**inferential statistics**).

The appropriate statistical method for describing and analyzing the data will depend on whether the data are **quantitative** or **qualitative**. These methods allow us to make inferences about a population and also provide a **measure of reliability** for the inference.

Descriptive statistics is the topic of Chapter 2. The remaining chapters are devoted to inferential statistics.

SUPPLEMENTARY EXERCISES

1.11   The reliability of a computer system is measured in terms of the lifelength of a specified hardware component (for example, the disk drive). To estimate the reliability of a particular system, 100 computer components are tested until they fail, and their lifelengths are recorded.
   a. What is the population of interest?
   b. What is the sample?
   c. Are the data quantitative or qualitative?
   d. How could the sample information be used to estimate the reliability of the computer system?

1.12   Hundreds of sea turtle hatchlings, instinctively following the bright lights of condominiums, wandered to their deaths across a coastal highway in Florida (*Tampa Tribune*, Sept. 16, 1990). This incident led researchers to begin experimenting with special low-pressure sodium lights. One night, 60 turtle hatchlings were released on a dark beach and their direction of travel noted. The next night, the special lights were installed and the same 60 hatchlings were released. Finally, on the third night, tar paper was placed over the sodium

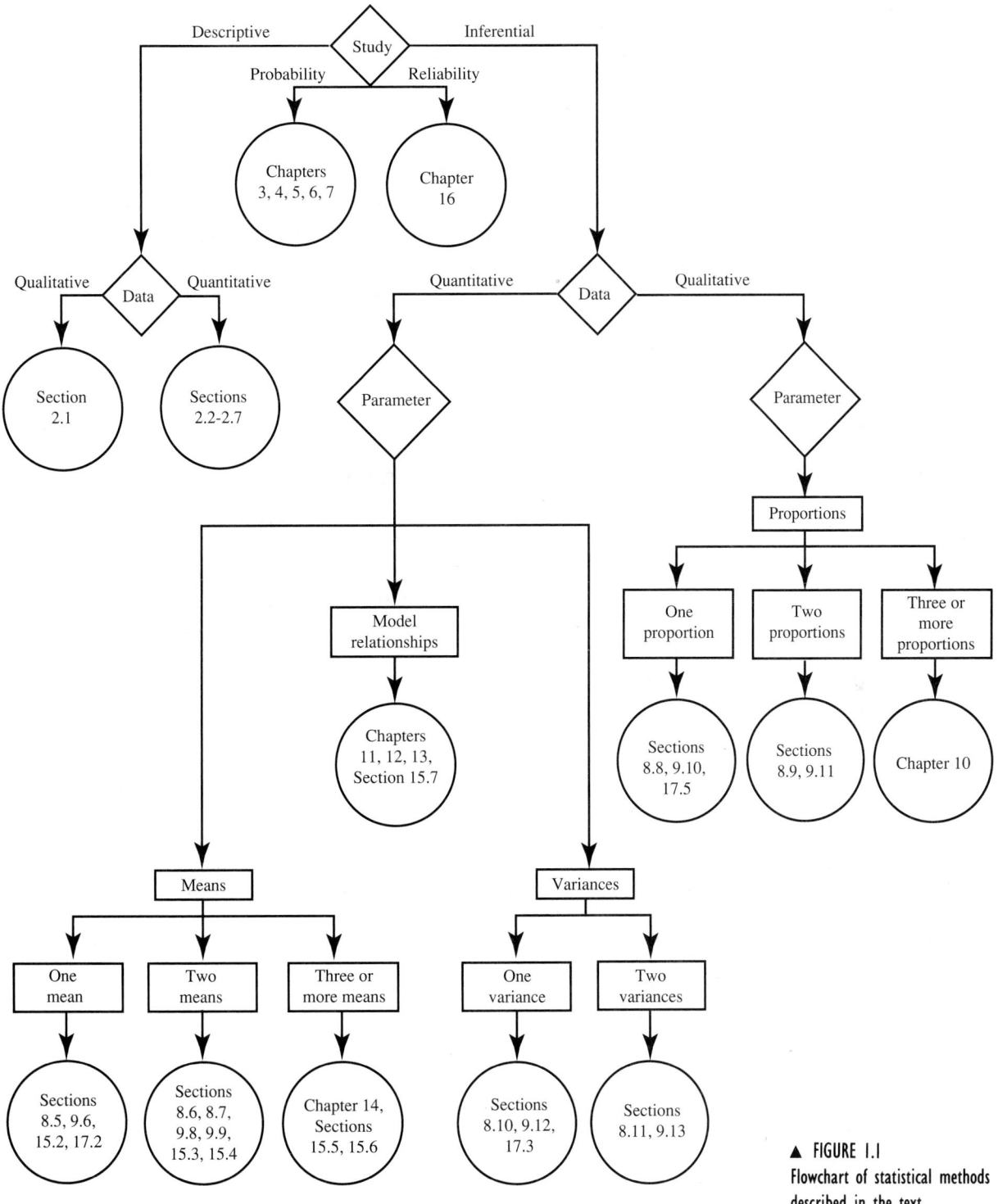

▲ FIGURE 1.1
Flowchart of statistical methods described in the text

lights. Consequently, the direction of travel was recorded for each hatchling under three experimental conditions—darkness, sodium lights, and sodium lights covered with tar paper.
a. Identify the population of interest to the researchers.
b. Identify the sample.
c. What type of data were collected, quantitative or qualitative?

1.13   Every 5 years the Mechanics Division of the American Society of Engineering Education (ASEE) conducts a nationwide survey on undergraduate mechanics education at colleges and universities. In the latest survey, 66 out of the 100 colleges sampled covered fluid statics in their undergraduate engineering program (*Engineering Education*, April 1986).
a. What is the population of interest to the ASEE? The sample?
b. What type of data, quantitative or qualitative, are collected?
c. Use the sample information to make an inference about the population.

1.14   State whether each of the following data sets is quantitative or qualitative.
a. Arrival times of 16 reflected seismic waves
b. Types of computer software used in a database management system
c. Brands of calculator used by 100 engineering students on campus
d. Ash contents in pieces of coal from three different mines
e. Mileages attained by 12 automobiles powered by alcohol
f. Numbers of print characters per line of computer output for 20 line printers
g. Shift supervisors in charge of computer operations at an airline company
h. Accident rates at 46 machine shops

1.15   The data in the accompanying table were obtained from the Environmental Protection Agency (EPA) *1993 Gas Mileage Guide* for new automobiles. State whether each of the variables measured is quantitative or qualitative.

Model Name	Manufacturer	Transmission	Engine Size (liters)	Number of Cylinders	Estimated City Miles/Gallon	Estimated Highway Miles/Gallon
NSX	Acura	Automatic	3.0	6	18	23
Colt	Dodge	Manual	1.5	4	32	40
318i	BMW	Automatic	1.8	4	22	30
Aerostar	Ford	Automatic	4.0	6	16	22
Camry	Toyota	Manual	2.2	4	22	30

Source: *1993 Gas Mileage Guide*, EPA Fuel Economy Estimates, Oct. 1992.

COMPUTER LAB: Entering and Listing Data

In the Computer Lab sections of this text, we give the commands necessary to conduct a statistical analysis of data using one of two statistical software packages—SAS or MINITAB. These two packages were selected because of their current popularity, ease of use, and availability at most university computing centers. In addition, both packages have versions available for large mainframe computers and for personal computers (PCs).

Both software packages utilize the following three basic types of instructions:

1. **Data entry commands:**   Instructions on how the data will be entered
2. **Input data values:**   The values of the variables in the data set
3. **Statistical analysis commands:**   Instructions on what type of analysis is to be conducted on the data

In this section we give the **data entry commands** for each package. That is, we give the commands that will enable you to create a data set ready for analysis. (The appropriate statistical analysis commands are provided in the relevant sections of the text.) The data set of interest from Appendix III consists of location, species, length, weight, and DDT levels of a sample of five fish. The data are listed in Table 1.1.

Note: With few exceptions, the commands provided in the following sections are appropriate for the large mainframe and PC versions of both software packages. When a mainframe computer is being used, however, these statements must be preceded by the job control language (JCL) commands required at your institution.

TABLE 1.1   Five Measurements Selected from Appendix III

Observation	Location	Species	Length	Weight	DDT Concentration
1	FCM5	Catfish	42.5	732	10.00
8	LCM3	Catfish	48.0	1,151	7.70
31	TRM280	Buffalo	49.0	1,763	4.50
43	TRM285	Bass	28.5	778	.48
73	TRM300	Buffalo	35.5	1,300	1.30

SAS

Command
line

```
1    DATA FISH;
2    INPUT LOCATION $ SPECIES $ LENGTH WEIGHT DDT;   } Data entry
3    LWRATIO = LENGTH/WEIGHT;                           instructions
4    CARDS;
5    FCM5    CATFISH 42.5 732 10.00
6    LCM3    CATFISH 48.0 1151 7.70
7    TRM280 BUFFALO 49.0 1763 4.50    } Input data values
8    TRM285 BASS    28.5  778 0.48      (1 observation per line)
9    TRM300 BUFFALO 35.5 1300 1.30
10   PROC PRINT;                       Print instruction
```

COMMAND 1   FISH is an arbitrarily chosen name used to identify the data set. (Data set names are restricted to a maximum length of eight characters.)

COMMAND 2   LOCATION, SPECIES, LENGTH, WEIGHT, and DDT are arbitrarily chosen names for the variables in the data set. (Variable names are also restricted to a maximum length of eight characters.) A dollar sign ($) must follow the name of any nonnumeric variable in the data set.

COMMAND 3   LWRATIO (length-to-weight ratio) is calculated by dividing LENGTH by WEIGHT. (The standard arithmetic operations symbols, $+$, $-$, $*$, and $/$, are used for addition, subtraction, multiplication, and division, respectively.)

COMMAND 4   CARDS signals SAS that the input data values are to follow.

COMMANDS 5–9   Each data line gives the values of the variables in the data set for a single observation (fish) in the order in which the variables are listed in the INPUT command. Input data values must be separated by at least one blank space; commas are not permitted in numeric values.

COMMAND 10   The PRINT procedure (PROC) will produce a listing of the entire data set (see Figure 1.2). In addition to the INPUT variables, the data set will contain any variables created using the standard arithmetic operations (e.g., LWRATIO) in command line 3.

GENERAL   All SAS commands must end with a semicolon; the only exceptions to this rule are the input data values.

FIGURE 1.2 ▶

SAS output: Listing of the data in Table 1.1

OBS	LOCATION	SPECIES	LENGTH	WEIGHT	DDT	LWRATIO
1	fcm5	catfish	42.5	732	10.00	0.058060
2	lcm3	catfish	48.0	1151	7.70	0.041703
3	trm280	buffalo	49.0	1763	4.50	0.027794
4	trm285	bass	28.5	778	0.48	0.036632
5	trm300	buffalo	35.5	1300	1.30	0.027308

MINITAB

Command line

```
 1    READ C1 C2 C3 C4 C5       Data entry instructions
 2    1 1 42.5  732 10.00  ⎫
 3    2 1 48.0 1151  7.70  ⎪  Input data values
 4    3 2 49.0 1763  4.50  ⎬  (1 observation per line)
 5    4 3 28.5  778  0.48  ⎪
 6    5 2 35.5 1300  1.30  ⎭
 7    DIVIDE C3 BY C4 PUT INTO C6
 8    NAME C1 = 'LOCATION' C2 = 'SPECIES'     Data entry instructions
 9    NAME C3='LENGTH' C4='WEIGHT' C5='DDT' C6='LWRATIO'
10    PRINT C1-C6           Print instruction
11    STOP
```

COMMAND 1   The five variables to be read onto the MINITAB "worksheet" are identified by the "columns" into which they are placed: C1, C2, C3, C4, and C5. (MINITAB does not, in general, recognize variable names.) Thus, location will be read in column 1, species in column 2, etc.

COMMANDS 2–6   Each data line gives the values of the variables read in the worksheet columns for a single observation (fish). Input data values must be separated by at least one blank space; commas are not permitted. MINITAB also requires all data used in statistical analysis to be numerical. For example, the values of the nonnumeric variable *location* are converted to numbers in C1. (Arbitrarily let 1 represent FCM5, 2 represent LCM3, etc.)

COMMAND 7   MINITAB uses the word commands ADD, SUBTRACT, MULTIPLY, and DIVIDE to perform the usual arithmetic operations on variables. The ratio of length (C3) to weight (C4) is stored in C6.

COMMANDS 8–9   For labeling printed output, the NAME command can be used to give names to the variables stored in the worksheet columns. If the NAME command is omitted, the columns will be labeled C1, C2, etc., on the MINITAB printouts.

COMMAND 10   The PRINT command will produce a listing of the data in the MINITAB worksheet for the specified variables (columns). (See Figure 1.3.)

COMMAND 11   All MINITAB programs terminate with the STOP command.

GENERAL   MINITAB permits you to insert extraneous words within each command to help you follow the logic of the program. For example, command line 1 could be entered as follows:

```
READ LOCATION IN C1, SPECIES IN C2, LENGTH IN C3, WEIGHT IN C4, DDT IN C5
```

FIGURE 1.3 ►
MINITAB output: Listing of data in Table 1.1

ROW	Location	Species	Length	Weight	DDT	LWRatio
1	1	1	42.5	732	10.00	0.0580601
2	2	1	48.0	1151	7.70	0.0417029
3	3	2	49.0	1763	4.50	0.0277935
4	4	3	28.5	778	0.48	0.0366324
5	5	2	35.5	1300	1.30	0.0273077

COMPUTER LAB: Accessing an External Data File (Optional)

Data created by other software and saved in an external file as an ASCII data set can also be accessed and analyzed by SAS and MINITAB. For example, the full data set of Appendix III (DDT measurements and other data for 144 fish specimens) is saved in an ASCII file called FISH.DAT on a 3.5″ micro disk or 5.25″ floppy disk available from the publisher (see the Preface). The program lines shown here give the commands for reading and listing the data on this external file.

SAS

Command
line

```
1    DATA FISH;
2    INFILE 'FISH.DAT';
3    INPUT LOCATION $ SPECIES $ LENGTH WEIGHT DDT;
4    LWRATIO=LENGTH/WEIGHT;
5    PROC PRINT;
```

MINITAB

Command
line

```
1    READ 'FISH.DAT' C1-C5
2    DIVIDE C3 C4 C6
3    NAME C1='LOCATION' C2='SPECIES' C3='LENGTH'
        C4='WEIGHT' C5='DDT' C6='LWRATIO'
5    PRINT C1-C6
```

References

Careers in Statistics. American Statistical Association and the Institute of Mathematical Statistics, 1974.

Huff, D. *How to Lie with Statistics*. New York: W. W. Norton and Co., 1978.

Ryan, B. F., Joiner, B. L., and Ryan, T. A. *Minitab Handbook*, 2nd ed. Boston: PWS-Kent, 1990.

SAS Procedures Guide for Personal Computers, Version 6 ed. Cary, N.C.: SAS Institute, Inc., 1986.

SAS User's Guide: Basics, Version 6 ed. Cary, N.C.: SAS Institute, Inc., 1991.

Tanur, J. M., Mosteller, F., Kruskal, W. H., Link, R. F., Pieters, R. S., and Rising, G. R., eds. *Statistics: A Guide to the Unknown*, 3rd ed. Pacific Grove, California: Wadsworth, Brooks/Cole, 1989.

CHAPTER TWO
Descriptive Statistics

To present graphical and numerical methods for exploring, summarizing, and describing data

Contents

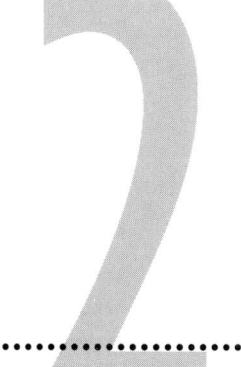

2.1   Graphical and Numerical Methods for Describing Qualitative Data

Assuming you have collected a data set of interest to you, how can you make sense out of it? That is, how can you organize and summarize the data set to make it more comprehensible and meaningful? In this chapter, we look at several basic statistical tools for describing data. These involve graphs and charts that rapidly convey a visual picture of the data, and numerical measures that describe certain features of the data. The proper procedure to use depends on the type of data (quantitative or qualitative) that we want to describe.

When describing qualitative observations, we define the categories in such a way that each observation can fall in one and only one category. The data set is then described numerically by giving the number of observations, or the proportion of the total number of observations, that fall in each of the categories.

Definition 2.1

The **category frequency** for a given category is the number of observations that fall in that category.

Definition 2.2

The **category relative frequency** for a given category is the proportion of the total number of observations that fall in that category.

To illustrate, consider a problem of interest to researchers writing in the *Nuclear Engineering Journal*. The researchers located 98 large nuclear reactors operating in the world and listed the country of each. Table 2.1 summarizes the researcher's findings. In this problem, the qualitative variable of interest is the country in which the nuclear reactor is located. You can see from Table 2.1 that the data for the 98 nuclear reactors fall into nine categories (countries). The summary table gives both the frequency and relative frequency of nuclear reactors in each country. Clearly, the United States dominates the other eight countries, with 47 of the 98 nuclear reactors (or approximately 48%).

Graphical descriptions of qualitative data sets are usually achieved using bar graphs or pie charts; these figures are often constructed by a computer. **Bar graphs** give the frequency (or relative frequency) corresponding to each category, with the height or length of the bar proportional to the category frequency (or relative frequency). **Pie charts** divide a complete circle (a pie) into slices, one corresponding to each category, with the central angle of the slice proportional to the category relative frequency. Examples of these familiar graphical methods are shown in Figures 2.1 and 2.2.

TABLE 2.1	Summary Frequency Table for Largest Nuclear Reactors Worldwide	
Category	Frequency	Relative Frequency
Country	Number of Nuclear Reactors	Proportion
Belgium	4	.0408
France	22	.2245
Finland	2	.0204
Germany	7	.0714
Holland	1	.0102
Japan	11	.1123
Sweden	3	.0306
Switzerland	1	.0102
United States	47	.4796
TOTALS	98	1.0000

Source: Plews, M. J., Wakerly, M. W., and Winyard, R. A. "Comparing PWR exposures worldwide." *Nuclear Engineering International*, Vol. 31, No. 381, Apr. 1986, p. 46 (Table 1).

FIGURE 2.1 ▶
Vertical bar graph showing the number of large nuclear reactors for nine countries

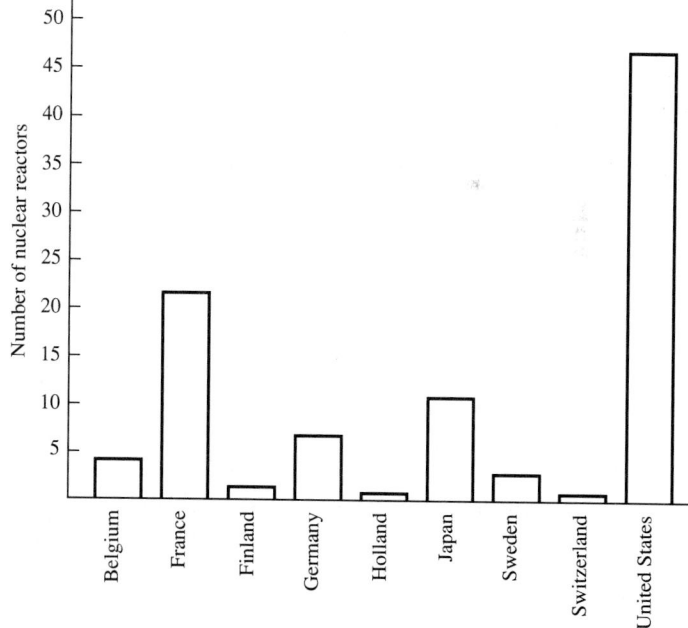

Figure 2.1 is a vertical bar graph that describes the data in Table 2.1. (Bar graphs can be vertical or horizontal.) Each bar corresponds to one of the nine countries, and the height of the bar is proportional to the number of large nuclear reactors in that country.

FIGURE 2.2 ►
Pie chart showing percentages of
industrial robots assigned to
various tasks

U.S. Robot Applications in 1990 (33,600 units)

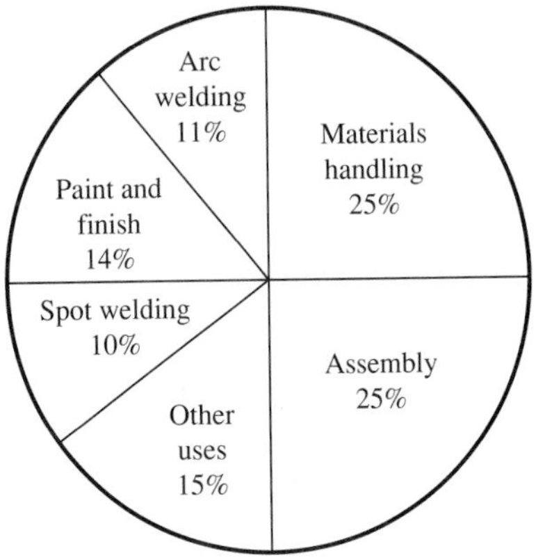

Source: Info Graphics, News America Syndicate.

Figure 2.2 shows the percentages of the 33,600 computer-generated industrial robots assigned to each of six categories at U.S. industrial plants in 1990: (1) arc welding, (2) paint and finish, (3) spot welding, (4) materials handling, (5) assembly, and (6) other uses. The pie chart not only enables you to determine the exact percentage of industrial robots assigned to a given application, but it also provides a rapid visual comparison of the relative percentages (sizes of the slices) assignable to the various application types.

EXAMPLE 2.1

Refer to the fish sample data in Appendix III (see Case Study 1.1). Construct a summary table and a horizontal bar graph for the proportion of fish specimens captured for each of the three species: channel catfish, largemouth bass, and smallmouth buffalo.

Solution

The fish data were analyzed using the computer (SAS). Figure 2.3 is a SAS summary table for the three species. The analysis reveals that 36 are smallmouth buffalo, 12 are largemouth bass, and the remaining 96 are channel catfish. The corresponding proportions (or relative frequencies) are $\frac{36}{144} = .25$, $\frac{12}{144} = .083$, and $\frac{96}{144} = .667$. This same information is displayed on the (SAS) horizontal bar graph shown in Figure 2.4.

Vertical bar graphs like Figure 2.1 can be enhanced by arranging the bars on the graph in the form of a **Pareto diagram**. A Pareto diagram (named for the Italian economist Vilfredo Pareto) is a frequency bar graph with the bars displayed in order of height, starting with the tallest bar on the left. Pareto diagrams are popular graphical tools in process and quality control, where the heights of the bars often represent frequencies of problems (e.g., defects, accidents, breakdowns, and failures) in the production process. Because the bars are arranged in descending order of height, it is easy to identify the areas with the most severe problems.

For example, consider a problem of interest to the Business Economics Division (BED) of the U.S. Department of Labor. Each year, the BED monitors business failures and classifies each failure into one of the following six categories: (1) lack of

FIGURE 2.3 ▶

SAS summary frequency table for the three fish species

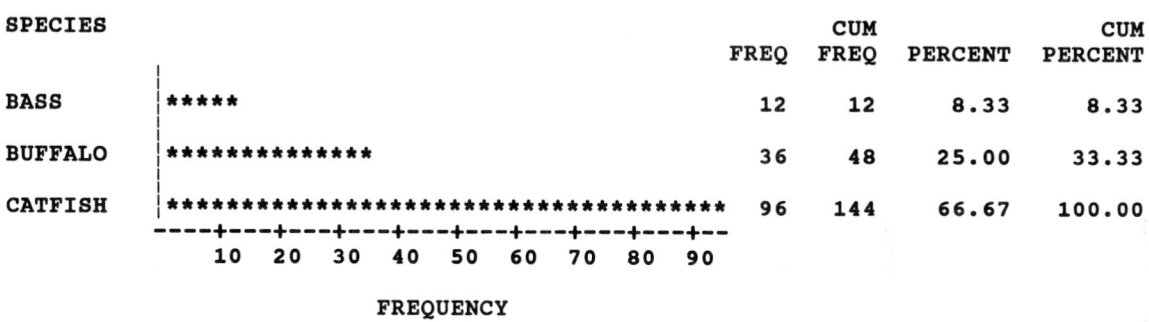

SPECIES	Frequency	Percent	Cumulative Frequency	Cumulative Percent
BASS	12	8.3	12	8.3
BUFFALO	36	25.0	48	33.3
CATFISH	96	66.7	144	100.0

```
                              FREQUENCY OF SPECIES

SPECIES                                              CUM                    CUM
                                        FREQ        FREQ      PERCENT     PERCENT

BASS       |*****                        12          12        8.33        8.33
           |
BUFFALO    |*************                36          48       25.00       33.33
           |
CATFISH    |*******************************************    96     144    66.67      100.00
           ----+---+---+---+---+---+---+---+---+--
              10  20  30  40  50  60  70  80  90

                          FREQUENCY
```

FIGURE 2.4 ▲

SAS horizontal bar graph for the three fish species

experience in the production line, (2) lack of managerial experience, (3) unbalanced experience, (4) incompetence, (5) other causes (such as neglect, fraud, and natural disaster), and (6) unknown reasons. These classifications are based on the opinions of informed creditors and information in BED reports. Recently, the BED determined the cause of 1,463 failures of construction enterprises. The 1,463 construction failures are summarized in Table 2.2. Note that the categories (underlying causes) are arranged in decreasing order of frequency of failures. These frequencies are shown in the Pareto diagram displayed in Figure 2.5 (page 20). In addition to the bars with decreasing heights, the Pareto diagram also shows a plot of the cumulative proportion of construction failures (called a "cum" line) superimposed over the bars. The cum line scale

TABLE 2.2   Reasons of 1,463 Construction Failures Rearranged in Order of Frequency, with Cumulative Proportions

Underlying Cause	Frequency	Relative Frequency	Cumulative Proportion
Incompetence	698	.477	.477
Unbalanced experience	314	.215	.692
Lack of managerial experience	236	.161	.853
Lack of line experience	111	.076	.929
Reason unknown	83	.057	.986
Other causes	21	.014	1.000
TOTALS	1,463	1.000	

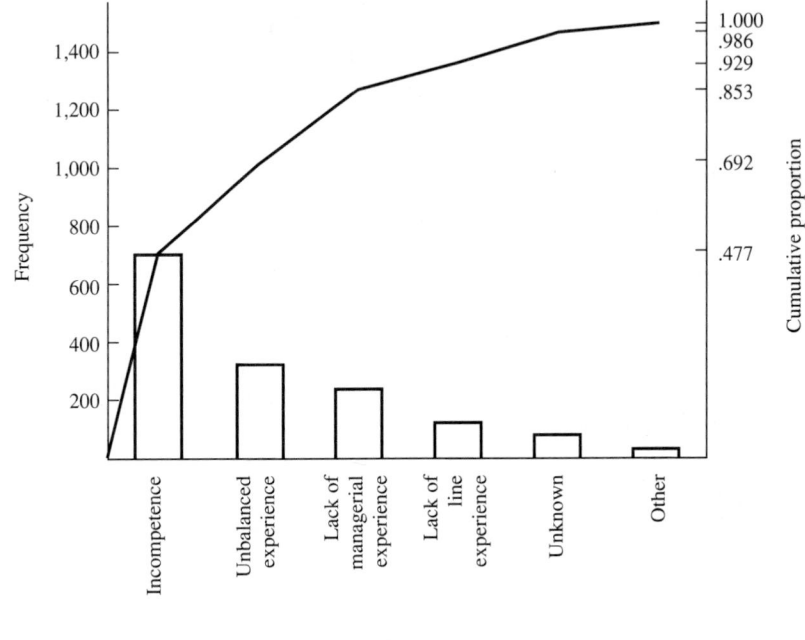

FIGURE 2.5 ▶
Pareto diagram of construction
failures for six underlying causes

appears on the right side of the Pareto diagram. From Figure 2.5, you can see that almost 70% of the construction failures are due to the first two causes listed in Table 2.2, incompetence and unbalanced experience.

EXERCISES

2.1   The accompanying pie chart describes the fate of the (estimated) 242 million automobile tires that are scrapped in the United States each year.

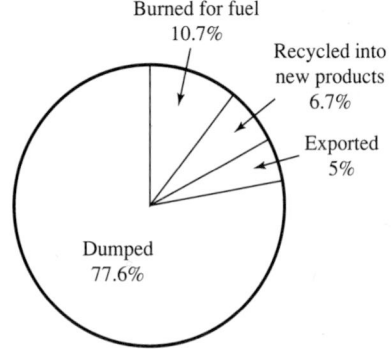

Source: U.S. Environmental Protection Agency and
National Solid Waste Management Association. *Tampa Tribune*, June 29, 1992.

a. Interpret the pie chart.
b. Convert the pie chart into a relative frequency bar chart.
c. Convert the pie chart into a frequency bar chart.

2.2   The cornrake is a European species of bird in danger of worldwide extinction. A census of singing cornrakes on agricultural land in Britain and Ireland was recently conducted (*Journal of Applied Ecology*, Vol. 30, 1993). The table gives the total number of cornrakes inhabiting each of 10 geographical areas.

Area	Number of Cornrakes
1. Mainland Scotland	12
2. Highland region of Scotland	15
3. Orkney and Shetland	34
4. Lewis and Harris	76
5. N. Uist and Benbecula	82
6. S. Uist and Barra	155
7. Inner Hebrides	76
8. Coll and Tirce	121
9. Northern Ireland	128
10. Republic of Ireland	789
TOTAL	1,488

Source: Stowe, T. J., et al. "The decline of the cornrake *Crex crex* in Britain and Ireland in relation to habitat." *Journal of Applied Ecology*, Vol. 30, 1993, p. 55 (Table 1).

a. Summarize the data with a graphical technique.
b. On the island of Barra, the cornrake census was carried out during the daytime when only a small proportion of male birds are expected to call. A total of 99 cornrakes were observed on Barra. Eliminate the Barra results from the census in area 6 and redo the graph.

2.3   In Florida, civil engineers are designing roads with the latest safety-oriented construction methods in response to the fact that in 1988, more people in Florida were killed by bad roads than by guns. A total of 135 traffic accidents that occurred during the year have been attributed to poorly constructed roads (*Tampa Tribune*, Nov. 14, 1989). A breakdown of the poor road conditions that caused the accidents is shown in the following table. Construct and interpret a Pareto diagram for the data.

Poor Road Condition	Number of Fatalities
Obstructions without warning	7
Road repairs/Under construction	39
Loose surface material	13
Soft or low shoulders	20
Holes, ruts, etc.	8
Standing water	25
Worn road surface	6
Other	17
TOTAL	135

Source: Florida Department of Highway Safety and Motor Vehicles, 1989.

2.4   The total employment and the percentage of women employed in construction occupations in 1990 are summarized in the accompanying table.

Construction Occupation	Total Employment thousands	Percent Women
Brickmasons/stonemasons	152	.2
Carpenters	1,057	1.3
Carpet installers	73	2.1
Concrete/terrazzo finishers	113	.6
Drywall installers	143	1.0
Electricians	548	1.7
Glaziers	42	.4
Hard tile setters	28	2.0
Insulation workers	70	1.5
Painters/paperhangers/construction and maintenance	453	6.9
Plumbers/pipefitters/steamfitters	379	.9
Roofers	138	.3
Structural metal workers	80	.2

Source: Green, K. "Should you build a future as a construction tradeswoman?" *Occupational Outlook Quarterly*, Vol. 37, No. 1 (Spring 1993), p. 4.

a. Construct a relative frequency bar chart for total employment in the 13 construction occupations. Interpret the result.

b. Construct a frequency table for the number of women employed in the 13 construction occupations. Interpret the result.

2.5   In the United States, dyes are used in coloration products, such as textiles, paper, leather, and foodstuffs, and are required by law to be in gasoline to indicate the presence of lead. The long-term effects of dyes and their degradation products, however, are unknown. To monitor environmental contamination, analytical methods must be developed to identify and quantify these dyes. In one study, thermospray high-performance liquid chromatography/mass spectrometry was used to characterize dyes in wastewater and gasoline. The accompanying table gives the relative abundance (relative frequency of occurrence) of commerical Diazo Red dye components in gasoline. Describe the relative abundance of red dye compounds with a bar graph. Interpret the graph.

Red Dye Compound	Relative Abundance	Red Dye Compound	Relative Abundance
H	.021	C_8H_{17}	.127
CH_3	.210	C_9H_{19}	.118
C_2H_5	.354	$C_{10}H_{21}$	.025
C_3H_7	.072	Others	.019
C_7H_{15}	.054		

Source: Voyksner, R. D. "Characterization of Dyes in Environmental Samples by Thermospray High-performance Liquid Chromatography/Mass Spectrometry." *Analytical Chemistry*, Vol. 57, No. 13, Nov. 1985, p. 2601 (Table I). Reprinted with permission. Copyright 1985 American Chemical Society.

2.6   Some scientists claim that global climate warming—caused by smoke stacks, gas-powered automobiles, power-generating stations, forest fires, etc.—will threaten the habitability of the Earth by the end of the 20th century. *Scientific American* (July 1990) reported on computer models designed to assess the causes of global warming. The accompanying horizontal relative frequency bar chart shows a breakdown of the potential causes of global warming into five general categories: (1) energy use and production, (2) chlorofluorocarbons, (3) agriculture, (4) land-use modification, and (5) other industrial causes. Interpret the bar chart.

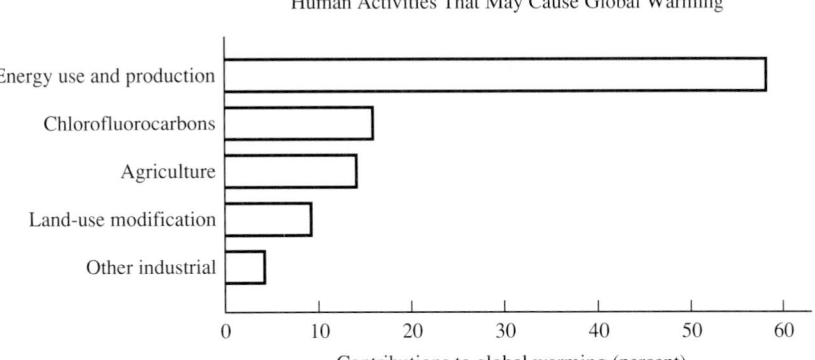

Human Activities That May Cause Global Warming

Source: White, R.M. "The Great Climate Debate." *Scientific American*, Vol. 263, No. 1, July 1990, p. 43.

2.7   Stainless steels are frequently used in chemical plants to handle corrosive fluids. However, in certain environments these steels are especially susceptible to stress corrosion cracking. One study identified stress corrosion cracking as the greatest single cause of steel alloy failure in Japanese chemical plants. The accompanying table lists the various modes of failure and their corresponding percentages of the total for 295 cases of alloy failures that occurred in oil refineries and petrochemical plants in Japan over the last 10 years.

Cause of Failure	Percentage
Wet environment	
General corrosion	12.5%
Localized corrosion	15.9
Stress corrosion cracking	39.9
Miscellaneous	3.8
Dry environment	
Corrosion	8.2
Cracking	10.9
Decrease of mechanical properties	1.7
Miscellaneous	1.7
Material defects	2.0
Welding defects	3.4

Source: Yamamoto, K., and Kagawa, N. "Ferritic Stainless Steels Have Improved Resistance to SCC in Chemical Plant Environments." *Materials Performance*, June 1981, Vol. 20, No. 6, pp. 32–35.

a. Construct a Pareto diagram for the causes of steel alloy failure in Japanese chemical plants.

b. Does the bar graph of part **a** support the claim made by the researchers?

2.8   Researchers have been creating thin films of tiny diamonds since the early 1950s, but industry has only recently utilized diamond thin films in the manufacture of such products as cutting tools, stereo loudspeaker tweeters, heat sinks, sunglasses, and components for scientific instruments. According to the Philadelphia Institute for Scientific Information (ISI), the United States and Japan are preeminent in current research on diamond thin films (*The Scientist*, June 11, 1990). Each of 251 published papers was categorized according to the author's country of residence. The results are shown in the accompanying table. Use an appropriate graphical technique to summarize the data. Do you agree with ISI's assessment of the United States and Japan with regard to diamond thin film research?

Country	Number of Papers on Diamond Thin Film Research
United States	105
Japan	63
United Kingdom	20
Germany	17
Italy	7
Others	39
TOTAL	251

Source: Grissom, A. "U.S. and Japan Sparkle in Diamond Thin Film Research." *The Scientist*, June 11, 1990, p. 17 (Table 1).

2.9   Wayne State University is one of the few U.S. universities that offers a graduate program in hazardous-waste management. For future planning, a survey was taken to determine the background and goals of the 223 students currently enrolled in the program (*Journal of Professional Issues in Engineering*, Apr. 1990). The pie chart gives a breakdown of the undergraduate majors of the 223 students. Interpret the chart.

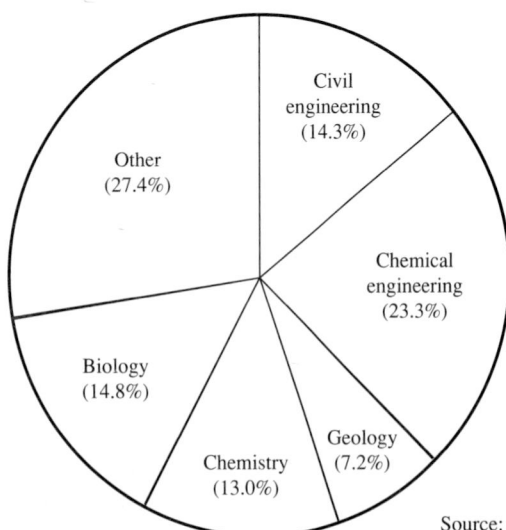

Source: Miller, C.J., et al. "Educational Program for Hazardous Waste Management." *Journal of Professional Issues in Engineering*, Vol. 116, No. 2, April 1990, p. 226 (Figure 2).

2.2   Graphical Methods for Describing Quantitative Data

In this section, we consider graphs that describe quantitative data. For small quantitative data sets, the simplest graph is the **dot plot**. A dot plot is constructed by first drawing a horizontal scale that spans the range of the data. The numerical values of the observations are located on the horizontal scale by placing a dot over the appropriate value. If data values repeat, then the dots are placed on top of each other, forming a pile at that particular numerical location.

For example, suppose we want to describe graphically the data shown in Table 2.3. The CPU times given in the table are the amounts of time (in seconds) 25 jobs were in control of a large mainframe computer's central processing unit (CPU). These 25 values represent a sample selected from the 1,000 CPU times listed in Appendix IV.

TABLE 2.3   A Sample of $n = 25$ Job CPU Times (in seconds) Selected from Appendix IV

1.17	1.61	1.16	1.38	3.53
1.23	3.76	1.94	.96	4.75
.15	2.41	.71	.02	1.59
.19	.82	.47	2.16	2.01
.92	.75	2.59	3.07	1.40

Figure 2.6 is a MINITAB dot plot for the data in Table 2.3. For small data sets, the dot plot provides a quick and easy way to obtain a visual picture of how the quantitative data are distributed along the horizontal scale. Figure 2.6 shows that most of the CPU times lie between 1 and 2 seconds, and that several extreme values (e.g., 3.76 and 4.75 seconds) occur.

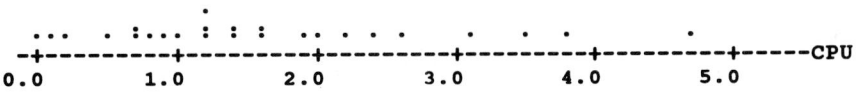

FIGURE 2.6 ▲
MINITAB dot plot for CPU times data of Table 2.3

The most popular and traditional graphical method for describing quantitative data is the **histogram**. The steps to follow in constructing a histogram for the CPU data of Table 2.3 are listed in the box.

Steps to Follow in Constructing a Histogram

STEP 1   Calculate the **range** of the data:

Range = Largest observation − Smallest observation

The range for the data of Table 2.1 is

Range = 4.75 − .02 = 4.73

STEP 2   Divide the range into between 5 and 20 **classes** of equal width. The number of classes is arbitrary, but you will obtain a better graphical description if you use a small number of classes for a small amount of data and a larger number of classes for larger data sets (see the Rule of Thumb in the next box). The lowest (or first) class boundary should be located below the smallest measurement, and the class width should be chosen so that no observation can fall on a class boundary.

We will use seven classes for the data of Table 2.3. Then the approximate class width is

$$\text{Approximate class width} = \frac{\text{Range}}{7} = \frac{4.73}{7} = .676$$

We will round this width upward and use a class width of .7. The first class will be located at .015, just below the smallest CPU time. The resulting seven class intervals are shown in Table 2.4.

STEP 3   For each class, count the number of observations that fall in that class. This number is called the **class frequency**.

STEP 4   Calculate each **class relative frequency**:

$$\text{Class relative frequency} = \frac{\text{Class frequency}}{\text{Total number of measurements}}$$

The class frequencies and relative frequencies for the data of Table 2.3 are shown in columns 4 and 5, respectively, of Table 2.4.

STEP 5   The **histogram** is essentially a bar graph in which the categories are classes. In a **frequency histogram**, the heights of the bars are determined by the class frequency. Similarly, in a **relative frequency histogram**, the heights of the bars are determined by the class relative frequency.

The relative frequency histogram for the data of Table 2.3 is shown in Figure 2.7.

TABLE 2.4   Calculating Class Relative Frequencies for the CPU Data of Table 2.3

Class	Class Interval	Data Tabulation	Class Frequency	Class Relative Frequency
1	.015–.715	ЖHT	5	.20
2	.715–1.415	ЖHT IIII	9	.36
3	1.415–2.115	IIII	4	.16
4	2.115–2.815	III	3	.12
5	2.815–3.515	I	1	.04
6	3.515–4.215	II	2	.08
7	4.215–4.915	I	1	.04
		TOTALS $n = 25$		1.00

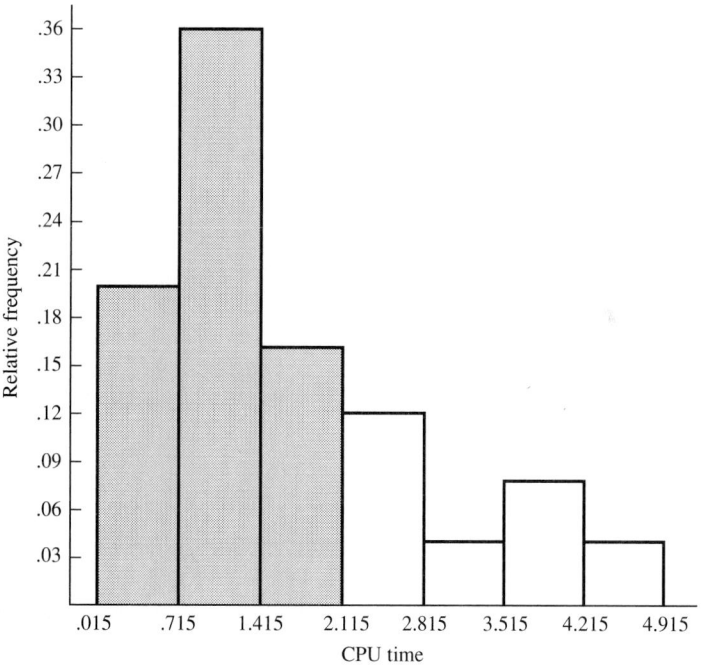

FIGURE 2.7 ▲
Relative frequency histogram
for the $n = 25$ CPU times of
Table 2.3

Rule of Thumb for Determining the Number of Classes in a Histogram

Number of Observations in a Data Set	*Number of Classes*
Less than 25	5 or 6
25–50	7–14
More than 50	15–20

Since the bars in a histogram are of equal width, the area of a particular bar is proportional to the corresponding class relative frequency. If we let the total area of the bars equal 1, then the area of a particular bar is *equal* to its corresponding class relative frequency. Furthermore, if we select one observation from among the $n = 25$ observations in Table 2.3, then the likelihood (or *probability**) that the observation will fall in a particular class is equal to the relative frequency of that class. The probability that the observation will fall in one of two or more specific classes is equal to the sum of their respective relative frequencies and is proportional to the total area of the bars corresponding to those classes. For example, the probability that the observation will be a CPU time less than 2.115 seconds is equal to .72, the sum of the relative frequencies for classes 1, 2, and 3 of Table 2.4. This probability is proportional to the shaded area of Figure 2.7.

Interpreting a Relative Frequency Distribution

The percentage of the total number of measurements falling within a particular interval is proportional to the area of the bar that is constructed above the interval. For example, if 30% of the area under the distribution lies over a particular interval, then 30% of the observations fall in that interval.

Another graphical method for describing quantitative data is the **stem-and-leaf display**, which is widely used in exploratory data analysis when the data set is small. The next box contains the steps to follow in constructing a stem-and-leaf display for the 25 CPU times in Table 2.3.

---

*A more formal definition of probability is given in Chapter 3.

Steps to Follow in Constructing a Stem-and-Leaf Display

STEP 1 Divide each observation in the data set into two parts, the **stem** and the **leaf**. We will designate the first digit of the CPU time (i.e., the digit to the left of the decimal point) as its stem; we will call the last two digits its leaf. For example, the stem and leaf of the CPU time 2.41 are 2 and 41, respectively:

Stem	Leaf
2	41

STEP 2 List the stems in order in a column, starting with the smallest stem and ending with the largest (see Figure 2.8).

STEP 3 Proceed through the data set, placing the leaf for each observation in the appropriate stem row. Arbitrarily, you may want to arrange the leaves in each row in ascending order. The completed **stem-and-leaf display** for the data of Table 2.3 is shown in Figure 2.8.

Notice that if you rotate the stem-and-leaf display on its side, you obtain the same type of bar graph as provided by the histogram. The stem-and-leaf display of Figure 2.8 partitions the data set into five classes corresponding to the five stems. The number of leaves in each class gives the class frequency.

FIGURE 2.8 ▶
Stem-and-leaf display for $n = 25$
CPU times of Table 2.3

Stems	Leaves	Frequency	Relative Frequency
0	02 15 19 47 71 75 82 92 96	9	.36
1	16 17 23 38 40 59 61 94	8	.32
2	01 16 41 59	4	.16
3	07 53 76	3	.12
4	75	1	.04
		TOTALS $n = 25$	1.00

A computer-generated (MINITAB) stem-and-leaf display for the data of Table 2.3 is shown in Figure 2.9. Note that the second column of the MINITAB printout gives the stems and the third column gives the leaves.* MINITAB uses only a single digit—

---

*The numbers in the first column of the MINITAB printout give the cumulative number of observations from the stem row to the nearest end of the distribution.

the number following the decimal point—to represent the leaf.* Thus, the leaf 4 in stem row 2 of Figure 2.9 represents the value 2.41 in Table 2.3.

FIGURE 2.9 ▶
MINITAB stem-and-leaf display for
CPU data

```
Stem-and-leaf of CPU       N  = 25
Leaf Unit = 0.10

    4        0 0114
    9        0 77899
   (5)       1 11234
   11        1 569
    8        2 014
    5        2 5
    4        3 0
    3        3 57
    1        4
    1        4 7
```

Like dot plots, stem-and-leaf displays are well-suited for small data sets. (One advantage of a stem-and-leaf display over a dot plot is that the original data are preserved. That is, you can look at the stem-and-leaf display and resurrect the exact values of the data.) Alternatively, histograms are better suited for the description of large data sets since they permit a greater flexibility in the choice of classes.

EXAMPLE 2.2

Appendix V contains data on percentage iron content for 390 iron-ore specimens collected in Japan. Figure 2.10 is a computer-generated (SAS) histogram for the 390 iron-ore measurements.

a. Interpret the graph.

b. Visually estimate the fraction of iron-ore measurements that lie between 64.6 and 65.8.

Solution

a. Note that the classes are marked off in intervals of .4 along the horizontal axis of the SAS histogram in Figure 2.10, with the midpoint (rather than the lower and upper boundaries) of each interval shown.[†] The histogram shows that the percentage iron-ore measurements tend to pile up near 66; that is, the class from 65.6 to 66.4 has the greatest relative frequency.

b. The bars that fall in the interval from 64.6 to 65.8 are shaded in Figure 2.10. This shaded portion represents approximately 40% of the total area of the bars for the complete distribution. Thus, about 40% of the 390 iron-ore measurements lie between 64.6 and 65.8.

---

*In MINITAB, the leaf will always be the digit immediately to the right of the stem.

†Note that the SAS-generated relative frequency histogram leaves gaps between the bars. However, the resulting figure should not be confused with a bar graph for qualitative data. When drawn by hand, the bars of a histogram are adjacent, with no gaps.

FIGURE 2.10 ▶
SAS histogram for iron-ore data in
Appendix V

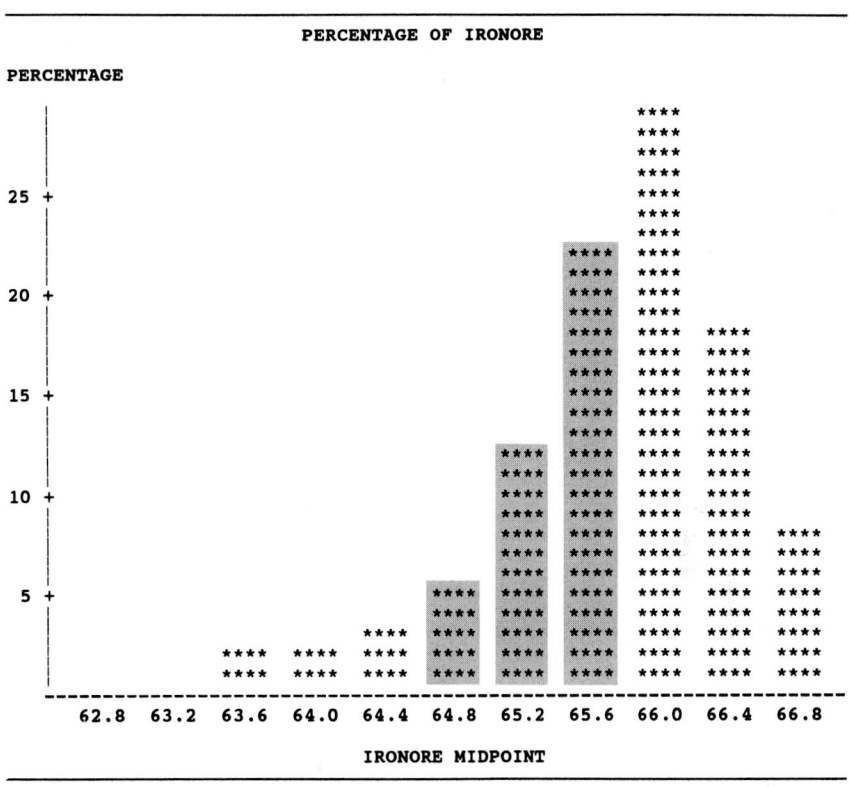

PERCENTAGE OF IRONORE

IRONORE MIDPOINT

EXERCISES

2.10   Researchers at the Massachusetts Institute of Technology (MIT) studied the spectroscopic properties of main-belt asteroids having diameters smaller than 10 kilometers. Asteroids were observed with the Hiltner telescope at the MIT Observatory; the number N of independent spectral image exposures for each observation was recorded. The data for 40 asteroid observations, obtained from *Science* (Apr. 9, 1993), are listed here.

Number of Independent Spectral Image Exposures for 40 Asteroid Observations

3	4	3	3	1	4	1	3	2	3
1	1	4	2	3	3	2	6	1	1
3	3	2	2	2	2	1	3	2	1
6	1	3	2	2	1	2	2	4	2

Source: Binzel, R. P., and Xu, S. "Chips off of Asteroid 4 Vesta: Evidence for the parent body of basaltic achondrite meteorites." *Science*, Vol. 260, Apr. 3, 1993, p. 187 (Table 1).

a. Summarize the data with a stem-and-leaf display.
b. What proportion of asteroid observations resulted in exactly one spectral image exposure?

2.11 Refer to the *Journal of Engineering for Industry* (May 1993) study of deep hole drilling described in Exercise 1.9. An analysis of drill chip congestion was performed using data generated via computer simulation. The simulated distribution of the length (in millimeters) of 50 drill chips is displayed here in a frequency histogram.

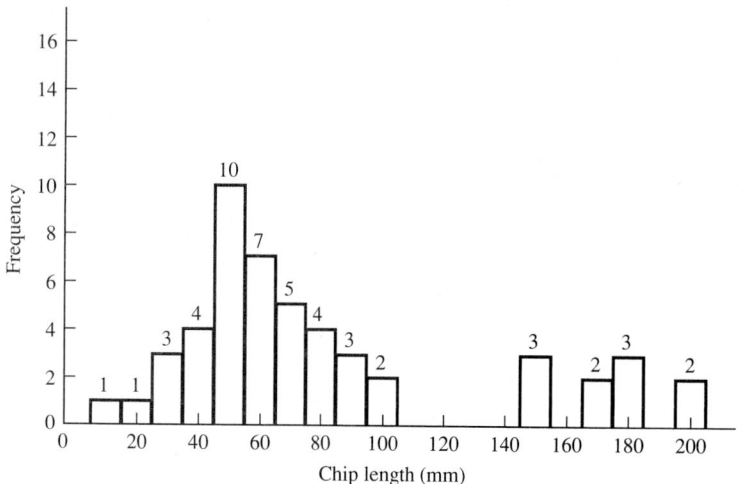

Source: Chin, Jih-Hua et al. "The computer simulation and experimental analysis of chip monitoring for deep hole drilling." *Journal of Engineering for Industry, Transactions of the ASME*, Vol. 115, May 1993, p. 187 (Figure 12).

a. Convert the frequency histogram into a relative frequency histogram.

b. Based on the graph in part **a**, would you expect to observe a drill chip with a length of at least 190 mm? Explain.

2.12 A Harris Corporation/University of Florida study was undertaken to determine whether a manufacturing process performed at a remote location can be established locally. Test devices (pilots) were set up at both the old and new locations and voltage readings on the process were obtained. A "good process" was considered to be one with voltage readings of at least 9.2 volts (with larger readings being better than smaller readings). The table contains voltage readings for 30 production runs at each location.

Old Location			New Location		
9.98	10.12	9.84	9.19	10.01	8.82
10.26	10.05	10.15	9.63	8.82	8.65
10.05	9.80	10.02	10.10	9.43	8.51
10.29	10.15	9.80	9.70	10.03	9.14
10.03	10.00	9.73	10.09	9.85	9.75
8.05	9.87	10.01	9.60	9.27	8.78
10.55	9.55	9.98	10.05	8.83	9.35
10.26	9.95	8.72	10.12	9.39	9.54
9.97	9.70	8.80	9.49	9.48	9.36
9.87	8.72	9.84	9.37	9.64	8.68

Source: Harris Corporation, Melbourne, Fla.

a. Construct a relative frequency histogram for the voltage readings of the old process.

b. Construct a stem-and-leaf display for the voltage readings of the old process. Which of the two graphs in parts **a** and **b** is more informative?

c. Construct a frequency histogram for the voltage readings of the new process.

d. Compare the two graphs in parts **a** and **c**. (You may want to draw the two histograms on the same graph.) Does it appear that the manufacturing process can be established locally (i.e., is the new process as good as or better than the old)?

2.13   Under a voluntary cooperative inspection program, all passenger cruise ships arriving at U.S. ports are subject to unannounced inspections. The purpose of these inspections is to achieve levels of sanitation that will minimize the potential for gastrointestinal disease outbreaks on these ships. Ships are rated on a scale of 0 to 100, depending on how well they meet the Centers for Disease Control sanitation standards. In general, the lower the score, the lower the level of sanitation. The table lists the sanitation inspection scores for 91 international cruise ships during 1992.

Ship	Score	Ship	Score	Ship	Score
Americana	89	Hanseatic Renaissance	82	Sea Princess	88
Amerikanis	97	Holiday	91	Seabourn Pride	99
Azure Seas	83	Horizon	94	Seabourn Spirit	92
Britanis	93	Island Princess	87	Seabreeze I	96
Caribbean Prince	84	Jubilee	89	Seaward	89
Caribe I	90	Mardi Gras	92	Sky Princess	97
Carla C	90	Meridian	95	Society Explorer	66
Carnivale	92	Nantucket Clipper	89	Song of America	95
Celebration	95	New Shoreham II	95	Song of Flower	99
Club Med 1	94	Nieuw Amsterdam	97	Song of Norway	92
Costa Classica	91	Noordam	92	Southward	89
Costa Marina	91	Nordic Empress	93	Sovereign of the Seas	93
Costa Riviera	91	Nordic Prince	92	Star Princess	94
Crown Monarch	94	Norway	84	Starship Atlantic	87
Crown Odyssey	88	Pacific Princess	88	Starship Majestic	94
Crown Princess	88	Pacific Star	70	Starship Oceanic	97
Crystal Harmony	99	Queen Elizabeth 2	98	Starward	96
Cunard Countess	96	Regent Sea	87	Stella Solaris	94
Cunard Princess	89	Regent Star	74	Sun Viking	90
Daphne	86	Regent Sun	95	Sunward	95
Dawn Princess	86	Rotterdam	92	Triton	86
Discovery I	93	Royal Princess	93	Tropicale	93
Dolphin IV	96	Royal Viking Sun	86	Universe	92
Ecstasy	94	Sagafjord	89	Victoria	96
Emerald Seas	95	Scandinavian Dawn	87	Viking Princess	90
Enchanted Isle	86	Scandinavian Song	90	Viking Serenade	96
Enchanted Seas	96	Scandinavian Sun	89	Vistafjord	94
Fair Princess	87	Sea Bird	86	Westerdam	91
Fantasy	97	Sea Goddess I	97	Wind Spirit	96
Festivale	94	Sea Lion	91	Yorktown Clipper	92
Golden Odyssey	89				

Source: Center of Environmental Health and Injury Control, Miami, Fla. (reported in *Tampa Tribune*, May 17, 1992).

a. A MINITAB stem-and-leaf display of the data is shown here. Identify the stems and leaves of the graph.

```
Stem-and-leaf of SanLevel   N  = 91
Leaf Unit = 1.0

     1      6 6
     1      6
     2      7 0
     2      7
     3      7 4
     3      7
     3      7
     3      8
     5      8 23
     7      8 44
    18      8 66666677777
    31      8 8888999999999
    42      9 00000111111
   (15)     9 222222222333333
    34      9 4444444445555555
    18      9 66666666777777
     4      9 8999
```

b. A score of 86 or higher at the time of inspection indicates the ship is providing an accepted standard of sanitation. Use the MINITAB graph to estimate the proportion of ships that have an accepted sanitation standard.

c. Locate the inspection score of 70 (Pacific Star) on the stem-and-leaf display.

2.14   Refer to the *Environmental Science & Technology* study of insecticides used on dormant orchards in the San Joaquin Valley, California, Exercise 1.1. Ambient air samples were collected and analyzed daily at an orchard site during the most intensive period of spraying. The thion and oxon levels (in ng/m^3) in the air samples are recorded in the table, as well as the oxon/thion ratios.

Date	Condition	Thion	Oxon	Oxon/Thion Ratio
Jan. 15	Fog	38.2	10.3	.270
17	Fog	28.6	6.9	.241
18	Fog	30.2	6.2	.205
19	Fog	23.7	12.4	.523
20	Fog	62.3	(Air sample lost)	—
20	Clear	74.1	45.8	.618
21	Fog	88.2	9.9	.112
21	Clear	46.4	27.4	.591
22	Fog	135.9	44.8	.330
23	Fog	102.9	27.8	.270
23	Cloud	28.9	6.5	.225
25	Fog	46.9	11.2	.239
25	Clear	44.3	16.6	.375

Source: Selber, J. N., et al. "Air and fog deposition residues of four organophosphate insecticides used on dormant orchards in the San Joaquin Valley, California." *Environmental Science & Technology*, Vol. 27, No. 10, Oct. 1993, p. 2240 (Table V).

a. Summarize the daily oxon/thion ratios with a stem-and-leaf display.
b. Comment on the statement, "The oxon/thion ratio for the insecticide chlorpyrifos is greater in the clear air than in fog air."

2.15   Refer to the *IEEE Transactions on Industry Applications* (July/Aug. 1990) survey on computer power system load capacities, Exercise 1.3. A relative frequency histogram for the load capacities (measured as a percentage) of the 146 sites in the sample is shown here.

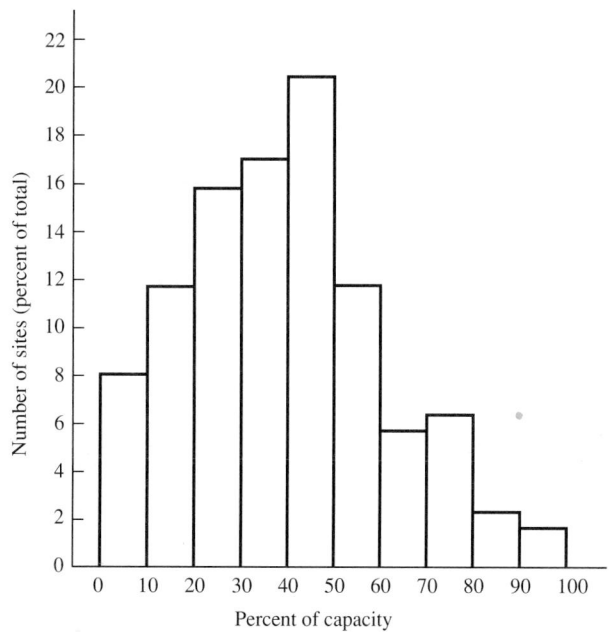

Source: Gruzs, T. M. "A survey of neutral currents in three-phase computer power systems." *IEEE Transactions on Industry Applications*, Vol. 26, No. 4, July/Aug. 1990, p. 722 (Figure 6).

a. Approximately what proportion of the 146 computer sites had a load capacity between 20% and 30%?
b. Approximately what proportion of the 146 computer sites had a load capacity of 50% or more?

2.16   Many Vietnam veterans have dangerously high levels of the dioxin 2,3,7,8-TCDD in blood and fat tissue as a result of their exposure to the defoliant Agent Orange. A study published in *Chemosphere* (Vol. 20, 1990) reported on the TCDD levels of 20 Massachusetts Vietnam veterans who were possibly exposed to Agent Orange. The amounts of TCDD (measured in parts per trillion) in blood plasma and fat tissue drawn from each veteran are shown in the table at the top of page 36. Use a graphical technique to compare the distributions of TCDD levels in plasma and fat tissue.

TCDD Levels in Plasma			TCDD Levels in Fat Tissue		
2.5	3.1	2.1	4.9	5.9	4.4
3.5	3.1	1.8	6.9	7.0	4.2
6.8	3.0	36.0	10.0	5.5	41.0
4.7	6.9	3.3	4.4	7.0	2.9
4.6	1.6	7.2	4.6	1.4	7.7
1.8	20.0	2.0	1.1	11.0	2.5
2.5	4.1		2.3	2.5	

Source: Schecter, A., et al. "Partitioning of 2,3,7,8-chlorinated dibenzo-p-dioxins and diben-zofurans between adipose tissue and plasma lipid of 20 Massachusetts Vietnam veterans." *Chemosphere*, Vol. 20, Nos. 7–9, 1990, pp. 954–955 (Tables I and II).

2.17   Scientists in India experimented with growing copper nanoparticles within a glass medium (*Journal of Applied Physics*, Sept. 1993). A glass ceramic was subjected to an alkali/copper ion exchange reaction followed by a reduction treatment in hydrogen. Upon drying, a sample of 255 copper particles were extracted from the glass surface. The diameters of the copper particles were measured and are described by the accompanying frequency histogram.

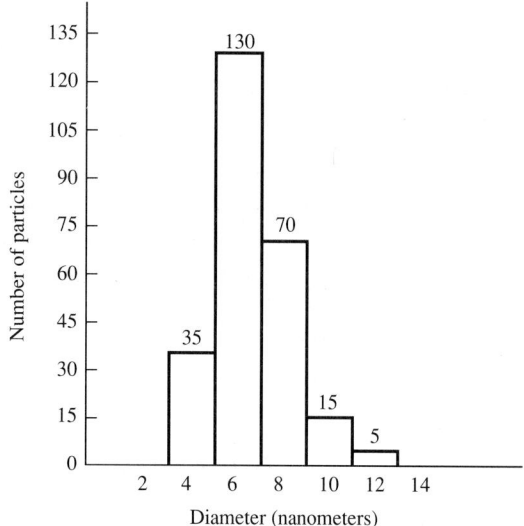

Source: Roy, B. and Chakravorty, D. "Ultrafine copper particles grown in a glass ceramic." *Journal of Applied Physics*, Vol. 74, No.6, Sept. 15, 1993, p. 4192 (Figure 3).

a. Approximately how many copper particles had a diameter between 5 and 7 nanometers?

b. Convert the frequency histogram to a relative frequency histogram.

c. Approximately what proportion of copper particles exceeded 9 nanometers in diameter?

2.18   Each year *U.S. News & World Report* surveys America's best graduate schools. The 1993 survey included a list of the top 25 graduate programs of engineering. The accompanying data include each school's overall score (based on a weighted average of rankings in five areas), total enrollment, dollar amount awarded for research, doctoral student-to-faculty ratio, and acceptance rate. MINITAB stem-and-leaf displays for each of the five quantitative variables measured follow. Interpret the results.

Rank/School	Overall Score	1992 Total Enrollment	1992 Eng. Research	Doctoral Student/ Faculty Ratio	1992 Acceptance Rate
1. Massachusetts Institute of Technology	100.0	2,315	$132,466,000	2.52	27.5%
2. Stanford University	87.2	2,688	59,875,828	5.24	49.6%
3. Univ. of Illinois at Urbana-Champaign	84.8	2,264	80,509,000	2.82	24.7%
4. University of California at Berkeley	81.6	1,527	53,300,000	4.66	27.7%
5. Purdue University (Ind.)	80.3	2,076	62,096,400	2.36	26.3%
6. University of Michigan	79.9	1,799	63,316,579	2.63	48.8%
7. Cornell University	76.3	999	58,720,000	3.27	24.4%
8. University of Texas at Austin	75.4	2,119	58,556,115	3.30	38.6%
9. Georgia Institute of Technology	72.3	2,511	44,040,000	2.32	43.1%
10. Carnegie Mellon University (Pa.)	71.8	819	63,866,000	2.23	13.7%
11. California Institute of Technology	70.7	469	23,998,785	3.70	12.4%
12. University of Wisconsin at Madison	67.6	1,567	52,449,700	2.51	40.9%
13. Pennsylvania State University	67.5	2,022	55,078,000	1.75	46.3%
14. Texas A&M University	66.7	2,056	49,907,596	2.04	38.1%
15. Ohio State University	66.3	1,296	42,805,005	1.96	20.1%
16. Rensselaer Polytechnic Institute	63.4	1,256	34,717,706	2.38	67.1%
17. Northwestern University	62.5	1,060	27,066,662	4.88	26.0%
18. University of California at Los Angeles	62.2	1,012	29,902,411	6.35	43.8%
19. University of Southern California	61.5	2,367	57,366,290	2.41	62.6%
20. Princeton University	59.1	380	22,087,000	2.46	23.4%
21. North Carolina State Univ. at Raleigh	57.0	1,268	40,593,970	1.27	48.3%
22. Virginia Tech	57.0	2,247	35,400,260	1.42	43.7%
23. University of Minnesota at Twin Cities	56.6	1,303	15,928,331	2.70	32.1%
24. University of Washington	56.0	1,292	21,230,881	1.85	26.5%
25. University of Florida	55.8	1,545	38,560,536	1.75	60.7%

Source: *U.S. News & World Report*, Mar. 22, 1993, p. 68.

▶

MINITAB printouts for Exercise 2.18

```
Stem-and-leaf of SCORE     N  = 25
Leaf Unit = 1.0

     6    5 566779
    10    6 1223
    (4)   6 6677
    11    7 012
     8    7 569
     5    8 014
     2    8 7
     1    9
     1    9
     1   10 0
```

(*continued*)

▶

MINITAB printouts for Exercise 2.18
(continued)

```
Stem-and-leaf of ENROLL     N  = 25
Leaf Unit = 100

     1      0 3
     2      0 4
     2      0
     4      0 89
     6      1 00
    11      1 22223
    (3)     1 555
    11      1 7
    10      1
    10      2 0001
     6      2 2233
     2      2 5
     1      2 6


Stem-and-leaf of RESEARCH  N  = 25
Leaf Unit = 1000000

     1      1 5
     6      2 12379
     9      3 458
    (4)     4 0249
    12      5 2357889
     5      6 233
     2      7
     2      8 0
     1      9
     1     10
     1     11
     1     12
     1     13 2


Stem-and-leaf of RATIO      N  = 25
Leaf Unit = 0.10

     2      1 24
     6      1 7789
    (7)     2 0233344
    12      2 55678
     7      3 23
     5      3 7
     4      4
     4      4 68
     2      5 2
     1      5
     1      6 3


Stem-and-leaf of ACCRATE    N  = 25
Leaf Unit = 1.0

     2      1 23
     2      1
     6      2 0344
    11      2 66677
    12      3 2
    (2)     3 88
    11      4 0333
     7      4 6889
     3      5
     3      5
     3      6 02
     1      6 7
```

2.3   Numerical Methods for Describing Quantitative Data

Numerical descriptive measures are numbers computed from a data set to help us create a mental image of its relative frequency histogram. The measures that we will present fall into three categories: (1) those that help to locate the *center* of the relative frequency distribution, (2) those that measure its *spread*, and (3) those that describe the *relative position* of an observation within the data set. These categories are called, respectively, **measures of central tendency, measures of variation**, and **measures of relative standing**. In the definitions that follow, we will denote the *variable* observed to create a data set by the symbol y and the n measurements of a data set by y_1, $y_2, \ldots , y_n$.

Numerical descriptive measures computed from sample data are often called **statistics**. In contrast, numerical descriptive measures of the population are called **parameters**. Their values are typically unknown and are usually represented by Greek symbols. For example, we will see that the average value of the population is represented by the Greek letter μ. Although we *could* calculate the value of this parameter if we actually had access to the entire population, we generally wish to avoid doing so, for economic or other reasons. Thus, as you will subsequently see, we will *sample* the population and then use the sample statistic to infer, or make decisions about, the value of the population parameter of interest.

Definition 2.3

A **statistic** is a numerical descriptive measure computed from sample data.

Definition 2.4

A **parameter** is a numerical descriptive measure of a population.

2.4   Measures of Central Tendency

The three most common measures of central tendency are the **arithmetic mean**, the **median**, and the **mode**. Of the three, the arithmetic mean (or **mean**, as it is commonly called) is used most frequently in practice.

Definition 2.5

The **arithmetic mean** of a set of n measurements, $y_1, y_2, \ldots, y_n$, is the average of the measurements:

$$\frac{\sum_{i=1}^{n} y_i}{n}$$

Typically, the symbol $\bar{y}$ is used to represent the **sample mean** (i.e., the mean of a sample of n measurements), whereas the Greek letter μ represents the **population mean**.

EXAMPLE 2.3

Calculate the mean for the set of $n = 5$ sample measurements: 4, 6, 1, 2, 3.

Solution

Substitution into the formula for $\bar{y}$ yields

$$\bar{y} = \frac{\sum_{i=1}^{n} y_i}{n} = \frac{4 + 6 + 1 + 2 + 3}{5} = 3.2$$

Definition 2.6

The **median** of a set of n measurements, $y_1, y_2, \ldots, y_n$, is the middle number when the measurements are arranged in ascending (or descending) order, i.e., the value of y located so that half the area under the relative frequency histogram lies to its left and half the area lies to its right. We will use the symbol m to represent the *sample median* and the symbol τ to represent the *population median*.

If the number of measurements in a data set is odd, the median is the measurement that falls in the middle when the measurements are arranged in increasing order. For example, the median of the $n = 5$ sample measurements of Example 2.2 is $m = 3$. If the number of measurements is even, the median is defined to be the mean of the two middle measurements when the measurements are arranged in increasing order. For example, the median of the $n = 6$ measurements, 1, 4, 5, 8, 10, 11, is

$$m = \frac{5 + 8}{2} = 6.5$$

Calculating the Median of Small Sample Data Sets

Let $y_{(i)}$ denote the ith value of y when the sample of n measurements are arranged in ascending order. Then the sample median is calculated as follows:

$$m = \begin{cases} y_{[(n+1)/2]} & \text{if } n \text{ is odd} \\[2mm] \dfrac{y_{(n/2)} + y_{(n/2+1)}}{2} & \text{if } n \text{ is even} \end{cases}$$

Definition 2.7

The **mode** of a set of n measurements, $y_1, y_2, \ldots, y_n$, is the value of y that occurs with the greatest frequency.

If the outline of a relative frequency histogram were cut from a piece of plywood, it would be perfectly balanced over the point that locates its mean, as illustrated in Figure 2.11a. As noted in Definition 2.6, half the area under the relative frequency distribution will lie to the left of the median, and half will lie to the right, as shown in Figure 2.11b. The mode will locate the point at which the greatest frequency occurs, i.e., the peak of the relative frequency distribution, as shown in Figure 2.11c.

FIGURE 2.11 ▶
Interpretations of the mean, median, and mode for a relative frequency distribution

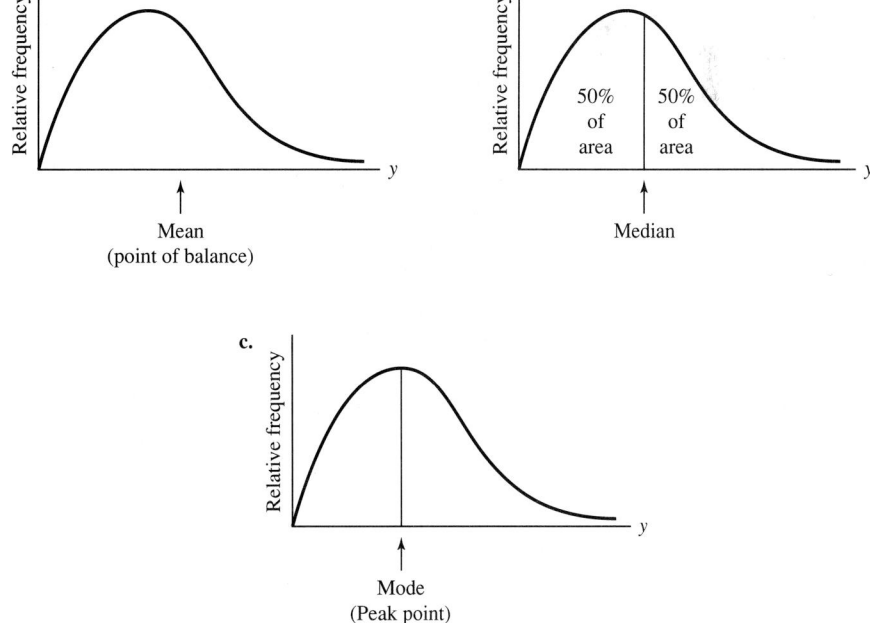

Although the mean is often the preferred measure of central tendency, it is sensitive to very large or very small observations. Consequently, the mean will shift toward the direction of **skewness** (i.e., the tail of the distribution) and may be misleading in some situations. For example, if a data set consists of the first-year starting salaries of civil engineering graduates, the high starting salaries of a few graduates will influence the mean more than the median. For this reason, the median is sometimes called a *resistant* measure of central tendency, since it, unlike the mean, is resistant to the influence of extreme observations. For data sets that are extremely skewed, (e.g., the starting salaries of civil engineering graduates), the median would better represent the "center" of the distribution data.

Rarely is the mode the preferred measure of central tendency. The mode is preferred over the mean or median only if the relative frequency of occurrence of *y* is of interest. For example, a supplier of carpenter's materials would be interested in the modal length (in inches) of nails he sells.

In summary, the best measure of central tendency for a data set depends on the type of descriptive information you want. Most of the inferential statistical methods discussed in this text are based, theoretically, on mound-shaped distributions of data with little or no skewness. For these situations, the mean and the median will be, for all practical purposes, the same. Since the mean has nicer mathematical properties than the median, it is the preferred measure of central tendency for these inferential techniques.

EXAMPLE 2.4

Consider the data on 144 contaminated fish specimens in Appendix III. One of the quantitative variables for each specimen is DDT level, measured in parts per million (ppm). Calculate the mean, median, and mode for this data set. Interpret the results.

Solution

Since the sample size is fairly large, we used the computer to calculate these measures of central tendency. Figure 2.12 is a SAS printout of the results. From Figure 2.12, the values of the sample mean, median, and mode (all shaded) are 24.355 ppm, 7.15 ppm, and 12 ppm, respectively.

The mean implies that the average DDT level of the fish specimens is 24.355 ppm. Fifty percent (or 72) of the specimens in the sample had DDT levels below 7.15 ppm. The DDT level that occurred most frequently in the sample was the mode, 12 ppm.

EXERCISES

2.19   Find the mean, median, and mode for each of the following data sets.
a. 4, 3, 10, 8, 5   **b.** 9, 6, 12, 4, 4, 2, 5, 6

2.20   Find and interpret the mean, median, and mode for the data set of spectral image exposures of asteroids in Exercise 2.10. Which is the preferred measure of central tendency? Explain.

FIGURE 2.12 ▶
SAS descriptive statistics for 144 DDT levels, Example 2.4

UNIVARIATE PROCEDURE

Variable=DDT

Moments

N	144	Sum Wgts	144
Mean	24.355	Sum	3507.12
Std Dev	98.37859	Variance	9678.346
Skewness	9.61166	Kurtosis	102.2388
USS	1469419	CSS	1384003
CV	403.9359	Std Mean	8.198215
T:Mean=0	2.970768	Prob>|T|	0.0035
Sgn Rank	5220	Prob>|S|	0.0001
Num ^= 0	144		
W:Normal	0.231228	Prob<W	0.0

Quantiles(Def=5)

100% Max	1100		99%	360
75% Q3	13		95%	61
50% Med	7.15		90%	28
25% Q1	3.35		10%	1.2
0% Min	0.11		5%	0.43
			1%	0.18
Range	1099.89			
Q3-Q1	9.65			
Mode	12			

Extremes

Lowest	Obs	Highest	Obs
0.11(	46)	140(	123)
0.18(	44)	150(	6)
0.22(	47)	180(	130)
0.25(	138)	360(	105)
0.3(	127)	1100(	115)

2.21 Refer to the Centers for Disease Control study of sanitation levels for 91 international cruise ships, Exercise 2.13. A MINITAB printout of the descriptive statistics for the data is shown here. (Recall that sanitation scores range from 0 to 100.) Interpret the numerical descriptive measures of central tendency displayed on the printout.

	N	MEAN	MEDIAN	TRMEAN	STDEV	SEMEAN
sanlevel	91	91.044	92.000	91.580	5.566	0.583

	MIN	MAX	Q1	Q3
sanlevel	66.000	99.000	89.000	95.000

2.22 Find and interpret the mean, median, and mode for each of the voltage readings data sets in Exercise 2.12. Which is the preferred measure of central tendency? Explain.

2.23 Find and interpret the mean, median, and mode for the oxon/thion ratio data set in Exercise 2.14. Which is the preferred measure of central tendency? Explain.

2.5   Measures of Variation

The most commonly used measures of data variation are the **range**, the **variance**, and the **standard deviation**.

Definition 2.8

The **range** is equal to the difference between the largest and the smallest measurements in a data set:

Range = Largest measurement − Smallest measurement

Definition 2.9

The **variance** of a **sample** of n measurements, $y_1, y_2, \ldots, y_n$, is defined to be

$$s^2 = \frac{\sum_{i=1}^{n}(y_i - \bar{y})^2}{n-1} = \frac{\sum_{i=1}^{n} y_i^2 - \frac{\left(\sum_{i=1}^{n} y_i\right)^2}{n}}{n-1}$$

The **population variance** is defined to be

$$\sigma^2 = \frac{\sum_{i=1}^{n}(y_i - \mu)^2}{n}$$

for a finite population with n measurements.

Definition 2.10

The **standard deviation** of a **sample** of n measurements is equal to the square root of the variance:

$$s = \sqrt{s^2} = \sqrt{\frac{\sum_{i=1}^{n}(y_i - \bar{y})^2}{n-1}}$$

The **population standard deviation** is $\sigma = \sqrt{\sigma^2}$.

EXAMPLE 2.5

Find the variance and standard deviation for the $n = 5$ sample observations: 1, 3, 2, 2, 4.

Solution

We must first calculate $\sum_{i=1}^{n} y_i$ and $\sum_{i=1}^{n} y_i^2$:

$$\sum_{i=1}^{n} y_i = 1 + 3 + 2 + 2 + 4 = 12 \qquad \sum_{i=1}^{n} y_i^2 = (1)^2 + (3)^2 + (2)^2 + (2)^2 + (4)^2 = 34$$

Then the sample variance is

$$s^2 = \frac{\sum_{i=1}^{n}(y_i - \bar{y})^2}{n-1} = \frac{\sum_{i=1}^{n} y_i^2 - \frac{\left(\sum_{i=1}^{n} y_i\right)^2}{n}}{n-1} = \frac{34 - \frac{(12)^2}{5}}{4} = 1.3$$

and the sample standard deviation is

$$s = \sqrt{s^2} = \sqrt{1.3} = 1.1402$$

It is possible that two different data sets could possess the same range but differ greatly in the amount of variation in the data. Consequently, the range is a relatively insensitive measure of data variation. It is used primarily in industrial quality control where the inferential procedures are based on small samples (i.e., small values of n). The variance has theoretical significance, but is difficult to interpret since the units of measurement on the variable y of interest are squared (e.g., feet^2, ppm^2, etc.). The units of measurement on the standard deviation, however, are the same as the units on y (e.g., feet, ppm). When combined with the mean of the data set, the standard deviation is easily interpreted. A useful rule of thumb is known as the **Empirical Rule**.

The Empirical Rule

If a data set has an approximately mound-shaped distribution, then the following rules of thumb may be used to describe the data set:

1. Approximately 68% of the measurements will lie within 1 standard deviation of their mean (i.e., within the interval $\bar{y} \pm s$ for samples and $\mu \pm \sigma$ for populations).

2. Approximately 95% of the measurements will lie within 2 standard deviations of their mean (i.e., within the interval $\bar{y} \pm 2s$ for samples and $\mu \pm 2\sigma$ for populations).

3. Almost all the measurements will lie within 3 standard deviations of their mean (i.e., within the interval $\bar{y} \pm 3s$ for samples and $\mu \pm 3\sigma$ for populations).

The Empirical Rule is the result of the practical experience of researchers in many fields who have observed many different types of real-life data sets. *

EXAMPLE 2.6   Refer to the data on 144 contaminated fish specimens in Appendix III. Another quantitative variable measured for each specimen is length (in centimeters). Use the Empirical Rule to describe the distribution of fish lengths.

Solution   Descriptive statistics for the sample of 144 fish lengths are displayed in the SAS printout, Figure 2.13. From the stem-and-leaf display shown at the bottom of the printout, you can see that the distribution of fish lengths is approximately mound-shaped; thus, we can apply the Empirical Rule. The mean,

$$\bar{y} = 42.81 \text{ cm}$$

and standard deviation,

$$s = 6.88 \text{ cm}$$

are shaded on the printout. Using these values, we form the intervals $\bar{y} \pm s$, $\bar{y} \pm 2s$, and $\bar{y} \pm 3s$. The proportions of the total number of measurements that we would expect to find in these intervals according to the Empirical Rule as well as the actual proportions are given in Table 2.5.

TABLE 2.5   Empirical Rule applied to fish length measurements in Appendix III

k	$\bar{y} \pm ks$	Expected Proportion of Measurements in the Interval	Actual Proportion of Measurements in the Interval
1	35.93–49.69	.68	.771
2	29.05–56.57	.95	.931
3	22.17–63.45	Almost 1.00	.993

You can see that, for each of the three intervals, the actual proportion of the $n = 144$ fish lengths that lie in the interval is very close to that specified by the Empirical Rule.

---

*Another rule, which applies to any and all data sets, is Tchebysheff's theorem. The theorem states that for $k \geq 1$, at least $(1 - 1/k^2)$ of a set of n measurements will lie within k standard deviations of their mean. (For example, at least $\frac{3}{4}$ will lie within the interval $\bar{y} \pm 2s$ and at least $\frac{8}{9}$ will lie within the interval $\bar{y} \pm 3s$.) The conservative nature of the theorem and the fact that many of the data sets encountered in engineering are approximately mound-shaped lead to the use of the Empirical Rule *in practice*.

FIGURE 2.13 ▶

SAS descriptive statistics for 144 fish lengths

UNIVARIATE PROCEDURE

Variable=LENGTH

Moments

N	144	Sum Wgts	144
Mean	42.8125	Sum	6165
Std Dev	6.882093	Variance	47.3632
Skewness	-1.30795	Kurtosis	1.483279
USS	270712	CSS	6772.938
CV	16.07496	Std Mean	0.573508
T:Mean=0	74.65026	Prob>$|T|$	0.0001
Sgn Rank	5220	Prob>$|S|$	0.0001
Num ^= 0	144		
W:Normal	0.877024	Prob<W	0.0

Quantiles(Def=5)

100% Max	52	99%	52
75% Q3	47.5	95%	51
50% Med	45	90%	49.5
25% Q1	40.5	10%	32.5
0% Min	17.5	5%	28
		1%	23
Range	34.5		
Q3-Q1	7		
Mode	46		

Extremes

Lowest	Obs	Highest	Obs
17.5(	143)	51.5(	104)
23(	47)	51.5(	123)
23.5(	140)	52(	6)
25(	46)	52(	24)
25.5(	45)	52(	33)

Stem	Leaf	#	Boxplot
52	000	3		
50	0005000055	10		
48	00000000005500000555	20		
46	000000000000555500000005555555	30	+-----+
44	00000055500000000055	20	*-----*
42	000555500055555	15	| + |
40	055550000055	12	+-----+
38	0005500	7		
36	0000000	7		
34	5005	4		
32	0555	4		
30	0	1		
28	0505	4	0
26	05	2	0
24	05	2	0
22	05	2	0
20			
18			
16	5	1	*

```
----+----+----+----+----+----+
```

Since many data sets encountered in engineering and the sciences are approximately mound-shaped, scientists often apply the Empirical Rule to estimate a range where most of the measurements fall. The interval $\bar{y} \pm 2s$ is typically selected since it captures about 95% of the data.

EXERCISES

2.24 Periodically, the Federal Trade Commission (FTC) ranks domestic cigarette brands according to tar, nicotine, and carbon monoxide content. The test results are obtained by using a sequential smoking machine to "smoke" cigarettes to a 23-millimeter butt length. The tar, nicotine, and carbon monoxide concentration (rounded to the nearest milligram) in the residual "dry" particulate matter of the smoke are then measured.

　　a. A SAS histogram of the tar contents of 372 cigarettes tested in 1991 is shown here.* Is the Empirical Rule useful for describing the distribution of tar contents?

▶

SAS histogram of tar contents for Exercise 2.24

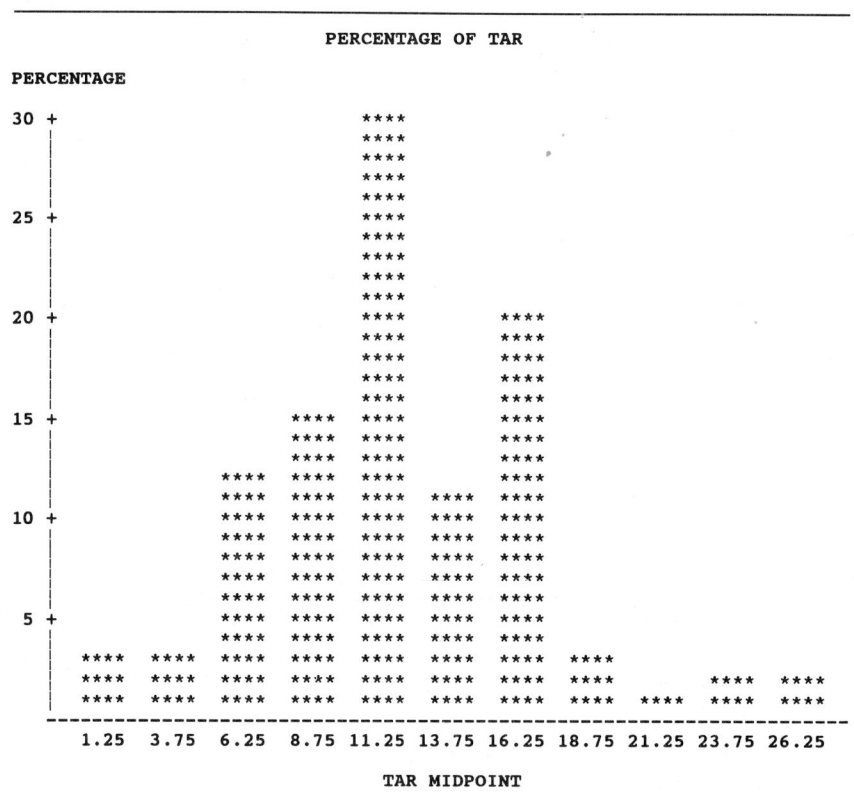

　　b. The mean and standard deviation of the 372 tar contents are 11.60 mg and 4.97 mg, respectively. Use this information to form an interval of 2 standard deviations around the mean.

　　c. Based on your answer to part **a**, estimate the percentage of cigarettes with tar contents in the interval formed in part **b**.

　　d. Use the information on the SAS histogram to determine the actual percentage of tar contents that fall within the interval formed in part **b**. Does your answer agree with your estimate of part **c**?

---

*Source: "Tar, nicotine, and carbon monoxide of the smoke of 475 varieties of domestic cigarettes."
Federal Trade Commission report, 1991.

2.25 Sixty-six bulk specimens of Chilean lumpy iron ore (95% particle size, 150 millimeters) were randomly sampled from a 35,325-long-ton shipload of ore, and the percentage of iron in each ore specimen was determined. The data are shown in the following table.

Ore Specimen	Percentage Iron	Ore Specimen	Percentage Iron	Ore Specimen	Percentage Iron
1	62.66	23	61.82	45	62.24
2	62.87	24	63.01	46	63.43
3	63.22	25	63.01	47	62.87
4	63.01	26	62.80	48	63.64
5	62.10	27	62.80	49	63.92
6	63.43	28	63.01	50	63.71
7	63.22	29	62.10	51	63.64
8	63.57	30	63.29	52	64.06
9	61.75	31	63.37	53	62.73
10	63.15	32	61.75	54	62.52
11	63.08	33	63.29	55	62.10
12	63.22	34	62.38	56	63.29
13	63.22	35	62.59	57	63.01
14	63.08	36	63.92	58	63.36
15	62.87	37	63.29	59	63.08
16	61.68	38	63.57	60	62.03
17	62.45	39	62.80	61	64.34
18	62.10	40	62.31	62	64.06
19	62.87	41	63.01	63	62.87
20	62.87	42	62.94	64	63.50
21	62.94	43	63.08	65	63.78
22	62.38	44	63.43	66	62.10

Source: Sato, T., Ito, K., Chujo, S., and Takahashi, U. "Example of experiments on systematic sampling of iron ore." *Reports of Statistical Application Research*, Union of Japanese Scientists and Engineers, Vol. 18, No. 1, 1971.

a. Describe the population from which the sample was selected.
b. Give one possible objective of this sampling procedure.
c. Construct a relative frequency histogram for the data.
d. Calculate $\bar{y}$ and s.
e. Find the percentage of the total number ($n = 66$) of observations that lie in the interval $\bar{y} \pm 2s$. Does this percentage agree with the Empirical Rule?

2.26 The means and standard deviations of the weight and DDT measurements for the data in Appendix III are shown in the accompanying table.

Variable	Mean	Standard Deviation
Weight (g)	1,049.72	376.55
DDT (ppm)	24.36	98.38

a. Use the information in the table, in conjunction with the Empirical Rule, to describe the relative frequency distributions of the measurements for the two variables.

b. Which of the two data sets is better described by the Empirical Rule?

2.27 The asteroid data of Exercise 2.10 are reproduced here, followed by a MINITAB printout giving descriptive statistics.

Number of Independent Spectral Image Exposures for 40 Asteroid Observations

3	4	3	3	1	4	1	3	2	3
1	1	4	2	3	3	2	6	1	1
3	3	2	2	2	2	1	3	2	1
6	1	3	2	2	1	2	2	4	2

Source: Binzel, R. P., and Xu, S. "Chips off of Asteroid 4 Vesta: Evidence for the parent body of basaltic achondrite meteorites." *Science*, Vol. 260, Apr. 3, 1993, p. 187 (Table 1).

▶
MINITAB printout for Exercise 2.27

	N	MEAN	MEDIAN	TRMEAN	STDEV	SEMEAN
EXPOSURE	40	2.425	2.000	2.306	1.259	0.199

	MIN	MAX	Q1	Q3
EXPOSURE	1.000	6.000	1.250	3.000

a. Locate $\bar{y}$ and s on the printout.
b. Construct the intervals $\bar{y} \pm s$, $\bar{y} \pm 2s$, and $\bar{y} \pm 3s$.
c. Count the number of observations that fall within each interval, and compare your results to the Empirical Rule.

2.28 Research has indicated that the inhabitants of some older cities in the United States may ingest small, but potentially harmful, amounts of lead introduced into their drinking water by the use of lead-lined pipes installed in some of the early city water systems. The data reported in the table are the mean lead, copper, and iron contents (milligrams per liter) for samples of water collected on each of 23 days from the Boston water system. The data were collected in 1977 after a sodium hydroxide water treatment system was installed. Each mean is based on approximately 40 measurements taken at different sites in the Boston water system where lead pipe was still being used.

Lead			Copper			Iron		
.035	.073	.030	.12	.07	.10	.20	.23	.17
.060	.047	.019	.18	.07	.04	.33	.18	.13
.055	.031	.021	.10	.08	.08	.22	.25	.15
.035	.016	.036	.07	.07	.05	.17	.14	.13
.031	.015	.016	.08	.04	.05	.15	.14	.14
.039	.015	.010	.09	.04	.04	.19	.12	.11
.038	.022	.020	.16	.05	.04	.17	.12	.11
.049	.043		.14	.07		.17	.16	

Source: Karalekas, P. C., Jr., Ryan, C. R., and Taylor, F. B. "Control of Lead, Copper, and Iron Pipe Corrosion in Boston." *Journal of the American Water Works Association*, Vol. 75, No. 2 (Feb. 1983), pp. 92–95. Reprinted by permission. Copyright © 1983, American Water Works Association.

a. Construct a relative frequency histogram for the 23 daily mean lead concentration measurements.
b. Calculate the mean and standard deviation for the sample of part **a**.

c. What percentage of the 23 daily mean lead concentrations lie in the interval $\bar{y} \pm 2s$?

d. Repeat parts **a–c**, using the copper concentration means.

e. Repeat parts **a–c**, using the iron concentration means.

2.29 Refer to the data on process voltage readings at two locations, Exercise 2.12. Descriptive statistics for both sample data sets are provided in the accompanying SAS printout. Use the Empirical Rule to compare the voltage reading distributions for the two locations.

▶

SAS printout for Exercise 2.29

```
          Analysis Variable : VOLTAGE


-------------------------------- LOCATION=NEW --------------------------------

 N Obs   N      Minimum       Maximum          Mean       Std Dev
 -----------------------------------------------------------------
    30   30    8.5100000    10.1200000     9.4223333     0.4788757
 -----------------------------------------------------------------


-------------------------------- LOCATION=OLD --------------------------------

 N Obs   N      Minimum       Maximum          Mean       Std Dev
 -----------------------------------------------------------------
    30   30    8.0500000    10.5500000     9.8036667     0.5409155
 -----------------------------------------------------------------


------------------------------- LOCATION=NEW --------------------------------
                          UNIVARIATE PROCEDURE

Variable=VOLTAGE

                                Moments

          N                  30    Sum Wgts          30
          Mean         9.422333    Sum           282.67
          Std Dev      0.478876    Variance    0.229322
          Skewness     -0.26699    Kurtosis    -0.89134
          USS          2670.061    CSS         6.650337
          CV           5.082347    Std Mean    0.08743
          T:Mean=0     107.7696    Prob>|T|      0.0001
          Sgn Rank        232.5    Prob>|S|      0.0001
          Num ^= 0           30


                            Quantiles(Def=5)

          100% Max      10.12       99%        10.12
          75%  Q3        9.75       95%         10.1
          50%  Med      9.455       90%        10.07
          25%  Q1        9.14       10%         8.73
          0%   Min       8.51        5%         8.65
                                     1%         8.51
          Range         1.61
          Q3-Q1         0.61
          Mode          8.82


                               Extremes

          Lowest    Obs      Highest    Obs
           8.51(    23)       10.03(    14)
           8.65(    22)       10.05(     7)
           8.68(    30)       10.09(     5)
           8.78(    26)        10.1(     3)
           8.82(    21)       10.12(     8)
```

(continued)

▶

SAS printout for Exercise 2.29
(continued)

```
------------------------------ LOCATION=OLD ------------------------------

                              UNIVARIATE PROCEDURE

Variable=VOLTAGE
                                    Moments

          N              30    Sum Wgts            30
          Mean     9.803667    Sum             294.11
          Std Dev  0.540915    Variance       0.29259
          Skewness -1.87787    Kurtosis      3.473528
          USS      2891.841    CSS           8.485097
          CV       5.517481    Std Mean      0.098757
          T:Mean=0 99.2704     Prob>|T|        0.0001
          Sgn Rank    232.5    Prob>|S|        0.0001
          Num ^= 0       30

                              Quantiles(Def=5)

          100% Max     10.55    99%      10.55
          75% Q3       10.05    95%      10.29
          50% Med      9.975    90%      10.26
          25% Q1         9.8    10%       8.76
          0% Min       8.05     5%       8.72
                                1%       8.05

          Range          2.5
          Q3-Q1         0.25
          Mode          8.72

                                 Extremes

          Lowest     Obs      Highest     Obs
          8.05(       6)      10.15(      22)
          8.72(      28)      10.26(       2)
          8.72(      20)      10.26(       8)
           8.8(      29)      10.29(       4)
          9.55(      17)      10.55(       7)
```

2.30 Refer to the *Journal of Performance of Constructed Facilities* (Feb. 1990) study of water distribution networks, Exercise 1.8. The internal pressure readings (measured in pounds per square inch, psi) for a sample of pipe sections had a mean of 7.99 psi and a standard deviation of 2.02 psi.
a. Use this information to construct an interval that captures about 95% of the pressure readings sampled.
b. Would you expect to observe an internal pressure reading of 20 psi? Explain.

2.31 The data on oxon/thion ratios from Exercise 2.14 are reproduced here. Use the Empirical Rule to describe the sample data.

Date	Condition	Thion	Oxon	Oxon/Thion Ratio
Jan. 15	Fog	38.2	10.3	.270
17	Fog	28.6	6.9	.241
18	Fog	30.2	6.2	.205
19	Fog	23.7	12.4	.523
20	Fog	62.3	(Air sample lost)	—
20	Clear	74.1	45.8	.618
21	Fog	88.2	9.9	.112
21	Clear	46.4	27.4	.591
22	Fog	135.9	44.8	.330

(continued)

Date	Condition	Thion	Oxon	Oxon/Thion Ratio
23	Fog	102.9	27.8	.270
23	Cloud	28.9	6.5	.225
25	Fog	46.9	11.2	.239
25	Clear	44.3	16.6	.375

Source: Selber, J. N., et al. "Air and fog deposition residues of four organophosphate insecticides used on dormant orchards in the San Joaquin Valley, California." *Environmental Science & Technology*, Vol. 27, No. 10, Oct. 1993, p. 2240 (Table V).

2.6 Measures of Relative Standing

Test scores and some types of sociological and health data are often reported in a manner that describes the location of an observation *relative* to the other scores in the distribution. Two measures of the relative standing of an observation are **percentiles** and **z-scores**.

Definition 2.11

The **100pth percentile** of a data set is a value of y located so that $100p\%$ of the area under the relative frequency distribution for the data lies to the left of the $100p$th percentile and $100(1 - p)\%$ of the area lies to its right. [*Note:* $0 \leq p \leq 1$.]

For example, if your grade in an industrial engineering class was located at the 84th percentile, then 84% of the grades were lower than your grade and 16% were higher.

The median is the 50th percentile. The 25th percentile, the median, and the 75th percentile are called the **lower quartile**, the **midquartile**, and the **upper quartile**, respectively, for a data set.

Definition 2.12

The **lower quartile**, Q_L, for a data set is the 25th percentile.

Definition 2.13

The **midquartile** (or median), m, for a data set is the 50th percentile.

Definition 2.14

The **upper quartile**, Q_U, for a data set is the 75th percentile.

For large data sets (e.g., populations), quartiles are found by locating the corresponding areas under the curve (relative frequency distribution). However, when the data set of interest is small, it may be impossible to find a measurement in the data set that exceeds, say, *exactly* 25% of the remaining measurements. Consequently, the 25th percentile (or lower quartile) for the data set is not well defined. The following box contains a few rules for finding quartiles and other percentiles with small data sets.

Finding Quartiles (and Percentiles) with Small Data Sets

STEP 1 Rank the measurements in the data set in increasing order of magnitude. Let $y_{(1)}, y_{(2)}, \ldots, y_{(n)}$ represent the ranked measurements.

STEP 2 Calculate the quantity $\ell = \frac{1}{4}(n + 1)$ and round to the nearest integer. The measurement with this rank, denoted $y_{(\ell)}$, represents the *lower quartile* or 25th percentile. [*Note:* If $\ell = \frac{1}{4}(n + 1)$ falls halfway between two integers, round up.]

STEP 3 Calculate the quantity $u = \frac{3}{4}(n + 1)$ and round to the nearest integer. The measurement with this rank, denoted $y_{(u)}$, represents the *upper quartile* or 75th percentile. [*Note:* If $u = \frac{3}{4}(n + 1)$ falls halfway between two integers, round down.]

GENERAL To find the pth percentile, calculate the quantity $i = p(n + 1)/100$ and round to the nearest integer. The measurement with this rank, denoted $y_{(i)}$, is the pth percentile.

EXAMPLE 2.7

Find the lower quartile for the 25 CPU times given in Table 2.3.

Solution

From the box, the lower quartile Q_L is the observation $y_{(\ell)}$ when the data are arranged in increasing order, where $\ell = \frac{1}{4}(n + 1)$. Since $n = 25$,

$$\ell = \frac{1}{4}(n + 1) = \frac{1}{4}(26) = 6.5$$

Rounding up, we obtain $\ell = 7$. Thus, the lower quartile, Q_L, will be the 7th observation when the data are arranged in order from smallest to largest, i.e., $Q_L = y_{(7)}$. For small data sets, a stem-and-leaf display is useful for finding quartiles and percentiles. The stem-and-leaf display for the 25 CPU times is reproduced in Figure 2.14. You can see that the seventh observation is the seventh leaf in stem row 0. This CPU value (circled in Figure 2.14) is $Q_L = .82$.

FIGURE 2.14 ▶
Stem-and-leaf display for $n = 25$
CPU times in Example 2.7

Stems	Leaves
0	02 15 19 47 71 75 ⟨82⟩ 92 96
1	16 17 23 38 40 59 61 94
2	01 16 41 59
3	07 53 76
4	75

Another useful measure of relative standing is a **z-score**. By definition, a z-score describes the location of an observation y relative to the mean in units of the standard deviation. Negative z-scores indicate that the observation lies to the left of the mean; positive z-scores indicate that the observation lies to the right of the mean. Also, we know from the Empirical Rule that most of the observations in a data set will be less than 2 standard deviations from the mean (i.e., will have z-scores less than 2 in absolute value) and almost all will be within 3 standard deviations of the mean (i.e., will have z-scores less than 3 in absolute value).

Definition 2.15

The **z-score** for a value y of a data set is the distance that y lies above or below the mean, measured in units of the standard deviation:

$$\text{Sample z-score:} \quad z = \frac{y - \bar{y}}{s}$$

$$\text{Population z-score:} \quad z = \frac{y - \mu}{\sigma}$$

EXAMPLE 2.8

Refer to the sample of $n = 25$ CPU times given in Table 2.3. Find and interpret the z-score for the CPU time of 3.76 seconds.

Solution

Figure 2.15 (page 56) is a MINITAB printout of descriptive statistics for the 25 CPU times. The mean and standard deviation of the sample, shaded in Figure 2.15, are $\bar{y} = 1.63$ and $s = 1.19$. Substituting $y = 3.76$ into the formula for z, we obtain

$$z = \frac{y - \bar{y}}{s} = \frac{3.76 - 1.63}{1.19} = 1.79$$

Since the z-score is positive, we conclude that the CPU time of 3.76 seconds lies a distance of 1.79 standard deviations above (to the right of) the sample mean of 1.63 seconds.

FIGURE 2.15 ▶
MINITAB descriptive statistics for
25 CPU times

	N	MEAN	MEDIAN	TRMEAN	STDEV	SEMEAN
CPU	25	1.630	1.380	1.564	1.193	0.239

	MIN	MAX	Q1	Q3		
CPU	0.020	4.750	0.785	2.285		

EXERCISES

2.32   Refer to the asteroid data given in Exercises 2.10 and 2.27.
  a. Find the lower and upper quartiles for the data set. Interpret these values.
  b. Find the z-score for an asteroid observation with 6 independent spectral image exposures. Interpret this value.

2.33   *Environmental Science & Technology* (Oct. 1993) reported on a study of contaminated soil in The Netherlands. A total of 72 400-gram soil specimens were sampled, dried, and analyzed for the contaminant cyanide. The cyanide concentration (milligrams per kilogram of soil) of each soil specimen was determined using an infrared microscopic method. The cyanide concentration levels are summarized in the accompanying table. Fully interpret the descriptive statistics shown in the table.

Summary Statistics for Cyanide Levels in Soil (mg/kg)

Sample size	72
Mean	84.0
Variance	6,400
Median	28.8
Lower quartile	13.8
Upper quartile	88.5
Minimum	2.0
Maximum	3,320.0

Source: Lamé, F. P. J., and Defize, P. R. "Sampling of contaminated soil: Sampling error in relation to sample size and segregation." *Environmental Science & Technology*, Vol. 27, No. 10, Oct. 1993, p. 2039 (Table II).

2.34   Refer to the data on percentage of iron to Chilean lumpy iron ore, Exercise 2.25. Find the 25th, 50th, 75th, and 90th percentiles for the data set. Interpret these values.

2.35   The relative frequency distribution of the 144 sample DDT measurements (ppm) (Appendix III) is summarized by the following numerical descriptive measures:

$$\bar{y} = 24.36 \qquad s = 98.38 \qquad m = 7.15$$

  a. Find the 50th percentile for the sample DDT measurements.
  b. Use Tchebysheff's theorem to find an upper bound for the 75th percentile of the sample of DDT measurements. (See footnote on page 46.)

2.36 A simulation study was conducted to investigate the rounding accuracies of several new algorithms for functions in the FORTRAN computer program library (*IBM Journal of Research and Development*, Mar. 1986). For each new FORTRAN function, the rounding error for each of 10,000 trials was calculated.
  a. The 99th percentile of the rounding errors for one particular FORTRAN function was found to be .53. Interpret this value.
  b. For the FORTRAN function of part **a**, the mean rounding error is $\bar{y} = .22$ and the standard deviation (estimated) is $s = .07$. Use this information to calculate the z-score for the 99th percentile value of .53. Interpret the z-score.

2.37 Refer to the Harris Corporation study on voltage readings at two locations, Exercise 2.12 and 2.29.
  a. Calculate the z-score for a voltage reading of 10.50 at the old location.
  b. Calculate the z-score for a voltage reading of 10.50 at the new location.
  c. Based on the results of parts **a** and **b**, at which location is a voltage reading of 10.50 more likely to occur? Explain.

2.38 Refer to the data on the top 25 graduate schools of engineering, Exercise 2.18. Descriptive statistics for the acceptance rate are shown in the accompanying MINITAB printout.

▶
MINITAB printout for Exercise 2.38

	N	MEAN	MEDIAN	TRMEAN	STDEV	SEMEAN
ACCRATE	25	36.66	38.10	36.39	14.80	2.96

	MIN	MAX	Q1	Q3
ACCRATE	12.40	67.10	25.35	47.30

  a. Locate the measures of relative standing on the printout, and interpret their values.
  b. Calculate a measure of relative standing for California Institute of Technology's acceptance rate of 12.4%. Interpret this value.

2.7 Methods for Detecting Outliers

Sometimes inconsistent observations are included in a data set. For example, when we discuss starting salaries for college graduates with bachelor's degrees, we generally think of traditional college graduates—those near 22 years of age with 4 years of college education. But suppose one of the graduates is a 34-year-old Ph.D. chemical engineer who has returned to the university to obtain a bachelor's degree in metallurgy. Clearly, the starting salary for this graduate could be much larger than the other starting salaries because of the graduate's additional education and experience, and we probably would not want to include it in the data set. Such an errant observation, which lies outside the range of the data values that we want to describe, is called an **outlier**.

> ### Definition 2.16
>
> An observation y that is unusually large or small relative to the other values in a data set is called an **outlier**. Outliers typically are attributable to one of the following causes:
>
> 1. The measurement is observed, recorded, or entered into the computer incorrectly.
> 2. The measurement comes from a different population.
> 3. The measurement is correct, but represents a rare (chance) event.

The most obvious method for determining whether an observation is an outlier is to calculate its z-score (Section 2.6).

EXAMPLE 2.9

Refer to the data on DDT levels of contaminated fish specimens, Appendix III. The fish specimen identified by observation 115 has a DDT measurement of 1,100 ppm. Is this observation an outlier?

Solution

In Example 2.4, descriptive statistics for the DDT levels were displayed in a SAS printout. A portion of the printout is reproduced in Figure 2.16. The mean and standard deviation of the DDT levels, shaded on the printout, are $\bar{y} = 24.36$ and $s = 98.38$ ppm, respectively. Therefore, the z-score for the DDT measurement of fish specimen 115 is

$$z = \frac{y - \bar{y}}{s} = \frac{1,100 - 24.36}{98.38} = 10.93$$

FIGURE 2.16 ►
SAS descriptive statistics for 144 DDT levels

UNIVARIATE PROCEDURE

Variable=DDT

Moments

N	144	Sum Wgts	144
Mean	24.355	Sum	3507.12
Std Dev	98.37859	Variance	9678.346
Skewness	9.61166	Kurtosis	102.2388
USS	1469419	CSS	1384003
CV	403.9359	Std Mean	8.198215
T:Mean=0	2.970768	Prob>|T|	0.0035
Sgn Rank	5220	Prob>|S|	0.0001
Num ^= 0	144		
W:Normal	0.231228	Prob<W	0.0

The Empirical Rule (Section 2.5) states that almost all the observations in a data set will have z-scores less than 3 in absolute value. Since a z-score as large as 10.93 is highly improbable, the DDT measurement of 1,100 ppm is called an *outlier*. Some research by the U.S. Army Corps of Engineers revealed that the DDT value for this fish specimen was correctly recorded, but that the fish was one of the few found at the exact location where the manufacturing plant was discharging its toxic waste materials into the river.

Another procedure for detecting outliers is to construct a **box plot** of the sample data. With this method, we construct intervals similar to the $\bar{y} \pm 2s$ and $\bar{y} \pm 3s$ intervals of the Empirical Rule; however, the intervals are based on a quantity called the **interquartile range** instead of the standard deviation s.

Definition 2.17

The **interquartile range**, IQR, is the distance between the upper and lower quartiles:

$$IQR = Q_U - Q_L$$

The procedure is especially easy to use for small data sets because the quartiles and interquartile range can be quickly determined. The steps to follow in constructing a box plot are given in the box.

Steps to Follow in Constructing a Box Plot

1. Calculate the median, m, lower and upper quartiles, Q_L and Q_U, and the interquartile range, IQR, for the y values in a data set.

2. Construct a box on the y-axis with Q_L and Q_U located at the lower corners (see Figure 2.17 on page 60). The base width will then be equal to the IQR. Draw a vertical line inside the box to locate the median, m.

3. Construct two sets of limits on the box plot. **Inner fences** are located a distance of $1.5(IQR)$ below Q_L and above Q_U; **outer fences** are located a distance of $3(IQR)$ below Q_L and above Q_U (see Figure 2.17).

4. Observations that fall between the inner and outer fences are called **suspect outliers**. Locate the suspect outliers on the box plot using asterisks (*). Observations that fall outside the outer fences are called **highly suspect outliers**. Use small circles (○) to locate highly suspect outliers.

5. To further highlight extreme values, **whiskers** are added to the box plot. Mark the y value in the region between Q_L and the lower inner fence that is closest to the inner fence with an ×, and join the × to the box with a dashed line— a whisker (see Figure 2.17). Similarly, use an × and attached whisker to locate the most extreme value between Q_U and the upper inner fence.

FIGURE 2.17 ▶
Box plot for the $n = 25$ CPU
times of Table 2.3

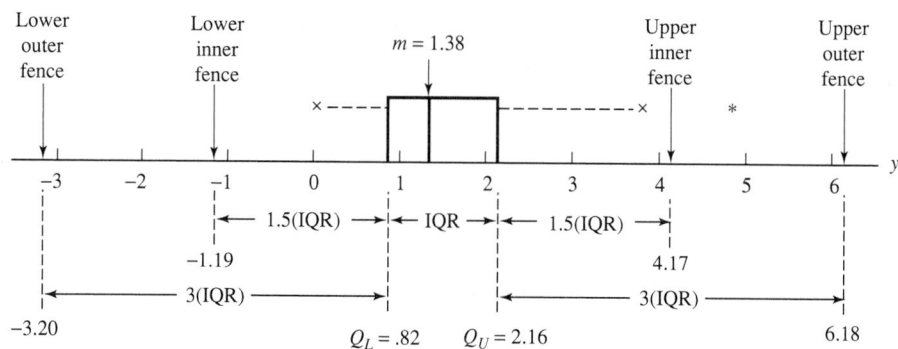

A box plot for the 25 CPU times in Table 2.3 is shown in Figure 2.17. From the plot you can see that $Q_L = .82$, $m = 1.38$, $Q_U = 2.16$, and

$$IQR = Q_U - Q_L = 2.16 - .82 = 1.34$$

The inner and outer fences are located a distance of $1.5(IQR) = 1.5(1.34) = 2.01$ and $3(IQR) = 3(1.34) = 4.02$ below Q_L and above Q_U, respectively. Note that the data set contains only one suspect outlier, indicated by the asterisk between the upper inner and outer fences. This is the CPU time of 4.75—the largest value in the data set.

EXAMPLE 2.10

Refer to the data on length (in centimeters) of contaminated fish species, Appendix III. Construct and interpret a box plot for the 144 fish lengths.

Solution

For large data sets, box plots can be constructed using a computer. A MINITAB box plot for the fish length data is displayed in Figure 2.18. The lower and upper quartiles, Q_L and Q_U, are indicated in the MINITAB box plot with the symbol I (called a **hinge**). These are (approximately), $Q_L = 40$ and $Q_U = 47$. The plus (+) symbol in the box locates the median, $m = 45$. Figure 2.18 shows that the data set contains several suspect outliers (indicated by asterisks) and one highly suspect outlier (indicated by a circle). The highly suspect outlier has a length of about 17 cm.

FIGURE 2.18 ▶
MINITAB box plot for 144 fish
lengths

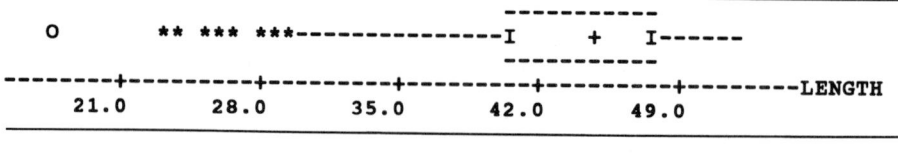

The z-score and box plot methods both establish rule-of-thumb limits outside of which a y value is deemed to be an outlier. Usually the two methods produce similar results. However, the presence of one or more outliers in a data set can inflate the value of s used to calculate the z-score. Consequently, it will be less likely that an errant observation would have a z-score larger than 3 in absolute value. In contrast, the values of the quartiles used to calculate the fences for a box plot are not affected by the presence of outliers.

Rule of Thumb for Detecting Outliers

1. **z-scores:** Observations with z-scores greater than 3 in absolute value are considered **outliers**.
2. **Box plots:** Observations falling between the inner and outer fences are deemed **suspect outliers**. Observations falling beyond the outer fences are deemed **highly suspect outliers**.

EXERCISES

2.39   Refer to the asteroid data given in Exercises 2.10 and 2.27.
  a. Construct a box plot for the data. Do you detect any outliers?
  b. Use the method of z-scores to detect outliers.

2.40   Refer to the voltage reading data supplied in Exercise 2.12.
  a. Construct a box plot for the data at the old location. Do you detect any outliers?
  b. Use the method of z-scores to detect outliers at the old location.
  c. Construct a box plot for the data at the new location. Do you detect any outliers?
  d. Use the method of z-scores to detect outliers at the new location.
  e. Compare the distributions of voltage readings at the two locations by placing the box plots, parts **a** and **c**, side by side vertically.

2.41   The data on TCDD levels in plasma of Vietnam veterans, Exercise 2.16, are reproduced here. Use the methods of this section to check for outliers in the data set.

TCDD Levels in Plasma

2.5	3.1	2.1	3.5	3.1	1.8	6.8	3.0	36.0	4.7
6.9	3.3	4.6	1.6	7.2	1.8	20.0	2.0	2.5	4.1

Source: Schecter, A., et al. "Partitioning of 2,3,7,8-chlorinated dibenzo-*p*-dioxins and dibenzofurans between adipose tissue and plasma lipid of 20 Massachusetts Vietnam veterans." *Chemosphere*, Vol. 20, Nos. 7–9, 1990, pp. 954–955 (Table 1).

2.42   Refer to the lead concentration data of Exercise 2.28.
  a. Construct a box plot for the data. Do you detect any outliers?
  b. Use the method of z-scores to detect outliers.

2.43   Refer to the 144 fish weight measurements in Appendix III.
  a. Construct a box plot for the data. Do you detect any outliers?
  b. Use the method of z-scores to detect outliers.

2.8 Summary

Data sets can be described using either **graphical** or **numerical methods**. **Pie charts, bar graphs**, and **Pareto diagrams** are used to describe **qualitative** data graphically. **Summary frequency tables** are commonly used to describe qualitative data numerically.

Quantitative data sets are graphically described using **dot plots, relative frequency histograms**, or **stem-and-leaf displays**. Numerical descriptive measures are numbers that enable us to create a mental image of these graphical descriptions. For example, in conjunction with the **Empirical Rule**, the **mean** and **standard deviation** of a data set enable us to visualize both the approximate location and spread of the relative frequency distribution for the data set. **Percentiles** and **z-scores** are numbers that measure the relative standing of a value within a data set. Errant observations or highly unusual values, called **outliers**, can be detected using either z-scores or **box plots**.

As you will subsequently see, we will employ sample numerical descriptive measures—**statistics**—to make inferences about the values of their population equivalents—the **parameters** of a population relative frequency distribution. The most important contribution of statistics is that our methodology will enable us to assess the uncertainty associated with an inference and, thereby, to evaluate its reliability.

In Chapter 3, we will turn to a study of probability, the vehicle that is used both in making inferences and in evaluating their reliabilities. Subsequent chapters will show how probability is used in statistical inference and will present some useful statistical methods.

SUPPLEMENTARY EXERCISES

2.44 Shore-based marine traffic systems have been proposed to improve the safety and efficiency of marine traffic. Prior to the installation of the traffic system, one study was conducted to assess the current level of risk of collision to vessels operating in European waters. Data on large-vessel collisions over the 5-year period 1978–1982 are presented in the table.

Collisions by Location		Collisions at Sea by Encounter Aspect	
Location	Number of Ships	Aspect	Number of Ships
At sea	376	Meeting	131
Restricted waters	273	Overtaking	29
In port	478	Crossing	73
TOTAL	1,127	Unknown	143
		TOTAL	376

Source: Kemp, J. F. and Goodwin, E. M. "Risk analysis within the Cost 301 Project." *The Dock and Harbour Authority*, Vol. 66, No. 775, Dec./Jan. 1985–1986.

a. Construct a bar graph for the locations of large-vessel collisions in European waters. Interpret the graph.

b. Construct a bar graph for the encounter aspects of large-vessel collisions at sea in European waters. Interpret the graph.

2.45 Refer to the *Chemosphere* (Feb. 1986) study to obtain information on the background levels of the toxic substance polychlorinated biphenyl (PCB) in soil samples in the United Kingdom, Exercise 1.10. Such information is used as a benchmark against which PCB levels at waste disposal facilities in the United Kingdom can be compared. The accompanying table contains the measured PCB levels of soil samples taken at 14 rural and 15 urban locations in the United Kingdom. (PCB concentration is measured in .0001 gram per kilogram of soil.) From these preliminary results, the researchers reported "a significant difference between (the PCB levels) for rural areas . . . and for urban areas."

Rural				Urban			
3.5	1.0	1.6	12.0	24.0	11.0	107.0	18.0
8.1	5.3	23.0	8.2	29.0	49.0	94.0	12.0
1.8	9.8	1.5	9.7	16.0	22.0	141.0	18.0
9.0	15.0			21.0	13.0	11.0	

Source: Badsha, K., and Eduljee, G. "PCB in the U.K. environment—A preliminary survey." *Chemosphere*, Vol. 15, No. 2, Feb. 1986, p. 213 (Table 1). Reprinted with permission. Copyright 1986, Pergamon Press, Ltd.

a. Construct a stem-and-leaf display for the PCB levels of rural soil samples.

b. Construct a stem-and-leaf display for the PCB levels of urban soil samples.

c. Combine the data for rural and urban soil samples and construct a stem-and-leaf display. Identify each of the urban PCB levels on the display with a circle. Does the graph support the researchers' conclusions?

2.46 Researchers at Northeastern University conducted a survey of U.S. residents "in an attempt to gauge their opinions concerning existing and proposed automobile safety standards" (*Transportation Journal*, Summer 1986). The following are results for the question "Would you purchase an optional automobile safety airbag at a price of $500 or $1,000?" Use an appropriate graphical method to summarize the results.

Response	Purchase Air Bag at	
	$500	$1,000
Definitely would	16%	5%
Probably would	17%	12%
Not Sure	18%	17%
Probably would not	21%	22%
Definitely would not	28%	44%
Number of responses	380	365

Source: Lieb, R. C., Wiseman, F., and Moore, T. E. "Automobile safety programs: The public viewpoint." *Transportation Journal*, Vol. 25, No. 4, Summer 1986, pp. 22–30. Permission to reprint the material for educational purposes has been granted by the American Society of Transportation and Logistics, publisher of the *Transportation Journal*.

2.47 *Scram* is the term used by nuclear engineers to describe a rapid emergency shutdown of a nuclear reactor. The nuclear industry has made a concerted effort to significantly reduce the number of unplanned scrams.

The accompanying table gives the number of scrams at each of 56 U.S. nuclear reactor units in a recent year. A MINITAB printout showing both a graphical and numerical description of the data is provided.

Number of Scrams

1	0	3	1	4	2	10	6	5	2	0	3	1	5
4	2	7	12	0	3	8	2	0	9	3	3	4	7
2	4	5	3	2	7	13	4	2	3	3	7	0	9
4	3	5	2	7	8	5	2	4	3	4	0	1	7

▶

Minitab printout for Exercise 2.47

```
Stem-and-leaf of SCRAMS     N = 56
Leaf Unit = 0.10

    6    0 000000
   10    1 0000
   19    2 000000000
  (10)   3 0000000000
   27    4 00000000
   19    5 00000
   14    6 0
   13    7 000000
    7    8 00
    5    9 00
    3   10 0
    2   11
    2   12 0
    1   13 0
```

```
                    ------------------
           --------I    +            I-------------------        *    *
                    ------------------
            +---------+---------+---------+---------+---------+------SCRAMS
          0.0       2.5       5.0       7.5      10.0      12.5
```

	N	MEAN	MEDIAN	TRMEAN	STDEV	SEMEAN
SCRAMS	56	4.036	3.000	3.820	3.027	0.404

	MIN	MAX	Q1	Q3
SCRAMS	0.000	13.000	2.000	5.750

a. Fully interpret the results.

b. Would you expect to observe a nuclear reactor in the future with 11 unplanned scrams? Explain.

2.48 Industrial engineers periodically conduct "work measurement" analyses to determine the time required to produce a single unit of output. At a large processing plant, the number of total worker-hours required per day to perform a certain task was recorded for 50 days. The data are shown here.

128	119	95	97	124	128	142	98	108	120
113	109	124	132	97	138	133	136	120	112
146	128	103	135	114	109	100	111	131	113
124	131	133	131	88	118	116	98	112	138
100	112	111	150	117	122	97	116	92	122

a. Compute the mean, median, and mode of the data set.

b. Find the range, variance, and standard deviation of the data set.

c. Construct the intervals $\bar{y} \pm s$, $\bar{y} \pm 2s$, and $\bar{y} \pm 3s$. Count the number of observations that fall within each interval and find the corresponding proportions. Compare the results to the Empirical Rule. Do you detect any outliers?

d. Construct a box plot for the data. Do you detect any outliers?

e. Find the 70th percentile for the data on total daily worker-hours. Interpret its value.

2.49 A marketing research study of consulting engineering services to industrial firms in the Midwest was recently conducted. The main goal of the study was to gather information that will enable consulting engineers to effectively market their services to industrial firms. Of the 70 firms surveyed, 40 indicated that they have no need for outside consulting engineering services. The accompanying table gives the primary reasons cited by the "nonneeders" and corresponding breakdown in percentages for both the large and small industrial firms in the survey.

Reason	Large Firms	Small Firms
Assistance obtained from corporate headquarters	62%	30%
No wastes, therefore, no need to improve	0	32
No improvements planned	0	24
Assistance obtained from staff engineers	19	6
Unfamiliar with consulting	10	2
Waiting for regulations	9	0
Other reasons	0	6
TOTALS	100%	100%

Source: Carey, R. J., and Brunner, J. A. "A study of marketing of consulting engineering services to industrial firms." *Journal of the Boston Society of Civil Engineers Section*, American Society of Civil Engineers, Vol. 71, Nos. 1 and 2, 1985, p. 152.

a. Construct a pie chart that describes the reasons cited for not needing consulting engineering services at large industrial firms.

b. Repeat part **a** for small industrial firms.

c. Compare the two pie charts in parts **a** and **b**. Do you detect major differences in the reasons cited by large and small firms?

2.50 The nuclear mishap on Three Mile Island near Harrisburg, Pennsylvania, on March 28, 1979, forced many local residents to evacuate their homes—some temporarily, others permanently. To assess the impact of the accident on the area population, a questionnaire was designed and mailed to a sample of 150 households within 2 weeks after the accident occurred. Two questions asked of the sampled residents were: (1) When did you learn about the accident? and (2) How did you learn about the accident? The responses to the two questions are illustrated in the frequency distributions shown at the top of page 66. Based on these graphical descriptions, find each of the following:

a. The percentage of the 150 respondents who learned about the accident on Wednesday afternoon

b. The percentage of the 150 respondents who learned about the accident on Friday

c. The percentage of the 150 respondents who learned about the accident from a radio report

d. The percentage of the 150 respondents who learned about the accident from television

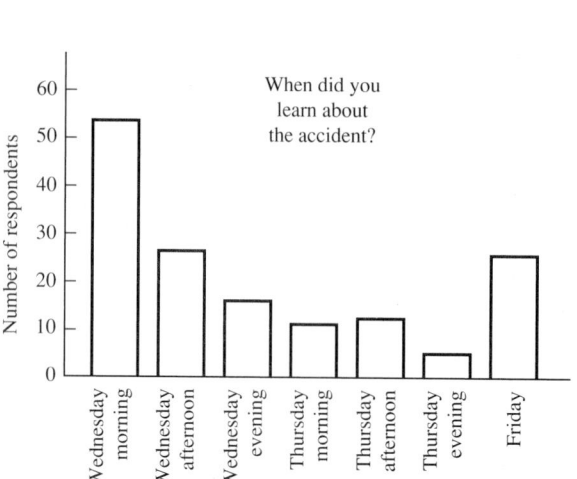

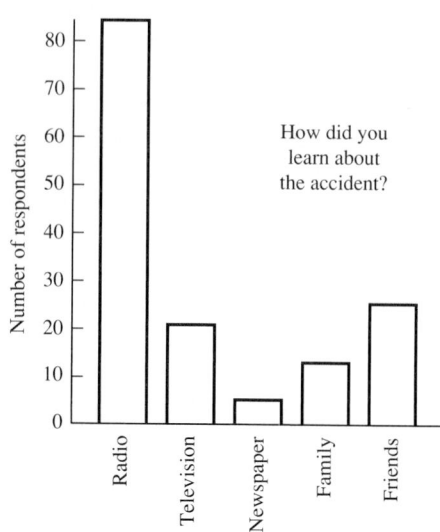

Source: Brown, S., et al. "Final Report on a Survey of Three Mile Island Area Residents." Department of Geography, Michigan State University, Aug. 1979.

2.51 The National Research Council's Committee on Underground Coal Mine Safety was established to determine "the factors that distinguish the safest from the most dangerous mines." To evaluate differences between the safest and most dangerous mines, the committee collected data on 19 of the largest underground coal companies. The "intermediate injury" rate (i.e., the number of disabling injuries resulting from falls of roof and sides, haulage, machinery, and explosive accidents per 200,000 worker hours) for each of the 19 companies is recorded in the table. Construct a stem-and-leaf display for the data. Interpret the results.

Company	Injury Rate	Company	Injury Rate
Old Ben	2.72	American Electric Power	5.11
Bethlehem	2.89	Rochester & Pittsburgh	5.12
Island Creek	2.97	Pittston	5.39
Consolidation	2.98	Ziegler	6.19
Mapco	3.17	Freeman United	6.83
U.S. Steel	3.58	Republic	6.84
Alabama By-Product	3.88	North American	7.47
Eastern Assoc.	4.66	West Moreland	7.68
Peabody	4.81	Valley Camp	8.71
Jones & Laughlin	4.87		

Source: Spokes, E. M. "New look at underground coal mine safety." *Mining Engineering*, Vol. 38, No. 4, Apr. 1986, p. 267 (Table 1).

2.52 Engineers have a term for unaided human acts of lifting, lowering, pushing, pulling, carrying, or holding and releasing an object—*manual materials handling activities* (*MMHA*). M. M. Ayoub et al. (1980) have attempted to develop strength and capacity guidelines for MMHA. The authors point out that a clear distinction between strength and capacity must be made: "Strength implies what a person can do in a single attempt, whereas capacity implies what a person can do for an extended period of time. Lifting strength, for example, determines the amount that can be lifted at frequent intervals." The accompanying table presents a portion of the recommendations of Ayoub et al. for the lifting capacities of males and females. It gives the means and standard deviations of the maximum weight (in kilograms) of a box 30 centimeters wide that can be safely lifted from the floor to knuckle height at two different lift rates—1 lift per minute and 4 lifts per minute.

Gender	Lifts/Minute	Mean	Standard Deviation
Male	1	30.25	8.56
	4	23.83	6.70
Female	1	19.79	3.11
	4	15.82	3.23

Source: Ayoub, M. M., Mital, A., Bakken, G. M., Asfour, S. S., and Bethea, N. J. "Development of strength capacity norms for manual materials handling activities: The state of the art." *Human Factors*, June 1980, Vol. 22, pp. 271–283. Copyright 1980 by the Human Factors Society, Inc. and reproduced by permission.

a. Roughly sketch the relative frequency distribution of maximum recommended weight of lift for each of the four gender/lifts-per-minute combinations. The Empirical Rule will help you do this.

b. Construct the interval $\bar{y} \pm 2s$ for each of the four data sets, and give the approximate proportion of measurements that fall within the interval.

c. Assuming the MMHA recommendations of Ayoub et al. are reasonable, would you expect that an average male could safely lift a box (30 centimeters wide) weighing 25 kilograms from the floor to knuckle height at a rate of 4 lifts per minute? An average female? Explain.

2.53 Prior to 1980, Egypt had no access to electronic databases, either at home or abroad. To provide Egyptians with access to existing U.S. databases, the Georgia Institute of Technology designed and tested the "delayed online database search service" (which operated for 38 months until a direct online service became available). As part of a performance study of the search service, the number of times each of the over 100 databases in the system was accessed during the 38-month period was recorded. The frequency of access for the 10 most requested databases is reported in the table. Summarize the data in the table using a graphical descriptive method. Interpret the graph.

Database	Frequency of Access	Relative Frequency
Medline	3,616	.343
Agricola	1,572	.149
Biosis	1,292	.123
CAB	1,113	.106
CA	742	.070
Compendex	239	.023
ERIC	213	.020
Food Science	201	.019
INSPEC	197	.019
PsychInfo	141	.013
All other databases	1,204	.114
TOTALS	10,530	.999

Source: Slamecka, V., El-Shishiny, N., and Bassit, A. A. "A longitudinal profile of a national database search service." *Information Processing & Management*, Vol. 22, No. 3, 1986, p. 208. Reprinted with permission. Copyright 1986, Pergamon Press, Ltd.

2.54   Refer to Exercise 2.53. Because of the large size of some databases in the "delayed online search service," users split some of them into "files"; therefore, in some cases, searching a database calls for accessing two or more files. The total number of times each of the 164 files in the system was accessed by Egyptian users over the 38-month period is recorded in the table.

213	2	3	201	1	10	1	481
5	3	112	6	1	6	3	4
11	13	1,505	4	213	2	5	3
14	1	11	7	1	1,603	1	2
2	8	34	3	504	4	1	4
14	10	1	1	575	1	12	7
86	7	8	6	2	3	2	52
2	17	2	12	3	13	6	3
1	1	15	2	14	4	4	1
9	1	12	19	5	239	2	1
12	2	4	1	1	4	2	1
1	2	6	12	64	1	1	2
1	1	1	905	5	1	12	1
43	1	1	32	1	1	141	2
1	5	1	8	1	1	11	1
1	90	4	18	2	6	1	3
1	1	66	1	107	65	2	8
3	1	3	1	3	138	4	32
2	6	4	9	1	5	15	1
188	55	36	9	1,113	42	1	667
6	8	1	241				

Source: Slamecka, V., El-Shishiny, N., and Bassit, A. A. "A longitudinal profile of a national database search service." *Information Processing & Management*, Vol. 22, No. 3, 1986, p. 209. Reprinted with permission. Copyright 1986, Pergamon Press, Ltd.

a. Use the computer to summarize the data with a graphical descriptive method.
b. Use the computer to generate descriptive statistics (e.g., mean, median, and standard deviation) for the data set. Interpret the results.
c. Identify any outliers in the data set.
d. Remove the outliers, part c, from the data set and recalculate the mean, median, and standard deviation.
e. Refer to part d. Comment on the sensitivity of the mean, median, and standard deviation to extreme observations.

2.55   The Airborne Toxic Elements and Organic Substances (ATEOS) project was designed to measure atmospheric levels of more than 50 toxic and carcinogenic chemicals within several areas in New Jersey. The accompanying pie chart shows the estimated contributions of various sources to the total inhalable particulate matter (IPM, measured in number of particles) at the Camden, New Jersey, site.

a. Which source contributes the most to the total IPM?
b. What percentage of the total IPM is due to industry, oil burning, or motor vehicles?

▶
Pie chart for
Exercise 2.55

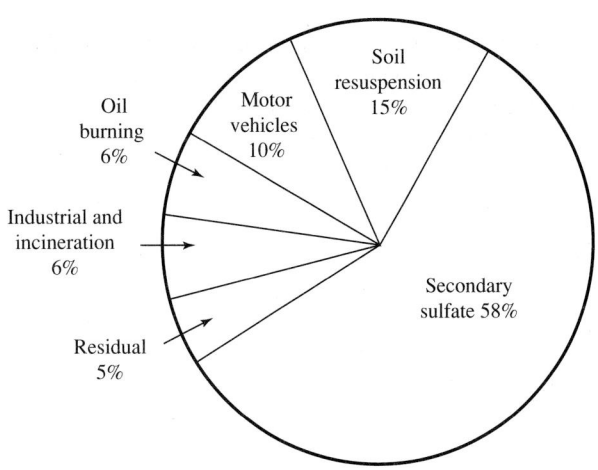

Source: Lioy, P. J., and Daisey, J. M. "Airborne toxic elements and organic substances." *Environmental Science & Technology*, Vol. 20, No. 1, Jan. 1986, p. 12. Reprinted with permission. Copyright 1986 American Chemical Society.

2.56   In his essay "Making Things Right," W. Edwards Deming considered the role of statistics in the quality control of industrial products.[*] In one example, Deming examined the quality control process for a manufacturer of steel rods. Rods produced with diameters smaller than 1 centimeter fit too loosely in their bearings and ultimately must be rejected (thrown out). To determine whether the diameter setting of the machine that produces the rods is correct, 500 rods are selected from the day's production and their diameters are recorded. The distribution of the 500 diameters for one day's production is shown in the figure. Note that the symbol LSL in the figure represents the 1-centimeter lower specification limit of the steel rod diameters.

▶
Histogram for Exercise 2.56

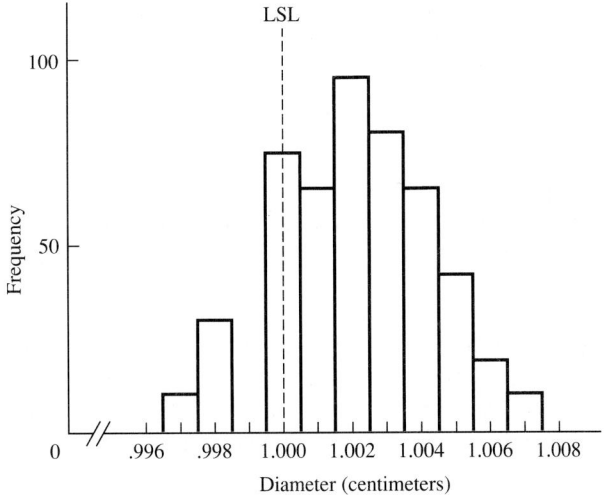

[*]From Tanur, J., et al., eds. *Statistics: A Guide to the Unknown.* San Francisco: Holden-Day, 1978, pp. 279–281.

a. What type of data, quantitative or qualitative, does the figure portray?

b. What type of graphical method is being used to describe the data?

c. Use the figure to estimate the proportion of rods with diameters between 1.0025 and 1.0045 centimeters.

d. There has been speculation that some of the inspectors are unaware of the trouble that an undersized rod diameter would cause later in the manufacturing process. Consequently, these inspectors may be passing rods with diameters that were barely below the lower specification limit, and recording them in the interval centered at 1.000 centimeter. According to the figure, is there any evidence to support this claim? Explain.

2.57   Snyder and Chrissis (1990) presented a hybrid algorithm for solving a polynomial zero–one mathematical programming problem. The algorithm incorporates a mixture of pseudo-Boolean concepts and time-proven implicit enumeration procedures. Fifty-two random problems were solved using the hybrid algorithm; the times to solution (CPU time in seconds) are listed in the accompanying table. Describe the data set graphically and numerically. Interpret the results.

.045	1.055	.136	1.894	.379	.136
.336	.258	1.070	.506	.088	.242
1.639	.912	.412	.361	8.788	.579
1.267	.567	.182	.036	.394	.209
.445	.179	.118	.333	.554	.258
.182	.070	3.985	.670	3.888	.136
.091	.600	.291	.327	.130	.145
4.170	.227	.064	.194	.209	.258
3.046	.045	.049	.079		

Source: Snyder, W. S., and Chrissis, J. W. "A hybrid algorithm for solving zero–one mathematical programming problems." *IIE Transactions*, Vol. 22, No. 2, June 1990, p. 166 (Table 1).

COMPUTER LAB: Graphical and Numerical Data Description

In this section we give the SAS and MINITAB commands for producing bar charts for qualitative data, and histograms, stem-and-leaf displays, box plots, and numerical descriptive measures for quantitative data. For purposes of illustration, we will use the computer to describe the data from Appendix III for a sample of 40 fish. Recall that the data set includes the quantitative variables length, weight, and DDT concentration, and the qualitative variables species and location. In particular, the programs below will produce (1) a bar chart for species, (2) a relative frequency histogram for length, (3) a stem-and-leaf display and box plot for DDT level, and (4) descriptive statistics for DDT level. [*Note:*   As in all Computer Lab sections, the commands given below (unless otherwise noted) are appropriate for both mainframe and personal computers. However, programs run on mainframe computers require JCL instructions. See your instructor for the appropriate JCL commands to use at your computing center.]

SAS

Command
line

1	DATA FISH;	
2	INPUT LOCATION $ SPECIES $ LENGTH WEIGHT DDT;	Data entry instructions
3	CARDS;	

{Input data values: 1 observation
per line (obs. 41–80 in Appendix III)}

4	PROC CHART;	Bar chart
5	VBAR SPECIES;	
6	PROC CHART;	Relative frequency histogram
7	VBAR LENGTH/TYPE=PERCENT;	
8	PROC UNIVARIATE PLOT;	Stem-and-leaf, box plot
9	VAR DDT;	Descriptive statistics

COMMANDS 4–5 The CHART procedure produces vertical and horizontal bar charts for qualitative data. The keyword VBAR followed by the variable name SPECIES produces a vertical bar chart for species (Figure 2.19). For horizontal bar charts, use the keyword HBAR.

FIGURE 2.19 ▶
SAS vertical bar graph for the three fish species

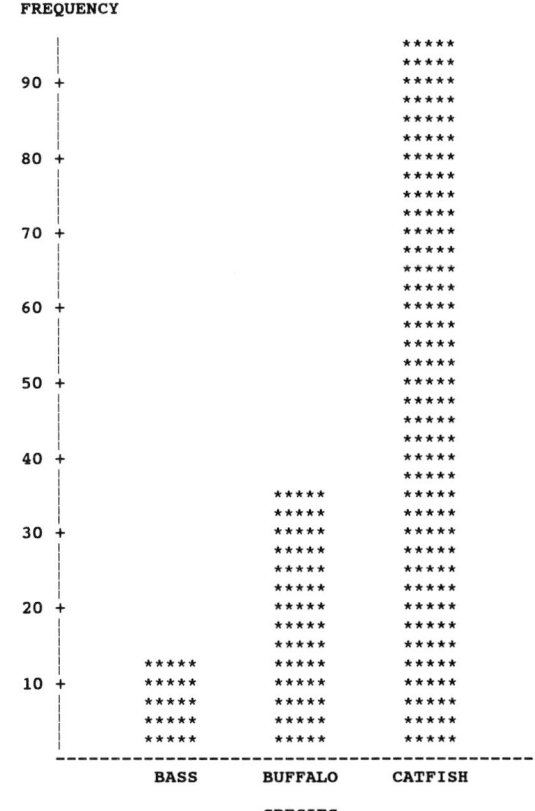

COMMANDS 6–7   The CHART procedure is also used to generate relative frequency and frequency histograms for quantitative data. The keyword VBAR followed by the variable name LENGTH produces a frequency histogram for the fish lengths. Relative frequency histograms are produced by adding the option TYPE=PERCENT (see Figure 2.20). SAS will automatically select suitable class intervals for the histogram.*

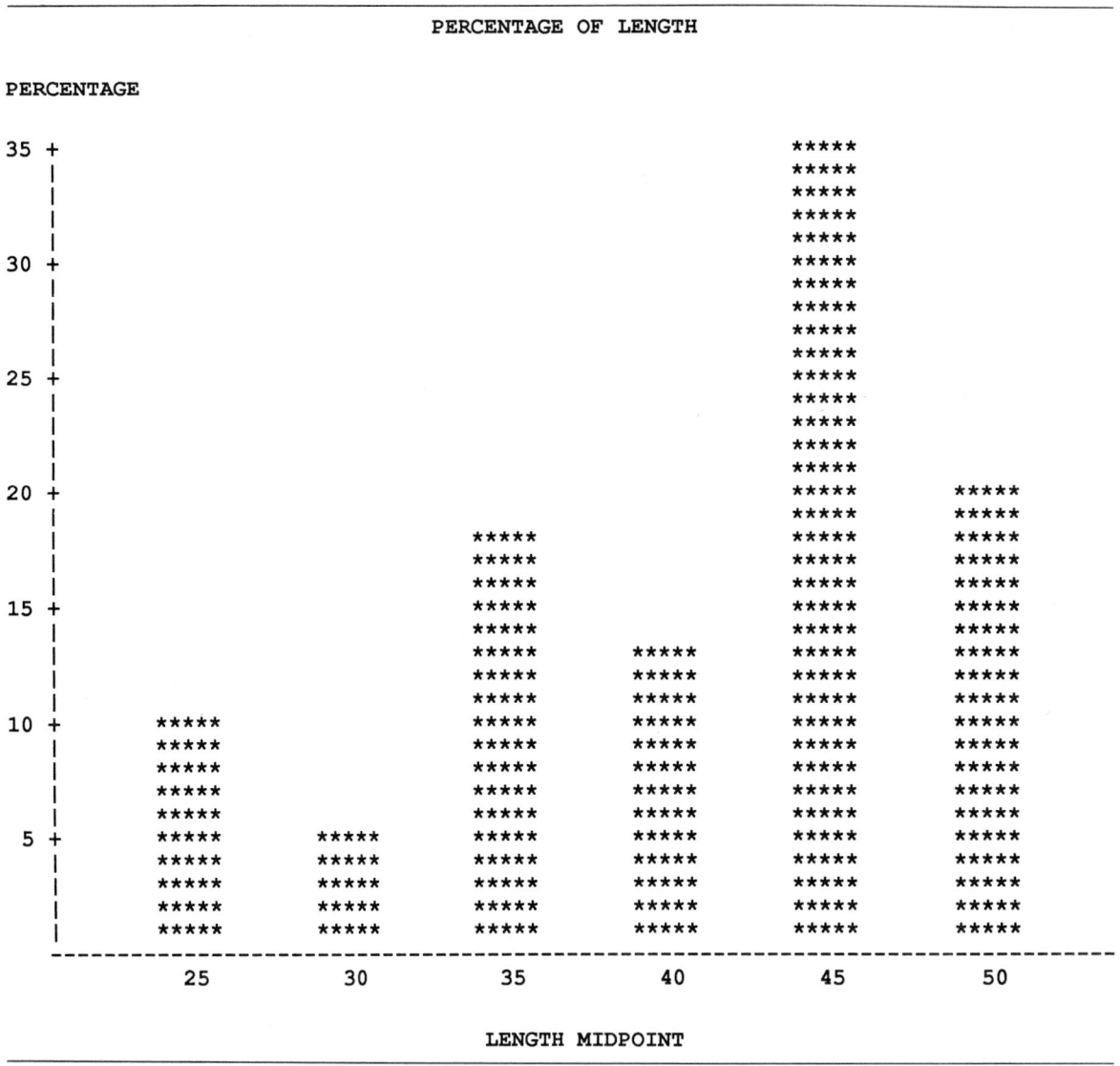

PERCENTAGE OF LENGTH

FIGURE 2.20 ▲
SAS relative frequency histogram
for fish lengths

*The MIDPOINTS option allows the user to select the class intervals. Consult the SAS references for details on how to use the MIDPOINTS option in PROC CHART.

COMMANDS 8-9   The UNIVARIATE procedure generates descriptive statistics—mean, median, mode, variance, standard deviation, lower quartile, upper quartile, etc.—for the variable DDT specified in the VAR statement in command 9 (see Figure 2.21). The PLOT option (command 8) will produce a stem-and-leaf display and a box plot for the data. [For large data sets (approximately 50 or more observations), a horizontal bar chart is produced rather than a stem-and-leaf display.]

UNIVARIATE PROCEDURE

Variable=DDT

	Moments				Quantiles(Def=5)			
N	40	Sum Wgts	40	100% Max	31	99%	31
Mean	9.28575	Sum	371.43	75% Q3	13	95%	24.5
Std Dev	7.860454	Variance	61.78674	50% Med	7.4	90%	21.5
Skewness	0.991654	Kurtosis	0.430665	25% Q1	3.45	10%	0.41
USS	5858.689	CSS	2409.683	0% Min	0.11	5%	0.2
CV	84.65072	Std Mean	1.242847			1%	0.11
T:Mean=0	7.471355	Prob>|T|	0.0001	Range	30.89		
Sgn Rank	410	Prob>|S|	0.0001	Q3-Q1	9.55		
Num ^= 0	40			Mode	12		

Extremes

Lowest	Obs	Highest	Obs
0.11(	6)	21(	19)
0.18(	4)	22(	10)
0.22(	7)	22(	40)
0.34(	5)	27(	26)
0.48(	3)	31(	24)

```
Stem Leaf                         #             Boxplot
 30 0                             1                0
 28
 26 0                             1                |
 24                                                |
 22 00                            2                |
 20 00                            2                |
 18 0                             1                |
 16                                                |
 14 0                             1                |
 12 0000000                       7             +-----+
 10 0                             1             |     |
  8 073                           3             |  +  |
  6 035                           3             *-----*
  4 0781126                       7             |     |
  2 8045                          4             +-----+
  0 1223583                       7                |
    ----+----+----+----+
```

FIGURE 2.21 ▲
SAS descriptive statistics and plots
for DDT levels

MINITAB

Command
line

1	READ C1 C2 C3 C4 C5	Data entry instruction
	$\begin{cases} \text{Input data values: 1 observation} \\ \text{per line (obs. 41–80 in Appendix III)} \end{cases}$	
2	NAME C1='LOCATION' C2='SPECIES'	
3	NAME C3='LENGTH' C4='WEIGHT' C5='DDT'	
4	HISTOGRAM OF SPECIES IN C2	Bar chart
5	HISTOGRAM OF LENGTH IN C3	Relative frequency histogram
6	STEM-AND-LEAF OF DDT IN C5	Stem-and-leaf plot
7	BOXPLOT OF DDT IN C5	Box plot
8	DESCRIBE DDT IN C5	Descriptive statistics

COMMAND 4   The HISTOGRAM command will generate horizontal bar charts for qualitative data and horizontal frequency histograms for quantitative data. Since MINITAB requires all data to be entered as numbers, the bar chart for the values of species located in C2 will look similar to a histogram with class interval midpoints identified by the values 1, 2, and 3 representing catfish, buffalo, and bass, respectively (see Figure 2.22).

FIGURE 2.22 ►
MINITAB bar graph for the three
fish species

```
Histogram of SPECIES    N = 40

Midpoint    Count
       1       22    **********************
       2       12    ************
       3        6    ******
```

COMMAND 5   MINITAB will automatically select suitable class intervals for the frequency histogram of the fish lengths located in C3* (see Figure 2.23).

FIGURE 2.23 ►
MINITAB frequency histogram for
fish lengths

```
Histogram of LENGTH    N = 40

Midpoint    Count
      24        3    ***
      28        3    ***
      32        0
      36        7    *******
      40        4    ****
      44        9    ********
      48       13    *************
      52        1    *
```

---

*The optional commands INCREMENT and START allow the user to select the class intervals. Consult the references for details on how to use these HISTOGRAM options.

COMMANDS 6–7   The STEM-AND-LEAF and BOXPLOT commands produce a stem-and-leaf display and a box plot, respectively, for the DDT levels located in C5 (see Figures 2.24 and 2.25).

FIGURE 2.24 ▶
MINITAB stem-and-leaf display for DDT levels

```
Stem-and-leaf of DDT        N  = 40
Leaf Unit = 1.0


      7      0 0000001
     11      0 2333
     18      0 4445555
     (3)     0 677
     19      0 889
     16      1 0
     15      1 2222333
      8      1 5
      7      1
      7      1 8
      6      2 11
      4      2 22
      2      2
      2      2 7
      1      2
      1      3 1
```

FIGURE 2.25 ▶
MINITAB box plot for DDT levels

```
                    -----------------
        ------I     +        I--------------------------        *
                    -----------------
      --+---------+---------+---------+---------+---------+----DDT
      0.0       6.0       12.0      18.0      24.0      30.0
```

COMMAND 8   The DESCRIBE command produces descriptive statistics—mean, median, standard deviation, lower quartile, and upper quartile—for the DDT levels located in C5 (see Figure 2.26).

FIGURE 2.26 ▶
MINITAB descriptive statistics for DDT levels

	N	MEAN	MEDIAN	TRMEAN	STDEV	SEMEAN
DDT	40	9.29	7.40	8.70	7.86	1.24

	MIN	MAX	Q1	Q3
DDT	0.11	31.00	3.43	13.00

References

Freedman, D., Pisani, R., and Purves, R. *Statistics*. New York: W. W. Norton and Co., 1978.

McClave, J. T., and Dietrich, F. H. II. *A First Course in Statistics*, 4th ed. New York: Macmillan, 1992.

Mendenhall, W. *Introduction to Probability and Statistics*, 8th ed. Boston: Duxbury Press, 1990.

Sincich, T. *Statistics by Example*, 5th ed. New York: Macmillan, 1993.

Tukey, J. W. *Exploratory Data Analysis*. Reading, Mass.: Addison-Wesley, 1977.

CHAPTER THREE

Probability

Objective

To present an introduction to the theory of probability and to suggest the role that probability will play in statistical inference

Contents

3.1   The Role of Probability in Statistics

If you play blackjack, a popular gambling game, you know that whether you win in any one game is an outcome that is very uncertain. Similarly, investing in bonds, stock, or an oil exploration company is a venture whose success is subject to uncertainty. (In fact, some would argue that investing is a form of educated gambling—one in which knowledge, experience, and good judgment can improve the odds of winning.)

Much like playing blackjack and investing, making inferences based on sample data is also subject to uncertainty. A sample rarely tells a perfectly accurate story about the population from which it was selected. There is always a margin of error (as the pollsters tell us) when sample data are used to estimate the proportion of people in favor of a particular political candidate or some consumer product. Similarly, there is always uncertainty about how far the sample estimate of the mean diameter of molded rubber expansion joints selected off an assembly line will depart from the true population mean. Consequently, a measure of the amount of uncertainty associated with an estimate (which we called *the reliability of an inference* in Chapter 1) plays a major role in statistical inference.

How do we measure the uncertainty associated with events? Anyone who has observed a daily newscast can answer that question. The answer is **probability**. For example, it may be reported that the probability of rain on a given day is 20%. Such a statement acknowledges that it is uncertain whether it will rain on the given day and indicates that the forecaster measures the likelihood of its occurrence as 20%.

Probability also plays an important role in decision making. To illustrate, suppose you have an opportunity to invest in an oil exploration company. Past records show that for 10 out of 10 previous oil drillings (a sample of the company's experiences), all 10 resulted in dry wells. What do you conclude? Do you think the chances are better than 50–50 that the company will hit a producing well? Should you invest in this company? We think your answer to these questions will be an emphatic "no." If the company's exploratory prowess is sufficient to hit a producing well 50% of the time, a record of 10 dry wells out of 10 drilled is an event that is just too improbable. Do you agree?

In this chapter, we will examine the meaning of probability and develop some properties of probability that will be useful in our study of statistics.

3.2   Events, Sample Spaces, and Probability

We will begin the discussion of probability with simple examples that are easily described, thus eliminating any discussion that could be distracting. With the aid of simple examples, important definitions are introduced and the notion of probability is more easily developed.

Suppose a coin is tossed once and the up face of the coin is recorded. This is an **observation**, or **measurement**. Any process of obtaining or generating an observation is called an **experiment**. Our definition of experiment is broader than that used in the physical sciences, where you would picture test tubes, microscopes, etc. Other practical examples of statistical experiments are recording whether a customer prefers one of two brands of electronic calculators, recording a voter's opinion on an important political issue, measuring the amount of dissolved oxygen in a polluted river, observing the closing price of a stock, counting the number of errors in an inventory, and observing the fraction of insects killed by a new insecticide. This list of statistical experiments could be continued, but the point is that our definition of an experiment is very broad.

Definition 3.1

An **experiment** is the process of obtaining an observation or taking a measurement.

Consider another simple experiment consisting of tossing a die and observing the number on the up face of the die. The six basic possible outcomes to this experiment are:

1. Observe a 1
2. Observe a 2
3. Observe a 3
4. Observe a 4
5. Observe a 5
6. Observe a 6

Note that if this experiment is conducted once, *you can observe one and only one of these six basic outcomes*. The distinguishing feature of these outcomes is that these possibilities *cannot be decomposed* into any other outcomes. These very basic possible outcomes to an experiment are called **simple events**.

Definition 3.2

A **simple event** is a basic outcome of an experiment; it cannot be decomposed into simpler outcomes.

EXAMPLE 3.1

Two coins are tossed and the up faces of both coins are recorded. List all the simple events for this experiment.

Solution

Even for a seemingly trivial experiment, we must be careful when listing the simple events. At first glance the basic outcomes seem to be Observe two heads, Observe two tails, Observe one head and one tail. However, further reflection reveals that the last of these, Observe one head and one tail, can be decomposed into Head on coin 1, Tail on coin 2 and Tail on coin 1, Head on coin 2.* Thus, the simple events are as follows:

1. Observe *HH*
2. Observe *HT*
3. Observe *TH*
4. Observe *TT*

(where *H* in the first position means "Head on coin 1," *H* in the second position means "Head on coin 2," etc.).

We will often wish to refer to the collection of all the simple events of an experiment. This collection will be called the **sample space** of the experiment. For example, there are six simple events in the sample space associated with the die-tossing experiment. The sample spaces for the experiments discussed thus far are shown in Table 3.1.

Definition 3.3

The **sample space** of an experiment is the collection of all its simple events.

TABLE 3.1   Experiments and Their Sample Spaces

Experiment: Toss a coin and observe the up face.

Sample space: 1. Observe a head
                  2. Observe a tail

This sample space can be represented in set notation as a set containing two simple events

   S: {*H, T*}

where *H* represents the simple event Observe a head and *T* represents the simple event Observe a tail.

(continued)

---

*Even if the coins are identical in appearance, there are, in fact, two distinct coins. Thus, the designation of one coin as "coin 1" and the other as "coin 2" is legitimate in any case.

TABLE 3.1   Continued

Experiment: Toss a die and observe the up face.

Sample space: 1. Observe a 1
                2. Observe a 2
                3. Observe a 3
                4. Observe a 4
                5. Observe a 5
                6. Observe a 6

This sample space can be represented in set notation as a set of six simple events

     S: {1, 2, 3, 4, 5, 6}

Experiment: Toss two coins and observe the up face on each.

Sample space: 1. Observe *HH*
                2. Observe *HT*
                3. Observe *TH*
                4. Observe *TT*

This sample space can be represented in set notation as a set of four simple events

     S: {*HH, HT, TH, TT*}

Just as graphs are useful in describing sets of data, a pictorial method for presenting the sample space and its simple events will often be useful. Figure 3.1 shows such a representation for each of the experiments in Table 3.1. In each case, the sample space is shown as a closed figure, labeled *S*, containing a set of points, called **sample points**, with each point representing one simple event. Note that the number of sample points in a sample space *S* is equal to the number of simple events associated with the respective experiment: two for the coin toss, six for the die toss, and four for the two-coin toss. These graphical representations are called **Venn diagrams**.

FIGURE 3.1 ▶
Venn diagrams for the three experiments from Table 3.1

a. Experiment: Observe the up face on a coin.

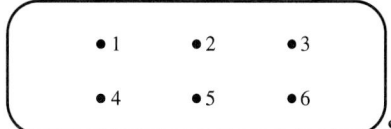

b. Experiment: Observe the up face on a die.

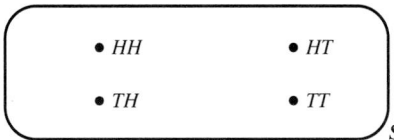

c. Experiment: Observe the up faces on two coins.

Now that we have defined simple events as the basic outcomes of the experiment and the sample space as the collection of all the simple events, we are prepared to discuss the probabilities of simple events. You have undoubtedly used the term *probability* and have some intuitive idea about its meaning. Probability is generally used synonymously with "chance," "odds," and similar concepts. We will begin our discussion of probability using these informal concepts. For example, if a fair coin is tossed, we might reason that both the simple events, Observe a head and Observe a tail, have the same chance of occurring. Thus, we might state that "the probability of observing a head is 50% or $\frac{1}{2}$," or "the odds of seeing a head are 50–50."

What do we mean when we say that the probability of a head is $\frac{1}{2}$? We mean that, in a very long series of tosses, approximately half would result in a head. Therefore, the number $\frac{1}{2}$ measures the likelihood of observing a head on a single toss.

Stating that the probability of observing a head is $\frac{1}{2}$ does *not* mean that exactly half of a number of tosses will result in heads. For example, we do not expect to observe exactly one head in two tosses of a coin or exactly five heads in ten tosses of a coin. Rather, we would expect the proportion of heads to vary in a random manner and to approach closer and closer the probability of a head, $\frac{1}{2}$, as the number of tosses increases. This property can be seen in the graph in Figure 3.2.

Figure 3.2 shows the proportion of heads observed after $n = 25, 50, 75, 100, 125, \ldots, 1{,}450, 1{,}475$, and $1{,}500$ simulated repetitions of a coin-tossing experiment. The number of tosses is marked along the horizontal axis of the graph, and the corresponding proportions of heads are plotted on the vertical axis above the values of n. We have connected the points to emphasize that the proportion of heads moves closer and closer to .5 as n gets larger (as you move to the right on the graph).

Definition 3.4

The **probability** of a simple event is a number that measures the likelihood that the event will occur when the experiment is performed. The probability can be approximated by the proportion of times that the simple event is observed when the experiment is repeated a very large number of times. For a simple event E, we denote the probability of E as $P(E)$.

Although we usually think of the probability of an event as the proportion of times the event occurs in a very long series of trials, some experiments can never be repeated. For example, if you invest in an oil-drilling venture, the probability that your venture will succeed has some unknown value that you will never be able to evaluate by repetitive experiments. The probability of this event occurring is a number that has some value, but it is unknown to us. The best that we could do, in estimating its value, would be to attempt to determine the proportion of similar ventures that succeeded and take this as an approximation to the desired probability. In spite of the fact that we may not be able to conduct repetitive experiments, the relative frequency definition for probability appeals to our intuition.

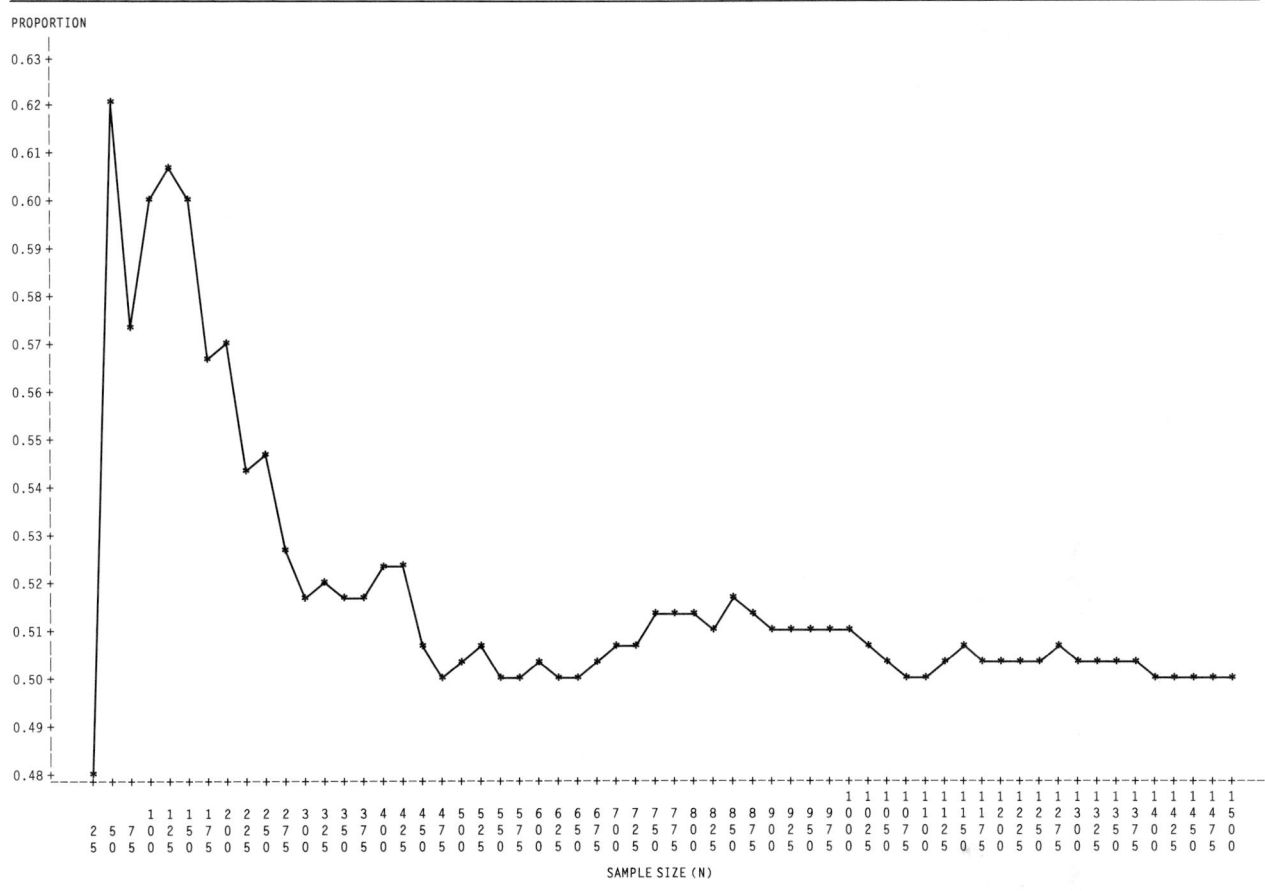

PROPORTION

SAMPLE SIZE (N)

FIGURE 3.2 ▲
The proportion of heads in *n* tosses of a coin

No matter how you assign probabilities to the simple events of an experiment, the probabilities assigned must obey the two rules (or axioms) given in the box.

Rules for Assigning Probabilities to Simple Events

Let $E_1, E_2, \ldots, E_k$ be the simple events in a sample space.

1. All simple event probabilities *must* lie between 0 and 1:

$$0 \le P(E_i) \le 1 \quad \text{for } i = 1, 2, \ldots, k$$

2. The sum of the probabilities of all the simple events within a sample space must be equal to 1:

$$\sum_{i=1}^{k} P(E_i) = 1$$

Sometimes we are interested in the occurrence of any one of a collection of simple events. For example, in the die-tossing experiment of Table 3.1, we may be interested in observing an odd number on the die. This will occur if any one of the following three simple events occurs:

1. Observe a 1
2. Observe a 3
3. Observe a 5

In fact, the event Observe an odd number is clearly defined if we specify the collection of simple events that imply its occurrence. Such specific collections of simple events are called **events**.

Definition 3.5

An **event** is a specific collection of simple events.

The probability of an event is computed by summing the probabilities of the simple events that comprise it. This rule agrees with the relative frequency concept of probability, as Example 3.2 illustrates.

The Probability of an Event

The **probability of an event** A is equal to the sum of the probabilities of the simple events in event A.

EXAMPLE 3.2

Consider the experiment of tossing two coins. If the coins are balanced, then the correct probabilities associated with the simple events are as follows:

Simple Event	Probability
HH	$\frac{1}{4}$
HT	$\frac{1}{4}$
TH	$\frac{1}{4}$
TT	$\frac{1}{4}$

Define the following events:

A: {Observe exactly one head}
B: {Observe at least one head}

Calculate the probability of A and the probability of B.

Solution

Note that each of the four simple events has the same probability since we expect each to occur with approximately equal relative frequency $\left(\frac{1}{4}\right)$ if the coin-tossing experiment were repeated a large number of times. Since the event A: {Observe exactly one head} will occur if either of the two simple events HT or TH occurs (see Figure 3.3), then approximately $\frac{1}{4} + \frac{1}{4} = \frac{1}{2}$ of the large number of experiments will result in event A. This additivity of the relative frequencies of simple events is consistent with our rule for finding $P(A)$:

$$P(A) = P(HT) + P(TH)$$
$$= \frac{1}{4} + \frac{1}{4} = \frac{1}{2}$$

FIGURE 3.3 ▶
Coin-tossing experiment showing events A and B as collections of simple events

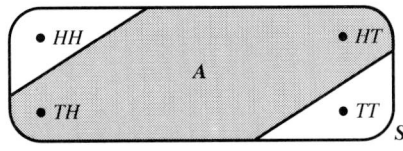

a. Event A

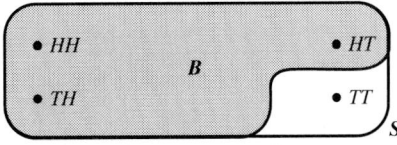

b. Event B

Applying this rule to find $P(B)$, we note that event B contains the simple events HH, HT, and TH—that is, B will occur if any one of these three simple events occurs. Therefore,

$$P(B) = P(HH) + P(HT) + P(TH)$$
$$= \frac{1}{4} + \frac{1}{4} + \frac{1}{4} = \frac{3}{4}$$

We can now summarize the steps for calculating the probability of any event:*

---

*A thorough treatment of this topic can be found in Feller (1968).

> ### Steps for Calculating Probabilities of Events
> ....
> 1. Define the experiment, i.e., describe the process used to make an observation and the type of observation that will be recorded.
> 2. List the simple events.
> 3. Assign probabilities to the simple events.
> 4. Determine the collection of simple events contained in the event of interest.
> 5. Sum the simple event probabilities to get the event probability.

....

EXAMPLE 3.3

A quality control engineer must decide whether an assembly line that produces manufactured items is "out of control"—that is, producing defective items at a higher rate than usual. At this stage of our study, we do not have the tools to solve this problem, but we can say that one of the important factors affecting the solution is the proportion of defectives manufactured by the line. To illustrate, what is the probability that an item manufactured by the line will be defective? What is the probability that the next two items produced by the line will be defective? What is the probability for the general case of k items? Explain how you might solve this problem.

Solution

STEP 1   Define the experiment. The experiment corresponding to the inspection of a single item is identical in underlying structure to the coin-tossing experiment illustrated in Figure 3.1a. An item, either a nondefective (call this a head) or a defective (call this a tail), is observed and its operating status is recorded.

Experiment: Observe the operating status of a single manufactured item.

STEP 2   List the simple events. There are only two possible outcomes of the experiment. These simple events are:

Simple events: 1. N: {Item is nondefective}
               2. D: {Item is defective}

STEP 3   Assign probabilities to the simple events. The difference between this problem and the coin-tossing problem becomes apparent when we attempt to assign probabilities to the two simple events. What probability should we assign to the simple event D? Some people might say .5, as for the coin-tossing experiment, but you can see that finding $P(D)$, the probability of simple event D, is not so easy. Suppose that when the assembly line is in control, 10% of the items produced will be defective. Then, at first glance, it would appear that $P(D)$ is .10. But this may not be correct, because the line may be out of control, producing defectives at a higher rate. So, the important point to note is that this is a case where equal probabilities are not assigned to the simple events. How can we find these probabilities? A good procedure might be to monitor the assembly line for a period of time, and record the number of defective and nondefective items produced. Then the proportions of the two types of items could be used to approximate the probabilities of the two simple events.

We could then continue with steps 4 and 5 to calculate any probability of interest for this experiment with two simple events.

The experiment, assessing the operating status of two items, is identical to the experiment of Example 3.2, tossing two coins, except that the probabilities of the simple events are not the same. We will learn how to find the probabilities of the simple events for this experiment, or for the general case of k items, in Section 3.6.

EXAMPLE 3.4

A computer programmer must select three jobs from among five jobs awaiting the programmer's attention. If, unknown to the programmer, the jobs vary in the length of programming time required, what is the probability that:

a. The programmer selects the two jobs that require the least amount of time?
b. The programmer selects the three jobs that require the most time?

Solution

STEP 1 The experiment consists of selecting three jobs from among the five that are available.

STEP 2 We will denote the available jobs by the symbols $J_1, J_2, \ldots, J_5$, where J_1 is the shortest job and J_5 is the longest. The notation $J_i J_j$ will denote the selection of jobs J_i and J_j. For example, $J_1 J_3$ denotes the selection of jobs J_1 and J_3. Then the 10 simple events associated with the experiment are as follows:

Simple Event	Probability	Simple Event	Probability
$J_1 J_2 J_3$	$\frac{1}{10}$	$J_1 J_4 J_5$	$\frac{1}{10}$
$J_1 J_2 J_4$	$\frac{1}{10}$	$J_2 J_3 J_4$	$\frac{1}{10}$
$J_1 J_2 J_5$	$\frac{1}{10}$	$J_2 J_3 J_5$	$\frac{1}{10}$
$J_1 J_3 J_4$	$\frac{1}{10}$	$J_2 J_4 J_5$	$\frac{1}{10}$
$J_1 J_3 J_5$	$\frac{1}{10}$	$J_3 J_4 J_5$	$\frac{1}{10}$

STEP 3 If we assume that the selection of any set of three jobs is as likely as any other, then the probability of each of the 10 simple events is $\frac{1}{10}$.

STEP 4 Define the events A and B as follows:

A: {The programmer selects the two jobs that require the least amount of time}

B: {The programmer selects the three jobs that require the most time}

Event A will occur for any simple events in which jobs J_1 and J_2 are selected—namely, the three simple events $J_1 J_2 J_3$, $J_1 J_2 J_4$, and $J_1 J_2 J_5$. Similarly, the event B is made up of the single event $J_3 J_4 J_5$.

STEP 5   We now sum the probabilities of the simple events in A and B to obtain

$$P(A) = P(J_1 J_2 J_3) + P(J_1 J_2 J_4) + P(J_1 J_2 J_5)$$
$$= \frac{1}{10} + \frac{1}{10} + \frac{1}{10} = \frac{3}{10}$$

and

$$P(B) = P(J_3 J_4 J_5) = \frac{1}{10}$$

[*Note:*   For the experiments discussed thus far, listing the simple events has been easy. For more complex experiments, the number of simple events may be so large that listing them is impractical. In solving probability problems for experiments with many simple events, we use the same principles as for experiments with few simple events. The only difference is that we need **counting rules** for determining the number of simple events without actually enumerating all of them. In Section 3.8, we present several of the more useful counting rules.]

EXERCISES

3.1   Environmental engineers classify U.S. consumers into five groups based on consumers' feelings about environmentalism:

1. *Basic browns* claim they don't have the knowledge to understand environmental problems.
2. *True-blue greens* use biodegradable products.
3. *Greenback greens* support requiring new cars to run on alternative fuel.
4. *Sprouts* recycle newspapers regularly.
5. *Grousers* believe industries, not individuals, should solve environmental problems.

The proportion of consumers in each group is shown in the table. Suppose a U.S. consumer is selected at random and his (her) feelings about environmentalism determined.

Basic browns	.28
True-blue greens	.11
Greenback greens	.11
Sprouts	.26
Grousers	.24

Source: *The Orange County* (Calif.) *Reporter*, Aug. 7, 1990.

a. List the simple events for the experiment.
b. Assign reasonable probabilities to the simple events.

c. Find the probability that the consumer is either a basic brown or a grouser.

d. Find the probability that the consumer supports environmentalism in some fashion (i.e., the consumer is a true-blue green, a greenback green, or a sprout).

3.2 The Commission of the European Communities initiated a research program to determine the influence of traffic noise on sleep, subjective assessment, and psychomotor performance. For one portion of the study, a team of German acoustical engineers monitored the sleep of 10 couples (one male and one female per couple) during 12 consecutive nights. All 10 couples slept under usual conditions on seven of the nights. (This represents the *control phase* of the study.) For the other five nights (the *experimental phase*), the 10 couples were divided into two groups of equal size. One group slept with the windows open and the other group slept with earplugs. The experimental setup is described in the following table.

	Control Phase Nights 1 2 3 4 5	*Experimental Phase* 6 7 8 9 10	*Control Phase* 11 12
Earplugs group (couples 1, 4, 6, 9, 10)	Without earplugs Windows open	With earplugs Windows open	Without earplugs Windows open
Windows group (couples 2, 3, 5, 7, 8)	Windows closed No earplugs	Windows open No earplugs	Windows closed No earplugs

Source: Griefahn, B., and Gros, E. "Noise and sleep at home, a field study on primary and after-effects." *Journal of Sound and Vibration*, Vol. 105, No. 3, Mar. 1986, p. 376 (Figure 2).

Suppose we randomly select one couple from the experiment on one randomly selected night and note whether the couple is wearing earplugs and whether the windows are open or closed.

a. List the simple events for the experiment.

b. Assign probabilities to the simple events.

c. What is the probability that the couple is wearing earplugs?

d. What is the probability that the windows are closed?

3.3 A Northwestern University Department of Pediatrics study of bicycle-related injuries over a 7-year period found that more than 2,500 babies and toddlers were hurt while riding in seats mounted on an adult's bike. The table gives a breakdown of the causes of the injuries.

Cause of Bike-Related Injuries to Children	*Percentage*
Fall out of seat	39
Accident with car	10
Stationary bike fell over	24
Seat falls off bike	6
Extremity caught in spoke	21
	100

Source: *Tampa Tribune*, July 10, 1988.

Suppose a child is injured in a bicycle accident.

a. What is the probability that the injury results from an extremity getting caught in the bicycle spoke?

b. What is the probability that the injury results from either the child falling out of the seat or the seat falling off the bike?

c. What is the probability that the injury did not occur as a result of an accident with a car?

3.4 An improved method for measuring the electrical resistivity of concrete has been developed that eliminates difficulties resulting from polarization effects and capacitive resistance (*Magazine of Concrete Research*, Dec. 1985). The method was tested on concrete specimens with different water–cement mixes. Three different water weight ratios (40%, 45%, and 50%) and three different mixes of cement (300, 350, and 400 kilograms per cubic meter) were examined.

a. List all possible combinations of water weight ratio and cement mix for this experiment.

b. Suppose we determine the combination of water weight ratio and cement mix that yields the highest electrical resistivity. Before the experiment is performed, should equal probabilities be assigned to the simple events? Why or why not?

3.5 The YES/MVS (Yorktown Expert System/MVS Manager) is an experimental expert system designed to exert active control over a computer system and provide advice to computer operators. YES/MVS is designed with a knowledge base consisting of 548 rules that are triggered in response to messages or queries from the computer operator. The accompanying table gives the number of rules allocated to different subdomains of the operator's actions. Periodically, the rules in the YES/MVS knowledge base are tested and adjusted, if necessary. Suppose a rule is selected at random for testing and its type (operator's action/query) noted.

Operator's Action/Query	Number of Rules
Batch scheduling	139
JES queue space	104
C-to-C links	68
Hardware errors	87
SMF management	25
Quiesce and IPL	52
Performance	41
Background monitor	32
TOTAL	548

Source: Ennis, R. L., et al., "A continuous real-time expert system for computer operations." *IBM Journal of Research and Development*, Vol. 30, No. 1, Jan. 1986, p. 19. Copyright 1986 by International Business Machines Corporation; reprinted with permission.

a. List the simple events for this experiment.

b. Assign probabilities to the simple events based on the information contained in the table.

c. What is the probability the rule is a C-to-C link or hardware error rule?

d. What is the probability the rule is not a performance rule?

3.6 *Science* magazine (Sept. 24, 1993) reported the results of a National Science Foundation (NSF) survey of graduate students in science and engineering. The NSF survey found that a large percentage of the Ph.D. degrees awarded go to students who are not U.S. citizens (i.e., foreign nationals). The accompanying table gives the number of engineering and science Ph.D. degrees awarded in 1991 to foreign nationals in several disciplines. Suppose a graduate student who earned a Ph.D. in one of the engineering and science disciplines listed in the table is randomly selected.

Discipline	Ph.D.'s Awarded to U.S. Citizens	Ph.D.'s Awarded to Foreign Nationals	Totals
Engineering	607	1,630	2,237
Astronomy	126	84	210
Chemistry	1,291	2,336	3,627
Physics	757	1,006	1,763
Earth/Ocean/Atmosphere	409	236	645
Mathematics	92	114	206
Computer Science	110	47	157
Agricultural Science	327	247	574
Biology	6,529	6,155	12,684
TOTALS	10,248	11,855	22,103

Source: *Science*, Vol. 26, Sept. 24, 1993, p. 1770.

a. Find the probability that the student was awarded a Ph.D. in engineering.
b. Find the probability that the student was a foreign national.

3.7 Biologists define a "hotspot" as a species-rich geographical area (10-kilometer square). *Nature* (Sept. 1993) reported on a study of hotspots for several rare British species, including butterflies, dragonflies, and breeding birds. The accompanying table gives the proportion of a particular species found in a hotspot for that or another species. For example, the value in the lower left corner, .70, implies that 70% of all British bird species inhabit a butterfly hotspot. [*Note:* It is possible for species hotspots to overlap.]

Proportion Found in

Species	Butterfly Hotspots	Dragonfly Hotspots	Bird Hotspots
Butterflies	.91	.91	1.00
Dragonflies	.82	.92	.92
Birds	.70	.73	.87

Source: Prendergast, J. R., et al. "Rare species, the coincidence of diversity hotspots and conservation strategies." *Nature*, Vol. 365, No. 6444, Sept. 23, 1993, p. 337 (Table 2c).

a. What is the probability that a dragonfly species will inhabit a dragonfly hotspot?
b. What is the probability that a butterfly species will inhabit a bird hotspot?
c. Explain why all butterfly hotspots are also bird hotspots.

3.3 Compound Events

An event can often be viewed as a composition of two or more other events. Such events are called **compound events**; they can be formed (composed) in two ways.

Definition 3.6

The **union** of two events A and B is the event that occurs if either A or B, or both, occur on a single performance of the experiment. We will denote the union of events A and B by the symbol A ∪ B.

Definition 3.7

The **intersection** of two events A and B is the event that occurs if both A and B occur on a single performance of the experiment. We will write A ∩ B for the intersection of events A and B.

EXAMPLE 3.5

Consider the die-tossing experiment. Define the following events:

A: {Toss an even number}
B: {Toss a number less than or equal to 3}

a. Describe A ∪ B for this experiment.
b. Describe A ∩ B for this experiment.
c. Calculate P(A ∪ B) and P(A ∩ B) assuming the die is fair.

Solution

a. The union of A and B is the event that occurs if we observe an even number, or a number less than or equal to 3, or both on a single throw of the die. Consequently, the simple events in the event A ∪ B are those for which A occurs, B occurs, or both A and B occur. Testing the simple events in the entire sample space, we find that the collection of simple events in the union of A and B is

$$A \cup B = \{1, 2, 3, 4, 6\}$$

as shown in the Venn diagram, Figure 3.4.

FIGURE 3.4 ▶
Venn diagram of A ∪ B,
Example 3.5

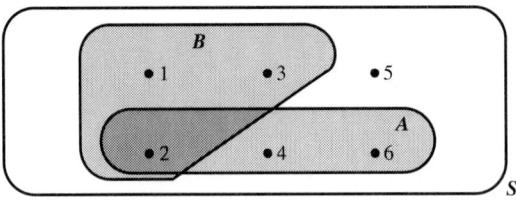

b. The intersection of A and B is the event that occurs if we observe both an even number and a number less than or equal to 3 on a single throw of the die. Testing the simple events to see which imply the occurrence of *both* events A and B, we see that the intersection contains only one simple event:

A ∩ B = {2}

In other words, the intersection of A and B is the simple event Observe a 2 (see Figure 3.4).

c. Recalling that the probability of an event is the sum of the probabilities of the simple events of which the event is composed, we have

$$P(A \cup B) = P(1) + P(2) + P(3) + P(4) + P(6)$$
$$= \frac{1}{6} + \frac{1}{6} + \frac{1}{6} + \frac{1}{6} + \frac{1}{6} = \frac{5}{6}$$

and

$$P(A \cap B) = P(2) = \frac{1}{6}$$

Unions and intersections also can be defined for more than two events. For example, the event A ∪ B ∪ C represents the union of three events, A, B, and C. This event, which includes the set of simple events in A, B, or C, will occur if any one or more of the events A, B, or C occurs. Similarly, the intersection A ∩ B ∩ C is the event that all three of the events A, B, and C occur. Therefore, A ∩ B ∩ C is the set of simple events that are in all three of the events A, B, and C.

EXAMPLE 3.6

Refer to Example 3.5 and define the event

C: {Toss a number greater than 1}

Find the simple events in

a. A ∪ B ∪ C   b. A ∩ B ∩ C

where

A: {Toss an even number}
B: {Toss a number less than or equal to 3}

Solution

a. Event C contains the simple events corresponding to tossing a 2, 3, 4, 5, or 6; event B contains the simple events 1, 2, and 3. Therefore, the event that A, B, or C occurs contains all six simple events in S, i.e., those corresponding to tossing a 1, 2, 3, 4, 5, or 6.

b. You can see that you will observe all of the events, A, B, and C, only if you observe a 2. Therefore, the intersection A ∩ B ∩ C contains the single simple event Toss a 2.

3.4   Complementary Events

A very useful concept in the calculation of event probabilities is the notion of **complementary events**.

Definition 3.8

The **complement*** of an event A is the event that A does not occur, i.e., the event consisting of all simple events that are not in event A. We will denote the complement of A by A^c. Note that $A \cup A^c = S$, the sample space.

An event A is a collection of simple events, and the simple events included in A^c are those that are not in A. Figure 3.5 demonstrates this. You will note from the figure that all simple events in S are included in *either* A or A^c, and that *no* simple event is in both A and A^c. This leads us to conclude that the probabilities of an event and its complement must sum to 1.

FIGURE 3.5 ▶
Venn diagram of complementary events

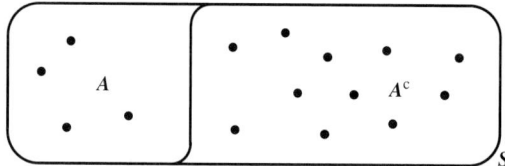

Complementary Relationship

The sum of the probabilities of complementary events equals 1. That is,

$$P(A) + P(A^c) = 1$$

In many probability problems, it will be easier to calculate the probability of the complement of the event of interest rather than the event itself. Then, since

$$P(A) + P(A^c) = 1$$

we can calculate $P(A)$ by using the relationship

$$P(A) = 1 - P(A^c)$$

---

*Some texts use the symbol A′ to denote the complement of an event A.

EXAMPLE 3.7

Consider the experiment of tossing two fair coins. Calculate the probability of event

A: {Observe at least one head}

by using the complementary relationship.

Solution

We know that the event A: {Observe at least one head} consists of the simple events

A: {HH, HT, TH}

The complement of A is defined as the event that occurs when A does not occur. Therefore,

A^c: {Observe no heads} = {TT}

This complementary relationship is shown in Figure 3.6. Assuming the coins are balanced, we have

$$P(A^c) = P(TT) = \frac{1}{4}$$

and

$$P(A) = 1 - P(A^c) = 1 - \frac{1}{4} = \frac{3}{4}$$

FIGURE 3.6 ▶
Complementary events in the toss of two coins

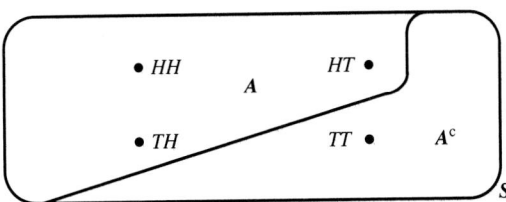

EXAMPLE 3.8

A fair coin is tossed 10 times and the up face is recorded after each toss. Find the probability of the event

A: {Observe at least one head}

Solution

We will solve this problem by following the five steps for calculating probabilities of events (see Section 3.2).

STEP 1   Define the experiment. The experiment is to record the results of the 10 tosses of the coin.

STEP 2   List the simple events. A simple event consists of a particular sequence of 10 heads and tails. Thus, one simple event is

HHTTTHTHTT

which denotes head on first toss, head on second toss, tail on third toss, etc. Others would be *HTHHHTTTTT* and *THHTHTHTTH*. There is obviously a very large number of simple events—too many to list. It can be shown (see Section 3.8) that there are $2^{10} = 1{,}024$ simple events for this experiment.

STEP 3   Assign probabilities. Since the coin is fair, each sequence of heads and tails has the same chance of occurring and therefore all the simple events are equally likely. Then

$$P(\text{Each simple event}) = \frac{1}{1{,}024}$$

STEP 4   Determine the simple events in event A. A simple event is in A if at least one *H* appears in the sequence of 10 tosses. However, if we consider the complement of A, we find that

A^c: {No heads are observed in 10 tosses}

Thus, A^c contains only the simple event

A^c: {*TTTTTTTTTT*}

and therefore

$$P(A^c) = \frac{1}{1{,}024}$$

STEP 5   Since we know the probability of the complement of A, we use the relationship for complementary events:

$$P(A) = 1 - P(A^c) = 1 - \frac{1}{1{,}024} = \frac{1{,}023}{1{,}024} = .999$$

That is, we are virtually certain of observing at least one head in 10 tosses of the coin.

EXERCISES

3.8   One game that is popular in many American casinos is roulette. Roulette is played by spinning a ball on a circular wheel that has been divided into 38 arcs of equal length; these bear the numbers 00, 0, 1, 2, . . . , 35, 36. The number on the arc at which the ball comes to rest is the outcome of one play of the game. The numbers are also colored in the following manner:

Red:	1	3	5	7	9	12	14	16	18
	19	21	23	25	27	30	32	34	36
Black:	2	4	6	8	10	11	13	15	17
	20	22	24	26	28	29	31	33	35
Green:	00	0							

Players may place bets on the table in a variety of ways, including bets on odd, even, red, black, low (1–18), and high (19–36) outcomes. Consider the following events (00 and 0 are considered neither odd nor even):

 A: {Outcome is an odd number}

 B: {Outcome is a black number}

 C: {Outcome is a high number}

Calculate the probabilities of the following events:
a. $A \cup B$ b. $A \cap C$ c. $B \cup C$ d. B^c e. $A \cap B \cap C$

3.9 An oil-drilling venture involves the drilling of six wildcat oil wells in different parts of the country. Suppose that each drilling will produce either a dry well or an oil gusher. Assuming that the simple events for this experiment are equally likely, find the probability that at least one oil gusher will be discovered.

3.10 Enhanced protection against corrosion of steel sheet is a top priority of automakers. At Mazda Motor Corporation (Japan), there is a strong preference for thin, plated alloy coatings to improve protection against rust and adhesion. The accompanying table gives the breakdown of steel sheet usage in Mazda 626's exported to the United States. Suppose a single steel sheet is randomly selected from among those sheets used in the production of a Mazda 626 and we are interested in the type of steel sheet that is selected.

Type of Steel Sheet	Percentage Used
Cold rolled, regular strength, nonplated	27
Cold rolled, high strength, nonplated	12
Cold rolled, regular strength, plated	30
Cold rolled, high strength, plated	15
Hot rolled, regular strength, nonplated	8
Hot rolled, high strength, nonplated	5
Hot rolled, regular strength, plated	3
Hot rolled, high strength, plated	0
TOTAL	100

Source: Chandler, H. E. "Materials trends at Mazda Motor Corporation." *Metal Progress*, Vol. 129, No. 6, May 1986, p. 57 (Figure 3).

a. Define the experiment.
b. List the simple events for the experiment.
c. Assign probabilities to the simple events based on Mazda's steel sheet usage.
d. What is the probability that the steel sheet will be of the hot-rolled, high-strength type?
e. What is the probability that the steel sheet will be of the cold-rolled type?
f. What is the probability that the steel sheet will not be plated?

3.11 The game of craps is played with two dice. A player throws both dice, winning unconditionally if he produces a *natural* (the sum of the numbers showing on the two dice is 7 or 11), and losing unconditionally if he throws *craps* (a 2, 3, or 12).
a. Find the probability that a player will throw a natural on the first toss of the dice.
b. Find the probability that a player does not throw craps on the first toss of the dice.

3.12   In the construction industry, disputes are common and are often settled through arbitration. A total of 4,940 construction disputes were filed for arbitration in 1988. A distribution of the dollar values of the 4,940 claims is provided in the table.

Value	Number of Claims
Under $10,000	1,439
$10,001–$50,000	1,769
$50,001–$100,000	590
$100,001–$500,000	739
$500,001–$1,000,000	129
$1,000,001 or over	80
Undisclosed	194
	4,940

Source: Riggs, L. S., and Schenk, R. M. "Arbitration: Survey on user satisfaction." *Journal of Performance of Constructed Facilities*, Vol. 4, No. 2, May 1990, p. 89.

a. Estimate the probability of an arbitrated claim with an undisclosed dollar amount.
b. Estimate the probability that the amount of the arbitration claim exceeds $1,000,000.
c. Estimate the probability that the amount of the arbitration claim is between $50,001 and $500,000.

3.5   Conditional Probability

The event probabilities we have discussed thus far give the relative frequencies of the occurrences of the events when the experiment is repeated a very large number of times. They are called **unconditional probabilities** because no special conditions are assumed other than those that define the experiment.

Sometimes we may wish to alter our estimate of the probability of an event when we have additional knowledge that might affect its outcome. This revised probability is called the **conditional probability** of the event. For example, we have shown that the probability of observing an even number (event A) on a toss of a fair die is $\frac{1}{2}$. However, suppose you are given the information that on a particular throw of the die the result was a number less than or equal to 3 (event B). Would you still believe that the probability of observing an even number on that throw of the die is equal to $\frac{1}{2}$? If you reason that making the assumption that B has occurred reduces the sample space from six simple events to three simple events (namely, those contained in event B), the reduced sample space is as shown in Figure 3.7.

FIGURE 3.7 ▶

Reduced sample space for the die-tossing experiment, given that event B has occurred

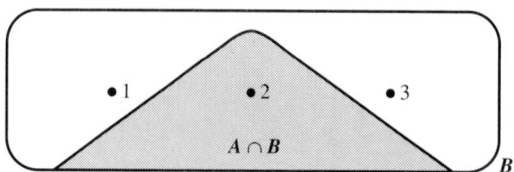

Since the only even number of the three numbers in the reduced sample space of event B is the number 2 and since the die is fair, we conclude that the probability that A occurs **given that B occurs** is one in three, or $\frac{1}{3}$. We will use the symbol $P(A \mid B)$ to represent the probability of event A given that event B occurs. For the die-tossing example, we write

$$P(A \mid B) = \frac{1}{3}$$

To get the probability of event A given that event B occurs, we proceed as follows: We divide the probability of the part of A that falls within the reduced sample space of event B, namely, $P(A \cap B)$, by the total probability of the reduced sample space, namely, $P(B)$. Thus, for the die-tossing example where event A: {Observe an even number} and event B: {Observe a number less than or equal to 3}, we find

$$P(A \mid B) = \frac{P(A \cap B)}{P(B)} = \frac{P(2)}{P(1) + P(2) + P(3)} = \frac{\frac{1}{6}}{\frac{3}{6}} = \frac{1}{3}$$

This formula for $P(A \mid B)$ is true in general.

Formula for Conditional Probability

To find the **conditional probability that event A occurs given that event B occurs**, divide the probability that *both* A and B occur by the probability that B occurs, that is,

$$P(A \mid B) = \frac{P(A \cap B)}{P(B)} \quad \text{where we assume that } P(B) \neq 0$$

EXAMPLE 3.9

Consider the following problem in process control. Suppose you are interested in the probability that a manufactured product (e.g., a small mechanical part) shipped to a buyer conforms to the buyer's specifications. Lots containing a large number of parts must pass inspection before they are accepted for shipment. [Assume that not all parts in a lot are inspected. For example, if the mean product characteristic (e.g., diameter) of a sample of parts selected from the lot falls within certain limits, the entire lot is accepted even though there may be one or more individual parts that fall outside specifications.] Let I represent the event that a lot passes inspection and let B represent the event that an individual part in a lot conforms to the buyer's specifications. Thus, $I \cap B$ is the simple event that the individual part is both shipped to the buyer (this happens when the lot containing the part passes inspection) and conforms to specifications, $I \cap B^c$ is the simple event that the individual part is shipped to the buyer but does not conform to specifications, etc. Assume that the probabilities associated with the four simple events are as shown in the accompanying table. Find the probability that an individual part conforms to the buyer's specifications given that it is shipped to the buyer.

Simple Event	Probability
$I \cap B$	.80
$I \cap B^c$	.02
$I^c \cap B$	.15
$I^c \cap B^c$	.03

Solution

If one part is selected from a lot of manufactured parts, what is the probability that the buyer will accept the part? To be accepted, the part must first be shipped to the buyer (i.e., the lot containing the part must pass inspection) *and* then the part must meet the buyer's specifications, so this *unconditional* probability is $P(I \cap B) = .80$.

In contrast, suppose you *know* that the selected part is from a lot that passes inspection. Now you are interested in the probability that the part conforms to specifications *given* that the part is shipped to the buyer, i.e., you want to determine the *conditional* probability $P(B \mid I)$. From the definition of conditional probability,

$$P(B \mid I) = \frac{P(I \cap B)}{P(I)}$$

where the event

I: {Part is shipped to the buyer}

contains the two simple events

$I \cap B$:   {Part is shipped to buyer and conforms to specifications}

and

$I \cap B^c$:   {Part is shipped to buyer but fails to meet specifications}

Recalling that the probability of an event is equal to the sum of the probabilities of its simple events, we obtain

$$P(I) = P(I \cap B) + P(I \cap B^c)$$
$$= .80 + .02 = .82$$

Then the conditional probability that a part conforms to specifications, given the part is shipped to the buyer, is

$$P(B \mid I) = \frac{P(I \cap B)}{P(I)} = \frac{.80}{.82} = .976$$

As we would expect, the probability that the part conforms to specifications, given that the part is shipped to the buyer, is higher than the unconditional probability that a part will be acceptable to the buyer.

EXAMPLE 3.10

The investigation of consumer product complaints by the Federal Trade Commission (FTC) has generated much interest by manufacturers in the quality of their products. A manufacturer of food processors conducted an analysis of a large number of consumer complaints and found that they fell into the six categories shown in Table 3.2. If a consumer complaint is received, what is the probability that the cause of the complaint was product appearance given that the complaint originated during the guarantee period?

TABLE 3.2   Distribution of Product Complaints

	Reason for Complaint			TOTALS
	Electrical	Mechanical	Appearance	
During guarantee period	18%	13%	32%	63%
After guarantee period	12%	22%	3%	37%
TOTALS	30%	35%	35%	100%

Solution

Let A represent the event that the cause of a particular complaint was product appearance, and let B represent the event that the complaint occurred during the guarantee period. Checking Table 3.2, you can see that $(18 + 13 + 32)\% = 63\%$ of the complaints occurred during the guarantee time. Hence, $P(B) = .63$. The percentage of complaints that were caused by appearance and occurred during the guarantee time (the event $A \cap B$) is 32%. Therefore, $P(A \cap B) = .32$.

Using these probability values, we can calculate the conditional probability $P(A \mid B)$ that the cause of a complaint is appearance given that the complaint occurred during the guarantee time:

$$P(A \mid B) = \frac{P(A \cap B)}{P(B)} = \frac{.32}{.63} = .51$$

Consequently, you can see that slightly more than half the complaints that occurred during the guarantee time were due to scratches, dents, or other imperfections in the surface of the food processors.

EXERCISES

3.13 An article in *IEEE Computer Applications in Power* (April 1990) describes "an unmanned watching system to detect intruders in real time without spurious detections, both indoors and outdoors, using video cameras and microprocessors." The system was tested outdoors under various weather conditions in Tokyo, Japan. The numbers of intruders detected and missed under each condition are provided in the table.

	Weather Condition				
	Clear	Cloudy	Rainy	Snowy	Windy
Intruders detected	21	228	226	7	185
Intruders missed	0	6	6	3	10
TOTALS	21	234	232	10	195

Source: Kaneda, K., et al. "An unmanned watching system using video cameras." *IEEE Computer Applications in Power*, Apr. 1990, p. 24.

a. Under cloudy conditions, what is the probability that the unmanned system detects an intruder?
b. Given that the unmanned system missed detecting an intruder, what is the probability that the weather condition was snowy?

3.14 Refer to the game of roulette and the events described in Exercise 3.8. Find
a. $P(A \mid B)$ b. $P(B \mid C)$ c. $P(C \mid A)$

3.15 Refer to the game of craps described in Exercise 3.11. A player casts the dice a single time.
a. Given that the sum of the dice is odd, what is the probability that craps is thrown?
b. Given that the player does not throw craps, what is the probability that the player throws a *double*— i.e., the same outcome on both dice?

3.16 Refer to the NSF survey on Ph.D.'s awarded in engineering and science disciplines, Exercise 3.6. The results of the survey are reproduced in the table. Again, assume you have randomly selected one of the 22,103 graduate students who earned a Ph.D. in one of these disciplines.

Discipline	Ph.D.'s Awarded to U.S. Citizens	Ph.D.'s Awarded to Foreign Nationals	Totals
Engineering	607	1,630	2,237
Astronomy	126	84	210
Chemistry	1,291	2,336	3,627
Physics	757	1,006	1,763
Earth/Ocean/Atmosphere	409	236	645
Mathematics	92	114	206
Computer Science	110	47	157
Agricultural Science	327	247	574
Biology	6,529	6,155	12,684
TOTALS	10,248	11,855	22,103

Source: *Science*, Vol. 26, Sept. 24, 1993, p. 1770.

a. Find the probability that the student was a foreign national and earned a Ph.D. in physics.
b. Given the student earned a Ph.D. in chemistry, what is the probability that he or she is a foreign national?
c. Repeat part b for a Ph.D. in engineering.

3.17   The probability that a data-communications system will have high selectivity is .72, the probability that it will have high fidelity is .59, and the probability that it will have both is .33. Find the probability that a system with high fidelity will also have high selectivity.

3.18   Refer to the U.S. Army Corps of Engineers study on the DDT contamination of fish in the Tennessee River in Alabama (see Case Study 1.1). Part of the investigation focused on how far upstream the contaminated fish have migrated. (A fish is considered to be contaminated if its measured DDT concentration is greater than 5.0 parts per million.) Recall that Appendix III gives the DDT concentration, species, and capture location (in miles from the river's mouth) for each in a sample of 144 fish specimens. The accompanying table gives the number of contaminated fish found for each species–location combination. Suppose a contaminated fish is captured from the river.

		Capture Location		
		275–300	305–325	330–350
	Smallmouth buffalo	9	7	0
Species	Largemouth bass	0	0	1
	Channel catfish	31	23	6

a. Given that the fish is a channel catfish, what is the probability that it is captured 330–350 miles upstream?

b. Given that the fish is captured 275–300 miles upstream, what is the probability that it is a smallmouth buffalo?

3.19   The United States Nuclear Regulatory Commission assesses the safety risks associated with nuclear power plants. The commission has concluded that the probability of less than one latent cancer fatality (per year) as a result of core melt of a nuclear reactor is .00005. Suppose the probability that a core melt occurs during a given year is 1 in 100,000. Find the probability that at least one latent cancer fatality (per year) will occur as a result of a core melt of a nuclear reactor.

3.6   Probability Rules for Unions and Intersections

Since unions and intersections of events are themselves events, we can always calculate their probabilities by adding the probabilities of the simple events that compose them. However, when the probabilities of certain events are known, it is easier to use one or both of two rules to calculate the probability of unions and intersections. How and why these rules work will be illustrated by example.

EXAMPLE 3.11

A loaded (unbalanced) die is tossed and the up face is observed. The following two events are defined:

A: {Observe an even number}

B: {Observe a number less than 3}

Suppose that $P(A) = .4$, $P(B) = .2$, and $P(A \cap B) = .1$. Find $P(A \cup B)$. [*Note*: Assuming that we would know these probabilities in a practical situation is not very realistic, but the example will illustrate a point.]

Solution   By studying the Venn diagram in Figure 3.8, we can obtain information that will help us find $P(A \cup B)$. We can see that

$$P(A \cup B) = P(1) + P(2) + P(4) + P(6)$$

Also, we know that

$$P(A) = P(2) + P(4) + P(6) = .4$$
$$P(B) = P(1) + P(2) = .2$$
$$P(A \cap B) = P(2) = .1$$

FIGURE 3.8 ▶
Venn diagram for die toss

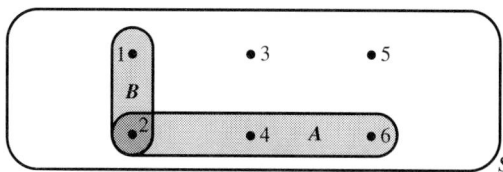

If we add the probabilities of the simple events that comprise events A and B, we find

$$P(A) + P(B) = \overbrace{P(2) + P(4) + P(6)}^{P(A)} + \overbrace{P(1) + P(2)}^{P(B)}$$
$$= \overbrace{P(1) + P(2) + P(4) + P(6)}^{P(A \cup B)} + \overbrace{P(2)}^{P(A \cap B)}$$

Thus, by subtraction, we have

$$P(A \cup B) = P(A) + P(B) - P(A \cap B)$$
$$= .4 + .2 - .1 = .5$$

By studying the Venn diagram in Figure 3.9, you can see that the method used in Example 3.11 may be generalized to find the union of two events for any experiment. The probability of the union of two events, A and B, can always be obtained by summing $P(A)$ and $P(B)$ and subtracting $P(A \cap B)$. Note that we must subtract $P(A \cap B)$ because the simple event probabilities in $(A \cap B)$ have been included twice—once in $P(A)$ and once in $P(B)$.

FIGURE 3.9 ▶
Venn diagram of union

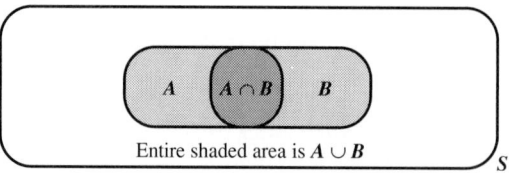

Entire shaded area is $A \cup B$

The formula for calculating the probability of the union of two events, often called the **additive rule of probability**, is given in the box.

> ## Additive Rule of Probability
>
> The probability of the union of events A and B is the sum of the probabilities of events A and B minus the probability of the intersection of events A and B:
>
> $$P(A \cup B) = P(A) + P(B) - P(A \cap B)$$

EXAMPLE 3.12

Records at an industrial plant show that 12% of all injured workers are admitted to a hospital for treatment, 16% are back on the job the next day, and 2% are both admitted to a hospital for treatment and back on the job the next day. If a worker is injured, what is the probability that the worker will be either admitted to a hospital for treatment, or back on the job the next day, or both?

Solution

Consider the following events:

A: {An injured worker is admitted to the hospital for treatment}

B: {An injured worker returns to the job the next day}

Then, from the information given in the statement of the example, we know that

$$P(A) = .12 \qquad P(B) = .16$$

and the probability of the event that an injured worker receives hospital treatment and returns to the job the next day is

$$P(A \cap B) = .02$$

The event that an injured worker is admitted to the hospital, or returns to the job the next day, or both, is the union, $A \cup B$. The probability of $A \cup B$ is given by the additive rule of probability:

$$P(A \cup B) = P(A) + P(B) - P(A \cap B)$$
$$= .12 + .16 - .02 = .26$$

Thus, 26% of all injured workers either are admitted to the hospital, or return to the job the next day, or both.

A very special relationship exists between events A and B when $A \cap B$ contains no simple events. In this case, we call the events A and B **mutually exclusive** events.

> ### Definition 3.9
>
> Events A and B are **mutually exclusive** if $A \cap B$ contains no simple events.

Figure 3.10 shows a Venn diagram of two mutually exclusive events. The events A and B have no simple events in common, i.e., A and B cannot occur simultaneously, and $P(A \cap B) = 0$. Thus, we have the important relationship shown in the next box.

FIGURE 3.10 ▶
Venn diagram of mutually exclusive events

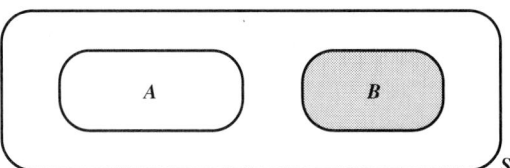

> ### Additive Rule for Mutually Exclusive Events
>
> **If two events A and B are mutually exclusive,** the probability of the union of A and B equals the sum of the probabilities of A and B:
>
> $$P(A \cup B) = P(A) + P(B)$$

. . . .

EXAMPLE 3.13

Consider the experiment of tossing two balanced coins. Find the probability of observing at least one head.

Solution

Define the events

   A: {Observe at least one head}
   B: {Observe exactly one head}
   C: {Observe exactly two heads}

Note that $A = B \cup C$ and that $B \cap C$ contains no simple events (see Figure 3.11). Thus, B and C are mutually exclusive, so that

$$P(A) = P(B \cup C) = P(B) + P(C)$$
$$= \frac{1}{2} + \frac{1}{4} = \frac{3}{4}$$

FIGURE 3.11 ▶
Venn diagram for coin toss
experiment

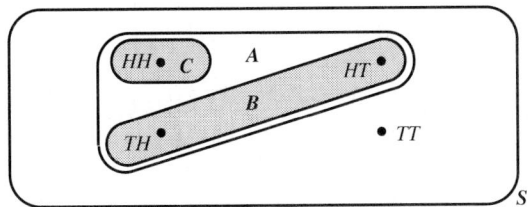

Although Example 3.13 is very simple, the concept of writing events with verbal descriptions that include the phrases "at least" or "at most" as unions of mutually exclusive events is a very useful one. This enables us to find the probability of the event by adding the probabilities of the mutually exclusive events.

The second rule of probability, which will help us find the probability of the intersection of two events, is illustrated by Example 3.14.

EXAMPLE 3.14

A data processor is interested in the event that a job will be processed immediately upon submission. This event is the intersection of the following two events:

A: {The computer is functional}

B: {The job will be processed immediately}

Based on available information, the data processor believes that the probability is .90 that the computer will be functional at any particular time and that the probability is .05 that the job will run immediately upon submission given that the computer is functional. That is,

$$P(A) = .90 \quad \text{and} \quad P(B \mid A) = .05$$

Based on the information provided, what is the probability that a submitted job will be processed immediately? That is, find $P(A \cap B)$.

Solution

As you will see, we have already developed a formula for finding the probability of an intersection of two events. Recall that the conditional probability of B given A is

$$P(B \mid A) = \frac{P(A \cap B)}{P(A)}$$

Multiplying both sides of this equation by $P(A)$, we obtain a formula for the probability of the intersection of events A and B. This is often called the **multiplicative rule of probability** and is given by

$$P(A \cap B) = P(A) P(B \mid A)$$

Thus,

$$P(A \cap B) = (.90)(.05) = .045$$

The probability that a submitted job will be processed immediately is .045.

> ### Multiplicative Rule of Probability
>
> $$P(A \cap B) = P(A \mid B)P(B) = P(B \mid A)P(A)$$

EXAMPLE 3.15

Consider the experiment of tossing a fair coin twice and recording the up face on each toss. The following events are defined:

A: {First toss is a head}

B: {Second toss is a head}

Does *knowing* that event A has occurred affect the probability that B will occur?

Solution

Intuitively the answer should be no, since what occurs on the first toss should in no way affect what occurs on the second toss. Let us check our intuition. Recall the sample space for this experiment:

1. Observe *HH*
2. Observe *HT*
3. Observe *TH*
4. Observe *TT*

Each of these simple events has a probability of $\frac{1}{4}$. Thus,

$$P(B) = P(HH) + P(TH) \quad \text{and} \quad P(A) = P(HH) + P(HT)$$
$$= \frac{1}{4} + \frac{1}{4} = \frac{1}{2} \qquad\qquad\qquad = \frac{1}{4} + \frac{1}{4} = \frac{1}{2}$$

Now, what is $P(B \mid A)$?

$$P(B \mid A) = \frac{P(A \cap B)}{P(A)} = \frac{P(HH)}{P(A)}$$
$$= \frac{\frac{1}{4}}{\frac{1}{2}} = \frac{1}{2}$$

We can now see that $P(B) = \frac{1}{2}$ and $P(B \mid A) = \frac{1}{2}$. Knowing that the first toss resulted in a head does not affect the probability that the second toss will be a head. The probability is $\frac{1}{2}$ whether or not we know the result of the first toss. When this occurs, we say that the two events A and B are **independent**.

Definition 3.10

Events A and B are **independent** if the occurrence of B does not alter the probability that A has occurred, i.e., events A and B are independent if

$$P(A \mid B) = P(A)$$

When events A and B are **independent**, it will also be true that

$$P(B \mid A) = P(B)$$

Events that are not independent are said to be **dependent**.

EXAMPLE 3.16

Consider the experiment of tossing a fair die and define the following events:

A: {Observe an even number}

B: {Observe a number less than or equal to 4}

Are events A and B independent?

Solution

The Venn diagram for this experiment is shown in Figure 3.12. We first calculate

$$P(A) = P(2) + P(4) + P(6) = \frac{1}{2}$$

$$P(B) = P(1) + P(2) + P(3) + P(4) = \frac{4}{6} = \frac{2}{3}$$

$$P(A \cap B) = P(2) + P(4) = \frac{2}{6} = \frac{1}{3}$$

FIGURE 3.12 ▶
Venn diagram for Example 3.16

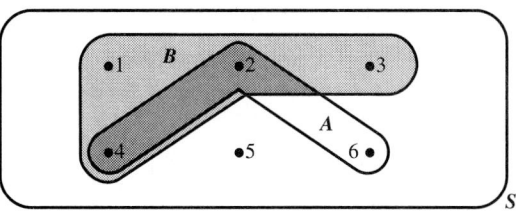

Now assuming B has occurred, the conditional probability of A given B is

$$P(A \mid B) = \frac{P(A \cap B)}{P(B)} = \frac{\frac{1}{3}}{\frac{2}{3}} = \frac{1}{2} = P(A)$$

Thus, assuming that event B occurs does not alter the probability of observing an even number—it remains $\frac{1}{2}$. Therefore, the events A and B are independent. Note that if we calculate the conditional probability of B given A, our conclusion is the same:

$$P(B \mid A) = \frac{P(A \cap B)}{P(A)} = \frac{\frac{1}{3}}{\frac{1}{2}} = \frac{2}{3} = P(B)$$

EXAMPLE 3.17

Refer to the consumer product complaint study in Example 3.10. The percentages of complaints of various types in the pre- and post-guarantee periods are shown in Table 3.2. Define the following events:

A: {Cause of complaint is product appearance}

B: {Complaint occurred during the guarantee term}

Are A and B independent events?

Solution

Events A and B are independent if $P(A \mid B) = P(A)$. We calculated $P(A \mid B)$ in Example 3.10 to be .51, and from Table 3.2 we can see that

$$P(A) = .32 + .03 = .35$$

Therefore, $P(A \mid B)$ is not equal to $P(A)$, and A and B are not independent events.

We will make three final points about independence. The first is that the property of independence, unlike the mutually exclusive property, cannot be shown on or gleaned from a Venn diagram, and you cannot trust your intuition. In general, the only way to check for independence is by performing the calculations of the probabilities in the definition.

The second point concerns the relationship between the mutually exclusive and independence properties. Suppose that events A and B are mutually exclusive, as shown in Figure 3.10. Are these events independent or dependent? That is, does the assumption that B occurs alter the probability of the occurrence of A? It certainly does, because if we assume that B has occurred, it is impossible for A to have occurred simultaneously. Thus, **mutually exclusive events are dependent events**.*

The third point is that the probability of the intersection of independent events is very easy to calculate. Referring to the formula for calculating the probability of an intersection, we find

$$P(A \cap B) = P(B)P(A \mid B)$$

Thus, since $P(A \mid B) = P(A)$ when A and B are independent, we have the useful rule stated in the following box.

---

*The result holds unless one of the events has zero probability.

Multiplicative Rule for Independent Events

If events A and B are independent, the probability of the intersection of A and B equals the product of the probabilities of A and B, i.e.,

$$P(A \cap B) = P(A)P(B)$$

In the die-tossing experiment, we showed in Example 3.16 that the events A: {Observe an even number} and B: {Observe a number less than or equal to 4} are independent if the die is fair. Thus,

$$P(A \cap B) = P(A)P(B) = \left(\frac{1}{2}\right)\left(\frac{2}{3}\right) = \frac{1}{3}$$

This agrees with the result

$$P(A \cap B) = P(2) + P(4) = \frac{2}{6} = \frac{1}{3}$$

that we obtained in the example.

....

EXAMPLE 3.18

In Example 3.3, a quality control engineer considered the problem of determining whether an assembly line is out of control. In the example, we discussed the problem of finding the probability that one, two, or, in general, k items arriving off the assembly line are defective. We are now ready to find the probability that both of two items arriving in succession off the line are defective. Suppose that the line is out of control and that 20% of the items being produced are defective.

a. If two items arrive in succession off the line, what is the probability that they are both defective?

b. If k items arrive in succession off the line, what is the probability that all are defective?

Solution

a. Let D_1 be the event that item 1 is defective, and let D_2 be a similar event for item 2. The event that *both* items will be defective is the intersection $D_1 \cap D_2$. Then, since it is not unreasonable to assume that the operating conditions of the items would be independent of one another, the probability that both will be defective is

$$P(D_1 \cap D_2) = P(D_1)P(D_2)$$
$$= (.2)(.2) = (.2)^2 = .04$$

b. Let D_i represent the event that the ith item arriving in succession off the line is defective. Then the event that all three of three items arriving in succession will be defective is the intersection of the event $D_1 \cap D_2$ (from part **a**) with the event D_3. Assuming independence of the events D_1, D_2, and D_3, we have

$$P(D_1 \cap D_2 \cap D_3) = P(D_1 \cap D_2)P(D_3)$$
$$= (.2)^2(.2) = (.2)^3 = .008$$

Noting the pattern, you can see that the probability that all k out of k arriving items are defective is the probability of $D_1 \cap D_2 \cap \cdots \cap D_k$, or

$$P(D_1 \cap D_2 \cap \cdots \cap D_k) = (.2)^k \quad \text{for } k = 1, 2, 3, \ldots$$

EXERCISES

3.20 The National Acid Precipitation Assessment Program (NAPAP) has recently concluded a 10-year study of acid rain. In its report, NAPAP estimates the probability of an Adirondack lake being acidic at .14. Given that the Adirondack lake is acidic, the probability that the lake comes naturally by its acidity is .25 (*Science News*, Sept. 15, 1990). Use this information to find the probability that an Adirondack lake is naturally acidic.

3.21 According to NASA, each space shuttle in the U.S. fleet has 1,500 "critical items" that could lead to catastrophic failure if rendered inoperable during flight. NASA estimates that the chance of at least one critical-item failure within the shuttle's main engines is about 1 in 63 for each mission (*Tampa Tribune*, Dec. 3, 1993). To build space station *Freedom*, NASA plans to fly eight shuttle missions a year during the remainder of the 1990s.
  a. Find the probability that at least one of the eight shuttle flights scheduled next year results in a critical-item failure.
  b. Find the probability that at least one of the 40 shuttle missions scheduled over the next 5 years results in a critical-item failure.

3.22 The merging process from an acceleration lane to the through lane of a freeway constitutes an important aspect of traffic operation at interchanges. A study of parallel and tapered interchange ramps in Israel revealed the accompanying information on traffic lags (where a *lag* is defined as an interval of time between arrivals of major streams of vehicles) accepted and rejected by drivers in the merging lane.

Type of Interchange Lane	Traffic Condition on Freeway	Number of Merging Drivers Accepting the First Available Lag	Number of Merging Drivers Rejecting the First Available Lag
Tapered	Heavy traffic	16	115
	Little traffic	67	121
Parallel	Heavy traffic	40	139
	Little traffic	144	331

Source: Polus, A., and Livneh, M. "Vehicle flow characteristics on acceleration lanes." *Journal of Transportation Engineering*, Vol. III, No. 6, Nov. 1985, pp. 600–601 (Table 4).

a. What is the probability that a driver in a tapered merging lane with heavy traffic will accept the first available lag?

b. What is the probability that a driver in a parallel merging lane will reject the first available lag in traffic?

c. Given that a driver accepts the first available lag in little traffic, what is the probability that the driver is in a parallel merging lane?

3.23 Managers of oil exploration portfolios make decisions on which prospects to pursue based, in part, on the level of risk associated with each venture. Kinchen (1986) examined the problem of risk analysis in oil exploration using the outcomes and associated probabilities for a single prospect, shown in the table.

Outcome barrels	Probability
0 (dry hole)	.60
50,000	.10
100,000	.15
500,000	.10
1,000,000	.05

Source: Kinchen, A. L. "Projected outcomes of exploration programs based on current program status and the impact of prospects under consideration." *Journal of Petroleum Technology*, Vol. 38, No. 4, Apr. 1986, p. 462.

a. What is the probability that a single oil well prospect will result in no more than 100,000 barrels of oil?

b. What is the probability that a single oil well prospect will strike oil?

c. Kinchen also considered two identical oil well prospects. List the possible outcomes (i.e., simple events) if the two wells are drilled. Assume the outcomes listed in the table are the only ones possible for any one well. [*Hint:* One possible simple event is two dry holes.]

d. Use the information in the table to calculate the probabilities of the simple events in part **c**. (Assume that the individual outcomes of the two wells are independent of each other.)

e. Refer to part **d**. Find the probability that at least one of the two oil prospects strikes oil.

3.24 Refer to Exercise 3.11 and the game of craps. Consider the following events:

    A: {Player throws craps}

    B: {Player throws a natural}

    C: {Player throws 9, 10, or 11}

a. Which pairs of events, if any, are mutually exclusive?

b. Which pairs of events, if any, are independent?

3.25 The transport of neutral particles in an evacuated duct is an important aspect of nuclear fusion reactor design. In one experiment, particles entering through the duct ends streamed unimpeded until they collided with the inner duct wall. Upon colliding, they were either scattered (reflected) or absorbed by the wall (*Nuclear Science and Engineering*, May 1986). The reflection probability (i.e., the probability that a particle is reflected off the wall) for one type of duct was found to be .16.

a. If two particles are released into the duct, find the probability that both will be reflected.

b. If five particles are released into the duct, find the probability that all five will be absorbed.

c. What assumption about the simple events in parts **a** and **b** is required to calculate the probabilities?

3.26 Based on data provided by the U.S. Department of Health and Human Resources, *U.S. News & World Report* (Sept. 28, 1992) estimates the probability of a kidney transplant failing within a year at .20.

   a. Consider three recent kidney transplant patients. Find the probability that all three kidney transplants fail within a year.

   b. In general, if k kidney transplants are performed, what is the probability that at least one will fail within a year?

3.27 Traditionally, geotechnical engineers have employed *working stress designs* (WSD) for designing structures safe from collapse. One study examined total safety of conventional WSD in three design areas: earthworks, earth-retaining structures and excavations, and foundations (*Canadian Geotechnical Journal*, Nov. 1985). The table gives the probability of failure in each of the design areas.

Design Area	Probability of Failure
Earthworks	.01
Earth-retaining structures and excavations	.001
Foundations	.0001

   Consider a WSD comprised of the three design areas. (Assume that the failure of any one design area is independent of the failure of the others.)

   a. What is the probability of failure in either the earthworks or earth-retaining structures and excavations design area?

   b. What is the probability of failure in all three design areas?

3.28 A two-component electronic system is connected in parallel so that it fails only if both of its components fail. The probability that the first component fails is .10. If the first component fails, the probability that the second component fails is .05. What is the probability that the two-component electronic system fails?

3.29 In 1987, Congress enacted the Surface Transportation and Uniform Act, which allowed states to increase the speed limit to 65 mph on interstate highways located outside of an urban area of 50,000 or more persons. In a study of traffic fatalities on interstate highways, the Fatal Accident Reporting System discovered that 96% of the interstate highway miles eligible to be posted at 65 mph are rural interstates, and 97% of these eligible miles were actually posted at 65 mph (*American Journal of Public Health*, Oct. 1989).

   a. For a particular 1-mile stretch of interstate highway eligible to be posted at 65 mph, estimate the probability that the 1-mile stretch is posted at 65 mph.

   b. For a particular 1-mile stretch of interstate highway eligible to be posted at 65 mph, estimate the probability that the 1-mile stretch is not rural.

   c. Are the events in parts **a** and **b** mutually exclusive? Explain.

3.30 An article in *Transportation Quarterly* (Jan. 1993) identified several studies on truck accidents that utilized misleading or inappropriate probability analysis. Consider the following excerpt from the article.* Can you find the flaw in the probability argument?

   For example, consider a situation where only two vehicle types are present in the traffic mix: trucks at 20% and cars at 80% of the total. If only two vehicle accidents are considered, the probability of occurrence for all events in the sample space would be as follows:

*Bowman, B. L., and Hummer, J. "Data validity barriers to determining magnitude of large truck accident problem." *Transportation Quarterly*, Vol. 47, No. 1, Jan. 1993, p. 40.

Probability of truck impacting truck $= P(TT) = .20 \times .20 = .04$
Probability of truck impacting car $\quad = P(TC) = .20 \times .80 = .16$
Probability of car impacting truck $\quad = P(CT) = .80 \times .20 = .16$
Probability of car impacting car $\quad\quad = P(CC) = .80 \times .80 = \underline{.64}$
$$1.00$$

Many analysts [used the calculation $P(TT) + P(TC) + P(CT) = .36$ to conclude] that trucks, constituting 20% of the traffic, are involved in 36% of all two-vehicle accidents. Hence cars, which constitute 80% of the traffic, are involved in $100\% - 36\% = 64\%$ of the accidents.

OPTIONAL EXERCISE

3.31   Writing in *Environmental Science & Technology* (May 1986), Joseph Fiksel researches the problem of compensating victims of chronic diseases (such as cancer and birth defects) who are exposed to hazardous and toxic substances. The key to compensation, as far as the U.S. judicial system is concerned, is the *probability of causation* (i.e., the likelihood, for a person developing the disease, that the cause is due to exposure to the hazardous substance). Usually, the probability of causation must be greater than .50 for the court to award compensation. Fiksel gives examples of how to calculate the probability of causation for several different scenarios.*

a. "*Ordinary causation*," as defined by Fiksel, "describes a situation in which the presence of a single factor, such as asbestos insulation, is believed to cause an effect, such as mesothelioma." For this situation, define the following events:

D: {Effect (disease) occurs}

A: {Factor A present}

Under ordinary causation, if A occurs, then D must occur. However, D can also occur when factor A is not present. The probability of causation for factor A, then, is the conditional probability $P(A \mid D)$. Show that the probability of causation for factor A is

$$P(A \mid D) = \frac{P_1 - P_0}{P_1}$$

where P_0 is the probability that the effect occurs when factor A is *not* present, and P_1 is the probability that the effect occurs when factor A is either present or not. [*Note:* To epidemiologists, P_1 is often called the *overall risk rate* for the disease and $P_1 - P_0$ is the *additional risk* attributable to the presence of factor A.] [*Hint:* The simple events for this experiment are $\{D^c \cap A^c, D \cap A, \text{ and } D \cap A^c\}$. Write P_0 and P_1 in terms of the simple events.]

b. Fiksel defines *simultaneous exclusive causation* as "a situation in which two or more causal factors are present but the resulting effect is caused by *one and only one* of these factors." Consider two factors, A and B, and let B be the event that factor B is present. In this situation, if either A or B occurs, then D must occur. However, both A and B cannot occur simultaneously (i.e., A and B are mutually exclusive).

*Fiksel, J. "Victim compensation: Understanding the problem of indeterminate causation." *Environmental Science and Technology*, May 1986. Copyright 1986 American Chemical Society. Reprinted with permission.

Assuming that D cannot occur when neither A nor B occurs, show that the probabilities of causations for factors A and B are, respectively,

$$P(A \mid D) = \frac{P_1}{P_1 + P_2} \quad \text{and} \quad P(B \mid D) = \frac{P_2}{P_1 + P_2}$$

where P_1 is the probability that the effect occurs when factor A is present and P_2 is the probability that the effect occurs when factor B is present. [*Hint:* The simple events for this experiment are $\{D^c \cap A^c \cap B^c, D \cap A \cap B^c, \text{ and } D \cap A^c \cap B\}$.]

c. *Simultaneous joint causation*, writes Fiksel, describes a more realistic situation "in which several factors can contribute in varying degrees to the occurrence of an effect. For example, a cigarette smoker who is exposed to radiation and chemical carcinogens in the workplace may develop a lung tumor. Whether the tumor was caused wholly by one factor or by a combination of factors is, at present, impossible to determine." For this case, consider two factors, A and B, which affect D independently. Also, assume that if either A or B, or both occur, then D must occur; D cannot occur if neither A nor B occurs. Show that the probabilities of causation for factors A and B are, respectively,

$$P(A \mid D) = \frac{P_1}{P_1 + P_2 - P_1 P_2} \quad \text{and} \quad P(B \mid D) = \frac{P_2}{P_1 + P_2 - P_1 P_2}$$

where P_1 is the probability that the effect occurs when factor A is present and P_2 is the probability that the effect occurs when factor B is present. [*Hint:* The simple events for this experiment are $\{D^c \cap A^c \cap B^c, D \cap A \cap B^c, D \cap A^c \cap B, \text{ and } D \cap A \cap B\}$.]

3.7   Bayes' Rule (Optional)

An early attempt to employ probability in making inferences is the basis for a branch of statistical methodology known as **Bayesian statistical methods**. The logic employed by the English philosopher, the Reverend Thomas Bayes (1702–1761) is illustrated by Example 3.19.

EXAMPLE 3.19

An unmanned monitoring system uses high-tech video equipment and microprocessors to detect intruders. A prototype system has been developed and is in use outdoors at a weapons munitions plant. The system is designed to detect intruders with a probability of .90. However, the design engineers expect this probability to vary with weather condition. The system automatically records the weather condition each time an intruder is detected. Based on a series of controlled tests, in which an intruder was released at the plant under various weather conditions, the following information is available: Given the intruder was, in fact, detected by the system, the weather was clear 75% of the time, cloudy 20% of the time, and raining 5% of the time. When the system failed to detect the intruder, 60% of the days were clear, 30% cloudy, and 10% rainy. Use this information to find the probability of detecting an intruder, given rainy weather conditions. (Assume that an intruder has been released at the plant.)

Solution

Define D to be the event that the intruder is detected by the system. Then D^c is the event that the system failed to detect the intruder. Our goal is to calculate the conditional probability, $P(D \mid \text{Rainy})$. From the statement of the problem, the following information is available:

$$P(D) = .90 \qquad\qquad P(D^c) = .10$$
$$P(\text{Clear} \mid D) = .75 \qquad P(\text{Clear} \mid D^c) = .60$$
$$P(\text{Cloudy} \mid D) = .20 \qquad P(\text{Cloudy} \mid D^c) = .30$$
$$P(\text{Rainy} \mid D) = .05 \qquad P(\text{Rainy} \mid D^c) = .10$$

Then

$$P(\text{Rainy} \cap D) = P(D)P(\text{Rainy} \mid D) = (.90)(.05) = .045$$

and

$$P(\text{Rainy} \cap D^c) = P(D^c)P(\text{Rainy} \mid D^c) = (.10)(.10) = .01$$

The event Rainy is the union of two mutually exclusive events, $(\text{Rainy} \cap D)$ and $(\text{Rainy} \cap D^c)$. Thus,

$$P(\text{Rainy}) = P(\text{Rainy} \cap D) + P(\text{Rainy} \cap D^c) = .045 + .01 = .055$$

We now apply the formula for conditional probability to obtain:

$$P(D \mid \text{Rainy}) = \frac{P(\text{Rainy} \cap D)}{P(\text{Rainy})} = \frac{P(\text{Rainy} \cap D)}{P(\text{Rainy} \cap D) + P(\text{Rainy} \cap D^c)}$$

$$= \frac{.045}{.055} = .818$$

Therefore, under rainy weather conditions, the prototype system can detect the intruder with a probability of .818—a value lower than the designed probability of .90.

The technique utilized in Example 3.19, called **Bayes' method**, can be applied when an observed event E occurs with any one of k mutually exclusive and exhaustive states of nature (or events), $A_1, A_2, \ldots, A_k$. The formula for finding the appropriate conditional probabilities is given in the box.

Bayes' Rule

Given k mutually exclusive and exhaustive states of nature (events), $A_1, A_2, \ldots, A_k$, and an observed event E, then $P(A_i \mid E)$, for $i = 1, 2, \ldots, k$, is

$$P(A_i \mid E) = \frac{P(A_i \cap E)}{P(E)}$$

$$= \frac{P(A_i)P(E \mid A_i)}{P(A_1)P(E \mid A_1) + P(A_2)P(E \mid A_2) + \cdots + P(A_k)P(E \mid A_k)}$$

In applying Bayes' rule to Example 3.19, the observed event E is {Rainy} and the mutually exclusive and exhaustive states of nature are D (intruder detected) and D^c (intruder not detected). Hence, the formula

$$P(D|\text{Rainy}) = \frac{P(D)P(\text{Rainy}|D)}{P(D)P(\text{Rainy}|D) + P(D^c)P(\text{Rainy}|D^c)}$$

$$= \frac{(.90)(.05)}{(.90)(.05) + (.10)(.10)} = .818$$

In Exercise 3.70, you use Bayes' rule to find $P(D|\text{Clear})$ and $P(D|\text{Cloudy})$.

EXERCISES

3.32   A construction company employs three sales engineers. Engineers 1, 2, and 3 estimate the costs of 30%, 20%, and 50%, respectively, of all jobs bid by the company. For $i = 1, 2, 3$, define A_i to be the event that a job is estimated by engineer i, and define E to be the event that a serious error is made in estimating the cost. The following probabilities are known to describe the error rates of the engineers:

$P(E|A_1) = .01$

$P(E|A_2) = .03$

$P(E|A_3) = .02$

If a particular bid results in a serious error in estimating the job costs, which engineer is most likely responsible?

3.33   Refer to the table in Exercise 3.18 describing the location and species for each of 77 contaminated fish. This information can be used to find the probability that a contaminated channel catfish (CC) is found in each of the three locations, 275–300 miles, 305–325 miles, and 330–350 miles upstream. These *conditional probabilities* are

$P(CC|275–300) = .775$ $P(CC|305–325) = .77$ $P(CC|330–350) = .86$

Also, the table shows that 52% of the 77 contaminated fish species are found 257–300 miles upstream, 39% are found 305–325 miles upstream, and 9% are found 330–350 miles upstream. Given that a contaminated channel catfish is captured from the Tennessee River, find the probability that it was located 275–300 miles upstream.

3.34   A manufacturing operation utilizes two production lines to assemble electronic fuses. Both lines produce fuses at the same rate and generally produce 2.5% defective fuses. However, production line 1 recently suffered mechanical difficulty and produced 6.0% defectives during a 3-week period. This situation was not known until several lots of electronic fuses produced in this period were shipped to customers. If one of two fuses tested by a customer was found to be defective, what is the probability that the lot from which it came was produced on malfunctioning line 1? (Assume all the fuses in the lot were produced on the same line.)

3.35   The computing system at a large university is currently undergoing shutdown for repairs. Previous shutdowns have been due to hardware failure, software failure, or power (electronic) failure. The system is forced to shut down 73% of the time when it experiences hardware problems, 12% of the time when it experiences software problems, and 88% of the time when it experiences electronic problems. Maintenance engineers have determined that the probabilities of hardware, software, and power problems are .01, .05, and .02, respectively. What is the probability that the current shutdown is due to hardware failure? Software failure? Power failure?

3.36   An important component of a personal computer (PC) is a microchip. The table gives the percentages of microchips that a certain PC manufacturer purchases from seven suppliers.

Supplier	Percentage
S_1	.15
S_2	.05
S_3	.10
S_4	.20
S_5	.12
S_6	.20
S_7	.18

   a. Suppose it is known that the proportions of defective microchips produced by the seven suppliers are .001, .0003, .0007, .006, .0002, .0002, and .001, respectively. If a single PC microchip failure is observed, which supplier is most likely responsible?

   b. Suppose the seven suppliers produce defective microchips at the same rate, .0005. If a single PC microchip failure is observed, which supplier is most likely responsible?

3.8   Some Counting Rules

In Section 3.2 we pointed out that experiments sometimes have so many simple events that it is impractical to list them all. However, many of these experiments possess simple events with identical characteristics. If you can develop a **counting rule** to count the number of simple events for such an experiment, it can be used to aid in the solution of the problems.

EXAMPLE 3.20   A product (e.g., hardware for a computer system) can be shipped by four different airlines, and each airline can ship via three different routes. How many distinct ways exist to ship the product?

Solution   A pictorial representation of the different ways to ship the product will aid in counting them. This representation, called a **decision tree**, is shown in Figure 3.13 (page 120). At the starting point (stage 1), there are four choices—the different airlines—to begin the journey. Once we have chosen an airline (stage 2), there are three choices—the different routes—to complete the shipment and reach the final destination. Thus, the decision tree clearly shows that there are (4)(3) = 12 distinct ways to ship the product.

FIGURE 3.13 ▶
Decision tree for shipping problem

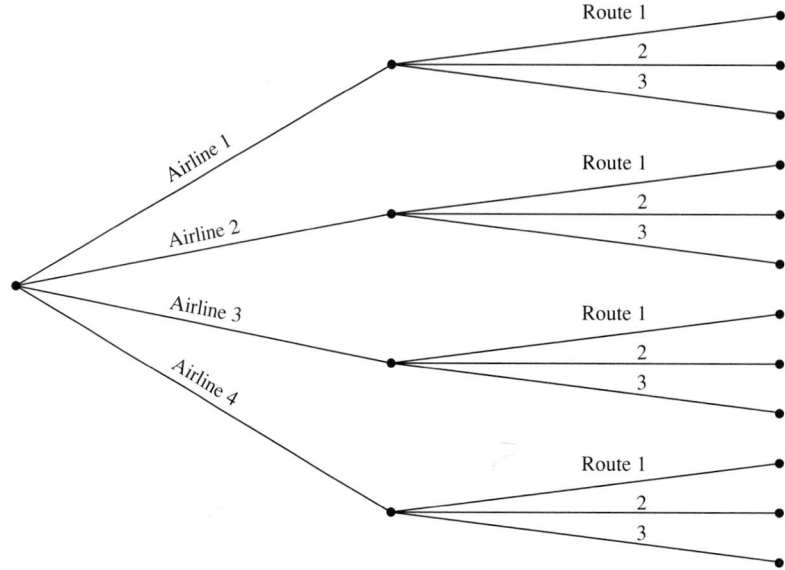

The method of solving Example 3.20 can be generalized to any number of stages with sets of different elements. The framework is provided by the **multiplicative rule**.

. . . .

Theorem 3.1
. . . .

THE MULTIPLICATIVE RULE   You have k sets of elements, n_1, in the first set, n_2 in the second set, . . . , and n_k in the kth set. Suppose you want to form a sample of k elements by taking one element from each of the k sets. The number of different samples that can be formed is the product

$$n_1 n_2 n_3 \cdot \cdot \cdot \cdot \cdot n_k$$

OUTLINE OF PROOF OF THEOREM 3.1   The proof of Theorem 3.1 can be obtained most easily by examining Table 3.3. Each of the pairs that can be formed from two sets of elements—$a_1, a_2, \ldots, a_{n_1}$ and $b_1, b_2, \ldots, b_{n_2}$—corresponds to a cell of Table 3.3.

TABLE 3.3   Pairings of $a_1, a_2, \ldots, a_{n_1}$ and $b_1, b_2, \ldots, b_{n_2}$

	b_1	b_2	b_3	$\cdots$	b_{n_2}
a_1	a_1b_1	a_1b_2	a_1b_3	$\cdots$	$a_1b_{n_2}$
a_2	a_2b_1	$\cdots$	$\cdots$	$\cdots$	$\cdots$
a_3	a_3b_1	$\cdots$	$\cdots$	$\cdots$	$\cdots$
$\vdots$	$\vdots$	$\vdots$	$\vdots$	$\vdots$	$\vdots$
a_{n_1}	$a_{n_1}b_1$	$\cdots$	$\cdots$	$\cdots$	$a_{n_1}b_{n_2}$

Since the table contains n_1 rows and n_2 columns, there will be n_1n_2 pairs corresponding to each of the n_1n_2 cells of the table. To extend the proof to the case in which $k = 3$, note that the number of triplets that can be formed from three sets of elements—$a_1, a_2, \ldots, a_{n_1}$; $b_1, b_2, \ldots, b_{n_2}$; and $c_1, c_2, \ldots, c_{n_3}$—is equal to the number of pairs that can be formed by associating one of the a_ib_j pairs with one of the c elements. Since there are (n_1, n_2) of the a_ib_j pairs and n_3 of the c elements, we can form $(n_1n_2)n_3 = n_1n_2n_3$ triplets consisting of one a element, one b element, and one c element. The proof of the multiplicative rule for any number, say, k, of sets is obtained by mathematical induction. We leave this proof as an exercise for the student.

EXAMPLE 3.21

There are 20 candidates for three different mechanical engineer positions, E_1, E_2, and E_3. How many different ways could you fill the positions?

Solution

This example consists of the following $k = 3$ sets of elements:

Set 1: Candidates available to fill position E_1
Set 2: Candidates remaining (after filling E_1) that are available to fill E_2
Set 3: Candidates remaining (after filling E_1 and E_2) that are available to fill E_3

The numbers of elements in the sets are $n_1 = 20$, $n_2 = 19$, $n_3 = 18$. Therefore, the number of different ways of filling the three positions is

$$n_1n_2n_3 = (20)(19)(18) = 6,840$$

EXAMPLE 3.22

Consider an experiment that consists of tossing a coin 10 times (recall Example 3.8). Show that there are $2^{10} = 1,024$ simple events for this experiment.

Solution

There are $k = 10$ sets of elements for this experiment. Each set contains two elements, a head and a tail. Thus, there are

$$(2)(2)(2)(2)(2)(2)(2)(2)(2)(2) = 2^{10} = 1{,}024$$

different outcomes (simple events) of this experiment.

EXAMPLE 3.23

Suppose there are five different space flights scheduled, each requiring one astronaut. Assuming that no astronaut can go on more than one space flight, in how many different ways can five of the country's top 100 astronauts be assigned to the five space flights?

Solution

We can solve this problem by using the multiplicative rule. The entire set of 100 astronauts is available for the first flight, and after the selection of one astronaut for that flight, 99 are available for the second flight, etc. Thus, the total number of different ways of choosing five astronauts for the five space flights is

$$n_1 n_2 n_3 n_4 n_5 = (100)(99)(98)(97)(96) = 9{,}034{,}502{,}400$$

The arrangement of elements in a distinct order is called a **permutation**. Thus, from Example 3.23, we see that there are more than 9 billion different *permutations* of five elements (astronauts) drawn from a set of 100 elements!

Theorem 3.2

PERMUTATIONS RULE   Given a single set of N distinctly different elements, you wish to select n elements from the N and arrange them within n positions. The number of different permutations of the N elements taken n at a time is denoted by P_n^N and is equal to

$$P_n^N = N(N - 1)(N - 2) \cdots (N - n + 1) = \frac{N!}{(N - n)!}$$

where $n! = n(n - 1)(n - 2) \cdots (3)(2)(1)$ and is called n **factorial**. (Thus, for example, $5! = 5 \cdot 4 \cdot 3 \cdot 2 \cdot 1 = 120$.) The quantity $0!$ is defined to be equal to 1.

PROOF OF THEOREM 3.2   The proof of Theorem 3.2 is a generalization of the solution to Example 3.23. There are N ways of filling the first position. After it is filled, there are $N - 1$ ways of filling the second, $N - 2$ ways of filling the third, . . . , and

$(N - n + 1)$ ways of filling the nth position. We apply the multiplicative rule to obtain

$$P_n^N = (N)(N - 1)(N - 2) \cdot \cdots \cdot (N - n + 1) = \frac{N!}{(N - n)!}$$

EXAMPLE 3.24

Consider the following transportation engineering problem: You want to drive, in sequence, from a starting point to each of five cities, and you want to compare the distances and average speeds of the different routings. How many different routings would have to be compared?

Solution

Denote the cities as $C_1, C_2, \ldots, C_5$. Then a route moving from the starting point to C_2 to C_1 to C_3 to C_4 to C_5 would be represented as $C_2C_1C_3C_4C_5$. The total number of routings would equal the number of ways you could rearrange the $N = 5$ cities in $n = 5$ positions. This number is

$$P_n^N = P_5^5 = \frac{5!}{(5 - 5)!} = \frac{5!}{0!} = \frac{5 \cdot 4 \cdot 3 \cdot 2 \cdot 1}{1} = 120$$

(recall that $0! = 1$).

EXAMPLE 3.25

There are four system analysts, and you must assign three to job 1 and one to job 2. In how many different ways can you make this assignment?

Solution

To begin, suppose that each system analyst is to be assigned to a distinct job. Then, using the multiplicative rule, we obtain $(4)(3)(2)(1) = 24$ ways of assigning the system analysts to four distinct jobs. The 24 ways are listed in four groups in Table 3.4 (where ABCD indicates that system analyst A was assigned the first job; system analyst B, the second; etc.).

TABLE 3.4   Ways to Assign System Analysts to Four Distinct Jobs

Group 1	Group 2	Group 3	Group 4
ABCD	ABDC	ACDB	BCDA
ACBD	ADBC	ADCB	BDCA
BACD	BADC	CADB	CBDA
BCAD	BDAC	CDAB	CDBA
CABD	DABC	DACB	DBCA
CBAD	DBAC	DCAB	DCBA

TABLE 3.5 Ways to Assign Three System Analysts to Job 1 and One System Analyst to Job 2	
Job 1	Job 2
ABC	D
ABD	C
ACD	B
BCD	A

Now, suppose the first three positions represent job 1 and the last position represents job 2. We can now see that all the listings in group 1 represent the same outcome of the experiment of interest. That is, system analysts A, B, and C are assigned to job 1 and system analyst D is assigned to job 2. Similarly, group 2 listings are equivalent, as are group 3 and group 4 listings. Thus, there are only four different assignments of four system analysts to the two jobs. These are shown in Table 3.5.

. . . .

To generalize the result obtained in Example 3.25, we point out that the final result can be found by

$$\frac{(4)(3)(2)(1)}{(3)(2)(1)(1)} = 4$$

The $(4)(3)(2)(1)$ is the number of different ways (*permutations*) the system analysts could be assigned four distinct jobs. The division by $(3)(2)(1)$ is to remove the duplicated permutations resulting from the fact that three system analysts are assigned the same jobs. And the division by (1) is associated with the system analyst assigned to job 2.

Theorem 3.3

. . . .

PARTITIONS RULE   There exists a single set of N distinctly different elements and you want to partition them into k sets, the first set containing n_1 elements, the second containing n_2 elements, . . . , and the kth set containing n_k elements. The number of different partitions is

$$\frac{N!}{n_1!n_2! \cdot \cdot \cdot \cdot \cdot n_k!} \quad \text{where } n_1 + n_2 + n_3 + \cdot \cdot \cdot + n_k = N$$

PROOF OF THEOREM 3.3   Let A equal the number of ways that you can partition N distinctly different elements into k sets. We want to show that

$$A = \frac{N!}{n_1!n_2! \cdot \cdot \cdot \cdot \cdot n_k!}$$

We will find A by writing an expression for arranging N distinctly different elements in N positions. By Theorem 3.2, the number of ways this can be done is

$$P_N^N = \frac{N!}{(N - N)!} = \frac{N!}{0!} = N!$$

But, by Theorem 3.1, P_N^N is also equal to the product

$$P_N^N = N! = (A)(n_1!)(n_2!) \cdot \cdot \cdot (n_k!)$$

where A is the number of ways of partitioning N elements into k groups of n_1, n_2, . . . , n_k elements, respectively; $n_1!$ is the number of ways of arranging the n_1 elements in group 1; $n_2!$ is the number of ways of arranging the n_2 elements in group 2; . . . ; and $n_k!$ is the number of ways of arranging the n_k elements in group k. We obtain the desired result by solving for A:

$$A = \frac{N!}{n_1!n_2! \cdot \cdots \cdot n_k!}$$

EXAMPLE 3.26

You have 12 system analysts and you want to assign three to job 1, four to job 2, and five to job 3. In how many different ways can you make this assignment?

Solution

For this example, $k = 3$ (corresponding to the $k = 3$ different jobs), $N = 12$, $n_1 = 3$, $n_2 = 4$, and $n_3 = 5$. Then the number of different ways to assign the system analysts to the jobs is

$$\frac{N!}{n_1!n_2!n_3!} = \frac{12!}{3!4!5!} = \frac{12 \cdot 11 \cdot 10 \cdot \cdots \cdot 3 \cdot 2 \cdot 1}{(3 \cdot 2 \cdot 1)(4 \cdot 3 \cdot 2 \cdot 1)(5 \cdot 4 \cdot 3 \cdot 2 \cdot 1)} = 27,720$$

EXAMPLE 3.27

How many samples of 4 tin-lead solder joints can be selected from a lot of 25 tin-lead solder joints available for strength tests?

Solution

For this example, $k = 2$ (corresponding to the $n_1 = 4$ solder joints you *do* choose and the $n_2 = 21$ solder joints you *do not* choose) and $N = 25$. Then, the number of different ways to choose the 4 solder joints from 25 is

$$\frac{N!}{n_1!n_2!} = \frac{25!}{(4!)(21!)} = \frac{25 \cdot 24 \cdot 23 \cdot \cdots \cdot 3 \cdot 2 \cdot 1}{(4 \cdot 3 \cdot 2 \cdot 1)(21 \cdot 20 \cdot \cdots \cdot 2 \cdot 1)} = 12,650$$

The special application of the partitions rule illustrated by Example 3.27—partitioning a set of N elements into $k = 2$ groups (the elements that appear in a sample and those that do not)—is very common. Therefore, we give a different name to the rule for counting the number of different ways of partitioning a set of elements into two parts—the **combinations rule**.

Theorem 3.4

THE COMBINATIONS RULE   A sample of n elements is to be chosen from a set of N elements. Then the number of different samples of n elements that can be

> selected from N is denoted by $\binom{N}{n}$ and is equal to
>
> $$\binom{N}{n} = \frac{N!}{n!(N-n)!}$$
>
> Note that the order in which the n elements are drawn is not important.

PROOF OF THEOREM 3.4   The proof of Theorem 3.4 follows directly from Theorem 3.3. Selecting a sample of n elements from a set of N elements is equivalent to partitioning the N elements into $k = 2$ groups—the n that are selected for the sample and the remaining $(N - n)$ that are not selected. Therefore, by applying Theorem 3.3 we obtain

$$\binom{N}{n} = \frac{N!}{n!(N-n)!}$$

EXAMPLE 3.28

Five sales engineers will be hired from a group of 100 applicants. In how many ways (*combinations*) can groups of five sales engineers be selected?

Solution

This is equivalent to sampling $n = 5$ elements from a set of N $= 100$ elements. Thus, the number of ways is the number of possible combinations of five applicants selected from 100, or

$$\binom{100}{5} = \frac{100!}{(5!)(95!)} = \frac{100 \cdot 99 \cdot 98 \cdot 97 \cdot 96 \cdot 95 \cdot 94 \cdots 2 \cdot 1}{(5 \cdot 4 \cdot 3 \cdot 2 \cdot 1)(95 \cdot 94 \cdots 2 \cdot 1)}$$
$$= \frac{100 \cdot 99 \cdot 98 \cdot 97 \cdot 96}{5 \cdot 4 \cdot 3 \cdot 2 \cdot 1} = 75{,}287{,}520$$

Compare this result with that of Example 3.23, where we found that the number of permutations of 5 elements drawn from 100 was more than 9 billion. **_Because the order of the elements does not affect combinations, there are fewer combinations than permutations._**

When working a probability problem, you should carefully examine the experiment to determine whether you can use one or more of the rules we have discussed in this section. We will illustrate in Examples 3.29 and 3.30 how these rules can help solve a probability problem.

EXAMPLE 3.29

A computer rating service is commissioned to rank the top three brands of EGA monitors. A total of 10 brands are to be included in the study.

a. In how many different ways can the computer rating service arrive at the final ranking?

b. If the rating service can distinguish no difference among the brands and therefore arrives at the final ranking by chance, what is the probability that company Z's brand is ranked first? In the top three?

Solution

a. Since the rating service is drawing three elements (brands) from a set of ten elements and arranging the three elements in a distinct order, we use the permutations rule to find the number of different results:

$$P_3^{10} = \frac{10!}{(10 - 3)!} = 10 \cdot 9 \cdot 8 = 720$$

Summary of Counting Rules

1. *Multiplicative rule:* If you are drawing one element from each of k sets of elements, with the sizes of the sets $n_1, n_2, \ldots, n_k$, the number of different results is

$$n_1 n_2 n_3 \cdot \cdots \cdot n_k$$

2. *Permutations rule:* If you are drawing n elements from a set of N elements and arranging the n elements in a distinct order, the number of different results is

$$P_n^N = \frac{N!}{(N - n)!}$$

3. *Partitions rule:* If you are partitioning the elements of a set of N elements into k groups consisting of $n_1, n_2, \ldots, n_k$ elements ($n_1 + n_2 + \cdots + n_k = N$), the number of different results is

$$\frac{N!}{n_1! n_2! \cdot \cdots \cdot n_k!}$$

4. *Combinations rule:* If you are drawing n elements from a set of N elements without regard to the order of the n elements, the number of different results is

$$\binom{N}{n} = \frac{N!}{n!(N - n)!}$$

[Note: The combinations rule is a special case of the partitions rule when $k = 2$.]

---

b. The steps for calculating the probability of interest are as follows:

STEP 1   The experiment is to select and rank three brands of EGA monitors from 10 brands.

STEP 2 There are too many simple events to list. However, we know from part **a** that there are 720 different outcomes (i.e., simple events) of this experiment.

STEP 3 If we assume the rating service determines the rankings by chance, each of the 720 simple events should have an equal probability of occurrence. Thus,

$$P(\text{Each simple event}) = \frac{1}{720}$$

STEP 4 One event of interest to company Z is that its brand receives top ranking. We will call this event A. The list of simple events that result in the occurrence of event A is long, but the *number* of simple events contained in event A is determined by breaking event A into two parts:

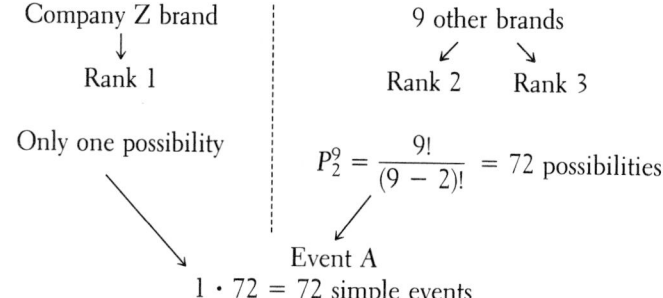

Thus, event A can occur in 72 different ways.

Now define B as the event that company Z's brand is ranked in the top three. Since event B specifies only that brand Z appear in the top three, we repeat the calculations above, fixing brand Z in position 2 and then in position 3. We conclude that the number of simple events contained in event B is $3(72) = 216$.

STEP 5 The final step is to calculate the probabilities of events A and B. Since the 720 simple events are equally likely to occur, we find

$$P(A) = \frac{\text{Number of simple events in } A}{\text{Total number of simple events}} = \frac{72}{720} = \frac{1}{10}$$

Similarly,

$$P(B) = \frac{216}{720} = \frac{3}{10}$$

EXAMPLE 3.30

Refer to Example 3.29. Suppose the computer rating service is to choose the top three EGA monitors from the group of 10, but is *not to rank the three*.

a. In how many different ways can the rating service choose the three to be designated as top-of-the-line EGA monitors?

b. Assuming that the rating service makes its choice by chance and that company X has two brands in the group of ten, what is the probability that exactly one of the company X brands is selected in the top three? At least one?

Solution

a. The rating service is selecting three elements (brands) from a set of ten elements *without regard to order*, so we can apply the combinations rule to determine the number of different results:

$$\binom{10}{3} = \frac{10!}{3!(10-3)!} = \frac{10 \cdot 9 \cdot 8}{3 \cdot 2 \cdot 1} = 120$$

b. We will follow the five-step procedure.

STEP 1 The experiment is to select (but *not rank*) three brands from ten.

STEP 2 There are 120 simple events for this experiment.

STEP 3 Since the selection is made by chance, each simple event is equally likely:

$$P(\text{Each simple event}) = \frac{1}{120}$$

STEP 4 Define events A and B as follows:

A: {Exactly one company X brand is selected}

B: {At least one company X brand is selected}

Since each of the simple events is equally likely to occur, we need to know only the number of simple events in A and B to determine their probabilities.

For event A to occur, exactly one company X brand must be selected, along with two of the remaining eight brands. We thus break A into two parts:

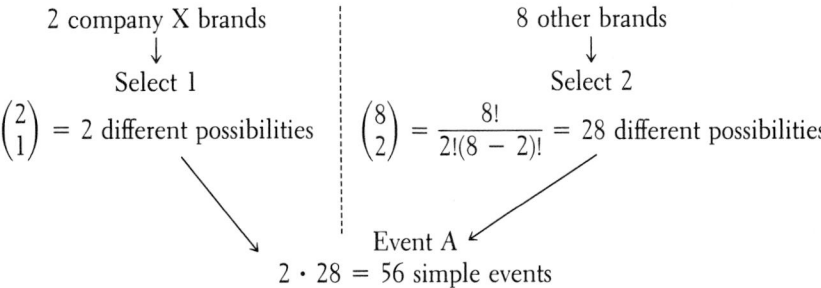

Note that the one company X brand can be selected in 2 ways, whereas the two other brands can be selected in 28 ways (we use the combinations rule because the order of selection is not important). Then, we use the multiplicative rule to combine one of the 2 ways to select a company X brand with one of the 28 ways to select two other brands, yielding a total of 56 simple events for event A.

The simple events in event B would include all simple events containing either one or two company X brands. We already know that the number containing exactly one company X brand is 56, the number of elements in event A. The number containing exactly two company X brands is equal to the product of the number of ways of selecting two company X brands out of a possible 2 and the number of ways of selecting the third brand from the remaining 8:

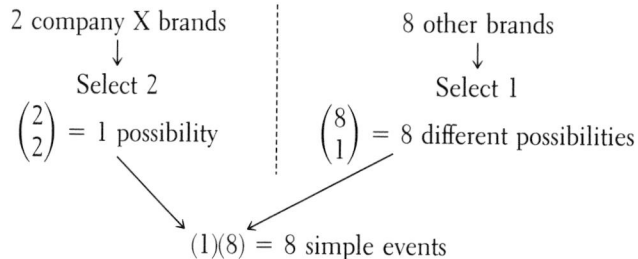

Then the number of simple events that imply the selection of either one *or* two company X brands is

$$\begin{pmatrix} \text{Number containing} \\ \text{one X brand} \end{pmatrix} + \begin{pmatrix} \text{Number containing} \\ \text{two X brands} \end{pmatrix}$$

or

$$56 + 8 = 64$$

STEP 5   Since all the simple events are equally likely, we have

$$P(A) = \frac{\text{Number of simple events in } A}{\text{Total number of simple events}} = \frac{56}{120} = \frac{7}{15}$$

and

$$P(B) = \frac{\text{Number of simple events in } B}{\text{Total number of simple events}} = \frac{64}{120} = \frac{8}{15}$$

Learning how to decide whether a particular counting rule applies to an experiment takes patience and practice. If you want to develop this skill, use the rules to solve the following exercises and some of the supplementary exercises given at the end of this chapter.

EXERCISES

3.37   The effect of global climate change on the U.S. economy was investigated by researchers at Carnegie Mellon University (*Environmental Science & Technology*, Oct. 1993). To gauge the opinions of the scientific community, the researchers set up several hypothetical scenarios. For one portion of the study, the scenarios were determined by varying perspectives on abatement costs and climate change damages. Perspective on abatement cost was "optimist," "moderate," or "pessimist." Similarly, perspective on climate change damages was "optimist," "moderate," or "pessimist."

a. Determine the number of different scenarios possible, where a scenario is a combination of abatement cost perspective and climate change damage perspective.

b. List the scenarios of part **a**.

c. In another portion of the study, five of the scenarios of part **a** were selected for further investigation. If the five scenarios are selected at random, how many different choices exist?

3.38 Can man communicate with a machine through brain-wave processing? This question was the topic of research reported in *IEEE Engineering in Medicine and Biology Magazine* (Mar. 1990). Volunteers were wired to both a computer and an electroencephalogram (EEG) monitor. Each subject performed five tasks under two conditions—eyes opened and eyes closed.

a. Determine the number of experimental conditions under which each subject was tested.

b. List the conditions of part **a**.

c. Two measurements were recorded for each subject—one after 2 seconds of artifact-free EEG and one after only .25 second of artifact-free EEG. What is the total number of measurements obtained for each subject?

3.39 A study was conducted by Union Carbide to identify the optimal catalyst preparation conditions in the conversion of monoethanolamine (MEA) to ethylenediamine (EDA), a substance used commercially in soaps.* The initial experimental plan was chosen to screen four metals (Fe, Co, Ni, and Cu) and four catalyst support classes (low acidity, high acidity, porous, and high surface area).

a. How many metal–support combinations are possible for this experiment?

b. All four catalyst supports are tested in random order with one of the metals. How many different orderings of the four supports are possible with each metal?

3.40 A security alarm system is activated and deactivated by correctly entering the appropriate three-digit numerical code in the proper sequence on a digital panel.

a. Compute the total number of possible code combinations if no digit may be used twice.

b. Compute the total number of possible code combinations if digits may be used more than once.

3.41 A full-scale reinforced concrete building was designed and tested under simulated earthquake loading conditions (*Journal of Structural Engineering*, Jan. 1986). After completion of the experiments, several design engineers were administered a questionnaire in which they were asked to evaluate two building parameters (size and reinforcement) for each of three parts (shear wall, columns, and girders). For each parameter–part combination, the design engineers were asked to choose one of the following three responses: too heavy, about right, and too light.

a. How many different responses are possible on the questionnaire?

b. Suppose the design engineers are also asked to select the three parameter–part combinations with the overall highest ratings and rank them from 1 to 3. How many different rankings are possible?

---

*Hansen, J. L., and Best, D. C. "How to Pick a Winner." Paper presented at Joint Statistical Meetings, American Statistical Association and Biometric Society, Aug. 1986, Chicago, Ill.

3.42   Suppose you need to replace 5 gaskets in a nuclear-powered device. If you have a box of 20 gaskets from which to make the selection, how many different choices are possible; i.e., how many different samples of 5 gaskets can be selected from the 20?

3.43   In high-volume machining centers, cutting tools are replaced at regular, heuristically chosen intervals. These intervals are generally untimely, i.e., either the tool is replaced too early or too late. The *Journal of Engineering for Industry* (Aug. 1993) reported on an automated real-time diagnostic system designed to replace the cutting tool of a drilling machine at optimum times. To test the system, data were collected over a broad range of machining conditions. The experimental variables were as follows:

1. Two workpiece materials (steel and cast iron)
2. Two drill sizes (.125 and .25 inch)
3. Six drill speeds (1,250, 1,800, 2,500, 3,000, 3,750, and 4,000 revolutions per minute)
4. Seven feed rates (.003, .005, .0065, .008, .009, .010, .011 inches per revolution)

a. How many different machining conditions are possible?
b. The eight machining conditions actually employed in the study are described in the table. Suppose one (and only one) of the machining combinations, part **a**, will detect a flaw in the system. What is the probability that the experiment conducted in the study will detect the system flaw?

Experiment	Workpiece Material	Drill Size in.	Drill Speed rpm	Feed Rate ipr
1	Cast iron	.25	1,250	.011
2	Cast iron	.25	1,800	.005
3	Steel	.25	3,750	.003
4	Steel	.25	2,500	.003
5	Steel	.25	2,500	.008
6	Steel	.125	4,000	.0065
7	Steel	.125	4,000	.009
8	Steel	.125	3,000	.010

c. Refer to part **b**. Suppose the system flaw occurs when drilling steel material with a .25 inch drill size at a speed of 2,500 rpm. Find the probability that the experiment conducted in the actual study will detect the system flaw.

3.44   To evaluate the traffic control systems of four facilities relying on computer-based equipment, the Federal Aviation Administration (FAA) formed a 16-member task force. If the FAA wants to assign 4 task force members to each facility, how many different assignments are possible?

3.45   The popularity of the state lottery has brought with it an avalanche of "experts" and "mathematical wizards" (such as the editors of the monthly publication *Lottery Buster*) who provide advice on how to win the lottery—for a fee, of course! These experts—the legitimate ones, anyway—base their "systems" of winning on their knowledge of probability and statistics. For example, consider the weekly Pick-6 Lotto game. To play Pick-6 Lotto, you select six numbers of your choice from a field of numbers ranging from 1 to N, where N depends on which state's game you are playing. Florida's Lotto game involves picking six numbers ranging from 1 to 49 (denoted 6/49). The cost of a ticket is $1 and the payoff, if your six numbers match the winning numbers drawn at the end of each week, is $6 million or more, depending on the number of tickets purchased. In addition to the grand prize, you can win second-, third-, and fourth-prize payoffs by matching five, four, and three of the six numbers drawn, respectively.

a. Calculate the number of possible ways in which you can choose the six numbers from the 49 available. If you purchase a single $1 ticket, what is the probability that you will win the grand prize (i.e., match all six numbers)?

b. One strategy used to increase your odds of winning a Lotto is to employ a *wheeling system*. In a complete wheeling system, you select more than six numbers, say, seven, and play every combination of six of those seven numbers. Suppose you choose to "wheel" the following seven numbers in a 6/49 game: 2, 7, 18, 23, 30, 32, 39. How many tickets would you need to purchase to have every possible combination of the seven numbers? List the six numbers on each of these tickets.

c. Refer to part **b**. What is the probability of winning the 6/49 Lotto when you wheel seven numbers? Does the strategy, in fact, increase your odds of winning?

d. Another strategy is to play neighboring pairs. "Neighboring pairs" are two consecutive numbers that come up together on the winning ticket. In one state lottery, for example, 79% of the winning tickets had at least one neighboring pair. Thus, some "experts" think you have a better chance of winning if you include at least one neighboring pair in your number selection. Calculate the probability of winning the 6/49 Lotto with the six numbers 2, 15, 19, 20, 27, 37. [*Note:* 19, 20 is a neighboring pair.] Compare this probability to the one in part **a**. Comment on the neighboring pairs strategy.

OPTIONAL EXERCISES

3.46 What is the probability that you will be dealt a 5-card poker hand of four aces?

3.47 Blackjack, a favorite game of gamblers, is played by a dealer and at least one opponent and uses a standard 52-card bridge deck. Each card is assigned a numerical value. Cards numbered from 2 to 10 are assigned the values shown on the card. For example, a 7 of spades has a value of 7; a 3 of hearts has a value of 3. Face cards (kings, queens, and jacks) are each valued at 10, and an ace can be assigned a value of either 1 or 11, at the discretion of the player holding the card. At the outset of the game, two cards are dealt to the player and two cards to the dealer. Drawing an ace and any card with a point value of 10 is called *blackjack*. In most casinos, if the dealer draws blackjack, he or she automatically wins.

a. What is the probability that the dealer will draw a blackjack?

b. What is the probability that a player will win with blackjack?

3.9 Probability and Statistics: An Example

We have introduced a number of new concepts in the preceding sections, and this makes the study of probability a particularly arduous task. It is, therefore, very important to establish clearly the connection between probability and statistics, which we will do in the remaining chapters. Although Bayes' rule demonstrates one way that probability can be used to make statistical inferences, traditional methods of statistical inference use probability in a slightly different way. In this section, we will present one brief example of this traditional approach to statistical inference so that you can begin to understand why some knowledge of probability is important in the study of statistics.

Suppose a firm that manufactures concrete studs is researching the hypothesis that its new chemically anchored studs achieve greater holding capacity and greater carrying load capacity than the more conventional, mechanically anchored studs. To test the hypothesis, three new chemical anchors are selected from a day's production and subjected to a durability test. Each of the three $\frac{1}{2}$-inch studs is drilled and set into a slab of 4,000 pounds-per-square-inch stone aggregate concrete, and their tensile load capacities (in pounds) are recorded. It is known from many previous durability tests of mechanically anchored studs that approximately 16% of mechanical anchors will have tensile strengths over 12,000 pounds. Suppose that all three of the chemically anchored studs tested have tensile strengths greater than 12,000 pounds. What can researchers for the firm conclude?

To answer these questions, define the events

A_1: {Chemically anchored stud 1 has tensile strength over 12,000 pounds}

A_2: {Chemically anchored stud 2 has tensile strength over 12,000 pounds}

A_3: {Chemically anchored stud 3 has tensile strength over 12,000 pounds}

We want to find $P(A_1 \cap A_2 \cap A_3)$, the probability that all three tested studs have tensile load capacities over 12,000 pounds.

Since the studs are selected by chance from a large production, it may be plausible to assume that the events A_1, A_2, and A_3 are independent. That is,

$$P(A_2 \mid A_1) = P(A_2)$$

In words, knowing that the first stud has a tensile strength over 12,000 pounds does not affect the probability that the second stud has a tensile strength over 12,000 pounds. With the assumption of independence, we can calculate the probability of the intersection by multiplying the individual probabilities:

$$P(A_1 \cap A_2 \cap A_3) = P(A_1)P(A_2)P(A_3)$$

If the new chemically anchored studs are no stronger or no weaker than the mechanically anchored studs, that is, *if the relative frequency distribution of tensile strengths for chemically anchored studs is no different from that for mechanically anchored studs*, then we would expect about 16% of the new studs to have tensile strengths over 12,000 pounds. Consequently, our estimate of $P(A)$ is .16 for all three studs, and

$$P(A_1 \cap A_2 \cap A_3) \approx (.16)(.16)(.16) = .004096$$

Thus, the probability that the firm's researchers will observe all three studs with tensile load capacity over 12,000 pounds is only about .004. If this event were to occur, the researchers might conclude that it lends credence to the theory that chemically anchored studs achieve greater carrying load capacity than mechanically anchored studs, *since it is so unlikely to occur if the distributions of tensile strength are the same*. Such a conclusion would be an application of the rare event approach to statistical inference. You can see that the basic principles of probability play an important role.

EXERCISES

3.48 *Sky & Telescope* (May 1993) reported that Noah Brosch of Tel Aviv University, Israel, discovered a new asterism in Virgo. "Five stars, all appearing brighter than about the 13th magnitude, comprise a diamond-shaped area with sides only 42 seconds long. The probability is small that five stars with similar brightnesses could be so closely aligned by chance, and Brosch suggests that the stars of the diamond . . . are physically associated." Assuming the "probability" mentioned in the article is small (say, less than .01), do you agree with the inference made by the astronomer?

3.49 Experience has shown that a manufacturer of micro 3.5″ diskettes for PCs produces, on the average, only one defective diskette in 100. Suppose that of the next four 3.5″ diskettes manufactured, at least one is defective. What would you infer about the claimed defective rate of .01? Explain.

3.50 Since 1961, parcels of land that may contain oil have been placed in a lottery with the winner receiving leasing rights (at $1 per acre per year) for a period of 10 years. United States citizens 21 years or older are eligible and are entitled to one entry per lottery by paying a $10 filing fee to the Bureau of Land Management (see *The Federal Oil & Gas Leasing System*, Federal Resource Registry, 1993). For several months in 1980, however, the lottery was suspended to investigate a player who won three parcels of land in 1 month. The numbers of entries for the three lotteries were 1,836, 1,365, and 495, respectively. An Interior Department audit stated that "federal workers did a poor job of shaking the drum before the drawing." Based on your knowledge of probability and rare events, would you make the same inference as that made by the auditor?

3.51 At the beginning of World War II, a group of British engineers and statisticians was formed in London to investigate the problem of the lethality of antiaircraft weapons.* One of the main goals of the research team was to assess the probability that a single shell would destroy (or cripple) the aircraft at which it was fired. Although a great deal of data existed at the time on ground-to-ground firing with artillery shells, little information was available on the accuracy of antiaircraft guns. Consequently, a series of trials was run in 1940 in which gun crews shot at free-flying (unpiloted) aircraft. When German aircraft began to bomb England later in that same year, however, the researchers found that the aiming errors of antiaircraft guns under battle stress were considerably greater than those estimated from trials. Let p be the probability that an antiaircraft shell strikes within a 30-foot radius of its target. Assume that under simulated conditions, $p = .45$.

a. In an actual attack by a single German aircraft, suppose that three antiaircraft shells are fired and all three miss their target by more than 30 feet. Is it reasonable to conclude that in battle conditions p differs from .45?

b. Answer part **a** assuming that you observe 10 consecutive shots that all miss their target by more than 30 feet.

---

*Pearson, E. S. "Statistics and probability applied to problems of antiaircraft fire in World War II." In *Statistics: A Guide to the Unknown*, 2nd ed. San Francisco: Holden-Day, 1978, pp. 474–482.

3.10   Summary

We have developed some of the basic tools of probability to enable us to assess the probabilities of various sample outcomes given a specific population structure. A summary of the probability rules is provided in the box.

Summary of Probability Rules

1. **Rule of Complements:** $P(A) + P(A^c) = 1$
2. **Conditional Probability:**

$$P(A \mid B) = \frac{P(A \cap B)}{P(B)}$$

3. **Additive Rule:**

$$P(A \cup B) = P(A) + P(B) - P(A \cap B)$$

If A and B are mutually exclusive, then

$$P(A \cup B) = P(A) + P(B)$$

4. **Multiplicative Rule:**

$$P(A \cap B) = P(A \mid B) \cdot P(B) = P(B \mid A) \cdot P(A)$$

If A and B are independent, then $P(A \cap B) = P(A) \cdot P(B)$.

5. **Bayes' Rule** (Optional):

$$P(A_i \mid E) = \frac{P(A_i) \cdot P(E \mid A_i)}{P(A_1) \cdot P(E \mid A_1) + \cdots + P(A_k) \cdot P(A_k \mid E_k)}$$

Although many of the examples we presented were of no practical importance, they accomplished their purpose if you now comprehend the concepts and definitions necessary for a basic understanding of probability.

In the next several chapters, we will present probability models that can be used to solve practical problems. You will see that for most applications, we will need to make inferences about unknown aspects of these probability models, i.e., we will need to apply inferential statistics to the problem.

SUPPLEMENTARY EXERCISES

3.52   A state Department of Transportation (DOT) recently claimed that each of five bidders received equal consideration in the awarding of two road construction contracts and that, in fact, the two contract recipients were randomly selected from among the five bidders. Three of the bidders were large construction conglomerates and two were small specialty contractors. Suppose that both contracts were awarded to large construction conglomerates.

a. What is the probability of this event occurring if, in fact, the DOT's claim is true?

b. Is the probability computed in part **a** inconsistent with the DOT's claim that the selection was random?

3.53 Refer to the study of automobile safety discussed in Exercise 2.46. The researchers also investigated the frequency of safety seat belt usage among automobile owners. Each in a sample of 387 drivers was classified according to frequency of use (always, frequently, infrequently, and never) and state of residence (states with mandatory safety seat belt laws, states with pending mandatory laws, and states without mandatory laws). The results are shown in the table.

State of Residence	Always	Frequently	Infrequently	Never	TOTALS
Mandatory seat belt law	67	24	18	19	128
Pending mandatory seat belt law	27	20	23	8	78
No mandatory seat belt law	63	42	38	38	181
TOTALS	157	86	79	65	387

Source: Lieb, R. C., Wiseman, F., and Moore, T. E. "Automobile safety programs: The public viewpoint." *Transportation Journal*, Vol. 25, No. 4, Summer 1986, p. 25. Permission to reprint this material for educational purposes has been granted by the American Society of Transportation and Logistics, publisher of the *Transportation Journal*.

Suppose we select one of the 387 drivers in the study.

a. Find the probability that the driver resides in a state with no mandatory seat belt law.

b. Find the probability that the driver uses safety seat belts infrequently.

c. Find the probability that the driver resides in a state with a pending mandatory seat belt law and never uses seat belts.

d. Find the probability that the driver either resides in a state with a mandatory seat belt law or always uses seat belts.

e. Given that the driver never uses seat belts, what is the probability that the driver resides in a state with no mandatory seat belt law?

f. Given that the driver resides in a state with a pending mandatory seat belt law, what is the probability that the driver frequently uses seat belts?

g. Are the events Mandatory seat belt law and Infrequent seat belt usage independent? Explain.

3.54 Two newly designed database management systems (DBMS), A and B, are being considered for marketing by a large computer software vendor. To determine whether DBMS users have a preference for one of the two systems, four of the vendor's customers are randomly selected and given the opportunity to evaluate the performances of each of the two systems. After sufficient testing, each user is asked to state which DBMS gave the better performance (measured in terms of CPU utilization, execution time, and disk access).

a. Count the possible outcomes for this marketing experiment.

b. If DBMS users actually have no preference for one system over the other (i.e., the performances of the two systems are identical), what is the probability that all four sampled users prefer system A?

c. If all four customers express their preference for system A, can the software vendor infer that DBMS users in general have a preference for one of the two systems?

3.55   Researchers at the Upjohn Company have developed a new sustained-release tablet for a prescription drug. To determine the effectiveness of the tablet, the following experiment was conducted. Six tablets were randomly selected from each of 30 production lots. Each tablet was submersed in water and the percent dissolved was measured at 2, 4, 6, 8, 10, 12, 16, and 20 hours. *

a. Find the total number of measurements (percent dissolved) recorded in the experiment.
b. For each lot, the measurements at each time period are averaged. How many averages are obtained?

3.56   A study was conducted to examine the relationship between the cost structure and the mechanical properties of equiaxed grains in unidirectionally solidified ingots (*Metallurgical Transactions*, May 1986). Ingots composed of copper alloys were poured into one of three mold types (columnar, mixed, or equiaxed) with either a transverse or a longitudinal orientation. From each ingot, five tensile specimens were obtained at varying distances (10, 35, 60, 85, and 100 millimeters) from the ingot chill face and yield strength was determined.

a. How many strength measurements will be obtained if the experiment includes one ingot for each mold type–orientation combination?
b. Suppose three of the ingots will be selected for further testing at the 100-mm distance. How many samples of three ingots can be selected from the total number of ingots in the experiment?
c. Use Table 6 of Appendix II to randomly select the three ingots for further testing.
d. Calculate the probability that the sample selected includes the three highest tensile strengths among all the ingots in the experiment.
e. Calculate the probability that the sample selected includes at least two of the three ingots with the highest tensile strengths.

3.57   A traffic engineer conducted a study of the urban mass transportation habits of a city's workers. The study revealed the following: Fifteen percent of the city workers regularly drive their own car to work. Of those who do drive their own car to work, 80% would gladly switch to public mass transportation if it were available. Forty percent of the city workers live more than 3 miles from the center of the city.
Suppose that one city worker is chosen at random. Define the events A, B, and C as follows:

A: {The person regularly drives his or her own car to work}
B: {The person would gladly switch to public mass transportation if it were available}
C: {The person lives within 3 miles of the center of the city}

a. Find $P(A)$.
b. Find $P(B \mid A)$.
c. Find $P(C)$.
d. Explain whether the pairs of events, A and B, A and C, B and C, are mutually exclusive.

3.58   A company specializing in data-communications hardware markets a computing system with two types of hard disk drives, four types of display stations, and two types of interfacing. How many systems would the company have to distribute if it received one order for each possible combination of hard disk drive, display station, and interfacing?

---

*Klassen, R. A. "The Application of Response Surface Methods to a Tablet Formulation Problem." Paper presented at Joint Statistical Meetings, American Statistical Association and Biometric Society, Aug. 1986, Chicago, Ill.

3.59   A brewery utilizes two bottling machines, but they do not operate simultaneously. The second machine acts as a backup system to the first machine, and operates only when the first breaks down during operating hours. The probability that the first machine breaks down during operating hours is .20. If, in fact, the first breaks down, then the second machine is turned on and has a probability of .30 of breaking down.
   a. What is the probability that the brewery's bottling system is not working during operating hours?
   b. The *reliability* of the bottling process is the probability that the system is working during operating hours. Find the reliability of the bottling process at the brewery.

3.60   Recently, the National Aeronautics and Space Administration (NASA) purchased a new solar-powered battery guaranteed to have a failure rate of only 1 in 20. A new system to be used in a space vehicle operates on one of these batteries. To increase the reliability of the system, NASA installed three batteries, each designed to operate if the preceding batteries in the chain fail. If the system is operated in a practical situation, what is the probability that all three batteries would fail?

3.61   The probability that a certain electronics component fails when first used is .10. If it does not fail immediately, the probability that it lasts for 1 year is .99. What is the probability that a new component will last 1 year?

3.62   Reports have recently surfaced regarding the shortage of college faculty in the field of civil engineering. One proposed solution is to hire more practicing civil engineers as faculty members. However, this idea has generally been met with resistance in the academic world. To investigate this problem, 200 College of Engineering deans were asked to give their opinions regarding the main barrier to the hiring of practitioners to college faculty. In addition, the deans were asked whether their colleges stress "theory" or "applications" more heavily. The accompanying table shows the proportions of responses that fall into the respective categories.

	Main Barrier to Hiring Practitioners		
	Lack of Ph.D.	Salary Demands Too High	Lack of Teaching Experience
Stress Theory	.13	.10	.02
Stress Applications	.37	.21	.17

Suppose one college dean is to be selected from the 200 surveyed. Find the probability that:
   a. The dean's college stresses applications.
   b. The dean's college stresses theory and considers lack of a Ph.D. as the main barrier to hiring practitioners.
   c. The dean's college stresses applications, or considers the salary demands of practitioners too high, or both.
   d. The dean does not consider lack of teaching experience as a barrier to hiring practitioners.

3.63   To ensure delivery of its raw materials, a company has decided to establish a pattern of purchases with at least two potential suppliers. If five suppliers are available, how many choices (options) are available to the company?

3.64   In an effort to assist the Occupational Safety and Health Administration in the development of federal safety standards, the Bureau of Labor Statistics conducted a survey of workers who suffer serious hand injuries on the job (*Engineering News-Record*, Mar. 3, 1983). The Bureau reported that, despite their relatively small numbers, carpenters account for 4% of all job-related hand injuries. The survey also indicated that 29% of the injured workers attributed their injuries to the pace at which they were working, and 13% of those injured workers wearing hand protection claimed their gloves actually caused the accident. Assume that the events described here are independent.

a. Find the probability that a worker with a job-related hand injury is a carpenter whose injury was caused by the pace at which he was working.

b. Find the probability that a worker with a job-related hand injury does not attribute the cause of the accident to his protective hand gloves.

OPTIONAL SUPPLEMENTARY EXERCISES

3.65 An assembler of computer terminals and modems uses parts from two sources. Company A supplies 80% of the parts and company B supplies the remaining 20% of the parts. From past experience, the assembler knows that 5% of the parts supplied by company A are defective and 3% of the parts supplied by company B are defective. An assembled modem selected at random is found to have a defective part. Which of the two companies is more likely to have supplied the defective part?

3.66 Refer to Exercise 3.11. In the two-dice game of craps, a player wins if he throws a *natural* (a 7 or 11) and loses if he throws *craps* (a 2, 3, or 12). However, if the sum of the two dice is 4, 5, 6, 8, 9, or 10 (each of these is known as a *point*), the player continues throwing the dice until the same outcome (point) is repeated (in which case the player wins), or the outcome 7 occurs (in which case the player loses). For example, if a player's first toss results in a 6, the player continues to toss the dice until a 6 or 7 occurs. If a 6 occurs first, the player wins. If a 7 occurs first, the player loses.

a. What is the probability that a player throws a point on the first toss?

b. If a player throws a point on the first toss, what is the probability the player wins the game on the next toss?

c. If a player throws a point on the first toss, what is the probability the player loses the game on the next toss?

d. Show that the probability a player wins the game (i.e., *makes a pass*) in two or fewer tosses is .299.

3.67 Five construction companies each offer bids on three distinct Department of Transportation (DOT) contracts. A particular company will be awarded at most one DOT contract.

a. How many different ways can the bids be awarded?

b. Under the assumption that the simple events are equally likely, find the probability that company 2 is awarded a DOT contract.

c. Suppose that companies 4 and 5 have submitted noncompetitive bids. If the contracts are awarded at random by the DOT, find the probability that both these companies receive contracts.

3.68 **a.** A professor asks his class to write a FORTRAN computer program that prints all three-letter sequences involving the five letters A, B, E, T, and O. How many different three-letter sequences will need to be printed?

b. Answer part **a** if the program is to be modified so that each three-letter sequence has at least one vowel, and no repeated letters.

3.69 Consider 5-card poker hands dealt from a standard 52-card bridge deck. Two important events are:

A: {You draw a flush}

B: {You draw a straight}

a. Find $P(A)$.   **b.** Find $P(B)$.

c. The event that both A and B occur, i.e., $A \cap B$, is called a *straight flush*. Find $P(A \cap B)$.

[*Note:* A *flush* consists of any five cards of the same suit. A *straight* consists of any five cards with values in sequence. In a straight, the cards may be of any suit and an ace may be considered as having a value of 1 or a value higher than a king.]

3.70   Refer to Example 3.13.

a. Find the probability that an intruder is detected, given a clear day.

b. Find the probability that an intruder is detected, given a cloudy day.

3.71   The U.S. Command, Control, Communication and Intelligence (C^3I) System includes sensors (e.g., satellites and radars), communication links, and computer systems that allow gathering and processing of information that a missile attack on the continental United States may be on the way. The C^3I System contains two basic components: a warning system, designed to detect missile attacks on the United States, and a response system, designed to launch a counterattack. The response system cannot launch a missile unless a signal is detected by the warning system. However, if a warning signal is received, it is possible the response system will fail to launch a counterattack.

Paté-Cornell and Neu conducted a probabilistic analysis of the reliability of the C^3I System (*Risk Analysis*, Vol. 5, No. 2, 1985). In particular, the researchers were interested in the probabilities of an accidental strike by the C^3I System, i.e., the probability that the system launches a nuclear missile toward Russia based on a false alert.

Suppose the conditional probability that the response system will launch a missile toward Russia, given a false alert from the warning system, is .90. Suppose also that the probability of false alert (i.e., the probability that the warning system sends a signal to the response system, given no Soviet attack is made) is .02. If the probability of a Soviet missile attack on the continental United States is .01, find the probability of an accidental strike by the C^3I System. [*Hint:* For three events, A, B, and C, the formula

$$P(A \cap B \cap C) = P(C \mid A \cap B) \cdot P(B \mid A) \cdot P(A)$$

gives the probability of their intersection.]

References

Feller, W. *An Introduction to Probability Theory and Its Applications*, 3rd ed. Vol. 1. New York: Wiley, 1968.

Mendenhall, W., Scheaffer, R. L., and Wackerly, D. *Mathematical Statistics with Applications*, 4th ed. Boston: Duxbury Press, 1989.

Parzen, E. *Modern Probability Theory and Its Applications*. New York: Wiley, 1960.

CHAPTER FOUR

Discrete Random Variables

Objective

To explain what is meant by a discrete random variable, its probability distribution, and corresponding numerical descriptive measures; to present some useful discrete probability distributions and show how they can be used to solve practical problems

Contents

4.1   Discrete Random Variables

As we noted in Chapter 1, the experimental events of greatest interest are often numerical, i.e., we conduct an experiment and observe the numerical value of some variable. If we repeat the experiment n times, we obtain a sample of quantitative data. To illustrate, suppose a manufactured product (e.g., a mechanical part) is sold in lots of 20 boxes of 12 items each. As a check on the quality of the product, a process control engineer randomly selects four from among the 240 items in a lot and checks to determine whether the items are defective. If more than one sampled item is found to be defective, the entire lot will be rejected.

The selection of four manufactured items from among 240 produces a sample space S that contains $\binom{240}{4}$ simple events, one corresponding to each possible combination of four items that might be selected from the lot. Although a description of a specific simple event would identify the four items acquired in a particular sample, the event of interest to the process control engineer is an observation on the variable y, the number of defective items among the four items that are tested. To each simple event in S, there corresponds one and only one value of the variable y. Therefore, a functional relation exists between the simple events in S and the values that y can assume. The event $y = 0$ is the collection of all simple events that contain no defective items. Similarly, the event $y = 1$ is the collection of all simple events in which one defective item is observed. Since the value that y can assume is a numerical event (i.e., an event defined by some number that varies in a random manner from one repetition of the experiment to another), it is called a **random variable**.

Definition 4.1

A **random variable** is a numerical-valued function defined over a sample space.

The number y of defective items in a selection of four items from among 240 is an example of a **discrete random variable**, one that can assume a countable number of values. For our example, the random variable y may assume any of the five values, $y = 0, 1, 2, 3,$ or 4. As another example, the number y of jobs received by a computer center in a day is also a discrete random variable which could, theoretically, assume a value that is large beyond all bound. The possible values for this discrete random variable correspond to the nonnegative integers, $y = 0, 1, 2, 3, \ldots, \infty$, and the number of such values is countable.

Random variables observed in nature often possess similar characteristics and consequently can be classified according to type. In this chapter, we will study seven different types of discrete random variables and will use the methods of Chapter 3 to derive the probabilities associated with their possible values. We will also begin to develop some intuitive ideas about how the probabilities of observed sample data can be used to make statistical inferences.

> **Definition 4.2**
>
> A **discrete random variable** y is one that can assume only a countable number of values.

4.2   The Probability Distribution for a Discrete Random Variable

Since the values that a random variable y can assume are numerical events, we will want to calculate their probabilities. A table, formula, or graph that gives these probabilities is called the **probability distribution** for the random variable y. We will illustrate this concept using a simple coin-tossing example.

EXAMPLE 4.1

A balanced coin is tossed twice, and the number y of heads is observed. Find the probability distribution for y.

Solution

Let H_i and T_i denote the observation of a head and a tail, respectively, on the ith toss, for $i = 1, 2$. The four simple events and the associated values of y are shown in Table 4.1.

TABLE 4.1   Outcomes of Coin-Tossing Experiment

Simple Event	Description	$P(E_i)$	Number of Heads y
E_1	H_1H_2	$\frac{1}{4}$	2
E_2	H_1T_2	$\frac{1}{4}$	1
E_3	T_1H_2	$\frac{1}{4}$	1
E_4	T_1T_2	$\frac{1}{4}$	0

The event $y = 0$ is the collection of all simple events that yield a value of $y = 0$, namely, the single simple event E_4. Therefore, the probability that y assumes the value 0 is

$$P(y = 0) = p(0) = P(E_4) = \frac{1}{4}$$

The event $y = 1$ contains two simple events, E_2 and E_3. Therefore,

$$P(y = 1) = p(1) = P(E_2) + P(E_3) = \frac{1}{4} + \frac{1}{4} = \frac{1}{2}$$

Finally,

$$P(y = 2) = p(2) = P(E_1) = \frac{1}{4}$$

The probability distribution $p(y)$ is displayed in tabular form in Table 4.2 and as a graph in Figure 4.1. Note that in Figure 4.1, the probabilities associated with y are illustrated with vertical lines; the height of the line is proportional to the value of $p(y)$. We show in Section 4.6 that this probability distribution can also be given by the formula

$$p(y) = \frac{\binom{2}{y}}{4}$$

where

$$p(0) = \frac{\binom{2}{0}}{4} = \frac{1}{4}$$

$$p(1) = \frac{\binom{2}{1}}{4} = \frac{2}{4} = \frac{1}{2}$$

$$p(2) = \frac{\binom{2}{2}}{4} = \frac{1}{4}$$

Any of these techniques—a table, graph, or formula—can be used to describe the probability distribution of a discrete random variable y.

· ·

TABLE 4.2   Probability Distribution for y, the Number of Heads in Two Tosses of a Coin

y	$p(y)$
0	$\frac{1}{4}$
1	$\frac{1}{2}$
2	$\frac{1}{4}$
$\sum_{y} p(y) =$	1

FIGURE 4.1 ▶

Probability distribution for y, the
number of heads in two tosses of
a coin

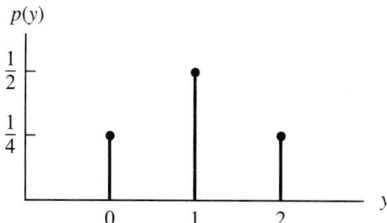

Definition 4.3

The **probability distribution** for a discrete random variable y is a table, graph, or formula that gives the probability $p(y)$ associated with each possible value of y.

The probability distribution $p(y)$ for a discrete random variable must satisfy two properties. First, because $p(y)$ is a probability, it must assume a value in the interval $0 \leq p(y) \leq 1$. Second, the sum of the values of $p(y)$ over all values of y must equal 1. This is true because we assigned one and only one value of y to each simple event in S. It follows that the values that y can assume represent different sets of simple events and are, therefore, mutually exclusive events. Summing $p(y)$ over all possible values of y is then equivalent to summing the probabilities of all simple events in S, and from Section 3.2, $P(S)$ is known to be equal to 1.

Requirements for a Discrete Probability Distribution

1. $0 \leq p(y) \leq 1$
2. $\sum_{\text{all } y} p(y) = 1$

To conclude this section, we will discuss the relationship between the probability distribution for a discrete random variable and the relative frequency distribution of data (discussed in Section 2.2). Suppose you were to toss two coins over and over again a very large number of times and record the number y of heads observed for each toss. A relative frequency histogram for the resulting collection of 0's, 1's, and 2's would have bars with heights of approximately $\frac{1}{4}$, $\frac{1}{2}$, and $\frac{1}{4}$, respectively. In fact, if it were possible to repeat the experiment an infinitely large number of times, the distribution would appear as shown in Figure 4.2 (page 148). Thus, the probability histogram of Figure 4.2 provides a **model** for a conceptual population of values of y—the values of y that would be observed if the experiment were to be repeated an infinitely large number of times.

FIGURE 4.2 ▶
Theoretical relative frequency
histogram for y, the number of
heads in two tosses of a coin

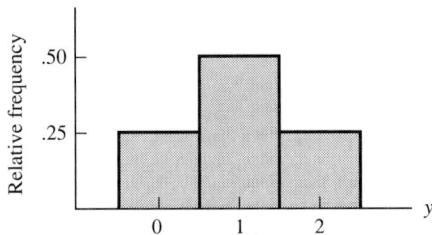

Beginning with Section 4.5, we will introduce a number of models for discrete random variables that occur in the physical, biological, social, and information sciences.

EXERCISES

4.1 The director of marketing for a small manufacturer of personal computers (PCs) believes that the discrete probability distribution shown in the accompanying figure characterizes the number, y, of new PCs the firm will lease next year.

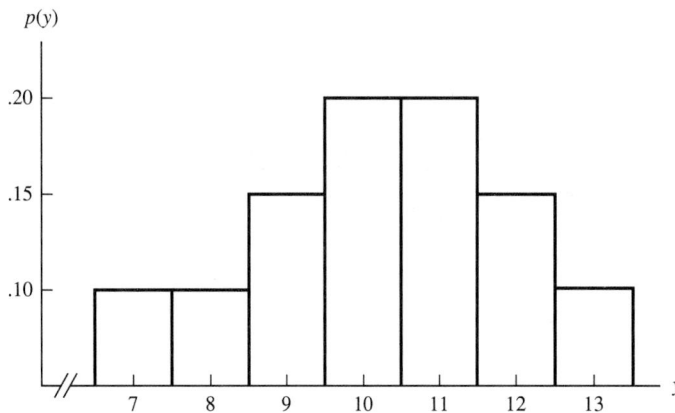

a. Is this a valid probability distribution? Explain.
b. Display the probability distribution in tabular form.
c. What is the probability that exactly 9 PCs will be leased?
d. What is the probability that fewer than 12 PCs will be leased?

4.2 Consider the segment of an electric circuit with three relays shown here. Current will flow from A to B if there is at least one closed path when the switch is thrown. Each of the three relays has an equally likely chance of remaining open or closed when the switch is thrown. Let y represent the number of relays that close when the switch is thrown.

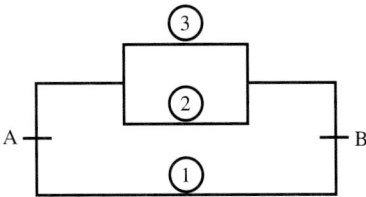

a. Find the probability distribution for *y* and display it in tabular form.
b. What is the probability that current will flow from A to B?

4.3   Refer to the *Journal of Applied Ecology* (1993) study of the nearly extinct singing cornrakes, Exercise 2.2. A census revealed that 12 cornrakes inhabit mainland Scotland. Suppose that two of these Scottish cornrakes are captured for mating purposes. Let *y* be the number of these captured cornrakes that are capable of mating. If exactly four of the original 12 cornrakes inhabiting Scotland are infertile and, consequently, unable to mate, find the probability distribution for *y*.

4.4   Refer to the *Metal Progress* (May 1986) study of steel sheet usage at Mazda Motor Corporation, introduced in Exercise 3.10. The table listing the seven steel types and percentages used in production is reproduced here. Suppose that three steel sheets are randomly selected (without replacement) from among those used in production of Mazda 626s. Find and graph the probability distribution of *y*, the number of cold rolled sheets in the sample.

Type of Steel Sheet	Percentage Used
Cold rolled, regular strength, nonplated	27
Cold rolled, high strength, nonplated	12
Cold rolled, regular strength, plated	30
Cold rolled, high strength, plated	15
Hot rolled, regular strength, nonplated	8
Hot rolled, high strength, nonplated	5
Hot rolled, regular strength, plated	3
Hot rolled, high strength, plated	0
TOTAL	100

Source: Chandler, H. E. "Materials trends at Mazda Motor Corporation." *Metal Progress*, Vol. 129, No. 6, May 1986, p. 57 (Figure 3).

4.5   A quality control engineer samples five from a large lot of manufactured firing pins and checks for defects. Unknown to the inspector, three of the five sampled firing pins are defective. The engineer will test the five pins in a randomly selected order until a defective is observed (in which case the entire lot will be rejected). Let *y* be the number of firing pins the quality control engineer must test. Find and graph the probability distribution of *y*.

4.6   Refer to the *Journal of Engineering for Industry* (Aug. 1993) study of an automated drilling machine, Exercise 3.43. The eight machining conditions employed in the study are reproduced here.

Experiment	Workpiece Material	Drill Size in.	Drill Speed rpm	Feed Rate ipr
1	Cast iron	.25	1,250	.011
2	Cast iron	.25	1,800	.005
3	Steel	.25	3,750	.003
4	Steel	.25	2,500	.003
5	Steel	.25	2,500	.008
6	Steel	.125	4,000	.0065
7	Steel	.125	4,000	.009
8	Steel	.125	3,000	.010

Suppose that two of the machining conditions listed here will detect a flaw in the automated system. Define *y* as the number of the three machining conditions with steel material and .25-inch drill size that detect the flaw. Prior to conducting the experiment, find the probability distribution for *y*. [*Hint:*   List all possible pairs of machining conditions that detect the flaw.]

OPTIONAL EXERCISE

4.7   Environmental engineers classify consumers into one of five categories (see Exercise 3.1 for a description of each group). The probabilities associated with the groups are listed in the following table.

Basic browns	.28
True-blue greens	.11
Greenback greens	.11
Sprouts	.26
Grousers	.24

Source: The *Orange County Register*, Aug. 7, 1990.

Let *y* equal the number of consumers that must be sampled until the first environmentalist is found. [*Note:*   From Exercise 3.1, an environmentalist is either a true-blue green, greenback green, or sprout.]
a. Specify the probability distribution for *y* in table form.
b. Give a formula for finding the probability distribution of *y*. (We will examine this random variable in Section 4.8.)

4.3   The Expected Value for a Random Variable y or for a Function $g(y)$ of y

The data we analyze in engineering and the sciences often result from observing a process. For example, in quality control a production process is monitored and the number of defective parts produced per hour is recorded. As noted earlier, a probability distribution for a random variable y is a model for a population relative frequency distribution, i.e., a model for the data produced by a process. Consequently, we can describe process data with numerical descriptive measures, such as its mean and standard deviation, and we can use the Empirical Rule to identify improbable values of y.

The **expected value** (or **mean**) of a random variable y, denoted by the symbol $E(y)$, is defined as follows:

Definition 4.4

Let y be a discrete random variable with probability distribution $p(y)$. Then the **mean** or **expected value of y** is

$$\mu = E(y) = \sum_{\text{all } y} y p(y)$$

EXAMPLE 4.2

Refer to the coin-tossing experiment of Example 4.1 and the probability distribution for the random variable y, shown in Table 4.1. Demonstrate that the formula for $E(y)$ yields the mean of the probability distribution for the discrete random variable y.

Solution

If we were to repeat the coin-tossing experiment a large number of times—say, 400,000 times—we would expect to observe $y = 0$ heads approximately 100,000 times, $y = 1$ head approximately 200,000 times, and $y = 2$ heads approximately 100,000 times. If we calculate the mean value of these 400,000 values of y, we obtain

$$\mu \approx \frac{\sum y}{n} = \frac{100,000(0) + 200,000(1) + 100,000(2)}{400,000}$$

$$= 0\left(\frac{100,000}{400,000}\right) + 1\left(\frac{200,000}{400,000}\right) + 2\left(\frac{100,000}{400,000}\right)$$

$$= 0\left(\frac{1}{4}\right) + 1\left(\frac{1}{2}\right) + 2\left(\frac{1}{4}\right) = \sum_{\text{all } y} y p(y)$$

If y is a random variable, so also is any function $g(y)$ of y. The **expected value of $g(y)$** is defined as follows:

Definition 4.5

Let y be a discrete random variable with probability distribution $p(y)$ and let $g(y)$ be a function of y. Then the **mean** or **expected value of $g(y)$** is

$$E[g(y)] = \sum_{\text{all } y} g(y) p(y)$$

One of the most important functions of a discrete random variable y is its **variance**, i.e., the expected value of the squared deviation of y from its mean μ.

> **Definition 4.6**
> ....
>
> Let y be a discrete random variable with probability distribution $p(y)$. Then the **variance of y** is
>
> $$\sigma^2 = E[(y - \mu)^2] = E(y^2) - \mu^2$$
>
> The **standard deviation of y** is the positive square root of the variance of y:
>
> $$\sigma = \sqrt{\sigma^2}$$

EXAMPLE 4.3

Refer to the coin-tossing experiment of Example 4.1 and the probability distribution for y, shown in Table 4.1. Find the variance and standard deviation of y.

Solution

In Example 4.2, we found that the mean value of y is $\mu = 1$. Then

$$\sigma^2 = E[(y - \mu)^2] = \sum_{y=0}^{2} (y - \mu)^2 p(y)$$

$$= (0 - 1)^2\left(\frac{1}{4}\right) + (1 - 1)^2\left(\frac{1}{2}\right) + (2 - 1)^2\left(\frac{1}{4}\right) = \frac{1}{2}$$

and

$$\sigma = \sqrt{\sigma^2} = \sqrt{\frac{1}{2}} = .707$$

EXAMPLE 4.4

Refer to Example 4.3 and find the probability that y will fall in the interval $\mu \pm 2\sigma$.

Solution

From Examples 4.2 and 4.3, we know that $\mu = 1$ and $\sigma = .707$. Then the interval $\mu \pm 2\sigma$ is $-.414$ to 2.414. Since y must assume one of only three values, $y = 0, 1,$ and 2, all of which fall in the computed interval, the probability that y falls in the interval $\mu \pm 2\sigma$ is 1.0. Clearly, the Empirical Rule (used in Chapter 2 to describe the variation for a finite set of data and the spread of its relative frequency histogram) provides an adequate description of the spread or variation in the probability distribution of Figure 4.2.

EXAMPLE 4.5

A panel of meteorological and civil engineers studying emergency evacuation plans for Florida's Gulf Coast in the event of a hurricane has estimated that it would take between 13 and 18 hours to evacuate people living in low-lying land with the probabilities shown in Table 4.3.

TABLE 4.3   Estimated Probability Distribution of Hurricane Evacuation Time

Time to Evacuate nearest hour	Probability
13	.04
14	.25
15	.40
16	.18
17	.10
18	.03

a. Calculate the mean and standard deviation of the probability distribution of the evacuation times.

b. Within what range would you expect the time to evacuate to fall?

Solution

a. Let y represent the time required to evacuate people in low-lying land. Using Definitions 4.4 and 4.6, we compute

$$\mu = E(y) = \sum yp(y) = 13(.04) + 14(.25) + 15(.40) + 16(.18) + 17(.10) + 18(.03)$$
$$= 15.14 \text{ hours}$$

$$\sigma^2 = E[(y - \mu)^2] = \sum (y - \mu)^2 p(y)$$
$$= (13 - 15.14)^2(.04) + (14 - 15.14)^2(.25) + \cdots + (18 - 15.14)^2(.03)$$
$$= 1.2404$$
$$\sigma = \sqrt{\sigma^2} = \sqrt{1.2404} = 1.11 \text{ hours}$$

b. Based on the Empirical Rule, we expect about 95% of the observed evacuation times (y's) to fall within $\mu \pm 2\sigma$, where

$$\mu \pm 2\sigma = 15.14 \pm 2(1.11) = 15.14 \pm 2.22 = (12.92, 17.36)$$

Consequently, we expect the time to evacuate to be between 12.92 hours and 17.36 hours. Based on the estimated probability distribution in Table 4.3, the actual probability that y falls between 12.92 and 17.36 is

$$P(12.92 \le y \le 17.36) = p(13) + p(14) + p(15) + p(16) + p(17)$$
$$= .04 + .25 + .40 + .18 + .10$$
$$= .97$$

Once again, the Empirical Rule provides a good approximation to the probability of a random variable y falling in the interval $\mu \pm 2\sigma$.

EXERCISES

4.8   Find the mean and variance of the probability distribution in Exercise 4.1.

4.9   Find the mean and variance of the probability distribution in Exercise 4.2.

4.10   Find the mean and variance of the probability distribution in Exercise 4.3.

4.11   Refer to the oil exploration study discussed in Exercise 3.23. Kinchen (1986) gives an example in which a $50,000 exploration budget is allocated to a single prospect. The well can result in a dry hole, 50,000 barrels (bbl), 100,000 bbl, 500,000 bbl, or 1,000,000 bbl, with probabilities and monetary outcomes shown in the table. Let y represent the monetary value of a single oil prospect. Find $E(y)$ and σ^2.

Possible Results bbl	Monetary Outcome $	Probability
Dry hole	−50,000	.60
50,000	−20,000	.10
100,000	30,000	.15
500,000	430,000	.10
1,000,000	950,000	.05

Source: Kinchen, A. L. "Projected outcomes of exploration programs based on current program status and the impact of prospects under consideration." *Journal of Petroleum Technology*, Vol. 38, No. 4, April 1986, p. 462 (Table 1).

4.12   Find the mean and variance of the probability distribution in Exercise 4.4.

4.13   Refer to Example 4.5. The probability distribution for the time to evacuate in the event of a hurricane, Table 4.3, is reproduced here. Weather forecasters say they cannot accurately predict a hurricane landfall more than 14 hours in advance. If the Gulf Coast Civil Engineering Department waits until the 14-hour warning before beginning evacuation, what is the probability that all residents of low-lying areas are evacuated safely (i.e., before the hurricane hits the Gulf Coast)?

Time to Evacuate nearest hour	Probability
13	.04
14	.25
15	.40
16	.18
17	.10
18	.03

4.14   Refer to Exercise 4.5. Suppose the cost of testing a single firing pin is $200.
   a. What is the expected cost of inspecting the lot?

b. What is the variance?

c. Within what range would you expect the inspection cost to fall?

4.4   Some Useful Expectation Theorems

We now present three theorems that are especially useful in finding the expected value of a function of a random variable. We will leave the proofs of these theorems as optional exercises.

Theorem 4.1

Let y be a discrete random variable with probability distribution $p(y)$ and let c be a constant. Then the expected value (or mean) of c is

$$E(c) = c$$

Theorem 4.2

Let y be a discrete random variable with probability distribution $p(y)$ and let c be a constant. Then the expected value (or mean) of cy is

$$E(cy) = cE(y)$$

Theorem 4.3

Let y be a discrete random variable with probability distribution $p(y)$, and let $g_1(y), g_2(y), \ldots, g_k(y)$ be functions of y. Then

$$E[g_1(y) + g_2(y) + \cdots + g_k(y)] = E[g_1(y)] + E[g_2(y)] + \cdots + E[g_k(y)]$$

Theorems 4.1–4.3 can be used to derive a simple formula for computing the variance of a random variable, as given by Theorem 4.4.

Theorem 4.4

$$\sigma^2 = E(y^2) - \mu^2$$

PROOF OF THEOREM 4.4   From Definition 4.6, we have the following expression for σ^2:

$$\sigma^2 = E[(y - \mu)^2] = E(y^2 - 2\mu y + \mu^2)$$

Applying Theorem 4.3 yields

$$\sigma^2 = E(y^2) + E(-2\mu y) + E(\mu^2)$$

We now apply Theorems 4.1 and 4.2 to obtain

$$\sigma^2 = E(y^2) - 2\mu E(y) + \mu^2 = E(y^2) - 2\mu(\mu) + \mu^2$$
$$= E(y^2) - 2\mu^2 + \mu^2$$
$$= E(y^2) - \mu^2$$

We will use Theorem 4.4 to derive the variances for some of the discrete random variables presented in the following sections. The method is demonstrated in Example 4.6.

EXAMPLE 4.6

Use Theorem 4.4 to find the variance for the random variable y of Example 4.1.

Solution

In Example 4.3, we found the variance of y, the number of heads observed in the tossing of two coins, by finding $\sigma^2 = E[(y - \mu)^2]$ directly. Since this can be a tedious procedure, it is usually easier to find $E(y^2)$ and then use Theorem 4.4 to compute σ^2. For our example,

$$E(y^2) = \sum_{\text{all } y} y^2 p(y) = (0)^2\left(\frac{1}{4}\right) + (1)^2\left(\frac{1}{2}\right) + (2)^2\left(\frac{1}{4}\right) = 1.5$$

Substituting the value $\mu = 1$ (obtained in Example 4.2) into the statement of Theorem 4.4, we have

$$\sigma^2 = E(y^2) - \mu^2$$
$$= 1.5 - (1)^2 = .5$$

Note that this is the value of σ^2 that we obtained in Example 4.3.

In Sections 4.6–4.10, we will present some useful models of discrete probability distributions and will state without proof the mean, variance, and standard deviation for each. Some of these quantities will be derived in optional examples; other derivations will be left as optional exercises.

EXERCISES

4.15   Refer to Exercises 4.1 and 4.8. The manufacturer leases new PCs at a cost of $15,000 per year. Find the mean and variance of the total amount the company will earn next year from leasing PCs.

4.16   Use Theorem 4.4 to calculate the variance of the probability distribution in Exercise 4.2. Verify that your result agrees with Exercise 4.9.

4.17   Use Theorem 4.4 to calculate the variance of the probability distribution in Exercise 4.3. Verify that your result agrees with Exercise 4.10.

4.18   Refer to Exercise 4.5, where y is the number of firing pins tested in a sample of five selected from a large lot. Suppose the cost of inspecting a single pin is \$300 if the pin is defective and \$100 if not. Then the total cost C (in dollars) of the inspection is given by the equation $C = 200 + 100y$. Find the mean and variance of C.

OPTIONAL EXERCISES

4.19   Prove Theorem 4.1. [*Hint:*   Use the fact that $\Sigma_{\text{all } y}\, p(y) = 1$.]

4.20   Prove Theorem 4.2. [*Hint:*   The proof follows directly from Definition 4.5.]

4.21   Prove Theorem 4.3.

4.5   Bernoulli Trials

Several of the discrete probability distributions discussed in this chapter are based on experiments or processes in which a sequence of trials, called **Bernoulli trials**, are conducted.

A Bernoulli trial results in one of two mutually exclusive outcomes, typically denoted S (for Success) and F (for Failure). For example, tossing a coin is a Bernoulli trial since only one of two different outcomes can occur, head (H) or tail (T).

The characteristics of a Bernoulli trial are stated in the box.

Characteristics of a Bernoulli Trial

1. The trial results in one of two mutually exclusive outcomes. (We denote one outcome by S and the other by F.)
2. The outcomes are exhaustive, i.e., no other outcomes are possible.
3. The probabilities of S and F are denoted by p and q, respectively. That is, $P(S) = p$ and $P(F) = q$. Note that $p + q = 1$.

A **Bernoulli random variable** y is defined as the numerical outcome of a Bernoulli trial, where $y = 1$ if a success occurs and $y = 0$ if a failure occurs. Consequently, the probability distribution for y is shown in Table 4.4 and the box on page 158.

TABLE 4.4   Bernoulli Probability Distribution

Outcome	y	$p(y)$
S	1	p
F	0	q

The Bernoulli Probability Distribution

Consider a Bernoulli trial where

$$y = \begin{cases} 1 & \text{if a success } (S) \text{ occurs} \\ 0 & \text{if a failure } (F) \text{ occurs} \end{cases}$$

The probability distribution for the Bernoulli random variable y is given by

$$p(y) = p^y q^{1-y} \qquad (y = 0, 1)$$

where

p = Probability of a success for a Bernoulli trial
$q = 1 - p$

The mean and variance of the Bernoulli random variable are, respectively,

$$\mu = p \qquad \text{and} \qquad \sigma^2 = pq$$

In the Bernoulli coin-tossing experiment, define H as a success and T as a failure. Then $y = 1$ if H occurs and $y = 0$ if T occurs. Since $P(H) = P(T) = .5$ if the coin is balanced, the probability distribution for y is

$$p(1) = p = .5$$
$$p(0) = q = .5$$

EXAMPLE 4.7

Show that for a Bernoulli random variable y, $\mu = p$ and $\sigma = \sqrt{pq}$.

Solution

We know that $P(y = 1) = p(1) = p$ and $P(y = 0) = p(0) = q$. Then, from Definition 4.4,

$$\mu = E(y) = \sum yp(y) = (1)p(1) + (0)p(0) = p(1) = p$$

Also, from Definition 4.5 and Theorem 4.4,

$$\sigma^2 = E(y^2) - \mu^2 = \sum y^2 p(y) - \mu^2 = (1)^2 p(1) + (0)^2 p(0) - \mu^2$$
$$= p(1) - \mu^2 = p - p^2 = p(1 - p) = pq$$

Consequently, $\sigma = \sqrt{\sigma^2} = \sqrt{pq}$.

A Bernoulli random variable, by itself, is of little interest in engineering and science applications. Conducting a *series* of Bernoulli trials, however, leads to some well-known and useful discrete probability distributions. One of these is described in the next section.

4.6   The Binomial Probability Distribution

Many real-life experiments result from conducting a series of Bernoulli trials and are analogous to tossing an *unbalanced* coin a number n of times. Suppose that 30% of the private wells that provide drinking water to a metropolitan area contain impurity A. Then selecting a random sample of ten wells and testing for impurity A would be analogous to tossing an unbalanced coin 10 times, with the probability of tossing a head (detecting impurity A) on a single trial equal to .30. Public opinion or consumer preference polls that elicit one of two responses—yes or no, approve or disapprove, etc.—are also analogous to the unbalanced coin tossing experiment if the number N in the population is large and if the sample size n is relatively small, say, .10N or less. All these experiments are particular examples of a **binomial experiment**. Such experiments and the resulting binomial random variables possess the characteristics stated in the box.

Characteristics That Define a Binomial Random Variable

1. The experiment consists of n identical Bernoulli trials.
2. There are only two possible outcomes on each trial: S (for Success) and F (for Failure).
3. $P(S) = p$ and $P(F) = q$ remain the same from trial to trial. (Note that $p + q = 1$.)
4. The trials are independent.
5. The binomial random variable y is the number of S's in n trials.

The binomial probability distribution, its mean, and its variance are shown in the box on page 160. Figure 4.3 shows the relative frequency histograms of binomial distributions for a sample of $n = 10$ and different values of p. Note that the probability distribution is skewed to the right for small values of p, skewed to the left for large values of p, and symmetric for $p = .5$.

The Binomial Probability Distribution

The probability distribution for a binomial random variable is given by

$$p(y) = \binom{n}{y} p^y q^{n-y} \qquad (y = 0, 1, 2, \ldots, n)$$

where

p = Probability of a success on a single trial

$q = 1 - p$

n = Number of trials

y = Number of successes in n trials

$$\binom{n}{y} = \frac{n!}{y!(n-y)!}$$

The mean and variance of the binomial random variable are, respectively,

$$\mu = np \quad \text{and} \quad \sigma^2 = npq$$

FIGURE 4.3 ▼
Binomial probability distributions
for $n = 10$, $p = .1, .3, .5, .7, .9$

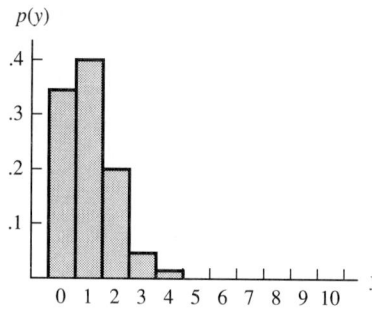

a. $p = .1$

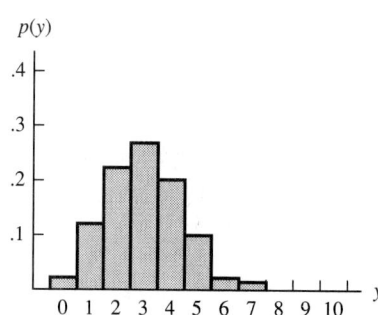

b. $p = .3$

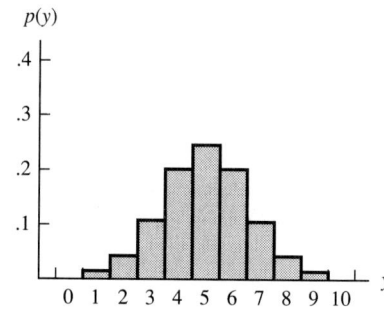

c. $p = .5$

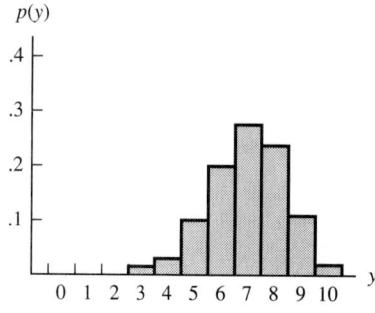

d. $p = .7$

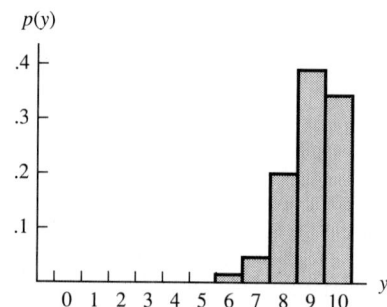

e. $p = .9$

The binomial probability distribution is derived as follows. A simple event for a binomial experiment consisting of n Bernoulli trials can be represented by the symbol

$$SFSFFFSSSF \ldots SFS$$

where the letter in the ith position, proceeding from left to right, denotes the outcome of the ith trial. Since we want to find the probability $p(y)$ of observing y successes in the n trials, we will need to sum the probabilities of all simple events that contain y successes (S's) and $(n - y)$ failures (F's). Such simple events would appear symbolically as

$$\overbrace{SSSS \ldots S}^{y} \overbrace{FF \ldots F}^{(n - y)}$$

or some different arrangement of these symbols.

Since the trials are independent, the probability of a *particular* simple event implying y successes is

$$P(\overbrace{SSS \ldots S}^{y} \overbrace{FF \ldots F}^{(n - y)}) = p^y q^{n-y}$$

The *number* of these equiprobable simple events is equal to the number of ways we can arrange the y S's and the $(n - y)$ F's in n positions corresponding to the n trials. This is equal to the number of ways of selecting y positions (trials) for the y S's from a total of n positions. This number, given by Theorem 3.4, is

$$\binom{n}{y} = \frac{n!}{y!(n - y)!}$$

We have determined the probability of each simple event that results in y successes, as well as the number of such events. We now sum the probabilities of these simple events to obtain

$$p(y) = \binom{\text{Number of simple events}}{\text{implying } y \text{ successes}} \binom{\text{Probability of one of these}}{\text{equiprobable simple events}}$$

or

$$p(y) = \binom{n}{y} p^y q^{n-y}$$

EXAMPLE 4.8

Electrical engineers recognize that high neutral current in computer power systems is a potential problem. A recent survey of computer power system load currents at U.S. sites found that 10% of the sites had high neutral to full-load current ratios (*IEEE Transactions on Industry Applications* (July/Aug. 1990). If a random sample of five computer power systems is selected from the large number of sites in the country, what is the probability that:

a. Exactly three will have a high neutral to full-current load ratio?

b. At least three?

c. Fewer than three?

Solution

The first step is to confirm that this experiment possesses the characteristics of a binomial experiment. The experiment consists of $n = 5$ Bernoulli trials, one corresponding to each randomly selected site. Each trial results in an S (the site has a computer power system with a high neutral to full-load current ratio) or an F (the system does not have a high ratio). Since the total number of sites with computer power systems in the country is large, the probability of drawing a single site and finding that it has a high neutral to full-load current ratio is .1, and this probability will remain approximately the same (for all practical purposes) for each of the five selected sites. Further, since the sampling was random, we assume that the outcome on any one site is unaffected by the outcome of any other and that the trials are independent. Finally, we are interested in the number y of sites in the sample of $n = 5$ that have high neutral to full-load current ratios. Therefore, the sampling procedure represents a binomial experiment with $n = 5$ and $p = .1$.

a. The probability of drawing exactly $y = 3$ sites containing a high ratio is

$$p(y) = \binom{n}{y} p^y q^{n-y}$$

where $n = 5$, $p = .1$, and $y = 3$. Thus,

$$p(3) = \frac{5!}{3!2!}(.1)^3(.9)^2 = .0081$$

b. The probability of observing at least three sites with high ratios is

$$P(y \geq 3) = p(3) + p(4) + p(5)$$

where

$$p(4) = \frac{5!}{4!1!}(.1)^4(.9)^1 = .00045$$

$$p(5) = \frac{5!}{5!0!}(.1)^5(.9)^0 = .00001$$

Since we found $p(3)$ in part **a**, we have

$$P(y \geq 3) = p(3) + p(4) + p(5)$$
$$= .0081 + .00045 + .00001 = .00856$$

c. Although $P(y < 3) = p(0) + p(1) + p(2)$, we can avoid calculating these probabilities by using the complementary relationship and the fact that $\sum_{y=0}^{n} p(y) = 1$.

Therefore,

$$P(y < 3) = 1 - P(y \geq 3) = 1 - .00856 = .99144$$

Tables that give partial sums of the form

$$\sum_{y=0}^{k} p(y)$$

for binomial probabilities are given in Table 1 of Appendix II, for $n = 5, 10, 15, 20,$ and 25. For example, you will find that the partial sum given in the table for $n = 5$, in the row corresponding to $k = 2$ and the column corresponding to $p = .1$, is

$$\sum_{y=0}^{2} p(y) = p(0) + p(1) + p(2) = .991$$

This answer, correct to three decimal places, agrees with our answer to part **c** of Example 4.8.

EXAMPLE 4.9

Find the mean, variance, and standard deviation for a binomial random variable with $n = 20$ and $p = .6$. Construct the interval $\mu \pm 2\sigma$ and compute $P(\mu - 2\sigma < y < \mu + 2\sigma)$.

Solution

Applying the formulas given previously, we have

$$\mu = np = 20(.6) = 12$$
$$\sigma^2 = npq = 20(.6)(.4) = 4.8$$
$$\sigma = \sqrt{4.8} = 2.19$$

The binomial probability distribution for $n = 20$ and $p = .6$ and the interval $\mu \pm 2\sigma$, or 7.62 to 16.38, are shown in Figure 4.4 (page 164). The values of y that lie in the interval $\mu \pm 2\sigma$ are 8, 9, . . . , 16. Therefore,

$$P(\mu - 2\sigma < y < \mu + 2\sigma) = P(y = 8, 9, 10, \ldots, \text{ or } 16)$$
$$= \sum_{y=0}^{16} p(y) - \sum_{y=0}^{7} p(y)$$

We obtain the values of these partial sums from Table 1 of Appendix II:

$$P(\mu - 2\sigma < y < \mu + 2\sigma) = \sum_{y=0}^{16} p(y) - \sum_{y=0}^{7} p(y)$$
$$= .984 - .021 = .963$$

FIGURE 4.4 ▶
Binomial probability distribution for y in Example 4.9 ($n = 20$, $p = .6$)

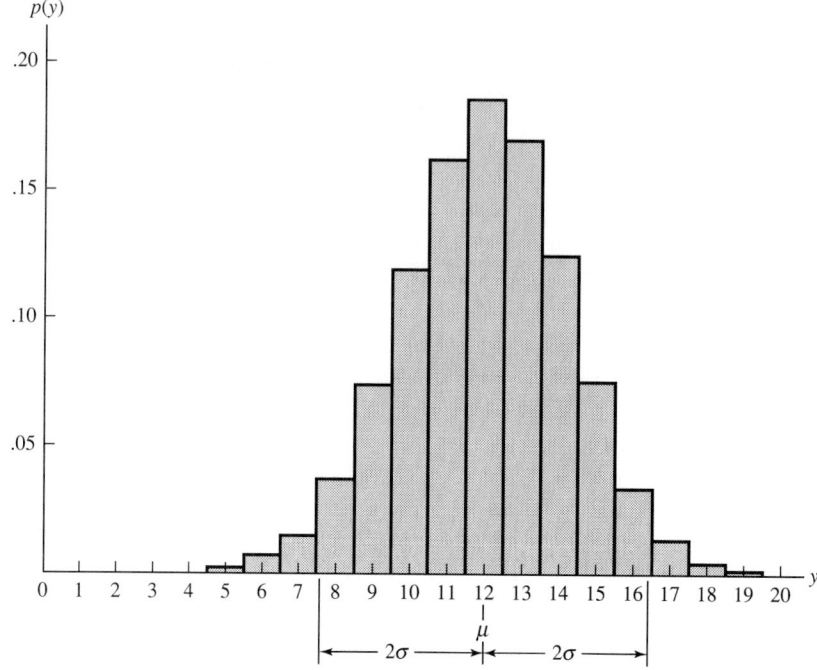

You can see that this result is close to the value of .95 specified by the Empirical Rule, discussed in Chapter 2.

EXAMPLE 4.10 (OPTIONAL)   Derive the formula for the expected value for the binomial random variable.

Solution   By Definition 4.4,

$$\mu = E(y) = \sum_{\text{all } y} yp(y) = \sum_{y=0}^{n} y \frac{n!}{y!(n-y)!} p^y q^{n-y}$$

The easiest way to sum these terms is to convert them into binomial probabilities and then use the fact that $\sum_{y=0}^{n} p(y) = 1$. Noting that the first term of the summation is equal to 0 (since $y = 0$), we have

$$\mu = \sum_{y=1}^{n} y \frac{n!}{[y(y-1)\cdots 3\cdot 2\cdot 1](n-y)!} p^y q^{n-y}$$

$$= \sum_{y=1}^{n} \frac{n!}{(y-1)!(n-y)!} p^y q^{n-y}$$

Because n and p are constants, we can use Theorem 4.2 to factor np out of the sum:

$$\mu = np \sum_{y=1}^{n} \frac{(n-1)!}{(y-1)!(n-y)!} p^{y-1} q^{n-y}$$

Let $z = (y - 1)$. Then when $y = 1$, $z = 0$ and when $y = n$, $z = (n - 1)$; thus,

$$\mu = np \sum_{y=1}^{n} \frac{(n - 1)!}{(y - 1)!(n - y)!} p^{y-1} q^{n-y}$$

$$= np \sum_{z=0}^{n-1} \frac{(n - 1)!}{z![(n - 1) - z]!} p^{z} q^{(n-1)-z}$$

The quantity inside the summation sign is $p(z)$, where z is a binomial random variable based on $(n - 1)$ Bernoulli trials. Therefore,

$$\sum_{z=0}^{n-1} p(z) = 1$$

and

$$\mu = np \sum_{z=0}^{n-1} p(z) = np(1) = np$$

EXERCISES

4.22 Use the formula for the binomial probability distribution to find the probabilities for $n = 4$, $p = .5$, and $y = 0, 1, 2, 3,$ and 4.

4.23 Use the binomial probabilities given in Table 1 of Appendix II to find $p(y)$ for $n = 10$ and
a. $p = .1$ **b.** $p = .5$ **c.** $p = .9$
d. Construct graphs (similar to Figure 4.2) of the three probability distributions in parts **a–c**. Note the symmetry of the distribution for $p = .5$ and the skewness for $p = .1$ and $p = .9$.

4.24 The National Science Foundation reports that 70% of the U.S. graduate students who earn Ph.D. degrees in engineering are foreign nationals (*Science*, Sept. 24, 1993). Consider the number of foreign students in a random sample of 25 engineering students who recently earned their Ph.D.
a. Find $P(y = 10)$.
b. Find $P(y \leq 5)$.
c. Find the mean μ and standard deviation σ for y.
d. Interpret the results, part **c**.

4.25 *Occupational Outlook Quarterly* (Spring 1993) reported that 1% of all the drywall installers employed in the construction industry are women. In a random sample of 10 drywall installers, find the probability that at most one is a woman.

4.26 Zoologists have discovered that animals spend a great deal of time resting, although this rest time can have functional importance (e.g., predators lying in wait for their prey). Discounting time spent in deep sleep, a University of Vermont researcher estimated the percentage of time various species spend at rest (*National Wildlife*, Aug.–Sept. 1993). For example, the probability that a female fence lizard will be resting at any given time is approximately .95.

a. In a random sample of 20 female fence lizards, what is the probability that at least 15 will be resting at any given time?

b. In a random sample of 20 female fence lizards, what is the probability that fewer than 10 will be resting at any given time?

c. In a random sample of 200 female fence lizards, would you expect to observe fewer than 190 at rest at any given time? Explain.

4.27   In a recent study, *Consumer Reports* (Feb. 1992) found widespread contamination and mislabeling of seafood in supermarkets in New York City and Chicago. The study revealed one alarming statistic: 40% of the swordfish pieces available for sale had a level of mercury above the Food and Drug Administration (FDA) minimum amount. For a random sample of three swordfish pieces, find the probability that:

a. All three swordfish pieces have mercury levels above the FDA minimum.

b. Exactly one swordfish piece has a mercury level above the FDA minimum.

c. At most one swordfish piece has a mercury level above the FDA minimum.

4.28   A study of 5-year trends in the logistics information systems of industries found that the greatest computerization advances were in transportation (*Industrial Engineering*, July 1990). Currently, 90% of all industries contain shipping open order files in their computerized database. In a random sample of 10 industries, let y equal the number that include shipping open order files in their computerized database.

a. Verify that the probability distribution of y can be modeled using the binomial distribution.

b. Find $P(y = 7)$.

c. Find $P(y > 5)$.

d. Find the mean and variance of y. Interpret the results.

4.29   Refer to the *IEEE Computer Applications in Power* study of an outdoor unmanned watching system designed to detect trespassers, Exercise 3.13. In snowy weather conditions, the system detected 7 out of 10 intruders; thus, the researchers estimated the system's probability of intruder detection in snowy conditions at .70.

a. Assuming the probability of intruder detection in snowy conditions is only .50, find the probability that the unmanned system detects at least 7 of the 10 intruders.

b. Based on the result, part **a**, comment on the reliability of the researcher's estimate of the system's detection probability in snowy conditions.

4.30   Refer to the neutral particle transport problem described in Exercise 3.25. Recall that particles released into an evacuated duct collide with the inner duct wall and are either scattered (reflected) with probability .16 or absorbed with probability .84 (*Nuclear Science and Engineering*, May 1986).

a. If four particles are released into the duct, what is the probability that all four will be absorbed by the inner duct wall? Exactly three of the four?

b. If 20 particles are released into the duct, what is the probability that at least 10 will be reflected by the inner duct wall? Exactly 10?

4.31   During the 1950s, a number of atomic weapons tests were conducted in the desert in Nevada. Since that time, estimates of radiation exposure to off-site populations, especially Utah, have been the subject of considerable scientific effort. The Surveillance, Epidemiology, and End Results (SEER) Registry collected data on incidence of thyroid cancer among Utah residents over the period 1973–1977. SEER found that the incidence rate of thyroid cancer among 50-year-old males is 3.89 per 100,000 population (*Health Physics*, Jan. 1986). This implies that the probability of a 50-year-old Utah male developing thyroid cancer is .0000389. In a random sample of 1,000 50-year-old Utah males, let y equal the number developing thyroid cancer.

a. Calculate the mean and variance of y.

b. Would you expect to observe at least one 50-year-old male with thyroid cancer among the 1,000?

4.32 *Organic Gardening* magazine conducted a poll to determine whether consumers would prefer organically grown fruits and vegetables over those grown with fertilizers and pesticides (*New York Times*, Mar. 21, 1989). If the costs of the two food types were the same, 85% said they would prefer the organic food. Surprisingly, 50% said they would prefer the organic food even if they had to pay more for it. Consider the preferences of a random sample of $n = 25$ consumers.

a. Assuming the percentages in the poll are reflective of the population, find the probability that at least 20 of the 25 consumers would prefer the organically grown food, if the costs were the same.

b. Assuming the percentages in the poll are reflective of the population, find the probability that at least 20 of the 25 consumers would prefer the organically grown food, even if the costs were higher than food grown with fertilizers and pesticides.

OPTIONAL EXERCISES

4.33 For the binomial probability distribution $p(y)$, show that $\sum_{y=0}^{n} p(y) = 1$. [*Hint:*   The binomial theorem, which pertains to the expansion of $(a + b)^n$, states that

$$(a + b)^n = \binom{n}{0}a^n + \binom{n}{1}a^{n-1}b + \binom{n}{2}a^{n-2}b^2 + \cdots + \binom{n}{n}b^n$$

Let $a = q$ and $b = p$.]

4.34 Show that, for a binomial random variable,

$$E[y(y - 1)] = npq + \mu^2 - \mu$$

[*Hint:*   Write the expected value as a sum, factor out $y(y - 1)$, and then factor terms until each term in the sum is a binomial probability. Use the fact that $\sum_y p(y) = 1$ to sum the series.]

4.35 Use the results of Exercise 4.34 and the fact that

$$E[y(y - 1)] = E(y^2 - y) = E(y^2) - E(y) = E(y^2) - \mu$$

to find $E(y^2)$ for a binomial random variable.

4.36 Use the results of Exercises 4.34 and 4.35, in conjunction with Theorem 4.4, to show that $\sigma^2 = npq$ for a binomial random variable.

4.7   The Multinomial Probability Distribution

Many types of experiments result in observations on a qualitative variable with more than two possible outcomes. For example, suppose that a particular personal computer (PC) is manufactured on one of five different production lines, A, B, C, D, or E. To compare the proportions of defective PCs that can be attributed to the five production lines, all defective computers located by quality control engineers are classified each

TABLE 4.5   Classification of the $n = 103$ Defective Personal Computers According to Production Line

Production Line				
A	B	C	D	E
15	27	31	19	11

day according to the production line. Each PC is an experimental unit and the observation is a letter that identifies the production line on which it was produced. Production line is clearly a qualitative variable.

Suppose that $n = 103$ computers are found to be defective in a given week. The $n = 103$ qualitative observations, each resulting in an A, B, C, D, or E, produce counts giving the numbers of defectives emerging from the five production lines. For example, if there were $y_1 = 15$ A's, $y_2 = 27$ B's, $y_3 = 31$ C's, $y_4 = 19$ D's, and $y_5 = 11$ E's, the classified data would appear as shown in Table 4.5, which shows the counts in each category of the classification. Note that the sum of the numbers of defective PCs produced by the five lines must equal the total number of defectives:

$$n = y_1 + y_2 + y_3 + y_4 + y_5 = 15 + 27 + 31 + 19 + 11 = 103$$

The classification experiment that we have just described is called a **multinomial experiment** and represents an extension of the binomial experiment discussed in Section 4.6. Such an experiment consists of n identical trials—that is, observations on n experimental units. Each trial must result in one and only one of k outcomes, the k classification categories (for the binomial experiment, $k = 2$). The probability that the outcome of a single trial will fall in category i is p_i ($i = 1, 2, \ldots, k$). Finally, the trials are independent and we are interested in the numbers of observations, y_1, $y_2, \ldots, y_k$, falling in the k classification categories.

Properties of the Multinomial Experiment

1. The experiment consists of n identical trials.
2. There are k possible outcomes to each trial.
3. The probabilities of the k outcomes, denoted by $p_1, p_2, \ldots, p_k$, remain the same from trial to trial, where $p_1 + p_2 + \cdots + p_k = 1$.
4. The trials are independent.
5. The random variables of interest are the counts $y_1, y_2, \ldots, y_k$ in each of the k classification categories.

The multinomial distribution, its mean, and its variance are shown in the following box.

The Multinomial Probability Distribution

$$p(y_1, y_2, \ldots, y_k) = \frac{n!}{y_1! \, y_2! \, \cdots \, y_k!} (p_1)^{y_1}(p_2)^{y_2} \cdots (p_k)^{y_k}$$

where

p_i = Probability of outcome i on a single trial

$p_1 + p_2 + \cdots + p_k = 1$

$n = y_1 + y_2 + \cdots + y_k$ = Number of trials

y_i = Number of occurrences of outcome i in n trials

The mean and variance of the multinomial random variable y_i are, respectively,

$$\mu_i = np_i \quad \text{and} \quad \sigma_i^2 = np_i(1 - p_i)$$

The procedure for deriving the **multinomial probability distribution** $p(y_1, y_2, \ldots, y_k)$ for the category counts, $n_1, n_2, \ldots, n_k$, is identical to the procedure employed for a binomial experiment. To simplify our notation, we will illustrate the procedure for $k = 3$ categories. The derivation of $p(y_1, y_2, \ldots, y_k)$ for k categories is similar.

Let the three outcomes corresponding to the $k = 3$ categories be denoted as A, B, and C, with respective category probabilities p_1, p_2, and p_3. Then any observation of the outcome of n trials will result in a simple event of the type shown in Table 4.6. The outcome of each trial is indicated by the letter that was observed. Thus, the simple event in Table 4.6 is one that results in C on the first trial, A on the second, A on the third, . . . , and B on the last.

TABLE 4.6   A Typical Simple Event for a Multinomial Experiment ($k = 3$)

			Trial				
1	2	3	4	5	6	$\cdots$	n
C	A	A	B	A	C	$\cdots$	B

Now consider a simple event that will result in y_1 A outcomes, y_2 B outcomes, and y_3 C outcomes, where $y_1 + y_2 + y_3 = n$. One of these simple events is shown in Figure 4.5. The probability of the simple event shown in the figure, which results in y_1 A outcomes, y_2 B outcomes, and y_3 C outcomes, is

$$(p_1)^{y_1}(p_2)^{y_2}(p_3)^{y_3}$$

FIGURE 4.5 ▶

A simple event containing y_1 A, y_2 B, and y_3 C outcomes

$$\underbrace{AAA \ldots A}_{y_1} \quad \underbrace{BBB \ldots B}_{y_2} \quad \underbrace{CCC \ldots C}_{y_3}$$

How many simple events will there be in the sample space S that will imply y_1 A's, y_2 B's, and y_3 C's? This number is equal to the number of different ways that we can arrange the y_1 A's, y_2 B's, and y_3 C's in the n distinct positions of Figure 4.5.

The number of ways that we would assign y_1 positions to A, y_2 positions to B, and y_3 to C is given by Theorem 3.3 as

$$\frac{n!}{y_1!y_2!y_3!}$$

Therefore, there are $n!/(y_1!y_2!y_3!)$ simple events resulting in y_1 A's, y_2 B's, and y_3 C's, each with probability $(p_1)^{y_1}(p_2)^{y_2}(p_3)^{y_3}$. It then follows that the probability of observing y_1 A's, y_2 B's, and y_3 C's in n trials is equal to the sum of the probabilities of these simple events:

$$p(y_1, y_2, y_3) = \frac{n!}{y_1!y_2!y_3!}(p_1)^{y_1}(p_2)^{y_2}(p_3)^{y_3}$$

You can verify that this is the expression obtained by substituting $k = 3$ into the formula for the multinomial probability distribution shown in the box.

The expected value, or mean, of the number of counts for a particular category, say, category i, follows directly from our knowledge of the properties of a binomial random variable. If we combine all categories other than category i into a single category, then the multinomial classification becomes a binomial classification with y_i observations in category i and $(n - y_i)$ observations in the combined category. Then, from our knowledge of the expected value and variance of a binomial random variable, it follows that

$$E(y_i) = np_i$$
$$V(y_i) = np_i(1 - p_i)$$

EXAMPLE 4.11

Refer to the study of neutral to full-load current ratios in computer power systems, Example 4.8. Suppose that the electrical engineers found that 10% of the systems have high ratios, 30% have moderate ratios, and 60% have low ratios. Consider a random sample of $n = 40$ computer power system sites.

a. Find the probability that 10 sites have high neutral to full-load current ratios, 10 sites have moderate ratios, and 20 sites have low ratios.

b. Find the mean and variance of the number of sites that have high neutral to full-load current ratios. Use this information to estimate the number of sites in the sample of 40 that will have high ratios.

Solution

In the solution to Example 4.8, we verified that the properties of a binomial experiment were satisfied. This example is simply an extension of the binomial experiment to one involving $k = 3$ possible outcomes—high, neutral, or low ratio—for each site. Thus, the properties of a multinomial experiment are satisfied, and we may apply the formulas given in the box.

a. Define the following:

y_1 = Number of sites with high ratios

y_2 = Number of sites with moderate ratios

y_3 = Number of sites with low ratios

p_1 = Probability of a site with a high ratio

p_2 = Probability of a site with a moderate ratio

p_3 = Probability of a site with a low ratio

Then we want to find the probability, $P(y_1 = 10, y_2 = 10, y_3 = 20)$, using the formula

$$p(y_1, y_2, y_3) = \frac{n!}{y_1! y_2! y_3!} (p_1)^{y_1}(p_2)^{y_2}(p_3)^{y_3}$$

where $n = 40$ and our estimates of p_1, p_2, p_3 are .1, .3, and .6, respectively. Substituting these values, we obtain

$$p(10, 10, 20) = \frac{40!}{10! 10! 20!} (.1)^{10}(.3)^{10}(.6)^{20} = .0005498$$

b. We want to find the mean and variance of y_1, the number of sites with high neutral to full-load current ratios. From the formula in the box, we have

$$\mu_1 = np_1 = 40(.1) = 4$$

and

$$\sigma_1^2 = np_1(1 - p_1) = 40(.1)(.9) = 3.6$$

From our knowledge of the Empirical Rule, we expect y_1, the number of sites in the sample with high ratios, to fall within 2 standard deviations of its mean, i.e., between

$$\mu_1 - 2\sigma_1 = 4 - 2\sqrt{3.6} = .21$$

and

$$\mu_1 + 2\sigma_1 = 4 + 2\sqrt{3.6} = 7.79$$

Since y_1 can take only whole-number values, 0, 1, 2, . . . , we expect the number of sites with high ratios to fall between 1 and 7.

EXERCISES

4.37 For the multinomial distribution with $n = 5$, $k = 3$, $p_1 = .2$, $p_2 = .5$, and $p_3 = .3$, find the following probabilities:

a. $p(3, 1, 1)$ b. $p(0, 5, 0)$ c. $p(1, 3, 1)$

4.38 Refer to the multinomial distribution, Exercise 4.37. Find the mean and variance for each of the three random variables, y_1, y_2, and y_3.

4.39 To compensate for disorientation in zero gravity, astronauts rely heavily on visual information to establish a top–down orientation. The potential of using color brightness as a body orientation clue was studied in *Human Factors* (Dec. 1988). Ninety college students, reclining on their backs in the dark, were disoriented when positioned on a rotating platform under a slowly rotating disk that blocked their field of vision. The subjects were asked to say "stop" when they felt as if they were right-side up. The position of the brightness pattern on the disk in relation to each student's body orientation was then recorded. Subjects selected only three disk brightness patterns as subjective vertical clues: (1) brighter side up, (2) darker side up, and (3) brighter and darker side aligned on either side of the subject's heads. Based on the study results, the probabilities of subjects selecting the three disk orientations are .65, .15, and .20, respectively. Suppose $n = 8$ subjects perform a similar experiment.

a. What is the probability that all eight subjects select the brighter-side-up disk orientation?

b. What is the probability that four subjects select the brighter-side-up orientation, three select the darker-side-up orientation, and one selects the aligned orientation?

c. On average, how many of the eight subjects will select the brighter-side-up orientation?

4.40 Piracy of popular computer software such as Lotus and WordStar is growing at a phenomenal rate. Recent court rulings have made companies liable for employees who make unauthorized copies of software purchased by the company, even if the employer is unaware of the copying. Are companies adopting tougher software copying policies, and do they enforce them? To answer this question, a researcher surveyed 121 industrial *Fortune 500* companies that use personal computers (PCs) in the workplace (*Journal of Systems Management*, July 1989). Of particular interest were the policy enforcement methods of the companies. The responses for the 121 companies are summarized in the table.

Policy Enforcement Method	Number of Companies
1. Do not take any action	10
2. Internal audits	49
3. Honor system	28
4. Manager audits/random checks	12
5. Others	22
TOTAL	121

Source: Athey, S. A. "Software copying policies of the *Fortune 500*," *Journal of Systems Management*, July 1989, p. 33 (Table 6).

a. Verify that the properties of a multinomial experiment are satisfied in this study.

b. A researcher has theorized that the companies are equally divided in the method of enforcement utilized. If so, assign values to the probabilities, p_1, p_2, p_3, p_4, and p_5, of the multinomial experiment.

c. Use the probabilities, part **b**, to calculate the probability of observing the results shown in the table.

4.41 An electrical current traveling through a resistor may take one of three different paths, with probabilities $p_1 = .25$, $p_2 = .30$, and $p_3 = .45$, respectively. Suppose we monitor the path taken in $n = 10$ consecutive trials.

    a. Find the probability that the electrical current will travel the first path $y_1 = 2$ times, the second path $y_2 = 4$ times, and the third path $y_3 = 4$ times.

    b. Find $E(y_2)$ and $V(y_2)$. Interpret the results.

4.42 Jobs submitted at a university computer center may run under one of four different priority classes: urgent, normal priority, low priority, and standby. The computer center estimates that 10% of the jobs are submitted as urgent, 50% as normal priority, 20% as low priority, and 20% as standby. Suppose that $n = 20$ jobs are submitted simultaneously.

    a. Find the probability that 2 jobs will be submitted as urgent, 12 as normal priority, 5 as low priority, and 1 as standby.

    b. Find the expected number of low priority jobs in the sample.

    c. Within what range would you expect the number of low priority jobs in the sample to fall?

4.43 A sample of size n is selected from a large lot of shear drill bits. Suppose that a proportion p_1 contains exactly one defect and a proportion p_2 contains more than one defect (with $p_1 + p_2 < 1$). The cost of replacing or repairing the defective drill bits is $C = 4y_1 + y_2$, where y_1 denotes the number of bits with one defect and y_2 denotes the number with two or more defects. Find the expected value of C.

4.44 In March 1981, a waterborne nonbacterial gastroenteritis outbreak occurred in Colorado as a result of a long-standing filter deficiency and malfunction of a sewage treatment plant. A study was conducted to determine whether the incidence of gastrointestinal disease during the epidemic was related to water consumption (*American Water Works Journal*, Jan. 1986). A telephone survey of households yielded the accompanying information on daily consumption of 8-ounce glasses of water for a sample of 40 residents who exhibited gastroenteritis symptoms during the epidemic.

	Daily Consumption of 8-Ounce Glasses of Water				
	0	*1–2*	*3–4*	*5 or more*	*Total*
Number of respondents with symptoms	6	11	13	10	40

Source: Hopkins, R. S., et. al. "Gastroenteritis: Case study of a Colorado outbreak." *Journal American Water Works Association*, Vol. 78, No. 1, Jan. 1986, p. 42, Table 1. Copyright © 1986, American Water Works Association. Reprinted with permission.

    a. If the number of respondents with symptoms *does not depend* on the daily amount of water consumed, assign probabilities to the four categories shown in the table.

    b. Use the information, part **a**, to find the probability of observing the sample result shown in the table.

OPTIONAL EXERCISE

4.45 For a multinomial distribution with $k = 3$ and $n = 2$, verify that

$$\sum_{y_1, \, y_2, \, y_3} p(y_1, y_2, y_3) = 1$$

[*Hint:* Use the binomial theorem (see Optional Exercise 4.33) to expand the sum $[a + (b + c)]^2$, then substitute the binomial expansion of $(b + c)^2$ in the resulting expression. Finally, substitute $a = p_1$, $b = p_2$, and $c = p_3$.]

4.8   The Negative Binomial and the Geometric Probability Distributions

Often we will be interested in measuring the length of time before some event occurs—for example, the length of time a customer must wait in line until receiving service, or the length of time until a piece of equipment fails.

For this application, we view each unit of time as a Bernoulli trial that can result in a success (S) or a failure (F), and consider a series of trials identical to those described for the binomial experiment (Section 4.6). Unlike the binomial experiment where y is the total number of successes, the random variable of interest here is y, the number of trials (time units) until the rth success is observed.

The probability distribution for the random variable y is known as a **negative binomial distribution**. Its formula is given in the next box, together with the mean and variance for a negative binomial random variable.

The Negative Binomial Probability Distribution

The probability distribution for a negative binomial random variable is given by

$$p(y) = \binom{y-1}{r-1} p^r q^{y-r} \qquad (y = r, r+1, r+2, \ldots)$$

where

p = Probability of success on a single Bernoulli trial

$q = 1 - p$

y = Number of trials until the rth success is observed

The mean and variance of a negative binomial random variable are, respectively,

$$\mu = \frac{r}{p} \quad \text{and} \quad \sigma^2 = \frac{rq}{p^2}$$

From the box, you can see that the negative binomial probability distribution is a function of two parameters, p and r. For the special case $r = 1$, the probability distribution of y is known as a **geometric probability distribution**.

The Geometric Probability Distribution

$$p(y) = pq^{y-1} \qquad (y = 1, 2, \ldots)$$

---

where

$$y = \text{Number of trials until the first success is observed}$$

$$\mu = \frac{1}{p}$$

$$\sigma^2 = \frac{q}{p^2}$$

To derive the negative binomial probability distribution, note that every simple event that results in y trials until the rth success will contain $(y - r)$ F's and r S's, as depicted here:

$$\overbrace{F \quad F \quad S \quad F \quad F \ldots S \quad F}^{(y - r) \text{ F's and } (r - 1) \text{ S's}} \quad \overbrace{S}^{r\text{th S}}$$

The number of different simple events that result in $(y - r)$ F's before the rth S is the number of ways that we can arrange the $(r - 1)$ S's and $(y - r)$ F's, namely,

$$\binom{(y - r) + (r - 1)}{r - 1} = \binom{y - 1}{r - 1}$$

Then, since the probability associated with each of these simple events is $p^r q^{y-r}$, we have

$$p(y) = \binom{y - 1}{r - 1} p^r q^{y-r}$$

Examples 4.12 and 4.13 demonstrate the use of the negative binomial and the geometric probability distributions, respectively.

. . . .

EXAMPLE 4.12

To attach the housing on a motor, a production line assembler must use an electrical hand tool to set and tighten four bolts. Suppose that the probability of setting and tightening a bolt in any 1-second time interval is $p = .8$. If the assembler fails in the first second, the probability of success during the second 1-second interval is .8, and so on.

a. Find the probability distribution of y, the length of time until a complete housing is attached.

b. Find $p(6)$.

c. Find the mean and variance of y.

Solution

a. Since the housing contains $r = 4$ bolts, we will use the formula for the negative binomial probability distribution. Substituting $p = .8$ and $r = 4$ into the formula for $p(y)$, we obtain

$$p(y) = \binom{y - 1}{r - 1} p^r q^{y-r} = \binom{y - 1}{3}(.8)^4(.2)^{y-4}$$

b. To find the probability that the complete assembly operation will require $y = 6$ seconds, we substitute $y = 6$ into the formula obtained in part **a** and find

$$p(y) = \binom{5}{3}(.8)^4(.2)^2 = (10)(.4096)(.04) = .16384$$

c. For this negative binomial distribution,

$$\mu = \frac{r}{p} = \frac{4}{.8} = 5 \text{ seconds}$$

and

$$\sigma^2 = \frac{rq}{p^2} = \frac{4(.2)}{(.8)^2} = 1.25$$

EXAMPLE 4.13

A manufacturer uses electrical fuses in an electronic system. The fuses are purchased in large lots and tested sequentially until the first defective fuse is observed. Assume that the lot contains 10% defective fuses.

a. What is the probability that the first defective fuse will be one of the first five fuses tested?

b. Find the mean, variance, and standard deviation for y, the number of fuses tested until the first defective fuse is observed.

Solution

a. The number y of fuses tested until the first defective fuse is observed is a geometric random variable with

$$p = .1 \quad \text{(probability that a single fuse is defective)}$$
$$q = 1 - p = .9$$

and

$$p(y) = pq^{y-1} \quad (y = 1, 2, \ldots)$$
$$= (.1)(.9)^{y-1}$$

The probability that the first defective fuse is one of the first five fuses tested is

$$P(y \le 5) = p(1) + p(2) + \cdots + p(5)$$
$$= (.1)(.9)^0 + (.1)(.9)^1 + \cdots + (.1)(.9)^4 = .41$$

b. The mean, variance, and standard deviation of this geometric random variable are

$$\mu = \frac{1}{p} = \frac{1}{.1} = 10$$

$$\sigma^2 = \frac{q}{p^2} = \frac{.9}{(.1)^2} = 90$$

$$\sigma = \sqrt{\sigma^2} = \sqrt{90} = 9.49$$

EXERCISES

4.46 Suppose y is a negative binomial random variable. Calculate $p(y)$ for each of the following situations:
  a. $p = .2$, $r = 2$, $y = 3$ **b.** $p = .5$, $r = 3$, $y = 5$ **c.** $p = .8$, $r = 3$, $y = 5$

4.47 Suppose y can be modeled by a negative binomial probability distribution with $p = .6$ and $r = 3$.
  a. Calculate $p(y)$ for $y = 6$, 7, 8, and 9.
  b. Construct a probability histogram for $p(y)$.
  c. Calculate μ and σ for the probability distribution.
  d. Locate the points $\mu + 2\sigma$ and $\mu - 2\sigma$ on the y-axis of the graph in part **b**. Find $P(\mu - 2\sigma \le y \le \mu + 2\sigma)$.

4.48 Let y be a geometric random variable with $p = .7$.
  a. Calculate $p(y)$ for $y = 1, 2, \ldots, 5$.
  b. Construct a probability histogram for $p(y)$.
  c. Calculate μ and σ for the geometric probability distribution.
  d. Locate the points $\mu + 2\sigma$ and $\mu - 2\sigma$ on the y-axis of the graph in part **b**. Find $P(\mu - 2\sigma \le y \le \mu + 2\sigma)$.

4.49 The negative binomial distribution was used to model the distribution of parasites (tapeworms) found in several species of Mediterranean fish (*Journal of Fish Biology*, Aug. 1990). Assume the event of interest is whether a parasite is found in the digestive tract of brill fish, and let y be the number of brill that must be sampled until a parasitic infection is found. The researchers estimate the probability of an infected fish at .544. Use this information to estimate the following probabilities:
  a. $P(y = 3)$ **b.** $P(y \le 2)$ **c.** $P(y > 2)$

4.50 The National Aeronautics and Space Administration (NASA) estimates that the chance of a "critical item" failure within a space shuttle's main engine is approximately 1 in 63 (*Tampa Tribune*, Dec. 3, 1993). The failure of a critical item during flight will lead directly to a shuttle catastrophe.
  a. On average, how many shuttle missions will fly before a critical item failure occurs?
  b. What is the standard deviation of the number of missions before a critical item failure occurs?
  c. Give an interval that will capture the number of missions before a critical item failure occurs with probability of approximately .95.

4.51 Environmental engineers classify consumers into one of five categories (see Exercise 3.1 for a description of each group). The probabilities associated with the groups follow.

Basic browns	.28
True-blue greens	.11
Greenback greens	.11
Sprouts	.26
Grousers	.24

Source: The *Orange County Register*, Aug. 7, 1990.

Let y equal the number of consumers that must be sampled until the first environmentalist is found. [*Note:* From Exercise 3.1, an environmentalist is a true-blue green, greenback green, or sprout.]

    a. Find μ and σ, the mean and standard deviation of y.

    b. Use the information, part a, to form an interval that will include y with a high probability.

4.52   Refer to the *Nuclear Science and Engineering* study, Exercise 4.30. If neutral particles are released one at a time into the evacuated duct, find the probability that more than five particles will need to be released until we observe two particles reflected by the inner duct wall.

4.53   Assume that hitting oil at one drilling location is independent of another, and that, in a particular region, the probability of success at an individual location is .3.

    a. What is the probability that a driller will hit oil on or before the third drilling?

    b. If y is the number of drillings until the first success occurs, find the mean and standard deviation of y.

    c. Is it likely that y will exceed 10? Explain.

    d. Suppose the drilling company believes that a venture will be profitable if the number of wells drilled until the second success occurs is less than or equal to 7. Find the probability that the venture will be successful.

4.54   Refer to Exercise 4.31. Let y represent the number of 50-year-old Utah males examined until the first incidence of thyroid cancer is detected.

    a. Find $P(y = 1,000)$.

    b. Find the mean and variance of y.

    c. Is it likely that y will exceed 100,000? Explain.

OPTIONAL EXERCISE

4.55   Let y be a negative binomial random variable with parameters r and p. Then it can be shown that $w = y - r$ is also a negative binomial random variable, where w represents the number of failures before the rth success is observed. Use the facts that

$$E(y) = \frac{r}{p} \quad \text{and} \quad \sigma_y^2 = \frac{rq}{p^2}$$

to show that

$$E(w) = \frac{rq}{p} \quad \text{and} \quad \sigma_w^2 = \frac{rq}{p^2}$$

[*Hint:* Use Theorems 4.1, 4.2, and 4.3.]

4.9 The Hypergeometric Probability Distribution

When we are sampling from a finite population of Successes and Failures (such as a finite population of consumer preference responses or a finite collection of observations in a shipment containing nondefective and defective manufactured products), the assumptions for a binomial experiment are satisfied exactly only if the result of each trial is observed and then replaced in the population before the next observation is made. This method of sampling is called **sampling with replacement**. However, in practice, we usually **sample without replacement**, i.e., we randomly select n different elements from among the N elements in the population. As noted in Section 4.6, when N is large and n/N is small (say, less than .05), the probability of drawing an S remains approximately the same from one trial to another, the trials are (essentially) independent, and the probability distribution for the number of successes, y, is *approximately* a binomial probability distribution. However, when N is small or n/N is large (say, greater than .05), we would want to use the exact probability distribution for y. This distribution, known as a **hypergeometric probability distribution**, is the topic of this section. The defining characteristics and probability distribution for a hypergeometric random variable are stated in the boxes.

Characteristics That Define a Hypergeometric Random Variable

1. The experiment consists of randomly drawing n elements without replacement from a set of N elements, r of which are S's (for Success) and $(N - r)$ of which are F's (for Failure).
2. The sample size n is large relative to the number N of elements in the population, i.e., $n/N > .05$.
3. The hypergeometric random variable y is the number of S's in the draw of n elements.

The Hypergeometric Probability Distribution

The hypergeometric probability distribution is given by

$$p(y) = \frac{\binom{r}{y}\binom{N - r}{n - y}}{\binom{N}{n}}, \qquad y = \text{Maximum } [0, n - (N - r)], \ldots, \text{Minimum } (r, n)$$

where

$N = $ Total number of elements

$r = $ Number of S's in the N elements

$n = $ Number of elements drawn

$y = $ Number of S's drawn in the n elements

The mean and variance of a hypergeometric random variable are, respectively,

$$\mu = \frac{nr}{N} \qquad \sigma^2 = \frac{r(N - r)n(N - n)}{N^2(N - 1)}$$

To derive the hypergeometric probability distribution, we first note that the total number of simple events in S is equal to the number of ways of selecting n elements from N, namely, $\binom{N}{n}$. A *simple event implying y successes* will be a selection of n elements in which y are S's and $(n - y)$ are F's. Since there are r S's from which to choose, the number of different ways of selecting y of them is $a = \binom{r}{y}$. Similarly, the number of ways of selecting $(n - y)$ F's from among the total of $(N - r)$ is $b = \binom{N - r}{n - y}$. We now apply Theorem 3.1 to determine the number of ways of selecting y S's and $(n - y)$ F's—that is, the number of simple events implying y successes:

$$a \cdot b = \binom{r}{y}\binom{N - r}{n - y}$$

Finally, since the selection of any one set of n elements is as likely as any other, all the simple events are equiprobable and thus,

$$p(y) = \frac{\text{Number of simple events that imply } y \text{ successes}}{\text{Number of simple events}} = \frac{\binom{r}{y}\binom{N - r}{n - y}}{\binom{N}{n}}$$

EXAMPLE 4.14

An experiment is conducted to select a suitable catalyst for the commercial production of ethylenediamine (EDA), a product used in soaps. Suppose a chemical engineer randomly selects three catalysts for testing from among a group of 10 catalysts, six of which have low acidity and four of which have high acidity.

a. Find the probability that no highly acidic catalyst is selected.

b. Find the probability that exactly one highly acidic catalyst is selected.

Solution

Let y be the number of highly acidic catalysts selected. Then y is a hypergeometric random variable with $N = 10$, $n = 3$, $r = 4$, and

$$p(y) = \frac{\binom{4}{y}\binom{6}{3 - y}}{\binom{10}{3}}$$

a. $p(0) = \dfrac{\binom{4}{0}\binom{6}{3}}{\binom{10}{3}} = \dfrac{(1)(20)}{120} = \dfrac{1}{6}$

b. $p(1) = \dfrac{\binom{4}{1}\binom{6}{2}}{\binom{10}{3}} = \dfrac{(4)(15)}{120} = \dfrac{1}{2}$

EXAMPLE 4.15

Refer to the EDA experiment, Example 4.14.

a. Find μ, σ^2, and σ for the random variable y.
b. Find $P(\mu - 2\sigma < y < \mu + 2\sigma)$. How does this result compare to the Empirical Rule?

Solution

a. Since y is a hypergeometric random variable with $N = 10$, $n = 3$, and $r = 4$, the mean and variance are

$$\mu = \frac{nr}{N} = \frac{(3)(4)}{10} = 1.2$$

$$\sigma^2 = \frac{r(N - r)n(N - n)}{N^2(N - 1)} = \frac{4(10 - 4)3(10 - 3)}{(10)^2(10 - 1)}$$

$$= \frac{(4)(6)(3)(7)}{(100)(9)} = .56$$

The standard deviation is

$$\sigma = \sqrt{.56} = .75$$

b. The probability distribution and the interval $\mu \pm 2\sigma$, or $-.3$ to 2.7, are shown in Figure 4.6 (page 182). The only possible value of y that falls outside the interval is $y = 3$. Therefore,

$$P(\mu - 2\sigma < y < \mu + 2\sigma) = 1 - p(3) = 1 - \frac{\binom{4}{3}\binom{6}{0}}{\binom{10}{3}}$$

$$= 1 - \frac{4}{120} = .967$$

FIGURE 4.6 ▶
Probability distribution for y in
Example 4.15

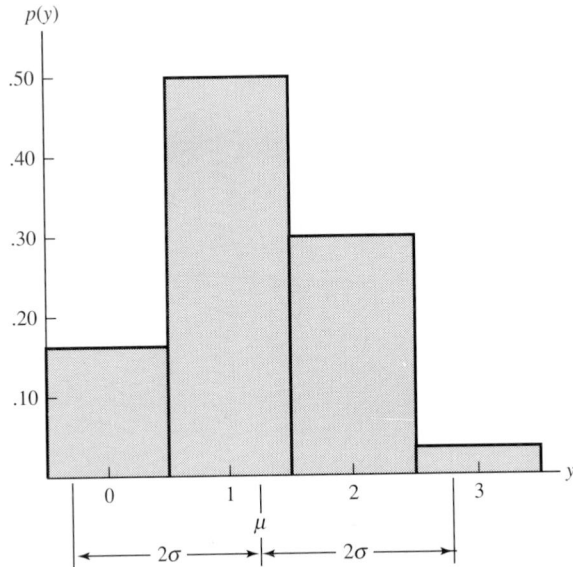

According to the Empirical Rule, we expect about 95% of the observed y's to fall in this interval. Thus, the Empirical Rule provides a good estimate of this probability.

EXAMPLE 4.16

Refer to Example 4.14. Find the mean, μ, of the random variable y.

Solution

By Definition 4.4,

$$\mu = E(y) = \sum_{\text{all } y} yp(y) = \sum_{y=0}^{3} y\frac{\binom{4}{y}\binom{6}{3-y}}{120}$$

Using the values of $p(y)$ calculated in Examples 4.14 and 4.15, and

$$p(2) = \frac{\binom{4}{2}\binom{6}{1}}{120} = \frac{(6)(6)}{120} = \frac{3}{10}$$

we obtain by substitution:

$$\mu = 0p(0) + 1p(1) + 2p(2) + 3p(3)$$
$$= 0 + 1\left(\frac{1}{2}\right) + 2\left(\frac{3}{10}\right) + 3\left(\frac{1}{30}\right) = 1.2$$

Note that this is the value we obtained in Example 4.15 by applying the formula given in the previous box.

EXERCISES

4.56 Suppose y is a hypergeometric random variable with $N = 12$, $n = 8$, and $r = 7$.
   a. Display the probability distribution for y in tabular form.
   b. Find $P(y < 3)$.
   c. Find $P(y \geq 5)$.
   d. Compute μ and σ for y.
   e. Graph $p(y)$ and locate μ and the interval $\mu \pm 2\sigma$ on the graph.
   f. What is the probability that y will fall within the interval $\mu \pm 2\sigma$?

4.57 Suppose that y is a hypergeometric random variable. Compute $p(y)$ for each of the following cases:
   a. $N = 5$, $n = 3$, $r = 4$, $y = 1$ b. $N = 10$, $n = 5$, $r = 3$, $y = 3$
   c. $N = 3$, $n = 2$, $r = 2$, $y = 2$ d. $N = 4$, $n = 2$, $r = 2$, $y = 0$

4.58 "Hotspots" are species-rich geographical areas (see Exercise 3.7). A *Nature* (Sept. 1993) study estimated the probability of a bird species in Great Britain inhabiting a butterfly hotspot at .70. Consider a random sample of 4 British bird species selected from a total of 10 tagged species. Assume that 7 of the 10 tagged species inhabit a butterfly hotspot.
   a. What is the probability that exactly half of the 4 bird species sampled inhabit a butterfly hotspot?
   b. What is the probability that at least 1 of the 4 bird species sampled inhabit a butterfly hotspot?

4.59 Based on data provided by the U.S. Department of Health and Human Resources, *U.S. News & World Report* (Sept. 28, 1992) estimates that 1 out of every 5 kidney transplants fails within a year. Suppose that exactly 3 of the next 15 kidney transplants will fail within a year. Consider a random sample of 3 of these 15 patients.
   a. Find the probability that all 3 sampled transplants fail within a year.
   b. Find the probability that at least 1 of the 3 sampled transplants fails within a year.

4.60 Refer to Exercise 4.29. As reported in *IEEE Computer Applications in Power* (Apr. 1990), an outdoor, unmanned computerized video monitoring system detected 7 out of 10 intruders in snowy conditions. Suppose that two of the intruders had criminal intentions. What is the probability that both of these intruders were detected by the system?

4.61 Suppose you are purchasing small lots of cathode ray tubes (CRTs) for computer terminals. Since it is very costly to test a single CRT, it may be desirable to test a sample of CRTs from the lot rather than every CRT in the lot. Such a sampling plan would be based on a hypergeometric probability distribution. For example, assume that each lot contains seven CRTs. You decide to sample three CRTs per lot and to reject the lot if you observe one or more defectives in the sample.
   a. If the lot contains one defective CRT, what is the probability that you will accept the lot?
   b. What is the probability that you will accept the lot if it contains three defective CRTs?

4.62 A task force established by the Environmental Protection Agency was scheduled to investigate 20 industrial firms to check for violations of pollution control regulations. However, budget cutbacks have drastically reduced the size of the task force, and they will be able to investigate only 3 of the 20 firms. If it is known that five of the firms are actually operating in violation of regulations, find the probability that:
   a. None of the three sampled firms will be found in violation of regulations.
   b. All three firms investigated will be found in violation of regulations.
   c. At least one of the three firms will be operating in violation of pollution control regulations.

4.63   An article in *The American Statistician* (May 1991) described the use of probability in a reverse cocaine sting. Police in a mid-size Florida city seized 496 foil packets in a cocaine bust. To convict the drug traffickers, police had to prove that the packets contained genuine cocaine. Consequently, the police lab randomly selected and chemically tested four of the packets; all four tested positive for cocaine. This result led to a conviction of the traffickers.

a. Of the 496 foil packets confiscated, suppose 331 contain genuine cocaine and 165 contain an inert (legal) powder. Find the probability that four randomly selected packets will test positive for cocaine.

b. Police used the 492 remaining foil packets (i.e., those not tested) in a reverse sting operation. Two of the 492 packets were randomly selected and sold by undercover officers to a buyer. Between the sale and the arrest, however, the buyer disposed of the evidence. Given that 4 of the original 496 packets tested positive for cocaine, what is the probability that the two packets sold in the reverse sting did not contain cocaine? Assume the information provided in part **a** is correct.

c. *The American Statistician* article demonstrates that the conditional probability, part **b**, is maximized when the original 496 packets consist of 331 packets containing genuine cocaine and 165 containing inert powder. Recalculate the probability, part **b**, assuming that 400 of the original 496 packets contain cocaine.

OPTIONAL EXERCISE

4.64   Show that the mean of a hypergeometric random variable is $\mu = nr/N$. [*Hint:* Show that

$$\frac{y\binom{r}{y}\binom{N-r}{n-y}}{\binom{N}{n}} = \frac{\frac{nr}{N}\binom{r-1}{y-1}\binom{N-1-(r-1)}{n-1-(y-1)}}{\binom{N-1}{n-1}}$$

and then use the fact that

$$\frac{\binom{r-1}{y-1}\binom{N-1-(r-1)}{n-1-(y-1)}}{\binom{N-1}{n-1}}$$

is the hypergeometric probability distribution for $z = (y - 1)$, where z is the number of S's in $(n - 1)$ trials, with a total of $(r - 1)$ S's in $(N - 1)$ elements.]

4.10   The Poisson Probability Distribution

The **Poisson probability distribution**, named for the French mathematician S. D. Poisson (1781–1840), provides a model for the relative frequency of the number of "rare events" that occur in a unit of time, area, volume, etc. The number of new jobs submitted to a computer in any one minute, the number of fatal accidents per month in a manufacturing plant, and the number of visible defects in a diamond are variables whose relative frequency distributions can be approximated well by Poisson probability distributions. The characteristics of a Poisson random variable are listed in the box.

Characteristics of a Poisson Random Variable

1. The experiment consists of counting the number y of times a particular event occurs during a given unit of time, or in a given area or volume (or weight, distance, or any other unit of measurement).
2. The probability that an event occurs in a given unit of time, area, or volume is the same for all the units.
3. The number of events that occur in one unit of time, area, or volume is independent of the number that occur in other units.
4. The mean (or expected) number of events in each unit will be denoted by the Greek letter lambda, λ.

The formulas for the probability distribution, the mean, and the variance of a Poisson random variable are shown in the next box. You will note that the formula involves the quantity $e = 2.71828\ldots$, the base of natural logarithms. Values of e^{-y}, needed to compute values of $p(y)$, are given in Table 2 of Appendix II.

The Poisson Probability Distribution

The probability distribution for a Poisson random variable is given by

$$p(y) = \frac{\lambda^y e^{-\lambda}}{y!} \qquad (y = 0, 1, 2, \ldots)$$

where

λ = Mean number of events during a given unit of time, area, or volume

$e = 2.71828\ldots$

The mean and variance of a Poisson random variable are, respectively,

$$\mu = \lambda \quad \text{and} \quad \sigma^2 = \lambda$$

The shape of the Poisson distribution changes as its mean μ changes. This fact is illustrated in Figure 4.7 (page 186), which shows relative frequency histograms for a Poisson distribution with $\mu = 1, 2, 3,$ and 4.

FIGURE 4.7 ▶
Histograms for the Poisson
distribution for $\mu = 1, 2, 3$,
and 4

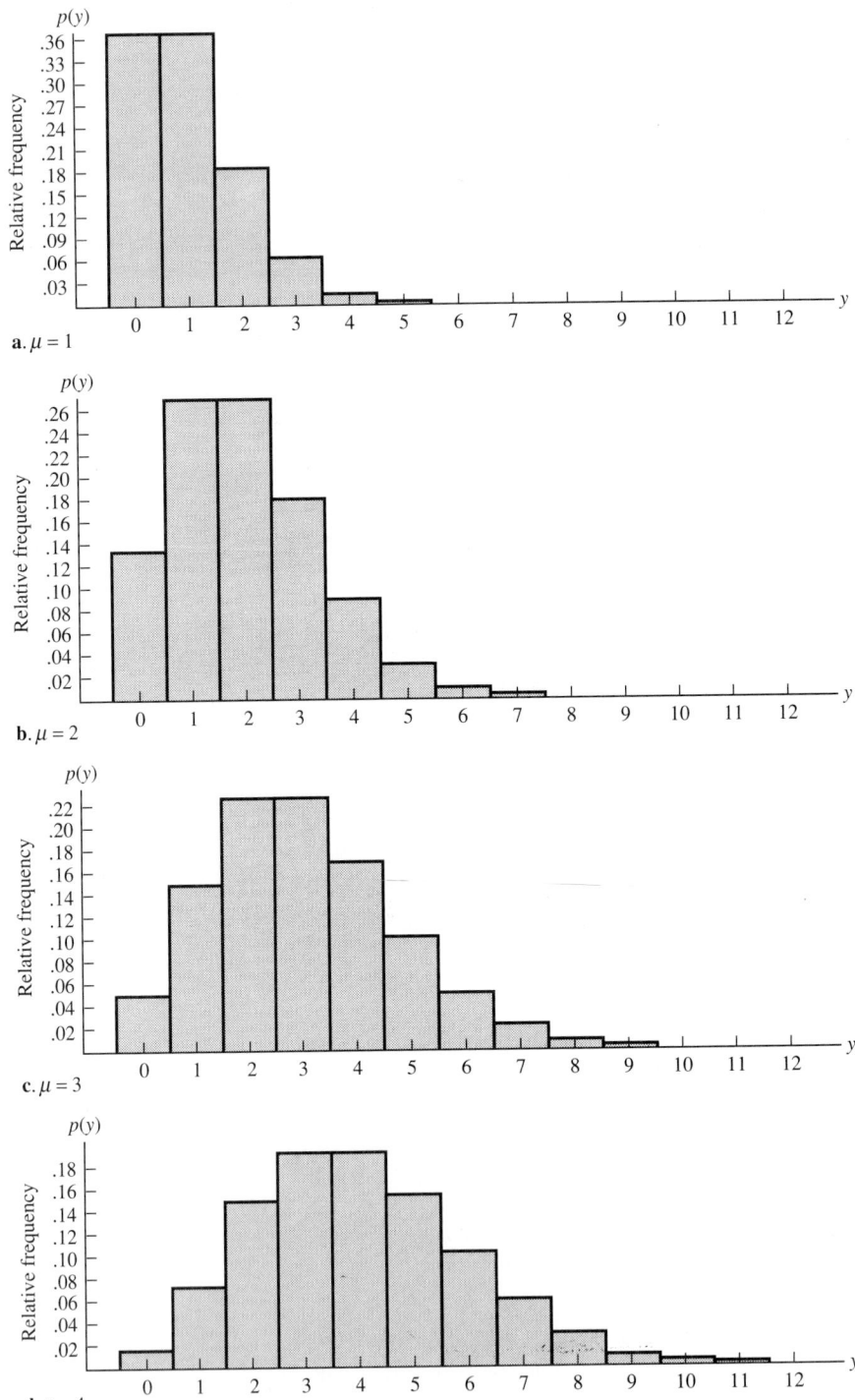

a. $\mu = 1$

b. $\mu = 2$

c. $\mu = 3$

d. $\mu = 4$

EXAMPLE 4.17

Suppose the number y of cracks per concrete specimen for a particular type of cement mix has approximately a Poisson probability distribution. Furthermore, assume that the average number of cracks per specimen is 2.5.

a. Find the mean and standard deviation of y, the number of cracks per concrete specimen.

b. Find the probability that a randomly selected concrete specimen has exactly five cracks.

c. Find the probability that a randomly selected concrete specimen has two or more cracks.

d. Find $P(\mu - 2\sigma < y < \mu + 2\sigma)$. Does the result agree with the Empirical Rule?

Solution

a. The mean and variance of a Poisson random variable are both equal to λ. Thus, for this example

$$\mu = \lambda = 2.5 \qquad \sigma^2 = \lambda = 2.5$$

Then the standard deviation is

$$\sigma = \sqrt{2.5} = 1.58$$

b. We want the probability that a concrete specimen has exactly five cracks. The probability distribution for y is

$$p(y) = \frac{\lambda^y e^{-\lambda}}{y!}$$

Then, since $\lambda = 2.5$, $y = 5$, and $e^{-2.5} = .082085$ (from Table 2 of Appendix II),

$$p(5) = \frac{(2.5)^5 e^{-2.5}}{5!} = \frac{(2.5)^5(.082085)}{5 \cdot 4 \cdot 3 \cdot 2 \cdot 1} = .067$$

c. To find the probability that a concrete specimen has two or more cracks, we need to find

$$P(y \geq 2) = p(2) + p(3) + p(4) + \cdots = \sum_{y=2}^{\infty} p(y)$$

To find the probability of this event, we must consider the complementary event. Thus,

$$P(y \geq 2) = 1 - P(y \leq 1) = 1 - [p(0) + p(1)]$$
$$= 1 - \frac{(2.5)^0 e^{-2.5}}{0!} - \frac{(2.5)^1 e^{-2.5}}{1!}$$
$$= 1 - \frac{1(.082085)}{1} - \frac{2.5(.082085)}{1}$$
$$= 1 - .287 = .713$$

According to our Poisson model, the probability that a concrete specimen has two or more cracks is .713.

FIGURE 4.8 ▶
Poisson probability distribution for
y in Example 4.17

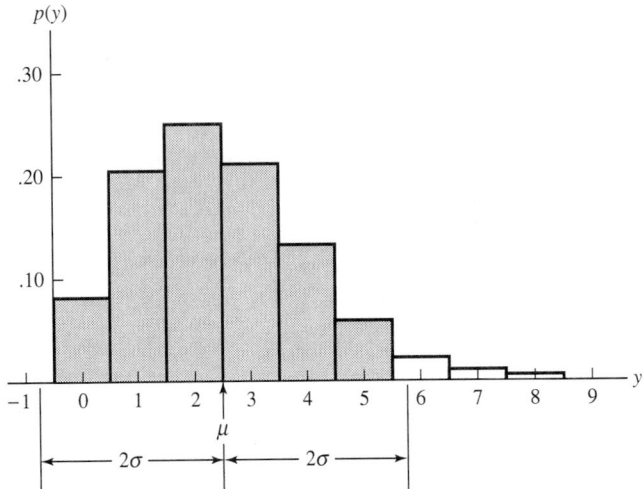

d. The probability distribution for y is shown in Figure 4.8 for y values between 0 and 9. The mean $\mu = 2.5$ and the interval $\mu \pm 2\sigma$, or $-.7$ to 5.7, are indicated. Consequently, $P(\mu - 2\sigma < y < \mu + 2\sigma) = P(y \leq 5)$. This probability is shaded in Figure 4.8.

The probabilities $p(0), p(1), \ldots, p(5)$ can be calculated and summed as in part **c**. However, we will use a table of cumulative Poisson probabilities to obtain the sum. Table 3 of Appendix II gives the partial sum, $\Sigma_{y=0}^{k} p(y)$, for different values of the Poisson mean λ. For $\lambda = 2.5$, the sum $\Sigma_{y=0}^{k} p(y) = p(0) + p(1) + \cdots + p(5)$ is given as $.9581$. Thus, $P(y \leq 5) = .9581$; note that this probability agrees with the Empirical Rule's approximation of $.95$.

The Poisson probability distribution is related to and can be used to approximate a binomial probability distribution when n is large and $\mu = np$ is small, say, $np \leq 7$. The proof of this fact is beyond the scope of this text, but it can be found in Feller (1968).

EXAMPLE 4.18   Let y be a binomial random variable with $n = 25$ and $p = .1$.

a. Use Table 1 of Appendix II to determine the exact value of $P(y \leq 1)$.

b. Find the Poisson approximation to $P(y \leq 1)$. [*Note:* Although we would prefer to compare the Poisson approximation to binomial probabilities for larger values of n, we are restricted in this example by the limitations of Table 1.]

Solution

a. From Table 3 of Appendix II, with $n = 25$ and $p = .1$, we have

$$P(y \le 1) = \sum_{y=0}^{1} p(y) = .271$$

b. Since $n = 25$ and $p = .1$, we will approximate $p(y)$ using a Poisson probability distribution with mean

$$\lambda = np = (25)(.1) = 2.5$$

Locating $\lambda = 2.5$ in Table 3 of Appendix II, we obtain the partial sum

$$P(y \le 1) = \sum_{y=0}^{1} p(y) = .2873$$

This approximation, .2873, to the exact value of $P(y \le 1) = .271$, is reasonably good considering that the approximation procedure is usually applied to binomial probability distributions for which n is much larger than 25.

EXAMPLE 4.19

Show that the expected value of a Poisson random variable is λ.

Solution

By Definition 4.4, we have

$$E(y) = \sum_{\text{all } y} yp(y) = \sum_{y=0}^{\infty} y \frac{\lambda^y e^{-\lambda}}{y!}$$

The first term of this series will equal 0, because $y = 0$. Therefore,

$$E(y) = \sum_{y=0}^{\infty} \frac{y\lambda^y e^{-\lambda}}{y!} = \sum_{y=1}^{\infty} \frac{\lambda^y e^{-\lambda}}{(y-1)!} = \sum_{y=1}^{\infty} \frac{\lambda \cdot \lambda^{y-1} e^{-\lambda}}{(y-1)!}$$

Factoring the constant λ outside the summation and letting $z = (y-1)$, we obtain

$$E(y) = \lambda \sum_{z=0}^{\infty} \frac{\lambda^z e^{-\lambda}}{z!} = \lambda \sum_{z=0}^{\infty} p(z)$$

where z is a Poisson random variable with mean λ. Hence,

$$E(y) = \lambda \sum_{z=0}^{\infty} p(z) = \lambda(1) = \lambda$$

EXERCISES

4.65   Suppose y is a random variable for which a Poisson probability distribution with $\lambda = 5.5$ provides a good characterization.

    a. Graph $p(y)$ for $y = 0, 1, 2, \ldots, 9, 10$.
    b. Find μ and σ for the random variable y, and locate μ and the interval $\mu \pm 2\sigma$ on the graph of part **a**.
    c. What is the probability that y will fall within the interval $\mu \pm 2\sigma$?

4.66   Suppose y is a random variable for which a Poisson probability distribution provides a good characterization. Compute the following:
    a. $P(y \leq 2)$, when $\lambda = 2$ **b.** $P(y = 1)$, when $\lambda = 5$
    c. $P(y \geq 1)$, when $\lambda = 3$ **d.** $P(y = 0)$, when $\lambda = 9$

4.67   Refer to the *Science* (Apr. 1993) study of the spectroscopic properties of main-belt asteroids, Exercise 2.10. Research revealed that, on average, 2.5 independent spectral image exposures are observed per asteroid.
    a. Assuming a Poisson distribution, find the probability that exactly one independent spectral image exposure is observed during a main-belt asteroid sighting.
    b. Assuming a Poisson distribution, find the probability that at most two independent spectral image exposures are observed during a main-belt asteroid sighting.
    c. Would you expect to observe seven or more independent spectral image exposures during a main-belt asteroid sighting? Explain.

4.68   A recent study of natural rock slope movements in the Canadian Rockies over the past 5,000 years revealed that the number of major rockslides per 100 square kilometers had an expected value of 1.57 (*Canadian Geotechnical Journal*, Nov. 1985).
    a. Find the mean and standard deviation of y, the number of major rockslides per 100 square kilometers in the Canadian Rockies over a 5,000-year period.
    b. What is the probability of observing three or more major rockslides per 100 square kilometers over a 5,000-year period?

4.69   The random variable y, the number of cars that arrive at an intersection during a specified period of time, often possesses (approximately) a Poisson probability distribution. When the mean arrival rate λ is known, the Poisson probability distribution can be used to aid a traffic engineer in the design of a traffic control system. Suppose you estimate that the mean number of arrivals per minute at the intersection is one car per minute.
    a. What is the probability that in a given minute, the number of arrivals will equal three or more?
    b. Can you assure the engineer that the number of arrivals will rarely exceed three per minute?

4.70   The Environmental Protection Agency (EPA) has established national ambient air quality standards in an effort to control air pollution. Currently, the EPA limit on ozone levels in air is 12 parts per hundred million (pphm). A 1990 study examined the long-term trend in daily ozone levels in Houston, Texas.* One of the variables of interest is y, the number of days in a year on which the ozone level exceeds the EPA 12 pphm threshold. The mean number of exceedances in a year is estimated to be 18. Assume that the probability distribution for y can be modeled with the Poisson distribution.
    a. Compute $P(y \geq 20)$.
    b. Compute $P(5 \leq y \leq 10)$.
    c. Estimate the standard deviation of y. Within what range would you expect y to fall in a given year?
    d. The study revealed a decreasing trend in the number of exceedances of the EPA threshold level over the past several years. The observed values of y for the past 6 years were 24, 22, 20, 15, 14, and 16.

---

*Shively, Thomas S. "An Analysis of the Trend in Ozone Using Nonhomogeneous Poisson Processes." Paper presented at annual meeting of the American Statistical Association, Anaheim, Calif., Aug. 1990.

Explain why this trend casts doubt on the validity of the Poisson distribution as a model for y. [*Hint:* Consider characteristic #3 of the Poisson random variable.]

4.71 The nuclear industry has made a concerted effort to significantly reduce the number of unplanned rapid emergency shutdowns of a nuclear reactor—called *scrams*. A decade ago, the mean annual number of unplanned scrams at U.S. nuclear reactor units was four (see Exercise 2.47). Assume that the annual number of unplanned scrams that occur at a nuclear reactor unit follows, approximately, a Poisson distribution.

    a. If the mean has not changed, compute the probability that a nuclear reactor unit will experience 10 or more unplanned scrams this year.

    b. Suppose a randomly selected nuclear reactor actually experiences 10 or more unplanned scrams this year. What can you infer about the true mean annual number of unplanned scrams? Explain.

4.72 Refer to the *American Journal of Public Health* (AJPH) report on traffic fatalities on rural interstate highways, Exercise 3.29. One year prior to the AJPH report, the American Automobile Association (AAA) sponsored an analysis of the effect of the 65-mph speed limit in the state of Indiana. The AAA study found that Indiana averaged 90 fatalities per year on rural interstates. For a given year, within what range would you expect the number of traffic fatalities on rural interstates in Indiana to fall?

4.73 A discharge (or response) rate of auditory nerve fibers [recorded as the number of spikes per 200 milliseconds (ms) of noise burst] is used to measure the effect of acoustic stimuli in the auditory nerve. An empirical study of auditory nerve fiber response rates in cats resulted in a mean of 15 spikes/ms (*Journal of the Acoustical Society of America*, Feb. 1986). Let y represent the auditory nerve fiber response rate for a randomly selected cat in the study.

    a. If y is approximately a Poisson random variable, find the mean and standard deviation of y.

    b. Assuming y is Poisson, what is the approximate probability that y exceeds 27 spikes/ms?

    c. In the study, the variance of y was found to be "substantially smaller" than 15 spikes/ms. Is it reasonable to expect y to follow a Poisson process? How will this affect the probability computed in part **b**?

4.74 Benzene, a solvent commonly used to synthesize plastics and found in consumer products such as paint strippers and high-octane unleaded gasoline, has been classified by scientists as a leukemia-causing agent. Let y be the level (in parts per million) of benzene in the air at a petrochemical plant. Then y can take on the values 0, 1, 2, 3, . . ., 1,000,000, and can be approximated by a Poisson probability distribution. In 1978, the federal government lowered the maximum allowable level of benzene in the air at a work place from 10 parts per million (ppm) to 1 ppm. Any industry in violation of these government standards is subject to severe penalties, including implementation of expensive measures to lower the benzene level.

    a. Suppose the mean level of benzene in the air at petrochemical plants is $\mu = 5$ ppm. Find the probability that a petrochemical plant exceeds the government standard of 1 ppm.

    b. Repeat part **a**, assuming that $\mu = 2.5$.

    c. The *Florida Times-Union* (Apr. 2, 1984) reported on a study by Gulf Oil that revealed that 88% of benzene-using industries expose their workers to 1 ppm or less of the solvent. Suppose you randomly sampled 55 of the benzene-using industries in the country and determined y, the number in violation of government standards. Use the Poisson approximation to the binomial to find the probability that none of the sampled industries violates government standards. Compare this probability to the exact probability computed using the binomial probability distribution. (You can compute the binomial probability using a hand calculator.)

    d. Refer to part **c**. Use the fact that 88% of benzene-using industries expose their workers to 1 ppm or less of benzene to approximate μ, the mean level of benzene in the air at these industries. [*Hint:* Search Table 4 of Appendix II for the value of μ that yields $P(y \le 1)$ closest to .88.]

OPTIONAL EXERCISES

4.75 Show that for a Poisson random variable y,
a. $0 \leq p(y) \leq 1$
b. $\displaystyle\sum_{y=0}^{\infty} p(y) = 1$
c. $E(y^2) = \lambda^2 + \lambda$

[*Hint:*   First derive the result $E[y(y - 1)] = \lambda^2$ from the fact that

$$E[y(y - 1)] = \sum_{y=0}^{\infty} y(y - 1)\frac{\lambda^y e^{-\lambda}}{y!} = \lambda^2 \sum_{y=2}^{\infty} \frac{\lambda^{y-2}e^{-\lambda}}{(y - 2)!} = \lambda^2 \sum_{z=0}^{\infty} \frac{\lambda^z e^{-\lambda}}{z!}$$

Then apply the result $E[y(y - 1)] = E(y^2) - E(y)$.]

4.76 Show that for a Poisson random variable y, $\sigma^2 = \lambda$. [*Hint:*   Use the result of Exercise 4.75 and Theorem 4.4.]

4.11   Moments and Moment Generating Functions (Optional)

The **moments** of a random variable can be used to completely describe its probability distribution.

Definition 4.7

The *k*th moment of a random variable y, **taken about the origin**, is denoted by the symbol μ_k' and defined to be

$$\mu_k' = E(y^k) \quad (k = 1, 2, \ldots)$$

Definition 4.8

The *k*th moment of a random variable y, **taken about its mean**, is denoted by the symbol μ_k and defined to be

$$\mu_k = E[(y - \mu)^k]$$

You have already encountered two important moments of random variables. The mean of a random variable is $\mu_1' = \mu$ and the variance is $\mu_2 = \sigma^2$. Other moments about the origin or about the mean can be used to measure the lack of symmetry or the tendency of a distribution to possess a large peak near the center. In fact, if all of the moments of a discrete random variable exist, they completely define its probability distribution. This fact is often used to prove that two random variables possess the same probability distributions. For example, if two discrete random variables, x and y, possess moments about the origin, $\mu'_{1x}, \mu'_{2x}, \mu'_{3x}, \ldots$ and $\mu'_{1y}, \mu'_{2y}, \mu'_{3y}, \ldots$, respectively, and if all corresponding moments are equal, i.e., if $\mu'_{1x} = \mu'_{1y}$, $\mu'_{2x} = \mu'_{2y}$, etc., then the two discrete probability distributions, $p(x)$ and $p(y)$, are identical.

The moments of a discrete random variable can be found directly using Definition 4.7, but as Examples 4.10 and 4.19 indicate, summing the series needed to find $E(y)$, $E(y^2)$, etc., can be tedious. Sometimes the difficulty in finding the moments of a random variable can be alleviated by using the **moment generating function** of the random variable.

Definition 4.9

The **moment generating function**, $m(t)$, of a discrete random variable y is defined to be

$$m(t) = E(e^{ty})$$

The moment generating function of a discrete random variable is simply a mathematical expression that condenses all the moments into a single formula. To extract specific moments from it, we first note that, by Definition 4.9,

$$E(e^{ty}) = \sum_{\text{all } y} e^{ty} p(y)$$

where

$$e^{ty} = 1 + ty + \frac{(ty)^2}{2!} + \frac{(ty)^3}{3!} + \frac{(ty)^4}{4!} + \cdots$$

Then, if μ'_i is finite for $i = 1, 2, 3, 4, \ldots$,

$$m(t) = E(e^{ty}) = \sum_{\text{all } y} e^{ty} p(y) = \sum_{\text{all } y} \left[1 + ty + \frac{(ty)^2}{2!} + \frac{(ty)^3}{3!} + \cdots \right] p(y)$$

$$= \sum_{\text{all } y} \left[p(y) + ty p(y) + \frac{t^2}{2!} y^2 p(y) + \frac{t^3}{3!} y^3 p(y) + \cdots \right]$$

Now apply Theorems 4.2 and 4.3 to obtain

$$m(t) = \sum_{\text{all } y} p(y) + t \sum_{\text{all } y} y p(y) + \frac{t^2}{2!} \sum_{\text{all } y} y^2 p(y) + \cdots$$

But, by Definition 4.7, $\sum_{\text{all } y} y^k p(y) = \mu'_k$. Therefore,

$$m(t) = 1 + t\mu'_1 + \frac{t^2}{2!} \mu'_2 + \frac{t^3}{3!} \mu'_3 + \cdots$$

This indicates that if we have the moment generating function of a random variable and can expand it into a power series in t, i.e.,

$$m(t) = 1 + a_1 t + a_2 t^2 + a_3 t^3 + \cdots$$

then it follows that the coefficient of t will be $\mu_1' = \mu$, the coefficient of t^2 will be $\mu_2'/2!$, and, in general, the coefficient of t^k will be $\mu_k'/k!$.

If we cannot easily expand $m(t)$ into a power series in t, we can find the moments of y by differentiating $m(t)$ with respect to t and then setting t equal to 0. Thus,

$$\frac{dm(t)}{dt} = \frac{d}{dt}\left(1 + t\mu_1' + \frac{t^2}{2!}\mu_2' + \frac{t^3}{3!}\mu_3' + \cdots\right)$$

$$= \left(0 + \mu_1' + \frac{2t}{2!}\mu_2' + \frac{3t^2}{3!}\mu_3' + \cdots\right)$$

Letting $t = 0$, we obtain

$$\frac{dm(t)}{dt}\bigg]_{t=0} = (\mu_1' + 0 + 0 + \cdots) = \mu_1' = \mu$$

Taking the second derivative of $m(t)$ with respect to t yields

$$\frac{d^2 m(t)}{dt^2} = \left(0 + \mu_2' + \frac{3!}{3!}t\mu_3' + \cdots\right)$$

Then, letting $t = 0$, we obtain

$$\frac{d^2 m(t)}{dt^2}\bigg]_{t=0} = (\mu_2' + 0 + 0 + \cdots) = \mu_2'$$

Theorem 4.5 describes how to extract μ_k' from the moment generating function $m(t)$.

Theorem 4.5
. . . .

If $m(t)$ exists, then the kth moment about the origin is equal to

$$\mu_k' = \frac{d^k m(t)}{dt^k}\bigg]_{t=0}$$

To illustrate the use of the moment generating function, consider the following examples.

EXAMPLE 4.20

Derive the moment generating function for a binomial random variable.

Solution

The moment generating function is given by

$$m(t) = E(e^{ty}) = \sum_{y=0}^{n} e^{ty}p(y) = \sum_{y=0}^{n} e^{ty}\binom{n}{y}p^y q^{n-y} = \sum_{y=0}^{n} \binom{n}{y}(pe^t)^y q^{n-y}$$

We now recall the binomial theorem (see Optional Exercise 4.33):

$$(a + b)^n = \sum_{y=0}^{n} \binom{n}{y} a^y b^{n-y}$$

Letting $a = pe^t$ and $b = q$ yields the desired result:

$$m(t) = (pe^t + q)^n$$

EXAMPLE 4.21

Use Theorem 4.5 to derive $\mu_1' = \mu$ and μ_2' for the binomial random variable.

Solution

From Theorem 4.5,

$$\mu_1' = \mu = \frac{dm(t)}{dt}\bigg]_{t=0} = n(pe^t + q)^{n-1}(pe^t)\bigg]_{t=0}$$

$$= n(pe^0 + q)^{n-1}(pe^0)$$

But $e^0 = 1$. Therefore,

$$\mu_1' = \mu = n(p + q)^{n-1}p = n(1)^{n-1}p = np$$

Similarly,

$$\mu_2' = \frac{d^2m(t)}{dt^2}\bigg]_{t=0} = np\frac{d}{dt}[e^t(pe^t + q)^{n-1}]\bigg]_{t=0}$$

$$= np[e^t(n - 1)(pe^t + q)^{n-2}pe^t + (pe^t + q)^{n-1}e^t]\bigg]_{t=0}$$

$$= np[(1)(n - 1)(1)p + (1)(1)] = np[(n - 1)p + 1]$$

$$= np(np - p + 1) = np(np + q) = n^2p^2 + npq$$

EXAMPLE 4.22

Use the results of Example 4.21, in conjunction with Theorem 4.4, to derive the variance of a binomial random variable.

Solution

By Theorem 4.4,

$$\sigma^2 = E(y^2) - \mu^2 = \mu_2' - (\mu_1')^2$$

Substituting the values of μ_2' and $\mu_1' = \mu$ from Example 4.21 yields

$$\sigma^2 = n^2p^2 + npq - (np)^2 = npq$$

TABLE 4.7   Some Useful Models for Discrete Random Variables

Random Variable	$p(y)$	μ	σ^2	$m(t)$
Bernoulli	$p(y) = p^y q^{1-y}$ where $q = 1 - p$, $y = 0, 1$	p	pq	$pe^t + q$
Binomial	$p(y) = \binom{n}{y} p^y q^{n-y}$ where $q = 1 - p$ $y = 0, 1, \ldots, n$	np	npq	$(pe^t + q)^n$
Hypergeometric	$p(y) = \dfrac{\binom{r}{y}\binom{N-r}{n-y}}{\binom{N}{n}}$	$\dfrac{nr}{N}$	$\dfrac{r(N-r)n(N-n)}{N^2(N-1)}$	Not given
Poisson	$p(y) = \dfrac{\lambda^y e^{-\lambda}}{y!}$ $y = 0, 1, 2, \ldots$	λ	λ	$e^{\lambda(e^t - 1)}$
Geometric	$p(y) = p(1-p)^{y-1}$ $y = 1, 2, \ldots$	$\dfrac{1}{p}$	$\dfrac{1-p}{p^2}$	$\dfrac{pe^t}{1 - (1-p)e^t}$
Negative binomial	$p(y) = \binom{y-1}{r-1} p^r (1-p)^{y-r}$ $y = r, r+1, \ldots$	$\dfrac{r}{p}$	$\dfrac{r(1-p)}{p^2}$	$\left(\dfrac{pe^t}{1 - (1-p)e^t}\right)^r$
Multinomial	$p(y_1, y_2, \ldots, y_k) = \dfrac{n!}{y_1! y_2! y_3!}(p_1)^{y_1}(p_2)^{y_2} \cdots (p_k)^{y_k}$	np_i	$np_i(1 - p_i)$	Not given

As demonstrated in Examples 4.21 and 4.22, it is easier to use the moment generating function to find μ_1' and μ_2' for a binomial random variable than to find $\mu_1' = E(y)$ and $\mu_2' = E(y^2)$ separately. You have to sum only a single series to find $m(t)$. This is also the best method for finding μ_1' and μ_2' for many other random variables, but not for all.

The probability distributions, means, variances, and moment generating functions for some useful discrete random variables are summarized in Table 4.7.

EXERCISES

4.77   Derive the moment generating function of the Poisson random variable. [*Hint:* Write

$$m(t) = E(e^{ty}) = \sum_{y=0}^{\infty} e^{ty} \frac{\lambda^y e^{-\lambda}}{y!}$$

$$= e^{-\lambda} \sum_{y=0}^{\infty} \frac{(\lambda e^t)^y}{y!} = e^{-\lambda} e^{\lambda e^t} \sum_{y=0}^{\infty} \frac{(\lambda e^t)^y e^{-\lambda e^t}}{y!}$$

Then note that the quantity being summed is a Poisson probability with parameter λe^t.]

4.78 Use the result of Exercise 4.77 to derive the mean and variance of the Poisson distribution.

4.79 Use the moment generating function given in Table 4.7 to derive the mean and variance of a geometric random variable.

4.12 Summary

This chapter introduces the concepts of numerical events and discrete random variables. A **random variable** is a rule that assigns one and only one value of a variable y to each simple event in the sample space. A random variable is said to be **discrete** if it can assume only a countable number of values.

The **probability distribution** of a discrete random variable is a table, graph, or formula that gives the probability associated with each value of y. The **expected value** $E(y) = \mu$ is the mean of this probability distribution and $E[(y - \mu)^2] = \sigma^2$ is its **variance**.

Seven discrete random variables—the **Bernoulli**, the **binomial**, the **multinomial**, the **negative binomial**, the **geometric**, the **hypergeometric**, and the **Poisson**—were presented, along with their probability distributions. We noted the physical characteristics of experiments that generate these random variables and identified some practical sampling situations that fit, to a reasonable degree of approximation, these experimental conditions. We gave the mean and variance for each of the random variables, showed how μ and σ provide measures of the location and variation of the probability distributions, and, in some cases, derived these quantities. Finally, we showed how the probability distribution can be used to calculate probabilities and, thereby, to evaluate the likelihood of the occurrence of some numerical events.

SUPPLEMENTARY EXERCISES

4.80 An engineering development laboratory conducted an experiment to investigate the life characteristics of a new solar heating panel, designed to have a useful life of at least 5 years with probability $p = .95$. A random sample of 20 such solar panels was selected, and the useful life of each was recorded.
a. What is the probability that exactly 18 will have a useful life of at least 5 years?
b. What is the probability that at most 10 will have a useful life of at least 5 years?
c. If only 10 of the 20 solar panels have a useful life of at least 5 years, what would you infer about the true value of p?

4.81 The economic risks taken by engineering-related businesses can be classified as being either *pure risks* or *speculative risks*. A pure risk is faced when there is a chance of incurring an economic loss but no chance of gain. A speculative risk is faced when there is a chance of gain as well as a chance of loss. Risk is sometimes measured by computing the variance or standard deviation of the probability distribution that describes the potential gains or losses of the firm. The two discrete probability distributions given in the table were developed from historical data. They describe the potential total physical damage losses next year to the computerized robots that operate at two different industrial engineering firms. Both firms have 10 industrial robots, and both have the same expected loss next year.

Firm A		Firm B	
Loss Next Year	Probability	Loss Next Year	Probability
$ 0	.01	$ 0	.00
500	.01	200	.01
1,000	.01	700	.02
1,500	.02	1,200	.02
2,000	.35	1,700	.15
2,500	.30	2,200	.30
3,000	.25	2,700	.30
3,500	.02	3,200	.15
4,000	.01	3,700	.02
4,500	.01	4,200	.02
5,000	.01	4,700	.01

a. Verify that both firms have the same expected total physical damage loss.
b. Compute the standard deviation of both probability distributions, and determine which firm faces the greater risk of physical damage to its industrial robots next year.
c. Was part **b** concerned with measuring speculative risk or pure risk? Explain.

4.82   The Environmental Protection Agency (EPA) issues standards on air and water pollution that vitally affect the safety of consumers and the operations of industry. For example, the EPA states that manufacturers of vinyl chloride and similar compounds must limit the amount of these chemicals in plant air emissions to 10 parts per million (ppm). Suppose you represent one of the manufacturers and you know that the mean emission of vinyl chloride for your plant is 4 ppm. Let y be the emission of vinyl chloride (in ppm) for a particular air sample at your plant; assume that the probability that an air sample is contaminated with the chemical is constant.
a. What is the standard deviation of y for your plant?
b. If the mean parts per million for your plant is, in fact, equal to 4, is it likely that a sample would yield a value of y that would exceed the EPA limits? Explain.

4.83   Refer to Exercise 4.82. Executives in the chemical industry claim that only 5% of all chemical plants in the United States discharge more than the EPA's suggested maximum amount of toxic waste into the air and water. Suppose that the EPA randomly samples 20 of the very large number of chemical plants for inspection. If the executives' claim is true, what is the probability that the number y of plants in violation of the EPA's standard is:
a. Less than 1?   b. Less than or equal to 1?   c. Less than 2?   d. More than 1?
e. What would you infer about the executives' claim if the observed value of y is 3?

4.84   Two of the five mechanical engineers employed by the county sanitation department have experience in the design of steam turbine power plants. You have been instructed to choose randomly two of the five engineers to work on a project for a new power plant.

a. What is the probability that you will choose the two engineers with experience in the design of steam turbine power plants?

b. What is the probability that you will choose at least one of the engineers with such experience?

4.85 *Engineering News-Record* (Dec. 23, 1982) reported on a survey about whether industry should be required to install best available technology (BAT) for pollution control. About 50% of those surveyed said they would rather endure factory shutdowns and lost jobs than waivers from BAT standards. Suppose 10 people are randomly selected and asked to give their opinion regarding BAT pollution control. Find the probability that:

a. None would prefer factory shutdowns and lost jobs to waiving BAT standards.

b. At least five would prefer factory shutdowns and lost jobs to waiving BAT standards.

c. At least one would prefer factory shutdowns and lost jobs to waiving BAT standards.

4.86 A particular system in a space vehicle must work properly for the spaceship to gain reentry into the earth's atmosphere. One component of the system operates successfully only 85% of the time. To increase the reliability of the system, four of the components will be installed in such a way that the system will operate successfully if at least one component is working successfully.

a. What is the probability that the system will fail? Assume the components operate independently.

b. If the system does fail, what would you infer about the claimed 85% success rate of a single component?

4.87 Lesser-developed countries experiencing rapid population growth often face severe traffic control problems in their large cities. Traffic engineers have determined that elevated rail systems may provide a feasible solution to these traffic woes. Studies indicate that the number of maintenance-related shutdowns of the elevated rail system in a particular country has a mean equal to 6.5 per month.

a. Find the probability that at least five shutdowns of the elevated rail system will occur next month in the country.

b. Find the probability that exactly four shutdowns will occur next month.

4.88 The scarce and essential metal, manganese, has been found in abundance in nodules on the deep-sea floor (*American Scientist*, Sept.–Oct. 1976). To investigate the relationship between the magnetic age of the earth's crust on the ocean floor and the abundance of manganese, several hundred manganese nodules were collected and the location (magnetic age) of each nodule determined. The data, converted to probabilities, are shown in the accompanying table.

Age	Probability
Oligocene	.20
Eocene	.15
Paleocene	.20
Cretaceous	.30
Jurassic	.10
Other	.05
Total	1.00

a. In a sample of 10 manganese nodules found on the ocean floor, find the probability that 1 is from the Oligocene, 2 are from the Eocene, 2 are from the Paleocene, 4 are from the Cretaceous, 1 is from the Jurassic, and none are from other divisions of geologic time.

b. In a future sample of 100 manganese nodules found on the ocean floor, find the mean and variance of the number of specimens from the Eocene epoch. Within what range would you expect the number to fall?

4.89 Refer to Exercise 4.11. Suppose a $100,000 exploration budget is divided equally between two identical and independent oil prospects, with probabilities and monetary outcomes as shown in the table given in Exercise 4.11.

a. Let x represent the sum of monetary values of the two oil prospects. Find the probability distribution for x.

b. Find $E(x)$ and σ^2. Compare these values to your results from part **a**.

c. What is the probability of doubling the $100,000 investment in the two oil prospects? Compare this to the probability of doubling the $50,000 investment in a single oil prospect in Exercise 4.11.

d. What is the probability of "gambler's ruin" (i.e., two dry holes) in the two oil prospects? Compare this to the probability of "gambler's ruin" in a single oil prospect in Exercise 4.11.

4.90 Refer to the *Mining Engineering* (Apr. 1986) study on underground coal mine safety, discussed in Exercise 2.51. Research revealed that "intermediate injuries," i.e., disabling injuries resulting from falls of roof and slides, haulage, machinery, and explosive accidents, constitute 41% of all disabling injuries and 98% of all fatal injuries in underground coal mines.

a. Find the probability that in a random sample of five disabling injuries, exactly three were intermediate injuries.

b. Find the probability that at least two of the five disabling injuries were intermediate injuries.

c. In a random sample of five fatal injuries, find the probability that at least two were intermediate injuries.

4.91 The manufacturer of a price-reading optical scanner claims that the probability it will misread the price of any product by misreading the "bar code" on a product's label is .001. At the time one of the scanners was installed in a supermarket, the store manager tested its performance. Let y be the number of trials (i.e., the number of prices read by the scanner) until the first misread price is observed.

a. If the manufacturer's claim is correct, find the probability distribution for y. (Assume the trials represent independent events.)

b. If the manufacturer's claim is correct, what is the probability that the scanner will not misread a price until after the fifth price is read?

c. If in fact the third price is misread, what inference would you make about the manufacturer's claim? Explain.

4.92 When radar was first introduced during World War II, it was very difficult for an operator manning the screen to distinguish a static interference blip from an actual enemy aircraft blip. Although the operator did not want to sound an alarm needlessly, failure to alert the defenses could have serious consequences. Records indicate that 60% of all observed blips represented enemy aircraft. Suppose that during a particular siege there were five blips spotted on the screen at different points in time and the radar operator alerted the defenses on each occasion. Assume that the events are independent; compute the probability of each of the following events:

a. Radar operator made the correct decision on all five occasions.

b. Radar operator made the correct decision on at least three occasions.

c. Radar operator was incorrect all five times (and therefore sounded five false alarms).

4.93 A study of vehicle flow characteristics on acceleration lanes (i.e., merging ramps) at a major freeway in Israel found that one out of every six vehicles uses less than one-third of the acceleration lane before merging into traffic (*Journal of Transportation Engineering*, Nov. 1985). Suppose we monitor the location of the merge for the next five vehicles that enter the acceleration lane.

a. What is the probability that none of the vehicles will use less than one-third of the acceleration lane?

b. What is the probability that exactly two of the vehicles will use less than one-third of the acceleration lane?

4.94 Refer to Exercise 4.93. Suppose that the number of vehicles using the acceleration lane per minute has a mean equal to 1.1.

a. What is the probability that more than two vehicles will use the acceleration lane in the next minute?

b. What is the probability that exactly three vehicles will use the acceleration lane in the next minute?

4.95 Today, most industrial robots are programmed to operate through microprocessors. The probability that one such computerized robot breaks down during any one 8-hour shift is .2. Find the probability that the robot will operate for at most five shifts before breaking down twice.

4.96 "The sufficiently prolonged continuation of a low probability makes a given outcome inevitable," writes A. J. Coale in *Population and Development Review* (Sept. 1985). The "inevitable" event Coale is specifically referring to is a nuclear war. Experts agree that the probability of a nuclear war occurring in a given year is small, but not 0. According to Coale, then, "over hundreds of years this makes nuclear war virtually certain." Suppose the probability of a nuclear war occurring in any given year is only .01.

a. What is the probability of a nuclear war occurring in the next 5 years?

b. What is the probability of a nuclear war occurring in the next 10 years?

c. What is the probability of a nuclear war occurring in the next 15 years?

d. What is the probability of a nuclear war occurring in the next 20 years?

e. What assumption must be made to answer parts **a–d**? How likely is this assumption to hold true?

4.97 A can company reports that the mean number of breakdowns per 8-hour shift on its machine-operated assembly line is 1.5. Assume that the probability of a breakdown is constant for all shifts.

a. What is the probability of exactly two breakdowns during the midnight shift?

b. What is the probability of fewer than two breakdowns during the afternoon shift?

c. What is the probability of no breakdowns during three consecutive 8-hour shifts? (Assume that the machine operates independently across shifts.)

OPTIONAL SUPPLEMENTARY EXERCISES

4.98 Suppose the random variable y has a moment generating function given by

$$m(t) = \frac{1}{5}e^t + \frac{2}{5}e^{2t} + \frac{2}{5}e^{3t}$$

a. Find the mean of y.

b. Find the variance of y.

4.99 Let y be a geometric random variable with the probability distribution given in Table 4.7. Show that $E(y) = 1/p$. [*Hint:* Write

$$E(y) = p \sum_{y=1}^{\infty} yq^{y-1} \quad \text{where } q = 1 - p$$

and note that

$$\frac{dq^y}{dq} = yq^{y-1}$$

Thus,

$$E(y) = p \sum_{y=1}^{\infty} yq^{y-1} = p\frac{d}{dq}\left(\sum_{y=1}^{\infty} q^y\right)$$

Then use the fact that

$$\sum_{y=1}^{\infty} q^y = \frac{q}{1-q}$$

(The sum of this infinite series is given in most mathematical handbooks.)]

4.100   The probability generating function $P(t)$ for a discrete random variable y is defined to be

$$P(t) = E(t^y) = p_0 + p_1 t + p_2 t^2 + \cdots$$

where $p_i = P(y = i)$.
a. Find $P(t)$ for the Poisson distribution. [*Hint:*   Write

$$E(t^y) = \sum_{y=0}^{\infty} \frac{(\lambda t)^y e^{-\lambda}}{y!} = e^{\lambda(t-1)} \sum_{y=0}^{\infty} \frac{(\lambda t)^y e^{-\lambda t}}{y!}$$

and note that the quantity being summed is a Poisson probability with mean λt.]
b. Use the facts that

$$E(y) = \frac{dP(t)}{dt}\bigg]_{t=1} \quad \text{and} \quad E[y(y-1)] = \frac{d^2P(t)}{dt^2}\bigg]_{t=1}$$

to derive the mean and variance of a Poisson random variable.

References

Feller, W. *An Introduction to Probability Theory and Its Applications*, Vol. I, 3rd ed. New York: Wiley, 1968.

Hogg, R. V., and Craig, A. T. *Introduction to Mathematical Statistics*, 4th ed. New York: Macmillan, 1978.

Mendenhall, W., Scheaffer, R. L., and Wackerly, D. *Mathematical Statistics with Applications*, 4th ed. Boston: Duxbury Press, 1989.

Mood, A. M., Graybill, F. A., and Boes, D. C. *Introduction to the Theory of Statistics*, 3rd ed. New York: McGraw-Hill, 1963.

Mosteller, F., Rourke, R. E. K., and Thomas, G. B. *Probability with Statistical Applications*, 2nd ed. Reading, Mass.: Addison-Wesley, 1970.

Parzen, E. *Modern Probability Theory and Its Applications.* New York: Wiley, 1964.

Parzen, E. *Stochastic Processes.* San Francisco: Holden-Day, 1962.

Standard Mathematical Tables, 17th ed. Cleveland: Chemical Rubber Company, 1969.

CHAPTER FIVE

Continuous Random Variables

Objective

To distinguish between continuous and discrete random variables and their respective probability distributions; to present some useful continuous probability distributions and show how they can be used to solve some practical problems

Contents

5.1   Continuous Random Variables

Many random variables observed in real life are not discrete random variables because the number of values that they can assume is not countable. For example, the waiting time y (in minutes) for a submitted data-processing job to be completed could, in theory, assume any of the uncountably infinite number of values in the interval $0 < y < \infty$. The daily rainfall at some location, the strength (in pounds per square inch) of a steel bar, and the intensity of sunlight at a particular time of the day are other examples of random variables that can assume any one of the uncountably infinite number of points in one or more intervals on the real line. In contrast to discrete random variables, such variables are called **continuous random variables**.

The preceding discussion identifies the difference between discrete and continuous random variables, but it fails to point to a practical problem. It is impossible to assign a finite amount of probability to each of the uncountable number of points in a line interval in such a way that the sum of the probabilities is 1. Therefore, the distinction between discrete and continuous random variables is usually based on the difference in their **cumulative distribution functions**.

Definition 5.1

The **cumulative distribution function $F(y_0)$** for a random variable y is equal to the probability

$$F(y_0) = P(y \leq y_0)$$

For a discrete random variable, the cumulative distribution function is the cumulative sum of $p(y)$, from the smallest value that y can assume, to a value of y_0. For example, from the cumulative sums in Table 1 of Appendix II, we obtain the following values of $F(y)$ for a binomial random variable with $n = 5$ and $p = .5$:

$$F(0) = P(y \leq 0) = \sum_{y=0}^{0} p(y) = p(0) = .031$$

$$F(1) = P(y \leq 1) = \sum_{y=0}^{1} p(y) = .188$$

$$F(2) = P(y \leq 2) = \sum_{y=0}^{2} p(y) = .500$$

$$F(3) = P(y \leq 3) = .812$$

$$F(4) = P(y \leq 4) = .969$$

$$F(5) = P(y \leq 5) = 1$$

A graph of $p(y)$ is shown in Figure 5.1. The value of $F(y_0)$ is equal to the sum of the areas of the probability rectangles from $y = 0$ to $y = y_0$. The probability $F(3)$ is shaded in the figure.

FIGURE 5.1 ▶
Probability distribution for a binomial random variable ($n = 5$, $p = .5$); shaded area corresponds to $F(3)$

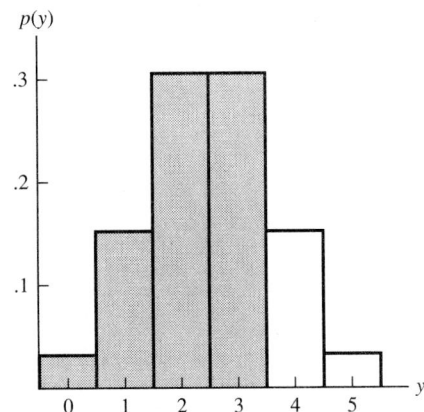

A graph of the cumulative distribution function for the binomial random variable with $n = 5$ and $p = .5$, shown in Figure 5.2, illustrates an important property of the cumulative distribution functions for all discrete random variables: *They are step functions*. For example, $F(y)$ is equal to .031 until, as y increases, it reaches $y = 1$. Then $F(y)$ jumps abruptly to $F(1) = .188$. The value of $F(y)$ then remains constant as y increases until y reaches $y = 2$. Then $F(y)$ rises abruptly to $F(2) = .500$. Thus, $F(y)$ is a discontinuous function that jumps upward at a countable number of points ($y = 0, 1, 2, 3,$ and 4).

FIGURE 5.2 ▶
Cumulative distribution function $F(y)$ for a binomial random variable ($n = 5$, $p = .5$)

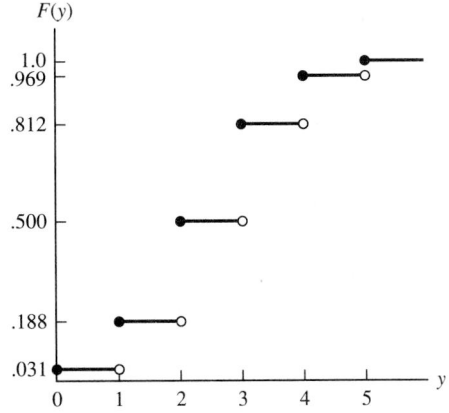

In contrast to the cumulative distribution function for a discrete random variable, the cumulative distribution function $F(y)$ for a continuous random variable is a **monotonically increasing continuous** function of y. This means that $F(y)$ is a continuous function such that if $y_a < y_b$, then $F(y_a) \leq F(y_b)$, i.e., as y increases, $F(y)$ never decreases. A graph of the cumulative distribution function for a continuous random variable might appear as shown in Figure 5.3.

FIGURE 5.3 ▶

Cumulative distribution function for a continuous random variable

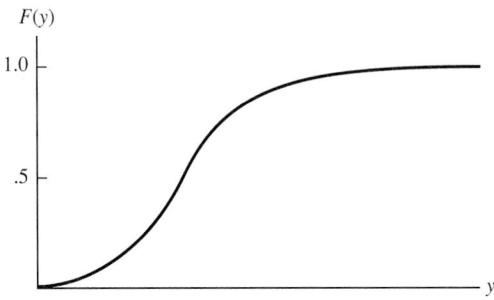

Definition 5.2

A **continuous random variable** y is one that has the following three properties:

1. y takes on an uncountably infinite number of values in the interval $(-\infty, \infty)$.
2. The cumulative distribution function, $F(y)$, is continuous.
3. The probability that y equals any one particular value is 0.

5.2 The Density Function for a Continuous Random Variable

In Chapter 1, we described a large set of data by means of a relative frequency distribution. If the data represent measurements on a continuous random variable and if the amount of data is very large, we can reduce the width of the class intervals until the distribution appears to be a smooth curve. A **probability density function** is a theoretical model for this distribution.

Definition 5.3

If $F(y)$ is the cumulative distribution function for a continuous random variable y, then the **density function** $f(y)$ for y is

$$f(y) = \frac{dF(y)}{dy}$$

The density function for a continuous random variable y, the model for some real-life population of data, will usually be a smooth curve as shown in Figure 5.4. It follows from Definition 5.3 that

$$F(y) = \int_{-\infty}^{y} f(t)dt$$

FIGURE 5.4 ▶
Density function $f(y)$ for a continuous random variable

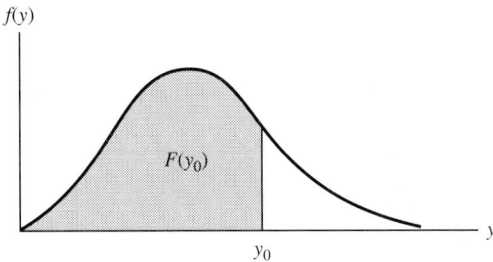

Thus, the cumulative area under the curve between $-\infty$ and a point y_0 is equal to $F(y_0)$.

The density function for a continuous random variable must always satisfy the three properties given in the following box.

Properties of a Density Function

1. $f(y) \geq 0$

2. $\int_{-\infty}^{\infty} f(y)dy = F(\infty) = 1$

3. $P(a < y < b) = \int_{a}^{b} f(y)dy$, where a and b are constants

---

EXAMPLE 5.1

Let c be a constant and consider the density function

$$f(y) = \begin{cases} cy & \text{if } 0 \leq y \leq 1 \\ 0 & \text{elsewhere} \end{cases}$$

a. Find the value of c.
b. Find $P(.2 < y < .5)$.

Solution

a. Since $\int_{-\infty}^{\infty} f(y)dy$ must equal 1, we have

$$\int_{-\infty}^{\infty} f(y)dy = \int_{0}^{1} cy \, dy = c\frac{y^2}{2}\Big]_{0}^{1} = c\left(\frac{1}{2}\right) = 1$$

Solving for c yields $c = 2$, and thus, $f(y) = 2y$. A graph of $f(y)$ is shown in Figure 5.5.

b. $P(.2 < y < .5) = \int_{.2}^{.5} f(y)dy$

$$= \int_{.2}^{.5} 2y \, dy$$

$$= y^2 \Big]_{.2}^{.5} = (.5)^2 - (.2)^2$$

$$= .25 - .04 = .21$$

This probability, shaded in Figure 5.5, is the area under the density function between $y = .2$ and $y = .5$.

FIGURE 5.5 ▶
Graph of the density function $f(y)$ for Example 5.1

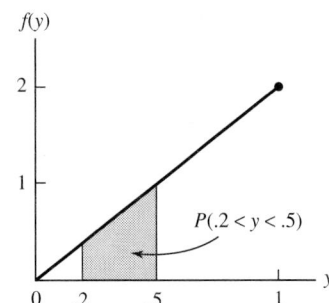

EXAMPLE 5.2

Refer to Example 5.1. Find the cumulative distribution function for the random variable y. Then find $F(.2)$ and $F(.7)$.

Solution

By Definition 5.3, it follows that

$$F(y) = \int_{-\infty}^{y} f(t)dt = \int_{0}^{y} 2t \, dt$$

$$= 2\left(\frac{t^2}{2}\right)\Big]_{0}^{y} = y^2$$

Then

$$F(.2) = P(y \le .2) = (.2)^2 = .04$$
$$F(.7) = P(y \le .7) = (.7)^2 = .49$$

The value of $F(y)$ when $y = .7$—i.e., $F(.7)$—is the shaded area in Figure 5.6.

FIGURE 5.6 ▶
Graph of the density function $f(y)$ for Example 5.2; shaded area corresponds to $F(.7)$

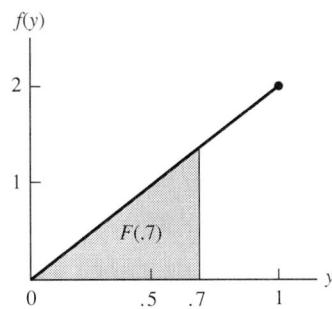

Many of the continuous random variables with applications in statistics have density functions whose integrals cannot be expressed in closed form. They can only be approximated by numerical methods. Tables of areas under several such density functions are presented in Appendix II and will be introduced as required.

EXERCISES

5.1   Let c be a constant and consider the density function

$$f(y) = \begin{cases} cy^2 & \text{if } 0 \le y \le 2 \\ 0 & \text{elsewhere} \end{cases}$$

a. Find the value of c.
b. Find the cumulative distribution function $F(y)$.
c. Compute $F(1)$.
d. Compute $F(.5)$.
e. Compute $P(1 \le y \le 1.5)$.

5.2   Let c be a constant and consider the density function

$$f(y) = \begin{cases} c(2 - y) & \text{if } 0 \le y \le 1 \\ 0 & \text{elsewhere} \end{cases}$$

a. Find the value of c.
b. Find the cumulative distribution function $F(y)$.
c. Compute $F(.4)$.
d. Compute $P(.1 \le y \le .6)$.

5.3   Let c be a constant and consider the density function

$$f(y) = \begin{cases} ce^{-y} & \text{if } y > 0 \\ 0 & \text{elsewhere} \end{cases}$$

a. Find the value of c.
b. Find the cumulative distribution function $F(y)$.

    c. Compute $F(2.6)$.
    d. Show that $F(0) = 0$ and $F(\infty) = 1$.
    e. Compute $P(1 \leq y \leq 5)$.

5.4   Let c be a constant and consider the density function

$$f(y) = \begin{cases} (1/c)e^{-y/2} & \text{if } y \geq 0 \\ (1/c)e^{y/2} & \text{if } y < 0 \end{cases}$$

    a. Find the value of c.
    b. Find the cumulative distribution function $F(y)$.
    c. Compute $F(1)$.
    d. Compute $P(y > .5)$.

5.5   Let c be a constant and consider the density function

$$f(y) = \begin{cases} c + y & \text{if } -1 < y < 0 \\ c - y & \text{if } 0 \leq y < 1 \end{cases}$$

    a. Find the value of c.
    b. Find the cumulative distribution function $F(y)$.
    c. Compute $F(-.5)$.
    d. Compute $P(0 \leq y \leq .5)$.

OPTIONAL EXERCISE

5.6   Continuous probability distributions provide theoretical models for the lifelength of a component (e.g., computer chip, light bulb, automobile, air-conditioning unit, and so on). Often, it is important to know whether or not it is better to periodically replace an old component with a new component. For example, for certain types of light bulbs, an old bulb that has been in use for a while tends to have a longer lifelength than a new bulb. Let y represent the lifelength of some component with cumulative distribution function $F(y)$. Then the "life" distribution $F(y)$ is considered **new better than used** (NBU) if

$$\bar{F}(x + y) \leq \bar{F}(x)\bar{F}(y) \quad \text{for all } x, y \geq 0$$

where $\bar{F}(y) = 1 - F(y)$ (*Microelectronics and Reliability*, Jan. 1986). Alternatively, a "life" distribution $F(y)$ is **new worse than used** (NWU) if

$$\bar{F}(x + y) \geq \bar{F}(x)\bar{F}(y) \quad \text{for all } x, y \geq 0$$

    a. Consider the density function

$$f(y) = \begin{cases} y/2 & \text{if } 0 < y < 2 \\ 0 & \text{elsewhere} \end{cases}$$

       Find the "life" distribution, $F(y)$.
    b. Determine whether the "life" distribution $F(y)$ is NBU or NWU.

5.3   Expected Values for Continuous Random Variables

You will recall from your study of calculus that integration is a summation process. Thus, finding the integral

$$F(y_0) = \int_{-\infty}^{y_0} f(t)dt$$

for a continuous random variable is analogous to finding the sum

$$F(y_0) = \sum_{y \leq y_0} p(y)$$

for a discrete random variable. Then it is natural to employ the same definitions for the expected value of a continuous random variable y, for the expected value of a function $g(y)$, and for the variance of y that were given for a discrete random variable in Section 4.3. The only difference is that we will substitute the integration symbol for the summation symbol. It also can be shown (proof omitted) that the expectation theorems of Section 4.4 hold for continuous random variables. We now summarize these definitions and theorems, and present some examples of their use.

Definition 5.4

Let y be a continuous random variable with density function $f(y)$, and let $g(y)$ be any function of y. Then the **expected values** of y and $g(y)$ are:

$$E(y) = \int_{-\infty}^{\infty} yf(y)dy$$

$$E[g(y)] = \int_{-\infty}^{\infty} g(y)f(y)dy$$

Theorem 5.1

Let c be a constant, let y be a continuous random variable, and let $g_1(y)$, $g_2(y), \ldots , g_k(y)$ be k functions of y. Then

$$E(c) = c$$
$$E(cy) = cE(y)$$
$$E[g_1(y) + g_2(y) + \cdots + g_k(y)] = E[g_1(y)] + E[g_2(y)] + \cdots + E[g_k(y)]$$

> ### Theorem 5.2
>
> Let y be a continuous random variable with $E(y) = \mu$. Then
> $$\sigma^2 = E[(y - \mu)^2] = E(y^2) - \mu^2$$

EXAMPLE 5.3

Refer to Example 5.1. Find the mean and standard deviation for the continuous random variable y.

Solution

Recall that $f(y) = 2y$. Therefore,

$$E(y) = \int_{-\infty}^{\infty} yf(y)dy = \int_0^1 y(2y)dy = \int_0^1 2y^2\,dy = \frac{2y^3}{3}\bigg]_0^1 = \frac{2}{3}$$

$$E(y^2) = \int_{-\infty}^{\infty} y^2 f(y)dy = \int_0^1 y^2(2y)dy = \int_0^1 2y^3\,dy = \frac{2y^4}{4}\bigg]_0^1 = \frac{1}{2}$$

Then, by Theorem 5.2,

$$\sigma^2 = E(y^2) - \mu^2 = \frac{1}{2} - \left(\frac{2}{3}\right)^2 = .0556$$

and thus

$$\sigma = \sqrt{.0556} = .24$$

EXAMPLE 5.4

Refer to Examples 5.1 and 5.3. The interval $\mu \pm 2\sigma$ is shown on the graph of $f(y)$ in Figure 5.7. Find $P(\mu - 2\sigma < y < \mu + 2\sigma)$.

Solution

From Example 5.3, we have $\mu = \frac{2}{3} \approx .67$ and $\sigma = .24$. Therefore, $\mu - 2\sigma = .19$ and $\mu + 2\sigma = 1.15$. Since $P(y > 1) = 0$, we want to find the probability $P(y > .19)$, corresponding to the shaded area in Figure 5.7:

$$P(\mu - 2\sigma < y < \mu + 2\sigma) = P(y > .19) = \int_{.19}^1 f(y)dy$$

$$= \int_{.19}^1 2y\,dy = y^2\bigg]_{.19}^1 = 1 - (.19)^2 = .96$$

FIGURE 5.7 ▶
Graph showing the interval
$\mu \pm 2\sigma$ for $f(y) = 2y$

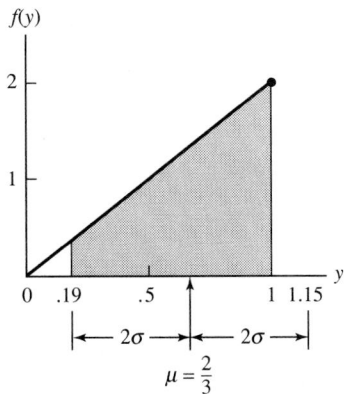

In Chapter 1, we applied the Empirical Rule to mound-shaped relative frequency distributions of data. The Empirical Rule may also be applied to mound-shaped theoretical—i.e., probability—distributions. As examples in the preceding chapters demonstrate, the percentage (or proportion) of a data set in the interval $\mu \pm 2\sigma$ is usually very close to .95, the value specified by the Empirical Rule. This is certainly true for the probability distribution considered in Example 5.4.

EXAMPLE 5.5

Let y be a continuous random variable with probability density function

$$f(y) = \begin{cases} \dfrac{e^{-y/2}}{2} & \text{if } 0 \leq y < \infty \\ 0 & \text{elsewhere} \end{cases}$$

Find the mean, variance, and standard deviation of y. (This density function is known as the **exponential probability distribution**.)

Solution

The mean of the random variable y is given by

$$\mu = E(y) = \int_{-\infty}^{\infty} yf(y)dy = \int_{0}^{\infty} \frac{ye^{-y/2}}{2} dy$$

To compute this definite integral, we use the following general formula, found in most mathematical handbooks:*

$$\int ye^{ay} dy = \frac{e^{ay}}{a^2}(ay - 1)$$

---

*See, for example, *Standard Mathematical Tables* (1969). Otherwise, the result can be derived using integration by parts:

$$\int ye^{ay} dy = \frac{ye^{ay}}{a} - \int \frac{e^{ay}}{a} dy$$

By substituting $a = -\frac{1}{2}$, we obtain

$$\mu = \frac{1}{2}(4) = 2$$

To find σ^2, we will first find $E(y^2)$ by making use of the general formula*

$$\int y^m e^{ay}\, dy = \frac{y^m e^{ay}}{a} - \frac{m}{a}\int y^{m-1} e^{ay}\, dy$$

Then with $a = -\frac{1}{2}$ and $m = 2$, we can write

$$E(y^2) = \int_{-\infty}^{\infty} y^2 f(y)dy = \int_{0}^{\infty} \frac{y^2 e^{-y/2}}{2}\, dy = \frac{1}{2}(16) = 8$$

Thus, by Theorem 5.2,

$$\sigma^2 = E(y^2) - \mu^2 = 8 - (2)^2 = 4$$

and

$$\sigma = \sqrt{4} = 2$$

EXAMPLE 5.6

A graph of the density function of Example 5.5 is shown in Figure 5.8. Find $P(\mu - 2\sigma < y < \mu + 2\sigma)$.

FIGURE 5.8 ▶
Graph of the density function of Example 5.5

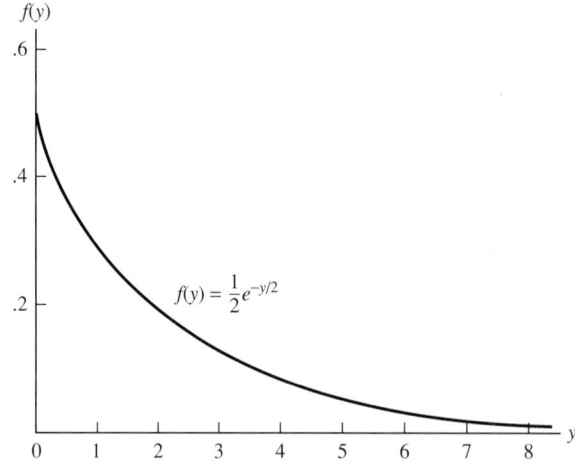

$$f(y) = \frac{1}{2}e^{-y/2}$$

---

*This result is also derived using integration by parts.

Solution

We showed in Example 5.5 that $\mu = 2$ and $\sigma = 2$. Therefore, $\mu - 2\sigma = 2 - 4 = -2$ and $\mu + 2\sigma = 6$. Since $f(y) = 0$ for $y < 0$,

$$P(\mu - 2\sigma < y < \mu + 2\sigma) = \int_0^6 f(y)dy = \int_0^6 \frac{e^{-y/2}}{2}\,dy$$

$$= -e^{-y/2}\Big]_0^6 = 1 - e^{-3}$$

$$= 1 - .049787 = .950213$$

The Empirical Rule of Chapter 2 would suggest that a good approximation to this probability is .95. You can see that for the exponential density function, the approximation is very close to the exact probability, .950213.

In many practical situations, we will know the variance (or standard deviation) of a random variable y and will want to find the standard deviation of $(c + y)$ or cy, where c is a constant. For example, we might know the standard deviation of the weight y in ounces of a particular type of computer chip and want to find the standard deviation of the weight in grams. Since 1 ounce = 28.349527 grams, we would want to find the standard deviation of cy, where $c = 28.349527$. The variances of $(c + y)$ and cy are given by Theorem 5.3.

Theorem 5.3

Let y be a random variable* with mean μ and variance σ^2. Then the variances of $(c + y)$ and cy are

$$\sigma^2_{(c+y)} = \sigma^2 \quad \text{and} \quad \sigma^2_{cy} = c^2\sigma^2$$

PROOF OF THEOREM 5.3   From Theorem 5.1, we know that $E(cy) = cE(y) = c\mu$. Using the definition of the variance of a random variable, we can write

$$\sigma^2_{cy} = E[(cy - c\mu)^2] = E\{[c(y - \mu)]^2\} = E[c^2(y - \mu)^2]$$

Then, by Theorem 5.1,

$$\sigma^2_{cy} = c^2E[(y - \mu)^2]$$

But, $E[(y - \mu)^2] = \sigma^2$. Therefore,

$$\sigma^2_{cy} = c^2\sigma^2$$

As an example of the application of this theorem, suppose that the variance of the weight y of a computer chip is 1.1 (ounces)^2. Then the variance of the weight of the chip in grams is equal to $(28.349527)^2(1.1) \approx 884.1$ (grams)^2. The standard deviation of the weight in grams is equal to $\sqrt{884.1} = 29.7$ grams.

---

*This theorem applies to discrete or continuous random variables.

EXERCISES

5.7   Find μ and σ^2 for the continuous random variable of Exercise 5.1. Then compute $P(\mu - 2\sigma < y < \mu + 2\sigma)$ and compare to the Empirical Rule.

5.8   Find μ and σ^2 for the continuous random variable of Exercise 5.2. Then compute $P(\mu - 2\sigma < y < \mu + 2\sigma)$ and compare to the Empirical Rule.

5.9   Find μ and σ^2 for the continuous random variable of Exercise 5.3. Then compute $P(\mu - 2\sigma < y < \mu + 2\sigma)$ and compare to the Empirical Rule.

5.10   Find μ and σ^2 for the continuous random variable of Exercise 5.4. Then compute $P(\mu - 2\sigma < y < \mu + 2\sigma)$ and compare to the Empirical Rule.

5.11   Find μ and σ^2 for the continuous random variable of Exercise 5.5. Then compute $P(\mu - 2\sigma < y < \mu + 2\sigma)$ and compare to the Empirical Rule.

5.12   The amount of time y (in minutes) that a commuter train is late is a continuous random variable with probability density

$$f(y) = \begin{cases} \dfrac{3}{500}(25 - y^2) & \text{if } -5 < y < 5 \\ 0 & \text{elsewhere} \end{cases}$$

[*Note:*   A negative value of y means that the train is early.]
a. Find the mean and variance of the amount of time in minutes the train is late.
b. Find the mean and variance of the amount of time in hours the train is late.
c. Find the mean and variance of the amount of time in seconds the train is late.

5.13   Researchers at the University of Rochester studied the friction that occurs in the paper-feeding process of a photocopier (*Journal of Engineering for Industry*, May 1993). The coefficient of fricton is a proportion that measures the degree of friction between two adjacent sheets of paper in the feeder stack. In one experiment, a triangular distribution was used to model the friction coefficient, y. (See the accompanying figure.)

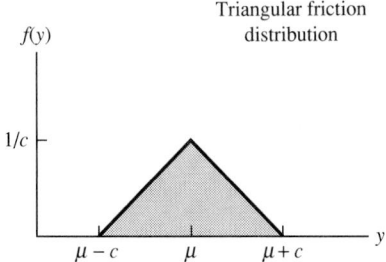

The density function for the triangular friction distribution is given by

$$f(y) = \begin{cases} \dfrac{(c - \mu) + y}{c^2} & \text{if } \mu - c < y < \mu,\ c > 0 \\[2mm] \dfrac{(c + \mu) - y}{c^2} & \text{if } \mu < y < \mu + c,\ c > 0 \\[2mm] 0 & \text{elsewhere} \end{cases}$$

a. Show that $\int_{-\infty}^{\infty} f(y)\,dy = 1$.
b. Find the mean of the triangular friction distribution.
c. Find the variance of the triangular friction distribution.

OPTIONAL EXERCISES

5.14   Prove Theorem 5.1.

5.15   Prove Theorem 5.2.

5.4   The Uniform Probability Distribution

Suppose you were to randomly select a number y represented by a point in the interval $a \le y \le b$. The density function of y is represented graphically by a rectangle, as shown in Figure 5.9. Notice that the height of the rectangle is $1/(b - a)$ to ensure that the area under the rectangle equals 1.

FIGURE 5.9 ▶
Uniform density function

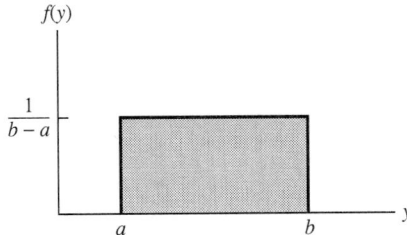

A random variable of the type shown in Figure 5.9 is called a **uniform random variable**; its density function, mean, and variance are shown in the next box.

The Uniform Probability Distribution

$$f(y) = \begin{cases} \dfrac{1}{b - a} & \text{if } a \leq y \leq b \\ 0 & \text{elsewhere} \end{cases}$$

$$\mu = \frac{a + b}{2} \qquad \sigma^2 = \frac{(b - a)^2}{12}$$

EXAMPLE 5.7

Suppose the research department of a steel manufacturer believes that one of the company's rolling machines is producing sheets of steel of varying thickness. The thickness is a uniform random variable with values between 150 and 200 millimeters. Any sheets less than 160 millimeters thick must be scrapped, since they are unacceptable to buyers.

a. Calculate the mean and standard deviation of y, the thickness of the sheets produced by this machine. Then graph the probability distribution, and show the mean on the horizontal axis. Also show 1 and 2 standard deviation intervals around the mean.

b. Calculate the fraction of steel sheets produced by this machine that have to be scrapped.

Solution

a. To calculate the mean and standard deviation for y, we substitute 150 and 200 millimeters for a and b, respectively, in the formulas. Thus,

$$\mu = \frac{a + b}{2} = \frac{150 + 200}{2} = 175 \text{ millimeters}$$

and

$$\sigma = \frac{b - a}{\sqrt{12}} = \frac{200 - 150}{\sqrt{12}} = \frac{50}{3.464} = 14.43 \text{ millimeters}$$

The uniform probability distribution is

$$f(y) = \frac{1}{b - a} = \frac{1}{200 - 150} = \frac{1}{50}$$

The graph of this function is shown in Figure 5.10. The mean and 1 and 2 standard deviation intervals around the mean are shown on the horizontal axis.

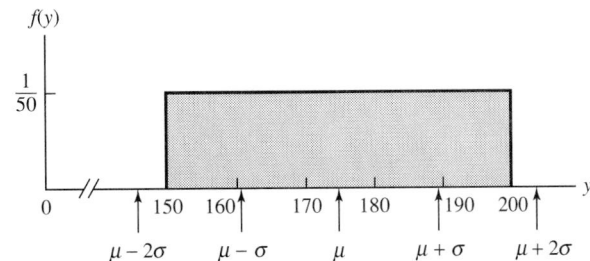

FIGURE 5.10 ▶
Frequency function for y in
Example 5.7

b. To find the fraction of steel sheets produced by the machine that have to be scrapped, we must find the probability that y, the thickness, is less than 160 millimeters. As indicated in Figure 5.11, we need to calculate the area under the frequency function $f(y)$ between the points $a = 150$ and $c = 160$. This is the area of a rectangle with base $160 - 150 = 10$ and height $\frac{1}{50}$. The fraction that has to be scrapped is then

$$P(y < 160) = (\text{Base})(\text{Height}) = (10)\left(\frac{1}{50}\right) = \frac{1}{5}$$

That is, 20% of all the sheets made by this machine must be scrapped.

FIGURE 5.11 ▶
The probability that the sheet
thickness, y, is between 150 and
160 millimeters

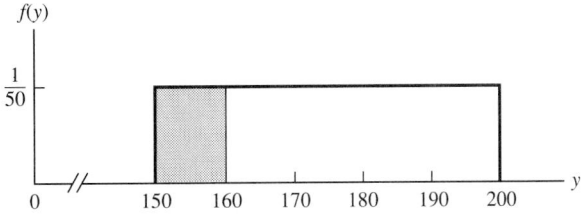

The random numbers in Table 6 of Appendix II were generated by a computer program that randomly selects values of y from a uniform distribution. (However, the random numbers are terminated at some specified decimal place.) One of the most important applications of the uniform distribution is described in Chapter 7, where, along with a computer program that generates random numbers, we will use it to simulate the sampling of many other types of random variables.

EXERCISES

5.16   Researchers at the University of California–Berkeley have designed, built, and tested a switched-capacitor circuit for generating random signals (*International Journal of Circuit Theory and Applications*, May–June 1990). The circuit's trajectory was shown to be uniformly distributed on the interval $(0, 1)$.
   a. Give the mean and variance of the circuit's trajectory.
   b. Compute the probability that the trajectory falls between .2 and .4.
   c. Would you expect to observe a trajectory that exceeds .995? Explain.

5.17   The amount of time y between pauses on a full-screen-edit terminal (i.e., the time required for the terminal to process an edit command and make the corrections on the screen) is uniformly distributed between .5 and 2.25 seconds.

   a. Find the mean and variance of y.

   b. Locate the interval $\mu \pm 2\sigma$ on a graph of the probability distribution and compute $P(\mu - 2\sigma < y < \mu + 2\sigma)$. Compare your result with the Empirical Rule.

   c. What is the probability the terminal will process an edit command and make the appropriate corrections on the screen in less than 1 second?

5.18   The Department of Transportation (DOT) has determined that the winning (low) bid y (in dollars) on a road construction contract has a uniform distribution with probability density function

$$f(y) = \begin{cases} \dfrac{5}{8d} & \text{if } \dfrac{2d}{5} \leq y \leq 2d \\ 0 & \text{elsewhere} \end{cases}$$

where d is the DOT estimate of the cost of the job.

   a. Find the mean and standard deviation of y. Then graph $f(y)$, showing the locations of the mean and 1 and 2 standard deviation intervals around the mean.

   b. What fraction of the winning bids on road construction contracts are less than the DOT estimate?

5.19   A manufacturing company has developed a fuel-efficient machine that combines pressure washing with steam cleaning. It is designed to deliver 7 gallons of cleaner per minute at 1,000 pounds per square inch for pressure washing. In fact, it delivers an amount at random anywhere between 6.5 and 7.5 gallons per minute. Assume that y, the amount of cleaner delivered, is a uniform random variable with probability density

$$f(y) = \begin{cases} 1 & \text{if } 6.5 \leq y \leq 7.5 \\ 0 & \text{elsewhere} \end{cases}$$

   a. Find the mean and standard deviation of y. Then graph $f(y)$, showing the locations of the mean and 1 and 2 standard deviation intervals around the mean.

   b. Find the probability that more than 7.2 gallons of cleaner are dispensed per minute.

OPTIONAL EXERCISES

5.20   Statistical software packages, such as SAS and MINITAB, are capable of generating random numbers from a uniform distribution. For example, the SAS function RANUNI uses a prime modulus multiplicative generator with modulus $2^{31} - 1$ and multiplier $397,204,094$ to generate a random variable y from a uniform distribution on the interval $(0, 1)$. This function can be used to generate a uniform random variable on any interval (a, b), where a and b are constants, using an appropriate transformation.

   a. Show that the random variable $w = by$ is uniformly distributed on the interval $(0, b)$.

   b. Find a function of y that will be uniformly distributed on the interval (a, b).

5.21   Assume that the random variable y is uniformly distributed over the interval $a \leq y \leq b$. Verify the following:

   a. $\mu = \dfrac{a + b}{2}$ and $\sigma^2 = \dfrac{(b - a)^2}{12}$

b. $F(y) = \begin{cases} \dfrac{y-a}{b-a} & \text{if } a \le y \le b \\ 0 & \text{if } y < a \\ 1 & \text{if } y > b \end{cases}$

5.22 Show that the uniform distribution is *new better than used* (NBU) over the interval $(0, 1)$. (See Optional Exercise 5.6 for the definition of NBU.)

5.23 Assume that y is uniformly distributed over the interval $0 \le y \le 1$. Show that, for $a \ge 0$, $b \ge 0$, and $(a + b) \le 1$,

$$P(a < y < a + b) = b$$

5.5 The Normal Probability Distribution

The **normal** (or **Gaussian**) **density function** was proposed by C. F. Gauss (1777–1855) as a model for the relative frequency distribution of *errors*, such as errors of measurement. Amazingly, this bell-shaped curve provides an adequate model for the relative frequency distributions of data collected from many different scientific areas and, as we will show in Chapter 7, it models the probability distributions of many statistics that we will use for making inferences.

The normal random variable possesses a density function characterized by two parameters. This density function, its mean, and its variance are shown in the box.

The Normal Probability Distribution

$$f(y) = \frac{1}{\sigma\sqrt{2\pi}} e^{-(y-\mu)^2/(2\sigma^2)} \qquad -\infty < y < \infty$$

The parameters μ and σ^2 are the mean and variance, respectively, of the normal random variable y.

There is an infinite number of normal density functions—one for each combination of μ and σ. The mean μ measures the location of the distribution and the standard deviation σ measures its spread. Several different normal density functions are shown in Figure 5.12 on page 222.

FIGURE 5.12 ▶
Several normal distributions, with
different means and standard
deviations

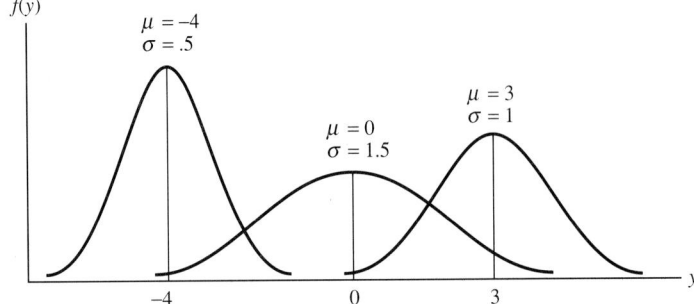

A closed-form expression cannot be obtained for the integral of the normal density function. However, areas under the normal curve can be obtained by using approximation procedures and Theorem 5.4.

Theorem 5.4

If y is a normal random variable with mean μ and variance σ^2, then $z = \dfrac{y - \mu}{\sigma}$ is a normal random variable with mean 0 and variance 1.[*] The random variable z is called a **standard normal variable**.

The areas for the **standard normal variable**,

$$z = \frac{y - \mu}{\sigma}$$

are given in Table 4 of Appendix II. Recall from Section 2.6 that z is the distance between the value of the normal random variable y and its mean μ, measured in units of its standard deviation σ.

The entries in Table 4 of Appendix II are the areas under the normal curve between the mean, $z = 0$, and a value of z to the right of the mean (see Figure 5.13). To find the area under the normal curve between $z = 0$ and, say, $z = 1.33$, move down the left column of Table 4 to the row corresponding to $z = 1.3$. Then move across the top of the table to the column marked .03. The entry at the intersection of this row and column gives the area A = .4082. Because the normal curve is symmetric about the mean, areas to the left of the mean are equal to the corresponding areas to the right of the mean. For example, the area A between the mean $z = 0$ and $z = -.68$ is equal to the area between $z = 0$ and $z = .68$. This area will be found in Table 4 at the intersection of the row corresponding to 0.6 and the column corresponding to .08 as A = .2517.

---

[*]The proof that the mean and variance of z are 0 and 1, respectively, is left as an optional exercise.

FIGURE 5.13 ▶
Standard normal density function
showing the tabulated areas given
in Table 4 of Appendix II

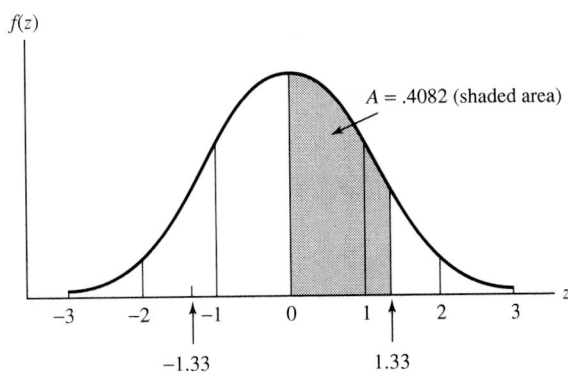

$A = .4082$ (shaded area)

-1.33

1.33

EXAMPLE 5.8

Suppose y is a normally distributed random variable with mean 10 and standard deviation 2.1.

a. Find $P(y \geq 11)$.

b. Find $P(7.6 \leq y \leq 12.2)$.

Solution

a. The value $y = 11$ corresponds to a z value of

$$z = \frac{y - \mu}{\sigma} = \frac{11 - 10}{2.1} = .48$$

FIGURE 5.14 ▶
Standard normal distribution for
Example 5.8; shaded area is
$P(y \geq 11)$

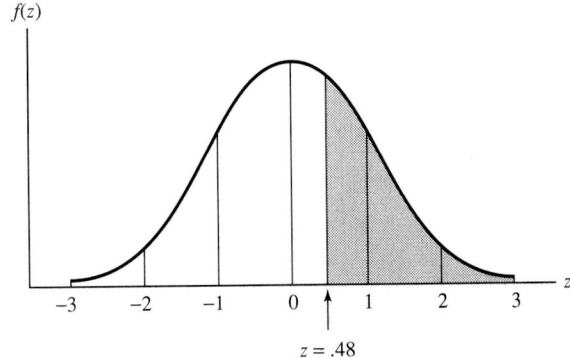

$z = .48$

and thus, $P(y \geq 11) = P(z \geq .48)$. The area under the standard normal curve corresponding to this probability is shaded in Figure 5.14. Since the normal curve is symmetric about $z = 0$ and the total area beneath the curve is 1, the area to the right of $z = 0$ is equal to .5. Thus, the shaded area is equal to $(.5 - A)$, where A is the tabulated area corresponding to $z = .48$. The area A, given in Table 4 of Appendix II, is .1844. Therefore,

$$P(y \geq 11) = .5 - A = .5 - .1844 = .3156$$

b. The values $y_1 = 7.6$ and $y_2 = 12.2$ correspond to the z values

$$z_1 = \frac{y_1 - \mu}{\sigma} = \frac{7.6 - 10}{2.1} = -1.14$$

$$z_2 = \frac{y_2 - \mu}{\sigma} = \frac{12.2 - 10}{2.1} = 1.05$$

The probability $P(7.6 \le y \le 12.2) = P(-1.14 \le z \le 1.05)$ is the shaded area shown in Figure 5.15. It is equal to the sum of A_1 and A_2, the areas corresponding to z_1 and z_2, respectively, where $A_1 = .3729$ and $A_2 = .3531$. Therefore,

$$P(7.6 \le y \le 12.2) = A_1 + A_2 = .3729 + .3531 = .7260$$

FIGURE 5.15 ▶
Standard normal distribution for
Example 5.8

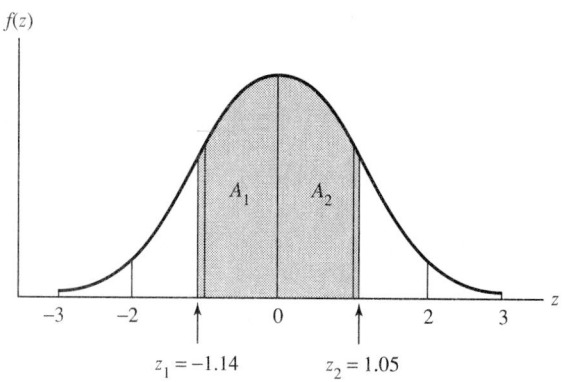

$f(z)$

$z_1 = -1.14$ $z_2 = 1.05$

EXAMPLE 5.9

The U.S. Department of Agriculture (USDA) has recently patented a process that uses a bacterium for removing bitterness from citrus juices (*Chemical Engineering*, Feb. 3, 1986). In theory, almost all the bitterness could be removed by the process, but for practical purposes the USDA aims at 50% overall removal. Suppose a USDA spokesman claims that the percentage of bitterness removed from an 8-ounce glass of freshly squeezed citrus juice is normally distributed with mean 50.1 and standard deviation 10.4. To test this claim, the bitterness removal process is applied to a randomly selected 8-ounce glass of citrus juice. Find the probability that the process removes less than 33.7% of the bitterness.

Solution

The value $y = 33.7$ corresponds to the value of the standard normal random variable:

$$z = \frac{y - \mu}{\sigma} = \frac{33.7 - 50.1}{10.4} = -1.58$$

Therefore, $P(y \le 33.7) = P(z \le -1.58)$, the shaded area in Figure 5.16, is equal to .5 minus the area A that corresponds to $z = 1.58$. Therefore, the probability that the process removes less than 33.7% of the bitterness is

$$P(y \le 33.7) = .5 - .4429 = .0571$$

FIGURE 5.16 ▶
The probability that percentage of bitterness removed is less than 33.7% in Example 5.9

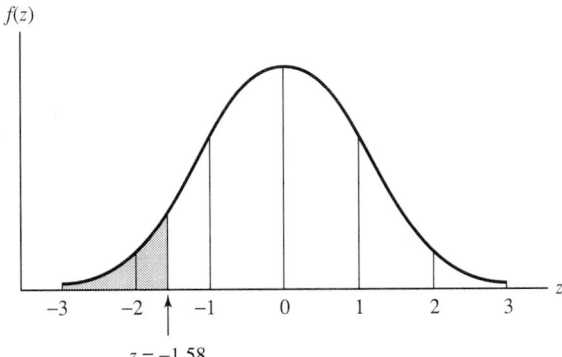

EXAMPLE 5.10

Refer to Example 5.9. If the test on the single glass of citrus juice yielded a bitterness removal percentage of 33.7, would you tend to doubt the USDA spokesman's claim?

Solution

Given the sample information, we have several choices. We could conclude that the spokesman's claim is true, i.e., that the mean percentage of bitterness removed for the new process is 50.1% and that we have just observed a *rare event*, one that would occur with a probability of only .0571. Or, we could conclude that the spokesman's claim for the mean percentage is too high, i.e., that the true mean is less than 50.1%. Or, perhaps the assumed value of σ or the assumption of normality may be in error. Given a choice, we think you will agree that there is reason to doubt the USDA spokesman's claim.

EXERCISES

5.24   Use Table 4 of Appendix II to find the following probabilities for a standard normal random variable:
a. $P(.5 < z < 1.5)$ b. $P(-1.75 < z < -.28)$ c. $P(-2.32 < z < .11)$
d. $P(z > .27)$ e. $P(z < -1.33)$ f. $P(z < 1.71)$

5.25   Find the value of the standard normal random variable z, call it z_0, such that:
a. $P(z > z_0) = .05$ b. $P(z > z_0) = .025$ c. $P(z > z_0) = .80$
d. $P(z < z_0) = .0013$ e. $P(z < z_0) = .97$ f. $P(z < z_0) = .5596$

5.26   Refer to the *Journal of Engineering for Industry* (May 1993) study of feed paper separation, Exercise 5.13. Assume the friction coefficient for a certain copier system is normally distributed, with $\mu = .55$ and $\sigma = .013$. (Higher coefficients correspond to a higher degree of friction.) During system operation, the friction coefficient is measured at a randomly selected time.
a. Find the probability that the friction coefficient falls between .53 and .56.
b. Is it likely to observe a friction coefficient below .50? Explain.

5.27   In a laboratory experiment, researchers at Barry University (Miami Shores, Florida) studied the rate at which sea urchins ingested turtle grass (*Florida Scientist*, Summer/Autumn 1991). The urchins, starved for 48 hours, were fed 5-cm. blades of green turtle grass. The mean ingestion time was found to be 2.83 hours and the standard deviation was .79 hour. Assume that green turtle grass ingestion time for the sea urchins has an approximate normal distribution.

    a. Find the probability that a sea urchin will require 4 or more hours to ingest a 5-cm. blade of green turtle grass.

    b. Find the probability that a sea urchin will require between 2 and 3 hours to ingest a 5-cm. blade of green turtle grass.

5.28   Paleomagnetic studies of Canadian volcanic rock known as the Carmacks Group have recently been completed. The studies revealed that the northward displacement of the rock units has an approximately normal distribution with standard deviation of 500 kilometers (*Canadian Journal of Earth Sciences*, Vol. 27, 1990). One group of researchers estimated the mean displacement at 1,500 km, whereas a second group estimated the mean at 1,200 km.

    a. Assuming the mean is 1,500 km, what is the probability of a northward displacement of less than 500 km?

    b. Assuming the mean is 1,200 km, what is the probability of a northward displacement of less than 500 km?

    c. If, in fact, the northward displacement is less than 500 km, which is the more plausible mean, 1,200 or 1,500 km?

5.29   Pacemakers are used to control the heartbeat of cardiac patients, with over 120,000 of the devices implanted each year. A single pacemaker is made up of several biomedical components that must be of a high quality for the pacemaker to work. It is vitally important for manufacturers of pacemakers to use parts that meet specifications. One particular plastic part, called a connector module, mounts on the top of the pacemaker. Connector modules are required to have a length between .304 inch and .322 inch to work properly. Any module with length outside these limits are "out-of-spec." *Quality* (Aug. 1989) reported on one supplier of connector modules that had been shipping out-of-spec parts to the manufacturer for 12 months.

    a. The lengths of the connector modules produced by the supplier were found to follow an approximate normal distribution with mean $\mu = .3015$ inch and standard deviation $\sigma = .0016$ inch. Use this information to find the probability that the supplier produces an out-of-spec part.

    b. Once the problem was detected, the supplier's inspection crew began to employ an automated data-collection system designed to improve product quality. After two months, the process was producing connector modules with mean $\mu = .3146$ inch and standard deviation $\sigma = .0030$ inch. Find the probability that an out-of-spec part will be produced. Compare your answer to part **a**.

5.30   Steel used for water pipelines is often coated on the inside with cement mortar to prevent corrosion. In a study of the mortar coatings of a pipeline used in a water transmission project in California (*Transportation Engineering Journal*, Nov. 1979), the mortar thickness was specified to be $\frac{7}{16}$ inch. A very large number of thickness measurements produced a mean equal to .635 inch and a standard deviation equal to .082 inch. If the thickness measurements were normally distributed, approximately what percentage were less than $\frac{7}{16}$ inch?

5.31   A standard fluorescent tube has a lifelength that is normally distributed with a mean of 7,000 hours and a standard deviation of 1,000 hours. A competitor has developed a compact fluorescent lighting system that will fit into incandescent sockets. It claims that the new compact tube has a normally distributed lifelength with a mean of 7,500 hours and a standard deviation of 1,200 hours.

a. Which fluorescent tube is more likely to have a lifelength greater than 9,000 hours?

b. Which tube is more likely to have a lifelength less than 5,000 hours?

5.32 The distribution of the demand (in number of units per unit time) for a product can often be approximated by a normal probability distribution. For example, a communication cable company has determined that the number of push-button terminal switches demanded daily has a normal distribution with mean 200 and standard deviation 50.

a. On what percentage of days will the demand be less than 90 switches?

b. On what percentage of days will the demand fall between 225 and 275 switches?

c. Based on cost considerations, the company has determined that its best strategy is to produce a sufficient number of switches so that it will fully supply demand on 94% of all days. How many terminal switches should the company produce per day?

5.33 Refer to the *Journal of the Acoustical Society of America* (Feb. 1986) study of auditory nerve response rates in cats, discussed in Exercise 4.73. A key question addressed by the research is whether rate changes (i.e., changes in number of spikes per burst of noise) produced by tones in the presence of background noise are large enough to detect reliably. That is, can the tone be detected reliably when background noise is present? In the theory of signal detection, the problem involves a comparison of two probability distributions. Let y represent the auditory nerve response rate (i.e., the number of spikes observed) under two conditions: when the stimulus is background noise only (N) and when the stimulus is a tone plus background noise (T). The probability distributions for y under the two conditions are represented by the density functions, $f_N(y)$ and $f_T(y)$, respectively, where we assume that the mean response rate under the background-noise-only condition is less than the mean response rate under the tone-plus-noise condition, i.e., $\mu_N < \mu_T$. In this situation, an observer sets a threshold C and decides that a tone is present if $y \geq C$ and decides that no tone is present if $y < C$. Assume that $f_N(y)$ and $f_T(y)$ are both normal density functions with means $\mu_N = 10.1$ spikes per burst and $\mu_T = 13.6$ spikes per burst, respectively, and equal variances $\sigma_N^2 = \sigma_T^2 = 2$.

a. For a threshold of $C = 11$ spikes per burst, find the probability of detecting the tone given that the tone is present. (This is known as the *detection probability.*)

b. For a threshold of $C = 11$ spikes per burst, find the probability of detecting the tone given that only background noise is present. (This is known as the *probability of false alarm.*)

c. Usually, it is desirable to maximize detection probability while minimizing false alarm probability. Can you find a value of C that will both increase the detection probability (part **a**) and decrease the probability of false alarm (part **b**)?

OPTIONAL EXERCISE

5.34 Let y be a normal random variable with mean μ and variance σ^2. Show that

$$z = \frac{y - \mu}{\sigma}$$

has mean 0 and variance 1. [*Hint:* Apply Theorems 5.1–5.2.]

5.6   Descriptive Methods for Assessing Normality

In the chapters that follow, we learn how to make inferences about the population based on information in the sample. Several of these techniques are based on the assumption that the population is approximately distributed. Consequently, it will be important to determine whether the sample data come from a normal population before we can properly apply these techniques.

Several descriptive methods can be used to check for normality. In this section, we consider the three methods summarized in the box.

Determining Whether the Data Are from an Approximately Normal Distribution

1. Construct either a **relative frequency histogram** or a **stem-and-leaf** display for the data. If the data are approximately normal, the shape of the graph will be similar to the normal curve, Figure 5.12 (i.e., mound-shaped and symmetric about the mean).

2. Find the **interquartile range, IQR**, and **standard deviation, s**, for the sample, then calculate the ratio IQR/s. If the data are approximately normal, then IQR/$s \approx 1.3$.

3. Construct a **normal probability plot** for the data. (See the following box.) If the data are approximately normal, the points will fall (approximately) on a straight line.

EXAMPLE 5.11

Each year the Federal Trade Commission (FTC) ranks American cigarette brands in terms of the amount of carbon monoxide, tar, and nicotine in their smoke. The FTC uses a 20-part sequential smoking machine to "smoke" cigarettes to a 23-millimeter butt length. Based on tests of 100 cigarettes per brand, the carbon monoxide, tar, and nicotine concentrations (in milligrams) in the residual *dry* particulate matter are determined. The results of the FTC's tests of 372 cigarette brands for a recent year are provided in Appendix VI. Numerical and graphical descriptive measures for the 372 tar contents are shown in the SAS printouts, Figures 5.17a–c. Determine whether the tar contents have an approximately normal distribution.

Solution

As a first check, we examine the horizontal frequency histogram of the data shown in Figure 5.17b. Clearly, the tar contents fall in an approximately mound-shaped, symmetric distribution centered around the mean of 11.60 milligrams. Thus, from check 1 in the box, the data appear to be approximately normal.

a. SAS descriptive statistics for tar contents of Appendix VI

FIGURE 5.17 ▶
SAS descriptive statistics for
Example 5.11

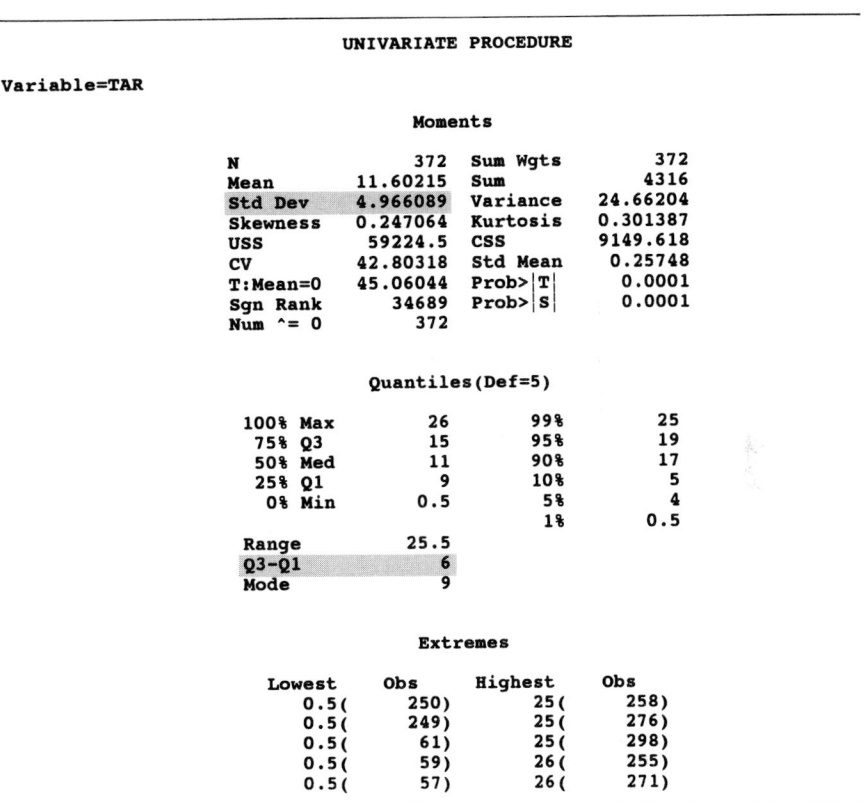

```
                         UNIVARIATE PROCEDURE

Variable=TAR

                              Moments

           N                372   Sum Wgts         372
           Mean        11.60215   Sum             4316
           Std Dev      4.966089   Variance    24.66204
           Skewness    0.247064   Kurtosis    0.301387
           USS          59224.5   CSS         9149.618
           CV          42.80318   Std Mean     0.25748
           T:Mean=0    45.06044   Prob>|T|      0.0001
           Sgn Rank       34689   Prob>|S|      0.0001
           Num ^= 0        372


                          Quantiles(Def=5)

           100% Max          26        99%          25
            75% Q3           15        95%          19
            50% Med          11        90%          17
            25% Q1            9        10%           5
             0% Min        0.5         5%           4
                                       1%         0.5

           Range          25.5
           Q3-Q1             6
           Mode             9


                             Extremes

           Lowest      Obs    Highest    Obs
            0.5(      250)        25(    258)
            0.5(      249)        25(    276)
            0.5(       61)        25(    298)
            0.5(       59)        26(    255)
            0.5(       57)        26(    271)
```

b. SAS histogram and box plot for tar contents of Appendix VI

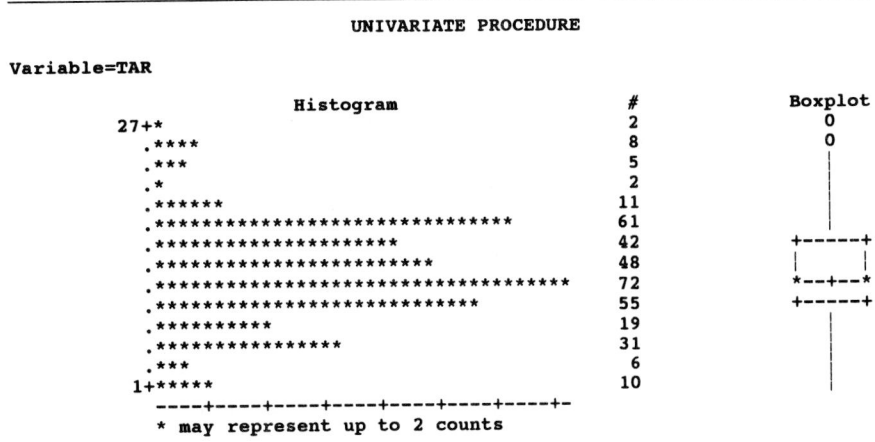

```
                         UNIVARIATE PROCEDURE

Variable=TAR

                   Histogram                    #         Boxplot
       27+*                                     2            0
         .****                                  8            0
         .***                                   5            |
         .*                                      2           |
         .******                                11           |
         .******************************       61           |
         .********************              42      +-----+
         .***********************           48      |     |
         .************************************ 72   *--+--*
         .****************************** 55         +-----+
         .*********                         19           |
         .****************                  31           |
         .***                                6           |
        1+*****                             10           |
         ----+----+----+----+----+----+----+-
         * may represent up to 2 counts
```

c. SAS normal probability plot for tar contents of Appendix VI

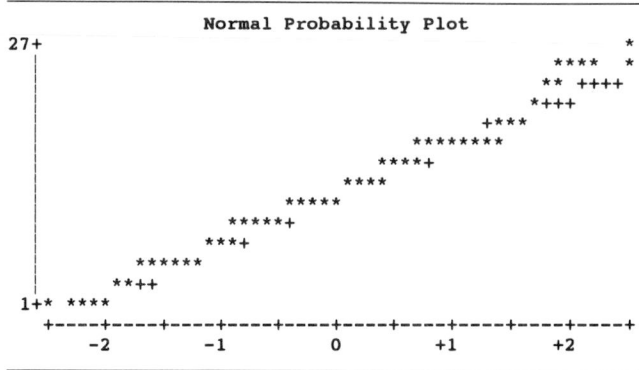

Check 2 in the box requires that we find the interquartile range (i.e., the difference between the 75th and 25th percentiles) and the standard deviation of the data set, and compute the ratio of these two numbers. The ratio IQR/s for a sample from a normal distribution will approximately equal 1.3.* The values of IQR and s, shaded in Figure 5.17a, are IQR $= Q_U - Q_L = 6$ and $s = 4.966$. Then the ratio is

$$\frac{IQR}{s} = \frac{6}{4.966} = 1.21$$

Since this value is approximately equal to 1.3, we have further confirmation that the data are approximately normal.

A third descriptive technique for checking normality is a **normal probability plot**. In a normal probability plot, the observations in the data set are ordered and then plotted against the sandardized expected values of the observations under the assumption that the data are normally distributed. When the data are, in fact, normally distributed, an observation will approximately equal its expected value. Thus, a linear (straight-line) trend on the normal probability plot suggests that the data are from an approximate normal distribution, whereas a nonlinear trend indicates that the data are nonnormal.

Normal probability plots can be constructed by hand, as shown in the box. However, it is easier to generate these plots by computer. A SAS normal probability plot for the 372 tar measurements is shown in Figure 5.17c. Notice that the ordered measurements (represented by the plotting symbol "*") fall reasonably close to a straight line (plotting symbol "+"). Thus, check 3 also suggests that the data are likely to be approximately normally distributed.

. . . .

---

*You can see that this property holds for normal distributions by noting that the z values (obtained from Table 4 in Appendix II) corresponding to the 75th and 25th percentiles are .67 and $-.67$, respectively. Since $\sigma = 1$ for a standard normal (z) distribution, IQR/$\sigma = [.67 - (-.67)]/1 = 1.34$.

Constructing a Normal Probability Plot for a Data Set

1. List the observations in the sample data set in ascending order, where x_i represents the ith ordered value.

2. For each observation, calculate the corresponding tail area of the standard normal (z) distribution,

$$A = \frac{i - .375}{n + .25}$$

where n is the sample size.

3. Calculate the estimated expected value of x_i under normality using the following formula:

$$E(x_i) = (s)[Z(A)]$$

where s is the sample standard deviation and $Z(A)$ is the z value that cuts off an area A in the lower tail of the standard normal distribution.

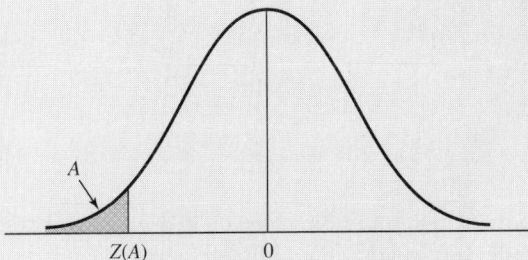

4. Plot the ordered observations x_i on the vertical axis and the corresponding estimated expected values, $E(x_i)$, on the horizontal axis.

The checks for normality given in the box are simple, yet powerful, techniques to apply, but they are only descriptive in nature. It is possible (although unlikely) that the data are nonnormal even when the checks are reasonably satisfied. Thus, we should be careful not to claim that the 372 tar measurements in Appendix VI are, in fact, normally distributed. We can only state that it is reasonable to believe that the data are from a normal distribution.*

---

*Statistical tests of normality that provide a measure of reliability for the inference are available. However, these tests tend to be very sensitive to slight departures from normality, i.e., they tend to reject the hypothesis of normality for any distribution that is not perfectly symmetrical and mound-shaped. Consult the references if you want to learn more about these tests.

EXERCISES

5.35   Foresters periodically "cruise" a forest to determine the size (usually measured as the diameter at breast height) of a certain species of trees. The breast height diameters (in meters) for a sample of 28 trembling aspen trees in British Columbia's boreal forest are listed here. Determine whether the sample data are from an approximately normal distribution.

12.4	17.3	27.3	19.1	16.9	16.2	20.0
16.6	16.3	16.3	21.4	25.7	15.0	19.3
12.9	18.6	12.4	15.9	18.8	14.9	12.8
24.8	26.9	13.5	17.9	13.2	23.2	12.7

Source: Scholz, H. "Fish Creek Community Forest: Exploratory statistical analysis of selected data," working paper, Northern Lights College, British Columbia, Canada.

5.36   The data on spectral image exposures of asteroids, Exercise 2.10, is reproduced here. Determine whether the data are approximately normal.

Number of Independent Spectral Image Exposures for 40 Asteroid Observations

3	4	3	3	1	4	1	3	2	3
1	1	4	2	3	3	2	6	1	1
3	3	2	2	2	2	1	3	2	1
6	1	3	2	2	1	2	2	4	2

Source: Binzel, R. P., and Xu, S. "Chips off of Asteroid 4 Vesta: Evidence for the parent body of basaltic achondrite meteorites." *Science*, Vol. 260, Apr. 3, 1993, p. 187 (Table 1).

5.37   A histogram describing the length (in millimeters) of 50 drill chips, Exercise 2.11, is reproduced here. Does it appear that the 50 drill chip lengths come from an approximately normal population?

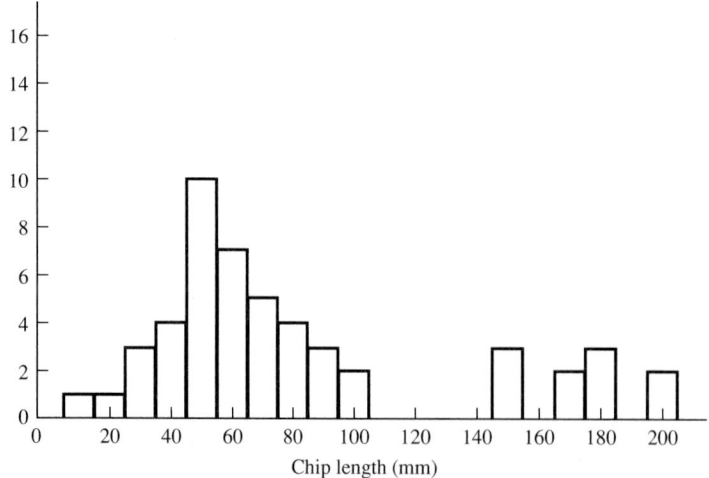

Source: Chin, Jih-Hua et al. "The computer simulation and experimental analysis of chip monitoring for deep hole drilling." *Journal of Engineering for Industry, Transactions of the ASME*, Vol. 115, May 1993, p. 187 (Figure 12).

5.38   The Harris Corporation data on voltage readings at two locations, Exercise 2.12, are reproduced here. Determine whether the voltage readings at each location are approximately normal.

Old Location			New Location		
9.98	10.12	9.84	9.19	10.01	8.82
10.26	10.05	10.15	9.63	8.82	8.65
10.05	9.80	10.02	10.10	9.43	8.51
10.29	10.15	9.80	9.70	10.03	9.14
10.03	10.00	9.73	10.09	9.85	9.75
8.05	9.87	10.01	9.60	9.27	8.78
10.55	9.55	9.98	10.05	8.83	9.35
10.26	9.95	8.72	10.12	9.39	9.54
9.97	9.70	8.80	9.49	9.48	9.36
9.87	8.72	9.84	9.37	9.64	8.68

Source: Harris Corporation, Melbourne, Fla.

5.39   Refer to the *U.S. News & World Report* survey of the top 25 graduate schools of engineering, Exercise 2.18. MINITAB stem-and-leaf displays for the five variables recorded in the survey (overall score, enrollment, research funds, student/faculty ratio, and acceptance rate) are reproduced here. Which of the variables appears to have an approximately normal distribution?

```
Stem-and-leaf of SCORE      N  = 25
Leaf Unit = 1.0

    6      5  566779
   10      6  1223
   (4)     6  6677
   11      7  012
    8      7  569
    5      8  014
    2      8  7
    1      9
    1      9
    1     10  0



Stem-and-leaf of ENROLL     N  = 25
Leaf Unit = 100

    1      0  3
    2      0  4
    2      0
    4      0  89
    6      1  00
   11      1  22223
   (3)     1  555
   11      1  7
   10      1
   10      2  0001
    6      2  2233
    2      2  5
    1      2  6
```

(*continued*)

Stem-and-leaf displays
for Exercise 5.39
(continued)

```
Stem-and-leaf of RESEARCH   N  = 25
Leaf Unit = 1000000

    1     1 5
    6     2 12379
    9     3 458
   (4)    4 0249
   12     5 2357889
    5     6 233
    2     7
    2     8 0
    1     9
    1    10
    1    11
    1    12
    1    13 2
```

```
Stem-and-leaf of RATIO      N  = 25
Leaf Unit = 0.10

    2     1 24
    6     1 7789
   (7)    2 0233344
   12     2 55678
    7     3 23
    5     3 7
    4     4
    4     4 68
    2     5 2
    1     5
    1     6 3
```

```
Stem-and-leaf of ACCRATE    N  = 25
Leaf Unit = 1.0

    2     1 23
    2     1
    6     2 0344
   11     2 66677
   12     3 2
   (2)    3 88
   11     4 0333
    7     4 6889
    3     5
    3     5
    3     6 02
    1     6 7
```

5.40   The data on percentage iron in 66 bulk specimens of Chilean lumpy iron ore, Exercise 2.25, are reproduced here. Assess whether the data are approximately normal.

Ore Specimen	Percentage Iron	Ore Specimen	Percentage Iron	Ore Specimen	Percentage Iron
1	62.66	23	61.82	45	62.24
2	62.87	24	63.01	46	63.43
3	63.22	25	63.01	47	62.87
4	63.01	26	62.80	48	63.64
5	62.10	27	62.80	49	63.92
6	63.43	28	63.01	50	63.71
7	63.22	29	62.10	51	63.64
8	63.57	30	63.29	52	64.06
9	61.75	31	63.37	53	62.73
10	63.15	32	61.75	54	62.52
11	63.08	33	63.29	55	62.10
12	63.22	34	62.38	56	63.29
13	63.22	35	62.59	57	63.01
14	63.08	36	63.92	58	63.36
15	62.87	37	63.29	59	63.08
16	61.68	38	63.57	60	62.03
17	62.45	39	62.80	61	64.34
18	62.10	40	62.31	62	64.06
19	62.87	41	63.01	63	62.87
20	62.87	42	62.94	64	63.50
21	62.94	43	63.08	65	63.78
22	62.38	44	63.43	66	62.10

Source: Sato, T., Ito, K., Chujo, S., and Takahashi, U. "Example of experiments on systematic sampling of iron ore." *Reports of Statistical Application Research*, Union of Japanese Scientists and Engineers, Vol. 18, No. 1, 1971.

5.7   Gamma-Type Probability Distributions

Many random variables, such as the length of the useful life of a computer, can assume only nonnegative values. The relative frequency distributions for data of this type can often be modeled by **gamma-type density functions**. The formulas for a gamma density function, its mean, and its variance are shown in the box.

The formula for the gamma density function contains two parameters, α and β. The parameter β, known as a **scale parameter**, reflects the size of the units in which y is measured. (It performs the same function as the parameter σ that appears in the formula for the normal density function.) The parameter α is known as a **shape parameter**. Changing its value changes the shape of the gamma distribution. This enables us to obtain density functions of many different shapes to model relative frequency distributions of experimental data. Computer graphs of the gamma density function for $\alpha = 1$, 3, and 5, with $\beta = 1$, are shown in Figure 5.18 on page 236.

The Gamma Probability Distribution

The probability density function for a gamma-type random variable is given by

$$f(y) = \begin{cases} \dfrac{y^{\alpha-1}e^{-y/\beta}}{\beta^{\alpha}\Gamma(\alpha)} & \text{if } 0 \le y < \infty; \ \alpha > 0; \ \beta > 0 \\ 0 & \text{elsewhere} \end{cases}$$

where

$$\Gamma(\alpha) = \int_{0}^{\infty} y^{\alpha-1}e^{-y}\, dy$$

The mean and variance of a gamma-type random variable are, respectively,

$$\mu = \alpha\beta \qquad \sigma^2 = \alpha\beta^2$$

It can be shown (proof omitted) that $\Gamma(\alpha) = (\alpha - 1)\Gamma(\alpha - 1)$ and that $\Gamma(\alpha) = (\alpha - 1)!$ when α is a positive integer. Values of $\Gamma(\alpha)$ for $1.0 \le \alpha \le 2.0$ are presented in Table 5 of Appendix II.

FIGURE 5.18 ▼
Graphs of gamma density functions for $\alpha = 1$, 3, and 5; $\beta = 1$

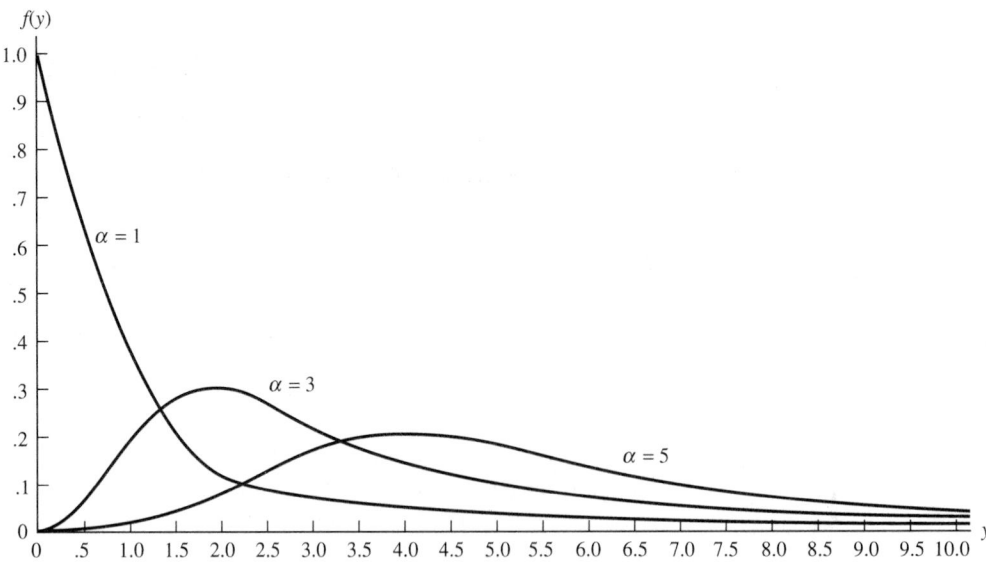

Except for the special case where α is an integer, we cannot obtain a closed-form expression for the integral of the gamma density function. Consequently, the cumulative distribution function for a gamma random variable, called an **incomplete gamma function**, must be obtained using approximation procedures with the aid of a computer. Values of this function are given in *Tables of the Incomplete Gamma Function* (1956).

A gamma-type random variable that plays an important role in statistics is the **chi-square random variable**. Chi-square values and corresponding areas under the chi-square density function are given in Table 8 of Appendix II. We will discuss the use of this table in Chapter 8.

When $\alpha = 1$, the gamma density function is known as an *exponential distribution*.* This important density function is employed as a model for the relative frequency distribution of the length of time between arrivals at a service counter (computer center, supermarket checkout counter, hospital clinic, etc.) when the probability of a customer arrival in any one unit of time is equal to the probability of arrival during any other. It is also used as a model for the length of life of industrial equipment or products when the probability that an "old" component will operate at least t additional time units, given it is now functioning, is the same as the probability that a "new" component will operate at least t time units. Equipment subject to periodic maintenance and parts replacement often exhibits this property of "never growing old."

The Chi-Square Probability Distribution

A **chi-square (χ^2) random variable** is a gamma-type random variable with $\alpha = \nu/2$ and $\beta = 2$:

$$f(\chi^2) = c(\chi^2)^{(\nu/2)-1}e^{-\chi^2/2} \qquad (0 \le \chi^2 < \infty)$$

where

$$c = \frac{1}{2^{\nu/2}\Gamma\left(\dfrac{\nu}{2}\right)}$$

The mean and variance of a chi-square random variable are, respectively,

$$\mu = \nu \qquad \sigma^2 = 2\nu$$

The parameter ν is called the **number of degrees of freedom** for the chi-square distribution.

The exponential distribution is related to the Poisson probability distribution. In fact, it can be shown (proof omitted) that if the number of arrivals at a service counter follows a Poisson probability distribution with the mean number of arrivals per unit time equal to $1/\beta$, then the density function for the length of time y between any pair of successive arrivals will be an exponential distribution with mean equal to β, i.e.,

$$f(y) = \frac{e^{-y/\beta}}{\beta} \qquad (0 \le y < \infty)$$

---

*The exponential distribution was encountered in Examples 5.5 and 5.6 of Section 5.3.

> ## The Exponential Probability Distribution
>
> An **exponential distribution** is a gamma density function with $\alpha = 1$:
>
> $$f(y) = \frac{e^{-y/\beta}}{\beta} \qquad (0 \leq y < \infty)$$
>
> with mean and variance
>
> $$\mu = \beta \qquad \sigma^2 = \beta^2$$

EXAMPLE 5.12

From past experience, a manufacturer knows that the relative frequency distribution of the length of time (in months) between major customer product complaints can be modeled by a gamma density function with $\alpha = 2$ and $\beta = 4$. Fifteen months after the manufacturer tightened its quality control requirements, the first complaint arrived. Does this suggest that the mean time between major customer complaints may have increased?

Solution

We want to determine whether the observed value of $y = 15$ months, or some larger value of y, would be improbable if, in fact, $\alpha = 2$ and $\beta = 4$. We do not give a table of areas under the gamma density function in this text, but we can obtain some idea of the magnitude of $P(y \geq 15)$ by calculating the mean and standard deviation for the gamma density function when $\alpha = 2$ and $\beta = 4$. Thus,

$$\mu = \alpha\beta = (2)(4) = 8$$
$$\sigma^2 = \alpha\beta^2 = (2)(4)^2 = 32$$
$$\sigma = 5.7$$

Since $y = 15$ months lies barely more than 1 standard deviation beyond the mean ($\mu + \sigma = 8 + 5.7 = 13.7$ months), we would not regard 15 months as an unusually large value of y. Consequently, we would conclude that there is insufficient evidence to indicate that the company's new quality control program has been effective in increasing the mean time between complaints. We will present formal statistical procedures for answering this question in later chapters.

EXAMPLE 5.13 (OPTIONAL)   Show that the mean for a gamma-type random variable is equal to $\mu = \alpha\beta$.

Solution

We first write

$$E(y) = \int_{-\infty}^{\infty} yf(y)dy = \int_{0}^{\infty} y\frac{y^{\alpha-1}e^{-y/\beta}}{\beta^{\alpha}\Gamma(\alpha)}\,dy = \int_{0}^{\infty} \frac{y^{(\alpha+1)-1}e^{-y/\beta}}{\beta^{\alpha}\Gamma(\alpha)}\,dy$$

Multiplying and dividing the integrand by $\alpha\beta$ and using the fact that $\Gamma(\alpha) = (\alpha - 1)\Gamma(\alpha - 1)$, we obtain

$$E(y) = \alpha\beta \int_0^\infty \frac{y^{(\alpha+1)-1}e^{-y/\beta}}{(\alpha\beta)\beta^\alpha\Gamma(\alpha)} \, dy = \alpha\beta \int_0^\infty \frac{y^{(\alpha+1)-1}e^{-y/\beta}}{\beta^{\alpha+1}\Gamma(\alpha + 1)} \, dy$$

The integrand is a gamma density function with parameters $(\alpha + 1)$ and β. Therefore, since the integral of any density function over $-\infty < y < \infty$ is equal to 1, we conclude

$$E(y) = \alpha\beta(1) = \alpha\beta$$

EXERCISES

5.41   Suppose a random variable y has a probability distribution given by

$$f(y) = \begin{cases} cy^2e^{-y/2} & \text{if } y > 0 \\ 0 & \text{elsewhere} \end{cases}$$

Find the value of c that makes $f(y)$ a density function.

5.42   Researchers have discovered that the maximum flood level (in millions of cubic feet per second) over a 4-year period for the Susquehanna River at Harrisburg, Pennsylvania, follows approximately a gamma distribution with $\alpha = 3$ and $\beta = .07$ (*Journal of Quality Technology*, Jan. 1986).
   a.   Find the mean and variance of the maximum flood level over a 4-year period for the Susquehanna River.
   b.   The researchers arrived at their conclusions about the maximum flood level distribution by observing maximum flood levels over 20 4-year periods, from 1890–1969. Suppose that over the 4-year period 1982–1985 the maximum flood level was observed to be .60 million cubic feet per second. Would you expect to observe a value this high from a gamma distribution with $\alpha = 3$ and $\beta = .07$? What can you infer about the maximum flood level distribution for the 4-year period 1982–1985?

5.43   The lifetime y (in hours) of the central processing unit of a certain type of microcomputer is an exponential random variable with parameter $\beta = 1,000$.
   a.   Find the mean and variance of the lifetime of the central processing unit.
   b.   What is the probability that a central processing unit will have a lifetime of at least 2,000 hours?
   c.   What is the probability that a central processing unit will have a lifetime of at most 1,500 hours?

5.44   A part processed in a flexible manufacturing system (FMS) is routed through a set of operations, some of which are sequential and some of which are parallel. In addition, an FMS operation can be processed by alternative machines. An article in *IEEE Transactions* (Mar. 1990) gave an example of an FMS with four machines operating independently. The repair rates for the machines (i.e., the time, in hours, it takes to repair a failed machine) are exponentially distributed with means $\mu_1 = 1$, $\mu_2 = 2$, $\mu_3 = .5$, and $\mu_4 = .5$, respectively.
   a.   Find the probability that the repair time for machine 1 exceeds 1 hour.
   b.   Repeat part **a** for machine 2.

c. Repeat part **a** for machines 3 and 4.

d. If all four machines fail simultaneously, find the probability that the repair time for the entire system exceeds 1 hour.

5.45   In finding and correcting errors in a computer program (*debugging*) and determining the program's reliability, computer software experts have noted the importance of the distribution of the time until the next program error is found. Suppose that this random variable has a gamma distribution with parameter $\alpha = 1$. One computer programmer believes that the mean time between finding program errors is $\beta = 24$ days. Suppose that a programming error is found today.

a. Assuming that $\beta = 24$, find the probability that it will take at least 60 days to discover the next programming error.

b. If the next programming error takes at least 60 days to find, what would you infer about the programmer's claim that the mean time between the detection of programming errors is $\beta = 24$ days? Why?

5.46   The length of time y (in minutes) required to generate a human reaction to tear gas formula A has a gamma distribution with $\alpha = 2$ and $\beta = 2$. The distribution for formula B is also gamma, but with $\alpha = 1$ and $\beta = 4$.

a. Find the mean length of time required to generate a human reaction to tear gas formula A. Find the mean for formula B.

b. Find the variances for both distributions.

c. Which tear gas has a higher probability of generating a human reaction in less than 1 minute? [*Hint:*   You may use the fact that

$$\int ye^{-y/2}\, dy = -2ye^{-y/2} + \int 2e^{-y/2}\, dy$$

This result is derived by integration by parts.]

5.47   Vardeman and Ray (*Technometrics*, May 1985) suggest that the number of industrial accidents can be modeled by an exponential distribution. Suppose the number of accidents per hour at an industrial plant is exponentially distributed with mean $\beta = .5$.

a. What is the probability that at least one accident will occur in a randomly selected hour at the industrial plant?

b. What is the probability that less than two accidents will occur in a randomly selected hour at the industrial plant?

OPTIONAL EXERCISES

5.48   Show that the variance of a gamma distribution with parameters α and β is $\alpha\beta^2$.

5.49   Let y have an exponential distribution with mean β. Show that $P(y > a) = e^{-a/\beta}$. [*Hint:*   Find $F(a) = P(y \le a)$.]

5.50   Refer to the concepts of *new better than used* (NBU) and *new worse than used* (NWU) in Optional Exercise 5.6. Show that the exponential distribution satisfies both the NBU and NWU properties. (Such a "life" distribution is said to be *new same as used* or *memoryless*.)

5.51   Show that $\Gamma(\alpha) = (\alpha - 1)\Gamma(\alpha - 1)$.

5.52   We have stated that a chi-square random variable has a gamma-type density with $\alpha = \nu/2$ and $\beta = 2$. Find the mean and variance of a chi-square random variable.

5.8   The Weibull Probability Distribution

In Section 5.7, we noted that the gamma density function can be used to model the distribution of the length of life (failure time) of manufactured components, equipment, etc. Another distribution used by engineers for the same purpose is known as the **Weibull distribution.** *

The Weibull Probability Distribution

$$f(y) = \begin{cases} \dfrac{\alpha}{\beta} y^{\alpha-1} e^{-y^{\alpha}/\beta} & \text{if } 0 \le y < \infty; \quad \alpha > 0; \quad \beta > 0 \\ 0 & \text{elsewhere} \end{cases}$$

$$\mu = \beta^{1/\alpha} \Gamma\left(\frac{\alpha + 1}{\alpha}\right)$$

$$\sigma^2 = \beta^{2/\alpha}\left[\Gamma\left(\frac{\alpha + 2}{\alpha}\right) - \Gamma^2\left(\frac{\alpha + 1}{\alpha}\right)\right]$$

The Weibull density function contains two parameters, α and β. The **scale parameter**, β, reflects the size of the units in which the random variable y is measured. The parameter α is the shape parameter. By changing the value of the shape parameter α, we can generate a widely varying set of curves to model real-life failure time distributions. For the case $\alpha = 1$, we obtain the exponential distribution of Section 5.7. The graphs of Weibull density functions for different values of α and β are shown in Figure 5.19 on page 242.

In addition to providing a good model for the failure time distributions of many manufactured items, the Weibull distribution is easy to use. A closed-form expression for its cumulative distribution function exists and can be used to obtain areas under the Weibull curve. Example 5.14 will illustrate the procedure.

---

*See Weibull (1951).

FIGURE 5.19 ▼
Graphs of Weibull density functions

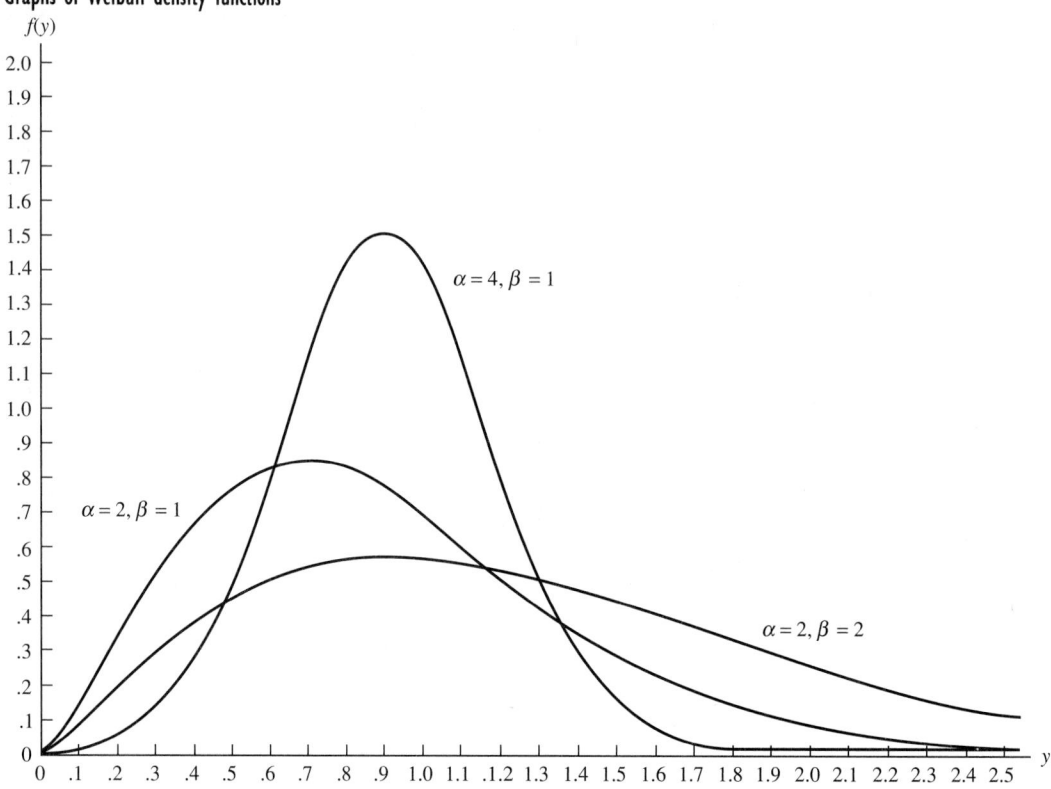

EXAMPLE 5.14

The length of life (in hours) of a drill bit used in a manufacturing operation has a Weibull distribution with $\alpha = 2$ and $\beta = 100$. Find the probability that a drill bit will fail before 8 hours of usage.

Solution

The cumulative distribution function for a Weibull distribution is

$$F(y_0) = \int_0^{y_0} f(y)dy = \int_0^{y_0} \frac{\alpha}{\beta} y^{\alpha-1} e^{-y^\alpha/\beta} \, dy$$

By making the transformation $z = y^\alpha$, we have $dz = \alpha y^{\alpha-1} \, dy$ and the integral reduces to

$$F(y_0) = 1 - e^{-z/\beta} = 1 - e^{-y_0^\alpha/\beta}$$

To find the probability that y is less than 8 hours, we calculate

$$P(y < 8) = F(8) = 1 - e^{-(8)^\alpha/\beta}$$
$$= 1 - e^{-(8)^2/100} = 1 - e^{-.64}$$

Interpolating between $e^{-.60}$ and $e^{-.65}$ in Table 2 of Appendix II, or using a calculator with the e function, we find $e^{-.64} \approx .527$. Therefore, the probability that a drill bit will fail before 8 hours is

$$P(y < 8) = 1 - e^{-.64} = 1 - .527 = .473$$

EXAMPLE 5.15

Refer to Example 5.14. Find the mean life of the drill bits.

Solution

Substituting $\alpha = 2$ and $\beta = 100$ into the formula for the mean of a Weibull random variable yields

$$\mu = \beta^{1/\alpha}\Gamma\left(\frac{\alpha + 1}{\alpha}\right) = (100)^{1/2}\Gamma\left(\frac{2 + 1}{2}\right) = 10\Gamma(1.5)$$

From Table 5 of Appendix II, we find $\Gamma(1.5) = .88623$. Therefore, the mean life of the drill bits is

$$\mu = (10)\Gamma(1.5) = (10)(.88623) = 8.8623 \approx 8.86 \text{ hours}$$

EXERCISES

5.53 Refer to Example 5.14. Calculate the values of $f(y)$ for $y = 2, 5, 8, 11, 14$, and 17. Plot the points $(y, f(y))$ and construct a graph of the failure time distribution of the drill bits.

5.54 Refer to Examples 5.14 and 5.15. Calculate the variance of the failure time distribution. Then find the probability that the length of life of a drill bit will fall within 2 hours of its mean.

5.55 Suppose the random variable y has a Weibull density function with $\alpha = 4$ and $\beta = 100$.
  a. Find $F(5)$.
  b. Find $P(y \geq 3)$.
  c. Find μ and σ.
  d. Find $P(\mu - 2\sigma \leq y \leq \mu + 2\sigma)$.

5.56 Based on extensive testing, a manufacturer of washing machines believes that the distribution of the time (in years) until a major repair is required has a Weibull distribution with $\alpha = 2$ and $\beta = 4$.
  a. If the manufacturer guarantees all machines against a major repair for 2 years, what proportion of all new washers will have to be repaired under the guarantee?
  b. Find the mean and standard deviation of the length of time until a major repair is required.
  c. Find $P(\mu - 2\sigma \leq y \leq \mu + 2\sigma)$.
  d. Is it likely that y will exceed 6 years?

5.57 *Wind models* are used in engineering design for wind energy analysis and design-limit wind speeds. A widely used model of wind speed y (in miles per second) is the Weibull density function with parameters $\alpha = 1$

and $\beta = v/2$, where v (the characteristic speed) is the 63.21 percentile of the wind speed distribution (*Atmospheric Environment*, Vol. 18, No. 10, 1984). At a particular site in Great Britain, the characteristic wind speed is known to be $v = 11.3$ miles per second. Use the Weibull wind model to find:

a. $E(y)$ and σ^2.

b. The probability that wind speed y is less than 6 miles per second.

c. The probability that wind speed y is greater than 10 miles per second.

5.58   The length of time (in months after maintenance) until failure of a bank's surveillance television equipment has a Weibull distribution with $\alpha = 2$ and $\beta = 60$. If the bank wants the probability of a breakdown before the next scheduled maintenance to be .05, how frequently should the equipment receive periodic maintenance?

5.59   Japanese electrical engineers have developed a sophisticated radar system called the moving target detector (MTD), designed to reject ground clutter, rain clutter, birds, and other interference (*IEE Proceedings*, Aug. 1984). The researchers show that the magnitude y of the Doppler frequency of a radar-received signal obeys a Weibull distribution with parameters $\alpha = 2$ and β.

a. Find $E(y)$.

b. Find σ^2.

c. Give an expression for the probability that the magnitude y of the Doppler frequency exceeds some constant C.

OPTIONAL EXERCISES

5.60   Show that for the Weibull distribution,

$$\mu = \beta^{1/\alpha}\Gamma\left(\frac{\alpha + 1}{\alpha}\right)$$

5.61   Show that for the Weibull distribution,

$$E(y^2) = \beta^{2/\alpha}\Gamma\left(\frac{\alpha + 2}{\alpha}\right)$$

Then use the relationship $\sigma^2 = E[(y - \mu)^2] = E(y^2) - \mu^2$ to show that

$$\sigma^2 = \beta^{2/\alpha}\left[\Gamma\left(\frac{\alpha + 2}{\alpha}\right) - \Gamma^2\left(\frac{\alpha + 1}{\alpha}\right)\right]$$

5.62   Show that the Weibull distribution with $\alpha = 2$ and $\beta > 0$ is *new better than used* (NBU). (See Optional Exercise 5.6 for the definition of NBU.)

5.9   Beta-Type Probability Distributions

Recall from Section 5.7 that the gamma density function provides a model for the relative frequency distribution of a random variable that possesses a fixed lower limit, but which can become infinitely large. In contrast, the **beta density function**, also characterized by two parameters, possesses finite lower and upper limits. We will give these limits as 0 and 1, but the density function, with modification, can be defined over any specified finite interval. Graphs of beta density functions for ($\alpha = 2$, $\beta = 4$), ($\alpha = 2$, $\beta = 2$), and ($\alpha = 3$, $\beta = 2$) are shown in Figure 5.20. The probability density function, the mean, and the variance for a beta-type random variable are shown in the next two boxes.

FIGURE 5.20 ▶

Graphs of beta density functions

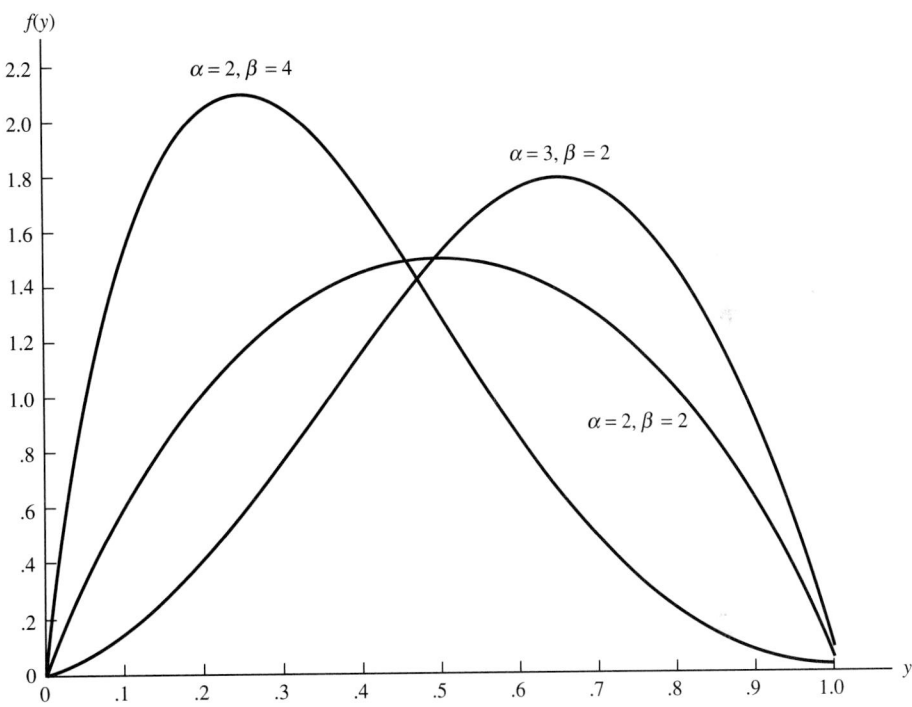

The Beta Probability Distribution

The probability density function for a beta-type random variable is given by

$$f(y) = \begin{cases} \dfrac{y^{\alpha-1}(1-y)^{\beta-1}}{B(\alpha,\ \beta)} & \text{if } 0 \le y \le 1;\ \alpha > 0;\ \beta > 0 \\ 0 & \text{elsewhere} \end{cases}$$

where

$$B(\alpha,\ \beta) = \int_0^1 y^{\alpha-1}(1-y)^{\beta-1}\ dy = \frac{\Gamma(\alpha)\Gamma(\beta)}{\Gamma(\alpha+\beta)}$$

(*continued*)

The mean and variance of a beta random variable are, respectively,

$$\mu = \frac{\alpha}{\alpha + \beta} \qquad \sigma^2 = \frac{\alpha\beta}{(\alpha + \beta)^2(\alpha + \beta + 1)}$$

[Recall that

$$\Gamma(a) = \int_0^\infty y^{a-1}e^{-y}\,dy$$

and $\Gamma(\alpha) = (\alpha - 1)!$ when α is a positive integer.]

EXAMPLE 5.16

Infrared sensors in a computerized robotic system send information to other sensors in different formats. The percentage y of signals sent that are directly compatible for all sensors in the system follows a beta distribution with $\alpha = \beta = 2$.

a. Find the probability that more than 30% of the infrared signals sent in the system are directly compatible for all sensors.

b. Find the mean and variance of y.

Solution

a. From the box, the probability density function for y is given as

$$f(y) = \frac{y^{\alpha-1}(1 - y)^{\beta-1}}{B(\alpha, \beta)} = \frac{\Gamma(\alpha + \beta)}{\Gamma(\alpha)\Gamma(\beta)} y^{\alpha-1}(1 - y)^{\beta-1}, \; 0 \le y \le 1$$

Substituting $\alpha = \beta = 2$ into the expression for $f(y)$, we obtain

$$f(y) = \frac{\Gamma(2 + 2)y^{2-1}(1 - y)^{2-1}}{\Gamma(2)\Gamma(2)} = \frac{(3!)y(1 - y)}{(1!)(1!)}$$

$$= 6y(1 - y)$$

The probability we seek is $P(y > .30)$. Integrating $f(y)$, we obtain

$$P(y > .30) = \int_{.30}^1 6y(1 - y)dy = 6\int_{.30}^1 (y - y^2)dy$$

$$= 6\left\{\int_{.30}^1 y\,dy - \int_{.30}^1 y^2\,dy\right\} = 6\left\{\left[y^2/2\right]_{.30}^1 - y^3/3\Big]_{.30}^1\right\}$$

$$= 6\left[\tfrac{1}{2} - (.3)^2/2 - \left(\tfrac{1}{3} - (.3)^3/3\right)\right]$$

$$= 6(.085667) = .514$$

b. From the box, the mean and variance of a beta random variable are

$$\mu = \frac{\alpha}{\alpha + \beta} \quad \text{and} \quad \sigma^2 = \frac{\alpha\beta}{(\alpha + \beta)^2(\alpha + \beta + 1)}$$

Substituting $\alpha = \beta = 2$, we obtain:

$$\mu = \frac{2}{2 + 2} = \frac{2}{4} = .5$$

$$\sigma^2 = \frac{(2)(2)}{(2 + 2)^2(2 + 2 + 1)} = \frac{4}{(16)(5)} = .05$$

The cumulative distribution function $F(y)$ of a beta density function is called an **incomplete beta function**. Values of this function for various values of y, α, and β are given in *Tables of the Incomplete Beta Function* (1956). For the special case where α and β are integers, it can be shown that

$$F(p) = \int_0^p \frac{y^{\alpha-1}(1 - y)^{\beta-1}}{B(\alpha, \beta)} \, dy = \sum_{y=\alpha}^n p(y)$$

where $p(y)$ is a binomial probability distribution with parameters p and $n = (\alpha + \beta - 1)$. Recall that tables giving the cumulative sums of binomial probabilities are given in Table 1 of Appendix II, for $n = 5$, 10, 15, 20, and 25. More extensive tables of these probabilities are listed in the references at the end of the chapter.

EXAMPLE 5.17

Data collected over time on the utilization of a computer core (as a proportion of the total capacity) were found to possess a relative frequency distribution that could be approximated by a beta density function with $\alpha = 2$ and $\beta = 4$. Find the probability that the proportion of the core being used at any particular time will be less than .20.

Solution

The probability that the proportion of the core being utilized will be less than $p = .2$ is

$$F(p) = \int_0^p \frac{y^{\alpha-1}(1 - y)^{\beta-1}}{B(\alpha, \beta)} \, dy = \sum_{y=\alpha}^n p(y)$$

where $p(y)$ is a binomial probability distribution with $n = (\alpha + \beta - 1) = (2 + 4 - 1) = 5$ and $p = .2$. Therefore,

$$F(.2) = \sum_{y=2}^5 p(y) = 1 - \sum_{y=0}^1 p(y)$$

From Table 1 of Appendix II for $n = 5$ and $p = .2$, we find that

$$\sum_{y=0}^1 p(y) = .737$$

Therefore, the probability that the computer core will be less than 20% occupied at any particular time is

$$F(.2) = 1 - \sum_{y=0}^1 p(y) = 1 - .737 = .263$$

EXERCISES

5.63 A continuous random variable y has a beta distribution with probability density

$$f(y) = \begin{cases} cy^5(1-y)^2 & \text{if } 0 \le y \le 1 \\ 0 & \text{elsewhere} \end{cases}$$

Find the value of c that will make $f(y)$ a density function.

5.64 The proportion y of a data-processing company's yearly hardware repair budget allocated to repair its tri-log color printer has an approximate beta distribution with parameters $\alpha = 2$ and $\beta = 9$.
  a. Find the mean and variance of y.
  b. Compute the probability that for any randomly selected year, at least 40% of the hardware repair budget is used to repair the color printer.
  c. What is the probability that at most 10% of the yearly repair budget is used for the color printer?

5.65 An investigation into pollution control expenditures of industrial firms found that the annual percentage of plant capacity shutdown attributable to environmental and safety regulation has an approximate beta distribution with $\alpha = 1$ and $\beta = 25$.
  a. Find the mean and variance of the annual percentage of plant capacity shutdown attributable to environmental and safety regulation.
  b. Find the probability that more than 1% of plant capacity shutdown is attributable to environmental and safety regulation.

5.66 An important property of certain products that are in powder or granular form is their particle size distribution. For example, refractory cements are adversely affected by too high a proportion of coarse granules, which can lead to weaknesses from poor packing. G. H. Brown (*Journal of Quality Technology*, July 1985) showed that the beta distribution provides an adequate model for the percentage y of refractory cement granules in bulk form that are coarse. Suppose you are interested in controlling the proportion y of coarse refractory cement in a lot, where y has a beta distribution with parameters $\alpha = \beta = 2$.
  a. Find the mean and variance of y.
  b. If you will accept the lot only if less than 10% of refractory cement granules are coarse, find the probability of lot acceptance.

5.67 Suppose the proportion of small data-processing firms that make a profit during their first year of operation possesses a relative frequency distribution that can be approximated by the beta density with $\alpha = 5$ and $\beta = 6$.
  a. Find the probability that at most 60% of all small data-processing firms make a profit during their first year of operation.
  b. Find the probability that at least 80% of all small data-processing firms make a profit during their first year of operation.

OPTIONAL EXERCISES

5.68 Verify that the mean of a beta density with parameters α and β is given by $\mu = \alpha/(\alpha + \beta)$.

5.69 Show that if y has a beta density with $\alpha = 1$ and $\beta = 1$, then y is uniformly distributed over the interval $0 \le y \le 1$.

5.70 Show that the beta distribution with $\alpha = 2$ and $\beta = 1$ is *new better than used* (NBU). (See Optional Exercise 5.6 for the definition of NBU.)

5.10 Moments and Moment Generating Functions (Optional)

The **moments** and **moment generating functions** for continuous random variables are defined in exactly the same way as for discrete random variables, except that the expectations involve integration.* The relevance and applicability of a moment generating function $m(t)$ are the same in the continuous case, as we now illustrate with two examples.

EXAMPLE 5.18

Find the moment generating function for a gamma-type random variable.

Solution

The moment generating function is given by

$$m(t) = E(e^{ty}) = \int_0^\infty e^{ty} \frac{y^{\alpha-1} e^{-y/\beta}}{\beta^\alpha \Gamma(\alpha)} \, dy$$

$$= \int_0^\infty \frac{y^{\alpha-1} e^{-y(1/\beta - t)}}{\beta^\alpha \Gamma(\alpha)} \, dy = \int_0^\infty \frac{y^{\alpha-1} e^{-y/[\beta/(1-\beta t)]}}{\beta^\alpha \Gamma(\alpha)} \, dy$$

An examination of this integrand indicates that we can convert it into a gamma density function with parameters α and $\beta/(1 - \beta t)$, by factoring $1/\beta^\alpha$ out of the integral and multiplying and dividing by $[\beta/(1 - \beta t)]^\alpha$. Therefore,

$$m(t) = \frac{1}{\beta^\alpha} \left(\frac{\beta}{1 - \beta t} \right)^\alpha \int_0^\infty \frac{y^{\alpha-1} e^{-y/[\beta/(1-\beta t)]}}{\left(\dfrac{\beta}{1 - \beta t} \right)^\alpha \Gamma(\alpha)} \, dy$$

The integral of this gamma density function is equal to 1. Therefore,

$$m(t) = \frac{1}{(1 - \beta t)^\alpha}(1) = \frac{1}{(1 - \beta t)^\alpha}$$

EXAMPLE 5.19

Refer to Example 5.18. Use $m(t)$ to find μ_1' and μ_2'. Use the results to derive the mean and variance of a gamma-type random variable.

---

*Moments and moment generating functions for discrete random variables are discussed in Optional Section 4.9.

Solution

The first two moments about the origin, evaluated at $t = 0$, are

$$\mu_1' = \mu = \frac{dm(t)}{dt}\bigg]_{t=0} = \frac{-\alpha(-\beta)}{(1 - \beta t)^{\alpha+1}}\bigg]_{t=0} = \alpha\beta$$

and

$$\mu_2' = \frac{d^2 m(t)}{dt^2}\bigg]_{t=0}$$

$$= -\frac{\alpha\beta(\alpha + 1)(-\beta)}{(1 - \beta t)^{\alpha+2}}\bigg]_{t=0} = \alpha(\alpha + 1)\beta^2$$

Then, applying Theorem 5.4, we obtain

$$\sigma^2 = E(y^2) - \mu^2 = \mu_2' - \mu^2$$
$$= \alpha(\alpha + 1)\beta^2 - \alpha^2\beta^2 = \alpha\beta^2$$

Some useful probability density functions, with their means, variances, and moment generating functions, are summarized in Table 5.1.

TABLE 5.1   Some Useful Continuous Random Variables

Random Variable	Probability Density Function	Mean	Variance	Moment Generating Function
Uniform	$f(y) = \dfrac{1}{b - a}$ $a \le y \le b$	$\dfrac{a + b}{2}$	$\dfrac{(b - a)^2}{12}$	$\dfrac{e^{tb} - e^{ta}}{t(b - a)}$
Normal	$f(y) = \dfrac{e^{-(y-\mu)^2/2\sigma^2}}{\sigma\sqrt{2\pi}}$ $-\infty < y < \infty$	μ	σ^2	$e^{\mu t + (t^2\sigma^2/2)}$
Gamma	$f(y) = \dfrac{y^{\alpha-1}e^{-y/\beta}}{\beta^\alpha\Gamma(\alpha)}$ $0 \le y < \infty$	$\alpha\beta$	$\alpha\beta^2$	$(1 - \beta t)^{-\alpha}$
Exponential	$f(y) = \dfrac{1}{\beta}e^{-y/\beta}$ $0 \le y < \infty$	β	β^2	$\dfrac{1}{(1 - \beta t)}$
Weibull	$f(y) = \dfrac{\alpha}{\beta}y^{\alpha-1}e^{-y^\alpha/\beta}$ $0 \le y < \infty$	$\beta^{1/\alpha}\Gamma\left(\dfrac{\alpha + 1}{\alpha}\right)$	$\beta^{2/\alpha}\left[\Gamma\left(\dfrac{\alpha + 2}{\alpha}\right) - \Gamma^2\left(\dfrac{\alpha + 1}{\alpha}\right)\right]$	$\beta^{t/\alpha}\Gamma(1 + t/\alpha)$

(continued)

Random Variable	Probability Density Function	Mean	Variance	Moment Generating Function
Chi-square	$f(\chi^2) = \dfrac{(\chi^2)^{(\nu/2)-1}e^{-\chi^2/2}}{2^{\nu/2}\Gamma\left(\dfrac{\nu}{2}\right)}$ $0 \le \chi^2 < \infty$	ν	2ν	$(1 - 2t)^{-\nu/2}$
Beta	$f(y) = \dfrac{\Gamma(\alpha + \beta)}{\Gamma(\alpha)\Gamma(\beta)}y^{\alpha-1}(1 - y)^{\beta-1}$ $0 \le y \le 1$	$\dfrac{\alpha}{\alpha + \beta}$	$\dfrac{\alpha\beta}{(\alpha + \beta)^2(\alpha + \beta + 1)}$	Closed-form expression does not exist.

EXERCISES

5.71   Use the moment generating function $m(t)$ of the normal density to find μ_1' and μ_2'. Then use these results to show that a normal random variable has mean μ and variance σ^2.

5.72   Verify that the moment generating function of a chi-square random variable with ν degrees of freedom is

$$m(t) = (1 - 2t)^{-\nu/2}$$

[*Hint:*   Use the fact that a chi-square random variable has a gamma-type density function with $\alpha = \nu/2$ and $\beta = 2$.]

5.73   Verify that the moment generating function of a uniform random variable on the interval $a \le y \le b$ is

$$m(t) = \frac{e^{tb} - e^{ta}}{t(b - a)}$$

5.74   Consider a continuous random variable y with density

$$f(y) = \begin{cases} e^y & \text{if } y < 0 \\ 0 & \text{elsewhere} \end{cases}$$

a. Find the moment generating function $m(t)$ of y.
b. Use the result of part **a** to find the mean and variance of y.

5.11   Summary

Continuous random variables are defined to be those that possess continuous **cumulative distribution functions**. From a practical point of view, they are variables that can assume values corresponding to the infinitely large number of points contained in one or more intervals on the real line.

The relative frequency distribution for a population of data associated with a continuous random variable can be modeled using a **probability density function**. A density function $f(y)$, usually a continuous smooth curve, must satisfy the following properties:

$$f(y) \geq 0 \quad \text{and} \quad \int_{-\infty}^{\infty} f(y)dy = 1$$

The **expected value** (or **mean**) of a continuous random variable y or of any function $g(y)$ of y is defined in the same manner as for discrete random variables, except that integration is substituted for summation.

Although there are many different types of continuous random variables, most relative frequency distributions of data in the engineering and computer sciences can be modeled by one of the five probability density functions presented in this chapter: the **uniform distribution**, the **normal distribution**, the **gamma distribution**, the **Weibull distribution**, and the **beta distribution**. We gave some practical examples of the use of these density functions, and will subsequently show that they play a very important role in statistical inference.

SUPPLEMENTARY EXERCISES

5.75 The continuous random variable y has a probability distribution given by

$$f(y) = \begin{cases} cye^{-y^2} & \text{if } y > 0 \\ 0 & \text{elsewhere} \end{cases}$$

   a. Find the value of c that makes $f(y)$ a probability density.
   b. Find $F(y)$.
   c. Compute $P(y > 2.5)$.

5.76 The problem of passenger congestion prompted a large international airport to install a monorail connecting its main terminal to the three concourses, A, B, and C. The engineers designed the monorail so that the amount of time a passenger at concourse B must wait for a monorail car has a uniform distribution ranging from 0 to 10 minutes.

   a. Find the mean and variance of y, the time a passenger at concourse B must wait for the monorail. (Assume that the monorail travels sequentially from concourse A, to concourse B, to concourse C, back to concourse B, and then returns to concourse A. The route is then repeated.)
   b. If it takes the monorail 1 minute to go from concourse to concourse, find the probability that a hurried passenger can reach concourse A less than 4 minutes after arriving at the monorail station at concourse B.

5.77 Many products are mass produced on automated assembly lines. The probability distribution of the length of time between the arrivals of successive manufactured components off the assembly line is often (approximately) exponential. Suppose the mean time between arrivals of magnetron tubes manufactured on an assembly line is 20 seconds.

   a. What is the probability that a particular interarrival time (the time between the arrivals of two magnetron tubes) is less than 10 seconds?
   b. What is the probability that the next four interarrival times are all less than 10 seconds?
   c. What is the probability that an interarrival time will exceed 1 minute?

5.78   The metropolitan airport commission is considering the establishment of limitations on the extent of noise pollution around a local airport. At the present time the noise level per jet takeoff in one neighborhood near the airport is approximately normally distributed with a mean of 100 decibels and a standard deviation of 6 decibels.
   a. What is the probability that a randomly selected jet will generate a noise level greater than 108 decibels in this neighborhood?
   b. What is the probability that a randomly selected jet will generate a noise level of exactly 100 decibels?
   c. Suppose a regulation is passed that requires jet noise in this neighborhood to be lower than 105 decibels 95% of the time. Assuming the standard deviation of the noise distribution remains the same, how much will the mean noise level have to be lowered to comply with the regulation?

5.79   The importance of modeling machine downtime correctly in simulation studies was discussed in *Industrial Engineering* (Aug. 1990). The paper presented simulation results for a single-machine-tool system with the following properties:

   • The interarrival times of jobs are exponentially distributed with a mean of 1.25 minutes.
   • The amount of time the machine operates before breaking down is exponentially distributed with a mean of 540 minutes.
   • The repair time (in minutes) for the machine has a gamma distribution with parameters $\alpha = 2$ and $\beta = 30$.

   a. Find the probability that two jobs arrive for processing at most 1 minute apart.
   b. Find the probability that the machine operates for at least 720 minutes (12 hours) before breaking down.
   c. Find the mean and variance of the repair time for the machine. Interpret the results.
   d. Find the probability that the repair time for the machine exceeds 120 minutes.

5.80   Suppose that the fraction of defective modems shipped by a data-communications vendor has an approximate beta distribution with $\alpha = 5$ and $\beta = 21$.
   a. Find the mean and variance of the fraction of defective modems per shipment.
   b. What is the probability that a randomly selected shipment will contain at least 30% defectives?
   c. What is the probability that a randomly selected shipment will contain no more than 5% defectives?

5.81   W. Nelson (*Journal of Quality Technology*, July 1985) suggests that the Weibull distribution usually provides a better representation for the lifelength of a product than the exponential distribution. Nelson used a Weibull distribution with $\alpha = 1.5$ and $\beta = 110$ to model the lifelength y of a roller bearing (in thousands of hours).
   a. Find the probability that a roller bearing of this type will have a service life of less than 12.2 thousand hours.
   b. Recall that a Weibull distribution with $\alpha = 1$ is an exponential distribution. Nelson claims that very few products have an exponential life distribution, although such a distribution is commonly applied. Calculate the probability from part **a** using the exponential distribution. Compare your answer to that obtained in part **a**.

5.82   Each year the top marlin fishermen from around the world compete in the Hawaiian International Bluefish Tournament. One year, a fisherman landed a 987-pound Pacific blue marlin—a world record until a check showed his fishing line was a few pounds over the 80-pound limit. The "80 pounds" refers to the strength of the fishing line—i.e., the weight the line is tested to hold outside water. Suppose the actual strength of manufactured "80-pound-test line" is normally distributed with a mean of 80 pounds and a standard deviation of .2 pound.

a. What is the probability that an "80-pound-test line" randomly selected from the production process will have a strength of at least 1 pound over the 80-pound limit?

b. Based on the probability computed in part **a**, is it likely that the fisherman actually used "80-pound-test line" to catch the 987-pound blue marlin? Explain.

5.83   Suppose we are counting events that occur according to a Poisson distribution, such as the number of data-processing jobs submitted to a computer center. If it is known that exactly one such event has occurred in a given interval of time, say $(0, t)$, then the actual time of occurrence is uniformly distributed over this interval. Suppose that during a given 30-minute period, one data-processing job was submitted. Find the probability that the job was submitted during the last 5 minutes of the 30-minute period.

5.84   The length of time between breakdowns of an essential piece of equipment is an important factor in deciding on the amount of auxiliary equipment needed to assure continuous service. A machine room foreman believes the time between breakdowns of a particular electrical generator is best approximated by an exponential distribution with mean equal to 10 days.

a. What is the standard deviation of this exponential distribution?

b. Assuming that the foreman has correctly characterized the distribution for the time between breakdowns and that the generator broke down today, what is the probability that the generator will break down again within the next 14 days?

c. What is the probability that the generator will operate for more than 20 days without a breakdown?

5.85   The percentage y of impurities per batch in a certain chemical product is a beta random variable with probability density

$$f(y) = \begin{cases} 90y^8(1 - y) & \text{if } 0 \le y \le 1 \\ 0 & \text{elsewhere} \end{cases}$$

a. What are the values of α and β?

b. Compute the mean and variance of y.

c. A batch with more than 80% impurities cannot be sold. What is the probability that a randomly selected batch cannot be sold because of excessive impurities?

5.86   The lifelength y (in years) of a memory chip in a mainframe computer is a Weibull random variable with probability density

$$f(y) = \begin{cases} \frac{1}{8}ye^{-y^2/16} & \text{if } 0 \le y < \infty \\ 0 & \text{elsewhere} \end{cases}$$

a. What are the values of α and β?

b. Compute the mean and variance of y.

c. Find the probability that a new memory chip will not fail before 6 years.

5.87   *System downtime* is defined as the fraction of time a computer system is inoperative because of hardware and/or software failure. Suppose that system downtime y (in hours) at a university computer center has a Weibull distribution with $\alpha = 2$ and $\beta = 2$. When the system is down for longer than 1 hour, all current working files are lost. If the system goes down while a user is accessing a working file, what is the probability that the file will be recovered?

OPTIONAL SUPPLEMENTARY EXERCISES

5.88 Let $m_y(t)$ be the moment generating function of a continuous random variable y. If a and b are constants, show that:

a. $m_{y+a}(t) = E[e^{(y+a)t}] = e^{at}m_y(t)$

b. $m_{by}(t) = E[e^{(by)t}] = m_y(bt)$

c. $m_{[(y+a)/b]}(t) = E[e^{(y+a)t/b}] = e^{at/b}m_y\left(\dfrac{t}{b}\right)$

5.89 To aid engineers seeking to predict the efficiency of a solar-powered device, Olseth and Skartveit (*Solar Energy*, Vol. 33, No. 6, 1984) developed a model for daily insolation y at sea-level locations within the temperate storm belt. To account for both "clear sky" and "overcast" days, the researchers constructed a probability density function for y (measured as a percentage) using a linear combination of two modified gamma distributions:

$$f(y) = wg(y, \lambda_1) + (1 - w)g(1 - y, \lambda_2), \qquad (0 < y < 1)$$

where

$$g(y) = \frac{(1 - y)e^{\lambda y}}{\int_0^1 (1 - y)e^{\lambda y}\, dy}$$

λ_1 = mean insolation of "clear sky" days

λ_2 = mean insolation of "cloudy" days

and w is a weighting constant, $0 \le w \le 1$. Show that

$$\int_0^1 f(y)dy = 1$$

References

Hogg, R. V., and Craig, A. T. *Introduction to Mathematical Statistics*, 4th ed. New York: Macmillan, 1978.

Mendenhall, W., Wackerly, D. D., and Scheaffer, R. L. *Mathematical Statistics with Applications*, 4th ed. Boston: PWS-Kent, 1989.

Mood, A. M., Graybill, F. A., and Boes, D. *Introduction to the Theory of Statistics*, 3rd ed. New York: McGraw-Hill, 1974.

Parzen, E. *Modern Probability Theory and Its Applications*. New York: Wiley, 1964.

Pearson, K. *Tables of the Incomplete Beta Function*. New York: Cambridge University Press, 1956.

Pearson, K. *Tables of the Incomplete Gamma Function*. New York: Cambridge University Press, 1956.

Standard Mathematical Tables, 17th ed. Cleveland: Chemical Rubber Company, 1969.

Tables of the Binomial Probability Distribution. Department of Commerce, National Bureau of Standards, Applied Mathematics Series 6, 1950.

Weibull, W. "A Statistical Distribution Function of Wide Applicability." *Journal of Applied Mechanics*, Vol. 18 (1951), pp. 293–297.

CHAPTER SIX

Bivariate Probability Distributions

Objective

To introduce the concepts of a bivariate probability distribution, covariance, and independence; to show you how to find the expected value and variance of a linear function of random variables

Contents

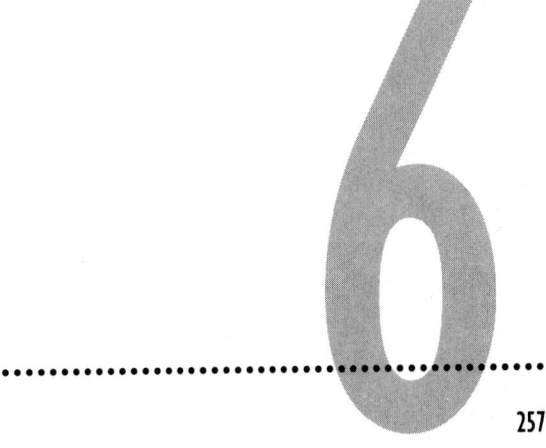

6.1 Bivariate Probability Distributions for Discrete Random Variables

Engineers responsible for estimating the cost of road construction utilize many variables to derive the estimate. For example, two important discrete random variables are x, the number of bridges that must be constructed, and y, the number of structures that need to be leveled. Assessing the probability of x and y taking specific values is key to developing an accurate estimate.

In Chapter 3, we learned that the probability of the intersection of two events (i.e., the event that both A and B occur) is equal to

$$P(A \cap B) = P(A)P(B \mid A) = P(B)P(A \mid B)$$

If we assign two numbers to each point in the sample space—one corresponding to the value of a discrete random variable x (e.g., the number of bridges built) and the second to a discrete random variable y (e.g., the number of structures leveled)—then specific values of x and y represent two numerical events. The probability of the intersection of these two events is obtained by replacing the symbol A by x and the symbol B by y:

$$
\begin{aligned}
P(A \cap B) &= p(x, y) \\
&= p_1(x)p_2(y \mid x) \\
&= p_2(y)p_1(x \mid y)
\end{aligned}
$$

[*Note:* To distinguish between the probability distributions, we will always use the subscript 1 (as in p_1) when we refer to the probability distribution of x and the subscript 2 (as in p_2) when we refer to the probability distribution of y.]

A table, graph, or formula that gives the probability of the intersection (x, y) for all values of x and y is called the **joint probability distribution** of x and y. The probability distribution of $p_1(x)$ gives the probabilities of observing specific values of x; similarly, $p_2(y)$ gives the probabilities of the discrete random variable y. Thus, $p_1(x)$ and $p_2(y)$, called **marginal probability distributions** for x and y, respectively, are the familiar unconditional probability distributions for discrete random variables encountered in Chapter 4.

Definition 6.1

The **joint probability distribution** $p(x, y)$ for two discrete random variables, x and y—called a **bivariate distribution**—is a table, graph, or formula that gives the values of $p(x, y)$ for every combination of values of x and y.

Requirements for a Discrete Bivariate Probability Distribution

1. $0 \le p(x, y) \le 1$ for all values of x and y

2. $\sum_y \sum_x p(x, y) = 1$

[*Note:*   The symbol $\sum_y \sum_x$ denotes summation over all values of both x and y.]

EXAMPLE 6.1

Consider two discrete random variables, x and y, where $x = 1$ or $x = 2$, and $y = 0$ or $y = 1$. The bivariate probability distribution for x and y is defined as follows:

$$p(x, y) = \frac{.25 + x - y}{5}$$

Verify that the properties (requirements) of a discrete bivariate probability distribution are satisfied.

Solution

Since x takes on two values (1 or 2) and y takes on two values (0 or 1), there are $2 \times 2 = 4$ possible combinations of x and y. These four (x, y) pairs are $(1, 0)$, $(1, 1)$, $(2, 0)$, and $(2, 1)$. Substituting these possible values of x and y into the formula for $p(x, y)$, we obtain the following joint probabilities:

$$p(1, 0) = \frac{.25 + 1 - 0}{5} = .25$$

$$p(1, 1) = \frac{.25 + 1 - 1}{5} = .05$$

$$p(2, 0) = \frac{.25 + 2 - 0}{5} = .45$$

$$p(2, 1) = \frac{.25 + 2 - 1}{5} = .25$$

Note that each of these joint probabilities is between 0 and 1 (satisfying requirement 1 given in the box) and the sum of these four probabilities equals 1 (satisfying requirement 2).

EXAMPLE 6.2

Consider the bivariate joint probability distribution shown in Table 6.1. The numbers in the cells are the values of $p(x, y)$ corresponding to pairs of values of the discrete random variables x and y, for $x = 1, 2, 3, 4$ and $y = 0, 1, 2, 3$. For example, in a flexible manufacturing system, x might represent the number of machines available and y might represent the number of sequential operations required to process a part. Find the marginal probability distribution $p_1(x)$ for the discrete random variable x.

TABLE 6.1   Bivariate probability distribution for x and y

		x		
	1	2	3	4
y 0	0	.10	.20	.10
1	.03	.07	.10	.05
2	.05	.10	.05	0
3	0	.10	.05	0

Solution

To find the marginal probability distribution for x, we need to find $P(x = 1)$, $P(x = 2)$, $P(x = 3)$, and $P(x = 4)$. Since $x = 1$ can occur when $y = 0, 1, 2,$ or 3 occurs, then $P(x = 1) = p_1(1)$ is calculated by summing the probabilities of four mutually exclusive events:

$$P(x = 1) = p_1(1) = p(1, 0) + p(1, 1) + p(1, 2) + p(1, 3)$$

Substituting the values for $p(x, y)$ given in Table 6.1, we obtain

$$P(x = 1) = p_1(1) = 0 + .03 + .05 + 0 = .08$$

Similarly,

$$P(x = 2) = p_1(2) = p(2, 0) + p(2, 1) + p(2, 2) + p(2, 3)$$
$$= .10 + .07 + .10 + .10 = .37$$
$$P(x = 3) = p_1(3) = p(3, 0) + p(3, 1) + p(3, 2) + p(3, 3)$$
$$= .20 + .10 + .05 + .05 = .40$$
$$P(x = 4) = p_1(4) = p(4, 0) + p(4, 1) + p(4, 2) + p(4, 3)$$
$$= .10 + .05 + 0 + 0 = .15$$

The marginal probability distribution $p_1(x)$ is given in the following table:

x	1	2	3	4
$p_1(x)$	.08	.37	.40	.15

Note from the table that $\sum_{x=1}^{4} p_1(x) = 1$.

Example 6.2 shows that the marginal probability distribution for a discrete random variable x may be obtained by summing $p(x, y)$ over all values of y. The result is summarized in the next box.

Definition 6.2

Let x and y be discrete random variables and let $p(x, y)$ be their joint probability distribution. Then the **marginal (unconditional) probability distributions** of x and y are, respectively,

$$p_1(x) = \sum_y p(x, y) \quad \text{and} \quad p_2(y) = \sum_x p(x, y)$$

[*Note*: We will use the symbol $\sum_y$ to denote summation over all values of y.]

The probability of the numerical event x, given that the event y occurred, is the conditional probability of x given y. A table, graph, or formula that gives these probabilities for all values of y is called the **conditional probability distribution** for x given y and is denoted by the symbol $p_1(x \mid y)$.

EXAMPLE 6.3

Refer to Example 6.2. Find the conditional probability distribution of x given $y = 2$.

Solution

There are four conditional probability distributions of x—one for each value of y. From Chapter 3, we know that

$$P(A \mid B) = \frac{P(A \cap B)}{P(B)}$$

If we let a value of x correspond to the event A and a value of y to the event B, then it follows that

$$p_1(x \mid y) = \frac{p(x, y)}{p_2(y)}$$

or, when $y = 2$,

$$p_1(x \mid 2) = \frac{p(x, 2)}{p_2(2)}$$

Therefore,

$$p_1(1 \mid 2) = \frac{p(1, 2)}{p_2(2)}$$

From Table 6.1, we obtain $p(1, 2) = .05$ and $P(y = 2) = p_2(2) = .2$. Therefore,

$$p_1(1 \mid 2) = \frac{p(1, 2)}{p_2(2)} = \frac{.05}{.20} = .25$$

Similarly,

$$p_1(2 \mid 2) = \frac{p(2, 2)}{p_2(2)} = \frac{.10}{.20} = .50$$

$$p_1(3 \mid 2) = \frac{p(3, 2)}{p_2(2)} = \frac{.05}{.20} = .25$$

$$p_1(4 \mid 2) = \frac{p(4, 2)}{p_2(2)} = \frac{0}{.20} = 0$$

Therefore, the conditional probability distribution of x, given that $y = 2$, is as shown in the following table:

x	1	2	3	4
$p_1(x \mid 2)$	.25	.50	.25	0

Note from Example 6.3 that the sum of the conditional probabilities $p_1(x \mid 2)$ over all values of x is equal to 1. Thus, a conditional probability distribution satisfies the requirements that all probability distributions must satisfy:

$$p_1(x \mid y) \geq 0 \quad \text{and} \quad \sum_x p_1(x \mid y) = 1$$

Similarly,

$$p_2(y \mid x) \geq 0 \quad \text{and} \quad \sum_y p_2(y \mid x) = 1$$

Definition 6.3

Let x and y be discrete random variables and let $p(x, y)$ be their joint probability distribution. Then the **conditional probability distributions** for x and y are defined as follows:

$$p_1(x \mid y) = \frac{p(x, y)}{p_2(y)} \quad \text{and} \quad p_2(y \mid x) = \frac{p(x, y)}{p_1(x)}$$

In the preceding discussion, we defined the bivariate joint marginal and conditional probability distributions for two discrete random variables, x and y. The concepts can be extended to any number of discrete random variables. Thus, we could define a third random variable w to each point in the sample space. The joint probability distribution $p(x, y, w)$ would be a table, graph, or formula that gives the values of $p(x, y, w)$, the event that the intersection (x, y, w) occurs, for all combinations of values of x, y, and w. In general, the joint probability distribution for two or more discrete random variables is called a **multivariate probability distribution**. Although the remainder of this chapter is devoted to bivariate probability distributions, the concepts apply to the general multivariate case also.

EXERCISES

6.1 The joint probability distribution $p(x, y)$ for two discrete random variables, x and y, is given in the accompanying table.

					x		
		0	1	2	3	4	5
	0	0	.050	.025	0	.025	0
y	1	.200	.050	0	.300	0	0
	2	.100	0	0	0	.100	.150

a. Verify that the properties of a joint probability distribution hold.
b. Find the marginal probability distribution $p_1(x)$ for x.
c. Find the marginal probability distribution $p_2(y)$ for y.
d. Find the conditional probability distribution $p_1(x \mid y)$.
e. Find the conditional probability distribution $p_2(y \mid x)$.

6.2 Consider the experiment of tossing a pair of dice. Let x be the outcome (i.e., the number of dots appearing face up) on the first die and let y be the outcome on the second die.
a. Find the joint probability distribution $p(x, y)$.
b. Find the marginal probability distributions $p_1(x)$ and $p_2(y)$.
c. Find the conditional probability distributions $p_1(x \mid y)$ and $p_2(y \mid x)$.
d. Compare the probability distributions of parts b and c. What phenomenon have you observed?

6.3 Refer to the *Journal of Engineering for Industry* (Aug. 1993) study of an automated drilling machine, Exercise 3.43. The eight machining conditions used in the study are reproduced at the top of page 264.

Experiment	Workpiece Material	Drill Size in.	Drill Speed rpm	Feed Rate ipr
1	Cast iron	.25	1,250	.011
2	Cast iron	.25	1,800	.005
3	Steel	.25	3,750	.003
4	Steel	.25	2,500	.003
5	Steel	.25	2,500	.008
6	Steel	.125	4,000	.0065
7	Steel	.125	4,000	.009
8	Steel	.125	3,000	.010

Suppose that two of the machining conditions listed will detect a flaw in the automated system. Define x as the number of these two conditions with steel material, and define y as the number of these two conditions with .25-inch drill size.

a. Find the bivariate probability distribution $p(x, y)$.
b. Find the marginal probability distribution $p_2(y)$.
c. Find the conditional probability distribution $p_1(x \mid y)$.

6.4 The joint probability distribution for two discrete random variables, x and y, is given by the formula

$$p(x, y) = p^{x+y}q^{2-(x+y)}, \quad x = 0, 1, \quad 0 \le p \le 1, \quad q = 1 - p, \quad y = 0, 1$$

Verify that the properties of a bivariate probability distribution are satisfied.

6.5 A special delivery truck travels from point A to point B and back over the same route each day. There are three traffic lights on this route. Let x be the number of red lights the truck encounters on the way to delivery point B and let y be the number of red lights the truck encounters on the way back to delivery point A. A traffic engineer has determined the joint probability distribution of x and y shown in the table.

		x			
		0	1	2	3
	0	.01	.02	.07	.01
y	1	.03	.06	.10	.06
	2	.05	.12	.15	.08
	3	.02	.09	.08	.05

a. Find the marginal probability distribution of y.
b. Given that the truck encounters $x = 2$ red lights on the way to delivery point B, find the probability distribution of y.

OPTIONAL EXERCISES

6.6 From a group of three data-processing managers, two senior systems analysts, and two quality control engineers, three people are to be randomly selected to form a committee that will study the feasibility of adding computer graphics at a consulting firm. Let x denote the number of data-processing managers and y the number of senior systems analysts selected for the committee.

a. Find the joint probability distribution of x and y.

b. Find the marginal distribution of x.

6.7 Let x and y be two discrete random variables with joint probability distribution $p(x, y)$. Define

$$F_1(a) = P(x \leq a) \quad \text{and} \quad F_1(a \mid y) = P(x \leq a \mid y)$$

Verify each of the following:

a. $F_1(a) = \sum_{x \leq a} \sum_{y} p(x, y)$

b. $F_1(a \mid y) = \dfrac{\sum_{x \leq a} p(x, y)}{p_2(y)}$

6.2 Bivariate Probability Distributions for Continuous Random Variables

As we have noted in Chapters 4 and 5, definitions and theorems that apply to discrete random variables apply as well to continuous random variables. The only difference is that the probabilities for discrete random variables are summed, whereas those for continuous random variables are integrated. As we proceed through this chapter, we will define and develop concepts in the context of discrete random variables and will use them to justify equivalent definitions and theorems pertaining to continuous random variables.

Definition 6.4

The **bivariate joint probability density function** $f(x, y)$ for two continuous random variables x and y is one that satisfies the following properties:

1. $f(x, y) \geq 0$ for all values of x and y

2. $\displaystyle\int_{-\infty}^{\infty} \int_{-\infty}^{\infty} f(x, y) = 1$

3. $P(a \leq x \leq b, c \leq y \leq d) = \displaystyle\int_{c}^{d} \int_{a}^{b} f(x, y)dx \, dy$ for all constants a, b, c, and d

Definition 6.5

Let $f(x, y)$ be the joint density function for x and y. Then the **marginal density functions** for x and y are

$$f_1(x) = \int_{-\infty}^{\infty} f(x, y)dy \quad \text{and} \quad f_2(y) = \int_{-\infty}^{\infty} f(x, y)dx$$

Definition 6.6

Let $f(x, y)$ be the joint density function for x and y. Then the **conditional density functions** for x and y are

$$f_1(x \mid y) = \frac{f(x, y)}{f_2(y)} \quad \text{and} \quad f_2(y \mid x) = \frac{f(x, y)}{f_1(x)}$$

EXAMPLE 6.4

Suppose the joint density function for two continuous random variables, x and y, is given by

$$f(x, y) = \begin{cases} cx & \text{if } 0 \le x \le 1;\ 0 \le y \le 1 \\ 0 & \text{elsewhere} \end{cases}$$

Determine the value of the constant c.

Solution

A graph of $f(x, y)$ traces a three-dimensional, wedge-shaped figure over the unit square $(0 \le x \le 1$ and $0 \le y \le 1)$ in the (x, y)-plane, as shown in Figure 6.1. The value of c is chosen so that $f(x, y)$ satisfies the property

$$\int_{-\infty}^{\infty}\int_{-\infty}^{\infty} f(x, y)dx\ dy = 1$$

FIGURE 6.1 ▶
Graph of the joint density function for Example 6.4

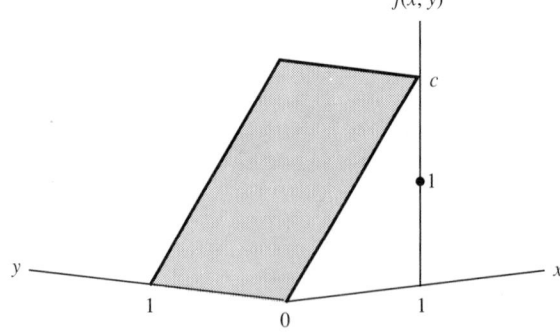

Performing this integration yields

$$\int_{-\infty}^{\infty}\int_{-\infty}^{\infty} f(x,\ y)dx\ dy = \int_{0}^{1}\int_{0}^{1} cx\ dx\ dy$$

$$= c\int_{0}^{1}\int_{0}^{1} x\ dx\ dy = c\int_{0}^{1} \frac{x^2}{2}\Big]_{0}^{1} dy$$

$$= c\int_{0}^{1} \frac{1}{2}\ dy = \left(\frac{c}{2}\right)y\Big]_{0}^{1} = \frac{c}{2}$$

Setting this quantity equal to 1 and solving for c, we obtain

$$1 = \frac{c}{2} \quad \text{or} \quad c = 2$$

Therefore,

$$f(x,\ y) = 2x \quad \text{for } 0 \le x \le 1 \text{ and } 0 \le y \le 1$$

EXAMPLE 6.5

Refer to Example 6.4 and find the marginal density function for x. Show that

$$\int_{-\infty}^{\infty} f_1(x) = 1$$

Solution

By Definition 6.5,

$$f_1(x) = \int_{-\infty}^{\infty} f(x,\ y)dy = 2\int_{0}^{1} x\ dy = 2xy\Big]_{y=0}^{y=1} = 2x$$

Thus,

$$\int_{-\infty}^{\infty} f_1(x)dx = 2\int_{0}^{1} x\ dx = 2\left(\frac{x^2}{2}\right)\Big]_{0}^{1} = 1$$

EXAMPLE 6.6

Refer to Example 6.4 and show that the marginal density function for y is a uniform distribution.

Solution

The marginal density function for y is given by

$$f_2(y) = \int_{-\infty}^{\infty} f(x,\ y)dx = 2\int_{0}^{1} x\ dx = 2\left(\frac{x^2}{2}\right)\Big]_{0}^{1} = 1$$

Thus, $f_2(y)$ is a uniform distribution defined over the interval $0 \le y \le 1$.

EXAMPLE 6.7

Refer to Examples 6.4–6.6. Find the conditional density function for x given y, and show that it satisfies the property

$$\int_{-\infty}^{\infty} f_1(x \mid y)dx = 1$$

Solution

Using the marginal density function $f_2(y) = 1$ (obtained in Example 6.6) and Definition 6.6, we derive the conditional density function as follows:

$$f_1(x \mid y) = \frac{f(x, y)}{f_2(y)} = \frac{2x}{1} = 2x$$

We now show that the integral of $f_1(x \mid y)$ over all values of x is equal to 1:

$$\int_0^1 f_1(x \mid y)dx = 2 \int_0^1 x \, dx = 2\left(\frac{x^2}{2}\right)\Big]_0^1 = 1$$

EXAMPLE 6.8

Suppose the joint density function for x and y is

$$f(x, y) = \begin{cases} cx & \text{if } 0 \le x \le y;\ 0 \le y \le 1 \\ 0 & \text{elsewhere} \end{cases}$$

Find the value of c.

Solution

Refer to Figure 6.1. If we pass a plane through the wedge, diagonally between the points $(0, 0)$ and $(1, 1)$, and perpendicular to the (x, y)-plane, then the slice lying along the y-axis will have a shape similar to that of the given density function (graphed in Figure 6.2). The value of c will be larger than the value found in Example 6.4 because the volume of the solid shown in Figure 6.2 must equal 1.

FIGURE 6.2 ▶
Graph of the joint density function for Example 6.8

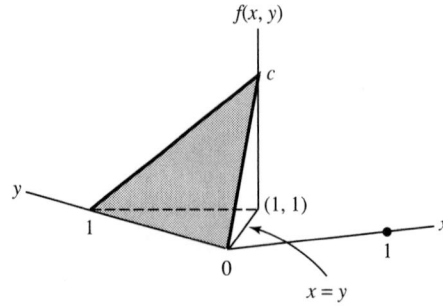

We find c by integrating $f(x, y)$ over the triangular region (shown in Figure 6.3) defined by $0 \le x \le y$ and $0 \le y \le 1$, setting this integral equal to 1, and solving for c:

$$\int_{-\infty}^{\infty} \int_{-\infty}^{\infty} f(x, y)dx\, dy = \int_{0}^{1} \int_{0}^{y} cx\, dx\, dy = c \int_{0}^{1} \frac{x^2}{2} \Big]_{0}^{y} dy$$

$$= c \int_{0}^{1} \frac{y^2}{2}\, dy = c \left(\frac{y^3}{6}\right) \Big]_{0}^{1} = \frac{c}{6}$$

Setting this quantity equal to 1 and solving for c yields $c = 6$; thus, $f(x, y) = 6x$ over the region of interest.

FIGURE 6.3 ▶
Region of integration for
Example 6.8

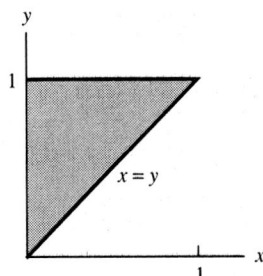

The joint density function for more than two random variables, say, $y_1, y_2, \ldots, y_n$, is denoted by the symbol $f(y_1, y_2, \ldots, y_n)$. Marginal and conditional density functions are defined in a manner similar to that employed for the bivariate case.

EXERCISES

6.8   Let x and y have the joint density

$$f(x, y) = \begin{cases} x + cy & \text{if } 1 \le x \le 2;\, 0 \le y \le 1 \\ 0 & \text{elsewhere} \end{cases}$$

where c is a constant.
a. Find the value of c that makes $f(x, y)$ a probability density function.
b. Find the marginal density for y and show that

$$\int_{-\infty}^{\infty} f_2(y)dy = 1$$

c. Find $f_1(x \mid y)$, the conditional density for x given y.

6.9   Let x and y have the joint density

$$f(x, y) = \begin{cases} cxy & \text{if } 0 \le x \le 1;\, 0 \le y \le 1 \\ 0 & \text{elsewhere} \end{cases}$$

a. Find the value of c that makes $f(x, y)$ a probability density function.
b. Find the marginal densities $f_1(x)$ and $f_2(y)$.
c. Find the conditional densities $f_1(x \mid y)$ and $f_2(y \mid x)$.

6.10 The joint density of x, the total time (in minutes) between a computer job's arrival in the job queue and its leaving the system after execution, and y, the time (in minutes) the job waits in the queue before being executed, is

$$f(x, y) = \begin{cases} ce^{-x^2} & \text{if } 0 \le y \le x; \, 0 \le x < \infty \\ 0 & \text{elsewhere} \end{cases}$$

a. Find the value of c that makes $f(x, y)$ a probability density function.
b. Find the marginal density for x and show that

$$\int_{-\infty}^{\infty} f_1(x)dx = 1$$

c. Show that the conditional density for y given x is a uniform distribution over the interval $0 \le y \le x$.

6.11 Refer to the *Journal of Engineering for Industry* (May 1993) study of friction feed paper separation, Exercises 5.13 and 5.26. Consider a system that utilizes two interrelated feed paper separators. The joint density of x and y, the friction coefficients of the two machines, is given by

$$f(x, y) = \begin{cases} xy & \text{if } 0 \le x \le 1; \, 0 \le y \le 1 \\ (2 - x)y & \text{if } 1 \le x \le 2; \, 0 \le y \le 1 \\ x(2 - y) & \text{if } 0 \le x \le 1; \, 1 \le y \le 2 \\ (2 - x)(2 - y) & \text{if } 1 \le x \le 2; \, 1 \le y \le 2 \end{cases}$$

a. Verify that $f(x, y)$ is a bivariate joint probability distribution function. [Show that Definition 6.4 holds for $f(x, y)$.]
b. Find the probability that both friction coefficients exceed .8.

OPTIONAL EXERCISES

6.12 Let x and y be two continuous random variables with joint probability density $f(x, y)$. The joint distribution function $F(a, b)$ is defined as follows:

$$F(a, b) = P(x \le a, y \le b) = \int_{-\infty}^{a}\int_{-\infty}^{b} f(x, y)dy \, dx$$

Verify each of the following:
a. $F(-\infty, -\infty) = F(-\infty, y) = F(x, -\infty) = 0$
b. $F(\infty, \infty) = 1$
c. If $a_2 \ge a_1$ and $b_2 \ge b_1$, then

$$F(a_2, b_2) - F(a_1, b_2) \ge F(a_2, b_1) - F(a_1, b_1)$$

6.13   Let x and y be two continuous random variables with joint probability density

$$f(x, y) = \begin{cases} ce^{-(x+y)} & \text{if } 0 \le x < \infty;\ 0 \le y < \infty \\ 0 & \text{elsewhere} \end{cases}$$

a. Find the value of c.
b. Find $f_1(x)$.
c. Find $f_2(y)$.
d. Find $f_1(x \mid y)$.
e. Find $f_2(y \mid x)$.
f. Find $P(x \le 1 \text{ and } y \le 1)$.

6.3   The Expected Value of Functions of Two Random Variables

The statistics that we will subsequently use for making inferences are computed from the data contained in a sample. The sample measurements can be viewed as observations on n random variables, $y_1, y_2, \ldots, y_n$, where y_1 represents the first measurement in the sample, y_2 represents the second measurement, etc. Since the sample statistics are functions of the random variables $y_1, y_2, \ldots, y_n$, they also will be random variables and will possess probability distributions. To describe these distributions, we will define the expected value (or mean) of functions of two or more random variables and present three expectation theorems that correspond to those given in Chapter 5. The definitions and theorems will be given in the bivariate context, but they can be written in general for any number of random variables by substituting corresponding multivariate functions and notation.

Definition 6.7

Let $g(x, y)$ be a function of the random variables x and y. Then the **expected value (mean)** of $g(x, y)$ is defined to be

$$E[g(x, y)] = \begin{cases} \displaystyle\sum_y \sum_x g(x, y)p(x, y) & \text{if } x \text{ and } y \text{ are discrete} \\ \displaystyle\int_{-\infty}^{\infty}\int_{-\infty}^{\infty} g(x, y)f(x, y)dx\,dy & \text{if } x \text{ and } y \text{ are continuous} \end{cases}$$

Suppose $g(x, y)$ is a function of only one of the random variables, say, x. We will show that, in the discrete situation, the expected value of this function possesses the same meaning as in Chapter 5. Let $g(x, y)$ be a function of x only, i.e., $g(x, y) = g(x)$. Then

$$E[g(x)] = \sum_x \sum_y g(x)p(x, y)$$

Summing first over y (in which case, x is regarded as a constant that can be factored outside the summation sign), we obtain

$$E[g(x)] = \sum_x g(x) \sum_y p(x, y)$$

However, by Definition 6.2, $\sum_y p(x, y)$ is the marginal probability distribution for x. Therefore,

$$E[g(x)] = \sum_x g(x) p_1(x)$$

You can verify that this is the same expression given for $E[g(x)]$ in Definition 4.5. An analogous result holds (proof omitted) if x and y are continuous random variables. Thus, if (μ_x, σ_x^2) and (μ_y, σ_y^2) denote the means and variances of x and y, respectively, then the bivariate expectations for functions of either x or y will equal the corresponding expectations given in Chapter 5, i.e., $E(x) = \mu_x$, $E[(x - \mu_x)^2] = \sigma_x^2$, etc.

It can be shown (proof omitted) that the three expectation theorems of Chapter 5 hold for bivariate and, in general, for multivariate probability distributions. We will use these theorems in Sections 6.5 and 6.7.

Theorem 6.1

Let c be a constant. Then the expected value of c is

$$E(c) = c$$

Theorem 6.2

Let c be a constant and let $g(x, y)$ be a function of the random variables x and y. Then the expected value of $cg(x, y)$ is

$$E[cg(x, y)] = cE[g(x, y)]$$

Theorem 6.3

Let $g_1(x, y), g_2(x, y), \ldots, g_k(x, y)$ be k functions of the random variables x and y. Then the expected value of the sum of these functions is

$$E[g_1(x, y) + g_2(x, y) + \cdots + g_k(x, y)]$$
$$= E[g_1(x, y)] + E[g_2(x, y)] + \cdots + E[g_k(x, y)]$$

EXERCISES

6.14 Refer to Exercise 6.3.
  a. Find $E(x)$.
  b. Find $E(y)$.

6.15 Refer to Exercise 6.5.
  a. On the average, how many red lights should the truck expect to encounter on the way to delivery point B, i.e., what is $E(x)$?
  b. The total number of red lights encountered over the entire route—that is, going to point B and back to point A—is $(x + y)$. Find $E(x + y)$.

6.16 Refer to Exercise 6.9.
  a. Find $E(x - y)$.   **b.** Find $E(3y)$.

OPTIONAL EXERCISES

6.17 Refer to Exercise 6.8.
  a. Find $E(x)$.   **b.** Find $E(y)$.
  c. Find $E(x + y)$.   **d.** Find $E(xy)$.

6.18 Refer to Exercise 6.13.
  a. Find $E(x)$.   **b.** Find $E(y)$.
  c. Find $E(x + y)$.   **d.** Find $E(xy)$.

6.19 Let x and y be two continuous random variables with joint probability distribution $f(x, y)$. Consider the function $g(x)$. Show that

$$E[g(x)] = \int_{-\infty}^{\infty} g(x)f_1(x)dx$$

6.20 Prove Theorems 6.1–6.3 for discrete random variables x and y.

6.21 Prove Theorems 6.1–6.3 for continuous random variables x and y.

6.4 Independence

In Chapter 3 we learned that two events A and B are said to be independent if $P(A \cap B) = P(A)P(B)$. Then, since the values assumed by two discrete random variables, x and y, represent two numerical events, it follows that x and y are **independent** if $p(x, y) = p_1(x)p_2(y)$. Two continuous random variables are said to be independent if they satisfy a similar criterion.

Definition 6.8

Let x and y be discrete random variables with joint probability distribution $p(x, y)$ and marginal probability distributions $p_1(x)$ and $p_2(y)$. Then x and y are said to be **independent** if and only if

$$p(x, y) = p_1(x)p_2(y) \quad \text{for all pairs of values of } x \text{ and } y$$

Definition 6.9

Let x and y be continuous random variables with joint density function $f(x, y)$ and marginal density functions $f_1(x)$ and $f_2(y)$. Then x and y are said to be **independent** if and only if

$$f(x, y) = f_1(x)f_2(y) \quad \text{for all pairs of values of } x \text{ and } y$$

EXAMPLE 6.9   Refer to Example 6.4 and determine whether x and y are independent.

Solution   From Examples 6.4–6.6, we have the following results:

$$f(x, y) = 2x \qquad f_1(x) = 2x \qquad f_2(y) = 1$$

Therefore,

$$f_1(x)f_2(y) = (2x)(1) = 2x = f(x, y)$$

and, by Definition 6.9, x and y are independent random variables.

EXAMPLE 6.10   Refer to Example 6.8 and determine whether x and y are independent.

Solution   From Example 6.8, we determined that $f(x, y) = 6x$ when $0 \leq x \leq y$ and $0 \leq y \leq 1$. Therefore,

$$f_1(x) = \int_{-\infty}^{\infty} f(x, y)dy = \int_{x}^{1} 6x \, dy = 6xy \Big]_{x}^{1}$$
$$= 6x(1 - x) \quad \text{where } 0 \leq x \leq 1$$

Similarly,

$$f_2(y) = \int_{-\infty}^{\infty} f(x, y)dx = \int_{0}^{y} 6x \, dx = \frac{6x^2}{2} \Big]_{0}^{y}$$
$$= 3y^2 \quad \text{where } 0 \leq y \leq 1$$

You can see that $f_1(x)f_2(y) = 18x(1 - x)y^2$ is *not* equal to $f(x, y)$. Therefore, x and y are *not* independent random variables.

Theorem 6.4 points to a useful consequence of independence.

Theorem 6.4

If x and y are independent random variables, then

$$E(xy) = E(x)E(y)$$

PROOF OF THEOREM 6.4 We will prove the theorem for the discrete case. The proof for the continuous case is identical, except that integration is substituted for summation. By the definition of expected value, we have

$$E(xy) = \sum_y \sum_x xyp(x, y)$$

But, since x and y are independent, we can write $p(x, y) = p_1(x)p_2(y)$. Therefore,

$$E(xy) = \sum_y \sum_x xyp_1(x)p_2(y)$$

If we sum first with respect to x, then we can treat y and $p_2(y)$ as constants and apply Theorem 6.2 to factor them out of the sum as follows:

$$E(xy) = \sum_y yp_2(y) \sum_x xp_1(x)$$

But,

$$\sum_x xp_1(x) = E(x) \quad \text{and} \quad \sum_y yp_2(y) = E(y)$$

Therefore

$$E(xy) = E(x)E(y).$$

EXERCISES

6.22   Refer to Exercise 6.1. Are x and y independent?

6.23   Refer to Exercise 6.2. Are x and y independent?

6.24   Refer to Exercise 6.3. Are x and y independent?

6.25   Refer to Exercise 6.4. Are x and y independent?

6.26   Refer to Exercise 6.8. Are x and y independent?

6.27   Refer to Exercise 6.9. Are x and y independent?

6.28   The lifelength y (in hundreds of hours) for fuses used in a televideo computer terminal has an exponential distribution with mean $\beta = 5$. Each terminal requires two such fuses—one acting as a backup that comes into use only when the first fuse fails.
  a. If two such fuses have independent lifelengths x and y, find the joint density $f(x, y)$.
  b. The total effective lifelength of the two fuses is $(x + y)$. Find the expected total effective lifelength of a pair of fuses in a televideo computer terminal.

OPTIONAL EXERCISES

6.29   Prove Theorem 6.4 for the continuous case.

6.30   Let x and y denote the lifetimes of two different types of components in an electronic system. The joint density of x and y is given by

$$f(x, y) = \begin{cases} \frac{1}{8}\, xe^{-(x+y)/2} & \text{if } x > 0;\, y > 0 \\ 0 & \text{elsewhere} \end{cases}$$

Show that x and y are independent. [*Hint:* A theorem in multivariate probability theory states that x and y are independent if we can write

$$f(x, y) = g(x)h(y)$$

where $g(x)$ is a nonnegative function of x only and $h(y)$ is a nonnegative function of y only.]

6.31   Refer to Exercise 6.11. Show that x and y are independent. [Use the hint, Exercise 6.30.]

6.5   The Covariance of Two Random Variables

When we think of two variables x and y being related, we usually imagine a relationship in which y increases as x increases or y decreases as x increases. In other words, we tend to think in terms of **linear relationships**.

If x and y are random variables and we collect a sample of n pairs of values (x, y), it is unlikely that the plotted data points would fall exactly on a straight line. If the points lie very close to a straight line, as in Figures 6.4a and 6.4b, we think of the linear relationship between x and y as being very strong. If they are widely scattered about a line, as in Figures 6.4c and 6.4d, we think of the linear relationship as weak.

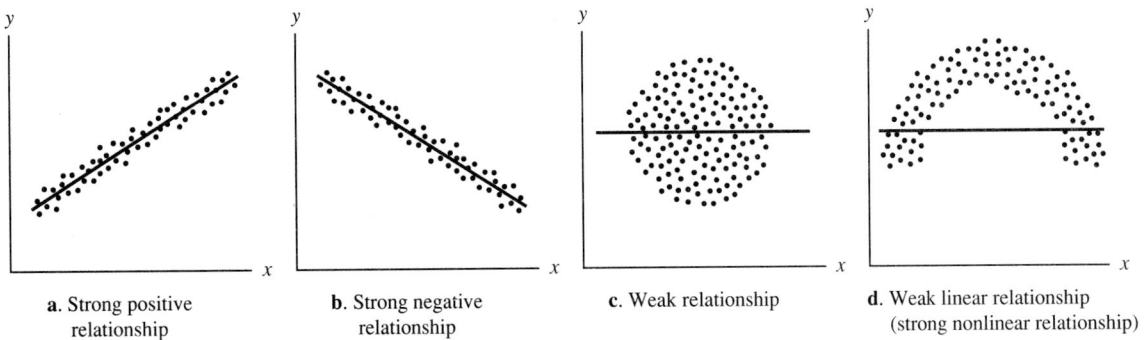

a. Strong positive
relationship

b. Strong negative
relationship

c. Weak relationship

d. Weak linear relationship
(strong nonlinear relationship)

FIGURE 6.4 ▲
Linear relationships between x
and y

(Note that the relationship between x and y in Figure 6.4d is strong in a curvilinear manner.) How can we measure the strength of the linear relationship between two random variables, x and y?

One way to measure the strength of a linear relationship is to calculate the cross-product of the deviations $(x - \mu_x)(y - \mu_y)$ for each data point. These cross-products will be positive when the data points are in the upper right or lower left quadrant of Figure 6.5 and negative when the points are in the upper left or lower right quadrant. If all the points lie close to a line with positive slope, as in Figure 6.4a, almost all the cross-products $(x - \mu_x)(y - \mu_y)$ will be positive and their mean value will be relatively large and positive. Similarly, if all the points lie close to a line with a negative slope, as in Figure 6.4b, the mean value of $(x - \mu_x)(y - \mu_y)$ will be a relatively large negative number. However, if the linear relationship between x and y is relatively weak, as in Figure 6.4c, the points will fall in all four quadrants, some cross-products $(x - \mu_x)(y - \mu_y)$ will be positive, some will be negative, and their mean value will be relatively small—perhaps very close to 0. This leads to the following definition of a measure of the strength of the linear relationship between two random variables.

FIGURE 6.5 ▶
Signs of the cross-products
$(x - \mu_x)(y - \mu_y)$

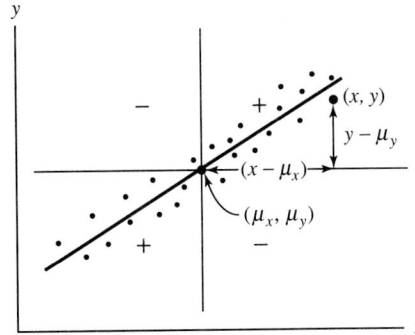

Definition 6.10

The **covariance** of two random variables, x and y, is defined to be

$$\text{Cov}(x, y) = E[(x - \mu_x)(y - \mu_y)]$$

Theorem 6.5

$$\text{Cov}(x, y) = E(xy) - \mu_x \mu_y$$

PROOF OF THEOREM 6.5 By Definition 6.10, we can write

$$\text{Cov}(x, y) = E[(x - \mu_x)(y - \mu_y)]$$
$$= E(xy - \mu_x y - \mu_y x + \mu_x \mu_y)$$

Applying Theorems 6.1, 6.2, and 6.3 yields

$$\text{Cov}(x, y) = E(x, y) - \mu_x E(y) - \mu_y E(x) + \mu_x \mu_y$$
$$= E(x, y) - \mu_x \mu_y - \mu_x \mu_y + \mu_x \mu_y$$
$$= E(x, y) - \mu_x \mu_y$$

EXAMPLE 6.11

Find the covariance of the random variables x and y of Example 6.4.

Solution

The variables have joint density function $f(x, y) = 2x$ when $0 \le x \le 1$ and $0 \le y \le 1$. Then

$$E(xy) = \int_0^1 \int_0^1 (xy)2x \, dx \, dy$$

$$= \int_0^1 2\left(\frac{x^3}{3}\right)\Big]_0^1 y \, dy = \frac{2}{3} \int_0^1 y \, dy = \frac{2}{3}\left(\frac{y^2}{2}\right)\Big]_0^1 = \frac{1}{3}$$

In Examples 6.5 and 6.6, we obtained the marginal density functions $f_1(x) = 2x$ and $f_2(y) = 1$. Therefore,

$$\mu_x = E(x) = \int_0^1 x f_1(x)dx = \int_0^1 x(2x)dx = 2\left(\frac{x^3}{3}\right)\Big]_0^1 = \frac{2}{3}$$

Furthermore, since y is a uniform random variable defined over the interval $0 \le y \le 1$ (see Example 6.6), it follows from Section 5.4 that $\mu_y = \frac{1}{2}$. Then

$$\text{Cov}(x, y) = E(x, y) - \mu_x \mu_y = \frac{1}{3} - \left(\frac{2}{3}\right)\left(\frac{1}{2}\right) = 0$$

Example 6.11 demonstrates an important result: If x and y are independent, then their covariance will equal 0. However, *the converse is not true*.

Theorem 6.6

If two random variables x and y are independent, then

$$\text{Cov}(x, y) = 0$$

The proof of Theorem 6.6, which follows readily from Theorem 6.5, is left as an optional exercise.

6.6   The Correlation Coefficient ρ

If the covariance between two random variables is positive, then y tends to increase as x increases. If the covariance is negative, then y tends to decrease as x increases. But what can we say about the numerical value of the covariance? We know that a covariance equal to 0 means that there is no linear relationship between x and y, but when the covariance is nonzero, its absolute value will depend on the units of measurement of x and y. To overcome this difficulty, we define a standardized version of the covariance known as the **coefficient of correlation**.

Definition 6.11

The **coefficient of correlation** ρ for two random variables x and y is

$$\rho = \frac{\text{Cov}(x, y)}{\sigma_x \sigma_y}$$

where σ_x and σ_y are the standard deviations of x and y, respectively.

Since ρ is equal to the covariance divided by the product of two positive quantities, σ_x and σ_y, it will have the same sign as the covariance but, in addition, it will (proof omitted) assume a value in the interval $-1 \leq \rho \leq 1$. Values of $\rho = -1$ and $\rho = 1$ imply perfect straight-line relationships between x and y, the former with a negative slope and the latter with a positive slope. A value of $\rho = 0$ implies no linear relationship between x and y.

> ### Property of the Correlation Coefficient
>
> $$-1 \le \rho \le 1$$

EXERCISES

6.32   Find the covariance of the random variables x and y in Exercise 6.1.

6.33   Find the covariance of the random variables x and y in Exercise 6.2.

6.34   Find the correlation coefficient ρ for x and y in Exercise 6.3.

6.35   Refer to Exercise 6.5.
  a. Find the covariance of the random variables x and y.
  b. Find the coefficient of correlation ρ for x and y.

6.36   Refer to Exercise 6.8.
  a. Find the covariance of the random variables x and y.
  b. Find the coefficient of correlation ρ for x and y.

6.37   Refer to Exercise 6.9.
  a. Find the covariance of the random variables x and y.
  b. Find the coefficient of correlation ρ for x and y.

OPTIONAL EXERCISES

6.38   Commercial kerosene is stocked in a bulk tank at the beginning of each week. Because of limited supplies, the proportion x of the capacity of the tank available for sale and the proportion y of the capacity of the tank actually sold during the week are continuous random variables. Their joint distribution is given by

$$f(x,\ y) = \begin{cases} 4x^2 & \text{if } 0 \le y \le x; \quad 0 \le x \le 1 \\ 0 & \text{elsewhere} \end{cases}$$

Find the covariance of x and y.

6.39   Prove Theorem 6.6 for the discrete case.

6.40   Prove Theorem 6.6 for the continuous case.

6.41   As an illustration of why the converse of Theorem 6.6 is not true, consider the joint distribution of two discrete random variables, x and y, shown in the accompanying table. Show that $\text{Cov}(x, y) = 0$, but that x and y are dependent.

		x		
		-1	0	$+1$
	-1	$\frac{1}{12}$	$\frac{2}{12}$	$\frac{1}{12}$
y	0	$\frac{2}{12}$	0	$\frac{2}{12}$
	$+1$	$\frac{1}{12}$	$\frac{2}{12}$	$\frac{1}{12}$

6.42   Find the covariance of x and y for the random variables of Exercise 6.13.

6.7   The Expected Value and Variance of Linear Functions of Random Variables (Optional)

Many experiments are conducted in engineering and the sciences to develop a mathematical model explaining the relationship between two or more variables. The usual objective is to be able to predict the value of one of the variables, y, given specific values of the other variables. In the methodology most frequently employed for fitting a model to multivariable data sets—**regression analysis** (the topic of Chapters 11 and 12)—estimates of the model parameters are **linear functions** of the observed sample y values.

Definition 6.12

Let $y_1, y_2, \ldots, y_n$ be random variables and let $a_1, a_2, \ldots, a_n$ be constants. Then ℓ is a **linear function** of $y_1, y_2, \ldots, y_n$ if

$$\ell = a_1 y_1 + a_2 y_2 + \cdots + a_n y_n$$

The expected value (mean) and variance of a linear function of $y_1, y_2, \ldots, y_n$ may be computed using the formulas presented in Theorem 6.7.

Theorem 6.7

The Expected Value $E(\ell)$ and Variance $V(\ell)^*$ of a Linear Function of $y_1, y_2, \ldots, y_n$

Suppose the means and variances of $y_1, y_2, \ldots, y_n$ are (μ_1, σ_1^2), (μ_2, σ_2^2), $\ldots, (\mu_n, \sigma_n^2)$, respectively. If $\ell = a_1 y_1 + a_2 y_2 + \cdots + a_n y_n$, then

$$E(\ell) = a_1\mu_1 + a_2\mu_2 + \cdots + a_n\mu_n$$

and

$$\begin{aligned}
\sigma_\ell^2 = V(\ell) &= a_1^2\sigma_1^2 + a_2^2\sigma_2^2 + \cdots + a_n^2\sigma_n^2 \\
&\quad + 2a_1a_2\text{Cov}(y_1, y_2) + 2a_1a_3\text{Cov}(y_1, y_3) + \cdots \\
&\quad + 2a_1a_n\text{Cov}(y_1, y_n) + 2a_2a_3\text{Cov}(y_2, y_3) \\
&\quad + \cdots + 2a_2a_n\text{Cov}(y_2, y_n) + \cdots + 2a_{n-1}a_n\text{Cov}(y_{n-1}, y_n)
\end{aligned}$$

Note: If $y_1, y_2, \ldots, y_n$ are independent, then

$$\sigma_\ell^2 = V(\ell) = a_1^2\sigma_1^2 + a_2^2\sigma_2^2 + \cdots + a_n^2\sigma_n^2$$

PROOF OF THEOREM 6.7   By Theorem 6.3, we know

$$E(\ell) = E(a_1 y_1) + E(a_2 y_2) + \cdots + E(a_n y_n)$$

Then, by Theorem 6.2,

$$\begin{aligned}
E(\ell) &= a_1 E(y_1) + a_2 E(y_2) + \cdots + a_n E(y_n) \\
&= a_1\mu_1 + a_2\mu_2 + \cdots + a_n\mu_n
\end{aligned}$$

Similarly,

$$\begin{aligned}
V(\ell) &= E\{[\ell - E(\ell)]^2\} \\
&= E[(a_1 y_1 + a_2 y_2 + \cdots + a_n y_n - a_1\mu_1 - a_2\mu_2 - \cdots - a_n\mu_n)^2] \\
&= E\{[a_1(y_1 - \mu_1) + a_2(y_2 - \mu_2) + \cdots + a_n(y_n - \mu_n)]^2\} \\
&= E[a_1^2(y_1 - \mu_1)^2 + a_2^2(y_2 - \mu_2)^2 + \cdots + a_n^2(y_n - \mu_n)^2 \\
&\quad + 2a_1a_2(y_1 - \mu_1)(y_2 - \mu_2) + 2a_1a_3(y_1 - \mu_1)(y_3 - \mu_3) \\
&\quad + \cdots + 2a_{n-1}a_n(y_{n-1} - \mu_{n-1})(y_n - \mu_n)] \\
&= a_1^2 E[(y_1 - \mu_1)^2] + \cdots + a_n^2 E[(y_n - \mu_n)^2] \\
&\quad + 2a_1a_2 E[(y_1 - \mu_1)(y_2 - \mu_2)] + 2a_1a_3 E[(y_1 - \mu_1)(y_3 - \mu_3)] \\
&\quad + \cdots + 2a_{n-1}a_n E[(y_{n-1} - \mu_{n-1})(y_n - \mu_n)]
\end{aligned}$$

By the definitions of variance and covariance, we have

$$E[(y_i - \mu_i)^2] = \sigma_i^2 \quad \text{and} \quad E[(y_i - \mu_i)(y_j - \mu_j)] = \text{Cov}(y_i, y_j)$$

---

*In the preceding sections, we have used different subscripts on the symbol σ^2 to denote the variances of different random variables. This notation is cumbersome if the random variable is a function of several other random variables. Consequently, we will use the notation σ_0^2 or $V(\ )$ interchangeably to denote a variance.

Therefore,

$$V(\ell) = a_1^2\sigma_1^2 + a_2^2\sigma_2^2 + \cdots + a_n^2\sigma_n^2 + 2a_1a_2\text{Cov}(y_1, y_2) + 2a_1a_3\text{Cov}(y_1, y_3)$$
$$+ \cdots + 2a_2a_3\text{Cov}(y_2, y_3) + \cdots + 2a_{n-1}a_n\text{Cov}(y_{n-1}, y_n)$$

EXAMPLE 6.12

Suppose y_1, y_2, and y_3 are random variables with $(\mu_1 = 1, \sigma_1^2 = 2)$, $(\mu_2 = 3, \sigma_2^2 = 1)$, $(\mu_3 = 0, \sigma_3^2 = 4)$, $\text{Cov}(y_1, y_2) = -1$, $\text{Cov}(y_1, y_3) = 2$, and $\text{Cov}(y_2, y_3) = 1$. Find the mean and variance of

$$\ell = 2y_1 + y_2 - 3y_3$$

Solution

The linear function

$$\ell = 2y_1 + y_2 - 3y_3$$

has coefficients $a_1 = 2$, $a_2 = 1$, and $a_3 = -3$. Then by Theorem 6.7,

$$\begin{aligned}
E(\ell) &= a_1\mu_1 + a_2\mu_2 + a_3\mu_3 \\
&= (2)(1) + (1)(3) + (-3)(0) = 5 \\
V(\ell) &= a_1^2\sigma_1^2 + a_2^2\sigma_2^2 + a_3^2\sigma_3^2 \\
&\quad + 2a_1a_2\text{Cov}(y_1, y_2) + 2a_1a_3\text{Cov}(y_1, y_3) + 2a_2a_3\text{Cov}(y_2, y_3) \\
&= (2)^2(2) + (1)^2(1) + (-3)^2(4) \\
&\quad + 2(2)(1)(-1) + 2(2)(-3)(2) + 2(1)(-3)(1) \\
&= 11
\end{aligned}$$

These results indicate that the probability distribution of ℓ is centered about $E(\ell) = \mu_\ell = 5$ and that its spread is measured by $\sigma_\ell = \sqrt{V(\ell)} = \sqrt{11} = 3.3$. If we were to randomly select values of y_1, y_2, and y_3, we would expect the value of ℓ to fall in the interval $\mu_\ell \pm 2\sigma_\ell$, or -1.6 to 11.6, according to the Empirical Rule.

EXAMPLE 6.13

Let y_1, y_2, . . . , y_n be a sample of n independent observations selected from a population with mean μ and variance σ^2. Find the expected value and variance of the sample mean, $\bar{y}$.

Solution

The sample measurements, y_1, y_2, . . . , y_n, can be viewed as observations on n independent random variables, where y_1 corresponds to the first observation, y_2 to the second, etc. Therefore, the sample mean $\bar{y}$ will be a random variable with a probability distribution (or density function).

By writing

$$\bar{y} = \frac{\sum\limits_{i=1}^{n} y_i}{n} = \frac{y_1}{n} + \frac{y_2}{n} + \cdots + \frac{y_n}{n}$$

we see that $\bar{y}$ is a linear function of $y_1, y_2, \ldots, y_n$, with $a_1 = \frac{1}{n}$, $a_2 = \frac{1}{n}, \ldots$, $a_n = \frac{1}{n}$. Since $y_1, y_2, \ldots, y_n$ are independent, it follows from Theorem 6.6 that the covariance of y_i and y_j, for all pairs with $i \neq j$, will equal 0. Therefore, we can apply Theorem 6.7 to obtain

$$E(\bar{y}) = \left(\frac{1}{n}\right)\mu + \left(\frac{1}{n}\right)\mu + \cdots + \left(\frac{1}{n}\right)\mu = \frac{n\mu}{n} = \mu$$

$$V(\bar{y}) = \left(\frac{1}{n}\right)^2 \sigma^2 + \left(\frac{1}{n}\right)^2 \sigma^2 + \cdots + \left(\frac{1}{n}\right)^2 \sigma^2 = \left(\frac{n}{n^2}\right)\sigma^2 = \frac{\sigma^2}{n}$$

EXAMPLE 6.14

Suppose that the population of Example 6.13 has mean $\mu = 10$ and variance $\sigma^2 = 4$. Describe the probability distribution for a sample mean based on $n = 25$ observations.

Solution

From Example 6.13, we know that the probability distribution of the sample mean will have mean and variance

$$E(\bar{y}) = \mu = 10 \quad \text{and} \quad \sigma_{\bar{y}}^2 = V(\bar{y}) = \frac{\sigma^2}{n} = \frac{4}{25}$$

and thus,

$$\sigma_{\bar{y}} = \sqrt{V(\bar{y})} = \sqrt{\frac{4}{25}} = \frac{2}{5} = .4$$

Therefore, the probability distribution of $\bar{y}$ will be centered about its mean, $\mu = 10$, and most of the distribution will fall in the interval $\mu \pm 2\sigma_{\bar{y}}$, or $10 \pm 2(.4)$, or 9.2 to 10.8. We will learn more about the properties of the probability distribution of $\bar{y}$ in Chapter 7.

EXERCISES

6.43 Suppose that y_1, y_2, and y_3 are random variables with $(\mu_1 = 0, \sigma_1^2 = 2)$, $(\mu_2 = -1, \sigma_2^2 = 3)$, $(\mu_3 = 5, \sigma_3^2 = 9)$, $\text{Cov}(y_1, y_2) = 1$, $\text{Cov}(y_1, y_3) = 4$, and $\text{Cov}(y_2, y_3) = -2$. Find the mean and variance of

$$\ell = \frac{1}{2} y_1 - y_2 + 2y_3$$

6.44 Suppose that y_1, y_2, y_3, and y_4 are random variables with

$$
\begin{array}{llll}
E(y_1) = 2 & V(y_1) = 4 & \text{Cov}(y_1, y_2) = -1 & \text{Cov}(y_2, y_3) = 0 \\
E(y_2) = 4 & V(y_2) = 8 & \text{Cov}(y_1, y_3) = 1 & \text{Cov}(y_2, y_4) = 2 \\
E(y_3) = -1 & V(y_3) = 6 & \text{Cov}(y_1, y_4) = \frac{1}{2} & \text{Cov}(y_3, y_4) = 0 \\
E(y_4) = 0 & V(y_4) = 1 & &
\end{array}
$$

Find the mean and variance of

$$\ell = -3y_1 + 2y_2 + 6y_3 - y_4$$

6.45 Refer to Exercise 6.2. Find the mean and variance of $(x + y)$, the sum of the dots showing on the two dice.

6.46 Refer to Exercises 6.5 and 6.15. Find the variance of $(x + y)$. Within what range would you expect $(x + y)$ to fall?

6.47 Refer to Exercises 6.9 and 6.16. Find the variance of $(x - y)$.

OPTIONAL EXERCISES

6.48 A particular manufacturing process yields a proportion p of defective items in each lot. The number y of defectives in a random sample of n items from the process follows a binomial distribution. Find the expected value and variance of $\hat{p} = y/n$, the fraction of defectives in the sample. [*Hint:* Write $\hat{p}$ as a linear function of a single random variable y, i.e., $\hat{p} = a_1 y$, where $a_1 = 1/n$.]

6.49 Let y_1, y_2, . . . , y_n be a sample of n independent observations selected from a gamma distribution with $\alpha = 1$ and $\beta = 2$. Show that the expected value and variance of the sample mean $\bar{y}$ are identical to the expected value and variance of a gamma distribution with parameters $\alpha = n$ and $\beta = 2/n$.

6.8 Summary

In Chapter 4, we defined a single random variable over a sample space. In this chapter, we extend this concept by defining two or more random variables, y_1, y_2, . . . , y_n, over a sample space. The probability of the intersection of the discrete numerical events, y_1, y_2, . . . , y_n, is represented by a **joint probability distribution** $p(y_1, y_2, . . . , y_n)$. Analogously, we define a **joint density function**, $f(y_1, y_2, . . . , y_n)$, which enables us to calculate probabilities associated with continuous random variables y_1, y_2, . . . , y_n.

The final objective of this chapter was to enable us to obtain the mean and variance of a **linear function** of random variables. This will be particularly useful in subsequent chapters when the random variables represent independent sample observations from a single population.

SUPPLEMENTARY EXERCISES

6.50   The management of a bank must decide whether to install a commercial loan decision-support system (an on-line management information system) to aid its analysts in making commercial loan decisions. Past experience shows that x, the additional number (per year) of correct loan decisions—accepting good loan applications and rejecting those that would eventually be defaulted—attributable to the decision-support system, and y, the lifetime (in years) of the decision-support system, have the joint probability distribution shown in the table.

		0	10	20	30	40	50	60	70	80	90
	1	.001	.002	.002	.025	.040	.025	.005	.005	0	0
	2	.005	.005	.010	.075	.100	.075	.050	.030	.030	.025
y	3	0	0	0	.025	.050	.080	.050	.080	.040	.030
	4	0	.001	.002	.005	.010	.025	.010	.003	.001	.001
	5	0	.002	.005	.005	.020	.030	.015	0	0	0

a. Find the marginal probability distributions, $p_1(x)$ and $p_2(y)$.
b. Find the conditional probability distribution, $p_1(x \mid y)$.
c. Given that the decision-support system is in its third year of operation, find the probability that at least 40 additional correct loan decisions will be made.
d. Find the expected lifetime of the decision-support system, i.e., find $E(y)$.
e. Are x and y correlated? Are x and y independent?
f. Each correct loan decision contributes approximately \$25,000 to the bank's profit. Compute the mean and standard deviation of the additional profit attributable to the decision-support system. [*Hint:* Use the marginal distribution $p_1(x)$.]

6.51   Suppose that x and y, the proportions of an 8-hour workday that two gas station attendants actually spend on performing their assigned duties, have joint probability density

$$f(x, y) = \begin{cases} x + y & \text{if } 0 \le x \le 1; 0 \le y \le 1 \\ 0 & \text{elsewhere} \end{cases}$$

a. Find the marginal probability distributions, $f_1(x)$ and $f_2(y)$.
b. Verify that

$$\int_{-\infty}^{\infty} f_1(x)dx = 1 \quad \text{and} \quad \int_{-\infty}^{\infty} f_2(y)dy = 1$$

c. Find the conditional probability distributions, $f_1(x \mid y)$ and $f_2(y \mid x)$.
d. Verify that

$$\int_{-\infty}^{\infty} f_1(x \mid y)dx = 1 \quad \text{and} \quad \int_{-\infty}^{\infty} f_2(y \mid x)dy = 1$$

e. Are x and y correlated? Are x and y independent?

f. The proportion d of "dead" time (i.e., time when no assigned duties are performed) for the two attendants is given by the relation $d = 1 - (x + y)/2$. Find $E(d)$ and $V(d)$. Within what limits would you expect d to fall?

6.52 Concrete experiences a characteristic marked increase in "creep" when it is heated for the first time under load. An experiment was conducted to investigate the transient thermal strain behavior of concrete (*Magazine of Concrete Research*, Dec. 1985). Two variables thought to affect thermal strain are x, rate of heating (degrees Centigrade per minute), and y, level of load (percentage of initial strength). Concrete specimens are prepared and tested under various combinations of heating rate and load, and the thermal strain is determined for each. Suppose the joint probability distribution for x and y for those specimens that yielded acceptable results is as given in the table. Suppose a concrete specimen is randomly selected from among those in the experiment that yielded acceptable thermal strain behavior.

		.1	.2	.3	.4	.5
				x (°C/minute)		
y	0	.17	.11	.07	.05	.05
	10	.10	.06	.05	.02	.01
	20	.09	.04	.03	.01	0
	30	.08	.04	.02	0	0

a. Find the probability that the concrete specimen was heated at a rate of .3°C/minute.

b. Given that the concrete specimen was heated at .3°C/minute, find the probability that the specimen had a load of 20%.

c. Are rate of heating x and level of load y correlated?

d. Are rate of heating x and level of load y independent?

OPTIONAL SUPPLEMENTARY EXERCISES

6.53 Let x and y be two continuous random variables with joint density $f(x, y)$. Show that

$$f_2(y \mid x)f_1(x) = f_1(x \mid y)f_2(y)$$

6.54 Let x and y be uncorrelated random variables. Verify each of the following:

a. $V(x + y) = V(x - y)$

b. $\text{Cov}[(x + y), (x - y)] = V(x) - V(y)$

6.55 Suppose three continuous random variables have the joint distribution

$$f(y_1, y_2, y_3) = \begin{cases} c(y_1 + y_2)e^{-y_3} & \text{if } 0 \le y_1 \le 1; 0 \le y_2 \le 2; y_3 > 0 \\ 0 & \text{elsewhere} \end{cases}$$

a. Find the value of c that makes $f(y_1, y_2, y_3)$ a probability density.

b. Are the three variables independent? [*Hint:* If $f(y_1, y_2, y_3) = f_1(y_1)f_2(y_2)f_3(y_3)$, then y_1, y_2, and y_3 are independent.]

References

Hoel, P. G. *Introduction to Mathematical Statistics*, 4th ed. New York: Wiley, 1971.

Hogg, R. V., and Craig, A. T. *Introduction to Mathematical Statistics*, 4th ed. New York: Macmillan, 1978.

Mendenhall, W., Wackerly, D. D., and Scheaffer, R. L. *Mathematical Statistics with Applications*, 4th ed. Boston: PWS-Kent, 1989.

Mood, A. M., Graybill, F. A., and Boes, D. *Introduction to the Theory of Statistics*, 3rd ed. New York: McGraw-Hill, 1974.

CHAPTER SEVEN

Sampling Distributions

Objective

To present methods for finding the probability distribution (sampling distribution) of a statistic; to identify the sampling distributions for some useful statistics

Contents

7.1   Random Sampling

Recall from Chapter 1 that statistical inference involves sampling from a well-defined population. How a sample is selected from a population is of vital importance because the probability of an observed sample will be used to infer the characteristics of the sampled population.

To illustrate, suppose you deal yourself 4 cards from a deck of 52 cards and all 4 cards are aces. Do you conclude that your deck is an ordinary bridge deck, containing only 4 aces, or do you conclude that the deck is stacked with more than 4 aces? It depends on how the cards were drawn. If the 4 aces are always placed at the top of a standard bridge deck, drawing 4 aces is not unusual—it is certain. On the other hand, if the cards are thoroughly mixed, drawing 4 aces in a sample of 4 cards is highly improbable. The point, of course, is that in order to use the observed sample of 4 cards to draw inferences about the population (the deck of 52 cards), you need to know how the sample was selected from the deck.

One of the simplest and most frequently employed sampling procedures produces what is known as a **random sample**.

Definition 7.1

If n elements are selected from a population in such a way that every set of n elements in the population has an equal probability of being selected, the n elements are said to be a **random sample**.*

EXAMPLE 7.1

An experiment was conducted in which each of 10 different antiscalants was added to an aliquot of brine. One of the 10 brine solutions is to be selected, filtered, and the amount of silica determined. How would you select the brine solution so that the choice is random?

Solution

If the choice is to be random, each brine solution must have the same probability of being drawn. That is, each solution should have a probability of $\frac{1}{10}$ of being selected. A method to achieve the objective of equal selection probabilities is to *thoroughly mix* the 10 brine solutions and *blindly* pick one of the solutions. If this procedure were

---

*Strictly speaking, this is a **simple random sample**. There are many different types of random samples. For example, a **stratified random sample** is obtained by partitioning the population into groups (*strata*) and selecting a random sample of elements from each group; a **cluster sample** involves randomly selecting groups (or *clusters*) of elements from the population and sampling *all* elements in each cluster; and a **systematic sample** is collected by systematically selecting every kth element from the population. Since it is the most common, we focus our discussion on the random sample.

repeatedly used, each time replacing the selected solution, a particular solution should be chosen approximately $\frac{1}{10}$ of the time in a long series of draws. This method of sampling is known as **random sampling**.

....

How can a random sample be generated? If a population is not too large and the elements can be numbered on slips of paper, poker chips, etc., you can physically mix the slips of paper or chips and remove n elements from the total. The numbers that appear on the chips selected would indicate the population elements to be included in the sample. Such a procedure will not guarantee a random sample, because it is often difficult to achieve a thorough mix, but it provides a reasonably good approximation to random sampling.

Another, more formal, technique is to use a **table of random numbers**. Random number tables are generated by computer in such a way that every number of the same length (2-digit, 3-digit, 4-digit, etc.), occurs with equal probability. Further, the occurrence of any one number in the table is independent of any of the other numbers in the table. Consequently, the numbers that are selected from a random number table identify the elements to be included in the random sample.

Although this method of random sampling is easy to implement, it can become time-consuming and tedious if the number of observations in the sample is large. Therefore, large-sample scientific studies rely on computers (with built-in random number generators) to automatically select the random sample.

....

EXAMPLE 7.2

Suppose you want to randomly sample 5 (we will keep the number in the sample small to simplify our example) from a shipment of 100,000 bolts for quality control testing.

a. Use a random number table to select this random sample.

b. Use the computer to generate the random sample.

Solution

a. Since there are 100,000 bolts in the shipment (target population), we first number the bolts from 1 to 100,000. Then, we turn to a table of random numbers (see Table 6, Appendix II), and select a page, say, the first page. (A partial reproduction of the first page of Table 6 is shown in Table 7.1 on page 292.) Now, randomly select a starting number, say, the random number appearing in the third row, second column. This number is 48360. Proceed down the second column to obtain the remaining four random numbers. (Proceeding down or across is an arbitrary choice.) The five selected random numbers are shaded in Table 7.1. Using the first five digits to represent the bolts from 1 to 99,999 and the number 00000 to represent bolt 100,000, you can see that the bolts numbered

   48,360   93,093   39,975   6,907   72,905

should be included in your sample.

TABLE 7.1   Partial Reproduction of Table 6 of Appendix II

Row	Column 1	2	3	4	5	6
1	10480	15011	01536	02011	81647	91646
2	22368	46573	25595	85393	30995	89198
3	24130	48360	22527	97265	76393	64809
4	42167	93093	06243	61680	07856	16376
5	37570	39975	81837	16656	06121	91782
6	77921	06907	11008	42751	27756	53498
7	99562	72905	56420	69994	98872	31016
8	96301	91977	05463	07972	18876	20922
9	89579	14342	63661	10281	17453	18103
10	85475	36857	53342	53988	53060	59533
11	28918	69578	88231	33276	70997	79936
12	63553	40961	48235	03427	49626	69445
13	09429	93969	52636	92737	88974	33488
14	10365	61129	87529	85689	48237	52267
15	07119	97336	71048	08178	77233	13916

b. Almost all of the commercial statistical software packages available (e.g., SAS and MINITAB) have procedures for generating random samples. The output from a SAS program designed to generate a sample of size 5 from a population of 100,000 elements is displayed in Figure 7.1.* From the printout, you can see that bolts numbered

6,181   35,982   76,110   58,667   59,592

comprise the random sample of size 5.

FIGURE 7.1 ▶
SAS-generated random sample for
Example 7.2

OBS	SELECT
1	6181
2	35982
3	76110
4	58667
5	59592

Although random sampling represents one of the simplest of the multitude of sampling techniques available for research, most of the statistical methods presented

---

*The commands for generating a random sample in SAS and MINITAB are provided in the Computer Lab at the end of this chapter.

in this text assume that such a sample has been collected. If a researcher knows that a sample is nonrandom, any inferences derived from the analysis may be invalid.

EXERCISES

7.1 Refer to the DDT levels for 144 contaminated fish specimens, Appendix III. Use Table 6 of Appendix II or a computer to generate a random sample of $n = 10$ DDT levels from the data set.

7.2 Refer to the CPU times for 1,000 computer jobs, Appendix IV. Use Table 6 of Appendix II or a computer to generate a random sample of $n = 25$ CPU times from the data set.

7.3 Refer to the percentage iron contents for 390 iron-ore specimens, Appendix V. Use Table 6 of Appendix II or a computer to generate a random sample of $n = 5$ percentage iron measurements from the data set.

7.4 Laboratory tests were conducted to compare the permeability of open-graded asphalt concrete with asphalt contents of 3% and 7% (*Journal of Testing and Evaluation*, July 1981). Eight batches of cement were prepared—four with a 3% asphalt mix and four with a 7% asphalt mix. Use Table 6 of Appendix II to randomly select the four batches that receive the 3% asphalt mix.

7.5 One of the most infamous examples of improper sampling was conducted in 1936 by the *Literary Digest* to determine the winner of the Landon–Roosevelt presidential election. The poll, which predicted Landon to be the winner, was conducted by sending ballots to a random sample of persons selected from among the names listed in the telephone directories of that year. In the actual election, Landon won in Maine and Vermont but lost in the remaining 46 states. The *Literary Digest*'s erroneous forecast is believed to be the major reason for its eventual failure.

What was the cause of the *Digest*'s erroneous forecast? That is, why might the sampling procedure described above yield a sample of people whose opinions might be biased in favor of Landon?

7.6 Every 10 years the United States population census provides essential information about our nation and its people. The basic constitutional purpose of the census is to apportion the membership of the House of Representatives among the states. However, the census has many other important uses. For example, private business uses the census for plant location and marketing.

The 1990 census included questions on age, sex, race, marital status, family relationship, and income; this census was mailed to every household in the United States. In some cities, however, a series of questions was added for a 5% sample of the city's households. That is, each of a random sample of the city's households was mailed a census form that included additional questions. Suppose that a particular city contained 100,000 households and, of these, 5,000 were selected and mailed the longer census form.

a. If you worked for the Bureau of the Census and were assigned the task of selecting a random sample of 5,000 of the city's households, describe how you would proceed.

b. Suppose that one of the additional questions on the long form of the census concerned energy consumption. The city used this sample information to project the average energy consumption for the city's 100,000 households. Explain why it is important that the sample of 5,000 households be random.

c. Using the procedure you described in part **a**, randomly select a sample of 10 households from the 100,000 households in the city.

7.2   Sampling Distributions

Recall (Chapter 6) that the n measurements in a sample can be viewed as observations on n random variables, $y_1, y_2, \ldots, y_n$. Consequently, the sample mean $\bar{y}$, the sample variance s^2, and other statistics are functions of random variables—functions that we will use in the following chapters to make inferences about population parameters. Thus, a primary reason for presenting the theory of probability and probability distributions in the preceding chapters was to enable us to find and evaluate the properties of the probability distribution of a statistic. This probability distribution is often called the **sampling distribution** of the statistic. As is the case for a single random variable, its mean is the expected value of the statistic. Its standard deviation is called the **standard error** of the statistic.

Definition 7.2

....

The **sampling distribution** of a statistic is its probability distribution.

Definition 7.3

....

The **standard error** of a statistic is the standard deviation of its sampling distribution.

The mathematical techniques for finding the sampling distribution of a statistic are difficult to apply and, except for very simple examples, are beyond the scope of this text. We will introduce this topic in Section 7.3, where we will develop a procedure for using a computer to generate random samples from theoretical populations of data. We will use this simulated sampling procedure to draw many samples of a specified size, calculate the value of a statistic for each sample, and form a relative frequency histogram of these values. The resulting relative frequency histogram will be an approximation to the sampling distribution of the statistic.

Even if we are unable to find the exact mathematical form of the probability distribution of a statistic and are unable to approximate it using simulation, we can always find its mean and variance using the methods of Chapters 4–6. Then we can obtain an approximate description of the sampling distribution by applying the Empirical Rule.

7.3 Probability Distributions of Functions of Random Variables (Optional)

There are essentially three methods for finding the density function for a function of one or more random variables. Two of these—the moment generating function method and the transformation method—are beyond the scope of this text, but a discussion of them can be found in the references at the end of the chapter. The third method, which we will call the **cumulative distribution function method**, will be demonstrated with examples.

Suppose w is a function of one or more random variables. The cumulative distribution function method finds the density function for w by first finding the probability $P(w \leq w_0)$, which (dropping the subscript 0) is equal to $F(w)$. The density function $f(w)$ is then found by differentiating $F(w)$ with respect to w. We will demonstrate the method in Examples 7.3 and 7.4.

EXAMPLE 7.3

Suppose the random variable y has a density function

$$f(y) = \begin{cases} \dfrac{e^{-y/\beta}}{\beta} & \text{if } 0 \leq y < \infty \\ 0 & \text{elsewhere} \end{cases}$$

and let $w(y) = y^2$. Find the density function for the random variable w.

Solution

A graph of $w = y^2$ is shown in Figure 7.2 on page 296. We will denote the cumulative distribution functions of w and y as $G(w)$ and $F(y)$, respectively. We note from the figure that w will be less than w_0 whenever y is less than y_0; it follows that $P(w \leq w_0) = G(w_0) = F(y_0)$. Since $w = y^2$, we have $y_0 = \sqrt{w_0}$ and

$$F(y_0) = F(\sqrt{w_0}) = \int_{-\infty}^{\sqrt{w_0}} f(y)dy = \int_0^{\sqrt{w_0}} \frac{e^{-y/\beta}}{\beta}\,dy = -e^{-y/\beta}\Big]_0^{\sqrt{w_0}} = 1 - e^{-(\sqrt{w_0}/\beta)}$$

Therefore, the cumulative distribution function for w is

$$G(w) = 1 - e^{-(\sqrt{w}/\beta)}$$

Differentiating, we obtain the density function for w:

$$\frac{dG(w)}{dw} = f(w) = \frac{w^{-1/2}e^{-(\sqrt{w}/\beta)}}{2\beta}$$

FIGURE 7.2 ▶
A graph of $w = y^2$

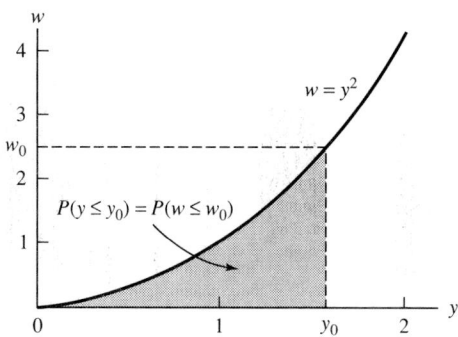

EXAMPLE 7.4

If the random variables x and y possess a uniform joint density function over the unit square, then $f(x, y) = 1$ for $0 \le x \le 1$ and $0 \le y \le 1$. Find the density function for the sum $w = x + y$.

Solution

Each value of w corresponds to a series of points on the line $w_0 = x + y$ (see Figure 7.3). Written in the slope–intercept form, $y = w_0 - x$, this is the equation of a line with slope equal to -1 and y-intercept equal to w_0. The values of w that are less than or equal to w_0 are those corresponding to points (x, y) below the line $w_0 = x + y$. (This area is shaded in Figure 7.3.) Then, for values of the y-intercept w_0, $0 \le w_0 \le 1$, the probability that w is less than or equal to w_0 is equal to the volume of a solid over the shaded area shown in the figure. We could find this probability by multiple integration, but it is easier to obtain it with the aid of geometry. Each of the two equal sides of the triangle has length w_0. Therefore, the area of the shaded triangular region is $w_0^2/2$, the height of the solid over the region is $f(x, y) = 1$, and the volume is

$$P(w \le w_0) = F(w_0) = w_0^2/2$$

We now drop the subscript to obtain

$$F(w) = w^2/2 \quad (0 \le w \le 1)$$

FIGURE 7.3 ▶
A graph showing the region of integration to find $F(w_0)$,
$0 \le w_0 \le 1$

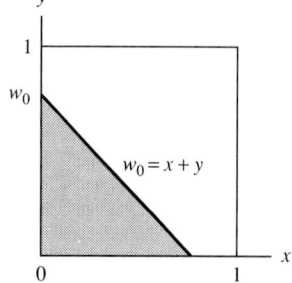

The equation for $F(w)$ is different over the interval $1 \leq w \leq 2$. The probability $P(w \leq w_0) = F(w_0)$ is the integral of $f(x, y) = 1$ over the shaded area shown in Figure 7.4. The integral can be found by subtracting from 1 the volume corresponding to the small triangular (nonshaded) area that lies above the line $w_0 = x + y$. To find the length of one side of this triangle, we need to locate the point where the line $w_0 = x + y$ intersects the line $y = 1$. Substituting $y = 1$ into the equation of the line, we find

$$w_0 = x + 1 \quad \text{or} \quad x = w_0 - 1$$

A graph showing the region of integration to find $F(w_0)$, $1 \leq w_0 \leq 2$

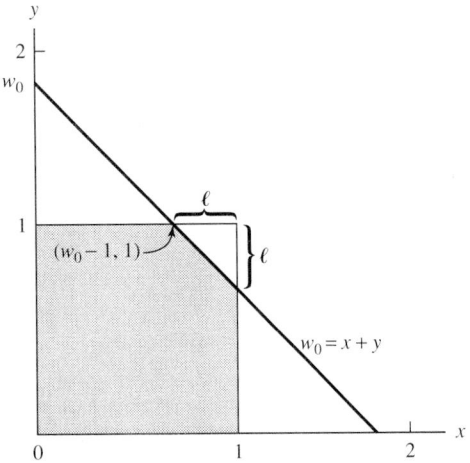

The point $(w_0 - 1, 1)$ is shown in Figure 7.4. The two equal sides of the triangle each have length $\ell = 1 - (w_0 - 1) = 2 - w_0$. The area of the triangle lying above the line $w_0 = x + y$ is then

$$\text{Area} = \frac{1}{2}(\text{Base})(\text{Height})$$

$$= \frac{1}{2}(2 - w_0)(2 - w_0) = \frac{(2 - w_0)^2}{2}$$

Since the height of the solid constructed over the triangle is $f(x, y) = 1$, the probability that w lies above the line $w_0 = x + y$ is $(2 - w_0)^2/2$. Subtracting this probability from 1, we find the probability that w lies below the line to be

$$F(w_0) = P(w \leq w_0) = 1 - \frac{(2 - w_0)^2}{2}$$

We drop the subscript and simplify to obtain

$$F(w) = -1 + 2w - w^2/2 \quad (1 \leq w \leq 2)$$

The density function for the sum of the two random variables x and y is now obtained by differentiating $F(w)$:

$$f(w) = \frac{dF(w)}{dw} = \frac{d(w^2/2)}{dw} = w \quad (0 \leq w \leq 1)$$

$$f(w) = \frac{dF(w)}{dw} = \frac{d(-1 + 2w - w^2/2)}{dw} = 2 - w \quad (1 \leq w \leq 2)$$

Graphs of the cumulative distribution function and the density function for $w = x + y$ are shown in Figures 7.5a and 7.5b, respectively. Note that the area under the density function over the interval $0 \leq w \leq 2$ is equal to 1.

FIGURE 7.5 ▶

Graphs of the cumulative distribution function and density function for $w = x + y$

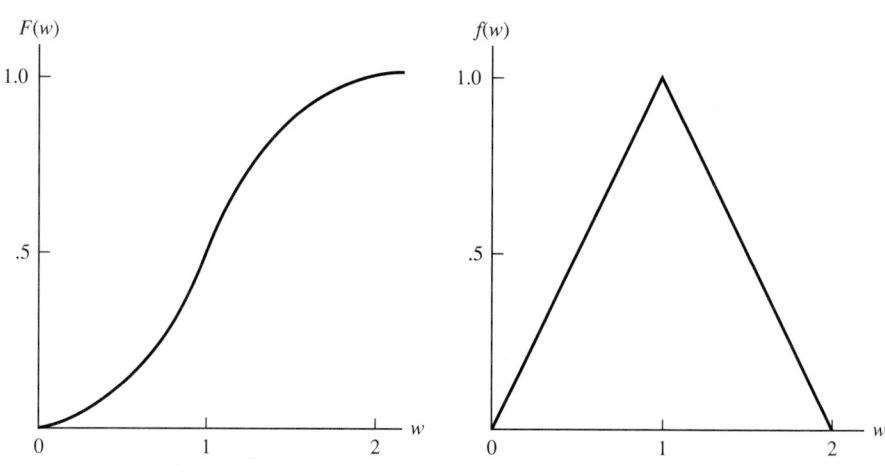

a. Cumulative distribution function   b. Density function

One of the most useful functions of a single continuous random variable is the cumulative distribution function itself. We will show that if y is a continuous random variable with density function $f(y)$ and cumulative distribution function $F(y)$, then $w = F(y)$ has a uniform probability distribution over the interval $0 \leq w \leq 1$. Using a computer program for generating random numbers, we can generate a random sample of w values. For each value of w, we can solve for the corresponding value of y using the equation $w = F(y)$ and, thereby, obtain a random sample of y values from a population modeled by the density function $f(y)$. We will present this important transformation as a theorem, prove it, and then demonstrate its use with an example.

> ### Theorem 7.1
> ....
>
> Let y be a continuous random variable with density function $f(y)$ and cumulative distribution $F(y)$. Then the density function of $w = F(y)$ will be a uniform distribution defined over the interval $0 \le w \le 1$, i.e.,
>
> $$f(w) = 1 \quad (0 \le w \le 1)$$

PROOF OF THEOREM 7.1   Figure 7.6 shows the graph of $w = F(y)$ for a continuous random variable y. You can see from the figure that there is a one-to-one correspondence between y values and w values, and that values of y corresponding to values of w in the interval $0 \le w \le w_0$ will be those in the interval $0 \le y \le y_0$. Therefore,

$$P(w \le w_0) = P(y \le y_0) = F(y_0)$$

But since $w = F(y)$, we have $F(y_0) = w_0$. Therefore, we can write

$$P(w \le w_0) = F(y_0) = w_0$$

The cumulative distribution function for w is obtained by dropping the subscript:

$$F(w) = w$$

FIGURE 7.6 ▶
Cumulative distribution function $F(y)$

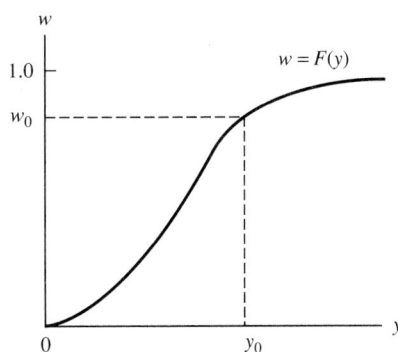

Finally, we differentiate over the range $0 \le w \le 1$ to obtain the density function:

$$f(w) = \frac{dF(w)}{dw} = 1$$

....

EXAMPLE 7.5   Use Theorem 7.1 to generate a random sample of $n = 3$ observations from an exponential distribution with $\beta = 2$.

Solution   The density function for the exponential distribution with $\beta = 2$ is

$$f(y) = \begin{cases} \dfrac{e^{-y/2}}{2} & \text{if } 0 \le y < \infty \\ 0 & \text{elsewhere} \end{cases}$$

and the cumulative distribution function is

$$F(y) = \int_{-\infty}^{y} f(t)dt = \int_{0}^{y} \frac{e^{-t/2}}{2} \, dt = -e^{-t/2} \Big]_{0}^{y} = 1 - e^{-y/2}$$

If we let $w = F(y) = 1 - e^{-y/2}$, then Theorem 7.1 tells us that w has a uniform density function over the interval $0 \le w \le 1$.

To draw a random number y from the exponential distribution, we first randomly draw a value of w from the uniform distribution. This can be done by drawing a random number from Table 6 of Appendix II or using a computer. Suppose, for example, that we draw the random number 10480. This corresponds to the random selection of the value $w_1 = .10480$ from a uniform distribution over the interval $0 \le w \le 1$. Substituting this value of w_1 into the formula for $w = F(y)$ and solving for y, we obtain

$$w_1 = F(y) = 1 - e^{-y_1/2}$$
$$.10480 = 1 - e^{-y_1/2}$$
$$e^{-y_1/2} = .8952$$
$$\frac{-y_1}{2} = -.111$$
$$y_1 = .222$$

If the next two random numbers selected are 22368 and 24130, then the corresponding values of the uniform random variable are $w_2 = .22368$ and $w_3 = .24130$. By substituting these values into the formula $w = 1 - e^{-y/2}$, you can verify that $y_2 = .506$ and $y_3 = .552$. Thus, $y_1 = .222$, $y_2 = .506$, and $y_3 = .552$ represent three randomly selected observations on an exponential random variable with mean equal to 2.

EXERCISES

7.7   Consider the density function

$$f(y) = \begin{cases} 2y & \text{if } 0 \le y \le 1 \\ 0 & \text{elsewhere} \end{cases}$$

Find the density function of w, where:
a. $w = y^2$ **b.** $w = 2y - 1$ **c.** $w = 1/y$

7.8   Consider the density function

$$f(y) = \begin{cases} e^{-(y-3)} & \text{if } y > 3 \\ 0 & \text{elsewhere} \end{cases}$$

Find the density function of w, where:
a. $w = e^{-y}$ **b.** $w = y - 3$ **c.** $w = y/3$

7.9 The amount y of paper used per day by a line printer at a university computing center has an exponential distribution with mean equal to five boxes (i.e., $\beta = 5$). The daily cost of the paper is proportional to $c = (3y + 2)$. Find the probability density function of the daily cost of paper used by the line printer.

7.10 An environmental engineer has determined that the amount y (in parts per million) of pollutant per water sample collected near the discharge tubes of an island power plant has probability density function

$$f(y) = \begin{cases} \dfrac{1}{10} & \text{if } 0 < y < 10 \\ 0 & \text{elsewhere} \end{cases}$$

A new cleaning device has been developed to help reduce the amount of pollution discharged into the ocean. It is believed that the amount a of pollutant discharged when the device is operating will be related to y by

$$a = \begin{cases} \dfrac{y}{2} & \text{if } 0 < y < 5 \\ \dfrac{2y - 5}{2} & \text{if } 5 < y < 10 \end{cases}$$

Find the probability density function of a.

7.11 Researchers at the University of California (Berkeley) have developed a switched-capacitor circuit for generating pseudorandom signals (*International Journal of Circuit Theory and Applications*, May/June, 1990). The intensity of the signal (voltage), y, is modeled using the Rayleigh probability distribution with mean μ. This continuous distribution has density function:

$$f(y) = \frac{y}{\mu} \exp^{-y^2/(2\mu)} \quad (y > 0)$$

Find the density function of the random variable $w = y^2$. Can you name the distribution?

7.12 Use Theorem 7.1 to draw a random sample of $n = 5$ observations from a distribution with probability density function

$$f(y) = \begin{cases} e^y & \text{if } y < 0 \\ 0 & \text{elsewhere} \end{cases}$$

7.13 Use Theorem 7.1 to draw a random sample of $n = 5$ observations from a beta distribution with $\alpha = 2$ and $\beta = 1$.

OPTIONAL EXERCISE

7.14 The total time x (in minutes) from the time a computer job is submitted until its run is completed and the time y the job waits in the job queue before being run have the joint density function

$$f(x, y) = \begin{cases} e^{-x} & \text{if } 0 \le y \le x < \infty \\ 0 & \text{elsewhere} \end{cases}$$

The CPU time for the job (i.e., the length of time the job is in control of the computer's central processing unit) is given by the difference $w = x - y$. Find the density function of a job's CPU time. [*Hint:* You may use the facts that

$$P(w \leq w_0) = P(w \leq w_0, x > w_0) + P(w \leq w_0, x \leq w_0)$$
$$= P(x - w_0 \leq y \leq x, w_0 < x < \infty) + P(0 \leq y \leq x, 0 \leq x \leq w_0)$$
$$= \int_{w_0}^{\infty} \int_{x-w_0}^{x} e^{-x} \, dy \, dx + \int_{0}^{w} \int_{0}^{x} e^{-x} \, dy \, dx$$

and $\int ye^{-y} \, dy = -ye^{-y} + \int e^{-y} \, dy$ in determining the density function.]

7.4   Approximating a Sampling Distribution by Simulation

We explained in Section 7.2 that a statistic w is a function of the n sample measurements, $y_1, y_2, \ldots, y_n$, and we have shown in Optional Section 7.3 how we can use probability theory and mathematics to find its sampling distribution. However, the mathematical problem of finding $f(w)$ is often very difficult to solve. When such a situation occurs, we may be able to find an approximation to $f(w)$ by computer simulation.

To illustrate the procedure, we will approximate the sampling distribution for the sum $w = y_1 + y_2$ of a sample of $n = 2$ observations from a uniform distribution over the interval $0 \leq y \leq 1$. Recall that we found an exact expression for this sampling distribution in Example 7.4. Thus, we will be able to compare our simulated sampling distribution with the exact form of the sampling distribution shown in Figure 7.5b.

To begin the simulation procedure, we used the computer to generate 10,000 pairs of random numbers, with each pair representing a sample (y_1, y_2) from the uniform distribution over the interval $0 \leq y \leq 1$. We then programmed the computer to calculate the sum $w = y_1 + y_2$ for each of the 10,000 pairs. A computer-generated relative frequency histogram for the 10,000 values of w is shown in Figure 7.7. By comparing Figures 7.5b and 7.7, you can see that the simulated sampling distribution provides a good approximation to the true probability distribution of the sum of a sample of $n = 2$ observations from a uniform distribution.

EXAMPLE 7.6

Simulate the sampling distribution of the sample mean

$$\bar{y} = \frac{y_1 + y_2 + y_3 + y_4 + y_5}{5}$$

for a sample of $n = 5$ observations drawn from the uniform probability distribution shown in Figure 7.8 on page 304. Note that the uniform distribution has mean $\mu = .5$. Repeat the procedure for $n = 15, 25, 50$, and 100. Interpret the results.

Solution

We first obtained 1,000 computer-generated random samples of size $n = 5$ from the uniform probability distribution, over the interval $(0, 1)$, and programmed the computer (using SAS) to compute the mean

$$\bar{y} = \frac{y_1 + y_2 + y_3 + y_4 + y_5}{5}$$

for each sample. The horizontal relative frequency histogram for the 1,000 values of $\bar{y}$ obtained from the uniform distribution is shown in Figure 7.9a on page 304. Note its shape for this small value of n.

The relative frequency histograms of $\bar{y}$ based on samples of size $n = 15, 25, 50,$ and 100, also simulated by computer, are shown in Figures 7.9b–e, respectively. Note that the values of $\bar{y}$ tend to cluster about the mean of the uniform distribution, $\mu = .5$. Furthermore, as n increases, there is less variation in the sampling distribution. You can also see from the figures that as the sample size increases, the shape of the sampling distribution of $\bar{y}$ tends toward the shape of the normal distribution (symmetric and mound-shaped).

FIGURE 7.7 ▶

Simulated sampling distribution for the sum of two observations from a uniform (0, 1) distribution

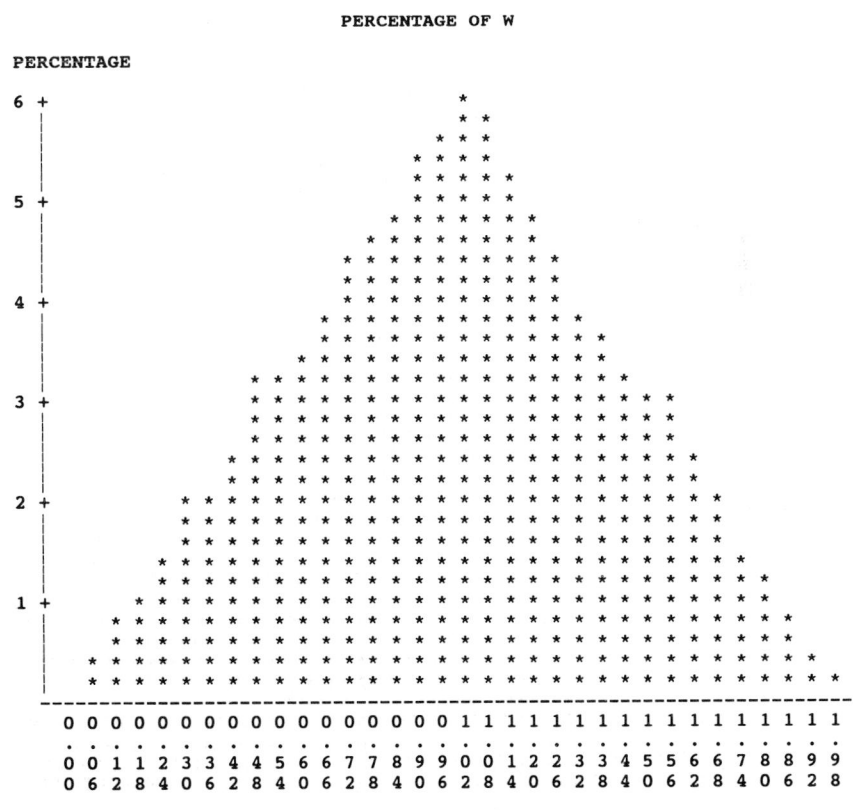

FIGURE 7.8 ▶
Uniform distribution of
Example 7.6

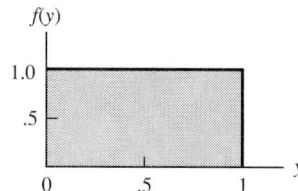

FIGURE 7.9 ▶
Distribution of a random sample
of 1,000 sample means from a
uniform (0, 1) distribution

a. $n = 5$

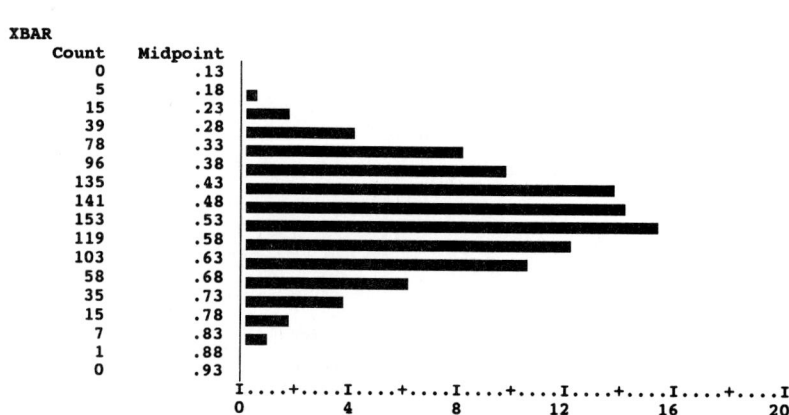

b. $n = 15$

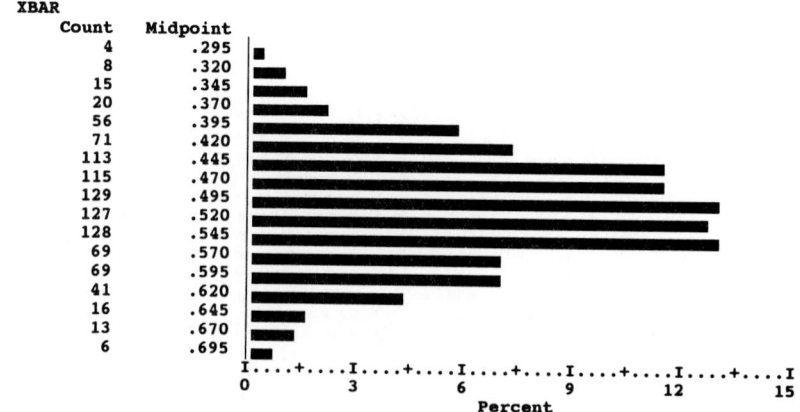

c. $n = 25$

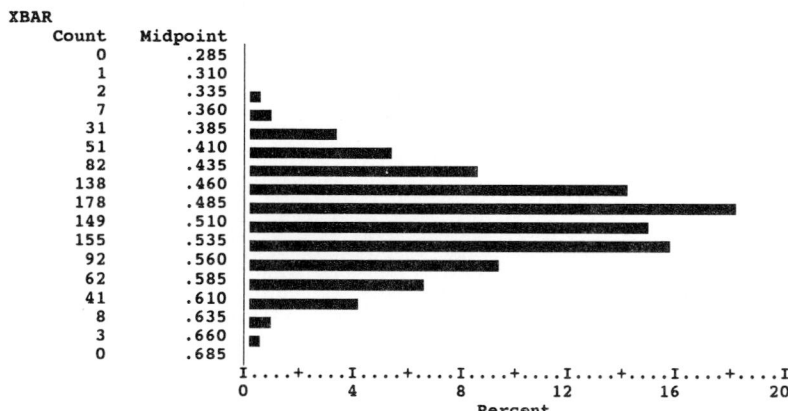

```
XBAR
   Count   Midpoint
      0     .285
      1     .310
      2     .335
      7     .360
     31     .385
     51     .410
     82     .435
    138     .460
    178     .485
    149     .510
    155     .535
     92     .560
     62     .585
     41     .610
      8     .635
      3     .660
      0     .685
            I....+....I....+....I....+....I....+....I....+....I
            0         4         8        12        16        20
                                  Percent
```

d. $n = 50$

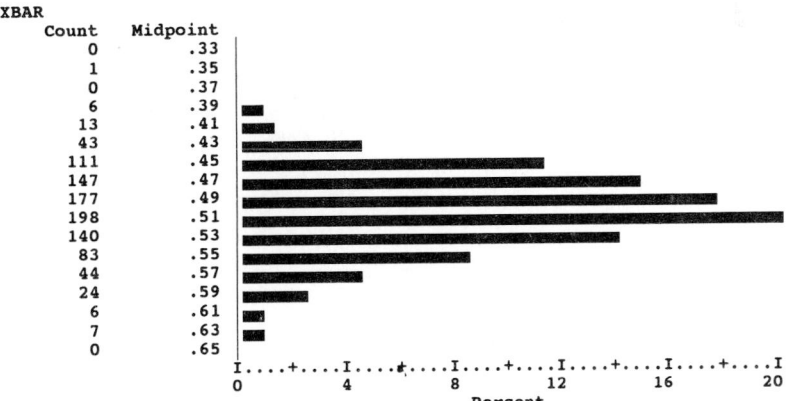

```
XBAR
   Count   Midpoint
      0     .33
      1     .35
      0     .37
      6     .39
     13     .41
     43     .43
    111     .45
    147     .47
    177     .49
    198     .51
    140     .53
     83     .55
     44     .57
     24     .59
      6     .61
      7     .63
      0     .65
            I....+....I....+....I....+....I....+....I....+....I
            0         4         8        12        16        20
                                  Percent
```

e. $n = 100$

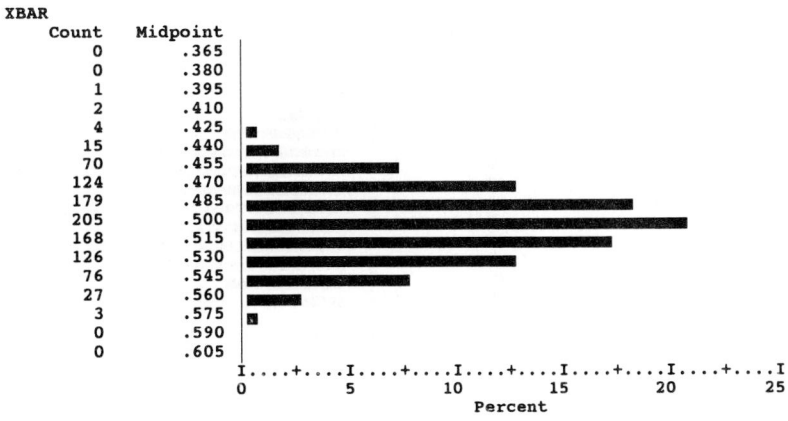

```
XBAR
   Count   Midpoint
      0     .365
      0     .380
      1     .395
      2     .410
      4     .425
     15     .440
     70     .455
    124     .470
    179     .485
    205     .500
    168     .515
    126     .530
     76     .545
     27     .560
      3     .575
      0     .590
      0     .605
            I....+....I....+....I....+....I....+....I....+....I
            0         5        10        15        20        25
                                  Percent
```

EXAMPLE 7.7

Repeat the instructions of Example 7.6, but sample from:

a. The normal probability distribution shown in Figure 7.10a.

b. The exponential probability distribution shown in Figure 7.10b.

FIGURE 7.10 ▶
Probability distributions for
Example 7.7

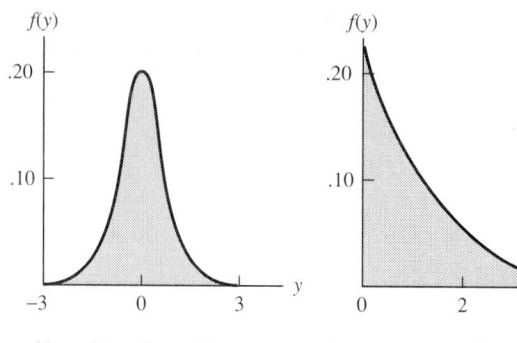

a. Normal ($\mu = 0$, $\sigma = 1$)   b. Exponential ($\beta = 1$)

Solution

a. The simulated sampling distributions of $\bar{y}$ for samples of size $n = 5$, 15, 25, 50, and 100 from a normal distribution are shown in Figures 7.11a–e, respectively. As in Example 7.6, the values of $\bar{y}$ tend to cluster about the mean of the normal probability distribution—in this case $\mu = 0$. Also the variance of the sampling distribution of $\bar{y}$ decreases as n increases.

FIGURE 7.11 ▶
Sampling distribution of $\bar{y}$:
Normal population

a. $n = 5$

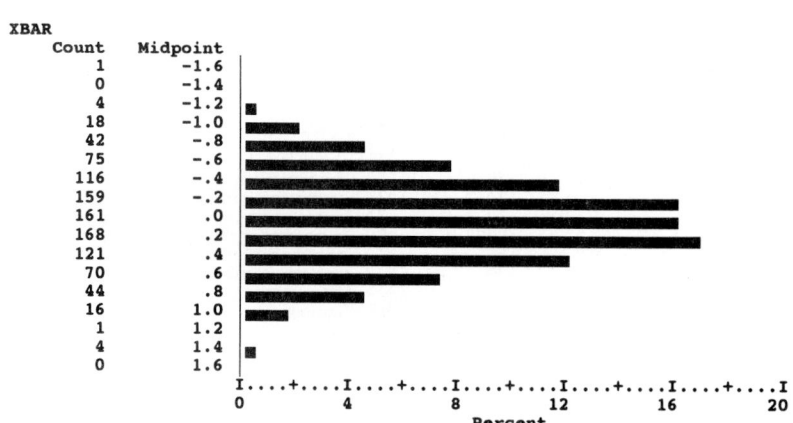

b. $n = 15$

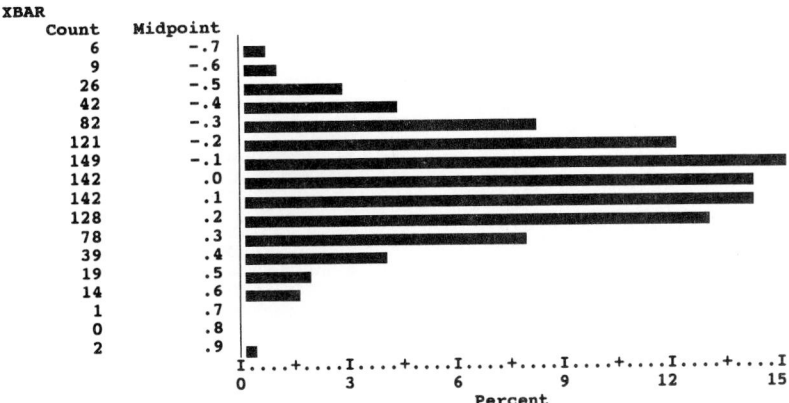

c. $n = 25$

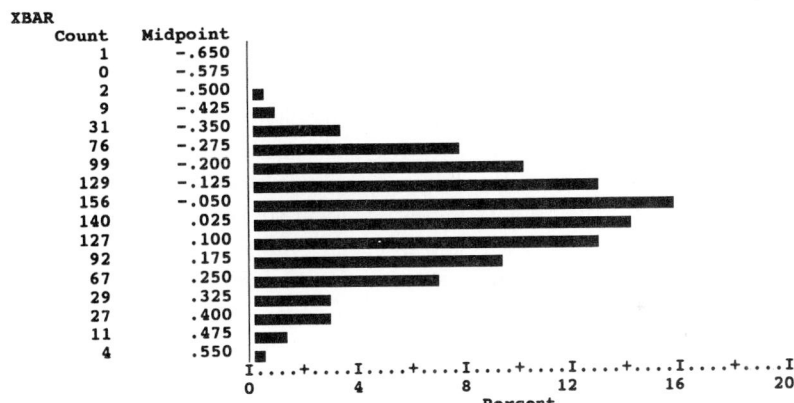

d. $n = 50$

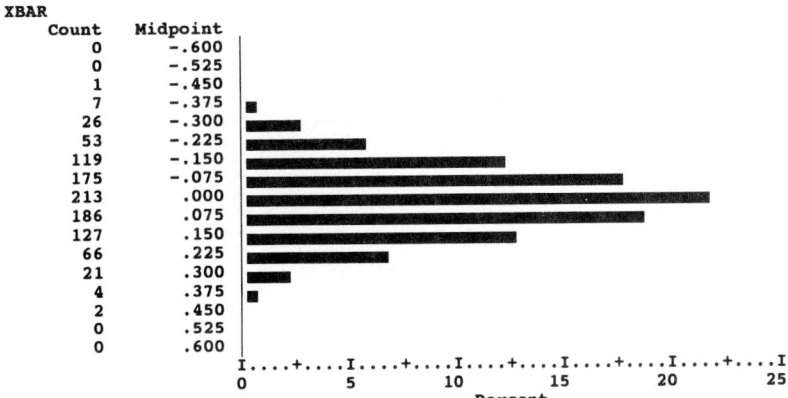

(continued)

FIGURE 7.11 ▶
Continued

e. $n = 100$

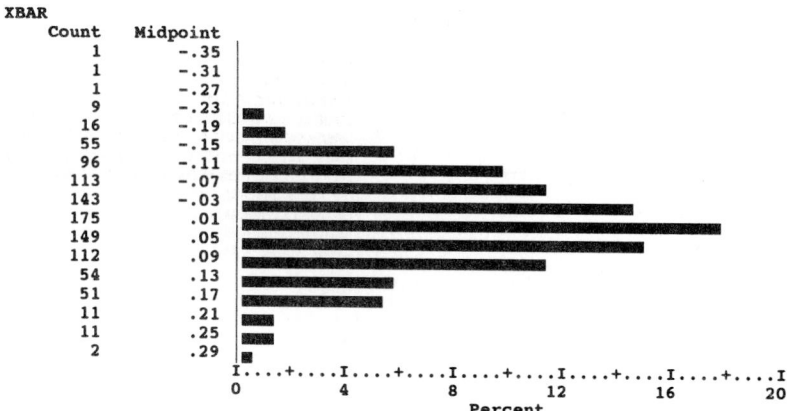

b. The simulated sampling distributions of $\bar{y}$ for samples of size $n = 5$, 15, 25, 50, and 100 from an exponential distribution are shown in Figures 7.12a–e, respectively. Note the three properties illustrated earlier: (1) values of $\bar{y}$ tend to cluster about the mean of the exponential probability distribution, $\mu = 1$; (2) the variance of $\bar{y}$ decreases as n increases; and, (3) the shape of the sampling distribution of $\bar{y}$ tends toward the shape of the normal distribution as n increases.

FIGURE 7.12 ▶
Sampling distributions of $\bar{y}$:
Exponential population

a. $n = 5$

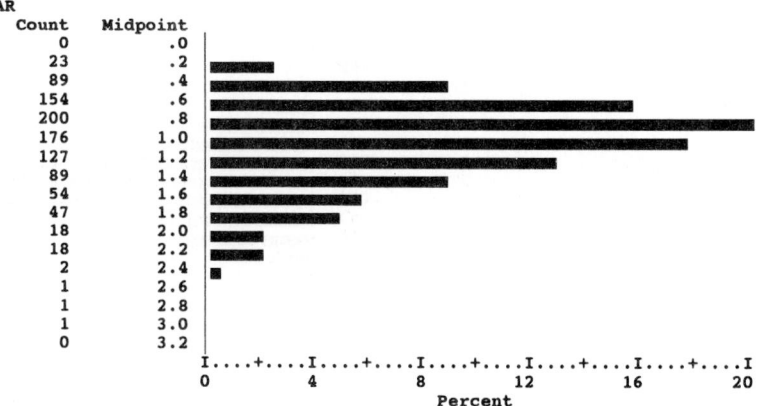

b. $n = 15$

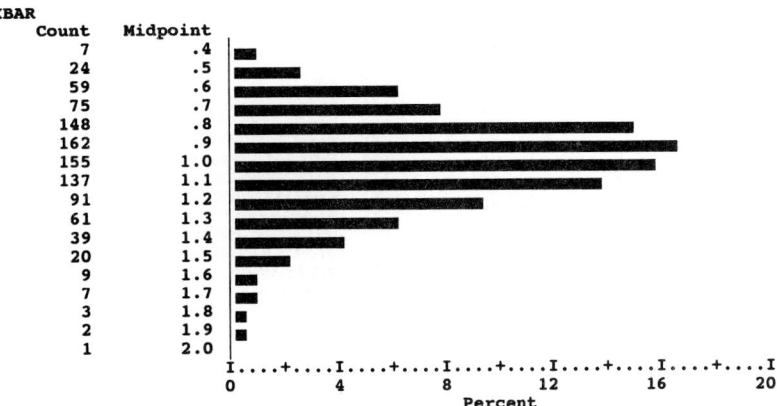

XBAR

Count	Midpoint
7	.4
24	.5
59	.6
75	.7
148	.8
162	.9
155	1.0
137	1.1
91	1.2
61	1.3
39	1.4
20	1.5
9	1.6
7	1.7
3	1.8
2	1.9
1	2.0

Percent: 0   4   8   12   16   20

c. $n = 25$

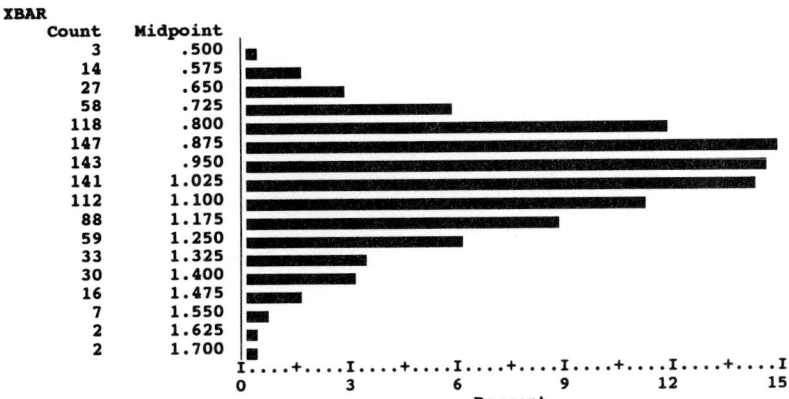

XBAR

Count	Midpoint
3	.500
14	.575
27	.650
58	.725
118	.800
147	.875
143	.950
141	1.025
112	1.100
88	1.175
59	1.250
33	1.325
30	1.400
16	1.475
7	1.550
2	1.625
2	1.700

Percent: 0   3   6   9   12   15

d. $n = 50$

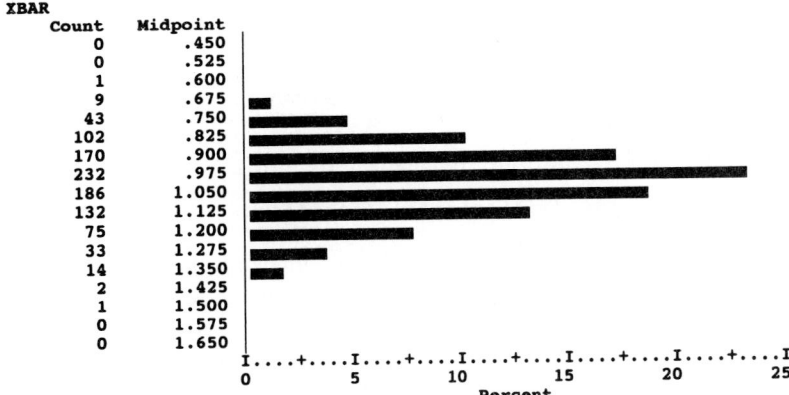

XBAR

Count	Midpoint
0	.450
0	.525
1	.600
9	.675
43	.750
102	.825
170	.900
232	.975
186	1.050
132	1.125
75	1.200
33	1.275
14	1.350
2	1.425
1	1.500
0	1.575
0	1.650

Percent: 0   5   10   15   20   25

(continued)

FIGURE 7.12 ▶
Continued

e. $n = 100$

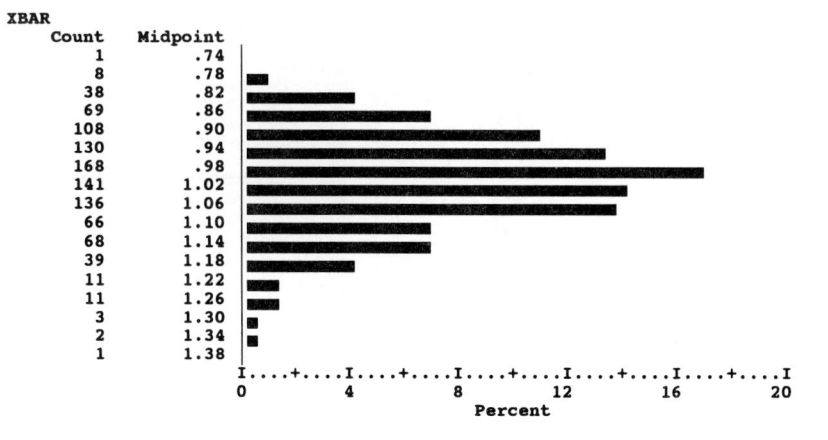

In Section 7.5, we generalize the results of Examples 7.6 and 7.7 in the form of a theorem.

EXERCISE

OPTIONAL EXERCISE

7.15   Use the computer to simulate the sampling distribution of s^2, the variance of a sample of $n = 100$ observations from a

    a. Uniform distribution on the interval $(0, 1)$
    b. Normal distribution, with mean 0 and variance 1
    c. Exponential distribution with mean 1

7.5 The Sampling Distributions of Means and Sums

The simulation of the sampling distribution of the sample mean based on independent random samples from uniform, normal, and exponential distributions in Examples 7.6 and 7.7 illustrates the ideas embodied in one of the most important theorems in statistics. The following version of the theorem applies to the sampling distribution of the sample mean, $\bar{y}$.

Theorem 7.2: The Central Limit Theorem

If a random sample of n observations, $y_1, y_2, \ldots, y_n$, is drawn from a population with finite mean μ and variance σ^2, then, when n is sufficiently large, the sampling distribution of the sample mean $\bar{y}$ can be approximated by a normal density function.

The sampling distribution of $\bar{y}$, in addition to being approximately normal for large n, has other known characteristics, which are given in Definition 7.4.

Definition 7.4

Let $y_1, y_2, \ldots, y_n$ be a random sample of n observations from a population with finite mean μ and finite standard deviation σ. Then, the **mean and standard deviation of the sampling distribution** of $\bar{y}$, denoted $\mu_{\bar{y}}$ and $\sigma_{\bar{y}}$, respectively, are:

$$\mu_{\bar{y}} = \mu \qquad \sigma_{\bar{y}} = \sigma/\sqrt{n}$$

The significance of the central limit theorem and Definition 7.4 is that we can use the normal distribution to approximate the sampling distribution of the sample mean $\bar{y}$ as long as the population possesses a finite mean and variance, and the number n of measurements in the sample is sufficiently large. How large the sample size must be will depend on the nature of the sampled population. You can see from our simulated experiments in Examples 7.6 and 7.7 that the sampling distribution of $\bar{y}$ tends to become very nearly normal for sample sizes as small as $n = 25$ for the uniform, normal, and exponential population distributions. When the population distribution is symmetric about its mean, the sampling distribution of $\bar{y}$ will be mound-shaped and nearly normal for sample sizes as small as $n = 15$. In addition, if the sampled population possesses a normal distribution, then the sampling distribution of $\bar{y}$ will be a normal density function, regardless of the sample size. (This may be seen in Figure 7.11.) In fact, it can be shown that *the sampling distribution of **any linear function** of normally distributed random variables, even those that are correlated and have different means and variances, is a normal distribution*. This important result is presented (without proof) in Theorem 7.3 and illustrated in an example.

Theorem 7.3

Let $a_1, a_2, \ldots, a_n$ be constants and let $y_1, y_2, \ldots, y_n$ be n normally distributed random variables with $E(y_i) = \mu_i$, $V(y_i) = \sigma_i^2$, and $\text{Cov}(y_i, y_j) = \sigma_{ij}$ $(i = 1, 2, \ldots, n)$. Then the sampling distribution of a linear combination of the normal random variables

$$\ell = a_1 y_1 + a_2 y_2 + \cdots + a_n y_n$$

possesses a normal density function with mean and variance[*]

$$E(\ell) = \mu = a_1 \mu_1 + a_2 \mu_2 + \cdots + a_n \mu_n$$

and

$$\begin{aligned}
V(\ell) = \ &a_1^2 \sigma_1^2 + a_2^2 \sigma_2^2 + \cdots + a_n^2 \sigma_n^2 \\
&+ 2a_1 a_2 \sigma_{12} + 2a_1 a_3 \sigma_{13} + \cdots + 2a_1 a_n \sigma_{1n} \\
&+ 2a_2 a_3 \sigma_{23} + \cdots + 2a_2 a_n \sigma_{2n} \\
&+ \cdots + 2a_{n-1} a_n \sigma_{n-1,n}
\end{aligned}$$

EXAMPLE 7.8

Suppose you select independent random samples from two normal populations, n_1 observations from population 1 and n_2 observations from population 2. If the means and variances for populations 1 and 2 are (μ_1, σ_1^2) and (μ_2, σ_2^2), respectively, and if $\bar{y}_1$ and $\bar{y}_2$ are the corresponding sample means, find the distribution of the difference $(\bar{y}_1 - \bar{y}_2)$.

Solution

Since $\bar{y}_1$ and $\bar{y}_2$ are both linear functions of normally distributed random variables, they will be normally distributed by Theorem 7.3. The means and variances of the sample means (see Example 6.13) are

$$E(\bar{y}_i) = \mu_i \quad \text{and} \quad V(\bar{y}_i) = \frac{\sigma_i^2}{n_i} \quad (i = 1, 2)$$

Then, $\ell = \bar{y}_1 - \bar{y}_2$ is a linear function of two normally distributed random variables, $\bar{y}_1$ and $\bar{y}_2$. According to Theorem 7.3, ℓ will be normally distributed with

$$E(\ell) = \mu_\ell = E(\bar{y}_1) - E(\bar{y}_2) = \mu_1 - \mu_2$$
$$V(\ell) = \sigma_\ell^2 = (1)^2 V(\bar{y}_1) + (-1)^2 V(\bar{y}_2) + 2(1)(-1)\text{Cov}(\bar{y}_1, \bar{y}_2)$$

But, since the samples were independently selected, $\bar{y}_1$ and $\bar{y}_2$ are independent and $\text{Cov}(\bar{y}_1, \bar{y}_2) = 0$. Therefore,

$$V(\ell) = \frac{\sigma_1^2}{n_1} + \frac{\sigma_2^2}{n_2}$$

---

[*]The formulas for the mean and variance of a linear function of any random variables, $y_1, y_2, \ldots, y_n$, were given in Theorem 6.7.

We have shown that $(\bar{y}_1 - \bar{y}_2)$ is a normally distributed random variable with mean $(\mu_1 - \mu_2)$ and variance $(\sigma_1^2/n_1 + \sigma_2^2/n_2)$.

Typical applications of the central limit theorem, however, involve samples selected from nonnormal or unknown populations, as illustrated in Examples 7.9 and 7.10.

EXAMPLE 7.9

Engineers responsible for the design and maintenance of aircraft pavements traditionally use pavement-quality concrete. A study was conducted at Luton Airport (United Kingdom) to assess the suitability of concrete blocks as a surface for aircraft pavements (*Proceedings of the Institute of Civil Engineers*, Apr. 1986). The original pavement-quality concrete of the western end of the runway was overlaid with 80-mm-thick concrete blocks. A series of plate-bearing tests was carried out to determine the load classification number (LCN)—a measure of breaking strength—of the surface. Let $\bar{y}$ represent the mean LCN of a sample of 25 concrete block sections on the western end of the runway.

a. Prior to resurfacing, the mean LCN of the original pavement-quality concrete of the western end of the runway was known to be $\mu = 60$, and the standard deviation was $\sigma = 10$. If the mean strength of the new concrete block surface is no different from that of the original surface, describe the sampling distribution of $\bar{y}$.

b. If the mean strength of the new concrete block surface is no different from that of the original surface, find the probability that $\bar{y}$, the sample mean LCN of the 25 concrete block sections, exceeds 65.

c. The plate-bearing tests on the new concrete block surface resulted in $\bar{y} = 73$. Based on this result, what can you infer about the true mean LCN of the new surface?

Solution

a. Although we have no information about the shape of the relative frequency distribution of the breaking strengths (LCNs) for sections of the new surface, we can apply Theorem 7.2 to conclude that the sampling distribution of $\bar{y}$, the mean LCN of the sample, is approximately normally distributed. In addition, if $\mu = 60$ and $\sigma = 10$, the mean, $\mu_{\bar{y}}$, and the standard deviation, $\sigma_{\bar{y}}$, of the sampling distribution are given by

$$\mu_{\bar{y}} = \mu = 60$$

and

$$\sigma_{\bar{y}} = \frac{\sigma}{\sqrt{n}} = \frac{10}{\sqrt{25}} = 2$$

b. We want to calculate $P(\bar{y} > 65)$. Since $\bar{y}$ has an approximate normal distribution, we have

$$P(\bar{y} > 65) = P\left(\frac{\bar{y} - \mu_{\bar{y}}}{\sigma_{\bar{y}}} > \frac{65 - \mu_{\bar{y}}}{\sigma_{\bar{y}}}\right)$$

$$\approx P\left(z > \frac{65 - 60}{2}\right) = P(z > 2.5)$$

where z is a standard normal random variable. Using Table 4 of Appendix II, we obtain

$$P(z > 2.5) = .5 - .4938 = .0062$$

Therefore, $P(\bar{y} > 65) = .0062$.

c. If there is no difference between the true mean strengths of the new and original surfaces (i.e., $\mu = 60$ for both surfaces), the probability that we would obtain a sample mean LCN for concrete block of 65 or greater is only .0062. Observing $\bar{y} = 73$ provides strong evidence that the true mean breaking strength of the new surface exceeds $\mu = 60$. Our reasoning stems from the rare event philosophy of Chapter 3, which states that such a large sample mean ($\bar{y} = 73$) is very unlikely to occur if $\mu = 60$.

EXAMPLE 7.10

Consider a binomial experiment with n Bernoulli trials and probability of success p on each trial. The number y of successes divided by the number n of trials is called the **sample proportion of successes** and is denoted by the symbol $\hat{p} = y/n$. Explain why the random variable

$$z = \frac{\hat{p} - p}{\sqrt{\dfrac{pq}{n}}}$$

has approximately a standard normal distribution for large values of n.

Solution

If we denote the outcome of the ith Bernoulli trial as y_i ($i = 1, 2, \ldots, n$), where

$$y_i = \begin{cases} 1 & \text{if outcome is a success} \\ 0 & \text{if outcome is a failure} \end{cases}$$

then the number y of successes in n trials is equal to the sum of n independent Bernoulli random variables:

$$\sum_{i=1}^{n} y_i$$

Therefore, $\hat{p} = y/n$ is a sample mean and, according to Theorem 7.2, $\hat{p}$ will be approximately normally distributed when the sample size n is large. To find the expected value and variance of $\hat{p}$, we can view $\hat{p}$ as a linear function of a single random variable y:

$$\hat{p} = \ell = a_1 y_1 = \left(\frac{1}{n}\right)y \qquad \text{where } a_1 = \frac{1}{n} \text{ and } y_1 = y$$

We now apply Theorem 6.7 to obtain $E(\ell)$ and $V(\ell)$:

$$E(\hat{p}) = \frac{1}{n}E(y) = \frac{1}{n}(np) = p$$

$$V(\hat{p}) = \left(\frac{1}{n}\right)^2 V(y) = \frac{1}{n^2}(npq) = \frac{pq}{n}$$

Therefore,

$$z = \frac{\hat{p} - p}{\sqrt{\dfrac{pq}{n}}}$$

is equal to the deviation between a normally distributed random variable $\hat{p}$ and its mean p, expressed in units of its standard deviation, $\sqrt{pq/n}$. This satisfies the definition of a standard normal random variable given in Section 5.5.

The central limit theorem also applies to the sum of a sample of n measurements subject to the conditions stated in Theorem 7.2. The only difference is that the approximating normal distribution will have mean $n\mu$ and variance $n\sigma^2$.

The Sampling Distribution of a Sum of Random Variables

If a random sample of n observations, $y_1, y_2, \ldots, y_n$, is drawn from a population with finite mean μ and variance σ^2, then, when n is sufficiently large, the sampling distribution of the sum

$$\sum_{i=1}^{n} y_i$$

can be approximated by a normal density function with mean $\mu_{\Sigma y_i} = n\mu$ and $\sigma^2_{\Sigma y_i} = n\sigma^2$.

In Section 7.6, we apply the central limit theorem for sums to show that the normal density function can be used to approximate the binomial probability distribution when the number n of trials is large.

EXERCISES

7.16 Let $\bar{y}_{25}$ represent the mean of a random sample of size $n = 25$ from a probability distribution with unknown density $f(y)$, mean $\mu = 17$, and standard deviation $\sigma = 10$. Similarly, let $\bar{y}_{100}$ represent the mean of a random sample of size $n = 100$ selected from the same probability distribution.

a. Describe the sampling distributions of $\bar{y}_{25}$ and $\bar{y}_{100}$.

b. Which of the probabilities, $P(15 < \bar{y}_{25} < 19)$ or $P(15 < \bar{y}_{100} < 19)$, would you expect to be larger?

c. Calculate approximations to the two probabilities of part **b**.

7.17 The National Institute for Occupational Safety and Health (NIOSH) recently completed a study to evaluate the level of exposure of workers to the chemical dioxin, 2,3,7,8-TCDD. The distribution of TCDD levels in parts per trillion (ppt) of production workers at a Newark, New Jersey, chemical plant had a mean of 293 ppt and a standard deviation of 847 ppt (*Chemosphere*, Vol. 20, 1990). A graph of the distribution is shown here.

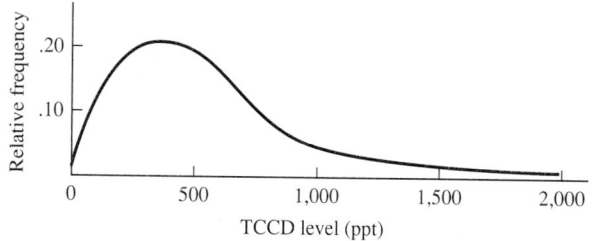

In a random sample of $n = 50$ workers selected at the New Jersey plant, let $\bar{y}$ represent the sample mean TCDD level.

a. Find the mean and standard deviation of the sampling distribution of $\bar{y}$.

b. Draw a sketch of the sampling distribution of $\bar{y}$. Locate the mean on the graph.

c. Find the probability that $\bar{y}$ exceeds 550 ppt.

7.18 Studies by neuroscientists at the Massachusetts Institute of Technology (MIT) reveal that melatonin, which is secreted by the pineal gland in the brain, functions naturally as a sleep-inducing hormone (*Tampa Tribune*, Mar. 1, 1994). Male volunteers were given various doses of melatonin or placebos and then placed in a dark room at midday and told to close their eyes and fall asleep on demand. Of interest to the MIT researchers is the time y (in minutes) required for each volunteer to fall asleep. With the placebo (i.e., no hormone), the researchers found that the mean time to fall asleep was 15 minutes. Assume that with the placebo treatment $\mu = 15$ and $\sigma = 5$.

a. Consider a random sample of $n = 20$ men who are given the sleep-inducing hormone, melatonin. Let $\bar{y}$ represent the mean time to fall asleep for this sample. If the hormone is *not* effective in inducing sleep, describe the sampling distribution of $\bar{y}$.

b. Refer to part **a**. Find $P(\bar{y} \leq 6)$.

c. In the actual study, the mean time to fall asleep for the 20 volunteers was $\bar{y} = 5$. Use this result to make an inference about the true value of μ for those taking the melatonin.

7.19 *Cost estimation* is the term used to describe the process by which engineers estimate the cost of work contracts (e.g., road construction, building construction) that are to be awarded to the lowest bidder. The engineers' estimate is the baseline against which the low (winning) bid is compared. A recent study investigated the factors that affect the accuracy of engineers' estimates (*Cost Engineering*, Oct. 1988), where accuracy is measured as the percentage difference between the low bid and the engineers' estimate. One of the most important factors is number of bidders—the more bidders on the contract, the more likely the engineers are to overestimate the cost. For building contracts with five bidders, the mean percentage error was -7.02 and the standard deviation was 24.66. Consider a sample of 50 building contracts, each with 5 bidders.

a. Describe the sampling distribution of $\bar{y}$, the mean percentage difference between the low bid and the engineers' estimate, for the 50 contracts.

b. Find $P(\bar{y} < 0)$. (This is the probability of an overestimate.)

c. Suppose you observe $\bar{y} = -17.83$ for a sample of 50 building contracts. Based on the information given, are all these contracts likely to have five bidders? Explain.

7.20 Many species of terrestrial frogs that hibernate at or near the ground surface can survive prolonged exposure to low winter temperatures. In freezing conditions, the frog's body temperature, called its *supercooling temperature*, remains relatively higher because of an accumulation of glycerol in its body fluids. Studies have shown that the supercooling temperature of terrestrial frogs frozen at $-6°C$ has a relative frequency distribution with a mean of $-2.18°C$ and a standard deviation of $.32°C$ (*Science*, May 1983). Consider the mean supercooling temperature, $\bar{y}$, of a random sample of $n = 42$ terrestrial frogs frozen at $-6°C$.

a. Find the probability that $\bar{y}$ exceeds $-2.05°C$.

b. Find the probability that $\bar{y}$ falls between $-2.20°C$ and $-2.10°C$.

7.21 General trace organic monitoring describes the process in which water engineers analyze water samples for various types of organic material (e.g., contaminants). One such contaminant, commonly found in treated surface water, is the pesticide trihalomethane (THM). General trace organic monitoring at the Bedford (England) water treatment works revealed a mean THM level of 51 μg/l and a standard deviation of 14 μg/l (*Journal of the Institution of Water Engineers and Scientists*, Feb. 1986). Assume that these figures represent the population mean μ and standard deviation σ, respectively. Suppose we collect 45 water samples (called water "profiles") at the Bedford plant and measure the THM level in each.

a. Describe the sampling distribution of $\bar{y}$, the mean THM level of the 45 water profiles.

b. Find the probability that $\bar{y}$ exceeds 52 μg/l.

c. Find the probability that $\bar{y}$ falls between 49.5 and 50.5 μg/l.

7.22 The U.S. Army Engineering and Housing Support Center recently sponsored a study of the reliability, availability, and maintainability (RAM) characteristics of small diesel and gas-powered systems at commercial and military facilities (*IEEE Transactions on Industry Applications*, July/Aug. 1990). The study revealed that the time, y, to perform corrective maintenance on continuous diesel auxiliary systems has an approximate exponential distribution with an estimated mean of 1,700 hours.

a. Assuming $\mu = 1,700$, find the probability that the mean time to perform corrective maintenance for a sample of 70 continuous diesel auxiliary systems exceeds 2,500 hours.

b. If you observe $\bar{y} > 2,500$, what inference would you make about the value of μ?

7.23 An article in *Industrial Engineering* (Aug. 1990) discussed the importance of modeling machine downtime correctly in simulation studies. As an illustration, the researcher considered a single-machine-tool system with repair times (in minutes) that can be modeled by a gamma distribution with parameters $\alpha = 1$ and $\beta = 60$. Of interest is the mean repair time, $\bar{y}$, of a sample of 100 machine breakdowns.

a. Find $E(\bar{y})$ and $\text{Var}(\bar{y})$.

b. What probability distribution provides the best model of the sampling distribution of $\bar{y}$? Why?

c. Calculate the probability that the mean repair time, $\bar{y}$, is no longer than 30 minutes.

7.24   A large freight elevator can transport a maximum of 10,000 pounds (5 tons). Suppose a load of cargo containing 45 boxes must be transported via the elevator. Experience has shown that the weight y of a box of this type of cargo follows a probability distribution with mean $\mu = 200$ pounds and standard deviation $\sigma = 55$ pounds. What is the probability that all 45 boxes can be loaded onto the freight elevator and transported simultaneously? [*Hint:*   Find $P(\Sigma_{i=1}^{45} y_i \leq 10,000).]$

OPTIONAL EXERCISES

7.25   Let $\hat{p}_1$ be the sample proportion of successes in a binomial experiment with n_1 trials and let $\hat{p}_2$ be the sample proportion of successes in a binomial experiment with n_2 trials, conducted independently of the first. Let p_1 and p_2 be the corresponding population parameters. Show that

$$z = \frac{\hat{p}_1 - \hat{p}_2 - (p_1 - p_2)}{\sqrt{\dfrac{p_1 q_1}{n_1} + \dfrac{p_2 q_2}{n_2}}}$$

has approximately a standard normal distribution for large values of n_1 and n_2.

7.26   If y has a χ^2 distribution with n degrees of freedom (see Section 5.7), then y could be represented by $y = \Sigma_{i=1}^n x_i$, where the x_i's are independent χ^2 distributions, each with 1 degree of freedom.
   a. Show that $z = (y - n)/\sqrt{2n}$ has approximately a standard normal distribution for large values of n.
   b. If y has a χ^2 distribution with 30 degrees of freedom, find the approximate probability that y falls within 2 standard deviations of its mean, i.e., find $P(\mu - 2\sigma < y < \mu + 2\sigma)$.

7.6   Normal Approximation to the Binomial Distribution

Consider the binomial random variable y with parameters n and p. Recall that y has mean $\mu = np$ and variance $\sigma^2 = npq$. We showed in Example 7.10 that the number y of successes in n trials can be regarded as a sum consisting of n values of 0 and 1, with each 0 and 1 representing the outcome (failure or success, respectively) of a particular trial, i.e.,

$$y = \sum_{i=1}^n y_i \qquad \text{where } y_i = \begin{cases} 1 & \text{if success} \\ 0 & \text{if failure} \end{cases}$$

Then, according to the central limit theorem for sums, the binomial probability distribution $p(y)$ should become more nearly normal as n becomes larger. The normal approximation to a binomial probability distribution is reasonably good even for small samples—say, n as small as 10—when $p = .5$ and the distribution of y is therefore symmetric about its mean $\mu = np$. When p is near 0 (or. 1), the binomial probability distribution will tend to be skewed to the right (or left), but this skewness will disappear as n becomes large. In general, the approximation will be good when n is large enough so that $\mu - 2\sigma = np - 2\sqrt{npq}$ and $\mu + 2\sigma = np + 2\sqrt{npq}$ both lie between 0 and n. It can be shown (proof omitted) that for both $\mu - 2\sigma$ and $\mu + 2\sigma$ to fall between 0 and n, both np and nq must be greater than or equal to 4.

> ### Condition Required to Apply a Normal Approximation to a Binomial Probability Distribution
>
> The approximation will be good if both $\mu - 2\sigma = np - 2\sqrt{npq}$ and $\mu + 2\sigma = np + 2\sqrt{npq}$ lie between 0 and n. This condition will be satisfied if both $np \geq 4$ and $nq \geq 4$.

EXAMPLE 7.11

Let y be a binomial probability distribution with $n = 10$ and $p = .5$.

a. Graph $p(y)$ and superimpose on the graph a normal distribution with $\mu = np$ and $\sigma = \sqrt{npq}$.

b. Use Table 1 of Appendix II to find $P(y \leq 4)$.

c. Use the normal approximation to the binomial probability distribution to find an approximation to $P(y \leq 4)$.

Solution

a. The graphs of $p(y)$ and a normal distribution with

$$\mu = np = (10)(.5) = 5$$

and

$$\sigma = \sqrt{npq} = \sqrt{(10)(.5)(.5)} = 1.58$$

are shown in Figure 7.13. Note that both $np = 5$ and $nq = 5$ both exceed 4. Thus, the normal density function with $\mu = 5$ and $\sigma = 1.58$ provides a good approximation to $p(y)$.

FIGURE 7.13 ▶
A binomial probability distribution ($n = 10$, $p = .5$) and the approximating normal distribution ($\mu = np = 5$ and $\sigma = \sqrt{npq} = 1.58$)

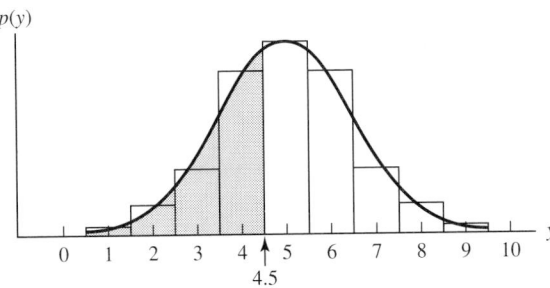

b. From Table 1 of Appendix II, we obtain

$$\sum_{y=0}^{4} p(y) = .377$$

c. By examining Figure 7.13, you can see that $P(y \leq 4)$ is the area under the normal curve to the left of $y = 4.5$. Note that the area to the left of $y = 4$ would *not* be appropriate because it would omit half the probability rectangle corresponding to

$y = 4$. We need to add $.5$ to 4 before calculating the probability to correct for the fact that we are using a continuous probability distribution to approximate a discrete probability distribution. The value $.5$ is called the **continuity correction factor** for the normal approximation to the binomial probability (see the box). The z value corresponding to the corrected value $y = 4.5$ is

$$z = \frac{y - \mu}{\sigma} = \frac{4.5 - 5}{1.58} = \frac{-.5}{1.58} = -.32$$

The area between $z = 0$ and $z = .32$, given in Table 4 of Appendix II, is $A = .1255$. Therefore,

$$P(y \leq 4) \approx .5 - A = .5 - .1255 = .3745$$

Thus, the normal approximation to $P(y \leq 4) = .377$ is quite good, although n is as small as 10. The sample size would have to be larger to apply the approximation if p were not equal to $.5$.

Continuity Correction for the Normal Approximation to a Binomial Probability

Let y be a binomial random variable with parameters n and p, and let z be a standard random variable. Then

$$P(y \leq a) \approx P\left(z < \frac{(a + .5) - np}{\sqrt{npq}}\right)$$

$$P(y \geq a) \approx P\left(z > \frac{(a - .5) - np}{\sqrt{npq}}\right)$$

$$P(a \leq y \leq b) \approx P\left(\frac{(a - .5) - np}{\sqrt{npq}} < z < \frac{(b + .5) - np}{\sqrt{npq}}\right)$$

EXERCISES

7.27 Let y be a binomial random variable with $n = 15$ and $p = .3$.
a. Use Table 1 of Appendix II to find $P(y \leq 8)$.
b. Use the normal approximation to the binomial probability distribution to find an approximation to $P(y \leq 8)$. Compare to your answer in part **a**.

7.28 *Consumer Reports* (Feb. 1992) found widespread contamination of seafood in New York and Chicago supermarkets. For example, 40% of the swordfish pieces available for sale have a level of mercury above the Food and Drug Administration (FDA) limit. Consider a random sample of 20 swordfish pieces from New York and Chicago supermarkets.

a. Use the normal approximation to the binomial to calculate the probability that less than 2 of the 20 swordfish pieces have mercury levels exceeding the FDA limit.

b. Use the normal approximation to the binomial to calculate the probability that more than half of the 20 swordfish pieces have mercury levels exceeding the FDA limit.

c. Use the binomial tables to calculate the exact probabilities in parts **a** and **b**. Does the normal distribution provide a good approximation to the binomial distribution?

7.29 The merging process from an acceleration lane to the through lane of a freeway constitutes an important aspect of traffic operation at interchanges. A study of parallel interchange ramps in Israel revealed that many drivers do not use the entire length of parallel lanes for acceleration, but seek as soon as possible an appropriate gap in the major stream of traffic for merging (*Transportation Engineering*, Nov. 1985). At one site (Yavneh), 54% of the drivers use less than half the lane length available before merging. Suppose we plan to monitor the merging patterns of a random sample of 330 drivers at the Yavneh site.

a. What is the approximate probability that fewer than 100 of the drivers will use less than half the acceleration lane length before merging?

b. What is the approximate probability that 200 or more of the drivers will use less than half the acceleration lane length before merging?

7.30 *Occupational Outlook Quarterly* (Spring 1993) reported that 1% of all drywall installers employed in the construction industry are women.

a. Approximate the probability that more than 100 of a random sample of 500 drywall installers are women.

b. Approximate the probability that five or fewer of a random sample of 500 drywall installers are women.

7.31 One of the keys to developing successful information systems is to implement structured design and programming techniques. Computer-aided software engineering (CASE) technology provides several automated tools (e.g., data flow diagrams) that can facilitate structured techniques. The *Journal of Systems Management* (July 1989) reported that 60% of information systems (IS) professionals make extensive use of data flow diagrams in their work. In a sample of 150 IS professionals, what is the approximate probability that at least half make extensive use of data flow diagrams?

7.32 Quality control is a problem with items that are mass produced. The production process must be monitored to ensure that the rate of defective items is kept at an acceptably low level. One method of dealing with this problem is **lot acceptance sampling**, in which a random sample of items produced is selected and each item in the sample is carefully tested. The entire lot of items is then accepted or rejected, based on the number of defectives observed in the sample. Suppose a manufacturer of pocket calculators randomly chooses 200 stamped circuits from a day's production and determines y, the number of defective circuits in the sample. If a sample defective rate of 6% or less is considered acceptable and, unknown to the manufacturer, 8% of the entire day's production of circuits is defective, find the approximate probability that the lot of stamped circuits will be rejected.

7.33 How well does a college engineering degree prepare you for the workplace? A 2-year nationwide survey of engineers and engineering managers in "specific high-demand" industries revealed that only 34% believe that their companies make good use of their learned skills (*Chemical Engineering*, Feb. 3, 1986). In a random sample of 50 engineers and engineering managers, consider the number y who believe that their employer makes good use of their college engineering background. Find the approximate probability that:

a. $y \leq 10$ b. $y \geq 25$ c. $20 \leq y \leq 30$

7.7   Sampling Distributions Related to the Normal Distribution

In this section, we present the sampling distributions of several well-known statistics that are based on random samples of observations from a normal population. These statistics are the χ^2, t, and F statistics. In Chapter 8, we show how to use these statistics to estimate the values of certain population parameters. The following results are stated without proof. Proofs using the methodology of Chapter 6 can be found in the references at the end of this chapter.

Theorem 7.4

If a random sample of n observations, $y_1, y_2, \ldots, y_n$, is selected from a normal distribution with mean μ and variance σ^2, then the sampling distribution of

$$\chi^2 = \frac{(n-1)s^2}{\sigma^2}$$

has a chi-square density function (see Section 5.7) with $\nu = (n-1)$ degrees of freedom.

Theorem 7.5

If χ_1^2 and χ_2^2 are independent chi-square random variables with ν_1 and ν_2 degrees of freedom, respectively, then the sum $(\chi_1^2 + \chi_2^2)$ has a chi-square distribution with $(\nu_1 + \nu_2)$ degrees of freedom.

Definition 7.5

Let z be a standard normal random variable and χ^2 be a chi-square random variable with ν degrees of freedom. If z and χ^2 are independent, then

$$t = \frac{z}{\sqrt{\chi^2/\nu}}$$

is said to possess a **Student's t distribution** (or, simply, t **distribution**) with ν degrees of freedom.

> ## Definition 7.6
>
> Let χ_1^2 and χ_2^2 be chi-square random variables with ν_1 and ν_2 degrees of freedom, respectively. If χ_1^2 and χ_2^2 are independent, then
>
> $$F = \frac{\chi_1^2/\nu_1}{\chi_2^2/\nu_2}$$
>
> is said to have an **F distribution** with ν_1 numerator degrees of freedom and ν_2 denominator degrees of freedom.

Note: The sampling distributions for the t and F statistics can also be derived using the methods of Optional Section 7.3. Both sampling distributions are related to the density function for a beta-type random variable (see Section 5.9). It can be shown (proof omitted) that a t distribution with ν degrees of freedom is actually a special case of an F distribution with $\nu_1 = 1$ and $\nu_2 = \nu$ degrees of freedom. Neither of the cumulative distribution functions can be obtained in closed form. Consequently, we dispense with the equations of the density functions and present useful values of the statistics and corresponding areas in tabular form in Appendix II.

The following examples illustrate how these statistics can be used to make probability statements about population parameters.

EXAMPLE 7.12

Consider a cannery that produces 8-ounce cans of processed corn. Quality control engineers have determined that the process is operating properly when the true variation σ^2 of the fill amount per can is less than .0025. A random sample of $n = 10$ cans is selected from a day's production, and the fill amount (in ounces) recorded for each. Of interest is the sample variance, s^2. If, in fact, $\sigma^2 = .001$, find the probability that s^2 exceeds .0025. Assume that the fill amounts are normally distributed.

Solution

We want to calculate $P(s^2 > .0025)$. Assume the sample of 10 fill amounts is selected from a normal distribution. Theorem 7.4 states that the statistic

$$\chi^2 = \frac{(n-1)s^2}{\sigma^2}$$

has a chi-square probability distribution with $\nu = (n-1)$ degrees of freedom. Consequently, the probability we seek can be written

$$P(s^2 > .0025) = P\left[\frac{(n-1)s^2}{\sigma^2} > \frac{(n-1)(.0025)}{\sigma^2}\right]$$

$$= P\left[\chi^2 > \frac{(n-1)(.0025)}{\sigma^2}\right]$$

Substituting $n = 10$ and $\sigma^2 = .001$, we have

$$P(s^2 > .0025) = P\left(\chi^2 > \frac{9(.0025)}{.001}\right) = P(\chi^2 > 22.5)$$

Upper-tail areas of the chi-square distribution have been tabulated and are given in Table 8 of Appendix II, a portion of which is reproduced in Table 7.2. The table gives the values of χ^2, denoted χ_a^2, that locate an area (probability) a in the upper-tail of the distribution, i.e., $P(\chi^2 > \chi_a^2) = a$. In our example, we want to find the probability a such that $\chi_a^2 > 22.5$.

Now, for $n = 10$, we have $\nu = n - 1 = 9$ degrees of freedom. Searching Table 7.2 in the row corresponding to $\nu = 9$, we find that $\chi_{.01}^2 = 21.666$ and $\chi_{.005}^2 = 23.5893$. (These values are shaded in Table 7.2.) Consequently, the probability that we seek falls between $a = .01$ and $a = .005$, i.e.,

$$.005 < P(\chi^2 > 22.5) < .01 \quad \text{(see Figure 7.14)}$$

Thus, the probability that the variance of the sample fill amounts exceeds .0025 is small (between .005 and .01) when the true population variance σ^2 equals .001.

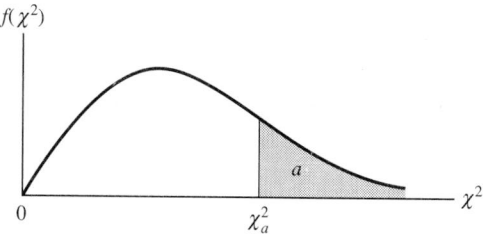

TABLE 7.2   Abbreviated Version of Table 8 of Appendix II: Tabulated Values of χ^2

Degrees of Freedom	$\chi_{.100}^2$	$\chi_{.050}^2$	$\chi_{.025}^2$	$\chi_{.010}^2$	$\chi_{.005}^2$
1	2.70554	3.84146	5.02389	6.63490	7.87944
2	4.60517	5.99147	7.37776	9.21034	10.5966
3	6.25139	7.81473	9.34840	11.3449	12.8381
4	7.77944	9.48773	11.1433	13.2767	14.8602
5	9.23635	11.0705	12.8325	15.0863	16.7496
6	10.6446	12.5916	14.4494	16.8119	18.5476
7	12.0170	14.0671	16.0128	18.4753	20.2777
8	13.3616	15.5073	17.5346	20.0902	21.9550
9	14.6837	16.9190	19.0228	21.6660	23.5893
10	15.9871	18.3070	20.4831	23.2093	25.1882
11	17.2750	19.6751	21.9200	24.7250	26.7569
12	18.5494	21.0261	23.3367	26.2170	28.2995
13	19.8119	22.3621	24.7356	27.6883	29.8194
14	21.0642	23.6848	26.1190	29.1413	31.3193
15	22.3072	24.9958	27.4884	30.5779	32.8013
16	23.5418	26.2962	28.8454	31.9999	34.2672
17	24.7690	27.5871	30.1910	33.4087	35.7185
18	25.9894	28.8693	31.5264	34.8053	37.1564
19	27.2036	30.1435	32.8523	36.1908	38.5822

FIGURE 7.14 ▶
Finding $P(\chi^2 > 22.5)$ in
Example 7.12

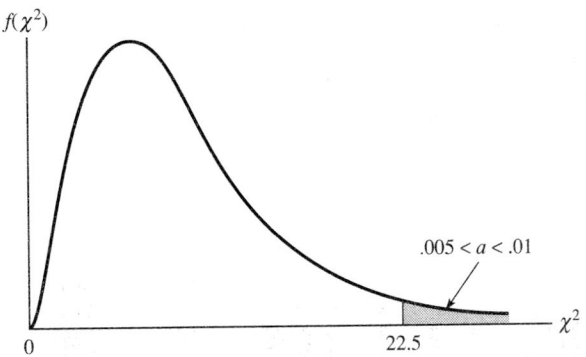

$f(\chi^2)$

$.005 < a < .01$

0   22.5 χ^2

EXAMPLE 7.13

Suppose that $\bar{y}$ and s^2 are the mean and variance of a random sample of n observations from a normally distributed population with mean μ and variance σ^2. It can be shown (proof omitted) that $\bar{y}$ and s^2 are statistically independent when the sampled population has a normal distribution. Use this result to show that

$$t = \frac{\bar{y} - \mu}{s/\sqrt{n}}$$

possesses a t distribution with $\nu = (n - 1)$ degrees of freedom.[*]

Solution

We know from Theorem 7.3 that $\bar{y}$ is normally distributed with mean μ and variance σ^2/n. Therefore,

$$z = \frac{\bar{y} - \mu}{\sigma/\sqrt{n}}$$

is a standard normal random variable. We also know from Theorem 7.4 that

$$\chi^2 = \frac{(n - 1)s^2}{\sigma^2}$$

is a χ^2 random variable with $\nu = (n - 1)$ degrees of freedom. Then, using Definition 7.4 and the information that $\bar{y}$ and s^2 are independent, we conclude that

$$t = \frac{z}{\sqrt{\chi^2/\nu}} = \frac{\dfrac{\bar{y} - \mu}{\sigma/\sqrt{n}}}{\sqrt{\dfrac{(n - 1)s^2}{\sigma^2} \Big/ (n - 1)}} = \frac{\bar{y} - \mu}{s/\sqrt{n}}$$

has a Student's t distribution with $\nu = (n - 1)$ degrees of freedom. As we will learn in Chapter 8, the t distribution is useful for making inferences about the population

---

[*]The result was first published in 1908 by W. S. Gosset, who wrote under the pen name of Student. Thereafter, this statistic became known as Student's t.

mean μ when the population standard deviation σ is unknown (and must be estimated by s^2).

Theorem 7.4 and Examples 7.12 and 7.13 identify the sampling distributions of two statistics that will play important roles in statistical inference. Others are presented without proof in Tables 7.3a and 7.3b. All are based on random sampling from normally distributed populations. The results contained in Table 7.3 will be needed in Chapter 8.

TABLE 7.3a.   Sampling Distributions of Statistics Based on Independent Random Samples of n_1 and n_2 Observations, Respectively, from Normally Distributed Populations with Parameters (μ_1, σ_1^2) and (μ_2, σ_2^2)

Statistic	Sampling Distribution	Additional Assumptions	Basis of Derivation of Sampling Distribution
$\chi^2 = \dfrac{(n_1 + n_2 - 2)s_p^2}{\sigma^2}$ where $s_p^2 = \dfrac{(n_1 - 1)s_1^2 + (n_2 - 1)s_2^2}{n_1 + n_2 - 2}$	Chi-square with $\nu = (n_1 + n_2 - 2)$ degrees of freedom	$\sigma_1^2 = \sigma_2^2 = \sigma^2$	Theorems 7.4–7.5
$t = \dfrac{(\bar{y}_1 - \bar{y}_2) - (\mu_1 - \mu_2)}{s_p\sqrt{\dfrac{1}{n_1} + \dfrac{1}{n_2}}}$ where $s_p^2 = \dfrac{(n_1 - 1)s_1^2 + (n_2 - 1)s_2^2}{n_1 + n_2 - 2}$	Student's t with $\nu = (n_1 + n_2 - 2)$ degrees of freedom	$\sigma_1^2 = \sigma_2^2 = \sigma^2$	Theorems 7.3–7.4 and Definition 7.4
$F = \left(\dfrac{s_1^2}{s_2^2}\right)\left(\dfrac{\sigma_2^2}{\sigma_1^2}\right)$	F distribution with $\nu_1 = (n_1 - 1)$ numerator degrees of freedom and $\nu_2 = (n_2 - 1)$ denominator degrees of freedom	None	Theorem 7.4 and Definition 7.6

TABLE 7.3b.   Sampling Distributions of Statistics Based on a Random Sample from a Single Normally Distributed Population with Mean μ and Variance σ^2

Statistic	Sampling Distribution	Additional Assumptions	Basis of Derivation of Sampling Distribution
$\chi^2 = \dfrac{(n-1)s^2}{\sigma^2}$	Chi-square with $\nu = (n-1)$ degrees of freedom	None	Methods of Section 7.2
$t = \dfrac{\bar{y} - \mu}{s/\sqrt{n}}$	Student's t with $\nu = (n-1)$ degrees of freedom	None	Theorems 7.3–7.4 and Definition 7.4

EXERCISES

7.34   Let $y_1, y_2, \ldots, y_n$, be a random sample of n observations from a normal distribution with mean μ and variance σ^2. Let s^2 be the variance of the sample. Use Table 8 of Appendix II to estimate the following probabilities:
   a. $P(s^2 > 8)$ when $n = 10$, $\sigma^2 = 5$
   b. $P(s^2 > 1.11)$ when $n = 5$, $\sigma^2 = .3$
   c. $P(s^2 > 199)$ when $n = 22$, $\sigma^2 = 107$

7.35   *IEEE Transactions* (June 1990) presented a hybrid algorithm for solving polynomial 0–1 mathematical programming problems. The solution time (in seconds) for a randomly selected problem solved using the hybrid algorithm has a normal probability distribution with mean $\mu = .8$ second and $\sigma = 1.5$ seconds. Consider a random sample of $n = 30$ problems solved with the hybrid algorithm.
   a. Describe the sampling distribution of s^2, the variance of the solution times for the 30 problems.
   b. Find the approximate probability that s^2 will exceed 3.30.

OPTIONAL EXERCISES

7.36   Let $y_1, y_2, \ldots, y_n$ be a random sample of n_1 observations from a normal distribution with mean μ_1 and variance σ_1^2. Let $x_1, x_2, \ldots, x_{n_2}$ be a random sample of n_2 observations from a normal distribution with mean μ_2 and variance σ_2^2. Assuming the samples were independently selected, show that

$$F = \left(\frac{s_1^2}{s_2^2}\right)\left(\frac{\sigma_2^2}{\sigma_1^2}\right)$$

has an F distribution with $\nu_1 = (n_1 - 1)$ numerator degrees of freedom and $\nu_2 = (n_2 - 1)$ denominator degrees of freedom.

7.37   Let s_1^2 and s_2^2 be the variances of independent random samples of sizes n_1 and n_2 selected from normally distributed populations with parameters (μ_1, σ^2) and (μ_2, σ^2), respectively. Thus, the populations have different means, but a common variance σ^2. To estimate the common variance, we can combine information from both samples and use the **pooled estimator**

$$s^2 = \frac{(n_1 - 1)s_1^2 + (n_2 - 1)s_2^2}{n_1 + n_2 - 2}$$

Use Theorems 7.4 and 7.5 to show that $(n_1 + n_2 - 2)s^2/\sigma^2$ has a chi-square distribution with $\nu = (n_1 + n_2 - 2)$ degrees of freedom.

7.38   Let $\bar{y}_1$ and $\bar{y}_2$ be the means of independent random samples of sizes n_1 and n_2 selected from normally distributed populations with parameters (μ_1, σ^2) and (μ_2, σ^2), respectively. If

$$s^2 = \frac{(n_1 - 1)s_1^2 + (n_2 - 1)s_2^2}{n_1 + n_2 - 2}$$

show that

$$t = \frac{(\bar{y}_1 - \bar{y}_2) - (\mu_1 - \mu_2)}{s\sqrt{\dfrac{1}{n_1} + \dfrac{1}{n_2}}}$$

has a Student's t distribution with $\nu = (n_1 + n_2 - 2)$ degrees of freedom.

7.39   The continuous random variable y is said to have a lognormal distribution with parameters μ and σ if its probability density function, $f(y)$, satisfies

$$f(y) = \frac{1}{\sigma y \sqrt{2\pi}} \exp\left\{ -\frac{(\ln y - \mu)^2}{2\sigma^2} \right\} \qquad (y > 0)$$

Show that $x = \ln(y)$ has a normal distribution with mean μ and variance σ^2.

7.8   Summary

In the following chapters, we will use sample statistics to make inferences about population parameters; the properties of these statistics will be determined by their probability distributions. The probability distribution of a statistic is called its **sampling distribution**.

A **simulation procedure** may be used to approximate the sampling distribution for a statistic. Random samples of a fixed size are drawn from a known population of data. The value of some statistic—say, the sample mean $\bar{y}$—is computed for each sample. The relative frequency distribution of the values of the statistic, generated by repeated sampling, approximates the probability distribution of the statistic.

Evidence of the major role that the normal distribution plays in statistical inference is given by the **central limit theorem**, Theorem 7.3, and the related χ^2, F, and t **distributions**. The central limit theorem explains why many statistics, especially those based on large samples, possess sampling distributions that can be approximated by a normal density function. Theorem 7.3, which states that linear functions of normally distributed random variables will be normally distributed, provides further explanation for the common occurrence of normally distributed sampling distributions. The χ^2, t, and F statistics are approximated when sampling from normally distributed populations. You will encounter them frequently in the statistical methodology to be developed in the following chapters.

SUPPLEMENTARY EXERCISES

7.40 Consider the density function

$$f(y) = \begin{cases} 3y^2 & \text{if } 0 \le y \le 1 \\ 0 & \text{elsewhere} \end{cases}$$

Find the density function of w, where:
a. $w = \sqrt{y}$ **b.** $w = 3 - y$ **c.** $w = -\ln(y)$

7.41 A supplier of home heating oil has a 250-gallon tank that is filled at the beginning of each week. Since the weekly demand for the oil increases steadily up to 100 gallons and then levels off between 100 and 250 gallons, the probability distribution of the weekly demand y (in hundreds of gallons) can be represented by

$$f(y) = \begin{cases} \dfrac{y}{2} & \text{if } 0 \le y \le 1 \\ \dfrac{1}{2} & \text{if } 1 \le y \le 2.5 \\ 0 & \text{elsewhere} \end{cases}$$

If the supplier's profit is given by $w = 10y - 2$, find the probability density function of w.

7.42 Dioxin, often described as the most toxic chemical known, is created as a by-product in the manufacture of herbicides such as Agent Orange. Scientists have found that .000005 gram (five-millionths of a gram) of dioxin—a dot barely visible to the human eye—is a lethal dose for experimental guinea pigs in more than half the animals tested, making dioxin 2,000 times more toxic than strychnine. Assume that the amount of dioxin required to kill a guinea pig has a relative frequency distribution with mean $\mu = .000005$ gram and standard deviation $\sigma = .000002$ gram. Consider an experiment in which the amount of dioxin required to kill each of $n = 50$ guinea pigs is measured, and the sample mean $\bar{y}$ is computed.
a. Calculate $\mu_{\bar{y}}$ and $\sigma_{\bar{y}}$.
b. Find the probability that the mean amount of dioxin required to kill the 50 guinea pigs is larger than .0000053 gram.

7.43 The determination of the percent canopy closure of a forest is essential for wildlife habitat assessment, watershed runoff estimation, erosion control, and other forest management activities. One way in which geoscientists estimate percent forest canopy closure is through the use of a satellite sensor called the Landsat Thematic Mapper. A study of the percent canopy closure in the San Juan National Forest (Colorado) was conducted by examining Thematic Mapper Simulator (TMS) data collected by aircraft at various forest sites (*IEEE Transactions on Geoscience and Remote Sensing*, Jan. 1986). The mean and standard deviation of the readings obtained from TMS Channel 5 were found to be 121.74 and 27.52, respectively.

a. Let $\bar{y}$ be the mean TMS reading for a sample of 32 forest sites. Assuming the figures given are population values, describe the sampling distribution of $\bar{y}$.

b. Use the sampling distribution of part **a** to find the probability that $\bar{y}$ falls between 118 and 130.

7.44 Refer to Exercise 7.43. Let s^2 be the variance of the TMS readings for the 32 sampled forest sites. Assuming the sample is from a normal population, estimate the probability that s^2 exceeds 1,311.

7.45 Use Theorem 7.1 to draw a random sample of $n = 5$ observations from a population with probability density function given by

$$f(y) = \begin{cases} 2ye^{-y^2} & \text{if } 0 < y < \infty \\ 0 & \text{elsewhere} \end{cases}$$

7.46 Use Theorem 7.1 to draw a random sample of $n = 5$ observations from a population with probability density function given by

$$f(y) = \begin{cases} 2(y - 1) & \text{if } 1 \leq y < 2 \\ 0 & \text{elsewhere} \end{cases}$$

7.47 This year a large architectural and engineering consulting firm began a program of compensating its management personnel for sick days not used. The firm decided to pay each manager a bonus for every unused sick day. In past years, the number y of sick days used per manager per year had a probability distribution with mean $\mu = 9.2$ and variance $\sigma^2 = 3.24$. To determine whether the compensation program has effectively reduced the mean number of sick days used, the firm randomly sampled $n = 80$ managers and recorded y, the number of sick days used by each at year's end.

a. Assuming the compensation program was *not* effective in reducing the average number of sick days used, find the probability that $\bar{y}$, the mean number of sick days used by the sample of 80 managers, is less than 8.80 days, i.e., find $P(\bar{y} < 8.80)$.

b. If you observe $\bar{y} < 8.80$, what inference would you make about the effectiveness of the compensation program?

7.48 To determine whether a metal lathe that produces machine bearings is properly adjusted, a random sample of 36 bearings is collected and the diameter of each is measured. Assume that the standard deviation of the diameter of the machine bearings measured over a long period of time is .001 inch.

a. What is the probability that the mean diameter $\bar{y}$ of the sample of 36 bearings will lie within .0001 inch of the population mean diameter of the bearings?

b. Suppose the mean diameter of the bearings produced by the machine is supposed to be .5 inch. The company decides to use the sample mean to decide whether the process is in control—i.e., whether it is producing bearings with a mean diameter of .5 inch. The machine will be considered out of control if the mean of the sample of $n = 36$ diameters is less than .4994 inch or larger than .5006 inch. If the true mean diameter of the bearings produced by the machine is .501 inch, what is the probability that the test will fail to imply that the process is out of control?

7.49 Refer to the problem of transporting neutral particles in a nuclear fusion reactor, described in Exercise 3.25. Recall that particles released into a certain type of evacuated duct collide with the inner duct wall and are either scattered (reflected) with probability .16 or absorbed with probability .84 (*Nuclear Science and Engineering*, May 1986). Suppose 2,000 neutral particles are released into an unknown type of evacuated duct in a nuclear fusion reactor. Of these, 280 are reflected. What is the approximate probability that as few as 280 (i.e., 280 or fewer) of the 2,000 neutral particles would be reflected off the inner duct wall if the reflection probability of the evacuated duct is .16?

7.50   Shear block tests on epoxy-repaired timber indicate that the probability distribution of the bond strengths of parallel grain, mill lumber specimens has a mean of 1,312 pounds per square inch (psi) and a standard deviation of 422 psi (*Journal of Structural Engineering*, Feb. 1986). Suppose a sample of 100 epoxy-repaired timber specimens is randomly selected and the bond strength of each is determined.
   a. Describe the sampling distribution of $\bar{y}$, the mean bond strength of the sample of 100 epoxy-repaired timber specimens.
   b. Compute $P(\bar{y} \geq 1,418)$.
   c. If the actual sample mean is computed to be $\bar{y} = 1,418$, what would you infer about the shear block test results?

7.51   Refer to Exercise 7.50.
   a. Describe the sampling distribution of s^2, the variance of the bond strengths of the 100 sampled epoxy-repaired timber specimens. Assume the sample is from a normal population.
   b. Estimate $P(s > 500)$.

OPTIONAL SUPPLEMENTARY EXERCISES

7.52   The waiting time y until delivery of a new component for a data-processing unit is uniformly distributed over the interval from 1 to 5 days. The cost c (in hundreds of dollars) of this delay to the purchaser is given by $c = (2y^2 + 3)$. Find the probability that the cost of delay is at least $2,000, i.e., compute $P(c \geq 20)$.

7.53   Let y_1 and y_2 be a sample of $n = 2$ observations from a gamma random variable with parameters $\alpha = 1$ and arbitrary β, and corresponding density function

$$f(y_i) = \begin{cases} \dfrac{1}{\beta} e^{-y_i/\beta} & \text{if } y_i > 0 \quad (i = 1, 2) \\ 0 & \text{elsewhere} \end{cases}$$

Show that the sum $w = (y_1 + y_2)$ is also a gamma random variable with parameters $\alpha = 2$ and β. [*Hint:*   You may use the result

$$P(w \leq w_0) = P(0 < y_2 \leq w - y_1, 0 \leq y_1 < w) = \int_0^w \int_0^{w-y_1} f(y_1, y_2) dy_2\, dy_1$$

Then use the fact that

$$f(y_1, y_2) = f(y_1)f(y_2)$$

since y_1 and y_2 are independent.]

7.54   Let y have an exponential density with mean β. Show that $w = 2y/\beta$ has a χ^2 density with $\nu = 2$ degrees of freedom.

7.55   The lifetime y of an electronic component of a home minicomputer has a *Rayleigh density*, given by

$$f(y) = \begin{cases} \left(\dfrac{2y}{\beta}\right) e^{-y^2/\beta} & \text{if } y > 0 \\ 0 & \text{elsewhere} \end{cases}$$

Find the probability density function for $w = y^2$, and identify the type of density function. [*Hint:* You may use the result

$$\int \frac{2y}{\beta} e^{-y^2/\beta} \, dy = -e^{-y^2/\beta}$$

in determining the density function for w.]

7.56   Let y_1 and y_2 be a random sample of $n = 2$ observations from a normal distribution with mean μ and variance σ^2.

a. Show that

$$z = \frac{y_1 - y_2}{\sqrt{2}\sigma}$$

has a standard normal distribution.

b. Given the result in part **a**, show that z^2 possesses a χ^2 distribution with 1 degree of freedom. [*Hint:* First show that $s^2 = (y_1 - y_2)^2/2$; then apply Theorem 7.4.]

7.57   Refer to Exercise 7.12. Use the computer to generate a random sample of $n = 100$ observations from a distribution with probability density

$$f(y) = \begin{cases} e^y & \text{if } y < 0 \\ 0 & \text{elsewhere} \end{cases}$$

Repeat the procedure 1,000 times and compute the sample mean $\bar{y}$ for each of the 1,000 samples of size $n = 100$. Then generate (by computer) a relative frequency histogram for the 1,000 sample means. Does your result agree with the theoretical sampling distribution described by the central limit theorem?

COMPUTER LAB: Generating Random Samples

Most statistical computer software packages have built-in algorithms for generating random samples of observations from a variety of probability distributions. The SAS and MINITAB commands for generating random samples of size 50 from the uniform distribution are given in the following programs. Table 7.4 gives the corresponding commands for generating samples from the normal, binomial, Poisson, exponential, and gamma distributions.

TABLE 7.4   Random Number Generators for SAS and MINITAB

Probability Distribution	SAS	MINITAB
Uniform (0, 1)	Y = RANUNI(seed);	UNIFORM.
Uniform (A, B)	Y = A+B*RANUNI(seed);	UNIFORM A B.
Normal (mean = 0, std.dev. = 1)	Y = RANNOR(seed);	NORMAL.
Normal (mean = M, std.dev. = S)	Y = M+S*RANNOR(seed);	NORMAL M S.
Binomial (N, P)	Y = RANBIN(seed,N,P);	BINOMIAL N P.
Exponential (mean = 1)	Y = RANEXP(seed);	EXPONENTIAL.
Exponential (mean = B)	Y = RANEXP(seed)/B;	EXPONENTIAL B.
Gamma (A, 1)	Y = RANGAM(seed,A);	GAMMA A 1.
Gamma (A, B)	Y = B*RANGAM(seed,A);	GAMMA A B.
Chi-square (df = V)	Y = 2*RANGAM(seed,V/2);	CHISQUARE V.
Poisson (mean = L)	Y = RANPOI(seed,L);	POISSON L.
Beta (A, B)	Y1 = RANGAM(seed,A);	BETA A B.
	Y2 = RANGAM(seed,B);	
	Y = Y1/(Y1+Y2);	
Weibull (A, B)	Not available	WEIBULL A B.

SAS

Command
line

```
1    DATA SAMPLE;               Data entry instruction
2    DO N = 1 TO 50;
3    Y = RANUNI(213);
4    X = 1 + 2000*RANUNI(6);    Generates 50 random numbers
5    X = ROUND(X, 1);
6    OUTPUT;
7    END;
8    PROC PRINT;                Prints the random numbers
```

COMMAND 3   RANUNI generates uniform random numbers in the interval (0, 1). The numerical "seed" (i.e., the number in parentheses following RANUNI) can be any integer value.

COMMANDS 4–5   Multiplying the uniform random number by 2,000 and adding 1 will generate a random number between 1 and 2,000. The ROUND function (Command 5) will round the resulting random number to the nearest integer.

NOTE: The output from this SAS program is displayed in Figure 7.15 on page 334. SAS commands for the random number generators of several other distributions are provided in Table 7.4.

MINITAB

Command
line

	Command line	
1	RANDOM 50 C1;	⎫
2	UNIFORM.	⎬ Generates 50 random numbers
3	RANDOM 50 C2;	⎪
4	UNIFORM 1 2000.	⎭
5	PRINT C1 C2	Prints the random numbers

COMMANDS 1–2 RANDOM with the UNIFORM subcommand generates uniform random numbers in the interval (0, 1).

COMMANDS 3–4 The UNIFORM subcommand followed by the values 1 and 2000 will generate a random number between 1 and 2000.

NOTE: The output from this MINITAB program is displayed in Figure 7.16. Minitab subcommands for the random number generators of several other probability distributions are provided in Table 7.4.

FIGURE 7.15 ▶

SAS printout for Computer Lab

N	Y	X
1	0.39703	1259
2	0.16258	505
3	0.30135	913
4	0.65456	502
5	0.60613	358
6	0.51486	1170
7	0.77299	622
8	0.84608	606
9	0.06631	1911
10	0.05092	493
11	0.59439	1838
12	0.97203	359
13	0.34312	1965
14	0.15364	1496
15	0.08987	609
16	0.14101	1814
17	0.34850	1806
18	0.59765	618
19	0.29204	1256
20	0.73898	1607
21	0.47006	1092
22	0.64217	158
23	0.80029	303
24	0.55323	1762
25	0.91071	546
26	0.51053	1306
27	0.22638	1059
28	0.59268	1011
29	0.44032	591
30	0.68000	1031
31	0.26740	275
32	0.83772	1691
33	0.59476	1994
34	0.69763	1696
35	0.99709	624
36	0.27695	1930
37	0.61072	561
38	0.35919	1072
39	0.43803	1035
40	0.67097	1067
41	0.26741	471
42	0.07262	1105
43	0.41368	10
44	0.87680	1626
45	0.68880	65
46	0.57243	1721
47	0.89295	965
48	0.64618	269
49	0.75235	180
50	0.68174	216

FIGURE 7.16 ►

MINITAB printout for Computer Lab

ROW	C1	C2
1	0.262667	170.25
2	0.833319	1166.89
3	0.164871	1808.98
4	0.608885	111.94
5	0.110577	1874.77
6	0.822181	339.32
7	0.772671	312.60
8	0.583832	969.61
9	0.978965	1137.29
10	0.370586	108.39
11	0.323264	1430.28
12	0.408010	750.34
13	0.001304	1714.99
14	0.163034	357.31
15	0.379198	561.50
16	0.399769	99.04
17	0.971068	262.59
18	0.383489	715.27
19	0.936076	1329.24
20	0.009521	113.97
21	0.190185	129.56
22	0.773176	78.92
23	0.646953	1745.57
24	0.869129	181.87
25	0.641075	620.47
26	0.134382	1472.91
27	0.797779	81.93
28	0.722374	121.72
29	0.296690	1097.71
30	0.086229	1157.76
31	0.778634	667.47
32	0.329307	1350.76
33	0.163365	805.58
34	0.420638	623.57
35	0.579784	1860.12
36	0.473011	506.76
37	0.126340	1251.50
38	0.792532	392.08
39	0.066484	909.82
40	0.310511	1659.03
41	0.813840	1358.03
42	0.729962	1713.86
43	0.245253	215.31
44	0.656617	802.93
45	0.077151	291.86
46	0.643837	376.03
47	0.479582	903.08
48	0.947811	817.06
49	0.476421	59.64
50	0.552677	1333.67

References

Freedman, D., Pisani, R., and Purves, R. *Statistics*. New York: W. W. Norton and Co., 1978.

Hogg, R. V., and Craig, A. T. *Introduction to Mathematical Statistics*, 4th ed. New York: Macmillan, 1978.

Mendenhall, W. *Introduction to Probability and Statistics*, 8th ed. Boston: Duxbury, 1990.

Mendenhall, W., Wackerly, D. D., and Scheaffer, R. L. *Mathematical Statistics with Applications*, 4th ed. Boston: Duxbury, 1989.

Snedecor, G. W., and Cochran, W. G. *Statistical Methods*, 7th ed. Ames, Iowa: Iowa State University Press, 1980.

CHAPTER EIGHT

Estimation

Objective

To explain the basic concepts of statistical estimation; to present some estimators and to illustrate their use in practical sampling situations involving one or two samples

Contents

337

8.1   Estimators

An inference about a population parameter can be made in either of two ways—we can estimate the unknown parameter value or we can make a decision about a hypothesized value of the parameter. To illustrate, we can estimate the mean number μ of jobs submitted per hour to a data-processing center or we might want to decide whether the mean μ exceeds some value—say, 60. The method for making a decision about one or more population parameters, called a **statistical test of a hypothesis**, is the topic of Chapter 9. This chapter will be concerned with **estimation**.

Suppose we want to estimate some population parameter, which we denote by θ. For example, θ could be a population mean μ, a population variance σ^2, or the probability $F(a)$ that an observation selected from the population is less than or equal to the value a. A **point estimator**, designated by the symbol $\hat{\theta}$ (i.e., we place a "hat" over the symbol of a parameter to denote its estimator), is a rule or formula that tells us how to use the observations in a sample to compute a single number (a point) that serves as an **estimate** of the value of θ. For example, the mean $\bar{y}$ of a random sample of n observations, $y_1, y_2, \ldots, y_n$, selected from a population is a point estimator of the population mean μ—i.e., $\hat{\mu} = \bar{y}$. Similarly, the sample variance s^2 is a point estimator of σ^2—i.e., $\hat{\sigma}^2 = s^2$.

Definition 8.1

A **point estimator** is a rule or formula that tells us how to calculate a numerical estimate based on the measurements contained in a sample. The single number that results from the calculation is called a **point estimate**.

Another way to estimate the value of a population parameter θ is to use an interval estimator. An **interval estimator** is a rule, usually expressed as a formula, for calculating two points from the sample data. The objective is to form an interval that contains θ with a high degree of confidence. For example, if we estimate the mean number μ of jobs submitted to a data-processing center to be between 40 and 60 jobs per hour, then the interval 40 to 60 is an interval estimate of μ.

Definition 8.2

An **interval estimator** is a formula that tells us how to use sample data to calculate an interval that estimates a population parameter.

In this chapter, we will identify desirable properties of point and interval estimators, explain how to compare two or more estimators for a single parameter, and show how to measure how good a single estimate actually is. In addition, we will present methods for finding both point and interval estimators, give the formulas for some useful estimators, and show how they can be used in practical situations.

8.2 Properties of Point Estimators

Since a point estimator is calculated from a sample, it possesses a sampling distribution. The sampling distribution of a point estimator completely describes its properties. For example, according to the central limit theorem, the sampling distribution for a sample mean will be approximately normally distributed for large sample sizes, say, $n = 30$ or more, with mean μ and standard error $\sigma/\sqrt{n}$ (see Figure 8.1). The figure shows that a sample mean $\bar{y}$ is equally likely to fall above or below μ and that the probability is approximately .95 that it will not deviate from μ by more than $2\sigma_{\bar{y}} = 2\sigma/\sqrt{n}$.

FIGURE 8.1 ▶
Sampling distribution of a sample mean for large samples

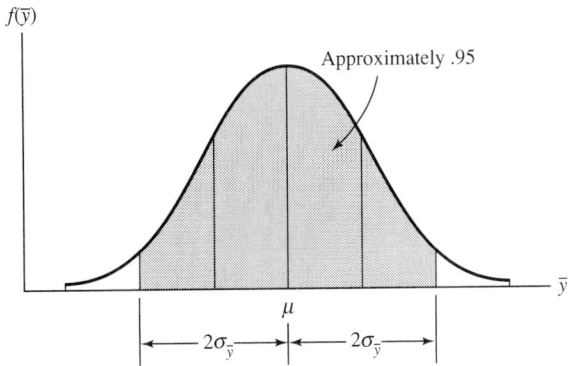

The characteristics exhibited in Figure 8.1 identify the two most desirable properties of estimators. First, we would like the sampling distribution of an estimator to be centered over the parameter being estimated. If the mean of the sampling distribution of an estimator $\hat{\theta}$ is equal to the estimated parameter θ, then the estimator is said to be **unbiased**. If not, the estimator is said to be **biased**. The sample mean is an unbiased estimator of the population mean μ. Sampling distributions for unbiased and biased estimators are shown in Figures 8.2a and 8.2b, respectively.

FIGURE 8.2 ▶
Sampling distributions for unbiased and biased estimators of θ

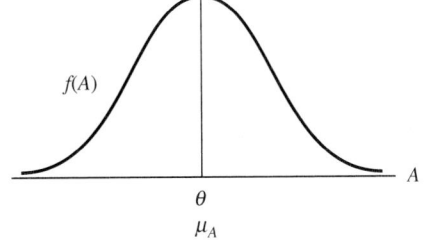

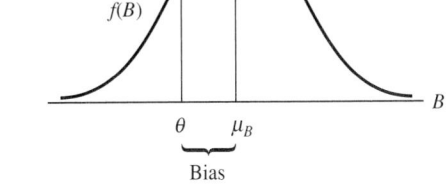

a. Estimator A is unbiased.

b. Estimator B is biased.

> ### Definition 8.3
>
> An estimator $\hat{\theta}$ of a parameter θ is **unbiased** if $E(\hat{\theta}) = \theta$. If $E(\hat{\theta}) \neq \theta$, the estimator is said to be **biased**.

> ### Definition 8.4
>
> The **bias** B of an estimator $\hat{\theta}$ is equal to the difference between the mean $E(\hat{\theta})$ of the sampling distribution of $\hat{\theta}$ and θ, i.e.,
>
> $$B = E(\hat{\theta}) - \theta$$

In addition to unbiasedness, we would like the sampling distribution of an estimator to have **minimum variance**, i.e., we want the spread of the sampling distribution to be as small as possible so that estimates will tend to fall close to θ.

Figure 8.3 portrays the sampling distributions of two unbiased estimators, A and B, with A having smaller variance than B. An unbiased estimator that has the minimum variance among all unbiased estimators is called the **minimum variance unbiased estimator (MVUE)**. For example, $\bar{y}$ is the MVUE for μ. That is, $\mathrm{Var}(\bar{y}) = \sigma^2/n$ is the smallest variance among all unbiased estimators of μ. (Proof omitted.)

FIGURE 8.3 ▶

Sampling distributions for two unbiased estimators of θ with different variances

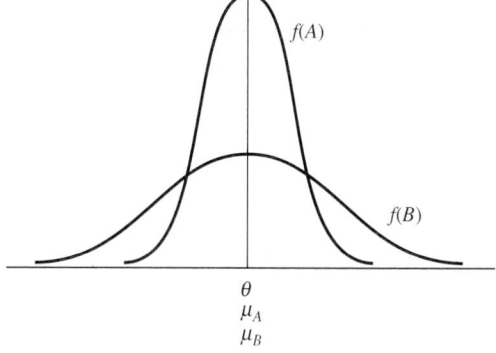

> ### Definition 8.5
>
> The **minimum variance unbiased estimator (MVUE)** of a parameter θ is the estimator $\hat{\theta}$ that has the smallest variance of all unbiased estimators.

Sometimes we cannot achieve both unbiasedness and minimum variance in the same estimator. For example, Figure 8.4 shows a biased estimator A with slight bias, but with a smaller variance than the MVUE B. In such a case, we prefer the estimator that minimizes the **mean squared error**, the mean of the squared deviations between $\hat{\theta}$ and θ:

Mean squared error for $\hat{\theta}$: $E[(\hat{\theta} - \theta)^2]$

It can be shown (proof omitted) that

$$E[(\hat{\theta} - \theta)^2] = V(\hat{\theta}) + B^2$$

Therefore, if $\hat{\theta}$ is unbiased, i.e., if $B = 0$, then the mean squared error is equal to $V(\hat{\theta})$. Furthermore, when $B = 0$, the estimator $\hat{\theta}$ that yields the smallest mean squared error is also the MVUE for θ.

FIGURE 8.4 ▶
Sampling distributions of biased estimator A and MVUE B

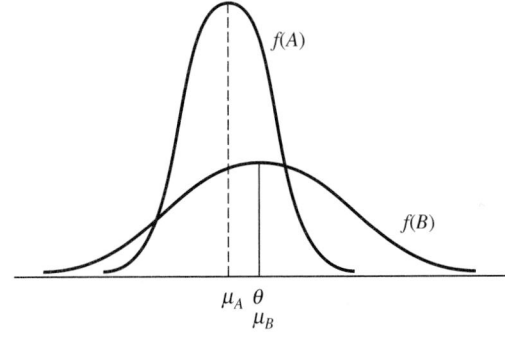

EXAMPLE 8.1

Let $y_1, y_2, \ldots, y_n$ be a random sample of n observations from a normal distribution with mean μ and variance σ^2. Show that the sample variance s^2 is an unbiased estimator of the population variance σ^2 when:

a. The sampled population has a normal distribution.

b. The distribution of the sampled population is unknown.

Solution

a. From Theorem 7.4, we know that when sampling from a normal distribution,

$$\frac{(n - 1)s^2}{\sigma^2} = \chi^2$$

where χ^2 is a chi-square random variable with $\nu = (n - 1)$ degrees of freedom. Rearranging terms yields

$$s^2 = \frac{\sigma^2}{(n - 1)}\chi^2$$

from which it follows that

$$E(s^2) = E\left[\frac{\sigma^2}{(n - 1)}\chi^2\right]$$

Applying Theorem 5.2, we obtain

$$E(s^2) = \frac{\sigma^2}{(n-1)}E(\chi^2)$$

We know from Section 5.6 that $E(\chi^2) = \nu$ and $V(\chi^2) = 2\nu$; thus

$$E(s^2) = \frac{\sigma^2}{(n-1)}\nu = \frac{\sigma^2}{(n-1)}(n-1) = \sigma^2$$

Therefore, by Definition 8.3, we conclude that s^2 is an unbiased estimator of σ^2.

b. By the definition of sample variance, we have

$$s^2 = \frac{1}{(n-1)}\left[\sum_{i=1}^{n} y_i^2 - \frac{\left(\sum y_i\right)^2}{n}\right] = \frac{1}{n-1}\left[\sum_{i=1}^{n} y_i^2 - n(\bar{y})^2\right]$$

From Theorem 4.4, $\sigma^2 = E(y^2) - \mu^2$. Consequently, $E(y^2) = \sigma^2 + \mu^2$ for a random variable y. Since each y value, $y_1, y_2, \ldots, y_n$, was randomly selected from a population with mean μ and variance σ^2, it follows that

$$E(y_i^2) = \sigma^2 + \mu^2 \quad (i = 1, 2, \ldots, n)$$

and

$$E(\bar{y}^2) = \sigma_{\bar{y}}^2 + (\mu_{\bar{y}})^2 = \sigma^2/n + \mu^2$$

Taking the expected value of s^2 and substituting these expressions, we obtain

$$E(s^2) = E\left\{\frac{1}{n-1}\left[\sum_{i=1}^{n} y_i^2 - n(\bar{y})^2\right]\right\}$$

$$= \frac{1}{n-1}\left\{E\left[\sum_{i=1}^{n} y_i^2\right] - E[n(\bar{y})^2]\right\}$$

$$= \frac{1}{n-1}\left\{\sum_{i=1}^{n} E[y_i^2] - nE[(\bar{y})^2]\right\}$$

$$= \frac{1}{n-1}\left\{\sum_{i=1}^{n} (\sigma^2 + \mu^2) - n\left(\frac{\sigma^2}{n} + \mu^2\right)\right\}$$

$$= \frac{1}{n-1}[(n\sigma^2 + n\mu^2) - \sigma^2 - n\mu^2]$$

$$= \frac{1}{n-1}[n\sigma^2 - \sigma^2]$$

$$= \left(\frac{n-1}{n-1}\right)\sigma^2 = \sigma^2$$

This shows that, regardless of the nature of the sampled population, s^2 is an unbiased estimator of σ^2.

EXERCISES

OPTIONAL EXERCISES

8.1 Let y_1, y_2, y_3 be a random sample from an exponential distribution with mean θ, i.e., $E(y_i) = \theta$, $i = 1, 2, 3$. Consider three estimators of θ:

$$\hat{\theta}_1 = \bar{y} \qquad \hat{\theta}_2 = y_1 \qquad \hat{\theta}_3 = \frac{y_1 + y_2}{2}$$

a. Show that all three estimators are unbiased.
b. Which of the estimators has the smallest variance? [*Hint:* Recall that, for an exponential distribution, $V(y_i) = \theta^2$.]

8.2 Let y_1, y_2, y_3, $\ldots$, y_n be a random sample from a Poisson distribution with mean λ, i.e., $E(y_i) = \lambda$, $i = 1, 2, \ldots, n$. Consider four estimators of λ:

$$\hat{\lambda}_1 = \bar{y} \qquad\qquad \hat{\lambda}_2 = n(y_1 + y_2 + \cdots + y_n)$$

$$\hat{\lambda}_3 = \frac{y_1 + y_2}{2} \qquad \hat{\lambda}_4 = \frac{y_1}{n}$$

a. Which of the four estimators are unbiased?
b. Of the unbiased estimators, which has the smallest variance? [*Hint:* Recall that, for a Poisson distribution, $V(y_i) = \lambda$.]

8.3 Suppose y has a binomial distribution with parameters n and p.
a. Show that $\hat{p} = y/n$ is an unbiased estimator of p.
b. Find the variance of $\hat{p}$.

8.4 Let y_1, y_2, $\ldots$, y_n be a random sample from a gamma distribution with parameters $\alpha = 2$ and β unknown.
a. Show that $\bar{y}$ is a biased estimator of β. Compute the bias.
b. Show that $\hat{\beta} = \bar{y}/2$ is an unbiased estimator of β.
c. Find the variance of $\hat{\beta} = \bar{y}/2$. [*Hint:* Recall that, for a gamma distribution, $E(y_i) = 2\beta$ and $V(y_i) = 2\beta^2$.]

8.5 Show that $E[(\hat{\theta} - \theta)^2] = V(\hat{\theta}) + B^2$, where the bias $B = E(\hat{\theta}) - \theta$. [*Hint:* Write $(\hat{\theta} - \theta) = [\hat{\theta} - E(\hat{\theta})] + [E(\hat{\theta}) - \theta]$.]

8.6 Let y_1 be a sample of size 1 from a uniform distribution over the interval from 2 to θ.
a. Show that y_1 is a biased estimator of θ and compute the bias.
b. Show that $2(y_1 - 1)$ is an unbiased estimator of θ.
c. Find the variance of $2(y_1 - 1)$.

8.7 Let y_1, y_2, $\ldots$, y_n be a random sample from a normal distribution, with mean μ and variance σ^2. Show that the variance of the sampling distribution of s^2 is $2\sigma^4/(n - 1)$.

8.3   Finding Point Estimators: Methods of Estimation

There are a number of different methods for finding point estimators of parameters. Two classical methods, the **method of moments** and the **method of maximum likelihood**, are the main topics of this section. These techniques produce the estimators of the population parameters encountered in Sections 8.5–8.11. A discussion of other methods for finding point estimators is beyond the scope of this text; we give a brief description of these other methods and refer you to the references given at the end of this chapter.

METHOD OF MOMENTS   The method of estimation that we have employed thus far is to use sample numerical descriptive measures to estimate their population parameters. For example, we used the sample mean $\bar{y}$ to estimate the population mean μ. From Definition 4.7, we know that the parameter $E(y) = \mu$ is the first moment about the origin or, as it is sometimes called, the **first population moment**. Similarly, we define the **first sample moment** as

$$\bar{y} = \frac{\sum_{i=1}^{n} y_i}{n}$$

The general technique of using sample moments to estimate their corresponding population moments is called the **method of moments**. For the parameters discussed in this chapter, the method of moments yields estimators that have the two desired properties mentioned earlier, i.e., unbiased estimators and estimators with minimum variance.

Definition 8.6

Let $y_1, y_2, \ldots, y_n$ represent a random sample of size n from some probability distribution (discrete or continuous). The **kth population moment** and **kth sample moment** are defined as follows:

kth population moment: $E(y^k)$

kth sample moment: $m^k = \dfrac{\sum_{i=1}^{n} y_i^k}{n}$

For the case $k = 1$, the first population moment is $E(y) = \mu$ and the first sample moment is $m = \bar{y}$.

> **Definition 8.7**
>
> Let $y_1, y_2, \ldots, y_n$ represent a random sample of size n from a probability distribution (discrete or continuous) with parameters $\theta_1, \theta_2, \ldots, \theta_m$. Then the **moment estimators**, $\hat{\theta}_1, \hat{\theta}_2, \ldots, \hat{\theta}_m$, are obtained by equating the first m sample moments to the corresponding first m population moments:
>
> $$E(y) = \frac{1}{n}\sum y_i$$
>
> $$E(y^2) = \frac{1}{n}\sum y_i^2$$
>
> $$\vdots$$
>
> $$E(y^m) = \frac{1}{n}\sum y_i^m$$
>
> and solving for $\theta_1, \theta_2, \ldots, \theta_m$. (Note that the first m population moments will be functions of $\theta_1, \theta_2, \ldots, \theta_m$.)
>
> For the special case $m = 1$, the moment estimator of θ is some function of the sample mean $\bar{y}$.

EXAMPLE 8.2

The response rate y of auditory nerve fibers in cats has an approximate Poisson distribution with unknown mean λ (*Journal of the Acoustical Society of America*, Feb. 1986). Suppose the auditory nerve fiber response rate (recorded as number of spikes per 200 milliseconds of noise burst) was measured in each of a random sample of 10 cats. The data follow:

15.1   14.6   12.0   19.2   16.1   15.5   11.3   18.7   17.1   17.2

Calculate a point estimate for the mean response rate λ using the method of moments.

Solution

We have only one parameter, λ, to estimate; therefore, the moment estimator is found by setting the first population moment, $E(y)$, equal to the first sample moment, $\bar{y}$. For the Poisson distribution, $E(y) = \lambda$; hence, the moment estimator is

$$\hat{\lambda} = \bar{y}$$

For this example,

$$\bar{y} = \frac{15.1 + 14.6 + \cdots + 17.2}{10} = 15.68$$

Thus, our estimate of the mean auditory nerve fiber response rate λ is 15.68 spikes per 200 milliseconds of noise burst.

EXAMPLE 8.3 (OPTIONAL)   The time y until failure from fatigue cracks for underground cable possesses an approximate gamma probability distribution with parameters α and β (*IEEE Transactions on Energy Conversion*, Mar. 1986). Let $y_1, y_2, \ldots, y_n$ be a random sample of n observations on the random variable y. Find the moment estimators of α and β.

Solution   Since we must estimate two parameters, α and β, the method of moments requires that we set the first two population moments equal to their corresponding sample moments. From Section 5.6, we know that for the gamma distribution

$$\mu = E(y) = \alpha\beta$$
$$\sigma^2 = \alpha\beta^2$$

Also, from Theorem 4.4, $\sigma^2 = E(y^2) - \mu^2$. Thus, $E(y^2) = \sigma^2 + \mu^2$. Then for the gamma distribution, the first two population moments are

$$E(y) = \alpha\beta$$
$$E(y^2) = \sigma^2 + \mu^2 = \alpha\beta^2 + (\alpha\beta)^2$$

Setting these equal to their respective sample moments, we have

$$\hat{\alpha}\hat{\beta} = \bar{y}$$
$$\hat{\alpha}\hat{\beta}^2 + (\hat{\alpha}\hat{\beta})^2 = \frac{\sum y_i^2}{n}$$

Substituting $\bar{y}$ for $\hat{\alpha}\hat{\beta}$ in the second equation, we obtain

$$\bar{y}\hat{\beta} + (\bar{y})^2 = \frac{\sum y_i^2}{n}$$

or,

$$\bar{y}\hat{\beta} = \frac{\sum y_i^2}{n} - (\bar{y})^2$$
$$= \frac{\sum y_i^2 - n(\bar{y})^2}{n} = \frac{\sum y_i^2 - \frac{\left(\sum y_i\right)^2}{n}}{n}$$
$$= \frac{(n-1)s^2}{n}$$

Our two equations are now reduced to

$$\hat{\alpha}\hat{\beta} = \bar{y}$$
$$\bar{y}\hat{\beta} = \left(\frac{n-1}{n}\right)s^2$$

Solving these equations simultaneously, we obtain the moment estimators

$$\hat{\beta} = \left(\frac{n-1}{n}\right)\frac{s^2}{\bar{y}} \quad \text{and} \quad \hat{\alpha} = \left(\frac{n}{n-1}\right)\frac{\bar{y}^2}{s^2} = \left(\frac{n}{n-1}\right)\left(\frac{\bar{y}}{s}\right)^2$$

METHOD OF MAXIMUM LIKELIHOOD   The method of maximum likelihood and an exposition of the properties of maximum likelihood estimators are the results of work by Sir Ronald A. Fisher (1890–1962). Fisher's logic can be seen by considering the following example: If we randomly select a sample of n observations, $y_1, y_2, \ldots, y_n$, of a discrete random variable y and if the probability distribution $p(y)$ is a function of a single parameter θ, then the probability of observing these n independent values of y is

$$p(y_1, y_2, \ldots, y_n) = p(y_1)p(y_2) \cdots p(y_n)$$

Fisher called this joint probability of the sample values, $y_1, y_2, \ldots, y_n$, the **likelihood** L of the sample, and suggested that one should choose as an estimate of θ the value of θ that maximizes L. If the likelihood L of the sample is a function of two parameters, say, θ_1 and θ_2, then the maximum likelihood estimates of θ_1 and θ_2 are the values that maximize L. The notion is easily extended to the situation in which L is a function of more than two parameters.

Definition 8.8

a. The **likelihood** L of a sample of n observations, $y_1, y_2, \ldots, y_n$, is the joint probability function $p(y_1, y_2, \ldots, y_n)$ when $y_1, y_2, \ldots, y_n$ are discrete random variables.

b. The **likelihood** L of a sample of n observations, $y_1, y_2, \ldots, y_n$, is the joint density function $f(y_1, y_2, \ldots, y_n)$ when $y_1, y_2, \ldots, y_n$ are continuous random variables.

Note: For fixed values of $y_1, y_2, \ldots, y_n$, L will be a function of θ.

Theorem 8.1 follows directly from the definition of independence and Definitions 6.8 and 6.9.

Theorem 8.1

a. Let $y_1, y_2, \ldots, y_n$ represent a random sample of n observations on a random variable y. Then $L = p(y_1)p(y_2) \cdots p(y_n)$ when y is a discrete random variable with probability distribution $p(y)$.

b. Let $y_1, y_2, \ldots, y_n$ represent a random sample of n observations on a random variable y. Then $L = f(y_1)f(y_2) \cdots f(y_n)$ when y is a continuous random variable with density function $f(y)$.

> ### Definition 8.9
>
> Let L be the likelihood of a sample, where L is a function of the parameters $\theta_1, \theta_2, \ldots, \theta_k$. Then the **maximum likelihood estimators** of $\theta_1, \theta_2, \ldots, \theta_k$ are the values of $\theta_1, \theta_2, \ldots, \theta_k$ that maximize L.

Fisher showed that maximum likelihood estimators of population means and proportions possess some very desirable properties. As the sample size n becomes larger and larger, the sampling distribution of a maximum likelihood estimator $\hat{\theta}$ tends to become more and more nearly normal, with mean equal to θ and a variance that is equal to or less than the variance of *any other* estimator. Although these properties of maximum likelihood estimators pertain only to estimates based on large samples, they tend to provide support for the maximum likelihood method of estimation. The properties of maximum likelihood estimators based on small samples can be acquired by using the methods of Chapters 4, 5, and 6 to derive their sampling distributions or, at the very least, to acquire their means and variances.

To simplify our explanation of how to find a maximum likelihood estimator, we will assume that L is a function of a single parameter θ. Then, from differential calculus, we know that the value of θ that maximizes (or minimizes) L is the value for which $\dfrac{dL}{d\theta} = 0$. Obtaining this solution, which always yields a maximum (proof omitted), can be difficult because L is usually the product of a number of quantities involving θ. Differentiating a sum is easier than differentiating a product, so we attempt to maximize the logarithm of L rather than L itself. Since the logarithm of L is a monotonically increasing function of L, L will be maximized by the same value of θ that maximizes its logarithm. We illustrate the procedure in Examples 8.4 and 8.5.

EXAMPLE 8.4

Let $y_1, y_2, \ldots, y_n$ be a random sample of n observations on a random variable y with the exponential density function

$$f(y) = \begin{cases} \dfrac{e^{-y/\beta}}{\beta} & \text{if } 0 \le y < \infty \\ 0 & \text{elsewhere} \end{cases}$$

Determine the maximum likelihood estimator of β.

Solution

Since $y_1, y_2, \ldots, y_n$ are independent random variables, we have

$$L = f(y_1)f(y_2) \cdots f(y_n)$$

$$= \left(\frac{e^{-y_1/\beta}}{\beta}\right)\left(\frac{e^{-y_2/\beta}}{\beta}\right) \cdots \left(\frac{e^{-y_n/\beta}}{\beta}\right)$$

$$= \frac{e^{-\sum_{i=1}^{n} y_i/\beta}}{\beta^n}$$

Taking the natural logarithm of L yields

$$\ln(L) = \ln(e^{-\sum_{i=1}^{n} y_i/\beta}) - n \ln(\beta) = -\frac{\sum_{i=1}^{n} y_i}{\beta} - n \ln(\beta)$$

Then

$$\frac{d \ln(L)}{d\beta} = \frac{\sum_{i=1}^{n} y_i}{\beta^2} - \frac{n}{\beta}$$

Setting this derivative equal to 0 and solving for $\hat{\beta}$, we obtain

$$\frac{\sum_{i=1}^{n} y_i}{\hat{\beta}^2} - \frac{n}{\hat{\beta}} = 0 \qquad \text{or} \qquad n\hat{\beta} = \sum_{i=1}^{n} y_i$$

This yields

$$\hat{\beta} = \frac{\sum_{i=1}^{n} y_i}{n} = \bar{y}$$

Therefore, the maximum likelihood estimator (MLE) of β is the sample mean $\bar{y}$, i.e., $\hat{\beta} = \bar{y}$.

EXAMPLE 8.5 (OPTIONAL)

Let $y_1, y_2, \ldots, y_n$ be a random sample of n observations on the random variable y, where $f(y)$ is a normal density function with mean μ and variance σ^2. Find the maximum likelihood estimators of μ and σ^2.

Solution

Since $y_1, y_2, \ldots, y_n$ are independent random variables, it follows that

$$L = f(y_1)f(y_2) \cdots f(y_n)$$

$$= \left(\frac{e^{-(y_1-\mu)^2/(2\sigma^2)}}{\sigma\sqrt{2\pi}}\right)\left(\frac{e^{-(y_2-\mu)^2/(2\sigma^2)}}{\sigma\sqrt{2\pi}}\right) \cdots \left(\frac{e^{-(y_n-\mu)^2/(2\sigma^2)}}{\sigma\sqrt{2\pi}}\right)$$

$$= \frac{e^{-\sum_{i=1}^{n}(y_i-\mu)^2/(2\sigma^2)}}{\sigma^n(2\pi)^{n/2}}$$

and

$$\ln(L) = -\frac{\sum_{i=1}^{n}(y_i - \mu)^2}{2\sigma^2} - \frac{n}{2}\ln(\sigma^2) - \frac{n}{2}\ln(2\pi)$$

Taking derivatives of $\ln(L)$ with respect to μ and σ and setting them equal to 0 yields

$$\frac{d\ln(L)}{d\mu} = \frac{\sum\limits_{i=1}^{n} 2(y_i - \hat{\mu})}{2\hat{\sigma}^2} - 0 - 0 = 0$$

and

$$\frac{d\ln(L)}{d\sigma^2} = \frac{\sum\limits_{i=1}^{n}(y_i - \hat{\mu})^2}{2\hat{\sigma}^4} - \frac{n}{2}\left(\frac{1}{\hat{\sigma}^2}\right) - 0 = 0$$

The values of μ and σ^2 that maximize L [and hence $\ln(L)$] will be the simultaneous solution of these two equations. The first equation reduces to

$$\sum_{i=1}^{n}(y_i - \hat{\mu}) = 0 \quad \text{or} \quad \sum_{i=1}^{n} y_i - n\hat{\mu} = 0$$

and it follows that

$$n\hat{\mu} = \sum_{i=1}^{n} y_i \quad \text{and} \quad \hat{\mu} = \bar{y}$$

Substituting $\hat{\mu} = \bar{y}$ into the second equation and multiplying by $2\hat{\sigma}^2$, we obtain

$$\frac{\sum\limits_{i=1}^{n}(y_i - \bar{y})^2}{\hat{\sigma}^2} = n \quad \text{or} \quad \hat{\sigma}^2 = \frac{\sum\limits_{i=1}^{n}(y_i - \bar{y})^2}{n}$$

Therefore, the maximum likelihood estimators of μ and σ^2 are

$$\hat{\mu} = \bar{y} \quad \text{and} \quad \hat{\sigma}^2 = \frac{\sum\limits_{i=1}^{n}(y_i - \bar{y})^2}{n}$$

Note that the maximum likelihood estimator of σ^2 is equal to the sum of squares of deviations $\sum_{i=1}^{n}(y_i - \bar{y})^2$ divided by n, whereas the sample variance s^2 uses a divisor of $(n-1)$. We showed in Example 8.1 that s^2 is an unbiased estimator of σ^2. Therefore, the maximum likelihood estimator

$$\hat{\sigma}^2 = \frac{\sum\limits_{i=1}^{n}(y_i - \bar{y})^2}{n} = \frac{(n-1)}{n}s^2$$

is a biased estimator of σ^2.

METHOD OF LEAST SQUARES   Another useful technique for finding point estimators is the **method of least squares**. This method finds the estimate of θ that minimizes the mean squared error (MSE):

$$\text{MSE} = E(\hat{\theta} - \theta)^2$$

The method of least squares—a widely used estimation technique—is discussed in detail in Chapter 11. Several other estimation methods are briefly described here; consult the references at the end of this chapter if you want to learn more about their use.

JACKKNIFE ESTIMATORS   Tukey (1958) developed a "leave-one-out-at-a-time" approach to estimation, called the **jackknife**,* that is gaining increasing acceptance among practitioners. Let $y_1, y_2, \ldots, y_n$ be a sample of size n from a population with parameter θ. An estimate $\hat{\theta}_{(i)}$ is obtained by omitting the ith observation (i.e., y_i) and computing the estimate based on the remaining $(n - 1)$ observations. This calculation is performed for each observation in the data set, and the procedure results in n estimates of θ: $\hat{\theta}_{(1)}, \hat{\theta}_{(2)}, \ldots, \hat{\theta}_{(n)}$. The **jackknife estimator** of θ is then some suitably chosen linear combination (e.g., a weighted average) of the n estimates. Application of the jackknife is suggested for situations where we are likely to have outliers or biased samples, or find it difficult to assess the variability of the more traditional estimators.

ROBUST ESTIMATORS   Many of the estimators discussed in Sections 8.5–8.11 are based on the assumption that the sampled population is approximately normal. When the distribution of the sampled population deviates greatly from normality, such estimators do not have desirable properties (e.g., unbiasedness and minimum variance). An estimator that performs well for a very wide range of probability distributions is called a **robust estimator**. For example, a robust estimate of the population mean μ, called the **M-estimator**, compares favorably to the sample mean $\bar{y}$ when the sampled population is normal and is considerably better than $\bar{y}$ when the population is heavy-tailed. See Mosteller and Tukey (1977) and Devore (1987) for a good practical discussion of robust estimation techniques.

BAYES ESTIMATORS   The classical approach to estimation is based on the concept that the unknown parameter θ is a constant. All the information available to us about θ is contained in the random sample $y_1, y_2, \ldots, y_n$ selected from the relevant population. In contrast, the **Bayesian** approach to estimation regards θ as a random variable with some known (**prior**) probability distribution $g(\theta)$. The sample information is used to modify the prior distribution on θ to obtain the **posterior** distribution, $f(\theta \mid y_1, y_2, \ldots, y_n)$. The **Bayes estimator** of θ is then the mean of the posterior probability distribution [see Mendenhall, Wackerly, and Scheaffer (1989)].

OPTIONAL EXERCISES

8.8   A binomial experiment consisting of n trials resulted in Bernoulli observations $y_1, y_2, \ldots, y_n$, where

$$y_i = \begin{cases} 1 & \text{if the } i\text{th trial was a success} \\ 0 & \text{if not} \end{cases}$$

and $P(y_i = 1) = p$, $P(y_i = 0) = 1 - p$. Let $y = \sum_{i=1}^{n} y_i$ be the number of successes in n trials.

---

*The procedure derives its name from the Boy Scout jackknife; like the jackknife, the procedure serves as a handy tool in a variety of situations when specialized techniques may not be available.

    a. Find the moment estimator of p.
    b. Is the moment estimator unbiased?
    c. Find the maximum likelihood estimator of p. [*Hint:* $L = p^y(1 - p)^{n-y}.$]
    d. Is the maximum likelihood estimator unbiased?

8.9   Let $y_1, y_2, \ldots, y_n$ be a random sample of n observations from a Poisson distribution with probability function

$$p(y) = \frac{e^{-\lambda}\lambda^y}{y!} \qquad (y = 0, 1, 2, \ldots)$$

    a. Find the maximum likelihood estimator of λ.
    b. Is the maximum likelihood estimator unbiased?

8.10   Let $y_1, y_2, \ldots, y_n$ be a random sample of n observations on a random variable y, where $f(y)$ is a gamma density function with $\alpha = 2$ and unknown β:

$$f(y) = \begin{cases} \dfrac{ye^{-y/\beta}}{\beta^2} & \text{if } y > 0 \\ 0 & \text{otherwise} \end{cases}$$

    a. Find the maximum likelihood estimator of β.
    b. Find $E(\hat{\beta})$ and $V(\hat{\beta})$.

8.11   Refer to Exercise 8.10.
    a. Find the moment estimator of β.
    b. Find $E(\hat{\beta})$ and $V(\hat{\beta})$.

8.12   Let $y_1, y_2, \ldots, y_n$ be a random sample of n observations from a normal distribution with mean 0 and unknown variance σ^2. Find the maximum likelihood estimator of σ^2.

8.13   Let $y_1, y_2, \ldots, y_n$ be a random sample of n observations from an exponential distribution with density

$$f(y) = \begin{cases} \dfrac{1}{\beta}e^{-y/\beta} & \text{if } y > 0 \\ 0 & \text{otherwise} \end{cases}$$

    a. Find the moment estimator of β.
    b. Is the moment estimator unbiased?
    c. Find $V(\hat{\beta})$.

8.4   Finding Interval Estimators: The Pivotal Method

In Section 8.1, we defined an interval estimator as a rule that tells how to use the sample observations to calculate two numbers that define an interval that will enclose the estimated parameter with a high degree of confidence. The resulting random interval (random, because the sample observations used to calculate the endpoints of the interval are random variables) is called a **confidence interval**, and the probability (prior to sampling) that it contains the estimated parameter is called its **confidence coefficient**. If a confidence interval has a confidence coefficient equal to .95, we call it a 95% confidence interval. If the confidence coefficient is .99, the interval is said to be a 99% confidence interval, etc. A more practical interpretation of the confidence coefficient for a confidence interval is given later in this section.

Definition 8.10

The **confidence coefficient** for a confidence interval is equal to the probability that the random interval, prior to sampling, will contain the estimated parameter.

One way to find a confidence interval for a parameter θ is to acquire a **pivotal statistic**, a statistic that is a function of the sample values and the single parameter θ. Because many statistics are approximately normally distributed when the sample size n is large (central limit theorem), we can construct confidence intervals for their expected values using the standard normal random variable z as a pivotal statistic.

To illustrate, let $\hat{\theta}$ be a statistic with a sampling distribution that is approximately normally distributed for large samples with mean $E(\hat{\theta}) = \theta$ and standard error $\sigma_{\hat{\theta}}$. Then,

$$z = \frac{\hat{\theta} - \theta}{\sigma_{\hat{\theta}}}$$

is a standard normal random variable. Since z is also a function of only the sample statistic $\hat{\theta}$ and the parameter θ, we will use it as a pivotal statistic. To derive a confidence interval for θ, we first make a probability statement about the pivotal statistic. To do this, we locate values $z_{\alpha/2}$ and $-z_{\alpha/2}$ that place a probability of $\alpha/2$ in each tail of the z distribution (see Figure 8.5), i.e., $P(z > z_{\alpha/2}) = \alpha/2$. It can be seen from Figure 8.5 that

$$P(-z_{\alpha/2} \leq z \leq z_{\alpha/2}) = 1 - \alpha$$

FIGURE 8.5 ▶
Locating $z_{\alpha/2}$ for a confidence interval

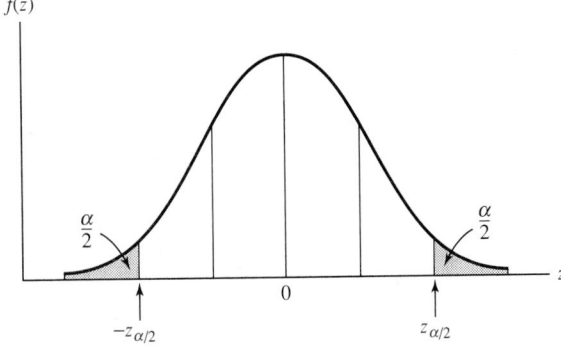

Substituting the expression for z into the probability statement and using some simple algebraic operations on the inequality, we obtain

$$P(-z_{\alpha/2} \le z \le z_{\alpha/2}) = P\left(-z_{\alpha/2} \le \frac{\hat{\theta} - \theta}{\sigma_{\hat{\theta}}} \le z_{\alpha/2}\right)$$

$$= P(-z_{\alpha/2}\sigma_{\hat{\theta}} \le \hat{\theta} - \theta \le z_{\alpha/2}\sigma_{\hat{\theta}})$$

$$= P(-\hat{\theta} - z_{\alpha/2}\sigma_{\hat{\theta}} \le -\theta \le -\hat{\theta} + z_{\alpha/2}\sigma_{\hat{\theta}})$$

$$= P(\hat{\theta} - z_{\alpha/2}\sigma_{\hat{\theta}} \le \theta \le \hat{\theta} + z_{\alpha/2}\sigma_{\hat{\theta}}) = 1 - \alpha$$

Therefore, the probability that the interval formed by

$$\text{LCL} = \hat{\theta} - z_{\alpha/2}\sigma_{\hat{\theta}} \quad \text{to} \quad \text{UCL} = \hat{\theta} + z_{\alpha/2}\sigma_{\hat{\theta}}$$

will enclose θ is equal to $(1 - \alpha)$. The quantities LCL and UCL are called the **lower** and **upper confidence limits,** respectively, for the confidence interval. The confidence coefficient for the interval will be $(1 - \alpha)$.

The derivation of a large-sample $(1 - \alpha)100\%$ confidence interval for θ is summarized in Theorem 8.2.

Theorem 8.2

Let $\hat{\theta}$ be normally distributed for large samples with $E(\hat{\theta}) = \theta$ and standard error $\sigma_{\hat{\theta}}$. Then a $(1 - \alpha)100\%$ confidence interval for θ is

$$\hat{\theta} - z_{\alpha/2}\sigma_{\hat{\theta}} \quad \text{to} \quad \hat{\theta} + z_{\alpha/2}\sigma_{\hat{\theta}}$$

The large-sample confidence interval can also be acquired intuitively by examining Figure 8.6. The z value corresponding to an area $A = .475$—i.e., the z value that places area $\alpha/2 = .025$ in the upper tail of the z distribution—is (see Table 4 of Appendix II) $z_{.025} = 1.96$. Therefore, the probability that $\hat{\theta}$ will lie within $1.96\sigma_{\hat{\theta}}$ of θ is .95. You can see from Figure 8.6 that whenever $\hat{\theta}$ falls within the interval $\theta \pm 1.96\sigma_{\hat{\theta}}$, then the interval $\hat{\theta} \pm 1.96\sigma_{\hat{\theta}}$ will enclose θ. Therefore, $\hat{\theta} \pm 1.96\sigma_{\hat{\theta}}$ yields a 95% confidence interval for θ.

FIGURE 8.6 ▶
The sampling distribution of θ for large samples

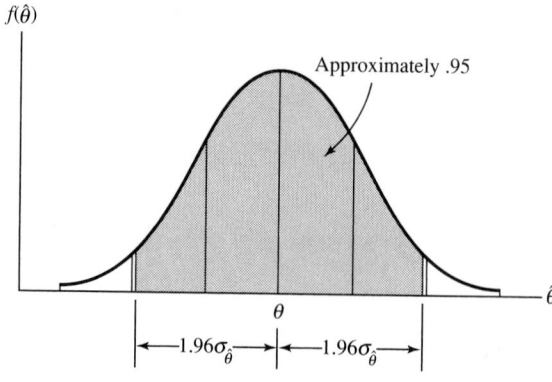

We may encounter one slight difficulty when we attempt to apply this confidence interval in practice. It is often the case that $\sigma_{\hat{\theta}}$ is a function of the parameter θ that we are attempting to estimate. However, when the sample size n is large (which we have assumed throughout the derivation), we can substitute the estimate $\hat{\theta}$ for the parameter θ to obtain an approximate value for $\sigma_{\hat{\theta}}$.

In Example 8.6 we will use a pivotal statistic to find a confidence interval for μ when the sample size is small, say, $n < 30$.

EXAMPLE 8.6

Let $\bar{y}$ and s^2 be the sample mean and variance based on a random sample of n observations ($n < 30$) from a normal distribution with mean μ and variance σ^2. Find a 95% confidence interval for μ.

Solution

A pivotal statistic for μ can be constructed using the t statistic of Chapter 7. By Definition 7.5,

$$t = \frac{z}{\sqrt{\chi^2/\nu}}$$

where z and χ^2 are independent random variables and χ^2 is based on ν degrees of freedom. We know that $\bar{y}$ is normally distributed and that

$$z = \frac{\bar{y} - \mu}{\sigma/\sqrt{n}}$$

is a standard normal random variable. From Theorem 7.4, it follows that

$$\frac{(n-1)s^2}{\sigma^2} = \chi^2$$

is a chi-square random variable with $\nu = (n-1)$ degrees of freedom. We state (without proof) that $\bar{y}$ and s^2 are independent when they are based on a random sample selected from a normal distribution. Therefore, z and χ^2 will be independent random variables. Substituting the expressions for z and χ^2 into the formula for t, we obtain

$$t = \frac{z}{\sqrt{\chi^2/\nu}} = \frac{\dfrac{\bar{y} - \mu}{\sigma/\sqrt{n}}}{\sqrt{\dfrac{(n-1)s^2}{\sigma^2} \Big/ (n-1)}} = \frac{\bar{y} - \mu}{s/\sqrt{n}}$$

Note that the pivotal statistic is a function only of μ and the sample statistics $\bar{y}$ and s^2.

The next step in finding a confidence interval for μ is to make a probability statement about the pivotal statistic t. We will select two values of t, call them $t_{\alpha/2}$ and $-t_{\alpha/2}$, that correspond to probabilities of $\alpha/2$ in the upper and lower tails, respectively, of the t distribution (see Figure 8.7). From Figure 8.7, it can be seen that

$$P(-t_{\alpha/2} \leq t \leq t_{\alpha/2}) = 1 - \alpha$$

FIGURE 8.7 ▶
The location of $t_{\alpha/2}$ and $-t_{\alpha/2}$
for a Student's t distribution

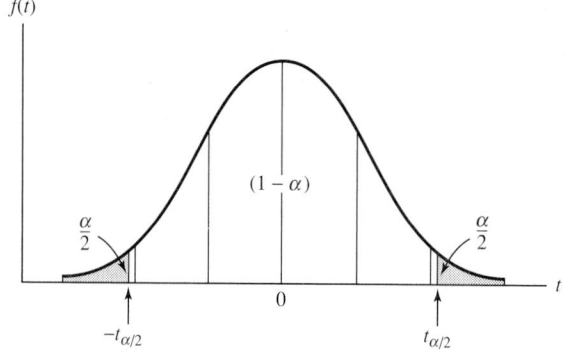

Substituting the expression for t into the probability statement, we obtain

$$P(-t_{\alpha/2} \le t \le t_{\alpha/2}) = P\left(-t_{\alpha/2} \le \frac{\bar{y} - \mu}{s/\sqrt{n}} \le t_{\alpha/2}\right) = 1 - \alpha$$

Multiplying the inequality within the brackets by $s/\sqrt{n}$, we obtain

$$P\left[-t_{\alpha/2}\left(\frac{s}{\sqrt{n}}\right) \le \bar{y} - \mu \le t_{\alpha/2}\left(\frac{s}{\sqrt{n}}\right)\right] = 1 - \alpha$$

Subtracting $\bar{y}$ from each part of the inequality yields

$$P\left[-\bar{y} - t_{\alpha/2}\left(\frac{s}{\sqrt{n}}\right) \le -\mu \le -\bar{y} + t_{\alpha/2}\left(\frac{s}{\sqrt{n}}\right)\right] = 1 - \alpha$$

Finally, we multiply each term of the inequality by (-1), thereby reversing the inequality signs. The result is

$$P\left[\bar{y} - t_{\alpha/2}\left(\frac{s}{\sqrt{n}}\right) \le \mu \le \bar{y} + t_{\alpha/2}\left(\frac{s}{\sqrt{n}}\right)\right] = 1 - \alpha$$

Therefore, a $(1 - \alpha)100\%$ confidence interval for μ when n is small is

$$\bar{y} - t_{\alpha/2}\left(\frac{s}{\sqrt{n}}\right) \quad \text{to} \quad \bar{y} + t_{\alpha/2}\left(\frac{s}{\sqrt{n}}\right)$$

We now apply the confidence interval derived in Example 8.6 to a practical situation.

EXAMPLE 8.7

Chemical plants must be regulated to prevent the poisoning of fish in nearby rivers or streams. One of the measurements made on fish to evaluate the potential toxicity of chemicals is the length of mature fish. If a river or stream is inhabited by an abundance of mature fish with lengths less than the average length of mature members of their species, we have strong evidence that the river is being chemically contaminated. A chemical plant, under investigation for chlorine poisoning of a stream, has hired a biologist to estimate the mean length of fathead minnows (the main inhabitants of the stream) exposed to 20 micrograms of chlorine per liter of water. The biologist captures 20 newborn fathead minnows from the stream and rears them in aquaria with this chlorine concentration. The length of each (in millimeters) is measured after a 10-week maturation period, with the following results:

$$\bar{y} = 27.5$$

$$s = 2.6$$

Construct a 95% confidence interval for the true mean length of fathead minnows reared in chlorine-contaminated water. Assume that the lengths of the fathead minnows are approximately normal.

Solution

Recall that the sampling distribution of the t statistic depends on its degrees of freedom, ν. The tabulated values t_a, such that $P(t \geq t_a) = a$, are given in Table 7 of Appendix II, for values of ν from 1 to 29, as well as the value of t_a when ν becomes infinitely large. An abbreviated version of this table is shown in Table 8.1 on page 358. For example, suppose a t statistic is based on $\nu = 4$ degrees of freedom (df) and we want to find the value t_a that places probability $a = .025$ in the upper tail of the t distribution. The appropriate value, shaded in Table 8.1, is $t_{.025} = 2.776$.

For our example, $n = 20$ and t will possess $(n - 1) = 19$ degrees of freedom. Since we want to find a $95\% = (1 - \alpha)100\%$ confidence interval for the mean length μ of fathead minnows, $\alpha = .05$; we must find the value $t_{.025}$ corresponding to $a = .025$ and 19 degrees of freedom. This value is given in Table 7 of Appendix II as $t_{\alpha/2} = t_{.025} = 2.093$. Then the confidence interval is

$$\bar{y} \pm t_{.025}\left(\frac{s}{\sqrt{n}}\right) = 27.5 \pm 2.093\left(\frac{2.60}{\sqrt{20}}\right)$$

$$= 27.5 \pm 1.22 \quad \text{or} \quad (26.28, 28.72)$$

Since the confidence coefficient is .95, we say that we are 95% confident that the interval from 26.28 to 28.72 millimeters contains the true mean length, μ, of fathead minnows reared in chlorine-contaminated water.

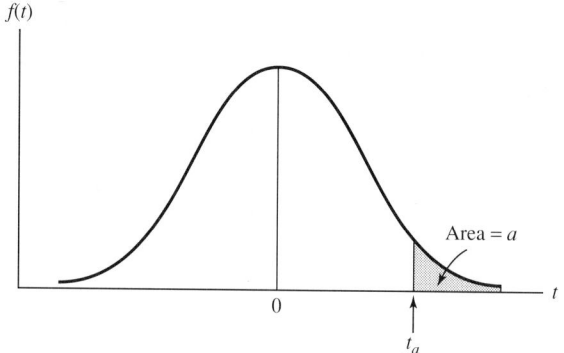

TABLE 8.I   An Abbreviated Version of Table 7 of Appendix II

Degrees of Freedom	$t_{.100}$	$t_{.050}$	$t_{.025}$	$t_{.010}$	$t_{.005}$
1	3.078	6.314	12.706	31.821	63.657
2	1.886	2.920	4.303	6.965	9.925
3	1.638	2.353	3.182	4.541	5.841
4	1.533	2.132	2.776	3.747	4.604
5	1.476	2.015	2.571	3.365	4.032
6	1.440	1.943	2.447	3.143	3.707
7	1.415	1.895	2.365	2.998	3.499
8	1.397	1.860	2.306	2.896	3.355
9	1.383	1.833	2.262	2.821	3.250
10	1.372	1.812	2.228	2.764	3.169
11	1.363	1.796	2.201	2.718	3.106
12	1.356	1.782	2.179	2.681	3.055
13	1.350	1.771	2.160	2.650	3.012
14	1.345	1.761	2.145	2.624	2.977
15	1.341	1.753	2.131	2.602	2.947

   To demonstrate the interpretation of a confidence interval, we programmed a computer to draw 1,000 samples of size $n = 10$ from a normal distribution with mean $\mu = 10$ and variance $\sigma^2 = 1$. A 95% confidence interval for μ was computed for each of the 1,000 samples. These are shown in Table 8.2. Only the 50 intervals that are starred (*) fail to enclose the mean $\mu = 10$. The proportion that enclose μ, .95, is exactly equal to the confidence coefficient. This explains why we are reasonably confident that the interval calculated in Example 8.7 (26.28, 28.72), encloses the true value of μ. *If we were to employ our interval estimator on repeated occasions, 95% of the intervals constructed would contain μ.*

TABLE 8.2 One Thousand 95% Confidence Intervals for the Mean of a Normal Distribution ($\mu = 10$, $\sigma^2 = 1$). [Note: Starred (*) intervals fail to include $\mu = 10$.]

SAMPLE	LCL	UCL	SAMPLE	LCL	UCL	SAMPLE	LCL	UCL	SAMPLE	LCL	UCL	SAMPLE	LCL	UCL
1	(9.574	11.183)	2	(9.370	11.137)	3	(9.425	10.403)	4	(9.356	10.777)	5	(9.956	11.455)
6	(8.807	10.589)	7	(9.188	10.588)	8	(9.798	11.390)	9	(10.057	11.561)*	10	(9.793	11.009)
11	(9.180	10.848)	12	(9.735	10.399)	13	(9.518	10.785)	14	(9.872	11.003)	15	(9.028	10.907)
16	(9.414	11.107)	17	(9.603	10.816)	18	(9.469	10.896)	19	(8.758	9.889)*	20	(9.617	11.285)
21	(8.926	10.389)	22	(9.710	10.512)	23	(8.847	10.667)	24	(9.148	10.675)	25	(9.722	11.017)
26	(9.575	11.221)	27	(8.820	10.664)	28	(9.222	11.015)	29	(9.525	10.717)	30	(9.036	10.802)
31	(8.758	10.151)	32	(9.043	10.650)	33	(9.819	10.958)	34	(9.085	10.610)	35	(8.847	10.692)
36	(9.590	10.551)	37	(9.826	11.063)	38	(9.506	10.615)	39	(9.322	10.401)	40	(8.892	10.239)
41	(9.519	10.812)	42	(9.023	10.640)	43	(9.560	10.651)	44	(8.885	10.327)	45	(9.901	11.353)
46	(9.348	10.324)	47	(9.188	10.766)	48	(9.173	10.563)	49	(9.039	10.567)	50	(9.234	10.864)
51	(8.799	10.503)	52	(9.870	11.382)	53	(8.706	10.830)	54	(9.690	11.002)	55	(9.340	10.864)
56	(9.244	10.666)	57	(9.910	11.487)	58	(8.690	10.111)	59	(9.149	10.661)	60	(9.320	10.740)
61	(9.052	11.085)	62	(9.593	10.985)	63	(9.103	10.768)	64	(9.429	10.023)	65	(9.275	10.032)
66	(9.139	11.033)	67	(9.621	10.916)	68	(9.464	10.571)	69	(9.717	10.938)	70	(8.895	10.638)
71	(9.496	11.260)	72	(9.124	10.437)	73	(9.416	10.718)	74	(8.516	10.296)	75	(8.991	10.290)
76	(9.225	10.554)	77	(8.641	10.451)	78	(9.598	11.359)	79	(9.443	11.217)	80	(9.384	11.055)
81	(9.088	10.592)	82	(9.777	11.142)	83	(9.160	10.683)	84	(8.969	10.122)	85	(9.275	10.372)
86	(9.676	10.772)	87	(9.075	10.507)	88	(8.425	10.059)	89	(9.382	10.761)	90	(8.646	10.648)
91	(9.414	10.410)	92	(9.661	10.909)	93	(9.240	10.679)	94	(9.138	10.469)	95	(9.497	10.824)
96	(8.871	10.627)	97	(9.402	10.923)	98	(9.241	10.695)	99	(8.832	10.790)	100	(9.546	10.472)
101	(9.604	10.705)	102	(9.315	10.519)	103	(9.306	10.572)	104	(9.129	10.750)	105	(9.566	10.658)
106	(9.490	10.558)	107	(9.052	10.387)	108	(9.464	10.969)	109	(9.899	10.919)	110	(9.045	10.284)
111	(9.112	10.341)	112	(9.593	10.836)	113	(8.726	10.515)	114	(9.511	10.916)	115	(9.535	10.938)
116	(9.526	10.690)	117	(8.848	10.395)	118	(8.765	10.126)	119	(9.151	10.696)	120	(8.764	10.382)
121	(9.598	10.578)	122	(8.988	10.286)	123	(9.435	10.890)	124	(8.833	10.335)	125	(9.644	10.744)
126	(9.589	10.533)	127	(9.284	10.174)	128	(9.110	10.522)	129	(9.502	10.728)	130	(9.144	11.044)
131	(9.344	10.851)	132	(9.915	11.372)	133	(9.252	10.399)	134	(9.833	11.188)	135	(9.268	10.219)
136	(9.681	10.804)	137	(9.082	10.719)	138	(9.374	10.198)	139	(9.303	10.781)	140	(9.046	10.329)
141	(9.191	10.640)	142	(9.777	10.812)	143	(8.622	10.513)	144	(9.175	10.931)	145	(9.227	10.863)
146	(9.167	10.455)	147	(9.323	11.067)	148	(9.148	10.282)	149	(9.169	10.360)	150	(9.635	10.989)
151	(9.877	10.723)	152	(8.950	10.546)	153	(8.911	9.986)*	154	(9.039	10.502)	155	(9.765	10.749)
156	(9.354	10.900)	157	(8.566	9.779)*	158	(9.218	10.508)	159	(9.312	10.971)	160	(9.262	10.390)
161	(9.584	10.838)	162	(9.621	11.306)	163	(9.114	10.142)	164	(8.680	10.564)	165	(9.249	10.030)
166	(9.518	10.579)	167	(9.740	10.844)	168	(9.183	10.795)	169	(8.686	10.580)	170	(9.442	10.740)
171	(9.129	11.088)	172	(9.542	11.062)	173	(9.201	10.730)	174	(9.485	11.251)	175	(8.640	10.463)
176	(9.382	10.690)	177	(9.241	10.585)	178	(9.495	10.810)	179	(9.859	11.136)	180	(9.356	10.975)
181	(9.385	10.516)	182	(8.884	10.759)	183	(9.011	10.829)	184	(9.401	10.731)	185	(8.637	10.468)
186	(8.769	10.727)	187	(9.925	11.065)	188	(9.427	11.199)	189	(9.550	11.040)	190	(9.729	10.887)
191	(9.157	10.439)	192	(9.277	10.485)	193	(9.691	10.611)	194	(9.358	10.997)	195	(9.229	10.976)
196	(9.014	11.275)	197	(8.475	10.120)	198	(9.390	10.469)	199	(9.485	11.083)	200	(9.238	10.721)
201	(9.153	10.465)	202	(9.121	10.960)	203	(9.596	10.440)	204	(9.595	11.125)	205	(9.136	10.383)
206	(8.930	10.040)	207	(9.045	10.714)	208	(8.894	10.830)	209	(9.029	10.821)	210	(9.320	10.355)
211	(9.380	10.707)	212	(9.283	10.236)	213	(9.280	10.681)	214	(8.606	10.343)	215	(9.585	11.183)
216	(8.958	9.899)*	217	(9.511	10.891)	218	(9.733	10.805)	219	(9.037	10.317)	220	(9.777	10.910)
221	(9.312	10.209)	222	(9.349	10.646)	223	(9.252	10.943)	224	(9.682	11.676)	225	(8.773	10.697)
226	(9.202	10.266)	227	(9.756	10.685)	228	(9.544	10.478)	229	(9.523	10.876)	230	(9.444	10.866)
231	(9.316	10.725)	232	(9.534	11.093)	233	(9.455	10.602)	234	(8.962	10.305)	235	(9.374	10.571)
236	(9.138	10.986)	237	(9.778	11.217)	238	(9.597	11.095)	239	(8.985	10.318)	240	(8.915	10.549)
241	(9.830	10.732)	242	(9.810	10.923)	243	(8.951	10.315)	244	(10.451	11.345)*	245	(9.170	10.339)
246	(9.020	10.123)	247	(9.296	10.288)	248	(9.510	10.359)	249	(9.031	10.354)	250	(9.428	11.241)
251	(9.445	10.761)	252	(9.697	10.937)	253	(9.494	11.246)	254	(9.200	10.861)	255	(8.904	10.378)
256	(9.129	10.713)	257	(9.383	10.142)	258	(9.879	10.792)	259	(8.852	10.912)	260	(9.725	10.517)
261	(9.626	11.264)	262	(8.700	10.547)	263	(8.911	10.488)	264	(9.289	10.694)	265	(9.229	10.756)
266	(9.188	10.753)	267	(9.396	11.143)	268	(9.225	11.391)	269	(9.005	10.153)	270	(9.196	10.505)
271	(9.208	10.526)	272	(8.902	10.389)	273	(8.742	11.019)	274	(9.069	10.410)	275	(9.501	10.632)
276	(9.324	10.635)	277	(9.488	11.056)	278	(9.277	10.547)	279	(9.408	10.679)	280	(9.329	10.839)
281	(8.636	9.820)*	282	(9.646	10.639)	283	(9.403	10.742)	284	(9.216	10.454)	285	(8.598	9.849)*
286	(9.266	11.348)	287	(9.208	10.449)	288	(9.113	10.901)	289	(8.934	10.334)	290	(9.306	10.454)
291	(9.373	11.202)	292	(9.063	10.685)	293	(10.229	11.040)*	294	(9.254	11.018)	295	(9.137	10.709)
296	(8.815	10.211)	297	(9.007	10.592)	298	(8.787	10.315)	299	(9.260	10.962)	300	(9.319	10.876)
301	(8.995	10.614)	302	(9.104	10.095)	303	(9.306	10.346)	304	(9.239	10.968)	305	(9.113	9.934)*
306	(9.390	10.522)	307	(9.639	10.848)	308	(9.209	10.601)	309	(8.866	11.200)	310	(9.597	11.396)
311	(8.391	10.287)	312	(8.964	10.791)	313	(9.645	10.769)	314	(9.373	10.817)	315	(9.420	10.751)
316	(9.312	11.081)	317	(8.901	10.141)	318	(9.730	10.525)	319	(9.636	11.284)	320	(9.291	10.781)
321	(9.723	10.775)	322	(9.249	10.688)	323	(9.113	10.160)	324	(9.109	10.434)	325	(9.329	11.007)
326	(8.959	10.226)	327	(9.664	10.516)	328	(9.856	11.101)	329	(9.345	10.956)	330	(8.908	10.843)
331	(9.693	11.499)	332	(9.423	11.238)	333	(8.978	10.768)	334	(9.534	11.050)	335	(9.576	11.082)
336	(9.371	10.638)	337	(8.950	11.271)	338	(9.276	10.557)	339	(9.310	10.619)	340	(9.073	10.076)
341	(9.281	10.795)	342	(9.744	10.505)	343	(9.542	10.813)	344	(8.913	10.316)	345	(9.414	11.246)
346	(9.661	10.722)	347	(8.724	10.361)	348	(9.224	11.179)	349	(9.354	10.569)	350	(9.318	10.665)
351	(9.174	10.895)	352	(9.615	11.003)	353	(9.121	10.696)	354	(9.517	10.884)	355	(8.730	10.328)
356	(8.942	10.684)	357	(8.890	10.399)	358	(9.640	11.146)	359	(9.349	11.253)	360	(9.522	10.452)
361	(9.136	10.555)	362	(8.923	10.764)	363	(9.737	11.513)	364	(9.159	10.257)	365	(9.736	11.236)
366	(9.156	10.699)	367	(9.515	11.037)	368	(9.175	10.724)	369	(9.475	10.408)	370	(9.108	10.933)
371	(9.135	10.924)	372	(9.144	10.631)	373	(8.854	10.319)	374	(8.680	10.513)	375	(9.529	10.391)

(continued)

TABLE 8.2 (continued)

SAMPLE	LCL	UCL	SAMPLE	LCL	UCL	SAMPLE	LCL	UCL	SAMPLE	LCL	UCL	SAMPLE	LCL	UCL
376	(9.886	11.506)	377	(9.633	10.961)	378	(9.252	11.411)	379	(9.218	10.469)	380	(8.648	10.653)
381	(9.193	10.900)	382	(9.331	10.868)	383	(9.072	10.634)	384	(8.974	10.078)	385	(9.170	10.652)
386	(9.063	10.490)	387	(9.047	10.484)	388	(9.202	10.194)	389	(9.475	10.655)	390	(9.553	10.720)
391	(9.396	11.115)	392	(9.236	10.644)	393	(8.785	10.183)	394	(9.145	10.765)	395	(9.340	11.055)
396	(9.123	10.534)	397	(9.828	11.058)	398	(9.386	10.229)	399	(9.234	10.500)	400	(9.072	10.405)
401	(9.680	10.752)	402	(9.487	10.849)	403	(9.539	11.137)	404	(9.795	11.293)	405	(9.566	10.792)
406	(8.983	10.842)	407	(9.410	10.964)	408	(9.892	10.949)	409	(9.097	11.117)	410	(9.229	11.201)
411	(9.451	10.924)	412	(9.530	10.756)	413	(9.328	11.021)	414	(9.512	10.590)	415	(9.027	10.805)
416	(8.982	10.591)	417	(9.059	10.856)	418	(8.971	10.620)	419	(9.236	10.456)	420	(9.085	10.768)
421	(8.900	10.358)	422	(9.604	11.044)	423	(10.265	11.443)*	424	(9.101	10.972)	425	(9.229	10.903)
426	(9.092	10.530)	427	(8.971	10.457)	428	(10.116	11.071)*	429	(9.579	11.107)	430	(9.066	10.596)
431	(8.892	10.710)	432	(9.684	11.258)	433	(8.919	10.350)	434	(9.226	11.093)	435	(9.012	10.969)
436	(8.582	10.107)	437	(9.106	9.925)*	438	(8.820	10.324)	439	(9.031	10.282)	440	(9.206	10.572)
441	(9.473	10.449)	442	(9.075	10.210)	443	(9.500	11.252)	444	(9.513	10.446)	445	(8.878	10.616)
446	(8.818	10.675)	447	(9.399	11.045)	448	(8.961	10.221)	449	(9.866	10.829)	450	(9.655	10.463)
451	(9.835	10.905)	452	(9.397	10.600)	453	(9.073	10.202)	454	(8.961	10.150)	455	(9.322	10.270)
456	(9.596	10.959)	457	(9.479	11.106)	458	(9.978	11.042)	459	(9.006	10.141)	460	(8.759	10.644)
461	(9.574	11.400)	462	(9.186	10.611)	463	(9.646	11.112)	464	(9.637	10.857)	465	(8.907	10.885)
466	(9.211	10.779)	467	(9.169	10.604)	468	(9.094	10.083)	469	(9.587	10.604)	470	(9.661	11.289)
471	(9.798	11.143)	472	(9.358	11.244)	473	(8.485	10.234)	474	(8.755	10.473)	475	(9.358	11.257)
476	(9.325	10.594)	477	(8.857	10.668)	478	(9.487	10.684)	479	(9.044	10.299)	480	(9.382	10.697)
481	(9.298	10.465)	482	(9.594	10.939)	483	(9.297	10.780)	484	(8.896	10.333)	485	(9.074	9.904)*
486	(9.284	10.777)	487	(9.125	10.438)	488	(9.081	10.442)	489	(9.242	10.483)	490	(9.420	10.687)
491	(9.284	10.471)	492	(9.462	10.845)	493	(9.274	10.676)	494	(8.961	10.458)	495	(9.796	11.205)
496	(9.080	10.854)	497	(9.399	10.606)	498	(8.593	10.554)	499	(9.527	10.925)	500	(9.340	10.413)
501	(8.907	10.531)	502	(9.243	10.401)	503	(9.270	10.787)	504	(9.331	11.183)	505	(9.200	10.602)
506	(9.422	10.835)	507	(9.279	10.687)	508	(8.884	10.683)	509	(9.190	10.255)	510	(8.733	10.404)
511	(9.441	10.889)	512	(9.070	10.392)	513	(8.946	9.772)*	514	(8.799	10.236)	515	(9.070	10.830)
516	(8.984	10.365)	517	(9.183	10.387)	518	(9.236	10.863)	519	(9.826	11.197)	520	(8.906	10.672)
521	(9.755	10.996)	522	(9.400	10.880)	523	(9.374	11.276)	524	(9.288	11.211)	525	(9.412	11.000)
526	(9.028	10.300)	527	(8.647	10.285)	528	(9.190	10.072)	529	(9.238	10.465)	530	(10.003	11.190)*
531	(9.644	10.974)	532	(9.679	10.738)	533	(8.559	10.014)	534	(9.895	11.131)	535	(9.653	11.007)
536	(9.769	11.144)	537	(8.837	10.136)	538	(9.939	10.836)	539	(9.553	10.853)	540	(9.351	10.552)
541	(9.532	11.320)	542	(9.262	10.728)	543	(8.864	11.341)	544	(9.052	10.482)	545	(9.551	10.610)
546	(9.564	11.060)	547	(9.699	10.912)	548	(8.915	10.042)	549	(8.801	10.648)	550	(9.111	9.913)*
551	(9.811	11.558)	552	(8.593	10.128)	553	(8.612	9.854)*	554	(9.555	10.986)	555	(9.567	10.666)
556	(9.399	10.979)	557	(9.168	11.195)	558	(9.270	11.456)	559	(9.197	10.554)	560	(8.985	10.492)
561	(9.067	10.622)	562	(8.843	10.484)	563	(9.346	11.128)	564	(8.692	10.475)	565	(9.413	10.583)
566	(9.416	10.678)	567	(9.451	11.099)	568	(9.339	10.862)	569	(8.933	10.698)	570	(9.212	10.368)
571	(8.894	10.438)	572	(9.161	10.964)	573	(9.841	11.306)	574	(8.990	10.541)	575	(8.530	10.038)
576	(9.687	11.005)	577	(9.131	10.759)	578	(9.167	10.734)	579	(9.301	10.507)	580	(9.379	10.872)
581	(9.298	10.917)	582	(8.407	10.030)	583	(9.080	10.523)	584	(9.043	10.509)	585	(9.636	11.032)
586	(9.562	10.527)	587	(9.224	10.279)	588	(9.439	10.305)	589	(9.320	10.482)	590	(9.363	11.047)
591	(9.136	10.521)	592	(9.059	10.320)	593	(8.686	10.278)	594	(9.280	10.267)	595	(9.251	10.964)
596	(8.693	10.114)	597	(8.712	10.394)	598	(9.340	10.710)	599	(8.244	9.684)*	600	(9.583	10.992)
601	(9.232	10.346)	602	(9.014	10.458)	603	(9.861	11.485)	604	(9.139	11.097)	605	(9.060	10.269)
606	(9.712	11.648)	607	(8.963	10.055)	608	(8.991	10.548)	609	(9.540	10.769)	610	(9.822	11.243)
611	(9.338	10.357)	612	(8.632	10.201)	613	(9.371	10.898)	614	(9.155	10.582)	615	(8.806	10.919)
616	(9.182	10.488)	617	(9.403	10.755)	618	(9.199	10.527)	619	(9.016	10.844)	620	(9.321	11.077)
621	(9.475	10.651)	622	(9.481	10.701)	623	(9.661	10.590)	624	(9.358	10.812)	625	(9.046	10.679)
626	(9.948	10.907)	627	(8.649	9.996)*	628	(9.201	10.332)	629	(9.195	10.908)	630	(9.460	10.435)
631	(9.222	10.772)	632	(9.757	10.880)	633	(9.926	10.885)	634	(9.027	10.425)	635	(8.436	10.011)
636	(9.160	10.474)	637	(9.723	11.075)	638	(8.597	10.879)	639	(10.024	10.931)*	640	(8.475	10.397)
641	(8.712	10.702)	642	(10.038	11.678)*	643	(9.706	10.962)	644	(9.028	10.275)	645	(9.395	10.414)
646	(9.283	10.641)	647	(8.628	10.107)	648	(9.456	10.820)	649	(9.999	11.336)	650	(8.587	10.063)
651	(9.616	11.090)	652	(9.403	10.537)	653	(10.263	11.277)*	654	(9.325	10.717)	655	(9.795	10.737)
656	(9.669	11.778)	657	(9.739	10.636)	658	(9.285	10.965)	659	(9.210	10.552)	660	(9.384	10.962)
661	(9.041	10.347)	662	(9.380	10.846)	663	(9.950	10.597)	664	(9.602	10.584)	665	(9.092	10.439)
666	(9.475	10.844)	667	(9.192	10.844)	668	(10.134	11.385)*	669	(8.523	10.431)	670	(9.657	11.222)
671	(8.710	10.470)	672	(8.854	10.039)	673	(8.833	10.174)	674	(9.500	10.956)	675	(9.546	10.782)
676	(9.115	10.545)	677	(9.005	10.434)	678	(9.783	11.217)	679	(9.384	10.647)	680	(9.783	11.586)
681	(9.160	10.040)	682	(8.822	10.238)	683	(9.374	11.064)	684	(8.895	10.274)	685	(8.986	10.854)
686	(8.665	10.523)	687	(8.630	10.270)	688	(9.914	10.898)	689	(8.787	10.323)	690	(9.483	10.850)
691	(9.369	10.797)	692	(9.271	10.776)	693	(8.715	9.846)*	694	(8.764	10.481)	695	(8.934	10.053)
696	(9.280	10.143)	697	(8.354	9.985)*	698	(9.599	11.275)	699	(8.488	10.224)	700	(9.278	10.213)
701	(9.247	10.552)	702	(9.043	10.327)	703	(9.578	10.914)	704	(8.815	10.387)	705	(8.786	9.901)*
706	(9.029	10.654)	707	(9.731	10.545)	708	(9.143	10.562)	709	(9.254	10.501)	710	(9.045	10.718)
711	(9.552	10.664)	712	(10.039	11.511)*	713	(9.670	10.482)	714	(9.491	10.669)	715	(9.589	10.869)
716	(8.900	10.986)	717	(9.557	10.872)	718	(8.845	10.578)	719	(9.316	11.041)	720	(9.420	10.645)
721	(9.839	10.896)	722	(9.264	10.440)	723	(10.020	11.239)*	724	(9.235	11.200)	725	(9.194	11.026)
726	(9.497	10.654)	727	(9.212	10.904)	728	(9.328	10.619)	729	(9.563	10.672)	730	(9.646	11.070)
731	(9.082	10.194)	732	(9.171	10.781)	733	(9.016	10.914)	734	(8.944	10.604)	735	(9.028	10.664)
736	(9.074	9.924)*	737	(9.050	10.604)	738	(8.641	10.155)	739	(10.052	11.660)*	740	(9.806	10.831)
741	(9.051	10.307)	742	(9.180	10.632)	743	(9.181	10.306)	744	(9.751	10.867)	745	(9.162	10.229)
746	(9.088	10.658)	747	(9.184	9.982)*	748	(8.697	10.393)	749	(9.292	10.612)	750	(9.331	10.615)

(continued)

TABLE 8.2 (continued)

SAMPLE	LCL	UCL	SAMPLE	LCL	UCL	SAMPLE	LCL	UCL	SAMPLE	LCL	UCL	SAMPLE	LCL	UCL
751	(9.138 ,	10.361)	752	(9.604 ,	11.201)	753	(8.921 ,	10.326)	754	(8.943 ,	10.219)	755	(9.222 ,	10.216)
756	(9.530 ,	10.981)	757	(9.248 ,	10.720)	758	(9.646 ,	10.700)	759	(8.895 ,	10.036)	760	(9.618 ,	10.742)
761	(9.290 ,	10.929)	762	(9.504 ,	10.942)	763	(9.053 ,	10.474)	764	(9.754 ,	10.946)	765	(9.198 ,	10.351)
766	(9.146 ,	10.468)	767	(9.180 ,	10.399)	768	(9.177 ,	10.305)	769	(9.130 ,	10.580)	770	(9.960 ,	11.238)
771	(8.694 ,	10.742)	772	(9.463 ,	10.594)	773	(9.348 ,	11.102)	774	(9.224 ,	10.726)	775	(9.229 ,	11.217)
776	(9.082 ,	10.291)	777	(9.352 ,	10.366)	778	(9.604 ,	11.415)	779	(8.366 ,	9.595)*	780	(9.622 ,	11.160)
781	(10.024 ,	11.043)*	782	(9.247 ,	10.508)	783	(10.053 ,	11.078)*	784	(8.640 ,	10.792)	785	(9.278 ,	10.767)
786	(9.486 ,	11.021)	787	(9.215 ,	10.090)	788	(9.647 ,	11.227)	789	(8.559 ,	10.444)	790	(8.498 ,	10.529)
791	(9.867 ,	10.967)	792	(9.095 ,	10.364)	793	(8.815 ,	10.275)	794	(8.648 ,	10.216)	795	(9.859 ,	11.008)
796	(8.862 ,	10.274)	797	(9.218 ,	10.439)	798	(9.299 ,	10.668)	799	(9.015 ,	10.139)	800	(8.873 ,	10.581)
801	(9.502 ,	11.150)	802	(9.598 ,	11.290)	803	(9.843 ,	11.204)	804	(9.377 ,	10.387)	805	(9.388 ,	10.640)
806	(8.571 ,	9.804)*	807	(9.369 ,	10.523)	808	(8.432 ,	10.584)	809	(9.305 ,	10.629)	810	(9.263 ,	10.718)
811	(9.253 ,	9.991)*	812	(9.060 ,	10.301)	813	(9.323 ,	11.395)	814	(9.261 ,	10.791)	815	(9.655 ,	10.995)
816	(9.425 ,	10.722)	817	(9.166 ,	10.566)	818	(9.511 ,	10.630)	819	(9.185 ,	10.674)	820	(9.612 ,	10.713)
821	(9.795 ,	11.330)	822	(9.491 ,	11.104)	823	(9.133 ,	10.491)	824	(9.459 ,	10.787)	825	(9.197 ,	10.451)
826	(9.276 ,	10.493)	827	(9.528 ,	10.964)	828	(8.961 ,	10.897)	829	(8.814 ,	10.037)	830	(9.439 ,	10.769)
831	(9.430 ,	10.786)	832	(10.506 ,	11.206)*	833	(9.033 ,	10.450)	834	(9.641 ,	11.223)	835	(9.383 ,	10.561)
836	(9.046 ,	10.512)	837	(9.281 ,	10.414)	838	(8.707 ,	10.181)	839	(9.870 ,	11.157)	840	(9.321 ,	10.426)
841	(9.058 ,	10.378)	842	(9.480 ,	11.349)	843	(8.897 ,	10.717)	844	(9.611 ,	10.216)	845	(8.722 ,	9.934)*
846	(9.350 ,	10.886)	847	(9.411 ,	10.844)	848	(8.984 ,	10.566)	849	(8.968 ,	10.537)	850	(9.081 ,	10.380)
851	(9.054 ,	10.647)	852	(8.873 ,	9.791)*	853	(10.021 ,	11.515)*	854	(9.554 ,	11.099)	855	(8.524 ,	10.378)
856	(8.781 ,	10.739)	857	(9.385 ,	10.910)	858	(8.945 ,	10.416)	859	(9.183 ,	10.624)	860	(9.462 ,	10.607)
861	(9.099 ,	10.434)	862	(9.331 ,	10.806)	863	(9.771 ,	10.995)	864	(9.327 ,	10.731)	865	(8.963 ,	10.438)
866	(9.259 ,	11.270)	867	(9.211 ,	10.519)	868	(9.821 ,	11.420)	869	(9.335 ,	10.513)	870	(9.078 ,	10.210)
871	(10.080 ,	10.769)*	872	(9.375 ,	10.590)	873	(8.535 ,	9.890)*	874	(9.414 ,	10.751)	875	(8.877 ,	9.994)*
876	(9.587 ,	10.795)	877	(9.121 ,	10.960)	878	(9.486 ,	10.822)	879	(10.293 ,	11.456)*	880	(9.514 ,	10.926)
881	(9.058 ,	10.909)	882	(8.990 ,	10.079)	883	(9.580 ,	11.051)	884	(9.185 ,	10.505)	885	(8.812 ,	10.421)
886	(9.301 ,	10.096)	887	(9.194 ,	10.273)	888	(9.278 ,	11.004)	889	(8.658 ,	10.170)	890	(9.367 ,	10.074)
891	(8.630 ,	10.978)	892	(9.842 ,	11.724)	893	(9.504 ,	10.998)	894	(9.287 ,	10.866)	895	(9.234 ,	10.570)
896	(9.986 ,	10.907)	897	(9.758 ,	11.048)	898	(9.687 ,	10.993)	899	(9.381 ,	10.822)	900	(9.518 ,	10.493)
901	(9.114 ,	10.575)	902	(8.869 ,	10.508)	903	(9.363 ,	10.595)	904	(9.252 ,	10.618)	905	(9.784 ,	10.718)
906	(9.147 ,	10.241)	907	(9.448 ,	10.569)	908	(9.330 ,	10.693)	909	(9.096 ,	10.499)	910	(9.780 ,	10.687)
911	(9.047 ,	10.283)	912	(9.036 ,	10.381)	913	(9.655 ,	11.262)	914	(9.400 ,	9.964)*	915	(9.368 ,	11.079)
916	(9.456 ,	10.747)	917	(8.768 ,	10.250)	918	(9.270 ,	10.158)	919	(9.419 ,	10.101)	920	(9.159 ,	10.773)
921	(9.736 ,	11.113)	922	(9.445 ,	10.763)	923	(9.423 ,	10.674)	924	(8.777 ,	10.774)	925	(9.155 ,	10.204)
926	(9.087 ,	10.368)	927	(9.079 ,	10.049)	928	(9.245 ,	10.969)	929	(9.096 ,	10.402)	930	(9.106 ,	10.613)
931	(9.603 ,	10.961)	932	(9.511 ,	11.157)	933	(9.650 ,	10.768)	934	(9.149 ,	10.002)	935	(10.015 ,	11.540)*
936	(9.676 ,	10.788)	937	(9.700 ,	11.167)	938	(9.615 ,	11.085)	939	(9.555 ,	10.694)	940	(9.382 ,	10.570)
941	(8.498 ,	9.897)*	942	(9.216 ,	10.700)	943	(9.140 ,	10.459)	944	(9.543 ,	10.540)	945	(8.824 ,	10.129)
946	(9.523 ,	10.824)	947	(9.147 ,	10.406)	948	(9.068 ,	10.536)	949	(9.119 ,	10.172)	950	(8.709 ,	10.638)
951	(9.850 ,	11.410)	952	(9.729 ,	10.940)	953	(9.067 ,	10.090)	954	(9.599 ,	11.064)	955	(9.753 ,	10.920)
956	(9.501 ,	10.523)	957	(9.598 ,	10.705)	958	(9.220 ,	10.626)	959	(8.391 ,	9.950)*	960	(9.629 ,	10.594)
961	(9.105 ,	10.574)	962	(9.504 ,	10.543)	963	(9.137 ,	10.475)	964	(9.303 ,	10.910)	965	(9.563 ,	10.871)
966	(9.161 ,	10.453)	967	(9.487 ,	10.752)	968	(9.531 ,	11.014)	969	(8.920 ,	10.599)	970	(9.058 ,	10.440)
971	(9.409 ,	10.760)	972	(8.981 ,	10.788)	973	(9.097 ,	10.186)	974	(8.674 ,	10.776)	975	(9.010 ,	10.745)
976	(8.714 ,	10.521)	977	(9.176 ,	10.301)	978	(9.263 ,	10.555)	979	(8.700 ,	10.244)	980	(9.334 ,	10.959)
981	(9.577 ,	10.873)	982	(9.383 ,	10.970)	983	(9.462 ,	10.826)	984	(9.367 ,	10.726)	985	(8.657 ,	10.496)
986	(9.436 ,	10.970)	987	(9.532 ,	11.605)	988	(9.309 ,	10.876)	989	(9.536 ,	10.799)	990	(9.827 ,	10.698)
991	(8.834 ,	9.807)*	992	(8.672 ,	10.247)	993	(8.974 ,	10.373)	994	(9.169 ,	10.891)	995	(8.704 ,	10.044)
996	(9.713 ,	10.932)	997	(9.169 ,	10.769)	998	(9.595 ,	10.769)	999	(9.648 ,	10.762)	1000	(9.029 ,	10.684)

Theoretical Interpretation of the Confidence Coefficient $(1 - \alpha)$

If we were to repeatedly collect a sample of size n from the population and construct a $(1 - \alpha)100\%$ confidence interval for each sample, then we expect $(1 - \alpha)100\%$ of the intervals to enclose the true parameter value.

Confidence intervals for population parameters other than the population mean can be derived using the pivotal method outlined in this section. The estimators and pivotal statistics for many of these parameters are well known. In Sections 8.5–8.11, we give the confidence interval formulas for several population parameters that are commonly encountered in practice.

EXERCISES

8.14 Use Table 7 of Appendix II to determine the values of $t_{\alpha/2}$ that would be used in the construction of a confidence interval for a population mean for each of the following combinations of confidence coefficient and sample size:

a. Confidence coefficient .99, $n = 18$
b. Confidence coefficient .95, $n = 10$
c. Confidence coefficient .90, $n = 15$

8.15 It can be shown (proof omitted) that as the sample size n increases, the t distribution tends to normality and the value t_a, such that $P(t > t_a) = a$, approaches the value z_a, such that $P(z > z_a) = a$. Use Table 7 of Appendix II to verify that as the sample size n gets infinitely large, $t_{.05} = z_{.05}$, $t_{.025} = z_{.025}$, and $t_{.01} = z_{.01}$.

8.16 Let y be the number of successes in a binomial experiment with n trials and probability of success p. Assuming that n is large, use the sample proportion of successes $\hat{p} = y/n$ to form a confidence interval for p with confidence coefficient $(1 - \alpha)$. [*Hint:*   Start with the pivotal statistic

$$z = \frac{\hat{p} - p}{\sqrt{\dfrac{\hat{p}\hat{q}}{n}}}$$

and use the fact (proof omitted) that for large n, z is approximately a standard normal random variable.]

8.17 Let $y_1, y_2, \ldots, y_n$ be a random sample from a Poisson distribution with mean λ. Suppose we use $\bar{y}$ as an estimator of λ. Derive a $(1 - \alpha)100\%$ confidence interval for λ. [*Hint:*   Start with the pivotal statistic

$$z = \frac{\bar{y} - \lambda}{\sqrt{\lambda/n}}$$

and show that for large samples, z is approximately a standard normal random variable. Then substitute $\bar{y}$ for λ in the denominator (why can you do this?) and follow the pivotal method of Example 8.6.]

8.18 Let $y_1, y_2, \ldots, y_n$ be a random sample of n observations from an exponential distribution with mean β. Derive a large-sample confidence interval for β. [*Hint:*   Start with the pivotal statistic

$$z = \frac{\bar{y} - \beta}{\beta/\sqrt{n}}$$

and show that for large samples, z is approximately a standard normal random variable. Then substitute $\bar{y}$ for β in the denominator (why can you do this?) and follow the pivotal method of Example 8.6.]

OPTIONAL EXERCISES

8.19 Let $\bar{y}_1$ and s_1^2 be the sample mean and sample variance, respectively, of n_1 observations randomly selected from a population with mean μ_1 and variance σ_1^2. Similarly, define $\bar{y}_2$ and s_2^2 for an independent random sample of n_2 observations from a population with mean μ_2 and σ_2^2. Derive a large-sample confidence interval for $(\mu_1 - \mu_2)$. [*Hint:* Start with the pivotal statistic

$$z = \frac{(\bar{y}_1 - \bar{y}_2) - (\mu_1 - \mu_2)}{\sqrt{\dfrac{\sigma_1^2}{n_1} + \dfrac{\sigma_2^2}{n_2}}}$$

and show that for large samples, z is approximately a standard normal random variable. Substitute s_1^2 for σ_1^2 and s_2^2 for σ_2^2 (why can you do this?) and follow the pivotal method of Example 8.6.]

8.20 Let $(\bar{y}_1, s_1^2)$ and $(\bar{y}_2, s_2^2)$ be the means and variances of two independent random samples of sizes n_1 and n_2, respectively, selected from normal populations with different means, μ_1 and μ_2, but with a common variance, σ^2.
a. Show that $E(\bar{y}_1 - \bar{y}_2) = \mu_1 - \mu_2$.
b. Show that

$$V(\bar{y}_1 - \bar{y}_2) = \sigma^2\left(\frac{1}{n_1} + \frac{1}{n_2}\right)$$

c. Explain why

$$z = \frac{(\bar{y}_1 - \bar{y}_2) - (\mu_1 - \mu_2)}{\sigma\sqrt{\dfrac{1}{n_1} + \dfrac{1}{n_2}}}$$

is a standard normal random variable.

8.21 Refer to Exercise 8.20. According to Theorem 7.4,

$$\chi_1^2 = \frac{(n_1 - 1)s_1^2}{\sigma^2} \quad \text{and} \quad \chi_2^2 = \frac{(n_2 - 1)s_2^2}{\sigma^2}$$

are independent chi-square random variables with $(n_1 - 1)$ and $(n_2 - 1)$ df, respectively. Show that

$$\chi^2 = \frac{(n_1 - 1)s_1^2 + (n_2 - 1)s_2^2}{\sigma^2}$$

is a chi-square random variable with $(n_1 + n_2 - 2)$ df.

8.22 Refer to Exercises 8.20 and 8.21. The pooled estimator of the common variance σ^2 is given by

$$s_p^2 = \frac{(n_1 - 1)s_1^2 + (n_2 - 1)s_2^2}{n_1 + n_2 - 2}$$

Show that

$$t = \frac{(\bar{y}_1 - \bar{y}_2) - (\mu_1 - \mu_2)}{s_p\sqrt{\dfrac{1}{n_1} + \dfrac{1}{n_2}}}$$

has a Student's t distribution with $(n_1 + n_2 - 2)$ df. [*Hint:* Recall that $t = z/\sqrt{\chi^2/\nu}$ has a Student's t distribution with ν df and use the results of Exercises 8.20c and 8.21.]

8.23   Use the pivotal statistic t given in Exercise 8.22 to derive a $(1 - \alpha)100\%$ small-sample confidence interval for $(\mu_1 - \mu_2)$.

8.5   Estimation of a Population Mean

From our discussions in Section 8.3, we already know that a useful point estimate of the population mean μ is $\bar{y}$, the sample mean. According to the central limit theorem (Theorem 7.2), we also know that for sufficiently large n, the sampling distribution of the sample mean $\bar{y}$ is approximately normal with $E(\bar{y}) = \mu$ and $V(\bar{y}) = \sigma^2/n$. The fact that $E(\bar{y}) = \mu$ implies that $\bar{y}$ is an unbiased estimator of μ. Furthermore, it can be shown (proof omitted) that $\bar{y}$ has the smallest variance among all unbiased estimators of μ. Hence, $\bar{y}$ is the MVUE for μ. Therefore, it is not surprising that $\bar{y}$ is considered the best estimator of μ.

Since $\bar{y}$ is approximately normal for large n, we can apply Theorem 8.2 to construct a large-sample $(1 - \alpha)100\%$ confidence interval for μ. Substituting $\hat{\theta} = \bar{y}$ and $\sigma_{\hat{\theta}} = \sigma/\sqrt{n}$ into the confidence interval formula given in Theorem 8.2, we obtain the formula given in the following box.

Large-Sample $(1 - \alpha)100\%$ Confidence Interval for the Population Mean, μ

$$\bar{y} \pm z_{\alpha/2}\sigma_{\bar{y}} = \bar{y} \pm z_{\alpha/2}\left(\frac{\sigma}{\sqrt{n}}\right) \approx \bar{y} \pm z_{\alpha/2}\left(\frac{s}{\sqrt{n}}\right)$$

where $z_{\alpha/2}$ is the z value that locates an area of $\alpha/2$ to its right, σ is the standard deviation of the population from which the sample was selected, n is the sample size, and $\bar{y}$ is the value of the sample mean.

[Note: When the value of σ is unknown (as will usually be the case), the sample standard deviation s may be used to approximate σ in the formula for the confidence interval. The approximation is generally quite satisfactory when $n \geq 30$.]

Assumptions: None (since the central limit theorem guarantees that $\bar{y}$ is approximately normal regardless of the distribution of the sampled population)

Note: The value of the sample size n required for the sampling distribution of $\bar{y}$ to be approximately normal will vary depending on the shape (distribution) of the target population (see Examples 7.6 and 7.7). As a general rule of thumb, a sample size n of 30 or more will be considered *sufficiently large* for the central limit theorem to apply.

EXAMPLE 8.8

Suppose a regional computer center wants to evaluate the performance of its disk memory system. One measure of performance is the average time between failures of its disk drive. To estimate this value, the center recorded the time between failures for a random sample of 45 disk-drive failures. The following sample statistics were computed:

$$\bar{y} = 1,762 \text{ hours} \qquad s = 215 \text{ hours}$$

a. Estimate the true mean time between failures with a 90% confidence interval.

b. If the disk memory system is running properly, the true mean time between failures will exceed 1,700 hours. Based on the interval, part a, what can you infer about the disk memory system?

Solution

a. For a confidence coefficient of $1 - \alpha = .90$, we have $\alpha = .10$ and $\alpha/2 = .05$; therefore, a 90% confidence interval for μ is given by

$$\bar{y} \pm z_{\alpha/2}\left(\frac{\sigma}{\sqrt{n}}\right) = \bar{y} \pm z_{.05}\left(\frac{\sigma}{\sqrt{n}}\right)$$

$$\approx \bar{y} \pm z_{.05}\left(\frac{s}{\sqrt{n}}\right)$$

$$= 1,762 \pm z_{.05}\left(\frac{215}{\sqrt{45}}\right)$$

where $z_{.05}$ is the z value corresponding to an upper-tail area of .05. From Table 4 of Appendix II, $z_{.05} = 1.645$. Then the desired interval is

$$1,762 \pm z_{.05}\left(\frac{215}{\sqrt{45}}\right) = 1,762 \pm 1.645\left(\frac{215}{\sqrt{45}}\right)$$

$$= 1,762 \pm 52.7$$

or 1,709.3 to 1,814.7 hours. We are 90% confident that the interval (1,709.3, 1,814.7) encloses μ, the true mean time between disk failures.

b. Since all values within the 90% confidence interval exceed 1,700 hours, we can infer (with 90% confidence) that the disk memory system is running properly.

Sometimes, time or cost limitations may restrict the number of sample observations that may be obtained for estimating μ. In the case of small samples, (say, $n < 30$), the following two problems arise:

1. Since the central limit theorem applies only to large samples, we are not able to assume that the sampling distribution of $\bar{y}$ is approximately normal. Therefore, we cannot apply Theorem 8.2. For small samples, the sampling distribution of $\bar{y}$ depends on the particular form of the relative frequency distribution of the population being sampled.

2. The sample standard deviation s may not be a satisfactory approximation to the population standard deviation σ if the sample size is small.

Fortunately, we may proceed with estimation techniques based on small samples if we can assume that the population from which the sample is selected has an approximate normal distribution. If this assumption is valid, then we can use the procedure of Example 8.6 to construct a confidence interval for μ. The general form of a small-sample confidence interval for μ, based on the Student's t distribution, is as shown in the next box.

Small-Sample $(1 - \alpha)100\%$ Confidence Interval for the Population Mean, μ

$$\bar{y} \pm t_{\alpha/2}\left(\frac{s}{\sqrt{n}}\right)$$

where the distribution of t is based on $(n - 1)$ degrees of freedom.

Assumption: The population from which the sample is selected has an approximate normal distribution.

EXAMPLE 8.9

The Geothermal Loop Experimental Facility, located in the Salton Sea in southern California, is a U.S. Department of Energy operation for studying the feasibility of generating electricity from the hot, highly saline water of the Salton Sea. Operating experience has shown that these brines leave silica scale deposits on metallic plant piping, causing excessive plant outages. Jacobsen et al. (*Journal of Testing and Evaluation*, Mar. 1981) have found that scaling can be reduced somewhat by adding chemical solutions to the brine. In one screening experiment, each of five antiscalants was added to an aliquot of brine, and the solutions were filtered. A silica determination (parts per million of silicon dioxide) was made on each filtered sample after a holding time of 24 hours, with the following results:

229   255   280   203   229

Estimate the mean amount of silicon dioxide present in the five antiscalant solutions. Use a 99% confidence interval.

Solution

The first step in constructing the confidence interval is to compute the mean, $\bar{y}$, and standard deviation, s, of the sample of five silicon dioxide amounts. These values, $\bar{y} = 239.2$ and $s = 29.3$, are shaded in the MINITAB printout, Figure 8.8.

FIGURE 8.8 ►
MINITAB descriptive statistics for Example 8.9

	N	MEAN	MEDIAN	TRMEAN	STDEV	SEMEAN
PPM	5	239.2	229.0	239.2	29.3	13.1

	MIN	MAX	Q1	Q3
PPM	203.0	280.0	216.0	267.5

For a confidence coefficient of $1 - \alpha = .99$, we have $\alpha = .01$ and $\alpha/2 = .005$. Since the sample size is small ($n = 5$), our estimation technique requires the assumption that the amount of silicon dioxide present in an antiscalant solution has an approximately normal distribution (i.e., the sample of 5 silicon amounts is selected from a normal population).

Substituting the values for $\bar{y}$, s, and n into the formula for a small-sample confidence interval for μ, we obtain

$$\bar{y} \pm t_{\alpha/2}\left(\frac{s}{\sqrt{n}}\right) = \bar{y} \pm t_{.005}\left(\frac{s}{\sqrt{n}}\right)$$

$$= 239.2 \pm t_{.005}\left(\frac{29.3}{\sqrt{5}}\right)$$

where $t_{.005}$ is the value corresponding to an upper-tail area of .005 in the Student's t distribution based on $(n - 1) = 4$ degrees of freedom. From Table 7 of Appendix II, the required t value is $t_{.005} = 4.604$. Substitution of this value yields

$$239.2 \pm t_{.005}\left(\frac{29.3}{\sqrt{5}}\right) = 239.2 \pm (4.604)\left(\frac{29.3}{\sqrt{5}}\right)$$

$$= 239.2 \pm 60.3$$

or, 178.9 to 299.5 ppm. Thus, if the distribution of silicon dioxide amounts is approximately normal, we can be 99% confident that the interval (178.9, 299.5) encloses μ, the true mean amount of silicon dioxide present in an antiscalant solution.

The 99% confidence interval can also be obtained with a statistical software package. Figure 8.9 shows a MINITAB printout of the analysis. You can see that the computer-generated interval (shaded in Figure 8.9) is identical to the one we calculated.

FIGURE 8.9 ►
MINITAB confidence interval for
Example 8.9

```
TEST OF MU = 300.000 VS MU N.E. 300.000

              N     MEAN    STDEV   SE MEAN   99.0 PERCENT C.I.
ppm           5     239.2    29.3     13.1    (   178.9,    299.5)
```

Before we conclude this section, two comments are necessary. The first concerns the assumption that the sampled population is normally distributed. In the real world, we rarely know whether a sampled population has an exact normal distribution. However, empirical studies indicate that moderate departures from this assumption do not seriously affect the confidence coefficients for small-sample confidence intervals. For example, if the population of silicon dioxide amounts for the antiscalant solutions of Example 8.9 has a distribution that is mound-shaped but nonnormal, it is likely that the actual confidence coefficient for the 99% confidence interval will be close to .99—at least close enough to be of practical use. As a consequence, the small-sample confidence interval given in the box is frequently used by experimenters when estimating the population mean of a nonnormal distribution as long as the distribution is mound-shaped and only moderately skewed. For populations that depart greatly from normality, other estimation techniques (such as robust estimation) or methods that are distribution-free (called **nonparametrics**) are recommended. Nonparametric statistics are the topic of Chapter 15.

The second comment focuses on whether σ is known or unknown. We have shown (Example 7.7) that when σ is known and the sampled population is normally distributed, the sampling distribution of $\bar{y}$ is normal regardless of the size of the sample. That is, if you know the value of σ and you know that the sample comes from a normal population, then you can use the z distribution rather than the t distribution to form confidence intervals. In reality, however, σ is rarely (if ever) known. Consequently, you will always be using s in place of σ in the confidence interval formulas, and the sampling distribution of $\bar{y}$ will be a t distribution. This is why the formula for a large-sample confidence interval given earlier in this section is only approximate; in the large-sample case, $t \approx z$. Many statistical software packages give the results for *exact* confidence intervals when σ is unknown; thus, these results are based on the t distribution. For practical reasons, however, we will continue to distinguish between z and t confidence intervals based on whether the sample size is large or small.

EXERCISES

8.24   Chemical engineers at the University of Murcia (Spain) conducted a series of experiments to determine the most effective membrane to use in a passive sampler (*Environmental Science & Technology*, Vol. 27, 1993). The effectiveness of a passive sampler was measured by the sampling rate, recorded in cubic centimeters per minute. In one experiment, six passive samplers were positioned with their faces parallel to the air flow and with an air velocity of 90 centimeters per second. After 6 hours, the sampling rate of each was determined. Based on the results, a 95% confidence interval for the mean sampling rate was calculated to be (49.66, 51.48).
   a. What is the confidence coefficient for the interval?
   b. Give a theoretical interpretation of the confidence coefficient, part **a**.
   c. Give a practical interpretation of the confidence interval.
   d. What assumptions, if any, are required for the interval to yield valid inferences?

8.25   The theoretical relationship between heat flux and temperature gradient for homogeneous materials is well known and described by a Fourier equation. However, this relationship does not hold for nonhomogeneous materials such as porous-capillary bodies, cellular systems, suspensions, and pastes. An experiment was conducted to estimate the mean thermal relaxation time (defined as the mean time needed for accumulating the thermal energy required for propagative transfer of heat) for several nonhomogeneous materials (*Journal of Heat Transfer*, Aug. 1990). A 95% confidence interval for the mean thermal relaxation time of sand was found to be 20.0 ± 6.4 seconds.
   a. Give a practical interpretation of the 95% confidence interval.
   b. Give a theoretical interpretation of the 95% confidence interval.

8.26   Unusual rocks at "The Seven Islands," located along the lower St. Lawrence River in Canada, have attracted geologists to the area for over a century. A major geological survey of "The Seven Islands" was recently completed for the purpose of developing a three-dimensional gravity model of the area (*Canadian Journal of Earth Sciences*, Vol. 27, 1990). One of the keys to an objective model is obtaining an accurate estimate of the rock densities. Based on samples of several varieties of rock, the following information on rock density (grams per cubic centimeter) was obtained.

Type of Rock	Sample Size	Mean Density	Standard Deviation
Late gabbro	36	3.04	.13
Massive gabbro	148	2.83	.11
Cumberlandite	135	3.05	.31

Source: Loncarevic, B. D., Feninger, T., and Lefebvre, D. "The Sept-Îles layered mafic intrusion: Geophysical expression." *Canadian Journal of Earth Sciences*, Vol. 27, Aug. 1990, p. 505.

a. For each rock type, estimate the mean density with a 90% confidence interval.

b. Interpret the intervals, part **a**.

8.27 An evaluation of trace metal chemistry and cycling in an acidic Adirondack lake was reported in *Environmental Science & Technology* (Dec. 1985). Twenty-four (24) water samples were collected from Darts Lake, New York, and analyzed for concentration of both lead and aluminum particulates.

a. The lead concentration measurements had a mean of 9.9 nmol/l and a standard deviation of 8.4 nmol/l. Calculate a 99% confidence interval for the true mean lead concentration in water samples collected from Darts Lake.

b. The aluminum concentration measurements had a mean of 6.7 nmol/l and a standard deviation of 10.8 nmol/l. Calculate a 99% confidence interval for the true mean aluminum concentration in water samples collected from Darts Lake.

c. What assumptions are necessary for the intervals of parts **a** and **b** to be valid?

8.28 According to one study, "The majority of people who die from fire and smoke in compartmented fire-resistive buildings—the type used for hotels, motels, apartments, and other health care facilities—die in the attempt to evacuate" (*Risk Management*, Feb. 1986). The accompanying data represent the numbers of victims who attempted to evacuate for a sample of 14 recent fires at compartmented fire-resistive buildings reported in the study.

Fire	Died in Attempt to Evacuate
Las Vegas Hilton (Las Vegas)	5
Inn on the Park (Toronto)	5
Westchase Hilton (Houston)	8
Holiday Inn (Cambridge, Ohio)	10
Conrad Hilton (Chicago)	4
Providence College (Providence)	8
Baptist Towers (Atlanta)	7
Howard Johnson (New Orleans)	5
Cornell University (Ithaca, New York)	9
Wesport Central Apartments (Kansas City, Missouri)	4
Orrington Hotel (Evanston, Illinois)	0
Hartford Hospital (Hartford, Connecticut)	16
Milford Plaza (New York)	0
MGM Grand (Las Vegas)	36

Source: Macdonald, J. N. "Is evacuation a fatal flaw in fire fighting philosophy?" *Risk Management*, Vol. 33, No. 2, Feb. 1986, p. 37.

a. State the assumption, in terms of the problem, that is required for a small-sample confidence interval technique to be valid.

b. Use the information in the accompanying MINITAB printout to construct a 98% confidence interval for the true mean number of victims per fire who die in an attempt to evacuate compartmented fire-resistive buildings.

c. Interpret the interval constructed in part b.

	N	MEAN	STDEV	SE MEAN	98.0 PERCENT C.I.	
numdied	14	8.36	8.94	2.39	(2.02,	14.69)

8.29 The *Journal of the American Medical Association* (Apr. 21, 1993) reported on the results of a National Health Interview Survey designed to determine the prevalence of smoking among U.S. adults. Over 40,000 adults responded to questions such as "Have you smoked at least 100 cigarettes in your lifetime?" and "Do you smoke cigarettes now?" Current smokers (over 11,000 adults in the survey) were also asked: "On the average, how many cigarettes do you now smoke a day?" The results yielded a mean of 20.0 cigarettes per day with an associated 95% confidence interval of (19.7, 20.3).

a. Interpret the 95% confidence interval.

b. State any assumptions about the target population of current cigarette smokers that must be satisfied for inferences derived from the interval to be valid.

c. A tobacco industry researcher claims that the mean number of cigarettes smoked per day by regular cigarette smokers is less than 15. Comment on this claim.

8.30 Tropical swarm-founding wasps, like ants and bees, rely on workers to raise their offspring. Interestingly, the workers of this species of wasp are mostly female, capable of producing offspring of their own. Instead, they rear the young of others in the brood. One possible explanation for this strange behavior is inbreeding, which increases relatedness among the wasps and makes it easier for the workers to pick out and aid their closest relatives. To test this theory, 197 swarm-founding wasps were captured in Venezuela, frozen at $-70°C$, and then subjected to a series of genetic tests (*Science*, Nov. 1988). The data were used to generate an inbreeding coefficient, x, for each wasp specimen, with the following results: $\bar{x} = .044$ and $s = .884$.

a. Construct a 90% confidence interval for the mean inbreeding coefficient of this species of wasp.

b. A coefficient of 0 implies that the wasp has no tendency to inbreed. Use the confidence interval, part a, to make an inference about the tendency for this species of wasp to inbreed.

8.31 The data for Exercise 2.57 are reproduced here. The numbers in the table represent the CPU solution times (in seconds) for 52 random polynomial 0–1 mathematical problems solved using a hybrid algorithm. A stem-and-leaf display and descriptive statistics for the data set are provided in the accompanying SAS printout. Use this information to estimate, with 95% confidence, the mean solution time for the hybrid algorithm. Interpret the result.

.045	.136	8.788	.079	3.985	1.267	.379	.327
.136	.130	.036	.136	.600	.209	.506	.064
.088	.194	.118	.258	4.170	.554	.412	.045
.361	.049	.070	1.639	.258	.670	.567	
.182	1.055	.091	.579	1.894	.291	.445	
.179	.336	.145	.394	1.070	.227	.258	
.182	.242	.209	.333	.912	3.046	3.888	

Source: Snyder, W. S., and Chrissis, J. W. "A hybrid algorithm for solving zero–one mathematical programming problems." *IIE Transactions*, Vol. 22, No. 2, June 1990, p. 166 (Table 1).

UNIVARIATE PROCEDURE

Variable=SOLTIME

Moments

N	52	Sum Wgts	52
Mean	0.812192	Sum	42.234
Std Dev	1.50476	Variance	2.264303
Skewness	3.65356	Kurtosis	15.73264
USS	149.7816	CSS	115.4795
CV	185.2714	Std Mean	0.208673
T:Mean=0	3.892183	Prob>$\|T\|$	0.0003
Sgn Rank	689	Prob>$\|S\|$	0.0001
Num ^= 0	52		
W:Normal	0.530623	Prob<W	0.0

Quantiles(Def=5)

100% Max	8.788	99%	8.788	
75% Q3	0.5895	95%	3.985	
50% Med	0.2745	90%	1.894	
25% Q1	0.136	10%	0.07	
0% Min	0.036	5%	0.045	
		1%	0.036	
Range	8.752			
Q3-Q1	0.4535			
Mode	0.136			

Extremes

Lowest	Obs	Highest	Obs
0.036(	22)	3.046(	49)
0.045(	50)	3.888(	35)
0.045(	1)	3.985(	33)
0.049(	51)	4.17(	43)
0.064(	45)	8.788(	17)

```
Stem Leaf                                              #      Boxplot
   8 8                                                 1         *
   8
   7
   7
   6
   6
   5
   5
   4
   4 02                                                2         *
   3 9                                                 1         *
   3 0                                                 1         *
   2
   2
   1 69                                                2         0
   1 113                                               3         |
   0 5666679                                           7      +--+--+
   0 00001111111111112222222233333333344444           35     *-----*
     ----+----+----+----+----+----+----+
```

8.6 Estimation of the Difference Between Two Population Means: Independent Samples

In Section 8.5, we learned how to estimate the parameter μ from a single population. We now proceed to a technique for using the information in two samples to estimate the difference between two population means, $(\mu_1 - \mu_2)$, when the samples are collected independently. For example, we may want to compare the mean starting salaries for college graduates with mechanical engineering and civil engineering degrees, or the mean operating costs of automobiles with rotary engines and standard engines, or the mean failure times of two electronic components. The technique to be presented is a straightforward extension of that used for estimation of a single population mean.

Suppose we select independent random samples of sizes n_1 and n_2 from populations with means μ_1 and μ_2, respectively. Intuitively, we want to use the difference between the sample means, $(\bar{y}_1 - \bar{y}_2)$, to estimate $(\mu_1 - \mu_2)$. In Example 7.5, we showed that

$$E(\bar{y}_1 - \bar{y}_2) = \mu_1 - \mu_2$$

$$V(\bar{y}_1 - \bar{y}_2) = \frac{\sigma_1^2}{n_1} + \frac{\sigma_2^2}{n_2}$$

You can see that $(\bar{y}_1 - \bar{y}_2)$ is an unbiased estimator for $(\mu_1 - \mu_2)$. Further, it can be shown (proof omitted) that $V(\bar{y}_1 - \bar{y}_2)$ is smallest among all unbiased estimators, i.e., $(\bar{y}_1 - \bar{y}_2)$ is the MVUE for $(\mu_1 - \mu_2)$.

According to the central limit theorem, $(\bar{y}_1 - \bar{y}_2)$ will also be approximately normal for large n_1 and n_2 regardless of the distributions of the sampled populations. Thus, we can apply Theorem 8.2 to construct a large-sample confidence interval for $(\mu_1 - \mu_2)$. The procedure for forming a large-sample confidence interval for $(\mu_1 - \mu_2)$ appears in the box.

Large-Sample $(1 - \alpha)100\%$ Confidence Interval for $(\mu_1 - \mu_2)$: Independent Samples

$$(\bar{y}_1 - \bar{y}_2) \pm z_{\alpha/2}\sigma_{(\bar{y}_1-\bar{y}_2)} = (\bar{y}_1 - \bar{y}_2) \pm z_{\alpha/2}\sqrt{\frac{\sigma_1^2}{n_1} + \frac{\sigma_2^2}{n_2}}$$

$$\approx (\bar{y}_1 - \bar{y}_2) \pm z_{\alpha/2}\sqrt{\frac{s_1^2}{n_1} + \frac{s_2^2}{n_2}}$$

[*Note:* We have used the sample variances s_1^2 and s_2^2 as approximations to the corresponding population parameters.]

Assumptions: 1. The two random samples are selected in an independent manner from the target populations. That is, the choice of elements in one sample does not affect, and is not affected by, the choice of elements in the other sample.

2. The sample sizes n_1 and n_2 are sufficiently large for the central limit theorem to apply. (We recommend $n_1 \geq 30$ and $n_2 \geq 30$.)

EXAMPLE 8.10

We want to estimate the difference between the mean starting salaries for recent graduates with mechanical engineering and civil engineering degrees from the University of Florida (UF). The following information is available:*

1. A random sample of 59 starting salaries for UF mechanical engineering graduates produced a sample mean of $32,675 and a standard deviation of $4,430.
2. A random sample of 30 starting salaries for UF civil engineering graduates produced a sample mean of $27,460 and a standard deviation of $4,286.

Solution

We will let the subscript 1 refer to the mechanical engineering graduates and the subscript 2 to the civil engineering graduates. We will also define the following notation:

μ_1 = Population mean starting salary of all recent UF mechanical engineering graduates

μ_2 = Population mean starting salary of all recent UF civil engineering graduates

Similarly, let $\bar{y}_1$ and $\bar{y}_2$ denote the respective sample means; s_1 and s_2, the respective sample standard deviations; and n_1 and n_2, the respective sample sizes. The given information is summarized in Table 8.3.

TABLE 8.3 Summary of Information for Example 8.10

	Mechanical Engineers	Civil Engineers
Sample Size	$n_1 = 59$	$n_2 = 30$
Sample Mean	$\bar{y}_1 = 32,675$	$\bar{y}_2 = 27,460$
Sample Standard Deviation	$s_1 = \$4,430$	$s_2 = 4,286$

Source: Career Resource Center, University of Florida.

The general form of a 95% confidence interval for $(\mu_1 - \mu_2)$, based on large, independent samples from the target populations, is given by

$$(\bar{y}_1 - \bar{y}_2) \pm z_{.025} \sqrt{\frac{\sigma_1^2}{n_1} + \frac{\sigma_2^2}{n_2}}$$

Recall that $z_{.025} = 1.96$ and use the information in Table 8.3 to make the following substitutions to obtain the desired confidence interval:

$$(32,675 - 27,460) \pm 1.96\sqrt{\sigma_1^2/59 + \sigma_2^2/30}$$
$$\approx (32,675 - 27,460) \pm 1.96\sqrt{(4,430)^2/59 + (4,286)^2/30}$$
$$\approx 5,215 \pm 1,905$$

or ($3,310, $7,120).

*The information for this example was extracted from a 1990 survey of graduates conducted by the Career Resource Center, University of Florida.

If we were to use this method of estimation repeatedly to produce confidence intervals for $(\mu_1 - \mu_2)$, the difference between population means, we would expect 95% of the intervals to enclose $(\mu_1 - \mu_2)$. Hence, we can be reasonably confident that the mean starting salary of mechanical engineering graduates of UF was between $3,310 and $7,120 higher than the mean starting salary of civil engineering graduates.

A confidence interval for $(\mu_1 - \mu_2)$, based on small samples from each population, is derived using Student's t distribution. As was the case when estimating a single population mean from information in a small sample, we must make specific assumptions about the relative frequency distributions of the two populations, as indicated in the box. These assumptions are required if either sample is small (i.e., if either $n_1 < 30$ or $n_2 < 30$).

Small-Sample $(1 - \alpha)100\%$ Confidence Interval for $(\mu_1 - \mu_2)$: Independent Samples and $\sigma_1^2 = \sigma_2^2$

$$(\bar{y}_1 - \bar{y}_2) \pm t_{\alpha/2} \sqrt{s_p^2 \left(\frac{1}{n_1} + \frac{1}{n_2} \right)}$$

where

$$s_p^2 = \frac{(n_1 - 1)s_1^2 + (n_2 - 1)s_2^2}{n_1 + n_2 - 2}$$

and the value of $t_{\alpha/2}$ is based on $(n_1 + n_2 - 2)$ degrees of freedom.

Assumptions: 1. Both of the populations from which the samples are selected have relative frequency distributions that are approximately normal.

2. The variances σ_1^2 and σ_2^2 of the two populations are equal.

3. The random samples are selected in an independent manner from the two populations.

Note that this procedure requires that the samples be selected from two normal populations that have equal variances (i.e., $\sigma_1^2 = \sigma_2^2 = \sigma^2$). Since we are assuming the variances are equal, we construct an estimate of σ^2 based on the information contained in *both* samples. This **pooled estimate** is denoted by s_p^2 and is computed as shown in the previous box. You will notice that s_p^2 is a weighted average of the two sample variances, s_1^2 and s_2^2, with the weights proportional to the respective sample sizes.

EXAMPLE 8.11   The *Journal of Testing and Evaluation* (July 1981) reported on the results of laboratory tests conducted to investigate the stability and permeability of open-graded asphalt concrete. In one part of the experiment, four concrete specimens were prepared for asphalt contents of 3% and 7% by total weight of mix. The water permeability of each concrete specimen was determined by flowing deaerated water across the specimen and measuring the amount of water loss. The permeability measurements (recorded in inches per hour) for the eight concrete specimens are shown in Table 8.4. Find a 95% confidence interval for the difference between the mean permeabilities of concrete made with asphalt contents of 3% and 7%. Interpret the interval.

TABLE 8.4 Permeability Measurements for 3% and 7% Asphalt Concrete, Example 8.11

| Asphalt Content | 3% | 1,189 | 840 | 1,020 | 980 |
| | 7% | 853 | 900 | 733 | 785 |

Source: Woelfl, G., Wei, I., Faulstich, C., and Litwack, H. "Laboratory testing of asphalt concrete for porous pavements." *Journal of Testing and Evaluation*, Vol. 9, No. 4, July 1981, pp. 175–181. Copyright American Society for Testing and Materials.

Solution

First, we calculate the means and variances of the two samples, using the computer. A SAS printout giving descriptive statistics for the two samples is shown in Figure 8.10. For the 3% asphalt, $\bar{y}_1 = 1{,}007.25$ and $s_1^2 = 20{,}636.92$; for the 7% asphalt, $\bar{y}_2 = 817.75$ and $s_2^2 = 5{,}420.92$.

FIGURE 8.10 ▶
SAS descriptive statistics for Example 8.11

```
N Obs   Variable   N          Mean        Variance      Std Dev
-------------------------------------------------------------------
  4     ASPH3PCT   4         1007.25       20636.92    143.6555487
        ASPH7PCT   4       817.7500000      5420.92     73.6268746
-------------------------------------------------------------------
```

Since both samples are small ($n_1 = n_2 = 4$), the procedure requires the assumption that the two samples of permeability measurements are independently and randomly selected from normal populations with equal variances. The 95% small-sample confidence interval is

$$(\bar{y}_1 - \bar{y}_2) \pm t_{.025}\sqrt{s_p^2\left(\frac{1}{n_1} + \frac{1}{n_2}\right)}$$

$$= (1{,}007.25 - 817.75) \pm t_{.025}\sqrt{s_p^2\left(\frac{1}{4} + \frac{1}{4}\right)}$$

where $t_{.025} = 2.447$ is obtained from the t distribution (Table 7 of Appendix II) based on $n_1 + n_2 - 2 = 4 + 4 - 2 = 6$ degrees of freedom, and

$$s_p^2 = \frac{(n_1 - 1)s_1^2 + (n_2 - 1)s_2^2}{n_1 + n_2 - 2} = \frac{3(20{,}636.92) + 3(5{,}420.92)}{6}$$

$$= 13{,}028.92$$

is the pooled sample variance. Substitution yields the interval

$$(1{,}007.25 - 817.75) \pm 2.447\sqrt{13{,}028.92\left(\frac{1}{4} + \frac{1}{4}\right)}$$

$$= 189.5 \pm 197.50$$

or, -8.00 to 387.00. This interval could also be obtained using the computer. The MINITAB-generated 95% confidence interval is displayed in Figure 8.11. Our calculated interval agrees with the MINITAB result. The interval is interpreted as follows: We are 95% confident that the interval $(-8, 387)$ encloses the true difference between the mean permeabilities of the two types of concrete. Since the interval includes 0, we are unable to conclude that the two means differ.

FIGURE 8.11 ▶

MINITAB printout for Example 8.11

TWOSAMPLE T FOR asph3pct VS asph7pct				
	N	MEAN	STDEV	SE MEAN
asph3pct	4	1007	144	72
asph7pct	4	817.8	73.6	37

95 PCT CI FOR MU asph3pct - MU asph7pct: (-8, 387)

TTEST MU asph3pct = MU asph7pct (VS NE): T= 2.35   P=0.057   DF=   6

POOLED STDEV =   114

As with the one-sample case, the assumptions required for estimating $(\mu_1 - \mu_2)$ with small samples do not have to be satisfied exactly for the interval estimate to be useful in practice. Slight departures from these assumptions do not seriously affect the level of confidence in the procedure. For example, when the variances σ_1^2 and σ_2^2 of the sampled populations are unequal, researchers have found that the formula for the small-sample confidence interval for $(\mu_1 - \mu_2)$ still yields valid results in practice as long as the two populations are normal and the sample sizes are equal, i.e., $n_1 = n_2$.

This situation occurs in Example 8.11. The sample variances given in Figure 8.10 are $s_1^2 = 20{,}636.92$ and $s_2^2 = 5{,}420.92$. Thus, it is very likely that the population variances, σ_1^2 and σ_2^2, are unequal. * However, since $n_1 = n_2 = 4$, the inference derived from this interval is still valid if we use s_1^2 and s_2^2 as estimates for the population variances (rather than using the pooled sample variance, s_p^2).

In the case where $\sigma_1^2 \neq \sigma_2^2$ and $n_1 \neq n_2$, an approximate confidence interval for $(\mu_1 - \mu_2)$ can be constructed by modifying the degrees of freedom associated with the t distribution, and, again, substituting s_1^2 for σ_1^2 and s_2^2 for σ_2^2. These modifications are shown in the box.

*A method for comparing two population variances is presented in Section 8.11.

Approximate Small-Sample Inferences for $(\mu_1 - \mu_2)$ when $\sigma_1^2 \neq \sigma_2^2$

To obtain approximate confidence intervals and tests for $(\mu_1 - \mu_2)$ when $\sigma_1^2 \neq \sigma_2^2$, make the following modifications to the degrees of freedom ν used in the t distribution and the estimated standard error:

$$n_1 = n_2 = n: \quad \nu = n_1 + n_2 - 2 = 2(n-1) \quad \hat{\sigma}_{\bar{y}_1 - \bar{y}_2} = \sqrt{\frac{1}{n}(s_1^2 + s_2^2)}$$

$$n_1 \neq n_2: \quad \nu = \frac{(s_1^2/n_1 + s_2^2/n_2)^2}{\frac{(s_1^2/n_1)^2}{n_1 - 1} + \frac{(s_2^2/n_2)^2}{n_2 - 1}} \quad \hat{\sigma}_{\bar{y}_1 - \bar{y}_2} = \sqrt{\frac{s_1^2}{n_1} + \frac{s_2^2}{n_2}}$$

[Note: In the case of $n_1 \neq n_2$, the value of ν will not generally be an integer. Round ν down to the nearest integer to use the t table.

Assumptions:
1. Both of the populations from which the samples are selected have relative frequency distributions that are approximately normal.
2. The random samples are selected in an independent manner from the two populations.

EXERCISES

8.32 Epidemiologists have theorized that the risk of coronary heart disease can be reduced by an increased consumption of fish. One study, begun in 1960, monitored the diet and health of a random sample of middle-age Dutchmen (*New England Journal of Medicine*, May 1985). The men were divided into groups according to the number of grams of fish consumed per day. Twenty years later, the level of dietary cholesterol (one of the risk factors for coronary disease) present in each was recorded. The results for two groups of subjects, the "no fish consumption" group (0 grams per day) and the "high fish consumption" group (greater than 45 grams per day), are summarized in the table. (Dietary cholesterol is measured in milligrams per 1,000 calories.)

	No Fish Consumption 0 grams/day	High Fish Consumption 45 grams/day
Sample Size	159	79
Mean	146	158
Standard Deviation	66	75

Source: Kromhout, D., Bosschieter, E. B., and Coulander, C. L. "The inverse relationship between fish consumption and 20-year mortality from coronary heart disease." *New England Journal of Medicine*, May 9, 1985, Vol. 312, No. 19, pp. 1205–1209. Reprinted by permission.

> a. Calculate an approximate 99% confidence interval for the difference between the mean levels of dietary cholesterol present in the two groups.
> b. Based on the interval constructed in part **a**, what can you infer about the true difference? Explain.

8.33 Marine biochemists at the University of Tokyo studied the properties of crustacean skeletal muscles (*The Journal of Experimental Zoology*, Sept. 1993). It is well known that certain muscles contract faster than others. The main purpose of the experiment was to compare the biochemical properties of fast and slow muscles of crayfish. Using crayfish obtained from a local supplier, twelve fast-muscle fiber bundles were extracted and each fiber bundle tested for uptake of the protein Ca^{2+}. Twelve slow-muscle fiber bundles were extracted from a second sample of crayfish, and Ca^{2+} uptake measured. The results of the experiment are summarized here. (All Ca^{2+} measurements are in moles per milligram.) Analyze the data using a 95% confidence interval. Make an inference about the difference between the protein uptake means of fast and slow muscles.

Fast Muscle	Slow Muscle
$n_1 = 12$	$n_2 = 12$
$\bar{y}_1 = .57$	$\bar{y}_2 = .37$
$s_1 = .104$	$s_2 = .035$

Source: Ushio, H., and Watabe, S. "Ultra-structural and biochemical analysis of the sarcoplasmic reticulum from crayfish fast and slow striated muscles." The *Journal of Experimental Zoology*, Vol. 267, Sept. 1993, p. 16 (Table 1).

8.34 Refer to the Harris Corporation/University of Florida study to determine whether a manufacturing process performed at a remote location can be established locally, Exercise 2.12. Test devices (pilots) were set up at both the old and new locations and voltage readings on 30 production runs at each location were obtained. The data are reproduced in the table. Descriptive statistics are displayed in the accompanying SAS printout. [*Note:* Larger voltage readings are better than smaller voltage readings.]

Old Location			New Location		
9.98	10.12	9.84	9.19	10.01	8.82
10.26	10.05	10.15	9.63	8.82	8.65
10.05	9.80	10.02	10.10	9.43	8.51
10.29	10.15	9.80	9.70	10.03	9.14
10.03	10.00	9.73	10.09	9.85	9.75
8.05	9.87	10.01	9.60	9.27	8.78
10.55	9.55	9.98	10.05	8.83	9.35
10.26	9.95	8.72	10.12	9.39	9.54
9.97	9.70	8.80	9.49	9.48	9.36
9.87	8.72	9.84	9.37	9.64	8.68

Source: Harris Corporation, Melbourne, Fla.

```
Analysis Variable : VOLTAGE


---------------------------------- LOCATION=OLD -----------------------


N Obs    N      Minimum       Maximum           Mean       Std Dev
        ----------------------------------------------------------------
  30    30    8.0500000     10.5500000      9.8036667     0.5409155
        ----------------------------------------------------------------


---------------------------------- LOCATION=NEW -----------------------


N Obs    N      Minimum       Maximum           Mean       Std Dev
        ----------------------------------------------------------------
  30    30    8.5100000     10.1200000      9.4223333     0.4788757
        ----------------------------------------------------------------
```

a. Compare the mean voltage readings at the two locations using a 90% confidence interval.

b. Based on the interval, part **a**, does it appear that the manufacturing process can be established locally?

8.35 The methodology for conducting a stress analysis of newly designed timber structures is well known. However, few data are available on the actual or allowable stress for repairing damaged structures. Consequently, design engineers often propose a repair scheme (e.g., gluing) without any knowledge of its structural effectiveness. To partially fill this void, a stress analysis was conducted on epoxy-repaired truss joints (*Journal of Structural Engineering*, Feb. 1986). Tests were conducted on epoxy-bonded truss joints made of various species of wood to determine actual glue-line shear stress recorded in pounds per square inch (psi). Summary information for independent random samples of southern pine and ponderosa pine truss joints is given in the accompanying table. Estimate the difference between the mean shear strengths of epoxy-repaired truss joints for the two species of wood with a 90% confidence interval.

	Southern Pine	Ponderosa Pine
Sample Size	100	47
Mean Shear Stress, psi	1,312	1,352
Standard Deviation	422	271

Source: Avent, R. R. "Design criteria for epoxy repair of timber structures." *Journal of Structural Engineering*, Vol. 112, No. 2, Feb. 1986, pp. 232.

8.36 To investigate the possible link between fluoride content of drinking water and cancer, Yiamouyiannis and Burk (1977) recorded cancer death rates (number of deaths per 100,000 population) from 1952–1969 in 20 selected U.S. cities—the 10 largest fluoridated cities and the 10 largest cities not fluoridated by 1969. Maritz and Jarrett (*Applied Statistics*, Feb. 1983) used the data collected by Yiamouyiannis and Burk to calculate for each city the annual rate of increase in cancer death rate over this 18-year period for each of four age groups: under 25, 25–44, 45–64, and 65 or older. The data for the 45–64 age group are reproduced in the table at the top of page 380, followed by a MINITAB analysis of the data.

	Fluoridated		*Nonfluoridated*
City	*Annual Increase in Cancer Death Rate*	*City*	*Annual Increase in Cancer Death Rate*
Chicago	1.0640	Los Angeles	.8875
Philadelphia	1.4118	Boston	1.7358
Baltimore	2.1115	New Orleans	1.0165
Cleveland	1.9401	Seattle	.4923
Washington	3.8772	Cincinnati	4.0155
Milwaukee	−.4561	Atlanta	−1.1744
St. Louis	4.8359	Kansas City	2.8132
San Francisco	1.8875	Columbus	1.7451
Pittsburgh	4.4964	Newark	−.5676
Buffalo	1.4045	Portland	2.4471

Source: Maritz, J. S., and Jarrett, R. G. "The use of statistics to examine the association between fluoride in drinking water and cancer death rates." *Applied Statistics*, Vol. 32, No. 2, 1983, pp. 97–101.

```
TWOSAMPLE T FOR fluorat VS nonflrat
            N      MEAN     STDEV    SE MEAN
fluorat    10      2.26     1.66     0.52
nonflrat   10      1.34     1.56     0.49

95 PCT CI FOR MU fluorat - MU nonflrat: (-0.60, 2.43)

TTEST MU fluorat = MU nonflrat (VS NE): T= 1.27  P=0.22  DF=  18

POOLED STDEV =        1.61
```

a. Find a 95% confidence interval for the difference between the mean annual increases in cancer death rates for fluoridated and nonfluoridated cities.

b. Interpret the interval obtained in part **a.**

c. What assumptions are necessary for the validity of the interval estimation procedure and any inferences derived from it? Do you think these assumptions are satisfied?

8.37   Agricultural experts in Israel have developed a new method of irrigation, called *fertigation*, in which fertilizer is added to water and the mixture is dripped periodically onto the roots of the plants. Very little water—a precious commodity in Israel—is wasted, and the nutrients go directly where they are needed. To test this new process, 100 acres were randomly selected and their historical yields were recorded. The fertigation process was then applied to the new crop and the new yields were recorded. The accompanying table summarizes the results.

	Before Fertigation	*After Fertigation*
Sample Size	100	100
Mean Yield	40%	75%
Standard Deviation	8%	6%

a. Estimate the difference between the true mean yields before and after fertigation. Use a 90% confidence interval.

b. Interpret the confidence interval of part **a.**

8.38 *Sintering*, one of the most important techniques of materials science, is used to convert powdered material into a porous solid body. The following two measures characterize the final product:

V_V = Percentage of total volume of final product that is solid

$$= \left(\frac{\text{Solid volume}}{\text{Porous volume} + \text{Solid volume}}\right) \cdot 100$$

S_V = Solid-pore interface area per unit volume of the product

When V_V = 100%, the product is completely solid—i.e., it contains no pores. Both V_V and S_V are estimated by a microscopic examination of polished cross sections of sintered material. The accompanying table gives the mean and standard deviation of the values of S_V (in squared centimeters per cubic centimeter) and V_V (percentage) for n = 100 specimens of sintered nickel for two different sintering times.

	S_V		V_V	
Time	$\bar{y}$	s	$\bar{y}$	s
10 minutes	736.0	181.9	96.73	2.1
150 minutes	299.5	161.0	97.82	1.5

Data and experimental information provided by Guoquan Liu while visiting at the University of Florida in 1983.

a. Find a 95% confidence interval for the mean change in S_V between sintering times of 10 minutes and 150 minutes. What inference would you make concerning the difference in mean sintering times?

b. Repeat part a for V_V.

8.7 Estimation of the Difference Between Two Population Means: Matched Pairs

The large- and small-sample procedures for estimating the difference between two population means presented in Section 8.6 were based on the assumption that the samples were randomly and independently selected from the target populations. Sometimes we can obtain more information about the difference between population means, $(\mu_1 - \mu_2)$, by selecting **paired observations**.

For example, suppose you want to compare two methods for drying concrete using samples of five cement mixes with each method. One method of sampling would be to randomly select 10 mixes (say, A, B, C, D, . . . , J) from among all available mixes and then randomly assign five to drying method 1 and five to drying method 2 (see Table 8.5 on page 382). The strength measurements obtained after conducting a series of strength tests would represent independent random samples of strengths attained by concrete specimens dried by the two different methods. The difference between the mean strength measurements, $(\mu_1 - \mu_2)$, could be estimated using the confidence interval procedure described in Section 8.6.

TABLE 8.5   Independent Random Samples of Cement Mixes Assigned to Each Method

Method 1	Method 2
Mix A	Mix B
Mix E	Mix C
Mix F	Mix D
Mix H	Mix G
Mix J	Mix I

A better method of sampling would be to match the concrete specimens in pairs according to type of mix. From each mix pair, one specimen would be randomly selected to be dried by method 1; the other specimen would be assigned to be dried by method 2, as shown in Table 8.6. Then the differences between **matched pairs** of strength measurements should provide a clearer picture of the difference in strengths for the two drying methods because the matching would tend to cancel the effects of the factors that formed the basis of the matching (i.e., the effects of the different cement mixes).

TABLE 8.6   Set-up of the Matched-Pairs Design for Comparing Two Methods of Drying Concrete

Type of Mix	Method 1	Method 2
A	Specimen 2	Specimen 1
B	Specimen 2	Specimen 1
C	Specimen 1	Specimen 2
D	Specimen 2	Specimen 1
E	Specimen 1	Specimen 2

In a matched-pairs experiment, the symbol μ_d is commonly used to denote the mean difference between matched pairs of measurements, where $\mu_d = (\mu_1 - \mu_2)$. Once the differences in the sample are calculated, a confidence interval for μ_d is identical to the confidence interval for the mean of a single population given in Section 8.5.

The procedure for estimating the difference between two population means based on matched-pairs data for both large and small samples is given in the box.

$(1 - \alpha)100\%$ Confidence Interval for $\mu_d = (\mu_1 - \mu_2)$: Matched Pairs

Let $d_1, d_2, \ldots, d_n$ represent the differences between the pairwise observations in a *random sample* of n matched pairs, $\bar{d}$ = mean of the n sample differences, and s_d = standard deviation of the n sample differences.

Large Sample

$$\bar{d} \pm z_{\alpha/2}\left(\frac{\sigma_d}{\sqrt{n}}\right)$$

where σ_d is the population deviation of differences.

Assumption: $n \geq 30$

[Note: When σ_d is unknown (as is usually the case), use s_d to approximate σ_d.]

Small Sample

$$\bar{d} \pm t_{\alpha/2}\left(\frac{s_d}{\sqrt{n}}\right)$$

where $t_{\alpha/2}$ is based on $(n - 1)$ degrees of freedom.

Assumption: The population of paired differences is normally distributed.

EXAMPLE 8.12

One desirable characteristic of water pipes is that the quality of water they deliver be equal to or near the quality of water entering the system at the water treatment plant. A type of ductile iron pipe has provided an excellent water delivery system for the St. Louis County Water Company. The chlorine levels of water emerging from the South water treatment plant and at the Fire Station (Fenton Zone 13) were measured over a 12-month period, with the results shown in Table 8.7. Find a 95% confidence interval for the mean difference in monthly chlorine content between the two locations.

TABLE 8.7   Chlorine Content Data for Example 8.12

		Jan.	Feb.	Mar.	Apr.	May	June	July	Aug.	Sept.	Oct.	Nov.	Dec.
							Month						
Location	South Plant	2.0	2.0	2.1	1.9	1.7	1.8	1.7	1.9	2.0	2.0	2.1	2.1
	Fire Station	2.2	2.2	2.1	2.0	1.9	1.9	1.8	1.7	1.9	1.9	1.8	2.0
Difference		−.2	−.2	0	−.1	−.2	−.1	−.1	.2	.1	.1	.3	.1

Source: "St. Louis County Standardizes Pipe and Procedures for Reliability." Staff Report, Water and Sewage Works, Dec. 1980.

Solution

Since the chlorine levels at the two plants were recorded over the same 12 months, the data are collected as matched pairs. We want to estimate $\mu_d = (\mu_1 - \mu_2)$, where

μ_1 = Mean monthly chlorine level at the South Plant

μ_2 = Mean monthly chlorine level at the Fire Station

The differences between pairs of monthly chlorine levels are computed as

$$d = \text{(South Plant level)} - \text{(Fire Station level)}$$

and are shown in the last row of Table 8.7.

Since the number of differences, $n = 12$, is small, we must assume that these differences are from an approximately normal distribution in order to proceed. The mean and standard deviation of these sample differences are shown (shaded) on the SAS printout, Figure 8.12. From the printout, $\bar{d} = -.0083$ and $s_d = .1676$.

FIGURE 8.12 ▶

SAS descriptive statistics for matched pairs, Example 8.12

Analysis Variable : DIFF (Plant minus Station)

N Obs	N	Minimum	Maximum	Mean	Std Dev
12	12	-0.2000000	0.3000000	-0.0083333	0.1676486

The value of $t_{.025}$, based on $(n - 1) = (12 - 1) = 11$ degrees of freedom, is given in Table 7 of Appendix II as $t_{.025} = 2.201$. Substituting these values into the formula for the small-sample confidence interval, we obtain

$$\bar{d} \pm t_{.025}\left(\frac{s_d}{\sqrt{n}}\right)$$

$$= -.0083 \pm 2.201\left(\frac{.1676}{\sqrt{12}}\right)$$

$$= -.0083 \pm .1065$$

or $(-.1148, .0982)$.

We estimate, with 95% confidence, that the difference between the mean monthly chlorine levels of water at the two St. Louis locations falls within the interval from $-.1148$ to $.0982$. Since 0 is within the interval, there is insufficient evidence to conclude there is a difference between the two means.

. . . .

In an analysis of matched-pair observations, it is important to stress that the pairing of the experimental units (the objects upon which the measurements are taken) must be performed *before* the data are collected. Recall that the objective is to compare two methods of "treating" the experimental units. By using the matched pairs of units that have similar characteristics, we are able to cancel out the effects of the variables used to match the pairs.

EXERCISES

8.39   Pesticides applied to an extensively grown crop can result in inadvertent area-wide air contamination. *Environmental Science & Technology* (Oct. 1993) reported on air deposition residues of the insecticide diazinon used on dormant orchards in the San Joaquin Valley, California. Ambient air samples were collected and analyzed at an orchard site for each of 11 days during the most intensive period of spraying. The levels of diazinon residue (in ng/m³) during the day and at night are recorded in the table. The researchers want to know whether the mean diazinon residue levels differ from day to night.

Date	Diazinon Residue	
	Day	Night
Jan. 11	5.4	24.3
12	2.7	16.5
13	34.2	47.2
14	19.9	12.4
15	2.4	24.0
16	7.0	21.6
17	6.1	104.3
18	7.7	96.9
19	18.4	105.3
20	27.1	78.7
21	16.9	44.6

Source: Selber, J. N., et al. "Air and fog deposition residues for organophosphate insecticides used on dormant orchards in the San Joaquin Valley, California." *Environmental Science & Technology*, Vol. 27, No. 10, Oct. 1993, p. 2240 (Table IV).

a. Analyze the data using a 90% confidence interval.
b. What assumptions are necessary for the validity of the interval estimation procedure of part **a**?
c. Use the interval, part **a**, to answer the researchers' question.

8.40 The *Journal of Environmental Engineering* (Feb. 1986) reported on a heat transfer model designed to predict winter heat loss in wastewater treatment clarifiers. The analysis involved a comparison of clear-sky solar irradiation for horizontal surfaces at different sites in the midwest. The day-long solar irradiation levels (in BTU/sq. ft.) at two midwestern locations of different latitudes (St. Joseph, Missouri, and Iowa Great Lakes) were recorded on each of seven clear-sky winter days. The data are given in the table. Find a 95% confidence interval for the mean difference between the day-long clear-sky solar irradiation levels at the two sites. Interpret the results.

Date	St. Joseph, Mo.	Iowa Great Lakes
December 21	782	593
January 6	965	672
January 21	948	750
February 6	1,181	988
February 21	1,414	1,226
March 7	1,633	1,462
March 21	1,852	1,698

Source: Wall, D. J., and Peterson, G. "Model for winter heat loss in uncovered clarifiers." *Journal of Environmental Engineering*, Vol. 112, No. 1, Feb. 1986, p. 128.

8.41   A federal traffic safety researcher was hired to ascertain the effect of wearing safety devices (shoulder harnesses, seat belts) on reaction times to peripheral stimuli. To investigate this question, he randomly selected 15 subjects from the students enrolled in a driver education program. Each subject performed a simulated driving task that allowed reaction times to be recorded under two conditions, wearing a safety device (restrained condition) and no safety device (unrestrained condition). Thus, each subject received two reaction-time scores, one for the restrained condition and one for the unrestrained condition. The data (in hundredths of a second) are shown in the accompanying table, followed by a MINITAB printout of the analysis.

Driver	1	2	3	4	5	6	7	8	9	10	11	12	13	14	15
Restrained	36.7	37.5	39.3	44.0	38.4	43.1	36.2	40.6	34.9	31.7	37.5	42.8	32.6	36.8	38.0
Unrestrained	36.1	35.8	38.4	41.7	38.3	42.6	33.6	40.9	32.5	30.7	37.4	40.2	33.1	33.6	37.5

	N	MEAN	STDEV	SE MEAN	90.0 PERCENT C.I.	
RminusU	15	1.180	1.191	0.307	(0.638,	1.722)

a. Find a 90% confidence interval for the difference between mean reaction-time scores for the restrained and unrestrained drivers.
b. What assumptions are necessary for the validity of the interval estimation procedure of part **a**?
c. Based on the interval of part **a**, what would you infer about the mean reaction times for the driving conditions?

8.42   Medical researchers believe that exposure to dust from cotton bract induces respiratory disease in susceptible field workers. An experiment was conducted to determine the effect of air-dried green cotton bract extract (GBE) on the cells of mill workers not exposed to dust (*Environmental Research*, Feb. 1986). Blood samples taken on eight workers were incubated with varying concentrations of GBE. After a short period of time, the cyclic AMP level (a measure of cell activity expressed in picomoles per million cells) of each blood sample was measured. The data for two GBE concentrations, 0 mg/ml (salt buffer, control solution) and .2 mg/ml, are reproduced in the table. [Note that one blood sample was taken from each worker, with one aliquot exposed to the salt buffer solution and the other to the GBE.]

Worker	GBE Concentration, mg/ml	
	0	.2
A	8.8	4.4
B	13.0	5.7
C	9.2	4.4
D	6.5	4.1
F	9.1	4.4
H	17.0	7.9

Source: Butcher, B. T., Reed, M. A., and O'Neil, C. E. "Biochemical and immunologic characterization of cotton bract extract and its effect on *in vitro* cyclic AMP production." *Environmental Research*, Vol. 39, No. 1, Feb. 1986, p. 119.

a. Find a 95% confidence interval for the mean difference between the cyclic AMP levels of blood samples exposed to the two concentrations of GBE.
b. Based on the interval obtained in part **a**, is there evidence that exposure to GBE blocks cell activity?

8.43   Many Vietnam veterans have dangerously high levels of the dioxin 2,3,7,8-TCDD in blood and fat tissue as a result of their exposure to the defoliant Agent Orange. A study published in *Chemosphere* (Vol. 20, 1990) reported on the TCDD levels of 20 Massachusetts Vietnam veterans who were possibly exposed to Agent Orange. The amounts of TCDD (measured in parts per trillion) in blood plasma and fat tissue drawn from each veteran are shown in the table followed by a SAS printout giving summary statistics. Use the information on the printout to construct a confidence interval that will allow you to compare the mean TCDD level in plasma to the mean TCDD level in fat tissue for Vietnam veterans exposed to Agent Orange. Interpret the result.

Veteran	*TCDD Levels in Plasma*	*TCDD Levels in Fat Tissue*	Veteran	*TCDD Levels in Plasma*	*TCDD Levels in Fat Tissue*
1	2.5	4.9	11	6.9	7.0
2	3.1	5.9	12	3.3	2.9
3	2.1	4.4	13	4.6	4.6
4	3.5	6.9	14	1.6	1.4
5	3.1	7.0	15	7.2	7.7
6	1.8	4.2	16	1.8	1.1
7	6.0	10.0	17	20.0	11.0
8	3.0	5.5	18	2.0	2.5
9	36.0	41.0	19	2.5	2.3
10	4.7	4.4	20	4.1	2.5

Source: Schecter, A., et. al. "Partitioning of 2,3,7,8-chlorinated dibenzo-*p*-dioxins and dibenzofurans between adipose tissue and plasma lipid of 20 Massachusetts Vietnam veterans." *Chemosphere*, Vol. 20, Nos. 7–9, 1990, pp. 954–955 (Table I & II).

N Obs	Variable	N	Minimum	Maximum	Mean	Std Dev
20	PLASMA	20	1.6000000	36.0000000	5.9900000	8.1279829
	FAT	20	1.1000000	41.0000000	6.8600000	8.4656209
	DIFF	20	-5.0000000	9.0000000	-0.8700000	2.9773001

8.8   Estimation of a Population Proportion

We will now consider the method for estimating the binomial proportion p of successes—that is, the proportion of elements in a population that have a certain characteristic. For example, a quality control inspector may be interested in the proportion of defective items produced on an assembly line; or a supplier of heating oil may be interested in the proportion of homes in its service area that are heated by natural gas.

A logical candidate for a point estimate of the population proportion p is the sample proportion $\hat{p} = y/n$, where y is the number of observations in a sample of size n that have the characteristic of interest (i.e., y is the number of "successes"). In Example 7.7, we showed that for large n, $\hat{p}$ is approximately normal with mean

$$E(\hat{p}) = p$$

and variance

$$V(\hat{p}) = \frac{pq}{n}$$

Therefore, $\hat{p}$ is an unbiased estimator of p and (proof omitted) has the smallest variance among all unbiased estimators; that is, $\hat{p}$ is the MVUE for p. Since $\hat{p}$ is approximately normal, we can use it as a pivotal statistic and apply Theorem 8.2 to derive the formula for a large-sample confidence interval for p shown in the box.

Large-Sample $(1 - \alpha)100\%$ Confidence Interval for a Population Proportion, p

$$\hat{p} \pm z_{\alpha/2}\sigma_{\hat{p}} \approx \hat{p} \pm z_{\alpha/2}\sqrt{\frac{\hat{p}\hat{q}}{n}}$$

where $\hat{p}$ is the sample proportion of observations with the characteristic of interest, and $\hat{q} = 1 - \hat{p}$.

[Note: The interval is approximate since we must substitute the sample $\hat{p}$ and $\hat{q}$ for the corresponding population values for $\sigma_{\hat{p}}$.]

Assumption: The sample size n is sufficiently large so that the approximation is valid. As a rule of thumb, the condition of a "sufficiently large" sample size will be satisfied if $n\hat{p} \geq 4$ and $n\hat{q} \geq 4$.

Note that we must substitute $\hat{p}$ and $\hat{q}$ into the formula for $\sigma_{\hat{p}} = \sqrt{pq/n}$ to construct the interval. This approximation will be valid as long as the sample size n is sufficiently large. Many researchers adopt the rule of thumb that n is "sufficiently large" if the interval $\hat{p} \pm 2\sqrt{\hat{p}\hat{q}/n}$ does not contain 0 or 1. Recall (Section 7.6) that this rule is satisfied if $n\hat{p} \geq 4$ and $n\hat{q} \geq 4$.

EXAMPLE 8.13

Stainless steels are frequently used in chemical plants to handle corrosive fluids. However, these steels are especially susceptible to stress corrosion cracking in certain environments. In a sample of 295 steel alloy failures that occurred in oil refineries and petrochemical plants in Japan over the last 10 years, 118 were caused by stress corrosion cracking and corrosion fatigue (*Materials Performance*, June 1981). Construct a 95% confidence interval for the true proportion of alloy failures caused by stress corrosion cracking.

Solution

The sample proportion of alloy failures caused by corrosion is

$$\hat{p} = \frac{\text{Number of alloy failures in sample caused by corrosion}}{\text{Number of alloy failures in sample}}$$

$$= \frac{118}{295} = .4$$

Thus, $\hat{q} = 1 - .4 = .6$. The approximate 95% confidence interval is then

$$\hat{p} \pm z_{.025} \sqrt{\frac{\hat{p}\hat{q}}{n}} = .4 \pm 1.96 \sqrt{\frac{(.4)(.6)}{295}} = .4 \pm .056$$

or (.344, .456). [Note that the approximation is valid since $n\hat{p} = 118$ and $n\hat{q} = 177$ both exceed 4.]

We are 95% confident that the interval from .344 to .456 encloses the true proportion of alloy failures that were caused by corrosion. If we repeatedly selected random samples of $n = 295$ alloy failures and constructed a 95% confidence interval based on each sample, then we would expect 95% of the confidence intervals constructed to contain p.

Small-sample procedures are available for the estimation of a population proportion p. These techniques are similar to those small-sample procedures for estimating a population mean μ. (Recall that $\hat{p} = y/n$ can be thought of as a mean of a sample of 0–1 Bernoulli outcomes.) The details are not included in our discussion, however, because most surveys in actual practice use samples that are large enough to employ the procedure of this section.

EXERCISES

8.44 An American Housing Survey (AHS) conducted by the U.S. Department of Commerce revealed that 705 of 1,500 sampled homeowners are "do-it-yourselfers"—they did most the work themselves on at least one of their home improvements or repairs (Bureau of the Census, *Statistical Brief*, May 1992). Estimate the true proportion of American homeowners who do most of the home improvement or repair work themselves using a 95% confidence interval. Interpret the result.

8.45 The "Black Hole" survey, sponsored by the Professional Employment Research Council, reports on the toughest jobs to fill on recruiters lists. In the most recent survey, 95 of 285 recruiters listed engineering positions as the "toughest to fill" (*Industrial Engineering*, Aug. 1990). Estimate the true percentage of recruiters who find it toughest to fill engineering positions. Use a 99% confidence interval.

8.46 Refer to the *Journal of the Medical Association* (Apr. 21, 1993) report on the prevalence of cigarette smoking among U.S. adults, Exercise 8.29. Of the 43,732 survey respondents, 11,239 indicated that they were current smokers and 10,539 indicated they were former smokers.
   a. Construct and interpret a 90% confidence interval for the percentage of U.S. adults who currently smoke cigarettes.

b. Construct and interpret a 90% confidence interval for the percentage of U.S. adults who are former cigarette smokers.

8.47 According to a study conducted by the California Division of Labor Research and Statistics (*Engineering News Record*, Mar. 10, 1983), roofing is one of the most hazardous occupations. Of 2,514 worker injuries that caused absences for a full workday or shift after the injury, 23% were attributable to falls from high elevations on level surfaces, 21% to falling hand tools or other materials, 19% to overexertion, and 20% to burns or scalds. Assume that the 2,514 injuries can be regarded as a random sample from the population of all roofing injuries in California.
a. Construct a 95% confidence interval for the proportion of all injuries that are due to falls.
b. Construct a 95% confidence interval for the proportion of all injuries that are due to burns or scalds.

8.48 As part of a cooperative research agreement between the United States and Japan, a full-scale reinforced concrete building was designed and tested under simulated earthquake loading conditions in Japan (*Journal of Structural Engineering*, Jan. 1986). For one part of the study, several U.S. design engineers were asked to evaluate the new design. Of the 48 engineers surveyed, 36 believed the shear wall of the structure to be too lightly reinforced. Find a 95% confidence interval for the true proportion of U.S. design engineers who consider the shear wall of the building too lightly reinforced.

8.49 Astronauts often report episodes of disorientation as they move around the zero-gravity spacecraft. To compensate, crew members rely heavily on visual information to establish a top-down orientation. An empirical study was conducted to assess the potential of using color brightness as a body orientation cue (*Human Factors*, Dec. 1988). Ninety college students, reclining on their backs in the dark, were disoriented when positioned on a rotating platform under a slowly rotating disk that filled their entire field of vision. Half the disk was painted with a brighter level of color than the other half. The students were asked to say "stop" when they believed they were right-side up, and the brightness level of the disk was recorded. Of the 90 students, 58 selected the brighter color level.
a. Use this information to estimate the true proportion of subjects who use the bright color level as a cue to being right-side up. Construct a 95% confidence interval for the true proportion.
b. Can you infer from the result, part **a**, that a majority of subjects would select bright color levels over dark color levels as a cue to being right-side up? Explain.

8.50 The U.S. Food and Drug Administration (FDA) recently approved the marketing of a new chemical solution, Caridex, which dissolves cavities. In a study conducted by dental researchers at Northwestern University, 21 of 35 patients with cavities preferred treatment with Caridex to drilling (*Gainesville Sun*, Feb. 11, 1988). Estimate the true proportion of dental patients who prefer having their cavities dissolved with Caridex rather than drilled. Use a 99% confidence interval and interpret the result.

8.9 Estimation of the Difference Between Two Population Proportions

This section extends the method of Section 8.8 to the case in which we want to estimate the difference between two binomial proportions. For example, we may be interested in comparing the proportion p_1 of defective items produced by machine 1 to the proportion p_2 of defective items produced by machine 2.

Let y_1 and y_2 represent the numbers of successes in two independent binomial experiments with samples of size n_1 and n_2, respectively. To estimate the difference

$(p_1 - p_2)$, where p_1 and p_2 are binomial parameters—i.e., the probabilities of success in the two independent binomial experiments—consider the proportion of successes in each of the samples:

$$\hat{p}_1 = \frac{y_1}{n_1} \quad \text{and} \quad \hat{p}_2 = \frac{y_2}{n_2}$$

Intuitively, we would expect $(\hat{p}_1 - \hat{p}_2)$ to provide a reasonable estimate of $(p_1 - p_2)$. Since $(\hat{p}_1 - \hat{p}_2)$ is a linear function of the binomial random variables y_1 and y_2, where $E(y_i) = n_i p_i$ and $V(y_i) = n_i p_i q_i$, we have

$$E(\hat{p}_1 - \hat{p}_2) = E(\hat{p}_1) - E(\hat{p}_2) = E\left(\frac{y_1}{n_1}\right) - E\left(\frac{y_2}{n_2}\right)$$

$$= \frac{1}{n_1}E(y_1) - \frac{1}{n_2}E(y_2) = \frac{1}{n_1}(n_1 p_1) - \frac{1}{n_2}(n_2 p_2)$$

$$= p_1 - p_2$$

and

$$V(\hat{p}_1 - \hat{p}_2) = V(\hat{p}_1) + V(\hat{p}_2) - 2\,\text{Cov}(\hat{p}_1, \hat{p}_2)$$

$$= V\left(\frac{y_1}{n_1}\right) + V\left(\frac{y_2}{n_2}\right) - 0 \quad \text{since } y_1 \text{ and } y_2 \text{ are independent}$$

$$= \frac{1}{n_1^2}V(y_1) + \frac{1}{n_2^2}V(y_2)$$

$$= \frac{1}{n_1^2}(n_1 p_1 q_1) + \frac{1}{n_2^2}(n_2 p_2 q_2)$$

$$= \frac{p_1 q_1}{n_1} + \frac{p_2 q_2}{n_2}$$

Thus, $(\hat{p}_1 - \hat{p}_2)$ is an unbiased estimator of $(p_1 - p_2)$ and, in addition, it has minimum variance (proof omitted).

The central limit theorem also guarantees that, for sufficiently large sample sizes n_1 and n_2, the sampling distribution of $(\hat{p}_1 - \hat{p}_2)$ will be approximately normal. It follows (Theorem 8.2) that a large-sample confidence interval for $(p_1 - p_2)$ may be obtained as shown in the box on page 392.

Note that we must substitute the values of $\hat{p}_1$ and $\hat{p}_2$ for p_1 and p_2, respectively, to obtain an estimate of $\sigma_{(\hat{p}_1 - \hat{p}_2)}$. As in the one-sample case, this approximation is reasonably accurate when both n_1 and n_2 are sufficiently large, i.e., if the intervals

$$\hat{p}_1 \pm 2\sqrt{\frac{\hat{p}_1 \hat{q}_1}{n_1}} \quad \text{and} \quad \hat{p}_2 \pm 2\sqrt{\frac{\hat{p}_2 \hat{q}_2}{n_2}}$$

do not contain 0 or the sample size (n_1 or n_2). This will be true if $n_1 \hat{p}_1$, $n_2 \hat{p}_2$, $n_1 \hat{q}_1$, and $n_2 \hat{q}_2$ are all greater than or equal to 4.

> ### Large-Sample $(1 - \alpha)100\%$ Confidence Interval for $(p_1 - p_2)$
>
> $$(\hat{p}_1 - \hat{p}_2) \pm z_{\alpha/2}\sigma_{(\hat{p}_1 - \hat{p}_2)} \approx (\hat{p}_1 - \hat{p}_2) \pm z_{\alpha/2}\sqrt{\frac{\hat{p}_1\hat{q}_1}{n_1} + \frac{\hat{p}_2\hat{q}_2}{n_2}}$$
>
> where $\hat{p}_1$ and $\hat{p}_2$ are the sample proportions of observations with the characteristic of interest.
>
> [Note: We have followed the usual procedure of substituting the sample values $\hat{p}_1$, $\hat{q}_1$, $\hat{p}_2$, and $\hat{q}_2$ for the corresponding population values required for $\sigma_{(\hat{p}_1 - \hat{p}_2)}$.
>
> Assumption: The samples are sufficiently large that the approximation is valid. As a general rule of thumb, we will require that $n_1\hat{p}_1 \geq 4$, $n_1\hat{q}_1 \geq 4$, $n_2\hat{p}_2 \geq 4$, and $n_2\hat{q}_2 \geq 4$.

EXAMPLE 8.14

A traffic engineer conducted a study of vehicular speeds on a segment of street that had the posted speed limit changed several times. When the posted speed limit on the street was 30 miles per hour, the engineer monitored the speeds of 100 randomly selected vehicles traversing the street and observed 49 violations of the speed limit. After the speed limit was raised to 35 miles per hour, the engineer again monitored the speeds of 100 randomly selected vehicles and observed 19 vehicles in violation of the speed limit. Find a 99% confidence interval for $(p_1 - p_2)$, where p_1 is the true proportion of vehicles that (under similar driving conditions) exceed the lower speed limit (30 miles per hour) and p_2 is the true proportion of vehicles that (under similar driving conditions) exceed the higher speed limit (35 miles per hour). Interpret the interval.

Solution

In this example,

$$\hat{p}_1 = \frac{49}{100} = .49 \quad \text{and} \quad \hat{p}_2 = \frac{19}{100} = .19$$

Note that

$$n_1\hat{p}_1 = 49 \qquad n_1\hat{q}_1 = 51$$
$$n_2\hat{p}_2 = 19 \qquad n_2\hat{q}_2 = 81$$

all exceed 4. Thus, we can apply the approximation for a large-sample confidence interval for $(p_1 - p_2)$.

For a confidence interval of $(1 - \alpha) = .99$, we have $\alpha = .01$ and $z_{\alpha/2} = z_{.005} = 2.58$ (from Table 4 of Appendix II). Substitution into the confidence interval formula yields:

$$(\hat{p}_1 - \hat{p}_2) \pm z_{\alpha/2}\sqrt{\frac{\hat{p}_1\hat{q}_1}{n_1} + \frac{\hat{p}_2\hat{q}_2}{n_2}}$$

$$= (.49 - .19) \pm 2.58\sqrt{\frac{(.49)(.51)}{100} + \frac{(.19)(.81)}{100}}$$

$$= .30 \pm .164$$

Our interpretation is that the true difference, $(p_1 - p_2)$, falls between .136 and .464 with 99% confidence. Since the lower bound on our estimate is positive (.136), we are fairly confident that the proportion of all vehicles in violation of the lower speed limit (30 miles per hour) exceeds the corresponding proportion in violation of the higher speed limit (35 miles per hour) by at least .136.

Small-sample estimation procedures for $(p_1 - p_2)$ will not be discussed here for the reasons outlined at the end of Section 8.8.

EXERCISES

8.51   Geneticists at Duke University Medical Center have identified the E2F1 transcription factor as an important component of cell proliferation control (*Nature*, Sept. 23, 1993). The researchers induced DNA synthesis in two batches of serum-starved cells. Each cell in one batch was micro-injected with the E2F1 gene, whereas the cells in the second batch (the controls) were not exposed to E2F1. After 30 hours, the number of cells in each batch that exhibited altered growth was determined. The results of the experiment are summarized in the table.

	Control	E2F1 Treated Cells
Total Number of Cells	158	92
Number of Growth-Altered Cells	15	41

Source: Johnson, D. G., et al. "Expression of transcription factor E2F1 induces quiescent to enter S phase." *Nature*, Vol. 365, No. 6444, Sept. 23, 1993, p. 351 (Table 1).

a. Compare the percentages of cells exhibiting altered growth in the two batches with a 90% confidence interval.

b. Use the interval, part a, to make an inference about the ability of the E2F1 transcription factor to induce cell growth.

8.52   The nuclear mishap at Three Mile Island near Harrisburg, Pennsylvania, on March 28, 1979, forced many local residents to evacuate their homes—some temporarily, others permanently. To assess the impact of the accident on the area population, a questionnaire was designed and mailed to a sample of 150 households within 2 weeks after the accident occurred. Residents were asked how they felt both before and after the accident about having some of their electricity generated from nuclear power. The summary results are provided in the table on page 394.

	Attitude Toward Nuclear Power			*Totals*
	Favor	*Oppose*	*Indifferent*	
Before Accident	62	35	53	150
After Accident	52	72	26	150

Source: Brown, A., et al. Final Report on a Survey of Three Mile Island Area Residents. Department of Geography, Michigan State University, Aug. 1979.

a. Construct a 99% confidence interval for the difference in the true proportions of Three Mile Island residents who favor nuclear power before and after the accident.

b. Construct a 99% confidence interval for the difference in the true proportions of Three Mile Island residents who oppose nuclear power before and after the accident.

8.53 The *Journal of Fish Biology* (Aug. 1990) reported on a study comparing the prevalence of parasites (tapeworms) found in species of Mediterranean and Atlantic fish. In the Mediterranean Sea, 588 brill were captured and dissected, and 211 were found to be infected by the parasite. In the Atlantic Ocean, 123 brill were captured and dissected, and 26 were found to be infected. Compare the proportions of infected brill at the two capture sites using a 90% confidence interval. Interpret the interval.

8.54 The Egyptian National Scientific and Technical Information Network (ENSTINET) operates an on-line database search service of existing U.S. databases. A database "search" occurs when a specific request is executed by ENSTINET during a single session. In situations when the search produces irrelevant or no output, the search is "rerun." According to *Information Processing & Management* (Vol. 22, No. 3, 1986), ENSTINET performed 342 database searches in 1982, of which 40 were rerun. In 1985, 83 of 2,117 searches required reruns. Assuming that the two samples of database searches are independent and random, construct a 95% confidence interval for the difference between the proportions of database search reruns performed by ENSTINET in 1982 and 1985. Interpret the interval.

8.55 Refer to the marketing research study of consulting engineering services to industrial firms in the Midwest, Exercise 2.49. Forty of the firms surveyed (20 large and 20 small firms) indicated they have no need for outside consulting engineering services (*Journal of the Boston Society of Civil Engineers*, Vol. 71, 1985). The primary reason cited by the "nonneeders" was that they obtained consulting assistance from corporate headquarters whenever necessary. However, twice as many large firms (12) as small firms (6) cited this reason. Establish a 90% confidence interval for the difference in the percentages of large and small industrial firms that cite assistance from corporate headquarters as the primary reason why they have no need for outside consulting engineering services.

8.10   Estimation of a Population Variance

In the previous sections, we considered interval estimates for population means and proportions. In this section, we discuss confidence intervals for a population variance σ^2, and, in Section 8.11, confidence intervals for the ratio of two variances, σ_1^2/σ_2^2. Unlike means and proportions, the pivotal statistics for variances do not possess a normal (z) distribution or a t distribution. In addition, certain assumptions are required regardless of the sample size.

Let $y_1, y_2, \ldots, y_n$ be a random sample from a normal distribution with mean μ and variance σ^2. From Theorem 7.4, we know that

$$\chi^2 = \frac{(n-1)s^2}{\sigma^2}$$

possesses a chi-square distribution with $(n-1)$ degrees of freedom. Confidence intervals for σ^2 are based on the pivotal statistic, χ^2.

Recall that upper-tail areas of the chi-square distribution have been tabulated and are given in Table 8 of Appendix II. Unlike the z and t distributions, the chi-square distribution is not symmetric about 0. To find values of χ^2 that locate an area a in the lower tail of the distribution, we must find χ^2_{1-a}, where $P(\chi^2 > \chi^2_{1-a}) = 1 - a$. For example, the value of χ^2 that places an area $a = .05$ in the lower tail of the distribution when df $= 9$ is $\chi^2_{1-a} = \chi^2_{.95} = 3.32511$ (see Table 8 of Appendix II). We use this fact to write a probability statement for the pivotal statistic χ^2:

$$P(\chi^2_{1-\alpha/2} \le \chi^2 \le \chi^2_{\alpha/2}) = 1 - \alpha$$

where $\chi^2_{\alpha/2}$ and $\chi^2_{(1-\alpha/2)}$ are tabulated values of χ^2 that place a probability of $\alpha/2$ in each tail of the chi-square distribution (see Figure 8.13).

FIGURE 8.13 ▶
The location of $\chi^2_{(1-\alpha/2)}$ and $\chi^2_{\alpha/2}$ for a chi-square distribution

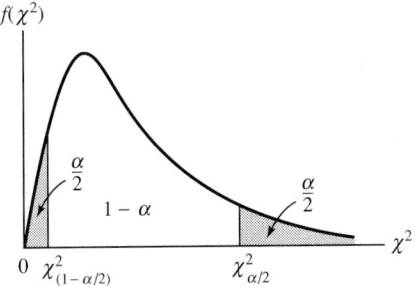

Substituting $[(n-1)s^2]/\sigma^2$ for χ^2 in the probability statement and performing some simple algebraic manipulations, we obtain

$$P\left(\chi^2_{(1-\alpha/2)} \le \frac{(n-1)s^2}{\sigma^2} \le \chi^2_{\alpha/2}\right)$$

$$= P\left(\frac{\chi^2_{(1-\alpha/2)}}{(n-1)s^2} \le \frac{1}{\sigma^2} \le \frac{\chi^2_{\alpha/2}}{(n-1)s^2}\right)$$

$$= P\left(\frac{(n-1)s^2}{\chi^2_{\alpha/2}} \le \sigma^2 \le \frac{(n-1)s^2}{\chi^2_{(1-\alpha/2)}}\right) = 1 - \alpha$$

Thus, a $(1-\alpha)100\%$ confidence interval for σ^2 is

$$\frac{(n-1)s^2}{\chi^2_{\alpha/2}} \le \sigma^2 \le \frac{(n-1)s^2}{\chi^2_{(1-\alpha/2)}}$$

> ### A $(1 - \alpha)100\%$ Confidence Interval for a Population Variance, σ^2
>
> $$\frac{(n - 1)s^2}{\chi^2_{\alpha/2}} \leq \sigma^2 \leq \frac{(n - 1)s^2}{\chi^2_{(1-\alpha/2)}}$$
>
> where $\chi^2_{\alpha/2}$ and $\chi^2_{(1-\alpha/2)}$ are values of χ^2 that locate an area of $\alpha/2$ to the right and $\alpha/2$ to the left, respectively, of a chi-square distribution based on $(n - 1)$ degrees of freedom.
>
> *Assumption:* The population from which the sample is selected has an approximate normal distribution.

Note that the estimation technique applies to either large or small n, and that the assumption of normality is required in either case.

EXAMPLE 8.15

A quality control supervisor in a cannery knows that the exact amount each can contains will vary, since there are certain uncontrollable factors that affect the amount of fill. The mean fill per can is important, but equally important is the variation σ^2 of the amount of fill. If σ^2 is large, some cans will contain too little and others too much. To estimate the variation of fill at the cannery, the supervisor randomly selects 10 cans and weighs the contents of each. The following weights (in ounces) are obtained:

7.96   7.90   7.98   8.01   7.97   7.96   8.03   8.02   8.04   8.02

Constuct a 90% confidence interval for the true variation in fill of cans at the cannery.

Solution

The supervisor wishes to estimate σ^2, the population variance of the amount of fill. A $(1 - \alpha)100\%$ confidence interval for σ^2 is

$$\frac{(n - 1)s^2}{\chi^2_{\alpha/2}} \leq \sigma^2 \leq \frac{(n - 1)s^2}{\chi^2_{(1-\alpha/2)}}$$

For the confidence interval to be valid, we must assume that the sample of observations (amounts of fill) is selected from a normal population.

To compute the interval, we need to calculate either the sample variance s^2 or the sample standard deviation s. Descriptive statistics for the sample data are provided in the SAS printout shown in Figure 8.14. The value of s, shaded in Figure 8.14, is $s = .043$.

Now, $(1 - \alpha) = .90$ and $\alpha/2 = .10/2 = .05$. Therefore, the tabulated values $\chi^2_{.05}$ and $\chi^2_{.95}$ for $(n - 1) = 9$ df (obtained from Table 8, Appendix II) are

$$\chi^2_{.05} = 16.9190 \quad \text{and} \quad \chi^2_{.95} = 3.32511$$

FIGURE 8.14 ▶
SAS descriptive statistics for Example 8.15

```
Variable=FILL

                    Moments

N                   10   Sum Wgts          10
Mean             7.989   Sum            79.89
Std Dev       0.043063   Variance    0.001854
Skewness       -0.8538   Kurtosis    0.479371
USS           638.2579   CSS          0.01669
CV            0.539032   Std Mean    0.013618
T:Mean=0      586.6587   Prob>|T|      0.0001
Sgn Rank          27.5   Prob>|S|      0.0020
Num ^= 0            10

                Quantiles(Def=5)

    100% Max        8.04      99%       8.04
     75% Q3         8.02      95%       8.04
     50% Med       7.995      90%      8.035
     25% Q1         7.96      10%       7.93
      0% Min         7.9       5%        7.9
                               1%        7.9

    Range          0.14
    Q3-Q1          0.06
    Mode           7.96
```

Substituting these values into the formula, we obtain

$$\frac{(10 - 1)(.043)^2}{16.9190} \le \sigma^2 \le \frac{(10 - 1)(.043)^2}{3.32511}$$

$$.00098 \le \sigma^2 \le .00500$$

We are 90% confident that the true variance in amount of fill of cans at the cannery falls between .00098 and .00500. The quality control supervisor could use this interval to check whether the variation of fill at the cannery is too large and in violation of government regulatory specifications.

EXAMPLE 8.16

Refer to Example 8.15. Find a 90% confidence interval for σ, the true standard deviation of the can weights.

Solution

A confidence interval for σ is obtained by taking the square roots of the lower and upper endpoints of a confidence interval for σ^2. Thus, the 90% confidence interval is

$$\sqrt{.00098} \le \sigma \le \sqrt{.00500}$$

$$.031 \le \sigma \le .071$$

We are 90% confident that the true standard deviation of can weights is between .031 and .071 ounce.

EXERCISES

8.56   For each of the following combinations of a and degrees of freedom (df), find the value of chi-square, χ_a^2, that places an area a in the upper tail of the chi-square distribution:
a. $a = .05$,   df $= 7$ b. $a = .10$,   df $= 16$ c. $a = .01$,   df $= 10$
d. $a = .025$,   df $= 8$ e. $a = .005$,   df $= 5$

8.57   *Jitter* is a term used to describe the variation in conduction time of a modular pulsed-water power system. Low throughput jitter is critical to successful waterline technology. An investigation of throughput jitter in the plasma opening switch of a prototype system (*Journal of Applied Physics*, Sept. 1993) yielded the following descriptive statistics on conduction time for $n = 18$ trials:

$\bar{y} = 334.8$ nanoseconds $s = 6.3$ nanoseconds

(Conduction time is defined as the length of time required for the downstream current to equal 10% of the upstream current.)
a. Construct a 95% confidence interval for the true standard deviation of conduction times of the prototype system.
b. A system is considered to have low throughput jitter if the true conduction time standard deviation is less than 7 nanoseconds. Does the prototype system satisfy this requirement? Explain.

8.58   Refer to the *IEEE Transactions* (June 1990) study of a new hybrid algorithm for solving polynomial 0–1 mathematical programs, Exercise 8.31. A SAS printout giving descriptive statistics for the sample of 52 solution times is reproduced here. Use this information to compute an approximate 95% confidence interval for the variance of the solution times. Interpret the result.

Analysis Variable : CPU				
N Obs	N	Mean	Variance	Std Dev
52	52	0.8121923	2.2643035	1.5047603

8.59   An interlaboratory study was conducted to determine the variation in the measured level of polychlorinated biphenyls (PCBs) in environmentally contaminated sediments (*Analytical Chemistry*, Nov. 1985). Samples of sediment from New Bedford Harbor (Massachusetts) known to be contaminated with PCBs were collected and aliquot solutions prepared. For one part of the study, the PCB concentration in each of a random sample of five aliquots was determined by a single laboratory using the Webb–McCall procedure. The analysis yielded a mean PCB concentration of 56 mg/kg and a standard deviation of .45 mg/kg. Find a 90% confidence interval for the variance in the PCB levels of contaminated sediment, determined using the Webb–McCall procedure.

8.60 An experiment was conducted to investigate the precision of measurements of a saturated solution of iodine after an extended period of continuous stirring. The data shown in the table represent $n = 10$ iodine concentration measurements on the same solution. The population variance σ^2 measures the variability— i.e., the precision—of a measurement. Use the information in the accompanying MINITAB printout to find a 95% confidence interval for σ^2. Interpret the result.

Run	Concentration	Run	Concentration
1	5.507	6	5.527
2	5.506	7	5.504
3	5.500	8	5.490
4	5.497	9	5.500
5	5.506	10	5.497

	N	MEAN	MEDIAN	TRMEAN	STDEV	SEMEAN
conctrat	10	5.5034	5.5020	5.5021	0.0098	0.0031

	MIN	MAX	Q1	Q3
conctrat	5.4900	5.5270	5.4970	5.5062

8.61 Geologists analyze fluid inclusions in rock to infer the compositions of fluids present when the rocks crystallized. A new technique, called laser Raman microprobe (LRM) spectroscopy, has been developed for this purpose. An experiment was conducted to estimate the precision of the LRM technique (*Applied Spectroscopy*, Feb. 1986). A chip of natural Brazilian quartz with several artificially produced fluid inclusions was subjected to LRM spectroscopy. The amount of liquid carbon dioxide (CO_2) present in the inclusion was recorded for the same inclusion on four different days. The data (in mole percentage) follow:

86.6   84.6   85.5   85.9

a. Obtain an estimate of the precision of the LRM technique by constructing a 99% confidence interval for the variation in the CO_2 concentration measurements.
b. What assumption is required for the interval estimate to be valid?

8.11 Estimation of the Ratio of Two Population Variances

The common statistical procedure for comparing two population variances, σ_1^2 and σ_2^2, makes an inference about the ratio σ_1^2/σ_2^2. This is because the sampling distribution of the estimator of σ_1^2/σ_2^2 is well known when the samples are randomly and independently selected from two normal populations. Under these assumptions, a confidence interval for σ_1^2/σ_2^2 is based on the pivotal statistic

$$F = \frac{\chi_1^2/\nu_1}{\chi_2^2/\nu_2}$$

where χ_1^2 and χ_2^2 are chi-square random variables with $\nu_1 = (n_1 - 1)$ and $\nu_2 = (n_2 - 1)$ degrees of freedom, respectively. Substituting $(n - 1)s^2/\sigma^2$ for χ^2 (see

Theorem 7.4), we may write

$$F = \frac{\chi_1^2/\nu_1}{\chi_2^2/\nu_2} = \frac{\dfrac{(n_1-1)s_1^2}{\sigma_1^2} \Big/ (n_1-1)}{\dfrac{(n_2-1)s_2^2}{\sigma_2^2} \Big/ (n_2-1)}$$

$$= \frac{s_1^2/\sigma_1^2}{s_2^2/\sigma_2^2}$$

$$= \left(\frac{s_1^2}{s_2^2}\right)\left(\frac{\sigma_2^2}{\sigma_1^2}\right)$$

From Definition 7.2 we know that F has an F distribution with $\nu_1 = (n_1 - 1)$ numerator degrees of freedom and $\nu_2 = (n_2 - 1)$ denominator degrees of freedom. An F distribution can be symmetric about its mean, skewed to the left, or skewed to the right; its exact shape depends on the degrees of freedom associated with s_1^2 and s_2^2, i.e., $(n_1 - 1)$ and $(n_2 - 1)$.

To establish lower and upper confidence limits for σ_1^2/σ_2^2, we need to be able to find tabulated F values corresponding to the tail areas of the distribution. The *upper-tail* F values can be found in Tables 9, 10, 11, and 12 of Appendix II for $a = .10$, .05, .025, and .01, respectively. Table 10 of Appendix II is partially reproduced in Table 8.8. The columns of Tables 9–12 of Appendix II correspond to various degrees of freedom for the numerator sample variance, s_1^2, in the pivotal statistic, whearas the rows correspond to the degrees of freedom for the denominator sample variance, s_2^2. For example, with numerator degrees of freedom $\nu_1 = 7$ and denominator degrees of freedom $\nu_2 = 9$, we have $F_{.05} = 3.29$ (shaded in Table 8.8). Thus, $a = .05$ is the tail area to the right of 3.29 in the F distribution with 7 numerator df and 9 denominator df, i.e., $P(F > F_{.05}) = .05$.

Lower-tail values of the F distribution are not given in Tables 9–12 of Appendix II. However, it can be shown (proof omitted) that

$$F_{1-a(\nu_1,\nu_2)} = \frac{1}{F_{a(\nu_2,\nu_1)}}$$

where $F_{1-a(\nu_1,\nu_2)}$ is the F value that cuts off an area a in the *lower* tail of an F distribution based on ν_1 numerator and ν_2 denominator degrees of freedom, and $F_{a(\nu_2,\nu_1)}$ is the F value that cuts off an area a in the *upper* tail of an F distribution based on ν_2 numerator and ν_1 denominator degrees of freedom. For example, suppose we want to find the value that locates an area $a = .05$ in the *lower* tail of an F distribution with $\nu_1 = 7$ and $\nu_2 = 9$. That is, we want to find $F_{1-a(\nu_1,\nu_2)} = F_{.95(7,9)}$. First, we find the upper-tail values, $F_{.05(9,7)} = 3.68$, from Table 8.8. (Note that we must switch the numerator and denominator degrees of freedom to obtain this value.) Then, we calculate

$$F_{.95(7,9)} = \frac{1}{F_{.05(9,7)}} = \frac{1}{3.68} = .272$$

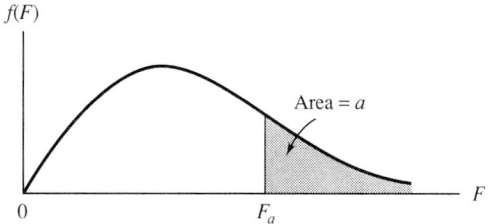

TABLE 8.8   Abbreviated Version of Table 10 of Appendix II: Tabulated Values of the F Distribution, $\alpha = .05$

ν_2	ν_1 Numerator Degrees of Freedom								
	1	**2**	**3**	**4**	**5**	**6**	**7**	**8**	**9**
1	161.4	199.5	215.7	224.6	230.2	234.0	236.8	238.9	240.5
2	18.51	19.00	19.16	19.25	19.30	19.33	19.35	19.37	19.38
3	10.13	9.55	9.28	9.12	9.01	8.94	8.89	8.85	8.81
4	7.71	6.94	6.59	6.39	6.26	6.16	6.09	6.04	6.00
5	6.61	5.79	5.41	5.19	5.05	4.95	4.88	4.82	4.77
6	5.99	5.14	4.76	4.53	4.39	4.28	4.21	4.15	4.10
7	5.59	4.74	4.35	4.12	3.97	3.87	3.79	3.73	3.68
8	5.32	4.46	4.07	3.84	3.69	3.58	3.50	3.44	3.39
9	5.12	4.26	3.86	3.63	3.48	3.37	3.29	3.23	3.18
10	4.96	4.10	3.71	3.48	3.33	3.22	3.14	3.07	3.02
11	4.84	3.98	3.59	3.36	3.20	3.09	3.01	2.95	2.90
12	4.75	3.89	3.49	3.26	3.11	3.00	2.91	2.85	2.80
13	4.67	3.81	3.41	3.18	3.03	2.92	2.83	2.77	2.71
14	4.60	3.74	3.34	3.11	2.96	2.85	2.76	2.70	2.65

(Denominator Degrees of Freedom)

Using the notation established previously, we can write a probability statement for the pivotal statistic F (see Figure 8.15):

$$P(F_{1-\alpha/2(\nu_1, \nu_2)} \leq F \leq F_{\alpha/2(\nu_1, \nu_2)}) = 1 - \alpha$$

FIGURE 8.15 ▶
F distribution with $\nu_1 = (n_1 - 1)$ and $\nu_2 = (n_2 - 1)$

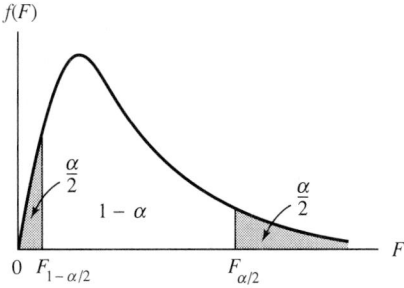

Letting $F_L = F_{1-\alpha/2}$ and $F_U = F_{\alpha/2}$, and substituting $(s_1^2/s_2^2)(\sigma_2^2/\sigma_1^2)$ for F, we obtain:

$$P(F_L \le F \le F_U) = P\left[F_L \le \left(\frac{s_1^2}{s_2^2}\right)\left(\frac{\sigma_2^2}{\sigma_1^2}\right) \le F_U\right]$$

$$= P\left(\frac{s_2^2}{s_1^2}F_L \le \frac{\sigma_2^2}{\sigma_1^2} \le \frac{s_2^2}{s_1^2}F_U\right)$$

$$= P\left(\frac{s_1^2}{s_2^2} \cdot \frac{1}{F_U} \le \frac{\sigma_1^2}{\sigma_2^2} \le \frac{s_1^2}{s_2^2} \cdot \frac{1}{F_L}\right) = 1 - \alpha$$

or

$$P\left(\frac{s_1^2}{s_2^2} \cdot \frac{1}{F_{\alpha/2(\nu_1, \nu_2)}} \le \frac{\sigma_1^2}{\sigma_2^2} \le \frac{s_1^2}{s_2^2} \cdot \frac{1}{F_{1-\alpha/2(\nu_1, \nu_2)}}\right) = 1 - \alpha$$

Replacing $F_{1-\alpha/2(\nu_1, \nu_2)}$ with $1/F_{\alpha/2(\nu_2, \nu_1)}$, we obtain the final form of the confidence interval:

$$P\left(\frac{s_1^2}{s_2^2} \cdot \frac{1}{F_{\alpha/2(\nu_1, \nu_2)}} \le \frac{\sigma_1^2}{\sigma_2^2} \le \frac{s_1^2}{s_2^2} \cdot F_{\alpha/2(\nu_2, \nu_1)}\right) = 1 - \alpha$$

A $(1 - \alpha)100\%$ Confidence Interval for the Ratio of Two Population Variances, σ_1^2/σ_2^2

$$\frac{s_1^2}{s_2^2} \cdot \frac{1}{F_{\alpha/2(\nu_1, \nu_2)}} \le \frac{\sigma_1^2}{\sigma_2^2} \le \frac{s_1^2}{s_2^2}F_{\alpha/2(\nu_2, \nu_1)}$$

where $F_{\alpha/2(\nu_1, \nu_2)}$ is the value of F that locates an area $\alpha/2$ in the upper tail of the F distribution with $\nu_1 = (n_1 - 1)$ numerator and $\nu_2 = (n_2 - 1)$ denominator degrees of freedom, and $F_{\alpha/2(\nu_2, \nu_1)}$ is the value of F that locates an area $\alpha/2$ in the upper tail of the F distribution with $\nu_2 = (n_2 - 1)$ numerator and $\nu_1 = (n_1 - 1)$ denominator degrees of freedom.

Assumptions: 1. Both of the populations from which the samples are selected have relative frequency distributions that are approximately normal.

2. The random samples are selected in an independent manner from the two populations.

As in the one-sample case, normal populations must be assumed regardless of the sizes of the two samples.

EXAMPLE 8.17   A firm has been experimenting with two different physical arrangements of its assembly line. It has been determined that both arrangements yield approximately the same average number of finished units per day. To obtain an arrangement that produces

TABLE 8.9 Summary Statistics for Example 8.17

Assembly Line 1	Assembly Line 2
$n_1 = 21$ days	$n_2 = 25$ days
$s_1^2 = 1,432$	$s_2^2 = 3,761$

greater process control, you suggest that the arrangement with the smaller variance in the number of finished units produced per day be permanently adopted. Two independent random samples yield the results shown in Table 8.9. Construct a 95% confidence interval for σ_1^2/σ_2^2, the ratio of the variances of the number of finished units for the two assembly line arrangements. Based on the result, which of the two arrangements would you recommend?

Solution

First, we must assume that the distributions of the numbers of finished units for the two assembly lines are both approximately normal. Since we want a 95% confidence interval, the value of $\alpha/2$ is .025, and we need to find $F_{.025(\nu_1, \nu_2)}$ and $F_{.025(\nu_2, \nu_1)}$. The sample sizes are $n_1 = 21$ and $n_2 = 25$; thus, $F_{.025(\nu_1, \nu_2)}$ is based on $\nu_1 = (n_1 - 1) = 20$ numerator df and $\nu_2 = (n_2 - 1) = 24$ denominator df. Consulting Table 11 of Appendix II, we obtain $F_{.025(20,24)} = 2.33$. In contrast, $F_{.025(\nu_2, \nu_1)}$ is based on $\nu_2 = (n_2 - 1) = 24$ numerator df and $\nu_1 = (n_1 - 1) = 20$ denominator df; hence (from Table 11 of Appendix II), $F_{.025(24,20)} = 2.41$. Substituting the values for s_1^2, s_2^2, $F_{.025(\nu_1, \nu_2)}$ and $F_{.025(\nu_2, \nu_1)}$ into the confidence interval formula, we have

$$\frac{1,432}{3,761}\left(\frac{1}{2.33}\right) \le \frac{\sigma_1^2}{\sigma_2^2} \le \frac{1,432}{3,761}(2.41)$$

$$.163 \le \frac{\sigma_1^2}{\sigma_2^2} \le .918$$

We estimate with 95% confidence that the ratio σ_1^2/σ_2^2 of the true population variances will fall between .163 and .918. Since all the values within the interval (.163,.918) are less than 1.0, we can be confident that the variance in the number of units finished on line 1 (as measured by σ_1^2) is less than the corresponding variance for line 2 (as measured by σ_2^2).

EXERCISES

8.62 Find F_a for an F distribution with 15 numerator df and 12 denominator df for the following values of a:
    a. $a = .025$ **b.** $a = .05$ **c.** $a = .10$

8.63 Find $F_{.05}$ for an F distribution with:
    a. Numerator df = 7,   denominator df = 25   **b.** Numerator df = 10,   denominator df = 8
    c. Numerator df = 30,   denominator df = 60   **d.** Numerator df = 15,   denominator df = 4

8.64 In *Environmental Science & Technology* (Oct. 1993), scientists reported on a study of the transport and transformation of PCDD, a pollutant emitted from solid waste incineration, motor vehicles, steel mills, and metal production. Ambient air specimens were collected over several different days at two locations in Swden: Rörvik (11 days) and Gothenburg (3 days). The level of PCDD (measured in pg/m^3) detected in each specimen is recorded here. Use interval estimation to compare the variation in PCDD levels at the two locations. Draw an inference from the analysis.

Rörvik				Gothenburg		
2.38	3.03	1.44	.47	.50	.61	.90
.50	.22	.26	.31			
.46	1.09	2.14				

Source: Tysklind, M., et al. "Atmospheric transport and transformation of poly-chlorinated dibenzo-p-dioxins and dibenzofurans." *Environmental Science & Technology*, Vol. 27, No. 10, Oct. 1993, p. 2193 (Table III).

8.65   Refer to the *Journal of Structural Engineering* (Feb. 1986) experiment with epoxy-repaired truss joints, Exercise 8.35. The data are reproduced here for convenience. Construct a 90% confidence interval for the ratio of the shear stress variances of epoxy-repaired truss joints for the two species of wood. Based on this interval, is there evidence to indicate that the two shear stress variances differ? Explain.

	Southern Pine	Ponderosa Pine
Sample Size	100	47
Mean Shear Stress, psi	1,312	1,352
Standard Deviation	422	271

Source: Avent, R. R. "Design criteria for epoxy repair of timber structures." *Journal of Structural Engineering*, Vol. 112, No. 2, Feb. 1986, pp. 232.

8.66   Refer to the strength and capacity guidelines for manual materials handling activities, Exercise 2.52. The guidelines were established by observing the maximum weight that random samples of men and women can safely lift from the floor to knuckle height (*Human Factors*, June 1980). When lifting at the rate of 1 lift per minute, males lifted a mean maximum weight of 30.25 kilograms (kg) with a standard deviation of 8.56 kg, whereas the mean and standard deviation for females was 19.79 kg and 3.11 kg, respectively.
   a. Assuming the sample consisted of 60 males and 60 females, construct a 90% confidence interval for the ratio of the variances of the maximum weights that can safely be lifted by males and females.
   b. What assumptions must be satisfied to ensure the validity of the interval estimate of part **a**?

8.67   Refer to the cancer death rate increases for fluoridated and nonfluoridated cities given in Exercise 8.36. The data are reproduced here for convenience. Find a 95% confidence interval for the ratio of the variances of the cancer death rate increases for the two groups of cities. Based on the interval, does it appear that the assumption of equal variances required to conduct the analysis of Exercise 8.36 is satisfied?

City	Fluoridated Annual Increase in Cancer Death Rate	City	Nonfluoridated Annual Increase in Cancer Death Rate
Chicago	1.0640	Los Angeles	.8875
Philadelphia	1.4118	Boston	1.7358
Baltimore	2.1115	New Orleans	1.0165
Cleveland	1.9401	Seattle	.4923
Washington	3.8772	Cincinnati	4.0155
Milwaukee	−.4561	Atlanta	−1.1744
St. Louis	4.8359	Kansas City	2.8132
San Francisco	1.8875	Columbus	1.7451
Pittsburgh	4.4964	Newark	−.5676
Buffalo	1.4045	Portland	2.4471

Source: Maritz, J. S., and Jarrett, R. G. "The use of statistics to examine the association between fluoride in drinking water and cancer death rates." *Applied Statistics*, Vol. 32, No. 2, 1983, pp. 97–101.

8.68 Refer to the PCB study described in Exercise 8.59. Recall that level of PCB was measured in each of a sample of five aliquots using the Webb–McCall procedure. Another sample of five aliquots of sediment was measured for PCBs using a diffferent procedure, called the Aroclor Standard comparison. Summary statistics on PCB concentration for the two samples are given in the table.

	Webb–McCall	Aroclor Standard
Sample Size	5	5
Mean PCB Concentration, mg/kg	56	60
Standard Deviation	.45	.89

Source: Alford-Stevens, A. L., Budde, W. L., and Bellar, T. A. "Interlaboratory study on determination of polychlorinated biphenyls in environmentally contaminated sediments." *Analytical Chemistry*, Vol. 57, No. 13, Nov. 1985, p. 2454. Reprinted with permission from *Analytical Chemistry*. Copyright 1985 American Chemical Society.

a. Construct a 90% confidence interval for the ratio of the variances in the PCB levels measured by the two techniques.
b. What assumptions are required for the interval estimate to be valid?

8.12 Choosing the Sample Size

One of the first problems encountered when applying statistics in a practical situation is to decide on the number of measurements to include in the sample(s). The solution to this problem depends on the answers to the following questions: Approximately how wide do you want your confidence interval to be? What confidence coefficient do you require?

You have probably noticed that the half-widths of many of the confidence intervals presented in Sections 8.5–8.11 are functions of the sample size and the estimated standard error of the point estimator involved. For example, the half-width H of the small-sample confidence interval for μ is

$$H = t_{\alpha/2}\left(\frac{s}{\sqrt{n}}\right)$$

where $t_{\alpha/2}$ depends on the sample size n, and s is a statistic computed from the sample data. Since we will not know s before selecting the sample and we have no control over its value, the easiest way to decrease the width of the confidence interval is to increase the sample size n. Generally speaking, the larger the sample size, the more information you will acquire and the smaller will be the width of the confidence interval. We illustrate the procedure for selecting the sample size in Examples 8.18 and 8.19.

EXAMPLE 8.18

As part of a Department of Energy (DOE) survey, American families will be randomly selected and questioned about the amount of money they spent last year on home heating oil or gas. Of particular interest to the DOE is the average amount μ spent last year on heating fuel. If the DOE wants the estimate of μ to be correct to within $10 with a confidence coefficient of .95, how many families should be included in the sample?

Solution

The DOE wants to obtain an interval estimate of μ, with confidence coefficient equal to $(1 - \alpha) = .95$ and half-width of the interval equal to 10. The half-width of a large-sample confidence interval for μ is

$$H = z_{\alpha/2}\sigma_{\bar{y}} = z_{\alpha/2}\left(\frac{\sigma}{\sqrt{n}}\right)$$

In this example, we have $H = 10$ and $z_{\alpha/2} = z_{.025} = 1.96$. To solve the equation for n, we need to know σ. But, as will usually be the case in practice, σ is unknown. Suppose, however, that the DOE knows from past records that the yearly amounts spent on heating fuel have a range of approximately $520. Then we could approximate σ by letting the range equal 4σ.* Thus,

$$4\sigma \approx 520 \quad \text{or} \quad \sigma \approx 130$$

Solving for n, we have

$$H = z_{\alpha/2}\left(\frac{\sigma}{\sqrt{n}}\right) \quad \text{or} \quad 10 = 1.96\left(\frac{130}{\sqrt{n}}\right)$$

---

*From the Empirical Rule, we expect about 95% of the observations to fall between $\mu - 2\sigma$ and $\mu + 2\sigma$. Thus,

$$\text{Range} \approx (\mu + 2\sigma) - (\mu - 2\sigma) = 4\sigma$$

or

$$n = \frac{(1.96)^2(130)^2}{(10)^2} \approx 650$$

Consequently, the DOE will need to elicit responses from 650 American families to estimate the mean amount spent on home heating fuel last year to within $10 with 95% confidence. Since this would require an extensive and costly survey, the DOE might decide to allow a larger half-width (say, $H = 15$ or $H = 20$) to reduce the sample size, or the DOE might decrease the desired confidence coefficient. The important point is that the experimenter can obtain an idea of the sampling effort necessary to achieve a specified precision in the final estimate by determining the approximate sample size *before* the experiment is begun.

EXAMPLE 8.19

A production supervisor suspects a difference exists between the proportions p_1 and p_2 of defective items produced by two different machines. Experience has shown that the proportion defective for each of the two machines is in the neighborhood of .03. If the supervisor wants to estimate the difference in the proportions correct to within .005 with probability .95, how many items must be randomly sampled from the production of each machine? (Assume that you want $n_1 = n_2 = n$.)

Solution

Since we want to estimate $(p_1 - p_2)$ with a 95% confidence interval, we will use $z_{\alpha/2} = z_{.025} = 1.96$. For the estimate to be correct to within .005, the half-width of the confidence interval must equal .005. Then, letting $p_1 = p_2 = .03$ and $n_1 = n_2 = n$, we find the required sample size per machine by solving the following equation for n:

$$H = z_{\alpha/2}\sigma_{(\hat{p}_1 - \hat{p}_2)} \quad \text{or} \quad H = z_{\alpha/2}\sqrt{\frac{p_1 q_1}{n_1} + \frac{p_2 q_2}{n_2}}$$

$$.005 = 1.96\sqrt{\frac{(.03)(.97)}{n} + \frac{(.03)(.97)}{n}}$$

$$.005 = 1.96\sqrt{\frac{2(.03)(.97)}{n}}$$

$$n = \frac{(1.96)^2(2)(.03)(.97)}{(.005)^2} \approx 8,944$$

You can see that this may be a tedious sampling procedure. If the supervisor insists on estimating $(p_1 - p_2)$ correct to within .005 with probability equal to .95, approximately 9,000 items will have to be inspected for each machine.

You can see from the calculations in Example 8.19 that $\sigma_{(\hat{p}_1 - \hat{p}_2)}$ (and hence the solution, $n_1 = n_2 = n$) depends on the actual (but unknown) values of p_1 and p_2. In fact, the required sample size $n_1 = n_2 = n$ is largest when $p_1 = p_2 = .5$. Therefore, if you have no prior information on the approximate values of p_1 and p_2, use $p_1 = p_2 = .5$ in the formula for $\sigma_{(\hat{p}_1 - \hat{p}_2)}$. If p_1 and p_2 are in fact close to $.5$, then the resulting values of n_1 and n_2 will be correct. If p_1 and p_2 differ substantially from $.5$, then your solutions for n_1 and n_2 will be larger than needed. Consequently, using $p_1 = p_2 = .5$ when solving for n_1 and n_2 is a conservative procedure because the sample sizes n_1 and n_2 will be at least as large as (and probably larger than) needed.

The formulas for calculating the sample size(s) required for estimating the parameters μ, $(\mu_1 - \mu_2)$, p, and $(p_1 - p_2)$ are summarized in the following boxes. Sample size calculations for variances require more sophisticated techniques and are beyond the scope of this text.

Choosing the Sample Size for Estimating a Population Mean μ to Within H Units with Probability $(1 - \alpha)$

$$n = \left(\frac{z_{\alpha/2}\sigma}{H}\right)^2$$

[*Note:* The population standard deviation σ will usually have to be approximated.]

Choosing the Sample Sizes for Estimating the Difference $(\mu_1 - \mu_2)$ Between a Pair of Population Means Correct to Within H Units with Probability $(1 - \alpha)$

$$n_1 = n_2 = \left(\frac{z_{\alpha/2}}{H}\right)^2 (\sigma_1^2 + \sigma_2^2)$$

where n_1 and n_2 are the numbers of observations sampled from each of the two populations, and σ_1^2 and σ_2^2 are the variances of the two populations.

Choosing the Sample Size for Estimating a Population Proportion p to Within H Units with Probability $(1 - \alpha)$

$$n = \left(\frac{z_{\alpha/2}}{H}\right)^2 pq$$

where p is the value of the population proportion that you are attempting to estimate and $q = 1 - p$.

[*Note:* This technique requires previous estimates of p and q. If none are available, use $p = q = .5$ for a conservative choice of n.]

> **Choosing the Sample Sizes for Estimating the Difference ($p_1 - p_2$) Between Two Population Proportions to Within H Units with Probability ($1 - \alpha$)**
>
> $$n_1 = n_2 = \left(\frac{z_{\alpha/2}}{H}\right)^2 (p_1 q_1 + p_2 q_2)$$
>
> where p_1 and p_2 are the proportions for populations 1 and 2, respectively, and n_1 and n_2 are the numbers of observations to be sampled from each population.

EXERCISES

8.69 *Cost Engineering* (Oct. 1988) reports on a study of the percentage difference between the low bid and the engineer's estimate of the cost for building contracts (see Exercise 7.19). For contracts with four bidders, the mean percentage error is $\mu = -7.02$ and the standard deviation is $\sigma = 24.66$. Suppose you want to estimate the mean percentage error for building contracts with five bidders. How many five-bidder contracts must be sampled to estimate with 90% confidence the mean to witihin 5 percentage points of its true value? Assume that the standard deviation for five-bidder contracts is approximately equal to the standard deviation for four-bidder contracts.

8.70 Refer to the *Human Factors* study on the use of color brightness as a body orientation cue, Exercise 8.49. How many subjects are required for a similar experiment to estimate the true proportion who use a bright color level as a cue to being right-side up to within .05 with 95% confidence? Use the sample proportion calculated in Exercise 8.49 as an estimate of p.

8.71 The federal government requires states to certify that they are enforcing the 55-miles-per-hour speed limit and that motorists are driving at that speed. A state is in jeopardy of losing millions of dollars in federal road funds if more than 60% of its vehicles on 55-miles-per-hour highways are exceeding the speed limit. The state highway patrol conducts 70 radar surveys each year at a total of 50 sites to estimate the proportion p of vehicles exceeding 55 miles per hour. Each sample survey involves at least 400 vehicles.
   a. How large a sample should be selected at a particular site to estimate p to within 3% with 90% confidence? Last year approximately 60% of all vehicles exceeded 55 miles per hour.
   b. The highway patrol also estimates μ, the average speed of vehicles on state highways. Accordingly, it wants to know whether the sample size determined in part **a** is large enough to also estimate μ to within .25 mile per hour with 90% confidence. Assume that the standard deviation of vehicle speeds is approximately 2 miles per hour. How large a sample should be taken at a particular site to estimate μ with the desired reliability?

8.72 A consumer protection agency wants to compare the work of two electrical contractors to evaluate their safety records. The agency plans to inspect residences in which each of these contractors has done the wiring to estimate the difference in the proportions of residences that are electrically deficient. Suppose the proportions of deficient work are expected to be about .10 for both contractors. How many homes should be inspected to estimate the difference in proportions to within .05 with 90% confidence?

8.73 A large steel corporation conducted an experiment to compare the average iron contents of two consignments of lumpy iron ore. In accordance with industrial standards, n increments of iron ore were randomly selected from each consignment and measured for iron content. From previous experiments, it is known that iron contents vary over a range of roughly 3%. How large should n be if the steel company wants to estimate the difference in mean iron contents of the two consignments correct to within .05% with 95% confidence? [*Hint:* To obtain an approximate value for σ_1 and σ_2, set $\sigma_1 = \sigma_2 = \sigma$ and set Range $= 4\sigma$. Then $3 \approx 4\sigma$ and $\sigma \approx \frac{3}{4}$.]

8.74 *Materials requirements planning (MRP) systems* are computerized planning and control systems for manufacturing operations. Since their introduction in the mid-1960s, MRP systems have been used to manage raw materials and work-in-process inventories while improving customer service. Suppose you want to estimate the proportion p of manufacturing firms that use MRP systems. Approximately how large a sample would be required to estimate p to within .02 with a confidence coefficient of .95? (Use a conservative estimate of $p \approx .5$ in your calculations.)

OPTIONAL EXERCISE

8.75 When determining the sample size required to estimate p, show that the sample size n is largest when $p = .5$.

8.13   Summary

Estimation is a procedure for inferring the value(s) of one (or more) population parameters. An **estimator**, a rule that tells how to calculate a particular **estimate** of a parameter based on information contained in a sample, can be one of two types. A **point estimator** uses the sample data to calculate a single number that serves as an estimate of a population parameter. An **interval estimator** uses the sample data to calculate two numbers that define an interval that is intended to enclose the estimated parameter with some predetermined probability.

Point and interval estimators can be acquired intuitively; it seems reasonable to use sample statistics to estimate the corresponding population parameters (the **method of moments**). In addition, point estimators can be acquired using the **method of maximum likelihood** (Section 8.3) or the **method of least squares** (Chapter 11); interval estimators can be constructed using **pivotal statistics** and the procedure illustrated in Section 8.4. In general, we prefer point estimators that are **unbiased** and possess **minimum variance**, i.e., **minimum variance unbiased estimators** (MVUE). For a given **confidence coefficient**, we prefer interval estimators with a mean interval width that is small and subject to a small amount of variation.

We presented a number of point and interval estimators and demonstrated how they can be applied in practical situations. (These results are summarized in Tables 8.10a and 8.10b.) By reviewing the examples, you can see that estimation as a method of inference attempts to answer the question, "What is the value of the parameter θ?" We will approach inference-making from a different point of view in Chapter 9.

TABLE 8.10a Summary of Estimation Procedures: One-Sample Case

Parameter θ	Estimator $\hat{\theta}$	$E(\hat{\theta})$	$\sigma_{\hat{\theta}}$	Approximation to $\sigma_{\hat{\theta}}$	$(1-\alpha)100\%$ Confidence Interval	Sample Size	Additional Assumptions
Mean μ	$\bar{y}$	μ	$\dfrac{\sigma}{\sqrt{n}}$	$\dfrac{s}{\sqrt{n}}$	$\bar{y} \pm z_{\alpha/2}\left(\dfrac{s}{\sqrt{n}}\right)$	$n \geq 30$	None
					$\bar{y} \pm t_{\alpha/2}\left(\dfrac{s}{\sqrt{n}}\right)$ where $t_{\alpha/2}$ is based on $(n-1)$ df	$n < 30$	Normal population
Binomial proportion p	$\hat{p} = \dfrac{y}{n}$	p	$\sqrt{\dfrac{pq}{n}}$	$\sqrt{\dfrac{\hat{p}\hat{q}}{n}}$	$\hat{p} \pm z_{\alpha/2}\sqrt{\dfrac{\hat{p}\hat{q}}{n}}$	n large enough so that the interval $\hat{p} \pm 2\sqrt{\dfrac{\hat{p}\hat{q}}{n}}$ does not contain 0 or 1	None
Variance σ^2	s^2	σ^2	Not needed	Not needed	$\dfrac{(n-1)s^2}{\chi_{\alpha/2}^2} \leq \sigma^2 \leq \dfrac{(n-1)s^2}{\chi_{(1-\alpha/2)}^2}$ where $\chi_{\alpha/2}^2$ and $\chi_{(1-\alpha/2)}^2$ are the tabulated values of χ^2, given in Table 8 of Appendix II, that locate $\alpha/2$ in each tail of the chi-square distribution with $(n-1)$ df, i.e., $P(\chi^2 \geq \chi_{\alpha/2}^2) = \alpha/2$ and $P(\chi^2 \geq \chi_{(1-\alpha/2)}^2) = 1 - \alpha/2$	All n	Normal population

TABLE 8.10b   Summary of Estimation Procedures: Two-Sample Case

Parameter θ	Estimator $\hat{\theta}$	$E(\hat{\theta})$	$\sigma_{\hat{\theta}}$	Approximation to $\sigma_{\hat{\theta}}$	$(1-\alpha)100\%$ Confidence Interval	Sample Sizes	Additional Assumptions
$(\mu_1 - \mu_2)$ Difference between population means: Independent samples	$(\bar{y}_1 - \bar{y}_2)$ Difference between sample means	$(\mu_1 - \mu_2)$	$\sqrt{\dfrac{\sigma_1^2}{n_1} + \dfrac{\sigma_2^2}{n_2}}$ $\sqrt{\sigma^2\left(\dfrac{1}{n_1} + \dfrac{1}{n_2}\right)}$	$\sqrt{\dfrac{s_1^2}{n_1} + \dfrac{s_2^2}{n_2}}$ $\sqrt{s_p^2\left(\dfrac{1}{n_1} + \dfrac{1}{n_2}\right)}$ where $s_p^2 = \dfrac{(n_1 - 1)s_1^2 + (n_2 - 1)s_2^2}{n_1 + n_2 - 2}$	$(\bar{y}_1 - \bar{y}_2) \pm z_{\alpha/2}\sqrt{\dfrac{s_1^2}{n_1} + \dfrac{s_2^2}{n_2}}$ $(\bar{y}_1 - \bar{y}_2) \pm t_{\alpha/2}\sqrt{s_p^2\left(\dfrac{1}{n_1} + \dfrac{1}{n_2}\right)}$ where $t_{\alpha/2}$ is based on $(n_1 + n_2 - 2)$ df	$n_1 \geq 30,\ n_2 \geq 30$ Either $n_1 < 30$ or $n_2 < 30$, or both	None Both populations normal with equal variances $(\sigma_1^2 = \sigma_2^2)$
$\mu_d = (\mu_1 - \mu_2)$ Difference between population means: Matched pairs	$\bar{d} = \Sigma d_i/n$ Mean of sample differences	μ_d	$\dfrac{\sigma_d}{\sqrt{n_d}}$	$\dfrac{s_d}{\sqrt{n_d}}$ where s_d is the standard deviation of the sample of differences	$\bar{d} \pm z_{\alpha/2}\left(\dfrac{s_d}{\sqrt{n_d}}\right)$ $\bar{d} \pm t_{\alpha/2}\left(\dfrac{s_d}{\sqrt{n_d}}\right)$ where $t_{\alpha/2}$ is based on $(n_d - 1)$ df	$n_d \geq 30$ $n_d < 30$	None Population of differences d_i is normal
$(p_1 - p_2)$ Difference between two binomial parameters	$(\hat{p}_1 - \hat{p}_2)$ Difference between the sample proportions $\hat{p}_1 = y_1/n_1$ and $\hat{p}_2 = y_2/n_2$	$(p_1 - p_2)$	$\sqrt{\dfrac{p_1 q_1}{n_1} + \dfrac{p_2 q_2}{n_2}}$	$\sqrt{\dfrac{\hat{p}_1\hat{q}_1}{n_1} + \dfrac{\hat{p}_2\hat{q}_2}{n_2}}$	$(\hat{p}_1 - \hat{p}_2) \pm z_{\alpha/2}\sqrt{\dfrac{\hat{p}_1\hat{q}_1}{n_1} + \dfrac{\hat{p}_2\hat{q}_2}{n_2}}$	n_1 and n_2 large enough so that the intervals $\hat{p}_1 \pm 2\sqrt{\dfrac{\hat{p}_1\hat{q}_1}{n_1}}$ and $\hat{p}_2 \pm 2\sqrt{\dfrac{\hat{p}_2\hat{q}_2}{n_2}}$ do not contain 0 or 1	Independent samples
σ_1^2/σ_2^2 Ratio of population variances	s_1^2/s_2^2 Ratio of sample variances	Not needed	Not needed	Not needed	$\left(\dfrac{s_1^2}{s_2^2}\right)\dfrac{1}{F_{\alpha/2(\nu_1,\nu_2)}} \leq \dfrac{\sigma_1^2}{\sigma_2^2} \leq \left(\dfrac{s_1^2}{s_2^2}\right)F_{\alpha/2(\nu_2,\nu_1)}$ where $F_{\alpha/2(\nu_1,\nu_2)}$ and $F_{\alpha/2(\nu_2,\nu_1)}$ are the tabulated values of F (Tables 9, 10, 11, and 12 of Appendix II) that place an area equal to $\alpha/2$ in the upper tail of the F distribution, where $F_{\alpha/2(\nu_1,\nu_2)}$ is based on $\nu_1 = (n_1 - 1)$ numerator degrees of freedom, and $F_{\alpha/2(\nu_2,\nu_1)}$ is based on $\nu_2 = (n_2 - 1)$ numerator and $\nu_1 = (n_1 - 1)$ denominator degrees of freedom	All n_1 and n_2	Independent samples from two normal populations

SUPPLEMENTARY EXERCISES

8.76 What do college recruiters think are the most important topics to be covered in a job interview? To answer this and other questions, Taylor and Sniezek elicited the opinions of recruiters interviewing at a small midwestern college and a large midwestern university (*Journal of Occupational Psychology*, 1984). Recruiters were asked to rate on a 105-point scale the importance of each in a list of 25 interview topics [where $0 =$ least important (can sometimes be omitted without hurting the interview), $52.5 =$ average importance (can sometimes be omitted without hurting the interview), and $105 =$ most important (can never be omitted without hurting the interview)]. The topic concerning "applicant's skill in communicating ideas to others" received the highest ratings of the $n = 58$ college recruiters who returned the questionnaire. The sample mean rating and sample standard deviation for this topic were $\bar{y} = 84.84$ and $s = 15.67$, respectively.

a. Give a point estimate for the true mean rating of the importance of "applicant's skill in communicating ideas to others" by all college recruiters.

b. Use the sample information to construct a 95% confidence interval for the true mean rating.

c. What is the confidence coefficient for the interval of part b? Interpret this value.

8.77 When new instruments are developed to perform chemical analyses of products (food, medicine, etc.), they are usually evaluated with respect to two criteria: accuracy and precision. *Accuracy* refers to the ability of the instrument to identify correctly the nature and amounts of a product's components. *Precision* refers to the consistency with which the instrument will identify the components of the same material. Thus, a large variability in the identification of a single sample of a product indicates a lack of precision. Suppose a pharmaceutical firm is considering two brands of an instrument designed to identify the components of certain drugs. As part of a comparison of precision, ten test-tube samples of a well-mixed batch of a drug are selected and then five are analyzed by instrument A and five by instrument B. The data shown in the table are the percentages of the primary component of the drug given by the instruments. A SAS printout giving descriptive statistics follows.

Instrument A	43	48	37	52	45
Instrument B	46	49	43	41	48

```
Analysis Variable : READING

------------------------- INSTRMNT=A -------------------------

N Obs    N      Minimum         Maximum            Mean         Std Dev
--------------------------------------------------------------------
  5      5    37.0000000      52.0000000      45.0000000      5.6124861
--------------------------------------------------------------------


------------------------- INSTRMNT=B -------------------------

N Obs    N      Minimum         Maximum            Mean         Std Dev
--------------------------------------------------------------------
  5      5    41.0000000      49.0000000      45.4000000      3.3615473
--------------------------------------------------------------------
```

a. Construct a 90% confidence interval to compare the precision of the two instruments.

b. Based on the interval estimate of part **a**, what would you infer about the precision of the two instruments?

c. What assumptions must be satisfied to ensure the validity of any inferences derived from the estimate?

8.78 A regional computer center wants to evaluate the performance of its disk memory system. One measure of performance is the average time between failures of a disk drive. Since the computer center operates two disk drives, it wants to compare the mean times between failures of the two disk drives. Independent random samples of $n_1 = 10$ and $n_2 = 15$ failures produced the following statistics:

Disk Drive 1	Disk Drive 2
$\bar{y}_1 = 92$ hours	$\bar{y}_2 = 108$ hours
$s_1 = 16$ hours	$s_2 = 12$ hours

Which of the two disk drives appears to give better performance?

8.79 According to a report by the U.S. surgeon general, electrical engineers have the lowest smoking rate among all workers surveyed (*IEEE Spectrum*, Apr. 1986). Only 16% of the male electrical engineers in the sample smoke cigarettes regularly. How many male electrical engineers must be sampled to estimate the proportion of all male electrical engineers who smoke regularly to within 3% of its true value with 95% confidence?

8.80 The pesticide Temik is used for controlling insects that feed on potatoes, oranges, and other crops. According to federal standards, drinking water wells with levels of Temik above 1 part per billion are considered contaminated. The accompanying table lists the results of tests for Temik contamination conducted in five states over the past few years. For each state, construct a 95% confidence interval for the true proportion of wells contaminated with Temik. Interpret the results.

State	Number of Wells Tested	Number of Contaminated Wells
New York	10,500	2,750
Wisconsin	700	105
Maine	124	82
Florida	825	4
Virginia	76	17

Source: *Orlando Sentinel*, July 4, 1983.

8.81 A machine used to fill beer cans must operate so that the amount of beer actually dispensed varies very little. If too much beer is released, the cans will overflow, causing waste. If too little beer is released, the cans will not contain enough beer, causing complaints from customers. A random sample of the fills for 20 cans yielded a standard deviation of .07 ounce. Estimate the true variance of the fills using a 95% confidence interval.

8.82 Refer to the LRM spectroscopy experiment described in Exercise 8.61. The amount of liquid CO_2 present in each of two different fluid inclusions (named FREO and FRITZ) was measured on each of four randomly selected days. The data are reproduced in the table. Use interval estimation to compare the mean difference between the CO_2 concentrations (in mole percentage) of the two fluid inclusions.

Day	Inclusion FREO	Inclusion FRITZ
1	86.6	83.8
2	84.6	85.3
3	85.5	84.6
4	85.9	83.4

Source: Wopenka, B., and Pasteris, J. D. "Limitations to quantitative analysis of fluid inclusions in geological samples by laser Raman microprobe spectroscopy." *Applied Spectroscopy*, Vol. 40, No. 2, Feb. 1986, p. 149.

8.83 Some power plants are located near rivers or oceans so that the available water can be used for cooling the condensers. As part of an environmental impact study, suppose a power company wants to estimate the difference in mean water temperature between the discharge of its plant and the offshore waters. How many sample measurements must be taken at each site to estimate the true difference between means to within .2°C with 95% confidence? Assume the range in readings will be about 4°C at each site and the same number of readings will be taken at each site.

8.84 A study was conducted to compare the attitudes of American and Soviet teenagers on nuclear war (*New England Journal of Medicine*, Aug. 18, 1988). A team of American and Soviet researchers surveyed 3,370 public school students in Maryland and 2,148 students in central Russia. One question asked whether the students believe a nuclear war will occur in their lifetime. Forty-two percent of the Maryland students and 9% of the Russian students responded affirmatively.

a. Calculate a 99% confidence interval for the difference between the proportions of Maryland and Russian students who believe that a nuclear war will occur in their lifetime. Interpret the interval.

b. How could the width of the interval of part **a** be reduced?

c. Although Maryland students were recruited randomly for the study, there is speculation that the Soviet students were selected much more carefully. How could the nonrandom Soviet sample bias the results obtained in part **a**?

8.85 Two alloys, A and B, are used in the manufacture of steel bars. Suppose a steel producer wants to compare the two alloys on the basis of average load capacity, where the load capacity of a steel bar is defined as the maximum load (weight in tons) it can support without breaking. Steel bars containing alloy A and steel bars containing alloy B were randomly selected and tested for load capacity. The results are summarized in the accompanying table.

Alloy A	Alloy B
$n_1 = 11$	$n_2 = 17$
$\bar{y}_1 = 43.7$	$\bar{y}_2 = 48.5$
$s_1^2 = 24.4$	$s_2^2 = 19.9$

a. Find a 99% confidence interval for the difference between the true average load capacities for the two alloys.

b. For the interval of part **a** to be valid, what assumptions must be satisfied?

c. Interpret the interval of part **a**. Can you conclude that the average load capacities for the two alloys are different?

d. How many steel bars of each type should be sampled to estimate the true difference in average load capacities to within 2 tons with 99% confidence? (Assume $n_1 = n_2 = n$.)

OPTIONAL SUPPLEMENTARY EXERCISES

8.86   Let $\bar{y}_1$ be the mean of a random sample of n_1 observations from a Poisson distribution with mean λ_1, and let $\bar{y}_2$ be the mean of a random sample of n_2 observations from a Poisson distribution with mean λ_2. Assume the samples are independent.
   a. Show that $(\bar{y}_1 - \bar{y}_2)$ is an unbiased estimator of $(\lambda_1 - \lambda_2)$.
   b. Find $V(\bar{y}_1 - \bar{y}_2)$. How could you estimate this variance?
   c. Construct a large-sample $(1 - \alpha)100\%$ confidence interval for $(\lambda_1 - \lambda_2)$. [*Hint:*   Consider

$$z = \frac{(\bar{y}_1 - \bar{y}_2) - (\lambda_1 - \lambda_2)}{\sqrt{\dfrac{\bar{y}_1}{n_1} + \dfrac{\bar{y}_2}{n_2}}}$$

   as a pivotal statistic.]

8.87   Let $y_1, y_2, \ldots, y_n$ denote a random sample from a uniform distribution with probability density

$$f(y) = \begin{cases} 1 & \text{if } \theta \le y \le \theta + 1 \\ 0 & \text{elsewhere} \end{cases}$$

   a. Show that $\bar{y}$ is a biased estimator of θ, and compute the bias.
   b. Find $V(\bar{y})$.
   c. What function of $\bar{y}$ is an unbiased estimator of θ?

8.88   Suppose y is a random sample of size $n = 1$ from a normal distribution with mean 0 and unknown variance σ^2.
   a. Show that y^2/σ^2 has a chi-square distribution with 1 degree of freedom. [*Hint:*   The result follows directly from Theorem 7.4.]
   b. Derive a 95% confidence interval for σ^2 using y^2/σ^2 as a pivotal statistic.

8.89   Suppose y is a random sample of size $n = 1$ from a gamma distribution with parameters $\alpha = 1$ and arbitrary β.
   a. Show that $2y/\beta$ has a gamma distribution with parameters $\alpha = 1$ and $\beta = 2$. [*Hint:*   Use the distribution function approach of Section 7.2.]
   b. Use the result of part **a** to show that $2y/\beta$ has a chi-square distribution with 2 degrees of freedom. [*Hint:*   The result follows directly from Section 5.7.]
   c. Derive a 95% confidence interval for β using $2y/\beta$ as a pivotal statistic.

8.90   Suppose y is a single observation from a normal distribution with mean μ and variance 1. Use y to find a 95% confidence interval for μ. [*Hint:*   Start with the pivotal statistic $z = (y - \mu)$. Since z is a standard normal random variable,

$$P(-z_{.025} \le y - \mu \le z_{.025}) = .95$$

   Follow the method of Example 8.6.]

8.91   A confidence interval for θ is said to be *unbiased* if the expected value of the interval midpoint is equal to θ.

a. Show that the small-sample confidence interval for μ,

$$\bar{y} - t_{\alpha/2}\left(\frac{s}{\sqrt{n}}\right) \leq \mu \leq \bar{y} + t_{\alpha/2}\left(\frac{s}{\sqrt{n}}\right)$$

is unbiased.

b. Show that the confidence interval for σ^2,

$$\frac{(n-1)s^2}{\chi^2_{\alpha/2}} \leq \sigma^2 \leq \frac{(n-1)s^2}{\chi^2_{(1-\alpha/2)}}$$

is biased.

8.92 Suppose y is a single observation from a uniform distribution defined on the interval from 0 to θ. Find a 95% confidence limit LCL for θ such that $P(LCL < \theta < \infty) = .95$. [*Hint:* Start with the pivotal statistic y/θ and show (using the method of Chapter 7) that y/θ is uniformly distributed on the interval from 0 to 1. Then observe that

$$P\left(0 < \frac{y}{\theta} < .95\right) = \int_0^{.95} (1)dy = .95$$

and proceed to obtain LCL.]

COMPUTER LAB: Confidence Intervals for Means

Most commercial statistical software packages (e.g., SAS) do not have modules for computing confidence intervals for the parameters discussed in this chapter. Those that do (e.g., MINITAB) are limited in scope. For example, MINITAB will produce confidence intervals for means but not for variances or proportions. The MINITAB programs presented here give the confidence interval commands for estimating the parameters μ, $\mu_1 - \mu_2$, and μ_d. The outputs of the programs are shown in Figures 8.16–8.18, on pages 418–419, respectively.

MINITAB

a. Confidence Interval for μ—Data from Example 8.9

Command
line

1	SET SILICON PPM IN C1	Data entry instruction
2	229 255 280 203 229	Input data (5 observations per line)
3	NAME C1 = 'PPM'	
4	TINTERVAL 99 C1	99% confidence interval

COMMAND 4 The TINTERVAL command produces a confidence interval for the mean of the data stored in C1. The confidence interval (in this case, 99%) is specified following TINTERVAL. (The default is a 95% confidence interval.)

NOTE When σ is unknown, as is usually the case, TINTERVAL uses the appropriate value from the t distribution to calculate the interval regardless of the size of the sample. For large samples, recall that $t_{\alpha/2} \approx z_{\alpha/2}$.

FIGURE 8.16 ▶
Output for MINITAB program a.

	N	MEAN	STDEV	SE MEAN	99.0 PERCENT C.I.
ppm	4	241.8	33.2	16.6	(144.8, 338.7)

b. Confidence Interval for $\mu_1 - \mu_2$, Independent Samples—Data from Example 8.11

Command
line

```
1    READ THREE IN C1, SEVEN IN C2    Data entry command
2    1189 853 ⎫
3     840 900 ⎪  Input data values
4    1020 733 ⎬  (1 observation per line)
5     980 785 ⎭
6    NAME C1 = '3%ASPH' C2 = '7%ASPH'
7    TWOSAMPLE 95 C1 C2; ⎫
8    POOLED.             ⎭  95% confidence interval
```

COMMAND 7   TWOSAMPLE produces a confidence interval on the difference between the mean of the data in C1 and the mean of the data in C2. By default, a 95% confidence interval is computed. To change the confidence level, specify 99, 90, etc., following the TWOSAMPLE command.

COMMAND 8   The POOLED subcommand instructs MINITAB to use s_p^2 in the calculation of a small-sample confidence interval. Omit the POOLED subcommand if you want MINITAB to compute a large sample confidence interval for $\mu_1 - \mu_2$.

NOTE   TWOSAMPLE uses the appropriate value from the t distribution to compute the confidence interval regardless of the sample size. For large samples, recall that $t_{\alpha/2} \approx z_{\alpha/2}$.

FIGURE 8.17 ▶
Output for MINITAB program b.

```
TWOSAMPLE T FOR 3%asph VS 7%asph
             N      MEAN     STDEV    SE MEAN
3%asph   4      1007      144       72
7%asph   4      817.8     73.6      37

95 PCT CI FOR MU 3%asph - MU 7%asph: (-8, 387)

TTEST MU 3%asph = MU 7%asph (VS NE): T= 2.35  P=0.057  DF=  6

POOLED STDEV =        114
```

c. Confidence Interval for $\mu_d = (\mu_1 - \mu_2)$, Paired Samples—Data from Example 8.12

Command
line

```
1    READ PLANT DATA IN C1, STATION DATA IN C2    Data entry instruction
2    2.0 2.2 ⎫
·       ·   ⎪
·       ·   ⎬  input data (1 observation per line)
·       ·   ⎪
13   2.1 2.0 ⎭
14   SUBTRACT C2 FROM C1, PUT IN C3
15   NAME C3 = "DIFF"
16   TINTERVAL 95 C3    95% confidence interval
```

COMMAND 14 Use the SUBTRACT command to calculate the differences for the paired observations in C1 and C2.

COMMAND 16 Use the TINTERVAL command to compute a 95% confidence interval for the mean of the differences in C3.

FIGURE 8.18 ▶
Output for MINITAB program c.

	N	MEAN	STDEV	SE MEAN	95.0 PERCENT C.I.
diff	12	-0.0083	0.1676	0.0484	(-0.1149, 0.0982)

References

Devore, J. *Probability and Statistics for Engineering and the Sciences*, 2nd ed. Monterey, California: Brooks/Cole, 1987.

Freedman, D., Pisani, R., and Purves, R. *Statistics*. New York: W. W. Norton and Co., 1978.

Hoel, P. G. *Introduction to Mathematical Statistics*, 4th ed. New York: Wiley, 1971.

Hogg, R. V., and Craig, A. T. *Introduction to Mathematical Statistics*, 4th ed. New York: Macmillan, 1978.

Mendenhall, W. *Introduction to Probability and Statistics*, 8th ed. Boston: Duxbury, 1990.

Mendenhall, W., Wackerly, D. D., and Scheaffer, R. L. *Mathematical Statistics with Applications*, 3rd ed. Boston: Duxbury, 1989.

Mood, A. M., Graybill, F. A., and Boes, D. *Introduction to the Theory of Statistics*, 3rd ed. New York: McGraw-Hill, 1974.

Mosteller, F., and Tukey, J. W. *Data Analysis and Regression*. Reading, Massachusetts: Addison-Wesley, 1977. Chapters 8 and 10.

Snedecor, G. W., and Cochran, W. G. *Statistical Methods*, 7th ed. Ames, Iowa: Iowa State University Press, 1980.

Tukey, J. W. "Bias and Confidence in Not-Quite Large Samples." *Annals of Mathematical Statistics*, Vol. 29, 1958, p. 614.

CHAPTER NINE

Tests of Hypotheses

Objective

To introduce the basic concepts of a statistical test of a hypothesis; to present statistical tests for several common population parameters and to illustrate their use in practical sampling situations

Contents

9.1   The Relationship Between Statistical Tests of Hypotheses and Confidence Intervals

As stated in Chapter 8, there are two general methods available for making inferences about population parameters. We can estimate their values using confidence intervals (the subject of Chapter 8) or we can make decisions about them. Making decisions about specific values of the population parameters—**testing hypotheses** about these values—is the topic of this chapter.

Confidence intervals and hypothesis tests are related and can be used to make decisions about parameters. For example, suppose an investigator for the Environmental Protection Agency (EPA) wants to determine whether the mean level μ of a certain type of pollutant released into the atmosphere by a chemical company meets the EPA guidelines. If 3 parts per million is the upper limit allowed by the EPA, the investigator would want to use sample data (daily pollution measurements) to decide whether the company is violating the law, i.e., to decide whether $\mu > 3$. If, say, a 99% confidence interval for μ contained only numbers greater than 3, then the EPA would be confident that the mean exceeds the established limit.

As a second example, consider a manufacturer that purchases terminal fuses in lots of 10,000, and suppose that the supplier of the fuses guarantees that no more than 1% of the fuses in any given lot are defective. Since the manufacturer cannot test each of the 10,000 fuses in a lot, he must decide whether to accept or reject a lot based on an examination of a sample of fuses selected from the lot. If the number y of defective fuses in a sample of, say, $n = 100$, is large, he will reject the lot and send it back to the supplier. Thus, he wants to decide whether the proportion p of defectives in the lot exceeds .01, based on information contained in a sample. If a confidence interval for p falls below .01, then the manufacturer will accept the lot and be confident that the proportion of defectives is less than 1%; otherwise, he will reject it.

The examples in the preceding paragraphs illustrate how a confidence interval can be used to make a decision about a parameter. Note that both applications are one-directional; the EPA wants to determine whether $\mu > 3$ and the manufacturer wants to know if $p > .01$. (In contrast, if the manufacturer is interested in determining whether $p > .01$ or $p < .01$, the inference would be two-directional.)

Recall, from Chapter 8, that to find the value of z (or t) used in a $(1 - \alpha)100\%$ confidence interval, the value of α is divided in half and $\alpha/2$ is placed in both the upper and lower tails of the z (or t) distribution. Consequently, confidence intervals are designed to be two-directional. Use of a two-directional technique in a situation where a one-directional method is desired will lead the researcher (e.g., the EPA or the manufacturer) to understate the level of confidence associated with the method. As we will explain in this chapter, hypothesis tests are appropriate for either one- or two-directional decisions about a population parameter.

9.2   Elements of a Statistical Test

We now return to the EPA example to introduce the concepts involved in a test of a hypothesis. We will use a method analogous to proof by contradiction. The theory the EPA wants to support, called the **alternative** (or **research**) **hypothesis**, is that $\mu > 3$, where μ is the true mean level of pollution in parts per million. The alternative hypothesis is denoted by the symbol H_a. The theory contradictory to the alternative hypothesis, that μ is at most equal to 3, say, $\mu = 3$, is called the **null hypothesis** and is denoted by the symbol H_0. Thus, the EPA hopes to show support for the alternative hypothesis, $\mu > 3$, by obtaining sample evidence indicating that the null hypothesis, $\mu = 3$, is false. That is, the EPA wants to test

$$H_0: \quad \mu = 3$$
$$H_a: \quad \mu > 3$$

The decision whether to reject the null hypothesis is based on a statistic, called a **test statistic**, computed from sample data. For example, suppose the EPA plans to base its decision on a sample of $n = 30$ daily pollution readings. If the sample mean $\bar{y}$ of the 30 pollution measurements is much larger than 3, the EPA would tend to reject the null hypothesis and conclude that $\mu > 3$. However, if $\bar{y}$ is smaller than 3, say, $\bar{y} = 2.8$ parts per million, there is insufficient evidence to refute the null hypothesis. Thus, the sample mean $\bar{y}$ serves as a test statistic.

The values that the test statistic $\bar{y}$ can assume will be divided into two sets. Those larger than some specified value, say, $\bar{y} \geq 3.1$, will imply rejection of the null hypothesis and acceptance of the alternative hypothesis. This set of values of the test statistic is known as the **rejection region** for the test. A test of the null hypothesis, $H_0: \mu = 3$, against the alternative hypothesis, $H_a: \mu > 3$, employing the sample mean $\bar{y}$ as a test statistic and $\bar{y} \geq 3.1$ as a rejection region, represents one particular test that possesses specific properties. If we change the rejection region to $\bar{y} \geq 3.2$, we obtain a different test with different properties.

The preceding discussion indicates that a statistical test consists of the four elements summarized in the box.

Elements of a Statistical Test

1. **Null hypothesis**, H_0, about one or more population parameters
2. **Alternative hypothesis**, H_a, that we will accept if we decide to reject the null hypothesis
3. **Test statistic**, computed from sample data
4. **Rejection region**, indicating the values of the test statistic that will imply rejection of the null hypothesis

In Section 9.3, we will show how to evaluate the reliability of a statistical test, how to compare one test with another, and how to evaluate the reliability of a particular test decision. We will apply the results to several practical examples.

9.3   Evaluating the Properties of a Statistical Test

Since a statistical test can result in one of only two outcomes—rejecting or not rejecting the null hypothesis—the test conclusion is subject to only two types of error. To illustrate, consider the EPA example of Section 9.2. Recall that the investigator wants to test H_0: $\mu = 3$ against H_a: $\mu > 3$, where μ = mean level of pollutant released into the atmosphere by a chemical company. If the investigator concludes that H_a is true (i.e., if he rejects H_0), then the EPA will charge the company with violating its pollution standards. The two errors that the EPA can make are shown in Table 9.1.

TABLE 9.1   Conclusions and Consequences for the EPA's Test of Hypothesis

	True State of Nature	
EPA Decision	Company Not in Violation (H_0 true)	Company in Violation (H_a true)
Company in Violation (Reject H_0)	Type I error	Correct decision
Company Not in Violation (Accept H_0)	Correct decision	Type II error

The EPA might reject the null hypothesis if, in fact, it is true. That is, the EPA might charge the company with violating its standards, when, in fact, the company is innocent (Type I error). Or the EPA might decide to accept the null hypothesis if, in fact, it is false. That is, the EPA may conclude that the company is not in violation of the pollution standards when, in fact, the company is in violation (Type II error). The probabilities of making these two types of errors measure the risks of making incorrect decisions when we perform a test of hypothesis and, consequently, provide measures of the goodness of this inferential decision-making procedure.

Definition 9.1

Rejecting the null hypothesis if it is true is a **Type I error**. The probability of making a Type I error is denoted by the symbol α.

> ### Definition 9.2
>
> Accepting the null hypothesis if it is false is a **Type II error**. The probability of making a Type II error is denoted by the symbol β.

Which of the two errors, Type I or Type II, is more serious? From the EPA's perspective, the Type I error is the more serious error. If the EPA falsely accuses the company of violating the pollution limits, a costly lawsuit will likely occur. On the other hand, the residents who live near the chemical company would probably view the Type II error as more serious; if this error occurs, the EPA is failing to charge the company when it is, in fact, polluting the surrounding air. In either case, it is important to compute the probabilities, α and β, to assess the reliability of inferences derived from the hypothesis test. The next four examples illustrate how to compute these probabilities.

EXAMPLE 9.1

A manufacturer of minicomputers believes that it can sell a particular software package to more than 20% of the buyers of its computers. Ten prospective purchasers of the computer were randomly selected and questioned about their interest in the software package. Of these, four indicated that they planned to buy the package. Does this sample provide sufficient evidence to indicate that more than 20% of the computer purchasers will buy the software package?

Solution

Let p be the true proportion of all prospective computer buyers who will purchase the software package. Since we want to show that $p > .2$, we choose $H_a: p > .2$ for the alternative hypothesis and $H_0: p = .2$ for the null hypothesis. We will use the binomial random variable y, the number of prospective purchasers in the sample who plan to buy the software, as the test statistic and will reject $H_0: p = .2$ if y is large. A graph of $p(y)$ for $n = 10$ and $p = .2$ is shown in Figure 9.1.

FIGURE 9.1 ▶
Graph of $p(y)$ for $n = 10$ and $p = .2$, i.e., if the null hypothesis is true

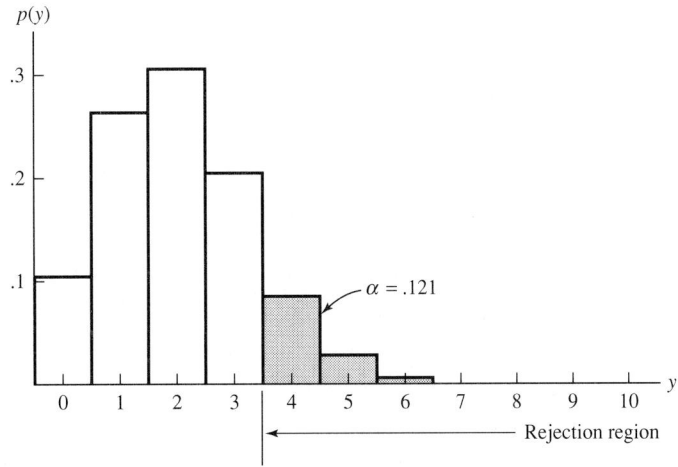

Large values of y will support the alternative hypothesis, $H_a: p > .2$, but what values of y should we include in the rejection region? Suppose that we select values of $y \geq 4$ as the rejection region. Then the elements of the test are:

H_0: $p = .2$

H_a: $p > .2$

Test statistic: y

Rejection region: $y \geq 4$

To conduct the test, we note that the observed value of y, $y = 4$, falls in the rejection region. Thus, for this test procedure, we reject the null hypothesis, $H_0: p = .2$, and conclude that the manufacturer is correct, i.e., $p > .2$.

EXAMPLE 9.2

What is the probability that the statistical test procedure of Example 9.1 would lead us to an incorrect decision if, in fact, the null hypothesis is true?

Solution

We will calculate the probability α that the test procedure would lead us to make a Type I error, i.e., to reject H_0 if, in fact, H_0 is true. This is the probability that y falls in the rejection region if in fact $p = .2$:

$$\alpha = P(y \geq 4 \text{ if in fact } p = .2) = 1 - \sum_{y=0}^{3} p(y)$$

The partial sum $\sum_{y=0}^{3} p(y)$ for a binomial random variable with $n = 10$ and $p = .2$ is given in Table 1 of Appendix II as .879. Therefore,

$$\alpha = 1 - \sum_{y=0}^{3} p(y) = 1 - .879 = .121$$

The probability that the test procedure would lead us to conclude that $p > .2$, if in fact it is not, is .121. This probability corresponds to the area of the shaded region in Figure 9.1.

In Example 9.1, we computed the probability α of committing a Type I error. *The probability β of making a Type II error, i.e., failing to detect a value of p greater than .2, depends on the value of p.* For example, if $p = .20001$, it will be very difficult to detect this small deviation from the null hypothesized value of $p = .2$. In contrast, if $p = 1.0$, then *every* prospective purchaser of the minicomputer will want to buy the software package, and in such a case it will be very evident from the sample information that $p > .2$. We will illustrate the procedure for calculating β in Example 9.3.

EXAMPLE 9.3

Refer to Example 9.2 and suppose that p is actually equal to .60. What is the probability β that the test procedure will fail to reject $H_0: p = .2$ if, in fact, $p = .6$?

Solution

The binomial probability distribution $p(y)$ for $n = 10$ and $p = .6$ is shown in Figure 9.2. The probability that we will fail to reject H_0 is equal to the probability that $y = 0, 1, 2,$ or 3, i.e., the probability that y does not fall in the rejection region. This probability, β, corresponds to the shaded area under the probability histogram in the figure. Therefore,

$$\beta = P(y \le 3 \text{ if in fact } p = .6) = \sum_{y=0}^{3} p(y) \quad \text{for } n = 10 \text{ and } p = .6$$

FIGURE 9.2 ▶

Graph of $p(y)$ for $n = 10$ and $p = .6$, i.e., if the alternative hypothesis is true

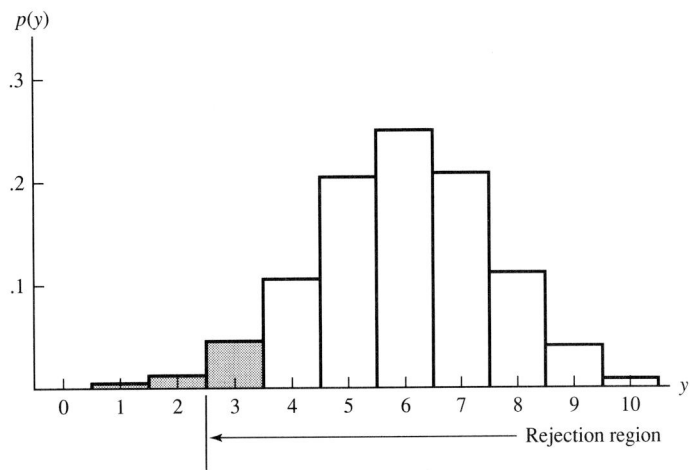

This partial sum, given in Table 1 of Appendix II for a binomial random variable with $n = 10$ and $p = .6$, is .055. Therefore, the probability that we will fail to reject $H_0: p = .2$ if p is as large as .6 is $\beta = .055$.

Another important property of a statistical test is its ability to detect departures from the null hypothesis when they exist. This is measured by the probability of rejecting H_0 when, in fact, H_0 is false. Note that this probability is simply $(1 - \beta)$:

$$P(\text{Reject } H_0 \text{ when } H_0 \text{ is false}) = 1 - P(\text{Accept } H_0 \text{ when } H_0 \text{ is false})$$
$$= 1 - P(\text{Type II error})$$
$$= 1 - \beta$$

The probability $(1 - \beta)$ is called the **power of the test**. The higher the power, the greater the probability of detecting departures from H_0 when they exist.

Definition 9.3

The **power** of a statistical test, $(1 - \beta)$, is the probability of rejecting the null hypothesis H_0 when, in fact, H_0 is false.

EXAMPLE 9.4

Refer to the test of hypothesis in Example 9.1. Find the power of the test if in fact $p = .3$.

Solution

From Definition 9.3, the power of the test is the probability $(1 - \beta)$. The probability of making a Type II error, i.e., failing to reject H_0: $p = .2$, if in fact $p = .3$, will be larger than the value of β calculated in Example 9.3 because $p = .3$ is much closer to the hypothesized value of $p = .2$. Thus,

$$\beta = P(y \leq 3 \text{ if in fact } p = .3) = \sum_{y=0}^{3} p(y) \quad \text{for } n = 10 \text{ and } p = .3$$

The value of this partial sum, given in Table 1 of Appendix II for a binomial random variable with $n = 10$ and $p = .3$, is .650. Therefore, the probability that we will fail to reject H_0: $p = .2$ if in fact $p = .3$ is $\beta = .650$ and the power of the test is $(1 - \beta) = (1 - .650) = .350$. You can see that the closer the actual value of p is to the hypothesized null value, the more unlikely it is that we will reject H_0: $p = .2$.

The preceding examples indicate how we can calculate α and β for a simple statistical test and thereby measure the risks of making Type I and Type II errors. These probabilities describe the properties of this inferential decision-making procedure and enable us to compare one test with another. For two tests, each with a rejection region selected so that α is equal to some specified value, say, .10, we would select the test that, for a specified alternative, has the smaller risk of making a Type II error, i.e., one that has the smaller value of β. This is equivalent to choosing the test with the higher power.

We will present a number of statistical tests in the following sections. In each case, the probability α of making a Type I error is known, i.e., α is selected by the experimenter and the rejection region is determined accordingly. In contrast, the value of β for a specific alternative is often difficult to calculate. This explains why we attempt to show that H_a is true by showing that the data do not support H_0. We hope that the sample evidence will support the alternative (or research) hypothesis. If it does, we will be concerned only about making a Type I error, i.e., rejecting H_0 if it is true. The probability α of committing such an error will be known.

EXERCISES

9.1   Define α and β for a statistical test of hypothesis.

9.2   Explain why each of the following statements is incorrect:
   a. The probability that the null hypothesis is correct is equal to α.
   b. If the null hypothesis is rejected, then the test proves that the alternative hypothesis is correct.
   c. In all statistical tests of hypothesis, $\alpha + \beta = 1$.

9.3 Pharmaceutical companies are continually searching for new drugs. Testing the thousands of compounds for the few that might be effective is known in the pharmaceutical industry as *drug screening*. Dunnett (1978) views the drug-screening procedure in its preliminary stage in terms of a statistical decision problem: "In drug screening, two actions are possible: (1) to 'reject' the drug, meaning to conclude that the tested drug has little or no effect, in which case it will be set aside and a new drug selected for screening; and (2) to 'accept' the drug provisionally, in which case it will be subjected to further, more refined experimentation."* Since it is the goal of the researcher to find a drug that effects a cure, the null and alternative hypotheses in a statistical test would take the following form:

H_0: Drug is ineffective in treating a particular disease

H_a: Drug is effective in treating a particular disease

Dunnett comments on the possible errors associated with the drug-screening procedure: "To abandon a drug when in fact it is a useful one (a *false negative*) is clearly undesirable, yet there is always some risk in that. On the other hand, to go ahead with further, more expensive testing of a drug that is in fact useless (a *false positive*) wastes time and money that could have been spent on testing other compounds."

a. A false negative corresponds to which type of error, Type I or Type II?

b. A false positive corresponds to which type of error, Type I or Type II?

c. Which of the two errors is more serious? Explain.

9.4 Pascal is a high-level programming language used frequently in minicomputers and microprocessors. An experiment was conducted to investigate the proportion of Pascal variables that are *array* variables (in contrast to *scalar* variables, which are less efficient in terms of execution time). Twenty variables are randomly selected from a set of Pascal programs and y, the number of array variables, is recorded. Suppose we want to test the hypothesis that Pascal is a more efficient language than Algol, in which 20% of the variables are array variables. That is, we will test H_0: $p = .20$ against H_a: $p > .20$, where p is the probability of observing an array variable on each trial. (Assume that the 20 trials are independent.)

a. Find α for the rejection region $y \geq 8$.

b. Find α for the rejection region $y \geq 5$.

c. Find β for the rejection region $y \geq 8$ if $p = .5$. [*Note:* Past experience has shown that approximately half the variables in most Pascal programs are array variables.]

d. Find β for the rejection region $y \geq 5$ if $p = .5$.

e. Which of the rejection regions, $y \geq 8$ or $y \geq 5$, is more desirable if you want to minimize the probability of a Type I error? Type II error?

f. Find the rejection region of the form $y \geq a$ so that α is approximately equal to .01.

g. For the rejection region determined in part **f**, find the power of the test, if in fact $p = .4$.

h. For the rejection region determined in part **f**, find the power of the test, if in fact $p = .7$.

9.5 A manufacturer of power meters, which are used to regulate energy thresholds of a data-communications system, claims that when its production process is operating correctly, only 10% of the power meters will be defective. A vendor has just received a shipment of 25 power meters from the manufacturer. Suppose the vendor wants to test H_0: $p = .10$ against H_a: $p > .10$, where p is the true proportion of power meters that are defective. Use $y \geq 6$ as the rejection region.

a. Determine the value of α for this test procedure.

---

*From Tanur, J. M., et al., eds. *Statistics: A Guide to the Unknown*. San Francisco: Holden-Day, 1978.

b. Find β if in fact $p = .2$. What is the power of the test for this value of p?

c. Find β if in fact $p = .4$. What is the power of the test for this value of p?

OPTIONAL EXERCISE

9.6   Show that for a fixed sample size n, α increases as β decreases, and vice versa.

9.4   Finding Statistical Tests: An Example of a Large-Sample Test

To find a statistical test about one or more population parameters, we must (1) find a suitable test statistic and (2) specify a rejection region. One method for finding a reasonable test statistic for testing a hypothesis was proposed by R. A. Fisher. For example, suppose we want to test a hypothesis about the sole parameter θ of a probability function $p(y)$ or density function $f(y)$, and let L represent the likelihood of the sample. Then to test the null hypothesis, $H_0: \theta = \theta_0$, Fisher's **likelihood ratio test statistic** is

$$\lambda = \frac{\text{Likelihood assuming } \theta = \theta_0}{\text{Likelihood assuming } \theta = \hat{\theta}} = \frac{L(\theta_0)}{L(\hat{\theta})}$$

where $\hat{\theta}$ is the maximum likelihood estimator of θ. Fisher reasoned that if θ differs from θ_0, then the value of the likelihood L when $\theta = \hat{\theta}$ will be larger than when $\theta = \theta_0$. Thus, the rejection region for the test contains values of λ that are small— say, smaller than some value λ_R.

If you are interested in learning more about Fisher's likelihood ratio test, consult the references at the end of this chapter. Fortunately, most of the statistics that we would choose intuitively for test statistics are functions of the corresponding likelihood ratio statistic λ. These are the pivotal statistics used to construct confidence intervals in Chapter 8.

Recall that most of the pivotal statistics in Chapter 8 have approximately normal sampling distributions for large samples. This fact allows us to easily derive a large-sample statistical test of hypothesis. To illustrate, suppose that we want to test a hypothesis, $H_0: \theta = \theta_0$, about a parameter θ and that the estimator $\hat{\theta}$ possesses a normal sampling distribution with mean θ and standard deviation $\sigma_{\hat{\theta}}$. We will further assume that $\sigma_{\hat{\theta}}$ is known or that we can obtain a good approximation for it when the sample size(s) is (are) large. It can be shown (proof omitted) that the likelihood ratio test statistic λ reduces to the standard normal variable z:

$$z = \frac{\hat{\theta} - \theta_0}{\sigma_{\hat{\theta}}}$$

The location of the rejection region for this test can be deduced by examining the formula for the test statistic z. The farther $\hat{\theta}$ departs from θ_0, i.e., the larger the absolute value of the deviation $|\hat{\theta} - \theta_0|$, the greater will be the weight of evidence to indicate that θ is not equal to θ_0. If we want to detect values of θ larger than θ_0, i.e., $H_a: \theta > \theta_0$, we locate the rejection region in the upper tail of the sampling distribution of the standard normal z test statistic (see Figure 9.3a). If we want to detect only values of θ less than θ_0, i.e., $H_a: \theta < \theta_0$, we locate the rejection region in the lower tail of the z distribution (see Figure 9.3b). These two tests are called **one-tailed statistical tests** because the entire rejection region is located in only one tail of the z distribution. However, if we want to detect *either* a value of θ larger than θ_0 or a value smaller than θ_0, i.e., $H_a: \theta \neq \theta_0$, we locate the rejection region in both the upper and the lower tails of the z distribution (see Figure 9.3c). This is called a **two-tailed statistical test**.

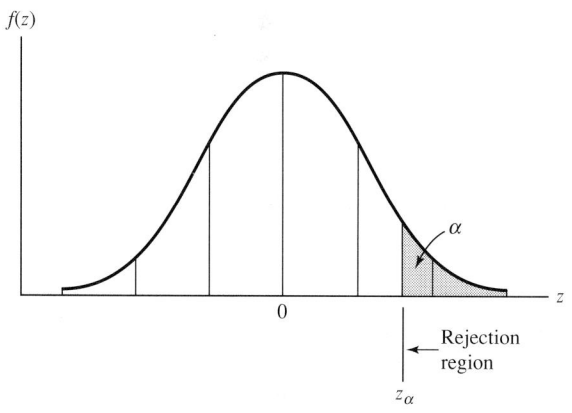

a. One-tailed test;
  $H_a: \theta > \theta_0$

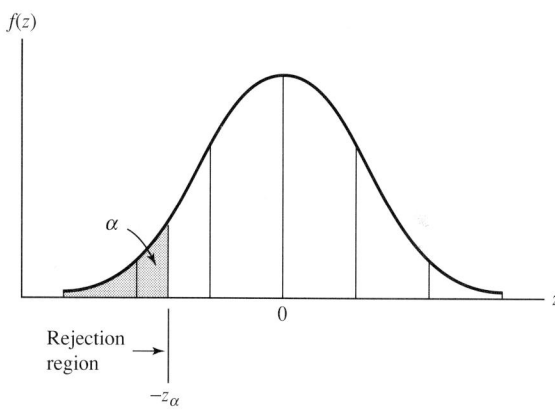

b. One-tailed test;
  $H_a: \theta < \theta_0$

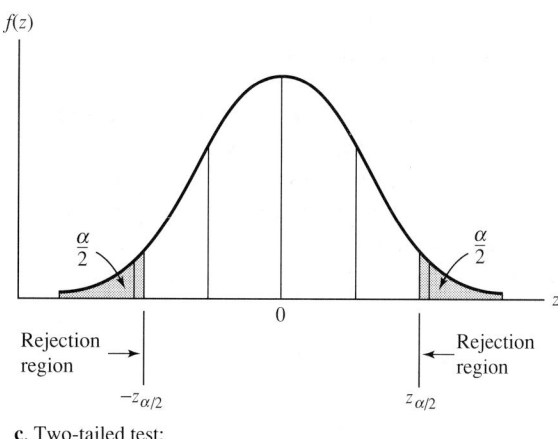

c. Two-tailed test;
  $H_a: \theta \neq \theta_0$

FIGURE 9.3 ▲
Rejection regions for one- and two-tailed tests

The large-sample statistical test that we have described is summarized in the box on page 432. Many of the population parameters and test statistics discussed in the remaining sections of Chapter 9 satisfy the assumptions of this test. We will illustrate the use of the test with a practical example on the population mean μ.

A Large-Sample Test Based on the Standard Normal z Test Statistic

One-Tailed Test

H_0: $\theta = \theta_0$

H_a: $\theta > \theta_0$
  (or H_a: $\theta < \theta_0$)

Test statistic: $z = \dfrac{\hat{\theta} - \theta_0}{\sigma_{\hat{\theta}}}$

Rejection region: $z > z_\alpha$
  (or $z < -z_\alpha$)

where $P(z > z_\alpha) = \alpha$

Two-Tailed Test

H_0: $\theta = \theta_0$

H_a: $\theta \neq \theta_0$

Test statistic: $z = \dfrac{\hat{\theta} - \theta_0}{\sigma_{\hat{\theta}}}$

Rejection region: $|z| > z_{\alpha/2}$

where $P(z > z_{\alpha/2}) = \alpha/2$

EXAMPLE 9.5

The Department of Highway Improvements, responsible for repairing a 25-mile stretch of interstate highway, wants to design a surface that will be structurally efficient. One important consideration is the volume of heavy freight traffic on the interstate. State weigh stations report that the average number of heavy-duty trailers traveling on a 25-mile segment of the interstate is 72 per hour. However, the section of highway to be repaired is located in an urban area and the department engineers believe that the volume of heavy freight traffic for this particular sector is greater than the average reported for the entire interstate. To validate this theory, the department monitors the highway for 50 1-hour periods randomly selected throughout the month. Suppose the sample mean and standard deviation of the heavy freight traffic for the 50 sampled hours are

$$\bar{y} = 74.1 \qquad s = 13.3$$

Do the data support the department's theory? Use $\alpha = .10$.

Solution

For this example, the parameter of interest is μ, the average number of heavy-duty trailers traveling on the 25-mile stretch of interstate highway. Recall that the sample mean $\bar{y}$ is used to estimate μ, and that for large n, $\bar{y}$ has an approximately normal sampling distribution. Thus, we can apply the large-sample test outlined in the box.

The elements of the test are

H_0: $\mu = 72$

H_a: $\mu > 72$

Test statistic: $z = \dfrac{\bar{y} - 72}{\sigma_{\bar{y}}} = \dfrac{\bar{y} - 72}{\sigma/\sqrt{n}} \approx \dfrac{\bar{y} - 72}{s/\sqrt{n}}$

Rejection region: $z > 1.28$
  (since $z_{.10} = 1.28$, from Table 4 of Appendix II)

We now substitute the sample statistics into the test statistic to obtain

$$z \approx \frac{74.1 - 72}{13.3/\sqrt{50}} = 1.12$$

Thus, although the average number of heavy freight trucks per hour in the sample exceeds the state's average by more than 2, the z value of 1.12 does not fall in the rejection region (see Figure 9.4). Therefore, this sample does not provide sufficient evidence at $\alpha = .10$ to support the Department of Highway Improvements' theory.

FIGURE 9.4 ▶
Location of the test statistic for Example 9.5

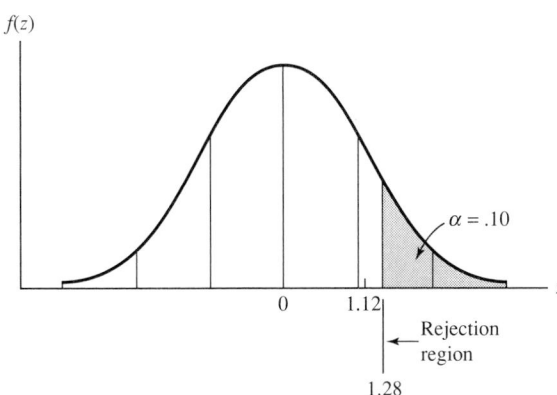

What is the risk of making an incorrect decision in Example 9.5? If we reject the null hypothesis then we know that the probability of making a Type I error (rejecting H_0 if it is true) is $\alpha = .10$. However, we failed to reject the null hypotheses in Example 9.5 and, consequently, we must be concerned about the possibility of making a Type II error (accepting H_0 if in fact it is false). We will evaluate the risk of making a Type II error in Example 9.6.

EXAMPLE 9.6

Refer to the one-tailed test for μ, Example 9.5. If the mean number μ of heavy freight trucks traveling a particular 25-mile stretch of interstate highway is in fact 78 per hour, what is the probability that the test procedure of Example 9.5 would fail to detect it? That is, what is the probability β that we would fail to reject H_0: $\mu = 72$ in this one-tailed test if μ is actually equal to 78?

Solution

To calculate β for the large-sample z test, we need to specify the rejection region in terms of the point estimator $\hat{\theta}$, where, for this example, $\hat{\theta} = \bar{y}$. From Figure 9.4, you can see that the rejection region consists of values of $z \geq 1.28$. To determine the value of $\bar{y}$ corresponding to $z = 1.28$, we substitute into the equation

$$z = \frac{\bar{y} - \mu_0}{\sigma/\sqrt{n}} \approx \frac{\bar{y} - \mu_0}{s/\sqrt{n}} \quad \text{or} \quad 1.28 = \frac{\bar{y} - 72}{13.3/\sqrt{50}}$$

Solving for $\bar{y}$, we obtain $\bar{y} = 74.41$. Therefore, the rejection region for the test is $z \geq 1.28$ or, equivalently, $\bar{y} \geq 74.41$.

The dotted curve in Figure 9.5 is the sampling distribution for $\bar{y}$ if $H_0: \mu = 72$ is true. This curve was used to locate the rejection region for $\bar{y}$ (and, equivalently, z), i.e., values of $\bar{y}$ contradictory to $H_0: \mu = 72$. The solid curve is the sampling distribution for $\bar{y}$ if $\mu = 78$. Since we want to find β if H_0 is in fact false and $\mu = 78$, we want to find the probability that $\bar{y}$ does not fall in the rejection region if $\mu = 78$. This probability corresponds to the shaded area under the solid curve for values of $\bar{y} <$ 74.41. To find this area under the normal curve, we need to find the area A corresponding to

$$z = \frac{\bar{y} - 78}{\sigma/\sqrt{n}} \approx \frac{74.41 - 78}{13.3/\sqrt{50}} = -1.91$$

FIGURE 9.5 ▶
The probability β of making a
Type II error if $\mu = 78$ in
Example 9.6

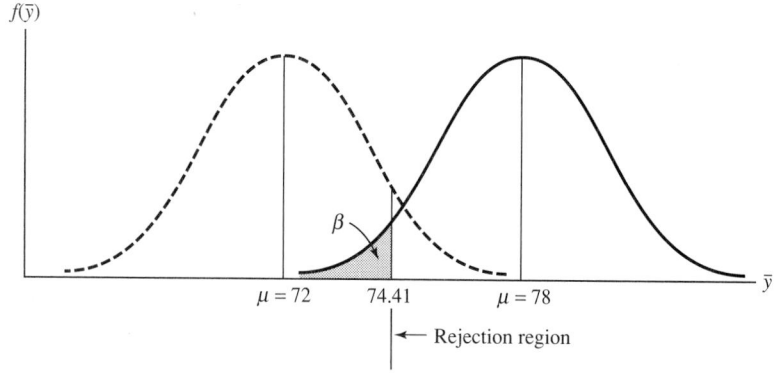

The value of A, given in Table 4 of Appendix II, is .4719. Then from Figure 9.5, it can be seen that

$$\beta = .5 - A = .5 - .4719 = .0281$$

Therefore, the probability of failing to reject $H_0: \mu = 72$ if μ is, in fact, as large as $\mu = 78$, is only .0281.

· ·

Example 9.6 illustrates that it is not too difficult to calculate β for various alternatives for the large-sample z test (see box). However, it may be extremely difficult to calculate β for other tests. Although sophisticated techniques are available for evaluating the risk of making a Type II error when the exact value of β is unavailable or is difficult to calculate, they are beyond the scope of this text. Consult the references at the end of this chapter if you are interested in learning about these methods.

Calculating β for a Large-Sample z Test

Consider a large-sample test of H_0: $\theta = \theta_0$ at significance level α. The value of β for a specific value of the alternative $\theta = \theta_a$ is calculated as follows:

Upper-tailed test: $\beta = P\left(z < \dfrac{\hat{\theta}_0 - \theta_a}{\sigma_{\hat{\theta}}}\right)$

where $\hat{\theta}_0 = \theta_0 + z_\alpha \sigma_{\hat{\theta}}$ is the value of the estimator corresponding to the border of the rejection region

Lower-tailed test: $\beta = P\left(z > \dfrac{\hat{\theta}_0 - \theta_a}{\sigma_{\hat{\theta}}}\right)$

where $\hat{\theta}_0 = \theta_0 - z_\alpha \sigma_{\hat{\theta}}$ is the value of the estimator corresponding to the border of the rejection region

Two-tailed test: $\beta = P\left(\dfrac{\hat{\theta}_{0,L} - \theta_a}{\sigma_{\hat{\theta}}} < z < \dfrac{\hat{\theta}_{0,U} - \theta_a}{\sigma_{\hat{\theta}}}\right)$

where $\hat{\theta}_{0,U} = \theta_0 + z_\alpha \sigma_{\hat{\theta}}$ and $\hat{\theta}_{0,L} = \theta_0 - z_\alpha \sigma_{\hat{\theta}}$ are the values of the estimator corresponding to the borders of the rejection region

EXERCISES

OPTIONAL EXERCISES

9.7 Suppose $y_1, y_2, \ldots, y_n$ is a random sample from a normal distribution with unknown mean μ and variance $\sigma^2 = 1$, i.e.,

$$f(y) = \frac{1}{\sqrt{2\pi}} e^{-(y-\mu)^2/2}$$

Show that the likelihood L of the sample is

$$L(\mu) = \left(\frac{1}{\sqrt{2\pi}}\right)^n e^{-\Sigma_{i=1}^n (y_i - \mu)^2/2}$$

9.8 Refer to Optional Exercise 9.7. Suppose we want to test H_0: $\mu = 0$ against the alternative H_a: $\mu > 0$. Since the estimator of μ is $\hat{\mu} = \bar{y}$, the likelihood ratio test statistic is

$$\lambda = \frac{L(\mu_0)}{L(\hat{\mu})} = \frac{L(0)}{L(\bar{y})}$$

Show that

$$\lambda = e^{-n(\bar{y})^2/2}$$

[*Hint:* Use the fact that $\Sigma_{i=1}^n (y_i - \bar{y})^2 = \Sigma_{i=1}^n y_i^2 - n\bar{y}^2$.]

9.9   Refer to Optional Exercises 9.7 and 9.8. Show that the rejection region $\lambda \leq \lambda_\alpha$ is equivalent to the rejection region $\bar{y} \geq \bar{y}_\alpha$, where $P(\lambda \leq \lambda_\alpha) = \alpha$ and $P(\bar{y} \geq \bar{y}_\alpha) = \alpha$. [*Hint:*   Use the fact that $e^{-a^2} \to 0$ as $a \to \infty$.]

9.5   Choosing the Null and Alternative Hypotheses

Now that you have conducted a large-sample statistical test of hypothesis and have seen how to calculate the value of β—the probability of failing to reject H_0: $\theta = \theta_0$ if θ is in fact equal to some alternative value, $\theta = \theta_a$—the logic for choosing the null and alternative hypotheses may make more sense to you. The theory that we want to support (or detect if true) is usually chosen as the alternative hypothesis because, if the data support H_a (i.e., if we reject H_0), we immediately know the value of α, the probability of incorrectly rejecting H_0 if it is true. For example, in Example 9.5, the Department of Highway Improvements theorized that the mean number of heavy-duty vehicles traveling a certain segment of interstate exceeds 72 per hour. Consequently, the department set up the alternative hypothesis as H_a: $\mu > 72$. In contrast, if we choose the null hypothesis as the theory that we want to support, and if the data support this theory, i.e., the test leads to nonrejection of H_0, then we would have to investigate the values of β for some specific alternatives. Clearly, we want to avoid this tedious and sometimes extremely difficult task, if possible.

Another issue that arises in a practical situation is whether to conduct a one- or a two-tailed test. The decision depends on what you want to detect. For example, suppose you operate a chemical plant that produces a variable amount y of product per day and that if μ, the mean value of y, is less than 100 tons per day, you will eventually be bankrupt. If μ exceeds 100 tons per day, you are financially safe. To determine whether your process is leading to financial disaster, you will want to detect whether $\mu < 100$ tons, and you will conduct a one-tailed test of H_0: $\mu = 100$ versus H_a: $\mu < 100$. If you were to conduct a two-tailed test for this situation, you would reduce your chance of detecting values of μ less than 100 tons, i.e., you would increase the values of β for alternative values of $\mu < 100$ tons.

As a different example, suppose you have designed a new drug so that its mean potency is some specific level, say, 10%. As the mean potency tends to exceed 10%, you lose money. If it is less than 10% by some specified amount, the drug becomes ineffective as a pharmaceutical (and you lose money). To conduct a test of the mean potency μ for this situation, you would want to detect values of μ either larger than or smaller than $\mu = 10$. Consequently, you would select H_a: $\mu \neq 10$ and conduct a two-tailed statistical test (or alternatively, construct a confidence interval).

These examples demonstrate that a statistical test is an attempt to detect departures from H_0; the key to the test is to define the specific *alternatives* that you want to detect. We must stress, however, that H_0 *and* H_a *should be constructed prior to obtaining and observing the sample data.* If you use information in the sample data to aid in selecting H_0 and H_a, the prior information gained from the sample biases the test results—specifically, the true probability of a Type I error will be larger than the preselected value of α.

EXAMPLE 9.7   A metal lathe is checked periodically by quality control inspectors to determine whether it is producing machine bearings with a mean diameter of .5 inch. If the mean diameter of the bearings is larger or smaller than .5 inch, then the process is out of control and needs to be adjusted. Formulate the null and alternative hypotheses that could be used to test whether the bearing production process is out of control.

Solution   The hypotheses must be stated in terms of a population parameter. Thus, we define

μ = True mean diameter (in inches) of all bearings produced by the lathe

If either $\mu > .5$ or $\mu < .5$, then the metal lathe's production process is out of control. Since we wish to be able to detect either possibility, the null and alternative hypotheses would be

H_0: $\mu = .5$ (i.e., the process is in control)

H_a: $\mu \neq .5$ (i.e., the process is out of control)

In Sections 9.6–9.13, we will present applications of the hypothesis-testing logic developed in this chapter. The cases to be considered are those for which we developed estimation procedures in Chapter 8. Since the theory and reasoning involved are based on the developments of Chapter 8 and Sections 9.1–9.5, we will present only a summary of the hypothesis-testing procedure for one-tailed and two-tailed tests in each situation.

EXERCISES

In Exercises 9.10–9.15, formulate the appropriate null and alternative hypotheses.

9.10   A herpetologist wants to determine whether the egg-hatching rate for a certain species of frog exceeds .5 when the eggs are exposed to ultraviolet radiation.

9.11   A manufacturer of fishing line wants to show that the mean breaking strength of a competitor's 22-pound line is really less than 22 pounds.

9.12   A craps player who has experienced a long run of bad luck at the craps table wants to test whether the casino dice are "loaded," i.e., whether the proportion of "sevens" occurring in many tosses of the two dice is different from $\frac{1}{6}$ (if the dice are fair, the probability of tossing a "seven" is $\frac{1}{6}$).

9.13   Each year, *Computerworld* magazine reports the Datapro ratings of all computer software vendors. Vendors are rated on a scale from 1 to 4 (1 = poor, 4 = excellent) in such areas as reliability, efficiency, ease of installation, and ease of use by a random sample of software users. A software vendor wants to determine whether its product has a higher mean Datapro rating than a rival vendor's product.

9.14   The Environmental Protection Agency wishes to test whether the mean amount of radium-226 in soil in a Florida county exceeds the maxium allowable amount, 4 pCi/L.

9.15   Industrial engineers want to compare two methods of real-time scheduling in a manufacturing operation. Specifically, they want to determine whether the mean number of items produced differs for the two methods.

9.6   Testing a Population Mean

In Example 9.5, we developed a large-sample test for a population mean based on the standard normal z statistic. The elements of this test are summarized in the box.

Large-Sample ($n \geq 30$) Test of Hypothesis About a Population Mean μ

One-Tailed Test

H_0: $\mu = \mu_0$

H_a: $\mu > \mu_0$
   (or H_a: $\mu < \mu_0$)

Test statistic:

$$z = \frac{\bar{y} - \mu_0}{\sigma_{\bar{y}}} \approx \frac{\bar{y} - \mu_0}{s/\sqrt{n}}$$

Rejection region:

$$z > z_\alpha \quad (\text{or } z < -z_\alpha)$$

Two-Tailed Test

H_0: $\mu = \mu_0$

H_a: $\mu \neq \mu_0$

Test statistic:

$$z = \frac{\bar{y} - \mu_0}{\sigma_{\bar{y}}} \approx \frac{\bar{y} - \mu_0}{s/\sqrt{n}}$$

Rejection region: $|z| > z_{\alpha/2}$

where z_α is the z value such that $P(z > z_\alpha) = \alpha$; and $z_{\alpha/2}$ is the z value such that $P(z > z_{\alpha/2}) = \alpha/2$. [*Note:* μ_0 is our symbol for the particular numerical value specified for μ in the null hypothesis.]

Assumptions: None (since the central limit theorem guarantees that $\bar{y}$ is approximately normal regardless of the distribution of the sampled population)

EXAMPLE 9.8

Humerus bones from the same species of animal tend to have approximately the same length-to-width ratios. When fossils of humerus bones are discovered, archeologists can often determine the species of animal by examining the length-to-width ratios of the bones. It is known that species A has a mean ratio of 8.5. Suppose 41 fossils of humerus bones were unearthed at an archeological site in East Africa, where species A is believed to have inhabited. (Assume that the unearthed bones are all from the same unknown species.) The length-to-width ratios of the bones were measured and are listed in Table 9.2.

TABLE 9.2   Length-to-Width Ratios of a Sample of Humerus Bones

10.73	8.89	9.07	9.20	10.33	9.98	9.84	9.59
8.48	8.71	9.57	9.29	9.94	8.07	8.37	6.85
8.52	8.87	6.23	9.41	6.66	9.35	8.86	9.93
8.91	11.77	10.48	10.39	9.39	9.17	9.89	8.17
8.93	8.80	10.02	8.38	11.67	8.30	9.17	12.00
9.38							

We wish to test the hypothesis that μ, the population mean ratio of all bones of this particular species, is equal to 8.5 against the alternative that it is different from 8.5, i.e., we wish to test whether the unearthed bones are from species A.

a. Suppose we want a very small chance of rejecting H_0, if, in fact, μ is equal to 8.5. That is, it is important that we avoid making a Type I error. Select an appropriate value of the significance level, α.

b. Test whether μ, the population mean length-to-width ratio, is different from 8.5, using the significance level selected in part **a**.

Solution

a. The hypothesis-testing procedure that we have developed gives us the advantage of being able to choose any significance level that we desire. Since the significance level, α, is also the probability of a Type I error, we will choose α to be very small. In general, researchers who consider a Type I error to have very serious practical consequences should perform the test at a very low α value—say, $\alpha = .01$. Other researchers may be willing to tolerate an α value as high as .10 if a Type I error is not deemed a serious error to make in practice. For this example, we will test at $\alpha = .01$.

b. We formulate the following hypotheses:

$$H_0: \quad \mu = 8.5$$
$$H_a: \quad \mu \neq 8.5$$

Note that this is a two-tailed test, since we want to detect departures from $\mu = 8.5$ in either direction. The sample size is large ($n = 41$); thus, we may proceed with the large-sample test about μ.

At significance level $\alpha = .01$, we will reject the null hypothesis for this two-tailed test if

$$|z| > z_{\alpha/2} = z_{.005}$$

i.e., if $z < -2.58$ or if $z > 2.58$. This rejection region is shown in Figure 9.6 on page 440.

FIGURE 9.6 ▶

Rejection region for Example 9.8

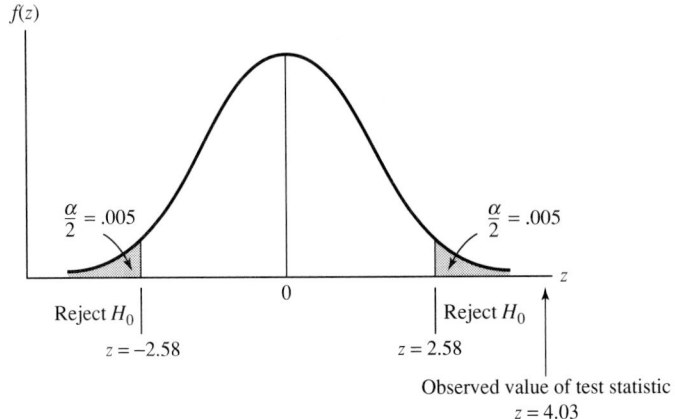

After entering the data of Table 9.2 into a computer, we obtained the summary statistics shown in the SAS printout, Figure 9.7. The values $\bar{y} = 9.257$ and $s = 1.203$ (shaded in the printout) are used to compute the test statistic

$$z \approx \frac{\bar{y} - \mu_0}{s/\sqrt{n}} = \frac{9.257 - 8.5}{1.203/\sqrt{41}} = 4.03$$

Since this value lies within the rejection region (see Figure 9.6), we reject H_0 and conclude that the mean length-to-width ratio of all humerus bones of this particular species is significantly different from 8.5. If the null hypothesis is in fact true (i.e., if $\mu = 8.5$), then the probability that we have incorrectly rejected it is equal to $\alpha = .01$.

FIGURE 9.7 ▶

SAS printout for Example 9.8

```
Analysis Variable : LWRATIO

N Obs        Minimum         Maximum            Mean           Std Dev
----------------------------------------------------------------------
  41        6.2300000      12.0000000       9.2575610         1.2035651
----------------------------------------------------------------------
```

The *practical* implications of the result obtained in Example 9.8 remain to be studied further. Perhaps the animal discovered at the archeological site is of some species other than A. Alternatively, the unearthed humerus bones may have larger than normal length-to-width ratios because of unusual feeding habits of species A. **It is not always the case that a statistically significant result implies a practically significant result.** The researcher must retain his or her objectivity and judge the practical significance using, among other criteria, his or her knowledge of the subject matter and the phenomenon under investigation.

A small-sample statistical test for making inferences about a population mean is (like its associated confidence interval of Section 8.5) based on the assumption that the sample data are independent observations on a normally distributed random variable. The test statistic is based on the *t* distribution given in Section 8.5.

The elements of the statistical test are listed in the accompanying box. As we suggested in Chapter 8, the small-sample test will possess the properties specified in the box even if the sampled population is moderately nonnormal. However, for data that departs greatly from normality (i.e., highly skewed data), we must resort to one of the nonparametric techniques discussed in Chapter 15.

Small-Sample Test of Hypothesis About a Population Mean μ

One-Tailed Test

H_0: $\mu = \mu_0$

H_a: $\mu > \mu_0$
   (or H_a: $\mu < \mu_0$)

Two-Tailed Test

H_0: $\mu = \mu_0$

H_a: $\mu \neq \mu_0$

Test statistic: $t = \dfrac{\bar{y} - \mu_0}{s/\sqrt{n}}$

Rejection region: $t > t_\alpha$
   (or $t < -t_\alpha$)

Rejection region: $|t| > t_{\alpha/2}$

where the distribution of t is based on $(n - 1)$ degrees of freedom; t_α is the t value such that $P(t > t_\alpha) = \alpha$; and $t_{\alpha/2}$ is the t value such that $P(t > t_{\alpha/2}) = \alpha/2$.

Assumption: The relative frequency distribution of the population from which the sample was selected is approximately normal.

Warning: If the data departs greatly from normality, this small-sample test may lead to erroneous inferences. In this case, use the nonparametric sign test that is discussed in Section 15.2.

EXAMPLE 9.9

Scientists have labeled benzene, a chemical solvent commonly used to synthesize plastics, as a possible cancer-causing agent. Studies have shown that people who work with benzene more than 5 years have 20 times the incidence of leukemia than the general population. As a result, the federal government has lowered the maximum allowable level of benzene in the workplace from 10 parts per million (ppm) to 1 ppm (reported in *Florida Times-Union*, Apr. 2, 1984). Suppose a steel manufacturing plant, which exposes its workers to benzene daily, is under investigation by the Occupational

Safety and Health Administration (OSHA). Twenty air samples, collected over a period of 1 month and examined for benzene content, yielded the following summary statistics:

$$\bar{y} = 2.1 \text{ ppm} \qquad s = 1.7 \text{ ppm}$$

Is the steel manufacturing plant in violation of the new government standards? Test the hypothesis that the mean level of benzene at the steel manufacturing plant is greater than 1 ppm, using $\alpha = .05$.

Solution

The OSHA wants to establish the research hypothesis that the mean level of benzene, μ, at the steel manufacturing plant exceeds 1 ppm. The elements of this small-sample one-tailed test are

$$H_0: \quad \mu = 1$$
$$H_a: \quad \mu > 1$$

Test statistic: $\quad t = \dfrac{\bar{y} - \mu_0}{s/\sqrt{n}}$

Assumption: The relative frequency distribution of the population of benzene levels for all air samples at the steel manufacturing plant is approximately normal.

Rejection region: For $\alpha = .05$ and df $= (n - 1) = 19$, reject H_0 if $t > t_{.05} = 1.729$ (see Figure 9.8)

FIGURE 9.8 ▶
Rejection region for Example 9.9

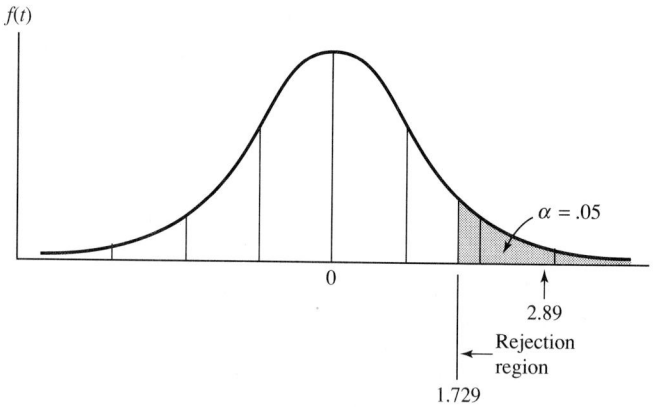

We now calculate the test statistic:

$$t = \frac{\bar{y} - 1}{s/\sqrt{n}} = \frac{2.1 - 1}{1.7/\sqrt{20}} = 2.89$$

Since the calculated t falls in the rejection region, the OSHA concludes that $\mu > 1$ part per million and the plant is in violation of the new government standards. The reliability associated with this inference is $\alpha = .05$. This implies that if the testing procedure was applied repeatedly to random samples of data collected at the plant, the OSHA would falsely reject H_0 for only 5% of the tests. Consequently, the OSHA is highly confident (95% confident) that the plant is violating the new standards.

EXERCISES

9.16   Radium-226 is a naturally occurring radioactive gas. Elevated levels of radium-226 in metropolitan Dade County (Florida) were recently investigated (*Florida Scientist*, Summer/Autumn 1991). The data in the table are radium-226 levels (measured in pCi/L) for 26 soil specimens collected in southern Dade County. The Environmental Protection Agency (EPA) has set maximum exposure levels of radium-226 at 4.0 pCi/L. Use the information in the accompanying MINITAB printout to determine whether the mean radium-226 level of soil specimens collected in southern Dade County is less than the EPA limit of 4.0 pCi/L. Use $\alpha = .10$.

1.46	.58	4.31	1.02	.17	2.92	.91	.43	.91
1.30	8.24	3.51	6.87	1.43	1.44	4.49	4.21	1.84
5.92	1.86	1.41	1.70	2.02	1.65	1.40	.75	

Source: Moore, H. E., and Gussow, D. G. "Radium and radon in Dade County ground water and soil samples." *Florida Scientist*, Vol. 54, No. 3/4, Summer/Autumn, 1991, p. 155 (portion of Table 3).

	N	MEAN	MEDIAN	TRMEAN	STDEV	SEMEAN
RadLevel	26	2.413	1.555	2.264	2.081	0.408

	MIN	MAX	Q1	Q3		
RadLevel	0.170	8.240	0.993	3.685		

9.17   The effect of machine breakdowns on the performance of a manufacturing system was investigated using computer simulation (*Industrial Engineering*, Aug. 1990). The simulation study focused on a single machine tool system with several characteristics, including a mean interarrival time of 1.25 minutes, a constant processing time of 1 minute, and a machine that breaks down 10% of the time. After $n = 5$ independent simulation runs of length 160 hours, the mean throughput per 40-hour week was $\bar{y} = 1,908.8$ parts. For a system with no breakdowns, the mean throughput for a 40-hour week will be equal to 1,920 parts. Assuming the standard deviation of the 5 sample runs was $s = 18$ parts per 40-hour week, test the hypothesis that the true mean throughput per 40-hour week for the system is less than 1,920 parts. Test using $\alpha = .05$.

9.18   Refer to the *Science* (Nov. 1988) study of inbreeding in tropical swarm-founding wasps, Exercise 8.30. A sample of 197 wasps, captured, frozen, and subjected to a series of genetic tests, yielded a sample mean inbreeding coefficient of $\bar{y} = .044$ with a standard deviation of $s = .884$. Recall that if the wasp has no tendency to inbreed, the true mean inbreeding coefficient μ for the species will equal 0.
   a. Test the hypothesis that the true mean inbreeding coefficient μ for this species of wasp exceeds 0. Use $\alpha = .05$.
   b. Compare the inference, part **a**, to the inference obtained in Exercise 8.28 using a confidence interval. Do the inferences agree? Explain.

9.19   Results of the second National Health and Nutrition Examination Survey indicate that the mean blood lead concentration of individuals between the ages of 6 months and 74 years is 14 μg/dl (*Analytical Chemistry*, Feb. 1986). However, the blood lead concentration in black children under the age of 5 years was found to be significantly higher than this figure. Suppose that in a random sample of 200 black children below the age of 5 years, the mean blood lead concentration is 21 μg/dl and the standard deviation is 10 μg/dl. Is there sufficient evidence to indicate that the true mean blood lead concentration in young black children is greater than 14 μg/dl? Test using $\alpha = .01$.

9.20   The EPA sets a limit of 5 parts per million on PCB (a dangerous substance) in water. A major manufacturing firm producing PCB for electrical insulation discharges small amounts from the plant. The company management, attempting to control the amount of PCB in its discharge, has given instructions to halt production if the mean amount of PCB in the effluent exceeds 3 parts per million. A random sampling of 50 water specimens produced the following statistics:

$\bar{y} = 3.1$ parts per million $s = .5$ part per million

a. Do these statistics provide sufficient evidence to halt the production process? Use $\alpha = .01$.
b. If you were the plant manager, would you want to use a large or a small value for α for the test in part **a**? Explain.

9.21   "Deep hole" drilling is a family of drilling processes used when the ratio of hole depth to hole diameter exceeds 10. Successful deep hole drilling depends on the satisfactory discharge of the drill chip. An experiment was conducted to investigate the performance of deep hole drilling when chip congestion exists (*Journal of Engineering for Industry*, May 1993). The length (in millimeters) of 50 drill chips resulted in the following summary statistics: $\bar{y} = 81.2$ mm, $s = 50.2$ mm. Conduct a test to determine whether the true mean drill chip length, μ, differs from 75 mm. Use a significance level of $\alpha = .01$.

9.22   *Environmental Science & Technology* (Oct. 1993) reported on a study of contaminated soil in The Netherlands. A total of 72 400-gram soil specimens were sampled, dried, and analyzed for the contaminant cyanide. The cyanide concentration (milligrams per kilogram of soil) of each soil specimen was determined using an infrared microscopic method. The sample resulted in a mean cyanide level of $\bar{y} = 84$ mg/kg and a standard deviation of $s = 80$ mg/kg. Use this information to test the hypothesis that the true mean cyanide level in soil in The Netherlands falls below 100 mg/kg. Test at $\alpha = .10$.

9.23   The building specifications in a certain city require that the sewer pipe used in residential areas have a mean breaking strength of more than 2,500 pounds per lineal foot. A manufacturer who would like to supply the city with sewer pipe has submitted a bid and provided the following additional information: An independent contractor randomly selected seven sections of the manufacturer's pipe and tested each for breaking strength. The results (pounds per lineal foot) follow:

2,610   2,750   2,420   2,510   2,540   2,490   2,680

Is there sufficient evidence to conclude that the manufacturer's sewer pipe meets the required specifications? Use a significance level of $\alpha = .10$.

9.24   Refer to Examples 9.5 and 9.6. Find the value of β for $\mu_a = 74$. What is the power of the test?

9.25   Refer to Example 9.9.
a. Find the value of β for $\mu_a = 1.015$.
b. Find the power of the test for $\mu_a = 1.045$.

9.26   Refer to Optional Exercises 9.7–9.9. Show that the rejection region for the likelihood ratio test is given by $z > z_\alpha$, where $P(z > z_\alpha) = \alpha$. [*Hint:*   Under the assumption that $H_0: \mu = 0$ is true, show that $\sqrt{n}(\bar{y})$ is a standard normal random variable.]

9.7   The Observed Significance Level for a Test

According to the statistical test procedures described in the preceding sections, the rejection region and the corresponding value of α are selected prior to conducting the test and the conclusion is stated in terms of rejecting or not rejecting the null hypothesis. A second method of presenting the result of a statistical test is one that reports the extent to which the test statistic disagrees with the null hypothesis and leaves the reader the task of deciding whether to reject the null hypothesis. This measure of disagreement is called the **observed significance level** (or *p*-value) for the test.[*]

> **Definition 9.4**
>
> The **observed significance level**, or *p*-value, for a specific statistical test is the probability (assuming H_0 is true) of observing a value of the test statistic that is at least as contradictory to the null hypothesis, and supportive of the alternative hypothesis, as the one computed from the sample data.

When publishing the results of a statistical test of hypothesis in journals, case studies, reports, etc., many researchers make use of *p*-values. Instead of selecting α a priori and then conducting a test as outlined in this chapter, the researcher may compute and report the value of the appropriate test statistic and its associated *p*-value. It is left to the reader of the report to judge the significance of the result, i.e., the reader must determine whether to reject the null hypothesis in favor of the alternative hypothesis, based on the reported *p*-value. Usually, *the null hypothesis will be rejected only if the observed significance level is **less** than the fixed significance level α chosen by the reader.* There are two inherent advantages of reporting test results in this manner: (1) Readers are permitted to select the maximum value of α that they would be willing to tolerate if they actually carried out a standard test of hypothesis in the manner outlined in this chapter, and (2) it is an easy way to present the results of test calculations performed by a computer. Most statistical software packages perform the calculations for a test, give the observed value of the test statistic, and leave it to the reader to formulate a conclusion. Others give the observed significance level for the test, a procedure that makes it easy for the user to decide whether to reject the null hypothesis.

---

[*]The term *p-value* or *probability value* was coined by users of statistical methods. The p in the expression *p-value* should not be confused with the binomial parameter p.

EXAMPLE 9.10

Find the observed significance level for the statistical test of Example 9.5 and interpret the result.

Solution

In Example 9.5, we tested a hypothesis about the mean μ of the number of heavy freight trucks per hour using a particular 25-mile stretch of interstate highway. Since we wanted to detect values of μ larger than $\mu_0 = 72$, we conducted a one-tailed test, rejecting H_0 for large values of $\bar{y}$, or equivalently, large values of z. The observed value of z, computed from the sample of $n = 50$ randomly selected 1-hour periods, was $z = 1.12$. Since any value of z larger than $z = 1.12$ would be even more contradictory to H_0, the observed significance level for the test is

$$p\text{-value} = P(z \geq 1.12)$$

FIGURE 9.9 ▶

Finding the p-value for an upper-tailed test when $z = 1.12$

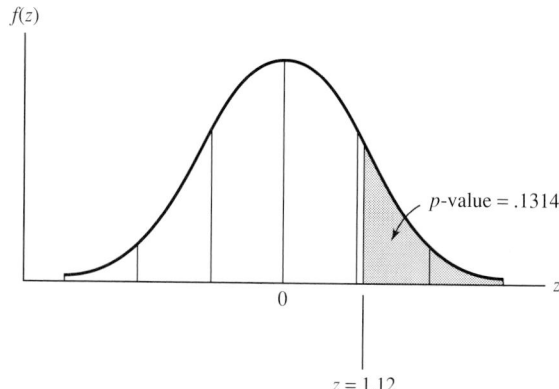

This value corresponds to the shaded area in the upper tail of the z distribution shown in Figure 9.9. The area A corresponding to $z = 1.12$, given in Table 4 of Appendix II, is .3686. Therefore, the observed significance level is

$$p\text{-value} = P(z \geq 1.12) = .5 - A = .5 - .3686 = .1314$$

This result indicates that the probability of observing a z value at least as contradictory to H_0 as the one observed in this test (if H_0 is in fact true) is .1314. Therefore, we will reject H_0 only for preselected values of α greater than .1314. Recall that the Department of Highway Improvements selected a Type I error probability of $\alpha = .10$. Since $\alpha = .10$ is *less* than the p-value, the department has insufficient evidence to reject H_0. Note that this conclusion agrees with that of Example 9.5.

EXAMPLE 9.11

Suppose that the test of Example 9.5 had been a two-tailed test, i.e., suppose that the alternative of interest had been $H_a: \mu \neq 72$. Find the observed significance level for the test and interpret the result. Assume that $\alpha = .10$, as in Example 9.5.

Solution

If the test were two-tailed, either very large or very small values of z would be contradictory to the null hypothesis H_0: $\mu = 72$. Consequently, values of $z \geq 1.12$ or $z \leq -1.12$ would be more contradictory to H_0 than the observed value of $z = 1.12$. Therefore, the observed significance level for the test (shaded in Figure 9.10) is

$$p\text{-value} = P(z \geq 1.12) + P(z \leq -1.12)$$
$$= 2(.1314) = .2628$$

Since we want to conduct the two-tailed test at $\alpha = .10$, and since the p-value exceeds α, we again have insufficient evidence to reject H_0.

FIGURE 9.10 ▶
Finding the p-value for a two-tailed test when $z = 1.12$

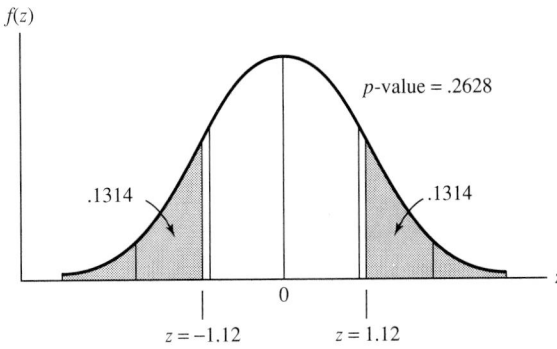

EXAMPLE 9.12

Find and interpret the observed significance level for the small-sample test described in Example 9.9. Recall that the test was conducted using $\alpha = .05$.

Solution

The test of Example 9.9 was a small-sample test of H_0: $\mu = 1$ versus H_a: $\mu > 1$. Since the value of t computed from the sample data was $t = 2.89$, the observed significance level (or p-value) for the test is equal to the probability that t would assume a value greater than or equal to 2.89, if in fact H_0 were true. This is equal to the area in the upper tail of the t distribution (shaded in Figure 9.11). To find this area, i.e., the p-value for the test, we consult the t table (Table 7 of Appendix II).

FIGURE 9.11 ▶
The observed significance level for the test of Example 9.12

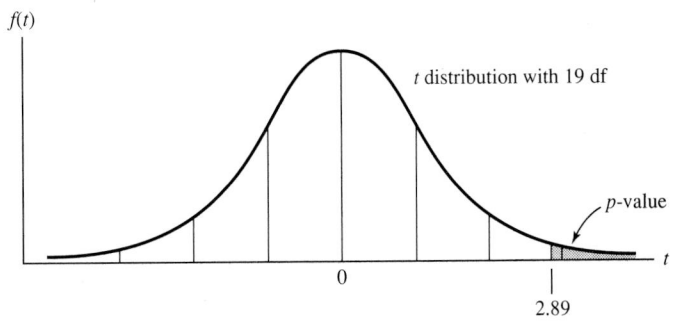

Unlike the table of areas under the normal curve, Table 7 gives only the t values corresponding to the areas .100, .050, .025, .010, .005, .001, and .0005. Therefore, we can only approximate the p-value for the test. Since the observed t value was based on 19 degrees of freedom, we use the df = 19 row in Table 7 and move across the row until we reach the t values that are closest to the observed $t = 2.89$. The t values corresponding to p-values of .001 and .005 are 3.579 and 2.861, respectively. Since the observed t value falls between $t_{.001}$ and $t_{.005}$, the p-value for the test lies between .001 and .005. We could interpolate to more accurately locate the p-value for the test, but it is easier and adequate for our purposes to choose the larger area as the p-value and report it as .005. Thus, we would reject the null hypothesis, $H_0: \mu = 1$ part per million, for any value of α larger than .005. Since $\alpha = .05$ for this test, the correct conclusion is to reject H_0.

Calculating p-Values

Large-sample tests: p-value $= P(z \geq z_c)$ if upper-tailed

p-value $= P(z \leq z_c)$ if lower-tailed

p-value $= 2P(z \geq |z_c|)$ if two-tailed

where z_c is the computed value of the test statistic.

Small-sample tests: p-value $= P(t \geq t_c)$ if upper-tailed

p-value $= P(t \leq t_c)$ if lower-tailed

p-value $= 2P(t \geq |t_c|)$ if two-tailed

where t_c is the computed value of the test statistic.

[Note: $|z_c|$ and $|t_c|$ denote the **absolute values** of z_c and t_c and will always be positive.]

Interpreting p-Values

1. Choose the maximum value of α that you are willing to tolerate.
2. If the observed significance level (p-value) of the test is less than the maximum value α, then reject the null hypothesis.

You can see from Example 9.12 that calculating a p-value for a t test by hand will rarely lead to an exact value. If we desire an exact p-value, we need to resort to the use of a computer. The SAS printout for the t test of Examples 9.9 and 9.12 is shown in Figure 9.12. The p-value for a two-tailed test (shaded) is given under the heading PROB > |T|. The p-value for a one-tailed test is equal to the reported value divided by 2. Thus, the p-value for the one-tailed test $H_0: \mu = 1$ versus $H_a: \mu > 1$ is

$$p\text{-value} = \frac{.0088}{2} = .0044$$

FIGURE 9.12 ▶
SAS printout for t test of
Example 9.12

```
Analysis Variable :  BENZLEV


N Obs                T   Prob>|T|
--------------------------------
   20     2.8937350    0.0088
--------------------------------
```

EXERCISES

9.27 For a large-sample test of $H_0: \theta = \theta_0$ versus $H_a: \theta > \theta_0$, compute the p-value associated with each of the following test statistic values:
a. $z = 1.96$ **b.** $z = 1.645$ **c.** $z = 2.67$ **d.** $z = 1.25$

9.28 For a large-sample test of $H_0: \theta = \theta_0$ versus $H_a: \theta \neq \theta_0$, compute the p-value associated with each of the following test statistic values:
a. $z = -1.01$ **b.** $z = -2.37$ **c.** $z = 4.66$ **d.** $z = 1.45$

9.29 Compute and interpret the p-value for the test of Example 9.8, assuming the test is two-tailed.

9.30 Compute and interpret the p-values for the tests conducted in the following exercises.
a. Exercise 9.16   **b.** Exercise 9.17   **c.** Exercise 9.18   **d.** Exercise 9.19   **e.** Exercise 9.20

9.31 A SAS printout for the t test of Exercise 9.23 is shown here. Find and interpret the p-value of the test. Does the result agree with your inference in Exercise 9.23?

```
Analysis Variable :  Y (strength - 2500)


N Obs              T   Prob>|T|
-------------------------------
   7    1.6419203    0.1517
-------------------------------
```

9.8 Testing the Difference Between Two Population Means: Independent Samples

Consider independent random samples from two populations with means μ_1 and μ_2, respectively. When the sample sizes are large (i.e., $n_1 \geq 30$ and $n_2 \geq 30$), a test of hypothesis for the difference between the population means $(\mu_1 - \mu_2)$ is based on the pivotal z statistic given in Section 8.6. A summary of the large-sample test is provided in the box.

Large-Sample Test of Hypothesis About $(\mu_1 - \mu_2)$: Independent Samples

One-Tailed Test

H_0: $(\mu_1 - \mu_2) = D_0$

H_a: $(\mu_1 - \mu_2) > D_0$
  [or H_a: $(\mu_1 - \mu_2) < D_0$]

Two-Tailed Test

H_0: $(\mu_1 - \mu_2) = D_0$

H_a: $(\mu_1 - \mu_2) \neq D_0$

Test statistic: $z = \dfrac{(\bar{y}_1 - \bar{y}_2) - D_0}{\sigma_{(\bar{y}_1 - \bar{y}_2)}} \approx \dfrac{(\bar{y}_1 - \bar{y}_2) - D_0}{\sqrt{\dfrac{s_1^2}{n_1} + \dfrac{s_2^2}{n_2}}}$

Rejection region:

$z > z_\alpha$ (or $z < -z_\alpha$)

Rejection region:

$|z| > z_{\alpha/2}$

[Note: D_0 is our symbol for the particular numerical value specified for $(\mu_1 - \mu_2)$ in the null hypothesis. In many practical applications, we wish to hypothesize that there is no difference between the population means; in such cases, $D_0 = 0$.]

Assumptions: 1. The sample sizes n_1 and n_2 are sufficiently large—say, $n_1 \geq 30$ and $n_2 \geq 30$.
  2. The two samples are selected randomly and independently from the target populations.

EXAMPLE 9.13

To reduce costs, a bakery has implemented a new leavening process for preparing commercial bread loaves. Loaves of bread were randomly sampled and analyzed for calorie content both before and after implementation of the new process. A summary of the results of the two samples is shown in the table. Do these samples provide sufficient evidence to conclude that the mean number of calories per loaf has decreased since the new leavening process was implemented? Test using $\alpha = .05$.

New Process	Old Process
$n_1 = 50$	$n_2 = 30$
$\bar{y}_1 = 1{,}255$ calories	$\bar{y}_2 = 1{,}330$ calories
$s_1 = 215$ calories	$s_2 = 238$ calories

Solution

We can best answer this question by performing a test of a hypothesis. Defining μ_1 as the mean calorie content per loaf manufactured by the new process and μ_2 as the mean calorie content per loaf manufactured by the old process, we will attempt to support the research (alternative) hypothesis that $\mu_2 > \mu_1$ [i.e., that $(\mu_1 - \mu_2) < 0$]. Thus, we will test the null hypothesis that $(\mu_1 - \mu_2) = 0$, rejecting this hypothesis if $(\bar{y}_1 - \bar{y}_2)$ equals a large negative value. The elements of the test are as follows:

H_0: $(\mu_1 - \mu_2) = 0$ (i.e., $D_0 = 0$)

H_a: $(\mu_1 - \mu_2) < 0$ (i.e., $\mu_1 < \mu_2$)

Test statistic: $z = \dfrac{(\bar{y}_1 - \bar{y}_2) - D_0}{\sigma_{(\bar{y}_1 - \bar{y}_2)}} = \dfrac{(\bar{y}_1 - \bar{y}_2) - 0}{\sigma_{(\bar{y}_1 - \bar{y}_2)}}$

(since both n_1 and n_2 are greater than or equal to 30)

Rejection region: $z < -z_\alpha = -1.645$ (see Figure 9.13)

Assumptions: The two samples of bread loaves are independently selected.

FIGURE 9.13 ►
Rejection region for Example 9.13

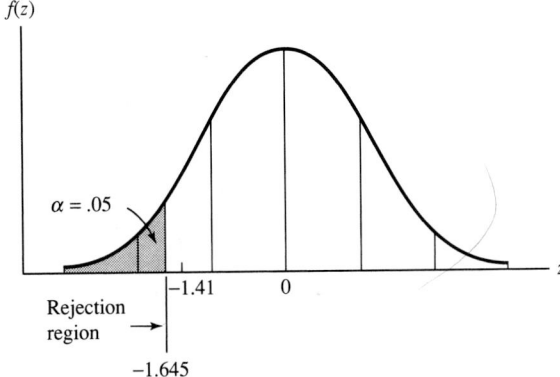

We now calculate

$$z = \frac{(\bar{y}_1 - \bar{y}_2) - 0}{\sigma_{(\bar{y}_1 - \bar{y}_2)}} = \frac{(1{,}255 - 1{,}330)}{\sqrt{\dfrac{\sigma_1^2}{n_1} + \dfrac{\sigma_2^2}{n_2}}}$$

$$\approx \frac{-75}{\sqrt{\dfrac{s_1^2}{n_1} + \dfrac{s_2^2}{n_2}}} = \frac{-75}{\sqrt{\dfrac{(215)^2}{50} + \dfrac{(238)^2}{30}}} = \frac{-75}{53.03} = -1.41$$

As you can see in Figure 9.13, the calculated z value does not fall in the rejection region. The samples do not provide sufficient evidence, with $\alpha = .05$, to conclude that the new process yields a loaf with fewer mean calories.

When the sample sizes n_1 and n_2 are inadequate to permit use of the large-sample procedure of Example 9.13, modifications may be made to perform a small-sample test of hypothesis about the difference between two population means. The test procedure is based on assumptions that are, again, more restrictive than in the large-sample case. The elements of the hypothesis test and the assumptions required are listed in the box. *Reminder:* When the assumption of normal population is grossly violated, the small-sample test outlined here will be invalid. In this case, we must resort to a nonparametric method.

Small-Sample Test of Hypothesis About $(\mu_1 - \mu_2)$: Independent Samples

One-Tailed Test

H_0: $(\mu_1 - \mu_2) = D_0$

H_a: $(\mu_1 - \mu_2) > D_0$
  [or H_a: $(\mu_1 - \mu_2) < D_0$]

Two-Tailed Test

H_0: $(\mu_1 - \mu_2) = D_0$

H_a: $(\mu_1 - \mu_2) \neq D_0$

Test statistic: $t = \dfrac{(\bar{y}_1 - \bar{y}_2) - D_0}{\sqrt{s_p^2\left(\dfrac{1}{n_1} + \dfrac{1}{n_2}\right)}}$

Rejection region: $t > t_\alpha$
  [or $t < -t_\alpha$]

Rejection region: $|t| > t_{\alpha/2}$

where

$$s_p^2 = \frac{(n_1 - 1)s_1^2 + (n_2 - 1)s_2^2}{n_1 + n_2 - 2}$$

and the distribution of t is based on $n_1 + n_2 - 2$ df.

Assumptions: 1. The populations from which the samples are selected both have approximately normal relative frequency distributions.

2. The variances of the two populations are equal, i.e., $\sigma_1^2 = \sigma_2^2$.

3. The random samples are selected in an independent manner from the two populations.

Warning: When the assumption of normal populations is violated, the test may lead to erroneous inferences. In this case, use the nonparametric Wilcoxon test described in Section 15.3.

EXAMPLE 9.14

Computer response time is defined as the length of time a user has to wait for the computer to access information on the disk. Suppose a data center wants to compare the average response times of its two computer disk drives. If μ_1 is the mean response time of disk 1 and μ_2 is the mean response time of disk 2, we want to detect a difference between μ_1 and μ_2—if such a difference exists. Therefore, we want to test the null hypothesis

H_0: $(\mu_1 - \mu_2) = 0$

against the alternative hypothesis

$$H_a: \quad (\mu_1 - \mu_2) \neq 0 \quad (\text{i.e., } \mu_1 > \mu_2 \text{ or } \mu_1 < \mu_2)$$

Independent random samples of 13 response times for disk 1 and 15 response times for disk 2 were selected. The data (recorded in milliseconds), as well as summary statistics, are given in Table 9.3. Is there sufficient evidence to indicate a difference between the mean response times of the two disk drives? Test using $\alpha = .05$.

TABLE 9.3   Response Times for Two Disk Drives

Disk 1 ($n_1 = 13$)				Disk 2 ($n_2 = 15$)			
59	73	74	61	71	63	40	34
92	60	84		38	48	60	75
54	73	47		47	41	44	86
102	75	33		53	68	39	
$\bar{y}_1 = 68.2$	$s_1 = 18.6$			$\bar{y}_2 = 53.8$	$s_2 = 15.8$		

Solution

We first calculate

$$
\begin{aligned}
s_p^2 &= \frac{(n_1 - 1)s_1^2 + (n_2 - 1)s_2^2}{n_1 + n_2 - 2} \\
&= \frac{(13 - 1)(18.6)^2 + (15 - 1)(15.8)^2}{13 + 15 - 2} \\
&= \frac{7{,}646.48}{26} = 294.09
\end{aligned}
$$

Then, if we can assume that the distributions of the response times for the two disk drives are both approximately normal with equal variances, the test statistic is

$$
t = \frac{(\bar{y}_1 - \bar{y}_2) - D_0}{\sqrt{s_p^2 \left(\dfrac{1}{n_1} + \dfrac{1}{n_2}\right)}} = \frac{(68.2 - 53.8) - 0}{\sqrt{294.09 \left(\dfrac{1}{13} + \dfrac{1}{15}\right)}}
$$

$$
= \frac{14.4}{6.5} = 2.22
$$

Since the observed value of t ($t = 2.22$) falls in the rejection region (see Figure 9.14 on page 454), the samples provide sufficient evidence to indicate that the mean response times differ for the two disk drives. Or, we say that the test results are statistically significant at the $\alpha = .05$ level of significance. Because the rejection was in the positive or upper tail of the t distribution, it appears that the mean response time for disk drive 1 exceeds that for disk drive 2.

FIGURE 9.14 ▶
Rejection region for Example 9.14

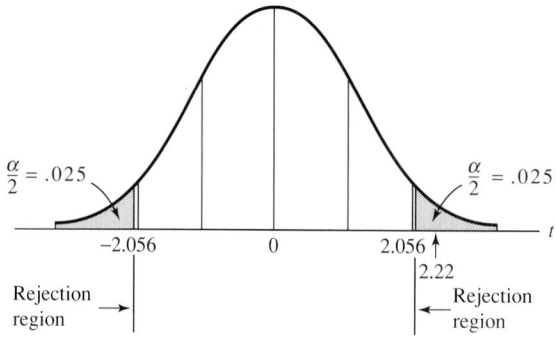

FIGURE 9.14 ▶

Rejection region for Example 9.14

Refer to Example 9.14. The same conclusion can be reached using the p-value approach. The SAS printout for the t test of Example 9.14 is shown in Figure 9.15. The test statistic and p-value for the test are both shaded on the printout. Note that the two-tailed p-value (for the equal variances case), $p = .0356$, is less than $\alpha = .05$; thus, there is sufficient evidence to reject H_0.

FIGURE 9.15 ▶

SAS printout for Example 9.14

TTEST PROCEDURE

Variable: Y

DISK	N	Mean	Std Dev	Std Error	Minimum	Maximum
1	13	68.23076923	18.65991178	5.17532836	33.00000000	102.0000000
2	15	53.80000000	15.80777386	4.08154966	34.00000000	86.0000000

Variances	T	DF	Prob>|T|
Unequal	2.1894	23.7	0.0387
Equal	2.2163	26.0	0.0356

For H0: Variances are equal, F' = 1.39   DF = (12,14)   Prob>F' = 0.5482

Recall from Section 8.6 that valid small-sample inferences about $(\mu_1 - \mu_2)$ can still be made when the assumption of equal variances is violated. We conclude this section by giving the modifications required to obtain approximate small-sample tests about $(\mu_1 - \mu_2)$ when $\sigma_1^2 \neq \sigma_2^2$ for the two cases described in Section 8.6: $n_1 = n_2$ and $n_1 \neq n_2$.

Modifications to Small-Sample Tests About $(\mu_1 - \mu_2)$ When $\sigma_1^2 \neq \sigma_2^2$: Independent Samples

$n_1 = n_2 = n$

Test statistic:

$$t = \frac{(\bar{y}_1 - \bar{y}_2) - D_0}{\sqrt{\dfrac{s_1^2}{n_1} + \dfrac{s_2^2}{n_2}}} = \frac{(\bar{y}_1 - \bar{y}_2) - D_0}{\sqrt{\dfrac{1}{n}(s_1^2 + s_2^2)}}$$

Degrees of freedom: $\nu = n_1 + n_2 - 2 = 2(n - 1)$

$n_1 \neq n_2$

Test statistic:

$$t = \frac{(\bar{y}_1 - \bar{y}_2) - D_0}{\sqrt{\dfrac{s_1^2}{n_1} + \dfrac{s_2^2}{n_2}}}$$

Degrees of freedom: $\nu = \dfrac{(s_1^2/n_1 + s_2^2/n_2)^2}{\left[\dfrac{(s_1^2/n_1)^2}{n_1 - 1} + \dfrac{(s_2^2/n_2)^2}{n_2 - 1}\right]}$

Note: The value of ν will generally not be an integer. Round down to the nearest integer to use the t table (Table 7 of Appendix II).

EXERCISES

9.32 Does competition between separate research and development (R&D) teams in the U.S. Department of Defense, working independently on the same project, improve performance? To answer this question, performance ratings were assigned to each of 58 multisource (competitive) and 63 sole source R&D contracts (*IEEE Transactions on Engineering Management*, Feb. 1990). With respect to quality of reports and products, the competitive contracts had a mean performance rating of 7.62, whereas the sole source contracts had a mean of 6.95.

a. Set up the null and alternative hypothesis for determining whether the mean quality performance rating of competitive R&D contracts exceeds the mean for sole source contracts.

b. Find the rejection region for the test using $\alpha = .05$.

c. The p-value for the test was reported to be between .02 and .03. What is the appropriate conclusion?

9.33 **a.** Use a random number table (Table 6 of Appendix II) to generate a random sample of $n = 40$ observations on DDT concentration in fish from the data of Appendix III. Compute $\bar{x}$ and s for the sample measurements.

b. The Food and Drug Administration (FDA) sets the limit for DDT content in individual fish at 5 parts per million (ppm). Does the sample of part **a** provide sufficient evidence to conclude that the average DDT content of individual fish inhabiting the Tennessee River and its creek tributaries exceeds 5 ppm? Test using a significance level of $\alpha = .01$.

c. Suppose the test of hypothesis, part **b**, was based on a random sample of only $n = 8$ fish. What are the disadvantages of conducting this small-sample test?

d. Repeat part **b** using only the information on the DDT contents of a sample of 8 fish (randomly selected from the 40 observations of part **a**). Compare the results of the large- and small-sample tests.

9.34   Many computer software packages utilize menu-driven user-interfaces to increase "user-friendliness." One feature that can be incorporated into the interface is a stacked menu display. Each time a menu item is selected, a submenu is displayed partially over the parent menu, thus creating a series of "stacked" menus. The *Special Interest Group on Computer Human Interaction Bulletin* (July 1993) reported on a study to determine the effects of the presence or absence of a stacked menu structure on search time. Twenty-two subjects were randomly placed into one of two groups, and each was asked to search a menu-driven software package for a particular item. In the experimental group ($n_1 = 11$), the stacked menu format was used; in the control group ($n_2 = 11$), only the current menu was displayed.

a. The researcher's initial hypothesis is that the mean time required to find a target item does not differ for the two menu displays. Describe the statistical method appropriate for testing this hypothesis.

b. What assumptions are required for inferences derived from the analysis to be valid?

c. The mean search times for the two groups were 11.02 seconds and 11.07 seconds, respectively. Is this enough information to conduct the test? Explain.

d. The observed significance level for the test, part **a**, exceeds .10. Interpret this result.

9.35   *Environmental Science & Technology* (Oct. 1993) reported on a study of insecticides used on dormant orchards in the San Joaquin Valley, California. Ambient air samples were collected and analyzed daily at an orchard site during the most intensive period of spraying. The thion and oxon levels (in ng/m^3) in the air samples are recorded in the table, as well as the oxon/thion ratios. Compare the mean oxon/thion ratios of foggy and clear/cloudy conditions at the orchard using a test of hypothesis. Use $\alpha = .05$.

Date	Condition	Thion	Oxon	Oxon/Thion Ratio
Jan. 15	Fog	38.2	10.3	.270
17	Fog	28.6	6.9	.241
18	Fog	30.2	6.2	.205
19	Fog	23.7	12.4	.523
20	Fog	62.3	(Air sample lost)	—
20	Clear	74.1	45.8	.618
21	Fog	88.2	9.9	.112
21	Clear	46.4	27.4	.591
22	Fog	135.9	44.8	.330
23	Fog	102.9	27.8	.270
23	Cloudy	28.9	6.5	.225
25	Fog	46.9	11.2	.239
25	Clear	44.3	16.6	.375

Source: Selber, J. N., et al. "Air and fog deposition residues of four organophosphate insecticides used on dormant orchards in the San Joaquin Valley, California." *Environmental Science & Technology*, Vol. 27, No. 10, Oct. 1993, p. 2240 (Table V).

9.36 Percentage of body fat can be a good indicator of an individual's energy metabolic status and general health. In an *American Journal of Physical Anthropology* (Jan. 1981) study of the percentage of body fat of college students in India, two groups of healthy male students, from urban and rural colleges in eastern India, were independently and randomly selected. The percentage of body fat in each was measured, with the results summarized in the table. Does the sample information provide sufficient evidence to conclude that the mean percentage of body fat in healthy male college students residing in urban areas of India differs from the corresponding mean for students residing in rural areas? Use a significance level of $\alpha = .05$.

Urban Students	Rural Students
$n_1 = 193$	$n_2 = 188$
$\bar{y}_1 = 12.07$	$\bar{y}_2 = 11.04$
$s_1 = 3.04$	$s_2 = 2.63$

Source: Bandyopadhyay, B., and Chattopadhyay, H. "Body fat in urban and rural male college students of eastern India." *American Journal of Physical Anthropology*, Jan. 1981, Vol. 54, pp. 119–122.

9.37 According to a popular model of managerial behavior, the current state of automation in a manufacturing firm influences managers' perceptions of problems of automation. To investigate this proposition, researchers at Concordia University (Montreal) surveyed managers at firms with a high level of automation and at firms with a low level of automation (*IEEE Transactions on Engineering Management*, Aug. 1990). Each manager was asked to give his/her perception of the problems of automation at the firm. Responses were measured on a 5-point scale (1: No problem, . . . 5: Major Problem). Summary statistics for the two groups of managers, provided in the table, were used to test the hypothesis of no difference in the mean perceptions of automation problems between managers of highly automated and less automated manufacturing firms.

	Sample Size	Mean	Standard Deviation
Low Level	17	3.274	.762
High Level	8	3.280	.721

Source: Farhoomand, A. F., Kira D., and Williams, J. "Managers' perceptions towards automation in manufacturing." *IEEE Transactions on Engineering Management*, Vol. 37, No. 3, Aug. 1990, p. 230.

a. Conduct the test for the researchers, assuming that the perception variances for the two groups of managers are equal. Use $\alpha = .01$.

b. Conduct the test for the researchers, if it is known that the perception variances differ for managers at low-level and high-level firms.

9.38 An industrial plant wants to determine which of two types of fuel—gas or electric—will produce more useful energy at the lower cost. One measure of economical energy production, called the *plant investment per delivered quad*, is calculated by taking the amount of money (in dollars) invested in the particular utility by the plant, and dividing by the delivered amount of energy (in quadrillion British thermal units). The smaller this ratio, the less an industrial plant pays for its delivered energy. Random samples of 11 plants using electrical utilities and 16 plants using gas utilities were taken, and the plant investment/quad wa: calculated for each. The data are listed in the table, followed by a MINITAB printout of the analysis of the data.

Electric

204.15	.57	62.76	89.72
.35	85.46	.78	.65
44.38	9.28	78.60	

Gas

.78	16.66	74.94	.01
.54	23.59	88.79	.64
.82	91.84	7.20	66.64
.74	64.67	165.60	.36

```
TWOSAMPLE T FOR electric VS gas
               N      MEAN     STDEV    SE MEAN
electric      11      52.4      62.4       19
gas           16      37.7      49.0       12

95 PCT CI FOR MU electric - MU gas: (-30, 59)

TTEST MU electric = MU gas (VS NE): T= 0.68   P=0.50   DF=  25

POOLED STDEV =        54.8
```

a. Do these data provide sufficient evidence at the $\alpha = .05$ level of significance to indicate a difference in the average investment/quad between the plants using gas and those using electrical utilities?

b. What assumptions are required for the procedure to be valid?

c. Check whether the assumptions, part b, are reasonably satisfied. How does this impact on the validity of the result, part a?

9.39   A field experiment was conducted to ascertain the impact of desert granivores (seed-eaters) on the density and distribution of seeds in the soil (*Ecology*, Dec. 1979). Since some desert rodents are known to hoard seeds in surface caches, the study was specifically designed to determine whether these caches eventually produce more seedlings, on the average, than an adjacent control area. Forty small areas excavated by rodents were located and covered with plastic cages to prevent rodents from reusing the caches. A caged control area was set up adjacent to each of the caged caches. The numbers of seedlings germinating from the caches and from the control areas were then observed. A summary of the data is provided in the accompanying table. Is there sufficient evidence (at $\alpha = .05$) to indicate that the average number of seedlings germinating from the seed caches of desert rodents is significantly higher than the corresponding average for the control areas?

Caches	Control Areas
$n_1 = 40$	$n_2 = 40$
$\bar{y}_1 = 5.3$	$\bar{y}_2 = 2.7$
$s_1 = 1.3$	$s_2 = .7$

Source: Reichman, O. J. "Desert granivore foraging and its impact on seed densities and distributions." *Ecology*, Dec. 1979, Vol. 60, pp. 1085–1092. Copyright 1979, the Ecological Society of America. Reprinted by permission.

9.9 Testing the Difference Between Two Population Means: Matched Pairs

It may be possible to acquire more information on the difference between two population means by using data collected in matched pairs instead of independent samples. Consider, for example, an experiment to investigate the effectiveness of cloud seeding in the artificial production of rainfall. Two farming areas with similar past meteorological records were selected for the experiment. One is seeded regularly; the other is left unseeded. The monthly precipitation at the farms will be recorded for 6 randomly selected months. The resulting data, matched on months, can be used to test a hypothesis about the difference between the mean monthly precipitation in the seeded and unseeded areas. The appropriate procedures are summarized in the boxes.

Large-Sample Test of Hypothesis About $(\mu_1 - \mu_2)$: Matched Pairs

One-Tailed Test

H_0: $(\mu_1 - \mu_2) = D_0$

H_a: $(\mu_1 - \mu_2) > D_0$
  [or H_a: $(\mu_1 - \mu_2) < D_0$]

Two-Tailed Test

H_0: $(\mu_1 - \mu_2) = D_0$

H_a: $(\mu_1 - \mu_2) \neq D_0$

$$\text{Test statistic:} \quad z = \frac{\bar{d} - D_0}{\sigma_d/\sqrt{n}} \approx \frac{\bar{d} - D_0}{s_d/\sqrt{n}}$$

where $\bar{d}$ and s_d represent the mean and standard deviation of the sample of differences.

Rejection region: $z > z_\alpha$
  [or $z < -z_\alpha$]

Rejection region: $|z| > z_{\alpha/2}$

[*Note:* D_0 is our symbol for the particular numerical value specified for $(\mu_1 - \mu_2)$ in H_0. In many applications, we want to hypothesize that there is no difference between the population means; in such cases, $D_0 = 0$.]

Small-Sample Test of Hypothesis About $(\mu_1 - \mu_2)$: Matched Pairs

One-Tailed Test

H_0: $(\mu_1 - \mu_2) = D_0$

H_a: $(\mu_1 - \mu_2) > D_0$

  [or H_a: $(\mu_1 - \mu_2) < D_0$]

Two-Tailed Test

H_0: $(\mu_1 - \mu_2) = D_0$

H_a: $(\mu_1 - \mu_2) \neq D_0$

$$\text{Test statistic:} \quad t = \frac{\bar{d} - D_0}{\sigma_d/\sqrt{n}} \approx \frac{\bar{d} - D_0}{s_d/\sqrt{n}}$$

where $\bar{d}$ and s_d represent the mean and standard deviation of the sample of differences.

Rejection region: $t > t_\alpha$

  [or $t > -t_\alpha$]

Rejection region: $|t| > t_{\alpha/2}$

where the t-distribution is based on $(n - 1)$ degrees of freedom.

[*Note:* D_0 is our symbol for the particular numerical value specified for $(\mu_1 - \mu_2)$ in the null hypothesis. In many practical applications, we want to hypothesize that there is no difference between the population means; in such cases, $D_0 = 0$.]

Assumptions: 1. The relative frequency distribution of the population of differences is approximately normal.

   2. The paired differences are randomly selected from the population of differences.

Warning: When the assumption of normality is grossly violated, the t test may lead to erroneous inferences. In this case, use the nonparametric Wilcoxon test described in Section 15.4.

EXAMPLE 9.15

Consider the cloud seeding experiment to compare monthly precipitation at the two farm areas. Do the data given in Table 9.4 provide sufficient evidence to indicate that the mean monthly precipitation at the seeded farm area exceeds the corresponding mean for the unseeded farm area? Test using $\alpha = .05$.

TABLE 9.4   Monthly Precipitation Data (in Inches) for Example 9.15

Farm Area	1	2	3	4	5	6
Seeded	1.75	2.12	1.53	1.10	1.70	2.42
Unseeded	1.62	1.83	1.40	.75	1.71	2.33
d	.13	.29	.13	.35	−.01	.09

Solution

Let μ_1 and μ_2 represent the mean monthly precipitation values for the seeded and unseeded farm areas, respectively. Since we want to be able to detect $\mu_1 > \mu_2$, we will conduct the one-tailed test:

$$H_0: \quad (\mu_1 - \mu_2) = 0$$
$$H_a: \quad (\mu_1 - \mu_2) > 0$$

Assuming the differences in monthly precipitation values for the two areas are from an approximately normal distribution, the test statistic will have a t distribution based on $(n - 1) = (6 - 1) = 5$ degrees of freedom. We will reject the null hypothesis if

$$t > t_{.05} = 2.015 \quad \text{(see Figure 9.16)}$$

FIGURE 9.16 ▶
Rejection region for Example 9.15

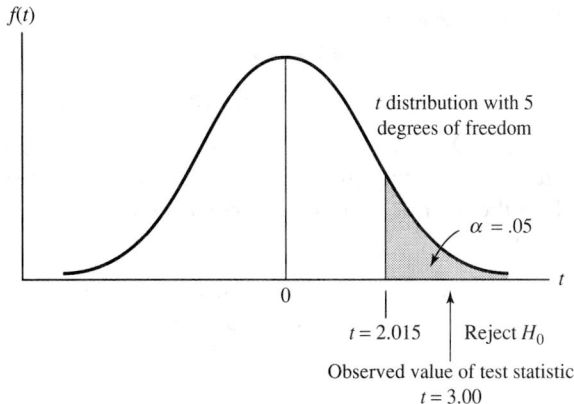

To conduct the test by hand, we must first calculate the difference d in monthly precipitation at the two farm areas for each month. These differences (where the observations for the unseeded farm area is subtracted from the observation for the seeded area within each pair) are shown in the last row of Table 9.4. Next, we would calculate the mean $\bar{d}$ and standard deviation s_d for this sample of $n = 6$ differences to obtain the test statistic.

Rather than perform these calculations, we will rely on the output from a computer. The MINITAB printout for the analysis is shown in Figure 9.17. The test statistic, shaded in Figure 9.17, is $t = 3.01$.

FIGURE 9.17 ▶
Minitab printout for Example 9.17

TEST OF MU = 0.0000 VS MU N.E. 0.0000

	N	MEAN	STDEV	SE MEAN	T	P VALUE
diff	6	0.1633	0.1331	0.0543	3.01	0.030

Substituting the values $\bar{d} = .1633$ and $s_d = .1331$ into the formula for the test statistic, we have

$$t = \frac{\bar{d} - D_0}{s_d/\sqrt{n}} = \frac{.1633 - 0}{.1331/\sqrt{6}} = 3.01$$

Since this value of the test statistic exceeds the critical value $t_{.05} = 2.015$, there is sufficient evidence (at $\alpha = .05$) to indicate that the mean monthly precipitation at the seeded farm area exceeds the mean for the unseeded farm area.

The same conclusion can be reached by examining the p-value of the test. The two-tailed p-value, shaded on the MINITAB printout, is .030. Consequently, the one-tailed p-value is $p = .030/2 = .015$. Since this value is less than the chosen α level (.05), we reject H_0.

In the experiment of Example 9.15, why did we collect the data in matched pairs rather than use independent random samples of months, with some assigned to only the seeded area and others to only the unseeded area? The answer is that we expected some months to have more rain than others. To cancel out this variation from month to month, the experiment was designed so that precipitation at both farm areas would be recorded during the same months. Then both farm areas would be subjected to the same weather pattern in a given month. By comparing precipitation *within* each month, we were able to obtain more information on the difference in mean monthly precipitation than we could have obtained by independent random sampling.

EXERCISES

9.40 Researchers at Purdue University compared human real-time scheduling in a processing environment to an automated approach that utilizes computerized robots and sensing devices (*IEEE Transactions*, Mar. 1993). The experiment consisted of eight simulated scheduling problems. Each task was performed by a human scheduler and by the automated system. Performance was measured by the *throughput rate*, defined as the number of good jobs produced weighted by product quality. The resulting throughput rates are shown in the accompanying table. Analyze the data using a test of hypothesis.

Task	Human Scheduler	Automated Method	Task	Human Scheduler	Automated Method
1	185.4	180.4	5	240.0	269.3
2	146.3	248.5	6	253.8	249.6
3	174.4	185.5	7	238.8	282.0
4	184.9	216.4	8	263.5	315.9

Source: Yih, Y., Liang, T., and Moskowitz, H. "Robot scheduling in a circuit board production line: A hybrid OR/ANN approach." *IEEE Transactions*, Vol. 25, No. 2, March 1993, p. 31 (Table 1).

9.41 For the perception of speech, profoundly deaf persons rely mainly on speechreading, i.e., they perceive spoken language by observing the articulatory movements, facial expressions, and gestures of the speaker. Can speech perception be improved by supplementing the speechreader with auditorily presented information about the prosody of the speech signal? To investigate this phenomenon, 10 normal-hearing subjects participated in an experiment in which they were asked to verbally reproduce sentences spoken but not heard on a video monitor (*Journal of the Acoustical Society of America*, Feb. 1986). The sentences were presented to the subjects under each of two conditions: (1) speechreading with information about the frequency and amplitude of the speech signal (denoted S + F + A), and (2) speechreading only (denoted S). For each of the 10 subjects, the difference between the percentage of correctly reproduced syllables under condition S + F + A and under condition S was calculated. The mean and standard deviation of the differences are as follows:

$$\bar{d} = 20.4 \qquad s_d = 17.44$$

Test the hypothesis that the mean percentage of correct syllables under condition S + F + A exceeds the corresponding mean under condition S. Use $\alpha = .05$.

9.42 Tetrachlorodibenzo-p-dioxin (TCDD) is a highly toxic substance found in industrial wastes. A study was conducted to determine the amount of TCDD present in the tissues of bullfrogs inhabiting the Rocky Branch Creek in central Arkansas, an area known to be contaminated by TCDD (*Chemosphere*, Feb. 1986). The level of TCDD (in parts per trillion) was measured in several specific tissues of four female bull frogs; the ratio of TCDD in the tissue to TCDD in the leg muscle of the frog was recorded for each. The relative ratios of contaminant for two tissues, the liver and the ovaries, are given for each of the four frogs in the accompanying table. According to the researchers, "the data set suggests that the [mean] relative level of TCDD in the ovaries of female frogs is higher than the [mean] level in the liver of the frogs." Test this claim using $\alpha = .05$.

Frog	A	B	C	D
Liver	11.0	14.6	14.3	12.2
Ovaries	34.2	41.2	32.5	26.2

Source: Korfmacher, W. A., Hansen, E. B., and Rowland, K. L. "Tissue distribution of 2,3,7,8-TCDD in bullfrogs obtained from a 2,3,7,8-TCDD-contaminated area." *Chemosphere*, Vol. 15, No. 2, Feb. 1986, p. 125. Reprinted with permission. Copyright 1986, Pergamon Press, Ltd.

9.43 Merck Research Labs conducted an experiment to evaluate the effect of a new drug using the Single-T Swim maze. Nineteen impregnated dam rats were captured and allocated a dosage of 12.5 milligrams of the drug. One male and one female pup were randomly selected from each resulting litter to perform in the swim maze. Each rat pup is placed in water at one end of the maze and allowed to swim until it successfully escapes at the opposite end. If the rat pup fails to escape after a certain period of time, it is placed at the beginning end of the maze and given another attempt to escape. The experiment is repeated until three successful escapes are accomplished by each rat pup. The number of swims required by each pup to perform three successful escapes is reported in the table on page 464. Is there sufficient evidence of a difference between the mean number of swims required by male and female rat pups? Use the MINITAB printout on page 464 to conduct the test (at $\alpha = .10$).

Litter	Male	Female	Litter	Male	Female
1	8	5	11	6	5
2	8	4	12	6	3
3	6	7	13	12	5
4	6	3	14	3	8
5	6	5	15	3	4
6	6	3	16	8	12
7	3	8	17	3	6
8	5	10	18	6	4
9	4	4	19	9	5
10	4	4			

Source: Thomas E. Bradstreet, Merck Research Labs, BL 3-2, West Point, Penn. 19486.

```
TEST OF MU = 0.000 VS MU N.E. 0.000

                N      MEAN    STDEV   SE MEAN       T    P VALUE
SwimDiff       19     0.368    3.515    0.806     0.46      0.65
```

9.44 Refer to the *Journal of Environmental Engineering* (Feb. 1986) study of winter heat loss in wastewater treatment clarifiers, Exercise 8.40. The data, reproduced in the table, were used to compare the mean day-long clear-sky solar radiation levels (in BTU/sq. ft.) at two midwest sites. A SAS printout for a test to compare the means follows. Interpret the results of the test.

Date	St. Joseph, Mo.	Iowa Great Lakes
December 21	782	593
January 6	965	672
January 21	948	750
February 6	1,181	988
February 21	1,414	1,226
March 7	1,633	1,462
March 21	1,852	1,698

Source: Wall, D. J., and Peterson, G. "Model for winter heat loss in uncovered clarifiers." *Journal of Environmental Engineering*, Vol. 112, No. 1, Feb. 1986, p. 128.

```
Analysis Variable : RADDIFF


N Obs          T    Prob>|T|
---------------------------------
    7   11.7649303     0.0001
---------------------------------
```

9.10   Testing a Population Proportion

In Section 9.3, we gave several examples of a statistical test of hypothesis for a population proportion p. When the sample size is large, the sample proportion of successes $\hat{p}$ is approximately normal and the general formulas for conducting a large-sample z test (given in Section 9.3) can be applied.

The procedure for testing a hypothesis about a population proportion p based on a large sample from the target population is described in the box. (Recall that p represents the probability of success in a binomial experiment.) For the procedure to be valid, the sample size must be sufficiently large to guarantee approximate normality of the sampling distribution of the sample proportion, $\hat{p}$. As with confidence intervals, a general rule of thumb for determining whether n is "sufficiently large" is that both $n\hat{p}$ and $n\hat{q}$ are greater than or equal to 4.

Large-Sample Test of Hypothesis About a Population Proportion

One-Tailed Test	Two-Tailed Test
H_0: $p = p_0$	H_0: $p = p_0$
H_a: $p > p_0$	H_a: $p \neq p_0$
[or H_a: $p < p_0$]	

Test statistic: $z = \dfrac{\hat{p} - p_0}{\sqrt{p_0 q_0 / n}}$

where $q_0 = 1 - p_0$

Rejection region: $z > z_\alpha$	Rejection region: $\lvert z \rvert > z_{\alpha/2}$
[or $z < -z_\alpha$]	

Assumption: The sample size n is sufficiently large so that the approximation is valid. As a rule of thumb, the condition of "sufficiently large" will be satisfied when $n\hat{p} \geq 4$ and $n\hat{q} \geq 4$.

EXAMPLE 9.16

Controversy surrounds the use of weathering steel in the construction of highway bridges. Critics have recently cited serious corrosive problems with weathering steel and are currently urging states to prohibit its use in bridge construction. On the other hand, the steel corporations claim that these charges are exaggerated and report that 95% of all weathering steel bridges in operation show "good" performance, with no major corrosive damage. To test this claim, a team of engineers and steel industry experts evaluated 60 randomly selected weathering steel bridges and found 54 of them showing "good" performance. Is there evidence, at $\alpha = .05$, that the true proportion of weathering steel highway bridges that show "good" performance is less than .95, the figure quoted by the steel corporations?

Solution

The parameter of interest is a population proportion, p. We want to test

$$H_0: \quad p = .95$$
$$H_a: \quad p < .95$$

where p is the true proportion of all weathering steel highway bridges that show "good" performance.

At significance level $\alpha = .05$, the null hypothesis will be rejected if

$$z < -z_{.05}$$

that is, H_0 will be rejected if

$$z < -1.645 \quad \text{(see Figure 9.18)}$$

The sample proportion of bridges that show "good" performance is

$$\hat{p} = \frac{54}{60} = .90$$

FIGURE 9.18 ▶
Rejection region for Example 9.16

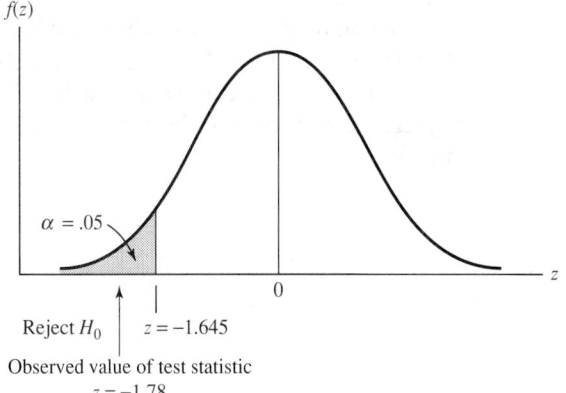

Thus, the test statistic has the value

$$z = \frac{\hat{p} - p_0}{\sqrt{p_0 q_0/n}} = \frac{.90 - .95}{\sqrt{(.95)(.05)/60}} = -1.78$$

The null hypothesis can be rejected (at $\alpha = .05$), since the computed value of z falls within the rejection region. There is sufficient evidence to support the hypothesis that the proportion of weathering steel highway bridges that show "good" performance is less than .95. [Note that both $n\hat{p} = 60(.90) = 54$ and $n\hat{q} = 60(.10) = 6$ exceed 4. Thus, the sample size is clearly large enough to guarantee the validity of the hypothesis test.]

Although small-sample procedures are available for testing hypotheses about a population proportion, the details are omitted from our discussion. It is our experience that they are of limited utility, since most surveys of binomial populations (for example, opinion polls) performed in the real world use samples that are large enough to employ the techniques of this section.

EXERCISES

9.45 Researchers at the University of Rochester studied the friction that occurs in the paper-feeding process of a photocopier (*Journal of Engineering for Industry*, May 1993). The experiment involved monitoring the displacement of individual sheets of paper in a stack fed through the copier. If no sheet except the top one moved more than 25% of the total stroke distance, the feed was considered successful. In a stack of 100 sheets of paper, the feeding process was successful 94 times. The success rate of the feeder is designed to be .90. Test to determine whether the true success rate of the feeder exceeds .90. Use $\alpha = .10$.

9.46 Staying too long in a spa pool can result in overheating, which in the case of a pregnant woman, may cause fetal malformation. But how long is too long? Based on their work in this area, several researchers hypothesize that 75% of women, immersed in a spa with water temperature of 40°C, will become uncomfortably hot when their ear canal (core) temperature reaches 40°C. As a result, subjective discomfort is suggested as a possible safeguard against overheating. This finding was apparently contradicted by an Australian study of 24 healthy, nonpregnant women (*New England Journal of Medicine*, Sept. 20, 1990). Only 11 of the 24 women (46%) were uncomfortably hot when their core temperature reached 40°C. Test the hypothesis that the true percentage of healthy, nonpregnant women who become uncomfortably hot when their core temperature reaches 40°C is less than 75%. Use $\alpha = .10$.

9.47 Distortions that occur on a computer graphics terminal screen are often due to data being lost in the communications linkage process between the terminal and the computer. A manufacturer of a new data-communications error controller claims that the chance of losing data with the controller in operation is only .01. To test this claim, the communications link between a graphics terminal and computer is monitored with the error controller in operation. Of a random sample of 200 on-screen graphic items, six were distorted because of data errors in the communications link. Does the sample evidence refute the manufacturer's claim? Use $\alpha = .05$.

9.48 The National Science Foundation, in a survey of 2,237 engineering graduate students who earned their Ph.D. degrees, found that 607 were U.S. citizens; the majority (1,630) of the Ph.D. degrees were awarded to foreign nationals (*Science*, Sept. 24, 1993). Conduct a test to determine whether the true proportion of engineering Ph.D. degrees awarded to foreign nationals exceeds .5. Use $\alpha = .01$.

9.49 Concerned about airport and airline security, the Federal Aviation Administration (FAA) has begun imposing sanctions against airlines that fail security tests. One series of tests conducted at Los Angeles International Airport (LAX) showed that security guards detected only 72 of the 100 mock weapons carried on by FAA inspectors or included in their carry-on luggage (*Gainesville Sun*, Dec. 11, 1987). According to the FAA, this "detection rate was well below the national rate of .80." Is there sufficient evidence to conclude that the mock weapon detection rate at LAX is less than the national rate of .80? Test using $\alpha = .10$.

9.50   As part of the evaluation for an environmental impact statement of proposed hydroelectric design on the Stikine River in British Columbia, researchers conducted preliminary investigations of the effects of human-induced disturbances on the behavior of the resident mountain goat population (*Environmental Management*, Mar. 1983). Goat responses to exploration activities, including close-flying helicopters, fixed-wing aircraft, human bipedal movement, and loud blasts from geological drilling activities, were recorded for $n = 804$ goats. The researchers observed that 265 goats displayed a severe flight response to local rock or plant cover. Test the hypothesis that over 30% of the resident mountain goats will show a severe response to human-induced disturbances. Use $\alpha = .05$.

9.51   Architects and engineers, faced with public-sector (i.e., government) cuts, are turning to private-sector clients to fill an increasing share of their workloads. According to some researchers, the decrease in popularity of public-sector work among small, medium, and large architecture–engineering (A–E) firms has been dramatic. Two years ago, one-third of all A–E firms reported they relied on public sector projects for most (if not all) of their work. In a recent survey of 60 A–E firms, 10 indicated that they depended so heavily on government contracts. Do the sample data provide sufficient evidence to conclude that the percentage of A–E firms that rely heavily on public-sector clients has declined during the past 2 years? Use $\alpha = .05$.

9.11   Testing the Difference Between Two Population Proportions

The method for performing a large-sample test of hypothesis about $(p_1 - p_2)$, the difference between two binomial proportions, is outlined in the accompanying box.

When testing the null hypothesis that $(p_1 - p_2)$ equals some specified difference— say, D_0—we make a distinction between the case $D_0 = 0$ and the case $D_0 \neq 0$. For the special case $D_0 = 0$, i.e., when we are testing $H_0: (p_1 - p_2) = 0$ or, equivalently, $H_0: p_1 = p_2$, the best estimate of $p_1 = p_2 = p$ is found by dividing the total number of successes in the combined samples by the total number of observations in the two samples. That is, if y_1 is the number of successes in sample 1 and y_2 is the number of successes in sample 2, then

$$\hat{p} = \frac{y_1 + y_2}{n_1 + n_2}$$

In this case, the best estimate of the standard deviation of the sampling distribution of $(\hat{p}_1 - \hat{p}_2)$ is found by substituting $\hat{p}$ for both p_1 and p_2:

$$\sigma_{(\hat{p}_1 - \hat{p}_2)} = \sqrt{\frac{p_1 q_1}{n_1} + \frac{p_2 q_2}{n_2}} \approx \sqrt{\frac{\hat{p}\hat{q}}{n_1} + \frac{\hat{p}\hat{q}}{n_2}} = \sqrt{\hat{p}\hat{q}\left(\frac{1}{n_1} + \frac{1}{n_2}\right)}$$

For all cases in which $D_0 \neq 0$ [for example, when testing $H_0: (p_1 - p_2) = .2$], we use $\hat{p}_1$ and $\hat{p}_2$ in the formula for $\sigma_{(\hat{p}_1 - \hat{p}_2)}$. However, in most practical situations, we will want to test for a difference between proportions—that is, we will want to test $H_0: (p_1 - p_2) = 0$.

Large-Sample Test of Hypothesis About $(p_1 - p_2)$: Independent Samples

One-Tailed Test

H_0: $(p_1 - p_2) = D_0$

H_a: $(p_1 - p_2) > D_0$

  [or H_a: $(p_1 - p_2) < D_0$]

Two-Tailed Test

H_0: $(p_1 - p_2) = D_0$

H_a: $(p_1 - p_2) \neq D_0$

$$\text{Test statistic:} \quad z = \frac{(\hat{p}_1 - \hat{p}_2) - D_0}{\sigma_{(\hat{p}_1 - \hat{p}_2)}}$$

Rejection region: $z > z_\alpha$

  [or $z < -z_\alpha$]

Rejection region: $|z| > z_{\alpha/2}$

When $D_0 \neq 0$,

$$\sigma_{(\hat{p}_1 - \hat{p}_2)} \approx \sqrt{\frac{\hat{p}_1 \hat{q}_1}{n_1} + \frac{\hat{p}_2 \hat{q}_2}{n_2}}$$

where $\hat{q}_1 = 1 - \hat{p}_1$ and $\hat{q}_2 = 1 - \hat{p}_2$.

When $D_0 = 0$,

$$\sigma_{(\hat{p}_1 - \hat{p}_2)} \approx \sqrt{\hat{p}\hat{q}\left(\frac{1}{n_1} + \frac{1}{n_2}\right)}$$

where the total number of successes in the combined sample is $(y_1 + y_2)$ and

$$\hat{p}_1 = \hat{p}_2 = \hat{p} = \frac{y_1 + y_2}{n_1 + n_2}$$

Assumption: The sample sizes, n_1 and n_2, are sufficiently large. This will be satisfied if $n_1 \hat{p}_1 \geq 4$, $n_1 \hat{q}_1 \geq 4$, and $n_2 \hat{p}_2 \geq 4$, $n_2 \hat{q}_2 \geq 4$.

The sample sizes n_1 and n_2 must be sufficiently large to ensure that the sampling distributions of $\hat{p}_1$ and $\hat{p}_2$, and hence of the difference $(\hat{p}_1 - \hat{p}_2)$, are approximately normal. The rule of thumb used to determine if the sample sizes are "sufficiently large" is the same as that given in Section 8.9, namely, that the quantities $n_1 \hat{p}_1$, $n_2 \hat{p}_2$, $n_1 \hat{q}_1$, and $n_2 \hat{q}_2$ are all greater than or equal to 4. [*Note:* If the sample sizes are not sufficiently large, p_1 and p_2 can be compared using a technique to be discussed in Chapter 10.]

EXAMPLE 9.17

Recently there have been intensive campaigns encouraging people to save energy by carpooling to work. Some cities have created an incentive for carpooling by designating certain highway traffic lanes as "car-pool only" (i.e., only cars with two or more passengers can use these lanes). To evaluate the effectiveness of this plan, toll booth personnel in one city monitored 2,000 randomly selected cars prior to establishing car-pool-only lanes, and 1,500 cars after the car-pool-only lanes were established. The results of the study are shown in Table 9.5, where y_1 and y_2 represent the numbers of cars with two or more passengers (i.e., car-pool riders) in the "before" and "after" samples, respectively. Do the data indicate that the fraction of cars with car-pool riders has increased over this period? Use $\alpha = .05$.

TABLE 9.5   Results of Carpooling Study, Example 9.16

	Before Car-Pool Lanes Established	After Car-Pool Lanes Established
Sample Size	$n_1 = 2,000$	$n_2 = 1,500$
Car-Pool Riders	$y_1 = 655$	$y_2 = 576$

Solution

If we define p_1 and p_2 as the true proportions of cars with car-pool riders before and after establishing car-pool lanes, respectively, the elements of our test are:

$$H_0: \quad (p_1 - p_2) = 0$$
$$H_a: \quad (p_1 - p_2) < 0$$

(The test is one-tailed since we are interested only in determining whether the proportion of cars with car-pool riders has increased, i.e., whether $p_2 > p_1$.)

Test statistic: $z = \dfrac{(\hat{p}_1 - \hat{p}_2) - 0}{\sigma_{(\hat{p}_1 - \hat{p}_2)}}$

Rejection region: $\alpha = .05$

$z < -z_\alpha = -z_{.05} = -1.645$ (see Figure 9.19)

We now calculate the sample proportions of cars with car-pool riders:

$$\hat{p}_1 = \frac{652}{2,000} = .326 \qquad \hat{p}_2 = \frac{576}{1,500} = .384$$

The test statistic is

$$z = \frac{(\hat{p}_1 - \hat{p}_2) - 0}{\sigma_{(\hat{p}_1 - \hat{p}_2)}} \approx \frac{(\hat{p}_1 - \hat{p}_2)}{\sqrt{\hat{p}\hat{q}\left(\dfrac{1}{n_1} + \dfrac{1}{n_2}\right)}}$$

FIGURE 9.19 ▶
Rejection region for Example 9.17

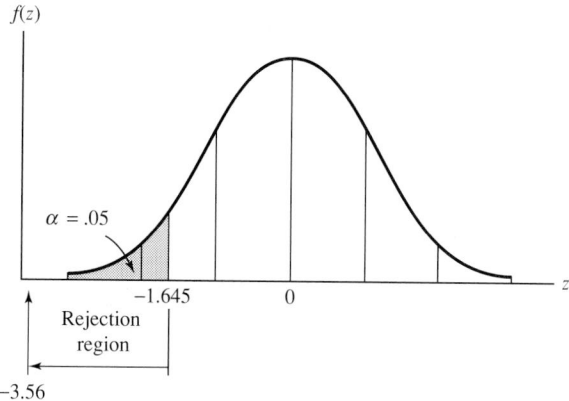

where

$$\hat{p} = \frac{y_1 + y_2}{n_1 + n_2} = \frac{652 + 576}{2{,}000 + 1{,}500} = .351$$

Thus,

$$z = \frac{.326 - .384}{\sqrt{(.351)(.649)\left(\dfrac{1}{2{,}000} + \dfrac{1}{1{,}500}\right)}} = \frac{-.058}{.0163} = -3.56$$

Since $z = -3.56$ falls in the rejection region, there is sufficient evidence at $\alpha = .05$ to conclude that the proportion of all cars with car-pool riders has increased after establishing car-pool lanes. We could place a confidence interval on $(p_1 - p_2)$ if we were interested in estimating the extent of the increase.

EXERCISES

9.52 Scientists have linked a catastrophic decline in the number of frogs inhabiting the world to ultraviolet radiation from the earth's tattered ozone layer (*Tampa Tribune*, Mar. 1, 1994). The Pacific tree frog, however, is not believed to be in decline because it produces an enzyme that appears to protect its eggs from ultraviolet radiation. Researchers at Oregon State University compared the hatching rates of two groups of Pacific tree frog eggs. One group of eggs was shielded with ultraviolet-blocking sun shades, whereas the second group was not. The number of eggs successfully hatched in each group is provided in the table. Compare the hatching rates of the two groups of Pacific tree frog eggs with a test of hypothesis. Use $\alpha = .01$.

	Sun-Shaded Eggs	*Unshaded Eggs*
Total Number	70	80
Number Hatched	34	31

9.53 Calcium blockers are among several classes of medicines commonly prescribed to relieve high blood pressure. A study in Denmark has found that calcium blockers may also be effective in reducing the risk of heart attacks (*Tampa Tribune*, Mar. 23, 1990). A total of 897 Danish patients, each recovering from a heart attack, were given a daily dose of the drug Verapamil, a calcium blocker. After 18 months of follow-up, 146 of these patients had recurring heart attacks. In a control group of 878 people—each of whom took placebos—180 had a heart attack. Do the data provide sufficient evidence to infer that calcium blockers are effective in reducing the risk of heart attacks? Test using $\alpha = .01$.

9.54 Every 10 years the Mechanics Division of ASEE conducts a nationwide survey on undergraduate mechanics education at colleges and universities. In 1985, 66 of the 100 colleges surveyed covered fluid statics in their undergraduate engineering program, compared to 43% in the 1975 survey (*Engineering Education*, Apr. 1986). Assuming that 100 colleges were also surveyed in 1975, conduct a test to determine whether the percentage of colleges covering fluid statics increased from 1975 to 1985. Use $\alpha = .01$.

9.55 A study was conducted to determine the impact of a multifunction workstation (MFWS) on the way managers work (*Datamation*, Feb. 15, 1986). Two groups of managers at a St. Louis-based defense agency took part in the survey: a test group consisting of 12 managers who currently use MFWS software and a control group of 25 non-MFWS users. One question on the survey concerned the information sources of the managers. In the test group (MFWS users), 4 of the 12 managers reported that their major source of information is the computer, whereas 2 of the 25 in the control group (non-MFWS users) rely on the computer as their major source of information.
    a. Is there evidence of a difference between the proportions of MFWS users and non-MFWS users who rely on the computer as their major information source? Test using $\alpha = .10$.
    b. Are the sample sizes large enough for the approximation procedure, part **a**, to be valid?

9.56 Home solar heating systems can be categorized into two groups, *passive* solar heating systems and *active* solar heating systems. In a passive solar heating system, the house itself is a solar energy collector, whereas in an active solar heating system, elaborate mechanical equipment is used to convert the sun's rays into heat. Consider the difference between the proportions of passive solar and active solar heating systems that require less than 200 gallons of oil per year in fuel consumption. Independent random samples of 50 passive and 50 active solar-heated homes are selected and the numbers that required less than 200 gallons of oil last year are noted, with the results given in the table. Is there evidence of a difference between the proportions of passive and active solar-heated homes that required less than 200 gallons of oil in fuel consumption last year? Test at a level of significance of $\alpha = .02$.

	Passive Solar	Active Solar
Number of homes	50	50
Number that required less than 200 gallons of oil last year	37	46

9.57 In 1982, 371 manufacturing and retailing companies were surveyed to determine the extent to which logistics information systems were implemented. A follow-up survey of 459 firms was conducted in 1987 to measure the 5-year trend in computerization of logistics information (*Industrial Engineering*, July 1990). One of the survey items focused on the percentage of firms that had computerized external market data. From 1982 to 1987, this percentage increased from 25% to 33%. Use this information to test for a significant increase in the percentage of firms with computerized external market data over the 5-year period. Test using $\alpha = .05$.

9.12   Testing a Population Variance

Recall from Section 8.10 that the pivotal statistic for estimating a population variance σ^2 does not possess a normal (z) distribution. Therefore, we cannot apply the procedure outlined in Section 9.4 when testing hypotheses about σ^2.

When the sample is selected from a normal population, however, the pivotal statistic possesses a chi-square (χ^2) distribution and the test can be conducted as outlined in the box. Note that the assumption of normality is required regardless of whether the sample size n is large or small.

Test of Hypothesis About a Population Variance σ^2

One-Tailed Test

H_0: $\sigma^2 = \sigma_0^2$

H_a: $\sigma^2 > \sigma_0^2$

   [or H_a: $\sigma^2 < \sigma_0^2$]

Two-Tailed Test

H_0: $\sigma^2 = \sigma_0^2$

H_a: $\sigma^2 \neq \sigma_0^2$

Test statistic: $\chi^2 = \dfrac{(n-1)s^2}{\sigma_0^2}$

Rejection region:

   $\chi^2 > \chi_\alpha^2$ (or $\chi^2 < \chi_{1-\alpha}^2$)

Rejection region:

   $\chi^2 < \chi_{1-\alpha/2}^2$ or $\chi^2 > \chi_{\alpha/2}^2$

where χ_α^2 and $\chi_{1-\alpha}^2$ are values of χ^2 that locate an area of α to the right and α to the left, respectively, of a chi-square distribution based on $(n-1)$ degrees of freedom.

[*Note:* σ_0^2 is our symbol for the particular numerical value specified for σ^2 in the null hypothesis.]

Assumption: The population from which the random sample is selected has an approximate normal distribution.

EXAMPLE 9.18

Refer to Example 8.15 concerning the variability of the amount of fill at a cannery. Suppose regulatory agencies specify that the standard deviation of the amount of fill should be less than .1 ounce. The quality control supervisor sampled $n = 10$ cans and mesured the amount of fill in each. The data are reproduced here. Does this information provide sufficient evidence to indicate that the standard deviation σ of the fill measurements is less than .1 ounce?

7.96   7.90   7.98   8.01   7.97   7.96   8.03   8.02   8.04   8.02

Solution

Since the null and alternative hypotheses must be stated in terms of σ^2 (rather than σ), we will want to test the null hypothesis that $\sigma^2 = .01$ against the alternative that $\sigma^2 < .01$. Therefore, the elements of the test are

H_0: $\sigma^2 = .01$ (i.e., $\sigma = .1$)

H_a: $\sigma^2 < .01$ (i.e., $\sigma < .1$)

Assumption: The populaton of fill amounts is approximately normal.

Test statistic: $\chi^2 = \dfrac{(n-1)s^2}{\sigma_0^2}$

Rejection region: The smaller the value of s^2 we observe, the stronger the evidence in favor of H_a. Thus, we reject H_0 for "small values" of the test statistic. With $\alpha = .05$ and 9 df, the χ^2 value for rejection is found in Table 8 of Appendix II and pictured in Figure 9.20. We will reject H_0 if $\chi^2 < 3.32511$. (Remember that the area given in Table 8 of Appendix II is the area to the *right* of the numerical value in the table. Thus, to determine the lower-tail value that has $\alpha = .05$ to its *left*, we use the $\chi^2_{.95}$ column in Table 8.)

FIGURE 9.20 ▶

Rejection region for Example 9.18

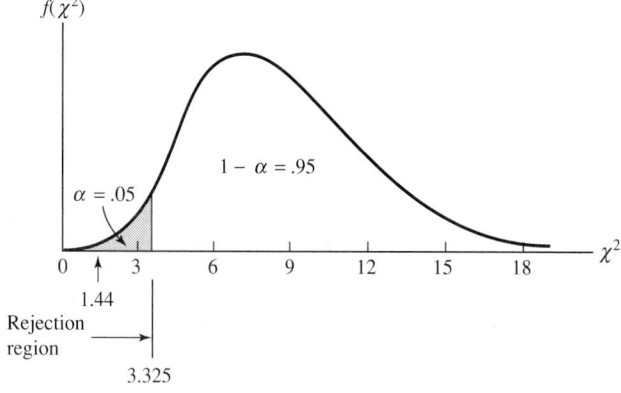

To compute the test statistic, we need to find the sample standard deviation, s. Numerical descriptive statistics for the sample data are provided in the SAS printout shown in Figure 9.21. The value of s, shaded in Figure 9.21, is $s = .043$. Substituting $s = .043$, $n = 10$, and $\sigma_0^2 = .01$ into the formula for the test statistic, we obtain

$$\chi^2 = \frac{(10-1)(.043)^2}{.01} = 1.66$$

Conclusion: Since the test statistic, $\chi^2 = 1.66$, is less than 3.32511, the supervisor can conclude (at $\alpha = .05$) that the variance of the population of all amounts of fill is less than .01 ($\sigma < .1$). If this procedure is repeatedly used, it will incorrectly reject H_0 only 5% of the time. Thus, the quality control supervisor is confident in the decision that the cannery is operating within the desired limits of variability.

FIGURE 9.21 ▶
SAS printout: Descriptive
statistics for Example 9.18

```
Variable=FILL
                              Moments

N                  10    Sum Wgts            10
Mean            7.989    Sum              79.89
Std Dev      0.043063    Variance      0.001854
Skewness      -0.8538    Kurtosis      0.479371
USS          638.2579    CSS            0.01669
CV           0.539032    Std Mean      0.013618
T:Mean=0     586.6587    Prob>|T|        0.0001
Sgn Rank         27.5    Prob>|S|        0.0020
Num  ^= 0          10

                       Quantiles(Def=5)

100% Max      8.04            99%         8.04
 75% Q3       8.02            95%         8.04
 50% Med     7.995            90%        8.035
 25% Q1       7.96            10%         7.93
  0% Min       7.9             5%          7.9
                               1%          7.9

Range         0.14
Q3-Q1         0.06
Mode          7.96
```

EXERCISES

9.58 Refer to the *Journal for Engineering for Industry* (May 1993) study of deep hole drilling under drill chip congestion, Exercise 9.21. Test to determine whether the true standard deviation of drill chip lengths differs from 75 mm. Recall that for $n = 50$ drill chips, $s = 50.2$.

9.59 Recording electrical activity of the brain is important in clinical problems as well as in neurophysiological research. To improve the signal-to-noise ratio (SNR) in the electrical activity, it is necessary to repeatedly stimulate subjects and average the responses—a procedure that assumes that single responses are homogeneous. A study was conducted to test the homogeneous signal theory (*IEEE Engineering in Medicine and Biology Magazine*, Mar. 1990). The null hypothesis is that the variance of the SNR readings of subjects equals the "expected" level under the homogeneous signal theory. For this study, the "expected" level was assumed to be .54. If the SNR variance exceeds this level, the researchers will conclude that the signals are nonhomogeneous.
a. Set up the null and alternative hypotheses for the researchers.
b. SNRs recorded for a sample of 41 normal children ranged from .03 to 3.0. Use this information to obtain an estimate of the sample standard deviation. [*Hint:* Assume that the distribution of SNRs is normal, and that most of the SNRs in the population will fall within $\mu \pm 2\sigma$, i.e., from $\mu - 2\sigma$ to $\mu + 2\sigma$. Note that the range of the interval equals 4σ.]
c. Use the estimate of s in part **b** to conduct the test of part **a**. Test using $\alpha = .10$.

9.60 The most common method of disinfecting water for potable use is free residual chlorination. Recently, preammoniation (i.e., the addition of ammonia to the water prior to applying free chlorine) has received considerable attention as an alternative treatment. In one study, 44 water specimens treated with pream-moniation were found to have a mean effluent turbidity of 1.8 and a standard deviation of .16 (*American Water Works Journal*, Jan. 1986). Is there sufficient evidence to indicate that the variance of the efflu-ent turbidity in water specimens disinfected by the preammoniation method exceeds .0016? (The value .0016 represents the known effluent turbidity variance of water specimens treated with free chlorine.) Test using $\alpha = .01$.

9.61 In any canning process, a manufacturer will lose money if the cans contain either significantly more or significantly less than is claimed on the label. Accordingly, canners pay close attention to the amount of their product being dispensed by the can-filling machines. Consider a company that produces a fast-drying rubber cement in 32-ounce aluminum cans. A quality control inspector is interested in testing whether the variance of the amount of rubber cement dispensed into the cans is more than .3. If so, the dispensing machine is in need of adjustment. Since inspection of the canning process requires that the dispensing machines be shut down, and shutdowns for any lengthy period of time cost the company thousands of dollars in lost revenue, the inspector is able to obtain a random sample of only 10 cans for testing. After measuring the weights of their contents, the inspector computes the following summary statistics:

$$\bar{x} = 31.55 \text{ ounces} \qquad s = .48 \text{ ounce}$$

a. Does the sample evidence indicate that the dispensing machines are in need of adjustment? Test at significance level $\alpha = .05$.

b. What assumption is necessary for the hypothesis test of part **a** to be valid?

9.62 Polychlorinated biphenyls (PCBs), used in the manufacture of large electrical transformers and capacitors, are extremely hazardous contaminants when released into the environment. The Environmental Protection Agency (EPA) is experimenting with a new device for measuring PCB concentration in fish. To check the precision of the new instrument, seven PCB readings were taken on the same fish sample. The data are recorded here (in parts per million):

> 6.2   5.8   5.7   6.3   5.9   5.8   6.0

Suppose the EPA requires an instrument that yields PCB readings with a variance of less than .1. Does the new instrument meet the EPA's specifications? Test at $\alpha = .05$.

9.13   Testing the Ratio of Two Population Variances

As in the one-sample case, the pivotal statistic for comparing two population vari-ances, σ_1^2 and σ_2^2, has a nonnormal sampling distribution. Recall from Section 8.11 that the ratio of the sample variances s_1^2/s_2^2 possesses, under certain conditions, an F distribution.

The elements of the hypothesis test for the ratio of two population variances, σ_1^2/σ_2^2, are given in the box.

Test of Hypothesis for the Ratio of Two Population Variances σ_1^2/σ_2^2: Independent Samples

One-Tailed Test

H_0: $\dfrac{\sigma_1^2}{\sigma_2^2} = 1$

H_a: $\dfrac{\sigma_1^2}{\sigma_2^2} > 1$

$\left[\text{or, } H_a: \dfrac{\sigma_1^2}{\sigma_2^2} < 1\right]$

Test statistic:

$F = \dfrac{s_1^2}{s_2^2} \quad \left[\text{or, } F = \dfrac{s_2^2}{s_1^2}\right]$

Two-Tailed Test

H_0: $\dfrac{\sigma_1^2}{\sigma_2^2} = 1$

H_a: $\dfrac{\sigma_1^2}{\sigma_2^2} \neq 1$

Test statistic:

$F = \dfrac{\text{Larger sample variance}}{\text{Smaller sample variance}}$

$= \begin{cases} \dfrac{s_1^2}{s_2^2} & \text{when } s_1^2 > s_2^2 \\[2ex] \dfrac{s_2^2}{s_1^2} & \text{when } s_2^2 > s_1^2 \end{cases}$

Rejection region:

$F > F_\alpha$

Rejection region:

$F > F_{\alpha/2}$

where F_α and $F_{\alpha/2}$ are values that locate area α and $\alpha/2$, respectively, in the upper tail of the F distribution with ν_1 = numerator degrees of freedom (i.e., the df for the sample variance in the numerator) and ν_2 = denominator degrees of freedom (i.e., the df for the sample variance in the denominator).

Assumptions: 1. Both of the populations from which the samples are selected have relative frequency distributions that are approximately normal.

2. The random samples are selected in an independent manner from the two populations.

EXAMPLE 9.19

Heavy doses of ethylene oxide (ETO) in rabbits have been shown to alter significantly the DNA structure of cells. Although it is a known mutagen and suspected carcinogen, ETO is used quite frequently in sterilizing hospital supplies. A study was conducted to investigate the effect of ETO on hospital personnel involved with the sterilization process. Thirty-one subjects were randomly selected and assigned to one of two tasks. Eighteen subjects were assigned the task of opening the sterilization package that contains ETO (task 1). The remaining 13 subjects were assigned the task of opening and unloading the sterilizer gun filled with ETO (task 2). After the tasks were performed, researchers measured the amount of ETO (in milligrams) present in the bloodstream of each subject. A summary of the results appears in Table 9.6. Do the data provide sufficient evidence to indicate a difference in the variability of the ETO levels in subjects assigned to the two tasks? Test using $\alpha = .10$.

TABLE 9.6   Summary Data for Example 9.19

	Task 1	Task 2
Sample Size	18	13
Mean	5.90	5.60
Standard Deviation	1.93	3.10

Solution

Let

σ_1^2 = Population variance of ETO levels in subjects assigned task 1

σ_2^2 = Population variance of ETO levels in subjects assigned task 2

For this test to yield valid results, we must assume that both samples of ETO levels come from normal populations and that the samples are independent.

The hypotheses of interest are then

$$H_0: \quad \frac{\sigma_1^2}{\sigma_2^2} = 1 \quad (\sigma_1^2 = \sigma_2^2)$$

$$H_a: \quad \frac{\sigma_1^2}{\sigma_2^2} \neq 1 \quad (\sigma_1^2 \neq \sigma_2^2)$$

The nature of the F tables given in Appendix II affects the form of the test statistic. To form the rejection region for a two-tailed F test we want to make certain that the upper tail is used, because only the upper-tail values of F are shown in Tables 9–12 of Appendix II. To accomplish this, **we will always place the larger sample variance in the numerator of the F test statistic**. This has the effect of doubling the tabulated value for α, since we double the probability that the F ratio will fall in the upper tail by always placing the larger sample variance in the numerator. That is, we make the test two-tailed by putting the larger variance in the numerator rather than establishing rejection regions in both tails.

Thus, for our example, we have a denominator s_1^2 with df $= n_1 - 1 = 17$ and a numerator s_2^2 with df $= n_2 - 1 = 12$. Therefore, the test statistic will be

$$F = \frac{\text{Larger sample variance}}{\text{Smaller sample variance}} = \frac{s_2^2}{s_1^2}$$

and we will reject $H_0: \sigma_1^2 = \sigma_2^2$ for $\alpha = .10$ when the calculated value of F exceeds the tabulated value:

$$F_{\alpha/2} = F_{.05} = 2.38$$

We can now calculate the value of the test statistic and complete the analysis:

$$F = \frac{s_2^2}{s_1^2} = \frac{(3.10)^2}{(1.93)^2} = \frac{9.61}{3.72} = 2.58$$

When we compare this to the rejection region shown in Figure 9.22, we see that $F = 2.58$ falls in the rejection region. Therefore, the data provide sufficient evidence to indicate that the population variances differ. It appears that hospital personnel involved with opening the sterilization package (task 1) have less variable ETO levels than those involved with opening and unloading the sterilizer gun (task 2).

FIGURE 9.22 ▶
Rejection region for Example 9.19

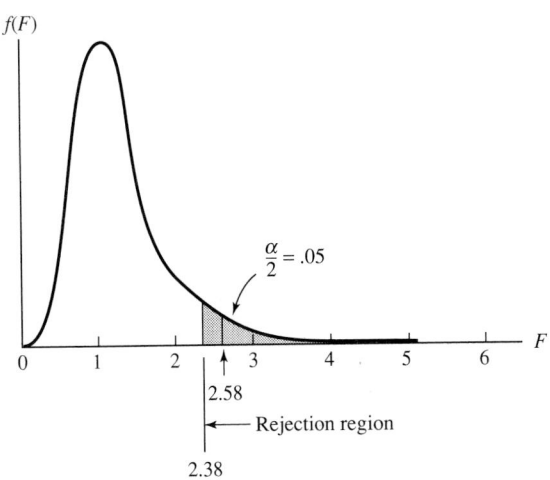

What would you have concluded in Example 9.19 if the value of F calculated from the samples had not fallen in the rejection region? Would you conclude that the null hypothesis of equal variances is true? No, because then you risk the possibility of a Type II error (failing to reject H_0 if H_a is true) without knowing the value of β, the probability of failing to reject H_0: $\sigma_1^2 = \sigma_2^2$ if in fact it is false. Since we will not consider the calculation of β for specific alternatives, when the F statistic does not fall in the rejection region, we simply conclude that insufficient sample evidence exists to refute the null hypothesis that $\sigma_1^2 = \sigma_2^2$.

Example 9.19 illustrates the technique for calculating the test statistic and rejection region for a two-tailed test to avoid the problem of locating an F value in the lower tail of the F distribution. In a one-tailed test this is much easier to accomplish since we can control how we specify the ratio of the population variances in H_0 and H_a. That is, we can always make a one-tailed test an *upper-tailed* test. For example, if we want to test whether σ_1^2 is greater than σ_2^2, then we write the alternative hypothesis as

$$H_a: \quad \frac{\sigma_1^2}{\sigma_2^2} > 1 \quad (\text{i.e., } \sigma_1^2 > \sigma_2^2)$$

and the appropriate test statistic is $F = s_1^2/s_2^2$. Conversely, if we want to test whether σ_1^2 is less than σ_2^2 (i.e, whether σ_2^2 is greater than σ_1^2), we write

$$H_a: \quad \frac{\sigma_2^2}{\sigma_1^2} > 1 \quad (\text{i.e., } \sigma_2^2 > \sigma_1^2)$$

and the corresponding test statistic is $F = s_2^2/s_1^2$.

EXERCISES

9.63 Refer to Exercise 9.35. Recall that an *Environmental Science & Technology* study was conducted to compare the mean oxon/thion ratios at a California orchard under two weather conditions—foggy and clear/cloudy. Test the assumption of equal variances required for the comparison of means to be valid. Use $\alpha = .05$.

Date	Condition	Thion	Oxon	Oxon/Thion Ratio
Jan. 15	Fog	38.2	10.3	.270
17	Fog	28.6	6.9	.241
18	Fog	30.2	6.2	.205
19	Fog	23.7	12.4	.523
20	Fog	62.3	(Air sample lost)	—
20	Clear	74.1	45.8	.618
21	Fog	88.2	9.9	.112
21	Clear	46.4	27.4	.591
22	Fog	135.9	44.8	.330
23	Fog	102.9	27.8	.270
23	Cloudy	28.9	6.5	.225
25	Fog	46.9	11.2	.239
25	Clear	44.3	16.6	.375

Source: Selber, J. N., et al. "Air and fog deposition residues of four organophosphate insecticides used on dormant orchards in the San Joaquin Valley, California." *Environmental Science & Technology*, Vol. 27, No. 10, Oct. 1993, p. 2240 (Table V).

9.64 Wet samplers are standard devices used to measure the chemical composition of precipitation. The accuracy of the wet deposition readings, however, may depend on the number of samplers stationed in the field. Experimenters in The Netherlands collected wet deposition measurements using anywhere from one to eight identical wet samplers (*Atmospheric Environment*, Vol. 24A, 1990). For each sampler (or sampler combination) data was collected every 24 hours for an entire year; thus, 365 readings were collected per sampler (or sampler combination). When one wet sampler was used, the standard deviation of the hydrogen readings (measured as percentage relative to the average reading from all eight samplers) was 6.3%. When three wet samplers were used, the standard deviation of the hydrogen readings (measured as percentage relative to the average reading from all eight samplers) was 2.6%. Conduct a test to compare the variation in hydrogen readings for the two sampling schemes (i.e., one wet sampler versus three wet samplers). Test using $\alpha = .05$.

9.65 An experiment was conducted to study the effect of reinforced flanges on the torsional capacity of reinforced concrete T-beams (*Journal of the American Concrete Institute*, Jan.–Feb. 1986). Several different types of

T-beams were used in the experiment, each type having a different flange width. The beams were tested under combined torsion and bending until failure (cracking). One variable of interest is the cracking torsion moment at the top of the flange of the T-beam. Cracking torsion moments for eight beams with 70-cm slab widths and eight beams with 100-cm slab widths follow:

70-cm slab width: 6.00, 7.20, 10.20, 13.20, 11.40, 13.60, 9.20, 11.20
100-cm slab width: 6.80, 9.20, 8.80, 13.20, 11.20, 14.90, 10.20, 11.80

a. Is there evidence of a difference in the variation in the cracking torsion moments of the two types of T-beams? Use $\alpha = .10$.

b. What assumptions are required for the test to be valid?

9.66 Refer to the general trace organic monitoring study discussed in Exercise 7.21. The total organic carbon (TOC) level was measured in water samples collected at two sewage treatment sites in England. The accompanying table gives the summary information on the TOC levels (measured in mg/l) found in the rivers adjacent to the two sewage facilities. Since the river at the Foxcote sewage treatment works was subject to periodic spillovers, not far upstream of the plant's intake, it is believed that the TOC levels found at Foxcote will have greater variation than the levels at Bedford. Does the sample information support this hypothesis? Test at $\alpha = .05$.

Bedford	Foxcote
$n_1 = 61$	$n_2 = 52$
$\bar{y}_1 = 5.35$	$\bar{y}_2 = 4.27$
$s_1 = .96$	$s_2 = 1.27$

Source: Pinchin, M. J. "A study of the trace organics profiles of raw and potable water systems." *Journal of the Institute of Water Engineers & Scientists*, Vol. 40, No. 1, Feb. 1986, p. 87.

9.67 Refer to the speechreading study introduced in Exercise 9.41. A second experiment was conducted to compare the variability in the sentence perception of normal-hearing individuals with no prior experience in speechreading to those with experience in speechreading. The sample consisted of 24 inexperienced and 12 experienced subjects. All subjects were asked to verbally reproduce sentences under several conditions, one of which was speechreading supplemented with sound-pressure information. A summary of the results (percentage of correct syllables) for the two groups is given in the table. Conduct a test to determine whether the variance in the percentage of correctly reproduced syllables differs between the two groups of speechreaders. Test using $\alpha = .10$.

Inexperienced Speechreaders	Experienced Speechreaders
$n_1 = 24$	$n_2 = 12$
$\bar{y}_1 = 87.1$	$\bar{y}_2 = 86.1$
$s_1 = 8.7$	$s_2 = 12.4$

Source: Breeuwer, M., and Plomp, R. "Speechreading supplemented with auditorily presented speech parameters." *Journal of the Acoustical Society of America*, Vol. 79, No. 2, Feb. 1986, p. 487.

OPTIONAL EXERCISES

9.68   Suppose we want to test $H_0: \sigma_1^2 = \sigma_2^2$ versus $H_a: \sigma_1^2 \neq \sigma_2^2$. Show that the rejection region given by

$$\frac{s_1^2}{s_2^2} > F_{\alpha/2} \quad \text{or} \quad \frac{s_1^2}{s_2^2} < F_{(1-\alpha/2)}$$

where F depends on $\nu_1 = (n_1 - 1)$ df and $\nu_2 = (n_2 - 1)$ df, is equivalent to the rejection region given by

$$\frac{s_1^2}{s_2^2} > F_{\alpha/2} \quad \text{where } F \text{ depends on } \nu_1 \text{ numerator df and } \nu_2 \text{ denominator df}$$

or

$$\frac{s_2^2}{s_1^2} > F_{\alpha/2}^* \quad \text{where } F^* \text{ depends on } \nu_2 \text{ numerator df and } \nu_1 \text{ denominator df}$$

[*Hint:* Use the fact (proof omitted) that

$$F_{(1-\alpha/2)} = \frac{1}{F_{\alpha/2}^*}$$

where F depends on ν_1 numerator df and ν_2 denominator df and F^* depends on ν_2 numerator df and ν_1 denominator df.]

9.69   Use the results of Optional Exercise 9.68 to show that

$$P\left(\frac{\text{Larger sample variance}}{\text{Smaller sample variance}} > F_{\alpha/2}\right) = \alpha$$

where F depends on numerator df = [(Sample size for numerator sample variance) − 1] and denominator df = [(Sample size for denominator sample variance) − 1]. [*Hint:* First write

$$P\left(\frac{\text{Larger sample variance}}{\text{Smaller sample variance}} > F_{\alpha/2}\right) = P\left(\frac{s_1^2}{s_2^2} > F_{\alpha/2} \quad \text{or} \quad \frac{s_2^2}{s_1^2} > F_{\alpha/2}\right)$$

Then use the fact that $P(F > F_{\alpha/2}) = \alpha/2$.]

9.14   Summary

This chapter presents the basic concepts of a statistical **test of a hypothesis** about one or more population parameters. Tests of hypotheses are used when the ultimate practical objective of an inference is to reach a decision about the value(s) of the parameter(s). We can evaluate the goodness of the inference in terms of α and β, the probabilities of making incorrect decisions.

The close relationship between estimation and hypothesis testing is apparent when we compare the statistics employed for these two purposes. The statistics used to construct confidence intervals for parameters in Chapter 8 were then used to test hypotheses about the same parameters in Chapter 9. These tests are summarized in Tables 9.7a and 9.7b.

In the following chapters, we will present some very useful methodology for analyzing multivariable experiments. As you will subsequently learn, the confidence intervals and tests that we will employ are based on an assumption of normality. Thus, the statistics that we will use to construct confidence intervals and test hypotheses possess sampling distributions that are the familiar t, χ^2, and F distributions of Chapters 7, 8, and 9.

TABLE 9.7a Summary of Hypothesis Tests: One-Sample Case

Parameter (θ)	Null Hypothesis (H_0)	Point Estimator ($\hat{\theta}$)	Test Statistic	Sample Size	Additional Assumptions
μ	$\mu = \mu_0$	$\bar{y}$	$z = \dfrac{\bar{y} - \mu_0}{\sigma/\sqrt{n}} \approx \dfrac{\bar{y} - \mu_0}{s/\sqrt{n}}$	$n \geq 30$	None
			$t = \dfrac{\bar{y} - \mu_0}{s/\sqrt{n}}$ where t is based on $\nu = (n-1)$ degrees of freedom	$n < 30$	Normal population
p	$p = p_0$	$\hat{p} = \dfrac{y}{n}$	$z = \dfrac{\hat{p} - p_0}{\sqrt{\dfrac{p_0 q_0}{n}}}$	n large enough so that $n\hat{p} \geq 4$ and $n\hat{q} \geq 4$	None
σ^2	$\sigma^2 = \sigma_0^2$	s^2	$\chi^2 = \dfrac{(n-1)s^2}{\sigma_0^2}$ where χ^2 has a chi-square distribution with $\nu = (n-1)$ degrees of freedom	All n	Normal population

TABLE 9.7b Summary of Hypothesis Tests: Two-Sample Case

Parameter (θ)	Null Hypothesis (H_0)	Point Estimator ($\hat{\theta}$)	Test Statistic	Sample Size	Additional Assumptions
$(\mu_1 - \mu_2)$ Independent samples	$(\mu_1 - \mu_2) = D_0$ (If we want to detect a difference between μ_1 and μ_2, then $D_0 = 0$.)	$(\bar{y} - \bar{y}_2)$	$z = \dfrac{(\bar{y}_1 - \bar{y}_2) - D_0}{\sqrt{\dfrac{\sigma_1^2}{n_1} + \dfrac{\sigma_2^2}{n_2}}}$ $\approx \dfrac{(\bar{y}_1 - \bar{y}_2) - D_0}{\sqrt{\dfrac{s_1^2}{n_1} + \dfrac{s_2^2}{n_2}}}$	$n_1 \geq 30,\ n_2 \geq 30$	None
			$t = \dfrac{(\bar{y}_1 - \bar{y}_2) - D_0}{\sqrt{s_p^2 \left(\dfrac{1}{n_1} + \dfrac{1}{n_2}\right)}}$ where t is based on $\nu = n_1 + n_2 - 2$ degrees of freedom and $s_p^2 = \dfrac{(n_1-1)s_1^2 + (n_2-1)s_2^2}{n_1 + n_2 - 2}$	Either $n_1 < 30$ or $n_2 < 30$ or both	Both populations normal with equal variances ($\sigma_1^2 = \sigma_2^2$) (For situations in which $\sigma_1^2 \neq \sigma_2^2$, see the modifications listed in the box on page 455.)

(continued)

TABLE 9.7b   Summary of Hypothesis Tests: Two-Sample Case, continued

Parameter (θ)	Null Hypothesis (H_0)	Point Estimator ($\hat{\theta}$)	Test Statistic	Sample Size	Additional Assumptions
$\mu_d =$ $(\mu_1 - \mu_2)$ Matched pairs	$\mu_d = D_0$ (If we want to detect a difference between μ_1 and μ_2, then $D_0 = 0$.)	$\bar{d} = \sum_{i=1}^{n} d_i/n$ Mean of sample differences	$t = \dfrac{\bar{d} - D_0}{s_d/\sqrt{n_d}}$ where t is based on $\nu = (n_d - 1)$ degrees of freedom	All n_d (If $n_d \geq 30$, then the standard normal (z) test may be used.)	Population of differences d_i is normal
$(p_1 - p_2)$	$(p_1 - p_2) = D_0$ (If we want to detect a difference between p_1 and p_2, then $D_0 = 0$.)	$(\hat{p}_1 - \hat{p}_2)$	For $D_0 = 0$: $z = \dfrac{(\hat{p}_1 - \hat{p}_2)}{\sqrt{\hat{p}\hat{q}\left(\dfrac{1}{n_1} + \dfrac{1}{n_2}\right)}}$ where $\hat{p} = \dfrac{y_1 + y_2}{n_1 + n_2}$ For $D_0 \neq 0$: $z = \dfrac{(\hat{p}_1 - \hat{p}_2) - D_0}{\sqrt{\dfrac{\hat{p}_1\hat{q}_1}{n_1} + \dfrac{\hat{p}_2\hat{q}_2}{n_2}}}$	n_1 and n_2 large enough so that $n_1\hat{p}_1 \geq 4$, $n_1\hat{q}_1 \geq 4$ and $n_2\hat{p}_2 \geq 4$, $n_2\hat{q}_2 \geq 4$	Independent samples
$\dfrac{\sigma_1^2}{\sigma_2^2}$	$\dfrac{\sigma_1^2}{\sigma_2^2} = 1$ (i.e., $\sigma_1^2 = \sigma_2^2$)	$\dfrac{s_1^2}{s_2^2}$	For $H_a: \sigma_1^2 > \sigma_2^2$: $F = \dfrac{s_1^2}{s_2^2}$ For $H_a: \sigma_2^2 > \sigma_1^2$: $F = \dfrac{s_2^2}{s_1^2}$ For $H_a: \sigma_1^2 \neq \sigma_2^2$: $F = \dfrac{\text{Larger } s^2}{\text{Smaller } s^2}$ where the distribution of F is based on $\nu_1 =$ numerator degrees of freedom and $\nu_2 =$ denominator degrees of freedom	All n_1 and n_2	Independent random samples from normal populations

SUPPLEMENTARY EXERCISES

9.70   One of the keys to occupational therapy is patient motivation. A study was conducted to determine whether *purposeful activity* (defined as tasks that are goal-directed) provides intrinsic motivation to exercise performance (*Journal of Occupational Therapy*, Mar. 1984). Twenty-six females were recruited to take part in the study. Each female subject was instructed to perform two similar exercises, jumping rope (the purposeful activity) and jumping without a rope (the nonpurposeful activity), until their perceived exertion level reached

17 on the RPE scale (i.e., until they had worked their bodies "very hard"). The length of time (in minutes) that each subject jumped was then recorded for each of the two exercises and the difference d_i (computed by subtracting the length of jumping time without rope from the length of jumping time with rope) was calculated. A summary of the 26 differences is provided here:

$$\bar{d} = 41.84 \text{ seconds}$$
$$s_d = 110.28 \text{ seconds}$$

One theory held by occupational therapists is that those performing a purposeful activity are more motivated, and hence, tend to fatigue less easily. Test the hypothesis that the mean exercise time for the purposeful activity (jumping with a rope) exceeds the mean exercise time for the nonpurposeful activity (jumping without a rope). Use $\alpha = .05$.

9.71 Suppose you want to determine whether users of data processors have a preference between word processors A and B. If users have no preference for either of the two word processors (i.e., if the two systems are identical), then the probability p that a user prefers system A is $p = .5$. Let y be the number of users in a sample of 10 who prefer system A, and suppose you want to test $H_0: p = .5$ against $H_a: p \neq .5$. One possible test procedure is to reject H_0 if $y \leq 1$ or $y \geq 8$.
   a. Find α for this test.
   b. Find β if $p = .4$. What is the power of the test?
   c. Find β if $p = .8$. What is the power of the test?

9.72 The quality control department of a paper company measures the brightness (a measure of reflectance) of finished paper on a periodic basis throughout the day. Two instruments that are available to measure the paper specimens are subject to error, but they can be adjusted so that the mean readings for a control paper specimen are the same for both instruments. Suppose you are concerned about the precision of the two instruments—namely, that instrument 2 is less precise than instrument 1. To check this theory, five measurements of a single paper sample are made on both instruments. The data are shown in the table. Do the data provide sufficient evidence to indicate that instrument 2 is less precise than instrument 1? Test using $\alpha = .05$.

Instrument 1	Instrument 2
29	26
28	34
30	30
28	32
30	28

9.73 The testing department of a tire and rubber company schedules truck and passenger tires for durability tests. Currently, tires are scheduled twice weekly on flexible processors (machines that can handle either truck or passenger tires) using the shortest processing time (SPT) approach. Under SPT, the tire with the shortest processing time is scheduled first. Company researchers have developed a new scheduling rule which they believe will reduce the average flow time (i.e., the average completion time of a test) and lead to a reduction in the average tardiness of a scheduled test. To compare the two scheduling rules, 64 tires were randomly selected and divided into two groups of equal size. One set of tires was scheduled using SPT, the other using the proposed rule. A summary of the flow times and tardiness (in hours) of the tire tests is provided in the table on page 486.

	Flow Time		Tardiness	
	Mean	Variance	Mean	Variance
SPT	158.28	8,532.80	5.26	452.09
Proposed Rule	117.07	5,208.53	4.52	319.41

a. Is there sufficient evidence at $\alpha = .05$ to conclude that the average flow time is less under the proposed scheduling rule than under the SPT approach?

b. Is there sufficient evidence at $\alpha = .05$ to conclude that the proposed scheduling rule will lead to a reduction in the average tardiness of tire tests?

9.74 Refer to the reinforced concrete T-beam cracking experiment described in Exercise 9.65. The experimental results were compared to the theoretical results obtained using the failure surface method of predicting ultimate load capacity. The actual and theoretical ultimate torsion moments for six T-beams with 40-cm slab widths are given in the table. Conduct a test to determine whether the experimental mean ultimate torsion moment differs from the theoretical mean ultimate torsion moment. Use $\alpha = .05$.

T-Beam	1	2	3	4	5	6
Experimental result	4.70	5.20	5.40	5.40	4.30	4.80
Theoretical result	4.63	4.65	5.60	5.60	3.62	3.62

Source: Zararis, P. D., and Penelis, G. Jr. "Reinforced concrete T-beams in torsion and bending." *Journal of the American Concrete Institute*, Vol. 83, No. 1, Jan.–Feb. 1986, p. 153.

9.75 A problem that occurs with certain types of mining is that some byproducts tend to be mildly radioactive and these products sometimes get into our freshwater supply. The EPA has issued regulations concerning a limit on the amount of radioactivity in supplies of drinking water. Particularly, the maximum level for naturally occurring radiation is 5 picocuries per liter of water. A random sample of 24 water specimens from a city's water supply produced the sample statistics $\bar{y} = 4.61$ picocuries per liter and $s = .87$ picocurie per liter.

a. Do these data provide sufficient evidence to indicate that the mean level of radiation is safe (below the maximum level set by the EPA)? Test using $\alpha = .01$.

b. Why should you want to use a small value of α for the test in part **a**?

c. Calculate the value of β for the test if $\mu_a = 4.5$ picocuries per liter of water.

d. Calculate and interpret the p-value for the test.

9.76 Usually, when trees grown in greenhouses are replanted in their natural habitat, there is only a 50% survival rate. However, a recent General Telephone and Electronics (GTE) advertisement claimed that trees grown in a particular environment ideal for plant growth have a 95% survival rate when replanted. These trees are grown inside a mountain in Idaho where the air temperature, carbon dioxide content, and humidity are all constant, and there are no major disease or insect problems. A key growth ingredient—light—is supplied by specially made GTE Sylvania Super-Metalarc lamps. These lights help the young trees develop a more fibrous root system that aids in the transplantation. Suppose that we want to challenge GTE's claim, i.e., we want to test whether the true proportion of all trees grown inside the Idaho mountain that survive when replanted in their natural habitat is less than .95. We randomly sample 50 of the trees grown in the controlled environment, replant the trees in their natural habitat, and observe that 46 of the trees survive. Perform the test at a level of significance of $\alpha = .01$.

9.77 A *parallel processor*, or *paracomputer*, consists of autonomous processing elements (PEs) sharing a central memory. Researchers at New York University have recently designed such a paracomputer, called the NYU

Ultracomputer. To assess the impact of network delay on overall ultracomputer performance, the researchers simulated central memory access time for sample instructions from a parallel version of a NASA weather program. Two sets of access times were simulated—one set processed with 16 processing elements, the other set with 48 processing elements. With 16 PEs, the average central memory access time was 8.94 seconds, whereas with 48 PEs the average central memory access time was 8.83 seconds. Assume that $n = 1,000$ instructions were simulated for each of the two programs, with standard deviations equal to 3.10 and 3.50, respectively. This information was not provided in the researchers' report. Is there sufficient evidence to indicate a difference between the average central memory access times of instructions processed with 16 and 48 PEs? Test using $\alpha = .05$.

9.78 In the manufacture of machinery, it is essential to utilize parts that conform to specifications. In the past, diameters of the ball bearings produced by a certain manufacturer had a variance of .00156. To cut costs, the manufacturer instituted a less expensive production method. The variance of the diameters of 100 randomly sampled bearings produced by the new process was .00211. Do the data provide sufficient evidence to indicate that diameters of ball bearings produced by the new process are more variable than those produced by the old process? Test at $\alpha = .05$.

9.79 The ion balance of our atmosphere has a significant effect on human health. A high concentration of positive ions in a room can induce fatigue, stress, and respiratory problems in the room's occupants. However, research has shown that introduction of additional negative ions into the room's atmosphere (through a negative ion generator), in combination with constant ventilation, restores the natural balance of ions that is conducive to human health. One experiment was conducted as follows. One hundred employees of a large factory were randomly selected and divided into two groups of 50 each. Both groups were told that they would be working in an atmosphere with an ion balance controlled through negative ion generators. However, unknown to the employees, the generators were switched on only in the experimental group's work area. At the end of the day, the number of employees reporting migraine, nausea, fatigue, faintness, or some other physical discomfort was recorded for each group. The results are summarized in the table.

	Experimental Group (Ion generators on)	Control Group (Ion generators off)
Number in Sample	$n_1 = 50$	$n_2 = 50$
Number in Sample Who Experience Some Type of Physical Discomfort	3	12

a. Perform a test of hypothesis to determine whether the proportion of employees in the experimental group who experience some type of physical discomfort at the end of the day is significantly less than the corresponding proportion for the control group. Use a significance level of $\alpha = .03$.

b. Compute the p-value for this test.

9.80 The use of computer equipment in business is growing at a phenomenal rate. A recent study revealed that 184 of 616 working adults now regularly use a personal computer, microcomputer, computer terminal, or word processor on the job (*Journal of Advertising Research*, Apr./May 1984). Is this sufficient evidence to indicate that the proportion of all working adults who regularly use computer equipment on the job exceeds 25%? Test using $\alpha = .05$.

9.81 The means and standard deviations shown in the table summarize information on the strengths (modules of rupture at ground line, in pounds per square inch) for two types of wooden poles used by the utility industry. Do the data provide sufficient evidence to indicate a difference in the variance of the strengths of wooden poles made from coastal Douglas fir and southern pine? Test using $\alpha = .02$.

Species	Sample Size	Sample Mean	Sample Standard Deviation
Coastal Douglas fir	118	8,380	644.62
Southern pine	147	8,870	611.72

Source: Goodman, J. R., Vanderbilt, M. D., and Criswell, M. E. "Reliability-based design of wood transmission line structures." *Journal of Structural Engineering*, Vol. 109, No. 3, 1983, pp. 690–704.

9.82   The accompanying table provides data on the theoretical (calculated) and experimental values of the vapor pressures for dibenzothiophene, a heterocycloaromatic compound similar to those found in coal tar. If the theoretical model for vapor pressure is a good model of reality, the true mean difference between the experimental and calculated values of vapor pressure for a given temperature will equal 0.

Temperature (°C)	Vapor Pressure Experimental	Calculated	Temperature (°C)	Vapor Pressure Experimental	Calculated
100.60	.282	.276	116.69	.669	.695
101.36	.314	.307	119.38	.834	.805
104.60	.335	.350	121.08	.890	.882
106.44	.404	.390	123.61	1.01	1.01
108.70	.422	.444	124.90	1.07	1.08
110.96	.513	.505	127.74	1.26	1.25
112.62	.554	.554	130.24	1.42	1.43
115.21	.642	.640	131.75	1.55	1.54

Source: Edwards, D. R., and Prausnitz, J. M. "Vapor pressures of some sulphur-containing, coal-related compounds." *Journal of Chemical and Engineering Data*, Vol. 26, 1981, pp. 121–124. Copyright 1981 American Chemical Society. Reprinted with permission.

a. Do the data provide sufficient evidence to indicate that the mean difference differs from 0? Test using $\alpha = .05$.

b. Calculate and interpret the p-value for the test.

9.83   A machine is set to produce bolts with a mean length of 1 inch. Bolts that are too long or too short do not meet the customer's specifications and must be rejected. To avoid producing too many rejects, the bolts produced by the machine are sampled from time to time and tested as a check to determine whether the machine is still operating properly, i.e., producing bolts with a mean length of 1 inch. Suppose 50 bolts have been sampled, and $\bar{y} = 1.02$ inches and $s = .04$ inch. Does the sample evidence indicate that the machine is producing bolts with a mean length not equal to 1 inch; i.e., is the production process out of control? Test using $\alpha = .01$.

9.84   Heat stress in dairy cows can have a dramatic negative effect on milk production. High temperatures tend to reduce a cow's food intake, which in turn reduces milk yield. Researchers in the IFAS Dairy Research Unit and the Department of Agricultural Engineering at the University of Florida have developed design criteria for the construction of shade structures that they believe will help alleviate heat stress for dairy cows. In one experiment, 31 Holstein cows in the last trimester of pregnancy were divided into two groups. Sixteen cows were given access to a shade structure and the remaining 15 cows were denied shade. Researchers recorded the 100-day milk yield (in pounds) of each cow after calving. The mean milk yields of the two groups are shown in the accompanying table. Is there sufficient evidence to indicate a difference between the mean milk yields of cows given access to shade and cows denied shade? Use $\alpha = .10$. (Assume the standard deviations of milk yields are equal to 40 pounds for both groups.)

	Shade	No Shade
Sample Size	16	15
Mean	367.4	330.8

Source: "Minimizing heat stress for dairy cows." *Florida Agricultural Research* 83, Vol. 2, No. 1, Winter 1983, pp. 10–13.

COMPUTER LAB: Testing Means

In this section, we present the computer commands for conducting tests of hypotheses concerning population means. Both packages, SAS and MINITAB, can perform t tests about μ, $(\mu_1 - \mu_2)$ for independent samples, and $(\mu_1 - \mu_2)$ for paired samples. (Remember, for large samples, the t and z statistics are nearly equivalent.) Tests about variances and proportions are not available in SAS or MINITAB.

SAS

a. One-Sample Test—Test H_0: $\mu = 8.5$ in Example 9.8

Command
line

1	`DATA BONES;`	
2	`INPUT RATIO @@;`	Data entry instructions
3	`TESTRAT=RATIO-8.5;`	
4	`CARDS;`	
	`10.73 8.48  8.52`	
	`  .    .     .`	Input data values
	`  .    .     .`	(3 observations per line)
	`9.93 8.17 12.00`	
5	`PROC MEANS T PRT;`	Student's t test
6	`VAR TESTRAT;`	

COMMAND 3   The transformed variable TESTRAT is computed by subtracting the hypothesized mean ($\mu = 8.5$) from each value of RATIO.

COMMANDS 5–6   The PROC MEANS statement commands SAS to conduct a t test on the values of the variable TESTRAT (specified in line 6). SAS will test the null hypothesis H_0: $\mu_{TESTRAT} = 0$, which is equivalent to testing H_0: $\mu_{RATIO} = 8.5$.

OUTPUT   The p-value reported in SAS is a *two-tailed* observed significance level. Divide this reported value in half to obtain the p-value for a one-tailed test. [*Note:*   The SAS output for this program is displayed in Figure 9.23a.]

b. Two-Sample Test, Independent Samples —Test $H_0: \mu_1 - \mu_2 = 0$ in Example 9.14

Command
line

1	`DATA DISKS;`	⎫
2	`INPUT DRIVE TIME @@;`	⎬ Data entry instructions
3	`CARDS;`	⎭
	`1 59 1 73 1 74 1 61`	⎫
	`. . . . . . . .`	⎬ Input data values
	`. . . . . . . .`	(4 observations per line)
	`2 86 2 53 2 68 2 39`	⎭
4	`PROC TTEST;`	⎫ Student's *t* test
5	`CLASS DRIVE; VAR TIME;`	⎭

COMMAND 2   TIME is the variable of interest. DRIVE is a grouping variable that takes on two values (e.g., 1 and 2).

COMMANDS 4–5   The TTEST procedure conducts a *t* test on the difference in means of the variable TIME for the two groups identified by DRIVE.

OUTPUT   SAS calculates the *t* value for both the equal population variances case and the unequal variances case. [*Note:*   The SAS output for this program is displayed in Figure 9.23b.]

c. Two-Sample Test, Paired Samples—Test $H_0: \mu_d = 0$ in Example 9.15

Command
line

1	`DATA CLOUD;`	⎫
2	`INPUT SEED UNSEED;`	⎬ Data entry instructions
3	`DIFF=SEED-UNSEED`	⎭
4	`CARDS;`	⎫
	`1.75 1.62`	
	`.    .`	⎬ Input data values
	`.    .`	(1 observation per line)
	`2.42 2.33`	⎭
5	`PROC MEANS T PRT;`	⎫ Student's *t* test
6	`VAR DIFF;`	⎭

COMMANDS 2–3   The variables SEED and UNSEED contain the measurements for each member of the matched pair. The difference, DIFF, is computed in line 3.

OUTPUT   [*Note:*   The SAS output for this program is displayed in Figure 9.23c.]

FIGURE 9.23 ▶
SAS output for computer Lab

a.

Analysis Variable : TESTRAT

N Obs	T	Prob>|T|
41	4.0303238	0.0002

b.

TTEST PROCEDURE

Variable: TIME

DRIVE	N	Mean	Std Dev	Std Error	Minimum	Maximum
1	13	68.23076923	18.65991178	5.17532836	33.00000000	102.0000000
2	15	53.80000000	15.80777386	4.08154966	34.00000000	86.0000000

Variances	T	DF	Prob>|T|
Unequal	2.1894	23.7	0.0387
Equal	2.2163	26.0	0.0356

For H0: Variances are equal, F' = 1.39   DF = (12,14)   Prob>F' = 0.5482

c.

Analysis Variable : DIFF

N Obs	T	Prob>|T|
6	3.0066442	0.0299

MINITAB

a. One-Sample t Test—Test H_0: $\mu = 8.5$ in Example 9.8

Command
line

1	`SET RATIOS IN C1`	Data entry instruction
2	`NAME C1='RATIO'`	
	`10.73 8.48  8.52`	
	$\vdots$ $\vdots$ $\vdots$	Input data values (3 observations per line)
	`9.93 8.17 12.00`	
3	`TTEST OF MU=50 ON C1;`	Student's t test
4	`ALTERNATIVE=+1.`	

COMMANDS 3–4 The TTEST procedure performs a t test on the difference between the mean of the variable read in C1 and the hypothesized value specified in the MU= subcommand (line 3). The subcommand ALTERNATIVE=+1 (line 4) requests that a one-tailed upper-tailed test be performed. Use ALTERNATIVE=−1 for a lower-tailed test. If the subcommand is not used, a two-tailed test is performed.

OUTPUT   [*Note:*   The MINITAB output for this program is displayed in Figure 9.24a on page 493.]

b. Two-Sample Test, Independent Samples—Test H_0: $\mu_1 - \mu_2 = 0$ in Example 9.14

Command
line

1	`SET DISK1 DATA IN C1`	Data entry instruction
	`59 73 74 61`	Input data values (4 observations per line)
2	`SET DISK2 DATA IN C2`	
	`71 63 40 34`	Input data values (4 observations per line)
3	`TWOSAMPLE T C1 C2;`	Student's t test
4	`  POOLED.`	

COMMANDS 3–4   TWOSAMPLE performs a t test on the difference between the means of the data in C1 and C2. The subcommand POOLED (line 4) requests that a pooled sample variance be used. (This is appropriate when the population variances are equal.) If you want MINITAB to adjust the t statistic and degrees of freedom for the unequal variances case, omit the POOLED subcommand.

GENERAL   Use the ALTERNATIVE subcommand to obtain a one-tailed test.

OUTPUT   [*Note:*   The MINITAB output for this program is displayed in Figure 9.24b.]

c. Two-Sample Test, Paired Samples—Test H_0: $\mu_d = 0$ in Example 9.15

Command
line

1	`READ DATA IN C1 C2`	Data entry instruction
	`1.75 1.62`	Input data values (1 observation per line)
	`2.42 2.33`	
2	`SUBTRACT C2 FROM C1, PUT IN C3`	
3	`NAME C3='DIFF'`	
4	`TTEST OF MU=0 ON DATA IN C3`	Student's t test

COMMANDS 1–2   The data in columns C1 and C2 are the measurements for each member of the matched pair. C3 contains the difference between the measurements.

COMMAND 4   TTEST performs a t test on the mean of the differences in C3.

GENERAL   Use the ALTERNATIVE subcommand to obtain a one-tailed test.

OUTPUT   [*Note:*   The MINITAB output for this program is displayed in Figure 9.24c.]

FIGURE 9.24 ▶
MINITAB output for Computer Lab

a.   TEST OF MU = 8.500 VS MU G.T. 8.500

	N	MEAN	STDEV	SE MEAN	T	P VALUE
RATIO	41	9.258	1.204	0.188	4.03	0.0001

b.   TWOSAMPLE T FOR disk1 VS disk2

	N	MEAN	STDEV	SE MEAN
disk1	13	68.2	18.7	5.2
disk2	15	53.8	15.8	4.1

95 PCT CI FOR MU disk1 - MU disk2: (1.0, 27.8)

TTEST MU disk1 = MU disk2 (VS NE): T= 2.22   P=0.036   DF=   26

POOLED STDEV =   17.2

c.   TEST OF MU = 0.0000 VS MU N.E. 0.0000

	N	MEAN	STDEV	SE MEAN	T	P VALUE
DIFF	6	0.1633	0.1331	0.0543	3.01	0.030

References

Freedman, D., Pisani, R., and Purves, R., *Statistics*. New York: W. W. Norton and Co., 1978.

Hoel, P. G. *Introduction to Mathematical Statistics*, 6th ed. New York: Wiley, 1987.

Hogg, R. V., and Craig, A. T. *Introduction to Mathematical Statistics*, 4th ed. New York: Macmillan, 1978.

McClave, J. T., and Dietrich, F. H. II. *Statistics*, 6th ed. San Francisco: Dellen, 1994.

Mendenhall, W. *Introduction to Probability and Statistics*, 8th ed. Boston: Duxbury, 1990.

Mendenhall, W., Wackerly, D. D., and Scheaffer, R. L. *Mathematical Statistics with Applications*, 3rd ed. Boston: Duxbury, 1989.

Mood, A. M., Graybill, F. A., and Boes, D. *Introduction to the Theory of Statistics*, 3rd ed. New York: McGraw-Hill, 1974.

Snedecor, G. W., and Cochran, W. G. *Statistical Methods*, 7th ed. Ames, Iowa: Iowa State University Press, 1980.

CHAPTER TEN

Categorical Data Analysis

Objective

To show how to analyze count data obtained by the classification of experimental observations from a multinomial experiment

Contents

10.1 Categorical Data and Multinomial Probabilities

In Chapters 8 and 9, we discussed how to make inferences about a proportion from a single population. Recall that the population proportion p is the probability of "success" in a binomial experiment—an experiment that results in one of two possible outcomes on any one trial. In this chapter, we are interested in making inferences about the unknown probabilities (or proportions) from a **multinomial experiment** with k possible outcomes. That is, we want to make inferences about p_1, p_2, . . . , p_k, where p_i is the probability of the ith outcome and $p_1 + p_2 + \cdots + p_k = 1$. (See Section 4.7 for a detailed discussion of multinomial experiments.)

To illustrate, consider a personal computer (PC) that is manufactured on one of five production lines, A, B, C, D, or E. In a sample of $n = 103$ PCs found to be defective, 15 were manufactured on line A, 27 on line B, 31 on line C, 19 on line D, and 11 on line E (see Table 10.1). For this multinomial experiment, there are five outcomes, or categories, into which each defective can be classified, one corresponding to each of the five production lines.

The practical question to be answered in the study is whether the proportions of defective PCs differ among the five production lines. Do the data provide evidence to contradict the null hypothesis $H_0\colon p_1 = p_2 = \cdots = p_5$, where p_i is the proportion of defectives manufactured on the ith production line? If the data in Table 10.1 contradict this hypothesis, the manufacturer would want to know why the rate of production of defectives is greater on some production lines than others and would take countermeasures to reduce the production of defectives.

This chapter is concerned with the analysis of categorical data—specifically, data that represent the counts for each category of a multinomial experiment. In Sections 10.2 and 10.3, we will learn how to make inferences about the category probabilities for data classified according to a single qualitative (or categorical) variable. In Sections 10.4 and 10.5, we consider inferences about the category probabilities for data classified according to two qualitative variables. The statistic used for most of these inferences is one that possesses, approximately, the familiar chi-square distribution. Although the proof of the adequacy of this approximation is beyond the scope of this text, some aspects of the theory can be deduced from what we have learned in earlier chapters.

TABLE 10.1   Classification of $n = 103$ Defective PCs According to Production Line

Production Line				
A	B	C	D	E
15	27	31	19	11

10.2 Estimating Category Probabilities in a One-Way Table

Consider a multinomial experiment with k outcomes that correspond to categories of a single qualitative variable. The data (i.e., category counts) for such an experiment would appear similar to that of Table 10.2, where n_1, n_2, . . . , n_k represent the category counts and $n = n_1 + n_2 + \cdots + n_k$. Such a table is often called a **one-way table** since only one qualitative variable is used to form the categories, or outcomes.

To estimate category probabilities in a one-way table, consider that a multinomial experiment can always be reduced to a binomial experiment by isolating one category,

EXAMPLE 10.2

Solution

EXERCISES

10.1 Piracy of pe
court ruling
by the com
copying po
Fortune 50(
July 1989).
for the 121

Poli

1. Do
2. Inter
3. Hon
4. Mar
5. Othe

Source:
Manageme

Let p_1, p_2, .
categories sl

TABLE 10.2 One-Way Table of Category Counts				
		Category		
1	2	3	$\cdots$	k
n_1	n_2	n_3	$\cdots$	n_k

say, category i, and then combining all others. Since we know that $\hat{p} = y/n$ is a good estimator of the binomial parameter p, it follows that

$$\hat{p}_i = \frac{n_i}{n}$$

is a good estimator of p_i, the probability associated with category i in a multinomial experiment. It also follows that $\hat{p}_i$ will possess the same properties as $\hat{p}$—namely, that when n is large, $\hat{p}_i$ will be approximately normally distributed (by the central limit theorem) with

$$E(\hat{p}_i) = p_i$$

and

$$V(\hat{p}_i) = \frac{p_i(1 - p_i)}{n}$$

Consequently, a large-sample confidence interval for p_i may be constructed as shown in the box.

A Large-Sample $(1 - \alpha)100\%$ Confidence Interval for p_i

$$\hat{p}_i \pm z_{\alpha/2} \sqrt{\frac{\hat{p}_i(1 - \hat{p}_i)}{n}}$$

Values of $z_{\alpha/2}$ can be found in Table 4 of Appendix II.

We will estimate the difference between a pair of category probabilities, say, categories i and j $(i \neq j)$, using $(\hat{p}_i - \hat{p}_j)$. This linear function of $\hat{p}_i$ and $\hat{p}_j$ will be approximately normally distributed with

$$E(\hat{p}_i - \hat{p}_j) = p_i - p_j$$

and

$$V(\hat{p}_i - \hat{p}_j) = V(\hat{p}_i) + V(\hat{p}_j) - 2 \, \text{Cov}(\hat{p}_i, \hat{p}_j)$$

Since the covariance of two category counts, say, n_i and n_j $(i \neq j)$, is given by

$$\text{Cov}(n_i, n_j) = -n p_i p_j$$

choose a test statistic based on the deviations of the observed category counts, n_1, n_2, . . . , n_5, from their expected values

$$E(n_i) = np_i = (103)(.2) = 20.6 \quad (i = 1, 2, \ldots , 5)$$

Large deviations between the observed and expected category counts would provide evidence to indicate that the hypothesized category probabilities are incorrect.

The statistic used to test hypotheses about the category probabilities of a k-category multinomial experiment, one based on the weighted sum of squared deviations between observed and expected cell counts, is

$$\chi^2 = \sum_{i=1}^{k} \frac{[n_i - E(n_i)]^2}{E(n_i)}$$

Substituting np_i for $E(n_i)$ and expanding the numerator, it can be shown (proof omitted) that

$$\chi^2 = \sum_{i=1}^{k} \frac{(n_i - np_i)^2}{np_i} = \left(\sum_{i=1}^{k} \frac{n_i^2}{np_i} \right) - n$$

When the number n of trials is large enough so that $E(n_i) \geq 5$ for $i = 1, 2,$ . . . , k, the statistic χ^2 will possess (proof omitted) approximately a chi-square sampling distribution.* The value of χ^2 will be larger than expected if the deviations $[n_i - E(n_i)]$ are large. Therefore, the rejection region for the test is $\chi^2 > \chi^2_\alpha$, where χ^2_α is the value of χ^2 that locates an area α in the upper tail of the chi-square distribution (see Figure 10.1).

FIGURE 10.1 ▶
Rejection region for the chi-square test

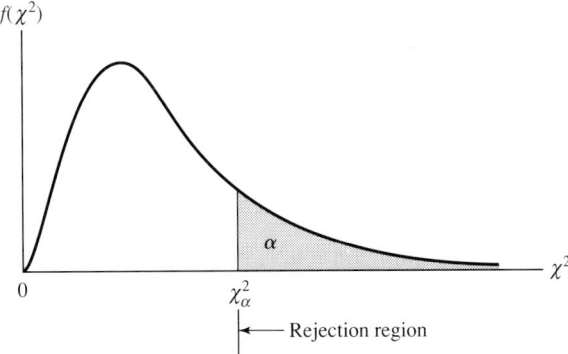

EXAMPLE 10.1

Solution

The number of degrees of freedom for the approximating chi-square distribution will always equal k less 1 degree of freedom for every linearly independent restriction placed on the category counts. For example, we always have at least one linear restriction on the category counts because their sum must equal the sample size, n:

$$n_1 + n_2 + \cdots + n_k = n$$

*For some applications, the expected cell counts can be less than 5. More on this subject can be found in the paper by Cochran (1952) listed in the references at the end of this chapter.

A Test of a Hypothesis About Multinomial Probabilities: One-Way Table

H_0: $p_1 = p_{1,0}$, $p_2 = p_{2,0}$, . . . , $p_k = p_{k,0}$, where $p_{1,0}$, $p_{2,0}$, . . . , $p_{k,0}$ represent the hypothesized values of the multinomial probabilities

H_a: At least one of the multinomial probabilities does not equal its hypothesized value

Test statistic: $\chi^2 = \sum_{i=1}^{k} \dfrac{[n_i - E(n_i)]^2}{E(n_i)} = \left(\sum_{i=1}^{k} \dfrac{n_i^2}{np_{i,0}} \right) - n$

where $E(n_i) = np_{i,0}$, the expected number of outcomes of type i assuming H_0 is true. The total sample size is n.

Rejection region: $\chi^2 > \chi_\alpha^2$, where χ_α^2 has $(k - 1)$ df

Assumption: $E(n_i) \geq 5$ for all n_i

Other restrictions arise if we must estimate the category probabilities. Since each estimate will involve a linear function of the category counts, the degrees of freedom for chi-square will be reduced by 1 for each category parameter that must be estimated.

A test of a hypothesis that the category probabilities assume specified values results in only a single linear restriction on the category counts—namely, $n_1 + n_2 + \cdots + n_k = n$. No category probabilities need to be estimated because their values are specified in H_0. The test procedure is described in the preceding box. We will illustrate this simple application of the chi-square test in Example 10.3.

EXAMPLE 10.3

Refer to the data provided in Table 10.1. Test the hypothesis that the proportions of all defective computers attributable to the five production lines are equal. Test using $\alpha = .05$.

Solution

We want to test H_0: $p_1 = p_2 = \cdots = p_5 = .2$ against the alternative hypothesis, H_a: At least two of the category probabilities are unequal. We have already calculated

$$E(n_i) = np_i = (103)(.2) = 20.16 \quad (i = 1, 2, \ldots, 5)$$

The observed and the expected category counts (in parentheses) are shown in Table 10.3 on page 504. Substituting the observed and expected values of the category counts into the formula for χ^2, we obtain

$$\chi^2 = \sum_{i=1}^{k} \frac{(n_i - np_i)^2}{np_i} = \frac{(15 - 20.6)^2}{20.6} + \frac{(27 - 20.6)^2}{20.6} + \cdots + \frac{(11 - 20.6)^2}{20.6}$$

$$= 13.36$$

The rejection region for the test is $\chi^2 > \chi^2_{.05}$, where $\chi^2_{.05}$ is based on $k - 1 = 5 - 1 = 4$ degrees of freedom. This value, found in Table 8 of Appendix II, is $\chi^2_{.05} = 9.48773$. Since the observed value of χ^2 exceeds this value, there is sufficient evidence (at $\alpha = .05$) to reject H_0. It appears that at least one production line is responsible for a higher proportion of defective computers than the other lines.

TABLE 10.3   Observed and Expected Category Counts for the Data of Table 10.1

Observed	15	27	31	19	11
Expected	(20.6)	(20.6)	(20.6)	(20.6)	(20.6)

EXERCISES

10.8 M&M's plain chocolate candies come in six different colors: brown, yellow, red, orange, green, and tan. According to the manufacturer (Mars, Inc.), the color ratio in each large production batch is 30% brown, 20% yellow, 20% red, 10% orange, 10% green, and 10% tan. To test this claim, a professor at Carleton College (Minnesota) had students count the colors of M&Ms found in "fun size" bags of the candy (*Teaching Statistics*, Spring 1993). The results for 370 M&M's are displayed in the table. Conduct a test to determine whether the true percentages of the colors produced differ from the manufacturer's stated percentages. Use $\alpha = .05$.

Color	Brown	Yellow	Red	Orange	Green	Tan	TOTAL
No. of M&M's	84	79	75	49	36	47	370

Source: Johnson, R. W. "Testing colour proportions of M&M's." *Teaching Statistics*, Vol. 15, No. 1, Spring 1993, p. 2 (Table 1).

10.9 Refer to the *Nature* (Sept. 1993) study of animal and plant species "hotspots" in Great Britain, Exercise 3.7. A hotspot if defined as a 10-km square area that is species-rich, i.e., that is heavily populated by the species of interest. Similarly, a coldspot is a 10-km square area that is species-poor. The following table gives the number of butterfly hotspots and number of butterfly coldspots in a sample of 2,588 10-km square areas. In theory, 5% of the areas should be butterfly hotspots, 5% should be butterfly coldspots, with the remaining areas (90%) neutral. Test the theory using $\alpha = .01$.

Butterfly Hotspots	123
Butterfly Coldspots	147
Neutral Areas	2,318
TOTAL	2,588

Source: Prendergast, J. R., et al. "Rare species, the coincidence of diversity hotspots and conservation strategies." *Nature*, Vol. 365, No. 6444, Sept. 23, 1993, p. 335 (Table 1).

10.10   Refer to the traffic study, Exercise 10.2.
   a. Do the data disagree with the hypothesis that the traffic is equally divided among the three directions? Test using $\alpha = .05$.
   b. Do the data provide sufficient evidence to indicate that more than one-third of all automobiles entering the intersection turn left? Test using $\alpha = .05$.

10.11   Refer to the gastroenteritis case study described in Exercise 10.3. Conduct a test to determine whether the incidence of gastrointestinal disease during the epidemic is related to water consumption. Use $\alpha = .01$.

10.12   The data for Exercise 10.4 follow. Conduct a test to compare the proportions of subjects that fall in the three disk orientation categories. Assume you want to determine whether the three proportions differ. Use $\alpha = .05$.

Disk Orientation		
Brighter Side Up	Darker Side Up	Bright and Dark Side Aligned
58	15	17

10.13   Refer to the survey of agricultural engineers, Exercise 10.5. Do the data present sufficient evidence to indicate a preference for one or more of the five water management strategies? Test using $\alpha = .05$.

10.14   Refer to the *New England Journal of Medicine* study of acute hospital care, Exercise 10.6. Recall that p_1, p_2, and p_3 represent the true percentages of hospital admissions in the three categories: appropriate, inappropriate, and avoidable by ambulatory surgery, respectively. Test the null hypothesis $H_0: p_1 = .8$, $p_2 = .1$, $p_3 = .1$. Use $\alpha = .10$.

OPTIONAL EXERCISE

10.15   A general proof of the fact that χ^2 possesses approximately a chi-square sampling distribution when n is large is beyond the scope of this text. However, it can be justified for the binomial case ($k = 2$). In Optional Exercise 7.56, we stated that if z is a standard normal random variable, then z^2 is a chi-square random variable with 1 degree of freedom. Denote the two cell counts for a binomial experiment as $n_1 = y$ and $n_2 = (n - y)$. Then, for large n,

$$z = \frac{y - np}{\sqrt{npq}}$$

has approximately a standard normal distribution and z^2 will be approximately distributed as a chi-square random variable with 1 degree of freedom. Show algebraically that for $k = 2$, $\chi^2 = z^2$.

10.4   Inferences About Category Probabilities in a Two-Way (Contingency) Table

The methods presented in Sections 10.2 and 10.3 are appropriate for a one-directional (or one-way) classification of the data. For example, the categories for the defective computer data of Example 10.3 correspond to the "values" assumed by the qualitative variable, production line. Often, we may want to classify data according to two directions of classification—that is, according to two qualitative variables. The objective of such a classification usually is to determine whether the two directions of classification are dependent.

To illustrate, consider a questionnaire that was mailed to a sample of 150 households within 2 weeks after a nuclear mishap occurred in 1979 on Three Mile Island near Harrisburg, Pennsylvania. One question concerned residents' attitudes toward a full evacuation: "Should there have been a full evacuation of the immediate area?" Residents were classified according to the distance (in miles) of the community in which they reside from Three Mile Island and their opinion on a full evacuation. A summary of the responses for the 150 households randomly selected is shown in the **two-way table** shown in Table 10.4. This table is called a **contingency table**; it presents multinomial count data classified on two scales, or dimensions, of classification, namely, distance from Three Mile Island and responses to the full evacuation question.

TABLE 10.4   Contingency Table for Three Mile Island Survey

		Distance from Three Mile Island, miles			
		1–6	7–12	13+	TOTALS
Full	Yes	18	15	33	66
Evacuation	No	20	19	45	84
TOTALS		38	34	78	150

Source: Brown, S., et al. Final report on a survey of Three Mile Island area residents." Department of Geography, Michigan State University, Aug. 1979.

Each cell of Table 10.4, located in a specific row and column, represents one of the $k = (2)(3) = 6$ categories of a two-directional classification of the $n = 150$ observations. The symbols representing the cell counts for the experiment in Table 10.4 are shown in Table 10.5a; the corresponding cell, row, and column probabilities are shown in Table 10.5b. Thus n_{11} represents the number of residents who live within 6 miles of the accident and supported full evacuation, and p_{11} represents the corresponding cell probability. The row totals (designated at $n_{1.}$ and $n_{2.}$) and column totals (designated at $n_{.1}$, $n_{.2}$, and $n_{.3}$) are shown in Table 10.5 a. The corresponding row and column probability totals are shown in Table 10.5b. The probability totals for the rows and columns are called **marginal probabilities**. For example, the marginal probability $p_{1.}$ is the probability that a resident favored full evacuation, and the marginal probability $p_{.1}$ is the probability that a respondent lives 1–6 miles from Three Mile Island. Thus,

$$p_{1.} = p_{11} + p_{12} + p_{13} = P(\text{favor full evacuation})$$

and

$$p_{.1} = p_{11} + p_{21} = P(\text{live 1–6 miles from Three Mile Island})$$

TABLE 10.5a Observed Counts for Contingency Table

		Distance from Three Mile Island, miles			
		1–6	7–12	13+	TOTALS
Full Evacuation	Yes	n_{11}	n_{12}	n_{13}	$n_{1.}$
	No	n_{21}	n_{22}	n_{23}	$n_{2.}$
TOTALS		$n_{.1}$	$n_{.2}$	$n_{.3}$	n

TABLE 10.5b Probabilities for Contingency Table

		Distance from Three Mile Island, miles			
		1–6	7–12	13+	TOTALS
Full Evacuation	Yes	p_{11}	p_{12}	p_{13}	$p_{1.}$
	No	p_{21}	p_{22}	p_{23}	$p_{2.}$
TOTALS		$p_{.1}$	$p_{.2}$	$p_{.3}$	1

You can see that the experiment we have described is a multinomial experiment with a total of 150 trials and $(2)(3) = 6$ categories. Since the 150 residents were randomly chosen, the trials are considered independent, and the probabilities are viewed as remaining constant from trial to trial.

The objective of the study is to determine whether the two classifications, distance from Three Mile Island and opinion on full evacuation, are dependent. That is, if we know the distance from Three Mile Island, does that information provide a clue about the resident's opinion on evacuation? In a probabilistic sense, we know (Chapter 3) that independence of events A and B implies $P(A \cap B) = P(A)P(B)$. Similarly, in the contingency table analysis, if the two classifications are independent, the probability that an item is classified in any particular cell of the table is the product of the corresponding marginal probabilities. Thus, under the hypothesis of independence, in Table 10.5b, we must have

$$p_{11} = p_{1.}\, p_{.1} \qquad p_{12} = p_{1.}\, p_{.2} \qquad p_{13} = p_{1.}\, p_{.3}$$

and so forth. Therefore, the null hypothesis that the directions of classification are independent is equivalent to the hypothesis that every cell probability is equal to the product of its respective row and column marginal probabilities. If the data disagree with the expected cell counts computed from these probabilities, there is evidence to indicate that the two directions of classification are dependent.

If we were to calculate the expected cell counts for our example, you would immediately perceive a difficulty. The marginal probabilities are unknown and must be estimated. The best estimate of the ith row marginal probability, call it $p_{i.}$, is

$$\hat{p}_{i.} = \frac{n_{i.}}{n} = \frac{\text{Row } i \text{ total}}{n}$$

Similarly, the best estimate of the jth marginal column probability is

$$\hat{p}_{.j} = \frac{n_{.j}}{n} = \frac{\text{Column } j \text{ total}}{n}$$

Therefore, the estimated expected cell count for the cell in the ith row and jth column of the contingency table is

$$\hat{E}(n_{ij}) = n\hat{p}_{i.}\hat{p}_{.j} = n\left(\frac{n_{i.}}{n}\right)\left(\frac{n_{.j}}{n}\right) = \frac{n_{i.}\,n_{.j}}{n}$$

$$= \frac{(\text{Row } i \text{ total})(\text{Column } j \text{ total})}{n}$$

The general form of an $r \times c$ contingency table (one containing r rows and c columns) is shown in Table 10.6. When n is large, the test statistic

$$\chi^2 = \sum_{j=1}^{c}\sum_{i=1}^{r}\frac{[n_{ij} - \hat{E}(n_{ij})]^2}{\hat{E}(n_{ij})} = \sum_{j=1}^{c}\sum_{i=1}^{r}\frac{\left(n_{ij} - \dfrac{n_{i.}\,n_{.j}}{n}\right)^2}{\left(\dfrac{n_{i.}\,n_{.j}}{n}\right)}$$

will possess approximately a chi-square distribution. The rejection region for the test will be $\chi^2 > \chi^2_\alpha$ (see Figure 10.2).

TABLE 10.6   General $r \times c$ Contingency Table

		Column 1	2	$\cdots$	c	Row Totals
Row	1	n_{11}	n_{12}	$\cdots$	n_{1c}	$n_{1.}$
	2	n_{21}	n_{22}	$\cdots$	n_{2c}	$n_{2.}$
	$\vdots$	$\vdots$	$\vdots$		$\vdots$	$\vdots$
	r	n_{r1}	n_{r2}	$\cdots$	n_{rc}	$n_{r.}$
Column Totals		$n_{.1}$	$n_{.2}$	$\cdots$	$n_{.c}$	n

To determine the number of degrees of freedom for the approximating chi-square distribution, note that $k = rc$. From this we must subtract 1 degree of freedom because the sum of all rc cell counts must equal n. We also subtract $(r - 1)$ because we must estimate the $(r - 1)$ row marginal probabilities. (The last row probability will then be determined because the sum of the row probabilities must equal 1.) Similarly, we

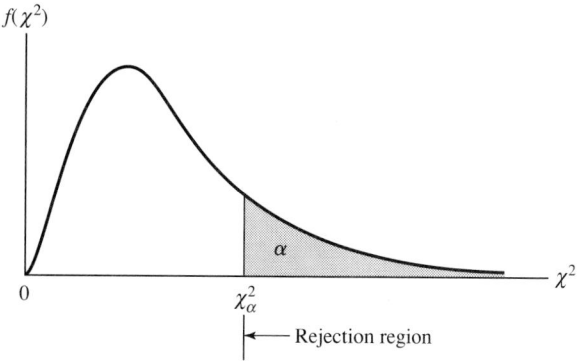

FIGURE 10.2 ▶
Rejection region for the chi-square test for dependence

$f(\chi^2)$

α

χ^2_α

χ^2

0

◀— Rejection region

must subtract $(c - 1)$ because we must estimate $(c - 1)$ column marginal probabilities. Therefore, the degrees of freedom for chi-square will be

$$
\text{df} = k - \begin{pmatrix} \text{number of linearly independent} \\ \text{restrictions on the cell counts} \end{pmatrix}
$$
$$
= rc - (1) - (r - 1) - (c - 1)
$$
$$
= rc - r - c + 1
$$
$$
= (r - 1)(c - 1)
$$

The chi-square test is summarized in the box; its use is illustrated in Example 10.4.

General Form of a Contingency Table Analysis: A Test for Independence

H_0:   The two classifications are independent

H_a: The two classifications are dependent

Test statistic: $\chi^2 = \displaystyle\sum_{j=1}^{c} \sum_{i=1}^{r} \frac{[n_{ij} - \hat{E}(n_{ij})]^2}{\hat{E}(n_{ij})}$

where

$$
\hat{E}(n_{ij}) = \frac{n_{i.}\, n_{.j}}{n}, \qquad
\begin{array}{l} n_{i.} = \text{total for row } i \\ n_{.j} = \text{total for column } j \end{array}
$$

Rejection region: $\chi^2 > \chi^2_\alpha$, where χ^2_α has $(r - 1)(c - 1)$ df.

Assumptions: 1. The n observed counts are a random sample from the population of interest. We may then consider this to be a multinomial experiment with $r \times c$ possible outcomes.

2. For the χ^2 approximation to be valid, we require that the estimated expected counts be greater than or equal to 5 in all cells.[*]

EXAMPLE 10.4

Use the data in Table 10.4 to decide whether a Harrisburg resident's opinion on full evacuation of Three Mile Island depends on how far (in miles) the resident lives from the nuclear plant.

Solution

The first step in the analysis of a contingency table is to calculate the estimated expected cell counts. For example,

$$E(n_{11}) = \frac{n_{1.}\, n_{.1}}{n}$$

$$= \frac{(66)(38)}{150} = 16.72$$

$$E(n_{12}) = \frac{n_{1.}\, n_{.2}}{n}$$

$$= \frac{(66)(34)}{150} = 14.96$$

$$\vdots$$

$$E(n_{23}) = \frac{n_{2.}\, n_{.3}}{n}$$

$$= \frac{(84)(78)}{150} = 43.68$$

The cell counts (top number in cell) and the corresponding estimated expected values (bottom number in cell) are shown in the SAS printout of the contingency table analysis, Figure 10.3.

For this study, the χ^2 test statistic is computed as follows:

$$\chi^2 = \frac{[n_{11} - \hat{E}(n_{11})]^2}{\hat{E}(n_{11})} + \frac{[n_{12} - \hat{E}(n_{12})]^2}{\hat{E}(n_{12})} + \cdots + \frac{[n_{23} - \hat{E}(n_{23})]^2}{\hat{E}(n_{23})}$$

$$= \sum_{j=1}^{3} \sum_{i=1}^{2} \frac{[n_{ij} - \hat{E}(n_{ij})]^2}{\hat{E}(n_{ij})}$$

Substituting the data of Figure 10.3 into this expression, we obtain

$$\chi^2 = \frac{(18 - 16.72)^2}{16.72} + \frac{(15 - 14.96)^2}{14.96} + \cdots + \frac{(45 - 43.68)^2}{43.68} = .266$$

---

*Exact tests are available for 2×2 or $n \times 2$ contingency tables. These tests can be applied regardless of the size of the sample or the magnitude of the estimated expected cell counts. Consult the references at the end of this chapter for details on these exact tests.

FIGURE 10.3 ▶

SAS printout for Example 10.4

TABLE OF EVAC BY DISTANCE

EVAC   DISTANCE

Frequency Expected	1-6	7-12	Over12	Total
No	20	19	45	84
	21.28	19.04	43.68	
Yes	18	15	33	66
	16.72	14.96	34.32	
Total	38	34	78	150

STATISTICS FOR TABLE OF EVAC BY DISTANCE

Statistic	DF	Value	Prob
Chi-Square	2	0.266	0.876
Likelihood Ratio Chi-Square	2	0.265	0.876
Mantel-Haenszel Chi-Square	1	0.259	0.611
Phi Coefficient		0.042	
Contingency Coefficient		0.042	
Cramer's V		0.042	

Sample Size = 150

Note that this value, $\chi^2 = .266$, is shaded at the bottom of the SAS printout, Figure 10.3. The rejection region for the test is $\chi^2 > \chi^2_{.05} = 5.99147$, where $\chi^2_{.05}$ is based on $(r - 1)(c - 1) = (1)(2) = 2$ degrees of freedom. Since the computed value of χ^2, .266, falls below this critical value, we fail to reject H_0; there is insufficient evidence to conclude that the two directions of data classification are dependent. It appears that opinion on full evacuation is independent of distance from Three Mile Island.

We can arrive at the same conclusion by observing that the p-value for the test, shaded in Figure 10.3, exceeds $\alpha = .05$.

Suppose we conclude that the two directions of classification in a contingency table are dependent. Practically speaking, this implies that the distribution of the percentages of observations falling in the categories for one of the qualitative variables depends on the level of the other variable. In the 2×3 table of Example 10.4, this means that the proportion p_i of residents that favored full evacuation differed for the three distance groups. To determine the magnitude of the differences, we could construct confidence intervals for the differences, $(p_{.1} - p_{.2})$, $(p_{.1} - p_{.3})$, and $(p_{.2} - p_{.3})$, using the method of Section 8.9.

EXERCISES

10.16 Find the rejection region for a test of independence of two directions of classification if the contingency table contains r rows and c columns and:
   a. $r = 2$, $c = 2$, $\alpha = .05$ **b.** $r = 3$, $c = 6$, $\alpha = .10$ **c.** $r = 3$, $c = 4$, $\alpha = .01$

10.17 According to research reported in the *Journal of the National Cancer Institute* (Apr. 1991), eating foods high in fiber may help protect against breast cancer. The researchers randomly divided 120 laboratory rats into four groups of 30 each. All rats were injected with a drug that causes breast cancer, then each rat was fed a diet of fat and fiber for 15 weeks. However, the levels of fat and fiber varied from group to group. At the end of the feeding period, the number of rats with cancer tumors was determined for each group. The data are summarized in the accompanying contingency table.

		High Fat/ No Fiber	*High Fat/ Fiber*	*Low Fat/ No Fiber*	*Low Fat/ Fiber*	*TOTALS*
Cancer Tumors	*Yes*	27	20	19	14	80
	No	3	10	11	16	40
TOTALS		30	30	30	30	120

Diet

Source: *Tampa Tribune*, Apr. 3, 1991.

   a. Does the sampling appear to satisfy the assumptions for a multinomial experiment? Explain.
   b. Calculate the expected cell counts for the contingency table.
   c. Calculate the χ^2 statistic.
   d. Is there evidence to indicate that diet and presence/absence of cancer are independent? Test using $\alpha = .05$.
   e. Compare the percentage of rats on a high fat/no fiber diet with cancer to the percentage of rats on a high fat/fiber diet with cancer using a 95% confidence interval. Interpret the result.

10.18 Four pesticides used in dormant California orchards are chlorpyrifos, diazinon, methidathion, and parathion. *Environmental Science & Technology* (Oct. 1993) reported the number of applications of these spray chemicals from January to June 1990 in California. The data for each of three types of fruit or nut orchards are shown in the accompanying table. (Parathion has since been banned for use on deciduous fruit and nut trees.)

		Fruit/Nut Trees	
Chemical	*Almonds*	*Peaches*	*Nectarines*
Chlorpyrifos	41,077	4,419	11,594
Diazinon	102,935	9,651	5,928
Methidathion	21,240	5,198	1,790
Parathion	136,064	53,384	24,417

Source: Selber, J. N., et al. "Air and fog deposition residues of four organophosphate insecticides used on dormant orchards in the San Joaquin Valley, California." *Environmental Science & Technology*, Vol. 27, No. 10, Oct. 1993, p. 2236 (Table I).

a. Use the information in the accompanying SAS printout to determine (at $\alpha = .01$) whether pesticide used depends on type of orchard.

b. Because of the large number of pesticide applications reported, the total sample size for the test, part **a**, is extremely large ($n = 417,697$). Consequently, a "statistically significant" result may not be "practically significant." Perform an analysis to show the magnitude of differences in the rates of methidathion application for the three orchard types.

TABLE OF CHEMICAL BY TREE

CHEMICAL   TREE

Frequency Expected	ALMONDS	NECTARS	PEACHES	Total
CHLORPYR	41077	11594	4419	57090
	41183	5976.8	9929.9	
DIAZINON	102935	5928	9651	118514
	85493	12407	20614	
METHIDON	21240	1790	5198	28228
	20363	2955.2	4909.8	
PARATHON	136064	24417	53384	213865
	154277	22390	37199	
Total	301316	43729	72652	417697

STATISTICS FOR TABLE OF CHEMICAL BY TREE

Statistic	DF	Value	Prob
Chi-Square	6	31000.416	0.000
Likelihood Ratio Chi-Square	6	32019.922	0.000
Mantel-Haenszel Chi-Square	1	16249.046	0.000
Phi Coefficient		0.272	
Contingency Coefficient		0.263	
Cramer's V		0.193	

Sample Size = 417697

10.19 Researchers at the Oak Ridge (Tennessee) National Laboratory have developed a computer program to estimate the numbers of expected and excess cases of thyroid cancer occurring in the lifetime of those exposed to atomic weapons tests at the Nevada Test Site in the 1950s (*Health Physics*, Jan. 1986). Of the approximately 23,000 people exposed to the weapons testing fallout, 58 were expected to develop thyroid cancer in their remaining lifetimes. According to the computer program, the 58 cases can be categorized by sex and level of radiation (dose) at the time of exposure as shown in the table on page 514.

Suppose that the data represent a random sample of 58 thyroid cancer patients selected from the target population. Conduct a test to determine whether the two directions of classification, sex and dose at time of exposure, are independent. Use $\alpha = .01$.

		Gender		TOTALS
		Male	Female	
	Less than 1	6	13	19
Dose, rad	1–10	8	18	26
	11 or more	3	10	13
TOTALS		17	41	58

Source: Zeighami, E. A., and Morris, M. D. "Thyroid cancer risk in the population around the Nevada test site." *Health Physics*, Vol. 50, No. 1, Jan. 1986, p. 26 (Table 2).

10.20 Refer to Exercise 7.31 and the user satisfaction study of computer-aided software engineering (CASE) technology (*Journal of Systems Management*, July 1989). A survey asked each in a sample of CASE users how often they use data flow diagrams on the job and how satisfied they are with the design charting techniques they are using. The percentages responding in each of the cells of the contingency table are given here. Analyze the survey data assuming 1,000 CASE users participated in the study.

Use of Data Flow Diagrams	User Satisfaction of Design Charting Techniques		TOTALS
	Satisfied	Unsatisfied	
Always	27.5	0.0	27.5
Most of the time	31.3	2.5	33.8
Occasionally	31.2	3.8	35.0
Never	2.5	1.2	3.7
TOTALS	92.5	7.5	100.0

Source: Kievit, K., and Martin, M. "Systems analysis tools—Who's using them?" *Journal of Systems Management*, July 1989, p. 29 (Table 6).

10.21 One criterion used to evaluate employees in the assembly section of a large factory is the number of defective pieces per 1,000 parts produced. The quality control department wants to find out whether there is a relationship between years of experience and defect rate. Since the job is rather repetitious, after the initial training period, any improvement as a result of learning might be offset by a decrease in the motivation of a worker. A defect rate is calculated for each worker for a yearly evaluation. The results for 100 workers are given in the table. An analysis of the data is provided in the MINITAB printout. Is there evidence of a relationship between defect rate and years of experience? Use $\alpha = .05$.

		Years of Experience (After Training Period)		
		1	2–5	6–10
	High	6	9	9
Defect Rate	Average	9	19	23
	Low	7	8	10

```
Expected counts are printed below observed counts

        Exp=1  Exp=2-5 Exp=6-10    Total
    1      6       9        9         24
         5.28    8.64    10.08

    2      9      19       23         51
        11.22   18.36    21.42

    3      7       8       10         25
         5.50    9.00    10.50

Total     22      36       42        100

ChiSq =  0.098 +  0.015 +  0.116 +
         0.439 +  0.022 +  0.117 +
         0.409 +  0.111 +  0.024 = 1.351

df = 4
```

10.22 In recent years, many companies have converted to the metric system of measurement. To investigate this phenomenon, B. D. Phillips, H. A. G. Lakhani, and S. L. George analyzed data collected on 757 small manufacturers for a U.S. Metric Board study (*Technological Forecasting and Social Change*, Apr. 1984). The firms were cross-classified according to metric conversion (converters or nonconverters) and level of technology (high or non–high technology). The contingency table for the data is shown here.

	High Tech	*Non-High Tech*
Metric converters	81	296
Nonconverters	80	300

Reprinted by permission of the publisher. Copyright 1984 by Elsevier Science Publishing Co., Inc.

a. Calculate the estimated expected number of firms in each of the four cells of the table.
b. Calculate the χ^2 statistic.
c. Is there sufficient evidence to indicate that the distributions of percentages of metric converters and nonconverters differ for high tech and non–high tech firms? Test using $\alpha = .01$.

10.5 Contingency Tables with Fixed Marginal Totals

In the analysis of contingency table data, one or more of the categories may contain an insufficient number of observations. To illustrate, we will consider the study (described in Section 10.4) of the relationship between a resident's opinion of full evacuation of the area surrounding a nuclear accident and the distance the resident lives from Three Mile Island. If the random sample contains only a small number of residents that live a certain distance away, this may cause the expected cell counts for that distance to be small—perhaps less than the required 5. To guard against this possibility, experimenters often fix either the row or column totals. For our example, we would fix the column totals by randomly and independently sampling a fixed number of residents in each distance group. This would increase the likelihood that the estimated expected cell counts would be of adequate size.

For example, suppose we obtain the evacuation opinion of random samples of 100 residents in each distance group. The results might appear as shown in Table 10.7. Note the difference between this sampling procedure and the one described in Section 10.4, where we assumed that a *single* random sample of $n = 150$ residents was selected from among the population of all people residing near Three Mile Island. In this section, we have randomly and independently selected three samples, 100 residents from each distance. Therefore, the data of Table 10.7 result from three multinomial experiments, each with $k = 2$ cells (support or do not support full evacuation), corresponding to the three distances, 1–6 miles, 7–12 miles, and 13 or more miles from Three Mile Island.

TABLE 10.7   Distance–Evacuation Contingency Table with Column Total Fixed

		Distance from Three Mile Island, miles			
		1–6	7–12	13+	TOTALS
Full	Yes	42	29	25	96
Evacuation	No	58	71	75	204
TOTALS		100	100	100	300

A chi-square test to detect dependence between row and column classifications, when either the column or the row totals are fixed, is conducted in exactly the same way as the test of Section 10.4. It can be shown (proof omitted) that the χ^2 statistic will possess a sampling distribution that is approximately a chi-square distribution with $(r - 1)(c - 1)$ degrees of freedom. The test procedure is summarized in the box. An application of the test to the comparison of two or more binomial proportions is illustrated in Example 10.5.

EXAMPLE 10.5

To compare the proportions of defective dishwashers produced by three production lines, an engineer randomly sampled 500 washers from each line. The numbers of defectives for the three lines were found to be 12, 17, and 7, respectively. Do the data

General Form of Contingency Table Analysis: A Test for Independence with Row* Totals Fixed

If row totals are fixed:

H_0: The row proportions in each cell do not depend on the row; that is, the distributions of observations in the column categories are the same for each row

H_a: The row proportions in some (or all) of the cells depend on the row; that is, the distributions of observations in the column categories differ for at least two of the rows

Test statistic: $\chi^2 = \sum\limits_{j=1}^{c} \sum\limits_{i=1}^{r} \dfrac{[n_{ij} - \hat{E}(n_{ij})]^2}{\hat{E}(n_{ij})}$

where

$$\hat{E}(n_{ij}) = \frac{n_{i.}\, n_{.j}}{n}$$

Rejection region: $\chi^2 > \chi_\alpha^2$, where χ_α^2 has $(r-1)(c-1)$ df

Assumptions: 1. A random sample is selected from each population for which the row totals are fixed.

2. The samples are independently selected.

3. We require the estimated expected value of each cell to be at least 5 to use the χ^2 approximation.

provide sufficient evidence to indicate differences in the proportions of defective washers produced by the three production lines? In other words, are the two directions of classification, production line and defective status, dependent?

The data are presented as a contingency table in Table 10.8 on page 518. The objective of this experiment is to compare three binomial proportions of defectives, p_1, p_2, and p_3, based on three independent binomial experiments, each containing 500 observations.

The null hypothesis is that the proportions of defectives for the three production lines are identical, i.e.,

H_0: $p_1 = p_2 = p_3$

---

*Note that to obtain the procedure for conducting a χ^2 analysis for fixed column totals, it is necessary only to interchange the words *column* and *row* in the box.

TABLE 10.8 Contingency Table for Example 10.5

	Production Line			TOTALS
	1	2	3	
Number of defectives	12	17	7	36
Number of nondefectives	488	483	493	1,464
TOTALS	500	500	500	1,500

against the alternative hypothesis

H_a: At least two of the proportions, p_1, p_2, and p_3, differ.

Note that the null hypothesis we have specified implies that the numbers of defectives and nondefectives are independent of the production line. Therefore, we test H_0: $p_1 = p_2 = p_3$ using the chi-square test for a contingency table analysis.

The estimated expected cell counts are computed using the formula

$$\hat{E}(n_{ij}) = \frac{n_{i.}\,n_{.j}}{n}$$

Therefore,

$$\hat{E}(n_{11}) = \frac{n_{i.}\,n_{.j}}{n} = \frac{(36)(500)}{1,500} = 12$$

and

$$\hat{E}(n_{12}) = \frac{n_{1.}\,n_{.2}}{n} = \frac{(36)(500)}{1,500} = 12$$

These, along with the remaining estimated expected cell counts (in parentheses), are shown in Table 10.9.

TABLE 10.9 Observed and Estimated Expected Cell Counts for Example 10.5

	Production Line		
	1	2	3
Number of Defectives	12 (12)	17 (12)	7 (12)
Number of Nondefectives	488 (488)	483 (488)	493 (488)

The computed value of χ^2 is

$$\chi^2 = \sum_{j=1}^{c} \sum_{i=1}^{r} \frac{[n_{ij} - \hat{E}(n_{ij})]^2}{\hat{E}(n_{ij})}$$

$$= \frac{(12 - 12)^2}{12} + \frac{(17 - 12)^2}{12} + \cdots + \frac{(493 - 488)^2}{488}$$

$$= 4.269$$

The rejection region for the test is $\chi^2 > \chi^2_{.05}$ where $\chi^2_{.05} = 5.99147$ is based on $(r - 1)(c - 1) = (1)(2) = 2$ degrees of freedom. Since the computed value of χ^2 does not exceed $\chi^2_{.05}$, there is insufficient evidence to indicate differences in the proportions of defective washers produced by the three production lines. Note that we do not accept H_0—that is, we do not conclude that $p_1 = p_2 = p_3$—because we would be concerned about the possibility of making a Type II error, failing to detect differences in the proportions of defectives if, in fact, differences exist. The test conclusion simply means that if differences exist, they were too small to detect using samples of 500 washers from each production line.

EXERCISES

10.23   Seldane-D, produced by Marion Merrell Dow, Inc., is an over-the-counter drug designed to relieve sneezing, nasal congestion, and other symptoms of allergic rhinitis. General adverse effects of Seldane-D were investigated in a double-blind, controlled study of over 500 patients suffering from allergic rhinitis. A sample of 374 patients were given Seldane-D, whereas a second sample of 193 patients were given a placebo (no drug). The number of patients reporting insomnia in each of the two groups are given in the table. Test to determine whether the proportion of patients taking Seldane-D who experience insomnia differs from the corresponding proportion for patients receiving the placebo. Use $\alpha = .10$.

	Seldane-D	Placebo
Insomnia	97	12
No Insomnia	277	181
TOTALS	374	193

Source: Marion Merrell Dow, Incorporated. Prescription Products Division, 1993.

10.24   The scarce and essential metal, manganese, has been found in abundance in nodules on the deep sea floor. To investigate the relationship between the magnetic age of the earth's crust on the ocean floor and the probability of finding manganese nodules in that location, crust specimens were selected from seven magnetic age locations and the percentage of specimens containing manganese nodules was recorded for each. The data are shown in the accompanying table. Is there sufficient evidence to indicate that the probability of finding manganese nodules in the deep sea earth's crust is dependent on the magnetic age of the crust? Test using $\alpha = .05$.

Age	Number of Specimens	Percentage with Manganese Nodules
Miocene–recent	389	5.9
Oligocene	140	17.9
Eocene	214	16.4
Paleocene	84	21.4
Late Cretaceous	247	21.1
Early and Middle Cretaceous	1,120	14.2
Jurassic	99	11.0

Source: Menard, H. W. "Time, chance, and the origin of manganese nodules." *American Scientist*, Sept.–Oct. 1976.

10.25 The use of high-level computer programming languages (for example, Fortran, Cobol, Algol, and Pascal) with microprocessors and minicomputers has increased dramatically over the past few years. This has increased the need for new and better methods of performance evaluation. In one study, a researcher developed a measurement system for evaluating two high-level programming languages, Algol and Pascal. The reported results include a distribution of the relative frequency of occurrence of the different types of statements used in typical Algol and Pascal programs of approximately the same size. The reported percentages were used to tabulate the information given in the table.

		Algol	Pascal
	IF	125	2,045
	FOR	968	350
Type of	IO	135	1,847
Statement	Assignment	8,923	4,763
	Other	261	465
TOTALS		10,412	9,470

Source: Adapted from De Prycker, M. "On the development of a measurement system for high-level language program statistics." *IEEE Transactions on Computers*, Vol. C-31, No. 9, Sept. 1982, pp. 888–890.

a. Assuming fixed marginals for the two programming languages, conduct a test to determine whether the percentages of the different types of programming statements differ for the two languages. Test using $\alpha = .05$.

b. Construct a 95% confidence interval for the difference in the percentages of assignment statements used in the two languages.

10.26 An electric utilities company must choose between two technology options for generating electricity for its customers in the future: coal or nuclear energy. To assess the attitudes of local citizens, the power company conducted a public opinion poll. Four sectors were considered: news media, coal miners' union, environmentalists and conservationists, and local groups. Fifty persons were randomly sampled from each sector and asked to give their opinions. The results of the survey are shown in the table, followed by a MINITAB analysis of the data.

	News Media	Coal Miners' Union	Environmentalist and Conservationists	Local Groups	TOTALS
Support Coal Option	21	42	11	25	99
Support Nuclear Option	18	2	16	13	49
Neutral	11	6	23	12	52
TOTALS	50	50	50	50	200

```
Expected counts are printed below observed counts

          News     Union      E&C     Local    Total
   1        21        42       11        25       99
          24.75     24.75    24.75     24.75

   2        18         2       16        13       49
          12.25     12.25    12.25     12.25

   3        11         6       23        12       52
          13.00     13.00    13.00     13.00

Total       50        50       50        50      200

ChiSq =   0.568 + 12.023 +   7.639 +   0.003 +
          2.699 +  8.577 +   1.148 +   0.046 +
          0.308 +  3.769 +   7.692 +   0.077 = 44.548
df = 6
```

a. Does public opinion regarding the choice of future technology options for generating electricity differ among the four groups? Test using $\alpha = .10$.

b. Does there appear to be more overall support for the coal option rather than the nuclear option? Test using $\alpha = .10$.

c. Construct a 90% confidence interval for the percentage of environmentalists and conservationists who support the nuclear option.

10.6   Summary

The use of **count data** to test hypotheses about **multinomial probabilities** represents a very useful statistical technique. In a **one-dimensional table**, we can use count data to test the hypothesis that the multinomial probabilities are equal to specified values. In a **two-dimensional contingency table**, we can test the independence of the two classifications. These by no means exhaust the uses of the χ^2 statistic. Many other applications can be found in the references at the end of this chapter.

Caution should be exercised to avoid misuse of the χ^2 procedure. The experiment must be multinomial.* Expected cell counts should be larger than or equal to 5 for the chi-square distribution to provide an adequate approximation to the sampling distribution of χ^2.

If the χ^2 value does not exceed the tabulated critical value of χ^2, *do not accept* the hypothesis of independence. You would be risking a Type II error (accepting H_0 if it is false), and the probability β of committing such an error is unknown. The usual alternative hypothesis is that the classifications are dependent. Because there is literally an infinite number of ways two classifications can be dependent, it is difficult to calculate one or even several values of β to represent such a broad research hypothesis. Therefore, we avoid concluding that two classifications are independent, even when χ^2 is small.

Finally, if a contingency table χ^2 value *does* exceed the critical value, we must be careful to avoid inferring that a causal relationship exists between the classifications. Our alternative hypothesis states that the two classifications are statistically dependent, and **statistical dependence does not imply causality**. Therefore, the existence of a causal relationship cannot be established by a contingency table analysis.

SUPPLEMENTARY EXERCISES

10.27   Employees' reactions to compressed work weeks were investigated in *Personnel Psychology* (Summer 1983). *Compressed work weeks* are defined as "alternative work schedules in which a trade is made between the number of hours worked per day, and the number of days worked per week, in order to work the standard number of weekly hours in less than 5 days." A field study was conducted at a large midwestern continuous-processing (7 days/24 hours) chemical plant that had experimented with four different work schedules, two of which were compressed:

Three 8-hour fixed shifts   Two 12-hour fixed shifts
(day, evening, midnight)   (12 A.M.–12 P.M., 12 P.M.–12 A.M.)
Three 8-hour rotating shifts   Two 12-hour rotating shifts

Six hundred seventy-one hourly employees were asked to rank the four work schedules in order of preference. The accompanying table gives the number of first-place rankings for each schedule. Is there sufficient evidence to indicate that the hourly employees have a preference for one of the work schedules? Test using $\alpha = .01$.

8-hour fixed	8-hour rotating	12-hour fixed	12-hour rotating
389	54	208	20

---

*When the row (or column) totals are fixed, each row (or column) represents a separate multinomial experiment.

10.28 A 4-year study of computer abuse was recently completed by researchers. The numbers of four types of abuse reported and verified by year are shown in the table, followed by a MINITAB printout of the analysis. Do the data provide sufficient evidence to indicate that the proportions of different types of abuse are changing over time? Test using $\alpha = .05$.

		Financial Fraud	Type of Abuse Theft of Information or Property	Unauthorized Use of Information	Vandalism	TOTAL
Year	1	7	5	9	8	29
	2	22	18	6	6	52
	3	12	15	6	12	45
	4	21	15	16	9	61
TOTAL		62	53	37	35	187

```
         Fraud    Theft    Use    Vandal   Total
  1        7        5       9       8        29
         9.61     8.22    5.74    5.43

  2       22       18       6       6        52
        17.24    14.74   10.29    9.73

  3       12       15       6      12        45
        14.92    12.75    8.90    8.42

  4       21       15      16       9        61
        20.22    17.29   12.07   11.42

Total     62       53      37      35       187

ChiSq =  0.711 +  1.261 +  1.854 +  1.219 +
         1.314 +  0.722 +  1.788 +  1.432 +
         0.571 +  0.396 +  0.947 +  1.520 +
         0.030 +  0.303 +  1.280 +  0.512 = 15.859

df = 9
```

10.29 One of the major problems confronting urban planners and design engineers is crime prevention. How should the buildings, sites, and neighborhoods in an urban (or urban renewal) area be physically designed to minimize crime levels? To assess the validity of several different planning perspectives, the *Journal of the American Planning Association* (Winter 1984) examined differences in physical characteristics and various dimensions of informal social control in six neighborhoods in Atlanta, Georgia. The neighborhoods were grouped into three pairs—white middle-income pair, black lower-middle income pair, and black lower-income pair—where one member of each pair had a relatively high crime rate, and the other had a relatively low crime rate. The number of census blocks in each neighborhood pair were then classified according to crime rate (high or low) and several physical characteristics. The classification for street-front characteristics is shown in the table on page 524. [*Note:* Greenberg and Rohe reported the results in terms of percentages. For the reader's convenience, we have converted all percentages to cell counts.]

   a. For each neighborhood pair, conduct a chi-square test for independence of classifications. Use $\alpha = .05$ and interpret your results.

b. For each neighborhood pair, construct a 95% confidence interval for the difference between the percentage of high-crime and low-crime neighborhood blocks that front a major thoroughfare.

Street Characteristics	White Middle-Income Pair		Black Lower-Middle Income Pair		Black Lower-Income Pair	
	High	Low	High	Low	High	Low
Major Thoroughfare	20	9	25	1	22	30
Small Neighborhood Street	7	9	25	27	8	42
Other	21	15	36	14	3	23
TOTALS	48	33	86	42	33	95

Source: Greenberg, S. W., and Rohe, W. M. "Neighborhood design and crime: A test of two perspectives." *Journal of the American Planning Association*, Vol. 50, No. 1, 1984, pp. 48–60.

10.30   Research has shown that there is a basic resistance on the part of managers to use information produced by a computer (*Journal of the Operational Research Society*, Mar. 1983). At one firm, over 40% of all computer-generated reports provided to managerial personnel were not used in any manner. A breakdown of the actual number of reports received and not used by each of three groups of employees is provided in the table. Is there sufficient evidence to conclude that the percentages of computer-generated reports not used differ among the three receiver groups? Test at $\alpha = .05$.

Receiver Group	Copies of Report Used	Copies Not Used
Directors and general managers	38	29
Middle managers	22	20
Clerks	138	42

Source: Edwards, C. "Encouraging usage of computer-produced management information." *The Journal of the Operational Research Society*, Vol. 34, No. 3, Mar. 1983, p. 201. Copyright 1983, Pergamon Press, Ltd. Reprinted with permission.

10.31   Refer to Exercise 10.30. Models were devised to encourage the usage of computer-generated reports by management. A flexible model, in which either the receiver or the producer can undertake the task of encouraging use, was tested at the firm. Forty-one receivers and 41 producers accepted the responsibility of encouraging the use of computer-generated reports. The number of times each group satisfied the conditions specified in the model is shown in the accompanying table. Test the hypothesis that the proportion of times the model conditions are satisfied is identical for the two groups. Use $\alpha = .01$.

	Receivers	Producers
Number of times model conditions satisfied	20	0
Number of times model conditions not satisfied	21	41

Source: Edwards, C. "Encouraging usage of computer-produced management information." *The Journal of the Operational Research Society*, Vol. 34, No. 3, Mar. 1983, p. 201. Copyright 1983, Pergamon Press, Ltd. Reprinted with permission.

10.32   *Dear enemy recognition* is the term used by naturalists and ecologists for the aggressive behavior of birds, mammals, and ants when their territorial boundaries are violated by one of their own species. Dear enemy recognition is often followed by escalated attacks on the invading animal. A recent study explored the possibility that the red-backed salamander employs dear enemy recognition by using chemical signals to distinguish familiar from unfamiliar salamanders. In escalated contests, a salamander will attempt to bite an opponent's snout—an injury that could reduce a salamander's ability to locate prey, mates, and territorial competitors. One part of the study focused on a comparison of the proportions of males and females exhibiting wounds in the snout. One hundred forty-four salamanders were collected from a forest, killed, and inspected for scar tissue in the snout. The results are shown in the table.

	Male	Female	TOTALS
Scar tissue in snout	5	12	17
No scar tissue in snout	76	51	127
TOTALS	81	63	

Source: Jaeger, R. G. "Dear enemy recognition and the costs of aggression between salamanders." *The American Naturalist*, June 1981, Vol. 117, pp. 962–973. Reprinted by permission of the University of Chicago Press. © 1981 The University of Chicago.

a. Use a chi-square test to determine whether there is a difference between the proportions of males and females with scar tissue in the snout. Use $\alpha = .01$.

b. Estimate the difference between the proportions of males and females with scar tissue in the snout. Use a 99% confidence interval. Interpret the result.

10.33   Video engineers have developed a new method of shortening the time required for broadcasting a television commercial. This technique, called *time compression*, has enabled television advertisers to cut the high costs of television commercials. But can shorter commercials be effective? To answer this question, 200 college students were randomly divided into three groups. The first group (57 students) was shown a videotape of a television program that included a 30-second commercial; the second group (74 students) was shown the same videotape but with the 24-second time-compressed version of the commercial; and the third group (69 students) was shown a 20-second time-compressed version of the commercial. Two days after viewing the tape, the three groups of students were asked to name the brand that was advertised. The numbers of students recalling the brand name for each of the three groups are given in the table.

		Normal Version (30 Seconds)	Time-Compressed Version 1 (24 Seconds)	Time-Compressed Version 2 (20 Seconds)	TOTALS
Recall of	Yes	15	32	10	57
Brand Name	No	42	42	59	143
TOTALS		57	74	69	200

a. Do the data provide sufficient evidence (at $\alpha = .05$) that the two directions of classification, type of commercial and recall of brand name, are dependent? Interpret your results.

b. Construct a 95% confidence interval for the difference between the proportions recalling brand name for viewers of normal and 24-second time-compressed commercials.

10.34   The air travel industry has long been concerned about the fear of flying; it is estimated that one of every six adult Americans is afraid to fly. To determine whether fear of flying is a significant problem for the airline industry, a series of national and special-purpose surveys was conducted. One question was posed to determine whether anxiety with respect to flying is dependent on flight experience on a commercial aircraft. Respondents were first classified as either flyers (those who have flown at least once), nonflyers likely to fly (those who have never flown but consider themselves likely to fly in the future), or nonflyers not likely to fly (those who have never flown and are not likely to fly in the future). The numbers of each group falling into each of three levels of anxiety with respect to flying are shown in the table.

		Flyers	Flight Experience Nonflyers Likely to Fly	Nonflyers Not Likely to Fly
Anxiety Level	No Anxiety	1,043	128	113
	Anxious	189	46	6
	Afraid	140	47	141

Source: Dean, R. D., and Whitaker, K. M. "Fear of flying: Impact on the U.S. air travel industry." *Journal of Travel Research*, Summer 1982, p. 10.

a. Does the anxiety level with respect to flying depend on flight experience? Use $\alpha = .05$.
b. Find a 95% confidence interval for the difference between the proportions of flyers and nonflyers likely to fly who have no anxiety toward flying. Interpret the interval.

10.35   A decision support system (DSS) is a computerized system designed to aid in the management and analysis of large data sets. Ideally, a DSS should include four components: (1) a data extraction system, (2) a relational database organization, (3) analysis models, and (4) a user-friendly interactive dialogue between the user and the system. A state highway agency recently installed a DSS to help monitor data on road construction contract bids. As part of a self-examination, the agency selected 151 of the most recently encountered problems that could be traced directly to the DSS and classified each according to the component of origination. Can it be concluded from the data in the table that the proportions of problems are different for at least two of the four DSS components? Test using $\alpha = .05$.

Component	1	2	3	4
Number of Problems	31	28	45	47

10.36   An experiment was conducted to compare the fidelity and selectivity of radio receivers. One hundred fifty receivers were tested and classified as low, medium, or high in each of the two categories. Do the data in the table provide sufficient evidence to indicate a dependence between fidelity and selectivity? Test using $\alpha = .025$.

		Selectivity Low	Medium	High
	Low	10	11	6
Fidelity	Medium	30	52	19
	High	12	8	2

10.37 A computer used by a 24-hour banking service is supposed to assign each transaction to one of five memory locations at random. A check at the end of a day's transactions gave the following counts to each of the five memory locations:

Memory Location	1	2	3	4	5
Number of Transactions	90	78	100	72	85

Is there evidence to indicate a difference among the proportions of transactions assigned to the five memory locations? Test using $\alpha = .025$.

10.38 Does the propensity for worker injuries depend on the length of time that a worker has been on the job? An analysis of 714 worker injuries by one manufacturer gave the results shown in the table for the distribution of injuries over the eight 1-hour time periods per shift.

Hour of Shift	1	2	3	4	5	6	7	8
Number of Accidents	93	71	79	72	98	89	102	110

a. Do the data imply that the probabilities of worker accidents are higher in some time periods than in others? Test using $\alpha = .10$.

b. Do the data provide sufficient evidence to indicate that the probability of an accident during the last 4 hours of a shift is greater than during the first 4 hours? Test using $\alpha = .10$. [*Hint:* Test $H_0: p_1 = .5$, where p_1 is the probability of an accident during the last 4 hours.]

COMPUTER LAB: Contingency Table Analysis

In this section, we give the SAS and MINITAB commands for testing multinomial probabilities from two-way (contingency) tables. The following programs analyze the data in the two-way table of Table 10.4. (Programs for one-way tables are not available in SAS or MINITAB.)

SAS

Command line

```
1    DATA TABLE;
2    INPUT EVAC $ DISTANCE $ NUMBER @@;        } Data entry instructions
3    CARDS;
     YES 1TO6 18 YES 7TO12 15 YES 13MORE 33
      .    .    .    .    .    .      .    .    } Input data values
      .    .    .    .    .    .      .    .      (3 observations per line)
     NO  1TO6 20  NO  7TO12 19  NO  13MORE 45
4    PROC FREQ;
5    TABLES EVAC*DISTANCE/EXPECTED CHISQ;       } Contingency table analysis
6    WEIGHT NUMBER;
```

COMMAND 4 The FREQ procedure generates a frequency (or contingency) table for the data.

COMMAND 5   The TABLES statement defines the two classification variables for the contingency table. Variable names are separated by an asterisk (*). The options EXPECTED and CHISQ (following the slash) request to print expected cell frequencies and the χ^2 statistic (and corresponding p-value) for the contingency table.

COMMAND 6   The WEIGHT statement defines the weighting variable of the contingency table (e.g., NUMBER). This statement is necessary when the cell counts have already been tabulated, as in Table 10.4. If the cell counts have *not* been pretabulated (i.e., if the data are "raw"), omit the WEIGHT statement.

NOTE   The printout for the SAS program is displayed in Figure 10.3 (Section 10.3).

MINITAB

Command
line

```
1     READ TABLE IN C1 C2 C3          Data entry instruction
2     18 15 33       ⎫  Input data values
3     20 19 45       ⎭  (Each row represents one row of the contingency table)
4     NAME C1='1TO6'  C2='7TO12'  C3='13MORE'
5     CHISQUARE TEST ON TABLE IN C1-C3          Contingency table analysis
```

COMMANDS 2–3   The pretabulated cell counts of the contingency table are read into the columns of the MINITAB worksheet. Each row represents one row and each column represents one column of the contingency table.

COMMAND 5   The CHISQUARE command generates expected cell frequencies and the χ^2 statistic for the contingency table stored in the columns specified.

NOTE   The MINITAB printout is displayed in Figure 10.4.

FIGURE 10.4 ▶
MINITAB contingency table analysis
for Computer Lab

```
Expected counts are printed below observed counts

              1to6      7to12     13More     Total
     1          18         15         33         66
            16.72      14.96      34.32

     2          20         19         45         84
            21.28      19.04      43.68

Total          38         34         78        150

ChiSq =   0.098 +   0.000 +   0.051 +
          0.077 +   0.000 +   0.040 = 0.266
df = 2
```

References

Agresti, A. *Categorical Data Analysis*. New York: Wiley, 1990.

Agresti, A., and Finlay, B. *Statistical Methods for the Social Sciences*, 2nd ed. San Francisco: Dellen, 1986.

Cochran, W. G. "The χ^2 Test of Goodness of Fit," *Annals of Mathematical Statistics*, Vol. 23, 1952.

Cochran, W. G. "Some Methods for Strengthening the Common χ^2 Tests," *Biometrics*, Vol. 10.

Davies, O. L. *The Design and Analysis of Industrial Experiments*, 2nd ed. New York: Hafner, 1956.

Johnson, N., and Leone, F. *Statistics and Experimental Design in Engineering and the Physical Sciences*, Vol. II, 2nd ed. New York: Wiley, 1977.

CHAPTER ELEVEN

Simple Linear Regression

Objective

To present the basic concepts of regression analysis based on a simple linear relation between a response y and a single predictor variable x

Contents

531

FIGURE 11.1 ▶
Scattergram for the data in
Table 11.1

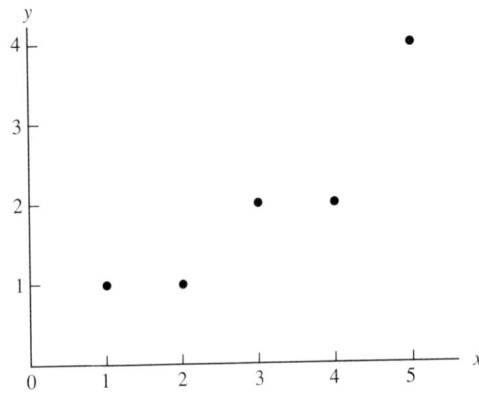

TABLE 11.1 Compression Versus Pressure for an Insulation Material

Specimen	Pressure	Compression
	x	y
1	1	1
2	2	1
3	3	2
4	4	2
5	5	4

of prediction—might be adequate if all of the points of Figure 11.1 fell on the fitted line. However, you can see that this idealistic situation will not occur for the data of Table 11.1. No matter how you draw a line through the points of Figure 11.1, at least some of the points will deviate substantially from the fitted line.

The solution to the preceding problem is to construct a **probabilistic model** relating y to x—one that acknowledges the random variation of the data points about a line. One type of probabilistic model, a **simple linear regression model,** makes the assumption that the mean value of y for a given value of x graphs as a straight line and that points deviate about this **line of means** by a random (positive or negative) amount equal to ε, i.e.,

$$y = \underbrace{\beta_0 + \beta_1 x}_{\substack{\text{Mean value of } y \\ \text{for a given } x}} + \underbrace{\varepsilon}_{\substack{\text{Random} \\ \text{error}}}$$

where β_0 and β_1 are unknown parameters of the deterministic (nonrandom) portion of the model. If we assume that the points deviate above and below the line of means, with some deviations positive, some negative, and with $E(\varepsilon) = 0$, then the mean value of y is

$$E(y) = E(\beta_0 + \beta_1 x + \varepsilon) = \beta_0 + \beta_1 x + E(\varepsilon) = \beta_0 + \beta_1 x$$

Therefore, the mean value of y for a given value of x, represented by the symbol $E(y),$* graphs as a straight line with y-intercept equal to β_0 and slope equal to β_1. A graph of the hypothetical line of means, $E(y) = \beta_0 + \beta_1 x$, is shown in Figure 11.2.

---

*The mean value of y for a given value of x should be denoted by the symbol $E(y \mid x)$. However, this notation becomes cumbersome when the model contains more than one independent variable. Consequently, we will abbreviate the notation and represent $E(y \mid x)$ by the symbol $E(y)$.

FIGURE 11.2 ▶

A graph of the data points of Table 11.1 and the hypothetical line of means,

$$E(y) = \beta_0 + \beta_1 x$$

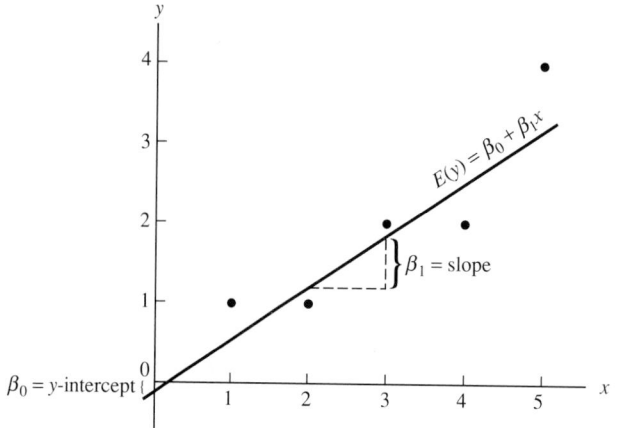

A Simple Linear Regression (Probabilistic) Model

$$y = \beta_0 + \beta_1 x + \varepsilon$$

where

y = Dependent variable

x = Independent variable

$E(y) = \beta_0 + \beta_1 x$ is the deterministic component (the equation of a straight line)

ε (epsilon) = Random error component

β_0 (beta-zero) = y-intercept of the line, i.e., point at which the line intercepts or cuts through the y-axis (see Figure 11.2)

β_1 (beta-one) = Slope of the line, i.e., amount of increase (or decrease) in the deterministic component of y for every 1-unit increase in x (see Figure 11.2)

To fit a simple linear regression model to a set of data, we must find estimators for the unknown parameters, β_0 and β_1, of the line of means, $E(y) = \beta_0 + \beta_1 x$. Valid inferences about β_0 and β_1 will depend on the sampling distributions of the estimators, which in turn depend on the probability distribution of the random error, ε; consequently, we must first make specific assumptions about ε. These assumptions, summarized here, are basic to every statistical regression analysis.

ASSUMPTION 1 The mean of the probability distribution of ε is 0. That is, the average of the errors over an infinitely long series of experiments is 0 for each setting of the independent variable x. This assumption implies that the mean value of y, $E(y)$, for a given value of x is $E(y) = \beta_0 + \beta_1 x$.

ASSUMPTION 2   The variance of the probability distribution of ε is constant for all settings of the independent variable x. For our straight-line model, this assumption means that the variance of ε is equal to a constant, say, σ^2, for all values of x.

ASSUMPTION 3   The probability distribution of ε is normal.

ASSUMPTION 4   The errors associated with any two different observations are independent. That is, the error associated with one value of y has no effect on the errors associated with other y values.

The implications of the first three assumptions can be seen in Figure 11.3, which shows distributions of errors for three particular values of x, namely, x_1, x_2, and x_3. Note that the relative frequency distributions of the errors are normal, with a mean of 0, and a constant variance σ^2 (all the distributions shown have the same amount of spread or variability). The straight line shown in Figure 11.3 is the mean value of y for a given value of x, $E(y) = \beta_0 + \beta_1 x$.

FIGURE 11.3 ▶
The probability distribution of ε

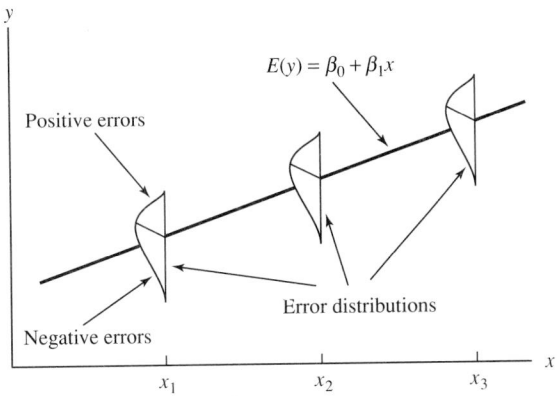

Various techniques exist for checking the validity of these assumptions, and there are remedies to be applied when they appear to be invalid. We discuss these techniques in detail in Chapter 12. In actual practice, the assumptions need not hold exactly for least squares estimators and test statistics (to be described subsequently) to possess the measures of reliability that we would expect from a regression analysis. The assumptions will be satisfied adequately for many practical applications.

11.3   Estimating β_0 and β_1: The Method of Least Squares

To choose the "best-fitting" line for a set of data, we must estimate the unknown parameters, β_0 and β_1, of the simple linear regression model. These estimators could be found using the method of maximum likelihood (Section 8.3), but the easiest method—and one that is intuitively appealing—is the **method of least squares**. When

the assumptions of Section 11.2 are satisfied, then the maximum likelihood and the least squares estimators of β_0 and β_1 are identical.*

The reasoning behind the method of least squares can be seen by examining Figure 11.4, which shows a line drawn on the scattergram of the data points of Table 11.1. The vertical line segments represent **deviations** of the points from the line. You can see by shifting a ruler around the graph that it is possible to find many lines for which the sum of deviations (or **errors**) is equal to 0, but it can be shown that there is one and only one line for which the **sum of squares of the deviations** is a minimum. The sum of squares of the deviations is called the **sum of squares for error** and is denoted by the symbol SSE. The line is called the **least squares line**, the **regression line**, or the **least squares prediction equation**.

FIGURE 11.4 ▶

Graph showing the deviations of the points about a line

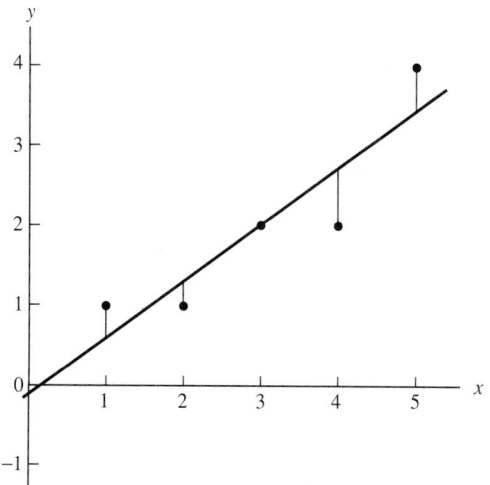

To find the least squares line for a set of data, assume that we have a sample of n data points which can be identified by corresponding values of x and y, say, (x_1, y_1), (x_2, y_2), . . . , (x_n, y_n). For example, the $n = 5$ data points shown in Table 11.1 are (1, 1), (2, 1), (3, 2), (4, 2), and (5, 4). The straight-line model for the response y in terms of x is

$$y = \beta_0 + \beta_1 x + \varepsilon$$

The line of means is $E(y) = \beta_0 + \beta_1 x$ and the fitted line, which we hope to find, is represented as $\hat{y} = \hat{\beta}_0 + \hat{\beta}_1 x$. Thus, $\hat{y}$ is an estimator of the mean value of y, $E(y)$, and a predictor of some future value of y; and $\hat{\beta}_0$ and $\hat{\beta}_1$ are estimators of β_0 and β_1, respectively.

---

*The method of least squares is a valid estimation technique even when one or more of the assumptions of Section 11.2 are violated. If the assumptions are not satisfied, it is the validity of inferences derived from the estimates that is in question.

For a given data point, say, the point (x_i, y_i), the observed value of y is y_i and the predicted value of y would be obtained by substituting x_i into the prediction equation:

$$\hat{y}_i = \hat{\beta}_0 + \hat{\beta}_1 x_i$$

And the deviation of the ith value of y from its predicted value is

$$(y_i - \hat{y}_i) = [y_i - (\hat{\beta}_0 + \hat{\beta}_1 x_i)]$$

Then the sum of squares of the deviations of the y values about their predicted values for all of the n data points is

$$\text{SSE} = \sum_{i=1}^{n} [y_i - (\hat{\beta}_0 + \hat{\beta}_1 x_i)]^2$$

The quantities $\hat{\beta}_0$ and $\hat{\beta}_1$ that make the SSE a minimum are called the **least squares estimates** of the population parameters β_0 and β_1, and the prediction equation $\hat{y} = \hat{\beta}_0 + \hat{\beta}_1 x$ is called the **least squares line**.

Definition 11.3

The **least squares line** is one that has a smaller SSE than any other straight-line model.

The values of $\hat{\beta}_0$ and $\hat{\beta}_1$ that minimize

$$\text{SSE} = \sum_{i=1}^{n} [y_i - (\hat{\beta}_0 + \hat{\beta}_1 x_i)]^2$$

are obtained by setting the two partial derivatives, $\partial \text{SSE}/\partial \hat{\beta}_0$ and $\partial \text{SSE}/\partial \hat{\beta}_1$, equal to 0 and solving the resulting simultaneous linear system of **least squares equations**. To illustrate, we first compute the partial derivatives:

$$\frac{\partial \text{SSE}}{\partial \hat{\beta}_0} = \sum_{i=1}^{n} 2[y_i - (\hat{\beta}_0 + \hat{\beta}_1 x_i)](-1)$$

$$\frac{\partial \text{SSE}}{\partial \hat{\beta}_1} = \sum_{i=1}^{n} 2[y_i - (\hat{\beta}_0 + \hat{\beta}_1 x_i)](-x_i)$$

Setting these partial derivatives equal to 0 and simplifying, we obtain the least squares equations:

$$\sum_{i=1}^{n} y_i - \sum_{i=1}^{n} \hat{\beta}_0 - \hat{\beta}_1 \sum_{i=1}^{n} x_i = \sum_{i=1}^{n} y_i - n\hat{\beta}_0 - \hat{\beta}_1 \sum_{i=1}^{n} x_i = 0$$

$$\sum_{i=1}^{n} x_i y_i - \hat{\beta}_0 \sum_{i=1}^{n} x_i - \hat{\beta}_1 \sum_{i=1}^{n} x_i^2 = 0$$

or

$$n\hat{\beta}_0 + \hat{\beta}_1 \sum_{i=1}^{n} x_i = \sum_{i=1}^{n} y_i$$

$$\hat{\beta}_0 \sum_{i=1}^{n} x_i + \hat{\beta}_1 \sum_{i=1}^{n} x_i^2 = \sum_{i=1}^{n} x_i y_i$$

Solving this pair of simultaneous linear equations for β_0 and β_1, we obtain (proof omitted) the formulas shown in the box.

Formulas for the Least Squares Estimates

Slope: $\hat{\beta}_1 = \dfrac{SS_{xy}}{SS_{xx}}$

y-intercept: $\hat{\beta}_0 = \bar{y} - \hat{\beta}_1 \bar{x}$

where

$$SS_{xy} = \sum_{i=1}^{n} (x_i - \bar{x})(y_i - \bar{y}) = \sum_{i=1}^{n} x_i y_i - \frac{\left(\sum_{i=1}^{n} x_i\right)\left(\sum_{i=1}^{n} y_i\right)}{n}$$

$$SS_{xx} = \sum_{i=1}^{n} (x_i - \bar{x})^2 = \sum_{i=1}^{n} x_i^2 - \frac{\left(\sum_{i=1}^{n} x_i\right)^2}{n}$$

$n = $ Sample size

EXAMPLE 11.1

a. Calculate the least squares estimates of β_0 and β_1 for the data of Table 11.1.

b. Give a practical interpretation of the results.

Solution

a. Preliminary computations for finding the least squares line for the insulation compression data are contained in Table 11.2. We can now calculate*

$$SS_{xy} = \sum x_i y_i - \frac{\left(\sum x_i\right)\left(\sum y_i\right)}{5} = 37 - \frac{(15)(10)}{5}$$

$$= 37 - 30 = 7$$

$$SS_{xx} = \sum x_i^2 - \frac{\left(\sum x_i\right)^2}{5} = 55 - \frac{(15)^2}{5}$$

$$= 55 - 45 = 10$$

TABLE 11.2   Preliminary Computations for the Insulation Compression Example

	x_i	y_i	x_i^2	$x_i y_i$	y_i^2
	1	1	1	1	1
	2	1	4	2	1
	3	2	9	6	4
	4	2	16	8	4
	5	4	25	20	16
TOTALS	$\sum x_i = 15$	$\sum y_i = 10$	$\sum x_i^2 = 55$	$\sum x_i y_i = 37$	$\sum y_i^2 = 26$

Then, the slope of the least squares line is

$$\hat{\beta}_1 = \frac{SS_{xy}}{SS_{xx}} = \frac{7}{10} = .7$$

and the y-intercept is

$$\hat{\beta}_0 = \bar{y} - \hat{\beta}_1 \bar{x} = \frac{\sum y_i}{5} - \hat{\beta}_1 \frac{\left(\sum x_i\right)}{5}$$

$$= \frac{10}{5} - (.7)\frac{(15)}{5}$$

$$= 2 - (.7)(3) = 2 - 2.1 = -.1$$

---

*Since summations will be used extensively from this point on, we will omit the limits on Σ when the summation includes all the measurements in the sample, i.e., when the symbol is $\Sigma_{i=1}^{n}$, we will write Σ.

The least squares line is thus

$$\hat{y} = \hat{\beta}_0 + \hat{\beta}_1 x = -.1 + .7x$$

The graph of this line is shown in Figure 11.5.

FIGURE 11.5 ▶
The line $\hat{y} = -.1 + .7x$ fit
to the data

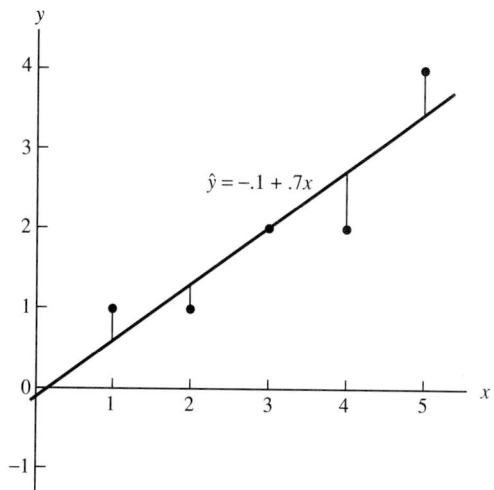

b. Our interpretation of the least squares slope, $\hat{\beta}_1 = .7$, is that compression y will increase .7 unit for every 1-unit increase in pressure x. Since y is measured in units of .1 inch and x in units of 10 pounds per square inch, our interpretation is that compression increases 07 inch for every 10-pound-per-square-inch increase in pressure. We will attach a measure of reliability to this inference in Section 11.6.

The least squares intercept, $\hat{\beta}_0 = -.1$, is our estimate of compression y when pressure is set at $x = 0$ pounds per square inch. Since level of compression can never be negative, why does such a nonsensical result occur? The reason is that we are attempting to use the least squares model to predict y for a value of x ($x = 0$) that is outside the range of the sample data and impractical. (We have more to say about predicting outside the range of the sample data—called **extrapolation**—in Section 11.9.) Consequently, $\hat{\beta}_0$ will not always have a practical interpretation. Only when $x = 0$ is within the range of the x values in the sample and is a practical value will $\hat{\beta}_0$ have a meaningful interpretation.

The observed and predicted values of y, the deviations of the y values about their predicted values, and the squares of these deviations for the data of Table 10.1 are shown in Table 11.3. Note that the sum of squares of the deviations, SSE, is 1.10. This is smaller than the value of SSE that would be obtained by fitting any other possible straight line to the data.

TABLE 11.3   Comparing Observed and Predicted Values for the Least Squares Model

x	y	$\hat{y} = -.1 + .7x$	$(y - \hat{y})$	$(y - \hat{y})^2$
1	1	.6	$(1 - .6) = \quad .4$	.16
2	1	1.3	$(1 - 1.3) = -.3$	.09
3	2	2.0	$(2 - 2.0) = \quad 0$	.00
4	2	2.7	$(2 - 2.7) = -.7$	.49
5	4	3.4	$(4 - 3.4) = \quad .6$	.36
			Sum of errors = $\quad 0$	SSE = 1.10

To summarize, we have defined the best-fitting straight line to be the one that satisfies the least squares criterion; that is, the sum of the squared errors will be smaller than for any other straight-line model. This line is called the **least squares line**, and its equation is called the **least squares prediction equation**.

EXERCISES

11.1   In each case graph the line that passes through the points.
  a. (0, 2)   and   (2, 6)
  b. (0, 4)   and   (2, 6)
  c. (0, −2)   and   (−1, −6)
  d. (0, −4)   and   (3, −7)

11.2   The equation for a straight line (deterministic) is

$$y = \beta_0 + \beta_1 x$$

If the line passes through the point (0, 1), then $x = 0$, $y = 1$ must satisfy the equation. That is,

$$1 = \beta_0 + \beta_1(0)$$

Similarly, if the line passes through the point (2, 3), then $x = 2$, $y = 3$ must satisfy the equation:

$$3 = \beta_0 + \beta_1(2)$$

Use these two equations to solve for β_0 and β_1, and find the equation of the line that passes through the points (0, 1) and (2, 3).

11.3 Find the equations of the lines passing through the points in Exercise 10.1.

11.4 Plot the following lines:
  a. $y = 3 + 2x$
  b. $y = 1 + x$
  c. $y = -2 + 3x$
  d. $y = 5x$
  e. $y = 4 - 2x$

11.5 Give the slope and y-intercept for each of the lines defined in Exercise 11.4.

11.6 Modern warehouses employ computerized and automated guided vehicles for materials handling. Consequently, the physical layout of the warehouse must be carefully designed to prevent vehicle congestion and optimize response time. Optimal design of an automated warehouse was studied in *The Journal of Engineering for Industry* (Aug. 1993). The layout employed assumes that vehicles do not block each other when they travel within the warehouse, i.e., that there is no congestion. The validity of this assumption was checked by simulating (on a computer) warehouse operations. In each simulation, the number of vehicles was varied and the congestion time (total time one vehicle blocked another) was recorded. The data are shown in the accompanying table. Of interest to the researchers is the relationship between congestion time (y) and number of vehicles (x).

Number of Vehicles	Congestion Time minutes	Number of Vehicles	Congestion Time minutes
1	0	9	.02
2	0	10	.04
3	.02	11	.04
4	.01	12	.04
5	.01	13	.03
6	.01	14	.04
7	.03	15	.05
8	.03		

Source: Pandit, R., and U. S. Palekar, "Response time considerations for optimal warehouse layout design." *Journal of Engineering for Industry*, Transactions of the ASME, Vol. 115, Aug. 1993, p. 326 (Table 2).

  a. Construct a scattergram for the data.
  b. Find the least squares line relating number of vehicles (x) to congestion time (y).
  c. Plot the least squares line on the graph, part **a**.
  d. Interpret the values of $\hat{\beta}_0$ and $\hat{\beta}_1$.

11.7   Two processes for hydraulic drilling of rock are dry drilling and wet drilling. In a dry hole, compressed air is forced down the drill rods to flush the cuttings and drive the hammer; in a wet hole, water is forced down. An experiment was conducted to determine whether the time y it takes to dry drill a distance of 5 feet in rock increases with depth x (*The American Statistician*, Feb. 1991). The results for one portion of the experiment are shown in the accompanying table.

Depth at Which Drilling Begins x, feet	Time to Drill 5 Feet y, minutes
0	4.90
25	7.41
50	6.19
75	5.57
100	5.17
125	6.89
150	7.05
175	7.11
200	6.19
225	8.28
250	4.84
275	8.29
300	8.91
325	8.54
350	11.79
375	12.12
395	11.02

Source: Penner, R., and Watts, D. G. "Mining information." *The American Statistician*, Vol. 45, No. 1, Feb. 1991, p. 6 (Table 1).

a. Construct a scattergram for the data.
b. Find the least squares prediction equation.
c. Graph the least squares line on the scattergram.
d. Interpret the values of $\hat{\beta}_0$ and $\hat{\beta}_1$.

11.8   A study was conducted to model the thermal performance of integral-fin tubes used in the refrigeration and process industries (*Journal of Heat Transfer*, Aug. 1990). Twenty-four specially manufactured integral-fin tubes having rectangular-shaped fins made of copper were used in the experiment. Vapor was released downward into each tube and the vapor-side heat transfer coefficient (based on the outside surface area of the tube) was measured. The dependent variable for the study is the heat transfer enhancement ratio y, defined as the ratio of the vapor-side coefficient of the fin-tube to the vapor-side coefficient of a smooth tube evaluated at the same temperature. Theoretically, heat transfer will be related to the area at the top of the tube that is "unflooded" by condensation of the vapor. The data in the table are the unflooded area ratio (x) and heat transfer enhancement (y) values recorded for the 24 integral-fin tubes.

Unflooded Area Ratio, x	Heat Transfer Enhancement, y	Unflooded Area Ratio, x	Heat Transfer Enhancement, y
1.93	4.4	2.00	5.2
1.95	5.3	1.77	4.7
1.78	4.5	1.62	4.2
1.64	4.5	2.77	6.0
1.54	3.7	2.47	5.8
1.32	2.8	2.24	5.2
2.12	6.1	1.32	3.5
1.88	4.9	1.26	3.2
1.70	4.9	1.21	2.9
1.58	4.1	2.26	5.3
2.47	7.0	2.04	5.1
2.37	6.7	1.88	4.6

Source: Marto, P. J., et. al. "An experimental study of R-113 film condensation on horizontal integral-fin tubes." *Journal of Heat Transfer*, Vol. 112, Aug. 1990, p. 763 (Table 2).

a. Find the least squares line relating heat transfer enhancement y to unflooded area ratio x.
b. Plot the data points and graph the least squares line as a check on your calculations.
c. Interpret the values of $\hat{\beta}_0$ and $\hat{\beta}_1$.

11.9 The Federal Communications Commission (FCC) specifies that radiated electromagnetic emissions from digital devices are to be measured in an open-field test site. To verify test-site acceptability, the site attenuation (i.e., the transmission loss from the input of one half-wave dipole to the output of another when both dipoles are positioned over the ground plane) must be evaluated. A study conducted at a test site in Fort Collins, Colorado, yielded the following data on site attenuation (in decibels) and transmission frequency (in megahertz) for dipoles at a distance of 3 meters.

Transmission Frequency x, MHz	Site Attenuation y, dBL
50	11.5
100	15.8
200	18.2
300	22.6
400	26.2
500	27.1
600	29.5
700	30.7
800	31.3
900	32.6
1,000	34.9

Source: Bennett, W. S. "An error analysis of the FCC site-attenuation approximation." *IEEE Transactions on Electromagnetic Compatibility*, Vol. EMC-27, No. 3, Aug. 1985, p. 113 (Table IV). © 1985 IEEE.

a. Construct a scattergram for the data. Does it appear that x and y are linearly related?
b. Find the least squares line relating site attenuation y to transmission frequency x.
c. Plot the least squares line on your scattergram as a check on your calculations.
d. Interpret the values of $\hat{\beta}_0$ and $\hat{\beta}_1$.

11.10 Amorphous alloys have been found to have superior corrosion resistance. *Corrosion Science* (Sept. 1993) reported on the resistivity of an amorphous iron–boron–silicon alloy after crystallization. Five alloy specimens were annealed at 700°C, each for a different length of time. The passivation potential—a measure of resistivity of the cystallized alloy—was then measured for each specimen. The experimental data are shown here.

Annealing Time x, minutes	Passivation Potential y, mV
10	−408
20	−400
45	−392
90	−379
120	−385

Source: Chattoraj, I., et al. "Polarization and resistivity measurements of post-crystallization changes in amorphous Fe–B–Si alloys." *Corrosion Science*, Vol. 49, No. 9, Sept. 1993, p. 712 (Table 1).

a. Construct a scattergram for the data.
b. Assuming the relationship between the variables is best described by a straight line, use the method of least squares to estimate the y-intercept and slope of the line.
c. Plot the least squares line on your scattergram.
d. According to your least squares line, what is the expected passivation potential, y, when annealing time is set at $x = 30$ minutes? [*Note:* A measure of the reliability of this prediction will be discussed in Section 11.9.]

11.11 Civil engineers often use the straight-line equation $E(y) = \hat{\beta}_0 + \hat{\beta}_1 x$ to model the relationship between the mean shear strength $E(y)$ of masonry joints and precompression stress x. To test this theory, a series of stress tests was performed on solid bricks arranged in triplets and joined with mortar (*Proceedings of the Institute of Civil Engineers*, Mar. 1990). The precompression stress was varied for each triplet and the ultimate shear load just before failure (called the shear strength) was recorded. The stress results for 7 triplets (measured in N/mm^2) are shown in the accompanying table.

Triplet Test	1	2	3	4	5	6	7
Shear Strength, y	1.00	2.18	2.24	2.41	2.59	2.82	3.06
Precompression Stress, x	0	.60	1.20	1.33	1.43	1.75	1.75

Source: Riddington, J. R., and Ghazali, M. Z. "Hypothesis for shear failure in masonry joints." *Proceedings of the Institute of Civil Engineers, Part 2*, Mar. 1990. Vol. 89, p. 96 (Fig. 7).

a. Plot the seven data points in a scattergram. Does the relationship between shear strength and precompression stress appear to be linear?
b. Use the method of least squares to estimate the parameters of the linear model.
c. Interpret the values of $\hat{\beta}_0$ and $\hat{\beta}_1$.

OPTIONAL EXERCISES

11.12 The maximum likelihood estimator of the mean μ of a normal distribution is the sample mean $\bar{y}$. Consider the model $E(y) = \mu$. Show that the least squares estimator of μ is also $\bar{y}$. [*Hint:* Minimize SSE $= \Sigma(y_i - \hat{\mu})^2$ with respect to $\hat{\mu}$.]

11.13 Consider the pair of simultaneous linear equations:

$$n\hat{\beta}_0 + \hat{\beta}_1 \sum x_i = \sum y_i$$

$$\hat{\beta}_0 \sum x_i + \hat{\beta}_1 \sum x_i^2 = \sum x_i y_i$$

Derive the formulas for the least squares estimates, $\hat{\beta}_0$ and $\hat{\beta}_1$.

11.4   Properties of the Least Squares Estimators

An examination of the formulas for the least squares estimators reveals that they are linear functions of the observed y values, $y_1, y_2, \ldots, y_n$. Since we have assumed (Section 11.2) that the random errors associated with these y values, $\varepsilon_1, \varepsilon_2, \ldots, \varepsilon_n$, are independent, normally distributed random variables with mean 0 and variance σ^2, it follows that the y values will be normally distributed with mean $E(y) = \beta_0 + \beta_1 x$ and variance σ^2 and that $\hat{\beta}_0$ and $\hat{\beta}_1$ will possess sampling distributions that are normally distributed (Theorem 7.3).

The mean and the variance of the sampling distribution of $\hat{\beta}_1$ are given in Section 11.6. We will illustrate how they are acquired in Example 11.2.

EXAMPLE 11.2

Find the mean and variance of the sampling distribution of $\hat{\beta}_1$.

Solution

The quantity SS_{xx} that appears in the formula for $\hat{\beta}_1$ involves only the x values, which are assumed to be known—i.e., nonrandom. Therefore, SS_{xx} can be treated as a constant when we find the expected value of $\hat{\beta}_1$. In contrast, SS_{xy} is a function of the random variables, $y_1, y_2, \ldots, y_n$. Thus,

$$SS_{xy} = \sum (x_i - \bar{x})(y_i - \bar{y}) = \sum [(x_i - \bar{x})(y_i) - (x_i - \bar{x})\bar{y}]$$

$$= \sum (x_i - \bar{x})y_i - \bar{y} \sum (x_i - \bar{x})$$

But

$$\sum (x_i - \bar{x}) = \sum x_i - n\bar{x} = \sum x_i - \sum x_i = 0$$

Therefore, $SS_{xy} = \Sigma(x_i - \bar{x})y_i$. Substituting this quantity into the formula for $\hat{\beta}_1$, we obtain

$$\hat{\beta}_1 = \frac{SS_{xy}}{SS_{xx}} = \frac{1}{SS_{xx}} \sum (x_i - \bar{x})y_i$$

$$= \frac{(x_1 - \bar{x})}{SS_{xx}}y_1 + \frac{(x_2 - \bar{x})}{SS_{xx}}y_2 + \cdots + \frac{(x_n - \bar{x})}{SS_{xx}}y_n$$

This shows that $\hat{\beta}_1$ is a linear function of the normally distributed random variables, $y_1, y_2, \ldots, y_n$. The coefficients, $a_1, a_2, \ldots, a_n$, of the random variables in the linear function are

$$a_1 = \frac{(x_1 - \bar{x})}{SS_{xx}} \qquad a_2 = \frac{(x_2 - \bar{x})}{SS_{xx}} \qquad \cdots \qquad a_n = \frac{(x_n - \bar{x})}{SS_{xx}}$$

The final step in finding the mean $E(\hat{\beta}_1)$ and the variance $V(\hat{\beta}_1)$ of the sampling distribution of $\hat{\beta}_1$ is to apply Theorem 6.7, which gives the rule for finding the mean and the variance of a linear function of random variables. Thus,

$$E(\hat{\beta}_1) = E\left[\frac{(x_1 - \bar{x})}{SS_{xx}} y_1 + \frac{(x_2 - \bar{x})}{SS_{xx}} y_2 + \cdots + \frac{(x_n - \bar{x})}{SS_{xx}} y_n\right]$$

where $y_1, y_2, \ldots, y_n$ are obtained by substituting the appropriate values of x into the formula for the linear model, i.e.,

$$y_1 = \beta_0 + \beta_1 x_1 + \varepsilon_1 \quad \text{and} \quad E(y_1) = \beta_0 + \beta_1 x_1$$
$$y_2 = \beta_0 + \beta_1 x_2 + \varepsilon_2 \quad \text{and} \quad E(y_2) = \beta_0 + \beta_1 x_2$$
$$\vdots \qquad\qquad\qquad\qquad \vdots$$
$$y_n = \beta_0 + \beta_1 x_n + \varepsilon_n \quad \text{and} \quad E(y_n) = \beta_0 + \beta_1 x_n$$

Therefore,

$$E(\hat{\beta}_1) = \frac{(x_1 - \bar{x})}{SS_{xx}} E(y_1) + \frac{(x_2 - \bar{x})}{SS_{xx}} E(y_2) + \cdots + \frac{(x_n - \bar{x})}{SS_{xx}} E(y_n)$$

$$= \frac{(x_1 - \bar{x})}{SS_{xx}} (\beta_0 + \beta_1 x_1) + \frac{(x_2 - \bar{x})}{SS_{xx}} (\beta_0 + \beta_1 x_2) + \cdots + \frac{(x_n - \bar{x})}{SS_{xx}} (\beta_0 + \beta_1 x_n)$$

$$= \frac{\beta_0}{SS_{xx}} \sum (x_i - \bar{x}) + \frac{\beta_1}{SS_{xx}} \sum (x_i - \bar{x}) x_i$$

But,

$$SS_{xx} = \sum (x_i - \bar{x})^2 = \sum [(x_i - \bar{x}) x_i - \bar{x}(x_i - \bar{x})]$$
$$= \sum (x_i - \bar{x}) x_i - \bar{x} \sum (x_i - \bar{x})$$

Since we have already shown that $\Sigma(x_i - \bar{x}) = 0$, we have $SS_{xx} = \Sigma(x_i - \bar{x})x_i$ and therefore,

$$E(\hat{\beta}_1) = 0 + \frac{\beta_1}{SS_{xx}}(SS_{xx}) = \beta_1$$

This shows that $\hat{\beta}_1$ is an unbiased estimator of β_1.

Applying the formula given in Theorem 6.7 for finding the variance of a linear function of random variables, and remembering that the covariance between any pair of y values will equal 0 because all pairs of y values are assumed to be independent, we have

$$V(\hat{\beta}_1) = \frac{(x_1 - \bar{x})^2}{(SS_{xx})^2} V(y_1) + \frac{(x_2 - \bar{x})^2}{(SS_{xx})^2} V(y_2) + \cdots + \frac{(x_n - \bar{x})^2}{(SS_{xx})^2} V(y_n)$$

According to the assumptions made in Section 11.2, $V(y_1) = V(y_2) = \cdots = V(y_n) = \sigma^2$. Therefore,

$$V(\hat{\beta}_1) = \frac{(x_1 - \bar{x})^2}{(SS_{xx})^2}\sigma^2 + \frac{(x_1 - \bar{x})^2}{(SS_{xx})^2}\sigma^2 + \cdots + \frac{(x_1 - \bar{x})^2}{(SS_{xx})^2}\sigma^2$$

$$= \frac{\sigma^2 \sum (x_i - \bar{x})^2}{(SS_{xx})^2} = \sigma^2 \frac{SS_{xx}}{(SS_{xx})^2} = \frac{\sigma^2}{SS_{xx}}$$

and

$$\sigma_{\hat{\beta}_1} = \frac{\sigma}{\sqrt{SS_{xx}}}$$

We will use the results of Example 11.2 in Section 11.6 to test hypotheses about and to construct a confidence interval for the slope β_1 of a regression line. The practical implications of these inferences will also be explained.

EXERCISES

OPTIONAL EXERCISES

11.14 Show that

$$\hat{\beta}_0 = \bar{y} - \hat{\beta}_1\bar{x} = \sum \left[\frac{1}{n} - \frac{\bar{x}(x_i - \bar{x})}{SS_{xx}}\right]y_i$$

[*Hint:* Note that

$$\hat{\beta}_1 = \frac{SS_{xy}}{SS_{xx}} = \frac{\sum (x_i - \bar{x})(y_i - \bar{y})}{SS_{xx}}$$

$$= \frac{\sum (x_i - \bar{x})y_i}{SS_{xx}} - \frac{\bar{y}\sum (x_i - \bar{x})}{SS_{xx}}$$

$$= \frac{\sum (x_i - \bar{x})y_i}{SS_{xx}}$$

since $\Sigma(x_i - \bar{x}) = 0$.]

11.15 We showed in Example 11.2 and $\hat{\beta}_1$, the least squares estimator of the slope β_1, is an unbiased estimator of β_1, i.e., $E(\hat{\beta}_1) = \beta_1$. Use the result from Optional Exercise 11.14 to show that $E(\hat{\beta}_0) = \beta_0$.

11.16 In Optional Exercise 11.14, you showed that $\hat{\beta}_0$ could be written as a linear function of independent random variables. Use Theorem 6.7 to show that

$$V(\hat{\beta}_0) = \frac{\sigma^2}{n}\left(\frac{\sum x_i^2}{SS_{xx}}\right)$$

11.5   An Estimator of σ^2

In most practical situations, the variance σ^2 of the random error ε will be unknown and must be estimated from the sample data. Since σ^2 measures the variation of the y values about the line $E(y) = \beta_0 + \beta_1 x$, it seems intuitively reasonable to estimate σ^2 by dividing SSE by an appropriate number. Theorem 11.1, an extension of Theorem 7.4, will be useful in obtaining an unbiased estimator.

Theorem 11.1

Let $s^2 = \text{SSE}/(n - 2)$. Then, when the assumptions of Section 11.2 are satisfied, the statistic

$$\chi^2 = \frac{\text{SSE}}{\sigma^2}$$

$$= \frac{(n - 2)s^2}{\sigma^2}$$

possesses a chi-square distribution with $\nu = (n - 2)$ degrees of freedom.

From Theorem 11.1, it follows that

$$s^2 = \frac{\chi^2 \sigma^2}{n - 2}$$

Then

$$E(s^2) = \frac{\sigma^2}{n - 2} E(\chi^2)$$

where $E(\chi^2) = \nu = (n - 2)$. Therefore,

$$E(s^2) = \frac{\sigma^2}{n - 2}(n - 2)$$

$$= \sigma^2$$

and we conclude that s^2 is an unbiased estimator of σ^2.

The procedure used in Table 11.3 to calculate SSE can lead to large rounding errors. The formula for s^2 and an appropriate method for calculating SSE are shown in the box at the top of the next page. We will illustrate the calculation of s^2 with Example 11.3.

Estimation of σ^2

$$s^2 = \frac{\text{SSE}}{\text{Degrees of freedom for error}} = \frac{\text{SSE}}{n-2}$$

where

$$\text{SSE} = \sum (y_i - \hat{y}_i)^2 = \text{SS}_{yy} - \hat{\beta}_1 \text{SS}_{xy}$$

$$\text{SS}_{yy} = \sum (y_i - \bar{y})^2 = \sum y_i^2 - \frac{\left(\sum y_i\right)^2}{n}$$

Warning: When performing these calculations, you may be tempted to round the calculated values of SS_{yy}, $\hat{\beta}_1$, and SS_{xy}. Be certain to carry at least six significant figures for each of these quantities to avoid substantial errors in the calculation of SSE.

EXAMPLE 11.3

Estimate σ^2 for the data of Table 11.1.

Solution

In the insulation compression example, we previously calculated SSE = 1.10 for the least squares line $\hat{y} = -.1 + .7x$. Recalling that there were $n = 5$ data points, we have $n - 2 = 5 - 2 = 3$ df for estimating σ^2. Thus,

$$s^2 = \frac{\text{SSE}}{n-2} = \frac{1.10}{3} = .367$$

is the estimated variance, and

$$s = \sqrt{.367} = .61$$

is the estimated standard deviation of ε.

You may be able to obtain an intuitive feeling for s by recalling the interpretation given to a standard deviation in Chapter 1 and remembering that the least squares line estimates the mean value of y for a given value of x. Since s measures the spread of the distribution of y values about the least squares line, we should not be surprised to find that most of the observations lie within $2s$ or $2(.61) = 1.22$ of the least squares line. For this simple example (only five data points), all five data points fall within $2s$ of the least squares line. In Section 11.9, we will use s to evaluate the error of prediction when the least squares line is used to predict a value of y to be observed for a given value of x.

> ### Interpretation of s, the Estimated Standard Deviation of ε
>
> We expect most of the observed y values to lie within $2s$ of their respective least squares predicted values, $\hat{y}$.

EXERCISES

11.17 Calculate SSE for the data of Table 11.1, using the formula $\text{SSE} = \text{SS}_{yy} - \hat{\beta}_1 \text{SS}_{xy}$, and verify that it equals the value (1.10) computed in Table 11.3.

11.18 Calculate SSE, s^2, and s for the least squares lines plotted in:
   a. Exercise 11.6   **b.** Exercise 11.7   **c.** Exercise 11.8
   d. Exercise 11.9   **e.** Exercise 11.10   **f.** Exercise 11.11
   Interpret the value of s for each line.

11.19 As part of a study on the rate of combustion of artificial graphite in humid air flow, an experiment was conducted to investigate oxygen diffusivity through a water vapor mixture (*Combustion and Flame*, Vol. 50, 1983). Sample mixtures of nitrogen and oxygen were prepared with .017 mole fraction of water at nine different temperatures, and the oxygen diffusivity was measured for each. The data are reproduced in the accompanying table.

Temperature x	Oxygen Diffusivity y	Temperature x	Oxygen Diffusivity y
1,000	1.69	1,500	3.39
1,100	1.99	1,600	3.79
1,200	2.31	1,700	4.21
1,300	2.65	1,800	4.64
1,400	3.01		

Source: Matsui, K., Tsuji, H., and Makino, A. "The effects of water vapor concentration on the rate of combustion of an artificial graphite in humid air flow." *Combustion and Flame*, Vol. 50, 1983, pp. 107–118. Copyright 1983 by The Combustion Institute. Reprinted by permission of Elsevier Science Publishing Co., Inc.

   a. Plot the data points on a scattergram.
   b. Fit a simple linear model relating mean oxygen diffusivity, $E(y)$, to the temperature, x. Interpret the estimates of the model parameters.
   c. Compute SSE and s^2.
   d. Compute s and interpret its value.

11.20 The thermogravimetric balance (TG) is a new technique developed to evaluate the thermal behavior of chemical compounds. Abou El Naga and Salem (1986) compared the TG technique to the standard method of evaluating the thermooxidation stability of base oils and their additive blends (for example, transformer oils, turbine oils and transmission oils). For each of a sample of 10 base oils, the amount y of oxidative compounds formed at the oxidation point was determined using the TG technique and the total percentage x of oxidation products determined by the standard method. The results of the experiment are shown in the accompanying table.

Base Oil	TG Technique: Amount of Oxidative Compounds y, % weight	Standard Method: Total Oxidation Products x, %
1	25.4	2.3
2	27.11	2.5
3	28.0	2.65
4	17.9	1.3
5	18.9	1.45
6	22.9	1.9
7	30.8	3.3
8	18.6	1.4
9	24.4	2.1
10	29.8	2.9

Source: Abou El Naga, H. H., and Salem, A. E. M. "Base oils thermooxidation." *Lubrication Engineering*, Vol. 24, No. 4, Apr. 1986, p. 213. Reprinted by permission of the American Society of Lubrication Engineers. All rights reserved.

a. Fit a simple linear model relating amount y of oxidative compounds determined by the TG technique to the total percentage x of oxidation products determined by the standard method.
b. Plot the data points and least squares line on a scattergram.
c. Interpret the values of $\hat{\beta}_0$ and $\hat{\beta}_1$.
d. Compute SSE, s^2, and s.
e. Interpret the value of s.

OPTIONAL EXERCISES

11.21 Show that $V(s^2) = 2\sigma^4/(n - 2)$. [*Hint:* The result follows from Theorem 11.1 and the fact that $V(\chi^2) = 2\nu$.]

11.22 Verify that SSE $= \Sigma(y_i - \hat{y}_i)^2 = SS_{yy} - \hat{\beta}_1 SS_{xy}$.

11.6 Assessing the Utility of the Model: Making Inferences About the Slope β_1

Refer again to the data of Table 11.1 and suppose that the compression of the insulation material is *completely unrelated* to the pressure. What could be said about the values of β_0 and β_1 in the hypothesized probabilistic model

$$y = \beta_0 + \beta_1 x + \varepsilon$$

if x contributes no information for the prediction of y? The implication is that the mean of y, i.e., the deterministic part of the model $E(y) = \beta_0 + \beta_1 x$, does not change as x changes. Regardless of the value of x, you always predict the same value of y. In the straight-line model, this means that the true slope, β_1, is equal to 0. Therefore, to test the null hypothesis that x contributes no information for the prediction of y against the alternative hypothesis that these variables are linearly related with a slope differing from 0, we test

$$H_0: \quad \beta_1 = 0$$
$$H_a: \quad \beta_1 \neq 0$$

If the data support the alternative hypothesis, we will conclude that x does contribute information for the prediction of y using the straight-line model [although the true relationship between $E(y)$ and x could be more complex than a straight line]. Thus, to some extent, this is a test of the utility of the hypothesized model.

The appropriate test statistic is found by considering the sampling distribution of $\hat{\beta}_1$, the least squares estimator of the slope β_1. The sampling distribution of this statistic (discussed in Section 10.4) is described in the box.

Sampling Distribution of $\hat{\beta}_1$

If we make the four assumptions about ε (see Section 11.2), then the sampling distribution of $\hat{\beta}_1$, the least squares estimator of slope, will be a normal distribution with mean β_1 (the true slope) and standard deviation

$$\sigma_{\hat{\beta}_1} = \frac{\sigma}{\sqrt{SS_{xx}}} \quad \text{(see Figure 11.6)}$$

FIGURE 11.6 ▶

Sampling distribution of $\hat{\beta}_1$

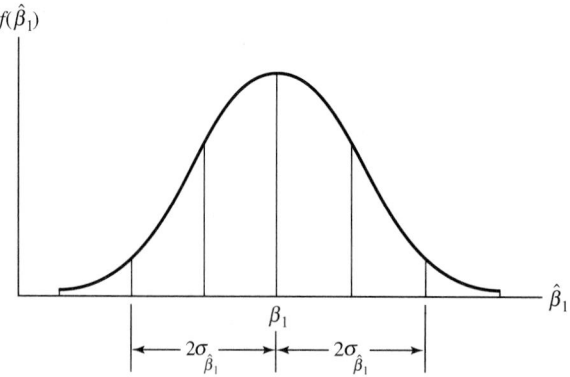

$f(\hat{\beta}_1)$

β_1

$\hat{\beta}_1$

$2\sigma_{\hat{\beta}_1}$ $2\sigma_{\hat{\beta}_1}$

Since σ will usually be unknown, the appropriate test statistic will generally be a Student's t statistic formed as follows:

$$t = \frac{\hat{\beta}_1 - \text{Hypothesized value of } \beta_1}{s_{\hat{\beta}_1}} \quad \text{where } s_{\hat{\beta}_1} = \frac{s}{\sqrt{SS_{xx}}}$$

$$= \frac{\hat{\beta}_1 - 0}{s/\sqrt{SS_{xx}}}$$

Note that we have substituted the estimator s for σ, and then formed $s_{\hat{\beta}_1}$ by dividing s by $\sqrt{SS_{xx}}$. The number of degrees of freedom associated with this t statistic is the same as the number of degrees of freedom associated with s. Recall that this will be $(n - 2)$ df when the hypothesized model is a straight line (see Section 11.5).

The setup of our test of the utility of the model is summarized in the box.*

A Test of Model Utility: Simple Linear Regression

One-Tailed Test	Two-Tailed Test
H_0: $\beta_1 = 0$	H_0: $\beta_1 = 0$
H_a: $\beta_1 < 0$	H_a: $\beta_1 \neq 0$
(or H_a: $\beta_1 > 0$)	

$$\text{Test statistic:} \quad t = \frac{\hat{\beta}_1}{s_{\hat{\beta}_1}} = \frac{\hat{\beta}_1}{s/\sqrt{SS_{xx}}}$$

Rejection region: $t < -t_\alpha$	Rejection region: $|t| > t_{\alpha/2}$
(or $t > t_\alpha$)	

where t_α and $t_{\alpha/2}$ are based on $(n - 2)$ df. The values of t_α such that $P(t \geq t_\alpha) = \alpha$ are given in Table 7 of Appendix II.

Assumptions: The four assumptions about ε are listed in Section 11.2

EXAMPLE 11.4

Refer to Examples 11.1 and 11.3, and test the hypothesis that $\beta_1 = 0$.

Solution

For the insulation compression example, we will choose $\alpha = .05$ and, since $n = 5$, df $= (n - 2) = 5 - 2 = 3$. Then the rejection region for the two-tailed test is

$$t < -t_{.025} \quad \text{or} \quad t > t_{.025}$$

where $t_{.025}$, given in Table 7 of Appendix II, is $t_{.025} = 3.182$. We previously calculated $\hat{\beta}_1 = .7$, $s = 61$, and $SS_{xx} = 10$. Thus,

$$t = \frac{\hat{\beta}_1}{s/\sqrt{SS_{xx}}} = \frac{.7}{.61/\sqrt{10}} = \frac{.7}{.19} = 3.7$$

Since this calculated t value falls in the upper-tail rejection region (see Figure 11.7 on page 556), we reject the null hypothesis and conclude that the slope β_1 is not 0.

---

*A test of hypothesis for β_0 is rarely of practical importance in simple linear regression. For the sake of completeness, the test statistic is

$$t = \frac{\hat{\beta}_0 - \text{Hypothesized value of } \beta_0}{s\sqrt{(1/n) + (\bar{x})^2/SS_{xx}}}$$

which, given the standard assumption on ε, follows a Student's t distribution with $(n - 2)$ df.

The sample evidence indicates that x contributes information for the prediction of y using a linear model for the relationship between compression and pressure.

FIGURE 11.7 ▶
Rejection region and calculated t
value for testing whether the slope
$\beta_1 = 0$

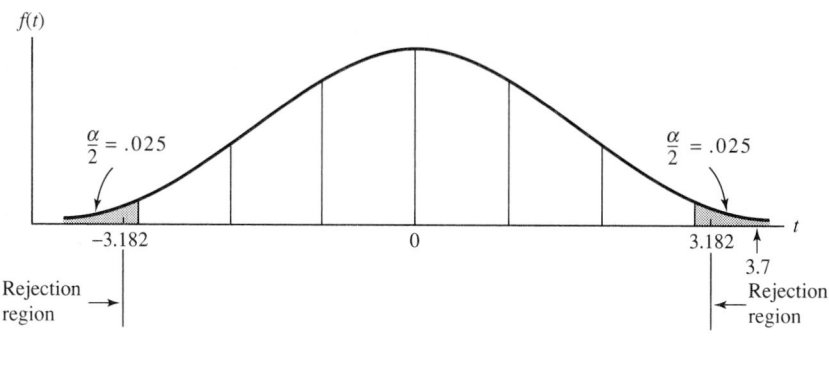

FIGURE 11.7 ▶
Rejection region and calculated t value for testing whether the slope $\beta_1 = 0$

Another way to make inferences about the slope β_1 is to estimate it using a confidence interval. This interval is formed as shown in the box.

A $(1 - \alpha)100\%$ Confidence Interval for the Slope β_1

$$\hat{\beta}_1 \pm t_{\alpha/2}s_{\hat{\beta}_1} \qquad \text{where} \qquad s_{\hat{\beta}_1} = \frac{s}{\sqrt{SS_{xx}}}$$

and $t_{\alpha/2}$ is based on $(n - 2)$ df

EXAMPLE 11.5

Find a 95% confidence interval for β_1 in Example 11.1. Interpret the result.

Solution

For the insulation compression example, a 95% confidence interval for the slope β_1 is

$$\hat{\beta}_1 \pm t_{.025}s_{\hat{\beta}_1} = .7 \pm 3.182\left(\frac{s}{\sqrt{SS_{xx}}}\right)$$

$$= .7 \pm 3.182\left(\frac{.61}{\sqrt{10}}\right) = .7 \pm .61$$

Thus, we estimate that the interval from .09 to 1.31 includes the slope parameter β_1. Remembering that y is recorded in units of .1 inch and x in units of 10 pounds per square inch, we can say, with 95% confidence, that the mean compression, $E(y)$, will increase between .009 and .1131 inch for every 10-pound-per-square-inch increase in pressure, x.

Since all the values in this interval are positive, it appears that β_1 is positive and that the mean of y, $E(y)$, increases as x increases. However, the rather large width of the confidence interval reflects the small number of data points (and, consequently, a lack of information) in the experiment. We would expect a narrower interval if the sample size were increased.

Before concluding this section, we call your attention to the similarity between the t statistic for testing hypotheses about β_1 and the t statistic for testing hypotheses about the means of normal populations in Chapter 9. Also note the similarity of the corresponding confidence intervals. In each case, the general form of the test statistic is

$$t = \frac{\hat{\theta} - \theta_0}{s_{\hat{\theta}}}$$

and the general form of the confidence interval is

$$\hat{\theta} \pm (t_{\alpha/2})s_{\hat{\theta}}$$

where $\hat{\theta}$ is the estimator of the population parameter θ, θ_0 is the hypothesized value of θ, and $s_{\hat{\theta}}$ is the estimatated standard error of $\hat{\theta}$.

In the optional exercises of this section, we outline the procedure for acquiring the t statistic for testing hypotheses about and constructing confidence intervals for β_1.

EXERCISES

11.23 Refer to the *Chemosphere* (Vol. 20, 1990) study of Vietnam veterans exposed to Agent Orange (and the dioxin 2,3,7,8-TCDD), Exercise 8.43. The data table, reproduced on page 558, gives the amounts of 2,3,7,8-TCDD (measured in parts per million) in both blood plasma and fat tissue drawn from each of the 20 veterans studied. One goal of the researchers is to determine the degree of linear association between the level of dioxin found in blood plasma and fat tissue. If a linear association between the two variables can be established, the researchers want to build models to (1) predict blood plasma level of 2,3,7,8-TCDD from the observed level of 2,3,7,8-TCDD in fat tissue and (2) predict fat tissue level from the observed blood plasma level.

Veteran	TCDD Levels in Plasma	TCDD Levels in Fat Tissue
1	2.5	4.9
2	3.1	5.9
3	2.1	4.4
4	3.5	6.9
5	3.1	7.0
6	1.8	4.2
7	6.0	10.0
8	3.0	5.5
9	36.0	41.0
10	4.7	4.4
11	6.9	7.0
12	3.3	2.9
13	4.6	4.6
14	1.6	1.4
15	7.2	7.7
16	1.8	1.1
17	20.0	11.0
18	2.0	2.5
19	2.5	2.3
20	4.1	2.5

Source: Schecter, A., et. al. "Partitioning of 2,3,7,8-chlorinated dibenzo-p-dioxins and dibenzofurans between adipose tissue and plasma lipid of 20 Massachusetts Vietnam veterans." *Chemosphere*, Vol. 20, Nos. 7–9, 1990, pp. 954–955 (Tables I & II).

a. Find the prediction equations for the researchers. Interpret the results.
b. Test the hypothesis that fat tissue level (x) is a useful linear predictor of blood plasma level (y). Use $\alpha = .05$.
c. Test the hypothesis that blood plasma level (x) is a useful linear predictor of fat tissue level (y). Use $\alpha = .05$.
d. Intuitively, why must the results of the tests, parts **b** and **c**, agree?

11.24 Refer to Exercise 11.23. The blood plasma and fat tissue levels of several other types of dioxin (called cogeners) were also measured for each of the 20 Vietnam veterans. For each cogener, a simple linear regression analysis was conducted to predict (1) fat tissue level from blood plasma level and (2) blood plasma level from fat tissue level. The results for three of these cogeners are shown in the table.

Cogener	y = Fat Tissue Level x = Blood Plasma Level	y = Blood Plasma Level x = Fat Tissue Level	t-value for Testing β_1
2,3,4,7,8-P_n CDF	$\hat{y} = .8109 + .9713x$	$\hat{y} = .9855 + .7605x$	7.13
H_x CDD	$\hat{y} = 18.1565 + .7377x$	$\hat{y} = 5.2009 + .9018x$	5.98
OCDD	$\hat{y} = 118.6057 + .3679x$	$\hat{y} = 167.723 + 1.5752x$	4.98

Source: Schecter, A., et. al. "Partitioning of 2,3,7,8-chlorinated dibenzo-p-dioxins and dibenzofurans between adipose tissue and plasma lipid of 20 Massachusetts Vietnam veterans." *Chemosphere*, Vol. 20, Nos. 7–9, 1990, pp. 954–955 (Table III).

a. For the cogener 2,3,4,7,8,-P_n CDF, are the two regression models statistically adequate for predicting y? Test both using $\alpha = .05$.

b. Repeat part **a** for the cogener H_x CDD.

c. Repeat part **a** for the cogener OCDD.

d. Use the regression results to predict the level of 2,3,4,7,8-P_n CDF in blood plasma for a veteran with a fat tissue level of 8.0 ppm.

e. Use the regression results to predict the level of H_x CDD in fat tissue for a veteran with a blood plasma level of 24.0 ppm.

f. Use the regression results to predict the level of OCDD in blood plasma for a veteran with a fat tissue level of 776 ppm.

11.25 Refer to the *Journal of Heat Transfer* study of the straight-line relationship between heat transfer enhancement, y, and unflooded area ratio, x, Exercises 11.8 and 11.18c. Construct a 95% confidence interval for β_1, the slope of the line. Interpret the result.

11.26 Refer to the *IEEE Transactions on Electromagnetic Compatibility* study of the straight-line relationship between site attenuation, y, and transmission frequency, x, Exercises 11.9 and 11.18d. Test the utility of the model using $\alpha = .05$.

11.27 Refer to the *Proceedings of the Institute of Civil Engineers* study of the straight-line relationship between shear strength, y, and precompression stress, x, Exercises 11.11 and 11.18f. Test the hypothesis that the slope of the line is positive. Use $\alpha = .10$.

11.28 Refer to the *Combustion and Flame* study of oxygen diffusivity of water vapor, Exercise 11.19. Do the data provide sufficient evidence to indicate that oxygen diffusivity, y, tends to increase as the temperature, x, increases? Test using $\alpha = .05$.

11.29 Refer to the *Lubrication Engineering* experiment comparing two methods of oxidation, Exercise 11.20. Do the data provide sufficient evidence to indicate that the amount, y, of oxidative compounds measured using the TG technique is positively linearly related to the total percentage, x, of oxidation products determined by the standard method? Support your inference with a 99% confidence interval for the slope of the line relating y to x.

11.30 Researchers at the University of North Carolina–Greensboro investigated a model for the rate of seed germination (*Journal of Experimental Botany*, Jan. 1993). In one experiment, alfalfa seeds were placed in a specially constructed germination chamber. Eleven hours later, the seeds were examined and the change in free energy (a measure of germination rate) recorded. The results for seeds germinated at seven different temperatures are given in the table on page 560. The data were used to fit a simple linear regression model, with y = change in free energy and x = temperature.

Change in Free Energy, kJ/mol	Temperature, K
7	295
6.2	297.5
9	291
9.5	289
8.5	301
7.8	293
11.2	286.5

Source: Hageseth, G. T., and Cody, A. L. "Energy-level model for isothermal seed germination." *Journal of Experimental Botany*, Vol. 44, No. 258, Jan. 1993, p. 123 (Figure 9).

a. Plot the points in a scattergram.
b. Find the least squares prediction equation.
c. Plot the least squares line, part **b**, on the scattergram of part **a**.
d. Conduct a test of model adequacy. Use $\alpha = .01$.
e. Use the plot, part **c**, to locate any unusual data points (outliers).
f. Eliminate the outlier, part **e**, from the data set, and repeat parts **a–d**.

11.31 An experiment was conducted to study the stress corrosion cracking of Type 304 stainless steel in a simulated boiling water reactor environment (*Transactions of the ASME*, Jan. 1986). Six specimens of stainless steel were annealed and sensitized in 289°C water with dissolved oxygen and sulfate under various stress intensity factors (i.e., loads). The table gives the maximum load and resulting crack growth rate (in meters per second) for the six specimens.

Maximum Load x, MPa $\cdot$ $m^{1/2}$	30.0	35.6	41.5	50.2	55.5	61.1
Crack Growth Rate y, m/s $\times$ 10^{10}	1.0	2.2	3.9	5.8	5.0	14.0

Source: Park, J. Y., Ruther, W. E., Kassner, T. F., and Shack, W. J. "Stress corrosion crack growth rates in Type 304 stainless steel in simulated BWR environments." *Transactions of the American Society of Mechanical Engineers*, Vol. 108, No. 1, Jan. 1986, p. 23 (Table 4).

a. Is there sufficient evidence to indicate that cracking growth rate increases linearly with maximum load? Test using $\alpha = .10$.
b. Estimate the mean increase in cracking growth rate for every 1-unit increase in maximum load using a 90% confidence interval. Interpret the result.

OPTIONAL EXERCISES

11.32 Explain why

$$z = \frac{\hat{\beta}_1 - \beta_1}{\sigma_{\hat{\beta}_1}} = \frac{\hat{\beta}_1 - \beta_1}{\sigma / \sqrt{SS_{xx}}}$$

is normally distributed with mean 0 and variance 1 when the four assumptions of Section 11.2 are satisfied.

11.33 It can be shown (proof omitted) that the least squares estimates, $\hat{\beta}_0$ and $\hat{\beta}_1$, are independent (in a probabilistic sense) of s^2. Use this fact, in conjunction with Theorem 11.1 and the result of Optional Exercise 11.32, to show that

$$t = \frac{\hat{\beta}_1 - \beta_1}{s/\sqrt{SS_{xx}}}$$

has a Student's t distribution with $\nu = (n - 2)$ df.

11.34 Use the t statistic in Optional Exercise 11.33 as a pivotal statistic to derive a $(1 - \alpha)100\%$ confidence interval for β_1.

11.7 The Coefficient of Correlation

In Section 11.6, we discovered that the least squares slope, $\hat{\beta}_1$, provides useful information on the linear relationship, or "association," between two variables y and x. Another way to measure association is to compute the **Pearson product moment correlation coefficient** r. The correlation coefficient, defined in the box, provides a quantitative measure of the strength of the linear relationship between x and y in the sample, as does the least squares slope $\hat{\beta}_1$. However, unlike the slope, the correlation coefficient r is *scaleless*. The value of r is always between -1 and $+1$, no matter what the units of x and y are.

Definition 11.4

The **Pearson product moment coefficient of correlation** r is a measure of the strength of the linear relationship between two variables x and y in the sample. It is computed (for a sample of n measurements on x and y) as follows:

$$r = \frac{SS_{xy}}{\sqrt{SS_{xx}SS_{yy}}}$$

Since both r and $\hat{\beta}_1$ provide information about the utility of the model, it is not surprising that there is a similarity in their computational formulas. In particular, note that SS_{xy} appears in the numerators of both expressions and, since both denominators are always positive, r and $\hat{\beta}_1$ will always be of the same sign (either both positive or both negative). A value of r near or equal to 0 implies little or no linear relationship between y and x. In contrast, the closer r is to 1 or -1, the stronger the linear relationship between y and x. And, if $r = 1$ or $r = -1$, all the points fall exactly on the least squares line. Positive values of r imply that y increases as x increases; negative values imply that y decreases as x increases. See Figure 11.8.

FIGURE 11.8 ▶

Values of r and their implications

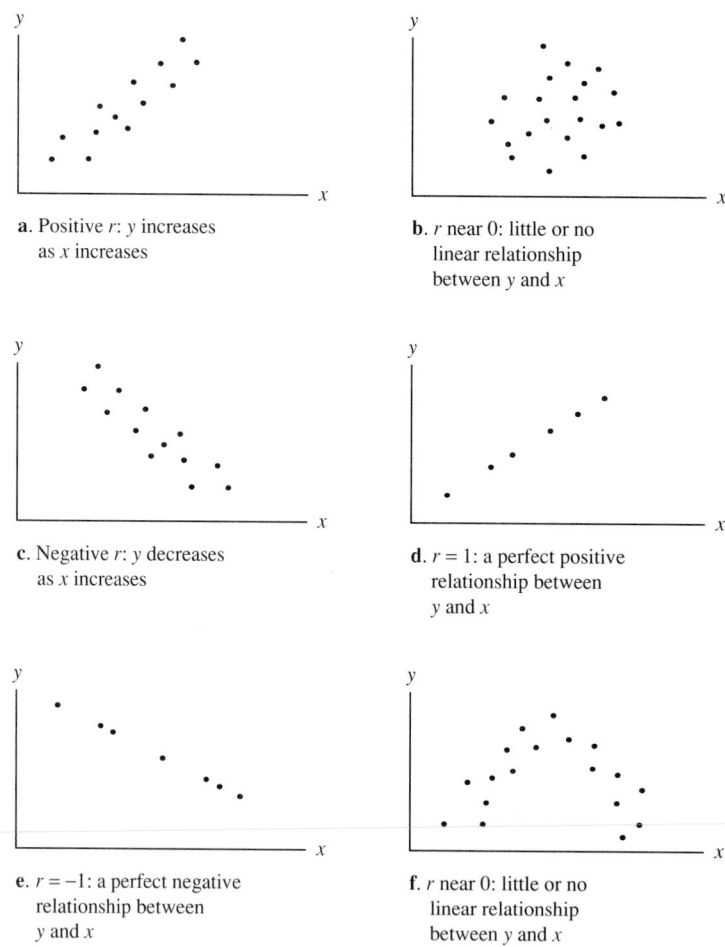

a. Positive r: y increases as x increases

b. r near 0: little or no linear relationship between y and x

c. Negative r: y decreases as x increases

d. $r = 1$: a perfect positive relationship between y and x

e. $r = -1$: a perfect negative relationship between y and x

f. r near 0: little or no linear relationship between y and x

EXAMPLE 11.6

The data for Example 11.1 are reproduced in Table 11.4. Calculate the coefficient of correlation r between pressure x and compression y.

TABLE 11.4 Compression Versus Pressure for an Insulation Material

Pressure	Compression
x, 10 pounds per square inch	y, .1 inch
1	1
2	1
3	2
4	2
5	4

Solution

From previous calculations (see Example 11.1), we found $SS_{xy} = 7$, $SS_{xx} = 10$, $\Sigma y_i = 10$, and $\Sigma y_i^2 = 26$. Then,

$$SS_{yy} = \sum y_i^2 - \frac{\left(\sum y_i\right)^2}{n} = 26 - \frac{(10)^2}{5} = 26 - 20 = 6$$

and the coefficient of correlation is

$$r = \frac{SS_{xy}}{\sqrt{SS_{xx}\, SS_{yy}}} = \frac{7}{\sqrt{(10)(6)}} = \frac{7}{7.746} = .904$$

Thus, the pressure and amount of compression are very highly correlated—at least for this sample of five pieces of insulation material. The implication is that a strong positive linear relationship exists between these variables. We must be careful, however, not to jump to any unwarranted conclusions. For instance, the developer of the new insulation material may be tempted to conclude that increasing pressure will always lead to a higher amount of compression. The implication of such a conclusion is that there is a **causal** relationship between the two variables. However, **high correlation does not imply causality**. Many other factors, such as temperature and humidity, may contribute to the increase in the amount of compression produced on the specimens.

Warning

High correlation does not imply causality. If a large positive or negative value of the sample correlation coefficient r is observed, it is incorrect to conclude that a change in x causes a change in y. The only valid conclusion is that a linear trend *may* exist between x and y.

Keep in mind that the correlation coefficient r measures the correlation between x values and y values in the sample, and that a similar linear coefficient of correlation exists for the population from which the data points were selected. The **population correlation coefficient** is denoted by the symbol ρ (rho). As you might expect, ρ is estimated by the corresponding sample statistic, r. Or, rather than estimating ρ, we might want to test the hypothesis $H_0: \rho = 0$ against $H_a: \rho \neq 0$, i.e., test the hypothesis that x contributes no information for the prediction of y using the straight-line model against the alternative that the two variables are at least linearly related. However, we have already performed this identical test in Section 11.6 when we tested $H_0: \beta_1 = 0$ against $H_a: \beta_1 \neq 0$.

It is easy to show that $r = \hat{\beta}_1 \cdot \sqrt{SS_{xx}/SS_{yy}}$. Thus, $\hat{\beta}_1 = 0$ implies $r = 0$, and vice versa. Consequently, the null hypothesis $H_0: \rho = 0$ is equivalent to the hypothesis $H_0: \beta_1 = 0$. When we tested the null hypothesis $H_0: \beta_1 = 0$ in connection with the insulation compression example, the data led to a rejection of the hypothesis for $\alpha = .05$. This implies that the null hypothesis of a zero linear correlation between the two variables (pressure and compression) can also be rejected at $\alpha = .05$. The only real difference between the least squares slope $\hat{\beta}_1$ and the coefficient of correlation r is the measurement scale. Therefore, the information they provide about the utility of the least squares model is to some extent redundant. Furthermore, the slope β_1 gives us additional information on the amount increase (or decrease) in y for every 1-unit increase in x. For this reason, we recommend using the slope to make inferences about the existence of a positive or negative linear relationship between two variables. For those who prefer to test for a linear relationship between two variables using the coefficient of correlation r, we outline the procedure in the box.

Test of Hypothesis for Linear Correlation

One-Tailed Test	*Two-Tailed Test*
H_0: $\rho = 0$	H_0: $\rho = 0$
H_a: $\rho > 0$	H_a: $\rho \neq 0$
(or $\rho < 0$)	

$$\text{Test statistic:} \quad t = \frac{r\sqrt{n-2}}{\sqrt{1-r^2}}$$

Rejection region: $t > t_\alpha$	Rejection region: $|t| > t_{\alpha/2}$
(or $t < -t_\alpha$)	

where the distribution of t depends on $(n - 2)$ df and t_α and $t_{\alpha/2}$ are the critical values obtained from Table 7 of Appendix II.

Assumptions: The sample of (x, y) values is randomly selected from a (bivariate) normal population.*

---

*The joint probability distribution of x and y will be bivariate normal if the marginal distributions of x and y are both normal.

The next example illustrates how the correlation coefficient r may be a misleading measure of the strength of the association between x and y in situations where the true relationship is nonlinear.

EXAMPLE 11.7

Underinflated or overinflated tires can increase tire wear and decrease gas mileage. A manufacturer of a new tire tested the tire for wear at different pressures with the results shown in Table 11.5. Calculate the coefficient of correlation r for the data. Interpret the result.

TABLE 11.5   Data for Example 11.7

Pressure	Mileage	Pressure	Mileage
x, pounds per sq. inch	y, thousands	x, pounds per sq. inch	y, thousands
30	29.5	33	37.6
30	30.2	34	37.7
31	32.1	34	36.1
31	34.5	35	33.6
32	36.3	35	34.2
32	35.0	36	26.8
33	38.2	36	27.4

Solution

Rather than perform the calculations by hand, we resort to the use of a computer to find the value of r. A SAS printout of the correlation analysis is shown in Figure 11.9. The value of r, shaded on the printout, is $r = -.114$. This relatively small value for r describes a weak linear relationship between pressure (x) and mileage (y). The manufacturer, however, would be remiss in concluding that tire pressure has little or no impact on wear of the tire. On the contrary, the relationship between pressure and wear is fairly strong, as the scattergram in Figure 11.10 illustrates. (See page 566.) Note that the relationship is not linear, but curvilinear; the underinflated tires (low pressure values) and overinflated tires (high pressure values) both lead to low mileages.

FIGURE 11.9 ▶
SAS printout of correlation analysis of data in Table 11.5

Pearson Correlation Coefficients / Prob > |R| under Ho: Rho=0 / N = 14

	X	Y
X	1.00000 0.0	-0.11371 0.6987
Y	-0.11371 0.6987	1.00000 0.0

FIGURE 11.10 ▶
Scattergram of data in Table 11.5

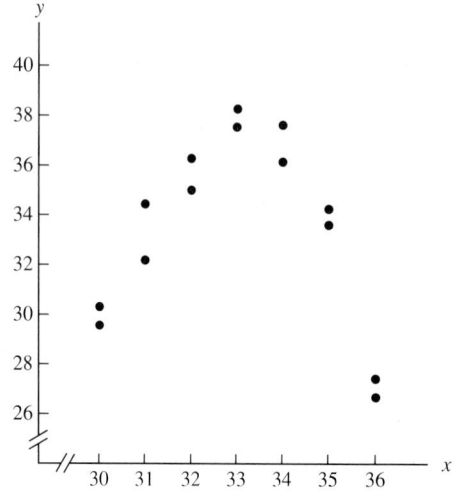

Example 11.7 points out the danger of using r to determine how well x predicts y: The correlation coefficient r describes only the *linear* relationship between x and y. For nonlinear relationships, the value of r may be misleading, and we need to resort to other methods for describing and testing such a relationship. Regression models for curvilinear relationships are presented in Chapter 12.

11.8   The Coefficient of Determination

Another way to measure the contribution of x in predicting y is to consider how much the errors of prediction of y can be reduced by using the information provided by x.

To illustrate, suppose a sample of data has the scattergram shown in Figure 11.11a. If we assume that x contributes no information for the prediction of y, the best prediction for a value of y is the sample mean $\bar{y}$, which graphs as the horizontal line shown in Figure 11.11b. The vertical line segments in Figure 11.11b are the deviations of the points about the mean $\bar{y}$. Note that the sum of squares of deviations for the model $\hat{y} = \bar{y}$ is $SS_{yy} = \Sigma (y_i - \bar{y})^2$.

Now suppose that you fit a least squares line to the same set of data and locate the deviations of the points about the line as shown in Figure 11.11c. Compare the deviations about the prediction lines in parts **b** and **c** in Figure 11.11. You can see that:

1. If x contributes little or no information for the prediction of y, then the sums of squares of deviations for the two lines,

$$SS_{yy} = \sum (y_i - \bar{y})^2 \quad \text{and} \quad SSE = \sum (y_i - \hat{y}_i)^2$$

will be nearly equal.

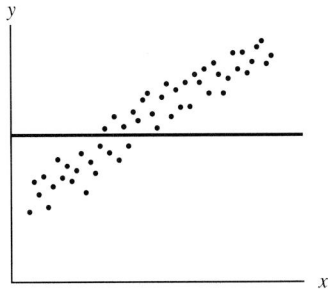

a. Scattergram of data

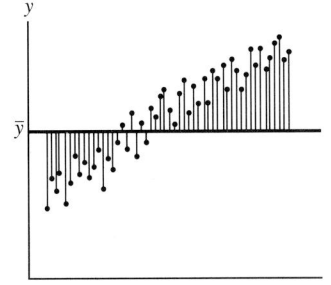

b. Assumption: x contributes no information for predicting y; $\hat{y} = \bar{y}$

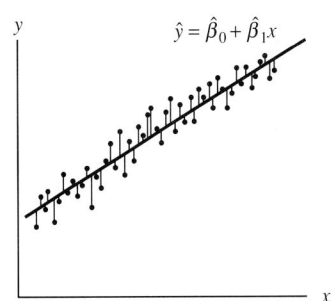

c. Assumption: x contributes information for predicting y; $\hat{y} = \hat{\beta}_0 + \hat{\beta}_1 x$

FIGURE 11.11 ▲
A comparison of the sum of squares of deviations for two models

2. If x does contribute information for the prediction of y, then SSE will be smaller than SS_{yy}. In fact, if all the points fall on the least squares line, then SSE = 0.

A convenient way of measuring how well the least squares equation $\hat{y} = \hat{\beta}_0 + \hat{\beta}_1 x$ performs as a predictor of y is to compute the reduction in the sum of squares of deviations that can be attributed to x, expressed as a proportion of SS_{yy}. This quantity, called the **coefficient of determination**, is

$$\frac{SS_{yy} - SSE}{SS_{yy}}$$

In simple linear regression it can be shown that this quantity is equal to the square of the simple linear coefficient of correlation r.

Definition 11.5

The **coefficient of determination** is

$$r^2 = \frac{SS_{yy} - SSE}{SS_{yy}} = 1 - \frac{SSE}{SS_{yy}}$$

It represents the proportion of the sum of squares of deviations of the y values about their predicted values ($\hat{y}$) that can be attributed to a linear relation between y and x. (In simple linear regression, it may also be computed as the square of the coefficient of correlation r.)

Note that r^2 is always between 0 and 1, because r is between -1 and $+1$. Thus, $r^2 = .60$ means that the sum of squares of deviations of the y values about their predicted values has been reduced 60% by the use of $\hat{y}$, instead of $\bar{y}$, to predict y. Or, more practically, $r^2 = .60$ implies that the straight-line model relating y to x can explain (or account for) 60% of the variation present in the sample of y values.

EXAMPLE 11.8

Calculate the coefficient of determination for the insulation compression example. The data are repeated in Table 11.6.

TABLE 11.6   Data for Example 11.8

Pressure	Compression
x, 10 pounds per square inch	y, .1 inch
1	1
2	1
3	2
4	2
5	4

Solution

We first calculate

$$SS_{yy} = \sum y_i^2 - \frac{\left(\sum y_i \right)^2}{5} = 26 - \frac{(10)^2}{5} = 26 - 20 = 6$$

From previous calculations, we have

$$SSE = \sum (y_i - \hat{y}_i)^2 = 1.10$$

Then, the coefficient of determination is given by

$$r^2 = \frac{SS_{yy} - SSE}{SS_{yy}} = \frac{6.0 - 1.1}{6.0} = \frac{4.9}{6.0} = .82$$

(Note that this value could also be obtained by squaring the correlation coefficient $r = .904$ found in Example 11.6.)

So we know that by using the pressure x to predict compression y with the least squares line $\hat{y} = -.1 + .7x$, the total sum of squares of deviations of the five sample y values about their predicted values has been reduced 82% by the use of the linear predictor $\hat{y}$. That is, 82% of the sample variation in compression values can be explained by the least squares line.

Practical Interpretation of the Coefficient of Determination, r^2

About $100(r^2)\%$ of the total sum of squares of deviations of the sample y values about their mean $\bar{y}$ can be explained by (or attributed to) using x to predict y in the straight-line model.

In situations where a straight-line regression model is found to be a statistically adequate predictor of y, the value of r^2 can help guide the regression analyst in the search for better, more useful models. For example, Crandall and Cedercreutz (1976) use a simple linear model to relate cost of mechanical work (heating, ventilating, and plumbing) in construction to floor area. Based on the data associated with 26 factory and warehouse buildings, the least squares prediction equation given in Figure 11.12 was found. It was concluded that floor area and mechanical cost are linearly related, since the t statistic (for testing $H_0: \beta_1 = 0$) was found to equal 3.61, which is significant with an α as small as .002. Thus, floor area should be useful when predicting the mechanical cost of a factory or warehouse. However, the value of the coefficient of determination r^2 was found to be .35. This tells us that only 35% of the variation among mechanical costs is accounted for by the differences in floor areas. This relatively small r^2 value led Crandall and Cedercreutz to include other independent variables (e.g., volume, amount of glass) in the model in an attempt to account for a significant portion of the remaining 65% of the variation in mechanical cost not explained by floor area. In the next chapter, we discuss this important aspect of relating a response to more than one independent variable.

FIGURE 11.12 ▶
Simple linear model relating cost to floor area

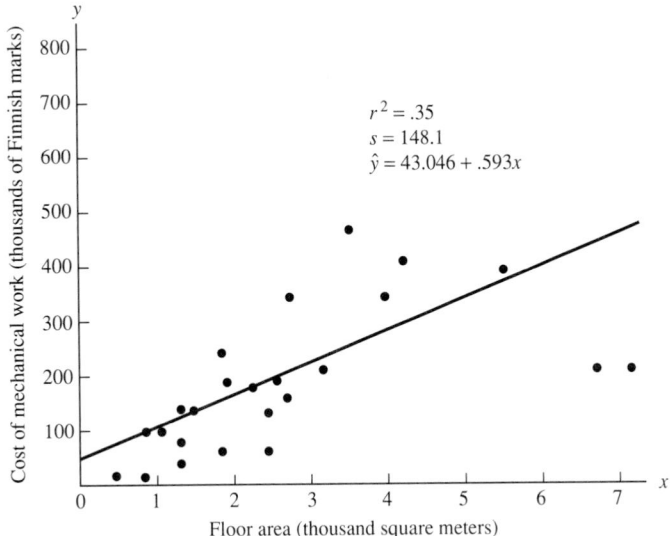

Floor area (thousand square meters)

EXERCISES

11.35 Find the correlation coefficient and the coefficient of determination for the sample data of each of the following exercises. Interpret your results.
    a. Exercise 11.6   **b.** Exercise 11.7   **c.** Exercise 11.8
    d. Exercise 11.9   **e.** Exercise 11.10   **f.** Exercise 11.11

11.36 A robust and highly adopted model of human movement is Fitts' Law. According to Fitts' Law, the time T required to move and select a target of width W that lies at a distance (or amplitude) A is

$$T = a + b \log_2(2A/W)$$

where a and b are constants estimated using simple linear regression. The quantity $\log_2(2A/W)$ is termed the Index of Difficulty (ID) and represents the independent variable (measured in "bits") in the model. Research reported in the *Special Interest Group on Computer–Human Interaction Bulletin* (July 1993) used Fitts' Law to model the time (in milliseconds) required to perform a certain task on a computer. Based on data collected for $n = 160$ trials (using different values of A and W), the following least squares prediction was obtained:

$$\hat{T} = 175.4 + 133.2(\text{ID})$$

    a Interpret the estimates, 175.4 and 133.2.
    b. The coefficient of correlation for the analysis is $r = .951$. Interpret this value.
    c. Conduct a test to determine whether the Fitts' Law model is statistically adequate for predicting performance time. Use $\alpha = .05$.
    d. Calculate the coefficient of determination, r^2. Interpret the result.

11.37 Refer to the *Combustion and Flame* oxygen diffusivity experiment described in Exercise 11.19. The data for the nine sample mixtures of nitrogen and oxygen are reproduced in the accompanying table.

Temperature x	Oxygen Diffusivity y
1,000	1.69
1,100	1.99
1,200	2.31
1,300	2.65
1,400	3.01
1,500	3.39
1,600	3.79
1,700	4.21
1,800	4.64

    a. Calculate r and r^2. Interpret their values.
    b. Conduct a test to determine whether temperature and oxygen diffusivity are positively correlated. Use $\alpha = .05$. Do your results agree with Exercise 11.28?

11.38 The electroencephalogram (EEG) is a device used to measure brain waves. Neurologists have found that the peak EEG frequency in normal children increases with age. In a study reported in *Science* (Vol. 215, 1982), 287 normal children ranging from 2 to 16 years were instructed to hold a 65-gram weight in the palm of their outstretched hand for a brief but unspecified time. The peak EEG frequency (measured in hertz) was then recorded for each child. The data were grouped according to age of the children, and the average peak frequency was calculated for each age group. The data appear in the accompanying table.

Age x, years	Average Peak EEG Frequency y, hertz	Age x, years	Average Peak EEG Frequency y, hertz
2	5.33	10	7.28
3	5.75	11	7.06
4	5.80	12	7.60
5	5.60	13	7.45
6	6.00	14	8.23
7	5.78	15	8.50
8	5.90	16	9.38
9	6.23		

Source: Tryon, W. W. "Developmental equations for postural tremor." *Science*, Vol. 215, No. 2, pp. 300–301, 1982. Copyright 1982 by the AAAS.

a. Construct a scattergram for the data. After examining the scattergram, do you think that x and y are correlated? If correlation is present, is it positive or negative?

b. Find the correlation coefficient r and interpret its value.

c. Do the data provide sufficient evidence to indicate that x and y are linearly correlated? Test using $\alpha = .05$.

11.39 Passive exposure to environmental tobacco smoke has been associated with growth suppression and an increased frequency of respiratory tract infections in normal children. Is this association more pronounced in children with cystic fibrosis? To answer this question, 43 children (18 girls and 25 boys) attending a 2-week summer camp for cystic fibrosis patients were studied (*New England Journal of Medicine*, Sept. 20, 1990). Among several variables measured were the child's weight percentile (y) and the number of cigarettes smoked per day in the child's home (x).

a. For the 18 girls, the coefficient of correlation between y and x was reported as $r = -.50$. Interpret this result.

b. Refer to part a. The p-value for testing $H_0: \rho = 0$ against $H_a: \rho \neq 0$ was reported as $p = .03$. Interpret this result.

c. For the 25 boys, the coefficient of correlation between y and x was reported as $r = -.12$. Interpret this result.

d. Refer to part c. The p-value for testing $H_0: \rho = 0$ against $H_a: \rho \neq 0$ was reported as $p = .57$. Interpret this result.

11.40 The Mixed Arithmetic-Perceptual (MA-P) model is a componential model of graphic interaction that was developed based on analyses of humans interacting with graphical displays on the computer. The assumptions of the MA-P model were tested in a research article reported in the *SIGCHI Bulletin* (July 1993). Using simple linear regression, the researcher modeled response time y (in milliseconds) in a standard graph problem as a function of the number x of processing steps required to solve the problem. A summary of the regression results for $n = 8$ problems follows:

$$\hat{y} = 1,346 + 450x \qquad r^2 = .91$$

a. Interpret the value of $\hat{\beta}_1$.
b. Interpret the value of r^2.
c. Conduct a test of model adequacy at $\alpha = .01$. [*Hint:*   Base the test on the value of r, the correlation coefficient.]

11.41   In New York state, common maize rust is a serious disease of sweet corn. Although fungicides are effective in controlling maize rust, the timing of the application is crucial. Researchers have developed an action threshold for initiation of fungicide applications based on a regression equation relating maize rust incidence to severity of the disease (*Phytopathology*, Vol. 80, 1990). In one particular field, data were collected on over 100 plants of the sweet corn hybrid Jubilee. For each plant, incidence was measured as the percentage of leaves infected (x) and severity as the log (base 10) of the average number of infections per leaf (y). A simple linear regression analysis of the data produced the following results:

$$\hat{y} = -.939 + .020x \qquad r^2 = .816 \qquad s = .288$$

a. Interpret the value of $\hat{\beta}_1$.
b. Interpret the value of r^2.
c. Interpret the value of s.
d. Calculate the value of r and interpret its value.
e. Use the result, part **d**, to test the utility of the model. Use $\alpha = .05$. (Assume $n = 100$.)
f. Predict the severity of the disease when the incidence of maize rust for a plant is 80%. [*Note:*   Take the antilog (base 10) of $\hat{y}$ to obtain the predicted average number of infections per leaf.]

OPTIONAL EXERCISES

11.42   Verify that

$$\hat{\beta}_1 = r\sqrt{\frac{SS_{yy}}{SS_{xx}}} \quad \text{and} \quad SSE = SS_{yy}(1 - r^2)$$

11.43   Use the result of Optional Exercise 11.42 to show that

$$\frac{\hat{\beta}_1}{s/\sqrt{SS_{xx}}} = \frac{r\sqrt{n-2}}{\sqrt{1-r^2}}$$

11.9   Using the Model for Estimation and Prediction

If we are satisfied that a useful model has been found to describe the relationship between the compression of the insulation material and compressive pressure, we are ready to accomplish the original objectives for building the model: using it to estimate or to predict the amount of compression for a particular level of compressive pressure.

The most common uses of a probabilistic model can be divided into two categories. **The first is the use of the model for estimating the mean value of y, $E(y)$, for a specific value of x.** For our example, we may want to estimate the mean amount of compression for all specimens of insulation subjected to a compressive pressure of 40 ($x = 4$) pounds per square inch. **The second use of the model entails predicting a particular y value for a given x.** That is, if we decide to install the insulation in a particular piece of equipment in which we think it will be subjected to a pressure of 40 pounds per square inch, we will want to predict the insulation compression for this particular specimen of insulation material.

In the case of estimating a mean value of y, we are attempting to estimate the mean result of a very large number of experiments at the given x value. In the second case, we are trying to predict the outcome of a single experiment at the given x value. In which of these model uses do you expect to have more success, i.e., which value—the mean or individual value of y—can we estimate (or predict) with greater accuracy?

Before answering this question, we first consider the problem of choosing an estimator (or predictor) of the mean (or individual) y value. We will use the least squares model

$$\hat{y} = \hat{\beta}_0 + \hat{\beta}_1 x$$

both to estimate the mean value of y and to predict a particular value of y for a given value of x. For our example, we found

$$\hat{y} = -.1 + .7x$$

so that the estimated mean compression of all specimens of insulation when $x = 4$ (compressive pressure of 40 pounds per square inch) is

$$\hat{y} = -.1 + .7(4) = 2.7$$

or .27 inch (the units of y are tenths of an inch). The identical value is used to predict the y value when $x = 4$. That is, both the estimated mean value and the predicted value of y equal $\hat{y} = 2.7$ when $x = 4$, as shown in Figure 11.13.

The difference in these two model uses lies in the relative accuracy of the estimate and the prediction. These accuracies are best measured by the repeated sampling errors of the least squares line when it is used as an estimator and as a predictor, respectively. These errors are given in the box on page 574.

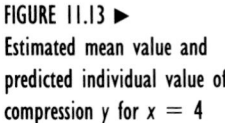

FIGURE 11.13 ▶
Estimated mean value and predicted individual value of compression y for x = 4

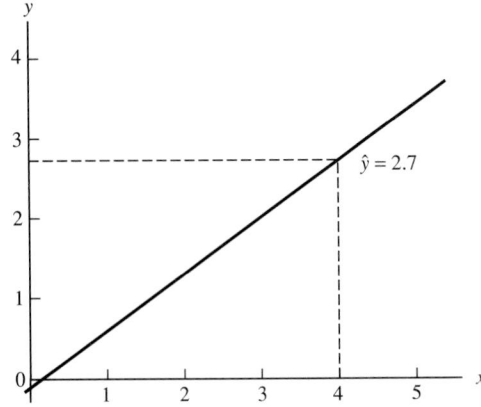

Sampling Errors for the Estimator of the Mean of y and the Predictor for an Individual y

1. The standard deviation of the sampling distribution of the estimator $\hat{y}$ of the mean value of y at a particular value of x, say, x_p, is

$$\sigma_{\hat{y}} = \sigma\sqrt{\frac{1}{n} + \frac{(x_p - \bar{x})^2}{SS_{xx}}}$$

where σ is the standard deviation of the random error ε.

2. The standard deviation of the prediction error for the predictor $\hat{y}$ of an individual y value for $x = x_p$ is

$$\sigma_{(y-\hat{y})} = \sigma\sqrt{1 + \frac{1}{n} + \frac{(x_p - \bar{x})^2}{SS_{xx}}}$$

where σ is the standard deviation of the random error ε.

The true value of σ will rarely be known. Thus, we estimate σ by s and calculate the estimation and prediction intervals as shown in the following boxes.

A $(1 - \alpha)100\%$ Confidence Interval for the Mean Value of y for $x = x_p$

$$\hat{y} \pm t_{\alpha/2}(\text{Estimated standard deviation of } \hat{y})$$

or

$$\hat{y} \pm t_{\alpha/2}s\sqrt{\frac{1}{n} + \frac{(x_p - \bar{x})^2}{SS_{xx}}}$$

where $t_{\alpha/2}$ is based on $(n - 2)$ df

A $(1 - \alpha)100\%$ Prediction Interval for an Individual y for $x = x_p$

$$\hat{y} \pm t_{\alpha/2}[\text{Estimated standard deviation of } (y - \hat{y})]$$

or

$$\hat{y} \pm t_{\alpha/2}s\sqrt{1 + \frac{1}{n} + \frac{(x_p - \bar{x})^2}{SS_{xx}}}$$

where $t_{\alpha/2}$ is based on $(n - 2)$ df

EXAMPLE 11.9

Find a 95% confidence interval for the mean insulation compression when the pressure is 40 pounds per square inch.

Solution

For a compressive pressure of 40 pounds per square inch, $x_p = 4$ and, since $n = 5$, df $= n - 2 = 3$. Then the confidence interval for the mean value of y is

$$\hat{y} \pm t_{\alpha/2}s\sqrt{\frac{1}{n} + \frac{(x_p - \bar{x})^2}{SS_{xx}}}$$

or

$$\hat{y} \pm t_{.025}s\sqrt{\frac{1}{5} + \frac{(4 - \bar{x})^2}{SS_{xx}}}$$

Recall that $\hat{y} = 2.7$, $s = .61$, $\bar{x} = 3$, and $SS_{xx} = 10$. From Table 7 of Appendix II, $t_{.025} = 3.182$. Thus, we have

$$2.7 \pm (3.182)(.61)\sqrt{\frac{1}{5} + \frac{(4 - 3)^2}{10}} = 2.7 \pm (3.182)(.61)(.55)$$

$$= 2.7 \pm 1.1$$

We estimate that the interval from .16 inch to .38 inch encloses the mean amount of compression when the insulation is subjected to a compressive pressure of 40 pounds per square inch. Note that we used a small amount of data for purposes of illustration in fitting the least squares line and that the width of the interval could be decreased by using a larger number of data points.

EXAMPLE 11.10

Predict the amount of compression for an individual piece of insulation material subjected to a compressive pressure of 40 pounds per square inch. Use a 95% prediction interval.

Solution

To predict the compression for a particular piece of insulation material for which $x_p = 4$, we calculate the 95% prediction interval as

$$\hat{y} \pm t_{\alpha/2}s\sqrt{1 + \frac{1}{n} + \frac{(x_p - \bar{x})^2}{SS_{xx}}} = 2.7 \pm (3.182)(.61)\sqrt{1 + \frac{1}{5} + \frac{(4 - 3)^2}{10}}$$

$$= 2.7 \pm (3.182)(.61)(1.14) = 2.7 \pm 2.2$$

Therefore, we predict that the compression for the piece of insulation material will fall in the interval from .05 inch to .49 inch. As in the case for the confidence interval for the mean value of y, the prediction interval for y is quite large. This is because we have chosen a simple example (only five data points) to fit the least squares line. The width of the prediction interval could be reduced by using a larger number of data points.

A comparison of the confidence limits for the mean value of y and the prediction limits for some future value of y for various values of compressive pressure x is illustrated in Figure 11.14. It is important to note that the prediction interval for an individual value of y will always be wider than the confidence interval for a mean value of y. You can see this by examining the formulas for the two intervals and you can see it in Figure 11.14.

FIGURE 11.14 ▶

Comparison of widths of 95% confidence and prediction intervals

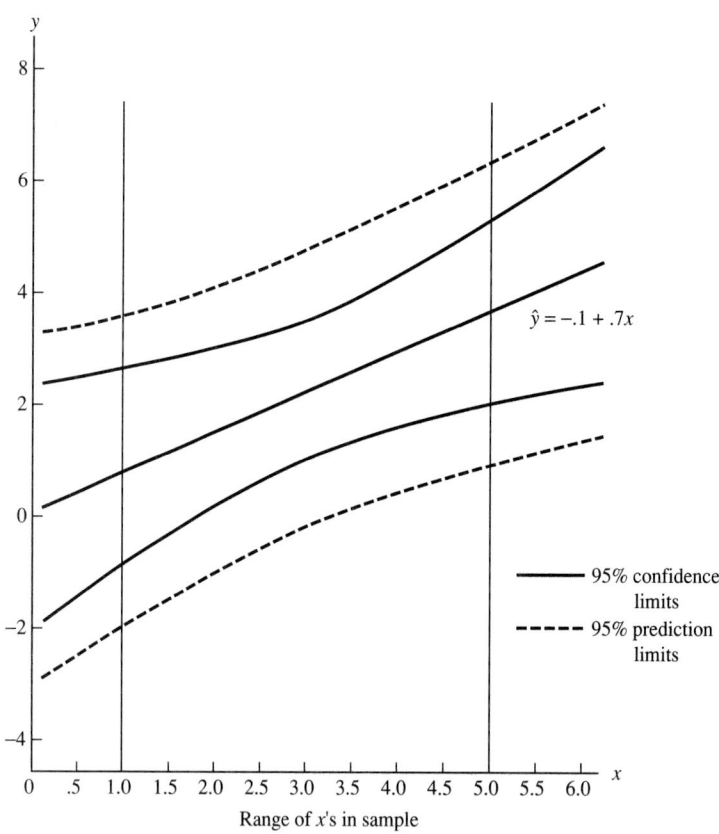

Additionally, over the range of the sample data, the widths of both intervals increase as the value of x gets farther from x̄. (See Figure 11.14.) Thus, the more x deviates from x̄, the less useful the interval will be in practice. In fact, when x is selected far enough away from x̄ so that it falls outside the range of the sample data, it is dangerous to make any inferences about $E(y)$ or y, as explained in the following box.

> **Warning**
> ....
>
> Using the least squares prediction equation to estimate the mean value of y or to predict a particular value of y for values of x that fall *outside* the range of values of x contained in your sample data may lead to errors of estimation or prediction that are much larger than expected. Although the least squares model may provide a very good fit to the data over the range of x values contained in the sample, **it could give a poor representation of the true model for values of x outside this region.**

To conclude this section, we will find the variance of the value of $\hat{y}$ when $x = x_p$. This variance plays an important role in developing the confidence interval for $E(y)$ when $x = x_p$ and the prediction interval for a particular value of y when $x = x_p$.

EXAMPLE 11.11

Find the variance of $\hat{y}$ when $x = x_p$.

Solution

When $x = x_p$, we have $\hat{y} = \hat{\beta}_0 + \hat{\beta}_1 x_p$, where $\hat{\beta}_0 = \bar{y} - \hat{\beta}_1 \bar{x}$. Substituting this value of $\hat{\beta}_0$ into the expression for $\hat{y}$, we obtain

$$\hat{y} = (\bar{y} - \hat{\beta}_1 \bar{x}) + \hat{\beta}_1(x_p)$$
$$= \bar{y} + \hat{\beta}_1(x_p - \bar{x})$$

The next step is to express $\hat{y}$ as a linear function of the random y values, $y_1, y_2, \ldots, y_n$, so that we can obtain $V(\hat{y})$ as the variance of a linear function of independent random variables. We now write

$$\hat{y} = \bar{y} + \hat{\beta}_1(x_p - \bar{x})$$
$$= \sum \frac{y_i}{n} + \frac{(x_p - \bar{x})}{SS_{xx}} \sum (x_i - \bar{x}) y_i$$
$$= \sum \frac{y_i}{n} + \sum \frac{(x_p - \bar{x})(x_i - \bar{x})}{SS_{xx}} y_i$$

We can now express $\hat{y}$ as a single summation:

$$\hat{y} = \sum \left[\frac{1}{n} + \frac{(x_p - \bar{x})(x_i - \bar{x})}{SS_{xx}} \right] y_i$$

i.e., $\hat{y}$ is a linear function of the independent random variables, $y_1, y_2, \ldots, y_n$, where the coefficient of y_i is

$$\left[\frac{1}{n} + \frac{(x_p - \bar{x})(x_i - \bar{x})}{SS_{xx}}\right]$$

Then, by Theorem 6.7,

$$V(\hat{y}) = \sum \left[\frac{1}{n} + \frac{(x_p - \bar{x})(x_i - \bar{x})}{SS_{xx}}\right]^2 V(y_i)$$

where $V(y_i) = \sigma^2$, $i = 1, 2, \ldots, n$. Therefore,

$$V(\hat{y}) = \sum \left[\frac{1}{n^2} + \frac{2}{n}\frac{(x_p - \bar{x})(x_i - \bar{x})}{SS_{xx}} + \frac{(x_p - \bar{x})^2(x_i - \bar{x})^2}{(SS_{xx})^2}\right]\sigma^2$$

$$= \left[\frac{n}{n^2} + \frac{2}{n}\frac{(x_p - \bar{x})}{SS_{xx}}\sum(x_i - \bar{x}) + \frac{(x_p - \bar{x})^2}{(SS_{xx})^2}\sum(x_i - \bar{x})^2\right]\sigma^2$$

$$= \left[\frac{1}{n} + \frac{(x_p - \bar{x})^2}{(SS_{xx})^2}SS_{xx}\right]\sigma^2 \quad \text{since } \sum(x_i - \bar{x}) = 0$$

$$= \sigma^2\left[\frac{1}{n} + \frac{(x_p - \bar{x})^2}{SS_{xx}}\right]$$

You can see that this agrees with the formula for $V(\hat{y})$ given previously in this section.

EXERCISES

11.44 Explain why for a particular x value, the prediction interval for an individual y value will always be wider than the confidence interval for the mean value of y.

11.45 Explain why the confidence interval for the mean value of y for a particular x value, say, x_p, gets wider the farther x_p is from $\bar{x}$. What are the implications of this phenomenon for estimation and prediction?

11.46 In forestry, the diameter of a tree at breast height (which is fairly easy to measure) is used to predict the height of the tree (a difficult measurement to obtain). Silviculturists working in British Columbia's boreal forest conducted a series of spacing trials to predict the heights of several species of trees. The data in the accompanying table are the breast height diameters (in centimeters) and heights (in meters) for a sample of 36 white spruce trees.

Breast Height Diameter x, cm	Height y, m	Breast Height Diameter x, cm	Height y, m
18.9	20.0	16.6	18.8
15.5	16.8	15.5	16.9
19.4	20.2	13.7	16.3
20.0	20.0	27.5	21.4
29.8	20.2	20.3	19.2
19.8	18.0	22.9	19.8
20.3	17.8	14.1	18.5
20.0	19.2	10.1	12.1
22.0	22.3	5.8	8.0
23.6	18.9	20.7	17.4
14.8	13.3	17.8	18.4
22.7	20.6	11.4	17.3
18.5	19.0	14.4	16.6
21.5	19.2	13.4	12.9
14.8	16.1	17.8	17.5
17.7	19.9	20.7	19.4
21.0	20.4	13.3	15.5
15.9	17.6	22.9	19.2

Source: Scholz, H., Northern Lights College, British Columbia.

a. Construct a scattergram for the data.
b. Assuming the relationship between the variables is best described by a straight line, use the method of least squares to estimate the y-intercept and slope of the line.
c. Plot the least squares line on your scattergram.
d. Do the data provide sufficient evidence to indicate that the breast height diamter x contributes information for the prediction of tree height y? Test using $\alpha = .05$.
e. Use your least squares line to find a 90% confidence interval for the average height of white spruce trees with a breast height diameter of 20 cm. Interpret the interval.

11.47   Refer to Exercise 11.8. Find a 99% prediction interval for the heat transfer coefficient of an integral-fin tube with an unflooded area ratio of 1.95. Interpret the result.

11.48   Refer to Exercise 11.9.
a. Find a 90% prediction interval for the site attenuation for dipoles with a transmission frequency of 350 megahertz.
b. Find a 90% confidence interval for the mean site attenuation for all sets of dipoles with transmission frequencies of 350 megahertz.
c. Compare and comment on the sizes of the intervals in parts a and b.
d. Could you reduce the size of either or both intervals by increasing your sample size? Explain.

11.49   Refer to Exercise 11.10. Find a 95% confidence interval for the mean passivation potential of crystallized alloy when annealing time is 30 minutes.

11.50   Refer to Exercise 11.30. Find a 90% confidence interval for the mean change in free energy for seeds germinated at a temperature of 290°K.

11.51 An automated system for marking large numbers of student computer programs, called AUTOMARK, has been used successfully at McMaster University in Ontario, Canada. AUTOMARK takes into account both program correctness and program style when marking student assignments. To evaluate the effectiveness of the automated system, AUTOMARK was used to grade the FORTRAN77 assignments of a class of 33 students (*Communications of the ACM*, Feb. 1986). These grades were then compared to the grades assigned by the instructor. The results are shown in the accompanying table.

AUTOMARK Grade x	Instructor Grade y	AUTOMARK Grade x	Instructor Grade y
12.2	10	17.8	17
10.6	11	18.0	17
15.1	12	18.2	17
16.2	12	18.4	17
16.6	12	18.6	17
16.6	13	19.0	17
17.2	14	19.3	17
17.6	14	19.5	17
18.2	14	19.7	17
16.5	15	18.6	18
17.2	15	19.0	18
18.2	15	19.2	18
15.1	16	19.4	18
17.2	16	19.6	18
17.5	16	20.1	18
18.6	16	19.2	19
18.8	16		

Source: Redish, K. A., and Smyth, W. F. "Program style analysis: A natural byproduct of program compilation." *Communications of the Association for Computing Machinery*, Vol. 29, No. 2, Feb. 1986, p. 132 (Figure 4). Copyright 1986, Association for Computing Machinery, Inc.

a. Find the least squares prediction equation for the straight-line model relating instructor grade y to AUTOMARK grade x.

b. Is there sufficient evidence to indicate that the model is useful for predicting y? Test using $\alpha = .10$.

c. Calculate a 95% prediction interval for the instructor-assigned grade of a FORTRAN77 assignment that received an AUTOMARK score of 17.5. Interpret the interval.

OPTIONAL EXERCISES

11.52 Suppose you want to predict some future value of y when $x = x_p$ using the prediction equation $\hat{y} = \hat{\beta}_0 + \hat{\beta}_1 x$. The error of prediction will be the difference between the actual value of y_p and the predicted value $\hat{y}$, i.e.,

Error of prediction $= y_p - \hat{y}$

a. Explain why the error of prediction will be normally distributed.

b. Find the expected value and the variance of the error of prediction.

11.53   Explain why

$$z = \frac{\text{Error of prediction}}{\text{Standard deviation of the error}}$$

$$= \frac{y_{\text{p}} - \hat{y}}{\sigma_{(y_{\text{p}} - \hat{y})}}$$

$$= \frac{y_{\text{p}} - \hat{y}}{\sigma\sqrt{1 + \dfrac{1}{n} + \dfrac{(x_{\text{p}} - \bar{x})^2}{\text{SS}_{xx}}}}$$

is a standard normal random variable.

11.54   Show that

$$t = \frac{\text{Error of prediction}}{\text{Estimated standard deviation of the error}}$$

$$= \frac{y_{\text{p}} - \hat{y}}{s\sqrt{1 + \dfrac{1}{n} + \dfrac{(x_{\text{p}} - \bar{x})^2}{\text{SS}_{xx}}}}$$

has a Student's t distribution with $\nu = (n - 2)$ df.

11.55   Use the t statistic in Optional Exercise 11.54 as a pivotal statistic to derive a $(1 - \alpha)100\%$ prediction interval for y_{p}.

11.10   Simple Linear Regression on the Computer

In the previous sections, we have presented the basic elements necessary to fit and use a straight-line regression model. In this section, we will assemble these elements by applying them in an example where we use the computer to perform the calculations.

Suppose a fire insurance company wants to relate the amount of fire damage in major residential fires to the distance between the residence and the nearest fire station. The study is to be conducted in a large suburb of a major city; a sample of 15 recent fires in this suburb is selected. The amount of damage y and the distance x between the fire and the nearest fire station are recorded for each fire. The results are given in Table 11.7 on page 582.

TABLE 11.7 Fire Damage Data	
Distance from Fire Station	Fire Damage
x, miles	y, thousands of dollars
3.4	26.2
1.8	17.8
4.6	31.3
2.3	23.1
3.1	27.5
5.5	36.0
.7	14.1
3.0	22.3
2.6	19.6
4.3	31.3
2.1	24.0
1.1	17.3
6.1	43.2
4.8	36.4
3.8	26.1

STEP 1 First, we hypothesize a model to relate fire damage y to the distance x from the nearest fire station. We will hypothesize a straight-line probabilistic model:

$$y = \beta_0 + \beta_1 x + \varepsilon$$

STEP 2 Next, we enter the data into a computer and use a statistical software package to estimate the unknown parameters in the deterministic component of the hypothesized model. The SAS printout for the simple linear regression analysis is shown in Figure 11.15.

The least squares estimates of β_0 and β_1 are found (shaded) under the column labeled **Parameter Estimate** (in the middle portion of the printout) in the rows labeled **INTERCEP** and **X**, respectively. Note that the estimate of the slope is

$$\hat{\beta}_1 = 4.919331$$

and the estimate of the y-intercept is

$$\hat{\beta}_0 = 10.277929$$

Thus, the least squares equation is

$$\hat{y} = 10.278 + 4.919x$$

This prediction equation is graphed in Figure 11.16 on page 584, along with a plot of the data points.

FIGURE 11.15 ▶
SAS printout for the fire damage linear regression

Model: MODEL1
Dep Variable: Y

Analysis of Variance

Source	DF	Sum of Squares	Mean Square	F Value	Prob>F
Model	1	841.76636	841.76636	156.886	0.0001
Error	13	69.75098	5.36546		
C Total	14	911.51733			

Root MSE	2.31635	R-Square	0.9235	
Dep Mean	26.41333	Adj R-Sq	0.9176	
C.V.	8.76961			

Parameter Estimates

Variable	DF	Parameter Estimate	Standard Error	T for H0: Parameter=0	Prob > |T|
INTERCEP	1	10.277929	1.42027781	7.237	0.0001
X	1	4.919331	0.39274775	12.525	0.0001

Obs	X	Y	Predict Value	Residual	Lower95% Predict	Upper95% Predict
1	3.4	26.2000	27.0037	-0.8037	21.8344	32.1729
2	1.8	17.8000	19.1327	-1.3327	13.8141	24.4514
3	4.6	31.3000	32.9068	-1.6068	27.6186	38.1951
4	2.3	23.1000	21.5924	1.5076	16.3577	26.8271
5	3.1	27.5000	25.5279	1.9721	20.3573	30.6984
6	5.5	36.0000	37.3342	-1.3342	31.8334	42.8351
7	0.7	14.1000	13.7215	0.3785	8.1087	19.3342
8	3	22.3000	25.0359	-2.7359	19.8622	30.2097
9	2.6	19.6000	23.0682	-3.4682	17.8678	28.2686
10	4.3	31.3000	31.4311	-0.1311	26.1908	36.6713
11	2.1	24.0000	20.6085	3.3915	15.3442	25.8729
12	1.1	17.3000	15.6892	1.6108	10.1999	21.1785
13	6.1	43.2000	40.2858	2.9142	34.5906	45:9811
14	4.8	36.4000	33.8907	2.5093	28.5640	39.2175
15	3.8	26.1000	28.9714	-2.8714	23.7843	34.1585
16 *	3.5	.	27.4956		22.3239	32.6672

Sum of Residuals	-3.73035E-14
Sum of Squared Residuals	69.7510
Predicted Resid SS (Press)	93.2117

FIGURE 11.16 ▶

Least squares model for the fire damage data

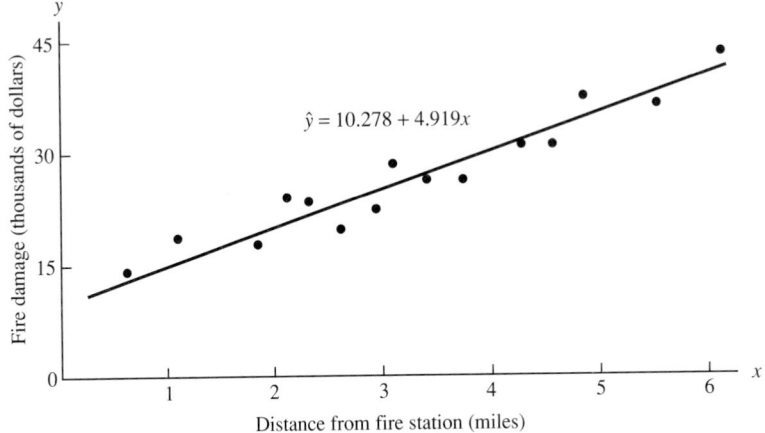

STEP 3   Now, we specify the probability distribution of the random error component ε. The assumptions about the distribution will be identical to those listed in Section 11.2. Although we know that these assumptions are not completely satisfied (they rarely are for any practical problem), we are willing to assume they are approximately satisfied for this example. The estimate of the variance σ^2 of ε is given (shaded) in the top portion of the printout in the column labeled **Mean Square** and the row labeled **Error**. This value is

$$s^2 = \text{MSE} = 5.36546$$

The estimated standard deviation of ε, given next to the heading **Root MSE**, is

$$s = \sqrt{5.36546} = 2.31635$$

The value of s implies that most of the observed fire damage (y) values will fall within approximately $2s = 4.64$ thousand dollars of their respective predicted values.

STEP 4

a. *Test of model utility*   We can now check the utility of the hypothesized model, that is, whether x really contributes information for the prediction of y using the straight-line model. First, test the null hypothesis that the slope β_1 is 0, i.e., that there is no linear relationship between fire damage and the distance from the nearest fire station, against the alternative that x and y are positively linearly related. We test:

$$H_0: \quad \beta_1 = 0$$
$$H_a: \quad \beta_1 > 0$$

The value of the test statistic is shaded in the middle portion of the printout under the column labeled **T for H0: Parameter=0** and the row corresponding to **X**. The value, a t statistic, is

$$t = 12.525$$

The p-value of the test is reported on the printout under the column heading **Prob > |T|** in the **X** row. This value (shaded) is a two-tailed p-value. The p-value for a one-tailed test of H_0: $\beta_1 = 0$ is found by dividing the value reported in the SAS printout in half. Thus, the p-value for our test is

$$p = \frac{.0001}{2} = .0005$$

This small p-value leaves little doubt that distance between the fire and the fire station contributes information for the prediction of fire damage and that fire damage increases as the distance increases.

b. *Confidence interval for slope*   We gain additional information about the relationship by forming a confidence interval for the slope β_1. A 95% confidence interval is $\hat{\beta}_1 \pm (t_{.025})s_{\hat{\beta}_1}$, where the value of $\hat{\beta}_1$ and its standard error, $s_{\hat{\beta}_1}$, are shown (shaded) on the printout. The value of $t_{.025}$, based on $n - 2 = 13$ df, is 2.160. Therefore, the 95% confidence interval is

$$\hat{\beta}_1 \pm (t_{.025})s_{\hat{\beta}_1} = 4.919 \pm (2.160)(.3927)$$
$$= 4.919 \pm .849 = (4.070, 5.768)$$

We estimate that the interval from \$4,070 to \$5,768 encloses the mean increase (β_1) in fire damage per additional mile distance from the fire station.

c. *Numerical descriptive measures of model adequacy*   The coefficient of determination is found next to the heading **R-Square** in the middle portion of the printout. This value (shaded) is

$$r^2 = .9235$$

which implies that about 92% of the sample variation in fire damage (y) is explained by the distance x between the fire and the fire station.

The coefficient of correlation r, which measures the strength of the linear relationship between y and x, is not shown on the SAS printout and must be calculated. Using the facts that $r = \sqrt{r^2}$ in simple linear regression and that r and $\hat{\beta}_1$ have the same sign, we find

$$r = +\sqrt{r^2} = \sqrt{.9235} = .96$$

The high correlation confirms our conclusion that β_1 differs from 0; it appears that fire damage and distance from the fire station are linearly correlated. All signs point to a strong linear relationship between x and y.

STEP 5   We are now prepared to use the least squares model. Suppose the insurance company wants to predict the fire damage if a major residential fire were to occur 3.5 miles from the nearest fire station, i.e., $x_p = 3.5$. The predicted value is shown (shaded) at the bottom of the SAS printout in the row corresponding to **X** = 3.5 and the column headed **Predict Value**. This value is

$$\hat{y} = 27.4956$$

Lower and upper prediction limits for this value are given under the columns labeled **Lower 95% Predict** and **Upper 95% Predict**, respectively. These values (shaded) are 22.3239 and 32.6672. Thus, the model yields a 95% prediction interval of $22,324 to $32,667 for fire damage in a major residential fire 3.5 miles from the nearest fire station.

Caution: We would not use this prediction model to make predictions for homes less than .7 mile or more than 6.1 miles from the nearest fire station. A look at the data in Table 11.7 reveals that all the x values fall between .7 and 6.1. Recall from Section 11.9 that it is dangerous to use the model to make predictions outside the region in which the sample data fall. A straight line might not provide a good model for the relationship between the mean value of y and the value of x when stretched over a wider range of x values.

11.11 Summary

We have introduced an extremely useful tool in this chapter—the **method of least squares** for fitting a prediction equation to a set of data. This procedure, along with associated statistical tests and estimations, is called a **regression analysis**. In five steps we showed how to use sample data to build a model relating a dependent variable y to a single independent variable x.

Steps to Follow in a Simple Linear Regression Analysis

1. The first step is to hypothesize a **probabilistic model**. In this chapter, we confined our attention to the **straight-line model**, $y = \beta_0 + \beta_1 x + \varepsilon$.

2. The second step is to use the method of least squares to estimate the unknown parameters in the **deterministic component**, $\beta_0 + \beta_1 x$. The least squares estimates yield a model $\hat{y} = \hat{\beta}_0 + \hat{\beta}_1 x$ with a **sum of squared errors (SSE)** that is smaller than the SSE for any other straight-line model.

3. The third step is to specify the probability distribution of the **random error component ε**.

4. The fourth step is to assess the utility of the hypothesized model. Included here are making inferences about the **slope β_1**, calculating the **coefficient of correlation r**, and calculating the **coefficient of determination r^2**.

5. Finally, if we are satisfied with the model, we are prepared to use it. We used the model to **estimate the mean y value**, $E(y)$, for a given x value and to **predict an individual y value** for a specific value of x.

The following chapter will develop more fully the concepts introduced in this chapter.

SUPPLEMENTARY EXERCISES

● ●

11.56   At temperatures approaching absolute zero (273 degrees below zero Celsius), helium exhibits traits that defy many laws of conventional physics. An experiment has been conducted with helium in solid form at various temperatures near absolute zero. The solid helium is placed in a dilution refrigerator along with a solid impure substance, and the proportion (by weight) of the impurity passing through the solid helium is recorded. (This phenomenon of solids passing directly through solids is known as *quantum tunneling*.) The data are given in the table.

Proportion of Impurity Passing Through Helium y	Temperature x, °C
.315	−262
.202	−265
.204	−256
.620	−267
.715	−270
.935	−272
.957	−272
.906	−272
.985	−273
.987	−273

a. Construct a scattergram of the data.
b. Find the least squares line for the data and plot it on your scattergram.
c. Define β_1 in the context of this problem.
d. Test the hypothesis (at $\alpha = .05$) that temperature contributes no information for the prediction of the proportion of impurity passing through helium when a linear model is used. Draw the appropriate conclusions.
e. Find a 90% confidence interval for β_1. Interpret your results.
f. Find the coefficient of correlation for the given data.
g. Find the coefficient of determination for the linear model you constructed in part **b**. Interpret your result.
h. Find a 99% prediction interval for the proportion of impurity passing through helium when the temperature is set at −270°C.
i. Estimate the mean proportion of impurity passing through helium when the temperature is set at −270°C. Use a 99% confidence interval.

11.57   A new computer software query package has been designed to achieve more efficient access and maintenance of large-scale data sets. Efficiency is measured in terms of the number of disk I/O's (called *storage blocks*) required to access and maintain the data set; the smaller the number of blocks that are read, the faster the operation takes place. To evaluate the performance of the new software system, the number of disk I/O's required to access a large-scale data set was recorded for each of a sample of 15 data sets of various sizes (where size is measured as the number of records in the data set). The results are shown in the table. Conduct a complete simple linear regression analysis of the data. (Use the information in the accompanying MINITAB printout to analyze the data.)

Data Set	Number of Records x, thousands	Number of Disk I/O's y, thousands
1	350	36
2	200	20
3	450	45
4	50	5
5	400	40
6	150	18
7	350	38
8	300	32
9	150	21
10	500	54
11	100	11
12	400	43
13	200	19
14	50	7
15	250	26

```
The regression equation is
DiskIOs = 1.40 + 0.101 Records

Predictor        Coef        Stdev      t-ratio        p
Constant        1.403       1.055         1.33    0.206
Records      0.101014    0.003570        28.30    0.000

s = 1.942       R-sq = 98.4%     R-sq(adj) = 98.3%

Analysis of Variance

SOURCE        DF          SS           MS        F        p
Regression     1      3020.3       3020.3   800.83    0.000
Error         13        49.0          3.8
Total         14      3069.3
```

11.58   A major portion of the effort expended in developing commercial computer software is associated with program testing. A study was undertaken to assess the potential usefulness of various product- and process-related variables in identifying error-prone software (*IEEE Transactions on Software Engineering*, Apr. 1985). A straight-line model relating the number y of module defects to the number x of unique operands in the module was fit to the data collected for a sample of software modules. The coefficient of determination for this analysis was $r^2 = .74$.

a. Interpret the value of r^2.
b. Based on this value, would you infer that the straight-line model is a useful predictor of number y of module defects? Explain.

11.59 An engineer conducted a study to determine whether there is a linear relationship between the breaking strength, y, of wooden beams and the specific gravity, x, of the wood. Ten randomly selected beams of the same cross-sectional dimensions were stressed until they broke. The breaking strength and the specific gravity of the wood are shown in the table for each of the 10 beams. Analyze the data for the engineer.

Beam	Breaking Strength y	Specific Gravity x	Beam	Breaking Strength y	Specific Gravity x
1	11.14	.499	6	12.60	.528
2	12.74	.558	7	11.13	.418
3	13.13	.604	8	11.70	.480
4	11.51	.441	9	11.02	.406
5	12.38	.550	10	11.41	.467

11.60 The accompanying table shows a portion of the experimental data obtained in a study of the radial tension strength of concrete pipe (*Journal of the American Concrete Institute*, 1983). The concrete pipe used for the experiment had an inside diameter of 84 inches and a wall thickness of approximately 8.75 inches. In addition, it was reinforced with cold drawn wire. The response y is the load (in pounds per foot) until the first crack in a pipe specimen was observed, and the independent variable x is the age of the specimen (in days) at the time of the test. The results of a simple linear regression analysis of the data are shown in the SAS printout reproduced on page 590.

Load lb/ft	Age days	Load lb/ft	Age days
11,450	20	10,540	25
10,420	20	9,470	31
11,142	20	9,190	31
10,840	25	9,540	31
11,170	25		

Source: Heger, F. J., and McGrath, T. J. "Radial tension strength of pipe and other curved flexural members." *Journal of the American Concrete Institute*, Vol. 80, No. 1, 1983, pp. 33–39.

```
Model: MODEL1
Dependent Variable: Y

                        Analysis of Variance

                          Sum of        Mean
        Source      DF    Squares       Square      F Value     Prob>F

        Model        1 4039390.0879 4039390.0879    19.030      0.0033
        Error        7 1485857.9121  212265.41601
        C Total      8 5525248.0000

           Root MSE      460.72271     R-square     0.7311
           Dep Mean    10418.00000     Adj R-sq     0.6927
           C.V.            4.42237

                        Parameter Estimates

                    Parameter     Standard    T for H0:
        Variable DF  Estimate       Error    Parameter=0   Prob > |T|

        INTERCEP  1      14192   878.68441059    16.152      0.0001
        X         1 -148.978022   34.15103944    -4.362      0.0033


                   Dep Var  Predict   Std Err  Lower95%  Upper95%
        Obs   X       Y      Value    Predict    Mean      Mean    Residual

         1    20   11450.0  11212.5   238.243  10649.2   11775.9    237.5
         2    20   10420.0  11212.5   238.243  10649.2   11775.9   -792.5
         3    20   11142.0  11212.5   238.243  10649.2   11775.9  -70.5495
         4    25   10840.0  10467.7   153.996  10103.5   10831.8    372.3
         5    25   11170.0  10467.7   153.996  10103.5   10831.8    702.3
         6    25   10540.0  10467.7   153.996  10103.5   10831.8   72.3407
         7    31    9470.0   9573.8   247.055   8989.6   10158.0   -103.8
         8    31    9190.0   9573.8   247.055   8989.6   10158.0   -383.8
         9    31    9540.0   9573.8   247.055   8989.6   10158.0  -33.7912
        10    28       .    10020.7   178.546   9598.5   10442.9       .

Sum of Residuals              5.456968E-12
Sum of Squared Residuals      1485857.9121
Predicted Resid SS (Press)    2405847.7272
```

a. Interpret the values of $\hat{\beta}_1$, $\hat{\beta}_0$, s, and r^2 shown on the printout.

b. Do the data provide sufficient evidence to indicate that the load required before the first crack is observed decreases linearly with the age of the pipe? Test using $\alpha = .05$.

c. Estimate the mean load required before the first crack is observed for 28-day-old pipe specimens. Use a 95% confidence interval.

11.61 As part of a computer system performance evaluation, a system manager is interested in predicting the response time for computer terminals. *Terminal response time* is defined as the length of time (in seconds) it takes the computer to respond to a command sent from a computer terminal by pressing one of the terminal's program function keys. Although many variables influence terminal response time, the system manager will model the response time as a function of the number of simultaneous users (i.e., the number of users who are accessing the computer's central processing unit at the same time the command was sent). The manager has collected the sample data given in the accompanying table. Conduct a complete simple linear regression analysis of the data.

Number of Simultaneous Users	Terminal Response Time
x	y, seconds
1	.22
2	.59
3	1.01
4	1.36
5	1.42

11.62 "In the analysis of urban transportation systems it is important to be able to estimate expected travel time between locations." Cook and Russell (*Transportation Research*, June 1980) collected data in the city of Tulsa on the urban travel times and distances between locations for two types of vehicles—large hoist compactor trucks and passenger cars. A simple linear regression analysis was conducted for both sets of data (y = urban travel time in minutes, x = distance between locations in miles) with the results shown in the accompanying table.

Passenger Cars	Trucks
$\hat{y} = 2.50 + 1.93x$	$\hat{y} = 1.85 + 3.86x$
$r^2 = .676$; p-value $< .05$	$r^2 = .758$; p-value $< .01$

Source: Cook, T. M., and Russell, R. A. "Estimating urban travel times: A comparative study." *Transportation Research*, 14A, June 1980, pp. 173–175. Copyright 1980, Pergamon Press, Ltd. Reprinted with permission.

a. Is there sufficient evidence to indicate that distance between locations is linearly related to urban travel time for passenger cars? Test at $\alpha = .05$.

b. Is there sufficient evidence to indicate that distance between locations is linearly related to urban travel time for trucks? Test at $\alpha = .01$.

c. Interpret the value of r^2 for the two prediction equations.

d. Estimate the mean urban travel time for all passenger cars traveling a distance of 3 miles on Tulsa's highways.

e. Predict the urban travel time for a particular truck traveling a distance of 5 miles on Tulsa's highways.

f. Explain how we could attach a measure of reliability to the inferences derived in parts **d** and **e**.

11.63 The Environmental Protection Agency establishes industrial and occupational standards for the ambient air quality of total suspended particulates. The high-volume air sampler—the standard device used for sampling total suspended particulates—collects suspended particulates on large filters. The name *high-volume* is derived from the fact that the air sampler has a high sampling flow rate (measured in standard cubic meters per minute). Because of this high flow rate, large quantities of particles are collected over a 24-hour sampling period. However, the flow rate will vary depending on the pressure drop (in inches of water) across the filter medium. An experiment was conducted to investigate the relationship between flow rate and pressure drop. Eight sampling environments in which the high-volume air sampler was implemented yielded the measurements on average flow rate (y) and pressure drop across filter (x) listed in the table on page 592.

Flow Rate	Pressure Drop	Flow Rate	Pressure Drop
y	x	y	x
.92	10	1.56	18
1.25	15	1.10	13
.60	8	.65	9
1.13	12	1.33	15

a. Use the data to develop a simple linear model for predicting the average flow rate of the high-volume air sampler based on the pressure drop of the filter.

b. Is the model of part **a** useful for predicting flow rate? (Use $\alpha = .05$.)

c. Using a 95% prediction interval, predict the flow rate in a sampling environment in which the pressure drop across the filter is 11 inches of water.

11.64 Passive and active solar energy systems are becoming viable options to home builders as installation and operating costs decrease. Laminated solar modules utilize high-quality, single crystal silicon solar cells, connected electrically in series, to deliver a specified power output. Research was conducted to investigate the relationship between the solar cell temperature (°C) rise above ambient and the amount of insulation (megawatts per square centimeter). Data collected for six solar cells sampled under identical experimental conditions are recorded in the table.

Temperature Rise Above Ambient	Insulation
y	x
9	25
25	70
20	50
12	30
15	45
22	60

a. Fit a least squares line to the data.

b. Plot the data and graph the line as a check on your calculations.

c. Calculate r and r^2. Interpret their values.

d. Is the model useful for predicting temperature rise above ambient? (Use $\alpha = .01$).

e. Estimate the mean temperature rise above ambient for solar cells with insulation of 35 megawatts per square centimeter. Use a 99% confidence interval.

11.65 A study was conducted to examine the inhibiting properties of the sodium salts of phosphoric acid on the corrosion of iron (*British Corrosion Journal*, 1979). The data shown in the table provide a measure of corrosion of Armco iron in tap water containing various concentrations of $NaPO_4$ inhibitor. The linear model $y = \beta_0 + \beta_1 x + \varepsilon$ is fit to the data using SAS (see accompanying printout). Fully interpret the results.

Concentration of NaPO$_4$ x, parts per million	Measure of Corrosion Rate y	Concentration of NaPO$_4$ x, parts per million	Measure of Corrosion Rate y
2.50	7.68	26.20	.93
5.03	6.95	33.00	.72
7.60	6.30	40.00	.68
11.60	5.75	50.00	.65
13.00	5.01	55.00	.56
19.60	1.43		

Source: Andrzejaczek, B. J. "Mechanism of action of acidified sodium phosphate solution as a corrosion inhibitor of iron in tap water." *British Corrosion Journal*, Vol. 14, No. 3, 1979, pp. 176–178.

Model: MODEL1
Dependent Variable: Y

Analysis of Variance

Source	DF	Sum of Squares	Mean Square	F Value	Prob>F
Model	1	67.84940	67.84940	30.939	0.0004
Error	9	19.73701	2.19300		
C Total	10	87.58642			

Root MSE	1.48088	R-square	0.7747	
Dep Mean	3.33273	Adj R-sq	0.7496	
C.V.	44.43444			

Parameter Estimates

Variable	DF	Parameter Estimate	Standard Error	T for H0: Parameter=0	Prob > |T|
INTERCEP	1	6.735099	0.75731292	8.893	0.0001
X	1	-0.142018	0.02553235	-5.562	0.0004

Obs	X	Dep Var Y	Predict Value	Std Err Predict	Lower95% Predict	Upper95% Predict	Residual
1	2.5	7.6800	6.3801	0.707	2.6681	10.0920	1.2999
2	5.03	6.9500	6.0207	0.658	2.3550	9.6865	0.9293
3	7.6	6.3000	5.6558	0.611	2.0315	9.2800	0.6442
4	11.6	5.7500	5.0877	0.547	1.5167	8.6587	0.6623
5	13	5.0100	4.8889	0.527	1.3331	8.4446	0.1211
6	19.6	1.4300	3.9515	0.460	0.4435	7.4595	-2.5215
7	26.2	0.9300	3.0142	0.450	-0.4871	6.5156	-2.0842
8	33	0.7200	2.0485	0.503	-1.4892	5.5862	-1.3285
9	40	0.6800	1.0544	0.606	-2.5652	4.6740	-0.3744
10	50	0.6500	-0.3658	0.801	-4.1744	3.4428	1.0158
11	55	0.5600	-1.0759	0.910	-5.0075	2.8557	1.6359

Sum of Residuals	-4.44089E-16
Sum of Squared Residuals	19.7370
Predicted Resid SS (Press)	29.8695

COMPUTER LAB: Simple Linear Regression and Correlation

The following sample programs give the SAS and MINITAB commands for analyzing the straight-line model, $E(y) = \beta_0 + \beta_1 x$, relating fire damage (y) to distance from fire station (x). (See Section 11.10.)

SAS

Command line		
1	DATA FIRE;	
2	INPUT X Y;	Data entry instructions
3	CARDS;	
4	3.4 26.2	
5	1.8 17.8	
.	. .	Input data values
.	. .	(1 observation per line)
.	. .	
18	3.8 26.1	
19	3.5 .	
20	PROC REG;	
21	MODEL Y = X/P CLI;	Regression analysis/prediction intervals
22	ID X;	
23	PROC CORR;	Correlation analysis
24	VAR X Y;	

COMMAND 20   The REG procedure fits linear models.

COMMAND 21   In the MODEL statement, the dependent variable is listed to the left of the equals sign and the independent variable to the right. The option P (following the slash) prints predicted values and residuals, and the option CLI prints corresponding lower and upper 95% prediction limits for all observations in the data set. Specify CLM to obtain 95% confidence intervals for $E(y)$. [Note: To predict y for a value of x that is not included in the data set (e.g., $x = 3.5$), you must include an "extra" observation in the data set. This observation has the specified value of x (e.g., 3.5), but a missing value for y (i.e., a single decimal point) as shown in line 19 of the SAS program.]

COMMANDS 23–24   The CORR procedure calculates the correlation coefficient between the variables specified in the VAR statement. The observed significance level for a test of 0 correlation in the population is also produced.

NOTE   The output for the SAS program is displayed in Figure 11.17.

FIGURE 11.17 ▶

SAS output for Computer Lab

Model: MODEL1
Dependent Variable: Y

Analysis of Variance

Source	DF	Sum of Squares	Mean Square	F Value	Prob>F
Model	1	841.76636	841.76636	156.886	0.0001
Error	13	69.75098	5.36546		
C Total	14	911.51733			

Root MSE	2.31635	R-square	0.9235
Dep Mean	26.41333	Adj R-sq	0.9176
C.V.	8.76961		

Parameter Estimates

Variable	DF	Parameter Estimate	Standard Error	T for H0: Parameter=0	Prob > |T|
INTERCEP	1	10.277929	1.42027781	7.237	0.0001
X	1	4.919331	0.39274775	12.525	0.0001

Obs	X	Dep Var Y	Predict Value	Std Err Predict	Lower95% Predict	Upper95% Predict	Residual
1	3.4	26.2000	27.0037	0.600	21.8344	32.1729	-0.8037
2	1.8	17.8000	19.1327	0.834	13.8141	24.4514	-1.3327
3	4.6	31.3000	32.9068	0.791	27.6186	38.1951	-1.6068
4	2.3	23.1000	21.5924	0.711	16.3577	26.8271	1.5076
5	3.1	27.5000	25.5279	0.602	20.3573	30.6984	1.9721
6	5.5	36.0000	37.3342	1.057	31.8334	42.8351	-1.3342
7	0.7	14.1000	13.7215	1.177	8.1087	19.3342	0.3785
8	3	22.3000	25.0359	0.608	19.8622	30.2097	-2.7359
9	2.6	19.6000	23.0682	0.655	17.8678	28.2686	-3.4682
10	4.3	31.3000	31.4311	0.720	26.1908	36.6713	-0.1311
11	2.1	24.0000	20.6085	0.757	15.3442	25.8729	3.3915
12	1.1	17.3000	15.6892	1.044	10.1999	21.1785	1.6108
13	6.1	43.2000	40.2858	1.259	34.5906	45.9811	2.9142
14	4.8	36.4000	33.8907	0.845	28.5640	39.2175	2.5093
15	3.8	26.1000	28.9714	0.632	23.7843	34.1585	-2.8714
16	3.5	.	27.4956	0.604	22.3239	32.6672	.

Sum of Residuals	-4.44089E-14
Sum of Squared Residuals	69.7510
Predicted Resid SS (Press)	93.2117

Pearson Correlation Coefficients / Prob > \|R\| under Ho: Rho=0
/ Number of Observations

	X	Y
X	1.00000	0.96098
	0.0	0.0001
	16	15
Y	0.96098	1.00000
	0.0001	0.0
	15	15

MINITAB

Command
line

1	READ X IN C1, Y in C2	Data entry instructions
2	3.4 26.2	
3	1.8 17.8	
	. .	Input data values
	: :	(1 observation per line)
	. .	
16	3.8 26.1	
17	NAME C1='Y' C2='X'	
18	REGRESS C2, USING 1 PREDICTOR C1;	Regression analysis
19	PREDICT 3.5.	
20	CORRELATION C1 C2	Correlation analysis

COMMAND 18   The REGRESS command fits linear models. The column number of the dependent variable is listed first, followed by the number of predictors in the model (1 for simple linear regression) and the column where the independent variable is located.

COMMAND 19   The PREDICT subcommand calculates the predicted value and corresponding 95% confidence and prediction intervals for the value of x specified.

COMMAND 20   The CORRELATION command computes the coefficient of correlation between the variables in the columns listed. [Note: MINITAB does not compute p-values for a test of 0 correlation in the population.]

NOTE   The output for the MINITAB program is displayed in Figure 11.18.

FIGURE 11.18 ▶
MINITAB output for Computer Lab

```
The regression equation is
X = 10.3 + 4.92 Y

Predictor       Coef       Stdev      t-ratio        p
Constant      10.278       1.420         7.24    0.000
Y             4.9193       0.3927       12.53    0.000

s = 2.316      R-sq = 92.3%      R-sq(adj) = 91.8%

Analysis of Variance

SOURCE        DF         SS          MS         F        p
Regression     1     841.77      841.77    156.89    0.000
Error         13      69.75        5.37
Total         14     911.52


      Fit   Stdev.Fit       95% C.I.           95% P.I.
   27.496       0.604   ( 26.190, 28.801)  ( 22.323, 32.669)


Correlation of Y and X = 0.961
```

References

Draper, N., and Smith, H. *Applied Regression Analysis,* 3rd ed. New York: Wiley, 1987.

Mendenhall, W., and Sincich, T. *A Second Course in Business Statistics: Regression Analysis,* 4th ed. New York: Macmillan, 1993.

Neter, J., Wasserman, W., and Kutner, M. H. *Applied Linear Statistical Models,* 2nd ed. Homewood, Ill.: Richard D. Irwin, 1988.

CHAPTER TWELVE

Multiple Regression Analysis

Objective

To extend the methods of Chapter 11 to develop a procedure for predicting a response y based on the values of two or more independent variables; to illustrate the types of practical inferences that can be drawn from this type of analysis

Contents

12.1   General Linear Models

The models for a **multiple regression analysis** are similar to the simple linear regression models except that they contain more terms and can be used to propose relationships more complex than a straight line. For example, suppose we think that the mean time $E(y)$ required to perform a data-processing job increases as the computer utilization increases and that the relationship is curvilinear. Instead of using the **straight-line model**, $E(y) = \beta_0 + \beta_1 x_1$, to model the deterministic component, we might use the **quadratic model**

$$E(y) = \beta_0 + \beta_1 x_1 + \beta_2 x_1^2$$

where x_1 is a variable that measures computer utilization. A quadratic model, often referred to as a **second-order model**, graphs as a parabola and allows for some curvature in the relationship (see Figure 12.1), in contrast to a straight-line or **first-order model**.

FIGURE 12.1 ▶

Graph of a second-order model

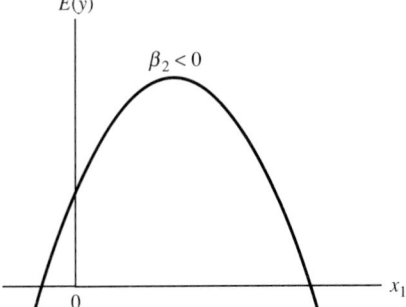

If, in addition, we think that the mean time required to process a job is also related to the size x_2 of the job, we could include x_2 in the model. A graph of $E(y)$ as a function of x_1 and x_2 traces a surface (called a **response surface**) over the (x_1, x_2)-plane. For example, the first-order model

$$E(y) = \beta_0 + \beta_1 x_1 + \beta_2 x_2$$

traces a planar surface over the (x_1, x_2)-plane (see Figure 12.2).

For our example (and for most real-life applications), we would expect curvature in the response surface and would use a second-order model

$$E(y) = \beta_0 + \beta_1 x_1 + \beta_2 x_2 + \beta_3 x_1 x_2 + \beta_4 x_1^2 + \beta_5 x_2^2$$

to model the relationship. A graph of a typical second-order response surface is shown in Figure 12.3.

All the models that we have written so far are called **general linear models** because $E(y)$ is a linear function of the unknown parameters, $\beta_0, \beta_1, \beta_2, \ldots$. The model

$$E(y) = \beta_0 e^{-\beta_1 x}$$

is *not* a linear model because $E(y)$ is not a *linear* function of the unknown model parameters, β_0 and β_1.

FIGURE 12.2 ▶
A response surface for two
quantitative independent variables

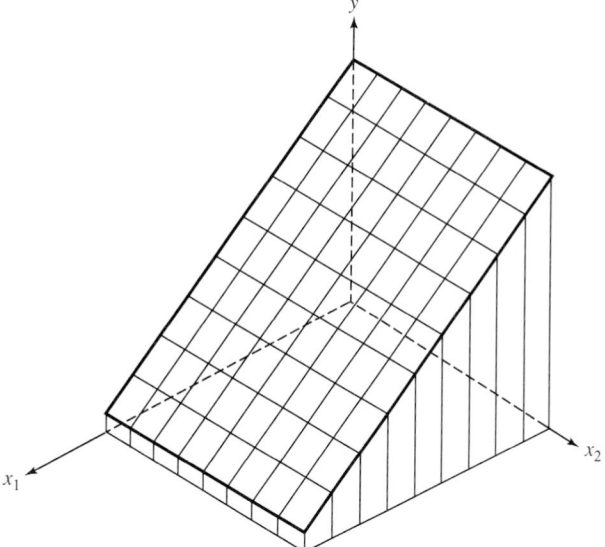

FIGURE 12.3 ▶
Graph of a second-order response
surface

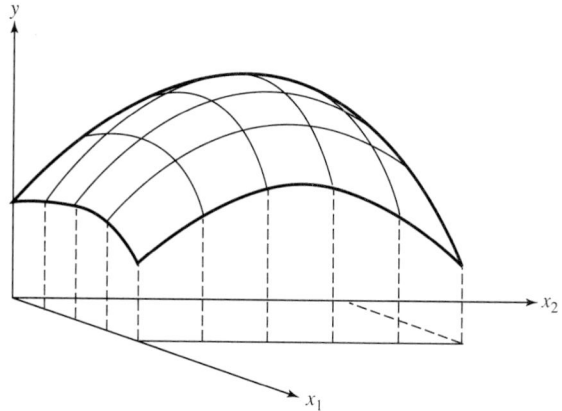

The independent variables that measure computer utilization (x_1) and size of job (x_2) are both quantitative variables—i.e., they measure the amount or quantity of something. We can also enter qualitative (nonquantitative) independent variables into the model. For example, suppose we expect the mean length of time required to process a job to be related to the day of the week that the job is processed. The qualitative independent variable, day of the week, can be entered into the model using **dummy** (or **index**) **variables**. Neglecting other terms (those corresponding to the quantitative independent variables) in the model, we would write

$$E(y) = \beta_0 + \beta_1 x_1 + \beta_2 x_2 + \beta_3 x_3 + \beta_4 x_4 + \beta_5 x_5 + \beta_6 x_6$$

where

$$x_1 = \begin{cases} 1 & \text{if the observation is made on Sunday} \\ 0 & \text{if not} \end{cases}$$

$$x_2 = \begin{cases} 1 & \text{if the observation is made on Monday} \\ 0 & \text{if not} \end{cases}$$

$$\vdots$$

$$x_6 = \begin{cases} 1 & \text{if the observation is made on Friday} \\ 0 & \text{if not} \end{cases}$$

The dummy variables enter the appropriate β parameter (which may be positive or negative), depending on the day of the week. Thus, on Sunday, $x_1 = 1$, $x_2 = x_3 = \cdots = x_6 = 0$ and the mean value of y is

$$E(y) = \beta_0 + \beta_1(1) = \beta_0 + \beta_1$$

Similarly, the mean value of y for Friday is

$$E(y) = \beta_0 + \beta_6$$

All of the dummy variables are assigned a value equal to 0 when an observation is made on Saturday. The mean value of y for Saturday is

$$E(y) = \beta_0$$

In general, qualitative variables are entered into a model using dummy variables—one fewer than the number of levels that the qualitative variable may assume. (We will have more to say about dummy variables in Chapter 13.)

Selecting an appropriate regression model for a particular situation is very important. If you try to fit a straight line (simple linear regression model) through a set of data points that plot as a curve, you will obtain a poor fit to the data. No statistical methods will compensate for poor model selection. We will defer further discussion of model construction until Chapter 13. In this chapter, we will assume that you have selected a reasonable model for your situation and will concentrate on the procedure for fitting the model to a set of data and on the associated methods of statistical inference.

Once a linear model has been chosen to relate $E(y)$ to a set of independent variables, the steps of a multiple regression analysis parallel those of a simple regression analysis. The only differences are that the mathematical theory is beyond the scope of this text and the computations are considerably more complex. In the following sections, we will summarize the assumptions underlying a multiple regression analysis, present the methods for estimating and testing hypotheses about the model parameters, and show how to find a confidence interval for $E(y)$ or a prediction interval for y for specific values of the independent variables. Since most multiple regression analyses are performed on a computer, we will demonstrate how to interpret the output produced by SAS and MINITAB.

12.2   Model Assumptions

After we have selected the deterministic portion of a regression model—i.e., a model for $E(y)$—we add a component ε to compensate for random error.

$$y = E(y) + \varepsilon$$

This component must obey the assumptions of the simple linear regression model—namely, that it is normally distributed with mean 0 and variance equal to σ^2. Further, we assume that the random errors associated with any pair of y values are independent.

To present formulas for the parameter estimates, we need to write $E(y)$ in a standard form. Thus, we will let

$$E(y) = \beta_0 + \beta_1 x_1 + \beta_2 x_2 + \cdots + \beta_k x_k$$

be the deterministic component of the model containing β_0 and k terms involving the predictor variables. The x values that appear in the model are those of Section 12.1. For example, x_2 could be x_1^2, x_3 could be $\sin(x_1)$, etc. *The essential points are that the quantities $x_1, x_2, \ldots, x_k$ can be measured without error when a value of y is observed and that they do not involve any unknown parameters.*

The linear regression model and associated assumptions are summarized in the box. In Section 12.11, we discuss how to use regression **residuals** to determine whether these assumptions are satisfied; a residual is the difference between the observed and predicted value of y (i.e., $y - \hat{y}$).

Assumptions for a Multiple Regression Analysis

1. The mean of ε is 0, i.e., $E(\varepsilon) = 0$. This implies that the mean of y is equivalent to the deterministic component of the model, i.e.,

$$E(y) = \beta_0 + \beta_1 x_1 + \beta_2 x_2 + \cdots + \beta_k x_k$$

2. For all settings of the independent variables $x_1, x_2, \ldots, x_k$, the variance of ε is constant.

3. The probability distribution of ε is normal.

4. The random errors are independent (in a probabilistic sense).

12.3   Fitting the Model: The Method of Least Squares

The method of fitting a multiple regression model is identical to that of fitting the first-order (straight-line) model. Thus, we will use the method of least squares and choose estimates of $\beta_0, \beta_1, \ldots, \beta_k$ that minimize

$$\text{SSE} = \sum_{i=1}^{n} (y_i - \hat{y}_i)^2 = \sum_{i=1}^{n} [y_i - (\hat{\beta}_0 + \hat{\beta}_1 x_{i1} + \hat{\beta}_2 x_{i2} + \cdots + \hat{\beta}_k x_{ik})]^2$$

As in the case of the straight-line model, the sample estimates $(\hat{\beta}_0, \hat{\beta}_1, \ldots, \hat{\beta}_k)$ that minimize SSE will be obtained as solutions to the system of simultaneous linear equations

$$\frac{\partial \text{SSE}}{\partial \hat{\beta}_0} = 0 \qquad \frac{\partial \text{SSE}}{\partial \hat{\beta}_1} = 0 \qquad \cdots \qquad \frac{\partial \text{SSE}}{\partial \hat{\beta}_k} = 0$$

To illustrate the nature of this system, we will examine the first equation. Taking the partial derivative of SSE with respect to $\hat{\beta}_0$, we obtain

$$\frac{\partial \text{SSE}}{\partial \hat{\beta}_0} = 2 \sum_{i=1}^{n} [y_i - (\hat{\beta}_0 + \hat{\beta}_1 x_{i1} + \hat{\beta}_2 x_{i2} + \cdots + \hat{\beta}_k x_{ik})] (-1)$$

Setting $\partial \text{SSE}/\partial \hat{\beta}_0$ equal to 0 yields

$$\sum y_i - \left(n\hat{\beta}_0 + \sum x_{i1} \hat{\beta}_1 + \sum x_{i2} \hat{\beta}_2 + \cdots + \sum x_{ik} \hat{\beta}_k \right) = 0$$

or

$$n\hat{\beta}_0 + \left(\sum x_{i1} \right) \hat{\beta}_1 + \left(\sum x_{i2} \right) \hat{\beta}_2 + \cdots + \left(\sum x_{ik} \right) \hat{\beta}_k = \sum y_i$$

As in the case of simple linear regression, this is a linear equation in $\hat{\beta}_0, \hat{\beta}_1, \ldots, \hat{\beta}_k$. The k remaining least squares equations, all linear equations in $\hat{\beta}_0, \hat{\beta}_1, \ldots, \hat{\beta}_k$, are

$$\left(\sum x_{i1} \right) \hat{\beta}_0 + \left(\sum x_{i1} \right)^2 \hat{\beta}_1 + \left(\sum x_{i1} x_{i2} \right) \hat{\beta}_2 + \cdots + \left(\sum x_{i1} x_{ik} \right) \hat{\beta}_k = \sum x_{i1} y_i$$

$$\left(\sum x_{i2} \right) \hat{\beta}_0 + \left(\sum x_{i1} x_{i2} \right) \hat{\beta}_1 + \left(\sum x_{i2} \right)^2 \hat{\beta}_2 + \cdots + \left(\sum x_{i2} x_{ik} \right) \hat{\beta}_k = \sum x_{i2} y_i$$

$$\vdots \qquad \qquad \vdots \qquad \qquad \qquad \qquad \vdots \qquad \qquad \vdots$$

$$\left(\sum x_{ik} \right) \hat{\beta}_0 + \left(\sum x_{i1} x_{ik} \right) \hat{\beta}_1 + \qquad \cdots \qquad + \left(\sum x_{ik} \right)^2 \hat{\beta}_k = \sum x_{ik} y_i$$

As you can see, writing the $(k + 1)$ least squares linear equations is a task; solving them simultaneously by hand is even more difficult. An easy way to express the equations and to solve them is to use matrix algebra, but the inevitable computations are best performed on a computer.

In the following sections, we use matrix algebra to give formulas for the least squares estimates, SSE, test statistics, confidence intervals, and prediction intervals. Their use will be illustrated with simple numerical examples. (You may want to review the concepts in Appendix I, Matrix Algebra, before reading the remainder of this chapter.) To conclude, we will examine and interpret the multiple regression computer printouts for the SAS and MINITAB software packages.

12.4 The Least Squares Equations and Their Solution

To apply matrix algebra to a regression analysis, we must place the data in matrices in a particular pattern. We will suppose that the model is

$$y = \beta_0 + \beta_1 x_1 + \beta_2 x_2 + \cdots + \beta_k x_k + \varepsilon$$

where $x_1, x_2, \ldots$ could actually represent the squares, cubes, cross products, or other functions of predictor variables, and ε is a random error. We will assume that we have collected n data points, i.e., n values of y and corresponding values of $x_1, x_2, \ldots, x_k$, and that these are denoted as shown in Table 12.1. Then the two data matrices Y and X are as shown in the box.

Notice that the first column in the X matrix is a column of 1's. Thus, we are inserting a value of x, namely, x_0, as the coefficient of β_0, where x_0 is a variable always equal to 1. Therefore, there is one column in the X matrix for each β parameter. Also, remember that a particular data point is identified by specific rows of the Y and X matrices. For example, the y value y_3 for data point 3 is in the third row of the Y matrix, and the corresponding values of $x_1, x_2, \ldots, x_k$ appear in the third row of the X matrix. Using this notation, the general linear model can be expressed in matrix form as

$$Y = X\beta + \varepsilon$$

TABLE 12.1 Notation for Multiple Regression

Data Point	y-value	x_1	x_2	$\cdots$	x_k	Unobservable Random Error
1	y_1	x_{11}	x_{12}	$\cdots$	x_{1k}	ε_1
2	y_2	x_{21}	x_{22}	$\cdots$	x_{2k}	ε_2
$\vdots$	$\vdots$	$\vdots$	$\vdots$		$\vdots$	$\vdots$
n	y_n	x_{n1}	x_{n2}	$\cdots$	x_{nk}	ε_n

The Data Matrices Y and X, the $\hat{\beta}$ Matrix, and the Error Matrix

$$Y = \begin{bmatrix} y_1 \\ y_2 \\ y_3 \\ \vdots \\ y_n \end{bmatrix} \quad X = \begin{bmatrix} 1 & x_{11} & x_{12} & \cdots & x_{1k} \\ 1 & x_{21} & x_{22} & \cdots & x_{2k} \\ 1 & x_{31} & x_{32} & \cdots & x_{3k} \\ \vdots & \vdots & \vdots & & \vdots \\ 1 & x_{n1} & x_{n2} & \cdots & x_{nk} \end{bmatrix} \quad \hat{\beta} = \begin{bmatrix} \hat{\beta}_0 \\ \hat{\beta}_1 \\ \hat{\beta}_2 \\ \vdots \\ \hat{\beta}_k \end{bmatrix} \quad \varepsilon = \begin{bmatrix} \varepsilon_1 \\ \varepsilon_2 \\ \varepsilon_3 \\ \vdots \\ \varepsilon_n \end{bmatrix}$$

(continued)

The $\hat{\boldsymbol{\beta}}$ matrix shown in the box contains the least squares estimates (which we are attempting to obtain) of the coefficients $\beta_0, \beta_1, \ldots, \beta_k$ of the linear model

$$y = \beta_0 + \beta_1 x_1 + \beta_2 x_2 + \cdots + \beta_k x_k + \varepsilon$$

Using the $\boldsymbol{Y}$ and $\boldsymbol{X}$ data matrices, their transposes, and the $\hat{\boldsymbol{\beta}}$ matrix, we can write the least squares equations as:

Least Squares Matrix Equation

$$(\boldsymbol{X'X})\hat{\boldsymbol{\beta}} = \boldsymbol{X'Y}$$

Thus, $(\boldsymbol{X'X})$ is the coefficient matrix of the least squares estimates $\hat{\beta}_0, \hat{\beta}_1, \ldots, \hat{\beta}_k$, and $\boldsymbol{X'Y}$ gives the matrix of constants that appear on the right-hand side of the equality signs.

The solution, which follows from Appendix I.3,* is

Least Squares Solution

$$\hat{\boldsymbol{\beta}} = (\boldsymbol{X'X})^{-1}\boldsymbol{X'Y}$$

Thus, to solve the least squares matrix equation, the computer calculates $(\boldsymbol{X'X})$, $(\boldsymbol{X'X})^{-1}$, $\boldsymbol{X'Y}$, and, finally, the product $(\boldsymbol{X'X})^{-1}\boldsymbol{X'Y}$. We will illustrate this process using the data for the insulation compression example from Section 11.2.

EXAMPLE 12.1

Find the least squares line for the insulation compression data repeated in Table 12.2.

Solution

The model is

$$y = \beta_0 + \beta_1 x_1 + \varepsilon$$

and the $\boldsymbol{Y}$, $\boldsymbol{X}$, $\hat{\boldsymbol{\beta}}$, and $\boldsymbol{\varepsilon}$ matrices are

$$Y = \begin{bmatrix} 1 \\ 1 \\ 2 \\ 2 \\ 4 \end{bmatrix} \qquad X = \begin{bmatrix} 1 & 1 \\ 1 & 2 \\ 1 & 3 \\ 1 & 4 \\ 1 & 5 \end{bmatrix} \qquad \hat{\boldsymbol{\beta}} = \begin{bmatrix} \hat{\beta}_0 \\ \hat{\beta}_1 \end{bmatrix} \qquad \boldsymbol{\varepsilon} = \begin{bmatrix} \varepsilon_1 \\ \varepsilon_2 \\ \varepsilon_3 \\ \varepsilon_4 \\ \varepsilon_5 \end{bmatrix}$$

(with column labels $x_0\ x_1$ over the X matrix)

---

*In the notation of Appendix I.3, $A = X'X$, $V = \hat{\boldsymbol{\beta}}$, and $G = X'Y$. Then the solution to the equation $AV = G$ is $V = A^{-1}G$.

TABLE 12.2 Compression Versus Pressure for an Insulation Material

Specimen	Pressure	Compression
	x	y
1	1	1
2	2	1
3	3	2
4	4	2
5	5	4

Then,

$$X'X = \begin{bmatrix} 1 & 1 & 1 & 1 & 1 \\ 1 & 2 & 3 & 4 & 5 \end{bmatrix} \begin{bmatrix} 1 & 1 \\ 1 & 2 \\ 1 & 3 \\ 1 & 4 \\ 1 & 5 \end{bmatrix} = \begin{bmatrix} 5 & 15 \\ 15 & 55 \end{bmatrix}$$

$$X'Y = \begin{bmatrix} 1 & 1 & 1 & 1 & 1 \\ 1 & 2 & 3 & 4 & 5 \end{bmatrix} \begin{bmatrix} 1 \\ 1 \\ 2 \\ 2 \\ 4 \end{bmatrix} = \begin{bmatrix} 10 \\ 37 \end{bmatrix}$$

The last matrix that we need is $(X'X)^{-1}$. This matrix can be found by using a packaged computer program or by using the method of Appendix I.4. Thus, you would find

$$(X'X)^{-1} = \begin{bmatrix} 1.1 & -.3 \\ -.3 & .1 \end{bmatrix}$$

Then the solution to the least squares equation is

$$\hat{\beta} = (X'X)^{-1}X'Y = \begin{bmatrix} 1.1 & -.3 \\ -.3 & .1 \end{bmatrix} \begin{bmatrix} 10 \\ 37 \end{bmatrix} = \begin{bmatrix} -.1 \\ .7 \end{bmatrix}$$

Thus, $\hat{\beta}_0 = -.1$, $\hat{\beta}_1 = .7$, and the prediction equation is

$$\hat{y} = -.1 + .7x$$

You can verify that this is the same answer as obtained in Section 11.3.

EXAMPLE 12.2

An electrical utility company wants to predict the monthly power usage of a home as a function of the size x of the home based on the model

$$y = \beta_0 + \beta_1 x + \beta_2 x^2 + \varepsilon$$

Find the least squares estimates of β_0, β_1, and β_2. The data are shown in Table 12.3.

TABLE 12.3 Data for Power Usage Study	
Size of Home	Monthly Usage
x, square feet	y, kilowatt-hours
1,290	1,182
1,350	1,172
1,470	1,264
1,600	1,493
1,710	1,571
1,840	1,711
1,980	1,804
2,230	1,840
2,400	1,956
2,930	1,954

Solution

The Y, X, and $\hat{\boldsymbol{\beta}}$ matrices are shown here:

$$
Y = \begin{bmatrix} 1,182 \\ 1,172 \\ 1,264 \\ 1,493 \\ 1,571 \\ 1,711 \\ 1,804 \\ 1,840 \\ 1,956 \\ 1,954 \end{bmatrix}
\qquad
X = \begin{matrix}
x_0 & x & x^2 \\
\begin{bmatrix} 1 & 1,290 & 1,664,100 \\ 1 & 1,350 & 1,822,500 \\ 1 & 1,470 & 2,160,900 \\ 1 & 1,600 & 2,560,000 \\ 1 & 1,710 & 2,924,100 \\ 1 & 1,840 & 3,385,600 \\ 1 & 1,980 & 3,920,400 \\ 1 & 2,230 & 4,972,900 \\ 1 & 2,400 & 5,760,000 \\ 1 & 2,930 & 8,584,900 \end{bmatrix}
\end{matrix}
$$

Then:

$$
X'X = \begin{bmatrix}
10 & 18,800 & 37,755,400 \\
18,800 & 37,755,400 & 8,093.9 \times 10^7 \\
37,755,400 & 8,093.9 \times 10^7 & 1.843 \times 10^{14}
\end{bmatrix}
$$

$$
X'Y = \begin{bmatrix}
15,947 \\
31,283,250 \\
6.53069 \times 10^{10}
\end{bmatrix}
$$

And, using a standard computer package, we obtain

$$(X'X)^{-1} = \begin{bmatrix} 26.9156 & -.027027 & 6.3554 \times 10^{-6} \\ -.027027 & 2.75914 \times 10^{-5} & -6.5804 \times 10^{-9} \\ 6.3554 \times 10^{-6} & -6.5804 \times 10^{-9} & 1.5934 \times 10^{-12} \end{bmatrix}$$

Finally, performing the multiplication, we obtain

$$\hat{\boldsymbol{\beta}} = (X'X)^{-1}X'Y$$

$$= \begin{bmatrix} 26.9156 & -.027027 & 6.3554 \times 10^{-6} \\ -.027027 & 2.75914 \times 10^{-5} & -6.5804 \times 10^{-9} \\ 6.3554 \times 10^{-6} & -6.5804 \times 10^{-9} & 1.5934 \times 10^{-12} \end{bmatrix} \begin{bmatrix} 15.947 \\ 31,283,250 \\ 6.53069 \times 10^{10} \end{bmatrix}$$

$$= \begin{bmatrix} -1,216.14389 \\ 2.39893 \\ -.00045 \end{bmatrix}$$

Thus, $\hat{\beta}_0 = -1,216.14389$, $\hat{\beta}_1 = 2.39893$, $\hat{\beta}_2 = -.00045$, and the prediction equation is

$$\hat{y} = -1,216.14389 + 2.39893x - .00045x^2$$

EXERCISES

12.1 Use the method of least squares to fit the model $E(y) = \beta_0 + \beta_1 x$ to the six data points given in the accompanying table.

x	1	2	3	4	5	6
y	1	2	2	3	5	5

a. Construct Y and X matrices for the data.
b. Find $X'X$ and $X'Y$.
c. Verify that

$$(X'X)^{-1} = \begin{bmatrix} \frac{13}{15} & -\frac{7}{35} \\ -\frac{7}{35} & \frac{2}{35} \end{bmatrix}$$

d. Find the $\hat{\boldsymbol{\beta}}$ matrix.
e. Give the prediction equation.

12.2 An experiment was conducted in which two y observations were collected for each of five values of x, as listed in the table. Use the method of least squares to fit the second-order model, $E(y) = \beta_0 + \beta_1 x + \beta_2 x^2$, to the 10 data points.

x	-2		-1		0		1		2	
y	1.1	1.3	2.0	2.1	2.7	2.8	3.4	3.6	4.1	4.0

a. Give the dimensions of the Y and X matrices.

b. Verify that

$$(X'X)^{-1} = \begin{bmatrix} \frac{17}{70} & 0 & -\frac{1}{14} \\ 0 & \frac{1}{20} & 0 \\ -\frac{1}{14} & 0 & \frac{1}{28} \end{bmatrix}$$

c. Find the $\hat{\boldsymbol{\beta}}$ matrix and the least squares prediction equation.

d. Plot the data points and graph the prediction equation.

12.3 Refer to the *Journal of Engineering for Industry* study of vehicle congestion in an automated warehouse, Exercise 11.6. The data on number of vehicles (x) and congestion time (y) are reproduced here. Consider the straight-line model $E(y) = \beta_0 + \beta_1 x$.

Number of Vehicles	Congestion Time minutes, hundredths	Number of Vehicles	Congestion Time minutes, hundredths
1	0	9	2
2	0	10	4
3	2	11	4
4	1	12	4
5	1	13	3
6	1	14	4
7	3	15	5
8	3		

Source: Pandit, R., and U. S. Palekar, "Response time considerations for optimal warehouse layout design." *Journal of Engineering for Industry*, Transactions of the ASME, Vol. 115, Aug. 1993, p. 326 (Table 2).

a. Construct Y and X matrices for the data.

b. Find $X'X$ and $X'Y$.

c. Find the least squares estimates $\hat{\boldsymbol{\beta}} = (X'X)^{-1}X'Y$. [*Note:* See Theorem I.1 in Appendix I for information on finding $(X'X)^{-1}$.]

d. Give the prediction equation.

12.4 A study was conducted to examine the relationship between the cast structure and the mechanical properties of equiaxed grains in unidirectionally solidified ingots (*Metallurgical Transactions*, May 1986). Ingots composed of aluminum, copper, and titanium alloys (the equiaxed structure) were poured into molds and cooled by water until solidification. From each ingot, five tensile specimens were obtained at varying distances from the ingot chill face, and the grain size (i.e., number of grains) was determined for each specimen. The data for one such ingot are given in the table at the top of the next page. Suppose we are interested in fitting the quadratic model

$$y = \beta_0 + \beta_1 x + \beta_2 x^2 + \varepsilon$$

where

y = Grain size
x = Distance from chill face

Distance from Chill Face x, cm	Grain Size y, mm
1.0	.24
3.5	.38
6.0	.44
8.5	.61
11.0	.75

Source: Kato, H., and Cahoon, J. R. "Tensile properties of directionally solidified Al-4 wt pct Cu alloys with columnar and equiaxed grains." *Metallurgical Transactions*, Vol. 17A, No. 5, May 1986, p. 830 (Table II).

a. Construct Y and X matrices for the data.
b. Find $X'X$ and $X'Y$.
c. Use the technique outlined in Appendix I.4 to find $(X'X)^{-1}$. (Be sure to carry out your calculations to six significant digits.)
d. Find the $\hat{\beta}$ matrix and the least squares prediction equation.
e. Plot the data points and graph the prediction equation.

12.5 Poly (perfluoropropyleneoxide), i.e., PPFPO, is a viscous liquid used extensively in the electronics industry as a lubricant. In a study reported in *Applied Spectroscopy* (Jan. 1986), the infrared reflectance spectra properties of PPFPO were examined. The optical density (y) for the prominent infrared absorption of PPFPO was recorded for different experimental settings of band frequency (x_1) and film thickness (x_2) in a Perkin–Elmer Model 621 infrared spectrometer. The results are given in the accompanying table. Consider the first-order model

$$E(y) = \beta_0 + \beta_1 x_1 + \beta_2 x_2$$

Optical Density y	Band Frequency x_1, cm^{-1}	Film Thickness x_2, milligrams
.231	740	1.1
.107	740	.62
.053	740	.31
.129	805	1.1
.069	805	.62
.030	805	.31
1.005	980	1.1
.559	980	.62
.321	980	.31
2.948	1,235	1.1
1.633	1,235	.62
.934	1,235	.31

Source: Pacansky, J., England, C. D., and Waltman, R. "Infrared spectroscopic studies of poly (perfluoropropyleneoxide) on gold substrates: A classical dispersion analysis for the refractive index." *Applied Spectroscopy*, Vol. 40, No. 1, Jan. 1986, p. 9 (Table I).

a. Construct Y and X matrices for the data.

b. Find $X'X$ and $X'Y$.

c. Use the technique outlined in Appendix I.4 to find $(X'X)^{-1}$. (Be sure to carry out your calculations to six significant digits.)

d. Find the $\hat{\boldsymbol{\beta}}$ matrix and the least squares prediction equation.

12.5   Properties of the Least Squares Estimators

In Section 12.4, we noted that the $\hat{\boldsymbol{\beta}}$ matrix is equal to the product of the $(X'X)^{-1}X'$ matrix and the Y matrix:

$$\hat{\boldsymbol{\beta}} = [(X'X)^{-1}X']Y$$

Since elements in the $\hat{\boldsymbol{\beta}}$ matrix (i.e., the estimators $\hat{\beta}_0, \hat{\beta}_1, \ldots, \hat{\beta}_k$) are obtained by multiplying the rows of $(X'X)^{-1}X'$ by the column matrix Y, it follows that $\hat{\beta}_0$ will equal the product of the first row of $(X'X)^{-1}X'$ and the Y matrix and, in general, $\hat{\beta}_i$ will equal the product of the $(i + 1)$st row of $(X'X)^{-1}X'$ and Y. Therefore, for $i = 0, 1, 2, \ldots, k$, $\hat{\beta}_i$ is a linear function of n normally distributed random variables, $y_1, y_2, \ldots, y_n$, and, by Theorem 7.3, $\hat{\beta}_i$ possesses a normal sampling distribution.

Derivation of the means and variances of the sampling distributions of $\hat{\beta}_0, \hat{\beta}_1, \ldots, \hat{\beta}_k$ is beyond the scope of this text. However, it can be shown that the least squares estimators provide unbiased estimates of $\beta_0, \beta_1, \ldots, \beta_k$, i.e.,

$$E(\hat{\beta}_i) = \beta_i \quad \text{for } i = 0, 1, 2, \ldots, k$$

The standard errors and covariances of the estimators $\hat{\beta}_0, \hat{\beta}_1, \ldots, \hat{\beta}_k$, are determined by the elements of the $(X'X)^{-1}$ matrix. Thus, if we denote the $(X'X)^{-1}$ matrix as

$$(X'X)^{-1} = \begin{bmatrix} c_{00} & c_{01} & \cdots & c_{0k} \\ c_{10} & c_{11} & \cdots & c_{1k} \\ c_{20} & c_{21} & c_{22} & \cdots & c_{2k} \\ \vdots & \vdots & \vdots & & \vdots \\ c_{k0} & \cdot & \cdot & \cdot & c_{kk} \end{bmatrix}$$

then it can be shown (proof omitted) that the standard errors of the sampling distributions of $\hat{\beta}_0, \hat{\beta}_1, \ldots, \hat{\beta}_k$ are

$$\sigma_{\hat{\beta}_0} = \sigma\sqrt{c_{00}}$$
$$\sigma_{\hat{\beta}_1} = \sigma\sqrt{c_{11}}$$
$$\sigma_{\hat{\beta}_2} = \sigma\sqrt{c_{22}}$$
$$\vdots$$
$$\sigma_{\hat{\beta}_k} = \sigma\sqrt{c_{kk}}$$

where σ is the standard deviation of the random error ε. In other words, the diagonal elements of $(X'X)^{-1}$ give the values of $c_{00}, c_{11}, \ldots, c_{kk}$ that are required for finding the standard errors of the estimators $\hat{\beta}_0, \hat{\beta}_1, \ldots, \hat{\beta}_k$.

The properties of the sampling distributions of the least squares estimators are summarized in the box.

Theorem 12.1

Properties of the Sampling Distribution of $\hat{\beta}_i$ ($i = 0, 1, 2, \ldots, k$)

The sampling distribution of $\hat{\beta}_i$ ($i = 0, 1, 2, \ldots, k$) is normal with

$$E(\hat{\beta}_i) = \beta_i \qquad V(\hat{\beta}_i) = c_{ii}\sigma^2 \qquad \sigma_{\hat{\beta}_i} = \sigma\sqrt{c_{ii}}$$

The off-diagonal elements of the $(X'X)^{-1}$ matrix determine the covariances of $\hat{\beta}_0, \hat{\beta}_1, \ldots, \hat{\beta}_k$. Thus, it can be shown that the covariance of two parameter estimators, say $\hat{\beta}_i$ and $\hat{\beta}_j$ (where $i \neq j$), is equal to

$$\text{Cov}(\hat{\beta}_i, \hat{\beta}_j) = c_{ij}\sigma^2 = c_{ji}\sigma^2$$

For example, $\text{Cov}(\hat{\beta}_0, \hat{\beta}_2) = c_{02}\sigma^2 = c_{20}\sigma^2$ and $\text{Cov}(\hat{\beta}_2, \hat{\beta}_3) = c_{23}\sigma^2 = c_{32}\sigma^2$. These covariances are necessary to determine the variance of the prediction equation

$$\hat{y} = \hat{\beta}_0 + \hat{\beta}_1 x_1 + \hat{\beta}_2 x_2 + \cdots + \hat{\beta}_k x_k$$

or of any other linear function of $\hat{\beta}_0, \hat{\beta}_1, \ldots, \hat{\beta}_k$. They will also play a role in finding a confidence interval for $E(y)$ and a prediction interval for y in Sections 12.9 and 12.10.

12.6   Estimating σ^2, the Variance of ε

You will recall that the variances of the estimators of all of the β parameters and of $\hat{y}$ will depend on the value of σ^2, the variance of the random error ε that appears in the linear model. Since σ^2 will rarely be known in advance, we must use the sample data to estimate its value.

Estimator of σ^2, the Variance of ε in a Multiple Regression Model

$$s^2 = \frac{\text{SSE}}{n - \text{Number of } \beta \text{ parameters in model}}$$

where

$$\text{SSE} = Y'Y - \hat{\beta}'X'Y$$

We will demonstrate the use of these formulas with the insulation compression data of Example 12.1.

EXAMPLE 12.3

Find SSE for the insulation compression data of Example 12.1.

Solution

From Example 12.1 we have

$$\hat{\boldsymbol{\beta}} = \begin{bmatrix} -.1 \\ .7 \end{bmatrix} \quad \text{and} \quad \boldsymbol{X'Y} = \begin{bmatrix} 10 \\ 37 \end{bmatrix}$$

Then,

$$\boldsymbol{Y'Y} = \begin{bmatrix} 1 & 1 & 2 & 2 & 4 \end{bmatrix} \begin{bmatrix} 1 \\ 1 \\ 2 \\ 2 \\ 4 \end{bmatrix} = 26 \quad \text{and} \quad \hat{\boldsymbol{\beta}}'\boldsymbol{X'Y} = \begin{bmatrix} -.1 & .7 \end{bmatrix} \begin{bmatrix} 10 \\ 37 \end{bmatrix} = 24.9$$

So

$$\text{SSE} = \boldsymbol{Y'Y} - \hat{\boldsymbol{\beta}}'\boldsymbol{X'Y} = 26 - 24.9 = 1.1$$

(Note that this is the same answer as was obtained in Section 11.3.)

Finally,

$$s^2 = \frac{\text{SSE}}{n - \text{Number of } \beta \text{ parameters in model}} = \frac{1.1}{5 - 2} = .367$$

This estimate is needed to construct a confidence interval for β_1, to test a hypothesis concerning its value, or to construct a confidence interval for the mean compression $E(y)$ for a given compressive pressure x.

You will not be surprised to learn that the sampling distribution of s^2 is related to the chi-square distribution. In fact, Theorems 7.4 and 11.1 are special cases of Theorem 12.2 (proof omitted).

Using Theorem 12.2 we can show that s^2 is an unbiased estimator of σ^2:

$$E(s^2) = E\left\{\frac{\chi^2\sigma^2}{[n - (k + 1)]}\right\} = \frac{\sigma^2}{[n - (k + 1)]}E(\chi^2)$$

where $E(\chi^2) = \nu = [n - (k + 1)]$. Therefore,

$$E(s^2) = \left(\frac{\sigma^2}{[n - (k + 1)]}\right)[n - (k + 1)] = \sigma^2$$

and we conclude that s^2 is an unbiased estimator of σ^2.

Theorem 12.2

Consider the linear model

$$y = \beta_0 + \beta_1 x_1 + \beta_2 x_2 + \cdots + \beta_k x_k + \varepsilon$$

which contains $(k + 1)$ unknown β parameters that must be estimated. If the assumptions of Section 12.2 are satisfied, then the statistic

$$\chi^2 = \frac{SSE}{\sigma^2} = \frac{[n - (k + 1)]s^2}{\sigma^2}$$

has a chi-square distribution with $\nu = [n - (k + 1)]$ degrees of freedom.

12.7   Confidence Intervals and Tests of Hypotheses for $\beta_0, \beta_1, \ldots, \beta_k$

A $(1 - \alpha)100\%$ confidence interval for a model parameter β_i $(i = 0, 1, 2, \ldots, k)$ can be constructed (see the Optional Exercises of this section) using the pivotal method and the t statistic

$$t = \frac{\hat{\beta}_i - \beta_i}{s\sqrt{c_{ii}}}$$

The quantity $s\sqrt{c_{ii}}$ is the estimated standard error of $\hat{\beta}_i$ and is obtained by replacing σ by s in the formula for the standard error. The resulting confidence interval for β_i takes the same form as the small-sample confidence interval for a population mean given in Section 8.7.

A $(1 - \alpha)100\%$ Confidence Interval for β_i

$$\hat{\beta}_i \pm t_{\alpha/2}(\text{Estimated standard error of } \hat{\beta}_i)$$

or

$$\hat{\beta}_i \pm t_{\alpha/2}s\sqrt{c_{ii}}$$

where $t_{\alpha/2}$ is based on the number of degrees of freedom associated with s.

Similarly, the test statistic for testing the null hypothesis H_0: $\beta_i = 0$ is

$$t = \frac{\hat{\beta}_i}{\text{Estimated standard error of } \hat{\beta}_i} = \frac{\hat{\beta}_i}{s\sqrt{c_{ii}}}$$

The test is summarized in the following box.

Test of an Individual Parameter Coefficient in the Multiple Regression Model

$$y = \beta_0 + \beta_1 x_1 + \beta_2 x_2 + \cdots + \beta_k x_k + \varepsilon$$

One-Tailed Test

H_0: $\beta_i = 0$

H_a: $\beta_i > 0$
      (or $\beta_i < 0$)

Two-Tailed Test

H_0: $\beta_i = 0$

H_a: $\beta_i \neq 0$

Test statistic:* $t = \dfrac{\hat{\beta}_i}{s_{\hat{\beta}_i}} = \dfrac{\hat{\beta}_i}{s\sqrt{c_{ii}}}$

Rejection region: $t > t_\alpha$
      (or $t < -t_\alpha$)

Rejection region:
      $|t| > t_{\alpha/2}$

where

n = Number of observations

k = Number of independent variables in the model

and $t_{\alpha/2}$ is based on $[n - (k + 1)]$ df

Assumptions: See Section 12.2 for the assumptions about the probability distribution of the random error component ε.

Either the confidence interval or the test can be used to determine whether a term in the model contributes information for the prediction of y. We illustrate with examples.

EXAMPLE 12.4

Refer to Example 12.1; find the estimated standard error for the sampling distribution of $\hat{\beta}_1$, the estimator of the slope of the line β_1. Then give a 95% confidence interval for β_1 and interpret the result.

Solution

The $(X'X)^{-1}$ matrix for the least squares solution of Example 12.1 was

$$(X'X)^{-1} = \begin{bmatrix} 1.1 & -3 \\ -.3 & .1 \end{bmatrix}$$

Therefore, $c_{00} = 1.1$, $c_{11} = .1$, and the estimated standard error for $\hat{\beta}_1$ is

$$s_{\hat{\beta}_1} = s\sqrt{c_{11}} = \sqrt{.367}(\sqrt{.1}) = .192$$

---

*To test the null hypothesis that a parameter β_i equals some value other than zero, say H_0: $\beta_i = \beta_{i0}$, use the test statistic $t = (\hat{\beta}_i - \beta_{i0})/s_{\hat{\beta}_i}$. All other aspects of the test will be described in the box.

The value for s, $\sqrt{.367}$, was obtained from Example 12.3.

A 95% confidence interval for β_1 is

$$\hat{\beta}_1 \pm t_{\alpha/2}s\sqrt{c_{11}}$$
$$.7 \pm (3.182)(.192) = (.09, \ 1.31)$$

The t value, $t_{.025}$, is based on $(n - 2) = 3$ df. Observe that this is the same confidence interval as the one obtained in Example 11.5 (Section 11.6). With 95% confidence, we say that compression y will increase between .09 and 1.31 units for every 1-unit increase in pressure x. Since the slope is significantly different from 0, the implication is that pressure x is a useful linear predictor of compression y.

The SAS and MINITAB printouts for a multiple regression analysis are identical to the printouts for a simple linear regression analysis, except that they contain estimates, test statistic values, etc. for all parameters of the multiple regression model. In Example 12.5, we will present a computer printout for the multiple regression analysis for the power usage data of Example 12.2, and we will compare some of our computed values with those shown on the printout.

EXAMPLE 12.5

Refer to Example 12.2 and the least squares solution for fitting power usage y to the size of a home x using the model

$$y = \beta_0 + \beta_1 x + \beta_2 x^2 + \varepsilon$$

A SAS printout of the multiple regression analysis is shown in Figure 12.4.

a. Compute the estimated standard error for $\hat{\beta}_1$ and compare this result with the printout value shown in Figure 12.4.

FIGURE 12.4 ▶
SAS computer printout for the power usage data of Examples 12.2 and 12.5

Dependent Variable: Y

Analysis of Variance

Source	DF	Sum of Squares	Mean Square	F Value	Prob>F
Model	2	831069.54637	415534.77319	189.710	0.0001
Error	7	15332.55363	2190.36480		
C Total	9	846402.10000			

Root MSE	46.80133	R-square	0.9819	
Dep Mean	1594.70000	Adj R-sq	0.9767	
C.V.	2.93480			

Parameter Estimates

Variable	DF	Parameter Estimate	Standard Error	T for H0: Parameter=0	Prob > |T|
INTERCEP	1	-1216.143887	242.80636850	-5.009	0.0016
X	1	2.398930	0.24583560	9.758	0.0001
XX	1	-0.000450	0.00005908	-7.618	0.0001

b. Compute the value of the test statistic for testing H_0: $\beta_2 = 0$. Compare this with the value given in the printout shown in Figure 12.4.

c. Test H_0: $\beta_2 = 0$ against H_a: $\beta_2 \neq 0$. State your conclusions.

Solution

The values of $\hat{\beta}_0$, $\hat{\beta}_1$, and $\hat{\beta}_2$ given in the **Parameter Estimate** column of the SAS printout shown in Figure 12.4 are the same as those obtained in Example 12.2. Therefore, the fitted model is

$$\hat{y} = -1,216.14389 + 2.39893x - .00045x^2$$

The $(X'X)^{-1}$ matrix, obtained in Example 12.2, is

$$(X'X)^{-1} = \begin{bmatrix} 26.9156 & -.027027 & 6.3554 \times 10^{-6} \\ -.027027 & 2.75914 \times 10^{-5} & -6.5804 \times 10^{-9} \\ 6.3554 \times 10^{-6} & -6.5804 \times 10^{-9} & 1.5934 \times 10^{-12} \end{bmatrix}$$

From $(X'X)^{-1}$ we see that

$$c_{00} = 26.9156$$
$$c_{11} = 2.75914 \times 10^{-5}$$
$$c_{22} = 1.5934 \times 10^{-12}$$

and from the printout, $s^2 = 2,190.3648$ (shaded under the column **Mean Square** in the row labeled **Error**), and $s = 46.801$ (shaded next to **Root MSE**).

a. The estimated standard error of $\hat{\beta}_1$ is

$$s_{\hat{\beta}_1} = s\sqrt{c_{11}}$$
$$= (46.801)\sqrt{2.75914 \times 10^{-5}} = .24583$$

Notice that this agrees with the value of $s_{\hat{\beta}_1}$ shaded in the SAS printout (Figure 12.4) under the column labeled **Standard Error** in the row labeled **X**.

b. The value of the test statistic for testing H_0: $\beta_2 = 0$ is

$$t = \frac{\hat{\beta}_2}{s\sqrt{c_{22}}} = \frac{-.00045}{(46.801)\sqrt{1.5934 \times 10^{-12}}} = -7.62$$

Notice that this value of the t statistic agrees with the value given in the column headed **T for H0: Parameter = 0** shown in the printout (Figure 12.4).

c. To test H_0: $\beta_2 = 0$ against the alternative hypothesis H_a: $\beta_2 \neq 0$, we will conduct a two-tailed t test and reject H_0 if $|t| > t_{\alpha/2}$. For our example, t has $[n - (k + 1)] = 10 - 3 = 7$ degrees of freedom. (This number of degrees of freedom is shaded in the **DF** column and **Error** row of the SAS printout shown in Figure 12.4.) Therefore, for $\alpha = .05$, we will reject H_0 (see Table 7 of

Appendix II) if $|t| > 2.365$. Since the observed value of $t = -7.62$ exceeds 2.365 in absolute value, there is evidence to indicate that $\beta_2 \neq 0$, i.e., that x^2 contributes information for the prediction of y. The parameter β_2 produces curvature in a graph of the second-order model. Therefore, the practical implication of the test conclusion is that there is evidence to indicate curvature in the model.

The SAS printout shown in Figure 12.4 (Example 12.5) also gives the two-tailed observed significance level (i.e., p-value) for each t test. These values appear under the column headed **Prob > |T|**. The shaded observed significance level .0001 corresponds to the quadratic term; this implies that we would reject H_0: $\beta_2 = 0$ in favor of H_a: $\beta_2 \neq 0$ at any α larger than .0001. [For one-sided alternatives (e.g., H_a: $\beta_2 < 0$), the p-value is half that given on the printout, i.e., p-value $= \frac{1}{2}(\textbf{Prob} > |\textbf{T}|)$, provided the sign of $\hat{\beta}_2$ agrees with the inequality in H_a.]

EXERCISES

12.6 Engineers at the University of Massachusetts studied the viability of using semiconductor lasers for solar lighting in spaceborne applications (*Journal of Applied Physics*, Sept. 1993). A series of $n = 8$ experiments with quantum-well lasers yielded the following observations on solar pumping threshold current (y) and waveguide Al mole fraction (x):

Threshold Current y, A/cm^{-2}	Waveguide Al Mole Fraction x
273	.15
175	.20
146	.25
166	.30
162	.35
165	.40
245	.50
314	.60

Source: Unnikrishnan, S., and Anderson, N. G. "Quantum-well lasers for direct solar photopumping." *Journal of Applied Physics*, Vol. 74, No. 6, Sept. 15, 1993, p. 4226 (data adapted from Figure 2).

a. The researchers theorize that the relationship between threshold current (y) and waveguide Al composition (x) will be represented by a U-shaped curve. Hypothesize a model that corresponds to this theory.

b. Plot the data points in a scattergram. Comment on the researchers' theory, part **a**.

c. Use the accompanying MINITAB printout to test the theory, part **a**.

```
The regression equation is
Y = 438 - 1684 X + 2502 X*X

Predictor        Coef        Stdev     t-ratio        p
Constant       438.31        60.54        7.24    0.001
X             -1684.3        357.3       -4.71    0.005
X*X            2502.3        470.6        5.32    0.003

s = 25.65        R-sq = 88.0%      R-sq(adj) = 83.2%

Analysis of Variance

SOURCE          DF           SS          MS         F         p
Regression       2        24163       12081     18.37     0.005
Error            5         3289         658
Total            7        27451
```

12.7 Refer to the *Metallurgical Transactions* study described in Exercise 12.4. Conduct a test to determine whether upward curvature exists in the relationship between grain size (y) and distance from chill face (x). Use $\alpha = .05$.

12.8 In a production facility, an accurate estimate of man-hours needed to complete a task is crucial to management in making such decisions as the proper number of workers to hire, an accurate deadline to quote a client, or cost-analysis decisions regarding budgets. A manufacturer of boiler drums wants to use regression to predict the number of man-hours needed to erect the drums in future projects. To accomplish this, data for 35 boilers were collected. In addition to man-hours (y), the variables measured were boiler capacity $(x_1 = \text{lb/hr})$, boiler design pressure $(x_2 = \text{pounds per square inch or psi})$, boiler type $(x_3 = 1$ if industry field-erected, 0 if utility field-erected), and drum type $(x_4 = 1$ if steam, 0 if mud). The data are provided in the accompanying table. A MINITAB printout for the model $E(y) = \beta_0 + \beta_1 x_1 + \beta_2 x_2 + \beta_3 x_3 + \beta_4 x_4$ follows on page 622.

a. Test the hypothesis that boiler capacity (x_1) is positively linearly related to man-hours (y). Use $\alpha = .05$.

b. Test the hypothesis that boiler pressure (x_2) is positively linearly related to man-hours (y). Use $\alpha = .05$.

c. Construct a 95% confidence interval for β_3.

d. In Chapter 13, we will learn that β_3 represents the difference between the mean number of man-hours required for industrial and utility field-erected boilers. Use this information to interpret the confidence interval of part **c**.

e. Construct a 95% confidence interval for β_4 and interpret the result. [*Hint:* $\beta_4 = \mu_{\text{Steam}} - \mu_{\text{Mud}}$, where μ_i represents the mean number of man-hours required for drum type i.]

Man-Hours	Boiler Capacity	Design Pressure	Boiler Type	Drum Type
y	x_1	x_2		
3,137	120,000	375	Industrial	Steam
3,590	65,000	750	Industrial	Steam
4,526	150,000	500	Industrial	Steam
10,825	1,073,877	2,170	Utility	Steam
4,023	150,000	325	Industrial	Steam
7,606	610,000	1,500	Utility	Steam
3,748	88,200	399	Industrial	Steam
2,972	88,200	399	Industrial	Steam
3,163	88,200	399	Industrial	Steam
4,065	90,000	1,140	Industrial	Steam
2,048	30,000	325	Industrial	Steam
6,500	441,000	410	Industrial	Steam
5,651	441,000	410	Industrial	Steam
6,565	441,000	410	Industrial	Steam
6,387	441,000	410	Industrial	Steam
6,454	627,000	1,525	Utility	Steam
6,928	610,000	1,500	Utility	Steam
4,268	150,000	500	Industrial	Steam
14,791	1,089,490	2,170	Utility	Steam
2,680	125,000	750	Industrial	Steam
2,974	120,000	375	Industrial	Mud
1,965	65,000	750	Industrial	Mud
2,566	150,000	500	Industrial	Mud
1,515	150,000	250	Industrial	Mud
2,000	150,000	500	Industrial	Mud
2,735	150,000	325	Industrial	Mud
3,698	610,000	1,500	Utility	Mud
2,635	90,000	1,140	Industrial	Mud
1,206	30,000	325	Industrial	Mud
3,775	441,000	410	Industrial	Mud
3,120	441,000	410	Industrial	Mud
4,206	441,000	410	Industrial	Mud
4,006	441,000	410	Industrial	Mud
3,728	627,000	1,525	Utility	Mud
3,211	610,000	1,500	Utility	Mud
1,200	30,000	325	Industrial	Mud

Source: Kelly Uscategui, former graduate student, University of South Florida

```
The regression equation is
Y = - 3783 + 0.00875 X1 + 1.93 X2 + 3444 X3 + 2093 X4

Predictor        Coef       Stdev     t-ratio        p
Constant         -3783       1205       -3.14     0.004
X1          0.0087490   0.0009035        9.68     0.000
X2             1.9265      0.6489        2.97     0.006
X3             3444.3       911.7        3.78     0.001
X4             2093.4       305.6        6.85     0.000


s = 894.6      R-sq = 90.3%     R-sq(adj) = 89.0%

Analysis of Variance

SOURCE       DF         SS          MS         F         p
Regression    4   230854848    57713712     72.11     0.000
Error        31    24809760      800315
Total        35   255664608

SOURCE       DF      SEQ SS
X1            1   175007136
X2            1      490357
X3            1    17813090
X4            1    37544264

Unusual Observations
Obs.      X1         Y       Fit Stdev.Fit  Residual   St.Resid
 19   1089490     14791     12022      523      2769      3.81R

R denotes an obs. with a large st. resid.

       Fit  Stdev.Fit      95% C.I.           95% P.I.
      1936        239   (  1449,   2424)  (    47,   3825)
```

12.9   Laboratory tests were conducted to determine the effect of asphalt content on the stability and permeability of open-graded asphalt concrete (*Journal of Testing and Evaluation*, July 1981). Four concrete specimens were prepared for each of the following asphalt contents (percentage by total weight of mix): 3, 4, 5, 6, 7, and 8. The water permeability of each concrete specimen was determined by flowing deaerated water across the specimen and measuring the amount of water loss. The permeability measurements (in inches per hour) for the 24 concrete specimens are shown in the table.

a. Plot the points in a scattergram.

b. Use the methods of Chapter 11 to fit the first-order model

$$y = \beta_0 + \beta_1 x + \varepsilon$$

What do you conclude about the utility of the model?

c. The SAS printout for the quadratic model

$$y = \beta_0 + \beta_1 x + \beta_2 x^2 + \varepsilon$$

follows the table. Is there sufficient evidence to indicate that the quadratic term should be included in the model? Test using $\alpha = .05$.

Asphalt Content x, %	Permeability y, in/hr	Asphalt Content x, %	Permeability y, in/hr
3	1,189	6	707
3	840	6	927
3	1,020	6	1,067
3	980	6	822
4	1,440	7	853
4	1,227	7	900
4	1,022	7	733
4	1,293	7	585
5	1,227	8	395
5	1,180	8	270
5	980	8	310
5	1,210	8	208

Source: Woelfl, G., Wei, I., Faulstich, C., and Litwack, H. "Laboratory testing of asphalt concrete for porous pavements." *Journal of Testing and Evaluation*, Vol. 9, No. 4, July 1981, pp. 175–181. Copyright American Society for Testing and Materials.

Analysis of Variance

Source	DF	Sum of Squares	Mean Square	F Value	Prob>F
Model	2	2203970.7494	1101985.3747	52.850	0.0001
Error	21	437878.20893	20851.34328		
C Total	23	2641848.9583			

Root MSE	144.39994	R-square	0.8343
Dep Mean	891.04167	Adj R-sq	0.8185
C.V.	16.20575		

Parameter Estimates

Variable	DF	Parameter Estimate	Standard Error	T for H0: Parameter=0	Prob > |T|
INTERCEP	1	-48.555357	337.93244741	-0.144	0.8871
X	1	560.463393	131.12226955	4.274	0.0003
XX	1	-64.611607	11.81649402	-5.468	0.0001

12.10 An experiment was conducted to investigate the effect of temperature (T) and pressure (P) on the yield y of a chemical. Each of the two factors, temperature and pressure, was held constant at two levels—T at $50°$ and $70°$, P at 10 pounds per square inch and 20 pounds per square inch—and the yield of each of the four combinations was measured. To simplify the calculations, the two factors were coded to produce two independent variables, x_1 and x_2:[*]

$$x_1 = \begin{cases} 1 & \text{if } T = 70 \\ -1 & \text{if } T = 50 \end{cases} \quad \text{and} \quad x_2 = \begin{cases} 1 & \text{if } P = 20 \\ -1 & \text{if } P = 10 \end{cases}$$

[*]The technique of coding quantitative independent variables is discussed in detail in Chapter 13.

The results are shown in the accompanying table.

		x_2	
		-1	1
x_1	-1	24.5	28.4
	1	22.1	16.7

a. Fit the linear model

$$E(y) = \beta_0 + \beta_1 x_1 + \beta_2 x_2$$

to the data.

b. Do the data provide sufficient evidence to indicate that temperature contributes information for the prediction of yield of chemical? Use $\alpha = .10$.

c. Do the data provide sufficient evidence to indicate that pressure contributes information for the prediction of yield of chemical? Use $\alpha = .10$.

d. Find a 90% confidence interval for β_1. Interpret the result.

e. Find a 90% confidence interval for β_2. Interpret the result.

12.11   The *Canadian Geotechnical Journal* (Aug. 1985) reported on a study to investigate the reliability of the use of fragmented Queenston Shale, a compaction shale, as a rockfill construction material. In particular, the researchers wanted to estimate the stress–strain relationship of the fragmented material. Based on a graph shown in the paper, the accompanying data were reproduced on deviatoric stress and axial strain for wet shale specimens.

Deviatoric Stress y, kPa	Axial Strain x, %	Deviatoric Stress y, kPa	Axial Strain x, %
500	1.0	6,000	13.5
2,000	2.8	6,625	16.7
2,750	4.3	7,000	19.8
3,500	6.0	7,125	23.0
4,375	7.5	7,000	26.0
4,875	9.0	7,125	27.5
5,250	10.5		

Source: Caswell, R. H., and Trak, B. "Some geotechnical characteristics of fragmented Queenston Shale."
Canadian Geotechnical Journal, Vol. 22, No. 3, Aug. 1985, pp. 403–408.

a. Plot the data on a scattergram. What type of relationship appears to exist?

b. The quadratic model $E(y) = \beta_0 + \beta_1 x + \beta_2 x^2$ was fit to the data, with the results shown in the accompanying SAS printout. Test the hypothesis that deviatoric stress y increases with axial strain x at a decreasing rate. Use $\alpha = .05$.

c. Give the observed significance level for the test of part b and interpret its value.

d. Locate the estimate of σ on the printout and interpret its value.

Dependent Variable: Y

Analysis of Variance

Source	DF	Sum of Squares	Mean Square	F Value	Prob>F
Model	2	57287428.971	28643714.485	802.791	0.0001
Error	10	356801.79868	35680.17987		
C Total	12	57644230.769			

Root MSE	188.89198	R-square	0.9938
Dep Mean	4932.69231	Adj R-sq	0.9926
C.V.	3.82939		

Parameter Estimates

Variable	DF	Parameter Estimate	Standard Error	T for H0: Parameter=0	Prob > |T|
INTERCEP	1	248.635810	147.80770576	1.682	0.1235
X	1	619.763109	25.80667772	24.016	0.0001
XX	1	-13.752316	0.87153259	-15.779	0.0001

OPTIONAL EXERCISES

12.12 If the assumptions of Section 12.2 are satisfied, it can be shown that s^2 is independent of $\hat{\beta}_i$, the least squares estimator of β_i. Use this fact, along with Theorems 12.1 and 12.2, to show that

$$t = \frac{\hat{\beta}_i - \beta_i}{s\sqrt{c_{ii}}}$$

has a t distribution with $[n - (k + 1)]$ degrees of freedom.

12.13 Use the t statistic given in Optional Exercise 12.12, in conjunction with the pivotal method, to derive the formula (given in Section 12.7) for a $(1 - \alpha)100\%$ confidence interval for β_i.

12.8   Assessing Model Adequacy

Conducting t tests on each β parameter in a model with a large number of terms is not a good way to determine whether a model is contributing information for the prediction of y. If we were to conduct a series of t tests to determine whether the independent variables are contributing to the predictive relationship, it is very likely that we would make one or more errors in deciding which terms to retain in the model and which to exclude. For example, suppose that all the β parameters (except β_0) are in fact equal to 0. Although the probability of concluding that any single parameter differs from 0 is only α, the probability of rejecting *at least one* true null hypothesis in a set of t tests is much higher. You can see why this is true by considering the following analogy: The probability of observing a head on a single toss of a coin is only .5, but the probability of observing *at least one* head in five tosses of a coin is .97. Thus, in multiple regression models for which a large number of independent variables are being considered, conducting a series of t tests may include a large number of insignificant variables and exclude some useful ones. If we want to test the overall adequacy of a multiple regression model, we will need a global test (one that encompasses all the β parameters). We would also like to find some statistical quantity that measures how well the model fits the data.

We begin with the easier problem—finding a measure of how well a multiple regression model fits a set of data. For this we use the multiple regression equivalent of r^2, the coefficient of determination for the straight-line model (Chapter 11). Thus, we define the **sample multiple coefficient of determination R^2** as

$$R^2 = 1 - \frac{\Sigma(y_i - \hat{y}_i)^2}{\Sigma(y_i - \bar{y})^2} = 1 - \frac{\text{SSE}}{\text{SS}_{yy}}$$

where $\hat{y}_i$ is the predicted value of y_i for the model. Just as for the simple linear model, R^2 is a sample statistic that represents the fraction of the sample variation of the y values (measured by SS_{yy}) that is attributable to the regression model. Thus, $R^2 = 0$ implies a complete lack of fit of the model to the data, and $R^2 = 1$ implies a perfect fit, with the model passing through every data point. In general, the larger the value of R^2, the better the model fits the data.

Definition 12.1

The **multiple coefficient of determination, R^2**, is defined as

$$R^2 = 1 - \frac{\text{SSE}}{\text{SS}_{yy}}$$

where $\text{SSE} = \Sigma(y_i - \hat{y}_i)^2$, $\text{SS}_{yy} = \Sigma(y_i - \bar{y})^2$, and $\hat{y}_i$ is the predicted value of y_i for the multiple regression model.

To illustrate, consider a production process in which one or more workers are engaged in a variety of tasks. For such a process, the total time spent in production varies as a function of the size of the workpool and the level of output of the various activities. For example, in a large metropolitan department store, the number of hours worked (y) per day by the clerical staff may depend on the following variables:

x_1 = Number of pieces of mail processed (open, sort, etc.)

x_2 = Number of money orders and gift certificates sold

x_3 = Number of window payments (customer charge accounts) transacted

x_4 = Number of change order transactions processed

x_5 = Number of checks cashed

x_6 = Number of pieces of miscellaneous mail processed on "as available" basis

x_7 = Number of bus tickets sold

Table 12.4 gives the output counts for these activities on each of 52 working days. The store's production engineer used the data in Table 12.4 to fit the multiple regression model

$$E(y) = \beta_0 + \beta_1 x_1 + \beta_2 x_2 + \beta_3 x_3 + \beta_4 x_4 + \beta_5 x_5 + \beta_6 x_6 + \beta_7 x_7$$

The results of the analysis are displayed in the SAS printout in Figure 12.5.

FIGURE 12.5 ▶
SAS printout for the Work
Measurement data

Dependent Variable: Y

Analysis of Variance

Source	DF	Sum of Squares	Mean Square	F Value	Prob>F
Model	7	6998.00941	999.71563	8.277	0.0001
Error	44	5314.50290	120.78416		
C Total	51	12312.51231			

Root MSE	10.99018	R-square	0.5684
Dep Mean	117.37692	Adj R-sq	0.4997
C.V.	9.36316		

Parameter Estimates

Variable	DF	Parameter Estimate	Standard Error	T for H0: Parameter=0	Prob > |T|
INTERCEP	1	60.553792	9.49521302	6.377	0.0001
X1	1	0.001350	0.00091684	1.472	0.1481
X2	1	0.087272	0.04825609	1.809	0.0774
X3	1	0.008688	0.00916813	0.948	0.3485
X4	1	-0.042778	0.01734491	-2.466	0.0176
X5	1	0.046790	0.01198080	3.905	0.0003
X6	1	0.209213	0.13022364	1.607	0.1153
X7	1	0.004819	0.00551050	0.875	0.3866

The value R^2 for the model (shaded on the printout) is $R^2 = .5684$. This value of R^2 implies that 57% of the sample variation in hours worked per day is attributable to, or explained by, one or more of the independent variables $x_1, x_2, \ldots, x_7$. Thus, R^2 is a sample statistic that tells how well the model fits the data, and thereby represents a measure of the adequacy of the overall model.

The fact that R^2 is a sample statistic implies that it can be used to make inferences about the statistical utility of the model for predicting y values for specific settings of the independent variables. In particular, for the work measurement data, the test

H_0: $\beta_1 = \beta_2 = \beta_3 = \beta_4 = \beta_5 = \beta_6 = 0$

H_a: At least one of the parameters $\beta_1 - \beta_7$ is nonzero

TABLE 12.4

Obs.	Day of Week	y	x_1	x_2	x_3	x_4	x_5	x_6	x_7
1	M	128.5	7,781	100	886	235	644	56	737
2	T	113.6	7,004	110	962	388	589	57	1,029
3	W	146.6	7,267	61	1,342	398	1,081	59	830
4	Th	124.3	2,129	102	1,153	457	891	57	1,468
5	F	100.4	4,878	45	803	577	537	49	335
6	S	119.2	3,999	144	1,127	345	563	64	918
7	M	109.5	11,777	123	627	326	402	60	335
8	T	128.5	5,764	78	748	161	495	57	962
9	W	131.2	7,392	172	876	219	823	62	665
10	Th	112.2	8,100	126	685	287	555	86	577
11	F	95.4	4,736	115	436	235	456	38	214
12	S	124.6	4,337	110	899	127	573	73	484
13	M	103.7	3,079	96	570	180	428	59	456
14	T	103.6	7,273	51	826	118	463	53	907
15	W	133.2	4,091	116	1,060	206	961	67	951
16	Th	111.4	3,390	70	957	284	745	77	1,446
17	F	97.7	6,319	58	559	220	539	41	440
18	S	132.1	7,447	83	1,050	174	553	63	1,133
19	M	135.9	7,100	80	568	124	428	55	456
20	T	131.3	8,035	115	709	174	498	78	968
21	W	150.4	5,579	83	568	223	683	79	660
22	Th	124.9	4,338	78	900	115	556	84	555
23	F	97.0	6,895	18	442	118	479	41	203
24	S	114.1	3,629	133	644	155	505	57	781
25	M	88.3	5,149	92	389	124	405	59	236
26	T	117.6	5,241	110	612	222	477	55	616
27	W	128.2	2,917	69	1,057	378	970	80	1,210
28	Th	138.8	4,390	70	974	195	1,027	81	1,452
29	F	109.5	4,957	24	783	358	893	51	616
30	S	118.9	7,099	130	1,419	374	609	62	957
31	M	122.2	7,337	128	1,137	238	461	51	968
32	T	142.8	8,301	115	946	191	771	74	719
33	W	133.9	4,889	86	750	214	513	69	489
34	Th	100.2	6,308	81	461	132	430	49	341
35	F	116.8	6,908	145	864	164	549	57	902
36	S	97.3	5,345	116	604	127	360	48	126
37	M	98.0	6,994	59	714	107	473	53	726
38	T	136.5	6,781	78	917	171	805	74	1,100
39	W	111.7	3,142	106	809	335	702	70	1,721
40	Th	98.6	5,738	27	546	126	455	52	502
41	F	116.2	4,931	174	891	129	481	71	737
42	S	108.9	6,501	69	643	129	334	47	473
43	M	120.6	5,678	94	828	107	384	52	1,083

(*continued*)

Obs.	Day of Week	y	x_1	x_2	x_3	x_4	x_5	x_6	x_7
44	T	131.8	4,619	100	777	164	834	67	841
45	W	112.4	1,832	124	626	158	571	71	627
46	Th	92.5	5,445	52	432	121	458	42	313
47	F	120.0	4,123	84	432	153	544	42	654
48	S	112.2	5,884	89	1,061	100	391	31	280
49	M	113.0	5,505	45	562	84	444	36	814
50	T	138.7	2,882	94	601	139	799	44	907
51	W	122.1	2,395	89	637	201	747	30	1,666
52	Th	86.6	6,847	14	810	230	547	40	614

Source: Adapted from *Work Measurement*, by G. L. Smith, Grid Publishing Co., Columbus, Ohio, 1978, (Table 3–1).

would formally test the utility of the overall model. The test statistic used to test this null hypothesis is

$$\text{Test statistic:}\quad F = \frac{\text{Mean square for model}}{\text{Mean square for error}}$$

$$= \frac{\text{SS(Model)}/k}{\text{SSE}/[n - (k + 1)]}$$

where n is the number of data points, k is the number of parameters in the model (not including β_0), and $\text{SS(Model)} = \text{SS}_{yy} - \text{SSE}$. Under the null hypothesis, this F test statistic has an F probability distribution with k df in the numerator and $[n - (k + 1)]$ df in the denominator. The upper-tail values of the F distribution are given in Tables 9–12 of Appendix II.

It can be shown (proof omitted) that an equivalent form of the test statistic for testing the overall adequacy of the model is

$$F = \frac{R^2/k}{(1 - R^2)/[n - (k + 1)]}$$

Therefore, the F test statistic becomes large as the coefficient of determination R^2 becomes large. To determine how large F must be before we can conclude at a given value of α that the model is useful for predicting y, we set up the rejection region as follows:

$$\text{Rejection region:}\quad F > F_\alpha$$

where

$$\nu_1 = k \text{ df},\quad \nu_2 = n - (k + 1) \text{ df}$$

This test procedure is summarized in the box at the top of page 630.

The Analysis of Variance F Test: Testing the Overall Adequacy of the Model
$$E(y) = \beta_0 + \beta_1 x_1 + \beta_2 x_2 + \cdots + \beta_k x_k$$

H_0: $\beta_1 = \beta_2 = \cdots = \beta_k = 0$

H_a: At least one of the parameters, $\beta_1, \beta_2, \ldots, \beta_k$, differs from 0

Test statistic: $F = \dfrac{R^2/k}{(1 - R^2)/[n - (k + 1)]}$

$$= \frac{\text{Mean square for model}}{\text{Mean square for error}} = \frac{\text{SS(Model)}/k}{\text{SSE}/[n - (k + 1)]}$$

Rejection region: $F > F_\alpha$, where $\nu_1 = k$ and $\nu_2 = [n - (k + 1)]$

Assumptions: See Section 12.2 for the assumptions about the probability distribution of the random error component ε.

EXAMPLE 12.6

Refer to the SAS printout (Figure 12.5) for the work measurement model. Test to determine whether the overall model contributes information for the prediction of y.

Solution

For this example, $n = 52$, $k = 7$, and $n - (k + 1) = 44$. At $\alpha = .05$, we will reject H_0: $\beta_1 = \beta_2 = \beta_3 = \beta_4 = \beta_5 = \beta_6 = \beta_7 = 0$ if $F > F_{.05}$, where $\nu_1 = 7$ and $\nu_2 = 44$ (the degrees of freedom are shaded on the printout in Figure 12.5). The critical F value from the Appendix is $F_{.05} \approx 2.25$. Therefore, we will reject H_0 if $F > 2.25$ (see Figure 12.6).

FIGURE 12.6 ▶
Rejection region for the F statistic with $\nu_1 = 7$, $\nu_2 = 44$, and $\alpha = .05$

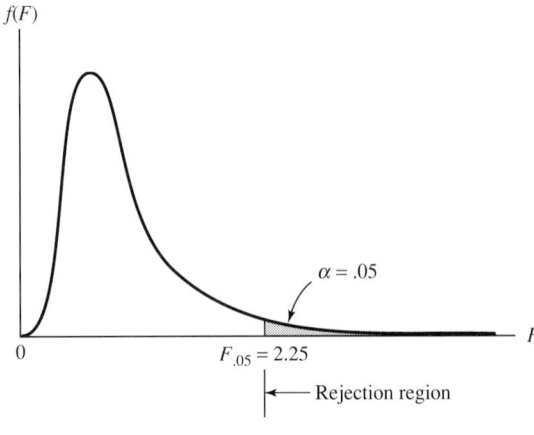

From the computer printout (Figure 12.5), we find that the computed F (shaded in the upper right region under **F Value**) is 8.277. Since this value exceeds the tabulated value of 2.25, we conclude that at least one of the model coefficients $\beta_1-\beta_7$ is nonzero. Therefore, this F test indicates that the multiple regression model $E(y) = \beta_0 + \beta_1x_1 + \cdots + \beta_7x_7$ is useful for predicting total number of hours worked per day.

We could arrive at the same decision by checking the observed significance level (p-value) of the F test, given as **Prob>F** in the SAS printout. This value (shaded in Figure 12.5) indicates that we will reject H_0 for any α greater than .0001.

To summarize the discussion so far, the value of R^2 is an indicator of how well the prediction equation fits the data. More importantly, it can be used (in the F statistic) to determine whether the data provide sufficient evidence to indicate that the overall model contributes information for the prediction of y. However, intuitive evaluations of the contribution of the model based on the computed value of R^2 must be examined with care. The value of R^2 will increase as more and more variables are added to the model. Consequently, you could force R^2 to take a value very close to 1 even though the model contributes no information for the prediction of y. In fact, R^2 will equal 1 when the number of terms in the model equals the number of data points.

As an alternative to using R^2 as a measure of model adequacy, the **adjusted multiple coefficient of determination**, denoted R_a^2, is often reported. The formula for R_a^2 is shown in the box.

The Adjusted Multiple Coefficient of Determination

The **adjusted multiple coefficient of determination** is given by

$$R_a^2 = 1 - \frac{(n-1)}{n-(k+1)}\left(\frac{\text{SSE}}{\text{SS}_{yy}}\right) = 1 - \frac{n-1}{n-(k+1)}(1 - R^2)$$

Unlike R^2, R_a^2 takes into account ("adjusts for") both the sample size n and the number of β parameters in the model. R_a^2 will always be smaller than R^2, and more importantly, cannot be "forced" to 1 by simply adding more and more independent variables to the model. Consequently, some analysts prefer the more conservative R_a^2 when choosing a measure of model adequacy.

The value of R_a^2 is shown on the SAS printout (Figure 12.5) directly underneath the value of R^2. Note that $R_a^2 = .4997$, a value only slightly smaller than R^2. Nevertheless, both R^2 and R_a^2 are only sample statistics, and **you should not rely solely on their values to tell you whether the model is useful for predicting** y. Use the F test (with supporting measure of reliability α) to make inferences about the overall adequacy of the multiple regression model.

EXERCISES

12.14 Personal computer (PC) technology is advancing at a phenomenal rate. As such, the retail price of a PC may vary dramatically depending on when it is purchased and what features it includes. Retail price data were recently collected for IBM and IBM-compatible PCs. The data for $n = 60$ PCs, shown in the accompanying table, were used to fit the multiple regression model

$$E(y) = \beta_0 + \beta_1 x_1 + \beta_2 x_2$$

where

$y =$ Retail price ($)

$x_1 =$ Microprocessor speed (megahertz)

$$x_2 = \begin{cases} 1 & \text{if 386 CPU chip} \\ 0 & \text{if 286 CPU chip} \end{cases}$$

A MINITAB printout of the analysis follows.

Retail Price y	Speed, MHz	Chip	Retail Price y	Speed, MHz	Chip
$5099	33	386	$3249	25	386
3995	25	386	2995	20	386
2230	20	386	3419	20	386
4395	33	386	1590	20	386
6299	25	386	3899	20	386
2549	16	386	2249	12	286
3499	16	386	5796	25	386
2995	16	386	4330	16	286
1649	10	286	2699	16	386
5499	20	386	5579	20	386
1695	12	286	2095	16	386
2595	20	386	2695	25	386
3695	33	386	2295	20	386
3499	33	386	3445	25	386
2845	20	386	2445	16	386
4195	33	386	3795	25	386
2895	20	386	2395	16	386
2195	12	286	1595	12	286
5625	25	386	2095	16	386
2495	20	386	2995	25	386
3795	33	386	2895	20	386
3295	25	386	3995	33	386
1995	16	386	2595	20	386
2795	25	386	4995	25	386
5795	33	386	2695	25	386

Retail Price y	Speed, MHz	Chip	Retail Price y	Speed, MHz	Chip
3995	33	386	3990	33	386
1850	12	286	2795	20	386
1895	16	386	1995	20	286
1795	16	286	1595	16	286
2645	16	386	2875	20	386

Source: *Computer Monthly*, *Computer Shopper*, and IBM Corporation flyers. Data compiled by Jerasimos N. Mantas, University of South Florida business student.

```
The regression equation is
Price = 648 + 105 Speed + 357 Chip

Predictor       Coef      Stdev     t-ratio        p
Constant       648.0      431.5        1.50    0.139
Speed         104.84      22.36        4.69    0.000
Chip           357.2      389.4        0.92    0.363

s = 953.7       R-sq = 40.0%    R-sq(adj) = 37.9%

Analysis of Variance

SOURCE        DF         SS          MS         F         p
Regression     2   34592104    17296052     19.02    0.000
Error         57   51840204      909477
Total         59   86432304

Unusual Observations
Obs.   Speed      Price     Fit Stdev.Fit  Residual   St.Resid
  5    25.0       6299     3626      142       2673      2.83R
 10    20.0       5499     3102      151       2397      2.55R
 19    25.0       5625     3626      142       1999      2.12R
 37    25.0       5796     3626      142       2170      2.30R
 38    16.0       4330     2325      306       2005      2.22R
 40    20.0       5579     3102      151       2477      2.63R

R denotes an obs. with a large st. resid.
```

a. Write the least squares prediction equation.
b. Is the model adequate for predicting y? Test using $\alpha = .10$.
c. Construct a 90% confidence interval for β_1. Interpret the interval.
d. Is CPU chip (x_2) a useful predictor of price (y) in this model? Test using $\alpha = .10$.

12.15 Refer to the *IEEE Transactions on Software Engineering* (Apr. 1985) study on identifying error-prone software, Exercise 11.58. A multiple regression analysis was conducted to identify the computer module-related variables (called metrics) useful for predicting the number y of discovered module defects. For a certain product written in PL/S language, the following model was fit to data collected for $n = 253$ modules:

$$E(y) = \beta_0 + \beta_1 x_1 + \beta_2 x_2$$

where

x_1 = Number of unique operands in the module

x_2 = Number of conditional statements, loops, and Boolean operators in the module

The multiple coefficient of determination for the model was $R^2 = .78$. Is there sufficient evidence to indicate that the model is useful for predicting the number y of defects in modules of the software product? Test using $\alpha = .05$.

12.16   "Zoning" is defined as the distribution of vacant land to residential and nonresidential uses via policy set by local governments. Although the negative effects of zoning have been studied (e.g., distorting urban property markets, creating barriers to residential mobility, and impeding economic and social integration), little empirical evidence exists identifying the factors that encourage restrictive zoning practices. A recent study, reported in the *Journal of Urban Economics* (Vol. 21, 1987), developed a series of multiple regression models that hypothesize several determinants of zoning. One of the models studied took the form

$$E(y) = \beta_0 + \beta_1 x_1 + \beta_2 x_1^2 + \beta_3 x_2$$

where

$y = $ Percentage of vacant land zoned for residential use

$x_1 = $ Proportion of existing land in nonresidential use

$x_2 = $ Proportion of total tax base derived from nonresidential property

The model was fit to data collected for $n = 185$ municipal communities in northeastern New Jersey, with the following results:

Independent Variable	Parameter Estimate	Standard Error of Estimate	t value	p-value
Intercept	92.26	3.07	30.05	$p < .01$
x_1	−96.35	46.59	−2.07	$p < .05$
x_1^2	166.80	120.88	1.38	$p > .10$
x_2	−75.51	13.35	−5.66	$p < .01$

Adjusted $R^2 = .25$ $F = 21.86$ $(p < .01)$

Source: Rolleston, B. S. "Determinants of restrictive suburban zoning: An empirical analysis." *Journal of Urban Economics*, Vol. 21, 1987, p. 15, Table 4.

a. Construct a 95% confidence interval for β_3. Interpret the result.
b. Test the hypothesis that a curvilinear relationship exists between percentage (y) of land zoned for residential use and proportion (x_1) of existing land in nonresidential use.
c. Is the overall model statistically useful for predicting y?
d. Interpret the adjusted R^2 value.

12.17   A study was conducted at Union Carbide to identify the optimal catalyst preparation conditions in the conversion of monoethanolamine (MEA) to ethylenediamine (EDA), a substance used commercially in soaps.* For each of 10 preselected catalysts, the following experimental variables were measured:

y = Rate of conversion of MEA to EDA

x_1 = Atom ratio of metal used in the experiment

x_2 = Reduction temperature

$x_3 = \begin{cases} 1 & \text{if high acidity support used} \\ 0 & \text{if low acidity support used} \end{cases}$

The data for the $n = 10$ experiments were used to fit the multiple regression model $E(y) = \beta_0 + \beta_1 x_1 + \beta_2 x_2 + \beta_3 x_3$. The results are summarized as follows:

$$\hat{y} = 40.2 - .808x_1 - 6.38x_2 - 4.45x_3 \qquad R^2 = .899$$

$$s_{\hat{\beta}_1} = .231 \qquad s_{\hat{\beta}_2} = 1.93 \qquad s_{\hat{\beta}_3} = .99$$

a. Is there sufficient evidence to indicate that the model is useful for predicting rate of conversion y? Test using $\alpha = .01$.

b. Conduct a test to determine whether atom ratio x_1 is a useful predictor of rate of conversion y. Use $\alpha = .05$.

c. Construct a 95% confidence interval for β_2. Interpret the interval.

12.18 Suppose you fit the model

$$y = \beta_0 + \beta_1 x_1 + \beta_2 x_2 + \beta_3 x_3 + \varepsilon$$

to $n = 20$ data points and obtain

$$\sum(y_i - \hat{y}_i)^2 = 225 \quad \text{and} \quad \sum(y_i - \bar{y})^2 = 305$$

a. Find R^2. Does the value of R^2 suggest that the model provides a good fit to the data? Explain.

b. Test the null hypothesis

$$H_0: \quad \beta_1 = \beta_2 = \beta_3 = 0$$

against the alternative hypothesis

$$H_a: \quad \text{At least one of the } \beta \text{ parameters is nonzero}$$

Use $\alpha = .05$.

12.19 Refer to Exercise 11.62. In an attempt to improve upon the ability of the model to predict urban travel times, Cook and Russell (*Transportation Research*, June 1980) added a second independent variable: weighted average speed limit between the two urban locations. The proposed model takes the form

$$y = \beta_0 + \beta_1 x_1 + \beta_2 x_2 + \varepsilon$$

where

y = Urban travel time (minutes)

x_1 = Distance between locations (miles)

x_2 = Weighted speed limit between locations (miles per hour)

---

*Source: Hansen, J. L., and Best, D. C. "How to Pick a Winner." Paper presented at Joint Statistical Meetings, American Statistical Association and Biometric Society, Aug. 1986, Chicago, Illinois.

This model was fitted to the data pertaining to passenger cars and to the data pertaining to trucks, with the results shown in the accompanying table.

Passenger Cars   *Trucks*

$\hat{y} = 5.46 + 2.15x_1 - .09x_2$ $\hat{y} = 4.84 + 3.92x_1 - .09x_2$

$R^2 = .687; n = 567$ $R^2 = .771; n = 918$

Source: Cook, T. M., and Russell, R. A. "Estimating urban travel times: A comparative study." *Transportation Research*, 14A, June 1980, pp. 173–175. Copyright 1980, Pergamon Press, Ltd. Reprinted with permission.

a. Is the model useful for predicting the urban travel times of passenger cars? Use $\alpha = .05$.
b. Is the model useful for predicting the urban travel times of trucks? Use $\alpha = .05$.

12.20 The Florida Department of Transportation (DOT) wants to develop a model relating bid price for a road construction project to length of the road to be built or repaired and number of bidders. Since the DOT believes that the bid price increases linearly with road length and number of bidders, the following model is hypothesized:

$$y = \beta_0 + \beta_1 x_1 + \beta_2 x_2 + \varepsilon$$

where

y = Bid price (thousands of dollars)

x_1 = Length of road (miles)

x_2 = Number of bidders

Dependent Variable: Y

Analysis of Variance

Source	DF	Sum of Squares	Mean Square	F Value	Prob>F
Model	2	4277159.7074	2138579.8517	120.651	0.0001
Error	29	514034.5153	17725.3281		
C Total	31	4791194.2187			

Root MSE	133.13650	R-square	0.8927
Dep Mean	665.00000	Adj R-sq	0.8853
C.V.	20.02053		

Parameter Estimates

Variable	DF	Parameter Estimate	Standard Error	T for H0: Parameter=0	Prob > |T|
INTERCEP	1	-1336.7220	173.35612607	-7.711	0.0001
X1	1	12.7362	0.90238048	14.114	0.0001
X2	1	85.8151	8.70575681	9.857	0.0001

Obs	X1	X2	Dep Var Y	Predict Value	Std Err Predict	Lower95% Mean	Upper95% Mean	Residual
32	100	7	601.5	537.6	138.771	253.81	821.39	63.9

Data collected on bid price, road length, and number of bidders for 32 randomly selected construction projects were used to fit the model, and a portion of the SAS printout is shown at the bottom of page 636.

a. Is the model useful for estimating mean bid price? Use $\alpha = .01$.
b. Test the hypothesis that the mean bid price increases as the number of bidders increases for road construction projects of the same length. Use $\alpha = .01$.

12.21 Because the coefficient of determination R^2 always increases when a new independent variable is added to the model, it is tempting to include many variables in a model to force R^2 to be near 1. However, doing so reduces the degrees of freedom available for estimating σ^2, which adversely affects our ability to make reliable inferences. As an example, suppose you want to predict the CPU time of a computer job using 18 predictor variables (such as size of job, time of submission, and estimated lines of print). You fit the model

$$y = \beta_0 + \beta_1 x_1 + \beta_2 x_2 + \cdots + \beta_{17} x_{17} + \beta_{18} x_{18} + \varepsilon$$

where y = CPU time and $x_1, x_2, \ldots, x_{18}$ are the predictor variables. Using the relevant information on $n = 20$ jobs to fit the model, you obtain $R^2 = .95$. Test to determine whether this value of R^2 is large enough for you to infer that this model is useful—i.e., that at least one term in the model is important for predicting CPU time. Use $\alpha = .05$.

12.22 Refer to the *Chemosphere* (1990) study of 103 production workers exposed to chemicals contaminated with the dioxin 2,3,7,8-TCDD, Exercise 7.17. Multiple regression analysis was used to relate the TCDD level (y) of a worker (measured in parts per trillion) to four independent variables in the model

$$E(y) = \beta_0 + \beta_1 x_1 + \beta_2 x_2 + \beta_3 x_3 + \beta_4 x_4$$

where

x_1 = Logarithm of years of exposure to TCDD
x_2 = Number of years since last exposure
x_3 = Age (in years)
x_4 = Body mass index

The results of the multiple regression analysis are summarized in the accompanying table. Interpret these results.

Independent Variable	Parameter Estimate	Standard Error of Estimate	t value	p-value
Intercept	1.721	.770	2.24	—
x_1	.566	.054	10.48	< .001
x_2	−.085	.018	−4.72	< .001
x_3	.044	.010	4.40	< .001
x_4	.075	.021	3.57	< .001

$R^2 = .742$

12.9   A Confidence Interval for $E(y)$

Suppose we were to postulate that the mean value of the productivity y of a company is related to the size of the company x and that the relationship could be modeled by the expression

$$E(y) = \beta_0 + \beta_1 x + \beta_2 x^2$$

A graph of $E(y)$ might appear as shown in Figure 12.7.

FIGURE 12.7 ▶
Graph of mean productivity $E(y)$

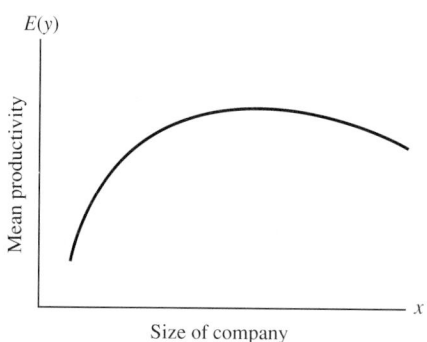

We might have several reasons for collecting data on the productivity and size of a set of n companies and finding the least squares prediction equation,

$$\hat{y} = \hat{\beta}_0 + \hat{\beta}_1 x + \hat{\beta}_2 x^2$$

For example, we might want to estimate the mean productivity for a company of a given size (say, $x = 2$). That is, we might want to estimate

$$
\begin{aligned}
E(y) &= \beta_0 + \beta_1 x + \beta_2 x^2 \\
&= \beta_0 + 2\beta_1 + 4\beta_2 \quad \text{where } x = 2
\end{aligned}
$$

Or we might want to estimate the marginal increase in productivity, the slope of a tangent to the curve, when $x = 2$ (see Figure 12.8). The marginal productivity for y when $x = 2$ is the rate of change of $E(y)$ with respect to x, evaluated at $x = 2$. For the quadratic model, the marginal productivity for a value of x, denoted by the symbol $dE(y)/dx$, is*

$$\frac{dE(y)}{dx} = \beta_1 + 2\beta_2 x$$

Therefore, the marginal productivity at $x = 2$ is

$$\frac{dE(y)}{dx} = \beta_1 + 2\beta_2(2) = \beta_1 + 4\beta_2$$

---

*Note that the marginal productivity for y given x is the first derivative of $E(y) = \beta_0 + \beta_1 x + \beta_2 x^2$ with respect to x.

FIGURE 12.8 ▶
Marginal productivity

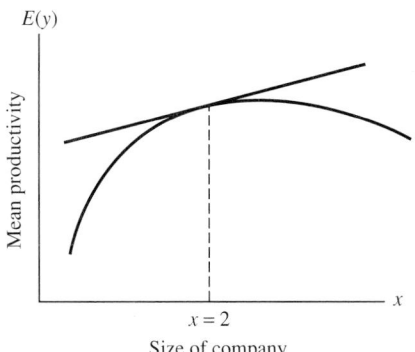

Note that for $x = 2$, both $E(y)$ and the marginal productivity are *linear* functions of the unknown parameters β_0, β_1, β_2 in the model. The problem we pose in this section is that of finding confidence intervals for linear functions of β parameters or testing hypotheses concerning their values. The information necessary to solve this problem is rarely given in a standard multiple regression analysis computer printout, but we can find these confidence intervals or values of the appropriate test statistics from knowledge of $(X'X)^{-1}$.

We will suppose that we have a model,

$$y = \beta_0 + \beta_1 x_1 + \cdots + \beta_k x_k + \varepsilon$$

and that we are interested in making an inference about a linear function of the β parameters, say,

$$a_0 \beta_0 + a_1 \beta_1 + \cdots + a_k \beta_k$$

where $a_0, a_1, \ldots, a_k$ are known constants. Further, we will use the corresponding linear function of least squares estimates,

$$\ell = a_0 \hat{\beta}_0 + a_1 \hat{\beta}_1 + \cdots + a_k \hat{\beta}_k$$

as our best estimate of $a_0 \beta_0 + a_1 \beta_1 + \cdots + a_k \beta_k$.

We recall from Section 12.5 that the least squares estimators, $\hat{\beta}_0, \hat{\beta}_1, \ldots, \hat{\beta}_k$, are normally distributed with

$$E(\hat{\beta}_i) = \beta_i$$
$$V(\hat{\beta}_i) = c_{ii} \sigma^2 \quad (i = 0, 1, 2, \ldots, k)$$

and covariances

$$\text{Cov}(\hat{\beta}_i, \hat{\beta}_j) = c_{ij} \sigma^2 \quad (i \neq j)$$

It then follows by Theorem 7.2 that

$$\ell = a_0 \hat{\beta}_0 + a_1 \hat{\beta}_1 + \cdots + a_k \hat{\beta}_k$$

is normally distributed with mean, variance, and standard deviation as given by Theorem 12.3.

Theorem 12.3

Properties of the Sampling Distribution of

$$\ell = a_0\hat{\beta}_0 + a_1\hat{\beta}_1 + \cdots + a_k\hat{\beta}_k$$

The sampling distribution of ℓ is normal with

$$E(\ell) = a_0\beta_0 + a_1\beta_1 + \cdots + a_k\beta_k$$
$$V(\ell) = [a'(X'X)^{-1}a]\sigma^2$$
$$\sigma_\ell = \sqrt{V(\ell)} = \sigma\sqrt{a'(X'X)^{-1}a}$$

where σ is the standard deviation of ε, $(X'X)^{-1}$ is the inverse matrix obtained in fitting the least squares model, and

$$a = \begin{bmatrix} a_0 \\ a_1 \\ a_2 \\ \cdot \\ \cdot \\ \cdot \\ a_k \end{bmatrix}$$

Theorem 12.3 indicates that ℓ is an unbiased estimator of

$$E(\ell) = a_0\beta_0 + a_1\beta_1 + \cdots + a_k\beta_k$$

and that its sampling distribution would appear as shown in Figure 12.9.

FIGURE 12.9 ▶
Sampling distribution for ℓ

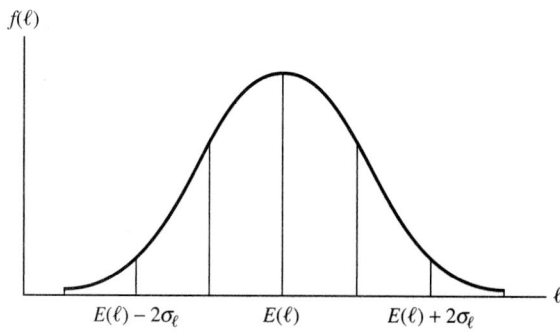

Therefore, a $(1 - \alpha)100\%$ confidence interval for $E(\ell)$ is as shown in the following box.

A $(1 - \alpha)100\%$ Confidence Interval for $E(\ell)$

$$\ell \pm (t_{\alpha/2})s\sqrt{a'(X'X)^{-1}a}$$

where

$$E(\ell) = a_0\beta_0 + a_1\beta_1 + \cdots + a_k\beta_k$$

$$\ell = a_0\hat{\beta}_0 + a_1\hat{\beta}_1 + \cdots + a_k\hat{\beta}_k$$

$$a = \begin{bmatrix} a_0 \\ a_1 \\ a_2 \\ \cdot \\ \cdot \\ \cdot \\ a_k \end{bmatrix}$$

s and $(X'X)^{-1}$ are obtained from the least squares procedure, and $t_{\alpha/2}$ is based on the number of degrees of freedom associated with s.

The linear function of the β parameters that is most often the focus of our attention is

$$E(y) = \beta_0 + \beta_1x_1 + \cdots + \beta_kx_k$$

That is, we want to find a confidence interval for $E(y)$ for specific values of x_1, x_2, . . . , x_k. For this special case, $\ell = \hat{y}$ and the a matrix is

$$a = \begin{bmatrix} 1 \\ x_1 \\ x_2 \\ \cdot \\ \cdot \\ \cdot \\ x_k \end{bmatrix}$$

where the symbols x_1, x_2, . . . , x_k in the a matrix indicate the specific numerical values assumed by these variables. Thus, the procedure for forming a confidence interval for $E(y)$ is as shown in the box on page 642.

> ### A $(1 - \alpha)100\%$ Confidence Interval for $E(y)$
>
> $$\ell \pm (t_{\alpha/2})s\sqrt{a'(X'X)^{-1}a}$$
>
> where
>
> $$E(y) = \beta_0 + \beta_1 x_1 + \cdots + \beta_k x_k$$
>
> $$\ell = \hat{y} = \hat{\beta}_0 + \hat{\beta}_1 x_1 + \cdots + \hat{\beta}_k x_k \qquad a = \begin{bmatrix} 1 \\ x_1 \\ x_2 \\ \vdots \\ x_k \end{bmatrix}$$
>
> s and $(X'X)^{-1}$ are obtained from the least squares analysis, and $t_{\alpha/2}$ is based on the number of degrees of freedom associated with s, namely, $[n - (k + 1)]$.

EXAMPLE 12.7

Refer to the data of Example 12.1 for insulation compression y and compressive pressure x. Find a 95% confidence interval for the mean compression $E(y)$ when the pressure is $x = 4$.

Solution

The confidence interval for $E(y)$ for a given value of x is

$$\hat{y} \pm t_{\alpha/2}s\sqrt{a'(X'X)^{-1}a}$$

Consequently, we need to find and substitute the values of $a'(X'X)^{-1}a$, $t_{\alpha/2}$, s, and $\hat{y}$ into this formula. Since we want to estimate

$$\begin{aligned} E(y) &= \beta_0 + \beta_1 x \\ &= \beta_0 + \beta_1(4) \quad \text{when } x = 4 \\ &= \beta_0 + 4\beta_1 \end{aligned}$$

it follows that the coefficients of β_0 and β_1 are $a_0 = 1$ and $a_1 = 4$, and thus,

$$a = \begin{bmatrix} 1 \\ 4 \end{bmatrix}$$

From Examples 12.1 and 12.3, we have $\hat{y} = -.1 + .7x$, $s^2 = .367$, $s = .61$, and

$$(X'X)^{-1} = \begin{bmatrix} 1.1 & -.3 \\ -.3 & .1 \end{bmatrix}$$

Then,

$$a'(X'X)^{-1}a = \begin{bmatrix} 1 & 4 \end{bmatrix} \begin{bmatrix} 1.1 & -.3 \\ -.3 & .1 \end{bmatrix} \begin{bmatrix} 1 \\ 4 \end{bmatrix}$$

We first calculate

$$a'(X'X)^{-1} = [1 \quad 4] \begin{bmatrix} 1.1 & -.3 \\ -.3 & .1 \end{bmatrix} = [-.1 \quad .1]$$

Then,

$$a'(X'X)^{-1}a = [-.1 \quad .1] \begin{bmatrix} 1 \\ 4 \end{bmatrix} = .3$$

The t value, $t_{.025}$, based on 3 df is 3.182. So, a 95% confidence interval for the mean compression of the insulation material when subjected to a pressure of 4 (that is, 40 pounds per square inch) is

$$\hat{y} \pm t_{\alpha/2}s\sqrt{a'(X'X)^{-1}a}$$

Since $\hat{y} = -.1 + .7x = -.1 + (.7)(4) = 2.7$, the 95% confidence interval for $E(y)$ when $x = 4$ is

$$2.7 \pm (3.182)(.61)\sqrt{.3}$$
$$2.7 \pm 1.1$$

or 1.6 to 3.8 inches. Notice that this is exactly the same result as obtained in Example 11.9.

EXAMPLE 12.8

An engineer recorded a measure of productivity y and the size x for each of 100 companies producing cement. A regression model,

$$y = \beta_0 + \beta_1 x + \beta_2 x^2 + \varepsilon$$

fit to the $n = 100$ data points produced the following results:

$$\hat{y} = 2.6 + .7x - .2x^2$$

where x is coded to take values in the interval $-2 < x < 2$, and

$$(X'X)^{-1} = \begin{bmatrix} .0025 & .0005 & -.0070 \\ .0005 & .0055 & 0 \\ -.0070 & 0 & .0050 \end{bmatrix} \qquad s = .14$$

Find a 95% confidence interval for the marginal increase in productivity given that the coded size of a plant is $x = 1.5$.

Solution

The mean value of y for a given value of x is

$$E(y) = \beta_0 + \beta_1 x + \beta_2 x^2$$

Therefore, the marginal increase in y for $x = 1.5$ is

$$\frac{dE(y)}{dx} = \beta_1 + 2\beta_2 x$$
$$= \beta_1 + 2(1.5)\beta_2$$

Or,

$$E(\ell) = \beta_1 + 3\beta_2 \quad \text{when } x = 1.5$$

Note from the prediction equation, $\hat{y} = 2.6 + .7x - .2x^2$, that $\hat{\beta}_1 = .7$ and $\hat{\beta}_2 = -.2$. Therefore,

$$\ell = \hat{\beta}_1 + 3\hat{\beta}_2 = .7 + 3(-.2) = .1$$

and

$$a = \begin{bmatrix} a_0 \\ a_1 \\ a_2 \end{bmatrix} = \begin{bmatrix} 0 \\ 1 \\ 3 \end{bmatrix}$$

We next calculate

$$a'(X'X)^{-1}a = \begin{bmatrix} 0 & 1 & 3 \end{bmatrix} \begin{bmatrix} .0025 & .0005 & -.0070 \\ .0005 & .0055 & 0 \\ -.0070 & 0 & .0050 \end{bmatrix} \begin{bmatrix} 0 \\ 1 \\ 3 \end{bmatrix} = .0505$$

Then, since s will be based on $n - (k + 1) = 100 - 3 = 97$ df, $t_{.025} \approx 1.96$, and a 95% confidence interval for the marginal increase in productivity when $x = 1.5$ is

$$\ell \pm t_{.025}s\sqrt{a'(X'X)^{-1}a}$$

or

$$.1 \pm (1.96)(.14)\sqrt{.0505}$$
$$.1 \pm .062$$

Thus, the marginal increase in productivity, the slope of the tangent to the curve

$$E(y) = \beta_0 + \beta_1 x + \beta_2 x^2$$

is estimated to lie in the interval $.1 \pm .062$ at $x = 1.5$. A graph of $\hat{y} = 2.6 + .7x - .2x^2$ is shown in Figure 12.10.

FIGURE 12.10 ▶
A graph of
$\hat{y} = 2.6 + .7x - .2x^2$

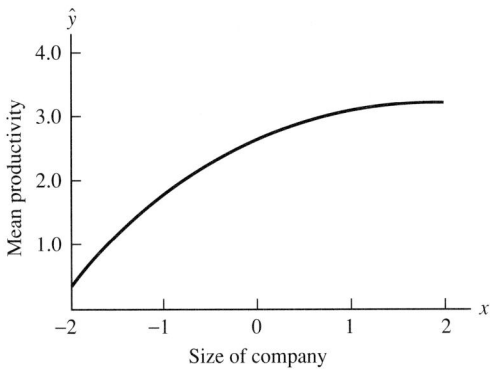

Confidence intervals for $E(y)$ or some other linear function of the β's are readily obtainable by computer. The Computer Lab section at the end of this chapter gives the SAS and MINITAB commands for producing the intervals.

12.10 A Prediction Interval for a Future Value of y

We have indicated that two of the most important applications of the least squares predictor $\hat{y}$ are estimating the mean value of y (the topic of the preceding section) and predicting a new value of y, yet unobserved, for specific values of $x_1, x_2, \ldots, x_k$. The difference between these two inferential problems (when each would be pertinent) was explained in Chapter 11, but we will give another example to make certain that the distinction is clear at this point.

Suppose you are the manager of a manufacturing plant and that y, the daily profit, is a function of various process variables $x_1, x_2, \ldots, x_k$. Suppose you want to know how much money you would make *in the long run* if the x's are set at specific values. For this case, you would be interested in finding a confidence interval for the mean profit per day, $E(y)$. In contrast, suppose you planned to operate the plant for only one more day! Then you would be interested in predicting the value of y, the profit associated with tomorrow's production.

We have indicated that the error of prediction is always larger than the error of estimating $E(y)$. You can see this by comparing the formula for the prediction interval (shown in the box on page 646) with the formula for the confidence interval for $E(y)$ that was given in Section 12.9.

> ## A $(1 - \alpha)100\%$ Prediction Interval for y
>
> $$\hat{y} \pm (t_{\alpha/2})s\sqrt{1 + a'(X'X)^{-1}a}$$
>
> where
>
> $$\hat{y} = \hat{\beta}_0 + \hat{\beta}_1 x_1 + \cdots + \hat{\beta}_k x_k$$
>
> s and $(X'X)^{-1}$ are obtained from the least squares analysis,
>
> $$a = \begin{bmatrix} 1 \\ x_1 \\ x_2 \\ \vdots \\ x_k \end{bmatrix}$$
>
> contains the numerical values of $x_1, x_2, \ldots, x_k$ and $t_{\alpha/2}$ is based on the number of degrees of freedom associated with s, namely, $[n - (k + 1)]$.

EXAMPLE 12.9

Refer to the insulation compression example (Example 12.7). Find a 95% prediction interval for the compression of a particular piece of insulation when it is to be subjected to a pressure of 40 pounds per square inch ($x = 4$).

Solution

The 95% prediction interval for the compression of this particular piece of insulation is

$$\hat{y} \pm t_{\alpha/2}s\sqrt{1 + a'(X'X)^{-1}a}$$

From Example 12.7, when $x = 4$, $\hat{y} = -.1 + .7x = -.1 + (.7)(4) = 2.7$, $s = .61$, $t_{.025} = 3.182$, and $a'(X'X)^{-1}a = .3$. Then the 95% prediction interval for y is

$$2.7 \pm (3.182)(.61)\sqrt{1 + .3}$$

$$2.7 \pm 2.2 \quad \text{or} \quad .05 \text{ to } .49 \text{ inch}$$

Consult the Computer Lab section at the end of this chapter for the SAS and MINITAB commands that produce prediction intervals for a future value of y.

EXERCISES

12.23 Refer to the *Metallurgical Transactions* study described in Exercise 12.4.
  a. Find a 90% confidence interval for the mean grain size of tensile specimens 7 centimeters from the ingot chill face. Interpret the interval.

b. Find a 90% prediction interval for the grain size of a tensile specimen to be observed in the future when the specimen is placed 7 centimeters from the ingot chill face.

c. Compare the width of the intervals, parts a and b. Which is wider? Why?

12.24 Refer to the manpower study of boiler drums, Exercise 12.8. A 95% prediction interval for the man-hours (y) required to erect an industrial field ($x_3 = 1$) boiler with capacity $x_1 = 150,000$ lb/hr, design pressure $x_2 = 500$ psi, and steam drum type ($x_4 = 0$) is shown at the bottom of the MINITAB printout, Exercise 12.8. Interpret the interval.

12.25 Refer to the chemical experiment, Exercise 12.10.

a. Find a 95% confidence interval for the mean yield $E(y)$ when the temperature is set at $50°$ ($x_1 = -1$) and pressure is set at 20 pounds per square inch ($x_2 = 1$). Interpret the interval.

b. Find a 95% prediction interval for a yield y to be observed in the future when the temperature is set at $50°$ ($x_1 = -1$) and pressure is set at 20 pounds per square inch ($x_2 = 1$). Interpret the interval.

c. Compare the width of the intervals, parts a and b. Which is wider? Why?

12.26 Refer to the DOT model of bid price for road construction projects, Exercise 12.20. A 95% confidence interval for the mean bid price of projects with roads of length 100 miles and with 7 bidders is shown at the bottom of the SAS printout, Exercise 12.20. Interpret the interval.

OPTIONAL EXERCISES

12.27 Since $\hat{\beta}_0, \hat{\beta}_1, \ldots, \hat{\beta}_k$ are independent of s^2, it follows that

$$\ell = a_0\hat{\beta}_0 + a_1\hat{\beta}_1 + \cdots + a_k\hat{\beta}_k$$

is independent of s^2. Use this fact and Theorems 12.2 and 12.3 to show that

$$t = \frac{\ell - E(\ell)}{s\sqrt{a'(X'X)^{-1}a}}$$

has a Student's t distribution with $[n - (k + 1)]$ degrees of freedom.

12.28 Let $\ell = \hat{y} = \hat{\beta}_0 + \hat{\beta}_1x_1 + \hat{\beta}_2x_2 + \cdots + \hat{\beta}_kx_k$. Use the t statistic of Optional Exercise 12.27, in conjunction with the pivotal method, to derive the formula (given in Section 12.9) for a $(1 - \alpha)100\%$ confidence interval for $E(y)$.

12.29 Let $\hat{y} = \hat{\beta}_0 + \hat{\beta}_1x_1 + \hat{\beta}_2x_2 + \cdots + \hat{\beta}_kx_k$ be the least squares prediction equation, and let y be some observation to be obtained in the future.

a. Explain why $(\hat{y} - y)$ is normally distributed.

b. Show that

$$E(\hat{y} - y) = 0$$

and

$$V(\hat{y} - y) = [1 + a'(X'X)^{-1}a]\sigma^2$$

12.30   Show that

$$t = \frac{\hat{y} - y}{s\sqrt{1 + a'(X'X)^{-1}a}}$$

has a Student's t distribution with $[n - (k + 1)]$ degrees of freedom.

12.31   Use the result of Optional Exercise 12.30 and the pivotal method to derive the formula (given in Section 12.10) for a $(1 - \alpha)100\%$ prediction interval for y.

12.11   Checking Assumptions: Residual Analysis

An analysis of **residuals**, the differences $(y - \hat{y})$ between the y values and their corresponding predicted values, often provides information that can lead to modifications and improvements in a regression model. These modifications may result from any one of three reasons: (1) the deterministic component of the model has been misspecified, (2) one or more of the assumptions about ε is violated, and (3) the data used to fit the model contain one or more unusual values.

Definition 12.2

A regression **residual** is defined as the difference between an observed y value and its corresponding predicted value:

$$\text{Residual} = y - \hat{y}$$

DETECTING MODEL MISSPECIFICATION   One method for analyzing the residuals in a regression analysis is to plot the value of each residual versus the corresponding value of the independent variable x. (If the model contains more than one independent variable, a plot would be constructed for each of the independent variables.) This plot will aid in detecting whether you have misspecified the deterministic component of the model, as the following example illustrates.

EXAMPLE 12.10   The first-order model $E(y) = \beta_0 + \beta_1 x$ is fit to the data shown in Table 12.5 using MINITAB. The MINITAB printout is shown in Figure 12.11. Calculate the residuals, plot them versus x, and analyze the plot.

TABLE 12.5   Data for Example 12.10

x	y
0	1
1	4
2	6
3	8
4	9
5	10
6	10
7	8

FIGURE 12.11 ▶
MINITAB printout for the simple linear model, Example 12.10

```
The regression equation is
Y = 3.17 + 1.10 X

Predictor       Coef       Stdev     t-ratio        p
Constant       3.167       1.167        2.71    0.035
X             1.0952      0.2790        3.93    0.008

s = 1.808       R-sq = 72.0%      R-sq(adj) = 67.3%

Analysis of Variance

SOURCE          DF          SS          MS        F        p
Regression       1      50.381      50.381    15.41    0.008
Error            6      19.619       3.270
Total            7      70.000

Unusual Observations
Obs.        X           Y       Fit Stdev.Fit  Residual   St.Resid
  8      7.00       8.000    10.833     1.167    -2.833     -2.05R

R denotes an obs. with a large st. resid.
```

Solution

The resulting prediction equation, obtained from Figure 12.11, is

$$\hat{y} = 3.167 + 1.095x$$

Substituting each value of x into this prediction equation, we can calculate $\hat{y}$ and the corresponding residual, $y - \hat{y}$. The value of x, the predicted value of $\hat{y}$, and the residual $(y - \hat{y})$ are shown in Table 12.6 for each of the data points. (See page 650.)

A plot of the residuals versus the independent variable x is shown in Figure 12.12a on page 650. If the model is correctly specified, we would expect the residuals to vary in a random pattern as x increases. Instead, the values of the residuals in Figure 12.12a cycle from negative to positive to negative as x increases. This cyclical behavior is

TABLE 12.6 Calculation of the Residuals for the Simple Linear Regression Analysis of Example 12.10

x	y	$\hat{y}$	$(y - \hat{y})$
0	1	3.167	−2.167
1	4	4.262	−.262
2	6	5.357	.643
3	8	6.452	1.548
4	9	7.548	1.452
5	10	8.643	1.357
6	10	9.738	.262
7	8	10.833	−2.833

present because we have fit a first-order (straight-line) model to data for which a second-order model is appropriate. A plot of the data points on a graph of $\hat{y}$ versus x is shown in Figure 12.12b. The residuals are represented by the vertical bars between the data points and the fitted line. Those below the $\hat{y}$ line are negative; those above it are positive. Figure 12.12 shows why fitting the wrong model to a set of data can produce patterns in the residuals when they are plotted versus an independent variable. For this simple example, the nonrandom (in this case, cyclical) behavior of the residuals can be eliminated by fitting a second-order model to the data. In general, certain patterns in the values of the residuals may suggest a need to modify the deterministic portion of the regression model, but the exact change that is needed may not always be obvious.

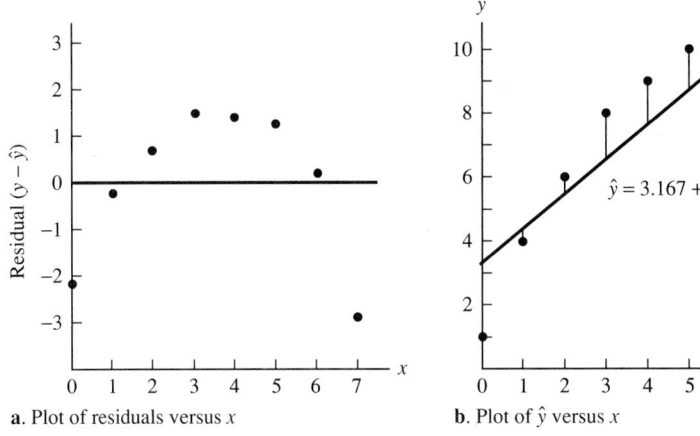

FIGURE 12.12 ▶
Analysis of residuals for Example 12.10

a. Plot of residuals versus x

b. Plot of $\hat{y}$ versus x

A check for model misspecification is equivalent to graphically testing the assumption that $E(\varepsilon) = 0$. To see this, suppose the true model for $E(y)$ is given by the second-order model

$$E(y) = \beta_0 + \beta_1 x + \beta_2 x^2$$

but we specify the first-order probabilistic model

$$y = \beta_0 + \beta_1 x + \varepsilon$$

For our model, we can write

$$\varepsilon = y - [\beta_0 + \beta_1 x]$$

Then it can be shown that

$$E(\varepsilon) = E(y) - [\beta_0 + \beta_1 x]$$

Substituting the expression for $E(y)$ above, we obtain

$$E(\varepsilon) = \beta_0 + \beta_1 x + \beta_2 x^2 - [\beta_0 + \beta_1 x]$$
$$= \beta_2 x^2$$

When $x \neq 0$, $E(\varepsilon)$ will be nonzero; consequently, the assumption that $E(\varepsilon) = 0$ will be violated.

DETECTING UNEQUAL VARIANCES   A plot of the residuals can also be used to check the assumption of a constant error variance. For example, a plot of the residuals versus an independent variable x may display a pattern as shown in Figure 12.13. In the figure, the range in values of the residuals increases as x increases, thus indicating that the variance of the response variable y becomes larger as x increases in value.

FIGURE 12.13 ▶
Residual plot showing changes in the variance of y

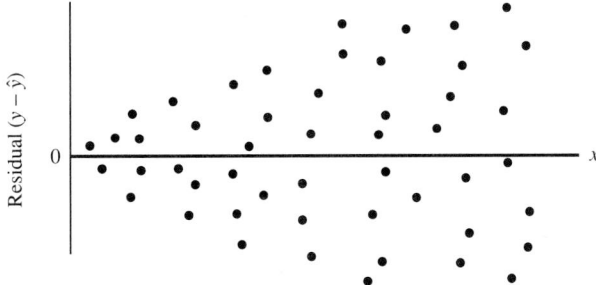

Residual plots of the type shown in Figure 12.13 are not uncommon because the variance of y often depends on the mean value of y. Variables that represent counts per unit of area, volume, time, etc. (i.e., Poisson random variables) are cases in point. For a Poisson random variable, the variance of y is equal to $E(y) = \mu$, i.e., $\sigma_y^2 = \mu$.

Since $\hat{y}$ is an estimator of $E(y)$, a plot of the residuals versus $\hat{y}$ may indicate how the range of the residuals (and hence, σ_y) varies as $E(y)$ increases. If the plot assumes the pattern shown in Figure 12.14a on page 652, and if you think it is possible that y is approximately a Poisson random variable, you may be able to stabilize the variance of the response by fitting $\sqrt{y}$ (instead of y) to the independent variables. Similarly, if y is a percentage or proportion, $\hat{p}$, we would expect $\sigma_{\hat{p}} = \sqrt{p(1 - p)/n}$ to be small when p is near 0 or 1 and to reach a maximum when p is equal to .5. A plot of the residuals versus $\hat{y}$ for this type of data would appear as shown in Figure 12.14b. To stabilize the variance of this type of data, fit $y^* = \sin^{-1} \sqrt{y}$, where y is expressed in radians.

A third situation that requires a variance-stabilizing transformation occurs when the response variable y follows a **multiplicative model**. Unlike the **additive** models discussed so far, in this model the dependent variable is written as the *product* of its mean and the random error component:

$$y = [E(y)] \cdot \varepsilon$$

The variance of this response will grow proportionally to the square of the mean, i.e., $\text{Var}(y) = [E(y)]^2\sigma^2$, where σ^2 is the variance of ε. Data subject to multiplicative errors produce a pattern of residuals about $\hat{y}$ like that shown in Figure 12.14c. The appropriate transformation for this type of data is $y^* = \log(y)$.

FIGURE 12.14 ▶

Plots of the residuals versus $\hat{y}$ for Poisson, binomial, and multiplicative response variables

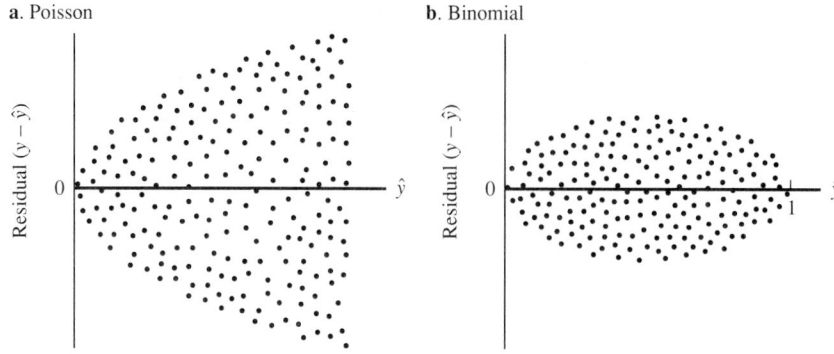

a. Poisson

b. Binomial

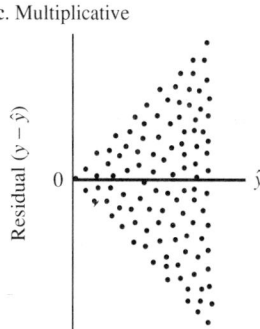

c. Multiplicative

The three variance-stabilizing transformations we have discussed are summarized in Table 12.7.

TABLE 12.7   Transformations to Stabilize the Variance of a Response

Residual Plot	Type of Data	Characteristics	Transformation
As shown in Figure 12.14a	Poisson	Counts per unit of time, distance, volume, etc.	$y^* = \sqrt{y}$
As shown in Figure 12.14b	Binomial	Proportions, percentages, or numbers of successes for a fixed number n of trials	$y^* = \sin^{-1}\sqrt{y}$ where y is proportion
As shown in Figure 12.14c	Multiplicative	Business and economic data	$y^* = \log(y)$

EXAMPLE 12.11

The data in Table 12.8 are the salaries, y, and years of experience, x, for a sample of 50 civil engineers. The first-order model $E(y) = \beta_0 + \beta_1 x$ was fit to the data using MINITAB. The MINITAB printout is shown in Figure 12.15, followed by a plot of the residuals versus $\hat{y}$ in Figure 12.16. (See page 654.) Interpret the results. Should the model be modified? If so, how?

TABLE 12.8   Salary Data for Example 12.11

Years of Experience	Salary	Years of Experience	Salary	Years of Experience	Salary
x	y	x	y	x	y
7	$26,075	21	$43,628	28	$99,139
28	79,370	4	16,105	23	52,624
23	65,726	24	65,644	17	50,594
18	41,983	20	63,022	25	53,272
19	62,308	20	47,780	26	65,343
15	41,154	15	38,853	19	46,216
24	53,610	25	66,537	16	54,288
13	33,697	25	67,447	3	20,844
2	22,444	28	64,785	12	32,586
8	32,562	26	61,581	23	71,235
20	43,076	27	70,678	20	36,530
21	56,000	20	51,301	19	52,745
18	58,667	18	39,346	27	67,282
7	22,210	1	24,833	25	80,931
2	20,521	26	65,929	12	32,303
18	49,727	20	41,721	11	38,371
11	33,233	26	82,641		

Solution

The MINITAB printout, Figure 12.15, suggests that the first-order model provides an adequate fit to the data. The R^2 value, .787, indicates that the model explains 78.7% of the sample variation in salaries. The t value for testing β_1, 13.31, is highly significant (p-value ≈ 0) and indicates that the model contributes information for the prediction of y. However, an examination of the residuals plotted against $\hat{y}$ (Figure 12.16) reveals a potential problem. Note the "cone" shape of the residual variability; the size of the residuals increases as the estimated mean salary increases.

FIGURE 12.15 ▶
MINITAB analysis for
Example 12.11

```
The regression equation is
Y = 11369 + 2141 X


Predictor        Coef       Stdev     t-ratio        p
Constant        11369        3160        3.60    0.001
X               2141.3       160.8      13.31    0.000


s = 8642        R-sq = 78.7%     R-sq(adj) = 78.2%


Analysis of Variance

SOURCE        DF         SS          MS         F         p
Regression     1 13238774784 13238774784    177.25    0.000
Error         48  3585073152    74689024
Total         49 16823847936


Unusual Observations
Obs.      X          Y      Fit Stdev.Fit  Residual   St.Resid
  31     1.0      24833    13511     3013     11322       1.40 X
  35    28.0      99139    71326     2005     27813       3.31R
  45    20.0      36530    54196     1259    -17666      -2.07R
R denotes an obs. with a large st. resid.
X denotes an obs. whose X value gives it large influence.
```

FIGURE 12.16 ▶
MINITAB residual plot for the data
of Example 12.11

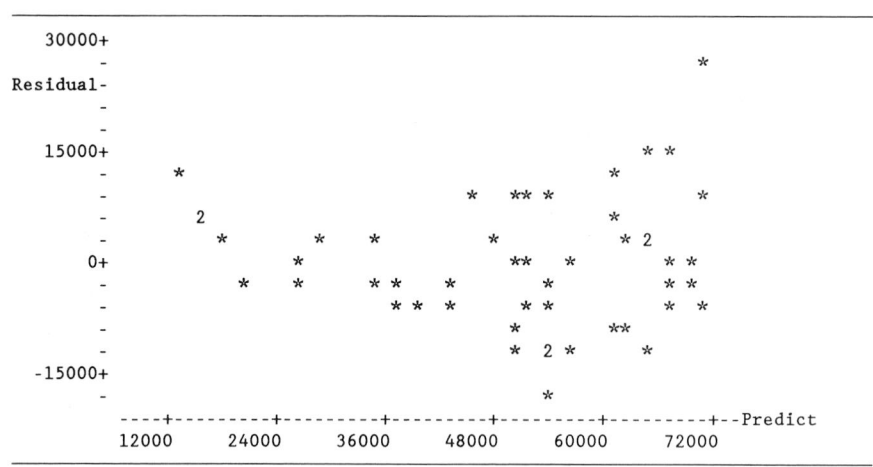

This residual plot indicates the possibility of a multiplicative model and suggests we use the variance-stabilizing transformation $y^* = \log(y)$. We explore this possibility further in the next example.

EXAMPLE 12.12

Consider the salary and experience data in Table 12.8. Use the logarithmic transformation on the dependent variable and relate $\log(y)$ to years of experience x with the linear model

$$\log(y) = \beta_0 + \beta_1 x + \varepsilon$$

a. Evaluate the adequacy of the model.
b. Interpret the value of $\hat{\beta}_1$.

Solution

a. The MINITAB printout in Figure 12.17 gives the regression analysis for the $n = 50$ measurements. The prediction equation is

$$\widehat{\log y} = 9.84 + .05x$$

with $R^2 = .863$ and $t = 17.43$ for testing $H_0: \beta_1 = 0$ is highly significant (p-value ≈ 0). Both imply that the model contributes significantly to the prediction of $\log(y)$.

FIGURE 12.17 ▶
MINITAB printout for the data in Example 12.12

```
The regression equation is
LOGY = 9.84 + 0.0500 X

Predictor        Coef        Stdev      t-ratio         p
Constant      9.84133     0.05636       174.63     0.000
X            0.049978    0.002868        17.43     0.000

s = 0.1541      R-sq = 86.3%      R-sq(adj) = 86.1%


Analysis of Variance

SOURCE        DF          SS           MS         F         p
Regression     1      7.2118       7.2118    303.65     0.000
Error         48      1.1400       0.0238
Total         49      8.3519


Unusual Observations
Obs.      X       LOGY        Fit  Stdev.Fit   Residual    St.Resid
 19     4.0     9.6869    10.0412     0.0460    -0.3544      -2.41R
 31     1.0    10.1199     9.8913     0.0537     0.2286       1.58 X
 45    20.0    10.5059    10.8409     0.0225    -0.3350      -2.20R
R denotes an obs. with a large st. resid.
X denotes an obs. whose X value gives it large influence.
```

The residual plot, shown in Figure 12.18 on page 656, indicates that the logarithmic transformation has stabilized the error variances. Note that the cone shape is gone; there is no apparent tendency of the residual variance to increase as mean salary increases. Therefore, we are confident that inferences using the logarithmic model are more reliable than those using the untransformed model.

FIGURE 12.18 ▶
MINITAB residual plot for the data in Example 12.12

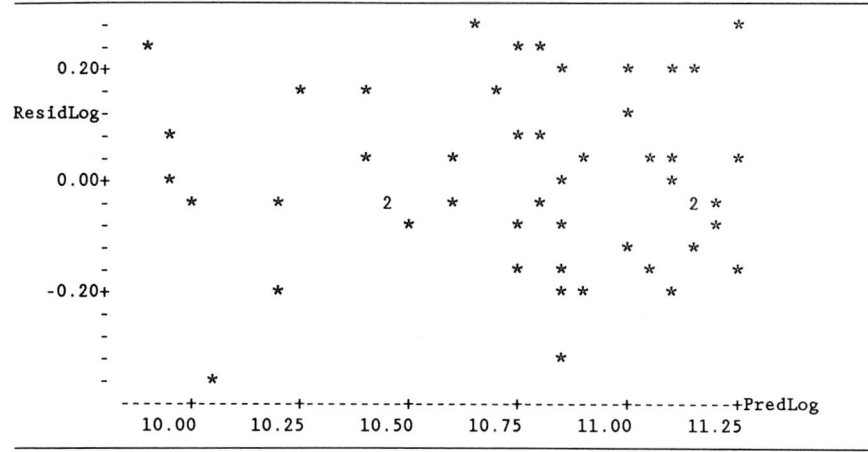

b. Because we are using the logarithm of salary as the dependent variable, the β estimates have slightly different interpretations than previously discussed. In general, a parameter β in a log-transformed model represents the percentage increase (or decrease) in the dependent variable for a 1-unit increase in the corresponding independent variable. The percentage change is calculated by taking the antilogarithm of the β estimate and subtracting 1, i.e., $e^{\hat{\beta}} - 1$.* For example, the percentage change in an engineer's salary associated with a 1-unit (i.e., 1-year) increase in years of experience x is $(e^{\hat{\beta}_1} - 1) = (e^{.05} - 1) = .051$. Thus, we estimate an engineer's salary to increase 5.1% for each additional year of experience.

· ·

DETECTING NONNORMALITY   Of the four standard regression assumptions about the random error ε, the assumption that ε is normally distributed is the least restrictive when we apply regression analysis in practice. That is, moderate departures from the assumption of normality have very little effect on the validity of the statistical tests, confidence intervals, and prediction intervals. In this case, we say that regression is **robust** with respect to nonnormality. However, great departures from normality cast doubt on any inferences derived from the regression analysis.

For moderate to large samples, the simplest way to determine whether the data grossly violate the assumption of normality is to construct a relative frequency histogram or a stem-and-leaf display of the residuals. If this distribution is mound-shaped and not badly skewed, you can be reasonably confident that the inferences derived from

---

*The result is derived by expressing the percentage change in salary y, as $(y_1 - y_0)/y_0$, where y_1 = the value of y when, say, $x = 1$, and y_0 = the value of y when $x = 0$. Now let $y^* = \log(y)$ and assume the log model is $y^* = \beta_0 + \beta_1 x$. Then

$$y = e^{y^*} = e^{\beta_0}e^{\beta_1 x} = \begin{cases} e^{\beta_0} & \text{when } x = 0 \\ e^{\beta_0}e^{\beta_1} & \text{when } x = 1 \end{cases}$$

Substituting, we have

$$\frac{y_1 - y_0}{y_0} = \frac{e^{\beta_0}e^{\beta_1} - e^{\beta_0}}{e^{\beta_0}} = e^{\beta_1} - 1$$

the regression analysis are valid. For small samples, box plots often provide more information about skewness in the data.

To illustrate, a SAS relative frequency histogram for the $n = 50$ residuals of Example 12.11 is shown in Figure 12.19. You can see that this distribution is mound-shaped and reasonably symmetric. Consequently, it is unlikely that the normality assumption is violated for this regression analysis.

When nonnormality of the random error term is detected, it can often be rectified by applying one of the transformations listed in Table 12.7. For example, if the relative frequency distribution (or stem-and-leaf display) of the residuals is highly skewed to the right (as it usually is for Poisson data), the square-root transformation on y will stabilize (approximately) the variance and, at the same time, will reduce skewness in the distribution of residuals. Nonnormality may also be due to outliers, discussed next.

FIGURE 12.19 ▶
SAS histogram for residuals of Example 12.11

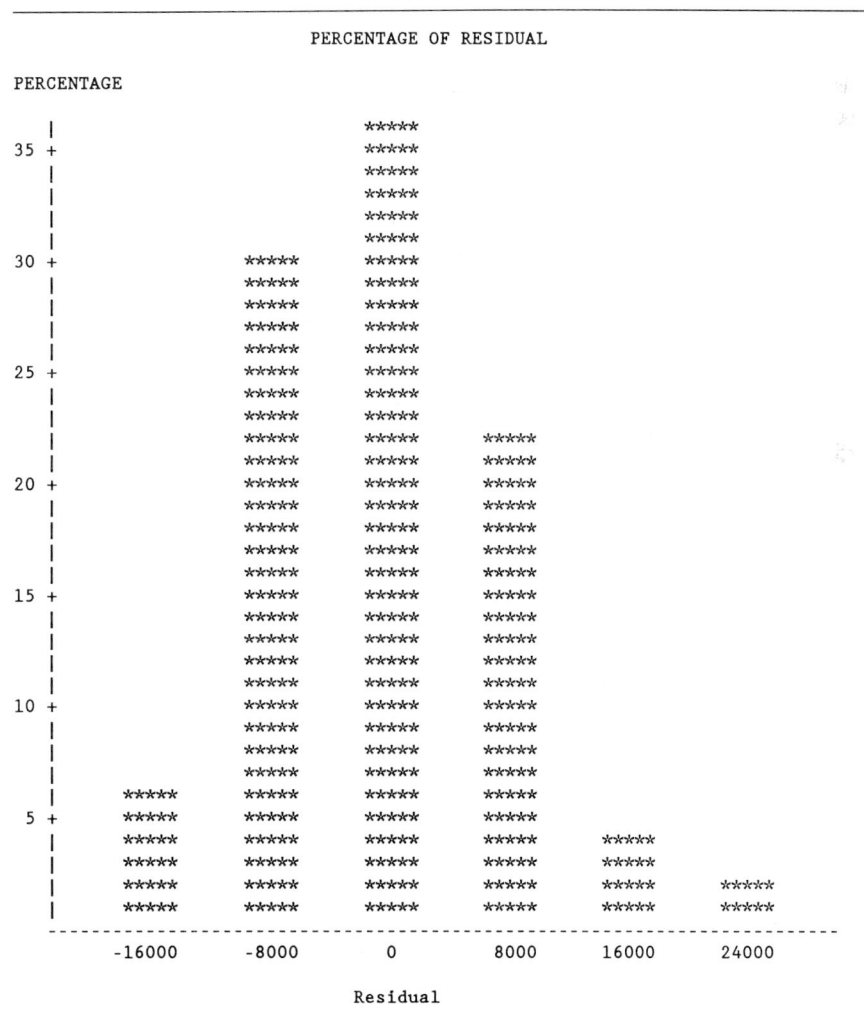

DETECTING OUTLIERS AND INFLUENTIAL OBSERVATIONS   Residual plots can also be used to detect **outliers**, values of y that appear to be in disagreement with the model. Since almost all values of y should lie within 3σ of $E(y)$, the mean values of y, we would expect most of them to lie within $3s$ of $\hat{y}$. If a residual is larger than $3s$ (in absolute value), we consider it an outlier and seek background information that might explain the reason for its large value.

Definition 12.3
....

A residual that is larger than $3s$ (in absolute value) is considered to be an **outlier**.

To detect outliers, we can construct horizontal lines located a distance of $3s$ above and below 0 (see Figure 12.20) on a residual plot. Any residual falling outside the band formed by these lines would be considered an outlier. We would then initiate an investigation to seek the cause of the departure of such observations from expected behavior.

FIGURE 12.20 ▶

3s lines used to locate outliers

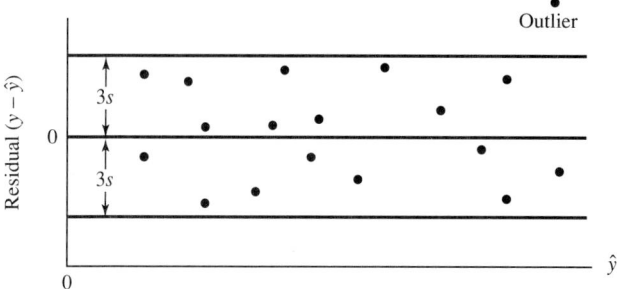

Although some analysts advocate elimination of outliers, regardless of whether cause can be assigned, others encourage the correction of only those outliers that can be traced to specific causes. The best philosophy is probably a compromise between these extremes. For example, before deciding the fate of an outlier you may want to determine how much influence it has on the regression analysis. When an accurate outlier (i.e., an outlier that is not due to recording or measurement error) is found to have a dramatic effect on the regression analysis, it may be the model and not the outlier that is suspect. Omission of important independent variables or higher-order terms could be the reason why the model is not predicting well for the outlying observation.

Several sophisticated numerical techniques are available for identifying outlying influential observations. One of these methods requires that you delete observations one at a time, each time refitting the regression model based on only the remaining

$n - 1$ observations. This method is based on a statistical procedure, called the **jackknife**,* that is gaining increasing acceptance among practitioners. The basic principle of the jackknife when applied to regression is to compare the regression results using all n observations to the results with the ith observation deleted, to ascertain how much influence a particular observation has on the analysis. Using the jackknife, several alternative influence measures can be calculated.

The **deleted residual**, $d_i = y_i - \hat{y}_{(i)}$, measures the difference between the observed value y_i and the predicted value $\hat{y}_{(i)}$, based on the model with the ith observation deleted. [The notation (i) is generally used to indicate that the observed value y_i was deleted from the regression analysis.] An observation with an unusually large (in absolute value) deleted residual is considered to have large influence on the fitted model.

A measure closely related to the deleted residual is the difference between the predicted value based on the model fit to all n observations and the predicted value obtained when y_i is deleted, i.e., $\hat{y}_i - \hat{y}_{(i)}$. When the difference $\hat{y}_i - \hat{y}_{(i)}$ is large relative to the predicted value $\hat{y}_i$, the observation y_i is said to influence the regression fit.

A third way to identify an influential observation using the jackknife is to calculate, for each β parameter in the model, the difference between the parameter estimate based on all n observations and the estimate based on only $n - 1$ observations (with the observation in question deleted). Consider, for example, the straight-line model $E(y) = \beta_0 + \beta_1 x$. The differences $\hat{\beta}_0 - \hat{\beta}_0^{(i)}$ and $\hat{\beta}_1 - \hat{\beta}_1^{(i)}$ measure how influential the ith observation y_i is on the parameter estimates. [Using the (i) notation defined earlier, $\hat{\beta}_j^{(i)}$ represents the estimate of the β_j coefficient when the ith observation is omitted from the analysis.] If the parameter estimates change drastically, i.e., if the absolute differences are large, y_i is deemed an influential observation.

DETECTING CORRELATED ERRORS   The assumption that the random errors are independent (uncorrelated) is most often violated when the data employed in a regression analysis are a **time series**. With time series data, the experimental units in the sample are time periods (e.g., years, months, or days) in consecutive time order.

For most business and economic time series, there is a tendency for the regression residuals to have positive and negative runs over time. For example, consider fitting a straight-line regression model to yearly time series data. The model takes the form

$$E(y) = \beta_0 + \beta_1 t$$

where y is the value of the time series in year t. A plot of the yearly residuals may appear as shown in Figure 12.21 on page 660. Note that if the residual for year t is positive (or negative) there is a tendency for the residual for year $(t + 1)$ to be positive (or negative). That is, neighboring residuals tend to have the same sign and appear to be correlated. Thus, the assumption of independent errors is likely to be violated and any inferences derived from the model are suspect.

---

*The procedure derives its name from the Boy Scout jackknife, which serves as a handy tool in a variety of situations when specialized techniques may not be applicable. [See Belsley, Kuh, and Welsch (1980).]

FIGURE 12.21 ▶
Residual plot for yearly time series model

Remedial measures for this problem involve proposing complex time series models that include a model for both the deterministic and the random error components. Time series models are beyond the scope of this text. Consult the references at the end of this chapter to learn more about these models.

A Summary of Steps to Follow in a Residual Analysis

1. Check for a **misspecified model** by plotting the residuals $(y - \hat{y})$ against each independent variable in the model. A curvilinear trend detected in a plot implies that a quadratic term for that particular x variable will probably improve model adequacy.

2. Check for **unequal variances** by plotting the residuals against the predicted values $(\hat{y})$. If you detect a pattern similar to one of those shown in Figure 12.14, refit the model using the appropriate variance-stabilizing transformation on y (see Table 12.7).

3. Check for **nonnormal errors** by constructing a stem-and-leaf display (or histogram) for the residuals. If you detect extreme skewness in the data, then either apply one of the transformations listed in Table 12.7 or look for one or more outliers (see step 4).

4. Check for **outliers** by locating residuals that lie a distance of $3s$ or more above or below 0 on a residual plot versus $\hat{y}$. Before eliminating an outlier from the analysis, you should conduct an investigation to determine its cause. If the outlier is found to be the result of a coding or recording error, fix it or remove it. Otherwise, you may want to determine how influential the outlier is before deciding its fate. Several measures of influence are available, including *deleted residuals*.

5. Check for **correlated errors** by plotting the residuals in time order. If you detect runs of positive and negative residuals, propose a time series model to account for the residual correlation.

EXERCISES

12.32   Identify the problem(s) in each of the following residual plots:

a.

b.

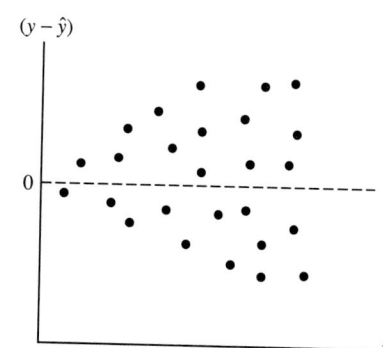

c.

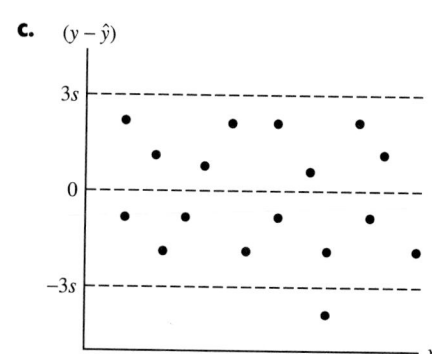

d.

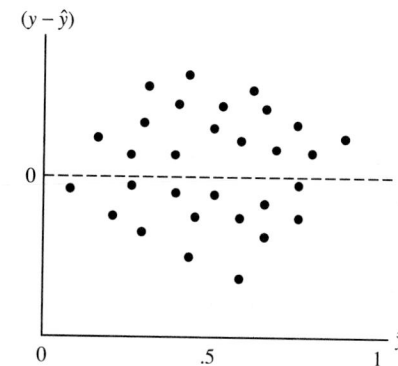

e.

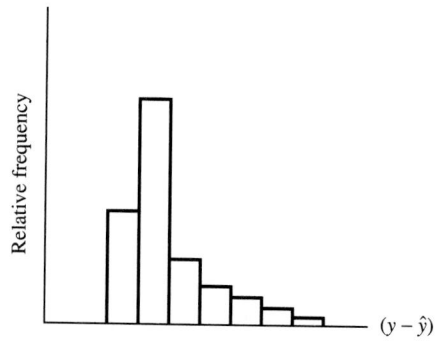

12.33   PCBs make up a family of hazardous chemicals that are often dumped, illegally, by industrial plants into the surrounding streams, rivers, or bays. The table on page 662 reports the 1984 and 1985 concentrations of PCBs (measured in parts per billion) in water samples collected from 37 U.S. bays and estuaries. An official from the Environmental Protection Agency wants to model the 1985 PCB concentration (y) of a bay as a function of the 1984 PCB concentration (x). Consider the first-order model $E(y) = \beta_0 + \beta_1 x$. A SAS printout of the analysis, with residuals, follows.

Bay	State	PCB Concentration 1984	1985
Casco Bay	ME	95.28	77.55
Merrimack River	MA	52.97	29.23
Salem Harbor	MA	533.58	403.1
Boston Harbor	MA	17,104.86	736
Buzzards Bay	MA	308.46	192.15
Narragansett Bay	RI	159.96	220.6
East Long Island Sound	NY	10	8.62
West Long Island Sound	NY	234.43	174.31
Raritan Bay	NJ	443.89	529.28
Delaware Bay	DE	2.5	130.67
Lower Chesapeake Bay	VA	51	39.74
Pamlico Sound	NC	0	0
Charleston Harbor	SC	9.1	8.43
Sapelo Sound	GA	0	0
St. Johns River	FL	140	120.04
Tampa Bay	FL	0	0
Apalachicola Bay	FL	12	11.93
Mobile Bay	AL	0	0
Round Island	MS	0	0
Mississippi River Delta	LA	34	30.14
Barataria Bay	LA	0	0
San Antonio Bay	TX	0	0
Corpus Christi Bay	TX	0	0
San Diego Harbor	CA	422.1	531.67
San Diego Bay	CA	6.74	9.3
Dana Point	CA	7.06	5.74
Seal Beach	CA	46.71	46.47
San Pedro Canyon	CA	159.56	176.9
Santa Monica Bay	CA	14	13.69
Bodega Bay	CA	4.18	4.89
Coos Bay	OR	3.19	6.6
Columbia River Mouth	OR	8.77	6.73
Nisqually Beach	WA	4.23	4.28
Commencement Bay	WA	20.6	20.5
Elliott Bay	WA	329.97	414.5
Lutak Inlet	AK	5.5	5.8
Nahku Bay	AK	6.6	5.08

Source: *Environmental Quality*, 1987–1988.

Analysis of Variance

Source	DF	Sum of Squares	Mean Square	F Value	Prob>F
Model	1	462349.85512	462349.85512	21.772	0.0001
Error	35	743254.18292	21235.83380		
C Total	36	1205604.0380			

Root MSE	145.72520	R-square	0.3835
Dep Mean	107.13351	Adj R-sq	0.3659
C.V.	136.02205		

Parameter Estimates

Variable	DF	Parameter Estimate	Standard Error	T for H0: Parameter=0	Prob > |T|
INTERCEP	1	85.013798	24.42159452	3.481	0.0014
PCB84	1	0.040454	0.00866978	4.666	0.0001

Obs	BAY	PCB84	Dep Var PCB85	Predict Value	Residual
1	Casco	95.28	77.5500	88.8682	-11.3182
2	Merrmack	52.97	29.2300	87.1566	-57.9266
3	Salem	533.58	403.1	106.6	296.5
4	Boston	17104.86	736.0	777.0	-40.9695
5	Buzzards	308.46	192.2	97.5	94.7
6	Narragan	159.96	220.6	91.4848	129.1
7	ELongIsl	10	8.6200	85.4183	-76.7983
8	WLongIsl	234.43	174.3	94.5	79.8126
9	Raritan	443.89	529.3	103.0	426.3
10	Delaware	2.5	130.7	85.1149	45.5551
11	LChesapk	51	39.7400	87.0769	-47.3369
12	Pamilico	0	0	85.0138	-85.0138
13	Charlest	9.1	8.4300	85.3819	-76.9519
14	Sapelo	0	0	85.0138	-85.0138
15	StJohns	140	120.0	90.6773	29.3627
16	Tampa	0	0	85.0138	-85.0138
17	Apalach	12	11.9300	85.4992	-73.5692
18	Mobile	0	0	85.0138	-85.0138
19	RoundIsl	0	0	85.0138	-85.0138
20	MissRiv	34	30.1400	86.3892	-56.2492
21	Baratara	0	0	85.0138	-85.0138
22	SanAnton	0	0	85.0138	-85.0138
23	CorpusCh	0	0	85.0138	-85.0138
24	SDiegoHa	422.1	531.7	102.1	429.6
25	SDiegoBa	6.74	9.3000	85.2865	-75.9865
26	DanaPt	7.06	5.7400	85.2994	-79.5594
27	SealBch	46.71	46.4700	86.9034	-40.4334
28	SanPedro	159.56	176.9	91.4686	85.4314
29	SantaMon	14	13.6900	85.5802	-71.8902
30	Bodega	4.18	4.8900	85.1829	-80.2929
31	Coos	3.19	6.6000	85.1428	-78.5428
32	Columbia	8.77	6.7300	85.3686	-78.6386
33	Nisquall	4.23	4.2800	85.1849	-80.9049
34	Commence	20.6	20.5000	85.8471	-65.3471
35	Elliot	329.97	414.5	98.4	316.1
36	Lutak	5.5	5.8000	85.2363	-79.4363
37	Nahku	6.6	5.0800	85.2808	-80.2008

a. Is the model adequate for predicting y? Explain.

b. Construct a residual plot for the data. Do you detect any outliers? If so, identify them.

c. Refer to part b. Although the residual for Boston Harbor is not, by definition, an outlier, the EPA believes that it has strong influence on the regression because of its large y value. Remove the observation for Boston Harbor from the data and refit the model. Has model adequacy improved?

d. An alternative approach is to use the log transformations $y^* = $ natural $\log(y + 1)$ and $x^* = $ natural $\log(x + 1)$, and fit the model $E(y^*) = \beta_0 + \beta_1 x^*$. A SAS printout for this model follows. Conduct a test for model adequacy and perform a residual analysis. Interpret the results. In particular, comment on the residual value for Boston Harbor.

Analysis of Variance

Source	DF	Sum of Squares	Mean Square	F Value	Prob>F
Model	1	145.58169	145.58169	251.172	0.0001
Error	35	20.28631	0.57961		
C Total	36	165.86800			

Root MSE	0.76132	R-square	0.8777	
Dep Mean	2.94451	Adj R-sq	0.8742	
C.V.	25.85556			

Parameter Estimates

Variable	DF	Parameter Estimate	Standard Error	T for H0: Parameter=0	Prob > |T|
INTERCEP	1	0.425110	0.20232699	2.101	0.0429
LNPCB84	1	0.850826	0.05368523	15.848	0.0001

Obs	BAY	LNPCB84	Dep Var LNPCB85	Predict Value	Residual
1	Casco	4.567261	4.3637	4.3111	0.0527
2	Merrmack	3.988428	3.4088	3.8186	-0.4097
3	Salem	6.281481	6.0017	5.7696	0.2321
4	Boston	9.747176	6.6026	8.7183	-2.1157
5	Buzzards	5.734829	5.2635	5.3045	-0.0410
6	Narragan	5.081156	5.4009	4.7483	0.6526
7	ELongIsl	2.397895	2.2638	2.4653	-0.2015
8	WLongIsl	5.461414	5.1666	5.0718	0.0947
9	Raritan	6.097827	6.2734	5.6133	0.6601
10	Delaware	1.252763	4.8803	1.4910	3.3893
11	LChesapk	3.951244	3.7072	3.7869	-0.0797
12	Pamilico	0	0	0.4251	-0.4251
13	Charlest	2.312535	2.2439	2.3927	-0.1488
14	Sapelo	0	0	0.4251	-0.4251
15	StJohns	4.94876	4.7961	4.6356	0.1605
16	Tampa	0	0	0.4251	-0.4251
17	Apalach	2.564949	2.5596	2.6074	-0.0479
18	Mobile	0	0	0.4251	-0.4251
19	RoundIsl	0	0	0.4251	-0.4251
20	MissRiv	3.555348	3.4385	3.4501	-0.0116
21	Baratara	0	0	0.4251	-0.4251
22	SanAnton	0	0	0.4251	-0.4251
23	CorpusCh	0	0	0.4251	-0.4251
24	SDiegoHa	6.047609	6.2779	5.5706	0.7073
25	SDiegoBa	2.046402	2.3321	2.1662	0.1659
26	DanaPt	2.086914	1.9081	2.2007	-0.2926
27	SealBch	3.865141	3.8601	3.7137	0.1464
28	SanPedro	5.078668	5.1812	4.7462	0.4351
29	SantaMon	2.70805	2.6872	2.7292	-0.0420
30	Bodega	1.644805	1.7733	1.8246	-0.0513
31	Coos	1.432701	2.0281	1.6441	0.3841
32	Columbia	2.279316	2.0451	2.3644	-0.3193
33	Nisquall	1.654411	1.6639	1.8327	-0.1688
34	Commence	3.072693	3.0681	3.0394	0.0286
35	Elliot	5.802028	6.0295	5.3616	0.6679
36	Lutak	1.871802	1.9169	2.0177	-0.1008
37	Nahku	2.028148	1.8050	2.1507	-0.3457

12.34 Moissanite is a popular abrasive material because of its extreme hardness. Another important property of moissanite is elasticity. The elastic properties of the material were investigated in the *Journal of Applied*

Physics (Sept. 1993). A diamond anvil cell was used to compress a mixture of moissanite, sodium chloride, and gold in a ratio of 33:99:1 by volume. The compressed volume, y, of the mixture (relative to the zero-pressure volume) was measured at each of 11 different pressures (GPa). The results are displayed in the table, followed by a MINITAB printout for the straight-line regression model $E(y) = \beta_0 + \beta_1 x$.

Compressed Volume y, %	Pressure x, GPa	Compressed Volume y, %	Pressure x, GPa
100	0	85.2	51.6
96	9.4	83.3	60.1
93.8	15.8	82.9	62.6
90.2	30.4	82.9	62.6
87.7	41.6	81.7	68.4
86.2	46.9		

Source: Bassett, W. A., Weathers, M. S., and Wu, T. C. "Compressibility of SiC up to 68.4 GPa." *Journal of Applied Physics*, Vol. 74, No. 6, Sept. 15, 1993, p. 3825 (Table I).

```
The regression equation is
Volume = 98.6 - 0.256 Pressure

Predictor        Coef       Stdev     t-ratio         p
Constant      98.6149      0.4037      244.26     0.000
Pressure    -0.255594    0.008646      -29.56     0.000

s = 0.6484      R-sq = 99.0%      R-sq(adj) = 98.9%

Analysis of Variance

SOURCE         DF          SS          MS         F         p
Regression      1      367.34      367.34    873.87     0.000
Error           9        3.78        0.42
Total          10      371.12

Unusual Observations
Obs.Pressure      Volume      Fit Stdev.Fit   Residual   St.Resid
   1      0.0     100.000   98.615     0.404      1.385      2.73R

R denotes an obs. with a large st. resid.
```

a. Calculate the regression residuals.
b. Plot the residuals against x. Do you detect a trend?
c. Propose an alternative model based on the plot, part b.
d. Fit and analyze the model, part c.

12.35 Chemical engineers at Tokyo Metropolitan University analyzed urban air specimens for the presence of low molecular weight dicarboxylic acid (*Environmental Science & Engineering*, Oct. 1993). The dicarboxylic acid (as a percent of total carbon) and oxidant concentrations for 19 air specimens collected from urban Tokyo are listed in the table on page 666. SAS printouts for the straight-line model relating dicarboxylic acid percentage (y) to oxidant concentration (x) follow. Conduct a complete residual analysis.

Dicarboxylic Acid %	Oxidant ppm	Dicarboxylic Acid %	Oxidant ppm
.85	78	.50	32
1.45	80	.38	28
1.80	74	.30	25
1.80	78	.70	45
1.60	60	.80	40
1.20	62	.90	45
1.30	57	1.22	41
.20	49	1.00	34
.22	34	1.00	25
.40	36		

Source: Kawamura, K., and Ikushima, K. "Seasonal changes in the distribution of dicarboxylic acids in the urban atmosphere." *Environmental Science & Technology*, Vol. 27, No. 10, Oct. 1993, p. 2232 (data extracted from Figure 4).

Dependent Variable: DICARBOX

Analysis of Variance

Source	DF	Sum of Squares	Mean Square	F Value	Prob>F
Model	1	2.41362	2.41362	17.080	0.0007
Error	17	2.40234	0.14131		
C Total	18	4.81597			

Root MSE	0.37592	R-square	0.5012
Dep Mean	0.92737	Adj R-sq	0.4718
C.V.	40.53600		

Parameter Estimates

Variable	DF	Parameter Estimate	Standard Error	T for H0: Parameter=0	Prob > |T|
INTERCEP	1	-0.023737	0.24576577	-0.097	0.9242
OXIDANT	1	0.019579	0.00473739	4.133	0.0007

Obs	Dep Var DICARBOX	Predict Value	Std Err Predict	Residual	Std Err Residual	Student Residual	-2-1-0 1 2
1	0.8500	1.5034	0.164	-0.6534	0.338	-1.931	***
2	0.5000	0.6028	0.117	-0.1028	0.357	-0.288	
3	1.4500	1.5425	0.172	-0.0925	0.334	-0.277	
4	0.3800	0.5245	0.130	-0.1445	0.353	-0.410	
5	1.8000	1.4251	0.148	0.3749	0.346	1.085	**
6	0.3000	0.4657	0.141	-0.1657	0.348	-0.476	
7	1.8000	1.5034	0.164	0.2966	0.338	0.877	*
8	0.7000	0.8573	0.088	-0.1573	0.365	-0.430	
9	1.6000	1.1510	0.102	0.4490	0.362	1.241	**
10	0.8000	0.7594	0.095	0.0406	0.364	0.112	
11	1.2000	1.1901	0.107	0.0099	0.360	0.027	
12	0.9000	0.8573	0.088	0.0427	0.365	0.117	
13	1.3000	1.0922	0.095	0.2078	0.364	0.571	*
14	1.2200	0.7790	0.093	0.4410	0.364	1.211	**
15	0.2000	0.9356	0.086	-0.7356	0.366	-2.010	****
16	1.0000	0.6419	0.110	0.3581	0.359	0.997	*
17	0.2200	0.6419	0.110	-0.4219	0.359	-1.174	**
18	1.0000	0.4657	0.141	0.5343	0.348	1.533	***
19	0.4000	0.6811	0.105	-0.2811	0.361	-0.779	*

(continued)

```
Sum of Residuals            1.110223E-15
Sum of Squared Residuals         2.4023
Predicted Resid SS (Press)       3.0590
```

Plot of RESIDUAL*PREDICT.   Symbol used is '*'.

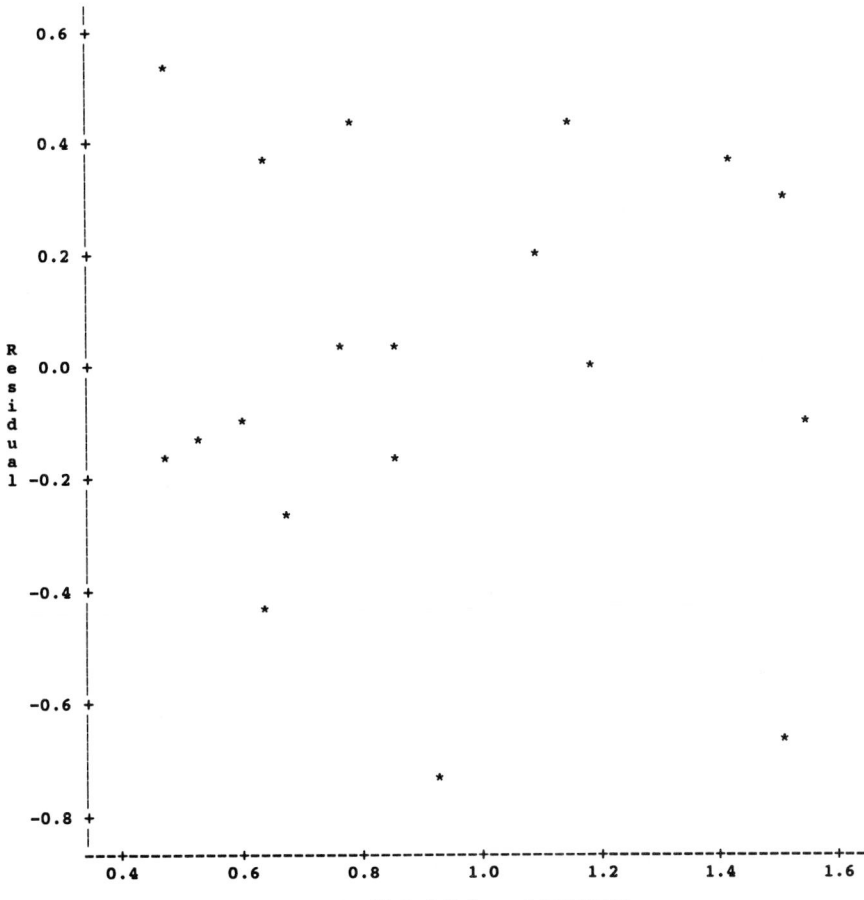

Predicted Value of DICARBOX

UNIVARIATE PROCEDURE

Variable=RESIDUAL   Residual

Moments

N	19	Sum Wgts	19
Mean	0	Sum	0
Std Dev	0.365327	Variance	0.133464
Skewness	-0.41391	Kurtosis	-0.43294
USS	2.402345	CSS	2.402345
CV	.	Std Mean	0.083812
T:Mean=0	0	Prob>$|T|$	1.0000
Sgn Rank	4	Prob>$|S|$	0.8906
Num ^= 0	19		
W:Normal	0.951334	Prob<W	0.4220

(continued)

```
                          Quantiles(Def=5)

            100% Max  0.534273      99%  0.534273
             75% Q3   0.358066      95%  0.534273
             50% Med  0.009867      90%  0.449024
             25% Q1  -0.16573       10% -0.65339
              0% Min -0.73561        5% -0.73561
                                     1% -0.73561
            Range     1.269885
            Q3-Q1     0.523793
            Mode     -0.73561

                             Extremes

            Lowest      Obs     Highest     Obs
          -0.73561(     15) 0.358066(      16)
          -0.65339(      1) 0.374924(       5)
          -0.42193(     17) 0.441016(      14)
          -0.28109(     19) 0.449024(       9)
          -0.16573(      6) 0.534273(      18)


     Stem Leaf                     #          Boxplot
        4 453                      3             |
        2 1067                     4          +-----+
        0 144                      3          *--+--*
       -0 76409                    5          +-----+
       -2 8                        1             |
       -4 2                        1             |
       -6 45                       2             |
          ----+----+----+----+
     Multiply Stem.Leaf by 10**-1



                         Normal Probability Plot
        0.5+                              *++*++ *
           |                           **+*+*+
           |                         **+*++
       -0.1+                 * ***+*
           |                +*+++
           |           ++++++*
       -0.7+     +++*+   *
           +----+----+----+----+----+----+----+----+----+----+
              -2        -1         0        +1        +2
```

12.36 Refer to *The New England Journal of Medicine* study of passive exposure to environmental tobacco smoke in children with cystic fibrosis, Exercise 11.39. Recall that the researchers investigated the correlation between a child's weight percentile (y) and the number of cigarettes smoked per day in the child's home (x). The accompanying table lists the data for the 25 boys.

a. A SAS regression printout (with residuals) for the straight-line model relating y to x is shown here. Examine the residuals. Do you detect any outliers?

b. Influence diagnostics are also given on the SAS printout. Interpret these results. [*Note:* "Studentized" deleted residuals, i.e., the deleted residuals divided by their standard errors, are given under the heading **Rstudent**; the difference between fits, $\hat{y}_i - \hat{y}_{(i)}$, is given under **Dffits**; and the difference between the estimated β's, $\hat{\beta}_1 - \hat{\beta}_1^{(i)}$, is given under **X Dfbetas**.]

Weight Percentile	No. of Cigarettes Smoked per Day	Weight Percentile	No. of Cigarettes Smoked per Day
y	x	y	x
6	0	43	0
6	15	49	0
2	40	50	0
8	23	49	22
11	20	46	30
17	7	54	0
24	3	58	0
25	0	62	0
17	25	66	0
25	20	66	23
25	15	83	0
31	23	87	44
35	10		

Source: Rubin, B. K. "Exposure of children with cystic fibrosis to environmental tobacco smoke." *The New England Journal of Medicine*, Sept. 20, 1990, Vol. 323, No. 12, p. 785 (data extracted from Figure 3).

SAS printout for Exercise 12.36

Dependent Variable: Y

Analysis of Variance

Source	DF	Sum of Squares	Mean Square	F Value	Prob>F
Model	1	304.88209	304.88209	0.500	0.4864
Error	23	14011.11791	609.17904		
C Total	24	14316.00000			

Root MSE	24.68155	R-square	0.0213
Dep Mean	37.80000	Adj R-sq	-0.0213
C.V.	65.29511		

Parameter Estimates

Variable	DF	Parameter Estimate	Standard Error	T for H0: Parameter=0	Prob > |T|
INTERCEP	1	41.152655	6.84296599	6.014	0.0001
X	1	-0.261926	C.37024180	-0.707	0.4864

(continued)

SAS printout for Exercise 12.36, continued

Obs	Dep Var Y	Predict Value	Std Err Predict	Residual	Std Err Residual	Student Residual	-2-1-0 1 2	Cook's D
1	6.0000	41.1527	6.843	-35.1527	23.714	-1.482	**|	0.091
2	43.0000	41.1527	6.843	1.8473	23.714	0.078	|	0.000
3	6.0000	37.2238	5.003	-31.2238	24.169	-1.292	**|	0.036
4	49.0000	41.1527	6.843	7.8473	23.714	0.331	|	0.005
5	2.0000	30.6756	11.215	-28.6756	21.986	-1.304	**|	0.221
6	50.0000	41.1527	6.843	8.8473	23.714	0.373	|	0.006
7	8.0000	35.1284	6.215	-27.1284	23.886	-1.136	**|	0.044
8	49.0000	35.3903	5.997	13.6097	23.942	0.568	|*	0.010
9	11.0000	35.9141	5.610	-24.9141	24.036	-1.037	**|	0.029
10	46.0000	33.2949	8.057	12.7051	23.329	0.545	|*	0.018
11	17.0000	39.3192	5.383	-22.3192	24.087	-0.927	*|	0.021
12	54.0000	41.1527	6.843	12.8473	23.714	0.542	|*	0.012
13	24.0000	40.3669	6.126	-16.3669	23.909	-0.685	*|	0.015
14	58.0000	41.1527	6.843	16.8473	23.714	0.710	|*	0.021
15	25.0000	41.1527	6.843	-16.1527	23.714	-0.681	*|	0.019
16	62.0000	41.1527	6.843	20.8473	23.714	0.879	|*	0.032
17	17.0000	34.6045	6.691	-17.6045	23.757	-0.741	*|	0.022
18	66.0000	41.1527	6.843	24.8473	23.714	1.048	|**	0.046
19	25.0000	35.9141	5.610	-10.9141	24.036	-0.454	|	0.006
20	66.0000	35.1284	6.215	30.8716	23.886	1.292	|**	0.057
21	25.0000	37.2238	5.003	-12.2238	24.169	-0.506	*|	0.005
22	83.0000	41.1527	6.843	41.8473	23.714	1.765	|***	0.130
23	31.0000	35.1284	6.215	-4.1284	23.886	-0.173	|	0.001
24	87.0000	29.6279	12.562	57.3721	21.246	2.700	|*****	1.275
25	35.0000	38.5334	5.044	-3.5334	24.161	-0.146	|	0.000

Obs	Rstudent	Hat Diag H	Cov Ratio	Dffits	INTERCEP Dfbetas	X Dfbetas
1	-1.5244	0.0769	0.9686	-0.4399	-0.4399	0.3046
2	0.0762	0.0769	1.1834	0.0220	0.0220	-0.0152
3	-1.3120	0.0411	0.9804	-0.2716	-0.1627	-0.0442
4	0.3244	0.0769	1.1727	0.0936	0.0936	-0.0648
5	-1.3255	0.2065	1.1812	-0.6762	0.2058	-0.6072
6	0.3660	0.0769	1.1697	0.1056	0.1056	-0.0731
7	-1.1433	0.0634	1.0398	-0.2975	-0.0453	-0.1808
8	0.5599	0.0590	1.1292	0.1403	0.0281	0.0797
9	-1.0383	0.0517	1.0474	-0.2424	-0.0741	-0.1152
10	0.5361	0.1066	1.1920	0.1852	-0.0195	0.1463
11	-0.9236	0.0476	1.0635	-0.2064	-0.1936	0.0823
12	0.5333	0.0769	1.1540	0.1539	0.1539	-0.1066
13	-0.6764	0.0616	1.1178	-0.1733	-0.1718	0.1027
14	0.7026	0.0769	1.1326	0.2027	0.2027	-0.1404
15	-0.6730	0.0769	1.1367	-0.1942	-0.1942	0.1345
16	0.8746	0.0769	1.1058	0.2524	0.2524	-0.1748
17	-0.7335	0.0735	1.1240	-0.2066	-0.0134	-0.1395
18	1.0501	0.0769	1.0737	0.3030	0.3030	-0.2099
19	-0.4461	0.0517	1.1319	-0.1041	-0.0318	-0.0495
20	1.3126	0.0634	1.0036	0.3415	0.0520	0.2075
21	-0.4974	0.0411	1.1146	-0.1030	-0.0617	-0.0168
22	1.8561	0.0769	0.8851	0.5356	0.5356	-0.3709
23	-0.1691	0.0634	1.1639	-0.0440	-0.0067	-0.0267
24	3.1959	0.2590	0.6880	1.8896	-0.6678	1.7376
25	-0.1431	0.0418	1.1385	-0.0299	-0.0253	0.0061

12.37 Breakdowns of machines that produce steel cans are very costly. The more breakdowns, the fewer cans produced, and the smaller the company's profits. To help anticipate profit loss, the owners of a can company would like to find a model that will predict the number of breakdowns on the assembly line. The model proposed by the company's statisticians is the following:

$$y = \beta_0 + \beta_1 x_1 + \beta_2 x_2 + \beta_3 x_3 + \beta_4 x_4 + \varepsilon$$

where y is the number of breakdowns per 8-hour shift,

$$x_1 = \begin{cases} 1 & \text{if afternoon shift} \\ 0 & \text{otherwise} \end{cases} \qquad x_2 = \begin{cases} 1 & \text{if midnight} \\ 0 & \text{otherwise} \end{cases}$$

x_3 is the temperature of the plant (°F), and x_4 is the number of inexperienced personnel working on the assembly line. After the model is fit using the least squares procedure, the residuals are plotted against $\hat{y}$, as shown in the accompanying figure.

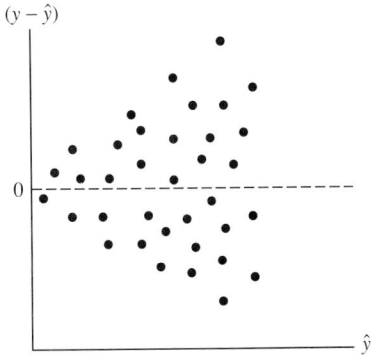

a. Do you detect a pattern in the residual plot? What does this suggest about the least squares assumptions?
b. Given the nature of the response variable y and the pattern detected in part **a**, what model adjustments would you recommend?

12.38 The data in the table on page 672 are sales, y, in thousands of dollars per week, for fast-food outlets in each of four cities. The objective is to model sales, y, as a function of traffic flow, adjusting for city-to-city variations that might be due to size or other market conditions. The model is

$$E(y) = \beta_0 + \beta_1 x_1 + \beta_2 x_2 + \beta_3 x_3 + \beta_4 x_4$$

where

$$x_1 = \begin{cases} 1 & \text{if city 1} \\ 0 & \text{if other} \end{cases} \qquad x_2 = \begin{cases} 1 & \text{if city 2} \\ 0 & \text{if other} \end{cases}$$

$$x_3 = \begin{cases} 1 & \text{if city 3} \\ 0 & \text{if other} \end{cases} \qquad x_4 = \text{Traffic flow}$$

See the SAS printout for the regression analysis.
a. Is the model statistically useful for predicting y? Explain.
b. A residual plot for the regression is shown. Examine the plot. Do you detect any outliers?

City	Traffic Flow thousands of cars	Weekly Sales y, thousands of dollars	City	Traffic Flow thousands of cars	Weekly Sales y, thousands of dollars
1	59.3	6.3	3	75.8	8.2
1	60.3	6.6	3	48.3	5.0
1	82.1	7.6	3	41.4	3.9
1	32.3	3.0	3	52.5	5.4
1	98.0	9.5	3	41.0	4.1
1	54.1	5.9	3	29.6	3.1
1	54.4	6.1	3	49.5	5.4
1	51.3	5.0	4	73.1	8.4
1	36.7	3.6	4	81.3	9.5
2	23.6	2.8	4	72.4	8.7
2	57.6	6.7	4	88.4	10.6
2	44.6	5.2	4	23.2	3.3

```
Dependent Variable: Y
                              Analysis of Variance

                           Sum of        Mean
            Source      DF  Squares       Square     F Value    Prob>F

            Model        4  1423.32470   355.83118    1.582     0.2199
            Error       19  4274.47488   224.97236
            C Total     23  5697.79958

            Root MSE     14.99908   R-square    0.2498
            Dep Mean      8.87917   Adj R-sq    0.0919
            C.V.        168.92440


                            Parameter Estimates

                      Parameter    Standard   T for H0:
            Variable DF  Estimate     Error   Parameter=0  Prob > |T|

            INTERCEP  1  -15.529711  13.28933470   -1.169    0.2570
            X1        1    0.471952   8.50276160    0.056    0.9563
            X2        1    5.789159  11.79117565    0.491    0.6291
            X3        1   14.223452   9.37682727    1.517    0.1458
            X4        1    0.349139   0.16950687    2.060    0.0534


         Dep Var  Predict  Std Err         Std Err  Student           Cook's
    Obs      Y     Value   Predict Residual Residual Residual -2-1-0 1 2   D

     1   6.3000   5.6462   5.001    0.6538  14.141   0.046   |    |    |  0.000
     2   6.6000   5.9953   5.007    0.6047  14.139   0.043   |    |    |  0.000
     3   3.0000  13.6065   6.380  -10.6065  13.575  -0.781   |   *|    |  0.027
     4   3.0000  -3.7806   6.712    6.7806  13.413   0.506   |    |*   |  0.013
     5   9.5000  19.1578   8.326   -9.6578  12.476  -0.774   |   *|    |  0.053
     6   5.9000   3.8306   5.061    2.0694  14.120   0.147   |    |    |  0.001
     7   6.1000   3.9354   5.053    2.1646  14.122   0.153   |    |    |  0.001
     8   5.0000   2.8531   5.156    2.1469  14.085   0.152   |    |    |  0.001
     9   3.6000  -2.2444   6.240    5.8444  13.640   0.428   |    |    |  0.008
    10   2.8000  -1.5009   9.200    4.3009  11.846   0.363   |    |    |  0.016
    11   6.7000  10.3698   9.058   -3.6698  11.955  -0.307   |    |    |  0.011
```

(continued)

12	5.2000	5.8310	8.672	-0.6310	12.238	-0.052	|	|	|	0.000
13	82.0000	25.1585	7.339	56.8415	13.081	4.345	|	|****** |	1.189
14	5.0000	15.5571	5.669	-10.5571	13.886	-0.760	|	*|	|	0.019
15	3.9000	13.1481	5.789	-9.2481	13.837	-0.668	|	*|	|	0.016
16	5.4000	17.0235	5.714	-11.6235	13.868	-0.838	|	*|	|	0.024
17	4.1000	13.0084	5.803	-8.9084	13.831	-0.644	|	*|	|	0.015
18	3.1000	9.0282	6.495	-5.9282	13.520	-0.438	|	|	|	0.009
19	5.4000	15.9761	5.673	-10.5761	13.885	-0.762	|	*|	|	0.019
20	8.4000	9.9923	6.770	-1.5923	13.384	-0.119	|	|	|	0.001
21	9.5000	12.8553	7.094	-3.3553	13.215	-0.254	|	|	|	0.004
22	8.7000	9.7479	6.755	-1.0479	13.392	-0.078	|	|	|	0.000
23	10.6000	15.3342	7.572	-4.7342	12.948	-0.366	|	|	|	0.009
24	3.3000	-7.4297	10.092	10.7297	11.096	0.967	|	|*	|	0.155

Obs	Rstudent	Hat Diag H	Cov Ratio	Dffits	INTERCEP Dfbetas	X1 Dfbetas	X2 Dfbetas	X3 Dfbetas	X4 Dfbetas
1	0.0450	0.1112	1.4734	0.0159	-0.0003	0.0094	0.0001	0.0001	0.0003
2	0.0416	0.1114	1.4740	0.0147	-0.0007	0.0088	0.0003	0.0003	0.0008
3	-0.7730	0.1809	1.3588	-0.3633	0.1948	-0.2077	-0.0835	-0.0791	-0.2257
4	0.4954	0.2003	1.5313	0.2479	0.1428	0.0790	-0.0612	-0.0579	-0.1654
5	-0.7656	0.3081	1.6136	-0.5110	0.3527	-0.2534	-0.1512	-0.1431	-0.4086
6	0.1427	0.1138	1.4704	0.0512	0.0068	0.0283	-0.0029	-0.0028	-0.0079
7	0.1493	0.1135	1.4691	0.0534	0.0067	0.0297	-0.0029	-0.0027	-0.0077
8	0.1485	0.1181	1.4769	0.0543	0.0114	0.0286	-0.0049	-0.0046	-0.0133
9	0.4191	0.1731	1.5095	0.1917	0.0990	0.0698	-0.0425	-0.0402	-0.1147
10	0.3546	0.3763	2.0290	0.2754	0.0803	-0.0166	0.1560	-0.0326	-0.0930
11	-0.2995	0.3647	2.0120	-0.2269	0.0574	-0.0119	-0.1840	-0.0233	-0.0665
12	-0.0502	0.3342	1.9669	-0.0356	0.0016	-0.0003	-0.0268	-0.0006	-0.0019
13	53.8929	0.2394	0.0000	30.2389	-16.5793	3.4296	7.1084	20.8497	19.2053
14	-0.7515	0.1429	1.3100	-0.3068	-0.0000	0.0000	0.0000	-0.1855	0.0000
15	-0.6583	0.1489	1.3670	-0.2754	-0.0480	0.0099	0.0206	-0.1436	0.0556
16	-0.8313	0.1451	1.2697	-0.3425	0.0368	-0.0076	-0.0158	-0.2204	-0.0427
17	-0.6339	0.1497	1.3800	-0.2659	-0.0490	0.0101	0.0210	-0.1372	0.0567
18	-0.4290	0.1875	1.5329	-0.2061	-0.0868	0.0180	0.0372	-0.0735	0.1006
19	-0.7530	0.1430	1.3095	-0.3076	0.0095	-0.0020	-0.0041	-0.1897	-0.0110
20	-0.1158	0.2038	1.6396	-0.0586	-0.0224	0.0444	0.0301	0.0387	-0.0080
21	-0.2475	0.2237	1.6596	-0.1329	-0.0261	0.0914	0.0555	0.0747	-0.0432
22	-0.0762	0.2028	1.6412	-0.0384	-0.0153	0.0293	0.0200	0.0257	-0.0046
23	-0.3571	0.2548	1.6975	-0.2089	-0.0098	0.1287	0.0694	0.0984	-0.0969
24	0.9652	0.4527	1.8603	0.8778	0.8607	-0.5774	-0.5747	-0.6471	-0.6558

c. Refer to part **b**. Are the outliers detected in the residual plot influential?

d. Note that the value of sales (y) for the 13th observation was incorrectly entered into the computer as 82.0; the correct value is 8.2. Make the correction and rerun the regression analysis. Interpret the results.

12.12 Some Pitfalls: Estimability, Multicollinearity, and Extrapolation

There are several problems you should be aware of when constructing a prediction model for some response y. A few of the most important will be discussed in this section.

PROBLEM 1: PARAMETER ESTIMABILITY   Suppose you want to fit a model relating the strength y of a new type of plastic fitting to molding temperature x. We propose the first-order model

$$E(y) = \beta_0 + \beta_1 x$$

Now, suppose we mold a sample of three plastic fittings, each at a temperature of 300°F. The data are graphed in Figure 12.22. You can see the problem: The parameters of the line cannot be estimated when all the data are concentrated at a single x value. Recall that it takes two points (x values) to fit a straight line. Thus, the parameters are not estimable when only one x value is observed.

FIGURE 12.22 ▶
Plastic strength and molding temperature data

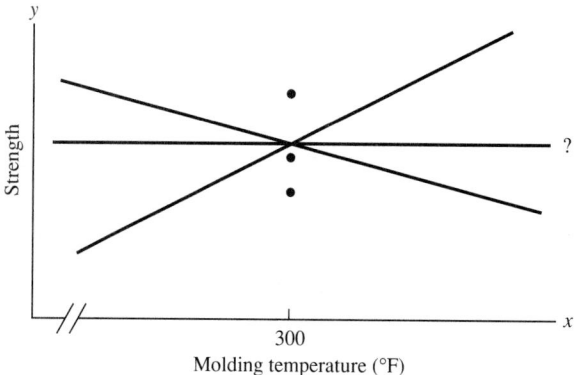

A similar problem would occur if we attempted to fit the second-order model

$$E(y) = \beta_0 + \beta_1 x + \beta_2 x^2$$

to a set of data for which only one or two different x values were observed (see Figure 12.23). At least three different x values must be observed before a second-order model can be fit to a set of data (that is, before all three parameters are estimable). In general, the number of levels of x must be at least one more than the order of the polynomial in x that you want to fit. Remember, also, that the sample size n must be sufficiently large to allow degrees of freedom for estimating σ^2.

FIGURE 12.23 ▶
Only two x values observed—second-order model is not estimable

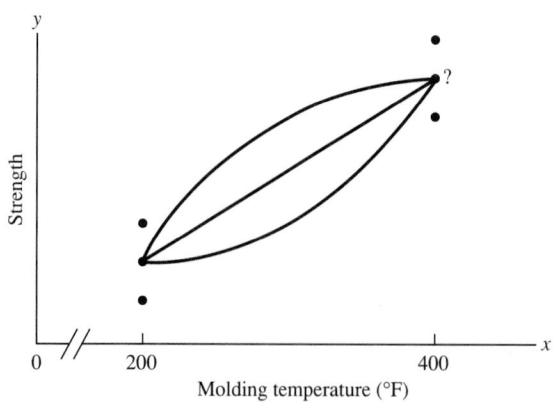

> ## Requirements for Fitting a pth-Order Polynomial Regression Model
>
> $$E(y) = \beta_0 + \beta_1 x + \beta_2 x^2 + \cdots + \beta_p x^p$$
>
> 1. The number of levels of x must be greater than or equal to $(p + 1)$.
> 2. The sample size n must be greater than $(p + 1)$ to allow sufficient degrees of freedom for estimating σ^2.

Since many variables observed in nature cannot be controlled by the researcher, the independent variables will almost always be observed at a sufficient number of levels to permit estimation of the model parameters. However, when the computer program you use suddenly refuses to fit a model, the problem is probably inestimable parameters.

PROBLEM 2: PARAMETER INTERPRETATION   Given that the parameters of the model are estimable, it is important to interpret the parameter estimates correctly. A typical misconception is that $\hat{\beta}_i$ *always* measures the effect of x_i on $E(y)$, *independent* of the other x variables in the model. This may be true for some models, but is not true in general. Generally, the interpretation of an individual β parameter becomes increasingly more difficult as the model becomes more complex. In Chapter 13, we give the β interpretations for a number of different multiple regression models.

Another misconception about parameter estimates is that a statistically significant $\hat{\beta}_i$ value establishes a *cause-and-effect* relationship between $E(y)$ and x_i. That is, if $\hat{\beta}_i$ is found to be significantly greater than 0, then some practitioners would infer that an increase in x_i *causes* an increase in the mean response, $E(y)$. However, we warned in Section 11.7 about the dangers of inferring a causal relationship between two variables. There may be many other independent variables (some of which we may have included in our model, some of which we may have omitted) that affect the mean response. Unless we can control the values of these other variables, we are uncertain about what is actually causing the observed increase in y. In Chapter 14, we introduce the notion of **designed experiments**, where the values of the independent variables are set in advance before the value of y is observed. Only with such an experiment can a cause-and-effect relationship be established.

PROBLEM 3: MULTICOLLINEARITY   Often, two or more of the independent variables used in the model for $E(y)$ will contribute redundant information. That is, the independent variables will be correlated with each other. For example, suppose we want to construct a model to predict the gasoline mileage rating, y, of a truck as a function of its load, x_1, and the horsepower, x_2, of its engine. In general, you would expect heavier loads to require greater horsepower and to result in lower mileage ratings. Thus, although both x_1 and x_2 contribute information for the prediction of mileage rating, some of the information is overlapping, because x_1 and x_2 are correlated. When the independent variables are correlated, we say that **multicollinearity** exists. In practice, it is not uncommon to observe correlations among the independent variables. However, a few problems arise when serious multicollinearity is present in the regression analysis.

First, high correlations among the independent variables increase the likelihood of rounding errors in the calculations of the β estimates, standard errors, and so forth.* Second, the regression results may be confusing and misleading.

To illustrate, if the gasoline mileage rating model

$$E(y) = \beta_0 + \beta_1 x_1 + \beta_2 x_2$$

were fit to a set of data, we might find that the t values for both $\hat{\beta}_1$ and $\hat{\beta}_2$ (the least squares estimates) are nonsignificant. However, the F test for H_0: $\beta_1 = \beta_2 = 0$ would probably be highly significant. The tests may seem to be contradictory, but really they are not. The t tests indicate that the contribution of one variable, say, x_1 = load, is not significant after the effect of x_2 = horsepower has been discounted (because x_2 is also in the model). The significant F test, on the other hand, tells us that at least one of the two variables is making a contribution to the prediction of y (i.e., either β_1, β_2, or both differ from 0). In fact, both are probably contributing, but the contribution of one overlaps with that of the other.

Multicollinearity can also have an effect on the signs of the parameter estimates. More specifically, a value of $\hat{\beta}_i$ may have the opposite sign from what is expected. For example, we expect the signs of both of the parameter estimates for the gasoline mileage rating model to be negative, yet the regression analysis for the model might yield the estimates $\hat{\beta}_1 = .2$ and $\hat{\beta}_2 = -.7$. The positive value of $\hat{\beta}_1$ seems to contradict our expectation that heavy loads will result in lower mileage ratings. However, it is dangerous to interpret a β coefficient when the independent variables are correlated. Because the variables contribute redundant information, the effect of load (x_1) on mileage rating is measured only partially by $\hat{\beta}_1$. Also, we warned in the discussion of Problem 2 that we cannot establish a cause-and-effect relationship between y and the predictor variables based on **observational data** (data for which the values of the independent variables are uncontrolled). By attempting to interpret the value $\hat{\beta}_1$, we are really trying to establish a cause-and-effect relationship between y and x_1 (by suggesting that a heavy load x_1 will *cause* a lower mileage rating y).

How can you avoid the problems of multicollinearity in regression analysis? One way is to conduct a designed experiment so that the levels of the x variables are uncorrelated. Unfortunately, time and cost constraints may prevent you from collecting data in this manner. For these and other reasons, most data collected in scientific studies are observational. Since observational data frequently consist of correlated independent variables, you will need to recognize when multicollinearity is present and, if necessary, make modifications in the regression analysis.

Several methods are available for detecting multicollinearity in regression. A simple technique is to calculate the coefficient of correlation r between each pair of independent variables in the model and use the procedure outlined in Section 11.7 to test for evidence of positive or negative correlation. If one or more of the r values

---

*The result is due to the fact that, in the presence of severe multicollinearity, the computer has difficulty inverting the $(X'X)$ matrix.

is statistically different from 0, the variables in question are correlated and a severe multicollinearity problem may exist.* Other indications of the presence of multicollinearity include those mentioned in the beginning of this section—namely, nonsignificant t tests for the individual β parameters when the F test for overall model adequacy is significant, and parameter estimates with opposite signs from what is expected. More formal methods for detecting multicollinearity exist, but are beyond the scope of this text. (Consult the references given at the end of the chapter if you want to learn more about these methods.)

The methods for detecting multicollinearity are summarized in the box. We illustrate the use of these statistics in Example 12.13.

Detecting Multicollinearity in the Regression Model

$$E(y) = \beta_0 + \beta_1 x_1 + \beta_2 x_2 + \cdots + \beta_k x_k$$

The following are indicators of multicollinearity:

1. Significant correlations between pairs of independent variables in the model
2. Nonsignificant t tests for the individual β parameters when the F test for overall model adequacy H_0: $\beta_1 = \beta_2 = \cdots = \beta_k = 0$ is significant
3. Opposite signs (from what is expected) in the estimated parameters

---

EXAMPLE 12.13

The Federal Trade Commission annually ranks varieties of domestic cigarettes according to their tar, nicotine, and carbon monoxide contents. The U.S. surgeon general considers each of these three substances hazardous to a smoker's health. Past studies have shown that increases in the tar and nicotine contents of a cigarette are accompanied by an increase in the carbon monoxide emitted from the cigarette smoke. Table 12.9 (page 678) contains the data on tar, nicotine, and carbon monoxide contents (in milligrams) and weight (in grams) for a sample of 25 (filter) brands tested in a recent year. Suppose we want to model carbon monoxide content, y, as a function of tar content, x_1, nicotine content, x_2, and weight, x_3, using the model

$$E(y) = \beta_0 + \beta_1 x_1 + \beta_2 x_2 + \beta_3 x_3$$

The model is fit to the 25 data points in Table 12.9 and a portion of the resulting SAS printout is shown in Figure 12.24 on page 679. Examine the printout. Do you detect any signs of multicollinearity?

---

*Remember that r measures only the pairwise correlation between x values. Three variables, x_1, x_2, and x_3, may be highly correlated as a group, but may not exhibit large pairwise correlations. Thus, multicollinearity may be present even when all pairwise correlations are not significantly different from 0.

TABLE 12.9   FTC Cigarette Data for Example

Brand	Tar	Nicotine	Weight	Carbon Monoxide
	x_1, milligrams	x_2, milligrams	x_3, grams	y, milligrams
Alpine	14.1	.86	.9853	13.6
Benson & Hedges	16.0	1.06	1.0938	16.6
Bull Durham	29.8	2.03	1.1650	23.5
Camel Lights	8.0	.67	.9280	10.2
Carlton	4.1	.40	.9462	5.4
Chesterfield	15.0	1.04	.8885	15.0
Golden Lights	8.8	.76	1.0267	9.0
Kent	12.4	.95	.9225	12.3
Kool	16.6	1.12	.9372	16.3
L&M	14.9	1.02	.8858	15.4
Lark Lights	13.7	1.01	.9643	13.0
Marlboro	15.1	.90	.9316	14.4
Merit	7.8	.57	.9705	10.0
Multifilter	11.4	.78	1.1240	10.2
Newport Lights	9.0	.74	.8517	9.5
Now	1.0	.13	.7851	1.5
Old Gold	17.0	1.26	.9186	18.5
Pall Mall Light	12.8	1.08	1.0395	12.6
Raleigh	15.8	.96	.9573	17.5
Salem Ultra	4.5	.42	.9106	4.9
Tareyton	14.5	1.01	1.0070	15.9
True	7.3	.61	.9806	8.5
Viceroy Rich Lights	8.6	.69	.9693	10.6
Virginia Slims	15.2	1.02	.9496	13.9
Winston Lights	12.0	.82	1.1184	14.9

Source: Federal Trade Commission.

Solution

First, notice that a test of H_0: $\beta_1 = \beta_2 = \beta_3 = 0$ is highly significant. The F value (shaded on the printout) is very large ($F = 78.984$), and the observed significance level of the test (also shaded) is small (p-value $= .0001$). Therefore, we can reject H_0 for any α greater than .0001 and conclude that at least one of the parameters, β_1, β_2, and β_3, is nonzero. The t tests for two of the three individual β's, however, are nonsignificant. (The p-values for these tests are shaded on the printout.) Unless tar is the only one of the three variables useful for predicting carbon monoxide content, these results are the first indication of a potential multicollinearity problem.

A second clue to the presence of multicollinearity is the negative value for both $\hat{\beta}_2$ and $\hat{\beta}_3$ (shaded on the printout). From past studies, we expect carbon monoxide content (y) to increase when nicotine content (x_2) increases or when weight (x_3) increases—that is, we expect a *positive* relationship between y and x_2 and a *positive* relationship between y and x_3, not a negative one.

FIGURE 12.24 ▶

SAS printout for analysis of FTC cigarette data

Dependent Variable: CO

Analysis of Variance

Source	DF	Sum of Squares	Mean Square	F Value	Prob>F
Model	3	495.25781	165.08594	78.984	0.0001
Error	21	43.89259	2.09012		
C Total	24	539.15040			

Root MSE	1.44573	R-square	0.9186	
Dep Mean	12.52800	Adj R-sq	0.9070	
C.V.	11.53996			

Parameter Estimates

Variable	DF	Parameter Estimate	Standard Error	T for H0: Parameter=0	Prob > |T|
INTERCEP	1	3.202190	3.46175473	0.925	0.3655
TAR	1	0.962574	0.24224436	3.974	0.0007
NICOTINE	1	-2.631661	3.90055745	-0.675	0.5072
WEIGHT	1	-0.130482	3.88534182	-0.034	0.9735

All signs indicate that a serious multicollinearity problem may exist. To confirm our suspicions, we calculated the coefficient of correlation r for each of the three pairs of independent variables in the model. These values are given in Table 12.10. You can see that tar content (x_1) and nicotine content (x_2) appear to be highly correlated $(r = .977)$, whereas weight (x_3) appears to be moderately correlated with both tar content $(r = .491)$ and nicotine content $(r = .500)$. In fact, all three sample correlations are significantly different from 0 when a two-tailed test of $H_0: \rho = 0$ is conducted at $\alpha = .05$.

TABLE 12.10   Correlation Coefficients for the Three Pairs of Independent Variables in Example 12.13

Pair	r
x_1, x_2	.977
x_1, x_3	.491
x_2, x_3	.500

Once you have detected that a multicollinearity problem exists, there are several alternative measures available for solving the problem. The appropriate measure to take depends on the severity of the multicollinearity and the ultimate goal of the regression analysis.

Some researchers, when confronted with highly correlated independent variables, choose to include only one of the correlated variables in the final model. One way of deciding which variable to include is by using **stepwise regression**, a topic discussed in Chapter 13. Generally, only one (or a small number) of a set of multicollinear independent variables will be included in the regression model by the stepwise regression procedure. This procedure tests the parameter associated with each variable in the presence of all the variables already in the model. For example, in fitting the gasoline mileage rating model introduced earlier, if at one step the variable representing truck load is included as a significant variable in the prediction of the mileage rating, the variable representing horsepower will probably never be added in a future step. Thus, if a set of independent variables is thought to be multicollinear, some screening by stepwise regression may be helpful.

If you are interested in using the model for estimation and prediction, you may decide not to drop any of the independent variables from the model. In the presence of multicollinearity, we have seen that it is dangerous to interpret the individual β's for the purpose of establishing cause and effect. However, confidence intervals for $E(y)$ and prediction intervals for y generally remain unaffected **as long as the values of the independent variables used to predict y follow the same pattern of multicollinearity exhibited in the sample data**. That is, you must take strict care to ensure that the values of the x variables fall within the experimental region. (We will discuss this problem in further detail in Problem 4.) Alternatively, if your goal is to establish a cause-and-effect relationship between y and the independent variables, you will need to conduct a designed experiment to break up the pattern of multicollinearity.

Solutions to Some Problems Created by Multicollinearity

1. Drop one or more of the correlated independent variables from the final model. A screening procedure such as stepwise regression (see Chapter 13) is helpful in determining which variables to drop.

2. If you decide to keep all the independent variables in the model:
   a. Avoid making inferences about the individual β parameters (such as establishing a cause-and-effect relationship between y and the predictor variables).
   b. Restrict inferences about $E(y)$ and future y values to values of the independent variables that fall within the experimental region (see Problem 4).

3. If your ultimate objective is to establish a cause-and-effect relationship between y and the predictor variables, use a designed experiment (see Chapter 14).

4. To reduce rounding errors in polynomial regression models, code the independent variables so that first-, second-, and higher-order terms for a particular x variable are not highly correlated (see Chapter 13).

When fitting a polynomial regression model [for example, the second-order model $E(y) = \beta_0 + \beta_1 x + \beta_2 x^2$], the independent variables $x_1 = x$ and $x_2 = x^2$ will often be correlated. If the correlation is high, the computer solution may result in extreme rounding errors. For this model, the solution is not to drop one of the independent variables but to transform the x variable in such a way that the correlation between the coded x and x^2 values is substantially reduced. Coding the independent quantitative variables in polynomial regression models is discussed in Chapter 13.

PROBLEM 4: PREDICTION OUTSIDE THE EXPERIMENTAL REGION   The fitted regression model enables us to construct a confidence interval for $E(y)$ and a prediction interval for y for values of the independent variable only within the region of experimentation, i.e., within the range of values of the independent variables used in the experiment. For example, suppose that you conduct experiments on the mean strength of the plastic fittings (see Figure 12.23) at several different temperatures in the interval 200°F to 400°F. The regression model that you fit to the data is valid for estimating $E(y)$ or for predicting values of y for values of x in the range 200°F $\leq x \leq$ 400°F. However, if you attempt to extrapolate beyond the experimental region, you risk the possibility that the fitted model is no longer a good approximation to the mean strength of the plastic (see Figure 12.25). For example, the plastic may become too brittle when formed at 500°F and possess no strength at all. Estimating and predicting outside of the experimental region are sometimes necessary. If you do so, keep in mind the possibility of a large extrapolation error.

FIGURE 12.25 ▶
Using a regression model outside the experimental region

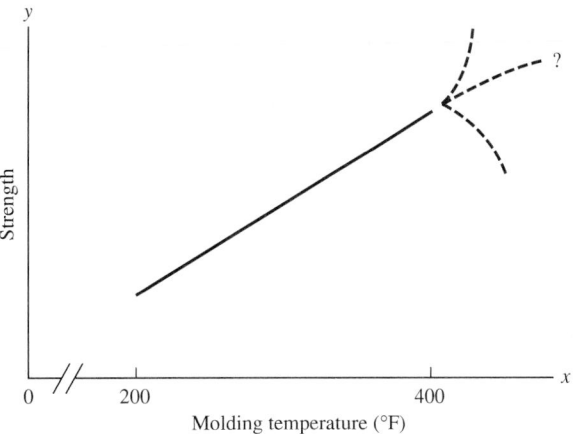

EXERCISES

12.39 Why is it dangerous to predict y for values of the independent variables that fall outside the experimental region?

12.40 The following questions pertain to multicollinearity.
   a. What problems result when multicollinearity is present in a regression analysis?
   b. How can you detect multicollinearity?
   c. What remedial measures are available when multicollinearity is detected?

12.41 To meet the increasing demand for new software products, many systems development experts have adopted a prototyping methodology. The effect of prototyping on the system development life cycle (SDLC) was investigated in the *Journal of Computer Information Systems* (Spring 1993). A survey of 500 randomly selected corporate level management information systems (MIS) managers was conducted. Three potential independent variables were: (1) *importance* of prototyping to each phase of the SDLC; (2) degree of *support* prototyping provides for the SDLC; and (3) degree to which prototyping *replaces* each phase of the SDLC. The accompanying table gives the pairwise correlations of the three variables in the survey data for one particular phase of the SDLC. Use this information to assess the degree of multicollinearity in the survey data. Would you recommend using all three independent variables in a regression analysis? Explain.

Variable Pairs	Correlation Coefficient, r
Importance–Replace	.2682
Importance–Support	.6991
Replace–Support	−.0531

Source: Hardgrave, B. C., Doke, E. R., and Swanson, N. E. "Prototyping effects of the system development life cycle: An empirical study." *Journal of Computer Information Systems*, Vol. 33, No. 3, Spring 1993, p. 16 (Table 1).

12.42 A bioengineer wants to model the amount (y) of carbohydrate solubilized during steam processing of peat as a function of temperature (x_1), exposure time (x_2), and pH value (x_3). Data collected for each of 15 peat samples were used to fit the model

$$E(y) = \beta_0 + \beta_1 x_1 + \beta_2 x_2 + \beta_3 x_3$$

A summary of the regression results follows:

$$\hat{y} = -3,000 + 3.2x_1 - .4x_2 - 1.1x_3 \qquad R^2 = .93$$

$$s_{\hat{\beta}_1} = 2.4 \qquad s_{\hat{\beta}_2} = .6 \qquad s_{\hat{\beta}_3} = .8$$

$$r_{12} = .92 \qquad r_{13} = .87 \qquad r_{23} = .81$$

Based on these results, the bioengineer concludes that none of the three independent variables, x_1, x_2, and x_3, is a useful predictor of carbohydrate amount, y. Do you agree with this statement? Explain.

12.43 The management of an engineering consultant firm is considering the possibility of setting up its own market research department rather than continuing to use the services of a market research firm. Management wants to know what salary should be paid to a market researcher, based on years of experience. An independent consultant has proposed the quadratic model

$$E(y) = \beta_0 + \beta_1 x + \beta_2 x^2$$

where

y = Annual salary (thousands of dollars)

x = Years of experience

To fit the model, the consultant randomly sampled three market researchers at other firms and recorded the information given in the accompanying table. Give your opinion regarding the adequacy of the proposed model.

	y	x
Researcher 1	40	2
Researcher 2	25	1
Researcher 3	42	3

12.44   Hamilton (1987) illustrated the multicollinearity problem with an example using the data shown in the accompanying table. The values of x_1, x_2, and y in the table represent appraised land value, appraised improvements value, and sale price, respectively, of a randomly selected residential property. (All measurements are in thousands of dollars.)

x_1	x_2	y	x_1	x_2	y
22.3	96.6	123.7	30.4	77.1	128.6
25.7	89.4	126.6	32.6	51.1	108.4
38.7	44.0	120.0	33.9	50.5	112.0
31.0	66.4	119.3	23.5	85.1	115.6
33.9	49.1	110.6	27.6	65.9	108.3
28.3	85.2	130.3	39.0	49.0	126.3
30.2	80.4	131.3	31.6	69.6	124.6
21.4	90.5	114.4			

Source: Hamilton, D. "Sometimes $R^2 > r_{yx_1}^2 + r_{yx_2}^2$: Correlated variables are not always redundant." *The American Statistician*, Vol. 41, No. 2, May 1987, pp. 129–132.

a. Calculate the coefficient of correlation between y and x_1. Is there evidence of a linear relationship between sale price and appraised land value?

b. Calculate the coefficient of correlation between y and x_2. Is there evidence of a linear relationship between sale price and appraised improvements?

c. Based on the results in parts **a** and **b**, do you think the model $E(y) = \beta_0 + \beta_1 x_1 + \beta_2 x_2$ will be useful for predicting sale price?

d. Use a statistical computer program package to fit the model in part **c**, and conduct a test of model adequacy. In particular, note the value of R^2. Does the result agree with your answer to part **c**?

e. Calculate the coefficient of correlation between x_1 and x_2. What does the result imply?

f. Many researchers avoid the problems of multicollinearity by always omitting all but one of the "redundant" variables from the model. Would you recommend this strategy for this example? Explain. (Hamilton notes that in this case, such a strategy "can amount to throwing out the baby with the bathwater.")

12.45   Refer to the FTC cigarette data of Example 12.13. The data are reproduced on page 684 for convenience.

a. Fit the model $E(y) = \beta_0 + \beta_1 x_1$ to the data. Is there evidence that tar content (x_1) is useful for predicting carbon monoxide content (y)?

b. Fit the model $E(y) = \beta_0 + \beta_2 x_2$ to the data. Is there evidence that nicotine content (x_2) is useful for predicting carbon monoxide content (y)?

c. Fit the model $E(y) = \beta_0 + \beta_3 x_3$ to the data. Is there evidence that weight (x_3) is useful for predicting carbon monoxide content (y)?

d. Compare the signs of $\hat{\beta}_1$, $\hat{\beta}_2$, and $\hat{\beta}_3$ in the models of parts **a**, **b**, and **c**, respectively, to the signs of the $\hat{\beta}$'s in the multiple regression model fit in Example 12.13. The fact that the $\hat{\beta}$'s change dramatically when the independent variables are removed from the model is another indication of a serious multi-collinearity problem.

Brand	Tar x_1, milligrams	Nicotine x_2, milligrams	Weight x_3, grams	Carbon Monoxide y, milligrams
Alpine	14.1	.86	.9853	13.6
Benson & Hedges	16.0	1.06	1.0938	16.6
Bull Durham	29.8	2.03	1.1650	23.5
Camel Lights	8.0	.67	.9280	10.2
Carlton	4.1	.40	.9462	5.4
Chesterfield	15.0	1.04	.8885	15.0
Golden Lights	8.8	.76	1.0267	9.0
Kent	12.4	.95	.9225	12.3
Kool	16.6	1.12	.9372	16.3
L&M	14.9	1.02	.8858	15.4
Lark Lights	13.7	1.01	.9643	13.0
Marlboro	15.1	.90	.9316	14.4
Merit	7.8	.57	.9705	10.0
Multifilter	11.4	.78	1.1240	10.2
Newport Lights	9.0	.74	.8517	9.5
Now	1.0	.13	.7851	1.5
Old Gold	17.0	1.26	.9186	18.5
Pall Mall Light	12.8	1.08	1.0395	12.6
Raleigh	15.8	.96	.9573	17.5
Salem Ultra	4.5	.42	.9106	4.9
Tareyton	14.5	1.01	1.0070	15.9
True	7.3	.61	.9806	8.5
Viceroy Rich Lights	8.6	.69	.9693	10.6
Virginia Slims	15.2	1.02	.9496	13.9
Winston Lights	12.0	.82	1.1184	14.9

Source: Federal Trade Commission.

12.13 Summary

We have discussed some of the methodology of **multiple regression analysis**, a technique for modeling a dependent variable y as a function of several independent variables x_1, x_2, . . . , x_k. The steps we follow in constructing and using multiple regression models are much the same as those for the simple straight-line models:

1. The form of the probabilistic model is hypothesized.
2. The model coefficients are estimated using least squares.

3. The probability distribution of ε is specified and σ^2 is estimated.

4. The utility of the model is checked using the analysis of variance F test and the multiple coefficient of determination R^2. The t tests on individual β parameters aid in deciding the final form of the model.

5. An analysis of residuals is conducted to determine if the data comply with the assumptions in step 3.

6. If the model is deemed useful and the assumptions are satisfied, it may be used to make estimates and to predict values of y to be observed in the future.

We have covered steps 2–6 in this chapter, assuming that the model was specified. Chapter 13 is devoted to step 1—model construction.

SUPPLEMENTARY EXERCISES

12.46 J. Vuorinen carried out a series of experiments to gather information on the coefficient of permeability of concrete (*Magazine of Concrete Research*, Sept. 1985). In one experiment, the outflow of water from the pores of a concrete specimen after it had been under saturating water pressure for a period of time was recorded for different combinations of concrete permeability and porosity. The resulting water quantities after different lapses of time for one permeability–porosity combination are given in the table.

Time t, seconds	Water Outflow w, grams per cylinder	Time t, seconds	Water Outflow w, grams per cylinder
201	3.88	775	7.80
325	4.93	975	8.72
525	6.42	1,200	9.60

Source: Vuorinen, J. "Applications of diffusion theory to permeability tests on concrete, Part II: Pressure-saturation test on concrete and coefficient of permeability." *Magazine of Concrete Research*, Vol. 37, No. 132, Sept. 1985, p. 156 (Table II.1).

a. According to Vuorinen, "the quantity of water discharged is approximately in linear relationship with the square root of time" for most of the permeability–porosity combinations. Using the formulas given in Section 11.3, fit the following model to the data in the table:

$$E(w) = \alpha_0 + \alpha_1\sqrt{t}$$

b. Is there sufficient evidence to indicate that quantity of water outflow and the square root of time are linearly related? Test using $\alpha = .10$.

12.47 Refer to Exercise 12.46. Vuorinen fit the water outflow–time model for each of nine permeability–porosity combinations and used the results to develop a model for the coefficient of permeability of concrete, y. Specifically, he fit the model*

$$E(y) = \beta_0 + \beta_1 x_1 + \beta_2 x_2$$

---

*In actuality, Vuorinen fit the logarithmic model

$$\log(y) = \beta_0 + \beta_1\log(x_1) + \beta_2\log(x_2) + \varepsilon$$

where

x_1 = Porosity of the cement

x_2 = Estimated slope coefficient ($\hat{\alpha}_1$) of the corresponding water outflow–time regression line

The data are reproduced here, followed by the SAS printout for the analysis.

Coefficient of Permeability y, (meters per second) $\times$ 10^{-11}	Porosity x_1	Estimated Water Outflow Time Slope Coefficient x_2
1.00	.050	.903
1.00	.035	.722
1.00	.025	.590
.10	.050	.345
.10	.035	.282
.10	.025	.233
.01	.050	.103
.01	.035	.091
.01	.025	.078

Source: Vuorinen, J. "Applications of diffusion theory to permeability tests on concrete, Part II: Pressure-saturation test on concrete and coefficient of permeability." *Magazine of Concrete Research*, Vol. 37, No. 132, Sept. 1985, p. 156 (Table II.1).

Dependent Variable: Y

Analysis of Variance

Source	DF	Sum of Squares	Mean Square	F Value	Prob>F
Model	2	1.65932	0.82966	35.843	0.0005
Error	6	0.13888	0.02315		
C Total	8	1.79820			

Root MSE	0.15214	R-square	0.9228
Dep Mean	0.37000	Adj R-sq	0.8970
C.V.	41.11920		

Parameter Estimates

Variable	DF	Parameter Estimate	Standard Error	T for H0: Parameter=0	Prob > |T|
INTERCEP	1	0.132021	0.19005130	0.695	0.5133
X1	1	-9.307122	5.05702529	-1.840	0.1153
X2	1	1.557563	0.18396157	8.467	0.0001

a. Give the least squares prediction equation.
b. Conduct a test of overall model utility. Interpret the p-value of the test.
c. Is there evidence that concrete porosity x_1 is a useful predictor of coefficient of permeability y? Test using $\alpha = .05$.

d. Is there evidence that the estimated water outflow–time slope is a useful predictor of coefficient of permeability y? Test using $\alpha = .05$.

e. Locate R^2 on the printout and interpret its value.

f. Locate the estimate of σ on the printout and interpret its value.

12.48   An experiment was conducted to investigate the effect of extrusion pressure P and temperature at extrusion T on the strength y of a new type of plastic. Two plastic specimens were prepared for each of five combinations of pressure and temperature. The specimens were then tested in random order, and the breaking strength for each specimen was recorded. The independent variables were coded as follows to simplify computations:

$$x_1 = \frac{P - 200}{10}$$

$$x_2 = \frac{T - 400}{25}$$

The $n = 10$ data points are listed in the table.

y	x_1	x_2
5.2; 5.0	-2	2
.3; $-.1$	-1	-1
-1.2; -1.1	0	-2
2.2; 2.0	1	-1
6.2; 6.1	2	2

a. Give the Y and X matrices needed to fit the model $y = \beta_0 + \beta_1 x_1 + \beta_2 x_2 + \varepsilon$.

b. Find the least squares prediction equation. Interpret the β estimates.

c. Find SSE, s^2, and s. Interpret the value of s.

d. Does the model contribute information for the prediction of y? Test using $\alpha = .05$.

e. Find R^2 and interpret its value.

f. Test the null hypothesis that $\beta_1 = 0$. Use $\alpha = .05$. What is the practical implication of the test?

g. Find a 90% confidence interval for the mean strength of the plastic for $x_1 = -2$ and $x_2 = 2$.

h. Suppose a single specimen of the plastic is to be installed in the engine mount of a Douglas DC-10 aircraft. Find a 90% prediction interval for the strength of this specimen if $x_1 = -2$ and $x_2 = 2$.

12.49   One of the best methods of improving the common resistance of chromium deposit on steel is to apply a uniformly porous layer. An experiment was conducted to investigate the relationship between porosity (number of pores per square centimeter) and chromium deposit thickness (μm). Here are the data, followed by the MINITAB printout on page 688 for fitting a second-order quadratic model to the data.

x	.10	.15	.25	.42	.53
y	50	30	20	13	4.5

```
The regression equation is
Y = 67.0 - 244 X + 246 XX

Predictor        Coef      Stdev    t-ratio      P
Constant        66.95      14.00       4.78    0.041
X              -243.5      111.4      -2.19    0.160
XX              246.0      174.9       1.41    0.295

s = 6.801        R-sq = 92.5%    R-sq(adj) = 84.9%

Analysis of Variance

SOURCE          DF         SS         MS         F        P
Regression       2    1135.48     567.74     12.27    0.075
Error            2      92.52      46.26
Total            4    1228.00

SOURCE          DF     SEQ SS
X                1    1043.95
XX               1      91.53


   Fit  Stdev.Fit        95% C.I.            95% P.I.
  16.03       5.58   ( -7.98,  40.05)  ( -21.83,  53.89)
```

a. Interpret the results of the regression analysis.
b. A 95% confidence interval for $E(y)$ when the thickness x is .3 is shown at the bottom of the printout. Interpret this interval. Why is it so wide?

12.50   A physiologist wanted to investigate the relationship between the physical characteristics of preadolescent boys and their maximal oxygen uptake (measured in milliliters of oxygen per kilogram of body weight). The data shown in the table were collected on a random sample of 10 preadolescent boys. As a first step in the data analysis, the researcher fit the regression model

$$y = \beta_0 + \beta_1 x_1 + \beta_2 x_2 + \beta_3 x_3 + \beta_4 x_4 + \varepsilon$$

to the data. The output for a SAS regression analysis follows the table.

Maximal Oxygen Uptake y	Age x_1, years	Height x_2, centimeters	Weight x_3, kilograms	Chest Depth x_4, centimeters
1.54	8.4	132.0	29.1	14.4
1.74	8.7	135.5	29.7	14.5
1.32	8.9	127.7	28.4	14.0
1.50	9.9	131.1	28.8	14.2
1.46	9.0	130.0	25.9	13.6
1.35	7.7	127.6	27.6	13.9
1.53	7.3	129.9	29.0	14.0
1.71	9.9	138.1	33.6	14.6
1.27	9.3	126.6	27.7	13.9
1.50	8.1	131.8	30.8	14.5

Dependent Variable: Y

Analysis of Variance

Source	DF	Sum of Squares	Mean Square	F Value	Prob>F
Model	4	0.20604	0.05151	37.204	0.0007
Error	5	0.00692	0.00138		
C Total	9	0.21296			

Root MSE	0.03721	R-square	0.9675
Dep Mean	1.49200	Adj R-sq	0.9415
C.V.	2.49391		

Parameter Estimates

Variable	DF	Parameter Estimate	Standard Error	T for H0: Parameter=0	Prob > |T|
INTERCEP	1	-4.774739	0.86281773	-5.534	0.0026
AGE	1	-0.035214	0.01538630	-2.289	0.0708
HEIGHT	1	0.051637	0.00621522	8.308	0.0004
WEIGHT	1	-0.023417	0.01342835	-1.744	0.1416
CHEST	1	0.034489	0.08523877	0.405	0.7025

a. Is the model adequate for predicting maximal oxygen uptake?

b. It seems reasonable to assume that the greater a child's chest depth, the greater should be the maximal oxygen uptake. But note that $\hat{\beta}_4$, the estimated coefficient of chest depth, x_4, is negative. Give an explanation for this result.

c. It would seem that the weight of a child should be positively correlated to lung volume and hence to maximal oxygen uptake. Can you explain the small t value associated with $\hat{\beta}_3$?

d. Calculate the coefficient of correlation r for each pair of independent variables. Does this information confirm your suspicions in parts **b** and **c**?

12.51 A naval base is considering modifying or adding to its fleet of 48 standard aircraft. The final decision regarding the type and number of aircraft to be added depends on a comparison of cost versus effectiveness of the modified fleet. Consequently, the naval base would like to model the projected percentage increase y in fleet effectiveness by the end of the decade as a function of the cost x of modifying the fleet. A first proposal is the quadratic model

$$E(y) = \beta_0 + \beta_1 x + \beta_2 x^2$$

The data provided in the table on page 690 were collected on 10 naval bases of similar size that recently expanded their fleets. The data were used to fit the model in the SAS printout of the multiple regression analysis. Interpret the results.

Percentage Improvement At End of Decade y	Cost of Modifying Fleet x, millions of dollars
18	125
32	160
9	80
37	162
6	110
3	90
30	140
10	85
25	150
2	50

Dependent Variable: Y

Analysis of Variance

Source	DF	Sum of Squares	Mean Square	F Value	Prob>F
Model	2	1368.77501	684.38750	33.079	0.0003
Error	7	144.82499	20.68928		
C Total	9	1513.60000			

Root MSE	4.54855	R-square	0.9043
Dep Mean	17.20000	Adj R-sq	0.8770
C.V.	26.44504		

Parameter Estimates

Variable	DF	Parameter Estimate	Standard Error	T for H0: Parameter=0	Prob > |T|
INTERCEP	1	10.659036	14.55009061	0.733	0.4876
X	1	-0.281606	0.28087588	-1.003	0.3494
XX	1	0.002672	0.00125383	2.131	0.0706

12.52 A large manufacturing firm wants to determine whether a relationship exists between the number of work-hours an employee misses per year and the employee's annual wages. A sample of 15 employees produced the data in the accompanying table. A first-order model was fit to the data with the results

$$\hat{y} = 222.64 - 9.60x \qquad r^2 = .073$$

a. Interpret the value of r^2.
b. Calculate and plot the regression residuals. What do you notice?
c. After searching through its employees' files, the firm has found that employee #13 had been fired but that his name had not been removed from the active employee payroll. This explains the large accumulation of work-hours missed (543) by that employee. In view of this fact, what is your recommendation concerning this outlier?

Employee	Work-Hours Missed y	Annual Wages x, thousands of dollars	Employee	Work-Hours Missed y	Annual Wages x, thousands of dollars
1	49	12.8	9	191	7.8
2	36	14.5	10	6	15.8
3	127	8.3	11	63	10.8
4	91	10.2	12	79	9.7
5	72	10.0	13	543	12.1
6	34	11.5	14	57	12.2
7	155	8.8	15	82	10.9
8	11	17.2			

d. Refit the model to the data, excluding the outlier, and find the least squares line. Calculate r^2 and comment on model adequacy.

12.53 The manager of a retail appliance store wants to model the proportion of appliance owners who decide to purchase a service contract for a specific major appliance. Since the manager believes that the proportion y decreases with age x of the appliance (in years), he will fit the first-order model

$$E(y) = \beta_0 + \beta_1 x$$

A sample of 50 purchasers of new appliances are contacted about the possibility of purchasing a service contract. Fifty owners of 1-year-old machines, and 50 owners each of 2-, 3-, and 4-year-old machines are also contacted. One year later, another survey is conducted in a similar manner. The proportion y of owners deciding to purchase the service policy is shown in the table.

Age of Appliance x, years	Proportion Buying Service Contract y
0	.94
0	.96
1	.7
1	.76
2	.6
2	.4
3	.24
3	.3
4	.12
4	.1

a. Fit the first-order model to the data.
b. Calculate the residuals and construct a residual plot versus $\hat{y}$.
c. What does the plot from part b suggest about the variance of y?
d. Explain how you could stabilize the variances.
e. Refit the model using the appropriate variance-stabilizing transformation. Plot the residuals for the transformed model and compare to the plot obtained in part b. Does the assumption of a constant error variance appear to be satisfied?

12.54 In an investigation of water relations in poplars (*Ecology*, Feb. 1981), two plants from each of two poplar clones (identified by the numbers 5263 and 5271) and three plants from each of two other poplar clones (identified by the numbers 5331 and 5319) were selected from a group of cuttings planted at the Hugo Sauer Nursery near Rhinelander, Wisconsin. (The four clones were chosen because of their differing growth rates.) Since clones of poplar trees may differ in root penetration, and thus in their capacity to extract water from the soil, the researchers examined the relationship between the soil water potential of the clones and their transpiration rates. For a period of approximately 2 weeks, the soil water potential y (in megapascals) and transpirational flux density x (in micrograms per centimeter squared per second) were measured each day for individually selected leaves of the plants. The data for each of the four clones were to be analyzed separately. The researchers fit the quadratic model

$$y = \beta_0 + \beta_1 x + \beta_2 x^2 + \varepsilon$$

to the four data sets using multiple regression. The results are summarized in the table.

Clone	Least Squares Prediction Method	$s_{\hat{\beta}_1}$	$s_{\hat{\beta}_2}$	R^2	n
5263	$\hat{y} = -1.47 - 2.53x + .12x^2$	.14	.01	.62	418
5319	$\hat{y} = -1.48 - 1.90x + .08x^2$	.14	.01	.59	417
5331	$\hat{y} = -1.11 - 2.43x + .14x^2$	.19	.02	.53	315
5271	$\hat{y} = -1.67 - 1.89x + .07x^2$	.10	.01	.68	315

Source: Pallardy, S. G., and Kozlowski, T. T. "Water relations of *Populus* clones." *Ecology*, Feb. 1981, Vol. 62, pp. 159–169. Copyright 1981, the Ecological Society of America.

For each of the four clones:
a. Interpret the value of R^2.
b. Test the hypothesis that the overall model is useful for predicting the soil water potential of leaves from the poplar clone. Use $\alpha = .05$.
c. Is there evidence of curvature in the response model relating soil water potential y to transpirational flux density x? Use $\alpha = .05$.
d. List any assumptions required for the validity of the tests conducted in parts **b** and **c**.

12.55 *Sintering*, one of the most important techniques of materials science, is used to convert a powdered material into a porous solid body. The following two measures characterize the final product:

V_v = Percentage of total volume of final product that is solid

$\quad = \left(\dfrac{\text{Solid volume}}{\text{Porous volume + Solid volume}} \right) \cdot 100$

S_v = Solid-pore interface area per unit volume of the product

When $V_v = 100\%$, the product is completely solid—i.e., it contains no pores. Both V_v and S_v are estimated by a microscopic examination of polished cross sections of sintered material. Generally, the longer a powdered material is sintered, the more solid will be the product. Thus, we would expect S_v to decrease and V_v to increase as the sintering time is increased. The accompanying table gives the mean and standard deviation of the values of S_v (in squared centimeters per cubic centimeter) and V_v (percentage) for 100 specimens of sintered nickel for six different sintering times.*

---

*Data and experimental information provided by Guoquan Liu while visiting at the University of Florida.

Sample	Time minutes	S_v Mean	S_v Standard Deviation	V_v Mean	V_v Standard Deviation
1	1.0	1,076.5	295.0	95.83	1.2
2	10.0	736.0	181.9	96.73	2.1
3	28.5	509.4	154.7	97.38	2.1
4	150.0	299.5	161.0	97.82	1.5
5	450.0	165.0	110.4	99.03	1.3
6	1,000.0	72.9	76.6	99.49	1.1

a. Plot the sample means of the S_v measurements versus sintering time. Hypothesize a linear model relating mean S_v to sintering time x.

b. Plot the sample means of the V_v measurements versus sintering time. Hypothesize a linear model relating mean V_v to sintering time x.

c. Suppose you were to fit a linear model relating $E(S_v)$ to sintering time x. Explain why the data may violate the assumptions of Section 12.2.

12.56 Ignoring the possible violation of assumptions (see part **c** of Exercise 12.55), we will fit a second-order model to the $n = 6$ sample means, i.e., we will fit

$$E(S_v) = \beta_0 + \beta_1 x + \beta_2 x^2$$

where x is the sintering time. The SAS printout for the regression analysis is shown here.

```
Dependent Variable: SV

                        Analysis of Variance

                           Sum of        Mean
        Source      DF     Squares       Square      F Value    Prob>F

        Model        2  548985.24236  274492.62118    4.824     0.1155
        Error        3  170691.61264   56897.20421
        C Total      5  719676.85500

             Root MSE    238.53135    R-square    0.7628
             Dep Mean    476.55000    Adj R-sq    0.6047
             C.V.         50.05379

                        Parameter Estimates

                    Parameter     Standard    T for H0:
     Variable   DF   Estimate       Error    Parameter=0   Prob > |T|

     INTERCEP    1   779.378350  139.41448552     5.590      0.0113
     TIME        1    -2.352000    1.08182944    -2.174      0.1180
     TIMESQ      1     0.001663    0.00107282     1.550      0.2188

                   Dep Var   Predict   Std Err  Lower95%  Upper95%
     Obs   TIME      SV       Value    Predict   Predict   Predict   Residual

      1       1    1076.5     777.0    138.771    -101.2    1655.3     299.5
      2      10     736.0     756.0    133.273    -113.6    1625.6   -20.0247
      3    28.5     509.4     713.7    123.740    -141.5    1568.9    -204.3
      4     150     299.5     464.0    122.247    -389.0    1317.0    -164.5
      5     450     165.0   57.8086    216.268    -966.9    1082.5     107.2
      6    1000   72.9000   90.7373    238.002    -981.6    1163.1   -17.8373
```

a. Graph the prediction equation and plot the data points.
b. Is the model adequate for predicting S_v? Test using $\alpha = .05$.
c. Confidence intervals for $E(S_v)$ are shown on the printout for each sintering time. Explain why some of the confidence intervals will be conservative and others will be nonconservative. Explain which confidence intervals might be expected to fall in each of the two categories.

12.57 Refer to Exercise 12.55. A second-order model relating V_v to sintering time x is given by

$$E(V_v) = \beta_0 + \beta_1 x + \beta_2 x^2$$

Refer to the accompanying SAS printout for the regression analysis.

Dependent Variable: VV

Analysis of Variance

Source	DF	Sum of Squares	Mean Square	F Value	Prob>F
Model	2	8.58051	4.29026	13.605	0.0313
Error	3	0.94602	0.31534		
C Total	5	9.52653			

Root MSE	0.56155	R-square	0.9007	
Dep Mean	97.71333	Adj R-sq	0.8345	
C.V.	0.57469			

Parameter Estimates

Variable	DF	Parameter Estimate	Standard Error	T for H0: Parameter=0	Prob > |T|
INTERCEP	1	96.550868	0.32821017	294.174	0.0001
TIME	1	0.008229	0.00254685	3.231	0.0482
TIMESQ	1	-0.000005316	0.00000253	-2.105	0.1260

Obs	TIME	Dep Var VV	Predict Value	Std Err Predict	Lower95% Predict	Upper95% Predict	Residual
1	1	95.8	96.6	0.327	94.5	98.6	-0.7291
2	10	96.7	96.6	0.314	94.6	98.7	0.0974
3	28.5	97.4	96.8	0.291	94.8	98.8	0.5989
4	150	97.8	97.7	0.288	95.7	99.7	0.1544
5	450	99.0	99.2	0.509	96.8	101.6	-0.1475
6	1000	99.5	99.5	0.560	96.9	102.0	0.0259

a. Graph the prediction equation and plot the data points.
b. Is there sufficient evidence to indicate that the quadratic term should be included in the model? Test using $\alpha = .05$.
c. Prediction intervals for V_v are shown on the printout. Find and interpret the prediction interval for V_v at sintering time 150 minutes.

12.58 Refer to Exercise 12.55. The unstable values of the standard deviations for S_v shown in the table indicate a strong possibility that the standard regression assumption of equal variances is violated for the second-order model of Exercise 12.56. We can satisfy this assumption by transforming the response to a new response that has a constant variance. For this exercise, consider the log transform* $S_v^* = \log(S_v)$ and fit the model

$$E(S_v^*) = \beta_0 + \beta_1 x$$

Refer to the SAS printout for the regression analysis of the log transform model shown here.

Dependent Variable: LOGSV

Analysis of Variance

Source	DF	Sum of Squares	Mean Square	F Value	Prob>F
Model	1	4.38661	4.38661	28.721	0.0058
Error	4	0.61093	0.15273		
C Total	5	4.99755			

Root MSE	0.39081	R-square	0.8778	
Dep Mean	5.81885	Adj R-sq	0.8472	
C.V.	6.71630			

Parameter Estimates

Variable	DF	Parameter Estimate	Standard Error	T for H0: Parameter=0	Prob > |T|
INTERCEP	1	6.467717	0.20028753	32.292	0.0001
TIME	1	-0.002375	0.00044310	-5.359	0.0058

Obs	TIME	Dep Var LOGSV	Predict Value	Std Err Predict	Lower95% Predict	Upper95% Predict	Residual
1	1	6.9815	6.4653	0.200	5.2464	7.6842	0.5161
2	10	6.6012	6.4440	0.198	5.2281	7.6599	0.1573
3	28.5	6.2332	6.4000	0.193	5.1900	7.6101	-0.1668
4	150	5.7021	6.1115	0.169	4.9298	7.2933	-0.4094
5	450	5.1059	5.3991	0.178	4.2071	6.5911	-0.2932
6	1000	4.2891	4.0931	0.359	2.6190	5.5672	0.1960

a. Graph the prediction equation and plot the data points.
b. Is the model adequate for predicting $\log(S_v)$? Test using $\alpha = .05$.
c. Prediction intervals for the transformed response $\log(S_v)$ are shown on the printout. The predicted value of S_v is the antilog,

$$\hat{S}_v = e^{\widehat{\log(S_v)}}$$

To obtain prediction intervals for S_v, take the antilogs of the endpoints of the intervals.[†] Find a 95% prediction interval for S_v when the sintering time is 150 minutes.

---

*To see the stabilizing effect of the log transform, use your calculator to take the logs of the standard deviations for S_v shown in the table. Note that the transformed values appear to be much less variable.

†Unfortunately, you cannot take antilogs to find the confidence interval for the mean response $E(y)$. This is because the mean value of $\log(y)$ is not equal to the logarithm of the mean of y.

OPTIONAL EXERCISE

12.59 Refer to Exercise 12.1. Suppose we obtained two replications of the experiment—i.e., two values of y were observed for each of the six values of x. The data are shown in the accompanying table.

x	1		2		3		4		5		6	
y	1.1	.5	1.8	2.0	2.0	2.9	3.8	3.4	4.1	5.0	5.0	5.8

a. Suppose (as in Exercise 12.1) you want to fit the model $E(y) = \beta_0 + \beta_1 x$. Construct Y and X matrices for the data. [*Hint:* Remember, the Y matrix must be of dimensions 12×1.]

b. Find $X'X$ and $X'Y$.

c. Compare the $X'X$ matrix for two replications of the experiment with the $X'X$ matrix obtained for a single replication (part **b** of Exercise 12.1). What is the relationship between the elements in the two matrices?

d. Observe the $(X'X)^{-1}$ matrix for a single replication (see part **c** of Exercise 12.1). Verify that the $(X'X)^{-1}$ matrix for two replications contains elements that are equal to $\frac{1}{2}$ of the values of the corresponding elements in the $(X'X)^{-1}$ matrix for a single replication of the experiment. [*Hint:* Show that the product of the $(X'X)^{-1}$ matrix (for two replications) and the $X'X$ matrix from part **c** equals I.]

e. Find the prediction equation.

COMPUTER LAB: Multiple Regression and Residual Analysis

In this section, we give the SAS and MINITAB commands for performing a multiple regression analysis and a graphical residual analysis. The sample programs below give the commands for analyzing the model

$$E(y) = \beta_0 + \beta_1 x_1 + \beta_2 x_2 + \beta_3 x_3 + \beta_4 x_4 + \beta_5 x_1^2$$

In all SAS and MINITAB programs, the higher-order terms specified in the model (e.g., x_1^2 in the above model) must be created through data transformation statements.

SAS

Command
line

```
1    DATA IN;                                              ⎫
2    INPUT Y X1 X2 X3 X4;                                  ⎬  Data entry instructions
3    X1SQ = X1*X1;                                         ⎭
4    CARDS;

           [Input data values]

5    PROC REG;                                             ⎫
6    MODEL Y = X1 X2 X3 X4 X1SQ/P CLI INFLUENCE;           ⎬  Regression analysis
7    ID X1 X2 X3 X4;                                       ⎭  and influence
                                                              diagnostics
8    OUTPUT OUT=RESIDS P=YHAT R=RESID;
9    PROC PLOT;                                               Residual plots
10   PLOT RESID*(YHAT X1);
11   PROC UNIVARIATE PLOT;                                    Histogram of residuals
12   VAR RESID;
```

COMMAND 5 The REG procedure fits general linear models.

COMMAND 6 In the MODEL statement, the dependent variable is listed to the left of the equals sign and the independent variables to the right. The option P (following the slash) prints predicted values and residuals, and the option CLI prints corresponding lower and upper 95% prediction limits. Specify CLM to obtain 95% confidence intervals for $E(y)$. The option INFLUENCE produces influence measures (e.g., deleted residuals) for the individual observations in the data set.

COMMANDS 9–10 Two plots are produced: residuals versus predicted ($\hat{y}$) and residuals versus quantitative x (x_1).

COMMANDS 11–12 The UNIVARIATE procedure with the PLOT option produces a histogram (or stem-and-leaf display) for the regression residuals.

MINITAB

Command
line

```
 1    READ Y IN C1, PREDICTORS IN C2-C5

          [Input data values]                              Data entry instructions

 2    NAME C1='Y' C2='X1' C3='X2' C4='X3' C5='X4'
 3    MULTIPLY C2 BY C2, PUT IN C6
 4    NAME C6='X1SQ'
 5    REGRESS C1, 5 XVARS ARE C2-C6, STDRES IN C7, PRED IN C8;
 6       RESIDUALS IN C9;                          Regression analysis
 7       TRESIDUALS IN C10;
 8       PREDICT FOR X-VALUES 10 2,3 4 15,7 100,
 9    NAME C8='PRED' C9='RESID' C10='DEL,RESID'
10    PLOT C9 VS, C8
11    PLOT C9 VS, C2                        Residual plots
12    STEM-AND-LEAF C9                      Stem-and-leaf display of residuals
13    PRINT C10                             List influence diagnostics
```

COMMAND 5 The REGRESS command fits general linear models. The column number of the dependent variable is listed first (C1), followed by the number of predictors in the model (5) and the columns where the independent variables are located (C2–C6). As an option, you can request MINITAB to store Studentized residuals and predicted values in the next two columns specified (C7 and C8, respectively).

COMMAND 6 The RESIDUALS subcommand stores (unstandardized) residuals in the assigned column (C9) for purposes of plotting.

COMMAND 7 The TRESIDUALS subcommand stores Studentized deleted residuals in the assigned column (C10) for checking for influential observations.

COMMAND 8 The PREDICT subcommand specifies the values of the independent variables (e.g., $x_1 = 10$, $x_2 = 2.3$, $x_3 = 4$, $x_4 = 15.7$, and $x_1^2 = 100$) to be used for confidence intervals for $E(y)$ and prediction intervals for y. The values specified must correspond to the order of the independent variable columns listed on the REGRESS command.

COMMANDS 10–11 Two residual plots are produced: residuals versus predicted (command 10) and residuals versus x_1 (command 11).

COMMAND 12   A stem-and-leaf display of the residuals is produced.

COMMAND 13   The Studentized deleted residuals are listed for each case to check for influential observations.

References

Barnett, V., and Lewis, T. *Outliers in Statistical Data*. New York: Wiley, 1978.

Belsley, D. A., Kuh, E., and Welsch, R. E. *Regression Diagnostics: Identifying Influential Data and Sources of Collinearity*. New York: Wiley, 1980.

Box, G. E. P., and Jenkins, G. M. *Time Series Analysis, Forecasting and Control*. San Francisco: Holden-Day, Inc., 1970.

Draper, N. R., and Smith, H. *Applied Regression Analysis*, 2nd ed. New York: Wiley, 1981.

Fuller, W. *Introduction to Statistical Time Series*. New York: Wiley, 1976.

Graybill, F. A. *Theory and Application of the Linear Model*. North Scituate, Mass.: Duxbury, 1976.

Mendenhall, W. *Introduction to Linear Models and the Design and Analysis of Experiments*. Belmont, Calif.: Wadsworth, 1968.

Mendenhall, W., and Sincich, T. *A Second Course in Business Statistics: Regression Analysis*, 4th ed. New York: Macmillan, 1993.

Neter, J., Wasserman, W., and Kutner, M. H. *Applied Linear Statistical Models*, 3rd ed. Homewood, Ill.: Richard D. Irwin, 1989.

Weisberg, S. *Applied Linear Regression*. New York: Wiley, 1980.

CHAPTER THIRTEEN

Model Building

Objective

To show you why the choice of the deterministic portion of a linear model is crucial to the acquisition of a good prediction equation; to present some basic concepts and procedures for constructing good linear models

Contents

13.1   Why Model Building Is Important

We have emphasized in Chapters 11 and 12 that the first step in the construction of a regression model is to hypothesize the form of the deterministic portion of the probabilistic model. This **model building**, or model construction, stage is the key to the success (or failure) of the regression analysis. If the hypothesized model does not reflect, at least approximately, the true nature of the relationship between the mean response $E(y)$ and the independent variables $x_1, x_2, \ldots, x_k$, the modeling effort will usually be unrewarded.

By *model building*, we mean writing a model that will provide a good fit to a set of data and that will give good estimates of the mean value of y and good predictions of future values of y for given values of the independent variables. To illustrate, suppose you want to relate the breaking strength y for a certain type of plastic to the amount of pressure x used to produce the plastic. Unknown to you, the second-order model

$$E(y) = \beta_0 + \beta_1 x + \beta_2 x^2$$

would permit you to predict y with a very small error of prediction (see Figure 13.1a). Unfortunately, you have erroneously chosen the first-order model

$$E(y) = \beta_0 + \beta_1 x$$

to explain the relationship between y and x (see Figure 13.1b).

FIGURE 13.1 ▶
Two models for relating breaking strength y to amount of pressure x

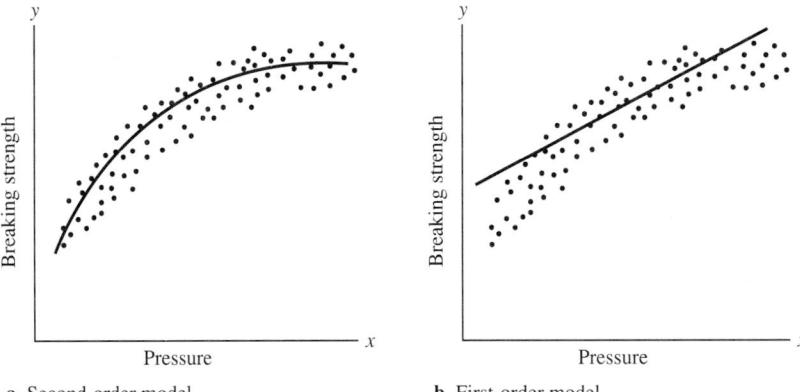

a. Second-order model   b. First-order model

The consequence of choosing the wrong model is clearly demonstrated by comparing Figures 13.1a and 13.1b. The errors of prediction for the second-order model are relatively small in comparison to those for the first-order model. The lesson to be learned from this simple example is clear. Choosing a good set of independent (predictor) variables $x_1, x_2, \ldots, x_k$ will not guarantee a good prediction equation. In addition to selecting independent variables that contain information about y, you must specify an equation relating y to $x_1, x_2, \ldots, x_k$ that will provide a good fit to your data.

In the following sections, we will present some useful models for relating a response y to one or more predictor variables.

13.2 The Two Types of Independent Variables: Quantitative and Qualitative

Recall from Chapter 1 the two types of data that arise in experimental situations: **quantitative** and **qualitative**. For the types of regression analyses considered in this text, the dependent variable will always be quantitative, but the independent variables may be either quantitative or qualitative. As you will see, the way an independent variable enters the model depends on its type.

> **Definition 13.1**
>
> A **quantitative** independent variable is one that assumes numerical values corresponding to the points on a line. An independent variable that is not quantitative is called **qualitative**.

The waiting time before a computer begins to process data, the number of defects in a product, and the kilowatt-hours of electricity used per day are all examples of quantitative independent variables. On the other hand, recall that three species of fish—channel catfish, largemouth bass, and smallmouth buffalo—were found in the contaminated Tennessee River (see Appendix III). The variable species is qualitative, since it is not measured on a numerical scale. Since it is likely that the different species have different mean levels of DDT contamination, we would want to include it as an independent variable in a model predicting the level of DDT contamination, y, in fish found in the Tennessee River.

> **Definition 13.2**
>
> The different intensity settings of an independent variable are called its **levels**.

For a quantitative independent variable, the levels correspond to the numerical values it assumes. For example, if the number of defects in a product ranges from 0 to 3, the independent variable has four levels: 0, 1, 2, and 3.

The levels of a qualitative variable are not numerical. They can be defined only by describing them. For example, the independent variable for the species of fish was observed at three levels: channel catfish, largemouth bass, and smallmouth buffalo.

EXAMPLE 13.1   Suppose our task is to predict the salary of a corporate executive at a high-technology firm as a function of the following four independent variables:

a. Experience of an employee (years)

b. Gender of the employee

c. Net asset value of the firm

d. Rank of the employee

For each of these independent variables, give its type and describe the levels you would expect to observe.

Solution   a. The independent variable, experience, is quantitative, since its values are numerical. We would expect to observe levels ranging from 0 to 40 (approximately) years.

b. The independent variable for gender is qualitative, since its levels can be described only by the nonnumerical labels "female" and "male."

c. The independent variable, net asset value of the firm, is quantitative, with a large number of possible levels corresponding to the range of dollar values representing the net asset values of the various firms.

d. Suppose the independent variable for the rank of the employee is observed at three levels: supervisor, assistant vice president, and vice president. Since we cannot assign a realistic numerical measure of relative importance to each position, rank is a qualitative independent variable.

Quantitative independent variables are treated differently from qualitative variables in regression modeling. In the next section, we will begin our discussion of how quantitative variables are used in the modeling effort.

EXERCISES

13.1   The *Journal of Human Stress* (Summer 1987) reported on a study of "psychological response of firefighters to a chemical fire." The researchers used multiple regression to predict emotional distress as a function of the following independent variables. Identify each independent variable as quantitative or qualitative. For qualitative variables, suggest several levels that might be observed. For quantitative variables, give a range of values (levels) for which the variable might be observed.

a. Number of preincident psychological symptoms

b. Years experience

c. Cigarette smoking behavior

d. Level of social support

e. Marital status

f. Age

g. Ethnic status

    h. Exposure to a chemical fire

    i. Educational level

    j. Distance lived from site of incident

    k. Gender

13.2 An experiment was conducted to investigate the sheet flow rate of a land waste treatment plant. Classify each of the following independent variables as quantitative or qualitative and describe the levels the variables might assume.

    a. Amount of rainfall

    b. Method of treatment

    c. Irrigation rate

    d. Slope of grass mat

    e. Type of sod

13.3 Consider the following variables related to running a computer job. Classify each variable as quantitative or qualitative and describe the levels each variable might assume.

    a. CPU time

    b. Software system

    c. Lines of output

    d. Job cost

    e. Date of submission

13.4 *Environmental Science & Technology* (Oct. 1993) published an article that investigated the variables that affect the sorption of organic vapors on clay minerals. The independent variables and levels considered in the study are listed here. Identify the type (quantitative or qualitative) of each.

    a. Temperature (50°F, 60°F, 75°F, 90°F)

    b. Relative humidity (30%, 50%, 70%)

    c. Organic compound (benzene, toluene, chloroform, methanol, anisole)

13.3 Models with a Single Quantitative Independent Variable

The most common linear models relating y to a single quantitative independent variable x are those derived from a polynomial expression of the type shown in the box. Specific models, obtained by assigning particular values to p, are listed subsequently.

Formula for a pth-Order Polynomial with One Independent Variable

$$E(y) = \beta_0 + \beta_1 x + \beta_2 x^2 + \beta_3 x^3 + \cdots + \beta_p x^p$$

where p is an integer and $\beta_0, \beta_1, \ldots, \beta_p$ are unknown parameters that must be estimated.

First-Order (Straight-Line) Model with One Independent Variable

$$E(y) = \beta_0 + \beta_1 x$$

Interpretation of model parameters

β_0: y-intercept; the value of $E(y)$ when $x = 0$

β_1:   Slope of the line; the change in $E(y)$ for a 1-unit increase in x

---

The first-order model is used when you expect the rate of change in y per unit change in x to remain fairly stable over the range of values of x for which you wish to predict y (see Figure 13.2). Most relationships between $E(y)$ and x are curvilinear, but the curvature over the range of values of x for which you wish to predict y may be very slight. When this occurs, a first-order (straight-line) model should provide a good fit to your data.

FIGURE 13.2 ▶
Graph of a first-order model

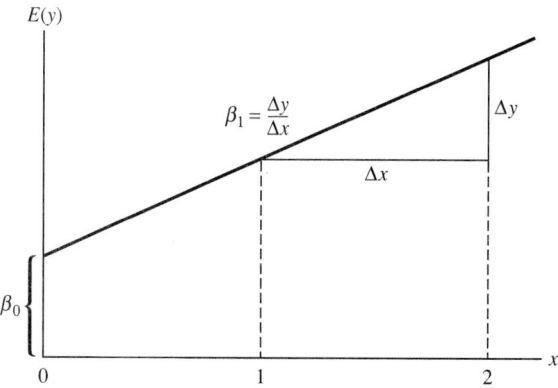

Second-Order (Quadratic) Model with One Independent Variable

$$E(y) = \beta_0 + \beta_1 x + \beta_2 x^2$$

Interpretation of model parameters

β_0: y-intercept; the value of $E(y)$ when $x = 0$

β_1:   Shift parameter; changing the value of β_1 shifts the parabola to the right or left (increasing the value of β_1 causes the parabola to shift to the right)

β_2:   Rate of curvature

A second-order model traces a parabola, one that opens either downward ($\beta_2 < 0$) or upward ($\beta_2 > 0$), as shown in Figure 13.3. Since most relationships will possess some curvature, a second-order model will often be a good choice to relate y to x.

FIGURE 13.3 ▶
The graphs of two second-order models

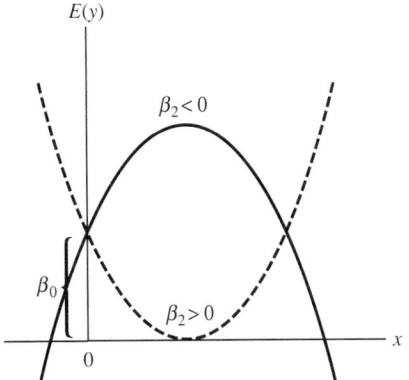

Third-Order Model with One Independent Variable

$$E(y) = \beta_0 + \beta_1 x + \beta_2 x^2 + \beta_3 x^3$$

Interpretation of model parameters

β_0: y-intercept; the value of $E(y)$ when $x = 0$

β_3:   The magnitude of β_3 controls the rate of reversal of curvature for the curve

---

Reversals in curvature are not common, but such relationships can be modeled by third- and higher-order polynomials. As can be seen in Figure 13.3, a second-order model contains no reversals in curvature. The slope continues to either increase or decrease as x increases and produces either a trough or a peak. A third-order model (see Figure 13.4 on page 706) contains one reversal in curvature and produces one peak and one trough. In general, the graph of a pth-order polynomial will contain a maximum of $(p - 1)$ peaks and troughs.

Most functional relationships in nature seem to be smooth (except for random error)—that is, they are not subject to rapid and irregular reversals in direction. Consequently, the second-order polynomial model is perhaps the most useful of those

FIGURE 13.4 ▶
The graphs of two third-order
models

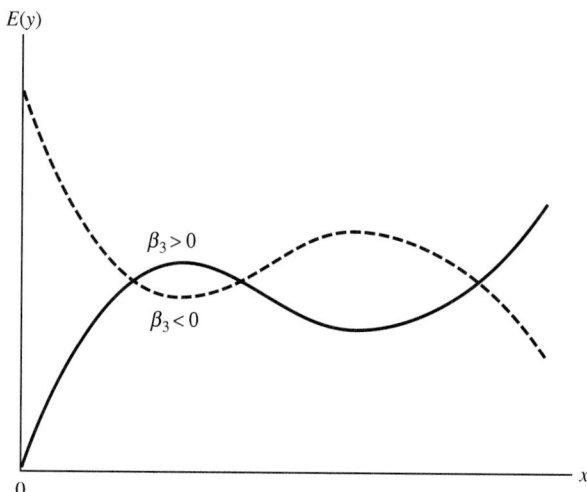

previously described. To develop a better understanding of how this model is used, consider the following example.

EXAMPLE 13.2

To operate efficiently, power companies must be able to predict the peak power load at their various stations. The peak power load is the maximum amount of power that must be generated each day to meet demand.

Suppose a power company located in the southern part of the United States decides to model daily peak power load, y, as a function of the daily high temperature, x, and the model is to be constructed for the summer months when demand is greatest. Although we would expect the peak power load to increase as the high temperature increases, the *rate* of increase in $E(y)$ might also increase as x increases. That is, a 1-unit increase in high temperature from 100°F to 101°F might result in a greater increase in power demand than would a 1-unit increase from 80°F to 81°F. Therefore, we postulate the second-order model

$$E(y) = \beta_0 + \beta_1 x + \beta_2 x^2$$

and we expect β_2 to be positive.

A random sample of 25 summer days is selected, and the data are shown in Table 13.1. Fit a second-order model using these data, and test the hypothesis that the power load increases at an increasing *rate* with temperature—i.e., that $\beta_2 > 0$. Use $\alpha = .05$.

TABLE 13.1	Power Load Data				
Temperature	Peak Load	Temperature	Peak Load	Temperature	Peak Load
°F	megawatts	°F	megawatts	°F	megawatts
94	136.0	106	178.2	76	100.9
96	131.7	67	101.6	68	96.3
95	140.7	71	92.5	92	135.1
108	189.3	100	151.9	100	143.6
67	96.5	79	106.2	85	111.4
88	116.4	97	153.2	89	116.5
89	118.5	98	150.1	74	103.9
84	113.4	87	114.7	86	105.1
90	132.0				

Solution

The SAS printout shown in Figure 13.5 on page 708 gives the least squares fit of the second-order model using the data in Table 13.1. The prediction equation is

$$\hat{y} = 385.048 - 8.293x + .05982x^2$$

A plot of this equation and the observed values is given in Figure 13.6 on page 708. Note that this curve passes through the data points and seems to produce (by visual examination) a set of deviations that are relatively small.

We now test to determine whether the sample value, $\hat{\beta}_2 = .05982$, is large enough to conclude *in general* that the power load increases at an increasing rate with temperature:

$$H_0: \quad \beta_2 = 0$$
$$H_a: \quad \beta_2 > 0$$

Test statistic:

$$t = \frac{\hat{\beta}_2}{s_{\hat{\beta}_2}}$$

$$= 7.925 \quad \text{(shaded in Figure 13.5)}$$

The two-tailed observed significance level of the test (shaded on the printout) is .0001. Consequently, the p-value for this one-tailed test is $.0001/2 = .00005$. Since this value is less than $\alpha = .05$, we reject H_0 and conclude that the mean power load increases at an increasing rate with temperature.

FIGURE 13.5 ▶
SAS printout for second-order
model of Example 13.2

Dependent Variable: LOAD

Analysis of Variance

Source	DF	Sum of Squares	Mean Square	F Value	Prob>F
Model	2	15011.77200	7505.88600	259.687	0.0001
Error	22	635.87840	28.90356		
C Total	24	15647.65040			

Root MSE	5.37620	R-square	0.9594	
Dep Mean	125.42800	Adj R-sq	0.9557	
C.V.	4.28629			

Parameter Estimates

Variable	DF	Parameter Estimate	Standard Error	T for H0: Parameter=0	Prob > |T|
INTERCEP	1	385.048093	55.17243578	6.979	0.0001
TEMP	1	-8.292527	1.29904502	-6.384	0.0001
TEMPSQ	1	0.059823	0.00754855	7.925	0.0001

FIGURE 13.6 ▶
Plot of the observations and the
second-order least squares fit
(Example 13.2)

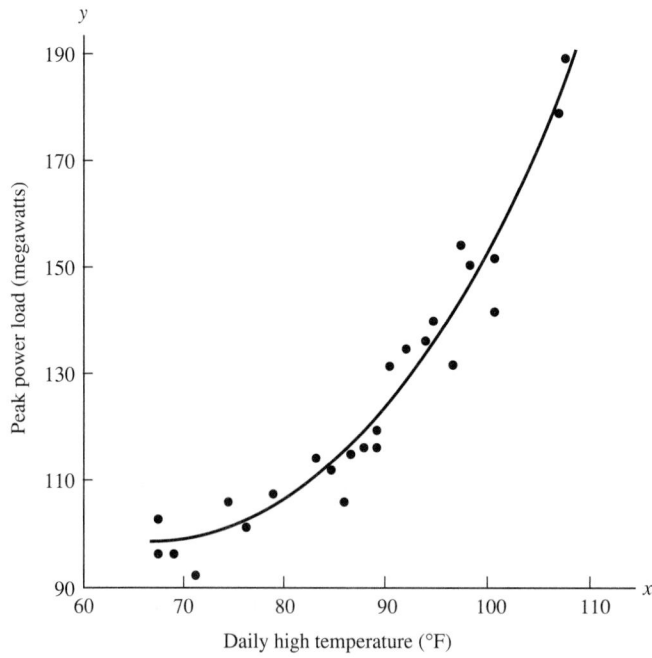

EXERCISES

13.5   Consider the following polynomial model:

$$E(y) = 2 - 4x$$

a. Give the order of this polynomial.
b. Sketch the curve corresponding to the equation for $E(y)$.
c. How would the graph change if the coefficient of x were positive instead of negative?

13.6   Consider the following polynomial model:

$$E(y) = 5 - 3x + x^2$$

a. Give the order of this polynomial.
b. Sketch the curve corresponding to the equation for $E(y)$.
c. How would the graph change if the coefficient of x^2 were negative rather than positive?

13.7   The accompanying graphs depict pth-order polynomials for one independent variable.

i. $E(y)$

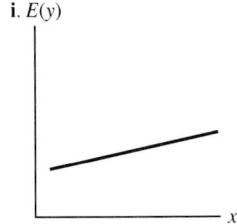

ii. $E(y)$

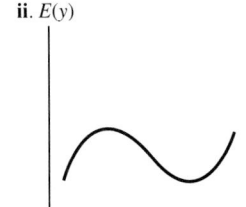

iii. $E(y)$

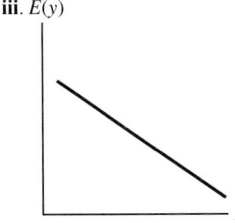

iv. $E(y)$

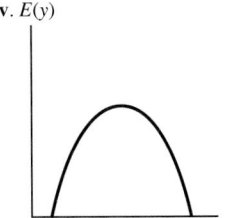

a. For each graph, identify the order of the polynomial.
b. Using the parameters β_0, β_1, β_2, etc., write an appropriate model relating $E(y)$ to x for each graph.
c. The signs (+ or −) of many of the parameters in the models of part **b** can be determined by examining the graphs. Give the signs of those parameters that can be determined.

13.8   Graph the following polynomials and identify the order of each on your graph:
a. $E(y) = 2 + 3x$ **b.** $E(y) = 2 + 3x^2$
c. $E(y) = 1 + 2x + 2x^2 + x^3$ **d.** $E(y) = 2x + 2x^2 + x^3$
e. $E(y) = 2 - 3x^2$ **f.** $E(y) = -2 + 3x$

13.9   Refer to the *Environmental Science & Technology* study of sorption of organic vapors, Exercise 13.4. Consider modeling the vapor retention coefficient y as a function of one of the two quantitative variables, temperature (x_1) and relative humidity (x_2).

  a. Propose a model that hypothesizes a curvilinear relationship between mean retention $E(y)$ and relative humidity x_2. Draw a sketch of the model.

  b. Propose a model that hypothesizes a third-order relationship between mean retention $E(y)$ and temperature x_1. Draw a sketch of the model.

13.10   The amount of pressure used to produce a certain plastic is thought to be related to the strength of the plastic. Researchers believe that, as pressure is increased, the strength of the plastic increases until, at some point, increases in pressure will have a detrimental effect on strength. Write a model to relate the strength, y, of the plastic to pressure, x, that would reflect the above beliefs. Sketch the model.

13.11   Does exercise improve the human immune system? An experiment was conducted by a physiologist at the University of Florida to determine whether such a relationship exists. Thirty subjects volunteered to participate in the study. The amount of immunoglobulin known as IgG (an indicator of long-term immunity) and the maximal oxygen uptake (a measure of aerobic fitness level) were recorded for each subject. The resulting data are given in the accompanying table.

Subject	IgG y	Maximal Oxygen Uptake x	Subject	IgG y	Maximal Oxygen Uptake x
1	881	34.6	16	1,660	52.5
2	1,290	45.0	17	2,121	69.9
3	2,147	62.3	18	1,382	38.8
4	1,909	58.9	19	1,714	50.6
5	1,282	42.5	20	1,959	69.4
6	1,530	44.3	21	1,158	37.4
7	2,067	67.9	22	965	35.1
8	1,982	58.5	23	1,456	43.0
9	1,019	35.6	24	1,273	44.1
10	1,651	49.6	25	1,418	49.8
11	752	33.0	26	1,743	54.4
12	1,687	52.0	27	1,997	68.5
13	1,782	61.4	28	2,177	69.5
14	1,529	50.2	29	1,965	63.0
15	969	34.1	30	1,264	43.2

  a. Construct a scattergram for the IgG–maximal oxygen uptake data.

  b. Hypothesize a probabilistic model relating IgG to maximal oxygen uptake.

13.12   The optomotor responses of tree frogs were studied in the *Journal of Experimental Zoology* (Sept. 1993). Microspectrophotometry was used to measure the threshold quantal flux (the light intensity at which the optomotor response was first observed) of tree frogs tested at different spectral wavelengths. The data revealed the following relationship between the log of quantal flux (y) and wavelength (x). Hypothesize a model for $E(y)$ that corresponds to the graph.

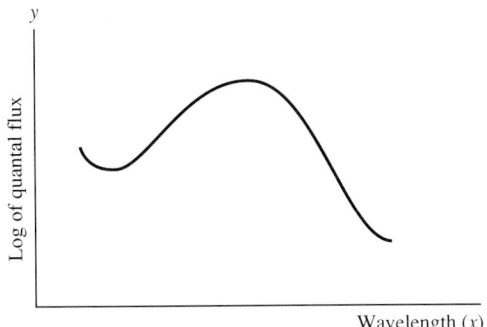

13.13 Air pollution regulations for power plants are often written so that the maximum amount of pollution that can be emitted increases as the plant's output increases. Assuming this is true, write a model relating the maximum amount of pollution permitted (in parts per million) to a plant's output (in megawatts).

13.14 Theophylline is a drug used to control asthma in children. To be effective, the blood concentration level of the drug must remain between 4 and 20 picograms per milliliter. Thus, frequent monitoring of theophylline concentrations is necessary for successful therapy. A study was conducted to compare the Ames Seralyzer assay system and the enzyme-multiplied immunoassay technique (EMIT), two methods of determining theophylline concentration (*American Journal of Hospital Pharmacy*, July 1986). A total of 102 blood serum samples were obtained from pediatric intensive-care unit patients who were receiving theophylline intra-venously. Each sample was analyzed for theophylline concentration using both methods. The data (recorded in picograms per milliliter) were used to fit the model $y = \beta_0 + \beta_1 x + \varepsilon$, where

   y = Theophylline concentration as determined by Ames Seralyzer

   x = Theophylline concentration as determined by EMIT

A summary of the results follows:

$$\hat{y} = 1.737 + .953x \qquad r = .97 \qquad s_{\hat{\beta}_1} = .025 \qquad s = 1.9$$

   a. Construct a 95% confidence interval for β_1.
   b. Interpret the interval, part **a**, and explain what it tells you about the relationship between the theophylline measurements of the two methods.

13.15 An engineer has proposed the following model to describe the relationship between the number of acceptable items produced per day (output) and the number of work-hours expended per day (input) in a particular production process:

$$y = \beta_0 + \beta_1 x + \beta_2 x^2 + \varepsilon$$

where

   y = Number of acceptable items produced per day

   x = Number of work-hours per day

A portion of the MINITAB computer printout that results from fitting this model to a sample of 25 weeks of production data is shown on page 712. Test the hypothesis that as amount of input increases, the amount of output also increases but at a decreasing rate. Do the data provide sufficient evidence to indicate that the *rate* of increase in output per unit increase of input decreases as the input increases? Test using $\alpha = .05$.

```
The regression equation is
Y = -6.17 + 2.04 X1 - .0323 X2


Predictor       Coef       Stdev      t-ratio         p
Constant       -6.173      1.666       -3.71       0.002
X1              2.036       .185       11.02       0.000
X2             -.03231     .00489      -6.60       0.000


s = 1.243        R-sq = 95.5%      R-sq(adj) = 95.1%


Analysis of Variance


SOURCE        DF         SS          MS          F         p
Regression     2      718.168     359.084     232.41     0.000
Error         22       33.992       1.545
Total         24      752.160
```

13.4   Models with Two Quantitative Independent Variables

Like models with a single quantitative independent variable, models with two quantitative independent variables are classified as first-order, second-order, and so forth. Since we rarely encounter third- or higher-order relationships in practice, we focus our discussion on first- and second-order models.

First-Order Model with Two Independent Variables

$$E(y) = \beta_0 + \beta_1 x_1 + \beta_2 x_2$$

Interpretation of model parameters

β_0: y-intercept; of a planar surface (see Figure 13.7); the value of $E(y)$ when $x_1 = x_2 = 0$

β_1:   Change in $E(y)$ for a 1-unit increase in x_1, when x_2 is held fixed

β_2:   Change in $E(y)$ for a 1-unit increase in x_2, when x_1 is held fixed

---

The graph in Figure 13.7 traces a **response surface** (in contrast to the **response curve** that is used to relate $E(y)$ to a *single* quantitative variable). In particular, a first-order model relating $E(y)$ to two independent quantitative variables, x_1 and x_2, graphs as a plane in a three-dimensional space. The plane traces the value of $E(y)$ for every combination of values (x_1, x_2) that correspond to points in the (x_1, x_2)-plane. Most response surfaces in the real world are well behaved (smooth) and they have curvature. Consequently, a first-order model is appropriate only if the response surface is fairly flat over the (x_1, x_2)-region that is of interest to you.

FIGURE 13.7 ▶
Response surface for first-order model with two independent variables

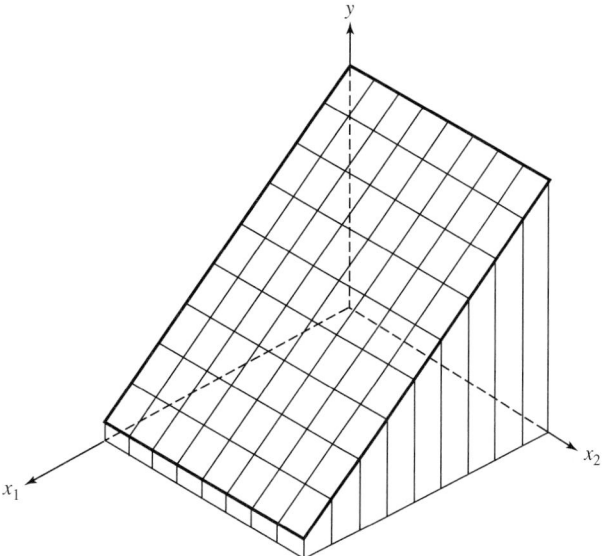

The assumption that a first-order model will adequately characterize the relationship between $E(y)$ and the variables x_1 and x_2 is equivalent to assuming that x_1 and x_2 do not "interact"; that is, you assume that the effect on $E(y)$ of a change in x_1 (for a fixed value of x_2) is the same regardless of the value of x_2 (and vice versa). Thus, "no interaction" is equivalent to saying that the effect of changes in one variable (say, x_1) on $E(y)$ is *independent* of the value of the second variable (say, x_2). For example, if we assign values to x_2 in a first-order model, the graph of $E(y)$ as a function of x_1 would produce parallel lines as shown in Figure 13.8 on page 714. These lines, called **contour lines**, show the contours of the surface when it is sliced by three planes, each of which is parallel to the $[E(y), x_1]$-plane, at distances $x_2 = 1, 2,$ and 3 from the origin.

Definition 13.3

Two variables x_1 and x_2 are said to **interact** if the change in $E(y)$ for a 1-unit change in x_1 (when x_2 is held fixed) is dependent on the value of x_2.

FIGURE 13.8 ▶
A graph indicating no
interaction between x_1 and x_2

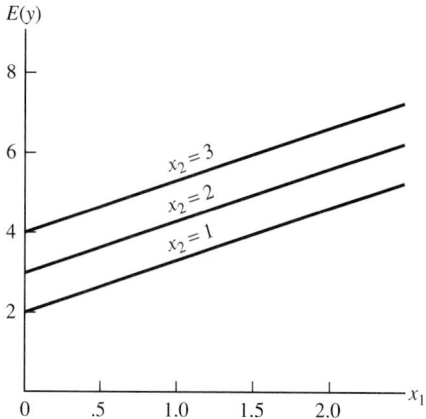

Interaction Model (Second-Order) with Two Independent Variables

$$E(y) = \beta_0 + \beta_1 x_1 + \beta_2 x_2 + \beta_3 x_1 x_2$$

Interpretation of model parameters

β_0: y-intercept; the value of $E(y)$ when $x_1 = x_2 = 0$

β_1 and β_2: Changing β_1 and β_2 causes the surface to shift along the x_1 and x_2 axes

β_3: Controls the rate of twist in the ruled surface (see Figure 13.9)

When one independent variable is held fixed, the model produces straight lines with the following slopes:

$\beta_1 + \beta_3 x_2$: Change in $E(y)$ for a 1-unit increase in x_1, when x_2 is held fixed

$\beta_2 + \beta_3 x_1$: Change in $E(y)$ for a 1-unit increase in x_2, when x_1 is held fixed

---

The interaction model is said to be second-order because the order of the highest-order ($x_1 x_2$) term in x_1 and x_2 is 2; i.e., the sum of the exponents of x_1 and x_2 equals 2. This model traces a ruled surface in a three-dimensional space (see Figure 13.9). You could produce such a surface by placing a pencil perpendicular to a line and moving it along the line, while rotating it around the line. The resulting surface would appear as a twisted plane. A graph of $E(y)$ as a function of x_1 for given values of x_2 (say, $x_2 = 1$, 2, and 3) produces nonparallel contour lines (see Figure 13.10), thus indicating that the change in $E(y)$ for a given change in x_1 is dependent on the

FIGURE 13.9 ▶
Response surface for an interaction
model (second-order)

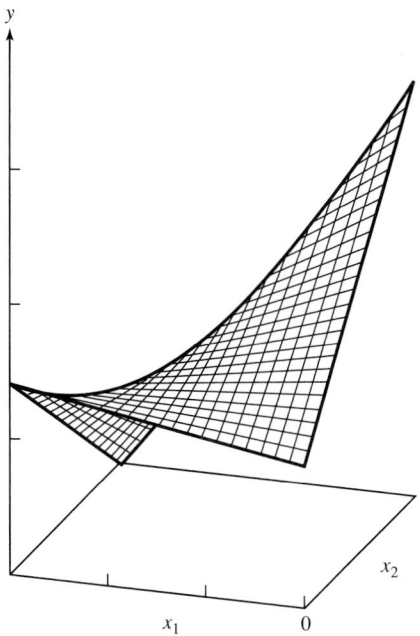

value of x_2 and, therefore, that x_1 and x_2 interact. Interaction is an extremely important concept because it is easy to get in the habit of fitting first-order models and individually examining the relationships between $E(y)$ and each of a set of independent variables, $x_1, x_2, \ldots, x_k$. Such a procedure is meaningless when interaction exists (which is, at least to some extent, almost always the case), and it can lead to gross errors in interpretation. For example, suppose that the relationship between $E(y)$ and x_1 and x_2 is as shown in Figure 13.10 and that you have observed y for each of the $n = 9$ combinations of values of x_1 and x_2, ($x_1 = 0$, 1, 2, and $x_2 = 1$, 2, 3). If you fit a

FIGURE 13.10 ▶
A graph indicating interaction
between x_1 and x_2

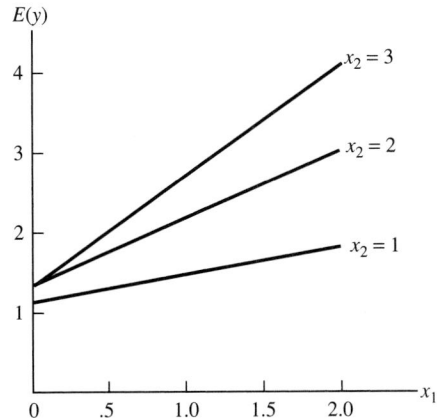

first-order model in x_1 and x_2 to the data, the fitted plane would be (except for random error) approximately parallel to the (x_1, x_2)-plane, thus suggesting that x_1 and x_2 contribute very little information about $E(y)$. That this is not the case is clearly indicated by Figure 13.10. Fitting a first-order model to the data would not allow for the twist in the true surface and would therefore give a false impression of the relationship between $E(y)$ and x_1 and x_2. The procedure for detecting interaction between two independent variables can be seen by examining the model. The interaction model differs from the noninteraction first-order model only in the inclusion of the $\beta_3 x_1 x_2$ term:

$$\text{Interaction model:} \quad E(y) = \beta_0 + \beta_1 x_1 + \beta_2 x_2 + \beta_3 x_1 x_2$$
$$\text{First-order model:} \quad E(y) = \beta_0 + \beta_1 x_1 + \beta_2 x_2$$

Therefore, to test for the presence of interaction, we test

$$H_0: \quad \beta_3 = 0 \quad \text{(no interaction)}$$

against the alternative hypothesis

$$H_a: \quad \beta_3 \neq 0 \quad \text{(interaction)}$$

using the familiar Student's t test of Section 12.7.

Complete Second-Order Model with Two Independent Variables

$$E(y) = \beta_0 + \beta_1 x_1 + \beta_2 x_2 + \beta_3 x_1 x_2 + \beta_4 x_1^2 + \beta_5 x_2^2$$

Interpretation of model parameters

β_0: y-intercept; the value of $E(y)$ when $x_1 = x_2 = 0$

β_1 and β_2:   Changing β_1 and β_2 causes the surface to shift along the x_1 and x_2 axes

β_3:   The value of β_3 controls the rotation of the surface

β_4 and β_5:   Signs and values of these parameters control the type of surface and the rates of curvature

The following three types of surfaces may be produced by a second-order model:*

A paraboloid that opens upward (Figure 13.11a)

A paraboloid that opens downward (Figure 13.11b)

A saddle-shaped surface (Figure 13.11c)

---

*The saddle-shaped surface (Figure 13.11c) is produced when $\beta_3^2 > 4\beta_4\beta_5$. For $\beta_3^2 < 4\beta_4\beta_5$, the paraboloid opens upward (Figure 13.11a) when $\beta_4 + \beta_5 > 0$ and opens downward (Figure 13.11b) when $\beta_4 + \beta_5 < 0$.

FIGURE 13.11 ▶
Graphs of three second-order
surfaces

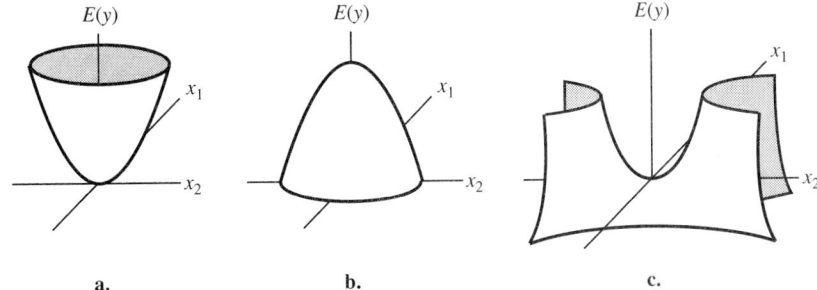

a.   b.   c.

A complete second-order model is the three-dimensional equivalent of a second-order model in a single quantitative variable. Instead of tracing parabolas, it traces paraboloids and saddle surfaces. Since you fit only a portion of the complete surface to your data, a complete second-order model provides a very large variety of gently curving surfaces. It is a good choice for a model if you expect curvature in the response surface relating $E(y)$ to x_1 and x_2.

EXAMPLE 13.3

Many companies manufacture products (e.g., steel, paint, gasoline) that are at least partially produced using chemicals. In many instances, the quality of the finished product is a function of the temperature and pressure at which the chemical reactions take place. Suppose you want to model the quality, y, of a product as a function of the temperature, x_1, and the pressure, x_2, at which it is produced. Four inspectors independently assign a quality score between 0 and 100 to each product, and then the quality, y, is calculated by averaging the four scores. An experiment is conducted by varying temperature between 80°F and 100°F and pressure between 50 and 60 pounds per square inch. The resulting data are given in Table 13.2.

TABLE 13.2   Temperature, Pressure, and Quality of the Finished Product

x_1, °F	x_2, psi	y	x_1, °F	x_2, psi	y	x_1, °F	x_2, psi	y
80	50	50.8	90	50	63.4	100	50	46.6
80	50	50.7	90	50	61.6	100	50	49.1
80	50	49.4	90	50	63.4	100	50	46.4
80	55	93.7	90	55	93.8	100	55	69.8
80	55	90.9	90	55	92.1	100	55	72.5
80	55	90.9	90	55	97.4	100	55	73.2
80	60	74.5	90	60	70.9	100	60	38.7
80	60	73.0	90	60	68.8	100	60	42.5
80	60	71.2	90	60	71.3	100	60	41.4

a. Fit a second-order model to the data.

b. Sketch the response surface.

c. Test the overall utility of the model.

Solution

a. The complete second-order model is

$$E(y) = \beta_0 + \beta_1 x_1 + \beta_2 x_2 + \beta_3 x_1 x_2 + \beta_4 x_1^2 + \beta_5 x_2^2$$

The data in Table 13.2 were used to fit this model, and a portion of the SAS output is shown in Figure 13.12.

FIGURE 13.12 ▶
SAS printout for complete second-order model

Dependent Variable: Y

Analysis of Variance

Source	DF	Sum of Squares	Mean Square	F Value	Prob>F
Model	5	8402.26454	1680.45291	596.324	0.0001
Error	21	59.17843	2.81802		
C Total	26	8461.44296			

Root MSE	1.67870	R-square	0.9930	
Dep Mean	66.96296	Adj R-sq	0.9913	
C.V.	2.50690			

Parameter Estimates

Variable	DF	Parameter Estimate	Standard Error	T for H0: Parameter=0	Prob > |T|
INTERCEP	1	-5127.899074	110.29601493	-46.492	0.0001
X1	1	31.096389	1.34441322	23.130	0.0001
X2	1	139.747222	3.14005412	44.505	0.0001
X1X2	1	-0.145500	0.00969196	-15.012	0.0001
X1SQ	1	-0.133389	0.00685325	-19.464	0.0001
X2SQ	1	-1.144222	0.02741299	-41.740	0.0001

The least squares prediction equation is

$$\hat{y} = -5,127.90 + 31.10x_1 + 139.75x_2 - .146x_1x_2 - .133x_1^2 - 1.14x_2^2$$

b. A three-dimensional graph of this prediction model is shown in Figure 13.13. Note that the mean quality seems to be greatest for temperatures of about 85–90°F and for pressures of about 55–57 pounds per square inch.* Further experimentation in these ranges might lead to a more precise determination of the optimal temperature–pressure combination.

c. A look at the coefficient of determination, $R^2 = .993$, the F value for testing the entire model, $F = 596.32$, and the p-value for the test, $p = .0001$ (in Figure 13.12), leaves little doubt that the complete second-order model is useful for

---

*We can estimate the values of temperature and pressure that maximize quality in the least squares model by solving $\partial\hat{y}/\partial x_1 = 0$ and $\partial\hat{y}/\partial x_2 = 0$ for x_1 and x_2. These estimated optimal values are $x_1 = 86.25$°F and $x_2 = 55.58$ pounds per square inch.

FIGURE 13.13 ▶

Plot of second-order least squares model for Example 13.3

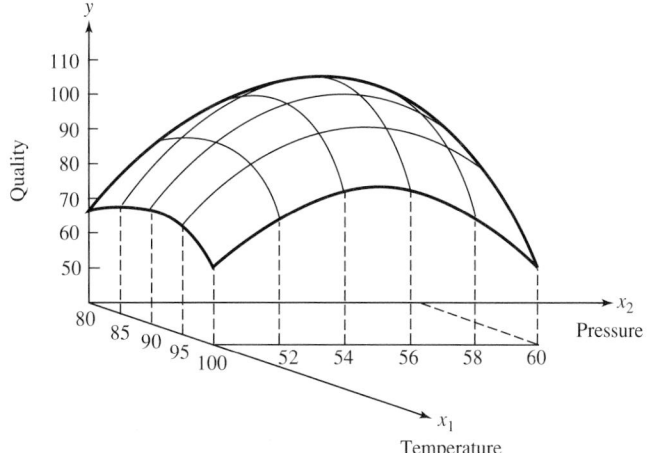

explaining mean quality as a function of temperature and pressure. This, of course, will not always be the case. The additional complexity of second-order models is worthwhile only if a better model results. Consequently, it is important to determine whether the higher-order terms in the model (e.g., the curvilinear terms) are statistically useful. A test for the curvilinear (quadratic terms) is presented in Section 13.6.

EXERCISES

13.16 Suppose the true relationship between $E(y)$ and the quantitative independent variables x_1 and x_2 is described by the following first-order model:

$$E(y) = 4 - x_1 + 2x_2$$

  a. Describe the corresponding response surface.
  b. Plot the contour lines of the response surface for $x_1 = 2, 3, 4$, where $0 \leq x_2 \leq 5$.
  c. Plot the contour lines of the response surface for $x_2 = 2, 3, 4$, where $0 \leq x_1 \leq 5$.
  d. Use the contour lines you plotted in parts **b** and **c** to explain how changes in the settings of x_1 and x_2 affect $E(y)$.
  e. Use your graph from part **b** to determine how much $E(y)$ changes when x_1 is changed from 4 to 2 and x_2 is simultaneously changed from 1 to 2.

13.17 Suppose the true relationship between $E(y)$ and the quantitative independent variables x_1 and x_2 is

$$E(y) = 4 - x_1 + 2x_2 + x_1x_2$$

Answer the questions posed in Exercise 13.16. Explain the effect of the interaction term on the mean response $E(y)$.

13.18 Refer to the *Environmental Science & Technology* study of sorption of organic vapors, Exercises 13.4 and 13.9. Consider modeling the retention coefficient y as a function of both

x_1 = Temperature (degrees)

x_2 = Relative humidity (percent)

a. Write a first-order model for $E(y)$.

b. Write a complete second-order model for $E(y)$.

c. Write a model for $E(y)$ that hypothesizes: (i) linear relationships, and (ii) the relationship between retention (y) and temperature (x_1) depends on relative humidity (x_2).

13.19 An energy conservationist wants to develop a model that will estimate the mean annual gasoline consumption in the United States (in millions of barrels), y, as a function of two independent variables:

x_1 = Number of cars (millions) in use during year

x_2 = Number of trucks (millions) in use during year

a. Identify the independent variables as quantitative or qualitative.

b. Write the first-order model for $E(y)$.

c. Write the complete second-order model for $E(y)$.

d. With respect to the model of part **c**, specify the null and alternative hypotheses you would employ in testing for the presence of interaction between x_1 and x_2.

13.20 The dissolved oxygen content, y, in rivers and streams is related to the amount, x_1, of nitrogen compounds per liter of water and the temperature, x_2, of the water. Write the complete second-order model relating $E(y)$ to x_1 and x_2.

13.21 An exploration seismologist wants to develop a model that will allow him to estimate the average signal-to-noise ratio of an earthquake's seismic wave, y, as a function of two independent variables:

x_1 = Frequency (cycles per second)

x_2 = Amplitude of the wavelet

a. Identify the independent variables as quantitative or qualitative.

b. Write the first-order model for $E(y)$.

c. Write a model for $E(y)$ that contains all first-order and interaction terms. Sketch typical response curves showing $E(y)$, the mean signal-to-noise ratio, versus x_2, the amplitude of the wavelet, for different values of x_1 (assume that x_1 and x_2 interact).

d. Write the complete second-order model for $E(y)$.

13.22 A study reported in *Human Factors* (Apr. 1990) investigated the effects of recognizer accuracy and vocabulary size on the performance of a computerized speech recognition device. Accuracy (x_1) of the device, measured as the percentage of correctly recognized spoken utterances, was set at three levels: 90%, 95%, and 99%. Vocabulary size (x_2), measured as the percentage of words needed for the task, was also set at three levels: 75%, 87.5%, and 100%. The dependent variable of primary interest was task completion time (y, in minutes), measured from when a user of the recognition device spoke the first input until the recognizer displayed the last spoken word of the task. Data collected for $n = 162$ trials was used to fit a complete second-order model for task completion time (y), as a function of the quantitative independent variables accuracy (x_1) and vocabulary (x_2). The coefficient of determination for the model was $R^2 = .75$.

a. Write the complete second-order model for $E(y)$.
b. Interpret the value of R^2.
c. Conduct a test of overall model adequacy. Use $\alpha = .05$.

3.23 Researchers at the Upjohn Company utilized multiple regression analysis in the development of a sustained-release tablet.* One of the objectives of the research was to develop a model relating the dissolution y of a tablet (i.e., the percentage of the tablet dissolved over a specified period of time) to the following independent variables:

x_1 = Excipient level (i.e., amount of nondrug ingredient in the tablet)

x_2 = Process variable (e.g., machine setting under which tablet is processed)

a. Write the complete second-order model for $E(y)$.
b. Write a model that hypothesizes straight-line relationships between $E(y)$, x_1, and x_2. Assume that x_1 and x_2 do not interact.
c. Repeat part **b**, but add interaction to the model.
d. For the model in part **c**, what is the slope of the linear relationship between $E(y)$ and x_1 for fixed x_2?
e. For the model in part **c**, what is the slope of the linear relationship between $E(y)$ and x_2 for fixed x_1?

13.5 Coding Quantitative Independent Variables (Optional)

In fitting higher-order polynomial regression models (e.g., second- or third-order models), it is often a good practice to code the quantitative independent variables. For example, suppose one of the independent variables in a regression analysis is temperature, T, and T is observed at three levels: 50°F, 100°F, and 150°F. We can code (or transform) the temperature measurements using the formula

$$x = \frac{T - 100}{50}$$

Then the coded levels $x = -1$, 0, and 1 correspond to the original levels 50°, 100°, and 150°.

In a general sense, **coding** means transforming a set of independent variables (qualitative or quantitative) into a new set of independent variables. For example, if we observe two independent variables,

T = Temperature

P = Pressure

then we can transform the two independent variables, T and P, into two new coded variables, x_1 and x_2, where x_1 and x_2 are related to T and P by two functional equations,

$$x_1 = f_1(T, P) \qquad x_2 = f_2(T, P)$$

---

*Source: Klassen, R. A. "The Application of Response Surface Methods to a Tablet Formulation Problem." Paper presented at Joint Statistical Meetings, American Statistical Association and Biometric Society, Aug. 1986, Chicago, Ill.

The functions f_1 and f_2 are algebraic relations that establish a one-to-one correspondence between combinations of levels of T and P with combinations of the coded values of x_1 and x_2.

Since qualitative independent variables are not numerical, it is necessary to code their values to fit the regression model. However, you might ask why we would bother to code the quantitative independent variables. There are two related reasons for coding quantitative variables. At first glance, it would appear that a computer would be oblivious to the values assumed by the independent variables in a regression analysis, but this is not the case. Recall from Section 12.3 that the computer must calculate the $(X'X)^{-1}$ matrix to obtain the least squares estimates of the model parameters. Considerable rounding error may occur during the inversion process if the numbers in the $(X'X)$ matrix vary greatly in absolute value. This can produce sizable errors in the computed values of the least squares estimates, $\hat{\beta}_0$, $\hat{\beta}_1$, $\hat{\beta}_2$, ... **Coding makes it computationally easier for the computer to invert the $(X'X)$ matrix, thus leading to more accurate estimates.**

A second reason for coding quantitative variables pertains to the problem of multicollinearity discussed in Section 12.12. When polynomial regression models (e.g., second-order models) are fit, the problem of multicollinearity is unavoidable, especially when higher-order terms are fit. For example, consider the quadratic model

$$E(y) = \beta_0 + \beta_1 x + \beta_2 x^2$$

If the range of the values of x is narrow, then the two variables, $x_1 = x$ and $x_2 = x^2$, will generally be highly correlated. As we pointed out in Section 12.12, the likelihood of rounding errors in the regression coefficients is increased in the presence of multicollinearity.

The best way to cope with the rounding error problem is to:

1. Code the quantitative variable so that the new coded origin is in the center of the coded values. For example, by coding temperature, T, as

$$x = \frac{T - 100}{50}$$

we obtain coded values -1, 0, 1. This places the coded origin, 0, in the middle of the range of coded values (-1 to 1).

2. Code the quantitative variable so that the range of the coded values is approximately the same for all coded variables. You need not hold exactly to this requirement. The range of values for one independent variable could be double or triple the range of another without causing any difficulty, but it would not be desirable to have a sizable disparity in the ranges, say, a ratio of 100 to 1.

When the data are observational (the values assumed by the independent variables are uncontrolled), the coding procedure described in the next box satisfies, reasonably well, these two requirements. The coded variable u is similar to the standardized normal z statistic of Section 5.5. Thus, the u value is the deviation (the distance) between an x value and the mean of the x values, $\bar{x}$, expressed in units of s_x.* Since we know that most (approximately 95%) measurements in a set will lie within 2 standard deviations of their mean, it follows that most of the coded u values will lie in the interval -2 to $+2$.

Coding Procedure for Observational Data

Let

x = Uncoded quantitative independent variable

u = Coded quantitative independent variable

Then if x takes values $x_1, x_2, \ldots, x_n$ for the n data points in the regression analysis, let

$$u_i = \frac{x_i - \bar{x}}{s_x}$$

where s_x is the standard deviation of the x values, i.e.,

$$s_x = \sqrt{\frac{\sum_{i=1}^{n} (x_i - \bar{x})^2}{n - 1}}$$

If you apply this coding to each quantitative variable, the range of values for each will be approximately -2 to $+2$. The variation in the absolute values of the elements of the coefficient matrix will be moderate, and rounding errors generated in finding the inverse of the matrix will be reduced. Additionally, the correlation between x and x^2 will be reduced.

EXAMPLE 13.4

Table 13.3 on page 724 gives monthly data on the index of building construction costs as a function of the index of the cost of construction materials (other components of construction costs would be labor, the cost of money, and so forth).

a. Give the equation relating the coded variable u to the index of construction materials x using the coding system for observational data.

b. Calculate the coded values, u, for the eight x values.

c. Find the sum of the $n = 8$ values for u.

---

*The divisor of the deviation, $x - \bar{x}$, need not equal s_x exactly. Any number approximately equal to s_x would suffice. Other candidate denominators are the range, range/2, and the interquartile range (IQR).

TABLE 13.3	Index of Building Construction Costs	
Month	Construction Cost[a]	Index of all Construction Materials[b]
	y	x
January	193.2	180.0
February	193.1	181.7
March	193.6	184.1
April	195.1	185.3
May	195.6	185.7
June	198.1	185.9
July	200.9	187.7
August	202.7	189.6

[a]Source: United States Department of Commerce, Bureau of the Census.
[b]Source: United States Department of Labor, Bureau of Labor Statistics.

Solution

a. We first find $\bar{x}$ and s_x. The MINITAB printout, Figure 13.14, provides summary statistics for construction index, x. From the printout, we obtain

$$\bar{x} = 185.0 \quad \text{and} \quad s_x = 3.08$$

FIGURE 13.14 ▶
MINITAB printout for Example 13.4

	N	MEAN	MEDIAN	TRMEAN	STDEV	SEMEAN
X	8	185.00	185.50	185.00	3.08	1.09

	MIN	MAX	Q1	Q3		
X	180.00	189.60	182.30	187.25		

Then the equation relating u and x is

$$u = \frac{x - 185.0}{3.08}$$

b. When $x = 180.0$,

$$u = \frac{x - 185.0}{3.08} = \frac{180.0 - 185.0}{3.08} = -1.62$$

Similarly, when $x = 181.7$,

$$u = \frac{x - 185.0}{3.08} = \frac{181.7 - 185.0}{3.08} = -1.07$$

Table 13.4 gives the coded values for all $n = 8$ observations. [*Note:* You can see that all the $n = 8$ values for u lie in the interval from -2 to $+2$.]

TABLE 13.4 Coded Values of x, Example 13.4			
Index	Coded Values	Index	Coded Values
x	u	x	u
180.0	−1.62	185.7	.23
181.7	−1.07	185.9	.29
184.1	−.29	187.7	.88
185.3	.10	189.6	1.49

c. If you ignore rounding error, the sum of the $n = 8$ values for u will equal 0. This is because the sum of the deviations of a set of measurements about their mean is always equal to 0.

To illustrate the advantage of coding, consider fitting the second-order model

$$E(y) = \beta_0 + \beta_1 x + \beta_2 x^2$$

to the data of Example 13.4. The coefficient of correlation between the two variables x and x^2, shown on the MINITAB printout displayed in Figure 13.15a, is $r = .999$. However, the coefficient of correlation between the corresponding coded values, u and u^2, shown in Figure 13.15b, is only $r = -.203$. Thus, we can avoid potential rounding error caused by multicollinearity by fitting, instead, the model

$$E(y) = \beta_0^* + \beta_1^* u + \beta_2^* u^2$$

Other methods of coding have been developed to reduce rounding errors and multicollinearity. One of the more complex coding systems involves fitting **orthogonal polynomials**. An orthogonal system of coding guarantees that the coded independent variables will be uncorrelated. For a discussion of orthogonal polynomials, consult the references given at the end of this chapter.

FIGURE 13.15 ▶
a. MINITAB printout: Correlation between x and x^2

```
Correlation of X and X*X = 0.999
```

b. MINITAB printout: Correlation between u and u^2

```
Correlation of U and U*U = −0.203
```

EXERCISES

13.24 Suppose you want to use the coding system for observational data to fit a second-order model to the tire pressure–automobile mileage data given in the table on page 726.

Pressure x, pounds per square inch	Mileage y, thousands
30	29
31	32
32	36
33	38
34	37
35	33
36	26

a. Give the equation relating the coded variable u to pressure, x, using the coding system for observational data.

b. Calculate the coded values, u.

c. Calculate the coefficient of correlation r between the variables x and x^2.

d. Calculate the coefficient of correlation r between the variables u and u^2. Compare this value to the value computed in part **c**.

e. If you have access to a statistical computer package, fit the model

$$E(y) = \beta_0 + \beta_1 u + \beta_2 u^2$$

13.25 Refer to the *Journal of Testing and Evaluation* study on permeability of open-graded asphalt, described in Exercise 12.7. The data for the analysis are repeated in the accompanying table.

Asphalt Content x, %	Permeability y, in/hr	Asphalt Content x, %	Permeability y, in/hr
3	1,189	6	707
3	840	6	927
3	1,020	6	1,067
3	980	6	822
4	1,440	7	853
4	1,227	7	900
4	1,022	7	733
4	1,293	7	585
5	1,227	8	395
5	1,180	8	270
5	980	8	310
5	1,210	8	208

Source: Woelfl, G., Wei, I., Faulstich, C., and Litwack, H. "Laboratory testing of asphalt concrete for porous pavements." *Journal of Testing and Evaluation*, Vol. 9, No. 4, July 1981, pp. 175–181. Copyright American Society for Testing and Materials.

a. Give the equation relating the coded variable u to asphalt content, x, using the coding system for observational data.

b. Calculate the coded values, u.

c. Calculate the coefficient of correlation r between the variables x and x^2.

d. Calculate the coefficient of correlation r between the variables u and u^2. Compare this value to the value computed in part **c**.

e. If you have access to a statistical computer package, fit the model

$$E(y) = \beta_0 + \beta_1 u + \beta_2 u^2$$

13.26 Refer to the *Applied Spectroscopy* study on the infrared reflectance spectra properties of poly (perfluoropropyleneoxide), described in Exercise 12.5. The data for the analysis are repeated in the table.

Optical Density y	Band Frequency x_1, cm^{-1}	Film Thickness x_2, milligrams
.231	740	1.1
.107	740	.62
.053	740	.31
.129	805	1.1
.069	805	.62
.030	805	.31
1.005	980	1.1
.559	980	.62
.321	980	.31
2.948	1,235	1.1
1.633	1,235	.62
.934	1,235	.31

Source: Pacansky, J., England, C. D., and Waltman, R. "Infrared spectroscopic studies of poly (perfluoropropyleneoxide) on gold substrates: A classical dispersion analysis for the refractive index." *Applied Spectroscopy*, Vol. 40, No. 1, Jan. 1986, p. 9 (Table I).

Suppose you want to fit the complete second-order model

$$E(y) = \beta_0 + \beta_1 x_1 + \beta_2 x_2 + \beta_3 x_1 x_2 + \beta_4 x_1^2 + \beta_5 x_2^2$$

using the coding system given in this section.
a. Give the coded values u_1 and u_2 for x_1 and x_2, respectively.
b. Compare the coefficient of correlation between x_1 and x_1^2 with the coefficient of correlation between u_1 and u_1^2.
c. Compare the coefficient of correlation between x_2 and x_2^2 with the coefficient of correlation between u_2 and u_2^2.
d. Give the prediction equation.

13.6 Tests for Comparing Nested Models

In regression analysis, we often want to determine (with a high degree of confidence) which one among a set of candidate models best fits the data. In this section, we present such a method for **nested models**.

> **Definition 13.4**
>
> Two models are **nested** if one model contains all the terms of the second model and at least one additional term.

To illustrate, suppose you have collected data on a response, y, and two quantitative independent variables, x_1 and x_2, and you are considering the use of either a first-order or a second-order model to relate $E(y)$ to x_1 and x_2. Will the second-order model provide better predictions of y than the first-order model? To answer this question, examine the two models, and note that the second-order model contains all terms contained in the first-order model plus three additional terms—those involving β_3, β_4, and β_5:

First-order model: $\quad E(y) = \beta_0 + \beta_1 x_1 + \beta_2 x_2$

$$\overbrace{}^{\text{Second-order terms}}$$

Second-order model: $\quad E(y) = \beta_0 + \beta_1 x_1 + \beta_2 x_2 + \beta_3 x_1 x_2 + \beta_4 x_1^2 + \beta_5 x_2^2$

Consequently, these are nested models. Since the first-order model is the simpler of the two, we say that the *first-order model is nested within the more complex second-order model*.

In general, the more complex of two nested models is called the **complete** (or **full**) **model**, and the simpler of the two is called the **reduced model**. Asking whether the second-order (or *complete*) model contributes more information for the prediction of y than the first-order (or *reduced*) model is equivalent to asking whether at least one of the parameters, β_3, β_4, or β_5, differs from 0—i.e., whether the terms involving β_3, β_4, and β_5 should be retained in the model. Therefore, to test whether the second-order terms should be included in the model, we test the null hypothesis

$$H_0: \quad \beta_3 = \beta_4 = \beta_5 = 0$$

(i.e., the second-order terms do not contribute information for the prediction of y) against the alternative hypothesis

$$H_a: \quad \text{At least one of the parameters, } \beta_3, \beta_4, \text{ or } \beta_5, \text{ differs from } 0$$

(i.e., at least one of the second-order terms contributes information for the prediction of y).

The procedure for conducting this test is intuitive: First, we use the method of least squares to fit the reduced model and calculate the corresponding sum of squares for error, SSE_R (the sum of squares of the deviations between observed and predicted y values). Next, we fit the complete model and calculate its sum of squares for error, SSE_C. Then, we compare SSE_R to SSE_C by calculating the difference $SSE_R - SSE_C$. If the second-order terms contribute to the model, then SSE_C should be much smaller than SSE_R, and the difference $SSE_R - SSE_C$ will be large. The larger the difference, the greater the weight of evidence that the complete model provides better predictions of y than does the reduced model.

The sum of squares for error will always decrease when new terms are added to the model. The question is whether this decrease is large enough to conclude that it is due to more than just an increase in the number of model terms and to chance. To test the null hypothesis that the parameters of the second-order terms, β_3, β_4, and β_5, simultaneously equal 0, we use an F statistic calculated as follows:

$$F = \frac{\text{Drop in SSE}/\text{Number of } \beta \text{ parameters being tested}}{s^2 \text{ for the second-order model}} = \frac{(\text{SSE}_R - \text{SSE}_C)/3}{\text{SSE}_C/[n - (5 + 1)]}$$

When the assumptions listed in Section 12.2 about the error term ε are satisfied and the β parameters for the second-order terms are all 0 (i.e., H_0 is true), this F statistic has an F distribution with $\nu_1 = 3$ and $\nu_2 = n - 6$ degrees of freedom. Note that ν_1 is the number of β parameters being tested and ν_2 is the number of degrees of freedom associated with s^2 in the second-order model.

If the second-order terms *do* contribute to the model (i.e., H_a is true), we expect the F statistic to be large. Thus, we use a one-tailed test and reject H_0 if F exceeds some critical value, F_α.

F Test for Comparing Nested Models

Reduced model: $E(y) = \beta_0 + \beta_1 x_1 + \cdots + \beta_g x_g$

Complete model:

$$E(y) = \beta_0 + \beta_1 x_1 + \cdots + \beta_g x_g + \beta_{g+1} x_{g+1} + \cdots + \beta_k x_k$$

H_0: $\beta_{g+1} = \beta_{g+2} = \cdots = \beta_k = 0$

H_a: At least one of the β parameters under test is nonzero

Test statistic: $F = \dfrac{(\text{SSE}_R - \text{SSE}_C)/(k - g)}{\text{SSE}_C/[n - (k + 1)]}$

$$= \frac{(\text{SSE}_R - \text{SSE}_C)/\# \text{ of } \beta\text{'s tested in } H_0}{\text{MSE}_C}$$

where

SSE$_R$ = Sum of squared errors for the reduced model

SSE$_C$ = Sum of squared errors for the complete model

MSE$_C$ = Mean square error (s^2) for the complete model

$k - g$ = Number of β parameters specified in H_0 (i.e., number of β parameters tested)

$k + 1$ = Number of β parameters in the complete model (including β_0)

n = Total sample size

Rejection region: $F > F_\alpha$

where F is based on $\nu_1 = k - g$ numerator degrees of freedom and $\nu_2 = n - (k + 1)$ denominator degrees of freedom

EXAMPLE 13.5

Refer to the second-order model relating temperature (x_1) and pressure (x_2) to the quality (y) of a finished product, Example 13.3. Do the data provide sufficient evidence to indicate that the quadratic terms, x_1^2 and x_2^2, contribute information for the prediction of y? Test at $\alpha = .05$.

Solution

To determine whether the quadratic (i.e., curvilinear) terms contribute information for the prediction of y, we test

$$H_0: \quad \beta_4 = \beta_5 = 0$$

against the alternative hypothesis

$$H_a: \quad \text{At least one of the parameters, } \beta_4 \text{ or } \beta_5, \text{ differs from 0}$$

The nested models to be compared are:

Completed model: $E(y) = \beta_0 + \beta_1 x_1 + \beta_2 x_2 + \beta_3 x_1 x_2 + \beta_4 x_1^2 + \beta_5 x_2^2$

Reduced model: $E(y) = \beta_0 + \beta_1 x_1 + \beta_2 x_2 + \beta_3 x_1 x_2$

The SAS printout for the reduced (interaction) model is shown in Figure 13.16.

FIGURE 13.16 ▶
SAS printout for reduced
(interaction) model

Dependent Variable: Y

Analysis of Variance

Source	DF	Sum of Squares	Mean Square	F Value	Prob>F
Model	3	2425.04194	808.34731	3.080	0.0475
Error	23	6036.40102	262.45222		
C Total	26	8461.44296			

Root MSE	16.20038	R-square	0.2866
Dep Mean	66.96296	Adj R-sq	0.1935
C.V.	24.19304		

Parameter Estimates

Variable	DF	Parameter Estimate	Standard Error	T for H0: Parameter=0	Prob > |T|
INTERCEP	1	-614.139815	466.16828161	-1.317	0.2007
X1	1	7.086389	5.15846283	1.374	0.1828
X2	1	13.882778	8.45253371	1.642	0.1141
X1X2	1	-0.145500	0.09353292	-1.556	0.1335

The sum of squares for error for the reduced model (shaded in Figure 13.16) is

$$SSE_R = 6,036.40102$$

To conduct the test, we also need the SSE and MSE for the complete model. These values, shown in Figure 13.12, are

$$SSE_C = 59.17843$$
$$MSE_C = 2.81802$$

For this test, $n = 27$, $k = 5$, $g = 3$, and the number of β's tested is $(k - g) = 2$. Therefore, the calculated value of the F statistic, based on $\nu_1 = k - g = 2$ and $\nu_2 = n - (k + 1) = 21$ degrees of freedom is

$$Test\ statistic:\quad F = \frac{(SSE_R - SSE_C)/\#\ \beta\text{'s tested in model}}{MSE_C}$$
$$= \frac{(6,036.40102 - 59.17843)/2}{2.81802} = 1,060.5$$

The final step in the test is to compare this computed value of F with the tabulated value based on $\nu_1 = 2$ and $\nu_2 = 21$ degrees of freedom. For $\alpha = .05$, $F_{.05} = 3.47$. Then the rejection region is

$$Rejection\ region:\quad F > 3.47\quad (\text{see Figure 13.17})$$

FIGURE 13.17 ▶
Rejection region for the F test
$H_0:\quad \beta_4 = \beta_5 = 0$

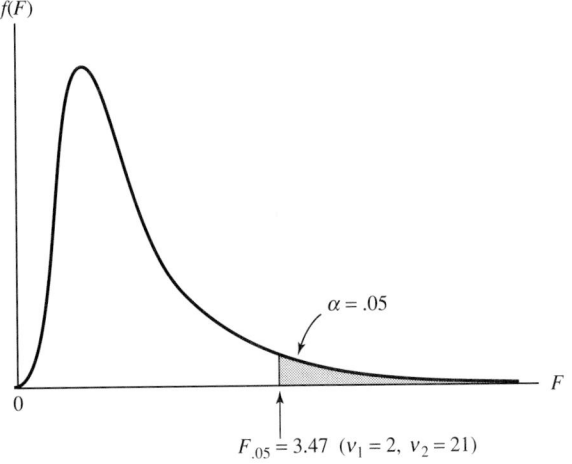

Since the computed value of F falls in the rejection region—i.e., it exceeds $F_{.05} = 3.47$—we reject H_0 and conclude (at $\alpha = .05$) that at least one of the quadratic terms contributes information for the prediction of y. In other words, the data support the contention that the curvature we see in the response surface is not due simply to random variation in the data. The complete second-order model appears to provide better predictions of y than does the reduced (interaction) model.

Suppose the F test in Example 13.5 yielded a test statistic that did not fall in the rejection region. That is, suppose there was insufficient evidence (at $\alpha = .05$) to say that the curvature terms contribute information for the prediction of product quality. As with any statistical test of hypothesis, we must be cautious about accepting H_0 since the probability of a Type II error is unknown. Nevertheless, most practitioners of regression analysis adopt the principle of **parsimony**. That is, in situations where two competing models are found to have essentially the same predictive power, the model with the fewest number of β's (i.e., the more **parsimonious model**) is selected. The principle of parsimony would lead us to choose the simpler (reduced) model over the more complex complete model when we fail to reject H_0 in the F test for nested models.

Definition 13.5

A **parsimonious model** is a general linear model with a small number of β parameters. In situations where two competing models have essentially the same predictive power (as determined by an F test), choose the more parsimonious of the two.

When the candidate models in model building are nested models, the F test developed in this section is the appropriate procedure to apply to compare the models. However, if the models are not nested, this F test is not applicable. In this situation, the analyst must base the choice of the best model on statistics such as R_a^2 and s. It is important to remember that decisions based on these and other numerical descriptive measures of model adequacy cannot be supported with a measure of reliability and are often very subjective in nature.

EXERCISES

13.27 Since 1978, when the U.S. airline industry was deregulated, researchers have questioned whether the deregulation has ensured a truly competitive environment. If so, the profitability of any major airline would be related only to overall industry conditions (e.g, disposable income and market share) but not to any unchanging feature of that airline. This profitability hypothesis was tested using multiple regression (*Transportation Journal*, Winter 1990). Data for $n = 234$ carrier-years were used to fit the model

$$E(y) = \beta_0 + \beta_1 x_1 + \beta_2 x_2 + \beta_3 x_3 + \cdots + \beta_{30} x_{30}$$

where

$$y = \text{Profit rate}$$
$$x_1 = \text{Real personal disposable income}$$
$$x_2 = \text{Industry market share}$$
$$x_3{-}x_{30} = \text{Dummy variables (coded 0–1) for the 29 air carriers investigated in the study}$$

The results of the regression are summarized in the table. Interpret the results. Is the profitability hypothesis supported?

Variable	β estimate	t value	p-value
Intercept	1.2642	.09	.9266
x_1	−.0022	−.99	.8392
x_2	4.8405	3.57	.0003
x_3–x_{30}	(not given)	—	—

$R^2 = .3402$ F (full model) $= 3.49$ p-value $= .0001$
F (for testing carrier dummies) $= 3.59$ p-value $= .0001$

Source: Leigh, L. E. "Contestability in deregulated airline markets: Some empirical tests." *Transportation Journal*, Winter 1990, p. 55 (Table 4). Reprinted from the Winter 1990 issue of *Transportation Journal* with the express permission of the publisher, the American Society of Transportation and Logistics, Inc., for educational purposes only.

13.28 Refer to Exercise 13.19, in which an energy conservationist wants to develop a regression model to forecast annual gasoline consumption in the United States. The complete and reduced models for the test that you described in part **d** of Exercise 13.19 were fit to $n = 25$ data points. The resulting values for SSE_1 and SSE_2 were 1,065.9 and 400.6, respectively.
   a. Conduct the test to determine whether the data present sufficient evidence to indicate interaction between x_1 and x_2. Test using $\alpha = .05$.
   b. Which model seems better for forecasting annual gasoline consumption? Why?

13.29 Refer to Exercise 13.21, in which an exploration seismologist wants to develop a regression model for estimating the mean signal-to-noise ratio of seismic waves from earthquakes. The model under consideration is a complete second-order model:

$$E(y) = \beta_0 + \beta_1 x_1 + \beta_2 x_2 + \beta_3 x_1 x_2 + \beta_4 x_1^2 + \beta_5 x_2^2$$

where

   $y =$ Signal-to-noise ratio
   $x_1 =$ Frequency of wavelet
   $x_2 =$ Amplitude of wavelet

Following is a portion of the computer printout that results from fitting this model to $n = 12$ data points:

SOURCE	DF	SUM OF SQUARES	MEAN SQUARE
MODEL	5	38638.97	7727.79
ERROR	6	159.94	26.66
TOTAL	11	38798.91	R-SQUARE
			0.996

The reduced first-order model

$$E(y) = \beta_0 + \beta_1 x_1 + \beta_2 x_2$$

was also fit to the same data; the resulting computer printout is partially reproduced here:

SOURCE	DF	SUM OF SQUARES	MEAN SQUARE
MODEL	2	36704.5	18352.2
ERROR	9	2094.4	232.7
TOTAL	11	38798.9	R-SQUARE
			0.946

Is there sufficient evidence to conclude that a second-order model contributes more information for the prediction of y than does a first-order model? Test using $\alpha = .05$.

13.30 Refer to the *Human Factors* study of the performance of a computerized speech recognizer, Exercise 13.22. Recall that the researchers built a complete second-order model for task completion time (y) as a function of accuracy (x_1) and vocabulary (x_2).

a. Give the null hypothesis for testing whether the quadratic terms in the model are useful predictors of y.

b. The test, part **a**, resulted in a p-value of less than .01. Interpret this result.

13.31 Consider the problem of modeling the price charged for motor transport service (such as trucking) in a particular state. In the early 1980s, several states removed regulatory constraints on the rate charged for intrastate trucking services. (Florida was the first state to embark on a deregulation policy on July 1, 1980.) One of the goals of the regression analysis is to assess the impact of state deregulation on the supply price y charged per ton-mile. The following independent variables were selected:

x_1 = Distance shipped

x_2 = Weight of product

$$x_3 = \begin{cases} 1 & \text{if deregulation in effect} \\ 0 & \text{if not} \end{cases} \qquad x_4 = \begin{cases} 1 & \text{if large market} \\ 0 & \text{if small market} \end{cases}$$

Data collected for $n = 132$ shipments were used to fit the three models shown here. The results are summarized in the table.

MODEL 1 $E(y) = \beta_0 + \beta_1 x_1 + \beta_2 x_2 + \beta_3 x_1 x_2 + \beta_4 x_1^2 + \beta_5 x_2^2 + \beta_6 x_3 + \beta_7 x_4 + \beta_8 x_3 x_4$
$+ \beta_9 x_1 x_3 + \beta_{10} x_1 x_4 + \beta_{11} x_1 x_3 x_4 + \beta_{12} x_2 x_3 + \beta_{13} x_2 x_4 + \beta_{14} x_2 x_3 x_4$
$+ \beta_{15} x_1 x_2 x_3 + \beta_{16} x_1 x_2 x_4 + \beta_{17} x_1 x_2 x_3 x_4 + \beta_{18} x_1^2 x_3 + \beta_{19} x_1^2 x_4$
$+ \beta_{20} x_1^2 x_3 x_4 + \beta_{21} x_2^2 x_3 + \beta_{22} x_2^2 x_4 + \beta_{23} x_2^2 x_4$

MODEL 2 $E(y) = \beta_0 + \beta_1 x_1 + \beta_2 x_2 + \beta_3 x_1 x_2 + \beta_4 x_3 + \beta_5 x_4 + \beta_6 x_3 x_4 + \beta_7 x_1 x_3$
$+ \beta_8 x_1 x_4 + \beta_9 x_1 x_3 x_4 + \beta_{10} x_2 x_3 + \beta_{11} x_2 x_4 + \beta_{12} x_2 x_3 x_4 + \beta_{13} x_1 x_2 x_3$
$+ \beta_{14} x_1 x_2 x_4 + \beta_{15} x_1 x_2 x_3 x_4$

MODEL 3 $E(y) = \beta_0 + \beta_1 x_1 + \beta_2 x_2 + \beta_3 x_1 x_2 + \beta_4 x_3 + \beta_5 x_4 + \beta_6 x_3 x_4$

Model	SSE	R^2	df(error)
1	203,570	.83	108
2	227,520	.81	116
3	395,165	.67	125

a. What null hypothesis would you test to compare models 1 and 2?

b. Conduct the test specified in part **a**. Use $\alpha = .05$.

c. Note that the terms tested in part **a** are all quadratic terms. Given the result of the test, would you recommend keeping these terms in the model?

d. What null hypothesis would you test to compare models 2 and 3?

e. Conduct the test specified in part **d**. Use $\alpha = .05$.

f. Based on the results of these tests, which of the three models would you recommend for predicting supply price y?

g. Based on the model you selected in part **f**, propose an alternative (simpler) model that will allow you to test for the impact of deregulation. How would you conduct this test?

13.7   Models with One Qualitative Independent Variable

Suppose we want to write a model for the mean performance, $E(y)$, of a diesel engine as a function of type of fuel. (For the purpose of explanation, we will ignore other independent variables that might affect the response.) Further, suppose there are three fuel types available: a petroleum-based fuel (P), a coal-based fuel (C), and a blended fuel (B). The fuel type is a single qualitative variable with three levels corresponding to fuels P, C, and B. Note that with a qualitative independent variable, we cannot attach a quantitative meaning to a given level. All we can do is describe it.

To simplify our notation, let μ_P be the mean performance for fuel P, and let μ_C and μ_B be the corresponding mean performances for fuels C and B. Our objective is to write a single prediction equation that will give the mean value of y for the three fuel types. This can be done as follows:

$$E(y) = \beta_0 + \beta_1 x_1 + \beta_2 x_2$$

where

$$x_1 = \begin{cases} 1 & \text{if fuel P is used} \\ 0 & \text{if not} \end{cases}$$

$$x_2 = \begin{cases} 1 & \text{if fuel C is used} \\ 0 & \text{if not} \end{cases}$$

The variables x_1 and x_2 are not meaningful independent variables as for the case of the models with quantitative independent variables. Instead, they are **dummy (indicator) variables** that make the model function. To see how they work, let $x_1 = 0$ and $x_2 = 0$. This condition will apply when we are seeking the mean response for fuel B (neither fuel P nor C is used; hence, it must be B). Then the mean value of y when fuel B is used is

$$\mu_B = E(y) = \beta_0 + \beta_1(0) + \beta_2(0) = \beta_0$$

This tells us that the mean performance level for fuel B is β_0. Or, it means that $\beta_0 = \mu_B$.

Now suppose we want to represent the mean response, $E(y)$, when fuel P is used. Checking the dummy variable definitions, we see that we should let $x_1 = 1$ and $x_2 = 0$:

$$\mu_P = E(y) = \beta_0 + \beta_1(1) + \beta_2(0) = \beta_0 + \beta_1$$

or, since $\beta_0 = \mu_B$,

$$\mu_P = \mu_B + \beta_1$$

Then it follows that the interpretation of β_1 is

$$\beta_1 = \mu_P - \mu_B$$

which is the difference in the mean performance levels for fuels P and B.

Finally, if we want the mean value of y when fuel C is used, we set $x_1 = 0$ and $x_2 = 1$:

$$\mu_C = E(y) = \beta_0 + \beta_1(0) + \beta_2(1) = \beta_0 + \beta_2$$

or, since $\beta_0 = \mu_B$,

$$\mu_C = \mu_B + \beta_2$$

Then it follows that the interpretation of β_2 is

$$\beta_2 = \mu_C - \mu_B$$

Note that we were able to describe *three levels* of the qualitative variable with only *two dummy variables*, because the mean of the base level (fuel B, in this case) is accounted for by the intercept β_0.

Since fuel type is a qualitative variable, we will use a bar graph to show the value of mean performance, $E(y)$, for the three levels of fuel type (see Figure 13.18). In particular, note that the height of the bar, $E(y)$, for each level of fuel type is equal to

FIGURE 13.18 ▶
Bar chart comparing E(y) for three diesel fuel types

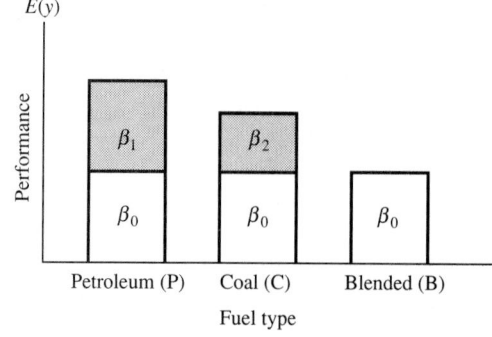

the sum of the model parameters shown in the preceding equations. You can see that the height of the bar corresponding to fuel B is β_0; i.e., $E(y) = \beta_0$. Similarly, the heights of the bars corresponding to P and C are $E(y) = \beta_0 + \beta_1$ and $E(y) = \beta_0 + \beta_2$, respectively.[*]

Now, carefully examine the model with a single qualitative independent variable at three levels, because we will use exactly the same pattern for any number of levels. Also, the interpretation of the parameters will always be the same.

One level is selected as the base level (we used fuel B). Then, for the one–zero system of coding[†] for the dummy variables,

$$\mu_A = \beta_0$$

The coding for all dummy variables is as follows: To represent the mean value of y for a particular level, let that dummy variable equal 1; otherwise, the dummy variable is set equal to 0. Using this system of coding, we have

$$\mu_B = \beta_0 + \beta_1$$
$$\mu_C = \beta_0 + \beta_2$$
$$\vdots$$

Because $\mu_A = \beta_0$, any other model parameter will represent the difference in means for that level and the base level:

$$\beta_1 = \mu_B - \mu_A$$
$$\beta_2 = \mu_C - \mu_A$$
$$\vdots$$

The general procedure is given in the accompanying box.

Procedure for Writing a Model with One Qualitative Independent Variable at k Levels

$$E(y) = \beta_0 + \beta_1 x_1 + \beta_2 x_2 + \cdots + \beta_{k-1} x_{k-1}$$

where x_i is the dummy variable for level i and

$$x_i = \begin{cases} 1 & \text{if } E(y) \text{ is the mean for level } i \\ 0 & \text{otherwise} \end{cases}$$

---

[*] Either β_1 or β_2, or both, could be negative. If, for example, β_1 were negative, the height of the bar corresponding to fuel P would be *reduced* (rather than increased) from the height of the bar for fuel B by the amount β_1. Figure 13.18 is constructed assuming that β_1 and β_2 are positive quantities.

[†] We do not have to use a one–zero system of coding for the dummy variables. Any two-value system will work, but the interpretation given to the model parameters will depend on the code. Using the one–zero system makes the model parameters easy to interpret.

General Interpretation of β's for 0–1 System of Coding

For the system of coding described in the previous box

$$\mu_A = \beta_0$$
$$\mu_B = \beta_0 + \beta_1$$
$$\mu_C = \beta_0 + \beta_2$$
$$\mu_D = \beta_0 + \beta_3$$
$$\vdots$$

where $\mu_i = E(y)$ for level i. Also, note that

$$\beta_1 = \mu_B - \mu_A$$
$$\beta_2 = \mu_C - \mu_A$$
$$\beta_3 = \mu_D - \mu_A$$
$$\vdots$$

EXAMPLE 13.6

A large consulting firm markets a computerized system for monitoring road construction bids to various state departments of transportation. Since the high cost of maintaining the system is partially absorbed by the firm, the firm wants to compare the mean annual maintenance costs accrued by system users in three different states: Kansas, Kentucky, and Texas. A sample of 10 users is selected from each state installation and the maintenance cost accrued by each is recorded, as shown in Table 13.5. Do the data provide sufficient evidence (at $\alpha = .05$) to indicate that the mean annual maintenance costs accrued by system users differ for the three state installations?

Solution

The model relating $E(y)$ to the single qualitative variable, state installation, is

$$E(y) = \beta_0 + \beta_1 x_1 + \beta_2 x_2$$

where

$$x_1 = \begin{cases} 1 & \text{if Kentucky} \\ 0 & \text{if not} \end{cases} \qquad x_2 = \begin{cases} 1 & \text{if Texas} \\ 0 & \text{if not} \end{cases}$$

and

$$\beta_1 = \mu_2 - \mu_1$$
$$\beta_2 = \mu_3 - \mu_1$$

where μ_1, μ_2, and μ_3 are the mean responses for Kansas, Kentucky, and Texas, respectively. Testing the null hypothesis that the means for the three states are equal,

TABLE 13.5   Annual Maintenance Costs

	State Installation		
	1: Kansas	2: Kentucky	3: Texas
	$ 198	$ 563	$ 385
	126	314	693
	443	483	266
	570	144	586
	286	585	178
	184	377	773
	105	264	308
	216	185	430
	465	330	644
	203	354	515
Totals	$2,796	$3,599	$4,778

i.e., $\mu_1 = \mu_2 = \mu_3$, is equivalent to testing

H_0: $\beta_1 = \beta_2 = 0$

because if $\beta_1 = \mu_2 - \mu_1 = 0$ and $\beta_2 = \mu_3 - \mu_1 = 0$, then μ_1, μ_2, and μ_3 must be equal. The alternative hypothesis is

H_a: At least one of the parameters, β_1 or β_2, differs from 0

There are two ways to conduct this test. We can fit the complete model shown above and the reduced model (deleting the terms involving β_1 and β_2),

$E(y) = \beta_0$

and conduct the F test described in the preceding section (we leave this as an exercise for you). Or, we can use the F test of the complete model (Section 12.8), which tests the null hypothesis that all parameters in the model, with the exception of β_0, equal 0. Either way you conduct the test, you will obtain the same computed value of F, the value shown on the SAS printout for a test of the complete model. The SAS printout for fitting the complete model,

$E(y) = \beta_0 + \beta_1 x_1 + \beta_2 x_2$

is shown in Figure 13.19 on page 740. The value of the F statistic for testing the complete model (shaded on Figure 13.19) is $F = 3.482$; the p-value for the test (also shaded) is $p = .0452$. Since our choice of α, $\alpha = .05$, exceeds the p-value, we reject H_0 and conclude that at least one of the parameters, β_1 or β_2, differs from 0. Or, equivalently, we conclude that the data provide sufficient evidence to indicate that the mean user maintenance cost does vary among the three state installations.

FIGURE 13.19 ▶
SAS printout for Example 13.6

Dependent Variable: Y

Analysis of Variance

Source	DF	Sum of Squares	Mean Square	F Value	Prob>F
Model	2	198772.46667	99386.23333	3.482	0.0452
Error	27	770670.90000	28543.36667		
C Total	29	969443.36667			

Root MSE	168.94782	R-square	0.2050
Dep Mean	372.43333	Adj R-sq	0.1462
C.V.	45.36324		

Parameter Estimates

Variable	DF	Parameter Estimate	Standard Error	T for H0: Parameter=0	Prob > |T|
INTERCEP	1	279.600000	53.42599243	5.233	0.0001
X1	1	80.300000	75.55576307	1.063	0.2973
X2	1	198.200000	75.55576307	2.623	0.0141

We make two additional comments about Example 13.6. If you choose to analyze the data by fitting complete and reduced models (Section 13.6), you will find that the least squares estimate of β_0 in the reduced model,

$$E(y) = \beta_0$$

is $\bar{y}$, the mean of all $n = 30$ observations, and that the sum of squares for error for the reduced model is

$$SSE_R = \sum(y_i - \hat{y}_i)^2 = \sum(y_i - \bar{y})^2 = 969,443.367$$

This value is shown in the SAS printout in Figure 13.19 as the **Sum of Squares** corresponding to **C Total**. We leave the remaining steps, calculating the drop in SSE and the resulting F statistic, to you. The value you obtain should be exactly the same as the value of F shown in the SAS printout in Figure 13.19.

A second method of analyzing the data of Table 13.5 is known as **analysis of variance**, or **ANOVA**. ANOVA is the topic of Chapter 14.

EXERCISES

13.32   Refer to the *Environmental Science & Technology* study of sorption of organic vapors, Exercise 13.4. Consider using the qualitative variable, organic compound, as a predictor of the retention coefficient y. Recall that five organic compounds were studied: benzene, toluene, chloroform, methanol, and anisole.

a. Write a model for $E(y)$ as a function of organic compound at two levels.

b. Interpret the β parameters in the model.

c. Explain how to test for differences among the mean retention coefficients of the five organic compounds.

13.33 The following model was used to relate $E(y)$ to a single qualitative variable with four levels:

$$E(y) = \beta_0 + \beta_1 x_1 + \beta_2 x_2 + \beta_3 x_3$$

where

$$x_1 = \begin{cases} 1 & \text{if level 2} \\ 0 & \text{if not} \end{cases} \qquad x_2 = \begin{cases} 1 & \text{if level 3} \\ 0 & \text{if not} \end{cases} \qquad x_3 = \begin{cases} 1 & \text{if level 4} \\ 0 & \text{if not} \end{cases}$$

This model was fit to $n = 30$ data points and the following result was obtained:

$$\hat{y} = 10.2 - 4x_1 + 12x_2 + 2x_3$$

a. Use the least squares prediction equation to find the estimate of $E(y)$ for each level of the qualitative independent variable.

b. Specify the null and alternative hypotheses you would employ to test whether $E(y)$ is the same for all four levels of the independent variable.

13.34 An electrical engineer wants to compare the mean lifelengths (in hours) of five different brands of magnetron tubes. Data are gathered on ten magnetron tubes selected at random from each of the five brands. Write a model that will give the mean lifelength for the five brands and interpret all the β parameters used in the model.

13.35 Because of the hot, humid weather conditions in Florida, the growth rates of beef cattle and the milk production of dairy cows typically decline during the summer. However, agricultural and environmental engineers have found that a well-designed shade structure can significantly increase the milk production of dairy cows. In one experiment, 30 cows were selected and divided into three groups of ten cows each. Group 1 cows were provided with a man-made shade structure, group 2 cows with tree shade, and group 3 cows with no shade. Of interest was the mean milk production (in gallons) of the cows in each group.

a. Identify the independent variables in the experiment.

b. Write a model relating the mean milk production, $E(y)$, to the independent variables. Identify and code all dummy variables.

c. Interpret the β parameters of the model.

13.36 TexaSoft, a manufacturer of video arcade and home computer games, wants to model weekly sales, y, as a function of game product. The firm markets four games: Trilogy, Set the Hostages Free, Queen of Hearts, and Squirm.

a. Write a model relating mean weekly sales, $E(y)$, to game product.

b. Interpret the β parameters of the model.

c. In terms of the β parameters, what are the mean weekly sales for the Queen of Hearts video game?

13.8   Comparing the Slopes of Two or More Lines

Suppose you want to relate the mean performance, $E(y)$, of a diesel engine to engine speed (rpm), x, for three different fuel types—petroleum, coal, and blended—and you wish to use first-order (straight-line) models to model the responses for all three fuels. Graphs of these three relationships might appear as shown in Figure 13.20 on page 742.

FIGURE 13.20 ▶
Graphs of the relationship between mean performance, $E(y)$, and engine speed, x

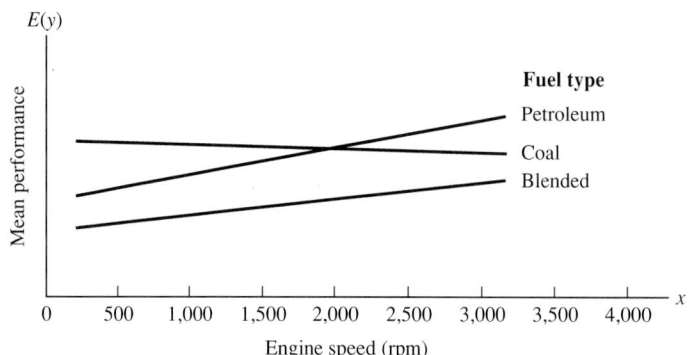

Since the lines in Figure 13.20 are hypothetical, a number of practical questions arise. Does one fuel type perform as well as any other; that is, do the three mean performance lines differ for the three fuel types? Does the rate of increase in mean performance level with engine speed differ for the three fuel types; that is, do the slopes of the three lines differ? Note that each of the two practical questions has been rephrased into a question about the parameters that define the three lines of Figure 13.20. To answer them, we must write a single linear statistical model that will characterize the three lines of Figure 13.20. Then the practical questions can be answered by testing hypotheses about the model parameters.

In the previous example, the response (engine performance) is a function of *two* independent variables: one quantitative (engine speed, x) and one qualitative (type of fuel). We will examine the different models that can be constructed relating $E(y)$ to these two independent variables.

1. The straight-line relationship between mean performance, $E(y)$, and engine speed is the same for all three fuels; that is, a single line will describe the relationship between $E(y)$ and speed, x_1, for all the fuel types (see Figure 13.21).

$$E(y) = \beta_0 + \beta_1 x_1$$
$$x_1 = \text{Engine speed}$$

FIGURE 13.21 ▶
The relationship between $E(y)$ and x_1 is the same for all fuel types

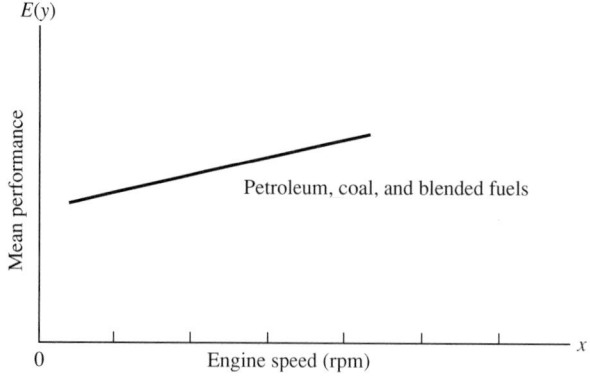

2. The straight lines relating mean performance, $E(y)$, to engine speed differ from one fuel to another, but the rate of increase in $E(y)$ per 1-rpm increase in speed, x_1, is the same for all fuel types. That is, the lines are parallel but possess different y-intercepts (see Figure 13.22).

$$E(y) = \beta_0 + \beta_1 x_1 + \beta_2 x_2 + \beta_3 x_3$$
$$x_1 = \text{Engine speed}$$
$$x_2 = \begin{cases} 1 & \text{if petroleum fuel} \\ 0 & \text{if not} \end{cases}$$
$$x_3 = \begin{cases} 1 & \text{if coal fuel} \\ 0 & \text{if not} \end{cases}$$

FIGURE 13.22 ▶
Parallel response lines for the three fuel types

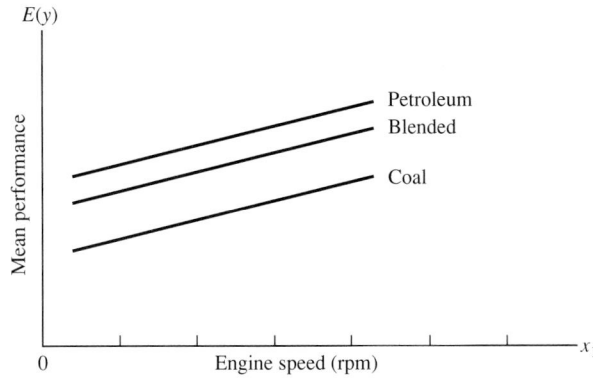

Notice that this model is essentially a combination of a first-order model with a single quantitative variable and the model with a single qualitative variable:

First-order model with a single
quantitative variable: $E(y) = \beta_0 + \boxed{\beta_1 x_1}$

Model with a single
qualitative variable
at three levels: $E(y) = \beta_0 + \boxed{\beta_2 x_2 + \beta_3 x_3}$

where x_1, x_2, and x_3 are defined as above. The model described implies no interaction between the two independent variables, engine speed x_1 and the qualitative variable, type of fuel. The change in $E(y)$ for a 1-unit change in x_1 is identical (i.e., the slopes of the lines are equal) for all three fuel types. The terms corresponding to each of the independent variables are called **main effect terms** because they imply no interaction.

> **Definition 13.6**
>
> All noninteraction terms in a regression model involving a particular variable (quantitative or qualitative) represent the **main effect** of that independent variable on y.

3. The straight lines relating mean performance, $E(y)$, to engine speed, x_1, differ for the three fuel types; that is, the intercepts and slopes differ for the three lines (see Figure 13.23). As you will see, this interaction model is obtained by adding interaction terms (those involving the cross product terms, one each from each of the two independent variables):

$$E(y) = \beta_0 + \overbrace{\beta_1 x_1}^{\substack{\text{Main effect,} \\ \text{engine} \\ \text{speed}}} + \overbrace{\beta_2 x_2 + \beta_3 x_3}^{\substack{\text{Main effect,} \\ \text{type of} \\ \text{fuel}}} + \overbrace{\beta_4 x_1 x_2 + \beta_5 x_1 x_3}^{\text{Interaction}}$$

FIGURE 13.23 ▶
Different response lines for the three fuel types

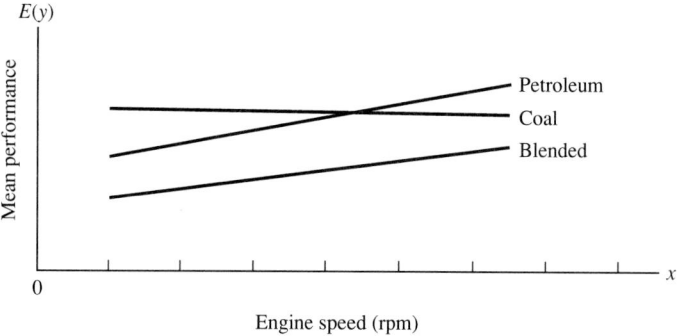

Note that each of the preceding models is obtained by adding terms to model 1, the single first-order model used to model the responses for all three fuels. Model 2 is obtained by adding the main effect terms for the qualitative variable, type of fuel; and model 3 is obtained by adding the interaction terms to model 2. Consequently, the models are nested (model 1 is nested within models 2 and 3; model 2 is nested within model 3) and can be compared using the F test of Section 13.6.

Will a single line (Figure 13.21) characterize the responses for all three fuels, or do the three response lines differ as shown in Figure 13.23? A test of the null hypothesis that a single first-order model adequately describes the relationship between $E(y)$ and engine speed x_1 for all three fuels is a test of the null hypothesis that the parameters of model 3, β_2, β_3, β_4, and β_5, equal 0, i.e.,

$$H_0: \quad \beta_2 = \beta_3 = \beta_4 = \beta_5 = 0$$

This hypothesis is tested by comparing the complete model (model 3) to the reduced model (model 1).

Suppose we assume that the response lines for the three fuels will differ, but we wonder whether the data present sufficient evidence to indicate differences in the slopes of the lines. To test the null hypothesis that model 2 adequately describes the relationship between $E(y)$ and engine speed x_1, we want to test

$$H_0: \quad \beta_4 = \beta_5 = 0$$

that is, that the two independent variables, engine speed x_1 and the qualitative variable, type of fuel, do not interact. This test can be conducted by comparing the complete model (model 3) to the reduced model (model 2).

EXAMPLE 13.7

Substitute the appropriate values of the dummy variables in model 3 to obtain the equations of the three response lines in Figure 13.23.

Solution

The complete model that characterizes the three lines in Figure 13.23 is

$$E(y) = \beta_0 + \beta_1 x_1 + \beta_2 x_2 + \beta_3 x_3 + \beta_4 x_1 x_2 + \beta_5 x_1 x_3$$

where

x_1 = Engine speed

$$x_2 = \begin{cases} 1 & \text{if petroleum fuel} \\ 0 & \text{if not} \end{cases}$$

$$x_3 = \begin{cases} 1 & \text{if coal fuel} \\ 0 & \text{if not} \end{cases}$$

Examining the coding, you can see that $x_2 = x_3 = 0$ when the fuel used is blended. Substituting these values into the expression for $E(y)$, we obtain the blended fuel line as:

Blended fuel line

$$\begin{aligned} E(y) &= \beta_0 + \beta_1 x_1 + \beta_2(0) + \beta_3(0) + \beta_4 x_1(0) + \beta_5 x_1(0) \\ &= \beta_0 + \beta_1 x_1 \end{aligned}$$

Similarly, we substitute the appropriate values of x_2 and x_3 into the expression for $E(y)$ to obtain:

Petroleum fuel line

$$E(y) = \beta_0 + \beta_1 x_1 + \beta_2(1) + \beta_3(0) + \beta_4 x_1(1) + \beta_5 x_1(0)$$

$$= \overbrace{(\beta_0 + \beta_2)}^{\text{y-intercept}} + \overbrace{(\beta_1 + \beta_4)}^{\text{Slope}} x_1$$

Coal fuel line

$$E(y) = \beta_0 + \beta_1 x_1 + \beta_2(0) + \beta_3(1) + \beta_4 x_1(0) + \beta_5 x_1(1)$$

$$= \overbrace{(\beta_0 + \beta_3)}^{\text{y-intercept}} + \overbrace{(\beta_1 + \beta_5)}^{\text{Slope}} x_1$$

EXERCISES

13.37   Refer to the *Environmental Science & Technology* study of sorption of organic vapors, Exercise 13.4. The independent variables used to model the retention coefficient y are:

x_1 = Temperature (degrees)

x_2 = Relative humidity (percent)

Organic compound = (benzene, toluene, chloroform, methanol, and anisole)

   a. Write a first-order, main effects model for $E(y)$ as a function of temperature and organic compound. Draw a sketch of the model.
   b. Interpret the β paramaters of the model, part **a**.
   c. Write a model for $E(y)$ as a function of relative humidity and organic compound that hypothesizes different retention–relative humidity slopes for the five compounds. Draw a sketch of the model.
   d. Give the slopes of the five compounds (in terms of the β's) for the model, part **c**.

13.38   Many companies are converting to the metric system of measurement. A U.S. Metric Board study was conducted to quantify some of the characteristics of companies that have converted to metric production (*Technological Forecasting and Social Change*, Apr. 1984). One of the research objectives was to investigate the relationship between the percentage y of metric work performed by a company, age x_1 of the company (in years), and cost x_2 of metric conversion, where

$$x_2 = \begin{cases} 1 & \text{if cost over } \$10,000 \\ 0 & \text{if not} \end{cases}$$

A first-order linear model was fit to data collected on $n = 350$ small manufacturers with the following results:[*]

$\hat{y} = 70.9770 - .2167x_1 - 13.2768x_2$

$R^2 = .0576 \qquad t \text{ (for } H_0: \beta_1 = 0) = -1.56 \qquad t \text{ (for } H_0: \beta_2 = 0) = -2.71$

   a. Sketch the least squares relationship between $\hat{y}$ and x_1 for the two levels of conversion cost.
   b. Is there evidence that the model is useful for predicting percentage y of metric work performed? Test using $\alpha = .01$.
   c. Is there evidence that percentage y of metric work performed decreases as age x_1 of the company increases, for companies with the same cost x_2 of conversion? Test using $\alpha = .05$.
   d. Write an interaction model for percentage y of metric work performed.
   e. How will interaction between age x_1 and cost x_2, if determined to be significant, affect the graphs constructed in part **a**?

---

[*]Reprinted by permission of the publisher. Copyright 1984 by Elsevier Science Publishing Co., Inc.

13.39 Eli Lilly and Company has developed three methods (G, R_1, and R_2) for estimating the shelf life of its drug products based on the potency of the drug.* One way to compare the three methods is to build a regression model for the dependent variable, estimated shelf life y (as a percent of true shelf life), with potency of the drug (x_1) as a quantitative predictor and method as a qualitative predictor.

  a. Write a first-order, main effects model for $E(y)$ as a function of potency (x_1) and method.
  b. Interpret the β coefficients of the model, part **a**.
  c. Write a first-order model for $E(y)$ that will allow the slopes to differ for the three methods.
  d. Refer to part **c**. For each method, write the slope of the y–x_1 line in terms of the β's.

13.40 The liquefaction of coal is a major contributor of synthetic fuels. An experiment was conducted to evaluate the performances of a diesel engine run on synthetic (coal-derived) and petroleum-derived fuel oil (*Journal of Energy Resources Technology*, Mar. 1990). The petroleum-derived fuel used was a number 2 diesel fuel (DF-2) obtained from Phillips Chemical Company. Two synthetic fuels were used: a blended fuel (50% coal-derived and 50% DF-2) and a blended fuel with advanced timing. The brake power (kW) and fuel type were varied in test runs, and engine performance was measured. The table gives the experimental results for the performance measure, mass burning rate per degree of crank angle.

Brake Power x_1	Fuel Type	Mass Burning Rate y	Brake Power x_1	Fuel Type	Mass Burning Rate y
4	DF-2	13.2	8	Blended	46.3
4	Blended	17.5	8	Advanced timing	45.6
4	Advanced timing	17.5	10	DF-2	30.7
6	DF-2	26.1	10	Blended	50.8
6	Blended	32.7	10	Advanced timing	68.9
6	Advanced timing	43.5	12	DF-2	32.3
8	DF-2	25.9	12	Blended	57.1

Source: Litzinger, T. A., and Buzza, T. G. "Performance and emissions of a diesel engine using a coal-derived fuel." *Journal of Energy Resources Technology*, Vol. 112, Mar. 1990, p. 32, Table 3.

a. Initially, the researchers fit the first-order, main effects model

$$E(y) = \beta_0 + \beta_1 x_1 + \beta_2 x_2 + \beta_3 x_3$$

where

y = Mass burning rate
x_1 = Brake power (kW)
$x_2 = \begin{cases} 1 & \text{if DF-2 fuel} \\ 0 & \text{if not} \end{cases}$
$x_3 = \begin{cases} 1 & \text{if Blended fuel} \\ 0 & \text{if not} \end{cases}$

---

*Murphy, J. R., and Weisman, D. "Using Random Slopes for Estimating Shelf Life." Paper presented at Joint Statistical Meetings, Anaheim, Calif., Aug. 1990.

Interpret the results shown in the accompanying MINITAB printout.

```
The regression equation is
Y = 13.3 + 4.36 X1 - 22.6 X2 - 7.36 X3

Predictor        Coef        Stdev      t-ratio          p
Constant       13.320        6.931         1.92      0.084
X1             4.3650        0.8057        5.42      0.000
X2            -22.600        5.464        -4.14      0.002
X3             -7.360        5.464        -1.35      0.208

s = 8.057      R-sq = 81.2%      R-sq(adj) = 75.6%

Analysis of Variance

SOURCE         DF          SS          MS         F         p
Regression      3      2807.90      935.97     14.42     0.001
Error          10       649.09       64.91
Total          13      3456.99

SOURCE         DF      SEQ SS
X1              1     1603.93
X2              1     1086.22
X3              1      117.76

Unusual Observations
Obs.      X1         Y        Fit  Stdev.Fit  Residual   St.Resid
  3      4.0     17.50      30.78       4.70    -13.28     -2.03R

R denotes an obs. with a large st. resid.
```

b. The interaction model

$$E(y) = \beta_0 + \beta_1 x_1 + \beta_2 x_2 + \beta_3 x_3 + \beta_4 x_1 x_2 + \beta_5 x_1 x_3$$

was fit using MINITAB, with the results shown in the accompanying printout. Conduct a test to determine whether brake power and fuel type interact. Test using $\alpha = .01$.

```
The regression equation is
Y = - 10.8 + 7.82 X1 + 19.4 X2 + 12.8 X3 - 5.68 X1X2 - 2.95 X1X3

Predictor        Coef        Stdev      t-ratio          p
Constant      -10.830        8.277        -1.31      0.227
X1             7.815         1.126         6.94      0.000
X2            19.35         10.69          1.81      0.108
X3            12.79         10.69          1.20      0.266
X1X2          -5.675         1.380        -4.11      0.003
X1X3          -2.950         1.380        -2.14      0.065

s = 5.037      R-sq = 94.1%      R-sq(adj) = 90.5%

Analysis of Variance

SOURCE         DF          SS          MS         F         p
Regression      5      3253.98      650.80     25.65     0.000
Error           8       203.01       25.38
Total          13      3456.99
```

(*continued*)

▶

SOURCE	DF	SEQ SS
X1	1	1603.93
X2	1	1086.22
X3	1	117.76
X1X2	1	330.04
X1X3	1	116.03

c. Refer to the model, part **b**. Give the estimates of the slope of the y–x_1 line for each of the three fuel types.

13.41 A building materials engineer is experimenting with three different cement mixes—dry, damp, and wet—for laying concrete. Since the compressive strength of a concrete slab varies as a function of hardening time and cement mix, the following main effects model is proposed:

$$E(y) = \beta_0 + \beta_1 x_1 + \beta_2 x_2 + \beta_3 x_3$$

where

y = Compressive strength (thousands of pounds per square inch)

x_1 = Hardening time of cement mix (days)

$x_2 = \begin{cases} 1 & \text{if damp cement} \\ 0 & \text{if not} \end{cases}$ $x_3 = \begin{cases} 1 & \text{if wet cement} \\ 0 & \text{if not} \end{cases}$

Dry cement is the base level.

a. What hypothesis would you test to determine whether mean compressive strength differs for the three cement mixes?

b. Using data collected for a sample of 50 batches of concrete, the main effects model is fit, with the result SSE = 140.5. Then the reduced model $E(y) = \beta_0 + \beta_1 x_1$ is fit to the same data, with the result SSE = 183.2. Test the hypothesis you formulated in part **a**. Use $\alpha = .05$

c. Explain how you would test the hypothesis that the slope of the linear relationship between mean compressive strength $E(y)$ and hardening time x_1 varies according to type of cement mix.

13.42 The Florida Citrus Commission is interested in evaluating the performance of two orange juice extractors, brand A and brand B. It is believed that the size of the fruit used in the test may influence the juice yield (amount of juice per pound of oranges) obtained by the extractors. The commission wants to find a regression model relating the mean yield, $E(y)$, to the type of orange juice extractor (brand A or brand B) and the size of orange (diameter), x_1.

a. Identify the independent variables as qualitative or quantitative.

b. Write a model that describes the relationship between $E(y)$ and size of orange as two parallel lines, one for each brand of extractor.

c. Modify the model of part **b** to permit the slopes of the two lines to differ.

d. Sketch typical response lines for the model of part **b**. Do the same for the model of part **c**. Label your graphs carefully.

e. Specify the null and alternative hypotheses you would employ to determine whether the model of part **c** provides more information for predicting yield than does the model of part **b**.

f. Explain how you would obtain the quantities necessary to compute the F statistic that would be employed in testing the hypotheses you described in part **e**.

13.43 Since glass is not prone to radiation damage, encapsulation of waste in glass is considered to be one of the most promising solutions to the problem of low-level nuclear waste in the environment. However, glass undergoes chemical changes when exposed to extreme environmental conditions and certain of its constituents leach into the surroundings. In addition, these chemical reactions may possibly weaken the glass. These concerns led to a study undertaken jointly by the Department of Materials Science and Engineering at the University of Florida and the U.S. Department of Energy to assess the utility of glass as a waste encapsulant material.* Corrosive chemical solutions (called corrosion baths) were prepared and applied directly to glass samples containing one of three types of waste (TDS-3A, FE, and AL); the chemical reactions were observed over time. A few of the key variables measured were:

y = Amount of silicon (in parts per million) found in solution at end of experiment. (This is both a measure of the degree of breakdown in the glass and a proxy for the amount of radioactive species released into the environment.)

x_1 = Temperature (°C) of the corrosion bath

$$x_2 = \begin{cases} 1 & \text{if waste type TDS-3A} \\ 0 & \text{if not} \end{cases} \qquad x_3 = \begin{cases} 1 & \text{if waste type FE} \\ 0 & \text{if not} \end{cases}$$

Waste type AL is the base level. Suppose we want to model amount y of silicon as a function of temperature (x_1) and type of waste (x_2, x_3).

a. Write a model that proposes parallel straight-line relationships between amount of silicon and temperature, one line for each of the three waste types.

b. Add terms for the interaction between temperature and waste type to the model of part **a**.

c. Refer to the model of part **b**. For each waste type, give the slope of the line relating amount of silicon to temperature.

d. Explain how you could test for the presence of temperature–waste type interaction.

13.44 As a result of the dramatic decline in the cost of computer hardware, it is becoming economically feasible to build computers with thousands of processors. However, the scheduling of computer jobs on these advanced computers can be a difficult task. Parallel scheduling algorithms have been designed to solve this problem. A *parallel algorithm* is a set of scheduling instructions designed to minimize the number of tardy jobs in the system and to minimize the mean finish time of the entire job stream. Suppose three different scheduling algorithms (A, B, and C) have been proposed for minimizing the mean finish time of n jobs in a system with a large number of processors.

a. Write a main effects model with interaction to relate the mean finish time, $E(y)$, to the number of jobs (x_1) and scheduling algorithm (A, B, or C).

b. The model of part **a** was fit to data collected on 12 simulated systems (four systems for each of the three algorithms) with the results shown in the accompanying SAS printout. Test whether the model is useful in predicting mean finish time. Use $\alpha = .05$.

c. Write the main effects model (with no interaction) relating mean finish time to number of jobs and scheduling algorithm.

*The background information for this exercise was provided by Dr. David Clark, Department of Materials Science and Engineering, University of Florida.

d. The main effects (reduced) model was fit to the data and produced SSE = 38.289. Does this provide sufficient evidence at the $\alpha = .05$ level of significance to indicate that the interaction terms should be kept in the model?

Analysis of Variance

Source	DF	Sum of Squares	Mean Square	F Value	Prob>F
Model	5	87.473	17.495	4.895	0.0394
Error	6	21.443	3.574		
C Total	11	108.916			

Root MSE	1.8905	R-square	0.8031
Dep Mean	12.604	Adj R-sq	0.6390
C.V.	14.999		

13.9   Comparing Two or More Response Curves

Suppose we think that the relationship between mean diesel engine performance, $E(y)$, and engine speed, x_1 (Section 13.8), is second-order. The scenario for writing the models for this situation is as follows:

1. The mean performance curves are identical for all three fuel types; that is, a single second-order curve will suffice to describe the relationship between $E(y)$ and x_1 for all the fuels (see Figure 13.27).

   MODEL I $E(y) = \beta_0 + \beta_1 x_1 + \beta_2 x_1^2$

   $x_1 = $ Engine speed

FIGURE 13.27 ►
The relationship between $E(y)$ and x_1 is the same for all fuel types

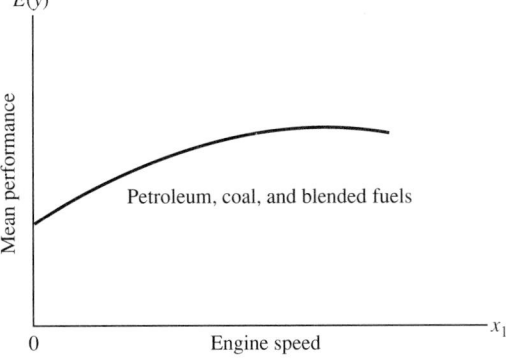

2. The response curves have the same shapes but different y-intercepts (see Figure 13.28 on page 756).

FIGURE 13.28 ▶
The response curves have the same
shapes but different y-intercepts

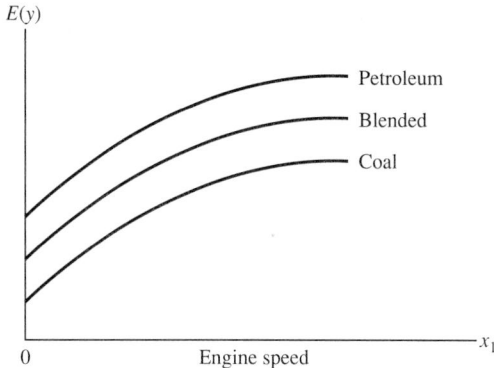

MODEL 2 $E(y) = \beta_0 + \beta_1 x_1 + \beta_2 x_1^2 + \beta_3 x_2 + \beta_4 x_3$

x_1 = Engine speed

$x_2 = \begin{cases} 1 & \text{if petroleum fuel} \\ 0 & \text{if not} \end{cases}$

$x_3 = \begin{cases} 1 & \text{if coal fuel} \\ 0 & \text{if not} \end{cases}$

3. The response curves for the three fuel types are different (i.e., engine speed and type of fuel interact), as shown in Figure 13.29.

MODEL 3 $E(y) = \beta_0 + \beta_1 x_1 + \beta_2 x_1^2 + \beta_3 x_2 + \beta_4 x_3 + \beta_5 x_1 x_2$
$+ \beta_6 x_1 x_3 + \beta_7 x_1^2 x_2 + \beta_8 x_1^2 x_3$

FIGURE 13.29 ▶
The response curves for the three
fuel types

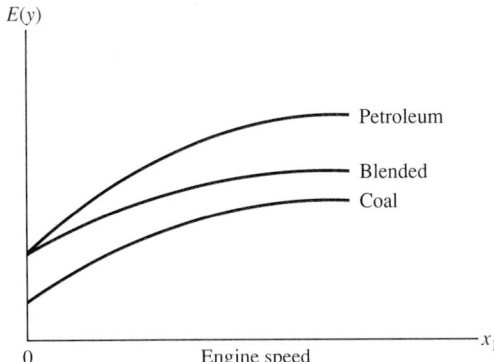

EXAMPLE 13.9   Give the equation of the complete second-order model for the petroleum fuel.

Solution   Model 3 characterizes the relationship between $E(y)$ and x_1 for the petroleum fuel (see the coding) when $x_2 = 1$ and $x_3 = 0$. Substituting these values into model 3, we obtain

$$E(y) = \beta_0 + \beta_1 x_1 + \beta_2 x_1^2 + \beta_3 x_2 + \beta_4 x_3 + \beta_5 x_1 x_2 + \beta_6 x_1 x_3 + \beta_7 x_1^2 x_2 + \beta_8 x_1^2 x_3$$

$$= \beta_0 + \beta_1 x_1 + \beta_2 x_1^2 + \beta_3(1) + \beta_4(0) + \beta_5 x_1(1) + \beta_6 x_1(0) + \beta_7 x_1^2(1) + \beta_8 x_1^2(0)$$

$$= \underbrace{(\beta_0 + \beta_3)}_{y\text{-intercept}} + \underbrace{(\beta_1 + \beta_5)}_{\text{Shift}} x_1 + \underbrace{(\beta_2 + \beta_7)}_{\text{Rate of curvature}} x_1^2$$

EXAMPLE 13.10

What null hypothesis about the parameters of model 3 would you test if you want to determine whether the second-order curves for the three fuel types are identical?

Solution

If the curves were identical, we would not need the independent variable Type of fuel in the model; that is, we would delete all terms involving x_2 and x_3. This would produce model 1,

$$E(y) = \beta_0 + \beta_1 x_1 + \beta_2 x_1^2$$

and the null hypothesis would be

$$H_0: \quad \beta_3 = \beta_4 = \beta_5 = \beta_6 = \beta_7 = \beta_8 = 0$$

The proper test to conduct is the nested F test where model 1 is nested within model 3.

EXAMPLE 3.11

Suppose we assume that the response curves for the three fuel types differ but we want to know whether the second-order terms contribute information for the prediction of y. Or, equivalently, will a second-order model give better predictions than a first-order model? Explain how to conduct the analysis.

Solution

The only difference between model 3 and a first-order model are those terms involving x_1^2. Therefore, the null hypothesis, "the second-order terms contribute no information for the prediction of y," is equivalent to

$$H_0: \quad \beta_2 = \beta_7 = \beta_8 = 0$$

To test this hypothesis, we would use the nested F test comparing model 3 to the reduced model

$$E(y) = \beta_0 + \beta_1 x_1 + \beta_3 x_2 + \beta_4 x_3 + \beta_5 x_1 x_2 + \beta_6 x_1 x_3$$

Examples 13.10 and 13.11 identify two nested F tests that answer practical questions concerning a collection of second-order models. Other comparisons among the curves can be made by testing appropriate sets of model parameters (see the exercises).

The models described in the preceding sections provide only an introduction to statistical modeling. Models can be constructed to relate $E(y)$ to any number of quantitative and/or qualitative independent variables. You can compare response curves and surfaces for different levels of a qualitative variable or for different combinations of levels of two or more qualitative independent variables.

EXERCISES

13.45   Refer to the *Journal of Human Stress* study of firefighters, Exercise 13.1. It is thought that a complete second-order model, shown here, will be adequate to describe the relationship between emotional distress and years of experience for two groups of firefighters—those exposed to a chemical fire and those unexposed. *

$$E(y) = \beta_0 + \beta_1 x_1 + \beta_2 x_1^2 + \beta_3 x_2 + \beta_4 x_1 x_2 + \beta_5 x_1^2 x_2$$

where

y = Emotional distress

x_1 = Experience (years)

$x_2 = \begin{cases} 1 & \text{if exposed to chemical fire} \\ 0 & \text{if not} \end{cases}$

a. What hypothesis would you test to determine whether the *rate* of increase of emotional distress with experience is different for the two groups of firefighters?

b. What hypothesis would you test to determine whether there are differences in mean emotional distress levels that are attributable to exposure group?

c. The following is a portion of the SAS printout that results from fitting the second-order model to a sample of 200 firefighters.

Analysis of Variance

Source	DF	Sum of Squares	Mean Square	F Value	Prob>F
Model	5	2351.70	470.34	116.42	0.0001
Error	194	783.90	4.04		
C Total	199	3135.60			

Root MSE	2.0102	R-square	0.7500	
Dep Mean	24.221	Adj R-sq	0.7436	
C.V.	8.299			

The reduced model $E(y) = \beta_0 + \beta_1 x_1 + \beta_2 x_1^2$ is fit to the same data, and the resulting computer printout is reproduced at the top of the next page. Is there sufficient evidence to support the claim that the mean emotional distress levels differ for the two groups of firefighters? Use $\alpha = .05$.

---

*In practice, we would include other variables in the model. We include only two here to simplify the exercise.

```
                    Analysis of Variance

                      Sum of        Mean
    Source      DF    Squares       Square      F Value     Prob>F

    Model        2    2340.37      1170.185      289.87      0.0001
    Error      197     795.23         4.037
    C Total    199    3135.60

       Root MSE    2.0092       R-square      0.7464
       Dep Mean   24.221        Adj R-sq      0.7438
       C.V.        8.295
```

13.46 Refer to the *Environmental Science & Technology* study of sorption of organic vapors, Exercise 13.37. Consider using the quantitative variable, relative humidity, and the qualitative variable, organic compound (at five levels), to model the retention coefficient y.

    a. Write a complete second-order model that relates $E(y)$ to relative humidity.

    b. Add the main effect terms for organic compound to the model of part **a**.

    c. Add terms to the model of part **b** to allow for interaction between relative humidity and organic compound.

    d. Under what circumstances will the response curves of the model of part **c** possess the same shape but have different y-intercepts?

    e. Under what circumstances will the response curves of the model of part **c** be parallel lines?

    f. Under what circumstances will the response curves of the model of part **c** be identical?

13.47 Refer to Exercise 13.41 in which a model relating mean compressive strength of concrete to hardening time and type of cement mix was proposed.

    a. Write a second-order model that allows different response curves for the three types of cement mixes.

    b. Explain how you would test the hypothesis that the three response curves have the same shape, but different y-intercepts.

13.48 Refer to Exercise 13.44 in which we considered models relating the mean finish time of a set of computer jobs to the number of jobs and scheduling algorithm.

    a. Write the complete second-order model. Sketch the response curves for this model.

    b. What hypothesis would you test to determine whether the response curves differ for the three scheduling algorithms?

    c. The complete second-order model of part **a** was fit to the 12 data points, with the result SSE = 16.225. The reduced model

$$E(y) = \beta_0 + \beta_1 x_1 + \beta_2 x_1^2$$

    was also fit, with the result SSE = 27.109. Conduct the test of part **b**. Use $\alpha = .05$.

13.49 An operations manager is interested in modeling $E(y)$, the expected length of time per month (in hours) that a machine will be shut down for repairs, as a function of the type of machine (001 or 002) and the age of the machine (in years). The manager has proposed the following model:

$$E(y) = \beta_0 + \beta_1 x_1 + \beta_2 x_1^2 + \beta_3 x_2$$

where

$$x_1 = \text{Age of machine}$$

$$x_2 = \begin{cases} 1 & \text{if machine type 001} \\ 0 & \text{if machine type 002} \end{cases}$$

Data were obtained on $n = 20$ machine breakdowns and were used to estimate the parameters of the model. A portion of the MINITAB printout is shown here.

```
s = 2.828        R-sq = 94.9%      R-sq(adj) = 94.0%

Analysis of Variance

SOURCE       DF        SS        MS        F         p
Regression    3       2396       799      99.83     0.000
Error        16        128         8
Total        19       2524
```

The reduced model $E(y) = \beta_0 + \beta_1 x_1 + \beta_2 x_2$ was fit to the same data. The MINITAB printout is partially reproduced here.

```
s = 3.272        R-sq = 92.8%      R-sq(adj) = 91.9%

Analysis of Variance

SOURCE       DF        SS        MS        F         p
Regression    2       2342      1171     109.38     0.000
Error        17        182        11
Total        19       2524
```

Is there sufficient evidence to conclude that the second-order (x_1^2) term in the model proposed by the operations manager is necessary? Test using $\alpha = .05$.

13.10   Stepwise Regression

In building a model to describe a response variable y, we must choose the important terms to be included in the model. The list of potentially important independent variables, with their associated main effect and interaction terms, may be extremely large. Therefore, we need some objective method of screening out those that are not important. The screening procedure that we present in this chapter is known as a **stepwise regression analysis**.

The most commonly used stepwise regression procedure, available in most popular statistical software packages, works as follows: The user first identifies the response, y, and the set of potentially important independent variables, $x_1, x_2, \ldots, x_k$, where k will generally be large. (Note that this set of variables could represent both first- and higher-order terms, as well as any interaction terms that might be important information contributors.) The response and independent variables are then entered into the computer, and the stepwise procedure begins.

STEP 1 The computer fits all possible one-variable models of the form

$$E(y) = \beta_0 + \beta_1 x_i$$

to the data. For each model, the test of the null hypothesis

$$H_0: \quad \beta_1 = 0$$

against the alternative hypothesis

$$H_a: \quad \beta_1 \neq 0$$

is conducted using the t (or the equivalent F) test for a single β parameter. The independent variable that produces the largest (absolute) t value is declared the best one-variable predictor of y.*

STEP 2 The stepwise program now begins to search through the remaining $(k - 1)$ independent variables for the best two-variable model of the form

$$E(y) = \beta_0 + \beta_1 x_1 + \beta_2 x_i$$

This is done by fitting all two-variable models containing x_1 and each of the other $(k - 1)$ options for the second variable x_i. The t values for the test H_0: $\beta_2 = 0$ are computed for each of the $(k - 1)$ models (corresponding to the remaining independent variables x_i, $i = 2, 3, \ldots, k$), and the variable having the largest t is retained. Call this variable x_2.

At this point, some software packages diverge in methodology. The better packages now go back and check the t value of $\hat{\beta}_1$ *after $\hat{\beta}_2 x_2$ has been added to the model*. If the t value has become nonsignificant at some specified α level (say, $\alpha = .10$), the variable x_1 is removed and a search is made for the independent variable with a β parameter that will yield the most significant t value in the presence of $\hat{\beta}_2 x_2$. Other packages do not recheck $\hat{\beta}_1$, but proceed directly to step 3.

The best-fitting model may yield a different value for $\hat{\beta}_1$ than that obtained in step 1, because x_1 and x_2 may be correlated. Thus, both the value of $\hat{\beta}_1$ and its significance usually change from step 1 to step 2. For this reason, the software packages that recheck the t values at each step are preferred.

STEP 3 The stepwise procedure now checks for a third independent variable to include in the model with x_1 and x_2. That is, we seek the best model of the form

$$E(y) = \beta_0 + \beta_1 x_1 + \beta_2 x_2 + \beta_3 x_i$$

To do this, we fit all the $(k - 2)$ models using x_1, x_2, and each of the $(k - 2)$ remaining variables, x_i, as a possible x_3. The criterion is again to

---

*Note that the variable with the largest t value will also be the one with the largest Pearson product moment correlation r with y.

include the independent variable with the largest t value. Call this best third variable x_3.

The better programs now recheck the t values corresponding to the x_1 and x_2 coefficients, replacing the variables that have t values that have become nonsignificant. This procedure is continued until no further independent variables can be found that yield significant t values (at the specified α level) in the presence of the variables already in the model.

The result of the stepwise procedure is a model containing only those terms with t values that are significant at the specified α level. Thus, in most practical situations, only several of the large number of independent variables will remain. However, it is very important *not* to jump to the conclusion that all the independent variables important for predicting y have been identified or that the unimportant independent variables have been eliminated. Remember, the stepwise procedure is using only *sample estimates* of the true model coefficients (β's) to select the important variables. An extremely large number of single β parameter t tests have been conducted, and the probability is very high that one or more errors have been made in including or excluding variables. That is, we have very probably included some unimportant independent variables in the model (Type I errors) and eliminated some important ones (Type II errors).

There is a second reason why we might not have arrived at a good model. When we choose the variables to be included in the stepwise regression, we may often omit high-order terms (to keep the number of variables manageable). Consequently, we may have initially omitted several important terms from the model. Thus, we should recognize stepwise regression for what it is: an objective screening procedure.

Now, we will consider interactions and quadratic terms (for quantitative variables) among variables screened by the stepwise procedure. It would be best to develop this response surface model with a second set of data independent of that used for the screening, so the results of the stepwise procedure can be partially verified with new data. However, this is not always possible, because in many practical modeling situations only a small amount of data is available.

Warning

Be cautious when using the results of stepwise regression to make inferences about the relationship between $E(y)$ and the independent variables in the resulting first-order model. First, an extremely large number of t tests have been conducted, leading to a high probability of making either one or more Type I or Type II errors. Second, the stepwise model does not include any higher-order or interaction terms. Stepwise regression should be used only when necessary, i.e., when you want to determine which of a large number of potentially important independent variables should be used in the model-building process.

Remember, do not be deceived by the impressive looking t values that result from the stepwise procedure—it has retained only the independent variables with the largest t values. Also, if you have used a main effects model for your stepwise procedure, remember that it may be greatly improved by the addition of interaction and quadratic terms.

EXAMPLE 13.12

Suppose a large civil engineering firm wants to use multiple regression to model an executive's salary as a function of experience, education, gender, and other factors. A preliminary step in the construction of the model is to determine the most important independent variables. Ten independent variables to be considered are listed in Table 13.7. Since it would be very difficult to perform a regression analysis on a complete second-order model using 10 independent variables, we need to eliminate those variables (or terms) that do not contribute much information for the prediction of salary. We will use the salary data for a sample of 100 executives to decide which of the 10 variables should be included in the construction of the final model. The computer printouts that we show in the solution are based on this data set.

TABLE 13.7   Independent Variables in Example 13.12

Independent Variable	Description
x_1	Experience (years)—quantitative
x_2	Education (years)—quantitative
x_3	Gender (1 if male, 0 if female)—qualitative
x_4	Number of employees supervised—quantitative
x_5	Corporate assets (millions of dollars)—quantitative
x_6	Board member (1 if yes, 0 if no)—qualitative
x_7	Age (years)—quantitative
x_8	Company profits (past 12 months, millions of dollars)—quantitative
x_9	Has international responsibility (1 if yes, 0 if no)—qualitative
x_{10}	Company's total sales (past 12 months, millions of dollars)—quantitative

Solution

We will use stepwise regression with the main effects of the 10 independent variables to identify the most important variables. The dependent variable y is the natural logarithm of the executive salaries. The SAS stepwise regression printout is shown in Figure 13.30 on page 764. SAS uses an F statistic, rather than a t statistic, in the stepwise procedure. It can be shown (proof omitted) that the square of a Student's t statistic with ν df is equal to an F statistic with 1 df in the numerator and ν df in the denominator. Thus, $t^2_{\alpha/2} = F_\alpha$, where t is based on ν df and F has 1 numerator df and ν denominator df.

Note that the first variable included in the model is x_4, number of employees supervised. At the second step, x_5, corporate assets, enters the model. At the sixth step, x_6, a dummy variable for the qualitative variable board member, is brought into the model. However, because the observed significance level (.2295) of the F statistic for x_6 is greater than the preassigned $\alpha = .10$, x_6 is removed from the model. Thus, at step 7 the procedure indicates that the five-variable model including x_1, x_2, x_3, x_4, and x_5 is best. That is, none of the other independent variables can meet the $\alpha = .10$ criterion for admission to the model. Therefore, in our final modeling effort, we will develop a model using these independent variables.

FIGURE 13.30 ▶

SAS stepwise regression printout for Example 13.12

STEP 1
Variable X4 Entered   R-Square = 0.42071677   C(P) = 1274.7576

	DF	Sum of Squares	Mean Square	F	Prob > F
Regression	1	11.46854285	11.46854285	71.17	0.0001
Error	98	15.79113802	0.16113696		
Total	99	27.25977087			

	B Value	Std Error	F	Prob > F
Intercept	10.20077500			
X4	0.00057284	0.00006790	71.17	0.0001

STEP 2
Variable X5 Entered   R-Square = 0.78299675   C(P) = 419.4947

	DF	Sum of Squares	Mean Square	F	Prob > F
Regression	2	21.34431198	10.67215599	175.00	0.0001
Error	97	5.91545889	0.06098411		
Total	99	27.25977087			

	B Value	Std Error	F	Prob > F
Intercept	9.87702903			
X4	0.00058353	0.00004178	195.06	0.0001
X5	0.00183730	0.00014438	161.94	0.0001

STEP 3
Variable X1 Entered   R-Square = 0.89667614   C(P) = 152.4952

	DF	Sum of Squares	Mean Square	F	Prob > F
Regression	3	24.44318616	8.14772872	277.71	0.0001
Error	96	2.81658471	0.02933942		
Total	99	27.25977087			

	B Value	Std Error	F	Prob > F
Intercept	9.66449288			
X4	0.00055251	0.00002914	359.59	0.0001
X5	0.00191195	0.00010041	362.60	0.0001
X1	0.01870784	0.00182032	105.62	0.0001

STEP 4
Variable X3 Entered   R-Square = 0.94815717   C(P) = 32.6757

	DF	Sum of Squares	Mean Square	F	Prob > F
Regression	4	25.84654710	8.46163678	434.37	0.0001
Error	95	1.41322377	0.01487604		
Total	99	27.25977087			

	B Value	Std Error	F	Prob > F
Intercept	9.40077349			
X4	0.00055288	0.00002075	710.15	0.0001
X5	0.00190876	0.00007150	712.74	0.0001
X1	0.02074868	0.00131310	249.68	0.0001
X3	0.30011726	0.03089939	94.34	0.0001

STEP 5
Variable X2 Entered   R-Square = 0.96039323   C(P) = 5.7215

	DF	Sum of Squares	Mean Square	F	Prob > F
Regression	5	26.18009940	5.23601988	455.87	0.0001
Error	94	1.07967147	0.01148587		
Total	99	27.25977087			

	B Value	Std Error	F	Prob > F
Intercept	8.85387930			
X4	0.00056061	0.00001829	939.84	0.0001
X5	0.00193684	0.00006304	943.98	0.0001
X1	0.02141724	0.00116047	340.61	0.0001
X3	0.31927842	0.02738298	135.95	0.0001
X2	0.03315807	0.00615303	29.04	0.0001

STEP 6
Variable X6 Entered   R-Square = 0.96100666   C(P) = 6.2699

	DF	Sum of Squares	Mean Square	F	Prob > F
Regression	6	26.19682148	4.36613691	382.00	0.0001
Error	93	1.06294939	0.01142956		
Total	99	27.25977087			

	B Value	Std Error	F	Prob > F
Intercept	8.87509152			
X4	0.00055820	0.00001835	925.32	0.0001
X5	0.00193764	0.00006289	949.31	0.0001
X1	0.02133460	0.00115963	338.48	0.0001
X3	0.31093801	0.02817264	121.81	0.0001
X2	0.03272195	0.00614851	28.32	0.0001
X6	0.03866226	0.03196369	1.46	0.2295

STEP 7
Variable X6 Removed   R-Square = 0.96039323   C(P) = 5.7215

	DF	Sum of Squares	Mean Square	F	Prob > F
Regression	5	26.18009940	5.23601988	455.87	0.0001
Error	94	1.07967147	0.01148587		
Total	99	27.25977087			

	B Value	Std Error	F	Prob > F
Intercept	8.85387930			
X4	0.00056061	0.00001829	939.84	0.0001
X5	0.00193684	0.00006304	943.98	0.0001
X1	0.02141724	0.00116047	340.61	0.0001
X3	0.31927842	0.02738298	135.95	0.0001
X2	0.03315807	0.00615303	29.04	0.0001

In addition to stepwise regression, other more subjective methods are designed to aid in the selection of the "most important" independent variables. For example, the **all-possible regressions selection procedure** considers regression models involving all possible subsets of the potentially important predictors. The "best" subset of variables is selected (by the researcher) based on model statistics, such as the familiar R^2 and MSE, and other statistics, such as PRESS (prediction sum of squares) and Mallows C_p. (Consult the references for details on the PRESS and C_p statistic.) These methods, however, lack the objectivity of stepwise regression, and (as with stepwise regression) analysts typically omit interactions and higher-order terms in the list of potential variables when using them.

EXERCISES

13.50   There are six independent variables, x_1, x_2, x_3, x_4, x_5, and x_6, that might be useful in predicting a response y. A total of $n = 50$ observations are available, and it is decided to employ stepwise regression to help in selecting the independent variables that appear to be useful. The computer fits all possible one-variable models of the form

$$E(y) = \beta_0 + \beta_1 x_i$$

where x_i is the ith independent variable, $i = 1, 2, \ldots, 6$. The information in the accompanying table is provided from the computer printout.

Independent Variable	$\hat{\beta}_1$	$s_{\hat{\beta}_1}$
x_1	1.6	.42
x_2	−.9	.01
x_3	3.4	1.14
x_4	2.5	2.06
x_5	−4.4	.73
x_6	.3	.35

a. Which independent variable is declared the best one-variable predictor of y? Explain.
b. Would this variable be included in the model at this stage? Explain.
c. Describe the next phase that a stepwise procedure would execute.

13.51   Many power plants dump hot wastewater into surrounding rivers, streams, and oceans, an action that may have an adverse effect on the marine life in the dumping areas. A marine biologist was hired by the EPA to determine whether the hot water runoff from a particular power plant located near a large gulf is having an adverse effect on the marine life in the area. In the initial phase of the study, the biologist's goal is to acquire a prediction equation for the number of marine animals located at certain predesignated areas, or stations, in the gulf. Based on past experience, the biologist considered the following environmental factors as predictors for the number of animals at a particular station:

x_1 = Temperature of water (TEMP)
x_2 = Salinity of water (SAL)
x_3 = Dissolved oxygen content of water (DO)
x_4 = Turbidity index, a measure of the turbidity of the water (TI)
x_5 = Depth of the water at the station (ST_DEPTH)
x_6 = Total weight of sea grasses in sampled area (TGRSWT)

STEP 1
  Variable ST_DEPTH Entered   R-Square = 0.1223

	DF	Sum of Squares	Mean Square	F	Prob > F
Regression	1	57.44	57.44	99.47	0.0001
Error	714	412.33	0.58		
Total	715	469.77			

	B Value	Std Error	F	Prob > F
Intercept	8.38559			
ST_DEPTH	-0.43678	0.04379	99.47	0.0001

STEP 2
  Variable TGRSWT Entered   R-Square = 0.1821

	DF	Sum of Squares	Mean Square	F	Prob > F
Regression	2	85.55	42.78	79.38	0.0001
Error	713	384.22	0.54		
Total	715	469.77			

	B Value	Std Error	F	Prob > F
Intercept	8.07682			
ST_DEPTH	-0.35355	0.04385	65.02	0.0001
TGRSWT	0.00271	0.00038	52.16	0.0001

STEP 3
  Variable TI Entered   R-Square = 0.1870

	DF	Sum of Squares	Mean Square	F	Prob > F
Regression	3	87.85	29.28	54.59	0.0001
Error	712	381.92	0.54		
Total	715	469.77			

	B Value	Std Error	F	Prob > F
Intercept	7.38864			
TI	0.65774	0.31783	4.28	0.0389
ST_DEPTH	-0.31451	0.47641	43.58	0.0001
TGRSWT	0.00261	0.00038	47.73	0.0001

STEP 4
  Variable DO Entered   R-Square = 0.1889

	DF	Sum of Squares	Mean Square	F	Prob > F
Regression	4	88.75	22.19	41.40	0.0001
Error	711	381.02	0.54		
Total	715	469.77			

	B Value	Std Error	F	Prob > F
Intercept	7.22576			
DO	0.01769	0.01363	1.69	0.1946
TI	0.67347	0.31791	4.49	0.0345
ST_DEPTH	-0.30417	0.04828	39.69	0.0001
TGRSWT	0.00267	0.00038	49.23	0.0001

(continued)

STEP 5
    Variable DO Removed   R-Square = 0.1870

	DF	Sum of Squares	Mean Square	F	Prob > F
Regression	3	87.85	29.28	54.59	0.0001
Error	712	381.92	0.54		
Total	715	469.77			

	B Value	Std Error	F	Prob > F
Intercept	7.38864			
TI	0.65774	0.31783	4.28	0.0389
ST_DEPTH	-0.31451	0.04764	43.58	0.0001
TGRSWT	0.00261	0.00038	47.73	0.0001

As a preliminary step in the construction of this model, the biologist used a stepwise regression procedure to identify the most important of these six variables. A total of 716 samples were taken at different stations in the gulf, producing the accompanying SAS printout. (The response measured was y, the log of the number of marine animals found in the sampled area.)

a. According to the SAS printout, which of the six independent variables should be used in the model? (Use $\alpha = .10$.)

b. Are we able to assume that the marine biologist has identified all the important independent variables for the prediction of y? Why?

c. Using the variables identified in part **a**, write the first-order model with interaction that may be used to predict y.

d. How would the marine biologist determine whether the model specified in part **c** was better than the first-order model?

e. Note the small value of R^2. What action might the biologist take to improve the model?

13.11   Model Building: An Example

The basic elements of multiple regression analysis have been presented in Chapters 12 and 13. Now we assemble these elements by applying them to a practical solution.

In the United States, commercial contractors bid for the right to construct state highways and roads. A state government agency, usually the Department of Transportation (DOT), notifies various contractors of the state's intent to build a highway. Sealed bids are submitted by the contractors, and the contractor with the lowest bid (building cost) is awarded the road construction contract. The bidding process works extremely well in competitive markets but has the potential to increase construction costs if the markets are noncompetitive or if collusive practices are present. The latter occurred in the 1970s and 1980s in Florida. Numerous contractors either admitted or were found guilty of price-fixing, i.e., setting the cost of construction above the fair, or competitive, cost through bid-rigging or other means.

In this section, we apply multiple regression to a data set obtained from the office of the Attorney General of Florida. Our objective is to build and test the adequacy of a model designed to predict the cost y of a road construction contract awarded using the sealed-bid system in Florida.

STEP 1   Based on the opinions of several experts in road construction and bid-rigging, a list of potential predictors of contract cost y is obtained. This list is shown in Table 13.8. Data collected on these eight potential predictors and contract cost for a sample of $n = 235$ contracts are shown in Table 13.9.

TABLE 13.8   Description of Several Potential Predictors of Contract Cost

Variable	Description
DOTEST (x_1)	DOT engineer's estimate of construction cost
B2B1RAT (x_2)	Ratio of second lowest bid to lowest bid
B3B1RAT (x_3)	Ratio of third lowest bid to lowest bid
BHB1RAT (x_4)	Ratio of highest bid to lowest bid
STATUS (x_5)	1 if "fixed' contract, 0 if competitive contract
DISTRICT (x_6)	1 if contract awarded in South Florida District, 0 if not
BTPRATIO (x_7)	Ratio of number of bidders to number of planholders
DAYSEST (x_8)	Engineer's estimate of number of work days required

TABLE 13.9   Data for Bid-Rigging Example

OBS	COST	DOTEST	B2B1RAT	B3B1RAT	BHB1RAT	STATUS	DISTRICT	BTPRATIO	DAYSEST
1	1379.43	1386.29	1.01397	1.03303	1.06121	1	0	0.33333	250
2	134.03	85.71	1.00995	1.01092	1.01092	1	1	0.75000	45
3	202.33	248.89	1.12084	1.22498	1.30546	0	0	0.50000	120
4	397.12	467.49	1.00588	1.11035	1.26733	0	0	0.50000	180
5	158.54	117.72	1.01053	1.10247	1.10247	1	0	0.37500	80
6	1128.11	1008.91	1.06208	1.09137	1.09137	1	0	0.60000	200
7	400.33	472.98	1.10275	1.13560	1.13560	1	1	0.60000	70
8	581.64	785.39	1.09346	1.16794	1.33349	0	0	0.50000	200
9	353.96	370.02	1.05063	1.28312	1.47836	0	1	0.57143	75
10	138.71	174.25	1.07047	1.19279	1.27559	0	0	0.83333	70
11	383.66	410.95	1.07508	1.13970	1.13970	1	1	0.42857	60
12	3910.94	3405.94	1.02768	1.04733	1.07683	1	1	0.45455	350
13	362.92	385.96	1.01691	1.04658	1.04658	0	1	0.37500	100
14	196.50	235.41	1.16398	1.19491	1.62532	0	0	0.70000	120
15	637.99	627.41	1.07043	1.16355	1.58125	0	0	0.50000	140
16	152.06	175.40	1.07504	1.24451	1.24451	1	1	0.50000	75
17	375.00	432.33	1.05025	1.20642	1.30949	0	0	0.57143	120
18	2284.56	1499.04	1.01600	1.20033	1.20033	1	0	0.60000	270
19	551.45	497.74	1.06668	1.10932	1.10932	1	1	0.60000	100
20	239.67	194.65	1.02302	1.21276	1.21276	1	1	0.60000	65
21	207.87	167.99	1.05143	1.08977	1.15240	1	1	0.66667	60
22	640.48	767.80	1.06059	1.08447	1.27066	0	0	0.40000	90
23	230.54	260.30	1.11029	1.12570	1.12570	1	1	0.42857	125
24	299.87	247.04	1.08411	1.10180	1.10180	1	1	0.60000	80
25	2368.84	2456.77	1.17209	1.18020	1.48550	0	0	0.30769	320
26	496.49	879.40	1.00453	1.17145	1.38498	0	0	0.58333	140
27	1564.87	1303.40	1.00374	1.04983	1.04983	1	0	0.33333	200
28	7387.03	6107.93	1.01878	1.05413	1.05718	0	1	0.66667	340
29	195.68	199.09	1.04290	1.27466	1.27466	0	1	0.60000	50
30	830.47	715.46	1.01755	1.02450	1.08833	1	0	0.57143	135
31	179.06	208.72	1.02474	1.03067	1.60580	0	1	0.62500	90
32	150.35	199.09	1.00893	1.06483	1.55218	0	0	0.63636	100

TABLE 13.9   Continued

OBS	COST	DOTEST	B2B1RAT	B3B1RAT	BHB1RAT	STATUS	DISTRICT	BTPRATIO	DAYSEST
177	1157.39	891.21	1.01295	1.09076	1.09076	1	0	0.75000	450
178	166.80	131.99	1.07707	1.08335	1.08335	1	0	0.42857	120
179	668.53	596.89	1.03133	1.05542	1.05542	1	1	0.75000	120
180	7622.16	7871.19	1.06781	1.08947	1.18429	0	1	0.37500	700
181	201.32	182.94	1.04814	1.07143	1.07143	0	0	0.42857	90
182	1270.08	1306.33	1.02258	1.07352	1.07352	1	1	0.75000	195
183	1055.14	1148.65	1.03627	1.10087	1.33284	0	1	0.45455	400
184	5212.23	5090.86	1.01774	1.01786	1.25398	0	1	0.56250	500
185	5654.86	5447.59	1.04491	1.06438	1.06438	1	1	0.37500	500
186	856.46	938.14	1.06181	1.15976	1.23706	0	1	0.50000	375
187	88.98	66.06	1.15552	1.18257	1.19208	1	1	0.50000	90
188	200.00	168.99	1.10151	1.12477	1.12477	1	1	0.75000	90
189	234.04	179.74	1.03977	1.04869	1.07225	0	0	0.80000	170
190	116.56	125.85	1.05611	1.07894	1.07894	0	1	0.75000	80
191	82.11	93.04	1.00000	1.15889	1.39368	0	0	0.75000	100
192	207.81	214.25	1.07698	1.09489	1.09489	0	0	0.50000	155
193	463.28	474.89	1.00903	1.04904	1.18654	0	0	0.88889	215
194	7385.55	8460.87	1.04472	1.05852	1.05852	0	0	0.23077	505
195	91.66	100.31	1.02867	1.12586	1.18879	0	1	0.57143	90
196	546.16	622.92	1.00235	1.07635	1.07635	0	0	0.37500	165
197	740.30	810.26	1.00000	1.03483	1.14590	0	0	0.44444	175
198	888.44	883.30	1.01844	1.03710	1.18272	1	0	0.83333	250
199	656.75	750.82	1.03327	1.06556	1.11905	1	1	0.44444	180
200	1884.39	1550.49	1.01914	1.08680	1.08680	1	1	0.42857	350
201	4448.13	4197.79	1.01046	1.02215	1.02215	1	0	0.50000	660
202	258.20	181.95	1.00732	1.02541	1.04932	1	1	0.80000	130
203	1949.63	1880.83	1.05165	1.10803	1.17919	1	1	0.44444	330
204	235.28	230.75	1.01587	1.08762	1.12906	1	0	0.83333	90
205	35.18	39.21	1.03338	1.39979	1.39979	0	1	0.60000	45
206	244.76	221.88	1.00543	1.02878	1.17723	1	0	0.80000	90
207	648.92	563.88	1.02119	1.02659	1.02659	1	0	0.60000	140
208	391.47	358.53	1.02829	1.09437	1.09437	1	0	0.60000	100
209	267.78	249.91	1.03914	1.06844	1.11820	1	0	0.36364	255
210	2130.04	2019.87	1.10956	1.16759	1.19220	0	1	0.71429	450
211	301.23	303.19	1.07610	1.10834	1.10834	1	0	0.60000	110
212	1077.90	878.72	1.04175	1.06434	1.06768	1	0	0.80000	190
213	927.38	902.03	1.11036	1.16285	1.16285	0	1	0.25000	400
214	241.70	243.97	1.04946	1.16941	1.16941	1	1	0.75000	45
215	65.79	82.36	1.18645	1.20456	1.22890	0	1	0.44444	60
216	1208.44	1230.33	1.00000	1.30919	1.49820	0	0	0.30769	295
217	9453.35	9479.73	1.02255	1.03217	1.14419	0	1	0.31579	500
218	7098.11	8296.80	1.00855	1.03726	1.19543	0	1	0.50000	510
219	912.06	1137.65	1.00000	1.28672	1.28672	0	0	0.33333	220
220	259.99	319.59	1.00717	1.06833	1.06854	1	0	0.80000	90
221	8992.25	10743.60	1.03058	1.05344	1.36599	0	1	0.45455	650
222	339.88	428.82	1.20245	1.23939	1.23939	0	1	0.37500	165
223	833.66	859.74	1.05191	1.06098	6.04598	1	0	0.33333	450
224	4833.82	6225.04	1.00000	1.06601	1.37437	0	0	0.53333	520
225	271.94	223.89	1.01232	1.03402	1.10971	− 1	1	0.66667	110
226	2966.28	4433.47	1.07730	1.30852	1.51367	0	0	0.25000	720
227	577.37	701.07	1.00000	1.25713	1.25713	0	0	0.25000	150
228	10480.32	10276.29	1.02502	1.03832	1.30423	0	1	0.68750	570
229	462.39	444.19	1.04262	1.04489	1.05778	0	1	0.80000	120
230	2558.19	2741.05	1.14482	1.16483	1.19685	0	1	0.44444	365
231	2814.91	2816.73	1.02002	1.11954	1.26368	0	0	0.54545	540
232	119.81	122.16	1.00000	1.06686	1.29526	0	0	0.66667	90
233	3184.86	3373.04	1.00000	1.02879	1.35838	0	1	0.58333	240
234	473.20	548.01	1.11100	1.12516	1.12516	0	0	0.37500	130
235	400.48	496.68	1.06915	1.08216	1.18507	0	1	0.50000	90

STEP 2   Since the number of potential predictors is large, we use stepwise regression to help us select the independent variables to include in the model. The SAS stepwise regression procedure applied to the sample data resulted in the printout shown in Figure 13.31. You can see that only two of the seven variables—DOTEST (x_1) and STATUS (x_5)—were selected by the stepwise routine. Our modeling effort will now focus on these two independent variables.

FIGURE 13.31 ▶

SAS stepwise regression printout for contract cost

```
            Stepwise Procedure for Dependent Variable COST

Step 1   Variable DOTEST Entered     R-square = 0.97424702   C(p) = 15.18496446

                    DF      Sum of Squares     Mean Square        F      Prob>F

Regression          1      864035547.29525   864035547.29525   8814.50   0.0001
Error             233       22839676.680072    98024.36343379
Total             234      886875223.97532

                    Parameter       Standard         Type II
Variable            Estimate          Error    Sum of Squares        F     Prob>F

INTERCEP          20.90684416     24.36729323     72159.98186400     0.74    0.3918
DOTEST             0.92628789      0.00986614    864035547.29525   8814.50   0.0001


---------------------------------------------------------------------------------

Step 2   Variable STATUS Entered     R-square = 0.97545236   C(p) =  5.66262181

                    DF      Sum of Squares     Mean Square        F      Prob>F

Regression          2      865104526.39042   432552263.19521   4609.50   0.0001
Error             232       21770697.584902    93839.21372803
Total             234      886875223.97532

                    Parameter       Standard         Type II
Variable            Estimate          Error    Sum of Squares        F     Prob>F

INTERCEP         -20.53871363     26.81797336     55040.06386988     0.59    0.4445
DOTEST             0.93077968      0.00974453    856162794.59683   9123.72   0.0001
STATUS           166.35513274     49.28829319   1068979.0951699     11.39    0.0009


---------------------------------------------------------------------------------

All variables in the model are significant at the 0.1500 level.
No other variable met the 0.0500 significance level for entry into the model.

            Summary of Stepwise Procedure for Dependent Variable COST

          Variable           Number   Partial    Model
Step    Entered Removed        In      R**2       R**2      C(p)        F       Prob>F

  1     DOTEST                  1      0.9742    0.9742    15.1850   8814.4979   0.0001
  2     STATUS                  2      0.0012    0.9755     5.6626     11.3916   0.0009
```

A good initial choice is the complete second-order model. For one quantitative and one qualitative variable, the model has the following form:

$$E(y) = \beta_0 + \beta_1 x_1 + \beta_2 x_1^2 + \beta_3 x_5 + \beta_4 x_1 x_5 + \beta_5 x_1^2 x_5$$

where $x_1 = \text{DOTEST}$ and $x_5 = \text{STATUS}$.

STEP 3   The SAS printout for the complete second-order model is shown in Figure 13.32 on page 774. The β estimates, shaded on the printout, yield the following least squares prediction equation:

$$\hat{y} = -2.975 + .9155 x_1 + .00000072 x_1^2 - 36.725 x_5$$
$$+ .324 x_1 x_5 - .0000358 x_1^2 x_5$$

FIGURE 13.32 ▶
SAS printout for complete second-order model

Dependent Variable: COST

Analysis of Variance

Source	DF	Sum of Squares	Mean Square	F Value	Prob>F
Model	5	866723465.17	173344693.03	1969.850	0.0001
Error	229	20151758.803	87998.94674		
C Total	234	886875223.98			

Root MSE	296.64616	R-square	0.9773	
Dep Mean	1268.70217	Adj R-sq	0.9768	
C.V.	23.38186			

Parameter Estimates

Variable	DF	Parameter Estimate	Standard Error	T for H0: Parameter=0	Prob > |T|
INTERCEP	1	-2.975454	30.89143173	-0.096	0.9234
DOTEST	1	0.915530	0.02917084	31.385	0.0001
DOTEST2	1	0.000000719	0.00000340	0.211	0.8330
STATUS	1	-36.724712	74.77308250	-0.491	0.6238
STA_DOT	1	0.324213	0.11917429	2.720	0.0070
STA_DOT2	1	-0.000035759	0.00002478	-1.443	0.1504

STEP 4   Before we can make inferences about model adequacy, we should be sure that the standard regression assumptions about the random error ε are satisfied. For given values of x_1 and x_5, the random error ε has a normal distribution with mean 0, constant variance σ^2, and the errors are independent. Residual plots (not shown here) verify that these assumptions are reasonably satisfied.

   The value of MSE, shaded on Figure 13.32, is MSE = s^2 = 87,998.9. The value of Root MSE (also shaded) is s = 296.65. Our interpretation is that the complete second-order model can predict contract costs to within $2s$ = 593.3 thousand dollars of the true value.

STEP 5   To check the adequacy of the complete second-order model, we conduct the global F test. The elements of the test follow:

H_0: $\beta_1 = \beta_2 = \beta_3 = \beta_4 = \beta_5 = 0$

H_a: At least one $\beta \neq 0$

Test statistic: $F = 1,969.85$ (shaded in Figure 13.32)

p-value: $p = .0001$ (shaded in Figure 13.32)

Conclusion: The extremely small p-value indicates that the model is statistically adequate for prediction contract cost, y

Are all the terms in the model statistically significant predictors? For example, is it necessary to include the curvilinear terms, $\beta_2 x_1^2$ and $\beta_5 x_1^2 x_5$, in the model? If not, the model can be simplified by dropping these curvature terms. The hypothesis we want to test is

$$H_0: \quad \beta_2 = \beta_5 = 0$$

$$H_a: \quad \text{At least one of the curvature } \beta\text{'s is nonzero}$$

To test this subset of β's, we need to fit a second (reduced) model. The reduced model takes the form:

$$E(y) = \beta_0 + \beta_1 x_1 + \beta_3 x_5 + \beta_4 x_1 x_5$$

The SAS printout for the reduced model is shown in Figure 13.33. The SSE for the reduced model, $\text{SSE}_R = 20{,}334{,}954$ (shaded in Figure 13.33), is compared to the SSE for the complete model, $\text{SSE}_C = 20{,}151{,}759$ (shaded in Figure 13.32), using the test statistic computed as follows:

$$\text{Test Statistic:} \quad F = \frac{(\text{SSE}_R - \text{SSE}_C)/\# \ \beta\text{'s tested}}{\text{MSE}_C}$$

$$= \frac{(20{,}334{,}954 - 20{,}151{,}759)/2}{87{,}999}$$

$$= 1.04$$

FIGURE 13.33 ▶
SAS printout for reduced model

Dependent Variable: COST

Analysis of Variance

Source	DF	Sum of Squares	Mean Square	F Value	Prob>I
Model	3	866540269.49	288846756.50	3281.227	0.000
Error	231	20334954.484	88030.10599		
C Total	234	886875223.98			

Root MSE	296.69868	R-square	0.9771
Dep Mean	1268.70217	Adj R-sq	0.9768
C.V.	23.38600		

Parameter Estimates

Variable	DF	Parameter Estimate	Standard Error	T for H0: Parameter=0	Prob > |T|
INTERCEP	1	-6.428954	26.20854879	-0.245	0.8064
DOTEST	1	0.921336	0.00972347	94.754	0.0001
STATUS	1	28.670505	58.66231493	0.489	0.6255
STA_DOT	1	0.163282	0.04043122	4.039	0.0001

Rejection region: Using $\alpha = .01$, $F_{.01} \approx 4.61$ (based on 2 numerator and 229 denominator degrees of freedom)

Conclusion: Since $F = 1.04$ falls below the critical value of 4.61, we fail to reject H_0. That is, there is insufficient evidence (at $\alpha = .01$) to indicate that the curvature terms are useful predictors of construction cost, y.

The results of the nested model F test lead us to select the reduced model as the better predictor of cost. The least squares prediction equation for the reduced model is

$$\hat{y} = -6.429 + .921x_1 + 28.671x_5 + .163x_1x_5$$

Note that we cannot simplify the model any further. The t test for the interaction term, $\beta_3 x_1 x_5$ is highly significant (p-value = .0001, shaded in Figure 13.33). Thus, our best model for construction cost proposes interaction between the DOT estimate (x_1) and status (x_5) of the contract, but only a linear relationship between cost and DOT estimate.

A plot of the least squares lines for the reduced model is shown in Figure 13.34. You can see that the model proposes two straight lines (one for fixed contracts and one for competitive contracts) with different slopes. The estimated slopes of the y–x_1 lines are computed and interpreted as follows:

Competitive contracts ($x_5 = 0$):   Estimated slope = $\hat{\beta}_1$ = .921
For every $1,000 increase in DOT estimate, we estimate contract cost to increase $921.

Fixed contracts ($x_5 = 1$):   Est. slope = $\hat{\beta}_1 + \hat{\beta}_4$ = .921 + .163 = 1.084

For every $1,000 increase in DOT estimate, we estimate contract cost to increase $1,084.

FIGURE 13.34 ▶
Plot of the least squares line for the reduced model

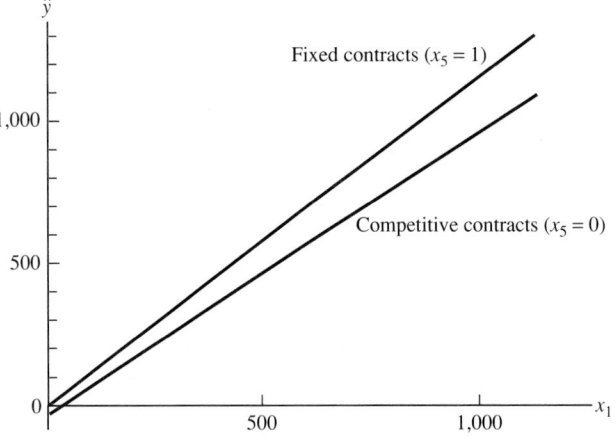

Before deciding to use the interaction model for estimation and/or prediction (step 6), we should check R^2 and s for the model. R^2 = .9771 (shaded on Figure 13.33) indicates that nearly 98% of the variation in the sample of construction costs can be "explained" by the model. The value of s (also shaded) implies that we can predict construction cost to within about $2s$ = $2(296.7)$ = 593.40 thousand dollars of its true value using the model. Although the R^2 value is high, the large $2s$ value suggests that the predictive ability of the model might be improved by additional independent variables.

13.12   Summary

Although this chapter provides only an introduction to the very important topic of **model building**, it will enable you to construct many interesting and useful models for engineering and science phenomena. You can build on this foundation and, with experience, develop competence in this fascinating area of statistics. Successful model building requires a delicate blend of knowledge of the process being modeled, geometry, and formal statistical testing.

The first step in model building is to **identify the response variable y and the set of independent variables**. Each independent variable is then classified as either **quantitative** or **qualitative**, and **dummy variables** are defined to represent the qualitative independent variables. If the total number of independent variables is large, you may want to use **stepwise regression** to screen out those that do not seem important for the prediction of y.

When the number of independent variables is manageable, the model builder is ready to begin a systematic effort. At least **second-order models**, those containing **two-way interactions and quadratic terms** in the quantitative variables, should be considered. Remember that a model with no interaction terms implies that each of the independent variables affects the response independently of the other independent variables. Quadratic terms add curvature to the contour curves when $E(y)$ is plotted as a function of the independent variable. The F test for comparing **nested models** aids in deciding the final form of the prediction model.

Many problems can arise in regression modeling, and the intermediate steps are often tedious and frustrating. However, the end result of a careful and determined modeling effort is very rewarding—you will have a better understanding of the process generating the dependent variable y and a predictive model for y.

SUPPLEMENTARY EXERCISES

13.52   Many service stations offer self-service gasoline at reduced prices when customers pay with cash rather than credit. Suppose an oil company wants to model the mean monthly gasoline sales, $E(y)$, of its affiliated stations as a function of the type of service they offer: cash only, cash or credit (same price), cash or credit (cash at reduced price).

 a. How many dummy variables will be needed to describe the qualitative independent variable Type of service?

 b. Write the main effects model relating $E(y)$ to the type of service. Describe the coding of the dummy variables.

13.53   To model the relationship between y, a dependent variable, and x, an independent variable, a researcher has taken one measurement on y at each of three different x values. Drawing on his mathematical expertise, the researcher realizes that he can fit the second-order polynomial model

$$E(y) = \beta_0 + \beta_1 x + \beta_2 x^2$$

and it will pass exactly through all three points, yielding SSE $= 0$. The researcher, delighted with the "excellent" fit of the model, eagerly sets out to use it to make inferences. What problems will he encounter in attempting to make inferences?

13.54   Many companies must accurately estimate their costs before a job is begun in order to acquire a contract and make a profit. For example, a heating and plumbing contractor may base cost estimates for new homes on the total area of the house and whether central air conditioning is to be installed.

   a. Write a main effects model relating the mean cost of material and labor, $E(y)$, to the area and central air conditioning variables.

   b. Write a complete second-order model for the mean cost as a function of the same two variables.

   c. What hypothesis would you test to determine whether the second-order terms are useful for predicting mean cost?

   d. Refer to part **c**. The contractor samples 25 recent jobs and fits both the complete second-order model (part **b**) and the reduced main effects model (part **a**), so that a test can be conducted to determine whether the additional complexity of the second-order model is necessary. The resulting SSE and R^2 values are shown in the table. Is there sufficient evidence to conclude that the second-order terms are important for predicting the mean cost? Use $\alpha = .05$.

	SSE	R^2
Main effects	8.548	.950
Second-order	6.133	.964

13.55   One factor that must be considered in developing a shipping system that is beneficial to both the customer and the seller is time of delivery. A manufacturer of farm equipment can ship its products by either rail or truck. Quadratic models are thought to be adequate in relating time of delivery to distance traveled for both modes of transportation. Consequently, it has been suggested that the following model be fit:

$$E(y) = \beta_0 + \beta_1 x_1 + \beta_2 x_1^2 + \beta_3 x_2 + \beta_4 x_1 x_2 + \beta_5 x_1^2 x_2$$

where

   $y = $ Shipping time

   $x_1 = $ Distance to be shipped

   $x_2 = \begin{cases} 1 & \text{if rail} \\ 0 & \text{if truck} \end{cases}$

   a. What hypothesis would you test to determine whether the data indicate that the quadratic distance terms are useful in the model, i.e., whether curvature is present in the relationship between mean delivery time and distance?

   b. What hypothesis would you test to determine whether there is a difference between mean delivery times by rail and truck?

c. Refer to part **b**. Suppose the model is fit to a total of 50 observations on delivery time. The sum of squared errors is SSE = 226.12. Then, the reduced model

$$E(y) = \beta_0 + \beta_1 x_1 + \beta_2 x_1^2$$

is fit to the same data, and SSE = 259.34. Test to determine whether the data indicate that the mean delivery time differs for rail and truck deliveries. Use $\alpha = .05$.

13.56 One of the most promising methods for extracting crude oil employs a carbon dioxide (CO_2) flooding technique. CO_2, when flooded into oil pockets, enhances oil recovery by displacing the crude oil. In a microscopic investigation of the CO_2 flooding process, flow tubes were dipped into sample oil pockets containing a known amount of oil (*Journal of Petroleum Technology*, Aug. 1982). The oil pockets were flooded with CO_2 and the percentage of oil displaced was recorded. The experiment was conducted at three different flow pressures and three different dipping angles. The displacement test data are recorded in the accompanying table.

Pressure x_1, pounds per square inch	Dipping Angle x_2, degrees	Oil Recovery y, percentage
1,000	0	60.58
1,000	15	72.72
1,000	30	79.99
1,500	0	66.83
1,500	15	80.78
1,500	30	89.78
2,000	0	69.18
2,000	15	80.31
2,000	30	91.99

Source: Wang, G. C. "Microscopic investigation of CO_2 flooding process." *Journal of Petroleum Technology*, Vol. 34, No. 8, Aug. 1982, pp. 1789–1797.

a. Write the complete second-order model relating percentage oil recovery y to pressure x_1 and dipping angle x_2.
b. Plot the sample data on a scattergram, with percentage oil recovery y on the vertical axis and pressure x_1 on the horizontal axis. Connect the points corresponding to the same value of dipping angle x_2. Based on the scattergram, do you believe a complete second-order model is appropriate?
c. The SAS printout for the interaction model

$$y = \beta_0 + \beta_1 x_1 + \beta_2 x_2 + \beta_3 x_1 x_2 + \varepsilon$$

is provided on page 780. Give the prediction equation for this model.
d. Construct a plot similar to the scattergram of part **b**, but use the predicted values from the interaction model on the vertical axis. Compare the two plots. Do you believe the interaction model will provide an adequate fit?
e. Check model adequacy using a statistical test with $\alpha = .05$.
f. Is there evidence of interaction between pressure x_1 and dipping angle x_2? Test using $\alpha = .05$.

SAS printout for Exercise 13.56

Dependent Variable: Y

Analysis of Variance

Source	DF	Sum of Squares	Mean Square	F Value	Prob>F
Model	3	843.19083	281.06361	44.670	0.0005
Error	5	31.45997	6.29199		
C Total	8	874.65080			

Root MSE	2.50838	R-square	0.9640
Dep Mean	76.90667	Adj R-sq	0.9425
C.V.	3.26160		

Parameter Estimates

Variable	DF	Parameter Estimate	Standard Error	T for H0: Parameter=0	Prob > |T|
INTERCEP	1	54.500000	5.03415841	10.826	0.0001
X1	1	0.007697	0.00323831	2.377	0.0634
X2	1	0.554111	0.25996282	2.132	0.0862
X1X2	1	0.000113	0.00016723	0.678	0.5280

13.57 A 40-year-old masonry duplex structure has recently undergone a passive solar retrofit with features including insulated exterior walls, heat distribution systems, storm sashes, and air-lock entries. To gauge the effectiveness of the improvements, architectural engineers monitored the winter energy usage of the structure for 2 years prior to the retrofit and for 2 years after the retrofit. The engineers want to use the data to fit a regression model relating monthly energy usage y (therms per billing day) to weather intensity x_1 (ddh/bd) and x_2, where

$$x_2 = \begin{cases} 1 & \text{if prior to retrofit} \\ 0 & \text{if after retrofit} \end{cases}$$

a. Write the complete second-order model for $E(y)$.
b. Graph the contour lines for the model of part **a**.
c. Hypothesize a first-order model that allows for a constant difference between the mean monthly usage prior to and after the retrofit at different levels of weather intensity.
d. Graph the contour lines for the model of part **c**.

13.58 Researchers conducted an analysis of bus travel demand in Albuquerque, New Mexico, a city selected because of its unique multicentered "Sun Tran" public transit system (*Transportation Quarterly*, Jan. 1983). One aspect of the study involved the development of a multiple regression model for predicting y, the home-origin trip rate (that is, the number of home-origin trips per 1,000 residents) of a Sun Tran subzone urban area. The following five independent variables, all designed to measure transit level of service (travel time), were entered into the model as main effects:

x_1 = Composite in-vehicle travel time to reach major destination (minutes)

x_2 = Composite transit wait time (minutes)

x_3 = Composite number of transfers required to reach major destination

x_4 = Number of transit routes serving the Sun Tran zone

$$x_5 = \begin{cases} 1 & \text{if Sun Tran zone at end of major regional transportation corridor} \\ 0 & \text{if not} \end{cases}$$

Data collected from a survey of the city's bus passengers in each of 298 Sun Tran planning analysis zones were used to fit the model

$$E(y) = \beta_0 + \beta_1 x_1 + \beta_2 x_2 + \beta_3 x_3 + \beta_4 x_4 + \beta_5 x_5$$

with the results shown in the accompanying SAS printout.

```
Dependent Variable: Y


                            Analysis of Variance

                            Sum of          Mean
         Source       DF    Squares        Square      F Value      Prob>F

         Model         5     32774        6554.80       87.533      0.0001
         Error       292     21866          74.88
         C Total     297     54660


            Root MSE        8.6535       R-square        0.5996
                                         Adj R-sq        0.5927

                            Parameter Estimates

                        Parameter      Standard     T for H0:
         Variable  DF    Estimate         Error     Parameter=0    Prob > |T|

         INTERCEP   1     22.0189
         X1         1     -0.1807        0.0389        -4.645        0.0001
         X2         1     -0.2498        0.1207        -2.070        0.0384
         X3         1     -4.6910        1.7020        -2.756        0.0058
         X4         1      3.6745        0.4027         9.125        0.0001
         X5         1     22.5201        3.5959         6.263        0.0001
```

a. Write the least squares prediction equation.
b. Compute and interpret the value of R^2.
c. Compute and interpret the value of s.
d. Is the model useful for predicting home-origin trip rate y? Test using $\alpha = .05$.
e. Is there evidence that home-origin trip rate y decreases as in-vehicle travel time x_1 increases and the remaining independent variables are held constant? Test using $\alpha = .05$.
f. Construct a 95% confidence interval for β_4. Interpret the interval.

13.59 A company is studying three different safety programs, A, B, and C, in an attempt to reduce the number of work-hours lost because of accidents. Each program is to be tried at three of the company's nine factories. The plan is to monitor the lost work-hours, y, for a 1-year period beginning 6 months after the new safety program is instituted.

a. Write a main effects model relating $E(y)$ to the lost work-hours, x_1, the year before the plan is instituted and to the type of program that is instituted.
b. In terms of the model parameters from part **a**, what hypothesis would you test to determine whether the mean work-hours lost differ for the three safety programs?

13.60 Refer to Exercise 13.59. After the three safety programs have been in effect for 18 months, the complete main effects model is fit to the $n = 9$ data points. Using safety program A as the base level, the following results are obtained:

$$\hat{y} = -2.1 + .88x_1 - 150x_2 + 35x_3 \qquad SSE = 1,527.27$$

Then the reduced model $E(y) = \beta_0 + \beta_1 x_1$ is fit, with the result

$$\hat{y} = 15.3 + .84x_1 \qquad SSE = 3,113.14$$

Test to determine whether the mean work-hours lost differ for the three programs. Use $\alpha = .05$.

OPTIONAL SUPPLEMENTARY EXERCISES

[*Note:* These exercises require the use of a computer.]

13.61   In any production process in which one or more workers are engaged in a variety of tasks, the total time spent in production varies as a function of the size of the workpool and the level of output of the various activities. For example, in a large metropolitan department store, the number of hours worked (y) per day by the clerical staff may depend on the following variables:

x_1 = Number of pieces of mail processed (open, sort, etc.)

x_2 = Number of money orders and gift certificates sold

x_3 = Number of window payments (customer charge accounts) transacted

x_4 = Number of change order transactions processed

x_5 = Number of checks cashed

x_6 = Number of pieces of miscellaneous mail processed on "as available" basis

x_7 = Number of bus tickets sold

The accompanying table gives the output counts for these activities on each of 52 working days.
a. Conduct a stepwise regression analysis of the data using the computer. (*Note:* The data are available on a 3½″ micro diskette from the publisher.)
b. Interpret the β estimates in the resulting stepwise model.
c. What are the dangers with drawing inferences from the stepwise model?

Obs.	Day of Week	y	x_1	x_2	x_3	x_4	x_5	x_6	x_7
1	M	128.5	7,781	100	886	235	644	56	737
2	T	113.6	7,004	110	962	388	589	57	1,029
3	W	146.6	7,267	61	1,342	398	1,081	59	830
4	Th	124.3	2,129	102	1,153	457	891	57	1,468
5	F	100.4	4,878	45	803	577	537	49	335
6	S	119.2	3,999	144	1,127	345	563	64	918
7	M	109.5	11,777	123	627	326	402	60	335
8	T	128.5	5,764	78	748	161	495	57	962
9	W	131.2	7,392	172	876	219	823	62	665
10	Th	112.2	8,100	126	685	287	555	86	577
11	F	95.4	4,736	115	436	235	456	38	214
12	S	124.6	4,337	110	899	127	573	73	484
13	M	103.7	3,079	96	570	180	428	59	456

(*continued*)

Obs.	Day of Week	y	x_1	x_2	x_3	x_4	x_5	x_6	x_7
14	T	103.6	7,273	51	826	118	463	53	907
15	W	133.2	4,091	116	1,060	206	961	67	951
16	Th	111.4	3,390	70	957	284	745	77	1,446
17	F	97.7	6,319	58	559	220	539	41	440
18	S	132.1	7,447	83	1,050	174	553	63	1,133
19	M	135.9	7,100	80	568	124	428	55	456
20	T	131.3	8,035	115	709	174	498	78	968
21	W	150.4	5,579	83	568	223	683	79	660
22	Th	124.9	4,338	78	900	115	556	84	555
23	F	97.0	6,895	18	442	118	479	41	203
24	S	114.1	3,629	133	644	155	505	57	781
25	M	88.3	5,149	92	389	124	405	59	236
26	T	117.6	5,241	110	612	222	477	55	616
27	W	128.2	2,917	69	1,057	378	970	80	1,210
28	Th	138.8	4,390	70	974	195	1,027	81	1,452
29	F	109.5	4,957	24	783	358	893	51	616
30	S	118.9	7,099	130	1,419	374	609	62	957
31	M	122.2	7,337	128	1,137	238	461	51	968
32	T	142.8	8,301	115	946	191	771	74	719
33	W	133.9	4,889	86	750	214	513	69	489
34	Th	100.2	6,308	81	461	132	430	49	341
35	F	116.8	6,908	145	864	164	549	57	902
36	S	97.3	5,345	116	604	127	360	48	126
37	M	98.0	6,994	59	714	107	473	53	726
38	T	136.5	6,781	78	917	171	805	74	1,100
39	W	111.7	3,142	106	809	335	702	70	1,721
40	Th	98.6	5,738	27	546	126	455	52	502
41	F	116.2	4,931	174	891	129	481	71	737
42	S	108.9	6,501	69	643	129	334	47	473
43	M	120.6	5,678	94	828	107	384	52	1,083
44	T	131.8	4,619	100	777	164	834	67	841
45	W	112.4	1,832	124	626	158	571	71	627
46	Th	92.5	5,445	52	432	121	458	42	313
47	F	120.0	4,123	84	432	153	544	42	654
48	S	112.2	5,884	89	1,061	100	391	31	280
49	M	113.0	5,505	45	562	84	444	36	814
50	T	138.7	2,882	94	601	139	799	44	907
51	W	122.1	2,395	89	637	201	747	30	1,666
52	Th	86.6	6,847	14	810	230	547	40	614

Source: Adapted from *Work Measurement*, by G. L. Smith, Grid Publishing Co., Columbus, Ohio, 1978, (Table 3–1).

13.62 The data in the table were obtained from an experiment designed to investigate the relationship between the yield, y, of potatoes and the levels of three minerals in the soil, x_1, x_2, and x_3. [*Note:* The mineral levels have been coded by subtracting an appropriate constant from each of the x values.]

y	x_1	x_2	x_3	y	x_1	x_2	x_3
16.40	−1	−1	−1	2.75	1	1	1
13.51	1	−1	−1	14.33	−1.682	0	0
14.41	−1	1	−1	5.44	1.682	0	0
9.38	1	1	−1	19.80	0	−1.682	0
10.77	−1	−1	1	20.00	0	1.682	0
11.78	1	−1	1	9.37	0	0	−1.682
4.11	−1	1	1	10.03	0	0	1.682

a. Fit a second-order polynomial,

$$y = \beta_0 + \beta_1 x_1 + \beta_2 x_2 + \beta_3 x_3 + \beta_4 x_1 x_2 + \beta_5 x_1 x_3 + \beta_6 x_2 x_3 + \beta_7 x_1^2 + \beta_8 x_2^2 + \beta_9 x_3^2 + \varepsilon$$

by least squares.

b. Test the hypothesis $H_0: \beta_4 = \beta_5 = \cdots = \beta_9 = 0$. That is, test whether the data provide sufficient evidence to indicate that a second-order model contributes more information for the prediction of yield than a first-order model. Test using $\alpha = .05$.

13.63 Five varieties of peas are currently being tested in Ohio to determine which is best suited for production in that state. A field was divided into 20 plots, with each variety of peas being planted in four plots. The yields in bushels of peas produced from each plot are shown in the accompanying table.

Variety of Peas

A	B	C	D	E
26.2	29.2	29.1	21.3	20.1
24.3	28.1	30.8	22.4	19.3
21.8	27.3	33.9	24.3	19.9
28.1	31.2	32.8	21.8	22.1

a. Write a model for the data to reflect the yield in bushels as a function of pea variety, and interpret all parameters in the model.

b. Fit the proposed model to the data.

c. Do the data provide sufficient evidence to indicate that the model is useful for predicting harvest yield? Use $\alpha = .05$.

13.64 Refer to Exercise 13.49. The data used to fit the operations manager's complete and reduced models are displayed in the table.

Down Time hours per month	Machine Age x_1, years	Machine Type	x_2	Down Time hours per month	Machine Age x_1, years	Machine Type	x_2
10	1.0	001	1	10	2.0	002	0
20	2.0	001	1	20	4.0	002	0
30	2.7	001	1	30	5.0	002	0
40	4.1	001	1	44	8.0	002	0
9	1.2	001	1	9	2.4	002	0
25	2.5	001	1	25	5.1	002	0

(continued)

Down Time hours per month	Machine Age x_1, years	Machine Type	x_2	Down Time hours per month	Machine Age x_1, years	Machine Type	x_2
19	1.9	001	1	20	3.5	002	0
41	5.0	001	1	42	7.0	002	0
22	2.1	001	1	20	4.0	002	0
12	1.1	001	1	13	2.1	002	0

a. Use these data to test the null hypothesis that $\beta_1 = \beta_2 = 0$. Test using $\alpha = .10$.
b. Interpret the results of the test in the context of the problem.

13.65 A firm has developed a new type of light bulb and is interested in evaluating its performance to decide whether to market the bulb. It is known that the level of light output of the bulb depends on the cleanliness of its surface area and the length of time the bulb has been in operation. The data are presented in the accompanying table. Use these data and the procedures you learned in this chapter to build a regression model that relates drop in light output to bulb surface cleanliness and length of operation.

Drop in Light Output percent original output	Bulb Surface C = Clean, D = Dirty	Length of Operation hours
0	C	0
16	C	400
22	C	800
27	C	1,200
32	C	1,600
36	C	2,000
38	C	2,400
0	D	0
4	D	400
6	D	800
8	D	1,200
9	D	1,600
11	D	2,000
12	D	2,400

COMPUTER LAB: Stepwise Regression

Both the SAS and MINITAB statistical software packages have routines for performing a stepwise regression. The sample programs in this section give the commands for conducting a stepwise regression in the bid-rigging example of Section 13.11.

SAS

Command
line

1	DATA BIDRIG;
2	INPUT COST DOTEST B2B1RAT B3B1RAT BHB1RAT 〉 Data entry commands
	STATUS DISTRICT BTPRATIO DAYSEST;
3	CARDS;
	1379.43 1386.29 1.01397 1.03303 1.06121 1 0 .333 250 ⎫
	. . . . ⎬ Input data values
	. . . . ⎪ (1 observation per line)
	400.48 496.68 1.06915 1.08216 1.18507 0 1 .500 90 ⎭
4	PROC REG;
5	MODEL COST=DOTEST B2B1RAT B3B1RAT BHB1RAT STATUS ⎫
	DISTRICT BTPRATIO DAYSEST/STEPWISE; ⎬ Stepwise regression

COMMANDS 4–5   The REG procedure with the /STEPWISE option conducts a stepwise regression analysis of the independent variables listed on the MODEL statement.

NOTE   The output for this SAS program is displayed in Figure 13.31.

MINITAB

Command
line

1	READ Y IN C1, PREDICTORS IN C2-C9 Data entry instruction
	1379.43 1386.29 1.01397 1.03303 1.06121 1 0 .333 250 ⎫
	. . . . ⎬ Input data values
	. . . . ⎪ (1 obs. per line)
	400.48 496.68 1.06915 1.08216 1.18507 0 1 .500 90 ⎭
2	NAME C1='COST' C2='DOTEST' C3='B2B1RAT' C4='B3B1RAT' C5='BHB1RAT'
3	NAME C6='STATUS' C7='DISTRICT' C8='BTPRATIO' C9='DAYSEST'
4	STEPWISE C1, ON PREDICTORS C2-C9 Stepwise regression

COMMAND 4   The STEPWISE command conducts a stepwise regression of the independent variables in the columns listed. Note that the column for the dependent variable must be listed first.

NOTE   The output for this MINITAB program is displayed in Figure 13.35.

FIGURE 13.35 ▶
MINITAB output for Computer Lab

```
STEPWISE REGRESSION OF    COST    ON   8 PREDICTORS, WITH N =   235

       STEP         1         2
   CONSTANT     20.91    -20.54

     DOTEST    0.9263    0.9308
    T-RATIO     93.89     95.52

     STATUS                 166
    T-RATIO                3.38

          S       313       306
       R-SQ     97.42     97.55
```

References

Daniel, C., and Wood, F. *Fitting Equations to Data*, 2nd ed. New York: Wiley, 1980.

Draper, N., and Smith, H. *Applied Regression Analysis*, 2nd ed. New York: Wiley, 1981.

Graybill, F. A. *Theory and Application of the Linear Model*. North Scituate, Mass.: Duxbury, 1976.

Mendenhall, W. *Introduction to Linear Models and the Design and Analysis of Experiments*. Belmont, Calif.: Wadsworth, 1968.

Mendenhall, W., and Sincich, T. *A Second Course in Business Statistics: Regression Analysis*, 4th ed. New York: Macmillan, 1993.

Neter, J., Wasserman, W., and Kutner, M. H. *Applied Linear Statistical Models*, 3rd ed. Homewood, Ill.: Irwin, 1988.

CHAPTER FOURTEEN

....

Analysis of Variance for Designed Experiments

Objective

....

To present a method for analyzing multivariable designed experiments; to identify its overlapping features with and its relation to regression analysis

Contents

....

14.1   Introduction

In Chapters 12–13, we learned how to analyze multivariable sample data using a multiple regression analysis. The data for regression can be collected **observationally** (where the values of the independent variables are uncontrolled) or **experimentally** (where the values of the *x*'s are controlled). With observational data, however, there is a caveat: A *statistically significant relationship between a response y and a predictor x does not imply a cause-and-effect relationship!* Since the values of other relevant independent variables—both those in the model and those omitted from the model— are uncontrolled, we are unsure whether it is these other variables or *x* that is causing the increase (or decrease) in *y*.

To illustrate, consider the data in Table 14.1 on monthly new home sales, *y*, of a residential builder and the number, *x*, of salespeople on staff. Obviously, sales (*y*) increases with number of salespeople (*x*) on staff. But does this imply that the builder need only hire more salespeople to increase new home sales? Common sense says no. More likely, there are other (unrecorded) variables that are causing the increase in new home sales (e.g., lower interest rates, lower sale prices), and the builder is hiring more salespeople to keep up with monthly demand. In other words, an unmeasured variable, demand, is causing both *y and x* to increase.

TABLE 14.1   New Home Sales Data

Month	Sales y	Number of Salespeople x
1	2	1
2	4	2
3	8	3
4	11	5
5	12	6
6	15	8

This caveat can be overcome by controlling the values of all the relevant *x*'s via a planned experiment. With experimental data, we usually select the *x*'s so that we can compare the mean responses, $E(y)$, for several different combinations of the *x* values. The procedure for selecting the sample data is called the **design of the experiment**. The statistical procedure for comparing the population means is called an **analysis of variance**.

14.2   Experimental Design: Terminology

The study of experimental design originated in England and, in its early years, was associated solely with agricultural experimentation. The need for experimental design in agriculture was very clear: It takes a full year to obtain a single observation on the yield of a new variety of wheat. Consequently, the need to save time and money led to a study of ways to obtain more information using smaller samples. Similar motivations led to its subsequent acceptance and wide use in all fields of scientific experimentation. Despite this fact, the terminology associated with experimental design clearly indicates its early association with the biological sciences.

Independent variables that may be related to a response variable y are called **factors**. The value—that is, the intensity setting—assumed by a factor in an experiment is called a **level**. For example, suppose that an experiment is conducted to measure the hardness y of a new type of plastic as a function of two factors, the pressure and temperature at the time of molding. If the hardness of the plastic is measured at pressures 200, 300, and 400 pounds per square inch (psi) and at temperatures 200 and 300 degrees Fahrenheit (°F), then pressure is at three levels and temperature is at two levels. The combinations of levels of the factors for which y will be observed are called **treatments**. For example, if the hardness of the new plastic is measured for each of the six pressure–temperature combinations, (200 psi, 200°F), (300 psi, 200°F), (400 psi, 200°F), (200 psi, 300°F), (300 psi, 300°F), and (400 psi, 300°F), then the experiment would involve six treatments. The term *treatments* is used to describe the factor–level combinations to be included in an experiment because many experiments involve treating or doing something to alter the nature of the **experimental unit**, the object upon which a measurement is made. Thus, we might view the six pressure–temperature combinations as treatments of the experimental units of plastic used in the hardness experiment.

Definition 14.1

The independent variables that are related to a response variable y are called **factors**.

Definition 14.2

The intensity setting of a factor is called a **level**.

> **Definition 14.3**
>
> A **treatment** is a particular combination of levels of the factors involved in an experiment.

The design of an experiment involves the following four steps:

STEP 1 Select the factors to be included in the experiment, and identify the parameters that are the object of the study. Usually, the target parameters are the population means associated with the factor–level combinations (i.e., treatments).

STEP 2 Choose the treatments (the factor–level combinations) to be included in the experiment.

STEP 3 Determine the number of observations (sample size) to be made for each treatment. (This will usually depend on the standard error(s) that you desire.)

STEP 4 Plan how the treatments will be assigned to the experimental units. That is, decide on which design to use.

By following these steps, you can control the quantity of information in an experiment. We shall explain how this is done in Section 14.3.

14.3   Controlling the Information in an Experiment

The problem of acquiring good experimental data is analogous to the problem faced by a communications engineer. The receipt of any signal, verbal or otherwise, depends on the volume of the signal and the amount of the background noise. The greater the volume of the signal, the greater will be the amount of information transmitted to the receiver. Conversely, the amount of information transmitted is reduced when the background noise is great. These intuitive thoughts about the factors that affect the information in an experiment are supported by the following fact: The standard errors of most estimators are proportional to σ (a measure of data variation or noise) and inversely proportional to the square root of the sample size (a measure of the volume of the signal). To illustrate, take the simple case where we wish to estimate a population mean μ by the sample mean $\bar{y}$. The standard error of the sampling distribution of $\bar{y}$ is

$$\sigma_{\bar{y}} = \frac{\sigma}{\sqrt{n}} \qquad \text{(See Section 7.5)}$$

Note that, for a fixed sample size n, the smaller the value of σ, which measures the **variability (noise)** in the population of measurements, the smaller will be the standard error $\sigma_{\bar{y}}$. Similarly, by increasing the sample size n (**volume of the signal**) in a given experiment, you decrease $\sigma_{\bar{y}}$.

Steps 1–3 in the design of an experiment (see Section 14.2) determine the volume of nature's signal. You must select the treatments so that the observed values of y provide information on the parameters of interest. Then the larger the treatment sample sizes, the greater will be the quantity of information in the experiment. (An example of a volume-increasing design is presented in Section 14.5.)

Is it possible to observe y and obtain no information on a parameter of interest? The answer is yes. To illustrate, suppose that you attempt to fit a first-order model

$$E(y) = \beta_0 + \beta_1 x$$

to a set of $n = 10$ data points, all of which were observed for a single value of x, say, $x = 5$. The data points might appear as shown in Figure 14.1. Clearly, there is no possibility of fitting a line to these data points. The only way to obtain information on β_0 and β_1 is to observe y for *different* values of x. Consequently, the $n = 10$ data points in this example contain absolutely no information on the parameters β_0 and β_1.

FIGURE 14.1 ▶
Data set with $n = 10$ responses, all at $x = 5$

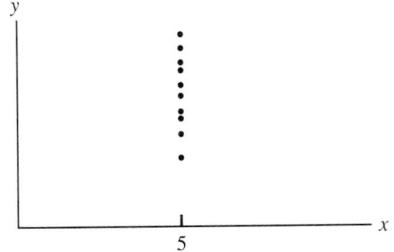

Step 4 in the design of an experiment provides an opportunity to reduce the noise (or experimental error) in an experiment. As we illustrate in Section 14.4, known sources of data variation can be reduced or eliminated by **blocking**—that is, observing all treatments within relatively homogeneous **blocks** of experimental material. When the treatments are compared within each block, any background noise produced by the block is canceled, or eliminated, allowing us to obtain better estimates of treatment differences.

Summary of Steps in Experimental Design

Volume-increasing: 1. Select the factors.
  2. Choose the treatments (factor–level combinations).
  3. Determine the sample size for each treatment.
Noise-reducing: 4. Assign the treatments to the experimental units.

In summary, it is useful to think of experimental designs as being either "noise reducers" or "volume increasers." We will learn, however, that most designs are multifunctional. That is, they tend to both reduce noise and increase the volume of the signal at the same time. Nevertheless, we will find that specific designs tend to lean heavily toward one or the other objective.

14.4   Noise-Reducing Designs

Noise reduction in an experimental design, i.e., the removal of extraneous experimental variation, can be accomplished by an appropriate assignment of treatments to the experimental units. The idea is to compare treatments within blocks of relatively homogeneous experimental units. The most common of this type is called a **randomized block design**.

To illustrate, suppose we want to compare the mean length of time required to assemble a digital watch using three different methods of assembly, A, B, and C. Thus, we want to compare the three means μ_A, μ_B, and μ_C, where μ_i is the mean assembly time for method i. One way to design the experiment is to select 15 workers (where the workers are the experimental units) and randomly assign one of the three assembly methods (treatments) to each worker. A diagram of this design, called a **completely randomized design** (since the treatments are randomly assigned to the experimental units) is shown in Table 14.2.

TABLE 14.2 Completely Randomized Design with $p = 3$ Treatments	
Worker	Treatment (Method) Assigned
1	B
2	A
3	B
4	C
5	C
6	A
7	B
8	C
9	A
10	A
11	C
12	A
13	B
14	C
15	B

> **Definition 14.4**
>
> A **completely randomized design** to compare p treatments is one in which the treatments are randomly assigned to the experimental units.

This design has the obvious disadvantage that the assembly times would vary greatly from worker to worker depending on manual dexterity, experience, etc. A better design—one that contains more information on the mean assembly times—would be to use only five workers and have each worker assemble three digital watches using each of the three methods. This *randomized block* procedure acknowledges the fact that the length of time required to assemble a watch varies substantially from worker to worker. By comparing the three assembly times for each worker, we eliminate worker-to-worker variation from the comparison.

The randomized block design that we have just described is shown diagrammatically in Figure 14.2. The figure shows that there are five workers. Each worker can be viewed as a **block** of three experimental units—watches assembled—one corresponding to the use of each of the assembly methods, A, B, and C. The blocks are said to be **randomized** because the treatments (assembly methods) are randomly assigned to the experimental units within a block. For our example, the watches would be assembled in a random order to avoid bias introduced by other unknown and unmeasured variables that may affect the assembly time.

In general, a randomized block design to compare p treatments will contain b relatively homogeneous blocks, with each block containing p experimental units. Each treatment appears once in every block with the p treatments randomly assigned to the experimental units within each block.

FIGURE 14.2 ▶

Diagram for a randomized block design containing $b = 5$ blocks and $p = 3$ treatments

Blocks (Workers)	Treatments (Methods)		
1	B	A	C
2	A	C	B
3	B	C	A
4	A	B	C
5	A	C	B

> **Definition 14.5**
> ....
>
> A **randomized block design** to compare p treatments involves b blocks, each containing p relatively homogeneous experimental units. The p treatments are randomly assigned to the experimental units within each block, with one experimental unit assigned per treatment.

EXAMPLE 14.1

Suppose you want to compare the abilities of four Department of Transportation (DOT) engineers, A, B, C, D, to estimate the cost of road construction contracts. One way to make the comparison would be to randomly allocate a number of road contracts— say, 40—10 to each of the four DOT engineers. Each engineer would then estimate the cost y of each contract. The treatment allocation to experimental units that we have described is a completely randomized design.

a. Discuss the problems that result when the completely randomized design is used for this experiment.

b. Explain how you would employ a randomized block design.

Solution

a. The problem with using a completely randomized design for the DOT experiment is that comparison of mean construction costs will be influenced by the nature of the road contracts. Some contracts will be easier to estimate than others, and the variation in costs that can be attributed to this fact will make it more difficult to compare treatment means.

b. To eliminate contract-to-contract variability in comparing mean engineers' estimates, you would select only 10 road contracts and require each DOT engineer to estimate the cost of each of the 10 contracts. Although in this case there is probably no need for randomization, it might be desirable to randomly assign the order (in time) of the estimates. This randomized block design, consisting of $p = 4$ treatments and $b = 10$ blocks would appear as shown in Figure 14.3.

FIGURE 14.3 ▶
Diagram for a randomized block design: Example 14.1

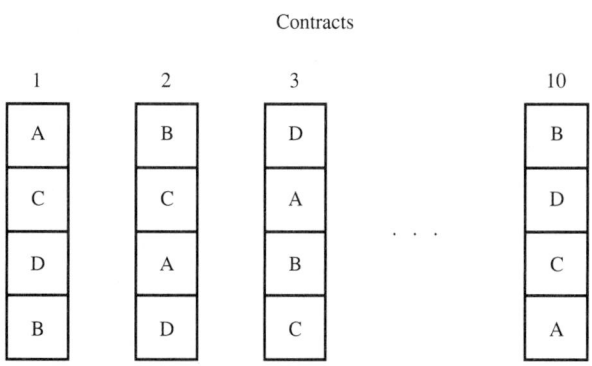

Contracts

Each experimental design can be represented by a general linear model relating the response y to the factors (treatments, blocks, etc.) in the experiment. When the factors are qualitative in nature (as is often the case), the model includes dummy variables. For example, consider the completely randomized design portrayed in Table 14.2. Since the experiment involves three treatments (methods), we require two dummy variables. The model for this completely randomized design would appear as follows:

$$y = \beta_0 + \beta_1 x_1 + \beta_2 x_2 + \varepsilon$$

where

$$x_1 = \begin{cases} 1 & \text{if method A} \\ 0 & \text{if not} \end{cases}$$

$$x_2 = \begin{cases} 1 & \text{if method B} \\ 0 & \text{if not} \end{cases}$$

Note that we have arbitrarily selected method C as the base level. From our discussion of dummy-variable models in Chapter 13 we know that the mean responses for the three methods are:

$$\mu_A = \beta_0 + \beta_1$$
$$\mu_B = \beta_0 + \beta_2$$
$$\mu_C = \beta_0$$

Recall that $\beta_1 = \mu_A - \mu_C$ and $\beta_2 = \mu_B - \mu_C$. Thus, to estimate the differences between the treatment means, we require estimates of β_1 and β_2.

Similarly, we can write the model for the randomized block design in Figure 14.2 as follows:

$$y = \beta_0 + \underbrace{\beta_1 x_1 + \beta_2 x_2}_{\substack{\text{Treatment} \\ \text{effects}}} + \underbrace{\beta_3 x_3 + \beta_4 x_4 + \beta_5 x_5 + \beta_6 x_6}_{\text{Block effects}} + \varepsilon$$

where

$$x_1 = \begin{cases} 1 & \text{if method A} \\ 0 & \text{if not} \end{cases} \qquad x_2 = \begin{cases} 1 & \text{if method B} \\ 0 & \text{if not} \end{cases} \qquad x_3 = \begin{cases} 1 & \text{if worker 1} \\ 0 & \text{if not} \end{cases}$$

$$x_4 = \begin{cases} 1 & \text{if worker 2} \\ 0 & \text{if not} \end{cases} \qquad x_5 = \begin{cases} 1 & \text{if worker 3} \\ 0 & \text{if not} \end{cases} \qquad x_6 = \begin{cases} 1 & \text{if worker 4} \\ 0 & \text{if not} \end{cases}$$

In addition to the treatment terms, the model includes four dummy variables representing the five blocks (workers). Note that we have arbitrarily selected worker 5 as the base level. Using this model, we can write each response y in the experiment of Figure 14.2 as a function of β's, as shown in Table 14.3 on page 798.

For example, to obtain the model for the response y for method A and worker 1 (denoted y_{A1}), we substitute $x_1 = 1$, $x_2 = 0$, $x_3 = 1$, $x_4 = 0$, $x_5 = 0$, and $x_6 = 0$ into the equation. The resulting model is

$$y_{A1} = \beta_0 + \beta_1 + \beta_3 + \varepsilon_{A1}$$

TABLE 14.3   The Response for the Randomized Block Design Shown in Figure 14.2

Blocks (Workers)	Treatments (Methods)		
	A $(x_1 = 1, x_2 = 0)$	B $(x_1 = 0, x_2 = 1)$	C $(x_1 = 0, x_2 = 0)$
1 $(x_3 = 1, x_4 = x_5 = x_6 = 0)$	$y_{A1} = \beta_0 + \beta_1 + \beta_3 + \varepsilon_{A1}$	$y_{B1} = \beta_0 + \beta_2 + \beta_3 + \varepsilon_{B1}$	$y_{C1} = \beta_0 + \beta_3 + \varepsilon_{C1}$
2 $(x_4 = 1, x_3 = x_5 = x_6 = 0)$	$y_{A2} = \beta_0 + \beta_1 + \beta_4 + \varepsilon_{A2}$	$y_{B2} = \beta_0 + \beta_2 + \beta_4 + \varepsilon_{B2}$	$y_{C2} = \beta_0 + \beta_4 + \varepsilon_{C2}$
3 $(x_5 = 1, x_3 = x_4 = x_6 = 0)$	$y_{A3} = \beta_0 + \beta_1 + \beta_5 + \varepsilon_{A3}$	$y_{B3} = \beta_0 + \beta_2 + \beta_5 + \varepsilon_{B3}$	$y_{C3} = \beta_0 + \beta_5 + \varepsilon_{C3}$
4 $(x_6 = 1, x_3 = x_4 = x_5 = 0)$	$y_{A4} = \beta_0 + \beta_1 + \beta_6 + \varepsilon_{A4}$	$y_{B4} = \beta_0 + \beta_2 + \beta_6 + \varepsilon_{B4}$	$y_{C4} = \beta_0 + \beta_6 + \varepsilon_{C4}$
5 $(x_3 = x_4 = x_5 = x_6 = 0)$	$y_{A5} = \beta_0 + \beta_1 + \varepsilon_{A5}$	$y_{B5} = \beta_0 + \beta_2 + \varepsilon_{B5}$	$y_{C5} = \beta_0 + \varepsilon_{C5}$

Now we will use Table 14.3 to illustrate how a randomized block design reduces experimental noise.

Since each treatment appears in each of the five blocks, there are five measured responses per treatment. Averaging the five responses for treatment A shown in Table 14.3, we obtain

$$\bar{y}_A = \frac{y_{A1} + y_{A2} + y_{A3} + y_{A4} + y_{A5}}{5}$$

$$= [(\beta_0 + \beta_1 + \beta_3 + \varepsilon_{A1}) + (\beta_0 + \beta_1 + \beta_4 + \varepsilon_{A2}) + (\beta_0 + \beta_1 + \beta_5 + \varepsilon_{A3})$$
$$+ (\beta_0 + \beta_1 + \beta_6 + \varepsilon_{A4}) + (\beta_0 + \beta_1 + \varepsilon_{A5})]/5$$

$$= \frac{5\beta_0 + 5\beta_1 + (\beta_3 + \beta_4 + \beta_5 + \beta_6) + (\varepsilon_{A1} + \varepsilon_{A2} + \varepsilon_{A3} + \varepsilon_{A4} + \varepsilon_{A5})}{5}$$

$$= \beta_0 + \beta_1 + \frac{(\beta_3 + \beta_4 + \beta_5 + \beta_6)}{5} + \bar{\varepsilon}_A$$

Similarly, the mean responses for treatments B and C are obtained:

$$\bar{y}_B = \frac{y_{B1} + y_{B2} + y_{B3} + y_{B4} + y_{B5}}{5}$$

$$= \beta_0 + \beta_2 + \frac{(\beta_3 + \beta_4 + \beta_5 + \beta_6)}{5} + \bar{\varepsilon}_B$$

$$\bar{y}_C = \frac{y_{C1} + y_{C2} + y_{C3} + y_{C4} + y_{C5}}{5}$$

$$= \beta_0 + \frac{(\beta_3 + \beta_4 + \beta_5 + \beta_6)}{5} + \bar{\varepsilon}_C$$

Since the objective is to compare treatment means, we are interested in the differences $\bar{y}_A - \bar{y}_B$, $\bar{y}_A - \bar{y}_C$, and $\bar{y}_B - \bar{y}_C$. These differences are calculated as follows:

$$\bar{y}_A - \bar{y}_B = [\beta_0 + \beta_1 + (\beta_3 + \beta_4 + \beta_5 + \beta_6)/5 + \bar{\varepsilon}_A]$$
$$- [\beta_0 + \beta_2 + (\beta_3 + \beta_4 + \beta_5 + \beta_6)/5 + \bar{\varepsilon}_B]$$
$$= (\beta_1 - \beta_2) + (\bar{\varepsilon}_A - \bar{\varepsilon}_B)$$

$$\bar{y}_A - \bar{y}_C = [\beta_0 + \beta_1 + (\beta_3 + \beta_4 + \beta_5 + \beta_6)/5 + \bar{\varepsilon}_A]$$
$$- [\beta_0 + (\beta_3 + \beta_4 + \beta_5 + \beta_6)/5 + \bar{\varepsilon}_C]$$
$$= \beta_1 + (\bar{\varepsilon}_A - \bar{\varepsilon}_C)$$
$$\bar{y}_B - \bar{y}_C = [\beta_0 + \beta_2 + (\beta_3 + \beta_4 + \beta_5 + \beta_6)/5 + \bar{\varepsilon}_B]$$
$$- [\beta_0 + (\beta_3 + \beta_4 + \beta_5 + \beta_6)/5 + \bar{\varepsilon}_C]$$
$$= \beta_2 + (\bar{\varepsilon}_B - \bar{\varepsilon}_C)$$

Note that for each pairwise comparison, the block β's (β_3, β_4, β_5, and β_6) cancel out, leaving only the treatment β's (β_1 and β_2). That is, the experimental noise resulting from differences between blocks is eliminated when treatment means are compared. The quantities $\bar{\varepsilon}_A - \bar{\varepsilon}_B$, $\bar{\varepsilon}_A - \bar{\varepsilon}_C$, and $\bar{\varepsilon}_B - \bar{\varepsilon}_C$ are the errors of estimation and represent the noise that tends to obscure the true differences between the treatment means.

What would occur if we employed the completely randomized design of Table 14.2 rather than the randomized block design? Since each worker assembles a watch using only one of the methods, each treatment does not appear in each block. Consequently, when we compare the treatment means, the worker-to-worker variation (i.e, the block effects) will not cancel. For example, the difference between $\bar{y}_A$ and $\bar{y}_C$ would be

$$\bar{y}_A - \bar{y}_C = \beta_1 + \underbrace{(\text{Block } \beta\text{'s that do not cancel}) + (\bar{\varepsilon}_A - \bar{\varepsilon}_C)}_{\text{Error of estimation}}$$

Thus, for the completely randomized design, the error of estimation will be increased by an amount involving the block effects (β_3, β_4, β_5, and β_6) that do not cancel. These effects, which inflate the error of estimation, cancel out for the randomized block design, thereby reducing the noise in the experiment.

EXAMPLE 14.2

Refer to Example 14.1 and the randomized block design used to compare the mean construction cost estimates of the four DOT engineers. The design is illustrated in Figure 14.3.

a. Write the model for the randomized block design.

b. Interpret the β parameters of the model, part **a**.

c. How can we use the model, part **a**, to test for differences among the mean estimates of the four engineers?

Solution

a. The experiment involves a qualitative factor, engineer, at four levels, which represents the treatments. The blocks for the experiment are the 10 road contracts. Therefore, the model is

$$E(y) = \beta_0 + \underbrace{\beta_1 x_1 + \beta_2 x_2 + \beta_3 x_3}_{\substack{\text{Treatments} \\ \text{(Engineers)}}} + \underbrace{\beta_4 x_4 + \beta_5 x_5 + \cdots + \beta_{12} x_{12}}_{\substack{\text{Blocks} \\ \text{(Contracts)}}}$$

where

$$x_1 = \begin{cases} 1 & \text{if engineer A} \\ 0 & \text{if not} \end{cases} \quad x_2 = \begin{cases} 1 & \text{if engineer B} \\ 0 & \text{if not} \end{cases} \quad x_3 = \begin{cases} 1 & \text{if engineer C} \\ 0 & \text{if not} \end{cases}$$

$$x_4 = \begin{cases} 1 & \text{if contract 1} \\ 0 & \text{if not} \end{cases} \quad x_5 = \begin{cases} 1 & \text{if contract 2} \\ 0 & \text{if not} \end{cases} \quad \cdots \quad x_{12} = \begin{cases} 1 & \text{if contract 9} \\ 0 & \text{if not} \end{cases}$$

b. Note that we have arbitrarily selected engineer D and contract 10 as the base levels. The interpretations of the β's follow:

$$\beta_1 = \mu_A - \mu_D \quad \text{for a given contract}$$
$$\beta_2 = \mu_B - \mu_D \quad \text{for a given contract}$$
$$\beta_3 = \mu_C - \mu_D \quad \text{for a given contract}$$
$$\beta_4 = \mu_1 - \mu_{10} \quad \text{for a given engineer}$$
$$\beta_5 = \mu_2 - \mu_{10} \quad \text{for a given engineer}$$
$$\vdots$$
$$\beta_{12} = \mu_9 - \mu_{10} \quad \text{for a given engineer}$$

c. One way to determine whether the means for the four engineers differ is to test the null hypothesis

$$H_0: \quad \mu_A = \mu_B = \mu_C = \mu_D$$

From our β interpretations in part **b**, this hypothesis is equivalent to testing

$$H_0: \quad \beta_1 = \beta_2 = \beta_3 = 0$$

To test this hypothesis, we drop the treatment β's (β_1, β_2, and β_3) from the complete model and fit the reduced model

$$E(y) = \beta_0 + \beta_4 x_4 + \beta_5 x_5 + \cdots + \beta_{12} x_{12}$$

Then we conduct the F test for nested models, where

$$F = \frac{(\text{SSE}_{\text{Reduced}} - \text{SSE}_{\text{Complete}})/3}{\text{MSE}_{\text{Complete}}}$$

· · · · · · · · · · · · · · · · · · · ·

The randomized block design represents one of the simplest types of noise-reducing designs. Other, more complex, designs that use the principle of blocking are available to remove trends or variation in two or more directions. The **Latin square design** is useful when you want to eliminate two sources of variation, i.e., when you want to block in two directions. **Latin cube designs** allow you to block in three directions. A further variation in blocking occurs when the block contains fewer experimental units than the number of treatments. By properly assigning the treatments to a specified number of blocks, one can still obtain an estimate of the difference between a pair of treatments free of block effects. These are known as **incomplete block designs**. Consult the references for details on how to set up these more complex block designs.

EXERCISES

14.1 What two factors affect the quantity of information in an experiment?

14.2 How do block designs increase the quantity of information in an experiment?

14.3 Researchers recently conducted an experiment to compare the mean job satisfaction rating $E(y)$ of workers using three types of work scheduling: flextime (which allows workers to set their individual work schedules), staggered starting hours, and fixed hours.
 a. Identify the treatments in the experiment.
 b. Suppose 60 workers are available for the study. Explain how you would employ a completely randomized design for this experiment.
 c. Write the linear model for the completely randomized design.

14.4 A commonly used index to estimate the reliability of a building subjected to lateral loads is the drift ratio. Sophisticated computer programs such as STAAD-III have been developed to estimate the drift ratio based on variables such as beam stiffness, column stiffness, story height, moment of inertia, etc. Civil engineers at SUNY, Buffalo, and the University of Central Florida performed an experiment to compare drift ratio estimates using STAAD-III with the estimates produced by a new, simpler microcomputer program called DRIFT (*Microcomputers in Civil Engineering*, 1993). Data for a 21-story building were used as input to the programs. Two runs were made with STAAD-III: Run 1 considered axial deformation of the building columns, and run 2 neglected this information. The goal of the analysis is to compare the mean drift ratios (where drift is measured as lateral displacement) estimated by the three computer runs.
 a. Identify the treatments in the experiment.
 b. Because lateral displacement will vary greatly across building levels (floors), a randomized block design will be used to reduce the level-to-level variation in drift. Explain, diagrammatically, the set-up of the design if all 21 levels are to be included in the study.
 c. Write the linear model for the randomized block design.

14.5 Refer to the randomized block design of Examples 14.1 and 14.2.
 a. Write the model for each observation of estimated cost y for engineer B. Sum the observations to obtain the average for engineer B.
 b. Repeat part **a** for engineer D.
 c. Show that $(\bar{y}_B - \bar{y}_D) = \beta_2 + (\bar{\varepsilon}_B - \bar{\varepsilon}_D)$. Note that the β's for blocks cancel when computing this difference.

14.5 Volume-Increasing Designs

In this section, we focus on how the proper choice of the treatments associated with two or more factors can increase the "volume" of information extracted from the experiment. The volume-increasing designs we will discuss are commonly known as **factorial designs** because they involve careful selection of the combinations of **factor levels** (i.e., treatments) in the experiment.

Consider a utility company that charges its customers a less expensive rate for using electricity during off-peak (less demanded) hours. The company is experimenting with several time-of-day pricing schedules. Two factors (i.e., independent variables) that the company can manipulate to form the schedule are price ratio, x_1, measured as the ratio of peak to off-peak prices, and peak period length, x_2, measured in hours. Suppose the utility company wants to investigate pricing ratio at two levels, 200% and 400%, and peak period length at two levels, 6 and 9 hours. The company will measure customer satisfaction, y, for several different schedules (i.e., combinations of x_1 and x_2) with the goal of comparing the mean satisfaction levels of the schedules. How should the company select the treatments for the experiment?

One method of selecting the price ratio–peak period length levels to be assigned to the experimental units (customers) would be to use the "one-at-a-time" approach. According to this procedure, one independent variable is varied while the remaining independent variables are held constant. This process is repeated for each of the independent variables in the experiment. This plan would *appear* to be extremely logical and consistent with the concept of blocking introduced in Section 14.4—that is, making comparisons within relatively homogeneous conditions—but this is not the case, as we will demonstrate.

The one-at-a-time approach applied to price ratio (x_1) and peak period length (x_2) is illustrated in Figure 14.4. When length is held constant at $x_2 = 6$ hours, we will observe the response y at a ratio of $x_1 = 200\%$ and $x_1 = 400\%$, thus yielding one pair of y values to estimate the average change in customer satisfaction as a result of changing the pricing ratio (x_1). Also, when pricing ratio is held constant at $x_1 = 200\%$, we observe the response y at a peak period length of $x_2 = 9$ hours. This observation, along with the one at (200%, 6 hours), allows us to estimate the average change in customer satisfaction as result of a change in peak period length (x_2). The three treatments just described, (200%, 6 hours), (400%, 6 hours), and (200%, 9 hours), are indicated as points in Figure 14.4. Note that the figure shows two measurements (points) for each treatment. This is necessary to obtain an estimate of the standard deviation of the differences of interest.

FIGURE 14.4 ▶
"One-at-a-time" approach to selecting treatments

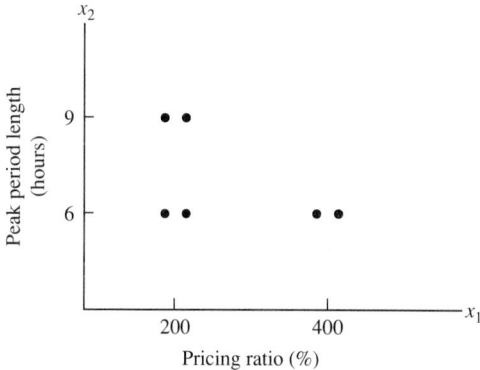

A second method of selecting the factor–level combinations would be to choose the same three treatments as implied by the one-at-a-time approach and then to choose the fourth treatment at (400%, 9 hours) as shown in Figure 14.5. In other words, we have varied both variables x_1 and x_2, at the same time.

FIGURE 14.5 ►

Selecting all possible treatments

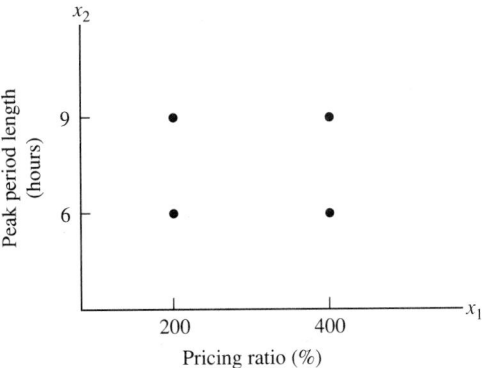

Which of the two designs yields the most information about the treatment differences? Surprisingly, the design of Figure 14.5, with only four observations, yields more accurate information than the one-at-a-time approach with its six observations. First, note that both designs yield two estimates of the difference between the mean response y at $x_1 = 200\%$ and $x_1 = 400\%$ when peak period length (x_2) is held constant, and both yield two estimates of the difference between the mean response y at $x_2 = 6$ hours and $x_2 = 9$ hours when pricing ratio (x_1) is held constant. But what if the difference between the mean response y at $x_1 = 200\%$ and at $x_1 = 400\%$ depends on which level of x_2 is held fixed, i.e., what if pricing ratio (x_1) and peak period length (x_2) *interact*? Then, we require estimates of the mean difference $(\mu_{200} - \mu_{400})$ when $x_2 = 6$ and the mean difference $(\mu_{200} - \mu_{400})$ when $x_2 = 9$. Estimates of both these differences are obtainable from the second design, Figure 14.5. However, since no estimate of the mean response for $x_1 = 400$ and $x_2 = 9$ is available from the one-at-a-time method, the interaction will go undetected for this design!

The importance of interaction between independent variables was emphasized in Chapter 13. If interaction is present, we cannot study the effect of one variable (or factor) on the response y independent of the other variable. Consequently, we require experimental designs that provide information on factor interaction.

Designs that accomplish this objective are called **factorial experiments**. A **complete factorial experiment** is one that includes all possible combinations of the levels of the factors as treatments. For the experiment on time-of-day pricing, we have two levels of pricing ratio (200% and 400%) and two levels of peak period length (6 and 9 hours). Hence, a complete factorial experiment will include $(2 \times 2) = 4$ treatments, as shown in Figure 14.5, and is called a **2 × 2 factorial design**.

Definition 14.6

A **factorial design** is a method for selecting the treatments (that is, the factor–level combinations) to be included in an experiment. A complete factorial experiment is one in which the treatments consist of all factor–level combinations.

If we were to include a third factor, say, season, at four levels, then a complete factorial experiment would include all $2 \times 2 \times 4 = 16$ combinations of pricing ratio, peak period length, and season. The resulting collection of data would be called a **$2 \times 2 \times 4$ factorial design**.

EXAMPLE 14.3

Suppose you want to conduct an experiment to compare the yield strengths of nickel alloy tensile specimens charged in a sulfuric acid solution. In particular, you want to investigate the effect on mean strength of three factors: nickel composition at three levels (A_1, A_2, and A_3), charging time at three levels (B_1, B_2, and B_3), and alloy type at two levels (C_1 and C_2). Consider a complete factorial experiment. Identify the treatments for this $3 \times 3 \times 2$ factorial design.

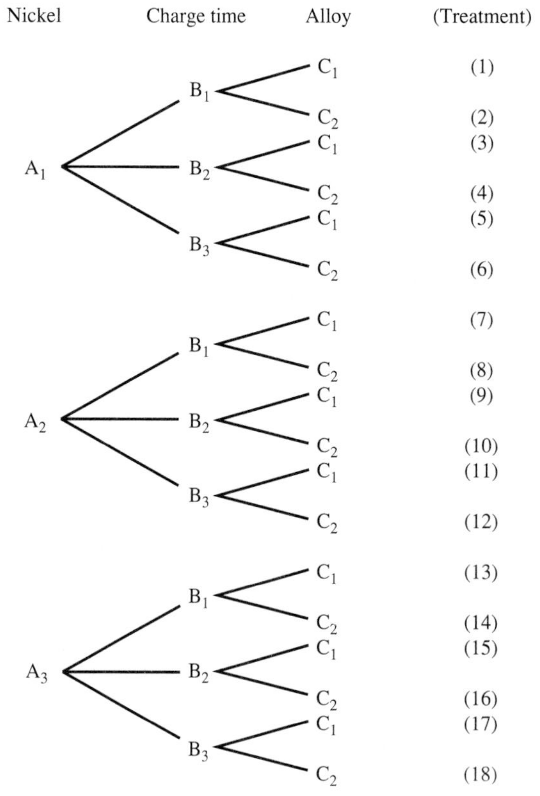

FIGURE 14.6 ▶
The 18 treatments for the
$3 \times 3 \times 2$ factorial of
Example 14.3

Solution

The complete factorial experiment includes all possible combinations of nickel composition, charging time, and alloy type. We therefore would include the following treatments: $A_1B_1C_1$, $A_1B_1C_2$, $A_1B_2C_1$, $A_1B_2C_2$, $A_1B_3C_1$, $A_1B_3C_2$, $A_2B_1C_1$, $A_2B_1C_2$, $A_2B_2C_1$, $A_2B_2C_2$, $A_2B_3C_1$, $A_2B_3C_2$, $A_3B_1C_1$, $A_3B_1C_2$, $A_3B_2C_1$, $A_3B_2C_2$, $A_3B_3C_1$, $A_3B_3C_2$. These 18 treatments are shown diagrammatically in Figure 14.6.

The linear model for a factorial design includes terms for each of the factors in the experiment—called **main effects**—and terms for factor interactions. For example, the model for the 2×2 factorial for the time-of-day pricing experiment includes a first-order term for the quantitative factor, pricing ratio (x_1), a first-order term for the quantitative factor, peak period length (x_2), and an interaction term:

$$y = \beta_0 + \underbrace{\beta_1 x_1 + \beta_2 x_2}_{\text{Main effects}} + \underbrace{\beta_3 x_1 x_2}_{\text{Interaction}} + \varepsilon$$

In general, the linear model for a complete factorial design for k factors contains terms for the following:

The main effects for each of the k factors

Two-way interaction terms for all pairs of factors

Three-way interaction terms for all combinations of three factors

$$\vdots$$

K-way interaction terms of all combinations of k factors

If the factors are qualitative, then we set up dummy variables and proceed as in the next example.

EXAMPLE 14.4

Write the model for the $3 \times 3 \times 2$ factorial experiment of Example 14.3.

Solution

Since the factors are qualitative, we set up dummy variables as follows:

$$x_1 = \begin{cases} 1 & \text{if nickel } A_1 \\ 0 & \text{if not} \end{cases} \qquad x_2 = \begin{cases} 1 & \text{if nickel } A_2 \\ 0 & \text{if not} \end{cases}$$

$$x_3 = \begin{cases} 1 & \text{if charge } B_1 \\ 0 & \text{if not} \end{cases} \qquad x_4 = \begin{cases} 1 & \text{if charge } B_2 \\ 0 & \text{if not} \end{cases}$$

$$x_5 = \begin{cases} 1 & \text{if alloy } C_1 \\ 0 & \text{if alloy } C_2 \end{cases}$$

Then the appropriate model is

$$y = \beta_0 + \underbrace{\beta_1 x_1 + \beta_2 x_2}_{\substack{\text{Nickel main} \\ \text{effects}}} + \underbrace{\beta_3 x_3 + \beta_4 x_4}_{\substack{\text{Charge main} \\ \text{effects}}} + \underbrace{\beta_5 x_5}_{\substack{\text{Alloy main} \\ \text{effect}}}$$

$$+ \underbrace{\beta_6 x_1 x_3 + \beta_7 x_1 x_4 + \beta_8 x_2 x_3 + \beta_9 x_2 x_4}_{\text{Nickel} \times \text{Charge}} + \underbrace{\beta_{10} x_1 x_5 + \beta_{11} x_2 x_5}_{\text{Nickel} \times \text{Alloy}}$$

$$+ \underbrace{\beta_{12} x_3 x_5 + \beta_{13} x_4 x_5}_{\text{Charge} \times \text{Alloy}}$$

$$+ \underbrace{\beta_{14} x_1 x_3 x_5 + \beta_{15} x_1 x_4 x_5 + \beta_{16} x_2 x_3 x_5 + \beta_{17} x_2 x_4 x_5}_{\text{Nickel} \times \text{Charge} \times \text{Alloy}}$$

Note that the number of parameters in the model for the $3 \times 3 \times 2$ factorial design of Example 14.4 is 18, which is equal to the number of treatments contained in the experiment. This is always the case for a complete factorial experiment. Consequently, if we fit the complete model to a single replication of the factorial treatments (i.e., one y observation measured per treatment), we will have no degrees of freedom available for estimating the error variance, σ^2. One way to solve this problem is to add additional data points to the sample. Researchers usually accomplish this by *replicating* the complete set of factorial treatments. That is, we collect two or more observed y values for each treatment in the experiment. This provides sufficient degrees of freedom for estimating σ^2.

One potential disadvantage of a complete factorial experiment is that it may require a large number of treatments. For example, an experiment involving 10 factors each at two levels would require $2^{10} = 1,024$ treatments! This might occur in an exploratory study where we are attempting to determine which of a large set of factors affect the response y. Several volume-increasing designs are available that employ only a fraction of the total number of treatments in a complete factorial experiment. For this reason, they are called **fractional factorial experiments**. Fractional factorials permit the estimation of the β parameters of lower-order terms (e.g., main effects and two-way interactions); however, β estimates of certain higher-order terms (e.g., three-way and four-way interactions) will be the same as some lower-order terms, thus confounding the results of the experiment. Consequently, a great deal of expertise is required to run and interpret fractional factorial experiments. Consult the references for details on fractional factorials and other more complex, volume-increasing designs.

EXERCISES

14.6   In what sense does a factorial experiment increase the quantity of information in an experiment?

14.7   Suppose you plan to investigate the effect of hourly pay rate and length of workday on some measure y of worker productivity. Both pay rate and length of workday will be set at three levels, and y will be observed for all combinations of these factors.
   a. What type of experiment is this?
   b. Identify the factors and state whether they are quantitative or qualitative.
   c. Identify the treatments to be employed in the experiment.

14.8   Many cognitively demanding jobs (e.g, air traffic controller, radar/sonar operator) require efficient processing of visual information. Researchers at Georgia Tech investigated the variables that affect the reaction time of subjects performing a visual search task (*Human Factors*, June 1993). College students were trained on microcomputers with one of two methods: continuously consistent or adjusted consistent. Each student was then assigned to one of six different practice sessions. Finally, the consistency of the search task was manipulated at four degrees: 100% consistency, 67%, 50%, or 33%. The goal of the researcher was to compare the mean reaction times of students assigned to each of the $2 \times 6 \times 4 = 48$ (training method) $\times$ (practice session) $\times$ (task consistency) experimental conditions.
   a. List the factors involved in the experiment.
   b. For each factor, state whether it is quantitative or qualitative.
   c. How many treatments are involved in the experiment? List them.

14.9   Consider a factorial design with two factors, A and B, each at three levels. Suppose we select the following treatment (factor–level) combinations to be included in the experiment: A_1B_1, A_2B_1, A_3B_1, A_1B_2, and A_1B_3.
   a. Is this a complete factorial experiment? Explain.
   b. Explain why it is impossible to investigate AB interaction in this experiment.

14.10 Write the complete factorial model for a 2×3 factorial experiment where both factors are qualitative.

14.11 Write the complete factorial model for a $2 \times 3 \times 3$ factorial experiment where the factor at two levels is quantitative and the other two factors are qualitative.

14.12 Suppose you wish to investigate the effect of three factors on a response y. Explain why a factorial selection of treatments is better than varying each factor, one at a time, while holding the remaining two factors constant.

14.13 Why is the randomized block design a poor design to use to investigate the effect of two qualitative factors on a response y?

14.6   Selecting the Sample Size

We demonstrated how to select the sample size for estimating a single population mean or comparing two population means in Chapter 8. We now show you how this problem can be solved for designed experiments.

As mentioned in Section 14.3, a measure of the quantity of information in an experiment that is pertinent to a particular population parameter is the standard error of the estimator of the parameter. A more practical measure is the half-width of the parameter's confidence interval, which will, of course, be a function of the standard error. For example, the half-width of a confidence interval for a population mean (given in Section 8.5) is:

$$t_{\alpha/2}s_{\bar{y}} = t_{\alpha/2}\left(\frac{s}{\sqrt{n}}\right)$$

Similarly, the half-width of a confidence interval for the slope β_1 of a straight-line model relating y to x (given in Section 11.6) is

$$(t_{\alpha/2})s_{\hat{\beta}_1} = t_{\alpha/2}\left(\frac{s}{\sqrt{SS_{xx}}}\right) = t_{\alpha/2}\left(\sqrt{\frac{SSE}{n-2}}\right)\left(\frac{1}{\sqrt{SS_{xx}}}\right)$$

In both cases, the half-width is a function of the total number of data points in the experiment; each interval half-width gets smaller as the total number of data points n increases. The same is true for a confidence interval for a parameter β_i of a general linear model, for a confidence interval for $E(y)$, and for a prediction interval for y. Since each designed experiment can be represented by a linear model, this result can be used to select, approximately, the number of replications (i.e., the number of observations measured for each treatment) in the experiment.

For example, consider a designed experiment consisting of three treatments, A, B, and C. Suppose we want to estimate $(\mu_B - \mu_C)$, the difference between the treatment means for B and C. From our knowledge of linear models for designed experiments, we know this difference will be represented by one of the β parameters in the model, say β_2. The confidence interval for β_2 for a single replication of the experiment is

$$\hat{\beta}_2 \pm (t_{\alpha/2})s_{\hat{\beta}_2}$$

If we repeat exactly the same experiment r times (we call this r **replications**), it can be shown (proof omitted) that the confidence interval for β_2 will be

$$\hat{\beta}_2 \pm \underbrace{t_{\alpha/2}\left(\frac{s_{\hat{\beta}_2}}{\sqrt{r}}\right)}_{B}$$

To find r, we first set the half-width of the interval to the largest value, B, we are willing to tolerate. Then we approximate $(t_{\alpha/2})$ and $s_{\hat{\beta}_2}$, and solve for the number of replications r.

EXAMPLE 14.5

Consider a 2×2 factorial experiment to investigate the effect of two factors on the light output y of flashbulbs used in cameras. The two factors (and their levels) are: $x_1 =$ Amount of foil contained in the bulb (100 and 200 milligrams) and $x_2 =$ Speed of sealing machine (1.2 and 1.3 revolutions per minute). The complete model for the 2×2 factorial experiment is

$$E(y) = \beta_0 + \beta_1 x_1 + \beta_2 x_2 + \beta_3 x_1 x_2$$

How many replicates of the 2×2 factorial are required to estimate β_3, the interaction β, to within .3 of its true value using a 95% confidence interval?

Solution

To solve for the number of replicates, r, we want to solve the equation

$$t_{\alpha/2}\left(\frac{s_{\hat{\beta}_3}}{\sqrt{r}}\right) = B$$

You can see that we need to have an estimate of $s_{\hat{\beta}_3}$, and standard error of $\hat{\beta}_3$ for a single replication. Suppose it is known from a previous experiment conducted by the manufacturer of the flashbulbs that $s_{\hat{\beta}_3} \approx .2$. For a 95% confidence interval, $\alpha = .05$ and $\alpha/2 = .025$. Since we want the half-width of the interval to be $B = .3$, we have

$$t_{.025}\left(\frac{.2}{\sqrt{r}}\right) = .3$$

The degrees of freedom for $t_{.025}$ will depend on the sample size $n = (2 \times 2)r = 4r$; consequently, we must approximate its value. In fact, since the model includes four parameters, the degrees of freedom for t will be df(Error) $= n - 4 = 4r - 4 = 4(r - 1)$. At minimum, we require two replicates; hence, we will have at least $4(2 - 1) = 4$ df. In Table 7 of Appendix II, we find $t_{.025} = 2.776$ for df $= 4$. We will use this conservative estimate of t in our calculations.

Substituting $t = 2.776$ into the equation, we have

$$\frac{2.776(.2)}{\sqrt{r}} = .3$$

$$\sqrt{r} = \frac{(2.776)(.2)}{.3} = 1.85$$

$$r = 3.42$$

Since we can run either three or four replications (but not 3.42), we should choose four replications to be reasonably certain that we will be able to estimate the interaction parameter, β_3, to within .3 of its true value. The 2×2 factorial with four replicates would be laid out as shown in Table 14.4.

TABLE 14.4   2 × 2 Factorial with Four Replicates

		Amount of Foil, x_1	
		100	200
Machine Speed, x_2	1.2	4 observations on y	4 observations on y
	1.3	4 observations on y	4 observations on y

EXERCISES

14.14 Why is replication important in a complete factorial experiment?

14.15 Consider a 2×2 factorial. How many replications are required to estimate the interaction β to within two units with a 90% confidence interval? Assume that the standard error of the estimate of the interaction β (based on a single replication) is approximately 3.

14.16 For a randomized block design with b blocks, the estimated standard error of the estimated difference between any two treatment means is $s\sqrt{2/b}$. Use this formula to determine the number of blocks required to estimate $(\mu_A - \mu_B)$, the difference between two treatment means, to within 10 units using a 95% confidence interval. Assume $s \approx 15$.

14.7 The Logic Behind an Analysis of Variance

Once the data for a designed experiment have been collected, we will want to use the sample information to make inferences about the population means associated with the various treatments. The method used to compare the treatment means is known as **analysis of variance**, or **ANOVA**. The concept behind an analysis of variance can be explained using the following simple example.

Consider an experiment with a single factor at two levels (that is, two treatments). Suppose we want to decide whether the two treatment means differ based on the means of two independent random samples, each containing $n_1 = n_2 = 5$ measurements, and that the y values appear as in Figure 14.7. Note that the five circles on the left are plots of the y values for sample 1 and the five solid dots on the right are plots of the y values for sample 2. Also, observe the horizontal lines that pass through the means for the two samples, $\bar{y}_1$ and $\bar{y}_2$. Do you think the plots provide sufficient evidence to indicate a difference between the corresponding population means?

FIGURE 14.7 ▶
Plots of data for two samples

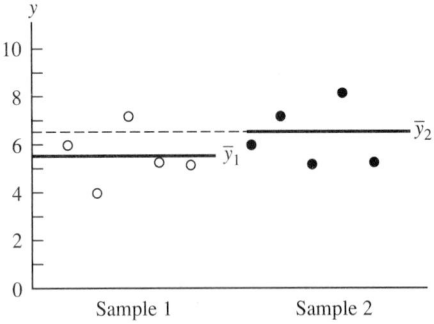

If you are uncertain whether the population means differ for the data in Figure 14.7, examine the situation for two different samples in Figure 14.8a. We think that you will agree that for these data, it appears that the population means differ. Examine a third case in Figure 14.8b. For these data, it appears that there is little or no difference between the population means.

FIGURE 14.8 ▶
Plots of data for two cases

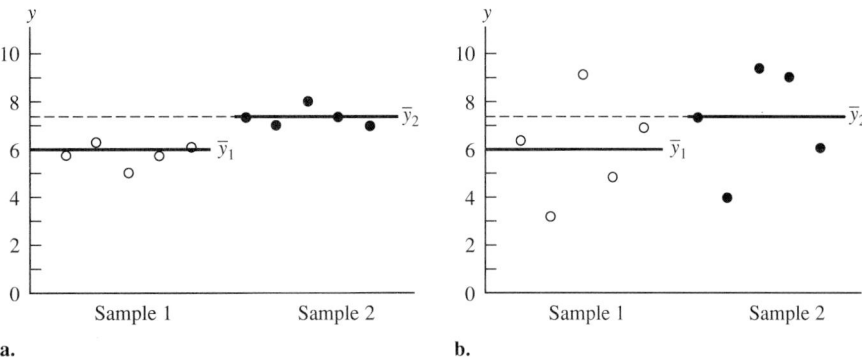

a.   b.

What elements of Figures 14.7 and 14.8 did we intuitively use to decide whether the data indicate a difference between the population means? The answer to the question is that we visually compared the distance (the variation) *between* the sample means to the variation *within* the y values for each of the two samples. Since the difference between the sample means in Figure 14.8a is large relative to the within-sample variation, we inferred that the population means differ. Conversely, in Figure 14.8b, the variation between the sample means is small relative to the within-sample variation and therefore there is little evidence to infer that the means are significantly different.

The variation within samples is measured by the pooled s^2 that we computed for the independent random samples t test of Section 9.6, namely,

$$\textit{Within-sample variation:}\quad s^2 = \frac{\sum_{i=1}^{n_1} (y_{i1} - \bar{y}_1)^2 + \sum_{i=1}^{n_2} (y_{i2} - \bar{y}_2)^2}{n_1 + n_2 - 2}$$

$$= \frac{\text{SSE}}{n_1 + n_2 - 2}$$

where y_{i1} is the ith observation in sample 1 and y_{i2} is the ith observation in sample 2. The quantity in the numerator of s^2 is often denoted **SSE**, the **sum of squared errors**. As with regression analysis, SSE measures unexplained variability. But in this case, it measures variability *unexplained* by the differences between the sample means.

A measure of the between-sample variation is given by the weighted sum of squares of deviations of the individual sample means about the mean for all 10 observations, $\bar{y}$, divided by the number of samples minus 1, i.e.,

$$\textit{Between-sample variation:}\quad \frac{n_1(\bar{y}_1 - \bar{y})^2 + n_2(\bar{y}_2 - \bar{y})^2}{2 - 1} = \frac{\text{SST}}{1}$$

The quantity in the numerator is often denoted **SST**, the **sum of squares for treatments**, since it measures the variability *explained* by the differences between the sample means of the two treatments.

For this experimental design, SSE and SST sum to a known total, namely,

$$SS(Total) = \sum (y_i - \bar{y})^2 \quad [\textit{Note:} \quad SS(Total) \text{ is equivalent to } SS_{yy} \text{ in regression.}]$$

Also, the ratio

$$F = \frac{\text{Between-sample variation}}{\text{Within-sample variation}} = \frac{SST/1}{SSE/(n_1 + n_2 - 2)}$$

has an F distribution with $\nu_1 = 1$ and $\nu_2 = n_1 + n_2 - 2$ degrees of freedom (df) and therefore can be used to test the null hypothesis of no difference between the treatment means. The additivity property of the sums of squares led early researchers to view this analysis as a **partitioning** of $SS(Total) = \Sigma(y_i - \bar{y})^2$ into sources corresponding to the factors included in the experiment and to SSE. The simple formulas for computing the sums of squares, the additivity property, and the form of the test statistic made it natural for this procedure to be called an **analysis of variance**.

We demonstrate the analysis of variance procedure and its relation to regression for several commonly used experimental designs in Sections 14.8–14.12.

EXERCISES

14.17   The *Journal of Testing and Evaluation* (July 1992) published an investigation of the mean compression strength of corrugated fiberboard shipping containers. Comparisons were made for boxes of five different sizes: A, B, C, D, and E. Twenty identical boxes of each size were tested and the peak compression strength (pounds) recorded for each box. The accompanying figure shows the sample means for the five box types as well as the variation around each sample mean.

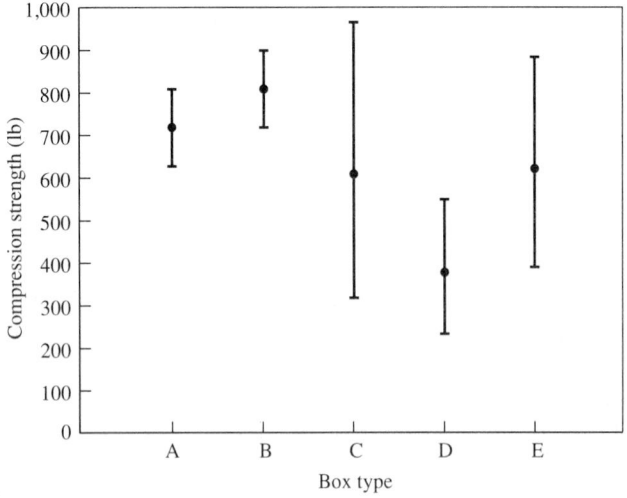

Source: Singh, S. P. et al. "Compression of single-wall corrugated shipping containers using fixed and floating test platens." *Journal of Testing and Evaluation*, Vol. 20, No. 4, July 1992, p. 319 (Figure 3).

a. Refer to box types B and D. Based on the graph, does it appear that the mean compressive strengths of these two box types are significantly different? Explain.
b. Based on the graph, does it appear that the mean compressive strengths of all five box types are significantly different? Explain.

14.8   ANOVA for Completely Randomized Designs

Recall (Section 14.2) the first two steps in designing an experiment: (1) decide on the factors to be investigated and (2) select the factor–level combinations (treatments) to be included in the experiment. For example, suppose you wish to compare the length of time to assemble a device in a manufacturing operation for workers who have completed one of three training programs, A, B, and C. Then this experiment involves a single factor, training program, at three levels, A, B, and C. Since training program is the only factor, these levels (A, B, and C) represent the treatments. Now we must decide the sample size for each treatment (step 3) and how to assign the treatments to the experimental units, namely, the specific workers (step 4).

As we learned in Section 14.4, the most common assignment of treatments to experimental units is called a **completely randomized design**. To illustrate, suppose we wish to obtain equal amounts of information on the mean assembly times for the three training procedures, i.e., we decide to assign equal numbers of workers to each of the three training programs. Also, suppose we determine the number of workers in each of the three samples to be $n_1 = n_2 = n_3 = 10$. Then a completely randomized design is one in which the $n_1 + n_2 + n_3 = 30$ workers are **randomly assigned**, ten to each of the three treatments. A *random assignment is one in which any one assignment is as probable as any other*. This eliminates the possibility of bias that might occur if the workers were assigned in some systematic manner. For example, a systematic assignment might accidentally assign most of the manually dexterous workers to training program A, thus tending to underestimate the true mean assembly time corresponding to A.

Example 14.6 illustrates how a **random number table** can be used to assign the 30 workers to the three treatments.

EXAMPLE 14.6

Use the random number table, Table 6 in Appendix II, to assign $n = 30$ experimental units to three treatment groups.

Solution

The first step is to number the 30 workers from 1 to 30. We will then use Table 6 in Appendix II to select two-digit numbers, discarding those that are larger than 30 or are identical, until we have a total of 20 two-digit numbers. We will then have 20 of the integers between 1 and 30 arranged in random order. The workers who have been assigned the first 10 numbers in the sequence are assigned to training program A, the second group of 10 workers are assigned to B, and the remaining workers are assigned to C.

To illustrate, suppose we start with the two-digit random number in row 5, column 6 of Table 6 and proceed down the column, selecting only two-digit numbers (the first two digits) less than or equal to 30 and deleting those that repeat. The first 20 are: 20, 18, 13, 16, 19, 04, 14, 06, 30, 25, 27, 17, 24, 21, 22, 02, 15, 05, 09, 08. The workers with the first 10 numbers are assigned to program A, the second 10 to B, and the remaining 10 to C. So the workers are assigned to the training program as shown in Table 14.5.

TABLE 14.5   Random Assignment of Workers to Treatments

A	B	C
20, 18, 13, 16, 19, 4, 14, 6, 30, 25	27, 17, 24, 21, 22, 2, 15, 5, 9, 8	1, 3, 7, 10, 11, 12, 23, 26, 28, 29

In some experimental situations, we are unable to randomly assign the treatment to the experimental units because of the nature of the experimental units themselves. For example, suppose we want to compare the mean annual salaries of professors in two College of Engineering departments, civil and industrial. Then the treatments—civil and industrial—cannot be "assigned" to the professors (experimental units). A professor is a member of either the civil engineering department or the industrial (or some other) engineering department and cannot be arbitrarily assigned one of the treatments. Rather, we view the treatments (departments) as populations from which we will select independent random samples of experimental units (professors). A **completely randomized design**, then, involves a comparison of the means for a number, say, p, of treatments, based on independent random samples of $n_1, n_2, \ldots, n_p$ observations, drawn from populations associated with treatments 1, 2, . . . , p, respectively. We repeat our definition of a completely randomized design (given in Section 14.4) with this modification.

> **Definition 14.7**
>
> A **completely randomized design** to compare p treatment means is one in which the treatments are randomly assigned to the experimental units, or in which independent random samples are drawn from each of the p populations.

After collecting the data from a completely randomized design, we want to make inferences about p population means where μ_i is the mean of the population of measurements associated with treatment i, for $i = 1, 2, \ldots, p$. The null hypothesis to be tested is that the p treatment means are equal, i.e., $H_0: \mu_1 = \mu_2 = \cdots = \mu_p$, and the alternative hypothesis we wish to detect is that at least two of the treatment means differ. The appropriate linear model for the response y is

$$E(y) = \beta_0 + \beta_1 x_1 + \beta_2 x_2 + \cdots + \beta_{p-1} x_{p-1}$$

where

$$x_1 = \begin{cases} 1 & \text{if treatment 2} \\ 0 & \text{if not} \end{cases} \qquad x_2 = \begin{cases} 1 & \text{if treatment 3} \\ 0 & \text{if not} \end{cases} \quad \cdots \quad x_p = \begin{cases} 1 & \text{if treatment } p \\ 0 & \text{if not} \end{cases}$$

and (arbitrarily) treatment 1 is the base level. Recall that this 0–1 system of coding implies that

$$\beta_0 = \mu_1$$
$$\beta_1 = \mu_2 - \mu_1$$
$$\beta_2 = \mu_3 - \mu_1$$
$$\vdots \qquad \vdots$$
$$\beta_{p-1} = \mu_p - \mu_1$$

The null hypothesis that the p population means are equal is equivalent to the null hypothesis that all the treatment differences equal 0, i.e.,

$$H_0: \quad \beta_1 = \beta_2 = \cdots = \beta_{p-1} = 0$$

To test this hypothesis using regression, we employ the technique of Section 13.6; that is, we compare the sum of squares for error, SSE_R, for the *reduced* model

$$E(y) = \beta_0$$

to the sum of squares for error, SSE_C, for the *complete* model

$$E(y) = \beta_0 + \beta_1 x_1 + \beta_2 x_2 + \cdots + \beta_{p-1} x_{p-1}$$

using the F statistic

$$\begin{aligned} F &= \frac{(SSE_R - SSE_C)/\text{Number of } \beta \text{ parameters in } H_0}{SSE_C/[n - (\text{Number of } \beta \text{ parameters in the complete model})]} \\ &= \frac{(SSE_R - SSE_C)/(p - 1)}{SSE_C/(n - p)} \\ &= \frac{(SSE_R - SSE_C)/(p - 1)}{MSE_C} \end{aligned}$$

where F is based on $\nu_1 = (p - 1)$ and $\nu_2 = (n - p)$ df. If F exceeds the upper critical value, F_a, we reject H_0 and conclude that at least one of the treatment differences, $\beta_1, \beta_2, \ldots, \beta_{p-1}$, differs from zero, i.e., we conclude that at least two treatment means differ.

EXAMPLE 14.7   Show that the F statistic for testing the equality of treatment means in a completely randomized design is equivalent to a global F test of the complete model.

Solution

Since the reduced model contains only the β_0 term, the least squares estimate of β_0 is $\bar{y}$, and it follows that

$$\text{SSE}_R = \sum (y - \bar{y})^2 = \text{SS}_{yy}$$

We called this quantity the sum of squares for total in Chapter 12. The difference $(\text{SSE}_R - \text{SSE}_C)$ is simply $(\text{SS}_{yy} - \text{SSE})$ for the complete model. Since in regression $(\text{SS}_{yy} - \text{SSE}) = \text{SS(Model)}$, and the complete model has $(p - 1)$ terms (excluding β_0),

$$F = \frac{(\text{SSE}_R - \text{SSE}_C)/(p - 1)}{\text{MSE}_C} = \frac{\text{SS(Model)}/(p - 1)}{\text{MSE}} = \frac{\text{MS(Model)}}{\text{MSE}}$$

Thus, it follows that the test statistic for testing the null hypothesis,

$$H_0: \quad \mu_1 = \mu_2 = \cdots = \mu_p$$

in a completely randomized design is the same as the F statistic for testing the global utility of the complete model for this design.

．．．．．．．．．．．．．．．．．．．

The regression approach to analyzing data from a completely randomized design is summarized in the box. Note that the test requires several assumptions about the distributions of the response y for the p treatments and that these assumptions are necessary regardless of the sizes of the samples. (We have more to say about these assumptions in Section 14.14.)

Model and F Test for a Completely Randomized Design with p Treatments

Complete model: $\quad E(y) = \beta_0 + \beta_1 x_1 + \beta_2 x_2 + \cdots + \beta_{p-1} x_{p-1}$

where

$$x_1 = \begin{cases} 1 & \text{if treatment 2} \\ 0 & \text{if not} \end{cases} \qquad x_2 = \begin{cases} 1 & \text{if treatment 3} \\ 0 & \text{if not} \end{cases} \cdots$$

$$x_{p-1} = \begin{cases} 1 & \text{if treatment } p \\ 0 & \text{if not} \end{cases}$$

$H_0: \quad \beta_1 = \beta_2 = \cdots = \beta_{p-1} = 0 \quad$ (i.e., $H_0: \quad \mu_1 = \mu_2 = \cdots = \mu_p$)
$H_a: \quad$ At least one of the β parameters listed in H_0 differs from 0
$\qquad$ (i.e., $H_a:$ At least two means differ)

Test statistic: $\quad F = \dfrac{\text{MS(Model)}}{\text{MSE}}$

Rejection region: $\quad F > F_\alpha$, where the distribution of F is based on $\nu_1 = p - 1$ and $\nu_2 = n - p$ degrees of freedom

Assumptions: $\quad$ 1. All p population probability distributions corresponding to the p treatments are normal.

$\qquad\qquad\qquad$ 2. The population variances of the p treatments are equal.

EXAMPLE 14.8

An experiment was conducted to compare the wearing qualities of three types of paint when subjected to the abrasive action of a slowly rotating cloth-surfaced wheel. Ten paint specimens were tested for each paint type, and the number of hours until visible abrasion was apparent was recorded for each specimen. The data (with totals) are shown in Table 14.6. Is there sufficient evidence to indicate a difference in the mean time until abrasion is visibly evident for the three paint types? Test using $\alpha = .05$.

TABLE 14.6 Wear Data for Three Types of Paint

	Paint Type		
	1	2	3
	148	513	335
	76	264	643
	393	433	216
	520	94	536
	236	535	128
	134	327	723
	55	214	258
	166	135	380
	415	280	594
	153	304	465
Totals	2,296	3,099	4,278

Solution

The experiment involves a single factor, paint type, at three levels. Thus, we have a completely randomized design with $p = 3$ treatments. Let μ_1, μ_2, and μ_3 represent the mean abrasion times for paint types 1, 2, and 3, respectively. Then we want to test

$$H_0: \quad \mu_1 = \mu_2 = \mu_3$$

against

$$H_a: \quad \text{At least two of the three means differ}$$

The appropriate linear model for $p = 3$ treatments is

$$\textit{Complete model:} \quad E(y) = \beta_0 + \beta_1 x_1 + \beta_2 x_2$$

where

$$x_1 = \begin{cases} 1 & \text{if paint type 1} \\ 0 & \text{if not} \end{cases} \quad \text{and} \quad x_2 = \begin{cases} 1 & \text{if paint type 2} \\ 0 & \text{if not} \end{cases}$$

Thus, we want to test $H_0: \beta_1 = \beta_2 = 0$.

The SAS regression analysis for the complete model is shown in Figure 14.9. The F statistic for testing the overall adequacy of the model (shaded on the printout) is $F = 3.48$, where the distribution of F is based on $\nu_1 = (p - 1) = 3 - 1 = 2$ and $\nu_2 = (n - p) = 30 - 3 = 27$ df. For $\alpha = .05$, the critical value (obtained from Table 10 of Appendix II) is $F_{.05} = 3.35$ (see Figure 14.10).

FIGURE 14.9 ▶
SAS printout for the completely randomized design, Example 14.8

Analysis of Variance

Source	DF	Sum of Squares	Mean Square	F Value	Prob>F
Model	2	198772.46667	99386.23333	3.482	0.0452
Error	27	770670.90000	28543.36667		
C Total	29	969443.36667			

Root MSE	168.94782	R-square	0.2050	
Dep Mean	322.43333	Adj R-sq	0.1462	
C.V.	52.39775			

Parameter Estimates

Variable	DF	Parameter Estimate	Standard Error	T for H0: Parameter=0	Prob > |T|
INTERCEP	1	427.800000	53.42599243	8.007	0.0001
X1	1	-198.200000	75.55576307	-2.623	0.0141
X2	1	-117.900000	75.55576307	-1.560	0.1303

FIGURE 14.10 ▶
Rejection region for Example 14.8; numerator df = 2, denominator df = 27, $\alpha = .05$

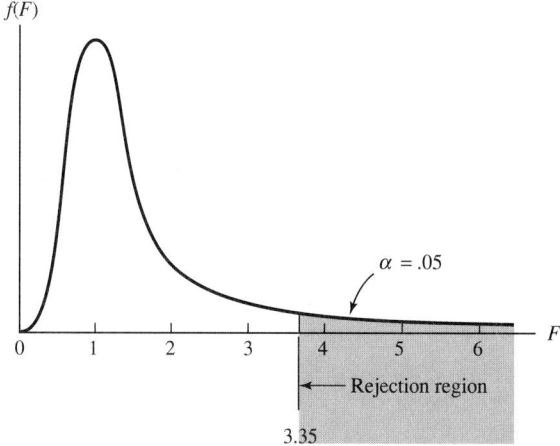

Since the computed value of F, 3.48, exceeds the critical value, $F_{.05} = 3.35$, we reject H_0 and conclude (at the $\alpha = .05$ level of significance) that the mean time to visible abrasion differs for at least two of the three paint types. We can arrive at the same conclusion by noting that $\alpha = .05$ is greater than the p-value (.0452) shaded on the printout.

The analysis of the data in Example 14.8 can also be accomplished using ANOVA computing formulas. In Section 14.7, we learned that an analysis of variance partitions SS(Total) = $\Sigma(y - \bar{y})^2$ into two components, SSE and SST (see Figure 14.11).

FIGURE 14.11 ▶
The partitioning of SS(Total) for a completely randomized design

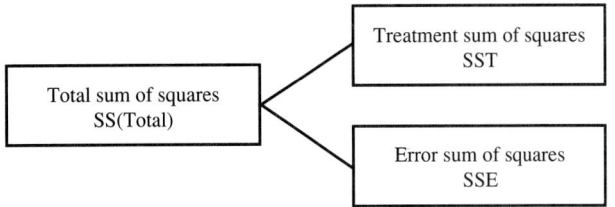

Recall that the quantity SST denotes the sum of squares for treatments and measures the variation explained by the differences between the treatment means. The sum of squares for error, SSE, is a measure of the unexplained variability, obtained by calculating a pooled measure of the variability *within* the p samples. If the treatment means truly differ, then SSE should be substantially smaller than SST. We compare the two sources of variability by forming an F statistic:

$$F = \frac{SST/(p-1)}{SSE/(n-p)} = \frac{MST}{MSE}$$

where n is the total number of measurements. The numerator of the F statistic, MST = SST/(p − 1), denotes **mean square for treatments** and is based on $(p - 1)$ degrees of freedom—one for each of the p treatments minus one for the estimation of the overall mean. The denominator of the F statistic, MSE = SSE/(n − p), denotes **mean square for error** and is based on $(n - p)$ degrees of freedom—one for each of the n measurements minus one for each of the p treatment means being estimated. We have already demonstrated that this F statistic is identical to the global F value for the regression model specified earlier.

For completeness, we provide the computing formulas for an analysis of variance in the box on page 820.

· ·

EXAMPLE 14.9

Refer to Example 14.8. Analyze the data of Table 14.6 using the ANOVA approach. Use $\alpha = .05$.

Solution

Rather than perform the tedious calculations by hand (we leave this for the student as an exercise), we resort to a statistical software package with an ANOVA routine. Both of the software packages discussed in this text (SAS and MINITAB) have procedures that automatically compute the ANOVA sums of squares and the ANOVA F statistic.

Computing Formulas for the Analysis of Variance for a Completely Randomized Design

Sum of all n measurements $= \sum_{i=1}^{n} y_i$

Mean of all n measurements $= \bar{y}$

Sum of squares of all n measurements $= \sum_{i=1}^{n} y_i^2$

CM = Correction for mean

$$= \frac{(\text{Total of all observations})^2}{\text{Total number of observations}} = \frac{\left(\sum_{i=1}^{n} y_i\right)^2}{n}$$

$SS(\text{Total})$ = Total sum of squares

$$= (\text{Sum of squares of all observations}) - CM$$

$$= \sum_{i=1}^{n} y_i^2 - CM$$

SST = Sum of squares for treatments

$$= \left(\begin{array}{c}\text{Sum of squares of treatment totals with}\\ \text{each square divided by the number of}\\ \text{observations for that treatment}\end{array}\right) - CM$$

$$= \frac{T_1^2}{n_1} + \frac{T_2^2}{n_2} + \cdots + \frac{T_p^2}{n_p} - CM$$

SSE = Sum of squares for error = $SS(\text{Total}) - SST$

MST = Mean square for treatments $= \dfrac{SST}{p-1}$

MSE = Mean square for error $= \dfrac{SSE}{n-p}$

The MINITAB ANOVA printout is shown in Figure 14.12. The value of the test statistic (shaded on the printout) is $F = 3.48$. Note that this is identical to the F value obtained using the regression approach in Example 14.8. The p-value of the test (also shaded) is $p = .045$. (Likewise, this quantity is identical to that in Example 14.8.) Since $\alpha = .05$ exceeds this p-value, we have sufficient evidence to conclude that the treatments differ.

The results of an analysis of variance are often summarized in tabular form. The general form of an ANOVA table for a completely randomized design is shown in Table 14.7. The column head **SOURCE** refers to the source of variation, and for

FIGURE 14.12 ▶
MINITAB ANOVA printout for
Example 14.9

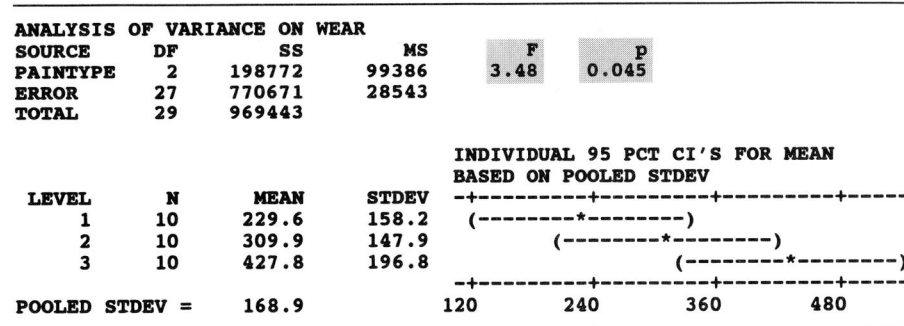

each source, **DF** refers to the degrees of freedom, **SS** to the sum of squares, **MS** to the mean square, and **F** to the F statistic comparing the treatment mean square to the error mean square. Table 14.8 is the ANOVA summary table corresponding to the analysis of variance data for Example 14.9, obtained from the MINITAB printout.

TABLE 14.7   ANOVA Summary Table for a Completely Randomized Design

Source	df	SS	MS	F
Treatments	$p - 1$	SST	MST	MST/MSE
Error	$n - p$	SSE	MSE	
Total	$n - 1$	SS(Total)		

TABLE 14.8   ANOVA Summary Table for Example 14.9

Source	df	SS	MS	F
Paint types	2	198,772	99,386	3.48
Error	27	770,671	28,543	
Total	29	969,443		

Once differences among treatment means are established in ANOVA, it is often important to rank the means from lowest to highest. Two useful methods for ranking treatment means in ANOVA are presented in Section 14.13.

EXERCISES

14.18 Refer to the completely randomized design of Exercise 14.3. Recall that the researchers want to compare the mean job satisfaction rating of workers using three types of work scheduling: flextime, staggered starting hours, and fixed hours. Use the random number table (Table 6 in Appendix II) to randomly assign the workers to the three work schedules.

14.19 Speech recognition technology has advanced to the point that it is now possible to communicate with a computer through verbal commands. A study was conducted to evaluate the value of speech recognition in human interactions with computer systems (*Special Interest Group on Computer-Human Interaction Bulletin*, July 1993). A sample of 45 subjects was randomly divided into three groups (15 subjects per group), and each subject was asked to perform tasks on a basic voice mail system. A different interface was employed in each group: (1) touch-tone, (2) human operator, or (3) simulated speech recognition. One of the variables measured was overall time (in seconds) to perform the assigned tasks. An analysis was conducted to compare the mean overall performance times of the three groups.

a. Identify the experimental design employed in this study.

b. Propose a regression model that will allow you to compare the three means.

c. In terms of means, give the appropriate null hypothesis to be tested.

d. In terms of the β's of the model, part **b**, give the appropriate null hypothesis to be tested.

e. The sample mean performance times for the three groups are given here. Despite differences among the sample means, the null hypothesis of part **c** could not be rejected at $\alpha = .05$. Explain how this is possible.

Group	Mean Performance Time (seconds)
Touch-tone	1,400
Human operator	1,030
Speech recognition	1,040

14.20 Vanadium (V) is a recently recognized essential trace element. An experiment was conducted to compare the concentrations of V in biological materials using isotope dilution mass spectrometry (*Analytical Chemistry*, Nov. 1985). The accompanying table gives the quantities of V (measured in nanograms per gram) in dried samples of oyster tissue, citrus leaves, bovine liver, and human serum. The data were used to fit the linear model

$$E(y) = \beta_0 + \beta_1 x_1 + \beta_2 x_2 + \beta_3 x_3$$

where

$$x_1 = \begin{cases} 1 & \text{if oyster tissue} \\ 0 & \text{if not} \end{cases} \quad x_2 = \begin{cases} 1 & \text{if citrus leaves} \\ 0 & \text{if not} \end{cases} \quad x_3 = \begin{cases} 1 & \text{if bovine liver} \\ 0 & \text{if not} \end{cases}$$

The SAS printout is presented on page 823.

Oyster Tissue	Citrus Leaves	Bovine Liver	Human Serum
2.35	2.32	.39	.10
1.30	3.07	.54	.17
.34	4.09	.30	.14
			.16
			.16

Source: Fassett, J. D., and Kingston, H. M. "Determination of nanogram quantities of vanadium in biological material by isotope dilution thermal ionization mass spectrometry with ion counting detection." *Analytical Chemistry*, Vol. 57, No. 13, Nov. 1985, p. 2475 (Table II). Copyright 1985 American Chemical Society. Reprinted with permission.

a. Identify the treatments in this experiment.

b. Is there sufficient evidence (at $\alpha = .05$) to indicate that the mean V concentrations differ among the four biological materials?

Dependent Variable: V

Analysis of Variance

Source	DF	Sum of Squares	Mean Square	F Value	Prob>F
Model	3	18.86832	6.28944	17.314	0.0003
Error	10	3.63252	0.36325		
C Total	13	22.50084			

Root MSE	0.60270	R-square	0.8386
Dep Mean	1.10214	Adj R-sq	0.7901
C.V.	54.68474		

Parameter Estimates

Variable	DF	Parameter Estimate	Standard Error	T for H0: Parameter=0	Prob > |T|
INTERCEP	1	0.146000	0.26953738	0.542	0.5999
X1	1	1.184000	0.44015270	2.690	0.0227
X2	1	3.014000	0.44015270	6.848	0.0001
X3	1	0.264000	0.44015270	0.600	0.5620

c. Use the β estimates of the model to estimate the mean V concentrations in each of the four biological materials.

14.21 The data for a completely randomized design with two treatments are shown in the accompanying table.

Treatment 1	Treatment 2
10	12
7	8
8	13
11	10
10	10
9	11
9	

a. Give the linear model appropriate for analyzing the data using regression.
b. Fit the model, part a, to the data and conduct the analysis. [*Hint:* You do not need a computer to fit the model. Use the formulas provided in Chapter 11.]

14.22 Refer to Exercise 14.21
a. Calculate MST for the data using the ANOVA formulas. What type of variability is measured by this quantity?
b. Calculate MSE for the data using the ANOVA formulas. What type of variability is measured by this quantity?
c. How many degrees of freedom are associated with MST?
d. How many degrees of freedom are associated with MSE?
e. Compute the test statistic appropriate for testing H_0: $\mu_1 = \mu_2$ against the alternative that the two treatment means differ, using a significance level of $\alpha = .05$. (Compare the value to the test statistic obtained using regression in Exercise 14.21b.)
f. Summarize the results from parts a–e in an ANOVA table.
g. Specify the rejection region, using a significance level of $\alpha = .05$.
h. State the proper conclusion.

14.23 Exercises 14.21 and 14.22 involve a test of the null hypothesis $H_0: \mu_1 = \mu_2$ based on independent random sampling (recall the definition of a completely randomized design). This test was conducted in Section 9.6 using a Student's t statistic.

a. Use the Student's t test to test $H_0: \mu_1 = \mu_2$ against the alternative hypothesis $H_a: \mu_1 \neq \mu_2$. Test using $\alpha = .05$.

b. It can be shown (proof omitted) that an F statistic with $\nu_1 = 1$ numerator degree of freedom and ν_2 denominator degrees of freedom is equal to t^2, where t is a Student's t statistic based on ν_2 degrees of freedom. Square the value of t calculated in part **a**, and show that it is equal to the value of F calculated in Exercises 14.21b and 14.22e.

c. Is the analysis of variance F test for comparing two population means a one- or a two-tailed test of $H_0: \mu_1 = \mu_2$? [*Hint:* Although the t test can be used to test for either $H_a: \mu_1 > \mu_2$ or $H_a: \mu_1 < \mu_2$, the alternative hypothesis for the F test is H_a: The two means are different.]

14.24 Epidemiologists have theorized that the risk of coronary heart disease can be reduced by an increased consumption of fish. One study, begun in 1960, monitored the diet and health of a random sample of middle-age Dutchmen. The men were divided into five groups according to the number of grams of fish consumed per day: 0 grams/day, 1–14 grams/day, 15–29 grams/day, 30–44 grams/day, and 45 or more grams/ day. One of the many variables measured on each subject was intake of polysaccharides (a substance linked to coronary heart disease). An analysis of variance on the levels of polysaccharides (measured as a percentage of energy) in the five groups of Dutchmen resulted in the partial ANOVA table given here.

Source	df	SS	MS	F
Groups	—	534.97	—	—
Error	—	23,659.45	—	
Total	851	24,194.42		

Source: Kromhout, D., Bosschieter, E. B., and Coulander, C. D. L. "The inverse relation between fish consumption and 20-year mortality from coronary heart disease." *New England Journal of Medicine*, May 9, 1985, Vol. 312, No. 19, pp. 1205–1209. Reprinted by permission.

a. Give the total number of Dutchmen included in this portion of the study.

b. Complete the ANOVA table.

c. Is there sufficient evidence of differences among the mean levels of polysaccharides in the five groups of Dutchmen? Test using $\alpha = .01$.

14.25 As oil drilling costs rise at unprecedented rates, the task of measuring drilling performance becomes essential to a successful oil company. One method of lowering drilling costs is to increase drilling speed. Researchers at Cities Service Co. have developed a drill bit, called the PD-1, which they believe penetrates rock at a faster rate than any other bit on the market. It is decided to compare the speed of the PD-1 with the two fastest drill bits known, the IADC 1-2-6 and the IADC 5-1-7, at 12 drilling locations in Texas. Four drilling sites were randomly assigned to each bit, and the rate of penetration (RoP) in feet per hour (fph) was recorded after drilling 3,000 feet at each site. The data are given in the table, followed by a MINITAB ANOVA printout. Based on this information, can Cities Service Co. conclude that the mean RoP differs for at least two of the three drill bits? Test at the $\alpha = .05$ level of significance.

PD-1	IADC 1-2-6	IADC 5-1-7
35.2	25.8	14.7
30.1	29.7	28.9
37.6	26.6	23.3
34.3	30.1	16.2

```
ANALYSIS OF VARIANCE ON ROP
SOURCE      DF        SS        MS       F         p
DRILLBIT     2      366.6     183.3    9.50     0.006
ERROR        9      173.7      19.3
TOTAL       11      540.2
                                    INDIVIDUAL 95 PCT CI'S FOR MEAN
                                    BASED ON POOLED STDEV
LEVEL        N       MEAN     STDEV   --------+---------+---------+--------
  1          4     34.300     3.127                        (------*------)
  2          4     28.050     2.167              (------*------)
  3          4     20.775     6.589   (------*------)
                                    --------+---------+---------+--------
POOLED STDEV =      4.393             21.0      28.0      35.0
```

14.26 The display consoles of modern computer-based systems use many abbreviated words to accommodate the large volume of information to be displayed. Therefore, operators must learn to decode each abbreviation quickly and accurately. An experiment was conducted to determine the optimal method for abbreviating any specific set of words on the sonar consoles used at the Naval Submarine Medical Research Laboratory in Groton, Connecticut (*Human Factors*, Feb. 1984). Of the 20 Navy and civilian personnel who took part in the study, five were highly familiar with the sonar system. The 15 subjects unfamiliar with the system were randomly divided into three groups of five. Thus, the study consisted of a total of four groups (one experienced and three inexperienced groups), with five subjects per group. The experienced group and one inexperienced group (denoted TE and TI, respectively) were assigned to learn the simple method of abbreviation. One of the remaining inexperienced groups was assigned the conventional single abbreviation method (denoted CS), whereas the other was assigned the conventional multiple abbreviation method (denoted CM). Each subject was then given a list of 75 abbreviations to learn, one at a time, through the display console of a minicomputer. The number of trials until the subject accurately decoded at least 90% of the words on the list was recorded. Do the data provide sufficient evidence to indicate differences among the mean numbers of trials required for the four groups? Test using $\alpha = .05$. (Use the SAS printout on page 826 to solve this problem.)

CM	CS	TE	TI
4	6	5	8
7	9	5	4
5	5	7	8
6	7	8	10
8	6	7	3

Source: Data are simulated values based on the group means reported in *Human Factors*, Feb. 1984. Copyright 1984 by the Human Factors Society, Inc. and reproduced by permission.

Analysis of Variance Procedure

Dependent Variable: TRIALS

Source	DF	Sum of Squares	Mean Square	F Value	Pr > F
Model	3	1.20000000	0.40000000	0.10	0.9566
Error	16	61.60000000	3.85000000		
Corrected Total	19	62.80000000			

R-Square	C.V.	Root MSE	TRIALS Mean
0.019108	30.658464	1.9621417	6.40000000

Source	DF	Anova SS	Mean Square	F Value	Pr > F
GROUP	3	1.20000000	0.40000000	0.10	0.9566

14.27 An excessive amount of ozone in the air is indicative of air pollution. Six air samples were collected from each of four locations in the industrial Midwest and measured for their content of ozone. The amounts of ozone (in parts per million) are shown in the accompanying table.

	Location		
1	2	3	4
.08	.15	.13	.05
.10	.09	.10	.11
.09	.11	.15	.07
.07	.10	.09	.09
.09	.08	.09	.11
.06	.13	.17	.08

a. Use the formulas provided in this section to construct an analysis of variance table for the data.
b. Do the data provide sufficient evidence to indicate differences in the mean ozone content among the four locations? Use $\alpha = .05$.
c. Suppose you want to estimate the difference in mean ozone content between two locations correct to within .01 part per million with probability approximately equal to .95. How many air samples would be required at each location? [*Hint:* Refer to Section 8.12.]

OPTIONAL EXERCISES

14.28 The small-sample estimation and test procedures for comparing two population means discussed in Chapters 8 and 9 were based on independent random sampling—that is, a completely randomized design. For both estimation and test procedures, we used a pooled estimate of σ^2, namely,

$$s^2 = \frac{(n_1 - 1)s_1^2 + (n_2 - 1)s_2^2}{n_1 + n_2 - 2}$$

$$= \frac{\sum_{i=1}^{n_1}(y_{i1} - \bar{y}_1)^2 + \sum_{i=2}^{n_2}(y_{i2} - \bar{y}_2)^2}{n_1 + n_2 - 2}$$

[*Note:* In the notation of this chapter, $\bar{y}_1 = \bar{T}_1$, $\bar{y}_2 = \bar{T}_2$, and, in general, $\bar{y}_i = \bar{T}_i$.] The numerator in this expression is SSE. In general, regardless of the number of treatments, it can be shown (proof omitted) that

$$SSE = (n_1 - 1)s_1^2 + (n_2 - 1)s_2^2 + \cdots + (n_p - 1)s_p^2$$

$$= \sum_{i=1}^{n_1} (y_{i1} - \bar{y}_1)^2 + \sum_{i=1}^{n_2}(y_{i2} - \bar{y}_2)^2 + \cdots + \sum_{i=1}^{n_p} (y_{ip} - \bar{y}_p)^2$$

Refer to Exercise 14.25. Calculate the sum of squares of deviations of the y values in each sample about their respective sample means. Then calculate SSE using the above formula and verify that it is the same value obtained in Exercise 14.25.

14.29 The means and standard deviations listed in the table provide information on the strengths (modules of rupture at ground line) for five types of wooden poles used by the utility industry. The data used to obtain the means and standard deviations (recorded in pounds per square inch) were collected according to a completely randomized design (independent random samples).

Species	Sample Size	Sample Mean	Sample Standard Deviation
Northern white cedar	28	3,660	203.33
Western red cedar	387	5,550	298.39
Pacific silver fir	103	5,420	313.29
Coastal Douglas fir	118	8,380	644.62
Southern pine	147	8,870	611.72

Source: Goodman, J. R., Vanderbilt, M. D., and Criswell, M. E. "Reliability-based design of wood transmission line structures." *Journal of Structural Engineering*, Vol. 109, No. 3, 1983, pp. 690–704.

a. Find the totals for each sample and the total for all 783 strength measurements. Then compute CM and SST.

b. Since we do not know the value of $\Sigma_{i=1}^n y_i^2$, calculate SSE using the pooled method:

$$SSE = \sum_{i=1}^{n_1} (y_{i1} - \bar{y}_1)^2 + \sum_{i=1}^{n_2} (y_{i2} - \bar{y}_2)^2 + \cdots + \sum_{i=1}^{n_5} (y_{i5} - \bar{y}_5)^2$$

$$= (n_1 - 1)s_1^2 + (n_2 - 1)s_2^2 + \cdots + (n_5 - 1)s_5^2$$

c. Find SS(Total).

d. Construct an analysis of variance table for the data.

e. Do the data provide sufficient evidence to indicate differences in the mean strengths among the five types of poles? Test using $\alpha = .05$.

f. Find a 90% confidence interval for the mean strength of Northern white cedar poles.

g. Find a 90% confidence interval for the difference in mean strengths between Northern white cedar and Southern pine poles.

14.30 Unlike most other commonly used engineering materials, concrete experiences a characteristic marked increase in "creep" when it is heated for the first time under load. To investigate this phenomenon, a study of the thermal strain behavior of concrete was conducted (*Magazine of Concrete Research*, Dec. 1985).

Concrete specimens were prepared and a constant load applied to each. The test specimens were then heated to a specified temperature at a rate of 1°C per minute, with the specimens randomly assigned to one of five temperature settings (100°, 200°, 300°, 400°, and 500°C). For each specimen, the difference between the free (unloaded) thermal strain and load-induced thermal strain, called the *total thermal strain*, was calculated. The sample size, mean, and standard deviation of the total thermal strain values for each temperature setting are given in the table. [*Note:* Thermal strain is recorded in units $\times 10^6$.]

Temperature	Number of Specimens	Mean	Standard Deviation
100	16	52	55
200	16	112	108
300	16	143	127
400	16	186	136
500	14	257	178

Source: Khoury, G. A., Grainger, B. N., and Sullivan, P. J. E. "Strain of concrete during first heating to 600°C under load." *Magazine of Concrete Research,* Vol. 37, No. 133, Dec. 1985, p. 198 (Table 2).

a. Use the technique of Exercise 14.28 to construct an ANOVA summary table for the data.
b. Is there sufficient evidence to indicate that heating temperature affects the mean total thermal strain of concrete? Test using $\alpha = .01$.

14.9 ANOVA for Randomized Block Designs

A commonly used noise-reducing design is the randomized block design. Recall (Definition 14.5) that a randomized block design employs groups of homogeneous experimental units (matched as closely as possible) to compare the means of the populations associated with p treatments. The general layout of a randomized block design is shown in Figure 14.13. Note that there are b blocks of relatively homogeneous experimental units. Since each treatment must be represented in each block, the blocks each contain p experimental units. Although Figure 14.13 shows the p treatments in order within the blocks, in practice they would be assigned to the experimental units in random order (thus the name **randomized block design**).

The complete model for a randomized block design contains $(p - 1)$ dummy variables for treatments and $(b - 1)$ dummy variables for blocks. Therefore, the total number of terms in the model, excluding β_0, is $(p - 1) + (b - 1) = p + b - 2$, as shown here.

Complete model:

$$E(y) = \beta_0 + \underbrace{\beta_1 x_1 + \beta_2 x_2 + \cdots + \beta_{p-1} x_{p-1}}_{\text{Treatment effects}} + \underbrace{\beta_p x_p + \cdots + \beta_{p+b-2} x_{p+b-2}}_{\text{Block effects}}$$

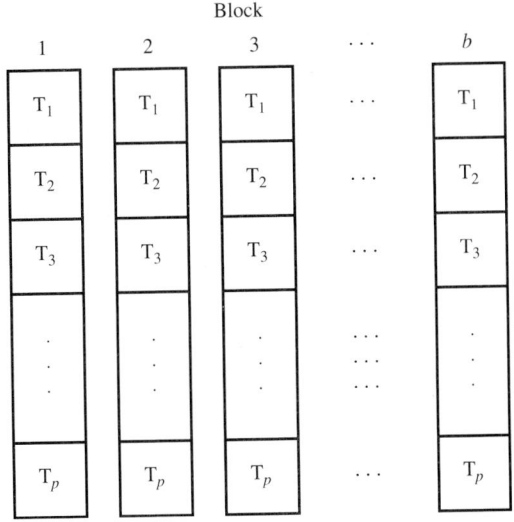

FIGURE 14.13 ▶
General form of a randomized block design (treatment is denoted by T_p)

where

$$x_1 = \begin{cases} 1 & \text{if treatment 2} \\ 0 & \text{if not} \end{cases} \qquad x_2 = \begin{cases} 1 & \text{if treatment 3} \\ 0 & \text{if not} \end{cases} \cdots \qquad x_{p-1} = \begin{cases} 1 & \text{if treatment } p \\ 0 & \text{if not} \end{cases}$$

$$x_p = \begin{cases} 1 & \text{if block 2} \\ 0 & \text{if not} \end{cases} \qquad x_{p+1} = \begin{cases} 1 & \text{if block 3} \\ 0 & \text{if not} \end{cases} \cdots \qquad x_{p+b-2} = \begin{cases} 1 & \text{if block } b \\ 0 & \text{if not} \end{cases}$$

Note that the model does *not* include terms for treatment–block interaction. The reasons are twofold. First, the addition of these terms would leave 0 degrees of freedom for estimating σ^2. Second, the failure of the mean difference between a pair of treatments to remain the same from block to block is, by definition, experimental error. In other words, in a randomized block design, treatment–block interaction and experimental error are synonymous.

The primary objective of the analysis is to compare the p treatment means, μ_1, $\mu_2, \ldots, \mu_p$. That is, we want to test the null hypothesis

$$H_0: \quad \mu_1 = \mu_2 = \mu_3 = \cdots = \mu_p$$

Recall (Section 10.3) that this is equivalent to testing whether all the treatment parameters in the complete model are equal to 0, i.e.,

$$H_0: \quad \beta_1 = \beta_2 = \cdots = \beta_{p-1} = 0$$

To perform this test using regression, we drop the treatment terms and fit the reduced model:

Reduced model for testing treatments:
$$E(y) = \beta_0 + \underbrace{\beta_p x_p + \beta_{p+1} x_{p+1} + \cdots + \beta_{p+b-2} x_{p+b-2}}_{\text{Block effects}}$$

Then we compare the SSEs for the two models, SSE_R and SSE_C, using the "partial" F statistic:

$$F = \frac{(SSE_R - SSE_C)/\text{Number of } \beta\text{'s tested}}{MSE_C}$$
$$= \frac{(SSE_R - SSE_C)/(p - 1)}{MSE_C}$$

A significant F value implies that the treatment means differ.

Occasionally, experimenters want to determine whether blocking was effective in removing the extraneous source of variation, i.e., whether there is evidence of a difference among block means. In fact, if there are no differences among block means, the experimenter will lose information by blocking because blocking reduces the number of degrees of freedom associated with the estimated variance of the model, s^2. If blocking is *not* effective in reducing the variability, then the block parameters in the complete model will all equal 0 (i.e., there will be no differences among block means). Thus, we want to test

$$H_0: \quad \beta_p = \beta_{p+1} = \cdots = \beta_{p+b-2} = 0$$

Another reduced model, with the block β's dropped, is fit:

Reduced model for testing blocks:
$$E(y) = \beta_0 + \underbrace{\beta_1 x_1 + \beta_2 x_2 + \cdots + \beta_{p-1} x_{p-1}}_{\text{Treatment effects}}$$

The SSE for this second reduced model is compared to the SSE for the complete model in the usual fashion. A significant F test implies that blocking is effective in removing (or reducing) the targeted extraneous source of variation.

These two tests are summarized in the following boxes.

Models and ANOVA F Tests for a Randomized Block Design with p Treatments and b Blocks

Complete model:

$$E(y) = \beta_0 + \overbrace{\beta_1 x_1 + \cdots + \beta_{p-1} x_{p-1}}^{(p-1) \text{ treatment terms}} + \overbrace{\beta_p x_p + \cdots + \beta_{p+b-2} x_{p+b-2}}^{(b-1) \text{ block terms}}$$

where

$$x_1 = \begin{cases} 1 & \text{if treatment 2} \\ 0 & \text{if not} \end{cases} \quad \cdots \quad x_{p-1} = \begin{cases} 1 & \text{if treatment } p \\ 0 & \text{if not} \end{cases}$$

$$x_p = \begin{cases} 1 & \text{if block 2} \\ 0 & \text{if not} \end{cases} \quad \cdots \quad x_{p+b-2} = \begin{cases} 1 & \text{if block } b \\ 0 & \text{if not} \end{cases}$$

Test for Comparing Treatment Means

H_0: $\beta_1 = \beta_2 = \cdots = \beta_{p-1} = 0$
(i.e., H_0: The p treatment means are equal)

H_a: At least one of the β parameters listed in H_0 differs from 0
(i.e., H_a: At least two treatment means differ)

Reduced model: $E(y) = \beta_0 + \beta_p x_p + \cdots + \beta_{p+b-2} x_{p+b-2}$

Test statistic: $F = \dfrac{(\text{SSE}_R - \text{SSE}_C)/(p-1)}{\text{SSE}_C/(n-p-b+1)}$

$\qquad\qquad\qquad = \dfrac{(\text{SSE}_R - \text{SSE}_C)/(p-1)}{\text{MSE}_C}$

where

SSE_R = SSE for reduced model

SSE_C = SSE for complete model

MSE_C = MSE for complete model

Rejection region: $F > F_\alpha$, where F is based on $\nu_1 = (p-1)$ and $\nu_2 = (n - p - b + 1)$ degrees of freedom

Test for Comparing Block Means

H_0: $\beta_p = \beta_{p+1} = \cdots = \beta_{p+b-2} = 0$
(i.e., H_0: The b block means are equal)

H_a: At least one of the β parameters listed in H_0 differs from 0
(i.e., H_a: At least two block means differ)

Reduced model: $E(y) = \beta_0 + \beta_1 x_1 + \beta_2 x_2 + \cdots + \beta_{p-1} x_{p-1}$

Test statistic: $F = \dfrac{(\text{SSE}_R - \text{SSE}_C)/(b-1)}{\text{SSE}_C/(n-p-b+1)}$

$\qquad\qquad\qquad = \dfrac{(\text{SSE}_R - \text{SSE}_C)/(b-1)}{\text{MSE}_C}$

Rejection region: $F > F_\alpha$, where F is based on $\nu_1 = (b-1)$ and $\nu_2 = (n - p - b + 1)$ degrees of freedom

Assumptions

1. The probability distribution of the difference between any pair of treatment observations within a block is approximately normal.

2. The variance of the difference is constant and the same for all pairs of observations.

EXAMPLE 14.10

Prior to submitting a bid for a construction job, cost engineers prepare a detailed analysis of the estimated labor and materials costs required to complete the job. This estimate will depend on the engineer who performs the analysis. An overly large estimate will reduce the chance of acceptance of a company's bid price, whereas an estimate that is too low will reduce the profit or even cause the company to lose money on the job. A company that employs three job cost engineers wanted to compare the mean level of the engineers' estimates. This was done by having each engineer estimate the cost of the same four jobs. The data (in hundreds of thousands of dollars) are shown in Table 14.9.

TABLE 14.9   Data for the Randomized Block Design of Example 14.10

		Job				Treatment Means
		1	2	3	4	
Engineer	1	4.6	6.2	5.0	6.6	5.60
	2	4.9	6.3	5.4	6.8	5.85
	3	4.4	5.9	5.4	6.3	5.50
Block Means		4.63	6.13	5.27	6.57	

a. Perform an analysis of variance on the data, and test to determine whether there is sufficient evidence to indicate differences among treatment means. Test using $\alpha = .05$.

b. Test to determine whether blocking on jobs was successful in reducing the job-to-job variation in the estimates. Use $\alpha = .05$.

Solution

a. The data for this experiment were collected according to a randomized block design because we would expect estimates of the same job to be more nearly alike than estimates between jobs. Thus, the experiment involves three treatments (engineers) and four blocks (jobs).

   The complete model for this design is

$$E(y) = \beta_0 + \underbrace{\beta_1 x_1 + \beta_2 x_2}_{\text{Treatments (engineers)}} + \underbrace{\beta_3 x_3 + \beta_4 x_4 + \beta_5 x_5}_{\text{Blocks (jobs)}}$$

   where

$$y = \text{Cost estimate}$$

$$x_1 = \begin{cases} 1 & \text{if engineer 2} \\ 0 & \text{if not} \end{cases} \qquad x_2 = \begin{cases} 1 & \text{if engineer 3} \\ 0 & \text{if not} \end{cases}$$

Base level = Engineer 1

$$x_3 = \begin{cases} 1 & \text{if block 2} \\ 0 & \text{if not} \end{cases} \qquad x_4 = \begin{cases} 1 & \text{if block 3} \\ 0 & \text{if not} \end{cases} \qquad x_5 = \begin{cases} 1 & \text{if block 4} \\ 0 & \text{if not} \end{cases}$$

Base level = Block 1

The SAS printout for the complete model is shown in Figure 14.14. Note that $SSE_C = .18667$ and $MSE_C = .03111$ (shaded on the printout).

FIGURE 14.14 ▶

SAS printout for complete model of Example 14.10

Dependent Variable: ESTCOST

Analysis of Variance

Source	DF	Sum of Squares	Mean Square	F Value	Prob>F
Model	5	7.02333	1.40467	45.150	0.0001
Error	6	0.18667	0.03111		
C Total	11	7.21000			

Root MSE	0.17638	R-square	0.9741	
Dep Mean	5.65000	Adj R-sq	0.9525	
C.V.	3.12183			

Parameter Estimates

Variable	DF	Parameter Estimate	Standard Error	T for H0: Parameter=0	Prob > |T|
INTERCEP	1	4.583333	0.12472191	36.748	0.0001
X1	1	0.250000	0.12472191	2.004	0.0919
X2	1	-0.100000	0.12472191	-0.802	0.4533
X3	1	1.500000	0.14401646	10.415	0.0001
X4	1	0.633333	0.14401646	4.398	0.0046
X5	1	1.933333	0.14401646	13.424	0.0001

To test for differences among treatment means, we will test

$$H_0: \quad \mu_1 = \mu_2 = \mu_3$$

where μ_i = mean cost estimate of engineer i. This is equivalent to testing

$$H_0: \quad \beta_1 = \beta_2 = 0$$

in the complete model. To proceed, we fit the reduced model

$$E(y) = \beta_0 + \underbrace{\beta_3 x_3 + \beta_4 x_4 + \beta_5 x_5}_{\text{Blocks (jobs)}}$$

The SAS printout for this reduced model is shown in Figure 14.15 on page 834. Note that $SSE_R = .44667$ (shaded on the printout).

FIGURE 14.15 ►
SAS printout for reduced model for
testing treatments, Example 14.10

Dependent Variable: ESTCOST

Analysis of Variance

Source	DF	Sum of Squares	Mean Square	F Value	Prob>F
Model	3	6.76333	2.25444	40.378	0.0001
Error	8	0.44667	0.05583		
C Total	11	7.21000			

Root MSE	0.23629	R-square	0.9380	
Dep Mean	5.65000	Adj R-sq	0.9148	
C.V.	4.18214			

Parameter Estimates

Variable	DF	Parameter Estimate	Standard Error	T for H0: Parameter=0	Prob > |T|
INTERCEP	1	4.633333	0.13642255	33.963	0.0001
X3	1	1.500000	0.19293062	7.775	0.0001
X4	1	0.633333	0.19293062	3.283	0.0111
X5	1	1.933333	0.19293062	10.021	0.0001

The remaining elements of the test follow:

Test statistic:

$$F = \frac{(SSE_R - SSE_C)/(p-1)}{MSE_C} = \frac{(.44667 - .18667)/2}{.03111} = 4.18$$

Rejection region: $F > 5.14$, where $F_{.05} = 5.14$ (obtained from Table 10, Appendix II) is based on $\nu_1 = (p-1) = 2$ df and $\nu_2 = (n - p - b + 1) = 6$ df

Conclusion: Since $F = 4.18$ is less than the critical value, 5.14, there is insufficient evidence, at the $\alpha = .05$ level of significance, to indicate the differences among the mean estimates for the three cost engineers.

b. To test for the effectiveness of blocking on jobs, we test

$$H_0: \quad \beta_3 = \beta_4 = \beta_5 = 0$$

in the complete model specified in part **a**. The reduced model is

$$E(y) = \beta_0 + \underbrace{\beta_1 x_1 + \beta_2 x_2}_{\text{Treatments (engineers)}}$$

The SAS printout for this second reduced model is shown in Figure 14.16. Note that $SSE_R = 6.95$ (shaded on the printout). The elements of the test follow.

Test statistic:

$$F = \frac{(SSE_R - SSE_C)/(b-1)}{MSE_C} = \frac{(6.95 - .18667)/3}{.03111} = 72.46$$

Rejection region: $F > 4.76$, where $F_{.05} = 4.76$ (from Table 10, Appendix II) is based on $\nu_1 = (b-1) = 3$ df and $\nu_2 = (n - p - b + 1) = 6$ df.

FIGURE 14.16 ▶

SAS printout for reduced model for testing blocks, Example 14.10

```
Dependent Variable: ESTCOST

                        Analysis of Variance

                         Sum of          Mean
    Source        DF     Squares        Square     F Value    Prob>F

    Model          2     0.26000       0.13000       0.168    0.8477
    Error          9     6.95000       0.77222
    C Total       11     7.21000

        Root MSE         0.87876      R-square       0.0361
        Dep Mean         5.65000      Adj R-sq      -0.1781
        C.V.            15.55331

                       Parameter Estimates

                      Parameter      Standard    T for H0:
    Variable   DF      Estimate         Error    Parameter=0    Prob > |T|

    INTERCEP    1      5.600000    0.43938088        12.745        0.0001
    X1          1      0.250000    0.62137840         0.402        0.6968
    X2          1     -0.100000    0.62137840        -0.161        0.8757
```

Conclusion: Since $F = 72.46$ exceeds the critical value, 4.76, there is sufficient evidence (at $\alpha = .05$) to indicate the differences among the block (job) means. It appears that blocking on jobs was effective in reducing the job-to-job variation in cost estimates.

· · · · · · · · · · · · · · · · · · · ·

Caution: The result of the test for the equality of block means must be interpreted with care, especially when the calculated value of the F test statistic does not fall in the rejection region. This does not necessarily imply that the block means are the same, i.e., that blocking is unimportant. Reaching this conclusion would be equivalent to accepting the null hypothesis, a practice we have carefully avoided because of to the unknown probability of committing a Type II error (that is, of accepting H_0 when H_a is true). In other words, even when a test for block differences is inconclusive, we may still want to use the randomized block design in similar future experiments. If the experimenter believes that the experimental units are more homogeneous within blocks than among blocks, he or she should use the randomized block design regardless of whether the test comparing the block means shows them to be different.

The traditional analysis of variance approach to analyzing the data collected from a randomized block design is similar to the completely randomized design. The partitioning of SS(Total) for the randomized block design is most easily seen by examining Figure 14.17 on page 836. Note that SS(Total) is now partitioned into *three* parts:

$$\text{SS(Total)} = \text{SSB} + \text{SST} + \text{SSE}$$

The formulas for calculating SST and SSB follow the same pattern as the formula for calculating SST for the completely randomized design.

FIGURE 14.17 ▶
Partitioning of the total sum of
squares for the randomized block
design

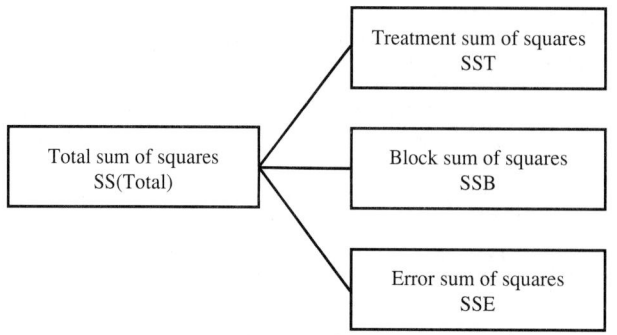

From these quantities, we obtain mean square for treatments, MST, mean square
for blocks, MSB, and mean square for error, MSE, as shown in the box. The test
statistics are

$$F = \frac{\text{MST}}{\text{MSE}} \quad \text{for testing treatments}$$

$$F = \frac{\text{MSB}}{\text{MSE}} \quad \text{for testing blocks}$$

These F values are equivalent to the "partial" F statistics of the regression approach.

EXAMPLE 14.11

Refer to Example 14.10. Perform an analysis of variance of the data in Table 14.9
using the ANOVA approach.

Computing Formulas for the Analysis of Variance for a Randomized Block Design

$$\sum_{i=1}^{n} y_i = \text{Sum of all } n \text{ measurements}$$

$$\sum_{i=1}^{n} y_i^2 = \text{Sum of squares of all } n \text{ measurements}$$

$$\begin{aligned}
\text{CM} &= \text{Correction for mean} \\
&= \frac{(\text{Total of all measurements})^2}{\text{Total number of measurements}} = \frac{\left(\sum_{i=1}^{n} y_i\right)^2}{n}
\end{aligned}$$

$$\begin{aligned}
\text{SS(Total)} &= \text{Total sum of squares} \\
&= \text{Sum of squares of all measurements} - \text{CM} \\
&= \sum_{i=1}^{n} y_i^2 - \text{CM}
\end{aligned}$$

(continued)

$$\text{SST} = \text{Sum of squares for treatments}$$

$$= \left(\begin{array}{c} \text{Sum of squares of treatment totals with} \\ \text{each square divided by } b \text{, the number of} \\ \text{measurements for that treatment} \end{array} \right) - \text{CM}$$

$$= \frac{T_1^2}{b} + \frac{T_2^2}{b} + \cdots + \frac{T_p^2}{b} - \text{CM}$$

$$\text{SSB} = \text{Sum of squares for blocks}$$

$$= \left(\begin{array}{c} \text{Sum of squares for block totals with} \\ \text{each square divided by } p \text{, the number} \\ \text{of measurements in that block} \end{array} \right) - \text{CM}$$

$$= \frac{B_1^2}{p} + \frac{B_2^2}{p} + \cdots + \frac{B_b^2}{p} - \text{CM}$$

$$\text{SSE} = \text{Sum of squares for error}$$

$$= \text{SS(Total)} - \text{SST} - \text{SSB}$$

$$\text{MST} = \text{Mean square for treatments}$$

$$= \frac{\text{SST}}{p - 1}$$

$$\text{MSB} = \text{Mean square for blocks}$$

$$= \frac{\text{SSB}}{b - 1}$$

$$\text{MSE} = \text{Mean square for error}$$

$$= \frac{\text{SSE}}{n - p - b + 1}$$

Solution

Rather than perform the calculations by hand (again, we leave this as an exercise for the student), we utilize a computer software package. The MINITAB printout of the ANOVA is displayed in Figure 14.18 on page 838. Unlike SAS, MINITAB does not calculate the F statistics—these must be calculated by hand. For example, the F statistic for testing treatment means is

$$F = \frac{\text{MST}}{\text{MSE}} = \frac{.130}{.0311}$$

$$= 4.18 \quad \text{(where MST and MSE are shaded on Figure 14.18)}$$

Note that this value agrees exactly with the F value for treatments obtained in Example 14.10.

FIGURE 14.18 ▶

MINITAB ANOVA for the data in
Table 14.9

```
ANALYSIS OF VARIANCE   Estimate

SOURCE          DF        SS          MS
Engineer         2     0.2600      0.1300
Job              3     6.7633      2.2544
ERROR            6     0.1867      0.0311
TOTAL           11     7.2100
```

As with a completely randomized design, the sources of variation and their respective degrees of freedom, sums of squares, and mean squares for a randomized block design are summarized in an analysis of variance table. The format of an ANOVA table for a randomized block design is shown in Table 14.10; the ANOVA table for the data for Table 14.9 is shown in Table 14.11. (These quantities were obtained from the printout, Figure 14.18.) Note that the degrees of freedom for the three sources of variation, treatments, blocks, and error, sum to the degrees of freedom for SS(Total). Similarly, the sums of squares for the three sources will always sum to SS(Total).

TABLE 14.10   Analysis of Variance Table for a Randomized Block Design

Source	df	SS	MS	F
Treatments	$p - 1$	SST	MST	MST/MSE
Blocks	$b - 1$	SSB	MSB	MSB/MSE
Error	$n - p - b + 1$	SSE	MSE	
Total	$n - 1$	SS(Total)		

TABLE 14.11   Analysis of Variance Table for Example 14.11

Source	df	SS	MS	F
Treatments (engineers)	2	.260	.130	4.18
Blocks (jobs)	3	6.763	2.254	72.46
Error	6	.187	.031	
Total	11	7.210		

There is one very important point to note when you block the treatments in an experiment. Recall from Section 14.4 that the block effects cancel. This fact enables us to calculate confidence intervals for the difference between treatment means. But, if a sample treatment mean is used to estimate a *single treatment mean*, the block effects do not cancel. *Therefore, the only way that you can obtain an unbiased estimate of a single treatment mean (and corresponding confidence interval) in a blocked design is to randomly select the blocks from a large collection (population) of blocks and to treat the block effect as a second random component, in addition to random error. Designs that contain two or more random components are called nested designs and are beyond the scope of this text. For more information on this topic, see the references at the end of this chapter.*

EXERCISES

14.31 *Physical Therapy* (Aug. 1986) reported on a study to "determine whether the medial rotation that accompanies flexion of the shoulder took place during the performance of the flexion-abduction-lateral-rotation proprioceptive neuromuscular facilitation pattern (D_2F)." Ten college students, who exhibited no evidence of disease or limitation of movement in their shoulders, served as the subjects for the study. For each subject, the medial rotation was measured (in degrees) at each of three positions in the D_2F pattern: (1) beginning position, (2) point at which rotation changed directions, and (3) ending position. The goal of the analysis is to compare the mean medial rotation measurements of the three positions.
a. Identify the treatments in this experiment.
b. Identify the blocks in this experiment.
c. Identify the response variable.
d. Explain why a randomized block design is appropriate for this experiment.
e. Give the linear model appropriate for analyzing the data.

14.32 Refer to the *Microcomputers in Civil Engineering* study of lateral drift in a building, Exercise 14.4. The lateral displacements (in inches) estimated by three different computer programs are recorded in the table for each of five building levels: 1, 5, 10, 15, and 21. Use the ANOVA formulas to analyze the data. Recall that the goal is to compare the mean drift ratios estimated by the three computer programs, STAAD-III (run 1), STAAD-III (run 2), and DRIFT. Use $\alpha = .05$.

Level	STAAD-III (1)	STAAD-III (2)	Drift
1	.17	.16	.16
2	1.35	1.26	1.27
3	3.04	2.76	2.77
4	4.54	3.98	3.99
5	5.94	4.99	5.00

Source: Valles, R. E., et al. "Simplified drift evaluation of wall-frame structures." *Microcomputers in Civil Engineering*, Vol. 8, 1993, p. 242 (Table 2).

14.33 The Perth (Australia) Metropolitan Water Authority recently completed construction of land pipeline for transporting domestic wastewaters from a primary treatment plant. During construction, the cement mortar lining of the pipeline was tested for cracking to determine whether autogenous healing will seal the cracks. Otherwise, expensive epoxy filling repairs would be necessary (*Proceedings of the Institute of Civil Engineers*, Apr. 1986). After cracks were observed in the pipeline, it was kept full of water for a period of 14 weeks. At each of 12 crack locations, crack widths were measured (in millimeters) after the 2nd, 6th, and 14th weeks of the wet period, as shown in the accompanying table. The data were subjected to an ANOVA using SAS. The SAS printout is shown on page 840.

Crack Location	Crack Width After Wetting				Crack Location	Crack Width After Wetting			
	0 Weeks	2 Weeks	6 Weeks	14 Weeks		0 Weeks	2 Weeks	6 Weeks	14 Weeks
1	.50	.20	.10	.10	7	.90	.25	.05	.05
2	.40	.20	.10	.10	8	1.00	.30	.05	.10
3	.60	.30	.15	.10	9	.70	.25	.10	.10
4	.80	.40	.10	.10	10	.60	.25	.10	.05
5	.80	.30	.05	.05	11	.30	.15	.10	.05
6	1.00	.40	.05	.05	12	.30	.14	.05	.05

Source: Cox, B. G., and Kelsall, K. J. "Construction of Cape Peron Ocean Outlet Perth, Western Australia." *Proceedings of the Institute of Civil Engineers*, Part 1, Vol. 80, Apr. 1986, p. 479 (Table 1).

```
                         Analysis of Variance Procedure

Dependent Variable: WIDTH
                                    Sum of           Mean
Source                  DF          Squares         Square     F Value     Pr > F

Model                   14        2.96188333     0.21156310     13.71      0.0001
Error                   33        0.50930833     0.01543359
Corrected Total         47        3.47119167

                    R-Square            C.V.        Root MSE          WIDTH Mean

                    0.853276         46.08296       0.124232          0.26958333

Source                  DF        Anova SS     Mean Square     F Value     Pr > F

PERIOD                   3      2.68489167     0.89496389       57.99      0.0001
LOCATION                11      0.27699167     0.02518106        1.63      0.1354
```

Conduct a test to determine whether the mean crack widths differ for the four time periods. Test using $\alpha = .05$.

14.34   Early full-screen video display terminals presented the viewer with white characters on a black background. Initially, viewers found the high degree of contrast easy on the eyes. However, after an extended period of use, black and white displays were frequently found to cause temporary eye irritations. Experimentation with other colors revealed that yellow/amber displays may be the easiest on the eyes. In one German study, video display terminals were produced with white/black and six different symbol colors. Thirty test subjects were asked to specify which color combination they preferred by ranking each of the seven color combinations on a scale from 0 (no preference) to 10. Based on the mean preference scores for each color provided by the researchers, we have simulated the individual preference scores for 10 subjects in the accompanying table. The data were subjected to an ANOVA for a randomized block design using MINITAB; the results are shown in the accompanying printout.
   a. Do the data provide sufficient evidence of a difference among the mean preference scores for the seven video display color combinations? Test using $\alpha = .05$.
   b. Perform the analysis, part a, by fitting and comparing the appropriate linear models. Verify that the results agree.

Subject	Green/ Black	White/ Black	Yellow/ White	Orange/ White	Yellow	Yellow/ Amber	Yellow/ Orange
1	7	6	7	2	8	9	3
2	8	6	9	4	9	8	1
3	5	5	7	1	6	8	2
4	3	4	2	0	2	6	0
5	9	8	8	3	9	9	2
6	7	5	6	2	7	7	1
7	6	7	8	4	6	9	5
8	6	5	8	1	8	9	1
9	9	9	8	2	9	8	0
10	9	8	8	3	9	10	1

Source: Adapted from Solomon, L., and Burawa, A. "Maximize your computing comfort and efficiency." *Computers & Electronics*, Apr. 1983, pp. 35–40.

```
ANALYSIS OF VARIANCE SCORE
SOURCE    DF      SS      MS
COLOR      6   421.34   70.22
SUBJECT    9   114.30   12.70
ERROR     54    71.80    1.33
TOTAL     69   607.44
```

14.35 An experiment was conducted to compare two different methods of sampling to determine the iron content of iron ore. The first method, *manual sampling*, involved stopping the ore conveyor belt and removing a 1-meter length of ore from the belt. The second method, *mechanical sampling*, involved collecting the sample of ore (an increment) from the stream of ore falling from the end of the belt. The samples were matched by making certain that the ore for the mechanical sample came from approximately the same increment on the conveyor belt as the ore obtained for the manual sample. The data shown in the table are measurements on the iron-ore content (percentage of increment) for 16 increments selected from a shipment of Chilean iron ore. (Only a portion of the experimental data is given here.)

Increment Number	Sampling Method Mechanical	Manual	Increment Number	Sampling Method Mechanical	Manual
1	62.66	63.92	9	61.75	62.03
2	62.87	63.64	10	63.15	62.17
3	63.22	63.64	11	63.08	64.34
4	63.01	63.27	12	63.22	62.30
5	62.10	62.94	13	63.22	63.50
6	63.43	64.61	14	63.08	62.73
7	63.22	62.87	15	62.87	61.89
8	63.57	64.20	16	61.68	62.10

Source: Sato, T., Ito, K., Chujo, S., and Takahashi, U. "Examples of experiments on systematic sampling of iron ore." *Reports of Statistical Application Research*, Union of Japanese Scientists and Engineers, Vol. 18, No. 1, 1971.

a. What type of experimental design was employed for this experiment?

b. Perform an analysis of variance for the data and display the results in an analysis of variance table.

c. Let μ_1 be the mean of the population of measurements obtained by the mechanical sampling method, and let μ_2 be the corresponding mean for the manual sampling method. Do the data provide sufficient evidence to indicate that μ_1 differs from μ_2? Test using $\alpha = .05$.

d. Compute the difference in the percentage iron measurements for each increment of ore. Then conduct the test of part **b** using a Student's t test for a matched-pairs experiment. [See Section 9.9.]

e. Show that the value of F computed in part **c** is equal to the square of the value of t computed in part **d**. Explain why the tests in parts **c** and **d** are equivalent.

14.36   A simulation study was conducted to investigate the machine performance of several new algorithms for functions in the FORTRAN computer program library (*IBM Journal of Research and Development*, Mar. 1986). The accompanying table gives the time per call (in microseconds) for several randomly selected scalar functions (averaged over 10,000 random arguments) on each of three different IBM System/370 machines. Treating the functions as blocks, the data were subjected to an ANOVA for a randomized block design using SAS. Use the accompanying SAS printout to answer the following questions.

Function	IBM 4331	IBM 4361	IBM 4341
EDUM	9.90	3.07	4.88
ACOS CIRC(O,PI)	179.62	33.28	33.23
SIN LINEAR($-$PI,PI)	105.72	24.13	27.08
EXP LINEAR($-16,16$)	254.82	39.14	37.46
D2DUM	13.47	4.63	5.72

Source: Agarwal, R. C., et al. "New scalar and vector elementary functions for the IBM System/370." *IBM Journal of Research and Development*, Vol. 30, No. 2, Mar. 1986, p. 139 (Table 4). Copyright 1986 by International Business Machines Corporation; reprinted with permission.

```
                       Analysis of Variance Procedure

Dependent Variable: TIME
                                   Sum of          Mean
Source                   DF        Squares         Square     F Value     Pr > F

Model                     6      53025.20409     8837.53402     3.21       0.0653
Error                     8      22016.91424     2752.11428
Corrected Total          14      75042.11833

                     R-Square          C.V.        Root MSE            TIME Mean

                     0.706606        101.3862      52.46060            51.7433333


Source                   DF       Anova SS      Mean Square    F Value     Pr > F

MACHINE                   2      27875.04789    13937.52395     5.06       0.0379
FUNCTION                  4      25150.15620     6287.53905     2.28       0.1487
```

a. Is there sufficient evidence to indicate that the mean function call times differ for the three IBM System/370 machines? Test using $\alpha = .10$.

b. Conduct a test to determine whether blocking on functions was effective in removing an extraneous source of variation. Use $\alpha = .10$.

14.37   An evaluation of diffusion bonding of zircaloy components is performed. The main objective is to determine which of three elements—nickel, iron, or copper—is the best bonding agent. A series of zircaloy components are bonded using each of the possible bonding agents. Since there is a great deal of variation in components machined from different ingots, a randomized block design is used, blocking on the ingots. A pair of components from each ingot are bonded together using each of the three agents, and the pressure (in units of 1,000 pounds per square inch) required to separate the bonded components is measured. The data are shown in the accompanying table, followed by a partial ANOVA summary table.

Ingot	Bonding Agent		
	Nickel	Iron	Copper
1	67.0	71.9	72.2
2	67.5	68.8	66.4
3	76.0	82.6	74.5
4	72.7	78.1	67.3
5	73.1	74.2	73.2
6	65.8	70.8	68.7
7	75.6	84.9	69.0

Source	df	SS	MS	F
Agent	2	131.90	—	—
Ingot	6	268.29	—	—
Error	12	124.46	—	
Total	20	524.65		

a. Identify the treatments in this experiment.
b. Identify the blocks in this experiment.
c. Is there evidence of a difference in pressure required to separate the components among the three bonding agents? Use $\alpha = .05$.

14.10   ANOVA for Two-Factor Factorial Experiments

In Section 14.5, we learned that factorial experiments are volume-increasing designs conducted to investigate the effect of two or more independent variables (factors) on the mean value of the response y. In this section, we focus on the analysis of two-factor factorial experiments.

For example, suppose we want to relate the mean number of defects on a finished item—say, a new desk top—to two factors, type of nozzle for the varnish spray gun and length of spraying time. Suppose further that we want to investigate the mean number of defects per desk for three types (three levels) of nozzles (N_1, N_2, and N_3) and for two lengths (two levels) of spraying time (S_1 and S_2). If we choose the treatments for the experiment to include all combinations of the three levels of nozzle type with the two levels of spraying time, i.e., we observe the number of defects for the factor–level combinations N_1S_1, N_1S_2, N_2S_1, N_2S_2, N_3S_1, N_3S_2, our design is called a **complete 3 × 2 factorial experiment**. Note that the design will contain $3 \times 2 = 6$ treatments.

Factorial experiments, you will recall, are useful methods for selecting treatments because they permit us to make inferences about factor interactions. The complete model for the 3×2 factorial experiment contains $(3 - 1) = 2$ main effect terms for nozzles, $(2 - 1) = 1$ main effect term for spray time, and $(3 - 1)(2 - 1) = 2$ nozzle–spray time interaction terms:

$$E(y) = \beta_0 + \underbrace{\beta_1 x_1 + \beta_2 x_2}_{\substack{\text{Nozzle} \\ \text{main effects}}} + \underbrace{\beta_3 x_3}_{\substack{\text{Spray time} \\ \text{main effect}}} + \underbrace{\beta_4 x_1 x_2 + \beta_5 x_1 x_3}_{\substack{\text{Nozzle} \times \text{spray time} \\ \text{interaction}}}$$

The independent variables (factors) in the model can be either quantitative or qualitative. If they are quantitative, the main effects are represented by terms such as x, x^2, x^3, etc.; if qualitative, the main effects are represented by dummy variables. In our 3×2 factorial experiment, nozzle type is qualitative and spraying time is quantitative; hence, the x variables in the model are defined as follows:

$$x_1 = \begin{cases} 1 & \text{if nozzle } N_1 \\ 0 & \text{if not} \end{cases} \qquad x_2 = \begin{cases} 1 & \text{if nozzle } N_2 \\ 0 & \text{if not} \end{cases} \qquad \text{Base level} = N_3$$

$x_3 = $ Length of spraying time (in minutes)

The model for the 3×2 factorial contains $3 \times 2 = 6$ β parameters. If we observe only a single value of the response y for each of the $3 \times 2 = 6$ treatments, then $n = 6$ and df(Error) for the complete model is $(n - 6) = 0$. Consequently, for a factorial experiment, *the number r of observations per factor–level combination (i.e., the number of replications of the factorial experiment) must always be 2 or more*. Otherwise, no degrees of freedom are available for estimating σ^2.

To test for factor interaction, we drop the interaction terms and fit the reduced model:

$$E(y) = \beta_0 + \underbrace{\beta_1 x_1 + \beta_2 x_2}_{\substack{\text{Main effect} \\ \text{Nozzle}}} + \underbrace{\beta_3 x_3}_{\substack{\text{Main effect} \\ \text{Spray time}}}$$

The null hypothesis of no interaction, $H_0: \beta_4 = \beta_5 = 0$, is tested by comparing the SSEs for the two models in a partial F statistic. This test for interaction is summarized, in general, in the accompanying box.

Models and ANOVA F Test for Interaction in a Two-Factor Factorial Experiment with Factor A at a Levels and Factor B at b Levels

....

Complete model:

$$E(y) = \beta_0 + \overbrace{\beta_1 x_1 + \cdots + \beta_{a-1} x_{a-1}}^{\text{Main effect A terms}} + \overbrace{\beta_a x_a + \cdots + \beta_{a+b-2} x_{a+b-2}}^{\text{Main effect B terms}}$$

$$+ \overbrace{\beta_{a+b-1} x_1 x_a + \beta_{a+b} x_1 x_{a+1} + \cdots + \beta_{ab-1} x_{a-1} x_{a+b-2}}^{\text{AB interaction terms}} \qquad \text{(continued)}$$

where*

$$x_1 = \begin{cases} 1 & \text{if level 2 of factor } A \ldots \\ 0 & \text{if not} \end{cases}$$

$$x_{a-1} = \begin{cases} 1 & \text{if level } a \text{ of factor } A \ldots \\ 0 & \text{if not} \end{cases}$$

$$x_a = \begin{cases} 1 & \text{if level 2 of factor } B \ldots \\ 0 & \text{if not} \end{cases}$$

$$x_{a+b-2} = \begin{cases} 1 & \text{if level } b \text{ of factor } B \ldots \\ 0 & \text{if not} \end{cases}$$

H_0: $\beta_{a+b-1} = \beta_{a+b} = \cdots = \beta_{ab-1} = 0$
(i.e., H_0:   No interaction between factors A and B)

H_a: At least one of the β parameters listed in H_0 differs from 0
(i.e., H_a: Factors A and B interact)

Reduced model:

$$E(y) = \overbrace{\beta_0 + \beta_1 x_1 + \cdots + \beta_{a-1} x_{a-1}}^{\text{Main effect } A \text{ terms}} + \overbrace{\beta_a x_a + \cdots + \beta_{a+b-2} x_{a+b-2}}^{\text{Main effect } B \text{ terms}}$$

Test statistic: $F = \dfrac{(\text{SSE}_R - \text{SSE}_C)/[(a-1)(b-1)]}{\text{SSE}_C/[ab(r-1)]}$

$$= \dfrac{(\text{SSE}_R - \text{SSE}_C)/[(a-1)(b-1)]}{\text{MSE}_C}$$

where

$\text{SSE}_R = $ SSE for reduced model

$\text{SSE}_C = $ SSE for complete model

$\text{MSE}_C = $ MSE for complete model

$r = $ Number of replications (i.e., number of y measurements per cell of the $a \times b$ factorial)

Rejection region: $F > F_\alpha$, where F is based on $\nu_1 = (a-1)(b-1)$ and $\nu_2 = ab(r-1)$ df

Assumptions: 1. The population probability distribution of the observations for any factor–level combination is approximately normal.

2. The variance of the probability distribution is constant and the same for all factor–level combinations.

*Note: The independent variables, $x_1, x_2, \ldots, x_{a+b-2}$, are defined for an experiment in which both factors represent *qualitative* variables. When a factor is *quantitative*, you may choose to represent the main effects with quantitative terms such as x, x^2, x^3, and so forth.

Tests for factor main effects are conducted in a similar manner. The main effect terms of interest are dropped from the complete model and the reduced model is fit. The SSEs for the two models are compared in the usual fashion.

Before we work through a numerical example of an analysis of variance for a factorial experiment, we need to understand the practical significance of the tests for factor interaction and factor main effects. We illustrate these concepts in Example 14.12.

···

EXAMPLE 14.12

A company that stamps gaskets out of sheets of rubber, plastic, and other materials, wants to compare the mean number of gaskets produced per hour for two different types of stamping machines. Practically, the manufacturer wants to determine whether one machine is more productive than the other and, even more important, whether one machine is more productive in making rubber gaskets whereas the other is more productive in making plastic gaskets. To answer these questions, the manufacturer decides to conduct a 2×3 factorial experiment using three types of gasket material, B_1, B_2, and B_3, with each of the two types of stamping machines, A_1 and A_2. Each machine is operated for three 1-hour time periods for each of the gasket materials, with the eighteen 1-hour time periods assigned to the six machine–material combinations in random order. (The purpose of the randomization is to eliminate the possibility that uncontrolled environmental factors might bias the results.) Suppose we have calculated and plotted the six treatment means. Two hypothetical plots of the six means are shown in Figures 14.19a and 14.19b. The three means for stamping machine A_1 are connected by solid line segments and the corresponding three means for machine A_2 by dashed line segments. What do these plots imply about the productivity of the two stamping machines?

Solution

Figure 14.19a suggests that machine A_1 produces a larger number of gaskets per hour, regardless of the gasket material, and is therefore superior to machine A_2. On the average, machine A_1 stamps more cork (B_1) gaskets per hour than rubber or plastic, but the *difference* in the mean numbers of gaskets produced by the two machines remains approximately the same, regardless of the gasket material. Thus, the difference in the mean number of gaskets produced by the two machines is *independent* of the gasket material used in the stamping process.

In contrast to Figure 14.19a, Figure 14.19b shows the productivity for machine A_1 to be greater than for machine A_2, when the gasket material is cork (B_1) or plastic (B_3). But the means are reversed for rubber (B_2) gasket material. For this material, machine A_2 produces, on the average, more gaskets per hour than machine A_1. Thus, Figure 14.19b illustrates a situation where the difference in the mean number of gaskets produced by the two machines *depends* on gasket material. When this situation occurs, we say that the factors *interact*. Thus, one of the most important objectives of a factorial experiment is to detect factor interaction if it exists.

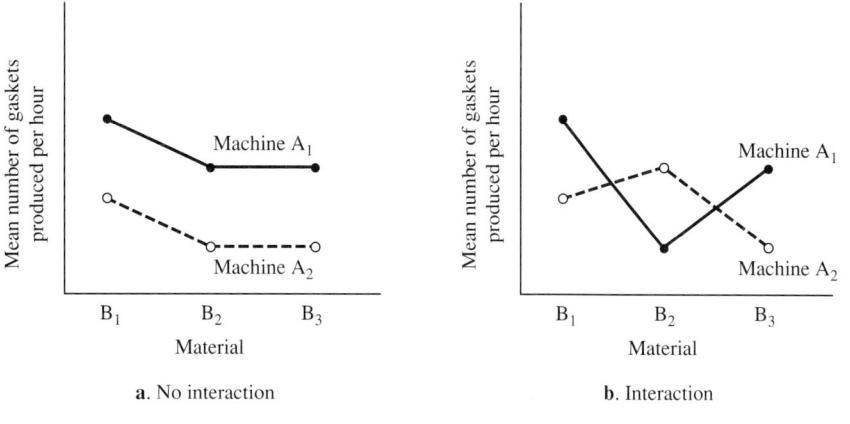

FIGURE 14.19 ►
Hypothetical plot of the means for the six machine–material combinations

a. No interaction   **b.** Interaction

Definition 14.8

In a factorial experiment, when the difference in the mean levels of factor A depends on the different levels of factor B, we say that the factors A and B **interact**. If the difference is independent of the levels of B, then there is **no interaction** between A and B.

Tests for main effects are relevant only when no interaction exists between factors. Generally, the test for interaction is performed first. *If there is evidence of factor interaction, then we will not perform the tests on the main effects.* Rather, we will want to focus attention on the individual cell (treatment) means, perhaps locating one that is the largest or the smallest.

EXAMPLE 14.13

A manufacturer, whose daily supply of raw materials is variable and limited, can use the material to produce two different products in various proportions. The profit per unit of raw material obtained by producing each of the two products depends on the length of a product's manufacturing run, and hence, on the amount of raw material assigned to it. Other factors, such as worker productivity and machine breakdown, affect the profit per unit as well, but their net effect on profit is random and uncontrollable. The manufacturer has conducted an experiment to investigate the effect of the level of supply of raw materials, S, and the ratio of its assignment, R, to the two product manufacturing lines on the profit y per unit of raw material. The ultimate goal would be to be able to choose the best ratio R to match each day's supply of raw materials, S. The levels of supply of the raw material chosen for the experiment were 15, 18, and 21 tons; the levels of the ratio of allocation to the two product lines were $\frac{1}{2}$, 1, and 2. The response was the profit (in dollars) per unit of raw material supply obtained from a single day's production. Three replications of a complete 3×3 factorial experiment were conducted in a random sequence (i.e., a completely randomized design). The data for the 27 days are shown in Table 14.12.

TABLE 14.12   Data for Example 14.13

		Raw Material Supply, tons (S)		
		15	18	21
Ratio of Raw Material Allocation (R)	$\frac{1}{2}$	23, 20, 21	22, 19, 20	19, 18, 21
	1	22, 20, 19	24, 25, 22	20, 19, 22
	2	18, 18, 16	21, 23, 20	20, 22, 24

a. Write the complete model for the experiment.

b. Do the data present sufficient evidence to indicate an interaction between supply S and ratio R? Use $\alpha = .05$.

c. Based on the result, part **b**, should we perform tests for main effects?

Solution

a. Both factors, supply and ratio, are quantitative. Accordingly, when the factors in a factorial experiment are quantitative, the main effects can be represented by terms such as x, x^2, x^3, and so forth. Since each factor has three levels, we require two main effects, x and x^2, for each factor. (In general, the number of main effect terms will be one less than the number of levels for a factor.) Consequently, the complete factorial model for this 3×3 factorial experiment is

$$y = \beta_0 + \underbrace{\beta_1 x_1 + \beta_2 x_1^2}_{\text{Supply main effects}} + \underbrace{\beta_3 x_2 + \beta_4 x_2^2}_{\text{Ratio main effects}}$$
$$+ \underbrace{\beta_5 x_1 x_2 + \beta_6 x_1 x_2^2 + \beta_7 x_1^2 x_2 + \beta_8 x_1^2 x_2^2}_{\text{Supply–Ratio interaction}} + \varepsilon$$

where

$x_1 = $ Supply of raw material (in tons)
$x_2 = $ Ratio of allocation

Note that the interaction terms for the model are constructed by taking the products of the various main effect terms, one from each factor. For example, we included terms involving the products of x_1 with x_2 and x_2^2. The remaining interaction terms were formed by multiplying x_1^2 by x_2 and by x_2^2.

b. To test the null hypothesis that supply and ratio do not interact, we must test the null hypothesis that the interaction terms are not needed in the linear model of part **a**:

$$H_0: \quad \beta_5 = \beta_6 = \beta_7 = \beta_8 = 0$$

This requires that we fit the reduced model

$$y = \beta_0 + \beta_1 x_1 + \beta_2 x_1^2 + \beta_3 x_2 + \beta_4 x_2^2$$

and perform the partial F test outlined in Section 13.6. The test statistic is

$$F = \frac{(\text{SSE}_R - \text{SSE}_C)/4}{\text{MSE}_C}$$

where

$$\text{SSE}_C = 43.33333 \quad \text{(see Figure 14.20a)}$$
$$\text{MSE}_C = 2.40741 \quad \text{(see Figure 14.20a)}$$
$$\text{SSE}_R = 89.55556 \quad \text{(see Figure 14.20b on page 850)}$$

The complete model of part **a** and the reduced model presented here were fit to the data in Table 14.12 using SAS. The SAS printouts are displayed in Figures 14.20a and 14.20b. The pertinent quantities, shaded on the printout, are

$$\text{SSE}_C = 43.33333 \quad \text{(see Figure 14.20a)}$$
$$\text{MSE}_C = 2.40741 \quad \text{(see Figure 14.20a)}$$
$$\text{SSE}_R = 89.55556 \quad \text{(see Figure 14.20b on page 850)}$$

Substituting these values into the formula for the test statistic, we obtain

$$F = \frac{(\text{SSE}_R - \text{SSE}_C)/4}{\text{MSE}_C} = \frac{(89.55556 - 43.33333)/4}{2.40741} = 4.80$$

FIGURE 14.20 ▶
a. SAS printout for complete factorial model

Analysis of Variance

Source	DF	Sum of Squares	Mean Square	F Value	Prob>F
Model	8	74.66667	9.33333	3.877	0.0081
Error	18	43.33333	2.40741		
C Total	26	118.00000			

Root MSE	1.55158	R-square	0.6328
Dep Mean	20.66667	Adj R-sq	0.4696
C.V.	7.50766		

Parameter Estimates

Variable	DF	Parameter Estimate	Standard Error	T for H0: Parameter=0	Prob > |T|
INTERCEP	1	245.333333	130.49665074	1.880	0.0764
X1	1	-25.074074	14.71842356	-1.704	0.1057
X1SQ	1	0.679012	0.40837272	1.663	0.1137
X2	1	-534.333333	252.45534989	-2.117	0.0485
X2SQ	1	192.666667	97.17010948	1.983	0.0629
X1X2	1	60.555556	28.47387077	2.127	0.0475
X1X2SQ	1	-22.148148	10.95959797	-2.021	0.0584
X1SQX2	1	-1.666667	0.79002700	-2.110	0.0492
X1SQX2SQ	1	0.617284	0.30408153	2.030	0.0574

FIGURE 14.20 ▶

b. SAS printout for reduced factorial model

Analysis of Variance

Source	DF	Sum of Squares	Mean Square	F Value	Prob>F
Model	4	28.44444	7.11111	1.747	0.1757
Error	22	89.55556	4.07071		
C Total	26	118.00000			

Root MSE	2.01760	R-square	0.2411	
Dep Mean	20.66667	Adj R-sq	0.1031	
C.V.	9.76258			

Parameter Estimates

Variable	DF	Parameter Estimate	Standard Error	T for H0: Parameter=0	Prob > |T|
INTERCEP	1	-43.481481	29.32960686	-1.483	0.1524
X1	1	6.814815	3.29853705	2.066	0.0508
X1SQ	1	-0.185185	0.09152016	-2.023	0.0553
X2	1	5.666667	4.35851270	1.300	0.2070
X2SQ	1	-2.296296	1.67759232	-1.369	0.1849

The rejection region for the test is $F > F_{.05}$, where $\nu_1 = 4$ (the number of β's tested in H_0), $\nu_2 = 18$ (the degrees of freedom for error for the complete model), and $F_{.05} = 2.93$ (obtained from Table 10, Appendix II). Since the computed test statistic, $F = 4.80$, exceeds $F_{.05}$, we reject H_0 and conclude that supply and ratio interact.

c. The presence of interaction tells you that the mean profit depends on the particular combination of levels of supply S and ratio R. Consequently, there is little point in checking to see whether the means differ for the three levels of supply or whether they differ for the three levels of ratio (i.e., we will not perform the tests for main effects). For example, the supply level that gave the highest mean profit (over all levels of R) might not be the same supply–ratio level combination that produces the largest mean profit per unit of raw material.

· ·

The traditional analysis of variance approach to analyzing a complete two-factor factorial with factor A at a levels and factor B at b levels utilizes the fact that the total sum of squares, SS(Total), can be partitioned into four parts, SS(A), SS(B), SS(AB), and SSE (see Figure 14.21). The first two sums of squares, SS(A) and SS(B), are called **main effect sums of squares** to distinguish them from the **interaction sum of squares**, SS(AB).

Since the sums of squares and the degrees of freedom for the analysis of variance are additive, the analysis of variance table appears as shown in Table 14.13.

Note that the F statistics for testing factor main effects and factor interaction are obtained by dividing the appropriate mean square by MSE. The numerator df for the test of interest will equal the df of the source of variation being tested; the denominator

TABLE 14.13   ANOVA Table for an $a \times b$ Factorial Design with r Observations per Cell (Note: $n = abr$)

Source	df	SS	MS	F
Main effects A	$(a - 1)$	SS(A)	MS(A) = SS(A)/(a - 1)	MS(A)/MSE
Main effects B	$(b - 1)$	SS(B)	MS(B) = SS(B)/(b - 1)	MS(B)/MSE
AB interaction	$(a - 1)(b - 1)$	SS(AB)	MS(AB) = SS(AB)/[(a - 1)(b - 1)]	MS(AB)/MSE
Error	$ab(r - 1)$	SSE	MSE = SSE/[ab(r - 1)]	
Total	$abr - 1$	SS(Total)		

FIGURE 14.21 ▶

Partitioning of the total sum of squares for a complete two-factor factorial experiment

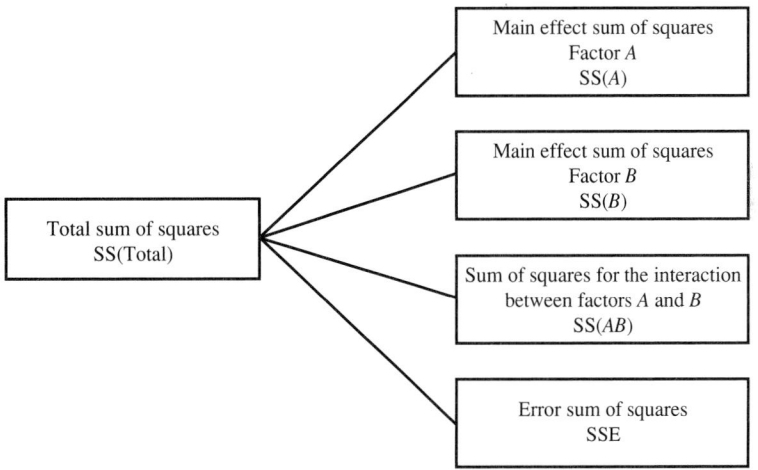

df will always equal df(Error). These F tests are equivalent to the F tests obtained by fitting complete and reduced models in regression.*

For completeness, the formulas for calculating the ANOVA sums of squares for a complete two-factor factorial experiment are given in the box.

EXAMPLE 14.14

Refer to Example 14.13.

a. Construct an ANOVA summary table for the analysis.

b. Conduct the test for supply $\times$ ratio interaction using the traditional analysis of variance approach.

---

*The ANOVA F tests for main effects shown in Table 14.13 are equivalent to those of the regression approach only when the reduced model includes interaction terms. Since we usually test for main effects only after determining that interaction is nonsignificant, some statisticians favor dropping the interaction terms from both the complete and reduced models prior to conducting the main effect tests. For example, to test for main effect A, the complete model includes terms for main effects A and B, whereas the reduced model includes terms for main effect B only. To obtain the equivalent result using the ANOVA approach, the sum of squares for AB interaction and error are "pooled" and a new MSE computed, where

$$MSE = \frac{SS(AB) + SSE}{n - a - b + 1}$$

Solution

a. Although the formulas given in the box are straightforward, they can become quite tedious to use. Therefore, we resort to a statistical software package to conduct the ANOVA. A SAS printout of the ANOVA is displayed in Figure 14.22. The value of SS(Total), given in the SAS printout under **Sum of Squares** in the **Corrected Total** row, is SS(Total) = 118. The sums of squares, mean squares, and F values for the factors, S, R, and $S \times R$ interaction are given under the **ANOVA SS**, **Mean Square**, and **F Value** columns, respectively, in the bottom portion of the printout. These values are shown in the ANOVA table given in Table 14.14.

FIGURE 14.22 ▶
SAS printout for ANOVA of data in Example 14.14

```
                        Analysis of Variance Procedure

Dependent Variable: PROFIT
                                      Sum of              Mean
Source                   DF           Squares            Square    F Value   Pr > F

Model                     8       74.66666667        9.33333333      3.88    0.0081
Error                    18       43.33333333        2.40740741
Corrected Total          26      118.00000000

                    R-Square            C.V.         Root MSE           PROFIT Mean

                    0.632768        7.507656         1.551582          20.6666667

Source                   DF          Anova SS      Mean Square   F Value   Pr > F

SUPPLY                    2       20.22222222      10.11111111      4.20    0.0318
RATIO                     2        8.22222222       4.11111111      1.71    0.2094
SUPPLY*RATIO              4       46.22222222      11.55555556      4.80    0.0082
```

TABLE 14.14   ANOVA Table for Example 14.14

Source	df	SS	MS
Supply	2	20.22	10.11
Ratio	2	8.22	4.11
Supply–Ratio interaction	4	46.22	11.56
Error	18	43.33	2.41
Total	26	118.00	

b. To test the hypothesis that supply and ratio interact, we use the test statistic

$$F = \frac{MS(SR)}{MSE} = \frac{11.56}{2.41} = 4.80 \quad \text{(shaded in the SAS printout)}$$

Note that this value is identical to the test statistic obtained in Example 14.13 using regression. The p-value of the test (also shaded on the SAS printout) is .0082. Since this value is less than the selected value of $\alpha = .05$, we conclude that supply and ratio interact.

Computing Formulas for the Analysis of Variance for a Two-Factor Factorial Experiment

$$CM = \text{Correction for the mean}$$

$$= \frac{(\text{Total of all } n \text{ measurements})^2}{n}$$

$$= \frac{\left(\sum_{i=1}^{n} y_i\right)^2}{n}$$

$$SS(\text{Total}) = \text{Total sum of squares}$$

$$= \text{Sum of squares of all } n \text{ measurements} - CM$$

$$= \sum_{i=1}^{n} y_i^2 - CM$$

$$SS(A) = \text{Sum of squares for main effects, independent variable 1}$$

$$= \left(\begin{array}{c} \text{Sum of squares of the totals } A_1, A_2, \ldots, A_a \\ \text{divided by the number of measurements} \\ \text{in a single total, namely, } br \end{array}\right) - CM$$

$$= \frac{\sum_{i=1}^{a} A_i^2}{br} - CM$$

$$SS(B) = \text{Sum of squares for main effects, independent variable 2}$$

$$= \left(\begin{array}{c} \text{Sum of squares of the totals } B_1, B_2, \ldots, B_b \\ \text{divided by the number of measurements} \\ \text{in a single total, namely, } ar \end{array}\right) - CM$$

$$= \frac{\sum_{i=1}^{b} B_i^2}{ar} - CM$$

$$SS(AB) = \text{Sum of squares for } AB \text{ interaction}$$

$$= \left(\begin{array}{c} \text{Sum of squares of the cell totals} \\ AB_{11}, AB_{12}, \ldots, AB_{ab} \text{ divided} \\ \text{by the number of measurements} \\ \text{in a single total, namely, } r \end{array}\right) - SS(A) - SS(B) - CM$$

$$= \frac{\sum_{i=1}^{b} \sum_{i=1}^{a} AB_{ij}^2}{r} - SS(A) - SS(B) - CM$$

(continued)

where

a = Number of levels of independent variable 1

b = Number of levels of independent variable 2

r = Number of measurements for each pair of levels of independent variables 1 and 2

n = Total number of measurements

= $a \times b \times r$

A_i = Total of all measurements of independent variable 1 at level i ($i = 1, 2, \ldots, a$)

B_j = Total of all measurements of independent variable 2 at level j ($j = 1, 2, \ldots, b$)

AB_{ij} = Total of all measurements at the ith level of independent variable 1 and at the jth level of independent variable 2 ($i = 1, 2, \ldots, a$; $j = 1, 2, \ldots, b$)

Throughout this chapter we have presented two methods for analyzing data from a designed experiment: the regression approach and the traditional ANOVA approach. In a factorial experiment, the two methods yield identical results when both factors are qualitative; however, regression will provide more information when at least one of the factors is quantitative. For example, the analysis of variance in Example 14.14 enables us to estimate the mean profit per unit of supply for *only* the nine combinations of supply–ratio levels. It will not permit us to estimate the mean response for some other combination of levels of the independent variables not included among the nine used in the factorial experiment. Alternatively, the prediction equation obtained from the regression analysis in Example 14.13 enables us to estimate the mean profit per unit of supply when ($S = 17$, $R = 1$). We could not obtain this estimate from the analysis of variance in Example 14.14.

The prediction equation found by regression analysis also contributes other information not provided by traditional analysis of variance. For example, we might wish to estimate the rate of change in the mean profit, $E(y)$, for unit changes in S, R, or both for specific values of S and R. Or, we might want to determine whether the third- and fourth-order terms in the complete model of Example 14.13 really contribute additional information for the prediction of profit, y.

We illustrate some of these applications in the final two examples of this section.

EXAMPLE 14.15

Do the data provide sufficient information to indicate that third- and fourth-order terms in the complete factorial model given in Example 14.13 contribute information for the prediction of y ? Use $\alpha = .05$.

Solution

If the response to the question is yes, then at least one of the parameters, β_6, β_7, or β_8, of the complete factorial model differs from 0 (i.e., they are needed in the model).

Consequently, the null hypothesis is

$$H_0: \quad \beta_6 = \beta_7 = \beta_8 = 0$$

and the alternative hypothesis is

$$H_a: \quad \text{At least one of the three } \beta\text{'s is nonzero.}$$

To test this hypothesis, we compute the drop in SSE between the appropriate reduced and complete model.

For this application the complete model is the complete factorial model of Example 14.13:

$$\text{Complete model:} \quad E(y) = \beta_0 + \beta_1 x_1 + \beta_2 x_1^2 + \beta_3 x_2 + \beta_4 x_2^2 + \beta_5 x_1 x_2 \\ + \beta_6 x_1 x_2^2 + \beta_7 x_1^2 x_2 + \beta_8 x_1^2 x_2^2$$

The reduced model is the complete model, minus the third- and fourth-order terms; i.e., the reduced model is the second-order model:

$$\text{Reduced model:} \quad E(y) = \beta_0 + \beta_1 x_1 + \beta_2 x_1^2 + \beta_3 x_2 + \beta_4 x_2^2 + \beta_5 x_1 x_2$$

Recall (from Figure 14.20a) that the SSE and MSE for the complete model are $\text{SSE}_C = 43.3333$ and $\text{MSE}_C = 2.4074$. A SAS printout of the regression analysis of the reduced model is shown in Figure 14.23. The SSE for the reduced model (shaded) is $\text{SSE}_R = 54.49206$.

FIGURE 14.23 ▶
SAS printout for the reduced (second-order) model

Dependent Variable: PROFIT

Analysis of Variance

Source	DF	Sum of Squares	Mean Square	F Value	Prob>F
Model	5	63.50794	12.70159	4.895	0.0040
Error	21	54.49206	2.59486		
C Total	26	118.00000			

Root MSE		1.61086	R-square	0.5382	
Dep Mean		20.66667	Adj R-sq	0.4283	
C.V.		7.79447			

Parameter Estimates

Variable	DF	Parameter Estimate	Standard Error	T for H0: Parameter=0	Prob > |T|
INTERCEP	1	-27.814815	23.80152168	-1.169	0.2557
S	1	5.944444	2.64418353	2.248	0.0354
R	1	-7.761905	5.04522969	-1.538	0.1389
SR	1	0.746032	0.20294890	3.676	0.0014
SS	1	-0.185185	0.07306996	-2.534	0.0193
RR	1	-2.296296	1.33939441	-1.714	0.1012

Consequently, the test statistic required to conduct the test is

Test statistic:

$$F = \frac{(\text{SSE}_R - \text{SSE}_C)/(\text{number of } \beta\text{'s tested})}{\text{MSE}_C} = \frac{(54.49206 - 43.3333)/3}{2.4074} = 1.54$$

The F statistic is based on $\nu_1 = 3$ numerator df, $\nu_2 = 18$ denominator df, and the critical value (obtained from Table 10 of Appendix II) is $F_{.05} = 3.16$. Thus, the rejection region is:

$$Rejection\ region:\ \ F > 3.16$$

Conclusion: Since the computed value of $F(1.54)$ is less than the critical value, $F_{.05} = 3.16$, we cannot reject the null hypothesis that $\beta_6 = \beta_7 = \beta_8 = 0$. That is, there is insufficient evidence (at $\alpha = .05$) to indicate that the third- and fourth-order terms associated with β_6, β_7, and β_8 contribute information for the prediction of y. Since the complete factorial model contributes no more information about y than the reduced (second-order) model, we recommend using the second-order model in practice.

EXAMPLE 14.16

Use the second-order model of Example 14.15 and find a 95% confidence interval for the mean profit per unit supply of raw material when $S = 17$ and $R = 1$.

Solution

The portion of the SAS printout for the second-order model with 95% confidence intervals for $E(y)$ is shown in Figure 14.24.

FIGURE 14.24 ▶
SAS printout of confidence intervals for mean profit

Obs	S	R	Dep Var PROFIT	Predict Value	Std Err Predict	Lower95% Mean	Upper95% Mean	Residual
1	15	0.5	23.0000	20.8254	0.803	19.1549	22.4959	2.1746
2	15	0.5	20.0000	20.8254	0.803	19.1549	22.4959	-0.8254
3	15	0.5	21.0000	20.8254	0.803	19.1549	22.4959	0.1746
4	18	0.5	22.0000	21.4444	0.693	20.0029	22.8860	0.5556
5	18	0.5	19.0000	21.4444	0.693	20.0029	22.8860	-2.4444
6	18	0.5	20.0000	21.4444	0.693	20.0029	22.8860	-1.4444
7	21	0.5	19.0000	18.7302	0.803	17.0596	20.4007	0.2698
8	21	0.5	18.0000	18.7302	0.803	17.0596	20.4007	-0.7302
9	21	0.5	21.0000	18.7302	0.803	17.0596	20.4007	2.2698
10	15	1	22.0000	20.8175	0.701	19.3605	22.2744	1.1825
11	15	1	20.0000	20.8175	0.701	19.3605	22.2744	-0.8175
12	15	1	19.0000	20.8175	0.701	19.3605	22.2744	-1.8175
13	18	1	24.0000	22.5556	0.693	21.1140	23.9971	1.4444
14	18	1	25.0000	22.5556	0.693	21.1140	23.9971	2.4444
15	18	1	22.0000	22.5556	0.693	21.1140	23.9971	-0.5556
16	21	1	20.0000	20.9603	0.701	19.5034	22.4173	-0.9603
17	21	1	19.0000	20.9603	0.701	19.5034	22.4173	-1.9603
18	21	1	22.0000	20.9603	0.701	19.5034	22.4173	1.0397
19	15	2	18.0000	17.3571	0.859	15.5707	19.1436	0.6429
20	15	2	18.0000	17.3571	0.859	15.5707	19.1436	0.6429
21	15	2	16.0000	17.3571	0.859	15.5707	19.1436	-1.3571
22	18	2	21.0000	21.3333	0.693	19.8918	22.7749	-0.3333
23	18	2	23.0000	21.3333	0.693	19.8918	22.7749	1.6667
24	18	2	20.0000	21.3333	0.693	19.8918	22.7749	-1.3333
25	21	2	20.0000	21.9762	0.859	20.1897	23.7627	-1.9762
26	21	2	22.0000	21.9762	0.859	20.1897	23.7627	0.0238
27	21	2	24.0000	21.9762	0.859	20.1897	23.7627	2.0238
28	17	1	.	22.3466	0.663	20.9687	23.7244	.

The confidence interval for $E(y)$ when $S = 17$ and $R = 1$ is shaded in the last row of the printout. You can see that the interval is (20.97, 23.72). Thus, we estimate (with confidence coefficient equal to .95) that the mean profit per unit of supply will lie between \$20.97 and \$23.72 when $S = 17$ tons and $R = 1$. Beyond this immediate result, you will note that this example illustrates the power and versatility of a regression analysis. In particular, there is no way to obtain this estimate from the analysis of variance in Example 14.14. However, a computerized regression package can be easily programmed to include the confidence interval automatically.

EXERCISES

14.38 Many temperate-zone animal species exhibit physiological and morphological changes when the hours of daylight begin to decrease during autumn months. A study was conducted to investigate the "short day" traits of collared lemmings (*The Journal of Experimental Zoology*, Sept. 1993). A total of 124 lemmings were bred in a colony maintained with a photoperiod of 22 hours of light per day. At weaning (19 days of age), the lemmings were weighed and randomly assigned to live under one of two photoperiods: 16 hours or less of light per day, more than 16 hours of light per day. (Each group was assigned the same number of males and females.) After 10 weeks, the lemmings were weighed again. The response variable of interest was the gain in body weight (measured in grams) over the 10-week experimental period. The researchers analyzed the data using an ANOVA for a 2×2 factorial design, where the two factors are photoperiod (at two levels) and gender (at two levels).

a. Construct an ANOVA table for the experiment, listing the sources of variation and associated degrees of freedom.

b. Give the models that will enable the researchers to test for photoperiod by gender interaction.

c. The F test for interaction was not significant. Interpret this result practically.

d. The p-values for testing for photoperiod and gender main effects were both smaller than .001. Interpret these results practically.

14.39 What is the optimal method of directing newcomers to a specific location in a complex building? Researchers at Ball State University (Indiana) investigated this "wayfinding" problem and reported their results in *Human Factors* (Mar. 1993). Subjects met in a starting room on a multilevel building and were asked to locate the "goal" room as quickly as possible. (Some of the subjects were provided directional aids, whereas others were not.) Upon reaching their destination, the subjects returned to the starting room and were given a second room to locate. (One of the goal rooms was located in the east end of the building, the other in the west end.) The experimentally controlled variables in the study were aid type at three levels (signs, map, no aid) and room order at two levels (east/west, west/east). Subjects were randomly assigned to each of the $3 \times 2 = 6$ experimental conditions; the travel time (in seconds) was recorded. The results of the analysis of the east room data for this 3×2 factorial design are provided in the table. Interpret the results.

Source	df	MS	F	p-value
Aid type	2	511,323.06	76.67	< .0001
Room order	1	13,005.08	1.95	> .10
Aid × Order	2	8,573.13	1.29	> .10
Error	46	6,668.94		

Source: Butler, D. L., et al. "Wayfinding by newcomers in a complex building." *Human Factors*, Vol. 35, No. 1, Mar. 1993, p. 163 (Table 2).

14.40   An important concern of designers and users of computer display monitors is readability of the text shown on the screen. Two factors thought to affect readability of scrolling texts is window size (i.e., number of characters displayed per line) and jump length (i.e., number of characters advanced per jump). To investigate this phenomenon, a 2×3 factorial experiment was conducted, with window size at two levels (20 and 40 characters) and jump length at three levels (1, 5, and 9 characters). The response variable of interest was reading rate (measured as number of words per minute) of Chinese college students who participated in the study (*Human Factors*, June 1988).

  a. The ANOVA F test for interaction between the two factors resulted in a p-value exceeding .10. Interpret this result.

  b. The ANOVA F test for the main effect of window size resulted in a p-value exceeding .10. Interpret this result.

  c. The ANOVA F test for the main effect of jump length resulted in a p-value less than .05. Interpret this result.

14.41   The chemical element antimony is sometimes added to tin–lead solder to replace the more expensive tin and to reduce the cost of soldering. A factorial experiment was conducted to determine how antimony affects the strength of the tin–lead solder joint (*Journal of Materials Science*, May 1986). Tin–lead solder specimens were prepared using one of four possible cooling methods (water-quenched, WQ; oil-quenched, OQ; air-blown, AB; and furnace-cooled, FC) and with one of four possible amounts of antimony (0%, 3%, 5%, and 10%) added to the composition. Three solder joints were randomly assigned to each of the $4 \times 4 = 16$ treatments and the shear strength of each measured. The experimental results, shown in the accompanying table, were subjected to an ANOVA using SAS. The SAS printout is reproduced at the top of page 859.

Amount of Antimony % weight	Cooling Method	Shear Strength MPa
0	WQ	17.6, 19.5, 18.3
0	OQ	20.0, 24.3, 21.9
0	AB	18.3, 19.8, 22.9
0	FC	19.4, 19.8, 20.3
3	WQ	18.6, 19.5, 19.0
3	OQ	20.0, 20.9, 20.4
3	AB	21.7, 22.9, 22.1
3	FC	19.0, 20.9, 19.9
5	WQ	22.3, 19.5, 20.5
5	OQ	20.9, 22.9, 20.6
5	AB	22.9, 19.7, 21.6
5	FC	19.6, 16.4, 20.5
10	WQ	15.2, 17.1, 16.6
10	OQ	16.4, 19.0, 18.1
10	AB	15.8, 17.3, 17.1
10	FC	16.4, 17.6, 17.6

Source: Tomlinson, W. J., and Cooper, G. A. "Fracture mechanism of brass/Sn-Pb-Sb solder joints and the effect of production variables on the joint strength." *Journal of Materials Science*, Vol. 21, No. 5, May 1986, p. 1731 (Table II). Copyright 1986 Chapman and Hall.

  a. Construct an ANOVA summary table for the experiment.

Analysis of Variance Procedure

Dependent Variable: STRENGTH

Source	DF	Sum of Squares	Mean Square	F Value	Pr > F
Model	15	157.95250000	10.53016667	6.10	0.0001
Error	32	55.24666667	1.72645833		
Corrected Total	47	213.19916667			

R-Square	C.V.	Root MSE	STRENGTH Mean
0.740868	6.7195275	1.3139476	19.55416667

Source	DF	Anova SS	Mean Square	F Value	Pr > F
AMOUNT	3	104.194167	34.731389	20.12	0.0001
METHOD	3	28.627500	9.542500	5.53	0.0036
AMOUNT*METHOD	9	25.130833	2.792315	1.62	0.1523

b. Conduct a test to determine whether the two factors, amount of antimony and cooling method, interact. Use $\alpha = .01$.

c. Interpret the result obtained in part b.

d. If appropriate, conduct the tests for main effects. Use $\alpha = .01$.

14.42 A study was conducted to investigate the effect of two factors on the mean level of sulfur content in coal: the laboratory conducting the analysis (seven levels) and the method of analysis (two levels). The 28 coal specimens used for the experiment, all from the same source, were randomly assigned, two to each of the 7×2 combinations of laboratory and method of analysis. The data, shown in the table, were subjected to an analysis of variance using MINITAB. The MINITAB printout is shown here.

		L_1	L_2	L_3	L_4	L_5	L_6	L_7
Method of Analysis	A_1	.107	.127	.115	.108	.097	.114	.155
		.105	.122	.112	.108	.096	.119	.145
	A_2	.105	.127	.109	.117	.110	.116	.164
		.103	.124	.111	.115	.097	.122	.160

Laboratory

Source: Taguchi, G. "Signal noise ratio and its application for testing material." *Reports of Statistical Application Research*, Union of Japanese Scientists and Engineers. Vol. 18, No. 4, 1971, pp. 21–33.

ANALYSIS OF VARIANCE SULFER

SOURCE	DF	SS	MS
ANALYSIS	1	0.0000893	0.0000893
LAB	6	0.0082432	0.0013739
INTERACTION	6	0.0001912	0.0000319
ERROR	14	0.0002030	0.0000145
TOTAL	27	0.0087267	

a. Identify the treatments in the experiment.

b. What is the practical significance of an interaction between method of analysis and laboratory?

c. Do the data provide sufficient evidence to indicate interaction between method of analysis and laboratory? Test using $\alpha = .05$.

d. Do the data provide sufficient evidence to indicate differences in the mean level of sulfur content readings from one laboratory to another? Test using $\alpha = .05$.

e. Do the data provide sufficient evidence to indicate a difference in the mean level of sulfur content between the two methods of analysis? Test using $\alpha = .05$.

14.43 A trade-off study regarding the inspection and test of transformer parts was conducted by the quality department of a major defense contractor. The investigation was structured to examine the effects of varying inspection levels and incoming test times to detect early part failure or fatigue. The levels of inspection selected were full military inspection (A), reduced military specification level (B), and commercial grade (C). Operational burn-in test times chosen for this study were at 1-hour increments from 1 hour to 9 hours. The response was failures per thousand pieces obtained from samples taken from lot sizes inspected to a specified level and burned-in over a prescribed time length. Three replications were randomly sequenced under each condition making this a complete 3×9 factorial experiment (a total of 81 observations). The data for the study (shown in the table) were subjected to an ANOVA using SAS. The SAS printout follows. Analyze and interpret the results.

Burn-in	Full Military			Inspection Levels Reduced Military			Commercial, C		
(hours)	Specification, A			Specification, B					
1	7.60	7.50	7.67	7.70	7.10	7.20	6.16	6.13	6.21
2	6.54	7.46	6.84	5.85	6.15	6.15	6.21	5.50	5.64
3	6.53	5.85	6.38	5.30	5.60	5.80	5.41	5.45	5.35
4	5.66	5.98	5.37	5.38	5.27	5.29	5.68	5.47	5.84
5	5.00	5.27	5.39	4.85	4.99	4.98	5.65	6.00	6.15
6	4.20	3.60	4.20	4.50	4.56	4.50	6.70	6.72	6.54
7	3.66	3.92	4.22	3.97	3.90	3.84	7.90	7.47	7.70
8	3.76	3.68	3.80	4.37	3.86	4.46	8.40	8.60	7.90
9	3.46	3.55	3.45	5.25	5.63	5.25	8.82	9.76	9.52

Source: Danny La Nuez, College of Business Administration, graduate student, University of South Florida, 1989–1990.

Analysis of Variance Procedure

Dependent Variable: FAILURES

Source	DF	Sum of Squares	Mean Square	F Value	Pr > F
Model	26	168.6120667	6.4850795	101.31	0.0001
Error	54	3.4565333	0.0640099		
Corrected Total	80	172.0686000			

R-Square	C.V.	Root MSE	FAILURE Mean
0.979912	4.405990	0.253002	5.74222222

Source	DF	Anova SS	Mean Square	F Value	Pr > F
BURNIN	8	27.97440000	3.49680000	54.63	0.0001
INSLEVEL	2	43.08411852	21.54205926	336.54	0.0001
BURNIN*INSLEVEL	16	97.55354815	6.09709676	95.25	0.0001

14.44 An experiment was conducted to determine the effect of sintering time (two levels) on the compressive strength of two different metals. Five test specimens were sintered for each metal at each of the two sintering times. The data (in thousands of pounds per square inch) are shown in the accompanying table.

<table>
<tr><td></td><td></td><td colspan="6" align="center">Sintering Time</td></tr>
<tr><td></td><td></td><td colspan="3" align="center">100 minutes</td><td colspan="3" align="center">200 minutes</td></tr>
<tr><td rowspan="4">Metal</td><td rowspan="2">1</td><td>17.1</td><td>16.5</td><td>14.9</td><td>19.4</td><td>18.9</td><td>20.1</td></tr>
<tr><td>15.2</td><td>16.7</td><td></td><td>17.2</td><td>20.7</td><td></td></tr>
<tr><td rowspan="2">2</td><td>12.3</td><td>13.8</td><td>10.8</td><td>15.6</td><td>17.2</td><td>16.7</td></tr>
<tr><td>11.6</td><td>12.1</td><td></td><td>16.1</td><td>18.3</td><td></td></tr>
</table>

a. Perform an analysis of variance for the data, and construct an analysis of variance table.
b. What is the practical significance of an interaction between sintering time and metal type?
c. Do the data provide sufficient evidence to indicate an interaction between sintering time and metal type? Test using $\alpha = .05$.

14.45 As part of a study on the rate of combustion of artificial graphite in humid air flow, researchers conducted an experiment to investigate oxygen diffusivity through a water vapor mixture. A 3×9 factorial experiment was conducted with mole fraction of water (H_2O) at three levels and temperature of the nitrogen–water mixture at nine levels. The data are shown in the table.

Temperature °K	Mole Fraction of H_2O		
	.0022	.017	.08
1,000	1.68	1.69	1.72
1,100	1.98	1.99	2.02
1,200	2.30	2.31	2.35
1,300	2.64	2.65	2.70
1,400	3.00	3.01	3.06
1,500	3.38	3.39	3.45
1,600	3.78	3.79	3.85
1,700	4.19	4.21	4.27
1,800	4.63	4.64	4.71

Source: Matsui, K., Tsuji, H., and Makino, A. "The effects of water vapor concentration on the rate of combustion of an artificial graphite in humid air flow." *Combustion and Flame*, Vol. 50, 1983, pp. 107–118. Copyright 1983 by The Combustion Institute. Reprinted by permission of Elsevier Science Publishing Co., Inc.

a. Explain why the traditional analysis of variance (using the ANOVA formulas) is inappropriate for the analysis of these data.
b. Write a second-order model relating mean oxygen diffusivity, $E(y)$, to temperature x_1 (in hundreds) and mole fraction x_2 (in thousandths).
c. The SAS computer printout for the regression analysis is shown on page 862. Find SSE, s^2, and SS(Total).

Dependent Variable: Y

Analysis of Variance

Source	DF	Sum of Squares	Mean Square	F Value	Prob>F
Model	5	24.85819	4.97164	696562.744	0.0001
Error	21	0.00015	0.00001		
C Total	26	24.85834			

Root MSE	0.00267	R-square	1.0000
Dep Mean	3.08852	Adj R-sq	1.0000
C.V.	0.08650		

Parameter Estimates

Variable	DF	Parameter Estimate	Standard Error	T for H0: Parameter=0	Prob > |T|
INTERCEP	1	-0.280150	0.01712523	-16.359	0.0001
X1	1	0.001000	0.00002477	40.388	0.0001
X2	1	-0.285549	0.13650623	-2.092	0.0488
X1X2	1	0.000733	0.00005903	12.411	0.0001
X1SQ	1	0.000000959	0.00000001	109.060	0.0001
X2SQ	1	0.551414	1.24232481	0.444	0.6617

Obs	X1	X2	Dep Var Y	Predict Value	Std Err Predict	Lower95% Mean	Upper95% Mean	Residual
1	1000	0.0022	1.6800	1.6796	0.002	1.6762	1.6830	0.000382
2	1000	0.017	1.6900	1.6864	0.001	1.6833	1.6895	0.00361
3	1000	0.08	1.7200	1.7179	0.002	1.7141	1.7217	0.00207
4	1100	0.0022	1.9800	1.9811	0.001	1.9786	1.9836	-0.00109
5	1100	0.017	1.9900	1.9890	0.001	1.9866	1.9913	0.00105
6	1100	0.08	2.0200	2.0251	0.001	2.0223	2.0280	-0.00511
7	1200	0.0022	2.3000	2.3017	0.001	2.2995	2.3040	-0.00174
8	1200	0.017	2.3100	2.3107	0.001	2.3086	2.3128	-0.00068
9	1200	0.08	2.3500	2.3515	0.001	2.3491	2.3538	-0.00145
10	1300	0.0022	2.6400	2.6416	0.001	2.6394	2.6438	-0.00156
11	1300	0.017	2.6500	2.6516	0.001	2.6494	2.6538	-0.00158
12	1300	0.08	2.7000	2.6970	0.001	2.6947	2.6992	0.00303
13	1400	0.0022	3.0000	3.0005	0.001	2.9983	3.0028	-0.00054
14	1400	0.017	3.0100	3.0117	0.001	3.0094	3.0139	-0.00165
15	1400	0.08	3.0600	3.0617	0.001	3.0594	3.0639	-0.00165
16	1500	0.0022	3.3800	3.3787	0.001	3.3765	3.3809	0.00130
17	1500	0.017	3.3900	3.3909	0.001	3.3887	3.3931	-0.0009
18	1500	0.08	3.4500	3.4455	0.001	3.4433	3.4477	0.00449
19	1600	0.0022	3.7800	3.7760	0.001	3.7738	3.7782	0.00397
20	1600	0.017	3.7900	3.7893	0.001	3.7872	3.7914	0.000692
21	1600	0.08	3.8500	3.8485	0.001	3.8462	3.8509	0.00146
22	1700	0.0022	4.1900	4.1925	0.001	4.1900	4.1951	-0.00253
23	1700	0.017	4.2100	4.2069	0.001	4.2045	4.2092	0.00311
24	1700	0.08	4.2700	4.2707	0.001	4.2679	4.2736	-0.00074
25	1800	0.0022	4.6300	4.6282	0.002	4.6248	4.6316	0.00181
26	1800	0.017	4.6400	4.6436	0.001	4.6405	4.6468	-0.00364
27	1800	0.08	4.7100	4.7121	0.002	4.7083	4.7159	-0.00210

d. Find R^2 and verify that

$$R^2 = 1 - \frac{\text{SSE}}{\text{SS(Total)}}$$

Interpret the value of R^2.

e. Suppose that temperature and mole fraction of H_2O do not interact. What does this imply about the relationship between $E(y)$ and x_1 and x_2?

f. Do the data provide sufficient information to indicate that temperature and mole fraction of H_2O interact? Test using $\alpha = .05$.

g. Give the least squares prediction equation for $E(y)$.

h. Substitute into the prediction equation to predict the mean diffusivity when the temperature of the process is 1,300°K and the mole fraction of water is .017.

i. The printout shows 95% confidence intervals for each of the 3 × 9 factor–level combinations. Find the 95% confidence interval for mean diffusivity when the temperature of the process is 1,300°K and the mole fraction of water is .017.

14.46 Suppose you plan to investigate the effect of hourly pay rate and length of workday on some measure y of worker productivity. Both pay rate and length of workday will be set at three levels, and y will be observed for all combinations of these factors. Thus, a 3 × 3 factorial experiment will be employed.

a. Identify the factors and state whether they are quantitative or qualitative.

b. Identify the treatments to be employed in the experiment.

c. Write a complete factorial model for the experiment. [*Hint:* When the factors are quantitative, main effect terms include x and x^2 terms for each factor.]

d. What is the order of the model specified in part **c**?

e. Suppose you want to fit a second-order model to the data. Give the appropriate model.

f. If you have only one observation for each combination and you fit a complete factorial model to the data, how many degrees of freedom will be available for estimating σ^2?

g. Refer to part **f**. If you fit a second-order model to the data, how many degrees of freedom will be available for estimating σ^2?

h. Suppose you replicated the experiment and hence obtained two observations for each treatment. How many degrees of freedom would be available for estimating σ^2 if you fit: (1) the complete factorial model? (2) a second-order model?

i. Which model—complete factorial or second-order—do you think would be more appropriate for this experiment?

j. Explain how to conduct a test for interaction between pay rate and length of workday using the complete factorial model.

k. Explain how to conduct a test for interaction between pay rate and length of workday using the second-order model.

OPTIONAL EXERCISE

14.47 How do women compare with men in their ability to perform laborious tasks that require strength? Some information on this question is provided in a study, by M. D. Phillips and R. L. Pepper, of the firefighting ability of men and women ("Shipboard fire-fighting performance of females and males," *Human Factors,* Vol. 24, 1982). Phillips and Pepper conducted a 2 × 2 factorial experiment to investigate the effect of the factor sex (male or female) and the factor weight (light or heavy) on the length of time required for a person to perform a particular firefighting task. Eight persons were selected for each of the 2 × 2 = 4 sex–weight categories of the 2 × 2 factorial experiment, and the length of time needed to complete the task was recorded for each of the 32 persons. The means and standard deviations of the four samples are shown in the table on page 864.

		Light Weight		Heavy Weight
	Mean	Standard Deviation	Mean	Standard Deviation
Female	18.30	6.81	14.50	2.93
Male	13.00	5.04	12.25	5.70

Source: *Human Factors*, 1982, Vol. 24. Copyright 1982 by the Human Factors Society, Inc. and reproduced by permission.

a. Calculate the total of the $n = 8$ time measurements for each of the four categories of the 2×2 factorial experiment.

b. Calculate CM.

c. Use the results of parts **a** and **b** to calculate the sums of squares for sex, weight, and for the sex–weight interaction.

d. Calculate each sample variance. Then calculate the sums of squares of deviations *within* each sample for each of the four samples.

e. Calculate SSE. [*Hint:* SSE is the pooled sum of squares of the deviations calculated in part **d**.]

f. Now that you know SS(Sex), SS(Weight), SS(Sex–Weight), and SSE, find SS(Total).

g. Summarize the calculations in an analysis of variance table.

h. Explain the practical significance of the presence (or absence) of sex–weight interaction. Do the data provide evidence of an interaction between sex and weight?

14.11   ANOVA for a k-Way Classification of Data (Optional)

In this optional section, we present some useful factorial designs that are more complex than the basic two-factor factorial of Section 14.10. These designs fall under the general category of a **k-way classification of data**. A k-way classification of data arises when we run all combinations of the levels of k independent variables. These independent variables can be factors or blocks.

For example, consider a replicated $2 \times 3 \times 3$ factorial experiment in which the $2 \times 3 \times 3 = 18$ treatments are assigned to the experimental units according to a completely randomized design. Since every combination of the three factors (a total of 18) is examined, the design is often called a three-way classification of data. Similarly, a k-way classification of data would result if we randomly assign the treatments of a $(k - 1)$-factor factorial experiment to the experimental units of a randomized block design. For example, if we assigned the $2 \times 3 = 6$ treatments of a complete 2×3 factorial experiment to blocks containing six experimental units each, the data would be arranged in a three-way classification, i.e., according to the two factors and the blocks.

The formulas required for calculating the sums of squares for main effects and interactions for an analysis of variance for a k-way classification of data are complicated and, therefore, are not given here. If you are interested in the computational formulas, see the references. As with the designs in the previous three sections, we provide the appropriate linear model for these more complex designs and use either regression or the standard ANOVA output of a statistical software package to analyze the data.

EXAMPLE 14.7

Consider a $2 \times 3 \times 3$ factorial experiment with qualitative factors and $r = 3$ experimental units randomly assigned to each treatment.

a. Write the appropriate linear model for the design.

b. Indicate the sources of variation and their associated degrees of freedom in a partial ANOVA table.

Solution

a. Denote the three qualitative factors as A, B, and C, with A at two levels, and B and C at three levels. Then the linear model for the experiment will contain one parameter corresponding to main effects for A, two each for B and C, $(1)(2) = 2$ each for the AB and AC interactions, $(2)(2) = 4$ for the BC interaction, and $(1)(2)(2) = 4$ for the three-way ABC interaction. Three-way interaction terms measure the failure of two-way interaction effects to remain the same from one level to another level of the third factor. The model is

$$E(y) = \beta_0 + \underbrace{\beta_1 x_1}_{\text{A main effect}} + \underbrace{\beta_2 x_2 + \beta_3 x_3}_{\text{B main effects}} + \underbrace{\beta_4 x_4 + \beta_5 x_5}_{\text{C main effects}} +$$

$$\underbrace{\beta_6 x_1 x_2 + \beta_7 x_1 x_3}_{\text{A}\times\text{B interaction}} + \underbrace{\beta_8 x_1 x_4 + \beta_9 x_1 x_5}_{\text{A}\times\text{C interaction}} +$$

$$\underbrace{\beta_{10} x_2 x_4 + \beta_{11} x_2 x_5 + \beta_{12} x_3 x_4 + \beta_{13} x_3 x_5}_{\text{B}\times\text{C interaction}} +$$

$$\underbrace{\beta_{14} x_1 x_2 x_4 + \beta_{15} x_1 x_3 x_4 + \beta_{16} x_1 x_2 x_5 + \beta_{17} x_1 x_3 x_5}_{\text{A}\times\text{B}\times\text{C interaction}}$$

where

$$x_1 = \begin{cases} 1 & \text{if level 1 of A} \\ 0 & \text{if level 2 of A} \end{cases} \qquad x_2 = \begin{cases} 1 & \text{if level 1 of B} \\ 0 & \text{if not} \end{cases}$$

$$x_3 = \begin{cases} 1 & \text{if level 2 of B} \\ 0 & \text{if not} \end{cases} \qquad x_4 = \begin{cases} 1 & \text{if level 1 of C} \\ 0 & \text{if not} \end{cases}$$

$$x_5 = \begin{cases} 1 & \text{if level 2 of C} \\ 0 & \text{if not} \end{cases}$$

b. The sources of variation and the respective degrees of freedom corresponding to these sets of parameters are shown in Table 14.15 on page 866.

TABLE 14.15   Analysis of Variance Table for Example 14.17

Source	df
Main effect A	1
Main effect B	2
Main effect C	2
AB interaction	2
AC interaction	2
BC interaction	4
ABC interaction	4
Error	36
Total	53

The degrees of freedom for SS(Total) will always equal $(n - 1)$—that is, n minus 1 degree of freedom for β_0. Since the degrees of freedom for all sources must sum to the degrees of freedom for SS(Total), it follows that the degrees of freedom for Error will equal the degrees of freedom for SS(Total), minus the sum of the degrees of freedom for main effects and interactions, i.e., $(n - 1) - 17$. Our experiment will contain three observations for each of the $2 \times 3 \times 3 = 18$ treatments; therefore, $n = (18)(3) = 54$, and the degrees of freedom for Error will equal $53 - 17 = 36$.

If data for this experiment were analyzed on a computer, the computer printout would show the analysis of variance table that we have constructed and would include the associated mean squares, values of the F test statistics, and their observed significance levels. Each F statistic would represent the ratio of the source mean square to MSE $= s^2$.

EXAMPLE 14.18

A transistor manufacturer conducted an experiment to investigate the effects of three factors on productivity (measured in thousands of dollars of items produced) per 40-hour week. The factors were as follows:

1. Length of work week (two levels): five consecutive 8-hour days or four consecutive 10-hour days

2. Shift (two levels): day or evening shift

3. Number of coffee breaks (three levels): 0, 1, or 2

The experiment was conducted over a 24-week period with the $2 \times 2 \times 3 = 12$ treatments assigned in a random manner to the 24 weeks. The data for this completely randomized design are shown in Table 14.16. Perform an analysis of variance for the data.

TABLE 14.16   Data for Example 14.18

		Day Shift			Night Shift		
		Coffee Breaks			Coffee Breaks		
		0	1	2	0	1	2
Length of Work Week	4 days	94 97	105 106	96 91	90 89	102 97	103 98
	5 days	96 92	100 103	82 88	81 84	90 92	94 96

Solution

The data were subjected to an analysis of variance. The SAS printout is shown in Figure 14.25.

FIGURE 14.25 ▶
SAS printout for ANOVA of data in Table 14.16

```
                    Analysis of Variance Procedure

Dependent Variable: DOLLARS
                                Sum of            Mean
Source                  DF      Squares           Square     F Value    Pr > F

Model                   11    1009.833333        91.803030    13.43     0.0001
Error                   12      82.000000         6.833333
Corrected Total         23    1091.833333


              R-Square            C.V.          Root MSE          DOLLARS Mean

          4   0.924897          2.768647     3   2.614065          94.4166667


Source                  DF      Anova SS      Mean Square    F Value    Pr > F

SHIFT                    1      48.1666667     48.1666667       7.05     0.0210
DAYS                     1     204.1666667    204.1666667      29.88  2  0.0001
SHIFT*DAYS               1       8.1666667      8.1666667       1.20     0.2958
BREAKS                   2     334.0833333    167.0416667      24.45     0.0001
SHIFT*BREAKS             2     385.5833333    192.7916667      28.21     0.0001
DAYS*BREAKS              2       8.0833333      4.0416667       0.59     0.5689
SHIFT*DAYS*BREAKS        2      21.5833333     10.7916667       1.58     0.2461
```

Pertinent sections of the SAS printout are boxed and numbered, as follows:

1. The value of SS(Total), shown in the **Corrected Total** row of box 1, is 1,091.833333. The degrees of freedom associated with this quantity is equal to $(n - 1) = (24 - 1) = 23$. Box 1 gives the partitioning (the analysis of variance) of this quantity into two sources of variation. The first source, **Model**, corresponds to the 11 parameters (all except β_0) in the model. The second source is **Error**. The degrees of freedom, sums of squares, and mean squares for these quantities are shown in their respective columns. For example, MSE = 6.833333. The F statistic for testing

$$H_0: \quad \beta_1 = \beta_2 = \cdots = \beta_{11} = 0$$

is based on $\nu_1 = 11$ and $\nu_2 = 12$ degrees of freedom and is shown on the printout as $F = 13.43$. The observed significance level, shown under **Pr > F**, is .0001.

This small observed significance level presents ample evidence to indicate that at least one of the three independent variables—shifts, number of days in a working week, or number of coffee breaks per day—contributes information for the prediction of mean productivity.

2. To determine which sets of parameters are actually contributing information for the prediction of y, we examine the breakdown (box 2) of SS(Model) into components corresponding to the sets of parameters for main effects SHIFTS, DAYS, and BREAKS, and two-way interactions, SHIFT*DAYS, SHIFT*BREAKS, and DAYS*BREAKS. The last **Model** source of variation corresponds to the set of all three-way SHIFT*DAYS*BREAKS parameters. Note that the degrees of freedom for these sources sum to 11, the number of degrees of freedom for **Model**. Similarly, the sum of the component sums of squares is equal to SS(Model). Box 2 does not give the mean squares associated with the sources, but it does give the F values associated with testing hypotheses concerning the set of parameters associated with each source. It also gives the observed significance levels of these tests. You can see that there is ample evidence to indicate the presence of a SHIFT*BREAKS interaction. The F tests associated with all three main-effect parameter sets are also statistically significant at the $\alpha = .05$ level of significance. The practical implication of these results is that there is evidence to indicate that all three independent variables, shift, number of work days per week, and number of coffee breaks per day, contribute information for the prediction of productivity. The presence of a SHIFT*BREAKS interaction means that the effect of the number of breaks on productivity is not the same from shift to shift. Thus, the specific number of coffee breaks that might achieve maximum productivity on one shift might be different from the number of breaks that will achieve maximum productivity on the other shift.

3. Box 3 gives the value of $s = \sqrt{\text{MSE}} = 2.614065$. This value will be used to construct confidence intervals for pairwise comparisons of the 12 treatment means. (Details of the procedure are provided in Section 14.13.)

4. Box 4 gives the value of R^2, a measure of how well the model fits the experimental data. It is of value primarily when the number of degrees of freedom for error is large—say, at least 5 or 6. The larger the number of degrees of freedom for error, the greater will be its practical importance. The value of R^2 for this analysis, .924897, indicates that the model provides a fairly good fit to the data. It also suggests that the model could be improved by adding new predictor variables or, possibly, by including higher-order terms in the variables originally included in the model.

EXAMPLE 14.19

In a manufacturing process, a plastic rod is produced by heating a granular plastic to a molten state and then extruding it under pressure through a nozzle. An experiment was conducted to investigate the effect of two factors, extrusion temperature (°F) and pressure (pounds per square inch), on the rate of extrusion (inches per second) of the molded rod. A complete 2×2 factorial experiment (that is, with each factor at two levels) was conducted. Three batches of granular plastic were used for the experiment, with each batch (viewed as a block) divided into four equal parts. The four portions of granular plastic for a given batch were randomly assigned to the four treatments; this was repeated for each of the three batches, resulting in a 2×2 factorial experiment laid out in three blocks. The data are shown in Table 14.17. Perform an analysis of variance for these data.

TABLE 14.17   Data for Example 14.19

		Batch (block)					
		1		2		3	
		Pressure		Pressure		Pressure	
		40	60	40	60	40	60
Temperature	200°	1.35	1.74	1.31	1.67	1.40	1.86
	300°	2.48	3.63	2.29	3.30	2.14	3.27

Solution

TABLE 14.18   Table of Sources and Degrees of Freedom for Example 14.19

Source	df
Pressure (P)	1
Temperature (T)	1
Blocks	2
Pressure–temperature interaction	1
Error	6
Total	11

This experiment consists of a three-way classification of the data corresponding to batches (blocks), pressure, and temperature. The analysis of variance for this 2×2 factorial experiment (four treatments) laid out in a randomized block design (three blocks) yields the sources and degrees of freedom shown in Table 14.18.

The linear model for the experiment is

$$E(y) = \beta_0 + \overbrace{\beta_1 x_1}^{\substack{\text{Main} \\ \text{effect} \\ P}} + \overbrace{\beta_2 x_2}^{\substack{\text{Main} \\ \text{effect} \\ T}} + \overbrace{\beta_3 x_1 x_2}^{\substack{PT \\ \text{inter-} \\ \text{action}}} + \overbrace{\beta_4 x_3 + \beta_5 x_4}^{\substack{\text{Block} \\ \text{terms}}}$$

where

$x_1 = $ Pressure $x_2 = $ Temperature

$x_3 = \begin{cases} 1 & \text{if block 2} \\ 0 & \text{otherwise} \end{cases}$ $x_4 = \begin{cases} 1 & \text{if block 3} \\ 0 & \text{otherwise} \end{cases}$

The SAS printout for the analysis of variance is shown in Figure 14.26 on page 870. You can see from the printout that the F test for the model was highly significant (observed significance level is .0001). Thus, there is ample evidence to indicate differences among the block means, or the treatment means, or both. Proceeding to the breakdown of the model sources, you can see that the values of the F statistics for pressure, temperature, and the temperature–pressure interaction are all highly significant (that is, their observed significance levels are very small). Therefore, all of the terms ($\beta_1 x_1$, $\beta_2 x_2$, and $\beta_3 x_1 x_2$) contribute information for the prediction of y.

a. How many treatments are associated with this four-way factorial experiment?

b. Write the complete factorial model for this experiment. [*Hint:* Use dummy variables to represent the factors.]

c. What hypothesis would you test to determine whether interaction exists among the four factors?

14.53 A 2×2 factorial experiment was conducted for each of 3 weeks to determine the effect of two factors, temperature and pressure, on the yield of a chemical. Temperature was set at 300° and 500°. The pressure maintained in the reactor was set at 100 and 200 pounds per square inch. Four days were randomly selected within each week, and the four factor–level combinations were randomly assigned to them.

a. What type of design was used for this experiment?

b. Construct an analysis of variance table showing all sources and their respective degrees of freedom.

14.54 Refer to Exercise 14.53. The yield data for the 2×2 factorial experiment, laid out in three blocks of time, are shown in the accompanying table. The SAS printout for the analysis of variance is also shown.

		Week 1 Temperature		Week 2 Temperature		Week 3 Temperature	
		300	500	300	500	300	500
Pressure	100	64	73	65	72	62	70
	200	69	81	71	85	67	83

```
                        Analysis of Variance Procedure

Dependent Variable: YIELD
                                      Sum of           Mean
Source                    DF          Squares         Square    F Value     Pr > F

Model                      5       613.5000000     122.7000000    72.41     0.0001
Error                      6        10.1666667       1.6944444
Corrected Total           11       623.6666667

                R-Square            C.V.          Root MSE            YIELD Mean

                0.983699          1.812123        1.301708           71.8333333


Source                    DF         Anova SS     Mean Square    F Value     Pr > F

PRESSURE                   1       208.3333333     208.3333333    122.95     0.0001
TEMP                       1       363.0000000     363.0000000    214.23     0.0001
PRESSURE*TEMP              1        27.0000000      27.0000000     15.93     0.0072
WEEK                       2        15.1666667       7.5833333      4.48     0.0646
```

a. Why does the analysis of variance table not include sources for the interaction of weeks with temperature and pressure?

b. Do the data provide sufficient evidence to indicate an interaction between temperature and pressure? Give the *p*-value for the test. What is the practical significance of this result?

c. Was blocking in time useful in increasing the amount of information in the experiment? That is, do the data provide sufficient evidence to indicate differences among the block means? Give the *p*-value for the test.

14.12   ANOVA for Nested Sampling Designs (Optional)

The random error ε in an ANOVA model is intended to represent the contribution of many variables (most of them unknown) that affect the response variable y. We hope that the net effect of these variables on the response will assume the properties described in the assumptions listed in Section 12.2. Sometimes the random sources of variation that enter into the sum of squares for error can be partitioned into two or more sources. The following example illustrates this situation.

Suppose a pharmaceutical manufacturer wants to estimate the mean potency of a batch of an antibiotic. The potency reading produced by a piece of equipment will vary from observation to observation as a result of at least two sources of random error. Antibiotic that is being produced in a vat is not a homogeneous substance; the potency varies slightly from one location in the batch to another. In addition, the potency reading produced in the measurement process will vary from observation to observation because of equipment error. Thus, repeated measurements on the same specimen vary from one reading to another.

One way to separate and to estimate the magnitudes of these two sources of variation is to perform the sampling in two stages. First, we randomly select n_1 specimens from the batch. Then we measure the potency of each specimen n_2 times. Because n_2 second-stage sampling units are obtained from each first-stage or **primary unit** (see Figure 14.27), the sampling procedure is called a **nested sampling design**. It is also referred to as **subsampling**—that is, sampling within a sample.

FIGURE 14.27 ▶

Diagrammatic representation of a two-stage nested sampling design

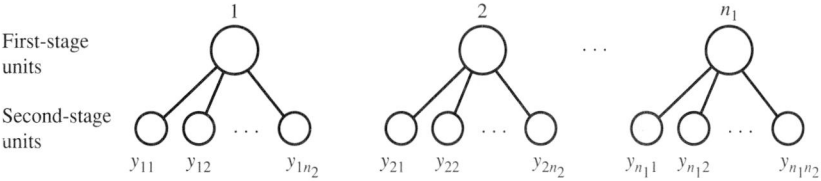

Definition 14.9

A **two-stage nested sampling design** involves the random selection of n_1 first-stage (primary) units from a population. Subsamples of n_2 second-stage units are then randomly selected from within each primary unit.

Nested sampling can be expanded to any number of stages. For example, suppose that after the equipment reacts to a specimen's potency, an operator must reset a gauge before taking an individual reading. Thus, repeated readings of the equipment's reaction to a specimen will vary from one observation to another as a result of the operator's recalibration process. The magnitude of this third source of sampling error can be evaluated using a three-stage sampling design. In addition to the two stages previously described, for each measurement produced by the equipment's reaction to a specimen, the operator would be required to recalibrate and read the meter n_3 times. This three-stage nested sampling experiment is shown diagrammatically in Figure 14.28.

FIGURE 14.28 ▶

Diagrammatic representation of a three-stage nested sampling design

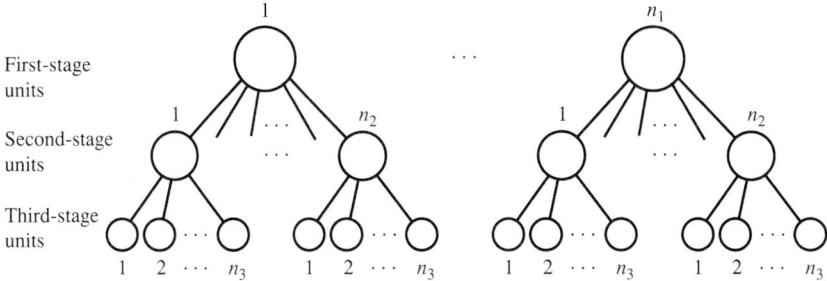

The probabilistic models for the ANOVA designs presented in previous sections are called *fixed-effect models* since the levels of all components in the model (e.g., treatments, factor interaction) other than the random error term are set or "fixed" prior to observing the response y. Conversely, models for nested sampling designs contain more than one random component; hence, they are called *nested models*. Models for nested designs and the corresponding ANOVAs are presented in this optional section.

Two-Stage Nested Sampling Designs

Consider a two-stage nested sampling design consisting of n_2 second-stage units for each of n_1 first-stage units. Since each second-stage unit will yield one observation, the experiment will yield $n = n_1 n_2$ values of the response variable y.

We will let y_{ii} denote the observation on the jth second-stage unit ($j = 1$, $2, \ldots, n_2$) within the ith first-stage unit ($i = 1, 2, \ldots, n_1$). The probabilistic model that we will use to describe this response is shown in the next box. From a practical point of view, this model implies that y is equal to a constant, μ, plus two random components, α_i and ε_{ij}. The response associated with every second-stage unit within the same first-stage unit i will read higher or lower than μ by the same random amount, α_i. The response y_{ij} associated with each second-stage unit will also be larger or smaller than $(\mu + \alpha_i)$ by an amount ε_{ij}. This random error will vary from one second-stage unit to another.

Because y_{ij} is equal to a constant (μ) plus the sum of two normally distributed random variables, it follows that y_{ij} is a normally distributed random variable with mean and variance

$$E(y_{ij}) = \mu + E(\alpha_i) + E(\varepsilon_{ij}) = \mu + 0 + 0 = \mu$$
$$V(y_{ij}) = V(\alpha_i) + V(\varepsilon_{ij}) + 2\text{Cov}(\varepsilon_{ij}, \alpha_i) = \sigma_\alpha^2 + \sigma^2 + 0$$
$$= \sigma_\alpha^2 + \sigma^2$$

The Probabilistic Model for a Two-Stage Nested Sampling Design

$$y_{ij} = \mu + \alpha_i + \varepsilon_{ij} \qquad (i = 1, 2, \ldots, n_1; \quad j = 1, 2, \ldots, n_2)$$

where α_i and ε_{ij} are independent normally distributed random variables with

$$E(\alpha_i) = E(\varepsilon_{ij}) = 0$$
$$V(\alpha_i) = \sigma_\alpha^2$$
$$V(\varepsilon_{ij}) = \sigma^2$$

In addition, every pair of values, α_i and α_j $(i \neq j)$, are independent. Similarly, pairs of values of ε are independent.

Note that although all the random components of the model are independent of one another, the y values within the same first-stage unit will be correlated. To illustrate, the correlation between two observations from the ith first-stage unit is

$$
\begin{aligned}
\text{Cov}(y_{ij}, y_{ik}) &= E\{[y_{ij} - E(y_{ij})][y_{ik} - E(y_{ik})]\} \\
&= E[(\mu + \alpha_i + \varepsilon_{ij} - \mu)(\mu + \alpha_i + \varepsilon_{ij} - \mu)] \\
&= E[(\alpha_i + \varepsilon_{ij})(\alpha_i + \varepsilon_{ik})] \\
&= E(\alpha_i^2 + \alpha_i\varepsilon_{ij} + \alpha_i\varepsilon_{ik} + \varepsilon_{ij}\varepsilon_{ik}) \\
&= E(\alpha_i^2) + E(\alpha_i\varepsilon_{ij}) + E(\alpha_i\varepsilon_{ik}) + E(\varepsilon_{ij}\varepsilon_{ik})
\end{aligned}
$$

The last three expectations, which are covariances, equal 0 because the random components of the model are assumed to be independent. Then, since $E(\alpha_i) = 0$, it follows that $E(\alpha_i^2) = \sigma_\alpha^2$ and the covariance between two y values in the same first-stage unit is

$$\text{Cov}(y_{ij}, y_{ik}) = \sigma_\alpha^2$$

The analysis of variance for a nested sampling design partitions SS(Total) into two parts (see Table 14.19), one measuring the variability *between* the first-stage means and the second measuring the variability of the y values *within* the individual first-stage units.

TABLE 14.19   An Analysis of Variance Table for a Two-Stage Nested Sampling Design

Source	df	SS	MS	E (MS)	F
First stage: A	$n_1 - 1$	SS(A)	MS(A)	$\sigma^2 + n_2\sigma_\alpha^2$	MS(A)/MS(B in A)
Second stage: B within A	$n_1(n_2 - 1)$	SS(B in A)	MS(B in A)	σ^2	
Total	$n_1 n_2 - 1$	SS(Total)			

The objectives of the analysis of variance are to obtain estimates of σ_α^2 and σ^2 and to determine whether $\sigma_\alpha^2 > 0$—that is, whether the variation among the first-stage (A) units exceeds the variation of the y values within first-stage units. The expected values of MS(A) and MS(B within A) are shown in the E(MS) column of Table 14.19. Unbiased estimates of σ_α^2 and σ^2 can be obtained from these mean squares. In addition, it can be shown (proof omitted) that when $\sigma_\alpha^2 = 0$,

$$F = \frac{\text{MS}(A)}{\text{MS}(B \text{ in } A)}$$

is an F statistic with $\nu_1 = n_1 - 1$ and $\nu_2 = n_1(n_2 - 1)$ degrees of freedom. The test of $H_0: \sigma_\alpha^2 = 0$ against $H_a: \sigma_\alpha^2 > 0$ is conducted in the same manner as the F tests of the previous sections.

The notation for an analysis of variance for a two-stage nested sampling design, the formulas for computing the mean squares, and the F test are shown in the accompanying boxes. When you examine the formulas for calculating the sums of squares, note their similarity to the corresponding formulas for the analysis of variance of a replicated two-factor factorial experiment. If the first-stage units are viewed as one direction of classification, then the main effect sum of squares for this direction is SS(A). Then SS(B in A) can be calculated as SS(B in A) = SS(Total) − SS(A).

Notation for the Analysis of Variance of a Two-Stage Nested Sampling Design

y_{ij} = Observation on the jth second-stage unit within the ith first-stage unit

n_1 = Number of first-stage units

n_2 = Number of second-stage units

$n = n_1 n_2$ = Total number of observations

A_i = Total of all observations in the ith first-stage unit

$\bar{A}_i$ = Mean of the n_2 observations in the ith first-stage unit

$\sum\limits_{i=1}^{n_1} \sum\limits_{j=1}^{n_2} y_{ij}$ = Total of all n observations

$\bar{y}$ = Mean of all n observations

Analysis of Variance F Test for a Two-Stage Nested Sampling Design

$H_0: \quad \sigma_\alpha^2 = 0$

$H_a: \quad \sigma_\alpha^2 > 0$

Test statistic: $\quad F = \dfrac{\text{MS}(A)}{\text{MS}(B \text{ in } A)}$

Rejection region: $\quad F > F_\alpha$, where F_α is the tabulated value for an F statistic with $\nu_1 = n_1 - 1$ and $\nu_2 = n_1(n_2 - 1)$ degrees of freedom

Although these formulas are easy to use, the calculations can become quite tedious. Therefore, we will use a statistical software package to perform the computations in the examples.

Calculation Formulas for a Two-Stage Nested Sampling Design

$$CM = \text{Correction for the mean}$$

$$= \frac{(\text{Total of all observations})^2}{n} = \frac{\left(\sum\limits_{i=1}^{n_1} \sum\limits_{j=1}^{n_2} y_{ij}\right)^2}{n}$$

$$SS(\text{Total}) = \sum_{i=1}^{n_1} \sum_{j=1}^{n_2} (y_{ii} - \bar{y})^2$$

$$= (\text{Sum of squares of all observations}) - CM$$

$$= \sum_{i=1}^{n_1} \sum_{j=1}^{n_2} y_{ij}^2 - CM$$

$$SS(A) = n_2 \sum_{i=1}^{n_1} (\bar{A}_i - \bar{y})^2 = \sum_{i=1}^{n_1} \frac{A_i^2}{n_2} - CM$$

$$SS(B \text{ in } A) = SS(\text{Total}) - SS(A)$$

$$MS(A) = \frac{SS(A)}{n_1 - 1}$$

$$MS(B \text{ in } A) = \frac{SS(B \text{ in } A)}{n_1(n_2 - 1)}$$

EXAMPLE 14.20

The compressive strength of concrete depends on the proportion of water mixed with the cement, the mixing time, the thoroughness of the mixing process, and so on. Even though these variables are presumed fixed at values that will produce maximum compressive strength, they vary slightly from batch to batch and the compressive strength of the concrete varies accordingly. A state highway department conducted an experiment to compare the strength variation between batches to the strength variation of concrete specimens prepared within the same batch. Five concrete specimens were prepared for each of six batches. The compressive strength measurements (in thousands of pounds per square inch) are shown in Table 14.20 on page 880. Perform an analysis of variance on the data and test $H_0: \sigma_\alpha^2 = 0$ against $H_a: \sigma_\alpha^2 > 0$, i.e., whether the batch-to-batch variation exceeds the within-batch variation.

TABLE 14.20 Compressive Strength Measurements for Concrete in Example 14.20

	Batch					
	1	2	3	4	5	6
	5.01	4.74	4.99	5.64	5.07	5.90
	4.61	4.41	4.55	5.02	4.93	5.27
	5.22	4.98	4.87	4.89	4.81	5.65
	4.93	4.26	4.19	5.51	5.19	4.96
	5.37	4.80	4.77	5.17	5.48	5.39
Totals	25.14	23.19	23.37	26.23	25.48	27.17

Solution

The SAS printout for the analysis of variance is shown in Figure 14.29. As in the case of fixed-effect models, the breakdown of SS(Total) is presented in two tables.

FIGURE 14.29 ▶
SAS printout for ANOVA of Example 14.20

```
                        Analysis of Variance Procedure

   Dependent Variable: STRENGTH
                                    Sum of          Mean
   Source                 DF        Squares         Square    F Value    Pr > F

① Model                   5        2.46974667     0.49394933    5.21     0.0022
   Error                 24        2.27624000     0.09484333
   Corrected Total       29        4.74598667


              R-Square            C.V.          Root MSE        STRENGTH Mean

              0.520386          6.135605        0.307966          5.01933333


   Source                 DF       Anova SS      Mean Square   F Value    Pr > F

② BATCH                   5        2.46974667     0.49394933    5.21     0.0022
```

The first table (box 1) shows the partitioning of SS(Total) into two sources of variation, **Model** and **Error**. The portion corresponding to **Error** is always associated with the variation in the units of the last stage of a nested sampling design. Thus, for a two-stage design, **Error** corresponds to specimen (B) within batch (A). The source designated as **Model** represents the variation for any fixed-effect sources and the variation associated with all other stages. Since there is only one other stage (A) for this two-stage design, **Model** corresponds to the variation within first-stage sampling units— that is, (A). The second table shown in Figure 14.29 (box 2) gives the breakdown of the **Model** source sum of squares into sums of squares corresponding to the stages not included in **Error**. Since we have only one other stage (A), it follows that the sum of squares for **Model** and the sum of squares for batch (A) are identical.

The sums of squares, mean squares (and their respective degrees of freedom), and the F value for testing H_0: σ_α^2 are extracted from the SAS printout and displayed in Table 14.21. The tabulated value of F_α for $\alpha = .05$ with $\nu_1 = 5$ and $\nu_2 = 24$ degrees of freedom (given in Table 10 of Appendix II) is $F_{.05} = 2.62$. Since the computed value of F exceeds this value, there is evidence to indicate that $\sigma_\alpha^2 > 0$, i.e., that the variation between batches exceeds the variation within batches. Note that the same conclusion can be reached by observing that the p-value of the test (shaded on the printout) is .0022.

TABLE 14.21   Analysis of Variance Table for Example 14.20

Source	df	SS	MS	F
Batch	5	2.46974667	.49394933	5.21
Specimens within batch	24	2.27624000	.09484333	
Total	29	4.74598667		

Three-Stage Nested Sampling Designs

We now assume that we have a three-stage sampling design containing n_1 first-stage units, n_2 second-stage units per first-stage unit, and n_3 third-stage units per second-stage unit. The total number of observations for this experiment is then $n = n_1 n_2 n_3$. The probabilistic model for a response obtained from a three-stage nested sampling design contains three random components, which represent the variation between first-, second-, and third-stage sampling units. We will let y_{ijk} denote the response on the kth third-stage unit within the jth second-stage and the ith first-stage units. The model for y_{ijk} is shown in the box.

The Probabilistic Model for a Three-Stage Nested Sampling Design

$$y_{ijk} = \mu + \alpha_i + \gamma_{ij} + \varepsilon_{ijk}$$

where α_i, γ_{ij}, and ε_{ijk} are independent, normally distributed random variables with

$$E(\alpha_i) = E(\gamma_{ij}) = E(\varepsilon_{ijk}) = 0$$
$$V(\alpha_i) = \sigma_\alpha^2$$
$$V(\gamma_{ij}) = \sigma_\gamma^2$$
$$V(\varepsilon_{ijk}) = \sigma^2$$

In addition, every pair of values, α_i and α_j $(i \neq j)$, are independent. Similarly, pairs of values of γ and ε are also independent.

The analysis of variance for a three-stage nested sampling design is an extension of the two-stage analysis. Before giving the computational formulas, we will examine the analysis of variance table shown in Table 14.22 on page 882.

TABLE 14.22 Analysis of Variance Table for a Three-Stage Nested Sampling Design

Source	df	SS	MS	E(MS)	F
First stage (A)	$n_1 - 1$	SS(A)	$\dfrac{\text{SS}(A)}{n_1 - 1}$	$\sigma^2 + n_3 \sigma_\gamma^2 + n_2 n_3 \sigma_\alpha^2$	$\dfrac{\text{MS}(A)}{\text{MS}(B \text{ in } A)}$
Second stage (B within A)	$n_1(n_2 - 1)$	SS(B in A)	$\dfrac{\text{SS}(B \text{ in } A)}{n_1(n_2 - 1)}$	$\sigma^2 + n_3 \sigma_\gamma^2$	$\dfrac{\text{MS}(B \text{ in } A)}{\text{MS}(C \text{ in } B)}$
Third stage (C within B)	$n_1 n_2(n_3 - 1)$	SS(C in B)	$\dfrac{\text{SS}(C \text{ in } B)}{n_1 n_2(n_3 - 1)}$	σ^2	
Total	$n_1 n_2 n_3 - 1$	SS(Total)			

When certain assumptions are made concerning σ_α^2 and σ_γ^2, the ratios of mean squares are F statistics with degrees of freedom, ν_1 and ν_2, corresponding to the numerator and denominator mean squares, respectively. For example, if $\sigma_\gamma^2 = 0$, then $E[\text{MS}(B \text{ in } A)] = E[\text{MS}(C \text{ in } B)]$ and

$$F = \frac{\text{MS}(B \text{ in } A)}{\text{MS}(C \text{ in } B)}$$

has an F distribution with $\nu_1 = n_1(n_2 - 1)$ and $\nu_2 = n_1 n_2(n_3 - 1)$ degrees of freedom. This statistic is used to test H_0: $\sigma_\gamma^2 = 0$ against H_a: $\sigma_\gamma^2 > 0$.

Similarly, if $\sigma_\alpha^2 = 0$, then $E[\text{MS}(A)] = E[\text{MS}(B \text{ in } A)]$ and

$$F = \frac{\text{MS}(A)}{\text{MS}(B \text{ in } A)}$$

has an F distribution with $\nu_1 = n_1 - 1$ and $\nu_2 = n_1(n_2 - 1)$ degrees of freedom. This statistic is used to test H_0: $\sigma_\alpha^2 = 0$ against H_a: $\sigma_\alpha^2 > 0$.

The notation used in the analysis of variance for a three-stage nested sampling design, the computational formulas, and statistical tests are shown in the accompanying boxes.

EXAMPLE 14.21

One job of computer scientists is to evaluate computer hardware and software systems. Computer performance evaluation for software involves monitoring the CPU times of processed jobs. In addition to job-to-job variability, the CPU time will vary depending on the day on which the job is submitted and the initiator (a hardware device that initiates job processing) on which the job runs. A three-stage nested sampling experiment was conducted to compare the three sources of variation. On each of five randomly selected days, two randomly selected initiators were monitored. Then four jobs of a particular type were randomly selected from each initiator. The CPU times (in seconds) are shown in Table 14.23. Perform an analysis of variance on the data, and test the hypotheses given on page 884.

Notation for the Analysis of Variance of a Three-Stage Nested Sampling Design

y_{ijk} = Observation on the kth third-stage unit within the jth second-stage and the ith first-stage unit

n_1 = Number of first-stage units

n_2 = Number of second-stage units

n_3 = Number of third-stage units

$n = n_1 n_2 n_3$ = Total number of observations

A_i = Total of all observations in the ith first-stage unit

$\bar{A}_i$ = Mean of all observations in the ith first-stage unit

B_{ij} = Total of all observations in the jth second-stage unit within ith first-stage unit

$\bar{B}_{ij}$ = Mean of all observations in the jth second-stage unit within ith first-stage unit

$\displaystyle\sum_{i=1}^{n_1} \sum_{j=1}^{n_2} \sum_{k=1}^{n_3} y_{ijk}$ = Total of all n observations

$\bar{y}$ = Mean of all n observations

Analysis of Variance F Tests for a Three-Stage Nested Sampling Design

A Test for First-Stage Variation

H_0: $\sigma_\alpha^2 = 0$

H_a: $\sigma_\alpha^2 > 0$

Test statistic: $F = \dfrac{\text{MS(A)}}{\text{MS(B in A)}}$

Rejection region: $F > F_\alpha$, where F_α is the tabulated value for an F statistic that possesses $\nu_1 = n_1 - 1$ and $\nu_2 = n_1(n_2 - 1)$ degrees of freedom.

A Test for Second-Stage Variation

H_0: $\sigma_\gamma^2 = 0$

H_a: $\sigma_\gamma^2 > 0$

Test statistic: $F = \dfrac{\text{MS(B in A)}}{\text{MS(C in B)}}$

Rejection region: $F > F_\alpha$, where F_α is the tabulated value for an F statistic that possesses $\nu_1 = n_1(n_2 - 1)$ and $\nu_2 = n_1 n_2(n_3 - 1)$ degrees of freedom.

Calculation Formulas for a Three-Stage Nested Sampling Design

$$CM = \text{Correction for the mean}$$

$$= \frac{(\text{Total of all observations})^2}{n} = \frac{\left(\sum\limits_{i=1}^{n_1} \sum\limits_{j=1}^{n_2} \sum\limits_{k=1}^{n_3} y_{ijk}\right)^2}{n}$$

$$SS(\text{Total}) = \sum\limits_{i=1}^{n_1} \sum\limits_{j=1}^{n_2} \sum\limits_{k=1}^{n_3} (y_{ijk} - \bar{y})^2$$

$$= (\text{Sum of squares of all observations}) - CM$$

$$= \sum\limits_{i=1}^{n_1} \sum\limits_{j=1}^{n_2} \sum\limits_{k=1}^{n_3} y_{ijk}^2 - CM$$

$$SS(A) = n_2 n_3 \sum\limits_{i=1}^{n_1} (\bar{A}_i - \bar{y})^2 = \sum\limits_{i=1}^{n_1} \frac{A_i^2}{n_2 n_3} - CM$$

$$SS(B \text{ in } A) = n_3 \sum\limits_{j=1}^{n_2} (\bar{B}_{1j} - \bar{A}_1)^2 + n_3 \sum\limits_{j=1}^{n_2} (\bar{B}_{2j} - \bar{A}_2)^2$$

$$+ \cdots + n_3 \sum\limits_{j=1}^{n_2} (\bar{B}_{n_1 j} - \bar{A}_{n_1})^2$$

$$= \sum\limits_{i=1}^{n_1} \sum\limits_{j=1}^{n_2} \frac{B_{ij}^2}{n_3} - \sum\limits_{i=1}^{n_1} \frac{A_i^2}{n_2 n_3}$$

Note: Whenever totals are squared and summed, the divisor is equal to the number of observations in a *single* total. Thus, there are n_3 observations in a second-stage total and $n_2 n_3$ in a first-stage total.

$$SS(C \text{ in } B) = SS(\text{Total}) - SS(A) - SS(B \text{ in } A)$$

$$MS(A) = \frac{SS(A)}{n_1 - 1}$$

$$MS(B \text{ in } A) = \frac{SS(B \text{ in } A)}{n_1(n_2 - 1)}$$

$$MS(C \text{ in } B) = \frac{SS(C \text{ in } B)}{n_1 n_2(n_3 - 1)}$$

---

a. H_0: $\sigma_\alpha^2 = 0$ against H_a: $\sigma_\alpha^2 > 0$ (i.e., whether the day-to-day variation exceeds the initiators-within-days variation)

b. H_0: $\sigma_\gamma^2 = 0$ against H_a: $\sigma_\gamma^2 > 0$ (i.e., whether the initiators-within-days variation exceeds the jobs-within-initiators variation)

Solution

The SAS printout for the analysis of variance for the three-stage nested design is shown in Figure 14.30. The printout is similar to that for the two-stage nested design (see Figure 14.29). However, the breakdown of SS(Total) is presented in three tables. The first table (box 1) shows the partitioning of SS(Total) into sources of variation due to

TABLE 14.23   CPU Times for Example 14.21

		Day				
		1	2	3	4	5
Initiator	1	5.61	1.22	.89	3.69	7.61
		3.44	1.86	1.26	10.84	6.02
		.66	.05	1.43	1.07	.52
		.29	2.11	1.90	2.46	1.98
	2	8.17	1.53	6.27	15.20	2.41
		.13	1.03	1.01	3.62	3.02
		4.22	3.67	2.55	10.22	1.77
		2.50	2.29	1.52	1.83	1.38

Model and **Error**. For a three-stage nested design, **Error** corresponds to jobs (C) in initiators (B), the last-stage source. The two remaining sources of variation, days (A) and initiators (B) in days (A), are included in **Model** variation. The second table (box 2) gives the individual sums of squares and computed F values for these first- and second-stage sources of variation, days (A) and initiators (B) within days (A). [*Warning*: Both F values are computed using MS(Error)—that is, MS(C in B)—in the denominator of the test statistic. Thus, the F value for source A is incorrect if we want to test $H_0: \sigma_{\alpha}^2 = 0$. However, SAS provides an option whereby the programmer may specify the appropriate mean square to be used in computing an F statistic. The correct F value for source A, computed using MS(B in A) in the denominator, is shown in the third table (box 3).] The key quantities on the SAS printout are displayed in the ANOVA table shown in Table 14.24 on page 886.

FIGURE 14.30 ▶

SAS printout for Example 14.21

```
                        Analysis of Variance Procedure

Dependent Variable: CPU
                                   Sum of          Mean
     Source              DF        Squares         Square     F Value    Pr > F
(1)  Model                9      131.7147125     14.6349681     1.55     0.1748
     Error               30      282.5627250      9.4187575
     Corrected Total     39      414.2774375

               R-Square          C.V.        Root MSE              CPU Mean

               0.317938       94.97871       3.068999             3.23125000


     Source              DF      Anova SS     Mean Square    F Value    Pr > F
(2)  DAY                  4     95.27542500   23.81885625      2.53     0.0612
     INIT(DAY)            5     36.43928750    7.28785750      0.77     0.5763

     Tests of Hypotheses using the Anova MS for INIT(DAY) as an error term
(3)  Source              DF      Anova SS     Mean Square    F Value    Pr > F

     DAY                  4     95.27542500   23.81885625      3.27     0.1131
```

TABLE 14.24   Analysis of Variance Table for Example 14.21

Source	df	SS	MS	F	p-value
Days (A)	4	95.2754	23.8188	3.27	.1131
Initiators within days (B in A)	5	36.4393	7.2879	.77	.5763
Jobs within initiators (C in B)	30	282.5627	9.4187		
Total	39	414.2774			

a. The F value for testing $H_0: \sigma_\alpha^2 = 0$ against $H_a: \sigma_\alpha^2 > 0$ is $F = 3.27$ and the corresponding p-value is .1131. Since the p-value exceeds $\alpha = .05$, there is insufficient evidence to indicate that $\sigma_\alpha^2 > 0$; that is, we cannot conclude that the variation between days exceeds the variation of initiators within days.

b. The F value for testing $H_0: \sigma_\gamma^2 = 0$ against $H_a: \sigma_\gamma^2 > 0$ is $F = .77$ and the corresponding p-value is .5763. Since the p-value exceeds $\alpha = .05$, there is insufficient evidence to indicate that $\sigma_\gamma^2 > 0$. We cannot conclude that initiators-within-days variation exceeds the jobs-within-initiators variation.

• •

More complex nested sampling designs (e.g., those involving factorial experiments and interaction effects) are beyond the scope of this text. Consult the references for more information on these complex, but useful, designs.

EXERCISES

• •

14.55   Large highwall failures at a strip mine in Queensland, Australia, occur by the sliding of soft, black bands of clay, called black clay planes, near the base of the highwall. A study was conducted to determine whether the chemical and mineralogical properties of the black clay planes are similar to mudstone (*Engineering Geology*, Oct. 1985). Black clay and mudstone specimens were randomly selected at each of three randomly selected sites within the siltstone faces in the ramp area of the mine. The densities of the specimens (in kilograms per cubic meter) are recorded in the table. A SAS printout of the nested ANOVA follows.

Site 1	Site 2	Site 3
2.06	2.09	2.07
1.84	2.03	2.04
2.47	2.01	1.90
2.12	2.04	2.00
2.00	2.41	2.64

Source: Seedsman, R. W., and Emerson, W. W. "The formation of planes of weakness in the highwall at Goonyella Mine, Queensland, Australia." *Engineering Geology*, Vol. 22, No. 2, Oct. 1985, p. 164 (Table I).

```
                    Analysis of Variance Procedure

Dependent Variable: DENSITY
                                  Sum of           Mean
Source                  DF        Squares         Square    F Value    Pr > F

Model                    2       0.00257333     0.00128667    0.02      0.9772
Error                   12       0.66960000     0.05580000
Corrected Total         14       0.67217333

                R-Square            C.V.        Root MSE         DENSITY Mean

                0.003828          11.17057      0.236220          2.11466667


Source                  DF        Anova SS     Mean Square    F Value    Pr > F

SITE                     2       0.00257333     0.00128667     0.02      0.9772
```

a. How many first-stage observations were included in the sample?
b. How many second-stage units were selected per first-stage unit?
c. Give the total number of observations obtained in the sample.
d. Write the probabilistic model for this sampling design.
e. Find estimates of σ_α^2 and σ^2 on the printout.
f. Conduct a test to determine whether the variation in black clay and mudstone specimen densities between sites exceeds the variation within sites. Use $\alpha = .10$.

14.56 A two-stage nested sampling design was used to collect data to estimate the mean porosity of paper emerging from a paper machine. Ten patches of paper were randomly selected from the end of the paper roll, and four porosity readings were made on each. The data are shown in the table. An analysis of variance for the data was performed using MINITAB; the results are displayed in the accompanying printout.

Paper Patch	Porosity Readings			
1	974	978	976	975
2	981	985	978	986
3	1,014	1,012	1,018	1,010
4	990	996	989	988
5	1,012	1,009	1,011	1,012
6	978	980	974	982
7	988	979	986	983
8	1,004	1,001	1,008	1,008
9	989	984	982	983
10	999	1,002	998	1,003

```
Factor      Type Levels Values
PATCH       fixed    10    1    2    3    4    5    6    7    8    9
                          10

Analysis of Variance for POROSITY

Source    DF        SS        MS       F      P
PATCH      9    6902.13    766.90   78.99  0.000
Error     30     291.25      9.71
Total     39    7193.38
```

a. Obtain the estimates of σ_α^2 and σ^2 from the printout.

b. Do the data provide sufficient evidence to indicate that the variation in porosity between patches exceeds the variation of porosity within patches? Test using $\alpha = .05$.

14.57 Quality control engineers at DuPont utilize nested sampling schemes to determine the percentage of a product shipped that conforms to specifications.[*] First, a random sample of n_1 production lots is selected; then, a random sample of n_2 batches is selected from each production lot. Finally, n_3 shipping lots are randomly selected from each batch for inspection. Suppose $n_1 = 10$, $n_2 = 5$, and $n_3 = 20$. Give the sources and degrees of freedom for an analysis of variance for the nested sampling design.

14.58 An experiment was conducted to estimate the mean level of sulfur content in coal produced by a particular mine. Five days were randomly selected and identified as coal sampling days. On each day, five coal cars were randomly selected and portions of coal were removed from each. Two specimens were prepared from each portion and analyzed for sulfur content. The data are shown in the accompanying table; a SAS printout of the analysis is given on page 889.

				Day		
		1	*2*	*3*	*4*	*5*
	1	.107	.091	.110	.088	.089
		.105	.089	.113	.092	.088
	2	.104	.093	.108	.091	.087
		.103	.090	.110	.093	.089
Coal Cars	3	.101	.092	.111	.092	.092
Within Days		.099	.093	.108	.089	.090
	4	.106	.091	.106	.088	.091
		.105	.091	.108	.087	.090
	5	.108	.092	.106	.091	.086
		.104	.090	.109	.088	.089

a. Construct an analysis of variance table to display the results.

b. Do the data provide sufficient evidence to indicate that the variation in sulfur content between days exceeds the variation within days? Test using $\alpha = .05$.

c. Do the data provide sufficient evidence to indicate that the variation of sulfur content between cars within a day exceeds the variation within the coal specimens? Test using $\alpha = .05$.

---

[*]Henderson, R. K. "On Making the Transition from Inspection to Process Control." Paper presented at Joint Statistical Meetings, American Statistical Association and Biometric Society, August 1986, Chicago, Ill.

```
                    Analysis of Variance Procedure

Dependent Variable: SULFER
                                  Sum of          Mean
Source                   DF       Squares         Square     F Value    Pr > F

Model                    24     0.00351872      0.00014661    53.51     0.0001
Error                    25     0.00006850      0.00000274
Corrected Total          49     0.00358722

                R-Square          C.V.         Root MSE         SULFER Mean

                0.980904        1.712492        0.001655         0.09666000


Source                   DF      Anova SS      Mean Square    F Value    Pr > F

DAY                       4     0.00339332      0.00084833    309.61     0.0001
CAR(DAY)                 20     0.00012540      0.00000627      2.29     0.0257

Tests of Hypotheses using the Anova MS for CAR(DAY) as an error term

Source                   DF      Anova SS      Mean Square    F Value    Pr > F

DAY                       4     0.00339332      0.00084833    135.30     0.0001
```

14.59 An experiment was conducted to monitor the resistivity of silicon monocrystals. The original data were collected according to a two-stage nested sampling design in which random samples of eight crystals were selected from among 30 lots. The measured resistivity of the crystals is recorded in the accompanying table for five of these lots. A SAS printout of the analysis follows.

Lot	Measured Values of Resistivity							
1	2.8	2.7	2.3	2.6	2.7	2.3	2.7	2.7
2	3.0	3.0	2.8	2.4	3.0	3.2	2.9	2.4
3	2.4	2.3	2.4	2.9	2.4	2.4	2.3	2.3
4	3.1	2.9	3.0	3.0	2.6	3.0	2.9	3.0
5	3.1	3.3	2.9	2.5	2.5	3.1	2.5	3.0

Source: Hoshide, M. "Optimization of lot size for quality assurance of silicon wafers." *Reports of Statistical Application Research*, Union of Japanese Scientists and Engineers, Vol. 19, No. 1, 1972, pp. 8–21.

```
                    Analysis of Variance Procedure

Dependent Variable: RESIST
                                  Sum of          Mean
Source                   DF       Squares         Square     F Value    Pr > F

Model                     4     1.45650000      0.36412500     6.34     0.0006
Error                    35     2.01125000      0.05746429
Corrected Total          39     3.46775000

                R-Square          C.V.         Root MSE         RESIST Mean

                0.420013        8.772812        0.239717         2.73250000


Source                   DF      Anova SS      Mean Square    F Value    Pr > F

LOT                       4     1.45650000      0.36412500     6.34     0.0006
```

a. Let σ_B^2 and σ_W^2 represent the components of between- and within-lot variances, respectively, of the resistivity readings. Obtain the estimates of σ_B^2 and σ_W^2 from the printout.

b. Do the data provide sufficient evidence to indicate that the variation in resistivity between lots exceeds the variation within lots? Test using $\alpha = .05$.

14.60 The strength of paper depends upon the length and other characteristics of the wood fiber stock entering the paper machine. Consequently, as the source of the fiber stock varies over time, we expect the strength of the produced paper to vary also. To test this theory, 6 days were randomly selected from within a 4-month period of time. On each of these days, an end-of-the-roll paper patch was selected from each of three randomly selected rolls. Two strength tests were conducted on each of the 18 patches of paper. The strength measurements (pounds per square inch) are shown in the table.

		Day					
		1	*2*	*3*	*4*	*5*	*6*
	1	20.7	22.1	19.0	20.6	23.2	20.7
		19.3	20.4	19.9	18.9	22.5	18.5
Rolls	2	21.2	21.6	18.8	19.8	24.2	19.6
Within Days		20.1	22.5	19.3	20.1	22.9	21.3
	3	19.9	20.9	20.2	20.7	23.4	20.0
		20.5	22.1	19.4	19.2	24.6	18.6

a. Perform an analysis of variance for the data using the formulas provided in this section. Construct an analysis of variance table to display the results.

b. Do the data provide sufficient evidence to indicate that the variation in paper strength between days exceeds the variation within days? Test using $\alpha = .05$.

c. Do the data provide sufficient evidence to indicate that the variation in strength from roll to roll exceeds the variation between strength tests within a roll? Test using $\alpha = .05$.

14.13 Procedures for Making Multiple Comparisons of Treatment Means

Many practical experiments are conducted to determine the largest (or the smallest) mean in a set. For example, suppose that a chemist has developed five chemical solutions for removing a corrosive substance from a metal fitting. The chemist would then want to determine the solution that will remove the greatest amount of the corrosive substance from the fitting in a single application. Similarly, a production engineer might want to determine which among six machines or which among three foremen achieves the highest mean productivity per hour. A mechanical engineer might want to choose one engine, from among five, that is most efficient, and so on.

Once differences among, say, five treatment means have been detected in an ANOVA, choosing the treatment with the largest mean might appear to be a simple matter. We could, for example, obtain the sample means $\bar{y}_1, \bar{y}_2, \ldots, \bar{y}_5$ and compare them by constructing a $(1 - \alpha)100\%$ confidence interval for the difference between each pair of treatment means. However, there is a problem associated with this procedure: **A confidence interval for $\mu_i - \mu_j$, with its corresponding value of α, is valid only when the two treatments (i and j) to be compared are selected prior to experimentation.** After you have looked at the data, you cannot use a confidence interval to compare the treatments for the largest and smallest sample means because they will always be farther apart, on the average, than any pair of treatments selected at random. Furthermore, if you construct a series of confidence intervals, each with a chance α of indicating a difference between a pair of means if in fact no difference exists, then the risk of making *at least one* Type I error in a series of inferences will be larger than the value of α specified for a single interval.

There are a number of procedures for comparing and ranking a group of treatment means. A popular method, known as **Tukey's method**, utilizes the Studentized range

$$q = \frac{\bar{y}_{\max} - \bar{y}_{\min}}{s/\sqrt{n}}$$

(where $\bar{y}_{\max}$ and $\bar{y}_{\min}$ are the largest and smallest sample means, respectively) to determine whether the difference in any pair of sample means implies a difference in the corresponding treatment means. The logic behind this **multiple comparisons procedure** is that if we determine a critical value for the difference between the largest and smallest sample means, $|\bar{y}_{\max} - \bar{y}_{\min}|$, one that implies a difference in their respective treatment means, then any other pair of sample means that differ by as much as or more than this critical value would also imply a difference in the corresponding treatment means. Tukey's (1949) procedure selects this critical distance, ω, so that the probability of making one or more Type I errors (concluding that a difference exists between a pair of treatment means if, in fact, they are identical) is α. Therefore, the risk of making a Type I error applies to the whole procedure, i.e., to the comparisons of all pairs of means in the experiment, rather than to a single comparison. Consequently, the value of α selected by the researchers is called an **experimentwise error rate** (in contrast to a **comparisonwise error rate**).

Tukey's procedure relies on the assumption that the p sample means are based on independent random samples, *each containing an equal number n_t of observations.* Then if $s = \sqrt{\text{MSE}}$ is the computed standard deviation for the analysis, the distance ω is

$$\omega = q(p,\ \nu)\frac{s}{\sqrt{n_t}}$$

The tabulated statistic $q_\alpha(p,\ \nu)$ is the critical value of the Studentized range, the value that locates α in the upper tail of the q distribution. This critical value depends on α, the number of treatment means involved in the comparison, and ν, the number of degrees of freedom associated with MSE, as shown in the box on page 892. Values of $q(p,\ \nu)$ for $\alpha = .05$ and $\alpha = .01$ are given in Tables 13 and 14 respectively, of Appendix II.

Tukey's Multiple Comparisons Procedure: Equal Sample Sizes

1. Select the desired experimentwise error rate, α.
2. Calculate

$$\omega = q_\alpha(p, \nu)\frac{s}{\sqrt{n_t}}$$

   where

$$p = \text{Number of sample means}$$
$$s = \sqrt{\text{MSE}}$$
$$\nu = \text{Number of degrees of freedom associated with MSE}$$
$$n_t = \text{Number of observations in each of the } p \text{ samples}$$
$$q_\alpha(p, \nu) = \text{Critical value of the Studentized range (Tables 13}$$
$$\text{and 14 of Appendix II)}$$

3. Calculate and rank the p sample means.

4. Place a bar over those pairs of treatment means that differ by less than ω. Any pair of treatments not connected by an overbar (i.e., differing by more than ω) implies a difference in the corresponding population means.

Note: The confidence level associated with all inferences drawn from the analysis is $(1 - \alpha)$.

EXAMPLE 14.22

Refer to the ANOVA for the completely randomized design, Example 14.8. Recall that, at $\alpha = .05$, we rejected the null hypothesis of no differences among the mean times until abrasion for the three paint types. Use Tukey's method to compare the three treatment means.

Solution

STEP 1 For this analysis, we will select an experimentwise error rate of $\alpha = .05$.

STEP 2 From previous examples, we have $p = 3$ treatments, $\nu = 27$ df for error, $s = \sqrt{\text{MSE}} = 168.95$, and $n_t = 10$ observations per treatment. The critical value of the Studentized range (obtained from Table 13, Appendix II) is $q_{.05}(3, 27) \approx 3.5$. Substituting these values into the formula for ω, we obtain

$$\omega = q_{.05}(3, 27)\left(\frac{s}{\sqrt{n_t}}\right) = 3.5\left(\frac{168.95}{\sqrt{10}}\right) = 187.0$$

STEP 3 The sample means for the three paint types (obtained from Figure 14.12) are:

$$\bar{y}_1 = 229.6 \qquad \bar{y}_2 = 309.8 \qquad \bar{y}_3 = 427.8$$

STEP 4 Based on the critical difference $\omega = 187$, the three treatment means are ranked as follows:

Sample Means:	229.6	309.9	427.8
Treatments:	Type 1	Type 2	Type 3

This same information can be obtained using a statistical software package. The SAS printout of the Tukey analysis is shown in Figure 14.31. Tukey's critical difference, $\omega = 187.33$, is shaded on the printout. (This value differs slightly from our calculated value because of rounding.) Note that SAS lists the treatment means vertically in descending order. Treatment means connected by the same letter (A, B, C, etc.) are *not* significantly different.

From this information we infer that the mean wear time for paint type 3 is significantly larger than the mean wear time for paint type 1, since $\bar{y}_3$ exceeds $\bar{y}_1$ by more than the critical value. However, the treatment pairs (1, 2) and (2, 3) are connected by a bar (or the same letter) since neither $(\bar{y}_2 - \bar{y}_1)$ nor $(\bar{y}_3 - \bar{y}_2)$ exceeds ω. This indicates that the sample means for these pairs of treatments are not significantly different. Practically, these results imply that paint type 3 has the highest mean time till abrasion and paint type 1 has the lowest. The mean for paint type 2, however, is not significantly different from either of the other two means. These inferences are made with an overall confidence level of $(1 - \alpha) = .95$.

FIGURE 14.31 ▶
SAS printout of Tukey analysis,
Example 14.22

```
                Analysis of Variance Procedure

        Tukey's Studentized Range (HSD) Test for variable: WEAR

     NOTE: This test controls the type I experimentwise error rate, but
           generally has a higher type II error rate than REGWQ.

              Alpha= 0.05   df= 27   MSE= 28543.37
            Critical Value of Studentized Range= 3.506
             Minimum Significant Difference= 187.33

     Means with the same letter are not significantly different.

          Tukey Grouping            Mean      N   PAINTYPE

                        A          427.80     10   TYPE_3
                        A
                  B     A          309.90     10   TYPE_2
                  B
                  B                229.60     10   TYPE_1
```

Remember that Tukey's multiple comparisons procedure requires the sample sizes associated with the treatments to be equal. This, of course, will be satisfied for the randomized block designs and factorial experiments described in Sections 14.9 and 14.10, respectively. The sample sizes, however, may not be equal in a completely randomized design (Section 14.8). In this case a modification of Tukey's method (sometimes called the Tukey–Kramer method) is necessary, as described in the box. The technique requires that the critical difference ω_{ij} be calculated for each pair of treatments (i, j) in the experiment and pairwise comparisons made based on the appropriate value of ω_{ij}. However, when Tukey's method is used with unequal sample sizes, the value of α selected a priori by the researcher only approximates the true experimentwise error rate. In fact, when applied to unequal sample sizes, the procedure has been found to be more conservative, i.e., less likely to detect differences between pairs of treatment means when they exist, than in the case of equal sample sizes. For this reason, researchers sometimes look to alternative methods of multiple comparisons when the sample sizes are unequal. One such method is *Bonferroni's procedure*.

Tukey's Approximate Multiple Comparisons Procedure for Unequal Sample Sizes

1. Select the desired experimentwise error rate, α.
2. Calculate for each treatment pair (i, j)

$$\omega_{ij} = q_\alpha(p, v)\frac{s}{\sqrt{2}}\sqrt{\frac{1}{n_i} + \frac{1}{n_j}}$$

where

p = Number of sample means

$s = \sqrt{MSE}$

v = Number of degrees of freedom associated with MSE

n_i = Number of observations in sample for treatment i

n_j = Number of observations in sample for treatment j

$q_\alpha(p, v)$ = Critical value of the Studentized range (Tables 13 and 14 of Appendix II)

3. Rank the p sample means and place a bar over any treatment pair (i, j) that differs by less than ω_{ij}. Any pair of sample means not connected by an overbar (i.e., differing by more than ω) implies a difference in the corresponding population means.

Note: This procedure is approximate, i.e., the value of α selected by the researcher approximates the true probability of making at least one Type I error.

The Bonferroni approach is based on the following result (proof omitted): If g comparisons are to be made, each with confidence coefficient $1 - \alpha/g$, then the overall probability of making one or more Type I errors (i.e., the experimentwise error rate) is at most α. That is, the set of intervals constructed using the Bonferroni method yields an overall confidence level of at least $1 - \alpha$. For example, if you want to construct $g = 2$ confidence intervals with an experimentwise error rate of at most

$\alpha = .05$, then each individual interval must be constructed using a confidence level of $1 - .05/2 = .975$.

When applied to pairwise comparisons of treatment means, the Bonferroni technique can be carried out by comparing the difference between two treatment means, $(\bar{y}_i - \bar{y}_j)$, to a critical difference B_{ij}, when B_{ij} depends on n_i, n_j, α, MSE, and the total number of treatments to be compared. If the difference between the sample means exceeds the critical difference, there is sufficient evidence to conclude that the population means differ. The steps to follow in carrying out the Bonferroni multiple comparisons procedure are described in the box.

Bonferroni Multiple Comparisons Procedure for Pairwise Comparisons of Treatment Means

1. Select the experimentwise error rate, α.
2. Calculate B_{ij} for each treatment pair (i, j):

$$B_{ij} = (t_{\alpha^*/2})(s)\sqrt{\frac{1}{n_i} + \frac{1}{n_j}}$$

where

p = Number of sample (treatment) means in the experiment

g = Number of pairwise comparisons [Note: If all pairwise comparisons are to be made, then $g = p(p - 1)/2$.]

$\alpha^* = \alpha/g$ = Comparisonwise error rate

$s = \sqrt{\text{MSE}}$

n_i = Number of observations in sample for treatment i

n_j = Number of observations in sample for treatment j

ν = Number of degrees of freedom associated with MSE

$t_{\alpha^*/2}$ = Critical value of t distribution with ν df and tail area $\alpha^*/2$ (Table 7, Appendix II)

3. Calculate and rank the sample means.

Place a bar over any treatment pair (i, j) that differs by less than B_{ij}. Any pair of means not connected by an overbar implies a difference in the corresponding population means.

Note: The level of confidence associated with all inferences drawn from the analysis is at least $(1 - \alpha)$.

EXAMPLE 14.23

Refer to the rankings of the mean wear times for three paint types, Example 14.22.

a. Use Bonferroni's method to compare the three treatment means.

b. Compare the results, part **a**, with Tukey's procedure.

Solution

a. We will follow the three steps outlined in the box.

STEP 1 As in Example 14.22, we will select an experimentwise error rate of $\alpha = .05$.

STEP 2 For $p = 3$ treatments, the number of pairwise comparisons is

$$g = p(p - 1)/2 = 3(2)/2 = 3$$

Hence, the adjusted α level (i.e., comparisonwise error rate) is $\alpha^* = \alpha/g = .05/3 \approx .017$. The critical value of the Student's t statistic with $\nu = 27$ df (obtained using a statistical software package) is $t_{\alpha/2} = t_{(.017)/2} = t_{.0083} \approx 2.55$. From Example 14.22, we have $s = \sqrt{MSE} = 168.95$, and $n_i = 10$ observations per treatment. Substituting these values into the formula for B, we obtain

$$B = t_{.0083}(s)/\sqrt{(1/n_i) + (1/(n_i))} = 2.55(168.95)/\sqrt{2/10} = 192.7$$

STEP 3 Based on the critical difference $B = 192.7$, the three treatment means are ranked as follows:

Sample Means:	229.6	309.9	427.8
Treatments:	Type 1	Type 2	Type 3

b. The conclusion reached by Bonferroni's method is identical to Tukey's method: At an overall significance level of .05, (1) the mean wear for paint type 3 is significantly higher than the corresponding mean for paint type 1, and (2) the mean for paint type 2 is not significantly different from either of the other two means. Note, however, that the Bonferroni critical difference, $B = 192.7$, is larger than the Tukey critical difference, $\omega = 187.33$, obtained in Exercise 14.22. Thus, for this example, the Tukey method will be able to detect smaller differences in the treatment means than Bonferroni's method using the same comparisonwise error rate α.

The result, Example 14.23b, reveals that the Bonferroni method produces wider confidence intervals on the differences between treatment means than Tukey's method. This will be true, in general, whenever the sample sizes are the same for the treatments. Consequently, *Tukey's method is the superior multiple comparisons procedure for balanced ANOVA designs* (i.e., designs with the same sample size per treatment). However, with unequal n's, the Bonferroni critical difference will usually be smaller than the Tukey critical difference. Hence, *the Bonferroni method is preferred over Tukey's method when the design is unbalanced* (i.e., when the sample sizes for the treatments are unequal). Keep in mind that the exact t value needed to calculate the Bonferroni critical difference may not be available in the t tables provided in most texts. If you do not have access to a software package that provides this information, you will have to estimate its value.

In general, multiple comparisons of treatment means should be performed only as a follow-up analysis to the ANOVA, i.e., only after we have conducted the appropriate analysis of variance F test(s) and determined that sufficient evidence exists of differences among the treatment means. Be wary of conducting multiple comparisons when the ANOVA F test indicates no evidence of a difference among a small number of treatment means—this may lead to confusing and contradictory results.*

> **Warning**
> ....
>
> In practice, it is advisable to avoid conducting multiple comparisons of a small number of treatment means when the corresponding ANOVA F test is nonsignificant; otherwise, confusing and contradictory results may occur.

EXERCISES

14.61 Refer to Exercise 14.20. Use Bonferroni's method to compare the mean Vanadium concentrations of the four biological materials. Use $\alpha = .06$.

14.62 Refer to Exercise 14.24. The mean levels of polysaccharides found in the five groups of Dutchmen are provided in the accompanying table. Use Tukey's method to rank the group means. Use $\alpha = .01$.

Fish Consumption grams/day	Sample Size	Mean Level of Polysaccharides percentage of energy
0	159	27.0
1–14	283	27.0
15–29	215	26.6
30–44	116	25.7
45 or more	79	24.4

14.63 Refer to Exercise 14.25. Use a multiple comparisons procedure to compare the mean rates of penetration for the three types of drill bits. Identify the means that appear to differ. Use $\alpha = .05$.

14.64 Refer to Exercise 14.33. Use a multiple comparisons procedure to compare the mean crack widths for the four wetting periods. Identify the means that appear to differ. Use $\alpha = .05$.

14.65 Refer to the *Human Factors* (Apr. 1990) study of recognizer accuracy at three levels (90%, 95%, and 99%) and vocabulary size at three levels (75%, 87.5%, and 100%) on the performance of a computerized speech recognizer, Exercise 13.22. The data on task completion times (minutes) were subjected to an analysis of

---

*When a large number of treatments are to be compared, a borderline, nonsignificant F value (e.g., $.05 < p$-value $< .10$) may mask differences between some of the means. In this situation, it is better to ignore the F test and proceed directly to a multiple comparisons procedure.

variance for a 3×3 factorial design. The F test for accuracy $\times$ vocabulary interaction resulted in a p-value less than .0003.

a. Interpret the result of the test for interaction.

b. As a follow-up to the test for interaction, the mean task completion times for the three levels of accuracy were compared under each level of vocabulary. Do you agree with this method of analysis? Explain.

c. Refer to part **b**. Tukey's multiple comparison method was used to compare the three accuracy means within each level of vocabulary at an experimentwise error rate of $\alpha = .05$. The results are summarized here. Interpret these results.

Mean Task Completion Time

Accuracy Level

Vocabulary Size	99%	95%	90%
75%	15.49	19.29	22.19
87.5%	12.77	14.31	16.48
100%	8.67	9.68	11.88

Source: Casali, S. P., Williges, B. H., and Dryden, R. D. "Effects of recognition accuracy and vocabulary size of a speech recognition system on task performance and user acceptance." *Human Factors*, Vol. 32, No. 2, April 1990, p. 190 (Figure 2).

14.66   Refer to Exercise 14.41. Use a multiple comparisons procedure to compare the mean shear strengths for the four antimony amounts. Identify the means that appear to differ. Use $\alpha = .01$.

14.14   Checking ANOVA Assumptions

For each of the experiments and designs discussed in this chapter, we listed in the relevant boxes the assumptions underlying the analysis in the terminology of ANOVA. For example, in the box on page 816, the assumptions for a completely randomized design are (1) the p probability distributions of the response y corresponding to the p treatments are normal, and (2) the population variances of the p treatments are equal. Similarly, for randomized block designs and factorial designs, the data for the treatments must come from normal probability distributions with equal variances.

These assumptions are equivalent to those required for a regression analysis (see Section 12.2). The reason, of course, is that the probabilistic model for the response y that underlies each design is the familiar general linear regression model of Chapters 12 and 13. Consequently, checks on the ANOVA assumptions can be performed by examining the regression residuals, as described in Section 12.11. A brief overview of these techniques follows.

Detecting Nonnormal Populations

1. For each treatment, construct a histogram or stem-and-leaf display of the residuals. Look for highly skewed distributions. (Remember, ANOVA, like regression, is robust with respect to the normality assumption. That is, slight departures from normality will have little impact on the validity of the inferences derived from the analysis.)

[*Note:*   If the sample size for each treatment is small, then these graphs will probably be of limited use.]

2. Formal statistical tests of normality (such as the Shapiro–Wilk test) are also available. The null hypothesis is that the probability distribution of the response is normal. These tests, however, are sensitive to slight departures from normality. Since in most scientific applications the normality assumption will not be satisfied exactly, these tests will likely result in a rejection of the null hypothesis and, consequently, are of limited use in practice. Consult the references for more information on these formal tests.

3. If the distribution of the residuals departs greatly from normality, a *normalizing transformation* may be necessary. For example, for highly skewed distributions, transformations on the response *y* such as $\log(y)$ or $\sqrt{y}$ tend to "normalize" the data since these functions "pull" the observations in the tail of the distribution back toward the mean.

Detecting Unequal Variances

1. For each treatment, construct a **residual frequency plot** and look for differences in the spread (variability) of the residuals shown in the plots. Residual frequency plots for the three paint types (treatments) in the completely randomized design ANOVA of Example 14.8 are shown in Figure 14.32. Note that the variability of the residuals in each plot is about the same; thus, the assumption of equal variances appears to be satisfied.

FIGURE 14.32 ▶
Residual frequency plots for ANOVA of Example 14.8

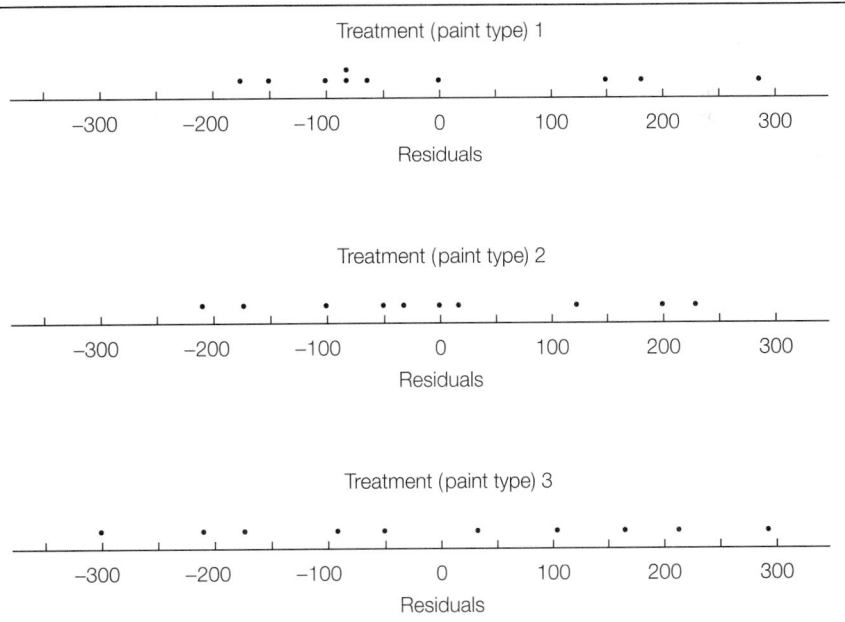

2. When the sample sizes are small for each treatment, only a few points are plotted on the residual frequency plots, making it difficult to detect differences in variation. In this situation, you may want to use one of several formal statistical tests of homogeneity of variances that are available. For p treatments, the null hypothesis is $H_0: \sigma_1^2 = \sigma_2^2 = \cdots = \sigma_p^2$, where σ_i^2 is the population variance of the response y corresponding to the ith treatment. If all p populations are approximately normal, **Bartlett's test for homogeneity of variances** can be applied. The elements of the test are shown in the box. Note that the test statistic depends on whether the sample sizes are equal or unequal.

Applying Bartlett's test to the ANOVA of Example 14.9, the null hypothesis is

$$H_0: \quad \sigma_1^2 = \sigma_2^2 = \sigma_3^2$$

where σ_1^2, σ_2^2, and σ_3^2 are the population wear variances for the three paint types, 1, 2, and 3, respectively. Since the sample sizes are the same ($n_1 = n_2 = n_3 = 10$), the formula for the test statistic is

$$B = \frac{(n - 1)[p \ln \bar{s}^2 - \Sigma \ln s_i^2]}{1 + \dfrac{(p + 1)}{3p(n - 1)}}$$

To obtain B, we first compute the sample variances, s_1^2, s_2^2, s_3^2, and their average, $\bar{s}^2$. The sample variances, shown (shaded) on the SAS printout displayed in Figure 14.33, are $s_1^2 = 25{,}026$, $s_2^2 = 21{,}867$, and $s_3^2 = 38{,}737$. Then, the average sample

FIGURE 14.33 ▶
SAS descriptive statistics for residuals of Example 14.9

```
                        Analysis Variable : RESID

-------------------------------- TYPE=1 --------------------------------

         N Obs          Mean       Variance        Std Dev
        ------------------------------------------------------
           10    -2.27374E-14      25026.04     158.1962213
        ------------------------------------------------------


-------------------------------- TYPE=2 --------------------------------

         N Obs          Mean       Variance        Std Dev
        ------------------------------------------------------
           10    -3.41061E-14      21866.77     147.8741582
        ------------------------------------------------------


-------------------------------- TYPE=3 --------------------------------

         N Obs          Mean       Variance        Std Dev
        ------------------------------------------------------
           10    -1.13687E-14      38737.29     196.8179079
        ------------------------------------------------------
```

Bartlett's Test of Homogeneity of Variance

H_0: $\sigma_1^2 = \sigma_2^2 = \cdots = \sigma_p^2$

H_a: At least two variances differ

Test statistic (equal sample sizes):

$$B = \frac{(n - 1)[p \ln \bar{s}^2 - \Sigma \ln s_i^2]}{1 + \dfrac{(p + 1)}{3p(n - 1)}}$$

where

$$n = n_1 = n_2 = \cdots = n_p$$

s_i^2 = Sample variance for sample i

$\bar{s}^2$ = Average of the p sample variances = $(\Sigma\, s_i^2)/p$

$\ln x$ = Natural logarithm (i.e., log to the base e) of the quantity x

Test statistic (unequal sample sizes):

$$B = \frac{[\Sigma(n_i - 1)]\ln \bar{s}^2 - \Sigma(n_i - 1)\ln s_i^2}{1 + \dfrac{1}{3(p - 1)}\left\{\Sigma\dfrac{1}{(n_i - 1)} - \dfrac{1}{\Sigma(n_i - 1)}\right\}}$$

where

n_i = Sample size for sample i

s_i^2 = Sample variance for sample i

$\bar{s}^2$ = Weighted average of the p sample variances = $\dfrac{\Sigma(n_i - 1)\, s_i^2}{\Sigma(n_i - 1)}$

$\ln x$ = Natural logarithm (i.e., log to the base e) of the quantity x

Rejection region: $B > \chi_\alpha^2$, where χ_α^2 locates an area α in the upper tail of a χ^2 distribution with $(k - 1)$ degrees of freedom

Assumptions: 1. Independent random samples are selected from the p populations.

2. All p populations are normally distributed.

variance is $\bar{s}^2 = (25{,}026 + 21{,}867 + 38{,}737)/3 = 28{,}543$. Substituting these values into the formula, we obtain

$$B = \frac{(10 - 1)\{3 \ln(28543) - [\ln(25026) + \ln(21867) + \ln(38737)]\}}{1 + \dfrac{(3 + 1)}{3(3)(10 - 1)}} = .79$$

Since this value is less than the critical value, $\chi^2_{.05} = 5.99147$ (based on $p - 1 = 2$ degrees of freedom), we fail to reject the null hypothesis of equal variances; there is insufficient evidence (at $\alpha = .05$) of differences among the variances in wear for the three treatments. This result supports our conclusion derived from the residual frequency plots of Figure 14.32.

Bartlett's test works well when the data come from normal (or near normal) distributions. The results, however, can be misleading for nonnormal data. In this case, we can apply a test that is much less sensitive to nonnormality in the data. See the references at the end of this chapter for more information on alternative tests.

3. When unequal variances are detected, use one of the **variance-stabilizing transformations** of the response y discussed in Section 12.11.

In most business applications, the assumptions will not be satisfied exactly. These analysis of variance procedures are flexible, however, in the sense that slight departures from the assumptions will not significantly affect the analysis or the validity of the resulting inferences. On the other hand, gross violations of the assumptions (e.g., a nonconstant variance) will cast doubt on the validity of the inferences. Therefore, you should make it standard practice to conduct an analysis of the residuals from the ANOVA using the techniques of Chapter 12 to verify that the assumptions are (approximately) satisfied.

EXERCISES

[*Note:* These exercises require the use of a computer to calculate and plot residuals.]

14.67 Check the assumptions for the completely randomized design ANOVA of Exercise 14.20.

14.68 Check the assumptions for the completely randomized design ANOVA of Exercise 14.25.

14.69 Check the assumptions for the completely randomized design ANOVA of Exercise 14.27.

14.70 Check the assumptions for the randomized block design ANOVA of Exercise 14.34.

14.71 Check the assumptions for the factorial design ANOVA of Exercise 14.41.

14.72 Check the assumptions for the factorial design ANOVA of Exercise 14.43.

14.15   Summary

Experimental design is a plan (or strategy) for collecting the experimental data. The goal is to increase the amount of information by controlling two factors:

1. **Volume** of the signal contained in the data

2. **Noise** or random variation in the data that is measured by σ^2

The first three steps in designing an experiment are as follows:

STEP 1 Select the **factors** (i.e., the independent variables) to be investigated.

STEP 2 Choose the factor–level combinations (**treatments**).

STEP 3 Determine the number of observations for each treatment (i.e., the number of **replications** of the experiment).

These steps affect the volume of the signal contained in the data because they enable us to shift the information in the experiment so that it focuses on the parameter(s) of interest. An example of a volume-increasing design is a **factorial experiment**, in which all possible treatments (factor–level combinations) are selected. With factorial designs, we shift the focus of the experiment to an investigation of factor interaction.

The fourth step in designing an experiment is

STEP 4 Decide how to assign the treatments to the experimental units.

Two basic methods of assigning the treatments to the experimental units are the **completely randomized design** and the **randomized block design**. The latter is a noise-reducing design; by assigning treatments to relatively homogeneous blocks of experimental units, we can reduce the variation of treatment differences. The net effect of this action is to reduce experimental noise, measured by the variance of the random error ε that appears in the linear model.

After the data have been collected using a designed experiment, inferences about the treatment means are obtained by conducting an **analysis of variance** (**ANOVA**). An analysis of variance partitions the total sum of squares, SS(Total), into SSE and, depending on the design, sums of squares for treatments (SST), blocks (SSB), and factor main effects and interaction. Tests for treatment means, block means, factor interactions, and so forth are obtained by calculating the ratio of the appropriate mean square to MSE and conducting an F test. These F tests can also be conducted by fitting the appropriate linear models to the data using regression. The models differ depending on the specific design employed.

Throughout this chapter we showed that an ANOVA and a regression analysis yield equivalent results. But an analysis of variance possesses both advantages and disadvantages compared with a regression analysis. One major advantage of an analysis of variance is that it is easy to perform on a pocket or desk calculator. Second, an analysis of variance is essential when y is affected by more than one source of random variation, and then the experimental design permits us to separate these sources and to estimate the variances of their respective random components. (A discussion of these models is not included in this text.) The disadvantages are its restrictions and limitations, as follows:

1. **The set of analysis of variance formulas appropriate for a particular experimental design applies only to that design**. If the data collected are observational (i.e., the independent variables are uncontrolled), an analysis of variance is inappropriate.

No deviations from the design are permitted. Consequently, the method is of value only for special types of designed experiments.

2. **In contrast to a regression analysis, the analysis of variance formulas change from one design to another**. (There is a pattern, as indicated in Section 14.7, but the pattern is usually not apparent to a beginner.)

3. **The ANOVA formulas for a factorial experiment and many other experimental designs can be used only when the sample sizes are equal.** However, the regression approach applies to both equal and unequal sample sizes for the various factor–level combinations.

4. **An analysis of variance does not give you a prediction equation**. This is a great handicap when one (or more) of the independent variables is quantitative.

5. **Although a linear model is always implied in an analysis of variance, it is rarely presented or discussed when analyses of data have been performed**. Consequently, the thrust of an analysis of variance is often counter (although it need not be) to the notion of modeling, which is the modern quantitative way of analyzing business phenomena.

In conclusion, perhaps the most important point for you to note in this chapter is the following: **If your data can be modeled using a linear model that contains a single random error component (which is the model used throughout this text), then a regression analysis can do everything that an analysis of variance can do and it can do more!** But you will probably need a computer to do it. Regression analysis is simple, uses the same formulas for all analyses, is programmed for both mainframe and personal computers, and can be used to analyze data obtained from both designed and undesigned experiments. Consequently, a beginner may be advised to stick to regression analyses for analyzing the relationship between a set of independent variables and a response y if a computer is available to perform the computations.

SUPPLEMENTARY EXERCISES

14.73 Video games have revolutionized children's leisure time activities. However, many parents, including the U.S. surgeon general, believe that video games are a bad influence on their children. A study was conducted to examine the effect of playing video games on fifth-graders' free play (*Journal of Applied Social Psychology*, Vol. 16, 1986). Eighty-four fifth-graders were paired randomly, and then each pair was randomly assigned to one of three types of games, an aggressive video game (Missile Command), a nonaggressive video game (Pac-Man), or a pen-and-paper maze-solving game (control) in equal numbers. One member of each pair was then randomly chosen to play the designated game (player) for 8 minutes while the other member watched (observer). Thus, 14 fifth-graders were assigned to each of the $3 \times 2 = 6$ experimental conditions.

After video play was concluded, the children were sent to a toy room for free play. The goal of the experiment was to investigate the effect of type of game (Missile Command, Pac-Man, and control) and position (player or observer) on degree of aggressive play in the toy room.

a. Identify the factors in this factorial experiment.
b. Identify the levels of the factors.
c. What are the treatments?
d. Give the complete model appropriate for analyzing the data.
e. Give the sources of variation and their respective degrees of freedom in an ANOVA table for this experiment.
f. A significant interaction was found between type of game and position (p-value $< .01$). Interpret this result in the words of the problem.

14.74 Polychlorinated biphenyls (PCBs), used in the manufacture of large electrical transformers and capacitors, are extremely hazardous contaminants when released into the environment. Samples of fish were taken from each of five rivers and analyzed for PCB concentration (in parts per million). The data are shown in the table. (Some of the analyses were unproductive, so the sample sizes vary from river to river.)

		River		
1	2	3	4	5
2	4	12	7	13
3	6	9	5	9
1	3	11	5	15
5	5	8	9	10
	7			11
				7

a. Use the formulas provided in this section to construct an analysis of variance table.
b. Do the data provide sufficient evidence to indicate differences in the mean PCB concentration in fish for the five rivers? Test using $\alpha = .05$.
c. Rank the mean PCB levels of the five rivers with an appropriate multiple comparisons procedure. Use $\alpha = .10$.

14.75 To reduce the time spent in transferring materials from one location to another, three methods have been devised. With no previous information available on the effectiveness of these three approaches, a study is performed. Each approach is tried several times, and the amount of time to completion (in hours) is recorded in the table. A MINITAB printout of the analysis follows. (See page 906.)

	Method	
A	B	C
8.2	7.9	7.1
7.1	8.1	7.4
7.8	8.3	6.9
8.9	8.5	6.8
8.8	7.6	
	8.5	

```
ANALYSIS OF VARIANCE ON TIME
SOURCE      DF        SS        MS        F        p
METHOD       2      3.579     1.789     7.02     0.010
ERROR       12      3.057     0.255
TOTAL       14      6.636
                                     INDIVIDUAL 95 PCT CI'S FOR MEAN
                                     BASED ON POOLED STDEV
LEVEL       N       MEAN      STDEV   --+---------+---------+---------+----
  1         5      8.1600    0.7436                        (-------*-------)
  2         6      8.1500    0.3564                        (-------*------)
  3         4      7.0500    0.2646   (---------*--------)
                                     --+---------+---------+---------+----
POOLED STDEV =     0.5047            6.60      7.20      7.80      8.40
```

a. What type of experimental design was used?

b. Is there evidence that the mean time to completion of the task differs for at least two of the three methods? Use $\alpha = .01$.

14.76 The steam explosion of peat renders fermentable carbohydrates that have a number of potentially important industrial uses. A study of the steam explosion process was initiated to determine the optimum conditions for the release of fermentable carbohydrate (*Biotechnology and Bioengineering*, Feb. 1986). Triplicate samples of peat were treated for .5, 1.0, 2.0, 3.0, and 5.0 minutes at 170°, 200°, and 215°C, in the steam explosion process. Thus, the experiment consists of two factors—temperature at three levels and treatment time at five levels. The accompanying table gives the percentage of carbohydrate solubilized for each of the $3 \times 5 = 15$ peat samples.

Temperature °C	Time minutes	Carbohydrate Solubilized %
170	.5	1.3
170	1.0	1.8
170	2.0	3.2
170	3.0	4.9
170	5.0	11.7
200	.5	9.2
200	1.0	17.3
200	2.0	18.1
200	3.0	18.1
200	5.0	18.8
215	.5	12.4
215	1.0	20.4
215	2.0	17.3
215	3.0	16.0
215	5.0	15.3

Source: Forsberg, C. W., et al. "The release of fermentable carbohydrate from peat by steam explosion and its use in the microbial production of solvents." *Biotechnology and Bioengineering*, Vol. 28, No. 2, Feb. 1986, p. 179 (Table I). Copyright 1986.

a. What type of experimental design was employed?

b. Explain why the traditional analysis of variance formulas are inappropriate for the analysis of these data.

c. Write a second-order model relating mean amount of carbohydrate solubilized, $E(y)$, to temperature (x_1) and time (x_2).

d. Explain how you could test the hypothesis that the two factors, temperature (x_1) and time (x_2), interact.

e. If you have access to a statistical software package, fit the model and perform the test for interaction.

14.77 *Acid rain* is considered by some environmentalists to be the nation's most serious environmental problem. It is formed by the combination of water vapor in clouds with nitrogen oxide and sulfuric dioxide emissions from the burning of coal, oil, and natural gas. The acidity of rain in central and northern Florida consistently ranges from 4.5 to 5 on the pH scale, a decidedly acid condition. To determine the effects of acid rain on the acidity of soils in a natural ecosystem, engineers at the University of Florida's Institute of Food and Agricultural Sciences irrigated experimental plots near Gainesville, Florida, with acid rain at two pH levels, 3.7 and 4.5. The acidity of the soil was then measured at three different depths, 0–15, 15–30, and 30–46 centimeters. Tests were conducted during three different time periods. The resulting soil pH values are shown in the table.

		April 3 Acid Rain pH		June 16 Acid Rain pH		June 30 Acid Rain pH	
		3.7	4.5	3.7	4.5	3.7	4.5
	0–15 cm	5.33	5.33	5.47	5.47	5.20	5.13
Soil Depth	15–30 cm	5.27	5.03	5.50	5.53	5.33	5.20
	30–46 cm	5.37	5.40	5.80	5.60	5.33	5.17

Source: "Acid rain linked to growth of coal-fired power." *Florida Agricultural Research* 83, Vol. 2, No. 1, Winter 1983.

Suppose we treat the experiment as a 2×3 factorial laid out in three blocks, where the factors are acid rain at two pH levels and soil depth at three levels, and the blocks are the three time periods. The SAS printout for the analysis of variance is provided here.

```
                    Analysis of Variance Procedure

Dependent Variable: SOILPH
                                Sum of          Mean
Source                  DF      Squares         Square     F Value     Pr > F

Model                    7      0.48685556      0.06955079    6.99      0.0034
Error                   10      0.09952222      0.00995222
Corrected Total         17      0.58637778

                R-Square            C.V.         Root MSE         SOILPH Mean

                0.830276          1.861595       0.0997608        5.35888889


Source                  DF      Anova SS      Mean Square    F Value     Pr > F

DEPTH                    2      0.06714444    0.03357222       3.37      0.0759
RAINPH                   1      0.03042222    0.03042222       3.06      0.1110
RAINPH*DEPTH             2      0.00781111    0.00390556       0.39      0.6854
DATE                     2      0.38147778    0.19073889      19.17      0.0004
```

a. Is there evidence of an interaction between pH level of acid rain and soil depth? Test using $\alpha = .05$.

b. Conduct a test to determine whether blocking over time was effective in removing an extraneous source of variation. Use $\alpha = .05$.

14.78 The data shown in the table are the results of an experiment conducted to investigate the effect of three factors on the percentage of ash in coal.

Sample Replication		A_1 Mojiri			A_2 Michel			A_3 Kairan			A_4 Met. Coke	
		x_1	x_2	x_3	x_1	x_2	x_3	x_1	x_2	x_3	x_1	x_2	x_3
	C_1	7.30	7.35	7.42	10.69	10.58	10.72	12.20	12.27	12.23	9.99	10.02	9.95
B_1	C_2	6.84	6.07	6.91	10.26	10.35	10.42	11.85	11.85	12.05	9.45	9.86	9.78
	C_3	7.05	6.49	7.24	10.61	10.08	10.31	12.34	11.74	11.44	9.76	9.79	9.77
	C_4	6.75	5.62	7.24	10.66	10.61	10.01	12.22	11.68	12.09	9.92	10.17	10.50
	C_1	7.56	7.44	7.51	10.86	10.88	10.90	12.47	12.42	12.44	9.87	9.81	9.79
B_2	C_2	7.10	7.37	7.32	10.45	10.62	10.87	12.47	12.28	12.04	9.46	9.60	9.62
	C_3	7.41	7.60	7.49	10.85	10.89	10.61	12.33	12.35	12.40	9.97	9.77	9.76
	C_4	7.29	7.62	7.43	10.68	11.58	10.60	12.04	12.21	12.51	9.76	10.10	9.61
	C_1	7.51	7.64	7.58	10.30	10.68	10.73	12.42	12.41	12.39	9.97	10.02	10.01
B_3	C_2	7.36	7.50	7.21	10.33	10.50	10.64	12.05	12.30	12.20	9.78	10.02	9.91
	C_3	7.56	7.55	7.47	10.73	10.75	10.84	12.44	12.30	12.26	9.88	9.90	10.06
	C_4	7.71	7.67	7.76	10.92	10.80	10.79	12.11	12.02	12.26	9.77	9.74	9.69
	C_1	7.45	7.49	7.47	10.85	10.89	10.85	12.23	12.30	12.17	10.06	10.07	10.11
B_4	C_2	7.15	7.68	7.18	10.37	10.79	10.71	11.52	12.17	11.82	9.71	9.86	9.78
	C_3	7.60	7.55	6.61	10.82	10.82	10.88	12.40	11.99	12.17	10.13	9.93	10.01
	C_4	8.06	7.05	7.57	11.26	10.56	10.31	11.96	11.87	12.06	10.01	9.98	9.84

Source: Fujimori, T., and Ishikawa, K. "Sampling error on taking analysis-sample of coal after the last stage of a reduction process." *Reports of Statistical Application Research,* Union of Japanese Scientists and Engineers, Vol. 19, No. 4, 1972, pp. 22–32.

The three factors, each at four levels, were:

Type of coal (factor A):   Mojiri, Michel, Kairan, and Metallurgical Coke

Maximum particle size (factor B):   246, 147, 74, and 48 microns

Weight of selected coal specimen (factor C):   1 gram, 100 milligrams, 20 milligrams, and 5 milligrams

Three specimens were prepared for each of the $4 \times 4 \times 4 = 64$ factor–level combinations, yielding three replications of a complete $4 \times 4 \times 4$ factorial experiment.

a. Set up an analysis of variance table showing the sources and degrees of freedom for each.

b. Refer to the SAS printout for the analysis of variance shown on page 909. Do the data provide evidence of any interactions among the factors? Test using $\alpha = .05$.

c. Does the mean level of coal ash obtained in the analysis depend on the weight of the coal specimen? Test using $\alpha = .05$.

d. Find 95% confidence intervals for the difference in the mean ash content between Mojiri and Michel coal at each of the four levels of maximum particle size.

```
                        Analysis of Variance Procedure

Dependent Variable: ASH
                                     Sum of           Mean
Source                     DF        Squares         Square    F Value    Pr > F

Model                      63     604.142383     9.58956163    167.10     0.0001
Error                     128       7.345867     0.05738958
Corrected Total           191     611.488250


                     R-Square              C.V.       Root MSE              ASH Mean

                     0.987987            2.3946      0.2395612              10.00411


Source                     DF      Anova SS     Mean Square    F Value    Pr > F

A                           3    594.413877       198.13796    3542.51    0.0001
B                           3      2.666018         0.88867      15.48    0.0001
A*B                         9      2.898196         0.32202       5.61    0.0001
C                           3      1.812881         0.60429      10.53    0.0001
A*C                         9      0.253451         0.02816       0.49    0.8791
B*C                         9      0.472142         0.05246       0.91    0.5159
A*B*C                      27      1.625818         0.06022       1.05    0.4106
```

14.79 An experiment was conducted to compare the compressive strengths of two types of plastic. Eight specimens of plastic were tested for each type, and the compressive strengths (in thousands of pounds per square inch) were recorded, with the results listed in the accompanying table.

Plastic	1	14.1	14.3	13.8	14.2	14.0	14.5	13.9	13.7
Type	2	14.2	13.9	13.8	14.3	14.1	13.4	13.8	14.0

a. Perform an analysis of variance for the data.

b. Do the data provide sufficient evidence to indicate a difference between the mean compressive strengths of the two plastics? Use an analysis of variance F test with $\alpha = .05$.

c. How many plastic specimens of each type would have to be tested if you wanted to estimate the difference in mean strength correct to within .1 with probability approximately equal to .95? [*Hint:* See Section 8.12.]

14.80 Refer to the 2×3 factorial experiment, Exercise 14.40. Results of a Tukey analysis of the three jump length means (using $\alpha = .05$) are shown here. Interpret the results.

Mean Reading Rate: (words/minute)	91	128	141
Jump Length: (# of characters)	1	5	9

14.81 The percentage of water removed from paper as it passes through a dryer depends on the temperature of the dryer and the speed of the paper passing through it. A laboratory experiment was conducted to investigate the relationship between dryer temperature T at three levels and exposure time E (which is related to speed). A 3×3 factorial experiment was conducted with temperature at $100°$, $120°$, and $140°F$ and for exposure time T at 10, 20, and 30 seconds. Four paper specimens were prepared for each condition. The data (percentages of water removed) are shown in the table on page 910.

		Temperature (T)					
		100		120		140	
	10	24	26	33	33	45	49
		21	25	36	32	44	45
Exposure Time (E)	20	39	34	51	50	67	64
		37	40	47	52	68	65
	30	58	55	75	71	89	87
		56	53	70	73	86	83

a. Perform an analysis of variance for the data and construct an analysis of variance table.
b. Do the data provide sufficient evidence to indicate that temperature and time interact? Test using $\alpha = .05$. What is the practical significance of this test?

14.82 Refer to Exercise 14.81. Because both factors are quantitative, it would be useful to fit a linear model to the data and acquire a prediction equation that can be used to predict the percentage of water removed for various combinations of temperature and drying time. The SAS printout for fitting the second-order model

$$E(y) = \beta_0 + \beta_1 E + \beta_2 T + \beta_3(E \times T) + \beta_4 E^2 + \beta_5 T^2$$

to the data is shown here.
a. Find the prediction equation.
b. Estimate the mean percentage of water removed when $T = 120$ and $E = 20$. Why does this value differ from the sample mean of the four observations obtained for this factor–level combination?
c. Find SSE on the computer printout. Why does this differ from the value of SSE found in part **a** of Exercise 14.81?

Dependent Variable: PCTWATER

Analysis of Variance

Source	DF	Sum of Squares	Mean Square	F Value	Prob>F
Model	5	12658.11111	2531.62222	501.219	0.0001
Error	30	151.52778	5.05093		
C Total	35	12809.63889			

Root MSE	2.24743	R-square	0.9882	
Dep Mean	52.30556	Adj R-sq	0.9862	
C.V.	4.29673			

Parameter Estimates

Variable	DF	Parameter Estimate	Standard Error	T for H0: Parameter=0	Prob > |T|
INTERCEP	1	-12.305556	29.14201560	-0.422	0.6758
E	1	-0.187500	0.46558448	-0.403	0.6900
T	1	0.100000	0.48059820	0.208	0.8366
ET	1	0.011250	0.00280928	4.005	0.0004
EE	1	0.017083	0.00794585	2.150	0.0397
TT	1	0.001458	0.00198646	0.734	0.4686

(*continued*)

Obs	E	T	Dep Var PCTWATER	Predict Value	Std Err Predict	Lower95% Mean	Upper95% Mean	Residual
1	10	100	24.0000	23.3611	1.009	21.3014	25.4209	0.6389
2	10	100	21.0000	23.3611	1.009	21.3014	25.4209	-2.3611
3	10	100	26.0000	23.3611	1.009	21.3014	25.4209	2.6389
4	10	100	25.0000	23.3611	1.009	21.3014	25.4209	1.6389
5	10	120	33.0000	34.0278	0.838	32.3173	35.7383	-1.0278
6	10	120	36.0000	34.0278	0.838	32.3173	35.7383	1.9722
7	10	120	33.0000	34.0278	0.838	32.3173	35.7383	-1.0278
8	10	120	32.0000	34.0278	0.838	32.3173	35.7383	-2.0278
9	10	140	45.0000	45.8611	1.009	43.8014	47.9209	-0.8611
10	10	140	44.0000	45.8611	1.009	43.8014	47.9209	-1.8611
11	10	140	49.0000	45.8611	1.009	43.8014	47.9209	3.1389
12	10	140	45.0000	45.8611	1.009	43.8014	47.9209	-0.8611
13	20	100	39.0000	37.8611	0.838	36.1506	39.5716	1.1389
14	20	100	37.0000	37.8611	0.838	36.1506	39.5716	-0.8611
15	20	100	34.0000	37.8611	0.838	36.1506	39.5716	-3.8611
16	20	100	40.0000	37.8611	0.838	36.1506	39.5716	2.1389
17	20	120	51.0000	50.7778	0.838	49.0673	52.4883	0.2222
18	20	120	47.0000	50.7778	0.838	49.0673	52.4883	-3.7778
19	20	120	50.0000	50.7778	0.838	49.0673	52.4883	-0.7778
20	20	120	52.0000	50.7778	0.838	49.0673	52.4883	1.2222
21	20	140	67.0000	64.8611	0.838	63.1506	66.5716	2.1389
22	20	140	68.0000	64.8611	0.838	63.1506	66.5716	3.1389
23	20	140	64.0000	64.8611	0.838	63.1506	66.5716	-0.8611
24	20	140	65.0000	64.8611	0.838	63.1506	66.5716	0.1389
25	30	100	58.0000	55.7778	1.009	53.7180	57.8375	2.2222
26	30	100	56.0000	55.7778	1.009	53.7180	57.8375	0.2222
27	30	100	55.0000	55.7778	1.009	53.7180	57.8375	-0.7778
28	30	100	53.0000	55.7778	1.009	53.7180	57.8375	-2.7778
29	30	120	75.0000	70.9444	0.838	69.2339	72.6550	4.0556
30	30	120	70.0000	70.9444	0.838	69.2339	72.6550	-0.9444
31	30	120	71.0000	70.9444	0.838	69.2339	72.6550	0.0556
32	30	120	73.0000	70.9444	0.838	69.2339	72.6550	2.0556
33	30	140	89.0000	87.2778	1.009	85.2180	89.3375	1.7222
34	30	140	86.0000	87.2778	1.009	85.2180	89.3375	-1.2778
35	30	140	87.0000	87.2778	1.009	85.2180	89.3375	-0.2778
36	30	140	83.0000	87.2778	1.009	85.2180	89.3375	-4.2778

d. Examine the computer printout and find the 95% confidence interval for the mean percentage of water removed when $T = 140$ and $E = 30$.

14.83 A chemist has run an experiment to study the effect of four treatments on the glass transition temperature (in degrees Kelvin) of a particular polymer compound. Raw material used to make this polymer is bought in small batches. The material is thought to be fairly uniform within a batch but variable between batches. Therefore, each treatment was run on samples from each batch with the results shown in the table.

		Treatment			
		1	2	3	4
	1	576	584	562	543
Batch	2	515	563	522	536
	3	562	555	550	530

a. Do the data provide sufficient evidence to indicate a difference in mean temperature among the four treatments? Use $\alpha = .05$.

b. Is there sufficient evidence to indicate a difference in mean temperature among the three batches? Use $\alpha = .05$.

c. If the experiment were to be conducted again in the future, would you recommend any changes in the design of the experiment?

14.84 The concentration of a catalyst used in producing grouted sand is thought to affect its strength. An experiment designed to investigate the effects of three different concentrations of the catalyst utilized five test specimens of grout per concentration. The strength of a grouted sand was determined by placing the test specimen in a press and applying pressure until the specimen broke. The pressures required to break the specimens, expressed in pounds per square inch, are shown in the table.

Concentration of Catalyst		
35%	40%	45%
5.9	6.8	9.9
8.1	7.9	9.0
5.6	8.4	8.6
6.3	9.3	7.9
7.7	8.2	8.7

Do the data provide sufficient evidence to indicate a difference in mean strength of the grouted sand among the three concentrations of catalyst? Test using $\alpha = .05$.

14.85 A $2 \times 2 \times 2 \times 2 = 2^4$ factorial experiment was conducted to investigate the effect of four factors on the light output, y, of flashbulbs. Two observations were taken for each of the factorial treatments. The factors are: amount of foil contained in a bulb (100 and 120 milligrams); speed of sealing machine (1.2 and 1.3 revolutions per minute); shift (day or night); machine operator (A or B). The data for the two replications of the 2^4 factorial experiment and the SAS printout for the regression analysis are shown here and on page 913.

		Amount of Foil			
		100 milligrams		120 milligrams	
		Speed of Machine			
		1.2 rpm	1.3 rpm	1.2 rpm	1.3 rpm
Day	Operator B	6; 5	5; 4	16; 14	13; 14
Shift	Operator A	7; 5	6; 5	16; 17	16; 15
Night	Operator B	8; 6	7; 5	15; 14	17; 14
Shift	Operator A	5; 4	4; 3	15; 13	13; 14

To simplify computations, we let

$$x_1 = \frac{\text{Amount of foil} - 110}{10} \qquad x_2 = \frac{\text{Speed of machine} - 1.25}{.05}$$

so that x_1 and x_2 will take values -1 and $+1$. Also,

$$x_3 = \begin{cases} -1 & \text{if night shift} \\ 1 & \text{if day shift} \end{cases} \qquad x_4 = \begin{cases} -1 & \text{if machine operator B} \\ 1 & \text{if machine operator A} \end{cases}$$

a. Do the data provide sufficient evidence to indicate that any of the factors contribute information for the prediction of y? Give the results of a statistical test to support your answer.

b. Identify the factors that appear to affect the amount of light y in the flashbulbs.

c. Give the complete factorial model for y. [Hint: For a factorial experiment with four factors, the complete model includes main effects for each factor, two-way cross-product terms, three-way cross-product terms, and four-way cross-product terms.]

d. How many degrees of freedom will be available for estimating σ^2?

Dependent Variable: Y

Analysis of Variance

Source	DF	Sum of Squares	Mean Square	F Value	Prob>F
Model	15	745.46875	49.69792	40.778	0.0001
Error	16	19.50000	1.21875		
C Total	31	764.96875			

Root MSE	1.10397	R-square	0.9745
Dep Mean	10.03125	Adj R-sq	0.9506
C.V.	11.00531		

Parameter Estimates

Variable	DF	Parameter Estimate	Standard Error	T for H0: Parameter=0	Prob > |T|
INTERCEP	1	10.031250	0.19515619	51.401	0.0001
X1	1	4.718750	0.19515619	24.179	0.0001
X2	1	-0.343750	0.19515619	-1.761	0.0973
X3	1	0.218750	0.19515619	1.121	0.2789
X4	1	-0.156250	0.19515619	-0.801	0.4351
X1X2	1	0.093750	0.19515619	0.480	0.6375
X1X3	1	0.156250	0.19515619	0.801	0.4351
X1X4	1	0.281250	0.19515619	1.441	0.1688
X2X3	1	-0.156250	0.19515619	-0.801	0.4351
X2X4	1	-0.031250	0.19515619	-0.160	0.8748
X3X4	1	0.781250	0.19515619	4.003	0.0010
X1X2X3	1	-0.218750	0.19515619	-1.121	0.2789
X1X2X4	1	-0.093750	0.19515619	-0.480	0.6375
X1X3X4	1	-0.031250	0.19515619	-0.160	0.8748
X2X3X4	1	0.156250	0.19515619	0.801	0.4351
X1X2X3X4	1	0.093750	0.19515619	0.480	0.6375

14.86 An automobile manufacturer conducted a study of the number of observed defects per new automobile delivered to its dealerships. Twenty-five days were randomly selected, and ten automobiles were randomly selected from each day's production. After the cars arrived at the dealerships, the number of defects observed during preparation for sale and during the first 1,000 miles of use after purchase was recorded for each automobile. The data for 3 production days are shown in the table.

Production Days

1	2	3
14	13	7
17	18	11
12	10	12
8	15	10
15	19	6
12	13	9
10	16	7
13	12	11
9	10	6
7	14	13

a. Perform an analysis of variance for the data using the formulas for a nested sampling design. Construct an analysis of variance table to display the results.

b. Do the data provide sufficient evidence to indicate that the variation between days in the number of defects per new automobile exceeds the variation within days? Test using $\alpha = .05$.

14.87 Aroni and Fletcher (1979) presented data on the compressive and tensile strength of mortar used to line steel water pipelines. They noted that mortar strength is expected to increase as the curing time of the mortar increases from 7 to 28 days. The compressive and tensile strength means and standard deviations, each based on the testing of samples of $n = 50$ specimens, are shown in the accompanying table.

	Compressive Strength Curing Time		Tensile Strength Curing Time	
	7 days	28 days	7 days	28 days
Sample Mean	$\bar{y}_1 = 8,477$	$\bar{y}_2 = 10,404$	$\bar{y}_1 = 621$	$\bar{y}_2 = 737$
Sample Standard Deviation	$s_1 = 820$	$s_2 = 928$	$s_1 = 48$	$s_2 = 55$
Sample Size	50	50	50	50

Source: Aroni, S., and Fletcher, G. "Observations on mortar lining of steel pipelines." *Transportation Engineering Journal*, Nov. 1979.

a. Refer to the compressive strength data and regard the two curing times as treatments. Find the total for all $n = 100$ observations. Then find CM and calculate SST.
b. Find SSE.
c. Find SS(Total).
d. Construct an analysis of variance table for the results of parts **a–c**.

14.88 Refer to Exercise 14.87. Suppose the researchers want to estimate the mean compressive strength of the mortar mix using a simple linear regression model to relate mean compressive strength $E(y)$ to curing time x over the time interval from 7 to 28 days.
a. Explain why the least squares line will pass through the points $(7, \bar{y}_1)$ and $(28, \bar{y}_2)$.
b. Find the least squares line.
c. Use the prediction equation of part **b** and the value of SSE found in Exercise 14.87 to find a 95% confidence interval for the mean compressive strength at $x = 20$ days.
d. Find r^2 and interpret its value.

14.89 Refer to Exercise 14.87.
a. Refer to the tensile strength data and regard the two curing times as treatments. Find the total for all $n = 100$ observations. Then find CM and calculate SST.
b. Find SSE.

14.90 Refer to Exercise 14.87. Suppose we use a simple linear regression model to relate mean tensile strength $E(y)$ to curing time x over the time interval from 7 to 28 days.
a. Explain why the least squares line will pass through the points $(7, \bar{y}_1)$ and $(28, \bar{y}_2)$.
b. Find the least squares line.

c. Use the prediction equation of part **b** and the value of SSE found in Exercise 14.89 to find a 95% confidence interval for the mean tensile strength at $x = 20$ days.

COMPUTER LAB: Analysis of Variance

In this section we give the ANOVA commands for analyzing data in SAS and MINITAB. Both SAS and MINITAB are capable of analyzing experimental designs ranging from simple one-way classifications of data (completely randomized designs) to the more sophisticated k-way classifications (factorial experiments).

As we noted in the previous sections, each experimental design possesses an underlying probabilistic model for the response variable y. These models can become quite complex, especially for large factorial experiments. Fortunately, neither software package requires that the exact model be specified. Rather, only the sources of variation for the analysis of variance need be given in the appropriate command lines. For example, for a 2×3 factorial with temperature at two levels and pressure at three levels, we need to specify three sources of variation: (1) temperature (main effect); (2) pressure (main effect); and (3) temperature–pressure interaction. The software package will automatically fit the complete factorial model that corresponds to these sources of variation and produce an ANOVA summary table.

SAS and MINITAB commands for the completely randomized design of Example 14.9, the randomized block design of Example 14.11, the 3×3 factorial design of Example 14.14, and the $2 \times 2 \times 3$ factorial design of Example 14.18 are presented here.

SAS

Command
line

	Completely Randomized Design, Example 14.9	
1	`DATA CRD;`	Data entry instructions
2	`INPUT PAINT HOURS @@;`	
3	`CARDS;`	
4	`1 148 1  76 1 393 1 520 1 236`	Input data values
.	. . . .	(4 observations per line)
.	. . . .	
.	. . . .	
9	`3 723 3 258 3 380 3 594 3 465`	
10	`PROC ANOVA;`	ANOVA instructions
11	`CLASSES PAINT;`	
12	`MODEL HOURS=PAINT;`	
13	`MEANS PAINT/TUKEY LINES;`	

	Randomized Block Design, Example 14.11	
14	`DATA RBD;`	Data entry instructions
15	`INPUT ENGINEER JOB DOLLARS @@;`	
16	`CARDS;`	
17	`1 1 4.6  1 2 6.2  1 3 5.0  1 4 6.6`	Input data values
18	`2 1 4.9  2 2 6.3  2 3 5.4  2 4 6.8`	(4 observations per line)
19	`3 1 4.4  3 2 5.9  3 3 5.4  3 4 6.3`	
20	`PROC ANOVA;`	ANOVA instructions
21	`CLASSES ENGINEER JOB;`	
22	`MODEL DOLLARS=ENGINEER JOB;`	
23	`MEANS ENGINEER/TUKEY LINES;`	

(continued)

Two-Way Factorial Experiment, Example 14.14

```
24    DATA FACTOR;                              Data entry instructions
25    INPUT R S PROFIT @@;
26    CARDS;
27    .5  15  23    .5  15  20    .5  15  21     Input data values
 .     .   .   .     .   .   .     .   .   .     (3 observations per line)
 .     .   .   .     .   .   .     .   .   .
 .     .   .   .     .   .   .     .   .   .
36    2  21  20    2  21  22    2  21  24
37    PROC ANOVA;                               ANOVA instructions
38    CLASSES R S;
39    MODEL PROFIT=R S R*S;
40    MEANS R*S/TUKEY LINES;
```

Three-Way Factorial Experiment, Example 14.18

```
41    DATA ITEMS;                               Data entry instructions
42    INPUT SHIFT $ BREAKS DAYS DOLLARS @@;
43    CARDS;
44    DAY   0  4  94   DAY   0  4  97           Input data values
 .     .   .   .          .   .   .            (2 observations per line)
 .     .   .   .          .   .   .
 .     .   .   .          .   .   .
53    NIGHT 2  5  94 NIGHT 2  5  96
54    PROC ANOVA;                               ANOVA instructions
55    CLASSES SHIFT BREAKS DAYS;
56    MODEL DOLLARS=SHIFT BREAKS DAYS SHIFT*BREAKS SHIFT*DAYS
57           BREAKS*DAYS SHIFT*BREAKS*DAYS;
```

COMMAND 10   The ANOVA procedure performs an analysis of variance for all designs.

COMMAND 11   The CLASSES statement identifies the independent variables (factors) for the experiment. *All* independent variables (quantitative and qualitative) should be included on this line.

COMMAND 12   The dependent variable and sources of variation for the ANOVA are specified in the MODEL statement. The dependent variable appears to the left of the equals sign; the sources of variation appear to the right.

COMMAND 13   The optional MEANS statement produces a multiple comparison of the means for the treatments (sources of variation) specified. Following the slash (/), two options are specified. TUKEY requests that Tukey's Studentized range method be employed to compare the means. LINES requests that the results be presented with line segments connecting the means that are not significantly different. To request the Bonferroni method, specify BON.

COMMAND 39   When the ANOVA includes interaction terms, the factors that comprise an interaction are separated by an asterisk (for example, R*S) on the MODEL statement.

MINITAB

Command
line

	Completely Randomized Design, Example 14.9	
1	READ C1 C2	Data entry instructions
2	1 148	
3	1 76	Input data values
		(1 observation per line)
.	. .	
.	. .	
31	3 465	
32	NAME C1='PAINT' C2='HOURS'	
33	ONEWAY C2 C1	ANOVA instruction

	Randomized Block Design, Example 14.11	
34	READ C1 C2 C3	Data entry instructions
35	1 1 4.6	
36	1 2 6.2	Input data values
		(1 observation per line)
.	. . .	
.	. . .	
46	3 4 6.3	
47	NAME C1='ENGINEER' C2='JOB' C3='DOLLARS'	
48	TWOWAY C3, C1-C2;	ANOVA instructions
49	ADDITIVE;	
50	MEANS C1.	

	Two-Way Factorial Experiment, Example 14.14	
51	READ C1 C2 C3	Data entry instructions
52	1 1 23	
53	1 1 20	Input data values
		(1 observation per line)
.	. . .	
.	. . .	
78	3 3 24	
79	NAME C1='R' C2='S' C3='PROFIT'	
80	TWOWAY C3, C1-C2	ANOVA instructions

	Three-Way Factorial Experiment, Example 14.18	
81	READ C1-C4	Data entry instructions
82	1 0 4 94	
83	1 0 4 97	Input data values
		(1 observation per line)
.	. . . .	
.	. . . .	
104	2 2 5 96	
105	NAME C1='SHIFT' C2='BREAKS' C3='DAYS' C4='DOLLARS'	
106	ANOVA C4=C1 C2 C3 C1*C2 C1*C3 C2*C3 C1*C2*C3;	
107	MEANS C1*C2*C3.	ANOVA instructions

GENERAL   MINITAB requires that the data for the independent variables (i.e., treatments, blocks, and factors) be numeric integers between $-9,999$ and $+9,999$.

COMMAND 33   The ONEWAY command conducts an analysis of variance for a completely randomized design. The response variable column is specified first, followed by the column for the treatments.

COMMAND 48 The TWOWAY command conducts an analysis of variance for two-factor experiments, i.e., randomized block designs and factorial designs. The response variable column is listed first, followed by the columns for the factors.

COMMAND 49 The ADDITIVE subcommand fits an ANOVA model *without* the interaction term. This is required for analysis of randomized block designs.

COMMAND 50 The MEANS subcommand produces 95% confidence intervals for the means of the factors specified. (Multiple comparisons methods such as Tukey's and Bonferroni's procedures are not available in MINITAB.)

COMMAND 80 For factorial experiments, the ADDITIVE subcommand is omitted to test the interaction term.

COMMAND 106 The ANOVA command conducts an analysis of variance for general k-way factorial designs. (It can also be used for completely randomized and randomized block designs.) The response variable column is specified to the left of the equals sign and the independent variable (i.e., factor) columns are specified to the right. Interaction terms are designated by placing an asterisk (*) between the factors.

References

Box, G. E. P., Hunter, W. G., and Hunter, J. S. *Statistics for Experimenters*. New York: Wiley, 1957.

Cochran, W. G., and Cox, G. M. *Experimental Designs*, 2nd ed. New York: Wiley, 1957.

Davies, O. L. *Statistical Methods in Research and Production*, 3rd ed. London: Oliver and Boyd, 1958.

Davies, O. L. *The Design and Analysis of Industrial Experiments*. New York: Hafner, 1956.

Dunn, O. J., and Clark, V. *Applied Statistics: Analysis of Variance and Regression*. New York: Wiley, 1974.

Johnson, N., and Leone, F. *Statistics and Experimental Design in Engineering and the Physical Sciences*, Vol. II, 2nd ed. New York: Wiley, 1977.

Mason, R. L., Gunst, R. F., and Hess, J. L. *Statistical Design and Analysis of Experiments*. New York: Wiley, 1989.

Mendenhall, W. *Introduction to Linear Models and the Design and Analysis of Experiments*. Belmont, Calif: Wadsworth, 1968.

Miller, R. G. *Simultaneous Statistical Inference*, 2nd ed. New York: Wiley, 1981.

Neter, J., Wasserman, W., and Kutner, M. H. *Applied Linear Statistical Models*, 3rd ed. Homewood, Ill.: Richard D. Irwin, 1988.

Scheffé, H. "A method for judging all contrasts in the analysis of variance." *Biometrika*, Vol. 40, 1953, pp. 87–104.

Scheffé, H. *The Analysis of Variance*. New York: Wiley, 1959.

Snedecor, G. W., and Cochran, W. G. *Statistical Methods*, 7th ed. Ames, Iowa: Iowa State University Press, 1980.

Tukey, J. W. "Comparing individual means in the analysis of variance." *Biometrics*, Vol. 5, 1949, pp. 99–114.

Winer, B. J. *Statistical Principles in Experimental Design*. New York: McGraw-Hill, 1962.

CHAPTER FIFTEEN

Nonparametric Statistics

Objective

To present some statistical tests that do not require the normality assumptions necessary for the Student's t and F tests of Chapters 9 and 11–14

Contents

15.1   Introduction

Confidence intervals and tests of hypotheses based on the t distribution are unsuitable for some types of data that fall into one of two categories. The first are data sets that do not satisfy the assumptions upon which the t test is based. For example, when making inferences about a population mean using small samples (Section 9.6), we assume that the random variable being measured has a normal probability distribution. Yet in practice, the population may be decidedly nonnormal. For example, the distribution might be very flat, peaked, or strongly skewed to the right or left (see Figure 15.1). When the normality assumption required for the t test is seriously violated, the computed t statistic may not follow the Student's t distribution. If this is true, the tabulated values of t given in Table 7 of Appendix II are not applicable, the correct value of α for the test (or confidence interval) is unknown, and the t test (or confidence interval) is of dubious value.

FIGURE 15.1 ▼
Some nonnormal distributions for which the t statistic is invalid

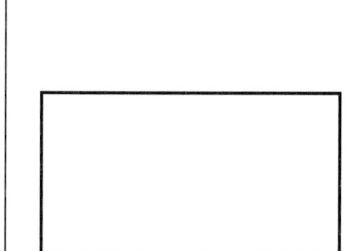

a. Flat distribution

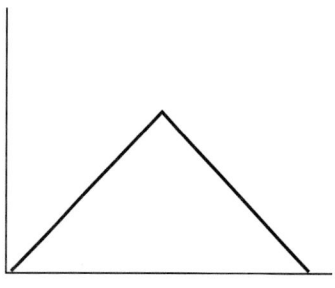

b. Peaked distribution

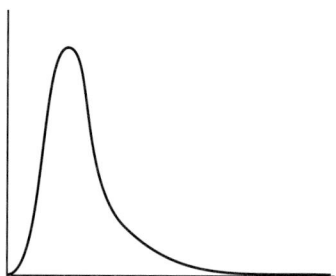

c. Skewed distribution

Responses that are not susceptible to measurement but that can be *ranked in order of magnitude* comprise the second type of data for which it is inappropriate to apply the t distribution. For example, suppose we want to compare the ease of operation of a new type of computer software against some industry standard based on subjective evaluations of trained observers. Although we cannot give an exact value to the variable "Ease of operation of the software package," we may be able to decide that the new software package is better than the standard. If the new software package is evaluated by each of 10 observers, we have the problem of comparing the mean ease of operation μ of the new software package to the known mean μ_0 of the industry standard. But the t test of Section 9.6 would be inappropriate, because the only data that can be recorded are preferences; that is, each observer decides whether the new software is better than the standard.

Consider another example of this type of data. Most firms that plan to purchase a new product first test the product to determine its acceptability. For a computer, an automobile, or some other piece of equipment, this may involve tests in which engineers rank the new product in order of preference with respect to one or more currently popular product types or makes. An engineer probably has a preference for each product, but the strength of the preference is difficult, if not impossible, to measure. Consequently, the best we can do is to have each engineer examine the new product along with a few established products and rank them according to preference: 1 for the product that is most preferred, 2 for the product with the second greatest preference, and so on.

A host of **nonparametric techniques** are available for analyzing data that do not follow a normal distribution. Nonparametric tests do not depend on the distribution of the sampled population, hence they are also called **distribution-free tests**. Also, nonparametric methods focus on the location of the probability distribution of the sampled population, rather than specific parameters of the population, such as the mean (hence, the name "nonparametrics"). For example, if it can be inferred that the distribution of preferences for a new product lies above (to the right of) the others, as illustrated in Figure 15.2, the implication is that the engineers tend to prefer the new product to the other products.

FIGURE 15.2 ▶
Probability distributions of strengths of preference measurements (new product is preferred)

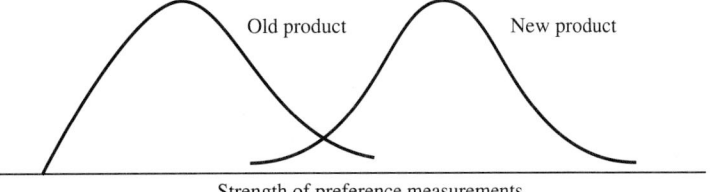

Strength of preference measurements

Definition 15.1

Distribution-free tests are statistical tests that do not rely on any underlying assumptions about the probability distribution of the sampled population.

Definition 15.2

The branch of inferential statistics devoted to distribution-free tests is called **nonparametrics**.

Many nonparametric methods use the **relative ranks** of the sample observations rather than their actual numerical values. These tests are particularly valuable when we are unable to obtain numerical measurements of some phenomenon but are able to rank the measurements relative to each other. Statistics based on the ranks of measurements are called **rank statistics**.

Definition 15.3

Nonparametric statistics (or tests) based on the ranks of measurements are called **rank statistics** (or **rank tests**).

In Section 15.2, we discuss a simple nonparametric test for the location of a single population. In Sections 15.3 and 15.5, we will present rank statistics for comparing two probability distributions using independent random samples. In Sections 15.4 and 15.6, we will use the matched-pairs and randomized block designs to make nonparametric comparisons of populations. Finally, in Section 15.7, we present nonparametric measure tests for simple linear regression. For a more complete discussion of tests based on rank statistics, see Lehmann (1975).

15.2   Testing for Location of a Single Population

Recall from Section 9.5 that small-sample procedures for testing a hypothesis about a population mean require that the population have an approximately normal distribution. For situations in which we collect a small sample from a decidedly nonnormal population (e.g., one of the populations shown in Figure 15.1), the t test is not valid, and we must resort to a nonparametric procedure. The simplest nonparametric technique to apply in this situation is the **sign test**. The sign test is specifically designed for testing hypotheses about the median of any continuous population. Like the mean, the median is a measure of the center, or location, of the distribution; consequently, the sign test is sometimes referred to as a **test for location**.

Let $y_1, y_2, \ldots, y_n$ be a random sample from a population with unknown median τ. Suppose we want to test the null hypothesis $H_0: \tau = 100$ against the one-sided alternative $H_a: \tau > 100$. From Definition 1.8 we know that the median is a number such that half the area under the probability distribution lies to the left of τ and half lies to the right (see Figure 15.3). Therefore, the probability that a y value selected

FIGURE 15.3 ▶
Location of the population median, τ

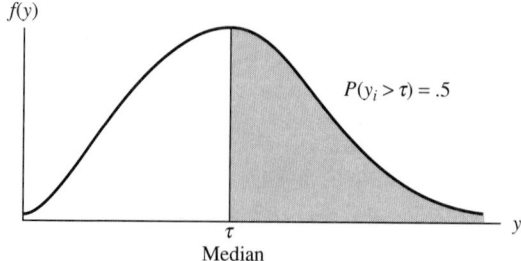

$f(y)$

$P(y_i > \tau) = .5$

τ
Median

y

from the population is larger than τ is .5, i.e., $P(y_i > \tau) = .5$. If, in fact, the null hypothesis is true, then we should expect to observe approximately half the sample y values greater than $\tau = 100$.

The sign test utilizes the test statistic S, where

S = Number of y_i's that exceed 100

Notice that S depends only on the *sign* (positive or negative) of the difference between each sample value y_i and 100. That is, we are simply counting the number of positive ($+$) signs among the sample differences $(y_i - 100)$. If S is "too large" (i.e., if we observe an unusually large number of y_i's exceeding 100), then we will reject H_0 in favor of the alternative H_a: $\tau > 100$.

The rejection region for the sign test is derived as follows. Let each sample difference $(y_i - 100)$ denote the outcome of a single trial in an experiment consisting of n identical trials. If we call a positive difference a "success" and a negative difference a "failure," then S is the number of successes in n trials. Under H_0, the probability of observing a success on any one trial is

$$p = P(\text{Success}) = P(y_i - 100 > 0) = P(y_i > 100) = .5$$

Since the trials are independent, the properties of a binomial experiment, listed in Chapter 4, are satisfied. Therefore, S has a binomial distribution with parameters n and $p = .5$. We can use this fact to calculate the observed significance level (p-value) of the sign test, as illustrated in the following example.

EXAMPLE 15.1

Bacteria are a most important component of microbial ecosystems in sewage treatment plants. Water management engineers have determined that the percentages of active bacteria in sewage specimens collected at a particular plant have a distribution with a median of 40 percent. If the median percentage is larger than 40, then adjustments in the sewage treatment process must be made. The percentages of active bacteria in a random sample of 10 sewage specimens are given here:

41	33	43	52	46
37	44	49	53	30

Do the data provide sufficient evidence to indicate that the median percentage of active bacteria in sewage specimens is greater than 40? Test using $\alpha = .05$.

Solution

We want to test

H_0: $\tau = 40$

H_a: $\tau > 40$

using the sign test. The test statistic is

S = Number of y_i's in the sample that exceed 40

    = 7

where S has a binomial distribution with parameters $n = 10$ and $p = .5$.

From Definition 9.4, the observed significance level (p-value) of the test is the probability that we observe a value of the test statistic S that is at least as contradictory to the null hypothesis as the computed value. For this one-sided case, the p-value is the probability that we observe a test statistic value greater than or equal to $S = 7$. We find this probability using the cumulative binomial table for $n = 10$ and $p = .5$ in Table 1 of Appendix II. If x has a binomial distribution with $n = 10$ and $p = .5$, then the p-value of the test is

$$p\text{-value} = P(x \geq S) = P(x \geq 7) = 1 - P(x \leq 6) = 1 - .828 = .172$$

This observed significance level is also shown (shaded) on the MINITAB printout of the analysis shown in Figure 15.4. Since the p-value, .1719, is larger than $\alpha = .05$, we cannot reject the null hypothesis. That is, there is insufficient evidence to indicate that the median percentage of active bacteria in sewage specimens exceeds 40.

FIGURE 15.4 ▶

MINITAB printout for Example 15.1

```
SIGN TEST OF MEDIAN = 40.00 VERSUS  G.T.   40.00

              N   BELOW  EQUAL  ABOVE   P-VALUE     MEDIAN
BACTPCT      10      3      0      7    0.1719      43.50
```

A summary of the sign test for both one-sided and two-sided alternatives is provided in the box.

For a two-tailed test, you may calculate the test statistic as either

S_1 = Number of y_i's greater than τ_0

    = Number of successes in n trials

or

S_2 = Number of y_i's less than τ_0

    = Number of failures in n trials

Note that $S_1 + S_2 = n$; therefore, $S_2 = n - S_1$. In either case, the p-value of the test is double the corresponding one-sided p-value. To simplify matters, we suggest using the larger of S_1 and S_2 as the test statistic and calculating the p-value as shown in the first box on page 925.

Recall from Section 7.6 that a normal distribution with mean $\mu = np$ and $\sigma = \sqrt{npq}$ can be used to approximate the binomial distribution for large n. When $p = .5$, the normal approximation performs reasonably well even for n as small as 10 (see Example 7.11). Thus, for $n \geq 10$, we can conduct the sign test using the familiar standard normal z statistic of Chapter 9. This large-sample sign test is summarized in the second box on page 925. Review Chapter 9 for examples of how to apply this test.

Sign Test for a Population Median, τ

One-Tailed Test

H_0: $\tau = \tau_0$

H_a: $\tau > \tau_0$ [or, H_a: $\tau < \tau_0$]

Test statistic:

S = Number of sample observations greater than τ_0

[or, S = Number of sample observations less than τ_0]

Observed significance level:

p-value = $P(x \geq S)$

Two-Tailed Test

H_0: $\tau = \tau_0$

H_a: $\tau \neq \tau_0$

Test statistic:

S = larger of S_1 and S_2

where

S_1 = Number of sample observations greater than τ_0

S_2 = Number of sample observations less than τ_0

[*Note:* By definition, $S_2 = n - S_1$.]

Observed significance level:

p-value = $2P(x \geq S)$

where x has a binomial distribution with parameters n and $p = .5$.

Rejection region: Reject H_0 if $\alpha > p$-value.

Assumption: The sample is randomly selected from a continuous probability distribution. [*Note:*   No assumptions have to be made about the shape of the probability distribution.]

Sign Test Based on a Large Sample ($n \geq 10$)

One-Tailed Test

H_0: $\tau = \tau_0$

H_a: $\tau > \tau_0$

[or, H_a: $\tau < \tau_0$]

Two-Tailed Test

H_0: $\tau = \tau_0$

H_a: $\tau \neq \tau_0$

Test statistic: $z = \dfrac{S - E(S)}{\sqrt{V(S)}} = \dfrac{S - .5n}{\sqrt{(.5)(.5)n}} = \dfrac{S - .5n}{.5\sqrt{n}}$

[*Note:*   The value of S is calculated as shown in the previous box.]

Rejection region:

$z > z_\alpha$

Rejection region:

$z > z_{\alpha/2}$

where tabulated values of z_α and $z_{\alpha/2}$ are given in Table 4 of Appendix II.

EXERCISES

15.1   Many Vietnam veterans have dangerously high levels of the dioxin 2,3,7,8-TCDD in blood and fat tissue as a result of their exposure to the defoliant Agent Orange. A study published in *Chemosphere* (Vol. 20, 1990) reported on the TCDD levels of 20 Massachusetts Vietnam veterans who were possibly exposed to Agent Orange. The amounts of TCDD (measured in parts per trillion) in blood plasma and fat tissue drawn from each veteran are shown in the table.

TCDD Levels in Plasma			TCDD Levels in Fat Tissue		
2.5	3.1	2.1	4.9	5.9	4.4
3.5	3.1	1.8	6.9	7.0	4.2
6.8	3.0	36.0	10.0	5.5	41.0
4.7	6.9	3.3	4.4	7.0	2.9
4.6	1.6	7.2	4.6	1.4	7.7
1.8	20.0	2.0	1.1	11.0	2.5
2.5	4.1		2.3	2.5	

Source: Schecter, A., et al. "Partitioning of 2,3,7,8-chlorinated dibenzo-*p*-dioxins and dibenzofurans between adipose tissue and plasma lipid of 20 Massachusetts Vietnam veterans." *Chemosphere*, Vol. 20, Nos. 7–9, 1990, pp. 954–955 (Tables I & II).

a. Test to determine whether the median TCDD level in plasma for Vietnam veterans exceeds 3.0 parts per trillion. Use $\alpha = .05$.

b. Test to determine whether the median level in fat tissue exceeds 3.0 parts per trillion. Use $\alpha = .05$.

15.2   A hybrid algorithm for solving a polynomial zero–one mathematical program was presented in *IIE Transactions* (June, 1990). The algorithm incorporates a mixture of pseudo-Boolean concepts and time-proven implicit enumeration procedures. Twenty-five random problems were solved using the hybrid algorithm; the times to solution (CPU time in seconds) are listed in the accompanying table. Conduct a test to determine if more than half of random polynomial zero–one mathematical problems will require a solution time of 1 CPU second or less. Use $\alpha = .01$.

.045	1.055	.136	1.894	.379
.136	.336	.258	1.070	.506
.088	.242	1.639	.912	.412
.361	8.788	.579	1.267	.567
.182	.036	.394	.209	.445

Source: Snyder, W. S., and Chrissis, J. W. "A hybrid algorithm for solving zero–one mathematical programming problems." *IIE Transactions*, Vol. 22, No. 2, June 1990, p. 166 (Table 1).

15.3   Radium-226 is a naturally occurring radioactive gas. Elevated levels of radium-226 in metro Dade County (Florida) were recently investigated (*Florida Scientist*, Summer/Autumn 1991). The data in the table are radium-226 levels (measured in pCi/L) for 26 soil specimens collected in southern Dade County. Utilize the nonparametric sign test to determine whether the median radium-226 level in soil in southern Dade County exceeds the Environmental Protection Agency limit of 4.0 pCi/L. Test at $\alpha = .10$.

1.46	.58	4.31	1.02	.17	2.92	.91	.43	.91
1.30	8.24	3.51	6.87	1.43	1.44	4.49	4.21	1.84
5.92	1.86	1.41	1.70	2.02	1.65	1.40	.75	

Source: Moore, H. E., and Gussow, D. G. "Radium and radon in Dade County ground water and soil samples." *Florida Scientist*, Vol. 54, No. 3/4, Summer/Autumn, 1991, p. 155 (portion of Table 3).

15.4 In zoology, the phenomenon of fish moving excessively from one confined area to another is known as excessive transitory migration (ETM). To investigate the ETM of guppy populations, 40 adult female guppies were placed into the left compartment of an experimental aquarium tank that was divided in half by a glass plate. After the plate was removed, the numbers of fish passing through the slit from the left compartment to the right one, and vice versa, was monitored every minute for 30 minutes (*Zoological Science*, Vol. 6, 1989). If an equilibrium is reached, the researchers would expect the median number of fish remaining in the left compartment to be 20. The data for the 30 observations (i.e., numbers of fish in left compartment at the end of the minute interval) are shown below. Use the large-sample sign test to determine whether the median is less than 20. Test using $\alpha = .05$.

16	11	12	15	14	16	18	15	13	15
14	14	16	13	17	17	14	22	18	19
17	17	20	23	18	19	21	17	21	17

Source: Terami, H., and Watanabe, M. "Excessive transitory migration of guppy populations. III. Analysis of perception of swimming space and a mirror effect." *Zoological Science*, Vol. 6, 1989, p. 977, (Figure 2).

15.5 An important property of certain products that are in powder or granular form is their particle size distribution. For example, refractory cements are adversely affected by too high a proportion of coarse granules, which can lead to weakness resulting from poor packing. The following data, extracted from the *Journal of Quality Technology* (July 1985), represent the percentages of coarse granules for a random sample of eight refractory cement specimens from a large lot:

| 1.7 | .9 | 3.4 | 2.5 | 3.1 | .6 | 1.0 | 2.1 |

Is there sufficient evidence to indicate that fewer than half of the cement specimens in the lot have more than 2% coarse granules? Test using $\alpha = .05$.

OPTIONAL EXERCISES

15.6 Suppose we want to test $H_0: \tau = \tau_0$ against $H_a: \tau \neq \tau_0$ using the sign test, where

S_1 = Number of sample observations greater than τ_0

and

S_2 = Number of sample observations less than τ_0

Show that $P(S_1 \geq c) = P(S_2 \leq n - c)$, where $0 \leq c \leq n$.

15.7 Refer to the two-tailed test of Exercise 15.6. Use the result of that exercise to show that the observed significance level for the test is

p-value $= 2P(S_1 \geq c)$

15.3   Comparing Two Populations: Independent Random Samples

Suppose two independent random samples are to be used to compare two populations, and the t test of Chapter 9 is inappropriate for making the comparison. Either we are unwilling to make assumptions about the form of the underlying probability distributions, or we are unable to obtain exact values of the sample measurements. For either of these situations, if the data can be ordered, we could apply a test to compare the medians of the two populations. A more powerful nonparametric test, however, is one that compares entire probability distributions and not just the medians. This test, called the **Wilcoxon rank sum test**, tests the null hypothesis that the probability distributions associated with the two populations are equivalent against the alternative hypothesis that one population probability distribution is shifted to the right (or left) of the other.

For example, suppose that an experiment is conducted to compare the ratings of a computer word-processing package by two groups of people—word-processing operators who must use the package and computer programming specialists who are trained to develop computer software. Independent random samples of $n_1 = 7$ word-processing operators and $n_2 = 7$ programming specialists were selected for the experiment. Each was asked to rate the package on a scale from 1 to 100, with 100 denoting the best rating. After the data were recorded, the fourteen ratings were ranked in order of magnitude, 1 for the smallest and 14 for the largest. Tied observations (if they occur) are assigned ranks equal to the average of the ranks of the tied observations. For example, if the second and third ranked observations were tied, each would be assigned the rank 2.5. The data for the experiment and their ranks are shown in Table 15.1.

TABLE 15.1   Ratings of a New Word-Processing Package by Word-Processing Operators and Programming Specialists

Word-Processing Operators		Programming Specialists	
Rating	Rank	Rating	Rank
35	5	45	7
50	8	60	10
25	3	40	6
55	9	90	13
10	1	65	11
30	4	85	12
20	2	95	14
$n_1 = 7$	$T_1 = 32$	$n_2 = 7$	$T_2 = 73$

> ## Wilcoxon Rank Sum Test for a Shift in Population Locations: Independent Random Samples*
> ....
> Let D_1 and D_2 represent the relative frequency distributions for populations 1 and 2, respectively.
>
> | *One-Tailed Test* | *Two-Tailed Test* |
> |---|---|
> | H_0: D_1 and D_2 are identical | H_0: D_1 and D_2 are identical |
> | H_a: D_1 is shifted to the right of D_2 | H_a: D_1 is shifted either to the left or to the right of D_2 |
> | [or H_a: D_1 is shifted to the left of D_2] | |
>
> Rank the $n_1 + n_2$ observations in the two samples from the smallest (rank 1) to the largest (rank $n_1 + n_2$). Calculate T_1 and T_2, the rank sums associated with sample 1 and sample 2, respectively. Then calculate the test statistic.
>
> | *Test statistic:* | *Test statistic:* |
> |---|---|
> | T_1, if $n_1 < n_2$; T_2, if $n_2 < n_1$ (Either rank sum can be used if $n_1 = n_2$.) | T_1, if $n_1 < n_2$; T_2, if $n_2 < n_1$ (Either rank sum can be used if $n_1 = n_2$.) We will denote this rank sum as T. |
>
> | *Rejection region:* | *Rejection region:* |
> |---|---|
> | T_1: $T_1 \geq T_U$ [or $T_1 \leq T_L$] | $T \leq T_L$ or $T \geq T_U$ |
> | T_2: $T_2 \leq T_L$ [or $T_2 \geq T_U$] | |
>
> where T_L and T_U are obtained from Table 15, Appendix II.
>
> *Note:*   Tied observations are assigned ranks equal to the average of the ranks that would have been assigned to the observations had they not been tied.

The Wilcoxon rank sum test is based on the sums of the ranks (called **rank sums**) for the two samples. The logic is that if the null hypothesis

H_0:   The two population probability distributions are identical

is true, then any one ranking of the $n = n_1 + n_2$ observations is just as likely as any other. Then, for equal sample sizes, we would expect the rank sums, T_1 and T_2, to be nearly equal.

In contrast, if the one-sided alternative hypothesis

H_a: Probability distribution for population 1 is shifted to the right of that for population 2

---

*Another statistic used for comparing two populations based on independent random samples is the *Mann–Whitney U statistic*. The U statistic is a simple function of the rank sums. It can be shown that the Wilcoxon rank sum test and the Mann–Whitney U test are equivalent.

is true, then, for equal sample sizes, we would expect the rank sum T_1 to be larger than the rank sum T_2. In fact, it can be shown (proof omitted) that, regardless of the sample sizes n_1 and n_2,

$$T_1 + T_2 = \frac{n(n + 1)}{2}$$

where $n = n_1 + n_2$. Therefore, as T_2 becomes smaller, T_1 will become larger and we would reject H_0 and accept H_a for large values of T_1. A summary of the Wilcoxon rank sum test for independent random samples is shown in the box.

In Example 15.3, we will illustrate the procedure for finding the rejection region for a specified value of α. First, we will use the rejection regions provided in Table 15 of Appendix II and a computer printout to compare the programmer and word-processor operator ratings of Table 15.1.

EXAMPLE 15.2

Refer to the data in Table 15.1.

a. Use Table 15 of Appendix II to test the null hypothesis that the probability distributions of the operator and programmer ratings are identical against the alternative hypothesis that one of the distributions is shifted to the right of the other. Test using $\alpha = .05$.

b. Use a computer to perform the Wilcoxon rank sum test and interpret the results.

Solution

a. We can use either rank sum as the test statistic for this two-tailed test and we will reject H_0 if that rank sum, say T_1, is very small or very large—that is, if $T_1 \leq T_L$ or $T_1 \geq T_U$. The tabulated values of T_L and T_U, the lower- and upper-tail values of the rank sum distribution, are given in Table 15 of Appendix II. The critical values of the rank sum for a one-tailed test with $\alpha = .025$ and for a two-tailed test with $\alpha = .05$ are given in Table 15a, which is reproduced in Table 15.2. Table 15b of Appendix II gives the critical values, T_L and T_U, for a one-tailed test with $\alpha = .05$ and for a two-tailed test with $\alpha = .10$. Examining Table 15.2, you will find that the critical values (shaded) corresponding to $n_1 = n_2 = 7$ are $T_L = 37$ and $T_U = 68$. Therefore, for $\alpha = .05$, we will reject H_0 if

$$T_1 \leq 37 \quad \text{or} \quad T_1 \geq 68$$

Since the observed value of the test statistic, $T_1 = 32$ (calculated in Table 15.1), is less than 37, we reject the hypothesis that the distributions of ratings are identical. There is sufficient evidence to indicate that one of the distributions is shifted to the right of the other.

b. A SAS printout of the identical analysis is shown in Figure 15.5. Both rank sums are shaded on the printout, as well as the two-tailed observed significance level (*p*-value) for the Wilcoxon rank sum test. Since the *p*-value, .0106, is less than $\alpha = .05$, we reach the same conclusion as in part **a**—namely, reject H_0 and conclude that the probability distributions have different locations.

TABLE 15.2   A Partial Reproduction of Table 15 of Appendix II

n_2 \ n_1	3 T_L	3 T_U	4 T_L	4 T_U	5 T_L	5 T_U	6 T_L	6 T_U	7 T_L	7 T_U	8 T_L	8 T_U	9 T_L	9 T_U
3	5	16	6	18	6	21	7	23	7	26	8	28	8	31
4	6	18	11	25	12	28	12	32	13	35	14	38	15	41
5	6	21	12	28	18	37	19	41	20	45	21	49	22	53
6	7	23	12	32	19	41	26	52	28	56	29	61	31	65
7	7	26	13	35	20	45	28	56	37	68	39	73	41	78
8	8	28	14	38	21	49	29	61	39	73	49	87	51	93
9	8	31	15	41	22	53	31	65	41	78	51	93	63	108
10	9	33	16	44	24	56	32	70	43	83	54	98	66	114

FIGURE 15.5 ▶
SAS printout of Wilcoxon rank sum test

```
                    N P A R 1 W A Y   P R O C E D U R E

              Wilcoxon Scores (Rank Sums) for Variable RATING
                        Classified by Variable USER


                           Sum of      Expected      Std Dev        Mean
        USER       N       Scores      Under H0      Under H0       Score

        wp         7        32.0     52.5000000    7.82623792    4.5714286
        prog       7        73.0     52.5000000    7.82623792   10.4285714

        Wilcoxon 2-Sample Test (Normal Approximation)
        (with Continuity Correction of .5)

        S=  32.0000     Z= -2.55551      Prob > |Z| =    0.0106

        T-Test approx. Significance =      0.0239

        Kruskal-Wallis Test (Chi-Square Approximation)
        CHISQ=  6.8612      DF=  1       Prob > CHISQ=      0.0088
```

EXAMPLE 15.3

Suppose that the alternative hypothesis in Example 15.2 had implied a one-tailed test. For example, suppose that we wanted to test H_0 against the alternative

H_a: Distribution 2 is shifted to the right of distribution 1

Locate the rejection region for the test using $\alpha = .025$.

Solution

We can use either T_1 or T_2 as the test statistic; small values of T_1 and large values of T_2 support the alternative hypothesis. If we use T_1 as the test statistic, we will reject H_0 if $T \le T_L$ where T_L is the lower-tail value of the rank sum, given in Table 15.2, for $n_1 = n_2 = 7$. This value is 37. Therefore, the rejection region for the one-tailed test with $\alpha = .025$ is $T_1 \le 37$.

If we choose T_2 as the test statistic, we would reject H_0 if T_2 is large, say, $T_2 \geq T_U$. The value of T_U given in Table 15.2 for $n_1 = n_2 = 7$ is $T_U = 68$. The two tests are equivalent.

EXAMPLE 15.4

Consider a Wilcoxon rank sum test for $n_1 = n_2 = 4$. Find the value of T_L such that $P(T_1 \leq T_L) \approx .05$. This value of T_L would be appropriate for a one-tailed test with $\alpha = .05$.

Solution

To solve this problem, we use the probability methods of Chapter 3. If H_0 is true— i.e., if the two population probability distributions are identical—then any one ranking of the $n_1 + n_2 = 8$ observations is as likely as any other and each would represent a simple event for the experiment. For example, suppose that the four observations associated with samples 1 and 2 are denoted as $y_{11}, y_{12}, y_{13}, y_{14}$ and $y_{21}, y_{22}, y_{23}, y_{24}$, respectively. One ranking of the data that will produce the smallest possible value for T_1 is shown in Table 15.3.

TABLE 15.3 One Ranking of the $n_1 + n_2 = 8$ Observations of Example 15.4

Sample 1		Sample 2	
Observation	Rank	Observation	Rank
y_{11}	4	y_{21}	6
y_{12}	1	y_{22}	5
y_{13}	3	y_{23}	7
y_{14}	2	y_{24}	8
	$T_1 = 10$		$T_2 = 26$

To find the value T_L such that $P(T_1 \leq T_L) \approx .05$, we find, $P(T_1 = 10)$, $P(T_1 = 11), \ldots,$ and sum these probabilities until

$$P(T_1 = 10) + P(T_1 = 11) + \cdots + P(T_1 = T_L) \approx .05$$

The number of simple events in the sample space S is equal to the number of ways that you can arrange the integers, $1, 2, \ldots, 8$—namely, $8!$. Since the simple events are equiprobable, the probability of each simple event E_i in the sample space is

$$P(E_i) = \frac{1}{8!}$$

The number of rankings that will result in $T_1 = 10$ is equal to the number of ways that you can arrange the four ranks for sample 1 and the four ranks for sample 2. The number of distinctly different arrangements of one sample of four ranks is 4!. Therefore, the number of ways that the two samples, each containing four ranks, can be arranged is

$$(4!)(4!)$$

Therefore, there will be $(4!)(4!)$ simple events in the event $T_1 = 10$, each with probability $P(E_i) = 1/8!$. Then,

$$P(T_1 = 10) = \frac{4!4!}{8!} = \frac{1}{70} = .0143$$

Next, consider the rank sum $T_1 = 11$. The only way that T_1 can equal 11 is if the ranks assigned to sample 1 are 1, 2, 3, and 5. Then

$$P(T_1 = 11) = \frac{4!4!}{8!} = \frac{1}{70} = .0143$$

and

$$P(T_1 \leq 11) = P(T_1 = 10) + P(T_1 = 11) = 2(.0143) = .0286$$

Since this value is less than $\alpha = .05$, we will calculate the probability of observing the next larger rank sum for T_1—namely, $T_1 = 12$. We can obtain a rank sum $T_1 = 12$ if either the ranks 1, 2, 3, and 6 or the ranks 1, 2, 4, and 5 are assigned to sample 1. The probability of each of these occurrences is $1/70$. Therefore,

$$P(T_1 = 12) = P\{1, 2, 3, 6\} + P\{1, 2, 4, 5\} = \frac{1}{70} + \frac{1}{70} = .0286$$

and

$$P(T_1 \leq 12) = P(T_1 = 10) + P(T_1 = 11) + P(T_1 = 12) = .0572$$

Since we want T_L to be the value such that $P(T_1 \leq T_L)$ is close to $\alpha = .05$, it follows that $T_L = 12$. This is the tabulated value for T_L given in Table 15b of Appendix II ($\alpha = .05$).

Like the sign test, the Wilcoxon rank sum test can be conducted using the familiar z test statistic of Section 9.4 when the samples are large. The following (which we state without proof) leads to a large-sample Wilcoxon rank sum test. It can be shown that the mean and variance of the rank sum T_1 are

$$E(T_1) = \frac{n_1 n_2 + n_1(n_1 + 1)}{2}$$

and

$$V(T_1) = \frac{n_1 n_2(n_1 + n_2 + 1)}{12}$$

Then, when n_1 and n_2 are large (say, $n_1 > 10$ and $n_2 > 10$), the sampling distribution of

$$z = \frac{T_1 - E(T_1)}{\sqrt{V(T_1)}} = \frac{T_2 - \left[\dfrac{n_1 n_2 + n_1(n_1 + 1)}{2}\right]}{\sqrt{\dfrac{n_1 n_2(n_1 + n_2 + 1)}{12}}}$$

will have, approximately, a standard normal distribution.

The Wilcoxon Rank Sum Test for Large Samples ($n_1 \geq 10$ and $n_2 \geq 10$)

Let D_1 and D_2 represent the relative frequency distributions for populations 1 and 2, respectively.

One-Tailed Test	*Two-Tailed Test*
H_0: D_1 and D_2 are identical	H_0: D_1 and D_2 are identical
H_a: D_2 is shifted to the right of D_2	H_a: D_1 is shifted either to the left or to the right of D_2
[or H_a: D_1 is shifted to the left of D_2]	

Test statistic: $z = \dfrac{T_1 - \left[\dfrac{n_1 n_2 + n_1(n_1 + 1)}{2}\right]}{\sqrt{\dfrac{n_1 n_2(n_1 + n_2 + 1)}{12}}}$

Rejection region:	*Rejection region:*
$z > z_\alpha$ (or $z < -z_\alpha$)	$\lvert z \rvert > z_{\alpha/2}$

[Note: The sample sizes n_1 and n_2 must both be at least 10.]

We summarize this large-sample test in the preceding box. The mechanics of the test can be seen by reconsidering one or more of the examples provided in Section 9.4.

EXERCISES

15.8 Type II collagen is a candidate drug for suppressing the symptoms of rheumatoid arthritis. Medical researchers at Harvard University conducted a clinical trial to test the ability of collagen to reduce swollen joints in rheumatoid arthritis sufferers (*Science*, Sept. 1993). Each of 59 patients with severe, active rheumatoid arthritis was randomly assigned to receive either a daily dose of collagen or an indistinguishable placebo, over a 30-day period. (Twenty-eight received collagen, 31 received the placebo.) The variable of interest was change in the number of swollen joints (after treatment minus before treatment) in each patient. The means and standard deviations for the two samples are reported here.

	Collagen	Placebo
Sample Size	28	31
Mean	−2.7	2.0
Standard Deviation	.5	1.4

Source: Trentham, D. E., et al. "Effects of oral administration of Type II collagen on rheumatoid arthritis." *Science*, Vol. 261, No. 5129, Sept. 24, 1993, p. 1727 (Table 1).

a. Although no information on the distribution of the variable of interest for the two patient groups was provided in the *Science* article, the researchers used the Wilcoxon rank sum test rather than a *t*-test to compare the two groups. Give two reasons why a nonparametric test may be more appropriate in this study.

b. Give the null hypothesis tested by the Wilcoxon rank sum procedure in this study.

c. The observed significance level of the test was reported to be smaller than .05 (i.e., *p*-value < .05). Make the appropriate conclusion.

15.9 *Environmental Science & Technology* (Oct. 1993) reported on a study of insecticides used on dormant orchards in the San Joaquin Valley, California. Ambient air samples were collected and analyzed daily at an orchard site during the most intensive period of spraying. The thion and oxon levels (in ng/m^3) in the air samples are recorded in the table, as well as the oxon/thion ratios. Compare the oxon/thion ratios of foggy days to the ratios on clear/cloudy days at the orchard using a nonparametric test. Use $\alpha = .05$.

Date	Condition	Thion	Oxon	Oxon/Thion Ratio
Jan. 15	Fog	38.2	10.3	.270
17	Fog	28.6	6.9	.241
18	Fog	30.2	6.2	.205
19	Fog	23.7	12.4	.523
20	Fog	62.3	(Air sample lost)	—
20	Clear	74.1	45.8	.618
21	Fog	88.2	9.9	.112
21	Clear	46.4	27.4	.591
22	Fog	135.9	44.8	.330
23	Fog	102.9	27.8	.270
23	Cloudy	28.9	6.5	.225
25	Fog	46.9	11.2	.239
25	Clear	44.3	16.6	.375

Source: Selber, J. N., et al. "Air and fog deposition residues of four organophosphate insecticides used on dormant orchards in the San Joaquin Valley, California." *Environmental Science & Technology*, Vol. 27, No. 10, Oct. 1993, p. 2240 (Table V).

15.10 The data in the table on page 936, extracted from *Technometrics* (Feb. 1986), represent daily accumulated streamflow and precipitation (in inches) for two U.S. Geological Survey stations in Colorado. Conduct a test to determine whether the distributions of daily accumulated streamflow and precipitation for the two stations differ in location. Use $\alpha = .10$.

	Station 1			Station 2	
127.96	108.91	100.85	114.79	85.54	280.55
210.07	178.21	85.89	109.11	117.64	145.11
203.24	285.37		330.33	302.74	95.36

Source: Gastwirth, J. L., and Mahmoud, H. "An efficient robust nonparametric test for scale change for data from a gamma distribution." *Technometrics*, Vol. 28, No. 1, Feb. 1986, p. 83 (Table 2).

15.11 An experiment was conducted to study the effect of reinforced flanges on the torsional capacity of reinforced concrete T-beams (*Journal of the American Concrete Institute*, Jan.–Feb. 1986). Several different types of T-beams were used in the experiment, each type having a different flange width. The beams were tested under combined torsion and bending until failure (i.e., cracking). One variable of interest is the cracking torsion moment at the top of the flange of the T-beam. Cracking torsion moments for eight beams with 70-cm slab widths and eight beams with 100-cm slab widths are recorded here:

70-cm slab width: 6.00, 7.20, 10.20, 13.20, 11.40, 13.60, 9.20, 11.20
100-cm slab width: 6.80, 9.20, 8.80, 13.20, 11.20, 14.90, 10.20, 11.80

Is there evidence of a difference in the locations of the cracking torsion moment distributions for the two types of T-beams? Test using $\alpha = .10$.

15.12 The presence of lead in drinking water is cause for alarm in some older cities, many of which used lead pipes for water service lines. In a study reported in the *American Water Works Journal* (Feb. 1983), researchers attempted to document the level of lead, copper, and iron in the Boston water supply for areas supplied by lead service lines. The data shown in the table are the mean concentrations of lead (milligrams per liter) for samples collected over the period from 1976 to 1981. In May 1977, the city began treating the water with sodium hydroxide to reduce traces of metal in the water. Compare the mean concentration levels of the samples before and after May 1977 using a Wilcoxon rank sum test. Do the data provide sufficient evidence to indicate a reduction in lead content in the city's water supply after the initiation of the sodium hydroxide water treatment? Test using $\alpha = .05$.

Date	Mean Concentration of Lead	Date	Mean Concentration of Lead
Feb. 1976	.074	June 1977	.035
Mar. 1976	.064	July 1977	.060
Apr. 1976	.069	Aug. 1977	.055
May 1976	.063	Oct. 1977	.035
July 1976	.077	Nov. 1977	.031
Sept. 1976	.095	Dec. 1977	.039
Oct. 1976	.092	Jan. 1978	.038
Nov. 1976	.091	Mar. 1978	.049
Dec. 1976	.067	Apr. 1978	.073
		May 1978	.047

Source: Karalekas, P. C., Jr., Ryan, C. R., and Taylor, F. B. "Control of lead, copper, and iron pipe corrosion in Boston." *American Water Works Journal*, Feb. 1983, pp. 92–95. Copyright © 1983, American Water Works Association. Reprinted by permission.

15.13 A preliminary study was conducted to obtain information on the background levels of the toxic substance polychlorinated biphenyl (PCB) in soil samples in the United Kingdom (*Chemosphere*, Feb. 1986). Such information could then be used as a benchmark against which PCB levels at waste disposal facilities in the United Kingdom can be compared. The accompanying table contains the measured PCB levels of soil samples taken at 14 rural and 15 urban locations in the United Kingdom (PCB concentration is measured in .0001 gram per kilogram of soil). From these preliminary results, the researchers reported "a significant difference between (the PCB levels) for rural areas . . . and for urban areas." Do the data support the researchers' conclusions? Test using $\alpha = .05$.

Rural		Urban	
3.5	5.3	24.0	11.0
8.1	9.8	29.0	49.0
1.8	15.0	16.0	22.0
9.0	12.0	21.0	13.0
1.6	8.2	107.0	18.0
23.0	9.7	94.0	12.0
1.5	1.0	141.0	18.0
		11.0	

Source: Badsha, K., and Eduljee, G. "PCB in the U.K. environment—A preliminary survey." *Chemosphere*, Vol. 15, No. 2, Feb. 1986, p. 213 (Table 1). Copyright 1986, Pergamon Press, Ltd. Reprinted with permission.

OPTIONAL EXERCISES

15.14 Use the formula for the sum of an arithmetic progression to show that

$$T_1 + T_2 = \frac{n(n + 1)}{2}$$

for the Wilcoxon rank sum test.

15.15 Show that for the special case where $n_1 = 2$ and $n_2 = 2$, the formula for the expected value of the Wilcoxon rank sum T_2 given in this section holds. [*Hint:* List the $(n_1 + n_2)! = 4!$ ways that the ranks can be assigned, and compute T_2 for each assignment. Then use the fact that the probability of any assignment is equally likely.]

15.16 Consider the Wilcoxon rank sum T_1 for the case where $n_1 = 3$ and $n_2 = 3$. Use the technique outlined in this section to find T_L such that $P(T_1 \leq T_L) \approx .05$.

15.4   Comparing Two Populations: Matched-Pairs Design

Nonparametric techniques can also be used to compare two probability distributions when a matched-pairs design (Section 9.9) is used. Recall that a **matched-pairs design** is a randomized block design with $k = 2$ treatments. In this section, we will show how the **Wilcoxon signed ranks test** can be used to test the hypothesis that two population probability distributions are identical against the alternative hypothesis that one is shifted to the right (or left) of the other.

For example, for some paper products, the softness of the paper is an important consideration in determining consumer acceptance. One method of assessing softness is to have judges give softness ratings to samples of the products. Suppose each of 10 judges is given a sample of two products that a company wants to compare. Each judge rates the softness of each product on a scale from 1 to 10, with higher ratings implying a softer product. The results of the experiment are shown in Table 15.4.

TABLE 15.4   Paper Softness Ratings

Judge	Product A	B	Difference (A − B)	Absolute Value of Difference	Rank of Absolute Value
1	6	4	2	2	5
2	8	5	3	3	7.5
3	4	5	−1	1	2
4	9	8	1	1	2
5	4	1	3	3	7.5
6	7	9	−2	2	5
7	6	2	4	4	9
8	5	3	2	2	5
9	6	7	−1	1	2
10	8	2	6	6	10

$$T_+ = \text{Sum of positive ranks} = 46$$
$$T_- = \text{Sum of negative ranks} = 9$$

Since this is a matched-pairs design, we analyze the differences between measurements within each pair. If almost all of the differences are positive (or negative), we have evidence to indicate that the population probability distributions differ in location—that is, one is shifted to the right or to the left of the other. The nonparametric approach requires us to calculate the ranks of the absolute values of the differences between the measurements (the ranks of the differences after removing any minus signs). Note that tied absolute differences are assigned the average of the ranks they would receive if they were unequal but successive measurements. After the absolute differences are ranked, the sum of the ranks of the positive differences, T_+, and the sum of the ranks of the negative differences, T_-, are computed.

To test the null hypothesis

H_0:   The probability distributions of the ratings for products A and B are identical

against the alternative hypothesis

H_a: The probability distribution of the ratings for product A is shifted to the right or left of the probability distribution for the ratings for product B

we use the test statistic

$T =$ Smaller of the positive and negative rank sums T_+ and T_-

The Wilcoxon Signed Ranks Test: Matched-Pairs

Let D_1 and D_2 represent the relative frequency distributions for populations 1 and 2, respectively.

<table>
<tr><td colspan="2">One-Tailed Test</td><td colspan="2">Two-Tailed Test</td></tr>
<tr><td>H_0:</td><td>D_1 and D_2 are identical</td><td>H_0:</td><td>D_1 and D_2 are identical</td></tr>
<tr><td>H_a:</td><td>D_1 is shifted to the right of D_2</td><td>H_a:</td><td>D_1 is shifted either to the left or to the right of D_2</td></tr>
<tr><td></td><td>[or H_a: D_1 is shifted to the left of D_2]</td><td></td><td></td></tr>
</table>

Calculate the difference within each of the n matched pairs of observations. Then rank the absolute values of the n differences from the smallest (rank 1) to the highest (rank n) and calculate the rank sum T_- of the negative differences and the rank sum T_+ of the positive differences.

Test statistic:

T_-, the rank sum of the negative differences

(or T_+, the rank sum of the positive differences)

Test statistic:

T, the smaller of T_- or T_+

Rejection region:

$T_- \le T_0$ (or $T_+ \le T_0$)

Rejection region:

$T \le T_0$

where T_0 is given in Table 16 of Appendix II

[*Note:* Differences equal to 0 are eliminated and the number n of differences is reduced accordingly. Tied absolute differences receive ranks equal to the average of the ranks they would have received had they not been tied.]

The rejection region for the test includes the smallest values of T and is located so that $P(T \le T_0) = \alpha$ for a one-tailed statistical test and $P(T \le T_0) = \alpha/2$ for a two-tailed test. Values of T_0 for $n = 5$ to $n = 50$ pairs are presented in Table 16 of Appendix II. The Wilcoxon signed ranks test is summarized in the box and demonstrated in Example 15.5.

EXAMPLE 15.5

Refer to the data shown in Table 15.4. Compare the judges' ratings of products 1 and 2, using a Wilcoxon signed ranks test. For $\alpha = .05$, test

H_0:   The distributions of product ratings are identical for products 1 and 2

against the alternative hypothesis

H_a: The distribution of ratings for one of the products is shifted to the left (or right) of the other distribution—that is, one of the products is rated higher than the other

Solution

The test statistic for this two-tailed test is the smaller rank sum, namely, $T_- = 9$. The rejection region is $T \le T_0$ where values of T_0 are given in Table 16 of Appendix II. A portion of this table is reproduced in Table 15.5. Examining Table 15.5 in the column corresponding to a two-tailed test, the row corresponding to $\alpha = .05$, and the column for $n = 10$ pairs, we read $T_0 = 8$. Therefore, we will reject H_0 if T is less than or equal to 8. Since the smaller rank sum, $T_- = 9$, is not less than or equal to 8, we cannot reject H_0. There is insufficient evidence to indicate a shift in the distributions of ratings for the two products.

TABLE 15.5   A Partial Reproduction of Table 16 of Appendix II

One-Tailed	Two-Tailed	$n = 5$	$n = 6$	$n = 7$	$n = 8$	$n = 9$	$n = 10$
$\alpha = .05$	$\alpha = .10$	1	2	4	6	8	11
$\alpha = .025$	$\alpha = .05$		1	2	4	6	8
$\alpha = .01$	$\alpha = .02$			0	2	3	5
$\alpha = .005$	$\alpha = .01$				0	2	3
		$n = 11$	$n = 12$	$n = 13$	$n = 14$	$n = 15$	$n = 16$
$\alpha = .05$	$\alpha = .10$	14	17	21	26	30	36
$\alpha = .025$	$\alpha = .05$	11	14	17	21	25	30
$\alpha = .01$	$\alpha = .02$	7	10	13	16	20	24
$\alpha = .005$	$\alpha = .01$	5	7	10	13	16	19
		$n = 17$	$n = 18$	$n = 19$	$n = 20$	$n = 21$	$n = 22$
$\alpha = .05$	$\alpha = .10$	41	47	54	60	68	75
$\alpha = .025$	$\alpha = .05$	35	40	46	52	59	66
$\alpha = .01$	$\alpha = .02$	28	33	38	43	49	56
$\alpha = .005$	$\alpha = .01$	23	28	32	37	43	49
		$n = 23$	$n = 24$	$n = 25$	$n = 26$	$n = 27$	$n = 28$
$\alpha = .05$	$\alpha = .10$	83	92	101	110	120	130
$\alpha = .025$	$\alpha = .05$	73	81	90	98	107	117
$\alpha = .01$	$\alpha = .02$	62	69	77	85	93	102
$\alpha = .005$	$\alpha = .01$	55	61	68	76	84	92

The MINITAB printout of the analysis is shown in Figure 15.6. Note that MINITAB uses $T_+ = 46$ as the test statistic. The two-tailed p-value of the test (shaded) is .067. Since this value exceeds $\alpha = .05$, our results agree—do not reject H_0.

FIGURE 15.6 ▶
MINITAB printout for Example 15.5

```
TEST OF MEDIAN = 0.000000 VERSUS MEDIAN N.E.  0.000000

                   N FOR   WILCOXON                ESTIMATED
            N      TEST    STATISTIC   P-VALUE      MEDIAN
AminusB    10      10        46.0       0.067        2.000
```

The Wilcoxon signed ranks procedure can also be used to test the location of a *single* population. That is, the Wilcoxon signed ranks test can be used as an alternative to the sign test of Section 15.2. For example, suppose we want to test the following hypotheses about a population median:

$$H_0: \quad \tau = 100$$
$$H_a: \quad \tau > 100$$

To conduct the test we calculate the differences $(y_i - 100)$ for the sample. Recall that the sign test depends only on the number of positive differences in the sample. The signed ranks test, on the other hand, requires that we first rank the differences, then sum the ranks of the positive differences. Thus, the Wilcoxon signed ranks test for a single sample is conducted exactly as the signed ranks procedure for matched pairs, except that the differences are calculated by subtracting the hypothesized value of the median from each observation. We summarize the procedure in the next box.

EXERCISES

15.17 Researchers at Purdue University compared human real-time scheduling in a processing environment to an automated approach that utilizes computerized robots and sensing devices (*IEEE Transactions*, Mar. 1993). The experiment consisted of eight simulated scheduling problems. Each task was performed by a human scheduler and by the automated system. Performance was measured by the *throughput rate*, defined as the number of good jobs produced weighted by product quality. The resulting throughput rates are shown in the accompanying table. Compare the throughput rates of tasks scheduled by a human and the automated method with a nonparametric test. Use $\alpha = .01$.

Task	Human Scheduler	Automated Method	Task	Human Scheduler	Automated Method
1	185.4	180.4	5	240.0	269.3
2	146.3	248.5	6	253.8	249.6
3	174.4	185.5	7	238.8	282.0
4	184.9	216.4	8	263.5	315.9

Source: Yih, Y., Liang, T., and Moskowitz, H. "Robot scheduling in a circuit board production line: A hybrid OR/ANN approach." *IEEE Transactions*, Vol. 25, No. 2, Mar. 1993, p. 31 (Table 1).

The Wilcoxon Signed Ranks Test for the Median, τ, of a Single Population

| One-Tailed Test | Two-Tailed Test |

H_0: $\tau = \tau_0$ H_0: $\tau = \tau_0$

H_a: $\tau > \tau_0$ H_a: $\tau \neq \tau_0$

          [or, H_a: $\tau < \tau_0$]

Test statistic:

    T_-, the negative rank sum
    [or, T_+, the positive rank
    sum]

Test statistic:

    T, the smaller of the positive and
    negative rank sums, T_+ and T_-

[*Note:*   The sample differences are computed as $(y_i - \tau_0)$.]

Rejection region:

    $T_- \leq T_0$
    [or, $T_+ \leq T_0$]

Rejection region:

    $T \leq T_0$

where T_0 is found in Table 16 of Appendix II.

Assumptions: 1. A random sample of observations has been selected from the population.

2. The absolute differences $y_i - \tau_0$ can be ranked. [No assumptions must be made about the form of the population probability distribution.]

3. Differences equal to 0 are eliminated and n is reduced accordingly. Tied differences are assigned ranks equal to the average of the ranks of the tied observations.

15.18   Refer to the *Chemosphere* (Vol. 20, 1990) study on the TCDD levels of 20 Massachusetts Vietnam veterans who were possibly exposed to Agent Orange, Exercise 15.1. The amounts of TCDD (measured in parts per trillion) in blood plasma and fat tissue drawn from each veteran are shown in the table. Is there sufficient evidence of a difference between the distributions of TCDD levels in plasma and fat tissue for Vietnam veterans exposed to Agent Orange? Test using $\alpha = .05$.

Veteran	TCDD Levels in Plasma	TCDD Levels in Fat Tissue	Veteran	TCDD Levels in Plasma	TCDD Levels in Fat Tissue
1	2.5	4.9	11	6.9	7.0
2	3.1	5.9	12	3.3	2.9
3	2.1	4.4	13	4.6	4.6
4	3.5	6.9	14	1.6	1.4
5	3.1	7.0	15	7.2	7.7
6	1.8	4.2	16	1.8	1.1
7	6.0	10.0	17	20.0	11.0
8	3.0	5.5	18	2.0	2.5
9	36.0	41.0	19	2.5	2.3
10	4.7	4.4	20	4.1	2.5

Source: Schecter, A., et al. "Partitioning of 2,3,7,8-chlorinated dibenzo-p-dioxins and dibenzofurans between adipose tissue and plasma lipid of 20 Massachusetts Vietnam veterans." *Chemosphere*, Vol. 20, Nos. 7–9, 1990, pp. 954–955 (Tables I and II).

15.19 Medical researchers believe that exposure to dust from cotton bract induces respiratory disease in susceptible field workers. An experiment was conducted to determine the effect of air-dried green cotton bract extract (GBE) on the cells of non–dust-exposed mill workers (*Environmental Research*, Feb. 1986). Blood samples taken on six workers were incubated with varying concentrations of GBE. After a short period of time, the cyclic AMP level (a measure of cell activity expressed in picomoles per million cells) of each blood sample was measured. The data for two GBE concentrations, 0 mg/ml (salt solution) and .2 mg/ml, are reproduced in the table. [Note that one blood sample was taken from each worker, with one aliquot exposed to the salt buffer solution and the other to the GBE.] Conduct a test to detect a shift in the locations of the cyclic AMP level distributions for the two GBE concentrations. Test using $\alpha = .10$.

Worker	GBE Concentration, mg/ml	
	0	.2
A	8.8	4.4
B	13.0	5.7
C	9.2	4.4
D	6.5	4.1
F	9.1	4.4
H	17.0	7.9

Source: Butcher, B. T., Reed, M. A., and O'Neil, C. E. "Biochemical and immunologic characterization of cotton bract extract and its effect on *in vitro* cyclic AMP production." *Environmental Research*, Vol. 39, No. 1, Feb. 1986, p. 119.

15.20 Tetrachlorodibenzo-p-dioxin (TCDD) is a highly toxic substance found in industrial wastes. A study was conducted to determine the amount of TCDD present in the tissues of bullfrogs inhabiting the Rocky Branch Creek in central Arkansas, an area known to be contaminated by TCDD (*Chemosphere*, Feb. 1986). The level of TCDD (in parts per trillion) was measured in several specific tissues of four female bullfrogs, and the ratio of TCDD in the tissue to TCDD in the leg muscle of the frog was recorded for each. The relative ratios of contaminant for two tissues, the liver and the ovaries, are given for each of the four frogs in the table on page 944. According to the researchers, "the data set suggests that the relative level of TCDD in the ovaries of female frogs is higher than the level in the liver of the frogs." Test this claim using $\alpha = .05$.

[*Hint:* Find the approximate rejection region by using the value of T_0 given in Table 16 of Appendix II for $n = 5$.]

| | *Frog* | | | |
	A	B	C	D
Liver	11.0	14.6	14.3	12.2
Ovaries	34.2	41.2	32.5	26.2

Source: Korfmacher, W. A., Hansen, E. B., and Rowland, K. L. "Tissue distribution of 2,3,7,8-TCDD in bullfrogs obtained from a 2,3,7,8-TCDD-contaminated area." *Chemosphere*, Vol. 15, No. 2, Feb. 1986, p. 125. Copyright 1986, Pergamon Press, Ltd. Reprinted with permission.

15.21 A heat transfer model for predicting winter heat loss in wastewater treatment clarifiers was investigated in the *Journal of Environmental Engineering* (Feb. 1986). Part of the analysis involved a comparison of clear-sky solar irradiation for horizontal surfaces at different sites in the Midwest. The day-long solar irradiation levels (in BTU/sq. ft.) at two midwestern locations of different latitudes—St. Joseph, Missouri, and Iowa Great Lakes—were recorded on each of seven clear-sky winter days. The data are given in the table. Conduct a nonparametric test to compare the distributions of daily irradiation levels of the two locations. Test using $\alpha = .02$.

Date	*St. Joseph, Missouri*	*Iowa Great Lakes*
December 21	782	593
January 6	965	672
January 21	948	750
February 6	1,181	988
February 21	1,414	1,226
March 7	1,633	1,462
March 21	1,852	1,698

Source: Wall, D. J., and Peterson, G. "Model for winter heat loss in uncovered clarifiers." *Journal of Environmental Engineering*, Vol. 112, No. 1, Feb. 1986, p. 128.

15.22 Synthetic fibers (such as rayon, nylon, and polyester) account for approximately 70% of all fibers used by American mills in their production of textile products. An experiment was conducted to compare the breaking tenacity of synthetic fibers produced using two methods of spinning: wet spinning and dry spinning. Specimens of 10 different synthetic fibers were selected, and each was split into two filaments. One filament was processed using the wet spinning method, and the other using the dry spinning method; the breaking tenacity (grams per denier) of each filament was then measured. Do the data shown in the table provide sufficient evidence to indicate a difference in the breaking tenacity of synthetic fibers produced by the two methods? Test using $\alpha = .05$.

Fiber	Dry Spinning	Wet Spinning
Acetate	1.3	1.0
Acrylic	2.7	2.5
Aramid	4.8	4.7
Modacrylic	2.6	2.8
Nylon	4.5	4.2
Olefin	5.9	5.8
Polyester	4.5	4.3
Rayon	1.6	1.1
Spandex	.7	.9
Triacetate	1.3	.9

OPTIONAL EXERCISES

15.23 For the Wilcoxon signed ranks test, show that

$$T_+ + T_- = \frac{n(n + 1)}{2}$$

where n is the number of nonzero differences that are ranked.

15.24 For the special case $n = 2$, with no ties in the data (that is, no differences of zero), list the eight different ways in which the two absolute differences can be ranked. [Note: The number of arrangements, 8, results from the general formula $2^n \cdot n!$.]

15.25 For the special case described in Optional Exercise 15.24, show that

$$E(T_+) = \frac{n(n + 1)}{4}$$

[Hint: Find T_+ for each of the eight arrangements of the ranks listed in Optional Exercise 15.24; use the fact that any particular arrangement will occur with probability $\frac{1}{8}$.]

15.5 Comparing Three or More Populations: Completely Randomized Design

In Section 14.8 we compare the means of k populations based on data collected according to a completely randomized design. The analysis of variance F test, used to test the null hypothesis of equality of means, is based on the assumption that the populations are normally distributed with common variance σ^2.

The **Kruskal–Wallis H test** is the nonparametric equivalent of the analysis of variance F test. It tests the null hypothesis that all k populations possess the same probability distribution against the alternative hypothesis that the distributions differ in location—that is, one or more of the distributions are shifted to the right or left of each other. The advantage of the Kruskal–Wallis H test over the F test is that we need make no assumptions about the nature of the sampled populations.

A completely randomized design specifies that we select independent random samples of $n_1, n_2, \ldots, n_k$ observations from the k populations. To conduct the test, we first rank all $n = n_1 + n_2 + \cdots + n_k$ observations and compute the rank sums, $T_1, T_2, \ldots, T_k$, for the k samples. The ranks of tied observations are averaged in the same manner as for the Wilcoxon rank sum test. Then, if H_0 is true, and if the sample sizes, $n_1, n_2, \ldots, n_k$, each equal 5 or more, then the test statistic

$$H = \frac{12}{n(n+1)} \sum_{i=1}^{k} \frac{T_i^2}{n_i} - 3(n+1)$$

will have a sampling distribution that can be approximated by a chi-square distribution with $(k-1)$ degrees of freedom. Large values of H imply rejection of H_0. Therefore, the rejection region for the test is $H > \chi_\alpha^2$ where χ_α^2 is the value that locates α in the upper tail of the chi-square distribution.

The test is summarized in the box and its use is illustrated in Example 15.6.

Kruskal–Wallis H Test for Comparing k Population Probability Distributions: Completely Randomized Design

H_0: The k population probability distributions are identical

H_a: At least two of the k population probability distributions differ in location

Test statistic: $H = \dfrac{12}{n(n+1)} \sum_{i=1}^{k} \dfrac{T_i^2}{n_i} - 3(n+1)$

where

n_i = Number of measurements in sample i

T_i = Rank sum for sample i, where the rank of each measurement is computed according to its relative magnitude in the totality of data for the k samples

n = Total sample size = $n_1 + n_2 + \cdots + n_k$

Rejection region: $H > \chi_\alpha^2$ with $(k-1)$ degrees of freedom

Assumptions: 1. The k samples are random and independent.

2. There are 5 or more measurements in each sample.

3. The observations can be ranked.

[*Note:* No assumptions have to be made about the shape of the population probability distributions.]

EXAMPLE 15.6

Independent random samples of three different brands of magnetron tubes (the key components in microwave ovens) were subjected to stress testing, and the number of hours each operated without repair was recorded. Although these times do not represent typical lifelengths, they do indicate how well the tubes can withstand extreme stress. The data are shown in Table 15.6. Experience has shown that the distributions of lifelengths for manufactured products are often nonnormal, thus violating the assumptions required for the proper use of an analysis of variance F test. Use the Kruskal–Wallis H test to determine whether evidence exists to conclude that the brands of magnetron tubes tend to differ in length of life under stress. Test using $\alpha = .05$.

TABLE 15.6   Lengths of Life for Magnetron Tubes in Example 15.6

Brand		
A	B	C
36	49	71
48	33	31
5	60	140
67	2	59
53	55	42

Solution

The first step in performing the Kruskal–Wallis H test is to rank the $n = 15$ observations in the complete data set. The ranks and rank sums for the three samples are shown in Table 15.7.

TABLE 15.7   Ranks and Rank Sums for Example 15.6

A	Rank	B	Rank	C	Rank
36	5	49	8	71	14
48	7	33	4	31	3
5	2	60	12	140	15
67	13	2	1	59	11
53	9	55	10	42	6
	$T_1 = 36$		$T_2 = 35$		$T_3 = 49$

We want to test the null hypothesis

H_0:   The population probability distributions of length of life under stress are identical for the three brands of magnetron tubes

against the alternative hypothesis

H_a: At least two of the population probability distributions differ in location

using the test statistic

$$H = \frac{12}{n(n + 1)} \sum_{i=1}^{k} \frac{T_i^2}{n_i} - 3(n + 1)$$

$$= \frac{12}{(15)(16)} \left[\frac{(36)^2}{5} + \frac{(35)^2}{5} + \frac{(49)^2}{5} \right] - 3(16) = 1.22$$

The rejection region for the H test is $H > \chi_\alpha^2$ where χ_α^2 is based on $(k - 2)$ degrees of freedom and the tabulated values of χ_α^2 are given in Table 8 of Appendix II. For $\alpha = .05$ and $(k - 1) = 2$ degrees of freedom, $\chi_{.05}^2 = 5.99147$. The rejection region for the test is $H > 5.99147$, as shown in Figure 15.7. Since the computed value of H, $H = 1.22$, is less than $\chi_{.05}^2$, we cannot reject H_0. There is insufficient evidence to indicate a difference in location among the distributions of lifelengths for the three brands of magnetron tubes.

FIGURE 15.7 ▶
Rejection region for the comparison of three probability distributions

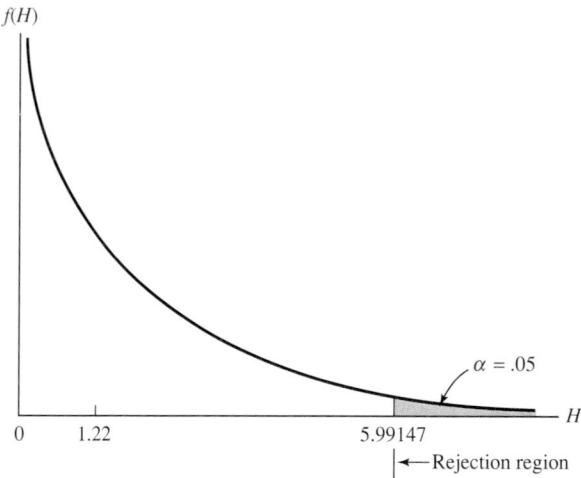

A SAS printout of the analysis is shown in Figure 15.8. The test statistic is shaded on the printout, as is the p-value of the test. Note that the p-value (.5434) exceeds $\alpha = .05$, resulting in a conclusion of "do not reject H_0."

FIGURE 15.8 ▶
SAS printout of Kruskal–Wallis test

```
                    N P A R 1 W A Y   P R O C E D U R E

            Wilcoxon Scores (Rank Sums) for Variable LIFE
                    Classified by Variable BRAND

                          Sum of      Expected      Std Dev         Mean
        BRAND     N       Scores      Under H0      Under H0        Score

        A         5        36.0         40.0       8.16496581    7.20000000
        B         5        35.0         40.0       8.16496581    7.00000000
        C         5        49.0         40.0       8.16496581    9.80000000

            Kruskal-Wallis Test (Chi-Square Approximation)
            CHISQ=  1.2200     DF=  2     Prob > CHISQ=      0.5434
```

EXERCISES

15.26 Refer to the data on DDT levels of contaminated fish, Appendix III. Suppose you want to compare the DDT levels of the three species of fish: (1) channel catfish, (2) smallmouth buffalo, and (3) largemouth bass. MINITAB stem-and-leaf displays for the DDT levels of the three species are provided here.

    a. Use the information provided in the MINITAB printouts to determine whether a parametric or non-parametric procedure is appropriate for analyzing the data. Explain.

```
Stem-and-leaf of DDTLevel  N  = 96     (CATFISH)
Leaf Unit = 10


  (90)    0 0000000000000000000000000000000000000000000000000001111111111111111+
    6     1 3458
    2     2
    2     3 6
    1     4
    1     5
    1     6
    1     7
    1     8
    1     9
    1    10
    1    11 0
```

```
Stem-and-leaf of DDTLevel  N  = 36     (BUFFALO)
Leaf Unit = 1.0


  (20)    0 00000111222233344444
   16     0 5555668
    9     1 00223
    4     1
    4     2 1
    3     2
    3     3 3
    2     3
    2     4 4
    1     4 8
```

```
Stem-and-leaf of DDTLevel  N  = 12     (BASS)
Leaf Unit = 0.10


   (8)    0 11233458
    4     1 9
    3     2 02
    1     3
    1     4
    1     5
    1     6
    1     7 4
```

    b. State the null and alternative hypothesis appropriate for analyzing the data nonparametrically.

    c. The data in Appendix III were analyzed using the Kruskal–Wallis H test. A MINITAB printout of the analysis is shown on page 950. Interpret the results.

LEVEL	NOBS	MEDIAN	AVE. RANK	Z VALUE
1	96	9.5500	85.8	5.42
2	36	4.6500	55.8	-2.77
3	12	0.5300	15.9	-4.91
OVERALL	144		72.5	

H = 37.64 d.f. = 2 p = 0.000
H = 37.65 d.f. = 2 p = 0.000 (adj. for ties)

15.27 The effectiveness of performance appraisal training in an organizational setting was evaluated in *Personnel Psychology* (Aug. 1984). Middle-level managers were randomly selected and assigned to one of three training conditions: no training, computer-assisted training, or computer-assisted training plus a behavior modeling workshop. After the formal training, the managers were administered a 25-question multiple-choice test of managerial knowledge and the number of correct answers was recorded for each. The data in the table are adapted from summary information provided in the article. Is there sufficient evidence to indicate that the relative frequency distributions of scores differ in location for the three types of performance appraisal training? Test using $\alpha = .01$.

No Training	Computer-Assisted Training	Computer Training Plus Workshop
16	19	12
18	22	19
11	13	18
14	15	22
23	20	16
	18	25
	21	

15.28 As oil drilling costs rise at unprecedented rates, the task of measuring drilling performance becomes essential to a successful oil company. One method of lowering drilling costs is to increase drilling speed. Researchers at Cities Service Co. have developed a drill bit, called the PD-1, which they believe penetrates rock at a faster rate than any other bit on the market. It is decided to compare the speed of the PD-1 with the two fastest drill bits known, the IADC 1-2-6 and the IADC 5-1-7, at 15 drilling locations in Texas. Five drilling sites were randomly assigned to each bit, and the rate of penetration (RoP) in feet per hour was recorded after drilling 3,000 feet at each site. Based on the information given in the table, can Cities Service Co. conclude that the RoP probability distributions differ for at least two of the three drill bits? Test at the $\alpha = .05$ level of significance.

PD-1	IADC 1-2-6	IADC 5-1-7
35.2	25.8	14.7
30.1	29.7	28.9
37.6	26.6	23.3
34.3	30.1	16.2
31.5	28.8	20.1

15.29 A *modulator/demodulator*, or *modem*, is a device that converts electrical impulses sent from a computer into audio tones that travel over telephone lines to a remote terminal. The performance of a modem varies, depending on the speed with which it can send and receive signals (called the *baud rate*) and whether it transmits and receives data at the same time (*full duplex*) or must take turns with the computer transmitting data (*half duplex*). A new type of modem, called a *smart modem*, has been developed. Smart modems have built-in microprocessors with advanced features that improve overall modem performance and efficiency. Four modems with self-contained microprocessors are on the market: Bizcomp 1012, Cermetek 212A, Hayes Smartmodem 1200, and Vadic 3451 Auto-Dial. Suppose that five users of each type of modem are randomly selected and asked to rate modem performance (measured on a scale from 1 to 100). Based on the data shown in the accompanying table, is there sufficient evidence to indicate a difference among the performance ratings of the four smart modems? Test using $\alpha = .10$.

Bizcomp 1012	Cermetek 212A	Smartmodem 1200	Vadic 3451
87	81	69	98
80	66	72	78
91	52	70	94
63	90	83	90
72	75	80	86

15.30 Vanadium (V) is a recently recognized essential trace element. An experiment was conducted to compare the concentrations of V in biological materials using isotope dilution mass spectrometry (*Analytical Chemistry*, Nov. 1985). The accompanying table gives the quantities of V (measured in nanograms per gram) in dried samples of oyster tissue, citrus leaves, bovine liver, and human serum. Conduct a nonparametric test to determine whether the distributions of V concentrations for the four biological materials differ in location. Test using $\alpha = .05$.

Oyster Tissue	Citrus Leaves	Bovine Liver	Human Serum
2.35	2.32	.39	.10
1.30	3.07	.54	.17
.34	4.09	.30	.14
			.16
			.16

Source: Fassett, J. D., and Kingston, H. M. "Determination of nanogram quantities of vanadium in biological material by isotope dilution thermal ionization mass spectrometry with ion counting detection." *Analytical Chemistry*, Vol. 57, No. 13, Nov. 1985, p. 2475 (Table II). Copyright 1985, American Chemical Society. Reprinted with permission.

15.31 Phosphoric acid is chemically produced by reacting phosphate rock with sulfuric acid. An important consideration in the chemical process is the length of time required for the chemical reaction to reach a specified temperature. The shorter the length of time, the higher the reactivity of the phosphate rock. An experiment was conducted to compare the reactivity of phosphate rock mined in north, central, and south Florida. Rock samples were collected from each location and placed in vacuum bottles with a 56% strength sulfuric acid solution. The time (in seconds) for the chemical reaction to reach 200°F was recorded for each sample. Do the data provide sufficient evidence to indicate a difference in the reactivity of phosphoric rock mined at the three locations? Test using $\alpha = .05$.

South		Central		North		
40.6	38.1	41.1	33.5	25.6	31.3	27.5
42.0	41.9	38.3	35.7	36.4	29.5	
37.5		40.2		28.2	22.8	

OPTIONAL EXERCISE

15.32   Use the sum of an arithmetic progression to show that for the Kruskal–Wallis H test,

$$T_1 + T_2 + \cdots + T_k = \frac{n(n + 1)}{2}$$

where k is the number of probability distributions being compared and n is the total sample size.

15.6   Comparing Three or More Populations: Randomized Block Design

In this section, we present the nonparametric equivalent of the analysis of variance F test for a randomized block design given in Section 14.9. The test, proposed by Milton Friedman (a Nobel prize winner in economics), is particularly appropriate for comparing the relative locations of k or more population probability distributions when the normality and common variance assumptions required for an analysis of variance are not (or may not be) satisfied.

To conduct the F_r test, we first rank the observations within each block and then compute the rank sums, $T_1, T_2, \ldots, T_k$, for the k treatments. If H_0 is true—that is, if the population probability distributions are identical—and if the number n of observations is large, then the F_r statistic

$$F_r = \frac{12}{bk(k + 1)} \sum_{i=1}^{k} T_i^2 - 3b(k + 1)$$

will possess a sampling distribution that can be approximated by a chi-square distribution with $(k - 1)$ degrees of freedom. For the approximation to be reasonably good, we require that either b, the number of blocks, or k, the number of treatments, exceed 5. The rejection region for the test consists of large values of F_r. Therefore, we reject H_0 if $F_r > \chi_\alpha^2$.

The **Friedman F_r test** is summarized in the box and its use is illustrated in Example 15.7.

The Friedman F_r Test for a Randomized Block Design

H_0:   The relative frequency distributions for the k populations are identical

H_a: At least two of k populations differ in location (shifted either to the left or to the right of one another)

Test statistic:

Rank each of the k observations within each block from the smallest (rank 1) to the largest (rank k). Calculate the treatment rank sums, $T_1, T_2, \ldots, T_k$. Then the test statistic is

$$F_r = \frac{12}{bk(k + 1)} \sum T_i^2 - 3b(k + 1)$$

(continued)

where

b = Number of blocks employed in the experiment

k = Number of treatments

T_i = Sum of the ranks for the ith treatment

Rejection region:

$F_r > \chi_\alpha^2$ where χ_α^2 is based on $(k-1)$ degrees of freedom

Assumptions: 1. The k treatments were randomly assigned to the k experimental units within each block.

2. For the chi-square approximation to be adequate, either the number b of blocks or the number k of treatments should exceed 5.

3. Tied observations are assigned ranks equal to the average of the ranks that would have been assigned to the observations had they not been tied.

EXAMPLE 15.7

The corrosion of different metals is a problem in many mechanical devices. Three sealers used to help retard corrosion were tested to determine whether there were any differences among them. Samples of 10 different metal compositions were treated with each of the three sealers, and the amount of corrosion was measured after exposure to the same environmental conditions for 1 month. The data and their associated ranks are shown in Table 15.8. Is there any evidence of a difference in the probability distributions of the amounts of corrosion among the three types of sealers? Test using $\alpha = .05$.

TABLE 15.8   Data and Ranks for the Randomized Block Design of Example 15.7

Metal	Sealer					
	1	Rank	2	Rank	3	Rank
1	21	2	23	3	15	1
2	29	2	30	3	21	1
3	16	1	19	3	18	2
4	20	3	19	2	18	1
5	13	2	10	1	14	3
6	5	1	12	3	6	2
7	18	2.5	18	2.5	12	1
8	26	2	32	3	21	1
9	17	2	20	3	9	1
10	4	2	10	3	2	1
		$T_1 = 19.5$		$T_2 = 26.5$		$T_3 = 14$

Solution

We want to test the null hypothesis

H_0: The probability distributions of the amounts of corrosion are identical for the three sealers

against the alternative hypothesis

H_a: At least two of the probability distributions differ in location

The ranks of the three treatments within each block and the treatment rank sums are shown in Table 15.8. Therefore, the calculated value of the F_r statistic is

$$F_r = \frac{12}{bk(k+1)} \sum_{i=1}^{k} T_i^2 - 3b(k+1)$$

$$= \frac{12}{10(3)(4)} [(19.5)^2 + (26.5)^2 + (14)^2] - 3(10)(4)$$

$$= 7.85$$

Note that this value agrees with the test statistic shaded on the MINITAB printout, Figure 15.9.

FIGURE 15.9 ▶

MINITAB printout for Example 15.7

```
Friedman test of Corros by Sealer blocked by Metal

S = 7.85   d.f. = 2   p = 0.020
S = 8.05   d.f. = 2   p = 0.018 (adjusted for ties)

                      Est.     Sum of
     Sealer    N    Median     RANKS
          1   10    16.583      19.5
          2   10    19.417      26.5
          3   10    12.750      14.0

Grand median  =   16.250
```

The rejection region for the test is $F_r > \chi^2_{.05}$, where the tabulated value (given in Table 8 of Appendix II) of $\chi^2_{.05}$, based on $k - 1 = 2$ degrees of freedom, is 5.99147. Thus, we will reject H_0 if $F_r > 5.99147$.

Since the computed value of the test statistic, $F_r = 7.85$, exceeds $\chi^2_{.05} = 5.99147$, there is sufficient evidence to reject H_0 and conclude that differences exist in the locations of two or more of the corrosion probability distributions. The p-value of the test (shaded in Figure 15.9) supports this result. The practical conclusion is that there is evidence to indicate a difference among the sealing abilities of the three sealers.

EXERCISES

15.33   Refer to the *Microcomputers in Civil Engineering* study of lateral drift in a building, Exercise 14.32. The data, reproduced in the table, are the lateral displacements (in inches) estimated by three different computer programs at each of five different building levels. Compare the distributions of lateral displacement estimated by the three computer programs with the appropriate nonparametric test. Use $\alpha = .05$.

Level	STAAD-III (1)	STAAD-III (2)	Drift
1	.17	.16	.16
2	1.35	1.26	1.27
3	3.04	2.76	2.77
4	4.54	3.98	3.99
5	5.94	4.99	5.00

Source: Valles, R. E., et al. "Simplified drift evaluation of wall-frame structures." *Microcomputers in Civil Engineering*, Vol. 8, 1993, p. 242 (Table 2).

15.34 An *optical mark reader* (OMR) is a machine that is able to "read" pencil marks that have been entered on a special form. A manufacturer of OMRs believes its product can operate equally well in a variety of temperature and humidity environments. To determine whether operating data contradict this belief, the manufacturer asks a well-known industrial testing laboratory to test its product. Five recently produced OMRs were randomly selected and each was operated in six different environments. The number of forms each was able to process in an hour was recorded and used as a measure of the OMR's operating efficiency. These data appear in the table. Use the Friedman F_r test to determine whether evidence exists to indicate that the probability distributions for the number of forms processed per hour differ in location for at least two of the environments. Test using $\alpha = .10$.

Machine Number	Environment					
	1	2	3	4	5	6
1	8,001	8,025	8,100	8,055	7,991	8,007
2	7,910	7,932	7,900	7,990	7,892	7,922
3	8,111	8,101	8,201	8,175	8,102	8,235
4	7,802	7,820	7,904	7,850	7,819	8,100
5	7,500	7,601	7,702	7,633	7,600	7,561

15.35 A topic of concern to computer terminal users is the color of the characters displayed on the video display screens. Early full-screen video display terminals presented the viewer with white characters on a black background. After an extended period of use, black and white displays were frequently found to cause temporary eye irritations. Experimentation with other colors revealed that yellow/amber displays may be the easiest on the eyes. In one German study, video display terminals were produced with white/black and six different symbol colors. (*Computers & Electronics*, Apr. 1983). Thirty test subjects were asked to specify which color combination they preferred by ranking each of the seven color combinations on a scale from 0 (no preference) to 10. Although the raw data were not revealed, the mean preference scores for each color were provided by the researchers. Based on these means, we have simulated the individual preference scores for ten subjects in the table on page 956.

   a. Do the data provide sufficient evidence to indicate a difference among the preference scores for the seven video display color combinations? Test using $\alpha = .05$.

   b. Do the data provide sufficient evidence to indicate that video display terminal users prefer a yellow/amber color combination over a green/black color combination? Test using $\alpha = .05$.

   c. Do the data provide sufficient evidence to indicate that video display terminal users prefer a yellow/amber color combination over yellow? Test using $\alpha = .05$.

Subject	Green/ Black	White/ Black	Yellow/ White	Orange/ White	Yellow	Yellow/ Amber	Yellow/ Orange
1	7	6	7	2	8	9	3
2	8	6	9	4	9	8	1
3	5	5	7	1	6	8	2
4	3	4	2	0	2	6	0
5	9	8	8	3	9	9	2
6	7	5	6	2	7	7	1
7	6	7	8	4	6	9	5
8	6	5	8	1	8	9	1
9	9	9	8	2	9	8	0
10	9	8	8	3	9	10	1

Source: Adapted from Solomon, L., and Burawa, A. "Maximize your computing comfort & efficiency." *Computers & Electronics*, Apr. 1983, pp. 35–40.

15.36 A study was conducted to explore the sources of occupational stress for engineers (*IEEE Transactions on Engineering Management*, Feb. 1986). One of the objectives was to determine "if there are consistent and significant differences among engineers at different levels of the organizational hierarchy in the degree to which they consider the different factors as sources of stress." A sample of male engineers from different types of organizations in Ontario, Canada, was administered the Stress Diagnostic Survey (SDS). The SDS provides stress ratings for each of 15 categories of work stressors. The researchers ranked 15 stress categories from 1 (highest stress) to 15 (lowest stress) for each of four groups of engineers—nonsupervisors, first-level supervisors, second-level supervisors, and third-level supervisors—as shown in the table. Conduct a test to determine whether the rank orderings of the stress categories differ among the four groups of engineers. Test using $\alpha = .01$.

Stress Category	Nonsupervisors	1st Level	2nd Level	3rd Level
Politics	5	6	4	7
Underutilization	3	5	7	5
Human resources development	4	3	2	3
Supervisory style	6	7	8	8
Rewards	1	1	1	4
Organizational structure	9	9	10	12
Participation	2	4	5	6
Role ambiguity	10	13	12	14
Overload/quantitative	15	15	15	15
Overload/qualitative	12	8	6	2
Time pressure	8	2	3	1
Role conflict	13	10	13	10
Career progression	7	10	9	13
Job scope	11	12	14	11
Responsibility for people	14	14	11	9

Source: Saleh, S. D., and Desai, K. "Occupational stress for engineers." *IEEE Transactions on Engineering Management*, Vol. EM-33, No. 1, Feb. 1986, p. 8 (Table II). © 1986, IEEE.

15.37   A serious, drought-related problem for farmers is the spread of aflatoxin, a highly toxic substance caused by mold, which contaminates field corn. In higher levels of contamination, aflatoxin is potentially hazardous to animal and possibly human health. (Officials of the FDA have set a maximum limit of 20 parts per billion aflatoxin as safe for interstate marketing.) Three sprays, A, B, and C, have been developed to control aflatoxin in field corn. To determine whether differences exist among the sprays, 10 ears of corn are randomly chosen from a contaminated corn field and each is divided into three pieces of equal size. The sprays are then randomly assigned to the pieces for each ear of corn, thus setting up a randomized block design. The table gives the amount (in parts per billion) of aflatoxin present in the corn samples after spraying. Use the Friedman test to determine whether there are differences among the probability distributions of the amounts of aflatoxin present for the three sprays. Test at the $\alpha = .05$ level of significance.

Ear	Spray			Ear	Spray		
	A	B	C		A	B	C
1	21	23	15	6	5	12	6
2	29	30	21	7	18	18	12
3	16	19	18	8	26	32	21
4	20	19	18	9	17	20	9
5	13	10	14	10	4	10	2

15.7   Nonparametric Regression

We learned in Section 12.11 how to modify the regression analysis when the assumptions about the random error term ε are violated. For example, if the variance σ^2 of ε is not constant, we transform the dependent variable y using one of the variance-stabilizing transformations discussed in Section 12.11. An alternative procedure is to conduct a nonparametric regression analysis of the data.

In nonparametric regression, tests of model adequacy do not require any assumptions about the probability distribution of ε; thus, they are distribution-free. Although the tests are intuitively appealing, they can become quite difficult to apply in practice, especially when the number of observations is large. For this reason, and the fact that residual diagnostics are readily available via the computer, most analysts prefer to use the techniques of Section 12.11 when the standard regression assumptions are violated.

For those who are interested, we provide brief descriptions of the nonparametric alternatives to the parametric simple linear regression tests of Chapter 11. Specifically, we discuss a nonparametric test for (1) rank correlation and (2) the slope parameter of the straight-line model.

SPEARMAN'S RANK CORRELATION   As an alternative to the Pearson product moment correlation coefficient r (Section 11.7), we can compute a correlation coefficient based on ranks. **Spearman's rank correlation coefficient**, denoted r_s, can then be used to test for rank correlation between two variables, y and x.

To illustrate, suppose a large manufacturing firm wants to determine whether the number y of work-hours an employee misses per year is correlated with the employee's annual wages x (in thousands of dollars). A sample of 15 employees produced the data shown in Table 15.9.

TABLE 15.9   Work-Hours Missed, Annual Wages, and Ranks for 15 Employees

Employee	Hours Missed, y	Annual Wages, x	y-Rank	x-Rank	Difference d_i	d_i^2
1	49	15.8	6	11	-5	25
2	36	17.5	4	12	-8	64
3	127	11.3	13	2	11	121
4	91	13.2	12	6	6	36
5	72	13.0	9	5	4	16
6	34	14.5	3	9	-6	36
7	155	11.8	14	3	11	121
8	11	20.2	2	14	-12	144
9	191	10.8	15	1	14	196
10	6	18.8	1	13	-12	144
11	63	13.8	8	7	1	1
12	79	12.7	10	4	6	36
13	43	15.1	5	10	-5	25
14	57	24.2	7	15	-8	64
15	82	13.9	11	8	3	9
					$\Sigma d_i^2 =$	1,038

Spearman's rank correlation coefficient is found by first ranking the values of each variable separately. (Ties are treated by averaging the tied ranks.) Then r_s is computed in exactly the same way as the Pearson correlation coefficient r—the only difference is that the values of x and y that appear in the formula for r are replaced by their ranks. That is, the *ranks* of the raw data are used to compute r_s rather than the raw data themselves. When there are no (or few) ties in the ranks, this formula reduces to the simple expression

$$r_s = 1 - \frac{6 \Sigma d_i^2}{n(n^2 - 1)}$$

where d_i is the difference between the rank of y and x for the ith observation.

The ranks of y and x, the differences between the ranks, and the squared differences for each of the 15 employees are also shown in Table 15.9. Note that the sum of the squared differences is $\Sigma d_i^2 = 1,038$. Substituting this value into the formula for r_s, we obtain

$$r_s = 1 - \frac{6 \Sigma d_i^2}{n(n^2 - 1)} = 1 - \frac{6(1,038)}{15(224)} = -.854$$

This large negative value of r_s implies that a fairly strong negative correlation exists between work-hours missed y and annual wages x in the sample.

To determine whether a negative rank correlation exists in the population, we would test $H_0: \rho = 0$ against $H_a: \rho < 0$ using r_s as a test statistic. As you would expect, we reject H_0 for small values of r_s. Upper-tailed critical values of Spearman's r_s are provided in Table 17 of Appendix II. This table is partially reproduced in Table 15.10. Since the distribution of r_s is symmetric around 0, the lower-tailed critical value is the negative of the corresponding upper-tailed critical value. For, say, $\alpha = .01$ and $n = 15$, the critical value (shaded in Table 15.10) is $r_{.01} = .623$. Thus, the rejection region for the test is

Reject H_0 if $r_s < -.623$

Since the test statistic, $r_s = -.854$, falls in the rejection region, there is sufficient evidence (at $\alpha = .01$) of negative correlation between work-hours missed y and annual wages x in the population.

TABLE 15.10   A Portion of the Spearman's r_s Table, Table 17 of Appendix II

The α values correspond to a one-tailed test of $H_0: \rho_s = 0$. The tabulated value of α should be doubled for two-tailed tests.

n	$\alpha = .05$	$\alpha = .025$	$\alpha = .01$	$\alpha = .005$
5	.900	—	—	—
6	.829	.886	.943	—
7	.714	.786	.893	—
8	.643	.738	.833	.881
9	.600	.683	.783	.833
10	.564	.648	.745	.794
11	.523	.623	.736	.818
12	.497	.591	.703	.780
13	.475	.566	.673	.745
14	.457	.545	.646	.716
15	.441	.525	.623	.689
16	.425	.507	.601	.666

Spearman's nonparametric test for rank correlation in the population is summarized in the box on page 960.

Spearman's Nonparametric Test for Rank Correlation

One-Tailed Test	*Two-Tailed Test*
H_0: $\rho = 0$	H_0: $\rho = 0$
H_a: $\rho > 0$	H_a: $\rho \neq 0$
(or H_a: $\rho < 0$)	

Test statistic: $r_s = 1 - \dfrac{6 \sum d_i^2}{n(n^2 - 1)}$

where d_i is the difference between the y rank and x rank for the ith observation.

[Note: In the case of ties, calculate r_s by substituting the ranks of the y's and the ranks of the x's for the actual y values and x values in the formula for r given in Section 11.7.]

Rejection region:	*Rejection region:*
$r_s > r_\alpha$ (or $r_s < -r_\alpha$)	$\lvert r_s \rvert > r_{\alpha/2}$

where the values of r_α and $r_{\alpha/2}$ are given in Table 17 of the Appendix.

Assumptions: None

THEIL TEST FOR ZERO SLOPE   Alternatively, we could test for linear correlation in the population by testing the slope parameter β_1 in the simple linear regression model

$$y = \beta_0 + \beta_1 x + \varepsilon$$

That is, we could test H_0: $\beta_1 = 0$ against H_a: $\beta_1 \neq 0$. A distribution-free test for the slope is the **Theil C test**.

To conduct this nonparametric test, we first rank the x values in increasing order and list the ordered (x, y) pairs, as shown in Table 15.11. Next, we calculate all possible differences $y_j - y_i$, $i < j$ (where i and j represent the ith and jth ranked observations), and note the sign (positive or negative) of each difference.

TABLE 15.11   Data of Table 15.9 Ranked by Annual Wages x

Employee Ranking	Hours Missed, y	Annual Wages, x	Differences, $y_j - y_i (i < j)$ # Negatives	# Positives
1	191	10.8	—	—
2	127	11.3	1	0
3	155	11.8	1	1
4	79	12.7	3	0
5	72	13.0	4	0
6	91	13.2	3	2
7	63	13.8	6	0

(continued)

(continued)

Employee Ranking	Hours Missed, y	Annual Wages, x	Differences, $y_j - y_i (i < j)$ # Negatives	# Positives
8	82	13.9	4	3
9	34	14.5	8	0
10	43	15.1	8	1
11	49	15.8	8	2
12	36	17.5	10	1
13	6	18.8	12	0
14	11	20.2	12	1
15	57	24.2	8	6
		Totals:	88	17

For example, the y value for employee ranked #2, $y_2 = 127$, is compared to the y value for each employee with a lower rank. In this case, the only employee ranked lower is employee #1, with $y_1 = 191$ (see Table 15.11). The difference

$$y_2 - y_1 = 127 - 191 = -64$$

is negative and is noted as such in Table 15.11.

Similarly, we compare the y value of employee ranked #3, $y_3 = 155$, to the y values of employees of lower rank, $y_2 = 127$ and $y_1 = 191$, by the differences

$$y_3 - y_2 = 155 - 127 = 28$$

and

$$y_3 - y_1 = 155 - 191 = -36$$

This results in one positive and one negative difference. Continuing in this manner, we obtain a total of 17 positive differences and 88 negative differences, as shown in Table 15.11.

The test statistic C is obtained by scoring each positive difference as a $+1$ and each negative difference as a -1 (differences of 0 are assigned a score of 0) and summing the scores. Therefore, for the data of Table 15.11, we obtain the test statistic

$$C = (+1)(17) + (-1)(88) = -71$$

The observed significance level (p-value) of the test is obtained from Table 18 of Appendix II. For this lower-tailed test, i.e., a test for a negative slope, the p-value is $P(C \le -71)$. Searching the $n = 15$ column and the $x = 81$ row of Table 18 of Appendix II, we obtain the p-value ≈ 0. Thus, there is strong evidence to reject H_0 and conclude that work-hours missed y is negatively linearly related to annual wages x at this firm.

Theil's test for the slope of a straight-line model is described, in general, in the box on page 962. A nonparametric confidence interval for the slope β_1 based on the Theil test can also be formed. Consult the references if you want to learn how to construct this interval.

Theil's Test for Zero Slope in the Straight-Line Model $y = \beta_0 + \beta_1 x + \varepsilon$

One-Tailed Test	*Two-Tailed Test*
H_0: $\beta_1 = 0$	H_0: $\beta_1 = 0$
H_a: $\beta_1 > 0$	H_a: $\beta_1 \neq 0$
(or H_a: $\beta_1 < 0$)	

Test statistic: $C = (-1)(\text{Number of negative } y_j - y_i \text{ differences})$
$+ (1)(\text{Number of positive } y_j - y_i \text{ differences})$

where y_i and y_j are the ith and jth observations ranked in increasing order of the x values, $i < j$.

Observed significance level:
$$p\text{-value} = \begin{cases} P(x \geq C) \text{ for } H_a\text{: } \beta_1 > 0 \\ P(x \leq C) \text{ for } H_a\text{: } \beta_1 < 0 \end{cases}$$

Observed significance level:
$$p\text{-value} = 2\min(p_1, p_2)$$
where
$$p_1 = P(x \geq C)$$
$$p_2 = P(x \leq C)$$

where the values of $P(x \geq C) = P(x \leq -C)$ are given in Table 18 of Appendix II.

Assumptions: The random error ε is independent.

Nonparametric tests are also available for multiple regression models. These tests are very sophisticated, however, and require the use of specialized statistical computer software not yet available on a commercial basis. Consult the references if you want to learn more about these nonparametric techniques.

EXERCISES

15.38 Modern warehouses employ computerized and automated guided vehicles for materials handling. Consequently, the physical layout of the warehouse must be carefully designed to prevent vehicle congestion and optimize response time. Optimal design of an automated warehouse was studied in the *Journal of Engineering for Industry* (Aug. 1993). The layout employed assumes that vehicles do not block each other when they travel within the warehouse, i.e., that there is no congestion. The validity of this assumption was checked by simulating (on a computer) warehouse operations. In each simulation, the number of vehicles was varied and the congestion time (total time one vehicle blocked another) was recorded. The data are shown in the accompanying table. Spearman's method was used to test for a correlation between congestion time (y) and number of vehicles (x). A MINITAB printout of the analysis follows. Interpret the results.

Number of Vehicles	Congestion Time, minutes	Number of Vehicles	Congestion Time, minutes
1	0	9	.02
2	0	10	.04
3	.02	11	.04
4	.01	12	.04
5	.01	13	.03
6	.01	14	.04
7	.03	15	.05
8	.03		

Source: Pandit, R., and Palekar, U. S., "Response time considerations for optimal warehouse layout design." *Journal of Engineering for Industry*, Transactions of the ASME, Vol. 115, Aug. 1993, p. 326 (Table 2).

```
Correlation of RankX and RankY = 0.898
```

15.39 Amorphous alloys have been found to have superior corrosion resistance. *Corrosion Science* (Sept. 1993) reported on the resistivity of an amorphous iron–boron–silicon alloy after crystallization. Five alloy specimens were annealed at 700°C, each for a different length of time. The passivation potential—a measure of resistivity of the crystallized alloy—was then measured for each specimen. The experimental data are shown here.

Annealing Time x, minutes	Passivation Potential y, mV
10	−408
20	−400
45	−392
90	−379
120	−385

Source: Chattoraj, I., et al. "Polarization and resistivity measurements of post-crystallization changes in amorphous Fe–B–Si alloys." *Corrosion Science*, Vol. 49, No. 9, Sept. 1993, p. 712 (Table 1).

a. Calculate Spearman's correlation coefficient between annealing time (x) and passivation potential (y). Interpret the result.

b. Use the result, part **a**, to test for a significant correlation between annealing time and passivation potential. Use $\alpha = .10$.

15.40 The Federal Communications Commission (FCC) specifies that radiated electromagnetic emissions from digital devices are to be measured in an open-field test site. To verify test-site acceptability, the site attenuation (i.e., the transmission loss from the input of one half-wave dipole to the output of another when both dipoles are positioned over the ground plane) must be evaluated. A study (*IEEE Transactions on Electromagnetic Compatibility*, Aug. 1985) conducted at a test site in Fort Collins, Colorado, yielded the accompanying data on site attenuation (in decibels) and transmission frequency (in megahertz) for dipoles at a distance of 3 meters. (See page 964.)

Transmission Frequency x, MHz	Site Attenuation y, db
50	11.5
100	15.8
200	18.2
300	22.6
400	26.2
500	27.1
600	29.5
700	30.7
800	31.3
900	32.6
1,000	34.9

Source: Bennett, W. S. "An error analysis of the FCC site-attenuation approximation." *IEEE Transactions on Electromagnetic Compatibility*, Vol. EMC-27, No. 3, Aug. 1985, p. 113 (Table IV). © 1985, IEEE.

a. Find the Spearman coefficient of correlation between transmission frequency (x) and site attenuation level (y). Interpret the result.

b. Conduct a test to determine if site attenuation level (y) is positively correlated with transmission frequency (x). Test using $\alpha = .10$.

15.41 An automated system for marking large numbers of student computer programs, called AUTOMARK, has been used successfully at McMaster University in Ontario, Canada. AUTOMARK takes into account both program correctness and program style when marking student assignments. To evaluate the effectiveness of the automated system, AUTOMARK was used to grade the FORTRAN77 assignments of a class of 33 students (*Communications of the ACM*, Feb. 1986). These grades were then compared to the grades assigned by the instructor. The results are shown in the accompanying table. Is there evidence to indicate that the AUTOMARK and instructor grade assignments are positively correlated? Use Spearman's test for rank correlation at $\alpha = .05$.

AUTOMARK Grade	Instructor Grade	AUTOMARK Grade	Instructor Grade
12.2	10	17.8	17
10.6	11	18.0	17
15.1	12	18.2	17
16.2	12	18.4	17
16.6	12	18.6	17
16.6	13	19.0	17
17.2	14	19.3	17
17.6	14	19.5	17
18.2	14	19.7	17
16.5	15	18.6	18
17.2	15	19.0	18
18.2	15	19.2	18
15.1	16	19.4	18

(continued)

AUTOMARK Grade	Instructor Grade	AUTOMARK Grade	Instructor Grade
17.2	16	19.6	18
17.5	16	20.1	18
18.6	16	19.2	19
18.8	16		

Source: Redish, K. A., and Smyth, W. F. "Program style analysis: A natural by-product of program compilation." *Communications of the Association for Computing Machinery*, Vol. 29, No. 2, Feb. 1986, p. 132 (Figure 4). Copyright 1986, Association for Computing Machinery, Inc.

15.42 Civil engineers often use the straight-line equation $E(y) = \beta_0 + \beta_1 x$ to model the relationship between the mean shear strength $E(y)$ of masonry joints and precompression stress, x. To test this model, a series of stress tests were performed on solid bricks arranged in triplets and joined with mortar (*Proceedings of the Institute of Civil Engineers*, Mar. 1990). The precompression stress was varied for each triplet, and the ultimate shear load just before failure (called the shear strength) was recorded. The stress results for seven triplets (measured in N/mm²) are shown in the accompanying table. Conduct a nonparametric test of H_0: $\beta_1 = 0$ against the alternative H_a: $\beta_1 > 0$. Test using $\alpha = .05$.

Triplet Test	1	2	3	4	5	6	7
Shear strength, y	1.00	2.18	2.24	2.41	2.59	2.82	3.06
Precompression stress, x	0	.60	1.20	1.33	1.43	1.75	1.75

Source: Riddington, J. R., and Ghazali, M. Z. "Hypothesis for shear failure in masonry joints." *Proceedings of the Institute of Civil Engineers*, Part 2, Mar. 1990, Vol. 89, p. 96 (Figure 7).

15.43 A study was conducted to model the thermal performance of integral-fin tubes used in the refrigeration and process industries (*Journal of Heat Transfer*, Aug. 1990). Twenty-four specially manufactured integral-fin tubes having rectangular-shaped fins made of copper were used in the experiment. Vapor was released downward into each tube and the vapor-side heat transfer coefficient (based on the outside surface area of the tube) was measured. The dependent variable for the study is the heat transfer enhancement ratio, y, defined as the ratio of the vapor-side coefficient of the fin-tube to the vapor-side coefficient of a smooth tube evaluated at the same temperature. Theoretically, heat transfer will be related to the area at the top of the tube that is "unflooded" by condensation of the vapor. The data in the table are the unflooded area ratio (x) and heat transfer enhancement (y) values recorded for the 24 integral-fin tubes. Conduct a nonparametric test for a positive linear relationship between heat transfer enhancement (y) and unflooded area ratio (x). Use $\alpha = .10$.

Unflooded Area Ratio, x	Heat Transfer Enhancement, y	Unflooded Area Ratio, x	Heat Transfer Enhancement, y
1.93	4.4	2.00	5.2
1.95	5.3	1.77	4.7
1.78	4.5	1.62	4.2
1.64	4.5	2.77	6.0
1.54	3.7	2.47	5.8
1.32	2.8	2.24	5.2
2.12	6.1	1.32	3.5

(*continued*)

Unflooded Area Ratio, x	Heat Transfer Enhancement, y	Unflooded Area Ratio, x	Heat Transfer Enhancement, y
1.88	4.9	1.26	3.2
1.70	4.9	1.21	2.9
1.58	4.1	2.26	5.3
2.47	7.0	2.04	5.1
2.37	6.7	1.88	4.6

Source: Marto, P. J., et al. "An experimental study of R-113 film condensation on horizontal integral-fin tubes." *Journal of Heat Transfer*, Vol. 112, Aug. 1990, p. 763 (Table 2).

OPTIONAL EXERCISES

15.44   Show that for the special case where $n = 3$, $-1 \leq r_s \leq 1$. [*Hint:*   List each of the $3! \times 3! = 36$ different arrangements of the x and y rankings and compute r_s for each.]

15.45   Show that for the special case where $n = 3$, $E(r_s) = 0$. (This fact is also true in general.) [*Hint:*   Use the results of Optional Exercise 15.44 and the fact that any of the arrangements has a probability of $\frac{1}{36}$ of occurring.]

15.8   Summary

We have presented several useful **nonparametric techniques** as alternatives to the parametric tests discussed in Chapters 9 and 11–14. Nonparametric techniques are useful when the underlying assumptions for their parametric counterparts are not justified or when it is impossible to assign specific values to the observations. Nonparametric methods provide more general comparisons of populations than parametric methods, because they compare the probability distributions of the populations rather than specific parameters. Consequently, they are **distribution-free**, i.e., they require no assumptions about the distributions of the sampled data.

Rank sums are the primary tools of nonparametric statistics. The **Wilcoxon rank sum test** can be used to compare two populations based on an independent sampling experiment, and the **Wilcoxon signed ranks test** can be used for a **matched-pairs experiment**. The **Kruskal–Wallis H test** is applied when comparing k populations using a **completely randomized design**. The **Friedman F_r test** is used to compare k populations when a randomized block design is conducted. Other nonparametric tests are the **sign test** for a single population, **Spearman's test** for correlation, and **Theil's slope test**.

The strength of nonparametric statistics lies in their general applicability. Few restrictive assumptions are required, and they may be used for observations that can be ranked but not exactly measured. Therefore, nonparametric methods provide useful alternatives to the parametric tests of Chapters 9 and 11–14.

SUPPLEMENTARY EXERCISES

15.46   The building specifications in a certain city require that the sewer pipe used in residential areas have a median breaking strength of more than 2,500 pounds per lineal foot. A manufacturer who would like to supply the city with sewer pipe has submitted a bid and provided the following additional information. An independent contractor randomly selected seven sections of the manufacturer's pipe and tested each for breaking strength. The results (pounds per lineal foot) are shown here:

   2,610   2,750   2,420   2,510   2,540   2,490   2,680

Is there sufficient evidence to conclude that the manufacturer's sewer pipe meets the required specifications? Use a significance level of $\alpha = .10$.

15.47   Weevils cause millions of dollars worth of damage each year to cotton crops. Three chemicals designed to control weevil populations were applied, one to each of three fields of cotton. After 3 months, 10 plots of equal size were randomly selected within each field and the percentage of cotton plants with weevil damage was recorded for each. Do the data in the table provide sufficient evidence to indicate a difference in location among the distributions of damage rates corresponding to the three treatments? Use $\alpha = .05$.

A	B	C
10.8	22.3	9.8
15.6	19.5	12.3
19.2	18.6	16.2
17.9	24.3	14.1
18.3	19.9	15.3
9.8	20.4	10.8
16.7	23.6	12.2
19.0	21.2	17.3
20.3	19.8	15.1
19.4	22.6	11.3

15.48   *Acid rain* is considered by some environmentalists to be the nation's most serious environmental problem. It is formed by the combination of water vapor in clouds with nitrogen oxide and sulfuric dioxide emissions from the burning of coal, oil, and natural gas. The acidity of rain in central and northern Florida consistently ranges from 4.5 to 5 on the pH scale, a decidedly acid condition. To determine the effects of acid rain on the acidity of soils in a natural ecosystem, engineers at the University of Florida's Institute of Food and Agricultural Sciences irrigated experimental plots near Gainesville, Florida, with acid rain at two pH levels: 3.7 and 4.5. The acidity of the soil was then measured at three different depths: 0–15, 15–30, and 30–46 centimeters. Tests were conducted during three different time periods. The resulting soil pH values are shown in the table on page 968. Suppose that the main objective of the experiment is to compare the acidity of soil irrigated with pH 4.5 acid rain to the acidity of soil irrigated with pH 3.7 acid rain, and that the different soil depths are to be treated as blocks.

| | | April 3 Acid Rain pH | | June 16 Acid Rain pH | | June 30 Acid Rain pH | |
		3.7	4.5	3.7	4.5	3.7	4.5
	0–15 cm	5.33	5.33	5.47	5.47	5.20	5.13
Soil Depth	15–30 cm	5.27	5.03	5.50	5.53	5.33	5.20
	30–46 cm	5.37	5.40	5.80	5.60	5.33	5.17

Source: "Acid rain linked to growth of coal-fired power." *Florida Agricultural Research* 83, Vol. 2, No. 1, Winter 1983.

a. Use a nonparametric test to compare the soil pH values of the two treatments on April 3.
b. Use a nonparametric test to compare the soil pH values of the two treatments on June 16.
c. Use a nonparametric test to compare the soil pH values of the two treatments on June 30.
d. Comment on the validity of the tests in parts a–c.

15.49 A new computer software query package has been designed to achieve more efficient access and maintenance of large-scale data sets. Efficiency is measured in terms of the number of disk I/O's (called *storage blocks*) required to access and maintain the data set. The smaller the number of blocks that are read, the faster the operation takes place. To evaluate the performance of the new software system, the number of disk I/O's required to access a large-scale data set was recorded for each of a sample of 15 data sets of various sizes (where size is measured as the number of records in the data set). The results are shown in the table.

Data Set	Number of Records x, thousands	Number of Disk I/O's y, thousands
1	350	36
2	200	20
3	450	45
4	50	5
5	400	40
6	150	18
7	350	38
8	300	32
9	150	21
10	500	54
11	100	11
12	400	43
13	200	19
14	50	7
15	250	26

a. Compute Spearman's rank correlation coefficient to measure the strength of the relationship between the number of records in a data set and the number of disk I/O's required to access the data set. Interpret the result.
b. Test the null hypothesis that the number of records and the number of disk I/O's are not correlated against the alternative that these variables are positively correlated. Use $\alpha = .01$.

15.50 Thermogravimetric balance (TG) is a technique developed to evaluate the thermal behavior of chemical compounds. Research reported in *Lubrication Engineering* (Apr. 1986) compared the TG technique to the standard method of evaluating the thermooxidation stability of base oils and their additive blends (e.g., transformer oils, turbine oils, transmission oils, and so forth). For each of a sample of 10 base oils, the amount of oxidative compounds formed at the oxidation point was determined using the TG technique and the total percentage of oxidation products was determined by the standard method. The results of the experiment are shown in the accompanying table. Do the data provide sufficient evidence to indicate that the oxidation measurements of the two methods are positively correlated? Test using $\alpha = .01$.

Base Oil	TG Technique Amount of Oxidative Compounds, % weight	Standard Method Total Oxidation Products, %
1	25.4	2.3
2	27.11	2.5
3	28.0	2.65
4	17.9	1.3
5	18.9	1.45
6	22.9	1.9
7	30.8	3.3
8	18.6	1.4
9	24.4	2.1
10	29.8	2.9

Source: Abou El Naga, H. H., and Salem, A. E. M. "Base oils thermooxidation." *Lubrication Engineering*, Vol. 24, No. 4, Apr. 1986, p. 213. Reprinted by permission of the American Society of Lubrication Engineers. All rights reserved.

15.51   Governmental agencies periodically monitor nuclear-powered electrical generating plants for the purpose of establishing radiation guidelines. These guidelines then permit the detection of any changes resulting from operation that may endanger the surrounding environment. In 1978–1979, the Department of Health and Rehabilitative Services (DHRS) monitored three nuclear power plants in Florida for radiation in air particulates. The data shown in the table represent mean gross beta values (pCi/m^3)—a measure of radioactive air particulates—recorded at each plant and an Orlando control site for the first 10 weeks in 1979.

Week	Orlando	Turkey Point	St. Lucie	Crystal River
1	.048	.023	.023	.041
2	.019	.025	.020	.032
3	.022	.026	.022	.025
4	.015	.026	.028	.027
5	.027	.034	.031	.030
6	.122	.035	.025	.033
7	.013	.033	.020	.080
8	.007	.022	.022	.026
9	.025	.021	.013	.015
10	.025	.027	.026	.042

Source: "Monitoring of nuclear power plant environs in Florida: 1978–79." Dept. of Health and Rehabilitative Services, Health & Technical Support Services, Radiological Health Services.

a. Do the data provide sufficient evidence to indicate a difference in the radioactivity of air particulates at the four Florida sites? Test using $\alpha = .05$.

b. Do the data provide sufficient evidence to indicate a difference in the radioactivity of air particulates at the Crystal River plant site and the Orlando control site? Test using $\alpha = .05$.

15.52 Bulk specimens of Chilean lumpy iron ore (95% particle size, 150 millimeters) were randomly sampled from a 35,325-long-ton shipload of ore; the percentage of iron in each ore specimen was determined (*Reports of Statistical Application Research*, Union of Japanese Scientists and Engineers, Vol. 18, 1971). The data for 10 bulk specimens are given here:

63.01	61.75	63.22	62.38	62.80
63.92	62.94	63.71	62.10	64.34

Is there sufficient evidence to indicate that the median percentage of iron in bulk specimens from the shipload of ore differs from 63? Test using $\alpha = .05$.

15.53 In the early 1960s, the air-conditioning systems of a fleet of Boeing 720 jet airplanes came under investigation. The accompanying table presents the lifelengths (in hours) of the air-conditioning systems in two different Boeing 720 planes. Assuming the data represent random samples from the respective populations, is there evidence of a shift in the location of the lifelength distributions of air-conditioning systems for the two Boeing 720 planes? Test using $\alpha = .05$.

Plane 1		Plane 2	
23	49	59	230
118	10	32	54
90	310	14	152
29	76	102	67
156	62	66	34

Source: Hollander, M., Park, D. H., and Proschan, F. "Testing whether F is 'more NBU' than is G." *Microelectronics and Reliability*, Vol. 26, No. 1, 1986, p. 43 (Table 1). Copyright 1986, Pergamon Press, Ltd. Reprinted with permission.

15.54 Nuclear power continues to be one of mankind's biggest fears. However, research has indicated that anti-smoking campaigns can save more lives each year than nuclear power plant safety programs (*Dun's Review*, Sept. 1979). In an effort to quantify the public's perception of risk, a research organization asked three groups of people to rank 30 products or activities from most risky to least risky. The three groups who took part in the survey were the League of Women Voters, college students, and business and professional club members. The accompanying table gives the rankings for the three groups and, in parentheses, the estimated number of deaths per year attributed to the 30 activities. Use the Friedman test to determine whether the three groups differ regarding their concepts of risk involved with these 30 activities. Test using $\alpha = .05$.

Activity and Deaths Per Year	League of Women Voters	College Students	Business and Professional Club Members
Smoking (150,000)	4	3	4
Alcoholic beverages (100,000)	6	7	5
Motor vehicles (50,000)	2	5	3
Handguns (17,000)	3	2	1
Electric power (14,000)	18	19	19
Motorcycles (3,000)	5	6	2
Swimming (3,000)	19	30	17
Surgery (2,800)	10	11	9
X-rays (2,300)	22	17	24
Railroads (1,950)	24	23	20
General (private) aviation (1,300)	7	15	11
Large construction (1,000)	12	14	13
Bicycles (1,000)	16	24	14
Hunting (800)	13	18	10
Home appliances (200)	29	27	27
Fire fighting (195)	11	10	6
Police work (160)	8	8	7
Contraceptives (150)	20	9	22
Commercial aviation (130)	17	16	18
Nuclear power (100)	1	1	8
Mountain climbing (30)	15	22	12
Power mowers (24)	27	28	25
High school & college football (23)	23	26	21
Skiing (18)	21	25	16
Vaccinations (10)	30	29	29
Food coloring[a]	26	20	30
Food preservatives[a]	25	12	28
Pesticides[a]	9	4	15
Prescription antibiotics[a]	28	21	26
Spray cans[a]	14	13	23

[a]Not available

Source: "What price safety? The 'zero-risk' debate." *Dun's Review*, Sept. 1979. Reprinted with permission, *Business Month* magazine. Copyright © 1979 by Business Magazine Corporation, 38 Commercial Wharf, Boston, Massachusetts 02110.

15.55 The oxygen supply of coastal marine sediments is of great importance to plant and animal communities in the ocean. An engineer wants to compare the mean depths of penetration of oxygen into coastal marine sediments at five different water depths: 5, 10, 15, 20, and 40 meters. Independent samples of marine sediments at each water depth were randomly selected and measured for depth of oxygen penetration by polarographic oxygen microelectrodes. The data are recorded (in millimeters) in the table on page 972. Is there evidence of a difference among the probability distributions of the depths of penetration of oxygen into marine sediments for the five water depths? Test using $\alpha = .05$.

	Water Depth, meters			
5	10	15	20	40
1.2	3.7	1.7	2.8	4.4
3.6	4.6	2.2	4.6	5.3
1.3	3.1	1.6	3.7	3.6
1.8	2.0	1.5	3.2	4.8
2.4	3.0	2.0	3.1	3.9

15.56 A team of research engineers has isolated a chemical that will speed the pulse of the corn earworm. The goal is to control these crop-damaging insects by inducing fatal heart attacks with the chemical. Tests of the new compound have been conducted in 10 different corn-producing states. Two fields were randomly selected from each state—one field was sprayed with the new chemical and the other field acted as the control. The crop yield per acre was recorded for all 20 farms, with the results shown in the accompanying table. Is there evidence that the new chemical will increase crop yield per acre? Test using $\alpha = .05$.

State	Yield Per Acre	
	New Chemical	Control
1	50.0	35.0
2	50.0	25.0
3	70.0	57.0
4	76.0	60.0
5	58.9	34.0
6	60.0	35.0
7	50.0	55.0
8	33.0	30.0
9	34.0	33.0
10	61.7	51.1

15.57 As part of a computer system performance evaluation, a system manager is interested in predicting the response time for computer terminals. *Terminal response time* is defined as the length of time (in seconds) required for the computer to respond to a command sent from a computer terminal by pressing one of the terminal's program function keys. One variable that influences terminal response time is the number of simultaneous users (that is, the number of users accessing the computer's central processing unit at the same time the command was sent). Refer to the sample data given in the table.

Number of Simultaneous Users x	Terminal Response Time y, seconds
1	.22
2	.59
3	1.36
4	1.01
5	1.42

a. Compute Spearman's rank coefficient of correlation between the number of simultaneous users and terminal response time.

b. Do the data provide sufficient evidence to indicate that there is a positive correlation between the two variables? Test using $\alpha = .10$.

15.58 The accompanying table shows a portion of the experimental data obtained in a study of the radial tension strength of concrete pipe. The concrete pipe used for the experiment had an inside diameter of 84 inches and a wall thickness of approximately 8.75 inches. In addition, it was reinforced with cold drawn wire. The table shows the load (in pounds per foot) until the first crack was observed and the age (in days) for each of nine pipe specimens. Do the data present sufficient evidence to indicate correlation between load and age? Test using $\alpha = .05$.

Load	Age	Load	Age
11,450	20	10,540	25
10,420	20	9,470	31
11,142	20	9,190	31
10,840	25	9,540	31
11,170	25		

Source: Heger, F. J., and McGrath, T. J. "Radial tension strength of pipe and other curved flexural members." *Journal of the American Concrete Institute*, Vol. 80, No. 1, 1983, pp. 33–39.

15.59 The EPA wants to determine whether temperature changes in the ocean's water caused by a nuclear power plant will have a significant effect on the animal life in the region. Recently hatched specimens of a certain species of fish are randomly divided into four groups. The groups are placed in separate simulated ocean environments that are identical in every way except for water temperature. Six months later, the specimens are weighed. The results (in ounces) are given in the table. Do the data provide sufficient evidence to indicate that one (or more) of the temperatures tend(s) to produce larger weight increases than the other temperatures? Test using $\alpha = .10$.

Water Temperature			
38°F	42°F	46°F	50°F
22	15	14	17
24	21	28	18
16	26	21	13
18	16	19	20
19	25	24	21
	17	23	

15.60 Oil producers are interested in finding high-strength nickel alloys that are corrosion-resistant. Nickel alloys are especially susceptible to hydrogen embrittlement, a process that results when the alloy is cathodically charged in a sulfuric acid solution. To rate the performance of two incoloy alloys, 800 and 902, hydrogen-charged tensile specimens of each alloy were measured for the amount of ductility loss (recorded as a percentage reduction of area). The measurements for eight tensile specimens of each type are given in the table. Conduct a test to determine whether the probability distributions of ductility losses differ for the two nickel alloys. Use $\alpha = .05$.

Alloy 800		Alloy 902	
59.2	66.3	67.2	61.3
78.8	69.8	46.8	58.7
79.2	66.2	50.2	40.9
75.0	70.7	44.5	55.4

OPTIONAL SUPPLEMENTARY EXERCISES

[*Note:* These exercises require the use of a computer and computer simulation techniques.]

15.61 Throughout this chapter we have omitted the theoretical derivations of the null distributions of the various nonparametric test statistics. However, we can use computer simulation to derive approximate rejection regions for the tests. Consider the problem of finding the approximate sampling distribution of the Wilcoxon rank sum statistic for the case $n_1 = n_2 = 10$.

 a. Write a computer program that will randomly order the $n = n_1 + n_2 = 20$ ranks and compute the corresponding Wilcoxon rank sum T_1. This can be accomplished using a random number generator.
 b. Write a computer program that will repeat the instructions of part **a** $N = 1,000$ times.
 c. Construct a relative frequency distribution for the $N = 1,000$ computer-generated values of T_1 (refer to Chapter 2). This simulated distribution represents an approximation to the sampling distribution of T_1.
 d. Use the simulated sampling distribution to determine the value $T_{.05}$, such that $P(T_1 \leq T_{.05}) = .05$. This value represents the one-tailed critical value of the Wilcoxon rank sum test for $\alpha = .05$.

15.62 Follow the steps outlined in Optional Exercise 15.61 to find the approximate critical value (at $\alpha = .05$) of Spearman's test for rank correlation for the case $n = 10$. [*Hint:* In part **a** you will need to randomly order the $n = 10$ y ranks and $n = 10$ x ranks.]

COMPUTER LAB: Nonparametric Tests

Several nonparametric tests are available in the current versions of SAS and MINITAB. In SAS, you can perform the Wilcoxon rank sum test, the Kruskal–Wallis test, and Spearman's test for rank correlation. In MINITAB, all the nonparametric tests discussed in this chapter are available except the Theil test for slope. The commands for accessing these tests are given in the following programs. For illustration, we analyze the data sets of the examples used in this chapter.

SAS

Command
line

Wilcoxon Rank Sum Test, Example 15.2

```
1    DATA WP;
2    INPUT USER $ RATING @@;
3    CARDS;
4    WP 35 WP 50 WP 25 WP 55 WP 10 WP 30 WP 20
5    PG 45 PG 60 PG 40 PG 90 PG 65 PG 85 PG 95
6    PROC NPAR1WAY WILCOXON;
7    VAR RATING;
8    CLASS USER;
```

(*continued*)

Kruskal–Wallis Test, Example 15.6

```
 9    DATA TUBE;
10    INPUT BRAND $ LIFE @@;
11    CARDS;
12    A 36 A 48 A  5 A 67 A 53
13    B 49 B 33 B 60 B  2 B 55
14    C 71 C 31 C 140 C 59 C 42
15    PROC NPAR1WAY WILCOXON;
16    VAR LIFE;
17    CLASS BRAND;
```

Spearman's Rank Correlation Test, Section 15.7

```
18    DATA FIRM;
19    INPUT HOURS WAGES @@;
20    CARDS;
21    49 15.8 36 17.5 127 11.3 51 13.2 72 13.0
 .     .   .    .   .     .     .   .    .   .    .
 .     .   .    .   .     .     .   .    .   .    .
 .     .   .    .   .     .     .   .    .   .    .
25    63 13.8 79 12.7  43 15.1 57 24.2 82 13.9
26    PROC RANK OUT=RANKS;
27    VAR HOURS WAGES;
28    PROC CORR DATA=RANKS;
29    VAR HOURS WAGES;
```

COMMAND 6 The NPAR1WAY procedure with the WILCOXON option performs a Wilcoxon rank sum test for comparing two populations.

COMMAND 7 The quantitative variable to be analyzed is specified in the VAR statement.

COMMAND 8 The qualitative variable containing the levels corresponding to the two different populations (treatments) is specified in the CLASS statement.

COMMAND 15 The WILCOXON option of NPAR1WAY is also used to conduct the Kruskal–Wallis test for a completely randomized design.

COMMANDS 26–27 The RANK procedure is used to rank the values of the variables specified on the VAR statement. These ranks are stored in the temporary SAS data set (RANKS) specified after OUT= and have the same names as the original variables.

COMMANDS 28–29 The CORR procedure calculates the correlation between the variables specified on the VAR statement. Since the data set RANKS is used, the correlation coefficient will equal Spearman's rank correlation coefficient.

NOTE The output for these SAS programs is displayed in Figure 15.10.

FIGURE 15.10 ▶
SAS printouts for Computer Lab

N P A R 1 W A Y   P R O C E D U R E

Wilcoxon Scores (Rank Sums) for Variable RATING
Classified by Variable USER

USER	N	Sum of Scores	Expected Under H0	Std Dev Under H0	Mean Score
WP	7	32.0	52.5000000	7.82623792	4.5714286
PG	7	73.0	52.5000000	7.82623792	10.4285714

(continued)

FIGURE 15.10 ▶
SAS printouts for Computer Lab
(continued)

```
Wilcoxon 2-Sample Test (Normal Approximation)
(with Continuity Correction of .5)

S=  32.0000     Z= -2.55551    Prob > |Z| =    0.0106

T-Test approx. Significance =      0.0239

Kruskal-Wallis Test (Chi-Square Approximation)
CHISQ=  6.8612     DF= 1     Prob > CHISQ=     0.0088
```

```
            N P A R 1 W A Y   P R O C E D U R E

        Wilcoxon Scores (Rank Sums) for Variable LIFE
                Classified by Variable BRAND

                       Sum of     Expected      Std Dev        Mean
   BRAND        N      Scores     Under H0      Under H0       Score

   A            5      36.0         40.0      8.16496581    7.20000000
   B            5      35.0         40.0      8.16496581    7.00000000
   C            5      49.0         40.0      8.16496581    9.80000000


       Kruskal-Wallis Test (Chi-Square Approximation)
       CHISQ=  1.2200     DF= 2     Prob > CHISQ=     0.5434
```

```
                   CORRELATION ANALYSIS

        2 'VAR' Variables:  HOURS    WAGES


Pearson Correlation Coefficients / Prob > |R| under Ho: Rho=0 / N = 15

                                    HOURS          WAGES

   HOURS                          1.00000        -0.85357
   VALUE OF HOURS REPLACED BY RANK  0.0            0.0001

   WAGES                         -0.85357         1.00000
   VALUE OF WAGES REPLACED BY RANK  0.0001         0.0
```

MINITAB

Command
line

Sign Test, Example 15.1

```
1      SET C1
2      41 33 43 52 46
3      37 44 49 53 30
4      NAME C1='PERCENT'
5      STEST MEDIAN=40 DATA IN C1;
6         ALTERNATIVE=+1.
```

(continued)

Wilcoxon Rank Sum Test, Example 15.2

```
 7    SET WP IN C1
 8    35 50 25 55 10 30 20
 9    SET PG IN C2
10    45 60 40 90 65 85 95
11    NAME C1='WPRATING' C2='PGRATING'
12    MANN-WHITNEY C1 C2
```

Wilcoxon Signed Ranks Test, Example 15.5

```
13    READ C1 C2 C3
14     1 6 4
15     2 8 5
 .     . . .
 .     . . .
 .     . . .
23    10 8 2
24    SUBTRACT C3 FROM C2, PUT IN C4
25    NAME C1='JUDGE' C2='A' C3='B' C4='AMINUSB'
26    WTEST C4
```

Kruskal–Wallis Test, Example 15.6

```
27    READ C1 C2
28    1 36
29    1 48
 .    . .
 .    . .
 .    . .
42    3 42
43    NAME C1='BRAND' C2='LIFE'
44    KRUSKAL-WALLIS C2 C1
```

Friedman's Test, Example 15.7

```
45    READ C1 C2 C3
46     1  1 21
47     2  1 29
 .     .  . .
 .     .  . .
 .     .  . .
75    10  3  2
76    NAME C1='METAL' C2='SEALER' C3='CORROS'
77    FRIEDMAN C3 C2 C1
```

Spearman's Rank Correlation Test, Section 15.7

```
78    READ C1 C2
79    49 15.8
80    36 17.5
 .     .   .
 .     .   .
 .     .   .
93    82 13.9
94    NAME C1='HOURS' C2='WAGES'
95    RANK DATA IN C1, PUT IN C3
96    RANK DATA IN C2, PUT IN C4
97    NAME C3='RANKHOUR' C4='RANKWAGE'
98    CORRELATION C3 C4
```

COMMAND 5   The STEST command performs a sign test on the data in the specified column. Optionally, the value of the hypothesized median (e.g., 40) is specified before the column. (If the median is not specified, the default is 0.)

COMMAND 6   The MINITAB default is to conduct a two-tailed test. If a one-tailed test is desired, specify either $+1$ (upper-tailed test) or -1 (lower-tailed test) in the ALTERNATIVE subcommand.

COMMAND 12   The MANN-WHITNEY command performs a two-sample Wilcoxon rank sum test on the data specified in the two columns. [*Note:*   Use the ALTERNATIVE subcommand to perform a one-tailed test.]

COMMAND 24   To perform a Wilcoxon signed ranks test, first compute the differences between the two samples.

COMMAND 26   The WTEST command performs a Wilcoxon signed ranks test on the differences in the specified column. [*Note:*   Use the ALTERNATIVE subcommand to perform a one-tailed test.]

COMMAND 44   The KRUSKAL-WALLIS command performs a Kruskal–Wallis test for a completely randomized design. The column containing the response variable (C2) is specified first, followed by the column containing the levels of the treatments (C1).

COMMAND 77   The FRIEDMAN command performs a Friedman test for a randomized block design. The column containing the response variable (C3) is specified first, followed by the treatment column (C2) and the block column (C1).

COMMANDS 95–96   The RANK command is used to rank the data in the specified columns. The second column listed will contain the ranks.

COMMAND 98   The CORRELATION command computes the correlation between the variables (columns) specified. When the ranks are specified, the result is Spearman's rank correlation coefficient.

NOTE   The output for these MINITAB programs is displayed in Figure 15.11.

FIGURE 15.11 ▶
MINITAB printouts for
Computer Lab

```
SIGN TEST OF MEDIAN = 40.00 VERSUS  G.T.   40.00

              N  BELOW  EQUAL  ABOVE   P-VALUE      MEDIAN
PERCENT      10    3      0      7     0.1719       43.50
```

```
Mann-Whitney Confidence Interval and Test

WPRating   N =   7     Median =       30.00
PGRating   N =   7     Median =       65.00
Point estimate for ETA1-ETA2 is      -35.00
95.9 pct c.i. for ETA1-ETA2 is (-65.01,-10.00)
W = 32.0
Test of ETA1 = ETA2  vs.  ETA1 n.e. ETA2 is significant at 0.0106
```

```
TEST OF MEDIAN = 0.000000 VERSUS MEDIAN N.E. 0.000000

                  N FOR   WILCOXON              ESTIMATED
            N     TEST    STATISTIC   P-VALUE    MEDIAN
AminusB    10      10        46.0      0.067      2.000
```

```
LEVEL     NOBS    MEDIAN   AVE. RANK   Z VALUE
    1       5     48.00       7.2       -0.49
    2       5     49.00       7.0       -0.61
    3       5     59.00       9.8        1.10
OVERALL    15                 8.0

H = 1.22   d.f. = 2   p = 0.544
```

(continued)

```
Friedman test of Corros by Sealer blocked by Metal

S = 7.85  d.f. = 2  p = 0.020
S = 8.05  d.f. = 2  p = 0.018 (adjusted for ties)

                     Est.    Sum of
     Sealer    N    Median    RANKS
         1    10    16.583     19.5
         2    10    19.417     26.5
         3    10    12.750     14.0

Grand median  =    16.250
```

```
Correlation of RankHour and RankWage = -0.854
```

References

Friedman, M. "The Use of Ranks to Avoid the Assumption of Normality Implicit in the Analysis of Variance." *Journal of the American Statistical Association*, Vol. 32, 1937.

Gibbons, J. D. *Nonparametric Statistical Inference*. New York: McGraw-Hill, 1971.

Hollander, M., and Wolfe, D. A. *Nonparametric Statistical Methods*. New York: Wiley, 1973.

Kruskal, W. H., and Wallis, W. A. "Use of Ranks in One-Criterion Variance Analysis." *Journal of the American Statistical Association*, Vol. 47, 1952.

Lehmann, E. L. *Nonparametrics: Statistical Methods Based on Ranks*. San Francisco: Holden-Day, 1975.

Siegel, S. *Nonparametric Statistics for the Behavioral Sciences*. New York: McGraw-Hill, 1956.

Wilcoxon, F., and Wilcox, R. A. "Some Rapid Approximate Statistical Procedures." The American Cyanamid Co., 1964.

CHAPTER SIXTEEN

Statistical Process and Quality Control

Objective

To present some statistical procedures for monitoring the quality of a manufactured product and for controlling the quality of products shipped to consumers

Contents

16.1 Total Quality Management

When we think of product quality, we think of a set of characteristics that we expect a product to possess. We want light bulbs to have a long life, paper towels to be strong and absorbent, and a quarter-pound hamburger to weigh at least one-quarter pound. But producing a quality product is not an easy job. Variations in the characteristics of raw materials and workmanship tend to produce variations in product quality. The length of life of a light bulb produced in an automated production line may differ markedly from the length of life of a bulb produced seconds later. Similarly, the strength of paper produced by a paper machine may vary from one point in time to another because of variations in the characteristics of the pulp fed into the machine. Consequently, it is vital that manufacturers monitor the quality of the product they produce.

Today, U.S. business leaders are promoting the concept of **total quality management (TQM)**. As shown in Figure 16.1, TQM has three key components: (1) concepts, (2) systems, and (3) tools. The concepts component of TQM includes a number of ideas that surround the total quality movement. These include *customer satisfaction, all work is a process, speak with data*, and *upstream management*. (Speaking with data is a particularly relevant concept for this text, since it involves measuring and monitoring process variables.)

FIGURE 16.1 ▶
TQM components

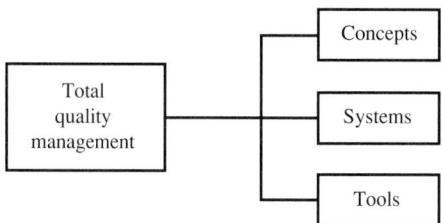

The second component, systems, involves the notion of systems management. Systems such as *general management, market creation, product creation*, and *product supply* must be responsibly managed by the company's owners.

Finally, several tools are avaiable to implement a TQM program. These include *flowcharts, cause-and-effect diagrams*, and *statistical process control charts*.

All three components of Figure 16.1 are necessary to successfully implement a TQM philosophy at a company. In this chapter, we focus on the statistical process control element of TQM. **Statistical process control (SPC)** allows engineers to understand and monitor process variation through **control charts**.

16.2 Variable Control Charts

Although TQM in U.S. business is a recent trend, the idea of a control chart to monitor process data was developed in 1924 by W. A. Shewhart.

Control charts are constructed by plotting a product's quality variable over time in a sequence plot, as shown in Figure 16.2. The variable plotted can be either a quantitative characteristic (e.g., diameter of an eyescrew) or a qualitative attribute (e.g., defective or nondefective light bulb) of a manufactured product. The power of this simple chart lies in its ability to separate two types of variation in a product quality characteristic: (1) variation due to **assignable causes** and (2) **random variation**.

Definition 16.1
....

A **control chart for a quality variable** is obtained by plotting the variable's measurements periodically over time.

FIGURE 16.2 ▶

Plots of a quality characteristic that suggest variation due to assignable causes

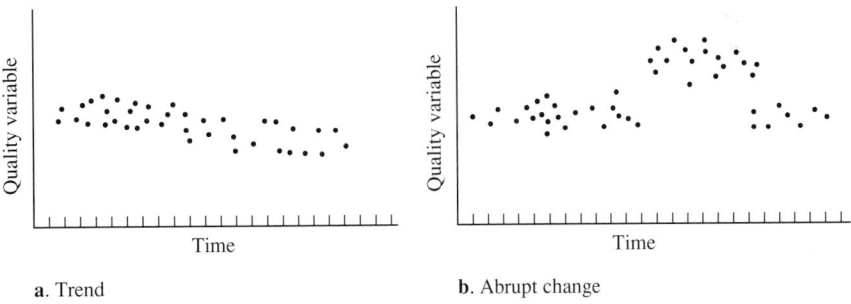

a. Trend   **b**. Abrupt change

Variations due to assignable causes are produced by such things as the wear in a metallic cutting machine, the wear in an abrasive wheel, changes in the humidity and temperature in the production area, worker fatigue, and so on. The effects of wear in cutting edges, abrasive surfaces, or changes in the environment are usually evidenced by gradual trends in a characteristic over time (see Figure 16.2a). In contrast, the raw material will often produce an abrupt change in the level of a quality characteristic (see Figure 16.2b). Quality control and production engineers attempt to identify trends or abrupt changes in a quality characteristic when they occur and to modify the process to reduce or eliminate this type of variation.

Even when variation due to assignable causes is accounted for, measurements taken on a product quality characteristic tend to vary in a random manner from one point in time to another. This second category of variation—random (or chance) variation—is caused by minute and random changes in raw materials, worker behavior, and so on. Since some stable system of chance causes is inherent in any production process, this type of variation is accepted as the normal variation of the process. When the quality characteristics of a product are subject only to random variation, the process is said to be **in control**.

> ### Definition 16.2
>
> The variation in a variable that measures a product quality characteristic is due to either an **assignable cause** or **random (chance) variation**.

> ### Definition 16.3
>
> A production process is said to be **in control** when the quality characteristics of a product are subject only to random variation.

To illustrate these ideas, consider a manufacturing process that produces shafts for an electrical motor. A quality control inspector might select one shaft every 10 minutes and measure its diameter. These measurements, plotted against time, provide visual evidence of the ability of the process to produce shafts with diameters that are subject only to random variation. For example, the diameters of 10 shafts might appear as shown in Figure 16.3. Although the diameters of these 10 shafts vary from one point in time to another, all fall within a set of *control limits* established by the manufacturer. The process appears to be "in control."

FIGURE 16.3 ▶

A plot of the diameters of 10 motor shafts

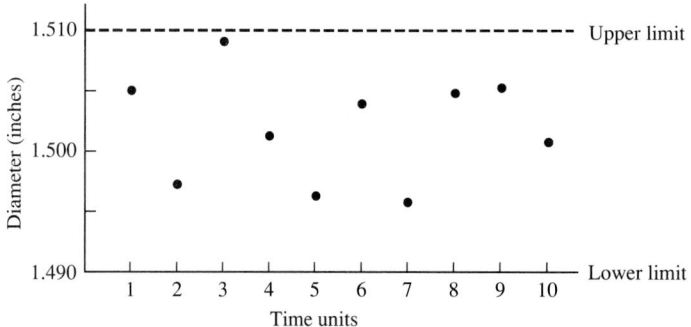

How are these **control limits** established? A widely used (and successful) technique is to monitor the process during a period when it is known to be in control and calculate the mean and standard deviation of the sample quality measurements. Then, for future measurements, apply the *z*-score rule for detecting outliers (Section 2.6). We know that it is highly unlikely that a sample measurement will fall more than 3 standard deviations away from the mean. Consequently, if a quality measurement falls below $\bar{x} - 3s$ or above $\bar{x} + 3s$, we say the process is "out of control" and modifications in the production process may be necessary.

EXAMPLE 16.1

A corporation that manufactures field rifles for the Department of Defense operates a production line that turns out finished firing pins. To monitor the process, an inspector randomly selects a firing pin from the production line every 30 minutes and measures its length (in inches). The lengths for a sample of 20 firing pins obtained in this manner are provided in Table 16.1. Construct a control chart for the length of the firing pins. Is the process out of control?

TABLE 16.1   Lengths of Firing Pins, Example 16.1

Pin	Length	Pin	Length
1	1.00	11	1.01
2	.99	12	.99
3	.98	13	.98
4	1.01	14	.99
5	1.01	15	.87
6	.99	16	1.01
7	1.06	17	.99
8	.99	18	.99
9	.99	19	.97
10	1.03	20	.99

Solution

The first step in constructing the control chart is to calculate the mean and standard deviation of the sample firing pin lengths. These values, obtained using a computer, are shown in the printout, Figure 16.4. You can see that the sample mean is $\bar{x} = .992$ and the sample standard deviation is $s = .035$.

FIGURE 16.4 ▶
SAS printout showing descriptive statistics for firing pin lengths

```
Analysis Variable : LENGTH

 N Obs   N      Minimum       Maximum          Mean       Std Dev
 -------------------------------------------------------------------
   20   20    0.8700000     1.0600000     0.9920000     0.0348833
 -------------------------------------------------------------------
```

Next, we plot the 20 sample measurements in time order, as shown in Figure 16.5 on page 986. Typically, three horizontal lines are drawn on the control chart. For variable control charts, the **center line** is the sample mean, $\bar{x}$. The center line estimates the mean value μ of the process. For this example, we estimate that the mean length of firing pins is .992 inch.

The two lines located above and below the center line on Figure 16.5 establish the **upper control limit (UCL)** and the **lower control limit (LCL)**, between which we expect the measurements to fall if the process is in control. For variable control charts, $LCL = \bar{x} - 3s$ and $UCL = \bar{x} + 3s$. Consequently, we have

$$LCL = .992 - 3(.035) = .887 \quad \text{and} \quad UCL = .992 + 3(.035) = 1.097$$

Note that the length measurement of firing pin #15 falls below the LCL. Thus, the process is "out of control," indicating possible trouble in the production line. In this situation, process engineers are usually assigned to determine the cause of the unusually small (or large) measurement.

FIGURE 16.5 ▶

Control chart for firing pin lengths, Example 16.1

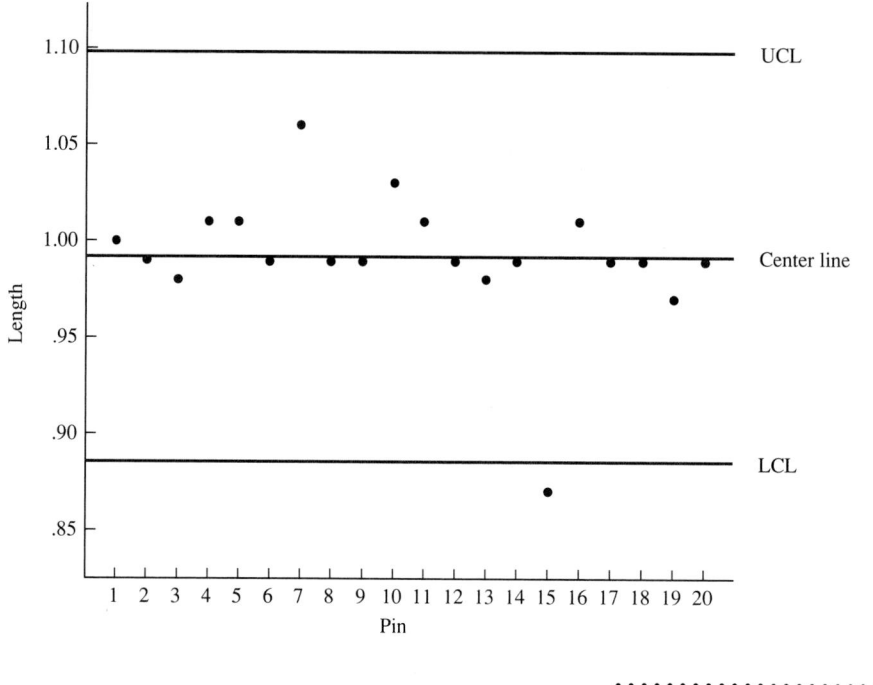

In concluding our discussion of an individual variable control chart (or, as it is often called, an **individuals control chart**), it is important to note that the chart describes the process as it is, not the way we want it to be. The process mean and control limits may differ markedly from the specifications set by the manufacturer of the product. For example, although a manufacturer may want to produce electrical motor shafts with a diameter of 1.5 inches, the actual process mean will usually differ from 1.5, at least by some small amount. Also, the control limits obtained from the control chart are appropriate only for analyzing past data—that is, the data that were used in their calculation. Thus, they may require modification before they are applied to future production data. For example, in cases where the process is found to be out of control (Example 16.1), the control limits and center line would be modified by recalculating their values using only the sample measurements that fell within the original control limits. If the cause of the problem has been corrected, these new values serve as control limits for future data.

> ### Definition 16.4
>
> The **center line** for a variable control chart is the mean of the sample measurements, $\bar{x}$.

> ### Definition 16.5
>
> The **lower control limit (LCL)** and **upper control limit (UCL)** for a variable control chart are calculated as follows:
>
> $$\text{LCL} = \bar{x} - 3s \qquad \text{UCL} = \bar{x} + 3s$$
>
> where s is the standard deviation of the sample measurements.

> ### Warning
>
> The control limits obtained from a control chart are appropriate only for analyzing past data—that is, the data that were used in their calculation. They can be applied to future data only when the process is in control and/or the control limits are modified.

In this section, we presented control charts for a single quality variable (e.g., firing pin length). Control charts can also be constructed for process means, process variation, percent defectives, and number of defects per item. We present these types of control charts in the sections that follow.

EXERCISES

16.1   Suppose the process for manufacturing electrical shafts is in control. At the end of each hour, for a period of 20 hours, the manufacturer randomly selects one shaft and measures the diameter. The measurements (in inches) for the 20 samples are recorded on page 988. Construct and interpret a control chart for shaft diameter.

Sample Number	Diameter, inches	Sample Number	Diameter, inches
1	1.505	11	1.491
2	1.496	12	1.486
3	1.516	13	1.510
4	1.507	14	1.495
5	1.502	15	1.504
6	1.502	16	1.499
7	1.489	17	1.501
8	1.485	18	1.497
9	1.503	19	1.503
10	1.485	20	1.494

16.2 Molded-rubber expansion joints, used in heating and air conditioning systems, are designed to have internal diameters of 5 inches. To monitor the manufacturing process, one joint was randomly selected each hour from the production line and its diameter (in inches) measured, for a period of 12 hours, as shown in the table. The data will be used to construct a variable control chart.

Hour	Molded-Rubber Expansion Joint Diameters
1	5.08
2	4.88
3	4.99
4	5.04
5	5.00
6	4.83
7	5.02
8	4.91
9	5.06
10	4.92
11	5.01
12	4.92

a. Locate the center line for the variable control chart.
b. Locate upper and lower control limits.
c. Does the process appear to be in control?

16.3 Each month, the quality control engineer at a bottle manufacturing company randomly selects one finished bottle from the production process at 20 points in time (days) and records the weight of each bottle (in ounces). The data for last month's inspection are provided in the table.

Day	Bottle Weight	Day	Bottle Weight
1	5.6	11	6.2
2	5.7	12	5.9
3	6.1	13	5.2
4	6.3	14	6.0
5	5.2	15	6.3
6	6.0	16	5.8
7	5.8	17	6.1

(continued)

Day	Bottle Weight	Day	Bottle Weight
8	5.8	18	6.2
9	6.4	19	5.3
10	6.0	20	6.0

a. Construct a variable control chart for the weights of the finished bottles.

b. Does the process appear to be in control for this particular month?

16.4 A rheostat knob, produced by plastic molding, contains a metal insert. The fit of this knob into its assembly is determined by the distance from the back of the knob to the far side of a pin hole. To monitor the molding operation, one knob from each hour's production was randomly sampled and the dimension measured on each. The accompanying table gives the distance measurements (in inches) for the first 27 hours the process was in operation.

Hour	Distance Measurements	Hour	Distance Measurements
1	.140	15	.144
2	.138	16	.140
3	.139	17	.137
4	.143	18	.137
5	.142	19	.142
6	.136	20	.136
7	.142	21	.142
8	.143	22	.139
9	.141	23	.140
10	.142	24	.134
11	.137	25	.138
12	.137	26	.140
13	.142	27	.145
14	.137		

a. Construct a variable control chart for the process.

b. Locate the center line, upper control limit, and lower control limit on the chart.

c. Does the process appear to be in control?

16.3 Control Chart for Means: x̄-Chart

A control chart constructed to monitor a quantitative quality characteristic is usually based on random samples of several units of the product rather than on the characteristics of individual industrial units as shown in Figure 16.3. For example, the manufacturer of electrical shafts in Section 16.2 might select a sample of five shafts at the end of each hour. A plot showing the mean diameters of the samples, one mean corresponding to each point in time, is called a **control chart for means** or an **x̄-chart**. *

---

*To be consistent with the symbols used in quality control literature, we will use x (rather than y) to denote a quantitative quality characteristic variable.

In practice, control charts are constructed after a process has been adjusted to correct for assignable causes of variation and the process is deemed to be in control. When the process is in control, an $\bar{x}$-chart would show only random variation in the sample mean over time. Theoretically, $\bar{x}$ should vary about the process mean, $E(x) = \mu$, and fall within the limits $\mu \pm 3\sigma_{\bar{x}}$ or $\mu \pm 3\sigma/\sqrt{n}$ with a high probability. A control chart constructed for the means of samples of $n = 5$ motor shafts taken each hour might appear as shown in Figure 16.6.

An $\bar{x}$-chart, such as that shown in Figure 16.6, contains three horizontal lines. The **center line** establishes the mean value μ of the process. Although this value is usually unknown, it can be estimated by averaging a large number (for example, 20) of sample means obtained when the process is in control. For example, if we average the values of k sample means, then

$$\text{Center line} = \bar{\bar{x}} = \frac{\sum_{i=1}^{k} \bar{x}_i}{k}$$

FIGURE 16.6 ▶
$\bar{x}$-chart for samples of $n = 5$ shaft diameters

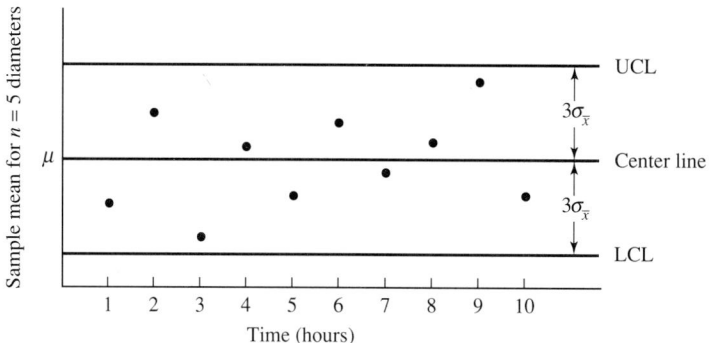

The two lines located above and below the center line establish the **upper control limit (UCL)** and the **lower control limit (LCL)**, between which we would expect the sample means to fall if the process is in control. They are located a distance of $3\sigma_{\bar{x}} = 3\sigma/\sqrt{n}$ above and below the center line.

The process standard deviation σ is usually unknown, but it can be estimated from a large sample of data collected while the process is in control. Prior to the advent of computers, it was common to estimate σ by first computing the sample range R, the difference between the largest and smallest sample measurements. The process standard deviation σ was then estimated by dividing the average $\bar{R}$ of k sample ranges by a constant d_2, the value of which depended on the sample size n:

$$\hat{\sigma} = \frac{\bar{R}}{d_2} = \frac{\sum_{i=1}^{k} R_i/k}{d_2}$$

Since the control limits are located a distance of $3\sigma_{\bar{x}} = 3\sigma/\sqrt{n}$ above and below the center line, this distance was estimated to be

$$3\hat{\sigma}_{\bar{x}} = \frac{3(\bar{R}/d_2)}{\sqrt{n}} = \frac{3}{d_2\sqrt{n}}\bar{R} = A_2\bar{R}$$

where

$$A_2 = \frac{3}{d_2\sqrt{n}}$$

Values of A_2 and d_2 for sample sizes $n = 2$ to $n = 25$ are given in Table 19 of Appendix II.

Location of Center Line and Control Limits for an $\bar{x}$-Chart

$$\text{Center line:} \quad \bar{\bar{x}} = \frac{\sum\limits_{i=1}^{k} \bar{x}_i}{k}$$

$$\text{UCL:} \quad \bar{\bar{x}} + A_2\bar{R}$$
$$\text{LCL:} \quad \bar{\bar{x}} - A_2\bar{R}$$

where

k = Number of samples, each of size n

$\bar{x}_i$ = Sample mean for the ith sample

R_i = Range of the ith sample

$$\bar{R} = \frac{\sum\limits_{i=1}^{k} R_i}{k}$$

and A_2 is given in Table 19 of Appendix II.

[Note: For large samples (say, $n > 15$) collected from a process with no time trend, the upper and lower control limits may be computed as follows:

$$\text{UCL:} \quad \bar{\bar{x}} + 3s/\sqrt{n} \qquad \text{LCL:} \quad \bar{\bar{x}} - 3s/\sqrt{n}$$

where s is the standard deviation of all nk sample measurements.]

Today, the sample measurements for quality control processes can be entered into a computer that is programmed to compute the means and standard deviations of the individual samples, as well as the means and standard deviations of the data contained in any set of k samples. When no time trend exists (see Section 16.5) and the samples are large, the best estimate of σ is then the standard deviation s of the data contained in the k sets of data.* The computer calculates $\bar{\bar{x}}$ and s and provides a printout of the control chart. However, the simplicity of calculating a sample range is not to be overlooked. Time, energy, and money often can be saved by reporting the sample ranges rather than s. Thus, in practice, $\bar{x}$-charts based on $\bar{R}$ remain the standard.

EXAMPLE 16.2

Suppose the process for manufacturing electrical shafts is in control. At the end of each hour, for a period of 20 hours, the manufacturer selected a random sample of four shafts and measured the diameter of each. The measurements (in inches) for the 20 samples are recorded in Table 16.2. Construct a control chart for the sample means and interpret the results.

Solution

The first step in constructing an $\bar{x}$-chart is to compute the sample mean, $\bar{x}$, and range, R, for each of the 20 samples. These values are shown in the last two columns of Table 16.2.

Next, we calculate $\bar{\bar{x}}$, the average of the 20 sample means, and $\bar{R}$, the average of the 20 sample ranges:

$$\bar{\bar{x}} = \frac{\sum_{i=1}^{20} \bar{x}_i}{20} = \frac{(1.4983 + 1.5055 + 1.4990 + \cdots + 1.5055)}{20}$$

$$= 1.50045$$

$$\bar{R} = \frac{\sum_{i=1}^{20} \bar{R}_i}{20} = \frac{(.017 + .017 + .031 + \cdots + .025)}{20}$$

The value of $\bar{\bar{x}} = 1.50045$ locates the center line on the control chart. To find upper and lower control limits, we need the value of the control limit factor A_2, found in Table 19 of Appendix II. For $n = 4$ measurements in each sample, $A_2 = .729$. Then

$$\text{UCL} = \bar{\bar{x}} + A_2\bar{R} = 1.50045 + (.729)(.01985)$$
$$= 1.51492$$
$$\text{LCL} = \bar{\bar{x}} - A_2\bar{R} = 1.50045 - (.729)(.01985)$$
$$= 1.48598$$

Using these limits, we construct the control chart for the sample means shown in Figure 16.7. Note that all 20 sample means fall within the control limits.

---

*Grant and Leavenworth (1980) suggest using s to estimate σ when the sample size n is greater than 15. For smaller samples, $\bar{R}/d_2$ will usually provide a better estimate.

TABLE 16.2   Samples of $n = 4$ Shaft Diameters, Example 16.2

Sample Number	Sample Measurements, inches				Sample Mean $\bar{x}$	Range R
1	1.505	1.499	1.501	1.488	1.4983	.017
2	1.496	1.513	1.512	1.501	1.5055	.017
3	1.516	1.485	1.492	1.503	1.4990	.031
4	1.507	1.492	1.511	1.491	1.5003	.020
5	1.502	1.491	1.501	1.502	1.4990	.011
6	1.502	1.488	1.506	1.483	1.4948	.023
7	1.489	1.512	1.496	1.501	1.4995	.023
8	1.485	1.518	1.494	1.513	1.5025	.033
9	1.503	1.495	1.503	1.496	1.4993	.008
10	1.485	1.519	1.503	1.507	1.5035	.034
11	1.491	1.516	1.497	1.493	1.4993	.025
12	1.486	1.505	1.487	1.492	1.4925	.019
13	1.510	1.502	1.515	1.499	1.5065	.016
14	1.495	1.485	1.493	1.503	1.4940	.018
15	1.504	1.499	1.504	1.500	1.5018	.005
16	1.499	1.503	1.508	1.497	1.5018	.011
17	1.501	1.493	1.509	1.491	1.4985	.018
18	1.497	1.510	1.496	1.500	1.5008	.014
19	1.503	1.526	1.497	1.500	1.5065	.029
20	1.494	1.501	1.508	1.519	1.5055	.025

FIGURE 16.7 ▶
$\bar{x}$-chart for shaft diameters, Example 16.2

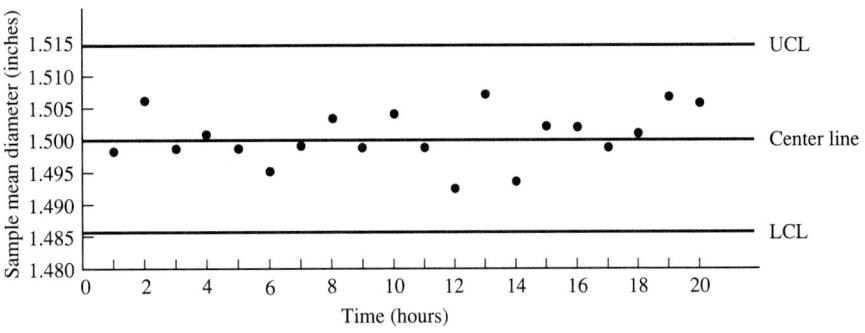

A computer-generated (MINITAB) control chart for the sample means is shown in Figure 16.8 on page 994. The upper and lower control limits in the MINITAB printout differ slightly from those in Figure 16.7, because the computer uses the standard deviation s of all 80 measurements to establish these limits.

FIGURE 16.8 ▶
Computer-generated $\bar{x}$-chart for
Example 16.2

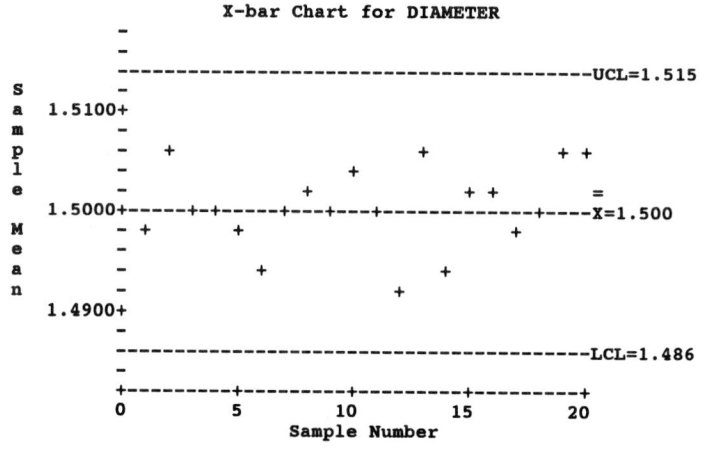

The purpose of the $\bar{x}$-chart is to detect departures from process control. If the process is in control, the probability that a sample mean will fall within the control limits is very high. This result is due to the Central Limit Theorem, which guarantees that the sampling distribution of $\bar{x}$ will be approximately normal for large samples. Consequently, the probability that $\bar{x}$ will fall within the control limits, i.e., $\pm 3\hat{\sigma}_{\bar{x}}$, is approximately .997. Therefore, a sample mean falling outside the control limits is taken as an indication of possible trouble in the production process. When this occurs, we say with a high degree of confidence that the process is out of control, and process engineers are usually assigned to determine the cause of the unusually large (or small) value of $\bar{x}$.

On the other hand, when all the sample means fall within the control limits (as in Figure 16.7) we say that the process is in control. However, we do not have the same degree of confidence in this statement as with the "out of control" conclusion above. In one sense, we are using the control chart to test the null hypothesis H_0: Process in control (i.e., no assignable causes of variation are present). As you recall from Chapter 9, we must be careful not to accept H_0 since the probability of a Type II error is unknown. In practice, when quality control engineers say "the process is in control," they really mean that "it pays to act as if no assignable causes of variation are present." In this situation, it is better to leave the process alone than to spend a great deal of time and money looking for trouble that may not exist.

Before concluding our discussion of the $\bar{x}$-chart, two important points must be made. First, in practice, the $\bar{x}$-chart is typically used in conjunction with a chart that monitors the variation of the process, called an R-chart. In fact, since the sample range (or standard deviation) is used the construct the $\bar{x}$-chart, it is essential to examine an R-chart first to be sure that the process variation is stable. The R-chart is the topic of the next section.

> ### Interpreting an x̄-Chart
>
> *Process "out of control":*   One or more of the sample means fall outside the control limits.* This indicates possible trouble in the production process and efforts should be made to determine the cause of the unusually large (or small) values of $\bar{x}$.
>
> *Process "in control":*   All sample means fall within the control limits. Although assignable causes of variation may be present, it is better to leave the process alone than to look for trouble that may not exist.

The second point to be made about $\bar{x}$-charts, and control charts in general, is the importance of the sampling plan. Ideally, we want to choose samples of items over time so that we maximize the chance of detecting process change, if it exists. To do this, we choose **rational subgroups** (samples) of items so that the change in the process mean (if it exists) occurs *between* samples, *not within* samples (i.e., not during the period that the sample is drawn). The next example illustrates this point.

> ### Definition 16.6
>
> **Rational subgroups** are samples of items collected that maximize the chance that (1) quality measurements within each sample are similar and (2) quality measurements between samples differ.

EXAMPLE 16.3

Refer to the discussion of the process for manufacturing electrical motor shafts in Example 16.2. Suppose that the operations manager suspects that workers on the night shift are producing shafts with larger mean diameters than workers on the morning and afternoon shifts. The manager wants to use an $\bar{x}$-chart to determine whether the process mean has changed. Suggest a sampling plan for the manager that follows rational subgrouping strategy. That is, how should the samples of four shafts be selected so that the chance of detecting the shift in means is maximized?

Solution

Obviously, the control chart should be constructed using samples of shafts that are drawn within each shift. For example, the manager could sample four shafts each

---

*In addition to this "one point beyond the control limits" rule, there are several other "pattern analysis" rules that help the analyst determine whether the process is out of control. For example, the process is also out of control if four of five consecutive points are beyond $\mu + 2\sigma_{\bar{x}}$ or $\mu - 2\sigma_{\bar{x}}$. Consult the references for a detailed discussion of these other rules of thumb.

hour for 24 consecutive hours. Then the first eight samples will come from the morning shift, the next eight from the afternoon shift, and the last eight from the night shift. In this way, none of the samples would span shifts. (This is in contrast to a sample of, say, two shafts from the afternoon shift, and two from the night shift.) These 24 samples represent rational subgroups of shafts designed to maximize the chance of detecting the change in mean shaft diameters attributable to the night shift workers.

EXERCISES

16.5   A corporation that manufactures field rifles for the Department of Defense operates a production line that turns out finished firing pins. To monitor the process, an inspector randomly selects five firing pins from the production line, measures their lengths (in inches), and repeats this process at 30-minute intervals over a 5-hour period.

a. Use the data for the 10 time periods listed in the table to calculate the center line for an $\bar{x}$-chart.

30-Minute Interval	Firing Pin Lengths				
1	1.05	1.03	.99	1.00	1.03
2	.93	.96	1.01	.98	.97
3	1.02	.99	.99	1.00	.98
4	.98	1.01	1.02	.99	.97
5	1.02	.99	1.04	1.07	.98
6	1.05	.98	.96	.91	1.02
7	.92	.95	1.00	.99	1.01
8	1.06	.98	.98	1.04	1.00
9	.97	.99	.99	.98	1.01
10	1.00	.96	1.02	1.03	.99

b. Compute upper and lower control limits.
c. Calculate and plot the 10 sample means to form an $\bar{x}$-chart for the firing pin lengths.
d. Suppose the Defense Department's specification for the firing pins is that they be 1.00 inch plus or minus .08 inch in length. Does the manufacturing process appear to be in control?

16.6   Refer to the production of molded-rubber expansion joints used in heating and air conditioning systems, Exercise 16.2. To monitor the mean of the manufacturing process, eight joints (rather than one joint) were randomly selected from the production line and their diameters (in inches) measured each hour, for a period of 12 hours, as shown in the table. The data for the 12 samples will be used to construct an $\bar{x}$-chart.

a. Locate the center line for the $\bar{x}$-chart.
b. Locate upper and lower control limits.
c. Calculate and plot the 12 sample means to produce an $\bar{x}$-chart for the joint diameters. Does the process appear to be in control?

Hour   *Molded-Rubber Expansion Joint Diameters*

Hour								
1	5.08	5.01	4.99	4.93	4.98	5.00	5.04	4.97
2	4.88	5.10	4.93	5.02	5.06	4.99	4.92	4.91
3	4.99	5.00	5.02	5.01	5.03	4.92	4.97	5.01
4	5.04	4.96	5.01	5.00	5.00	4.98	4.91	4.96
5	5.00	4.93	4.94	5.02	5.01	4.97	5.08	5.11
6	4.83	4.92	4.96	4.91	5.01	5.03	4.93	5.00
7	5.02	5.01	4.96	4.98	5.00	5.07	4.94	5.01
8	4.91	5.00	4.97	5.03	5.02	4.99	4.98	4.99
9	5.06	5.04	4.99	5.02	4.97	5.00	5.01	5.01
10	4.92	4.98	5.01	5.01	4.97	5.00	5.02	4.93
11	5.01	5.00	5.02	4.98	4.99	5.00	5.01	5.01
12	4.92	5.12	5.06	4.93	4.98	5.02	5.04	4.97

16.7 Refer to the bottle manufacturing process, Exercise 16.3. To monitor the process mean, three finished bottles are sampled from the production process at 20 points in time (days). The data (weight, in ounces) for last month's inspection are provided in the table.

Day	Bottle Weights			Day	Bottle Weights		
1	5.6	5.8	5.8	11	6.2	5.6	5.8
2	5.7	6.3	6.0	12	5.9	5.7	5.9
3	6.1	5.3	6.0	13	5.2	5.5	5.7
4	6.3	5.8	5.9	14	6.0	6.1	6.0
5	5.2	5.9	6.3	15	6.3	5.7	5.9
6	6.0	6.7	5.2	16	5.8	6.2	6.1
7	5.8	5.7	6.1	17	6.1	6.4	6.6
8	5.8	6.0	6.2	18	6.2	5.7	5.7
9	6.4	5.6	5.9	19	5.3	5.5	5.4
10	6.0	5.7	6.1	20	6.0	6.1	6.0

a. Construct an x̄-chart for the weights of the finished bottles.
b. Does the process appear to be in control for this particular month?

16.8 One of the operations in a plant consists of thread grinding a fitting for an aircraft hydraulic system. To monitor the process, a production supervisor randomly sampled five fittings for each hour, for a period of 20 hours, and measured the pitch diameters of the threads. The measurements, expressed in units of .0001 inch in excess of .4000 inch, are shown in the table on page 998. (For example, the value 36 represents .4036 inch.)

a. Construct an x̄-chart for the process.
b. Locate the center line, upper control limit, and lower control limit on the x̄-chart.
c. Does the process appear to be in control?
d. Eliminate the points that fall outside the control limits and recalculate their values. Would you recommend using these modified control limits for future data?

Hour	Pitch Diameters of Threads					Hour	Pitch Diameters of Threads				
1	36	35	34	33	32	11	34	38	35	34	38
2	31	31	34	32	30	12	36	38	39	39	40
3	30	30	32	30	32	13	36	40	35	26	33
4	32	33	33	32	35	14	36	35	37	34	33
5	32	34	37	37	35	15	30	37	33	34	35
6	32	32	31	33	33	16	28	31	33	33	33
7	33	33	36	32	31	17	33	30	34	33	35
8	23	33	36	35	36	18	27	28	29	27	30
9	43	36	35	24	31	19	35	36	29	27	32
10	36	35	36	41	41	20	33	35	35	39	36

Source: Grant, E. L., and Leavenworth, R. S. *Statistical Quality Control*, 5th ed. New York: McGraw-Hill, 1980 (Table 1-1). Reprinted with permission.

16.9   Refer to the manufacture of a rheostat knob, Exercise 16.4. To monitor the process mean, five knobs from each hour's production were randomly sampled and the distance from the back of the knob to the far side of a pin hole as measured on each. The measurements (in inches) for the first 27 hours the process was in operation are shown in the table.

Hour	Distance Measurements	Hour	Distance Measurements
1	.140, .143, .137, .134, .135	15	.144, .142, .143, .135, .145
2	.138, .143, .143, .145, .146	16	.140, .132, .144, .145, .141
3	.139, .133, .147, .148, .139	17	.137, .137, .142, .143, .141
4	.143, .141, .137, .138, .140	18	.137, .142, .142, .145, .143
5	.142, .142, .145, .135, .136	19	.142, .142, .143, .140, .135
6	.136, .144, .143, .136, .137	20	.136, .142, .140, .139, .137
7	.142, .147, .137, .142, .138	21	.142, .144, .140, .138, .143
8	.143, .137, .145, .137, .138	22	.139, .146, .143, .140, .139
9	.141, .142, .147, .140, .140	23	.140, .145, .142, .139, .137
10	.142, .137, .145, .140, .132	24	.134, .147, .143, .141, .142
11	.137, .147, .142, .137, .135	25	.138, .145, .141, .137, .141
12	.137, .146, .142, .142, .140	26	.140, .145, .143, .144, .138
13	.142, .142, .139, .141, .142	27	.145, .145, .137, .138, .140
14	.137, .145, .144, .137, .140		

Source: Grant, E. L., and Leavenworth, R. S. *Statistical Quality Control*, 5th ed. New York: McGraw-Hill, 1980 (Table 1-2). Reprinted with permission.

a. Construct an $\bar{x}$-chart for the process.
b. Locate the center line, upper control limit, and lower control limit on the $\bar{x}$-chart.
c. Does the process appear to be in control?

16.4   Control Chart for Process Variation: R-Chart

In quality control, we want to control not only the mean value of some quality characteristic, but also its variability. An increase in the process standard deviation σ means that the quality characteristic variable will vary over a wider range, thereby increasing the probability of producing an inferior product. Consequently, a process that is in control generates data with a relatively constant process mean μ and standard deviation σ.

The variation in a quality characteristic is monitored using a **range chart** or **R-chart**. Thus, in addition to calculating the mean $\bar{x}$ for each sample, we also calculate and plot the sample range R. As with an $\bar{x}$-chart, an R-chart also contains a center line and lines corresponding to the upper and lower control limits.

The expected value and standard deviation of the sample range are

$$E(R) = d_2\sigma \quad \text{and} \quad \sigma_R = d_3\sigma$$

where d_2 and d_3 are constants (see Table 19 of Appendix II) that depend on the sample size n. Therefore, we would locate the center line of the R-chart at $d_2\sigma$ where, if σ is unknown, $E(R)$ is estimated by the mean $\bar{R}$ of the ranges of k samples.[*]

Location of Center Line and Control Limits for an R-Chart

Center line: $\bar{R}$

UCL: $D_4\bar{R}$

LCL: $D_3\bar{R}$

where

k = Number of samples, each of size n

R_i = Range of the ith sample

$$\bar{R} = \frac{\sum_{i=1}^{k} R_i}{k}$$

and D_3 and D_4 are given in Table 19 of Appendix II for $n = 2$ to $n = 25$.

The upper and lower control limits are located a distance $3\sigma_R = 3d_3\sigma$ above and below the center line. Using $\bar{R}/d_2$ to estimate σ, we locate the upper and lower control

---

[*]As an alternative procedure, we could estimate σ using the standard deviation of all the data contained in the k samples.

limits as follows:

$$\text{UCL:} \quad \bar{R} + 3\frac{d_3}{d_2}\bar{R} = \left(1 + 3\frac{d_3}{d_2}\right)\bar{R} = D_4\bar{R}$$

where

$$D_4 = 1 + 3\frac{d_3}{d_2}$$

and

$$\text{LCL:} \quad \bar{R} - 3\frac{d_3}{d_2}\bar{R} = \left(1 - 3\frac{d_3}{d_2}\right)\bar{R} = D_3\bar{R}$$

where

$$D_3 = 1 - 3\frac{d_3}{d_2}$$

Values of D_3 and D_4 have been computed for sample sizes of $n = 2$ to $n = 25$, and appear in Table 19 of Appendix II.

EXAMPLE 16.4

Refer to the problem of monitoring the manufacturing of electrical shafts, Example 16.2. Recall that the manufacturer selected a sample of 4 shafts each hour, for a period of 20 hours, and measured the diameter of each. Assuming the process is in control, construct and interpret an R-chart for process variation.

Solution

In Example 16.2 we calculated the mean of the 20 sample ranges to be $\bar{R} = .01985$. This value is the center line. For $n = 4$, the values of D_3 and D_4 given in Table 19 of Appendix II are $D_3 = 0$ and $D_4 = 2.282$. Then the upper and lower control limits for the R-chart are:

$$\text{UCL} = D_4\bar{R} = (2.282)(.01985) = .045298$$

$$\text{LCL} = D_3\bar{R} = (0)(.01985) = 0$$

An $\bar{R}$-chart for the 20 sample ranges of Table 16.2 is shown in Figure 16.9.

FIGURE 16.9 ▶
R-chart for the $k = 20$ sample ranges of Table 16.2

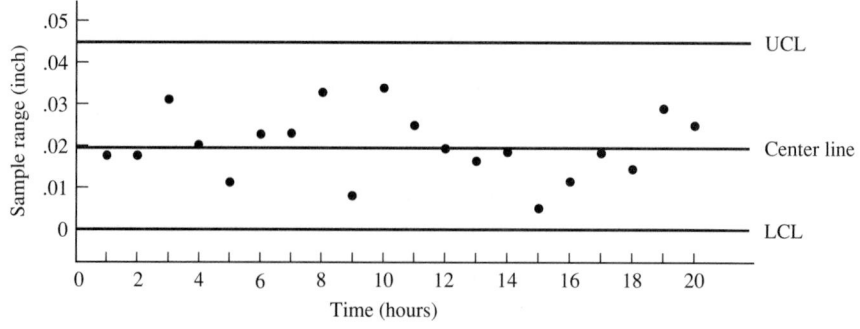

To monitor the variation in shaft diameters produced by the manufacturing process, a quality control engineer would check to determine that the sample range does not exceed the UCL of .045298 inch. (Since the LCL is 0, no diameter can fall below this value.)

The practical implications to be derived from an R-chart are similar to those associated with an $\bar{x}$-chart. Values of R that fall outside of the control limits are suspect and suggest a possible change in the process. Trends in the sample range may also indicate problems, such as wear within a machine. (We investigate this type of problem in the next section.) As in the case of the $\bar{x}$-chart, the R-chart can provide an indication of possible trouble in a process. A process engineer then attempts to locate the difficulty, if in fact it exists.

Interpreting an $\bar{R}$-Chart

Process "out of control":   One or more of the sample means fall outside the control limits. As with the $\bar{x}$-chart, this indicates a possible change in the production process and efforts should be made to locate the trouble.

Process "in control":   All sample means fall within the control limits. In this case, it is better to leave the process alone than to look for trouble that may not exist.

Remember, it is important to construct and interpret an R-chart before the $\bar{x}$-chart. When the R-chart indicates that process variation is in control, only then does it make sense to analyze the $\bar{x}$-chart.

EXERCISES

16.10 Refer to Exercise 16.5. Suppose the inspector wants to monitor the variation in firing pin lengths with an R-chart.
  a. Locate the center line for the R-chart.
  b. Locate upper and lower control limits for the R-chart.
  c. Calculate and plot the 10 sample ranges in an R-chart. Does the process variation appear to be in control?

16.11 Construct an R-chart for the data of Exercise 16.6 to monitor the variation in the diameters of the molded-rubber expansion joints produced by the manufacturing process. Does the process appear to be in control?

16.12 Construct an R-chart for the data of Exercise 16.7 to monitor the variation in the weights of the finished bottles. Does the process appear to be in control?

16.13   Construct an R-chart for the data of Exercise 16.8 to monitor the variation in pitch diameters of the threaded fittings. Does the process appear to be in control?

16.14   Refer to Exercise 16.13. Modify the control limits on the R-chart so it can be applied to future data.

16.15   Construct an R-chart for the data of Exercise 16.9. Does the process variation appear to be in control?

16.5   Detecting Trends in a Control Chart: Runs Analysis

As mentioned in the previous two sections, control charts are also examined for trends in the values of $\bar{x}$ or R collected over time. Even when the sample values fall within the control limits, such a trend may indicate the presence of one or more assignable causes of variation. For example, the true process mean may have shifted slightly as a result of wear in the machine.

Trends in the process can be detected by observing runs of points above or below the center line of a control chart. In quality control, a **run** is defined as a sequence of one or more consecutive points that all fall above (or all fall below) the center line.

Definition 16.7

A **run** is a sequence of one or more consecutive points that fall on the same side of the center line in a control chart.

The runs (indicated in brackets) for the R-chart of Figure 16.9 are shown in Figure 16.10. Sample ranges that fall above the center line are denoted by a "+" symbol, and ranges that fall below the center line by a "−" symbol.

FIGURE 16.10 ►
Runs for the $k = 20$ sample
ranges in the R-chart, Figure 16.9

− −	+ +	−	+ + +	−	+ +	− − − − − − −	+ +
Run: 1	2	3	4	5	6	7	8

Note that the sequence of 20 points consists of a total of eight runs, starting with a run of two "−", followed by a run of two "+", and so on. Considerable work has been done by researchers on the development of statistical tests based on the **theory of runs**. Many of these techniques are useful for testing whether the sample observations have been drawn at random from the target population. These tests require that the total number of runs, long and short alike, be determined. In quality control, however, a few simple rules have been developed for detecting trend that are based on only the *extreme (or longest) runs*, in the control chart.

To illustrate, consider the sequence of runs in Figure 16.10. The extreme run in the sequence is composed of seven "−" symbols. These represent the seven consecutive sample ranges that all fell below the center line during hours 12, 13, . . . , 18. How likely is it to observe seven consecutive points on the control chart, all on the same side of the center line, if in fact no assignable causes of variation are present? To answer this question, we use the laws of probability learned in Chapter 3.

First, note that the probability of any one point falling above (or below) the center line is $\frac{1}{2}$ when the process is in control. Then, from the Multiplicative Law of Probability for independent events (see Chapter 3), the probability of seven consecutive points falling, say, *above* the center line is

$$\left(\frac{1}{2}\right)\left(\frac{1}{2}\right)\left(\frac{1}{2}\right)\left(\frac{1}{2}\right)\left(\frac{1}{2}\right)\left(\frac{1}{2}\right)\left(\frac{1}{2}\right) = \left(\frac{1}{2}\right)^7 = \frac{1}{128}$$

Likewise, the probability of seven consecutive points falling *below* the center line is $(\frac{1}{2})^7 = \frac{1}{128}$. Therefore, the probability of seven consecutive points falling on the same side of the center line is, by the Additive Law of Probability,

$$P(7 \text{ consecutive points on the same side of the center line})$$
$$= P(7 \text{ consecutive points above the center line})$$
$$+ P(7 \text{ consecutive points below the center line})$$
$$= \frac{1}{128} + \frac{1}{128} = \frac{2}{128} = \frac{1}{64}$$

or .0156. Since it is very unlikely (probability of .0156) to observe such a pattern if the process is in control, the trend in the control chart is taken as a signal of possible trouble in the production process.

A probability such as the one above can be calculated for any run in the control chart, and, based on its value, a decision made about whether to look for trouble in the process. Grant and Leavenworth (1980) recommend looking for assignable causes of variation if any one of the following sequences of points occurs in the control chart:

Detecting Trend in a Control Chart: Runs Analysis

If any one of the following sequence of runs occurs in a control chart, assignable causes of variation (e.g., trend) are likely to be present:

- Seven or more consecutive points on the same side of the center line
- At least 10 out of 11 consecutive points on the same side of the center line
- At least 12 out of 14 consecutive points on the same side of the center line
- At least 14 out of 17 consecutive points on the same side of the center line

---

The rules in the box are easy to apply in practice since they simply require one to count consecutive points in the control chart. In each case, the probability of observing that sequence of points when the process is in control is approximately .01. (We leave proof of this result to you as an exercise.) Consequently, if one of these sequences occurs, we are highly confident that some problem in the production process, possibly a shift in the process mean, exists.

More formal statistical tests of runs are available. Consult the references at the end of this chapter if you want to learn more about these techniques.

EXERCISES

16.16 Examine the sequences of points in parts **a–f** for any trends.

    a. + + − − − − − + + + +   **b.** − + − − − + + − + + + +

    c. − − − − − + + + + + − −   **d.** − + + + + + − + + + + + + +

    e. + − + + + − − + + −   **f.** − + + + + + + + + + −

16.17 Refer to the $\bar{x}$- and R-charts, Exercises 16.5 and 16.10. Conduct a runs analysis to detect any trend in the process.

16.18 Refer to the $\bar{x}$- and R-charts, Exercises 16.6 and 16.11. Conduct a runs analysis to detect any trend in the process.

16.19 Refer to the $\bar{x}$- and R-charts, Exercises 16.7 and 16.12. Conduct a runs analysis to detect any trend in the process.

16.20 Refer to the $\bar{x}$- and R-charts, Exercises 16.8 and 16.13. Conduct a runs analysis to detect any trend in the process.

16.21 Refer to the $\bar{x}$- and R-charts, Exercises 16.9 and 16.15. Conduct a runs analysis to detect any trend in the process.

16.6 Control Chart for Percent Defectives: *p*-Chart

In addition to measuring quantitative quality characteristics, we are also interested in monitoring the binomial proportion p of the items produced that are defective. As in the case of the $\bar{x}$-chart, random samples of n items are selected from the production line at the end of some specified interval of time. For each sample, we compute the sample proportion

$$\hat{p} = \frac{y}{n}$$

where y is the number of defective items in the sample. The sample proportions are then plotted against time and displayed in a **p-chart**.

The center line for a p-chart is determined by combining the data contained in a large number k of samples. The estimate of the process proportion defective p is

$$\bar{p} = \frac{\text{Total number of defectives}}{\text{Total number inspected}} = \frac{n \sum_{i=1}^{k} \hat{p}_i}{nk} = \frac{\sum_{i=1}^{k} \hat{p}_i}{k}$$

The upper and lower control limits are located a distance of

$$3\sigma_{\hat{p}} = 3\sqrt{\frac{p(1-p)}{n}}$$

Location of Center Line and Control Limits for p-Chart

Center line: $\bar{p} = \dfrac{\text{Total number of defectives in } k \text{ samples}}{\text{Total number of items inspected}}$

$$= \frac{\sum_{i=1}^{k} \hat{p}_i}{k}$$

UCL: $\bar{p} + 3\sqrt{\dfrac{\bar{p}(1-\bar{p})}{n}}$

LCL: $\bar{p} - 3\sqrt{\dfrac{\bar{p}(1-\bar{p})}{n}}$

where

k = Number of samples, each of size n

y_i = Number of defectives in the ith sample

$\hat{p}_i = y_i/n$ is the proportion of defectives in the ith sample

---

above and below the center line. Using $\bar{p}$ to estimate the process proportion defective p, we find

$$\text{UCL} = \bar{p} + 3\sqrt{\frac{\bar{p}(1-\bar{p})}{n}}$$

$$\text{LCL} = \bar{p} - 3\sqrt{\frac{\bar{p}(1-\bar{p})}{n}}$$

The interpretation of a p-chart is similar to the interpretations of $\bar{x}$- and R-charts. We expect the sample proportions defective to fall within the control limits. Failure to do so suggests difficulties with the production process and should be investigated.

EXAMPLE 16.5

To monitor the manufacturing process of rubber support bearings used between the superstructure and foundation pads of nuclear power plants, a quality control engineer randomly samples 100 bearings from the production line each day over a 15-day period. The bearings were inspected for defects and the number of defectives found each day are recorded in Table 16.3 on page 1006. Construct a p-chart for the fraction of defective bearings.

TABLE 16.3   Defective Bearings in 15 Samples of $n = 100$, Example 16.5

Day	1	2	3	4	5	6	7	8
Number of Defectives	2	12	3	4	4	1	3	5
Proportion of Defectives	.02	.12	.03	.04	.04	.01	.03	.05

Day	9	10	11	12	13	14	15	Totals
Number of Defectives	3	2	10	3	3	2	3	60
Proportion of Defectives	.03	.02	.10	.03	.03	.02	.03	.04

Solution

The center line for the p-chart is the proportion of defective bearings in the combined sample of $nk = 1{,}500$ bearings:

$$\bar{p} = \frac{\text{Total number of defective bearings}}{\text{Total number inspected}} = \frac{60}{1{,}500} = .04$$

Upper and lower control limits are then computed as follows:

$$\text{UCL} = \bar{p} + 3\sqrt{\frac{\bar{p}(1-\bar{p})}{n}} = .04 + 3\sqrt{\frac{(.04)(.96)}{100}}$$

$$= .04 + .059 = .099$$

$$\text{LCL} = \bar{p} - 3\sqrt{\frac{\bar{p}(1-\bar{p})}{n}} = .04 - 3\sqrt{\frac{(.04)(.96)}{100}}$$

$$= .04 - .059 = -.019$$

Thus, if the process is in control, we expect the sample proportion of defective rubber bearings to fall between 0 (since no sample proportion can be negative) and .099 with a high probability.

A control chart for the percentage of defective bearings is shown in Figure 16.11.

FIGURE 16.11 ▶
p-chart for the percentage of defective bearings, Example 16.5

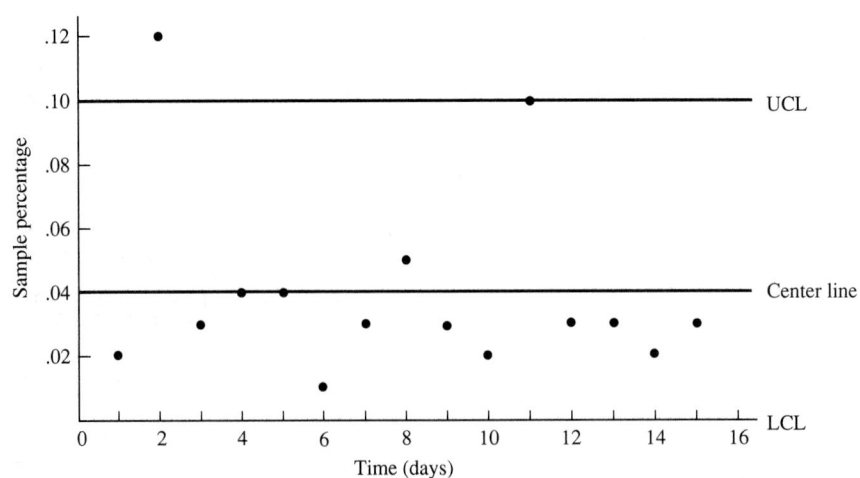

Note that on days 2 and 11, the sample proportion fell outside the control limits. This suggests possible problems with the manufacturing process and warrants further investigation.

······················

Interpreting a p-Chart
·····························

Process "out of control":   One or more of the sample proportions fall outside the control limits. This indicates possible trouble in the production process and warrants further investigation.

Process "in control":   All sample proportions fall within the control limits. In this case it is better to leave the process alone than to look for trouble that may not exist.

Once the problem that caused the two unusually large percentages of defectives in Example 16.5 has been identified and corrected, the control limits should be modified so that they can be applied to future data. As mentioned in Section 16.2, one method of adjusting is to recalculate their values based on only the sample points that fall within the control limits of Figure 16.11. Omitting the data for days 2 and 11, we obtain the modified values

$$\bar{p} = \frac{\text{Total number of defective bearings (excluding days 2 and 11)}}{\text{Total number inspected (excluding days 2 and 11)}}$$

$$= \frac{38}{1{,}300} = .029$$

$$\text{UCL} = \bar{p} + 3\sqrt{\frac{\bar{p}(1 - \bar{p})}{n}} = .029 + 3\sqrt{\frac{(.029)(.971)}{100}}$$

$$= .029 + .050 = .079$$

$$\text{LCL} = \bar{p} - 3\sqrt{\frac{\bar{p}(1 - \bar{p})}{n}} = .029 - 3\sqrt{\frac{(.029)(.971)}{100}}$$

$$= .029 - .050 = -.021$$

Now a control chart with center line $\bar{p} = .029$, UCL $= .079$, and LCL $= 0$ can be used to monitor the percentage defective produced in future days of the process.

EXERCISES
··

16.22   Prestressed concrete cylinder pipe (PCCP) is a rigid pipe designed to take optimum advantage of the tensile strength of steel and the compressive strength and corrosive inhibiting properties of concrete. PCCP, produced in laying lengths of 24 feet, is susceptible to major stress cracks during the manufacturing process. To monitor the process, 20 sections of PCCP were sampled each week for a 6-week period. The number of defective sections (i.e., sections with major stress cracks) in each sample is recorded in the table.

Week	1	2	3	4	5	6
Number of Defectives	1	0	2	2	3	1

a. Construct a p-chart for the sample percentage of defective PCCP sections manufactured.
b. Locate the center line on the p-chart.
c. Locate upper and lower control limits on the p-chart. Does the process appear to be in control?

16.23 A manufacturer of computer terminal fuses wants to establish a control chart to monitor the production process. Each hour, for a period of 25 hours, during a time when the process is known to be in control, a quality control engineer randomly selected and tested 100 fuses from the production line. The number of defective fuses found each hour is recorded in the table.

Hour	1	2	3	4	5	6	7	8	9	10
Number Defective	6	4	9	3	0	6	4	2	1	2
Hour	11	12	13	14	15	16	17	18	19	20
Number Defective	1	3	4	5	5	2	1	1	0	3
Hour	21	22	23	24	25					
Number Defective	7	9	2	10	3					

a. Construct a p-chart for the sample percentage of defective terminal fuses.
b. Locate the center line on the p-chart.
c. Locate upper and lower control limits on the p-chart. Does the process appear to be in control?
d. Conduct a runs analysis on the points on the p-chart. What does this imply?

16.24 Refer to Exercise 16.23. Suppose the next sample of 100 terminal fuses selected from the production line contains 11 defectives. Is the process now out of control? Explain.

16.25 An electronics company manufactures several types of cathode ray tubes on a mass production basis. To monitor the process, 50 tubes of a certain type were randomly sampled from the production line and inspected each day over a 1-month period. The number of defectives found each day is provided in the accompanying table.

Day	Number Defective	Day	Number Defective
1	11	12	23
2	15	13	15
3	12	14	12
4	10	15	11
5	9	16	11
6	12	17	16
7	12	18	15
8	14	19	10
9	9	20	13
10	13	21	12
11	15		

a. Construct a p-chart for the sample fraction of defective cathode ray tubes.
b. Locate the center line on the p-chart.
c. Locate the upper and lower control limits on the p-chart.
d. Does the process appear to be in control? If not, modify the control limits for future data.
e. Conduct a runs analysis to detect a trend in the production process.

16.7   Control Chart for the Number of Defects per Item: c-Chart

In addition to various other quality characteristics, we may be interested in the number of defects or blemishes contained in each single item of the product. For example, a manufacturer of office furniture might randomly sample one piece of furniture from the production line every 15 minutes and record the number of blemishes on the finish. Similarly, a textile manufacturer might inspect a randomly selected 1-square-foot piece of material each hour and count the number of minor defects that it contains. The objective of this procedure is to monitor the number of defects per item and to detect situations where this variable is out of control. In the notation used in quality control, the number of defects per item is denoted by the symbol c and a control chart used to monitor this variable over time is called a **c-chart**.

The Poisson probability distribution (Section 4.10) provides a good model for the probability distribution for the number c of defects contained in some manufactured product. From Section 4.10, we recall that if c possesses a Poisson probability distribution with parameter λ, then

$$E(c) = \lambda$$

and

$$\sigma_c = \sqrt{\lambda}$$

To construct a c-chart, we observe c over a reasonably large number, k, of equally spaced points in time and use the average value of c, $\bar{c}$, to estimate λ. Then since $E(c) = \lambda$, we would locate the center line of the c-chart at

$$\text{Center line:} \quad \bar{c} = \frac{\sum\limits_{i=1}^{k} c_i}{k}$$

The upper and lower control limits are located a distance of $3\sigma_c$ (estimated to be $3\sqrt{\bar{c}}$) above and below the center line. Thus, the upper and lower control limits are located at

$$UCL: \quad \bar{c} + 3\sqrt{\bar{c}}$$
$$LCL: \quad \bar{c} - 3\sqrt{\bar{c}}$$

Location of Center Line and Control Limits for a c-Chart

Center line: $\bar{c}$ UCL: $\bar{c} + 3\sqrt{\bar{c}}$ LCL: $\bar{c} - 3\sqrt{\bar{c}}$

where

k = Number of time periods sampled

c_i = Number of defects per item observed at time i

$\bar{c} = \dfrac{\sum\limits_{i=1}^{k} c_i}{k}$ = Average number of defects per item observed over all time periods

---

EXAMPLE 16.6

The number of noticeable defects found by quality control inspectors in a randomly selected 1-square-meter specimen of woolen fabric from a certain loom is recorded each hour for a period of 20 hours. The results are shown in Table 16.4. Assuming that the number of defects per square meter has an approximate Poisson probability distribution, construct a c-chart to monitor the textile production process.

TABLE 16.4   Number of Defects Observed in Specimens of Woolen Fabric over 20 Consecutive Hours, Example 16.6

Hour	1	2	3	4	5	6	7	8	9	10
Number of Defects	11	14	10	8	3	9	10	2	5	6

Hour	11	12	13	14	15	16	17	18	19	20
Number of Defects	12	3	4	5	6	8	11	8	7	9

Solution

The first step is to estimate λ, the mean number of defects per square meter of woolen fabric. This value, $\bar{c}$, also represents the center line for the control chart:

$$\bar{c} = \frac{\sum c_i}{n} = \frac{151}{20} = 7.55$$

Upper and lower control limits are then calculated as follows:

$$UCL = \bar{c} + 3\sqrt{\bar{c}} = 7.55 + 3\sqrt{7.55} = 15.79$$
$$LCL = \bar{c} - 3\sqrt{\bar{c}} = 7.55 - 3\sqrt{7.55} = -.69$$

Since a negative number of defects cannot be observed, the LCL is adjusted up to 0.

The control chart for the data appears in Figure 16.12. According to current standards, the textile process produces an allowable number of defects in woolen fabric if the number of defects per square meter does not exceed 15. At no time during the 20-hour period did the process appear to be out of control.

FIGURE 16.12 ▶
c-chart for the number of defects per square meter of woolen fabric, Example 16.6

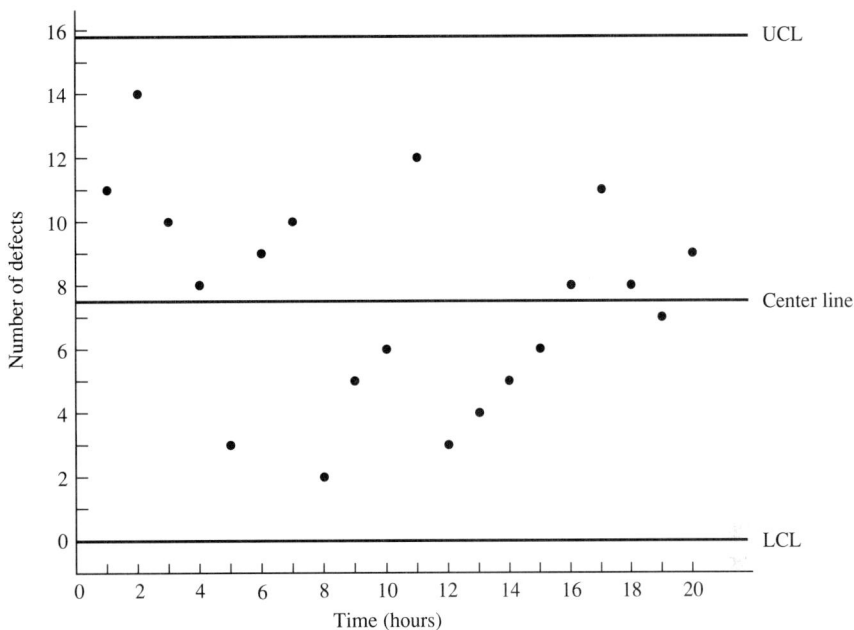

However, before we conclude that the process is in control, we should check for trends on the number of defects over time, i.e., we should perform a runs analysis as described in Section 16.5. Using the symbols "+" and "−" to denote points above and below the center line, respectively, we obtain the sequence of runs shown in Figure 16.13. Note that the extreme runs in the sequence (runs 1 and 6) include only four points. Also, none of the other unlikely sequences given in the box in Section 16.5 occurs. Therefore, it does not appear that any trend exists in the data. At this point in time, the process appears to be in control.

FIGURE 16.13 ▶
Runs for the $k = 20$ numbers of defects in the c-chart, Figure 16.12

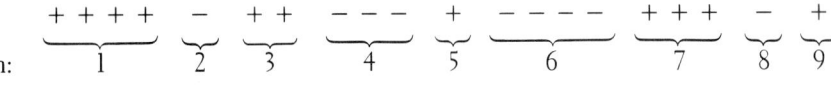

Interpreting a c-Chart

Process "out of control":   One or more of the sample numbers of defects fall outside the control limits. This indicates possible trouble in the production process and warrants further investigation.

Process "in control":   All of the sample numbers of defects fall within the control limits. In this case it is better to leave the process alone than to look for trouble that may not exist.

EXERCISES

16.26 The number of imperfections (scratches, chips, cracks, and blisters) in manufactured custom wood cabinet panels is important both to the customer and to the custom builder. To monitor the manufacturing process, each hour for 15 consecutive hours a finished panel 4 feet by 8 feet was selected and inspected for imperfections. The number of imperfections per panel is recorded in the table.

Panel	1	2	3	4	5	6	7	8	9	10	11	12	13	14	15
Number of Defects	4	2	3	3	9	4	5	3	8	7	3	6	5	7	3

a. Plot the number of defects per panel in a c-chart.
b. Locate the center line for the c-chart.
c. Locate upper and lower control limits for the c-chart. Is the process in control?
d. Conduct a runs analysis for the c-chart. What does this imply?

16.27 A quality control study was undertaken by the supervisor of a computer card keypunch operation. For each of the last 20 days' output, 25 punched cards were randomly selected and inspected for keypunching errors. The numbers of errors observed per day are recorded in the table.

Day	1	2	3	4	5	6	7	8	9	10
Number of Errors	7	3	9	8	2	5	10	5	7	6

Day	11	12	13	14	15	16	17	18	19	20
Number of Errors	1	4	11	8	6	6	9	2	12	9

a. Plot the number of keypunching errors per day in a c-chart.
b. Locate the center line for the c-chart.
c. Locate upper and lower control limits for the c-chart. Is the process in control?
d. Conduct a runs analysis for the c-chart. What does this imply?

16.28 A certain airplane model is susceptible to alignment errors in the manufacturing process. To monitor this process, the total number of alignment errors observed at final inspection for each of the first 25 aircraft produced were recorded, as shown in the accompanying table.

Airplane	Number of Alignment Errors	Airplane	Number of Alignment Errors
1	7	14	9
2	6	15	8
3	6	16	15
4	7	17	6
5	4	18	4
6	7	19	13
7	8	20	7
8	12	21	8
9	9	22	15

(continued)

Airplane	Number of Alignment Errors	Airplane	Number of Alignment Errors
10	9	23	6
11	8	24	6
12	5	25	10
13	5		

Source: Grant, E. L., and Leavenworth, R. S. *Statistical Quality Control*, 5th ed. New York: McGraw-Hill, 1980 (Table 8–1). Reprinted with permission.

a. Construct a c-chart for the number of alignment errors per aircraft.
b. Locate the center and upper and lower control limits on the c-chart.
c. Does the process appear to be in control? Would you recommend using these control limits for future data?

16.29 Refer to Exercise 16.28. The numbers of alignment errors observed for each of the next 25 aircraft produced are shown in the table.

Airplane	Number of Alignment Errors	Airplane	Number of Alignment Errors
26	7	39	11
27	13	40	8
28	4	41	10
29	5	42	8
30	9	43	7
31	3	44	16
32	4	45	13
33	6	46	12
34	7	47	9
35	14	48	11
36	18	49	11
37	11	50	8
38	11		

Source: Grant, E. L., and Leavenworth, R. S. *Statistical Quality Control*, 5th ed. New York: McGraw-Hill, 1980 (Table 8–1). Reprinted with permission.

a. Add these 25 points to the c-chart of Exercise 16.28. Does the process still appear to be in control?
b. Conduct a runs analysis for the revised c-chart. What do you detect?

16.8   Tolerance Limits

The Shewhart control charts described in the previous sections provide valuable information on the quality of the production process as a whole. Even if the process is deemed to be in control, however, an individual manufactured item may not always meet specifications. Therefore, in addition to process control, it is often important to know that a large proportion of the individual quality measurements fall within certain limits with a high degree of confidence. An interval that includes a certain percentage of measurements with a known probability is called a **tolerance interval** and the endpoints of the interval are called **tolerance limits**.

Tolerance intervals are identical to the confidence intervals of Chapter 8, except that we are attempting to capture a proportion γ of measurements in a population rather than a population parameter (e.g., the population mean μ). For example, a production supervisor may want to establish tolerance limits for 99% of the length measurements of eyescrews manufactured on the production line, using a 95% tolerance interval. Here, the confidence coefficient is $1 - \alpha = .95$ and the proportion of measurements the supervisor wants to capture is $\gamma = .99$. The confidence coefficient, .95, has the same meaning as in Chapter 8. That is, approximately 95 out of every 100 similarly constructed tolerance intervals will contain 99% of the length measurements in the population.

Definition 16.8

A $100(1 - \alpha)\%$ **tolerance interval** for $100(\gamma)\%$ of the quality measurements of a product is an interval that includes $100(\gamma)\%$ of the measurements with confidence coefficient $(1 - \alpha)$.

Definition 16.9

The endpoints of a tolerance interval are called **tolerance limits**.

When the population of measurements that characterize the product is normally distributed with known mean μ and known standard deviation σ, tolerance limits are easily constructed. In fact, such an interval is a 100% tolerance interval, i.e., the confidence coefficient is 1.0. For example, suppose the lengths of the eyescrews above have a normal distribution with $\mu = .50$ inch and $\sigma = .01$ inch. From our knowledge of the standard normal (z) distribution, we know with certainty (i.e., with probability $1 - \alpha = 1.0$) that 99% of the measurements will fall within $z = 2.58$ standard deviations of the mean (see Figure 16.14). Thus, a 100% tolerance interval for 99% of the length measurements is

$$\mu \pm 2.58\sigma = .50 \pm 2.58(.01)$$
$$= .50 \pm .0258$$

or $(.4742, .5258)$.

In practice, quality control engineers will rarely know the true values of μ and σ. Fortunately, tolerance intervals can be constructed by substituting the sample esti-

FIGURE 16.14 ▶
Normal distribution of eyescrew
lengths

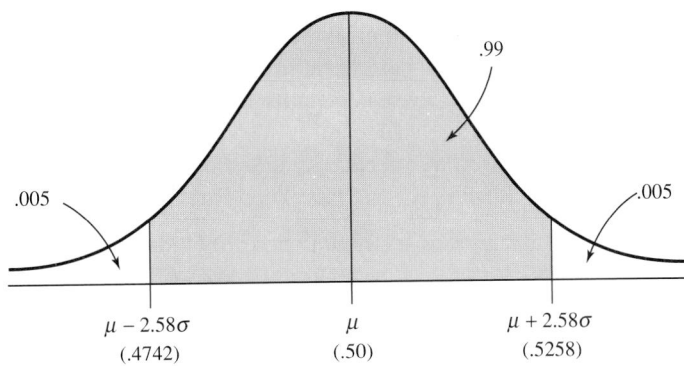

mates $\bar{x}$ and s for μ and σ, respectively. Due to the errors introduced by the sample estimators, however, the confidence coefficient for the tolerance interval will no longer equal 1.0. The procedure for constructing tolerance limits for a normal population of measurements is described in the following box.

A Tolerance Interval for the Measurements in a Normal Population

A $100(1 - \alpha)\%$ tolerance interval for $100\gamma\%$ of the measurements in a normal population is given by

$$\bar{x} \pm Ks$$

where

$\bar{x}$ = Mean of a sample of n measurements

s = Sample standard deviation

and K is found from Table 20 of Appendix II, based on the values of the confidence coefficient $(1 - \alpha)$, γ, and the sample size n.

Assumption: The population of measurements is approximately normal.

EXAMPLE 16.7

Refer to Example 16.2. Use the sample information provided in Table 16.2 to find a 95% tolerance interval for 99% of the shaft diameters produced by the manufacturing process. Assume that the distribution of shaft diameters is approximately normal.

Solution

Table 16.2 contains diameters for 20 samples of four shafts each, or a total of $n = 80$ shaft diameters. The mean diameter of the entire sample is

$$\bar{x} = \frac{\sum\limits_{i=1}^{80} x_i}{80} = \frac{(1.505 + 1.499 + 1.501 + 1.488 + \cdots + 1.519)}{80} = 1.50045$$

(Note that this is the same value as the center line, $\bar{\bar{x}}$, computed in Example 16.2.) The sample standard deviation (from a computer) is $s = .009244$.

Since we desire a tolerance interval for 99% of the shaft diameters, $\gamma = .99$. Also, the confidence coefficient is $1 - \alpha = .95$. Table 20 of Appendix II gives the values of K for several values of γ and $1 - \alpha$. For $\gamma = .99$, $1 - \alpha = .95$, and $n = 80$, Table 20 gives $K = 2.986$. Then, the 95% tolerance interval is

$$\bar{x} \pm 2.986s = 1.50045 \pm (2.986)(.009244)$$
$$= 1.50045 \pm .02760$$

or $(1.47285, 1.52805)$. Thus, the lower and upper 95% tolerance limits for 99% of the shaft diameters are 1.47285 inches and 1.52805 inches, respectively. Our confidence in the procedure is based on the premise that approximately 95 out of every 100 similarly constructed tolerance intervals will contain 99% of the shaft diameters in the population.

The technique applied in Example 16.7 gives tolerance limits for a normal distribution of measurements. If we are unwilling or unable to make the normality assumption, we must resort to a nonparametric method. Nonparametric tolerance limits are based on only the smallest and largest measurements in the sample data, as shown in the box. These tolerance intervals can be applied to any distribution of measurements.

A Nonparametric Tolerance Interval

Let $x_{\min}$ and $x_{\max}$ be the smallest and largest observations, respectively, in a sample of size n from any distribution of measurements. Then we can select n so that

$$(x_{\min}, x_{\max})$$

forms a $100(1 - \alpha)\%$ tolerance interval for at least $100\gamma\%$ of the population. Values of n for several values of the confidence coefficient $(1 - \alpha)$ and γ are given in Table 21 of Appendix II.

EXAMPLE 16.8

Refer to Example 16.7. Find the sample size required so that the interval $(x_{\min}, x_{\max})$ forms a 95% tolerance interval for at least 90% of the shaft diameters produced by the manufacturing process.

Solution

Here, the confidence coefficient is $1 - \alpha = .95$ and the proportion of measurements we want to capture is $\gamma = .90$. From Table 21 of Appendix II, the sample size corresponding to $1 - \alpha = .95$ and $\gamma = .90$ is $n = 46$. Therefore, if we randomly sample $n = 46$ shafts, the smallest and largest diameters in the sample will represent the lower and upper tolerance limits, respectively, for at least 90% of the shaft diameters with confidence coefficient .95.

The information provided by tolerance intervals is often used to determine whether product specifications are being satisfied. **Specification limits**, unlike tolerance or control limits, are not determined by sampling the process. Rather, they define acceptable values of the quality variable that are set by customers, management, and/or product designers. To determine whether the specifications are realistic, the specification limits are compared to the "natural" tolerance limits of the process, that is, the tolerance limits obtained from sampling. If the tolerance limits do not fall within the specification limits, a review of the production process is strongly recommended. An investigation may reveal that the specifications are tighter than necessary for the functioning of the production, and, consequently, should be widened. Or, if the specifications cannot be changed, a fundamental change in the production process may be necessary to reduce product variability.

EXERCISES

16.30 Refer to Exercise 16.7. Use all the sample information to find a 95% tolerance interval for 90% of the finished bottle weights. Assume the distribution of bottle weights is approximately normal.

16.31 Refer to Exercise 16.8.
a. Use all the sample information to find a 95% tolerance interval for 99% of all the pitch diameters. Assume the distribution of pitch diameters is approximately normal.
b. Specifications require the pitch diameter of the thread to fall within .4037 ± .0013 inch. Based on the "natural" tolerance limits of the process (i.e., the tolerance limits of part **a**), does it appear that the specifications are being met?
c. How large a sample is required to construct a nonparametric 95% tolerance interval for at least 95% of the pitch diameters? If n is large enough for this case, give the nonparametric tolerance limits.

16.32 Refer to Exercise 16.9. Find a 99% tolerance interval for at least 95% of the distance measurements assuming each of the following:
a. A normal distribution
b. A nonnormal distribution

16.33 J. Namias used the techniques of statistical quality control to determine when to conduct a search for specific causes of consumer complaints at a beverage company (*Journal of Marketing Research*, Aug. 1964). Namias discovered that when the process was in control, the biweekly complaint rate of a bottled product (i.e., the number of customer complaints per 10,000 bottles sold in a 2-week period) had an approximately normal distribution with $\mu = 26$ and $\sigma = 11.3$. Customer complaints primarily concerned chipped bottles that looked dangerous.
a. Find a tolerance interval for 99% of the complaint rates when the bottling process is assumed to be in control. What is the confidence coefficient for the interval? Explain.

b. In one 2-week period, the observed complaint rate was 93.12 complaints per 10,000 bottles sold. Based on your knowledge of statistical quality control, do you think the observed rate is due to chance or some specific cause? (In actuality, a search for a possible problem in the bottling process led to a discovery of rough handling of the bottled beverage in the warehouse by newly hired workers. As a result, a training program for new workers was instituted.)

16.34 Many hand tools used by mechanics involve attachments that fit into sockets (e.g., a socket wrench). In the manufacturing of the tools, specifications require that the inside diameter of the socket be larger than the outside diameter of the extension. That is, there must be enough clearance so that the extensions actually fit in the sockets. To establish tolerances for the tools, independent random samples of 50 sockets and 50 attachments were selected from the production process and the diameters (inside for sockets and outside for extensions) were measured. An analysis revealed that the distributions for both dimensions were approximately normal. The means and standard deviations (in inches) for the two samples are given in the accompanying table.

	Sockets (1)	Attachments (2)
Sample Mean	.5120	.5005
Standard Deviation	.0010	.0015

a. Find a 95% tolerance interval for 99% of the socket diameters.
b. Find a 95% tolerance interval for 99% of the attachment diameters.
c. Specifications require that the clearance between attachment and socket (i.e., the difference between the inside socket diameter and outside attachment diameter) be at least .004 inch. Based on the tolerance limits from parts **a** and **b**, is it likely to find an extension and socket with less than the desired minimum clearance of .004 inch?
d. Specifications also require a maximum of .015-inch clearance between attachment and socket, to prevent fits that are too loose. Based on the tolerance intervals from parts **a** and **b**, would you expect to find some attachment and socket pairs that fit too loosely?
e. Refer to part **d**. Calculate the approximate probability of observing a loose fit. [*Hint:*   Use the fact that the difference between the inside socket diameter and outside attachment diameter is approximately normal (since the two distributions are normal) with mean $\mu_1 - \mu_2$ and variance $\sigma_1^2 + \sigma_2^2$ (from Theorem 6.7).]

16.9   Acceptance Sampling for Defectives

In the preceding sections, we have learned how control charts can be used during the manufacturing process to monitor and improve the quality of a product. After manufacturing, items of the product are stored (and packaged) in *lots* containing anywhere from two to many thousands of items per lot, the *lot size* depending on the nature of the product. At this point, just prior to shipment, a second statistical tool—an **acceptance sampling plan**—is often employed to reduce the proportion of defective items shipped to customers.

An acceptance sampling plan works in the following way. A fixed number n of items is sampled from each lot, carefully inspected, and each item is judged to be either defective or nondefective. If the number y of defectives in the sample is less than or equal to a prespecified **acceptance number** *a*, the lot is accepted. If the number of defectives exceeds *a*, the lot is rejected and withheld for either a second sampling, a complete inspection, or some other procedure (see Figure 16.15). The objectives of the sampling plan are to accept and ship lots containing a small fraction *p* of defectives, to reject and withhold lots containing a high fraction of defectives, and to do both with a high probability.

FIGURE 16.15 ▶

Accepting or rejecting lots based on the number of defectives in a sample of *n* items

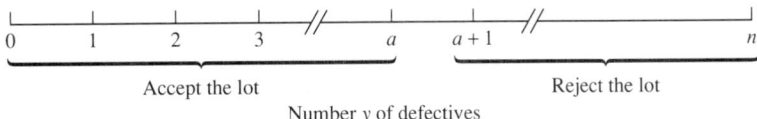

At this point you may wonder why quality control engineers resort to sampling rather than an inspection of all items in the lot. That is, why not 100% inspection? First, 100% inspection often turns out to be impractical or uneconomical. Second, studies have shown that the quality of the product shipped is often better with acceptance sampling than with 100% inspection, especially when there are a great many similar items of a product to be inspected. With 100% inspection, inspectors' fatigue on repetitive operations is always a danger. Also, psychologically, laborers have more of a tendency to make a quality product when only a few items are inspected.

Upon reflection, you can see that the decision procedure for accepting or rejecting a lot with acceptance sampling is simply a test of a hypothesis about the lot fraction defective *p*. The manufacturer (or customer) has in mind some lot fraction defective, say, p_0, called the **acceptable quality level** (**AQL**). If the lot fraction *p* is below p_0 = AQL, the lot is deemed acceptable. The probability α of rejecting

$$H_0: \quad p = p_0$$

if in fact $p = p_0$ (that is, if the lot is actually acceptable) is called the **producer's risk**. In other words, even if $p = p_0$, the manufacturer (the producer) will withhold $100\alpha\%$ of the acceptable lots from shipment and be subjected to the cost of resampling, and so on.

Definition 16.10

The **acceptable quality level** (**AQL**) is an upper limit, p_0, on the fraction defective that a producer is willing to tolerate.

Definition 16.11

The **producer's risk** is the probability α of rejecting lots if in fact the lot fraction defective is equal to p_0, the acceptable quality level. In the terminology of hypothesis testing, the producer's risk is the probability of a Type I error.

The consumer, the purchaser of the product, is also subject to a risk—namely, the risk of accepting lots containing a high fraction defective p. The consumer will usually have in mind a lot fraction defective p_1 which is the largest lot fraction defective that he or she will tolerate. The probability β of accepting lots containing fraction defective p_1 is called the **consumer's risk**.

Definition 16.12

The **consumer's risk** is the probability β of accepting lots containing fraction defective p_1 where p_1 is the upper limit in lot fraction defective acceptable to the consumer. In the terminology of hypothesis testing, the consumer's risk is the probability of a Type II error.

An **operating characteristic curve** is a graph of the probability of lot acceptance $P(A)$ versus lot fraction defective p. A typical operating characteristic curve, shown in Figure 16.16, completely characterizes a sampling plan and shows the probability of lot acceptance equal to 1 when $p = 0$ and equal to 0 when $p = 1$. As the lot fraction defective p increases, the probability $P(A)$ of lot acceptance decreases until it reaches 0. The producer's risk α is equal to $1 - P(A)$ when $p = p_0$. The consumer's risk β is equal to $P(A)$ when $p = p_1$.

FIGURE 16.16 ▶
A typical operating characteristic curve

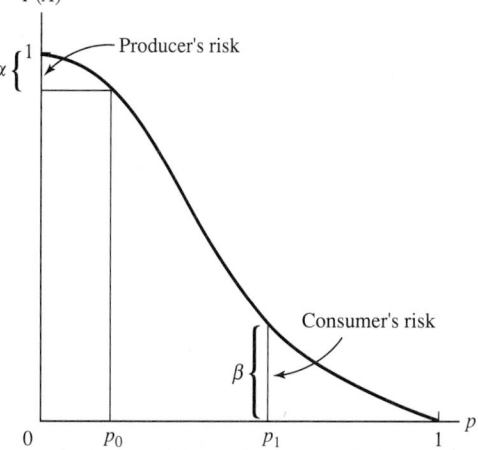

Definition 16.13

The **operating characteristic curve** for a sampling plan is a graph of the probability of lot acceptance, $P(A)$, versus the lot fraction defective, p.

The operating characteristic curve for a sampling plan can be constructed by calculating $P(A)$ for various values of the lot fraction defective p. As explained in Sections 4.6 and 4.9, the probability distribution for the number y of defectives in a sample of n items from a lot will depend on the lot size N. If N is large and n is small relative to N, then the probability distribution for y can be approximated by a **binomial probability distribution** (Section 4.6):

$$p(y) = \binom{n}{y} p^y q^{n-y} \qquad y = 0, 1, 2, \ldots, n$$

where

$$q = 1 - p$$

If N is small or n is large relative to N, then y will have a **hypergeometric probability distribution** (Section 4.9):

$$p(y) = \frac{\binom{r}{y}\binom{N-r}{n-y}}{\binom{N}{n}}$$

where

N = Lot size

r = Number of defectives in the lot

$p = \dfrac{r}{N}$ = Lot fraction defective

n = Sample size

y = Number of defectives in the sample

Using the appropriate probability distribution for a sampling plan with sample size n and acceptance number a, we can compute the probability of accepting a lot with lot fraction defective p:

$$P(A) = P(y \le a) = p(0) + p(1) + \cdots + p(a)$$

We will illustrate the procedure with the next example.

EXAMPLE 16.9

A manufacturer of metal gaskets ships a particular gasket in lots of 500 each. The acceptance sampling plan used prior to shipment is based on a sample size $n = 10$ and acceptance number $a = 1$.

a. Find the producer's risk if the AQL is .05.

b. Find the consumer's risk if the lot fraction defective is $p_1 = .20$.

c. Draw a rough sketch of the operating characteristic curve for the sampling plan.

Solution

a. The producer's risk is $\alpha = 1 - P(A)$ when $p = p_0 = .05$. For $N = 500$ and $n = 10$, y will possess approximately a binomial probability distribution. Then, if in fact $p = .05$,

$$P(A) = p(0) + p(1)$$

$$= \binom{10}{0}(.05)^0(.95)^{10} + \binom{10}{1}(.05)^1(.95)^9 = .914$$

and the producer's risk is

$$\alpha = 1 - P(A) = 1 - .914 = .086$$

This means that the producer will reject 8.6% of the lots, even if the lot fraction defective is as small as .05.

b. The consumer's risk is $\beta = P(A)$ when $p = .20$:

$$\beta = P(A) = p(0) + p(1)$$

$$= \binom{10}{0}(.2)^0(.8)^{10} + \binom{10}{1}(.2)^1(.8)^9 = .376$$

Thus, the consumer risks accepting lots containing a lot fraction defective equal to $p_1 = .20$ approximately 37.6% of the time. The fact that β is so large for $p_1 = .20$ indicates that this sampling plan would be of little value in practice. The plan needs to be based on a larger sample size.

c. A rough sketch of the operating characteristic curve for the sampling plan can be obtained using the two points calculated in parts **a** and **b** and the fact that $P(A) = 1$ when $p = 0$ and $P(A) = 0$ when $p = 1$. The sketch is shown in Figure 16.17.

FIGURE 16.17 ▶
A rough sketch of the operating characteristic curve of $n = 10$ and $a = 1$

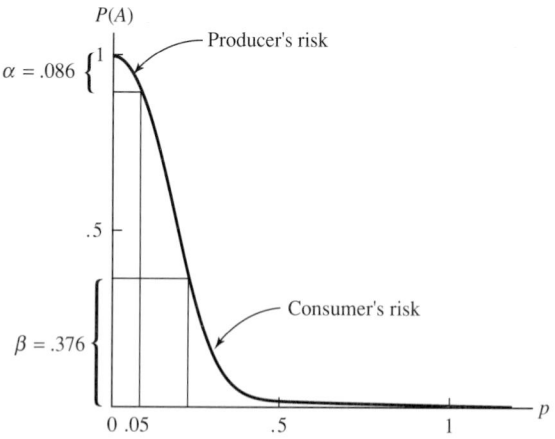

In practice, engineers do not construct sampling plans for specific lot sizes and AQLs because they have been constructed and have been in use for years. One of the most widely used collections of sampling plans is known as the **Military Standard 105D (MIL-STD-105D)**. The sampling plans contained in MIL-STD-105D employ a sample size n that varies with the lot size N. The sample sizes specified in the plans were chosen to give reasonable values of consumer risk. In addition, the plans have been constructed so that each falls into one of three levels of inspection categories: reduced (I), normal (II), or tightened (III). Lower consumer risks are associated with tighter plans.

Two of the MIL-STD-105D tables are reproduced in Tables 22 and 23 of Appendix II. The following example illustrates their use.

EXAMPLE 16.10

Find the appropriate MIL-STD-105D normal (level) general inspection sampling plan for a lot size of 500 items and an acceptable quality level of .065.

Solution

The first step in selecting the sampling plan is to identify the MIL-STD-105D code corresponding to a lot size of 500 and a normal inspection level—that is, level II. This code letter, H, is found in Table 22 of Appendix II, in the row corresponding to lot size 281–500 and in the column labeled II.

The second step in selecting the plan is to determine the sample size and acceptance number from Table 23 of Appendix II. The sample size code letters appear in the first column of the table. The recommended sample sizes are shown in the second column. Moving down column 1 to code letter H, we see that the recommended sample size (column 2) is $n = 50$. To find the acceptance number, move across the top row to 6.5%, or, equivalently, AQL $= .065$. The acceptance (Ac) number, $a = 7$, is shown at the intersection of the 6.5 column and the H row. The number 8 that also appears at this intersection is the rejection number for the sampling plan—that is, we reject a lot if y is greater than or equal to 8.

You can see that this MIL-STD-105D sampling plan uses a much larger sample ($n = 50$) than the plan of Example 16.9. Because of this larger sample size, the probability of lot acceptance, $P(A)$, calculated for a given lot fraction defective p, would be much smaller than for the plan of Example 16.9. We would say that the MIL-STD-105D plan is *tighter* than the plan of Example 16.9. The consumer risk is less or, equivalently, it allows fewer bad lots to be shipped.

The probability of acceptance $P(A)$ for the MIL-STD-105D sampling plan can be calculated as described earlier in this section. For example, for a lot fraction defective $p = .10$ in Example 16.10, we have

$$P(A) = P(y \leq 7)$$

$$= \sum_{y=0}^{7} p(y)$$

where $p(y)$ is a hypergeometric probability distribution with $N = 500$, $n = 50$, and the number r of defectives in the lot is $Np = (500)(.1) = 50$. The actual calculation of $P(A)$ is tedious and is best accomplished by using a computer.

EXERCISES

16.35 Consider a sampling plan with sample size $n = 5$ and acceptance number $a = 0$.
   a. Calculate the probability of lot acceptance for fractions defective $p = .1, .3,$ and $.5$. Sketch the operating characteristic curve for the plan.
   b. Find the producer's risk if AQL $= .01$.
   c. Find the consumer's risk if $p_1 = .10$.

16.36 Consider a sampling plan with sample size $n = 15$ and acceptance number $a = 1$.
   a. Calculate the probability of lot acceptance for fractions defective $p = .1, .2, .3, .4,$ and $.5$. Sketch the operating characteristic curve for the plan.
   b. Find the producer's risk if AQL $= .05$.
   c. Find the consumer's risk if $p_1 = .20$.

16.37 Find the appropriate MIL-STD-105D general inspection sampling plan for a lot size of 5,000 items and an AQL of 4% under each of the following inspection categories:
   a. Reduced (I) inspection level
   b. Normal (II) inspection level
   c. Tightened (III) inspection level

16.38 The tensile strengths of wires in a certain lot of size 400 are specified to exceed 5 kilograms. Consider an acceptance sampling plan based on a sample of $n = 10$ wires and acceptance number $a = 1$.
   a. Find the producer's risk if the AQL is 2.5%.
   b. Find the consumer's risk if the lot fraction failing to meet specifications is $p_1 = .15$.
   c. Draw a rough sketch of the operating characteristic curve for the sampling plan. Do you think the sampling plan is acceptable? Explain.

16.39 Refer to Exercise 16.38. Find the appropriate MIL-STD-105D normal (level) general inspection sampling plan for a lot size of 400 wires and an AQL of 2.5%.

16.10   Other Sampling Plans (Optional)

In Section 16.9, we presented a sampling plan based on the number of defectives contained in a single sample. A second type of acceptance sampling plan is one based on double or multiple sampling. A **double sampling plan** involves the selection of n_1 items from the lot. The lot is accepted if the number y_1 of defectives in the sample is $y_1 \leq a_1$ and rejected if $y_1 \geq r_1$ (where $r_1 > a_1$), as shown in Figure 16.18. If y_1 falls *between* a_1 and r_1, then a second sample of n_2 items is selected from the lot and the total number y of defectives in the $(n_1 + n_2)$ sampled items is recorded. If y is less than or equal to a second acceptance number a_2, the lot is accepted; otherwise, it is rejected.

The ultimate in multiple sampling is **sequential sampling**. In a sequential sampling plan, the items are selected from the lot, one by one. As each item is selected, a decision is made to accept the lot, to reject the lot, or to sample the next item from the lot. With this type of sampling, the decision to accept (or to reject) the lot might

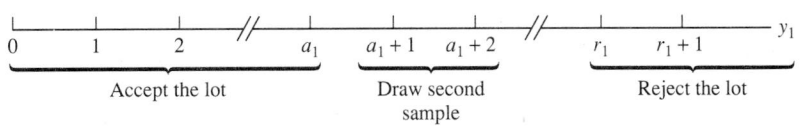

FIGURE 16.18 ▶
Location of the acceptance number a_1 and rejection number r_1 for the first sample in a double sampling plan

occur as early as the first, second, or third items sampled. It is also possible that the decision to accept or to reject the lot might require a very large sample. Thus, in sequential sampling, the sample size n is a random variable.

In addition to single, multiple, and sequential sampling plans based on the number y of defects observed, similar plans have been developed to utilize measurements on quantitative variables. Thus, instead of examining each item in a sample and rating it as defective or nondefective, we make our decision to reject or to accept the lot based on a quantitative measurement taken on each of the items. For example, a purchaser of 50-gallon barrels of acetone might be primarily concerned that each barrel contain at least 50 gallons. A typical sampling plan might involve sampling 10 barrels from each lot and measuring the exact number y of gallons in each barrel. We could classify each barrel that contains less than 50 gallons as defective and base our decision to reject or to accept the lot on the number of defective barrels in the sample. Alternatively, we could base our decision on the sample mean, $\bar{y}$, the average amount of acetone in the 10 barrels. A sampling plan based on the mean of a sample of quantitative measurements is called **acceptance sampling by variables**. One of the most widely used collections of such sampling plans is **Military Standard 414 (MIL-STD-414)**.

The literature on acceptance sampling plans is extensive. For collections of sampling plans and for more information on the subject, we refer you to the references at the end of the chapter. Before leaving this discussion, however, we leave you with this thought: *It does not always pay to sample.* There may be certain situations where the cost of sampling is so prohibitive that the only alternatives are either 100% inspection or no inspection at all. Thus, total cost plays an important role in the acceptance sampling plan selection process.

16.11 Evolutionary Operations (Optional)

An **evolutionary operation** is a technique designed to improve the yield and/or the quality of an industrial product by extracting information from an operating process. To illustrate the procedure, suppose that some quality characteristic of a chemical product—say, viscosity—is dependent on a number of variables, including the temperature of the raw materials and the pressure maintained within the vat in which they are mixed. To investigate the effect of these variables on the viscosity of a batch, we could simulate the process in a laboratory and conduct a multivariable experiment (for example, a factorial experiment) as described in Chapter 14. But this process would be costly and it is possible that the simulation would behave differently from the production process.

A second and less costly procedure is to concentrate on only two or three of the independent variables and to vary the settings of these variables according to a designed experiment. The key is to make the changes in the independent variables so small that there is no *observable* change in the quality of the product. To detect the effect of these small changes, we repeat the experiment over and over again until the sample sizes are so large that even small changes in the mean value of the quality variable are significant when tested statistically.

For example, suppose we know that a number of controllable process variables, including the temperature and pressure of raw materials, affect the viscosity of a batch-produced chemical. We are afraid to make experimental changes in these variables out of fear that we might produce a bad product and an accompanying financial loss. However, we know that very slight changes in temperature and pressure—say, changes of 2°F and 2 pounds per square inch (psi)—would have a negligible effect on product quality.

To investigate the effects of temperature and pressure, we will conduct an experiment in the operating process using the experimental design shown in Figure 16.19. The four temperature–pressure combinations at the corners of the design are the four factor–level combinations of a 2 × 2 factorial experiment. The pressure–temperature combination (50°F, 130 psi) was added at the center of the design region to enable us to detect a relatively high (or low) mean viscosity in the center of the experimental region, in case it exists.

FIGURE 16.19 ▶

An experimental design for an evolutionary operation

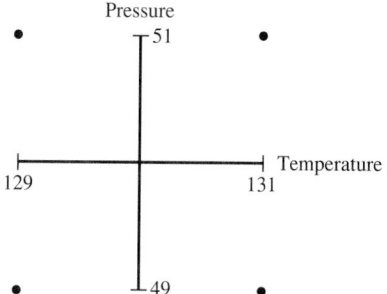

To conduct the evolutionary operation, we would assign one of the five pressure–temperature combinations to each batch of chemical and measure the viscosity *y* for each. If the manufacturer produces 10 batches per day, we would obtain two replications of the five treatments contained in the design shown in Figure 16.19. If we were to conduct statistical tests to detect changes in the mean viscosity based on the data for 1 day, or perhaps even for 100 days, it is conceivable that no changes in mean viscosity would be evident. However, if we continue to collect data over a long period of time, obtaining two replications of the experiment each day, we would eventually detect changes in mean viscosity (if they exist). Thus, the logic of an evolutionary operation is that a production process produces data at the same time that it generates a product. Why not utilize the information that is free (except for the cost of collection)? Although the individual observations contain very little information on the effect that pressure and temperature have on mean viscosity, the weight of huge amounts of data eventually will show us how to change these variables to produce desirable changes in mean viscosity. Thus, repeated experimentation over time enables the process to evolve to a higher level of quality and/or yield.

16.12   Summary

Chapter 16 introduced three statistical techniques useful in quality control: statistical control charts, acceptance sampling plans, and evolutionary operations. Although these methods involve relatively simple applications of statistical theory, they represent very powerful techniques for controlling and improving the quality of a manufactured product.

Control charts are used to monitor the quality characteristics of a product during the manufacturing process. Control charts indicate when something may be wrong with the manufacturing process. Although they do not specify what is wrong, the behavior of the plotted points on a control chart often provides clues that will lead a production engineer to the source of the trouble. The **x̄-charts** and **R-charts** monitor the mean and variability of a quantitative quality characteristic using the mean and range of samples selected at fixed intervals of time. A **p-chart** is used to monitor the fraction defective produced by a manufacturing process and a chart showing the **number of defects** tracks the mean number of defects per item.

Quality assurance sampling plans are utilized to prevent bad lots of product from being shipped to a manufacturer's customers. Thus, a sampling plan is intended to provide a screen at the door of the shipping department. The screen is supposed to pass good lots and withhold bad lots, both with a high probability. We described a single sampling plan for the number of defectives in a sample. We stated that a plan is completely described by its **operating characteristic curve**, a graph of the probability $P(A)$ of accepting a lot versus the lot fraction defective p $(0 \leq p \leq 1)$. **Acceptance sampling by variables**, and **double and sequential sampling plans** can also be used to withhold lots that contain an overly large fraction defective.

The third statistical technique presented was the concept of an **evolutionary operation**, the idea of experimenting and improving the quality of an industrial product during an ongoing manufacturing operation. Very small changes are made in the controllable process variables—changes so small that their effects would be undetectable using small to moderate sample sizes. The effects of these changes are detected by replicating the treatments of a simple experimental design, over and over again, until the effects of the small variable changes are clear. We then move the process control variable settings to the values that provide the best mean value for the quality characteristic and then repeat the experimentation using a new selection of design points. If the control variables really affect the quality characteristic, this process will lead to higher and higher levels of quality.

SUPPLEMENTARY EXERCISES

16.40 Specifications require the nickel content of manufactured stainless steel hydraulic valves to be 13% by weight. To monitor the production process, four valves were selected from the production line each hour over an 8-hour period and the percentage nickel content was measured for each, with the results recorded in the table.

Hour	Nickel Content			
1	13.1	12.8	12.7	12.9
2	12.5	13.0	13.6	13.1
3	12.9	12.9	13.2	13.3
4	12.4	13.0	12.1	12.6
5	12.8	11.9	12.7	12.4
6	13.0	13.6	13.2	12.9
7	13.5	13.5	13.1	12.7
8	12.6	13.9	13.3	12.8

a. Construct a control chart for the mean nickel content of the hydraulic valves.
b. Establish control limits for the mean using Table 19 of Appendix II.
c. Establish control limits for the mean using the standard deviation of the overall sample. Compare to the limits obtained in part **b.**
d. Do all observed sample means lie within the control limits? What are the consequences of this?
e. Find a 99% tolerance interval for 99% of the nickel contents in the hydraulic valves. Assume that the distribution of nickel contents is approximately normal.
f. Construct a control chart with control limits for the variability in the nickel contents of the hydraulic valves. Interpret your results.

16.41 A quality control inspector is studying the alternative sampling plans $(n = 5, a = 1)$ and $(n = 25, a = 5)$.
a. Sketch the operating characteristic curves for both plans, using lot fractions defective .05, .10, .20, .30, and .40.
b. As a seller producing lots with AQL $= .10$, which of the two sampling plans would you prefer? Why?
c. As a buyer wanting to protect against accepting lots with fraction defective exceeding $p_1 = .30$, which of the two sampling plans would you prefer? Why?

16.42 A company manufactures rolled steel for nuclear submarines. To monitor the production process, a quality control inspector sampled finished rolls of steel from the production line, one each hour for 12 consecutive hours. The number of imperfections discovered on each roll is recorded in the table.

Hour	1	2	3	4	5	6	7	8	9	10	11	12
Number of Imperfections	14	10	8	7	11	12	6	15	13	4	9	10

a. Construct a control chart for the number of imperfections per finished roll of steel.
b. Locate the center line and upper and lower control limits on the chart.
c. Does the manufacturing process appear to be in control?

16.43 For a lot of 250 electron tubes with an acceptance quality level of 10%, find the appropriate MIL-STD-105D general inspection sampling plan under each of the following inspection categories:

  a. Normal inspection level

  b. Tightened inspection level

16.44 High-level computer technology has developed bit-sized microprocessors for use in operating industrial "robots." To monitor the fraction of defective microprocessors produced by a manufacturing process, 50 microprocessors are sampled each hour. The results for 20 hours of sampling are provided in the table.

Sample	1	2	3	4	5	6	7	8	9	10
Number of Defectives	5	6	4	7	1	3	6	5	4	5
Sample	11	12	13	14	15	16	17	18	19	20
Number of Defectives	8	3	2	1	0	1	1	2	3	3

  a. Construct a control chart for the proportion of defective microprocessors.

  b. Locate the center line and upper and lower control limits on the chart. Does the process appear to be in control?

  c. Conduct a runs analysis for the control chart. Interpret the result.

16.45 A construction engineer buys steel cable in large rolls to use in supporting equipment and temporary structures during the process of erecting permanent structures. Specifications require the breaking strength of the steel cable to exceed 200 pounds. For a lot size of 1,500 large rolls of steel cable, consider an acceptance sampling plan based on a sample of $n = 20$ rolls and acceptance number $a = 2$.

  a. Find the producer's risk if the AQL is .05.

  b. Find the consumer's risk if the lot fraction failing to meet breaking strength specifications is $p_1 = .10$.

  c. Draw a rough sketch of the operating characteristic curve for the sampling plan. Is the sampling plan reasonable?

  d. Find the appropriate MIL-STD-105D normal (level) general inspection sampling plan for a lot size of 1,500 large rolls of steel cable and an AQL of .05.

  e. Refer to part **d**. Find the producer's risk under the inspection sampling plan. [*Hint:* Use the normal approximation to the binomial.]

  f. Refer to part **d**. Find the consumer's risk if the lot fraction failing to meet breaking strength specifications is $p_1 = .08$. [*Hint:* Use the normal approximation to the binomial.]

16.46 Refer to the stress analysis on epoxy-repaired truss joints described in Exercise 8.33. Tests were conducted on epoxy-bonded truss joints made of wood to determine tolerances for actual glue line shear stress (*Journal of Structural Engineering*, Feb. 1986). The mean and standard deviation of the shear strengths (pounds per square inch) for a random sample of 100 Southern pine truss joints are

$$\bar{x} = 1,312 \qquad s = 422$$

  a. Assuming the distribution of strength measurements is approximately normal, construct a 95% tolerance interval for 99% of the shear strengths.

  b. Interpret the interval obtained in part **b**.

  c. Explain how you could obtain a tolerance interval when the normality assumption is not satisfied.

COMPUTER LAB: Control Charts

In this lab section, we provide instructions on how to use the control charts available in MINITAB. MINITAB will automatically compute control limits and plot the points on a control chart. Specifically, the program statements generate a variable chart for the data of Table 16.1, an $\bar{x}$-chart and R-chart for the data of Table 16.2, a p-chart for the data of Table 16.3, and a c-chart for the data of Table 16.4. [*Note:* Although control chart routines are not available in SAS, you can generate these charts by using the SAS plotting commands.]

Command
line

1	SET C1	Data entry instructions
2	1.00 .99 .98 1.01 1.01	
	. . . . .	Input data values
	. . . . .	(5 observations per line)
	. . . . .	
	1.01 .99 .99 .97 .97	
3	NAME C1='LENGTH'	
4	ICHART C1	Individuals chart
1	SET C2	Data entry instruction
	1.505 1.499 1.501 1.488	
	. . . .	Input data values
	. . . .	(4 observations per line)
	. . . .	
6	1.494 1.501 1.508 1.519	
7	NAME C2='DIAMETER'	
8	XBARCHART C2 4	$\bar{x}$-chart
9	RCHART C2 4	R-chart
10	SET C3	Data entry instruction
	2 12 3 4 . . .	Input data values
11	NAME C3='DEFECTS'	
12	PCHART C3 100	p-chart
13	SET C4	Data entry instruction
	11 14 10 . . .	Input data values
14	NAME C4='DEFECTS'	
15	CCHART C4	c-chart

COMMAND 4   ICHART generates an individuals chart for the variable in the specified column.

COMMAND 8   XBARCHART generates an $\bar{x}$-chart for the variable in the specified column. The number of observations in each subgroup (sample) is specified after the column. (In this program, MINITAB reads the first four numbers as the first sample, the second four numbers as the second sample, etc.)

COMMAND 9   RCHART generates an R-chart for the variable in the specified column. The number of observations in each subgroup (sample) is specified after the column.

COMMAND 10   One observation is read for each sample (usually the observation represents the number of nonconformities).

COMMAND 12   PCHART produces a p-chart for the variable (number of nonconformities) in the column specified. The sample size is specified after the column.

COMMAND 15   CCHART produces a c-chart for the variable (number of defects) in the column specified.

NOTE   The output for this MINITAB program is displayed in Figure 16.20.

FIGURE 16.20 ▶

MINITAB output for Computer Lab

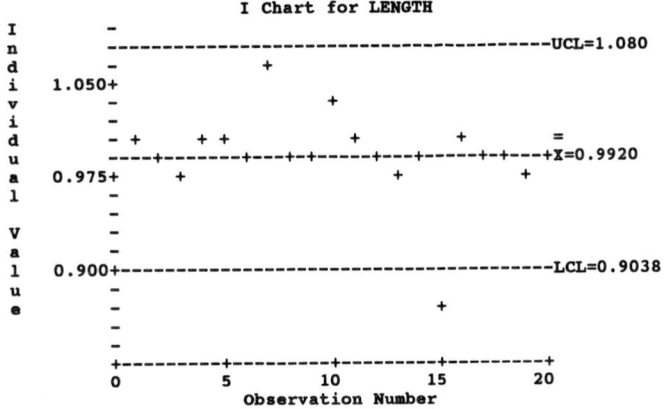

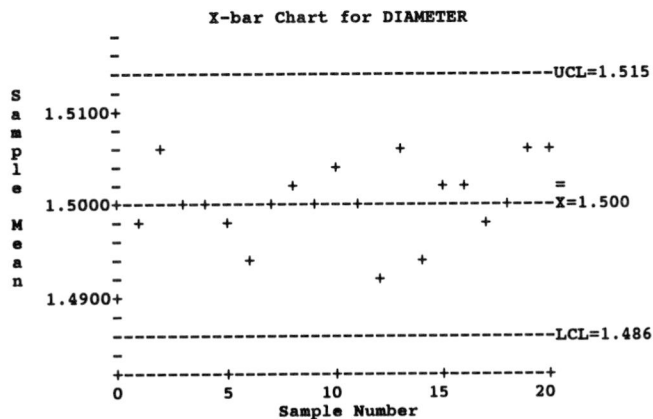

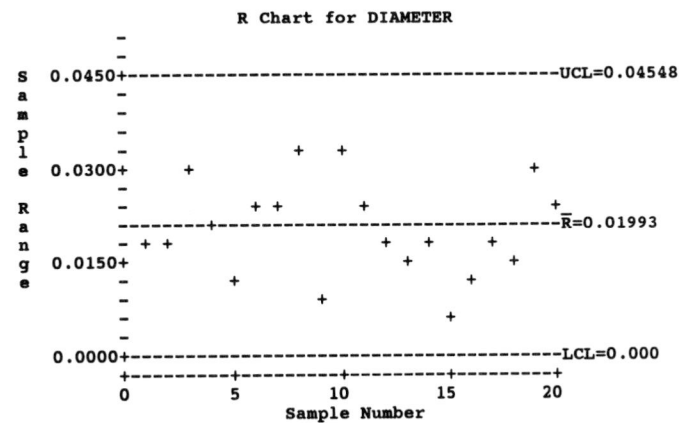

(continued)

FIGURE 16.20 ▶
Continued

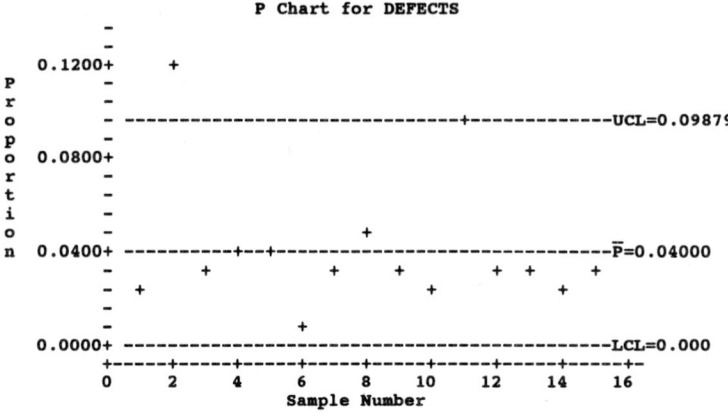

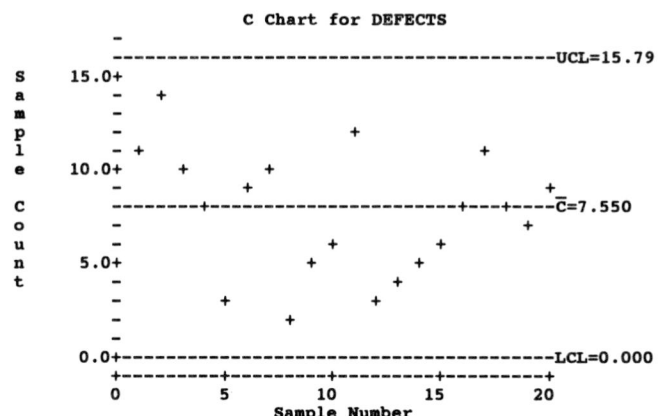

References

Box, G. E. P. "Evolutionary Operation: A Method for Increasing Industrial Productivity," *Applied Statistics*, Vol. 6, 1957, pp. 3–23.

Box, G. E. P., and Hunter, J. S. "Condensed Calculations for Evolutionary Operation Programs," *Technometrics*, Vol. 1, 1959, pp. 77–95.

Deming, W. E. *Quality, Productivity, and Competitive Position*. Cambridge, Mass.: MIT Press, 1982.

Grant, E. L., and Leavenworth, R. S. *Statistical Quality Control*, 5th ed. New York: McGraw-Hill, 1980.

Hald, A. *Statistical Theory of Sampling Inspection of Attributes*. New York: Academic Press, 1981.

Juran, J. M., and Gryna, F. M. *Quality Planning and Analysis*. New York: McGraw-Hill, 1970.

Mendenhall, W. *The Design and Analysis of Experiments*. Belmont, Calif.: Wadsworth, 1968.

Military Standard 105D. Washington, D. C.: U. S. Government Printing Office, 1963.

National Bureau of Standards, *Tables of the Binomial Distribution*. Washington, D. C.: U. S. Government Printing Office, 1950.

Ott, E. R. *Process Quality Control: Trouble-shooting and Interpretation of Data*. New York: McGraw-Hill, 1975.

Romig, H. G. 50–100 *Binomial Tables*. New York: Wiley, 1953.

Ryan, T. P. *Statistical Methods for Quality Improvement*. New York: Wiley, 1989.

Shewhart, W. A. *Economic Control of Quality of Manufactured Product*. Princeton, N. J.: Van Nostrand Reinhold, 1931.

CHAPTER SEVENTEEN

Product and System Reliability

Objective

To present some statistical methods for estimating the probability that a manufactured product or a system will perform satisfactorily for a specified period of time

Contents

17.1   Introduction

Do your stereo system and your automobile perform well for a reasonably long period of time? If they do, we would say that these products are *reliable*.

The **reliability** of a product is the probability that the product will meet certain specifications for a given period of time. For example, suppose we want a new automobile to perform without malfunction for a period of 2 years or for 20,000 miles. The probability that an automobile will meet these specifications is the *reliability* of the automobile.

> ### Definition 17.1
>
> The **reliability** of a product is the probability that the product will meet a set of specifications for a given period of time.

Some products need to function on a one-time basis. Others repeat a function over and over until they eventually fail. For example, a fuse either works or does not work when an electrical circuit is overloaded. The reliability of a fuse is the probability that it will work when subjected to a specific overload. In contrast, an automobile is used over and over again; its reliability is the probability that the automobile will perform without a major malfunction for some specified period of time.

17.2   Failure Time Distributions

The *length of life* of a product is the length of time until the product fails to perform according to specifications. When the product fails to perform according to specifications, it is said to have *failed*.

The time at which a single product item fails is called the **failure time** for the item. For example, the length of life of an abrasive grinding wheel is the length of time until the wheel fails to perform according to specifications. The specifications may have been determined by the manufacturer or the user may have written his or her own specifications. The length of time until failure is called the failure time of the wheel.

> ### Definition 17.2
>
> The **failure time** of a product is the length of time that the product performs according to specifications.

The failure time t for any product varies from one item to another and is, in fact, a random variable. The density function for a product failure time is called a **failure time distribution**. A typical failure time distribution might appear as shown in Figure 17.1.

> ## Definition 17.3
>
> The **failure time distribution** for a product is the density function of the failure time t.

FIGURE 17.1 ▶
A failure time distribution

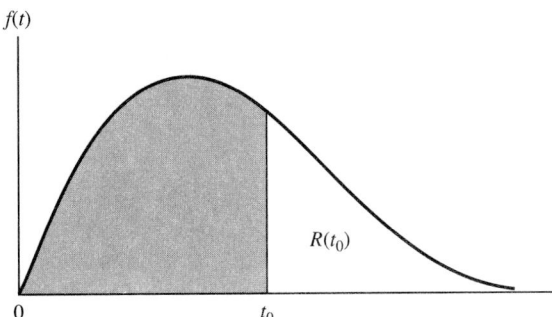

If we denote the failure time density function by the symbol $f(t)$, then the probability that the product will fail before time t_0 is

$$F(t_0) = \int_0^{t_0} f(t)dt$$

This probability is the shaded area under the density function shown in Figure 17.1.

Suppose that a product is said to be *reliable* if it survives until time t_0. Then the reliability of the product—that is, the probability that it will survive until time t_0—is

$$R(t_0) = 1 - F(t_0)$$

This probability, $R(t_0)$, is the unshaded area under the density function to the right of t_0 in Figure 17.1.

Realistically, the failure time distribution is a conceptual relative frequency distribution of the lengths of life of some group of product items of specific interest—say, those manufactured in a given week, month, or year. Based on an analysis of sample data, we may select one of the density functions described in Chapter 5 to model this distribution. The family of density functions represented by the Weibull distribution (discussed in Section 5.8) is often used for this purpose.

17.3   Hazard Rates

The failure time distribution for a product enables us to calculate the probability $F(t_0)$ that an item will fail before time t_0 and the probability $R(t_0) = 1 - F(t_0)$ that the item will survive until time t_0. The probability that an item will fail in the interval $(t, t + dt)$ is the shaded area shown in Figure 17.2. The density $f(t)$, the height of the shaded rectangle, is proportional to this probability.

Another way to describe the life characteristics of a product is to use a measure of the probability of failure as the product gets older—that is, the probability that the product will fail in the interval $(t, t + dt)$, given that the item has survived to time t.

If we define the events

A: Item fails in the interval $(t, t + dt)$

B: Item survives until time t

FIGURE 17.2 ▶

A failure time distribution showing the approximate probability of failure during the interval $(t, t + dt)$

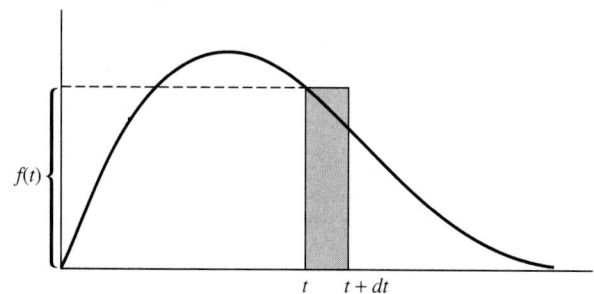

then the probability of failure in the time interval $(t, t + dt)$, given that the item has survived to time t, is

$$P(A \mid B) = \frac{P(A \cap B)}{P(B)}$$

But, the event $A \cap B$ is equivalent to the event A—that is, an item must have survived to time t for it to be able to fail in the interval $(t, t + dt)$. Therefore,

$$P(A \cap B) = P(A)$$

This probability is approximately equal to the shaded area in Figure 17.2. Then the probability of failure in the interval $(t, t + dt)$, given that the item has survived to time t, is

$$P(A \mid B) = \frac{P(A \cap B)}{P(B)} \approx \frac{f(t)dt}{1 - F(t)} = \frac{f(t)dt}{R(t)}$$

The quantity

$$z(t) = \frac{f(t)}{R(t)}$$

is proportional to this conditional probability and is called the **hazard rate** for the product.

Knowledge about a product's hazard rate often helps us to select the appropriate failure time density function for the product. The following example illustrates the point.

Definition 17.4

The **hazard rate** for a product is defined to be

$$z(t) = \frac{f(t)}{1 - F(t)} = \frac{f(t)}{R(t)}$$

where $f(t)$ is the density function of the product's failure time distribution.

EXAMPLE 17.1

The exponential distribution (discussed in Section 5.7) is often used in industry to model the failure time distribution of a product. Find the hazard rate for the exponential distribution.

Solution

The exponential density function and cumulative distribution function are, respectively,

$$f(t) = \frac{e^{-t/\beta}}{\beta} \qquad 0 \le t < \infty, \quad \beta > 0$$

and

$$F(t) = \int_{-\infty}^{t} f(y)dy = \int_{0}^{t} \frac{e^{-y/\beta}}{\beta}\,dy = 1 - e^{-t/\beta}$$

Then the hazard rate for the exponential distribution is

$$z(t) = \frac{f(t)}{1 - F(t)} = \frac{\dfrac{e^{-t/\beta}}{\beta}}{1 - (1 - e^{-t/\beta})} = \frac{1}{\beta}$$

Since $\beta = E(t)$ is the mean life of the product, it follows that the hazard rate is constant (see Figure 17.3 on page 1040). Therefore, a product that has an exponential failure time distribution never becomes fatigued. It is just as likely to survive any one unit of time as it is any other.

FIGURE 17.3 ▶
Hazard rate for the exponential
failure time distribution

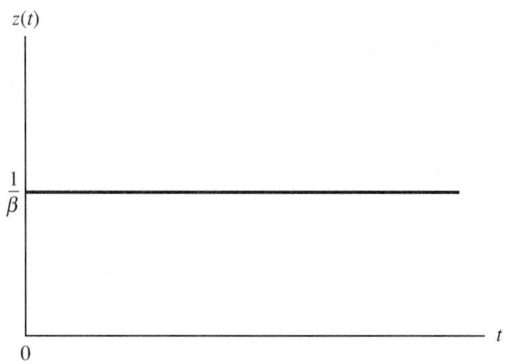

Clearly, the exponential distribution would not provide a good model for the failure time distribution of humans or for industrial products that become fatigued and more prone to failure as they get older. But it does provide a good model for some products, particularly for complex systems whose parts are replaced as they fail. After such systems have been in operation for a while, the probability of failure tends to be as likely in any one unit of time as in any other. Failure time distributions that exhibit this property (i.e., a constant hazard rate) are often called **memoryless distributions**.

The Weibull distribution density function (discussed in Section 5.8) and cumulative distribution function are, respectively,

$$f(t) = \frac{\alpha}{\beta}t^{\alpha-1}e^{-t^\alpha/\beta} \qquad 0 \le t < \infty; \quad \alpha > 0; \quad \beta > 0$$

and

$$F(t) = 1 - e^{-t^\alpha/\beta}$$

By changing the shape parameter α and the scale parameter β, we obtain a variety of density functions useful for modeling failure time distributions for many industrial products. For $\alpha = 1$, we obtain the exponential distribution.

EXAMPLE 17.2

Find the hazard rate for the Weibull distribution and graph $z(t)$ versus time for $\alpha = 1, 2,$ and 3.

Solution

Using the density function and cumulative distribution functions given above, we determine the hazard rate for the Weibull distribution:

$$z(t) = \frac{f(t)}{1 - F(t)} = \frac{\left(\frac{\alpha}{\beta}\right)t^{\alpha-1}e^{-t^\alpha/\beta}}{1 - (1 - e^{-t^\alpha/\beta})} = \frac{\alpha}{\beta}t^{\alpha-1}$$

When the shape parameter α is equal to 1, we obtain

$$z(t) = \frac{1}{\beta}$$

which is the constant hazard rate for the exponential distribution. For $\alpha = 2$,

$$z(t) = \frac{2}{\beta}t$$

the equation of a straight line passing through the origin. For $\alpha = 3$,

$$z(t) = \frac{3}{\beta}t^2$$

a second-order function of time t. Graphs of these hazard rates are shown in Figure 17.4. Note that the hazard rate increases more rapidly with time for larger values of the shape parameter α.

FIGURE 17.4 ▶
Graphs of the hazard rate for Weibull distributions with $\alpha = 1, 2, 3$

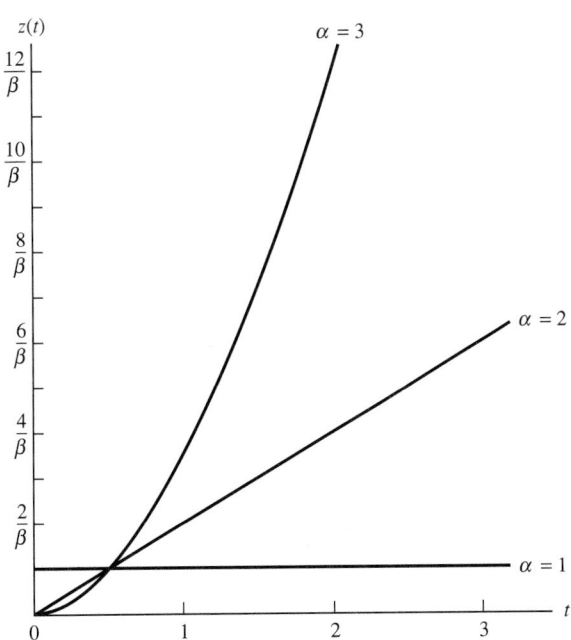

EXERCISES

17.1 Find and graph the hazard rate $z(t)$ for a Weibull distribution with:
   a. $\alpha = 1, \quad \beta = 4$ **b.** $\alpha = 2, \quad \beta = 2$ **c.** $\alpha = 3, \quad \beta = 6$

17.2 Graph the hazard rate $z(t)$ for Weibull distributions with $\beta = 1$ and $\alpha = 1, 2, 3$, and 4.

17.3 Suppose the failure time distribution for a product can be approximated by a normal distribution with $\mu = 3$ and $\sigma = 1$.
   a. Find $f(t)$, $F(t)$, and $z(t)$ for $t = 0, 1, 2, \ldots, 6$.
   b. Plot the values of $z(t)$ for corresponding values of t and obtain a graph of the hazard rate for this normal failure time distribution.

17.4   The lifetime t (in hours) of a certain electronic component is a random variable with density function

$$f(t) = \begin{cases} \dfrac{1}{100}e^{-t/100} & t > 0 \\ 0 & \text{elsewhere} \end{cases}$$

a. Find $F(t)$ and $R(t)$.
b. What is the reliability of the component at $t = 25$ hours?
c. Find $z(t)$ and interpret the result.

17.5   A drill bit has a failure time distribution given by the density

$$f(t) = \begin{cases} \dfrac{2te^{-t^2/100}}{100} & 0 \le t < \infty \\ 0 & \text{elsewhere} \end{cases}$$

a. Find $F(t)$.
b. Find expressions for the reliability $R(t)$ and the hazard rate $z(t)$ of the drill bit at time t.
c. Use the results of part **b** to find $R(8)$ and $z(8)$.

17.6   The failure of a computer disk pack is considered to be an *initial failure* if it occurs prior to time $t = \alpha$ and a *wear-out failure* if it occurs after time $t = \beta$. Suppose the failure time distribution during the useful life of the disk pack is given by

$$f(t) = \frac{1}{\beta - \alpha} \qquad \alpha \le t \le \beta$$

a. Find $F(t)$ and $R(t)$.
b. Find the hazard rate $z(t)$.
c. Graph the hazard rate of the disk pack for $\alpha = 100$ hours and $\beta = 1,500$ hours.
d. For $\alpha = 100$ and $\beta = 1,500$, what is the reliability of the disk pack at time $t = 500$ hours? What is the hazard rate?

17.4   Life Testing: Censored Sampling

A **life test** is an experiment conducted to obtain sample values of the lengths of life of some product items. Typically, a random sample of n items is placed on test under specified environmental conditions and left on test until they fail. The recorded times to failure, $t_1, t_2, \ldots, t_n$, provide a random sample of observations on the length of life t of the product. If for convenience we let t_1 represent the smallest failure time, t_2 the second smallest, $\ldots$, and t_n the largest, then the times might appear as points on a time line, as shown in Figure 17.5.

FIGURE 17.5 ▶
Failure times of n items of some product

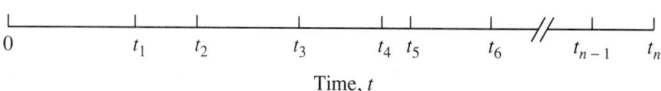

In many situations, life tests are conducted to determine the quality of a manufactured product prior to sale. Waiting for the last few items in a sample to fail can be time-consuming and expensive. To reduce the cost of waiting for some long-life items, tests are often concluded after a specified length T of test time. When we do this, we say that the life test is **censored** at time T. A second type of censored sampling occurs when we conclude the testing after a fixed number r of items have failed.

If a life test is censored at a fixed time T, the length of testing time is fixed. This makes it easier to schedule the life-testing equipment, but the number r of failures observed prior to time T is a random variable. Thus, r could assume any integer value in the interval $0 \le r \le n$, and it is possible that no failure times would be observed. If the test is censored after a fixed number r of failures have been observed, we know that we will always acquire the values of r failure times, but the length of the life test will be variable and equal to the length of time t_r until failure of the rth item.

There are many other types of life-testing procedures. In **life testing with replacement**, product items are replaced on the test equipment as soon as an item fails, a procedure that makes maximum use of the test equipment. Other tests are designed to investigate the effect of various stresses on a product by testing the items under varying stresses. Tests of this type are called **accelerated life tests**. Descriptions of these and other life test procedures, as well as methods for using the sample data to estimate the parameters of failure time distributions, are described in the references at the end of the chapter.

17.5 Estimating the Parameters of an Exponential Failure Time Distribution

The methods for finding estimators of the parameters of failure time distributions are those described in the preceding chapters. We can use the method of moments (Chapter 8), method of maximum likelihood (Chapter 8), or the method of least squares (Chapter 11). Depending on the failure time distribution and the number of parameters involved, finding the estimator may be easy or difficult. For example, finding the maximum likelihood estimator of the parameter of an exponential distribution based on simple random sampling is easy (see Example 8.5), but solving the maximum likelihood equations obtained for estimating the parameters of a Weibull distribution is relatively difficult.

It is also difficult to obtain estimators and their sampling distributions based on certain types of sampling, especially when the sampling has been censored at a fixed time T. Consequently, in this and the following sections, we will present estimation procedures for the exponential and the Weibull failure time distributions. Estimation procedures for these and other failure time distributions are discussed in the literature or in texts on product and system reliability.

We will first consider estimators for the mean failure time β for the exponential distribution. Estimators for β are the same regardless of whether the life test is censored or uncensored; the estimator is always equal to the total observed life divided by the number r of failures observed. For example, if a random sample of n items is selected from the population and the life test is concluded after the rth failure is observed $(r > 0)$, then

$$\hat{\beta} = \frac{\sum_{i=1}^{r} t_i + (n - r)t_r}{r} = \frac{\text{Total observed life}}{r}$$

If we wait until all n items fail, then $r = n$ and the estimator is the sample mean failure time:

$$\hat{\beta} = \frac{\sum_{i=1}^{n} t_i}{n} = \bar{t}$$

Note that for both the censored and uncensored sampling situations, the numerator in the above expressions is equal to the total length of life observed for the n items during the length of the life test.

For censored sampling with a fixed time of testing T,

$$\hat{\beta} = \frac{\sum_{i=1}^{r} t_i + (n - r)T}{r} = \frac{\text{Total observed life}}{r} \qquad \text{for } r \geq 1$$

Again, note that the numerator in this expression is the total length of life recorded for the n items until the life test is concluded at time T.

Point Estimators of the Mean Life β for an Exponential Distribution

For uncensored life testing:

$$\hat{\beta} = \frac{\sum_{i=1}^{n} t_i}{n}$$

For censored sampling with r fixed:

$$\hat{\beta} = \frac{\sum_{i=1}^{r} t_i + (n - r)t_r}{r}$$

For censored sampling with test time T fixed:

$$\hat{\beta} = \frac{\sum_{i=1}^{r} t_i + (n - r)T}{r}$$

The formulas for $(1 - \alpha)100\%$ confidence intervals for β are shown in the following boxes. The confidence interval based on sampling censored at a fixed point in time is only approximate.

A $(1 - \alpha)100\%$ Confidence Interval for β Based on Censored Sampling with r Fixed

$$\frac{2(\text{Total life})}{\chi^2_{\alpha/2}} \leq \beta \leq \frac{2(\text{Total life})}{\chi^2_{(1-\alpha/2)}}$$

where

$$\text{Total life} = \sum_{i=1}^{r} t_i + (n - r)t_r$$

and $\chi^2_{\alpha/2}$ and $\chi^2_{(1-\alpha/2)}$ are the tabulated values of a chi-square statistic, based on $2r$ degrees of freedom, that locate $\alpha/2$ in the upper and lower tails, respectively, of the chi-square distribution.

An Approximate $(1 - \alpha)100\%$ Confidence Interval for β Based on Censored Sampling with T Fixed

$$\frac{2(\text{Total life})}{\chi^2_{\alpha/2}} \leq \beta \leq \frac{2(\text{Total life})}{\chi^2_{(1-\alpha/2)}}$$

where

$$\text{Total life} = \sum_{i=1}^{r} t_i + (n - r)T$$

and $\chi^2_{\alpha/2}$ and $\chi^2_{(1-\alpha/2)}$ are the tabulated upper- and lower-tail values of a chi-square distribution based on $(2r + 2)$ degrees of freedom.

EXAMPLE 17.3

Suppose that the length of time between malfunctions for a particular type of aircraft engine has an exponential failure time distribution. Ten of the engines were tested until six of the engines malfunctioned. The times to malfunction were 48, 35, 91, 62, 59, and 77 hours, respectively. Find a 95% confidence interval for the mean time β between malfunctions for the engines.

Solution

Since this life test was concluded after the sixth failure was observed, it represents censored sampling with $r = 6$. The total observed life for the test was

$$\text{Total life} = \sum_{i=1}^{r} t_i + (n - r)t_r$$

$$= 372 + 364 = 736 \text{ hours}$$

The tabulated values of $\chi^2_{.025}$ and $\chi^2_{.975}$, based on $2r = 2(6) = 12$ degrees of freedom, are 23.3367 and 4.40379, respectively. Then the 95% confidence interval for β is

$$\frac{2(736)}{23.3367} \le \beta \le \frac{2(736)}{4.40379}$$

or $63.08 \le \beta \le 334.26$. Our interpretation is that the true mean time β between malfunctions of this particular type of aircraft engine falls between 63.08 hours and 334.26 hours, with 95% confidence.

EXAMPLE 17.4

Refer to Example 17.3.

a. Find a 95% confidence interval for the hazard rate of the aircraft engine.
b. Find a 95% confidence interval for the reliability of the system at time 50 hours.

Solution

a. Recall from Section 17.3 that the hazard rate for the exponential distribution is $1/\beta$. We therefore begin with the 95% confidence interval for β derived in Example 17.3 and transform it to a confidence interval for $1/\beta$:

$$63.08 \le \beta \le 334.26$$

$$\frac{1}{334.26} \le \frac{1}{\beta} \le \frac{1}{63.08}$$

$$.003 \le \frac{1}{\beta} \le .016$$

Thus, the hazard rate for the aircraft engine at time t (which is proportional to the probability that the engine will fail during a fixed small interval of time, given that the engine has survived to time t) falls between .003 and .016 with 95% confidence.

b. From Example 17.1, the cumulative distribution function for the exponential distribution is

$$F(t) = 1 - e^{-t/\beta}$$

By definition, the reliability of the aircraft engine at time t_0 is

$$R(t_0) = 1 - F(t_0)$$
$$= 1 - (1 - e^{-t_0/\beta}) = e^{-t_0/\beta}$$

or, for $t_0 = 50$ hours, $R(50) = e^{-50/\beta}$.

Then $63.08 \leq \beta \leq 334.26$ is equivalent to

$$e^{-50/63.08} \leq e^{-50/\beta} \leq e^{-50/334.26}$$

$$.453 \leq e^{-50/\beta} \leq .861$$

Therefore, the probability that the engine survives at least 50 hours may be as low as .453 or as high as .861, with 95% confidence.

EXERCISES

17.7   A wet-mix, steel-fiber reinforced microsilica concrete (called *shotcrete*), used extensively in Scandinavia, is now being marketed in the United States. The material is said to have a minimum 28-day breaking strength of 9,000 pounds per square inch (psi) of compression. To investigate the breaking strength of the new product, seven pieces of shotcrete were subjected to 9,000 psi of compression daily until they failed. The times to failure were 33, 35, 61, 38, 21, 41, and 52 days. Assuming that the shotcrete has an exponential failure time distribution when subjected to 9,000 psi of compression, find a 90% confidence interval for the mean time β until the shotcrete fails.

17.8   Refer to Exercise 17.7.
   a. Find a 90% confidence interval for the probability that the shotcrete will not fail before the 28-day specified minimum.
   b. Find a 90% confidence interval for the hazard rate of the shotcrete.

17.9   A study was conducted to estimate the mean life (in miles) of a certain type of locomotive using censored sampling (*Technometrics*, May 1985). Ninety-six locomotives were operated for either 135 thousand miles or until failure. Of these, 37 failed before the 135-thousand-mile period. The accompanying table contains the miles to failure for these locomotives. Assuming an exponential failure time distribution, construct a 95% confidence interval for the mean miles to failure of the locomotives.

Miles to Failure

22.5	57.5	78.5	91.5	113.5	122.5
37.5	66.5	80.0	93.5	116.0	123.0
46.0	68.0	81.5	102.5	117.0	127.5
48.5	69.5	82.0	107.0	118.5	131.0
51.5	76.5	83.0	108.5	119.0	132.5
53.0	77.0	84.0	112.5	120.0	134.0
54.5					

Source: Schmee, J., Gladstein, D., and Nelson, W. "Confidence limits for parameters of a normal distribution from singly-censored samples, using maximum likelihood." *Technometrics*, Vol. 27, No. 2, May 1985, p. 119.

17.10   Suppose that an integrated circuit chip possesses an exponential failure time distribution. Fifteen chips were put on accelerated life test until five of the chips failed. The first five failures occurred at 18.2, 19.5, 24.8, 31.0, and 45.6 (in thousands of hours).

a. Find a 95% confidence interval for the mean time between failures of the circuit chips.

b. Find a 95% confidence interval for the reliability of the circuit chips at 20,000 hours.

17.11   A sample of 100 high-reliability capacitors was placed on test for 2,000 hours. At the end of this period only three capacitors had malfunctioned, with failure times of 810, 1,422, and 1,816 hours. Assuming an exponential failure time distribution, construct a 99% confidence interval for the mean time between failures of the capacitors. Interpret the interval.

17.12   Refer to Exercise 17.11.

a. Find a 99% confidence interval for the hazard rate of the capacitors.

b. Find a 99% confidence interval for the reliability of the capacitors at 3,000 hours.

c. Find a 99% confidence interval for the probability that a capacitor will fail before 2,000 hours.

17.6   Estimating the Parameters of a Weibull Failure Time Distribution

The method of maximum likelihood (discussed in Section 8.3) can be used to obtain estimates of the shape and scale parameters of the Weibull distribution, but the procedure is difficult and beyond the scope of this text. The interested reader should consult the references listed at the end of the chapter. The disadvantage of the method of maximum likelihood is that the estimates of α and β are obtained by solving a complicated pair of simultaneous nonlinear equations. The advantage of the method is that when the sample size n is large, maximum likelihood estimators possess sampling distributions that are approximately normal with known means and variances. This fact can be used to form large-sample confidence intervals using the method described in Section 8.4.

Instead of using the method of maximum likelihood to estimate α and β, we will use the method of least squares. You will recall that the cumulative distribution function for the Weibull distribution is

$$F(t) = 1 - e^{-t^{\alpha}/\beta}$$

Then the probability of survival to time t is

$$R(t) = 1 - F(t)$$
$$= e^{-t^{\alpha}/\beta}$$

and

$$\frac{1}{R(t)} = e^{t^{\alpha}/\beta}$$

Taking the natural logarithms of both sides of this equation, we obtain

$$\ln\left[\frac{1}{R(t)}\right] = \frac{t^{\alpha}}{\beta}$$

$$-\ln R(t) = \frac{t^{\alpha}}{\beta}$$

$$\ln[-\ln R(t)] = -\ln \beta + \alpha \ln t$$

To use the method of least squares, we need to estimate the survival function based on life test data. One way to do this is to place a random sample of n items on life test and count the number of survivors at the end of one unit of time (for example, a week, or a month), after two units of time, and, in general, after i units of time, $i = 1, 2, \ldots$. The intervals of time are shown in Figure 17.6. An estimate of the proportion of survivors at time i is

$$\hat{R}(i) = \frac{n_i}{n}$$

where

n_i = Number of survivors at the end of the ith time unit

n = Total number of items placed on test

We would calculate $\hat{R}(i)$ for $i = 1, 2, \ldots$, and then fit the least squares line

$$\underbrace{\ln[-\ln \hat{R}(i)]}_{y} = \underbrace{-\ln \beta}_{\beta_0} + \underbrace{\alpha \ln i}_{\beta_1 \quad x}$$

to the data points (x_i, y_i), $i = 1, 2, \ldots$, where the ith data point is

$$y_i = \ln[-\ln \hat{R}(i)] \quad \text{and} \quad x_i = \ln i$$

FIGURE 17.6 ▶

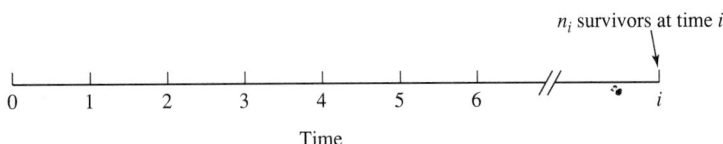

Time

EXAMPLE 17.5

A manufacturer of hydraulic seals conducted a life test during which the seals were subjected to a fluid pressure that was 200% of the pressure normally maintained in hydraulic systems in which the seal is used. One hundred seals were placed on test and the number of survivors was recorded at the end of each day for a period of 7 days, as listed in the following table.

Day	1	2	3	4	5	6	7
Number of Survivors	69	48	33	21	13	7	4

Use the data to estimate the parameters α and β for a Weibull distribution.

Solution

The first step is to calculate $\hat{R}(i)$ and $\ln[-\ln \hat{R}(i)]$ for each of the seven time intervals. These calculations are shown in Table 17.1. The SAS printout for a simple linear regression for the data is shown in Figure 17.7.

TABLE 17.1

i	$x_i = \ln i$	Number of Survivors	$\hat{R}(i)$	$-\ln \hat{R}(i)$	$y_i = \ln[-\ln \hat{R}(i)]$
1	0	69	.69	.37106	$-.99138$
2	.69315	48	.48	.73397	$-.30929$
3	1.09861	33	.33	1.10866	.10315
4	1.38629	21	.21	1.56065	.44510
5	1.60944	13	.13	2.04022	.71306
6	1.79176	7	.07	2.65926	.97805
7	1.94591	4	.04	3.21888	1.16903

FIGURE 17.7 ▶

SAS printout for Example 17.5

```
Dependent Variable: Y

                        Analysis of Variance

                              Sum of        Mean
        Source      DF       Squares       Square     F Value    Prob>F

        Model        1       3.46814      3.46814    1074.810    0.0001
        Error        5       0.01613      0.00323
        C Total      6       3.48428

            Root MSE      0.05680     R-square      0.9954
            Dep Mean      0.30110     Adj R-sq      0.9944
            C.V.         18.86544

                        Parameter Estimates

                     Parameter     Standard     T for H0:
        Variable  DF   Estimate       Error    Parameter=0    Prob > |T|

        INTERCEP   1   -1.050978   0.04649563    -22.604        0.0001
        X          1    1.110192   0.03386353     32.784        0.0001
```

From the printout, you can see that the least squares estimates (shaded) are

$$\hat{\beta}_0 = -1.05098 \quad \text{and} \quad \hat{\beta}_1 = 1.11019$$

Since $\beta_0 = -\ln \beta$ and $\beta_1 = \alpha$, we have

$$\hat{\alpha} = \hat{\beta}_1 = 1.11019$$

and

$$\hat{\beta}_0 = -\ln \hat{\beta} \quad \text{or} \quad \hat{\beta} = e^{-\hat{\beta}_0} = 2.86045$$

Therefore, based on the method of least squares, we would use a Weibull distribution with parameters $\alpha = 1.11019$ and $\beta = 2.86045$ to model the failure time distribution of the hydraulic seals.

Note that we could form confidence intervals for α and β using the confidence limits for β_0 and β_1. The confidence interval for α would be the usual regression confidence interval for β_1 because $\alpha = \beta_1$. The confidence limits for β would be computed by substituting the upper and lower confidence limits for β_0 into the relationship $\beta = e^{-\beta_0}$.

To illustrate, the formula for a $(1 - \alpha)100\%$ confidence interval for β_0 given in Section 11.6 is

$$\hat{\beta}_0 \pm (t_{\alpha/2})s_{\hat{\beta}_0}$$

where $t_{\alpha/2}$ depends on $(n - 2)$ degrees of freedom and $s_{\hat{\beta}_0}$ is the estimated standard error of the estimate $\hat{\beta}_0$. From the SAS printout (Figure 17.7), $\hat{\beta}_0 = -1.05098$ and $s_{\hat{\beta}_0} = .046496$, and for $n - 2 = 7 - 2 = 5$ degrees of freedom and $\alpha = .05$, $t_{\alpha/2} = t_{.025} = 2.571$. Then a 95% confidence interval for β_0 is given by

$$-1.05098 \pm (2.571)(.046496)$$
$$-1.05098 \pm .11954$$

or $(-1.17052, -.93144)$. Consequently, a 95% confidence interval for the Weibull parameter β is

$$(e^{.93144}, e^{1.17052})$$

or $(2.5382, 3.2237)$.

EXAMPLE 17.6

Use the estimates of α and β derived in Example 17.5 to find the probability that a hydraulic seal placed on test will survive at least 3 days.

Solution

Recall that the probability of survival to time t_0 under a Weibull distribution is given by

$$R(t_0) = 1 - F(t_0) = e^{-t_0^\alpha/\beta}$$

Substituting the estimates $\hat{\alpha} = 1.11019$ and $\hat{\beta} = 2.86045$ into the equation for $t_0 = 3$ days, we have

$$\hat{R}(3) = e^{-3^{1.11019}/2.86045} = e^{-1.18375} = .30613$$

Therefore, the probability that the hydraulic seal will survive at least 3 days is estimated to be $.30613$.

When n is small, we can still use the method of least squares to estimate the parameters of a Weibull distribution, but the preferred procedure is to estimate the probability of survival to time t, $R(t) = 1 - F(t)$, after each failure time has been observed. The data points used for the least squares methods are $[t_1, \hat{R}(t_1)]$, $[t_2, \hat{R}(t_2)]$, $\ldots$, $[t_r, \hat{R}(t_r)]$, where t_1 is the first observed failure, t_2 the second, and so on. When this method of defining the data points is used, the estimator of the survival rates used in Example 17.5 is modified to

$$\hat{R}(t_i) = \frac{n_i + 1}{n + 1}$$

where n_i is the number of survivors when the ith failure time t_i is observed and n is the sample size.*

In concluding, note that $\hat{\alpha}$ and $\hat{\beta}$ will not possess the properties of the usual least squares estimators of β_0 and β_1. The response variable

$$y = \ln[-\ln \hat{R}(t)]$$

is not a normally distributed random variable and, in addition, the observed values of y are correlated. This is because the number of survivors at one point in time is dependent on the number observed at some previous point in time. The extent to which these violations of the regression analysis assumptions affect the properties of the estimators is unknown, but it is probably slight when the sample size n and the number r of observed failures are large.

EXERCISES

17.13 Suppose the lifelength (in years) of a memory chip in a mainframe computer has a Weibull failure time distribution. To estimate the Weibull parameters, α and β, 50 chips were placed on test and the number of survivors was recorded at the end of each year, for a period of 8 years. The data are shown in the accompanying table.

Year	1	2	3	4	5	6	7	8
Number of Survivors	47	39	29	18	11	5	3	1

  a. Use the method of least squares to derive estimates of α and β.
  b. Construct a 95% confidence interval for α.
  c. If you have access to a linear regression computer package, construct a 95% confidence interval for β.

17.14 Refer to Exercise 17.13.
  a. Use the estimates of α and β to find the probability that a memory chip will fail before 5 years.
  b. Estimate the reliability of the memory chips at time $t = 7$ years.

17.15 Refer to Exercise 17.13.
  a. Using the least squares estimates of α and β, find and graph the hazard rate, $z(t)$.
  b. Compute the hazard rate at time $t = 4$ years and interpret its value.

17.16 Engineers often use a Weibull failure time distribution for a "weakest link" product, i.e., a product consisting of multiple parts (e.g., roller bearings) that fails when the first part (or weakest link) fails. Nelson (*Journal of Quality Technology*, July 1985) applied the Weibull distribution to the lifelengths of a sample of

---

*Some statisticians use $\hat{R}(t_i) = (n_i + 1/2)/n$. See Miller and Freund (1977).

$n = 138$ roller bearings. The accompanying table gives the number of bearings still in operation at the end of each 100-hour period until all bearings failed.

Hours (hundreds)	1	2	3	4	5	6	7	8	12	13	17	19	24	51
Number of Bearings	138	114	104	64	37	29	20	10	8	6	4	3	2	1

Source: Nelson, W. "Weibull analysis of reliability data with few or no failures." *Journal of Quality Technology*, Vol. 17, No. 3, July 1985, p. 141 (Table 1). © 1985 American Society for Quality Control. Reprinted by permission.

a. Use the method of least squares to estimate the Weibull parameters α and β.
b. Construct a 99% confidence interval for α. If you have access to a regression computer package, obtain a 99% confidence interval for β.
c. Estimate the reliability of the roller bearings at $t = 300$ hours.
d. Estimate the probability that a roller bearing will fail before 200 hours.

17.17 A manufacturer of washing machines conducted a life test during which he monitored 12 new machines for a period of 3 years and recorded the time to a major repair for each. At the end of the 3-year testing period, two machines had not yet required a major repair. The failure times (in months) of the remaining 10 washing machines were 14, 28, 9, 13, 6, 20, 10, 17, 30, and 20. Assume the lifelength (in years) of the machines has a Weibull failure time distribution with unknown parameters α and β.
a. Construct a table for the data listing the number of machines surviving (that is, without major repair) at the end of each year.
b. Apply the method of least squares to the data in the table of part **a** to derive estimates of α and β.
c. Find a 95% confidence interval for α. If you have access to a regression computer package, find a 95% confidence interval for β.
d. The manufacturer guarantees all machines against a major repair for 2 years. Using the least squares estimates of α and β, find the probability that a new washer will have to be repaired under the guarantee.

17.18 To evaluate the performance of rebuilt hydraulic pumps at an aircraft rework facility, 20 pumps were placed on test and the number of pumps still running at the end of each week was recorded for a period of 6 weeks, as listed in the accompanying table.

Week	1	2	3	4	5	6
Number of Pumps	14	11	9	7	5	4

a. Use the data to estimate the parameters, α and β, for a Weibull failure time distribution.
b. Construct a 90% confidence interval for α. If you have access to a regression computer package, find a 90% confidence interval for β.
c. Find the reliability of the rebuilt hydraulic pumps at time $t = 2$ weeks.

17.7 System Reliability

Systems—electronic, mechanical, or a combination of both—are composed of components, some of which are combined to form smaller subsystems. We will identify a component of a system by a capital letter and portray it graphically as a box. Two systems, each composed of three components, A, B, and C, are shown in Figure 17.8 on page 1054.

FIGURE 17.8 ▶

Two systems each composed of
three components, A, B, and C

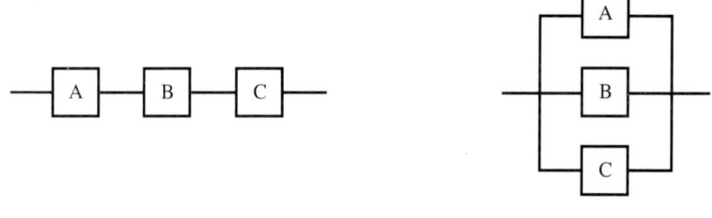

a. Series system   b. Parallel system

Suppose that a system is composed of k components. If the system fails when any one of the components fails, it is called a **series system**. A three-component series system is represented graphically in Figure 17.8a. If a system fails only when *all* of its components fail, it is called a **parallel system**. A three-component parallel system is represented graphically in Figure 17.8b.

Figure 17.9a shows a system composed of five components, A, B, C, D, and E. Components D and E form a two-component parallel subsystem. This subsystem is connected in series with components A, B, and C. Figure 17.9b represents a system containing two parallel subsystems connected in series. The first parallel subsystem contains three components, A, B, and C. The second contains two series subsystems—the first composed of components D and E, and the second composed of components F and G.

FIGURE 17.9 ▶

Two systems

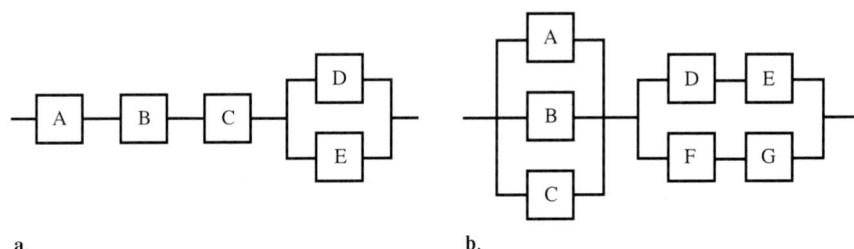

a.   b.

Definition 17.5

. . . .

A **series system** is one that fails if any one of its components fails.

Definition 17.6

. . . .

A **parallel system** is one that fails only if all of its components fail.

Suppose that the reliability of component i—the probability that it will function properly under specified conditions—is p_i and that the k components of a system are mutually independent. That is, we assume that the operation of one component does not affect the operation of any of the others. Then the reliability of a system can be calculated using the multiplicative rule of probability.

Since a series system will function only if all of its components function, the reliability of a series system is

$$P(\text{Series system functions}) = P(\text{All components function})$$

Then, because the components operate independently of each other, we can apply the multiplicative rule of probability:

$$P(\text{Series system functions})$$
$$= P(\text{A functions}) \, P(\text{B functions}) \cdots P(\text{K functions})$$
$$= p_A p_B p_C \cdots p_K$$

Theorem 17.1

The reliability of a series system consisting of k independently operating components, A, B, . . . , K, is

$$P(\text{Series system functions}) = p_A p_B \cdots p_K$$

where p_i is the probability that the ith component functions, $i = $ A, B, . . . , K.

The reliability of a parallel system containing k components can be calculated in a similar manner. Since a parallel system will fail only if all components fail,

$$P(\text{Parallel system fails}) = (1 - p_A)(1 - p_B) \cdots (1 - p_K)$$

and

$$P(\text{Parallel system functions}) = 1 - P(\text{Parallel system fails})$$
$$= 1 - (1 - p_A)(1 - p_B) \cdots (1 - p_K)$$

Theorem 17.2

The reliability of a parallel system consisting of k independently operating components is

$$P(\text{Parallel system functions}) = 1 - (1 - p_A)(1 - p_B) \cdots (1 - p_K)$$

where p_i is the probability that the ith component functions, $i = $ A, B, . . . , K.

Theorems 17.1 and 17.2 can be used to calculate the reliability of series systems, parallel systems, or any combinations thereof, as long as the systems satisfy the assumption that the components operate independently. The following examples illustrate the procedure.

EXAMPLE 17.7

Given that $p_A = .90$, $p_B = .95$, and $p_C = .90$, find the reliability of the series system shown in Figure 17.8a.

Solution

Since this is a series system consisting of three components, A, B, and C, it follows from Theorem 17.1 that the reliability of this system is

$$P(\text{System functions}) = p_A p_B p_C = (.90)(.95)(.90) = .7695$$

EXAMPLE 17.8

Suppose that the components in Example 17.7 were connected in parallel, as shown in Figure 17.8b. Find the reliability of the system.

Solution

To find the reliability of this parallel system, we apply Theorem 17.2:

$$
\begin{aligned}
P(\text{System functions}) &= 1 - (1 - p_A)(1 - p_B)(1 - p_C) \\
&= 1 - (.10)(.05)(.10) \\
&= 1 - .0005 \\
&= .9995
\end{aligned}
$$

Examples 17.7 and 17.8 demonstrate that the *reliability of a series system is always less than the reliability of its least reliable component. In contrast, the reliability of a parallel system is always greater than the reliability of its most reliable component.*

To find the reliability of a system containing subsystems, we first find the reliability of the smallest subsystems. Then we find the reliability of the systems in which they are contained.

EXAMPLE 17.9

Find the reliability of the system shown in Figure 17.9a, given the following component reliabilities: $p_A = .95$, $p_B = .99$, $p_C = .97$, $p_D = .90$, and $p_E = .90$.

Solution

The complete system is composed of three components, A, B, and C, and a subsystem connected in series. The parallel subsystem, comprised of components D and E, is shown here:

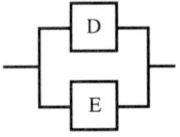

The reliability of this subsystem is

$$P(\text{Subsystem D and E functions}) = p_{DE}$$
$$= 1 - (1 - P_D)(1 - p_E)$$
$$= 1 - (.1)(.1) = .99$$

We now view the complete system as one consisting of four components: components A, B, and C and the subsystem (D, E), connected in series. To find its reliability, we apply Theorem 17.1. The reliability of the complete system is

$$P(\text{System functions}) = p_A p_B p_C p_{DE} = (.95)(.99)(.97)(.99)$$
$$= .9031622$$

EXAMPLE 17.10

Find the reliability of the system shown in Figure 17.9b, given that $p_A = .90$, $p_B = .95$, $p_C = .95$, $p_D = .92$, $p_E = .97$, $p_F = .92$, and $p_G = .97$.

Solution

An examination of Figure 17.9b shows that the system is a series of two parallel subsystems. The first parallel subsystem contains components A, B, and C. The second is a parallel subsystem of two series subsystems, the first containing components D and E, and the second containing components F and G.

Since the reliabilities of the pairs of components (D, E) and (F, G) are identical, it follows that the reliabilities of these two series subsystems are equal:

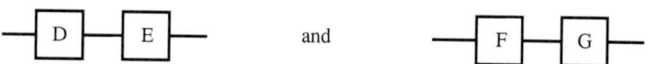

By Theorem 17.1, the reliability of these series subsystems is

$$p_{DE} = p_{FG} = p_D p_E = p_F p_G = (.92)(.97) = .8924$$

We now consider the reliability of the parallel subsystem containing these two series subsystems:

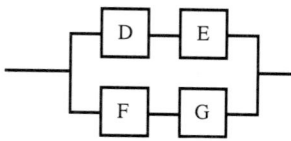

By Theorem 17.2, we have

$$p_{DEFG} = 1 - (1 - p_{DE})(1 - p_{FG})$$
$$= 1 - (1 - .8924)(1 - .8924)$$
$$= 1 - .0115778$$
$$= .9884222$$

Next, we compute the reliability of the parallel subsystem consisting of components A, B, and C:

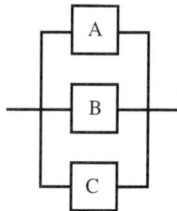

By Theorem 17.2,

$$
\begin{aligned}
p_{ABC} &= 1 - (1 - p_A)(1 - p_B)(1 - p_C) \\
&= 1 - (1 - .90)(1 - .95)(1 - .95) \\
&= 1 - .00025 \\
&= .99975
\end{aligned}
$$

We have calculated the reliabilities of the two parallel subsystems. These two subsystems are connected in series, as shown here:

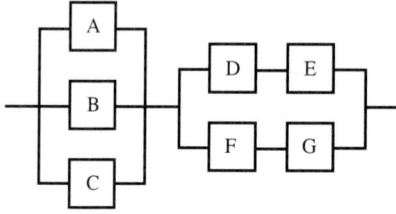

Thus, the reliability of the complete system is

$$
\begin{aligned}
P(\text{System functions}) &= p_{ABC}\,p_{DEFG} \\
&= (.99975)(.9884222) \\
&= .9881751
\end{aligned}
$$

EXERCISES

17.19   Consider a series system consisting of four components, A, B, C, and D, with probabilities of functioning given by $p_A = .88$, $p_B = .95$, $p_C = .90$, and $p_D = .80$. Find the reliability of the system.

17.20   Consider a parallel system consisting of four components, A, B, C, and D, with probabilities of functioning given by $p_A = .90$, $p_B = .99$, $p_C = .92$, and $p_D = .85$. Find the reliability of the system.

17.21   A system consists of eight components, as shown in the accompanying diagram. Find the reliability of the system, given that the individual probabilities of functioning are $p_A = .90$, $p_B = .95$, $p_C = .85$, $p_D = .85$, $p_E = .98$, $p_F = .80$, $p_G = .95$, and $p_H = .95$.

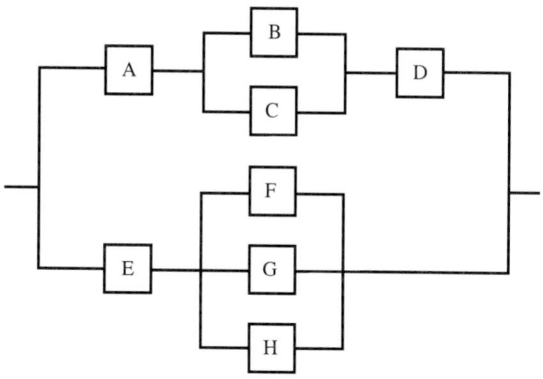

17.22   Consider an electrical circuit consisting of two subcircuits, the first of which involves components A, B, and C in parallel and the second of which involves components D and E in parallel. Suppose that the individual reliabilities of the components are given by $p_A = .95$, $p_B = .95$, $p_C = .90$, $p_D = .90$, and $p_E = .98$.
a. Find the reliability of the system if the two subcircuits are connected in series.
b. Find the reliability of the system if the two subcircuits are connected in parallel.

17.23   The reliability of a system consisting of three identical components is .95. What must be the probability of functioning for each component if:
a. The components are connected in series?
b. The components are connected in parallel?

17.8   Summary

This chapter presents statistical methods for evaluating the life characteristics of a manufactured product—whether a simple device such as a light bulb or a complex system composed of a number of components or subsystems.

The **reliability** of a product is the probability that the product will function a specified length of time under specified environmental conditions. The length of time that a unit of product performs satisfactorily is called its **length of life**. The time at which it fails is called its **failure time**.

If a population of product items was placed on test, they would fail at varying times and the relative frequency distribution of failure times would be called a **failure time distribution**. This distribution can often be modeled by one of the probability density functions presented in Chapter 5. The exponential distribution and the Weibull distribution are widely used as models for product failuretime distributions. The normal and gamma distributions are also used for some products.

Another way to describe the failure characteristics of a product is in terms of its hazard rate. The **hazard rate** $z(t)$ at time t is proportional to the probability that an item will fail during a fixed small interval of time, given that the item has survived to time t:

$$z(t) = \frac{f(t)}{1 - F(t)}$$

The hazard rate provides a measure of the propensity of the product to fail as it gets older.

To find an appropriate model for a product, we conduct a **life test**. That is, we place a random sample of product items on test and record the observed times to failure.

The length of time for a life test is often shortened by **censoring** the sample—that is, stopping the life test either after a specified number r of failures have been observed or after a specified amount of time T has elapsed. Regardless of how the sample data are collected, by censored or uncensored sampling, we employ the methods of Chapter 8 to find estimators of the parameters of the failure time distribution. Parameter estimates can then be substituted into the formula for the failure time distribution:

$$P(\text{Survival to time } t_0) = 1 - F(t_0)$$

In concluding, we learned how to calculate the reliability of systems of components, assuming that the components operate independently of each other and that the component reliabilities are known. We considered systems that can be viewed as **series systems**, **parallel systems**, or some combination of the two.

Because of its importance, much work has been done on life-testing methodology and on methods for evaluating system reliability. This chapter provides only an introduction to the topic. If you seek more information on the subject, consult the references at the end of this chapter.

SUPPLEMENTARY EXERCISES

17.24 A certain component has an exponential failure time distribution with mean $\beta = 3$ hours.
   a. Find the probability that the component will fail before time $t = 2$ hours.
   b. What is the reliability of the component at time $t = 5$ hours? Interpret this value.
   c. Find the hazard rate for the component and interpret its value.

17.25 Suppose the lifelength (in hours) of a fluorescent light has a Weibull failure time distribution with parameters $\alpha = .05$ and $\beta = .70$.
   a. Find the probability that the fluorescent light will fail before time $t = 1,000$ hours.
   b. Find the reliability of the fluorescent light at time $t = 500$ hours and interpret its value.
   c. Find the hazard rate for the fluorescent light at time $t = 500$ hours and interpret its value.

17.26 Consider the gamma failure time distribution with $\alpha = 2$ and $\beta = 1$ given by the density function

$$f(t) = \begin{cases} te^{-t} & 0 \le t < \infty \\ 0 & \text{elsewhere} \end{cases}$$

   a. Find $F(t)$. [*Hint:* $\int te^{-t}\, dt = -te^{-t} + \int e^{-t}\, dt$]
   b. Find expressions for the reliability $R(t)$ and the hazard rate $z(t)$.
   c. Use the results of part **b** to find $R(3)$ and $z(3)$. Interpret these values.

17.27 Consider the uniform failure time distribution given by the density function

$$f(t) = \begin{cases} \dfrac{1}{\beta} & 0 \le t \le \beta \\ 0 & \text{elsewhere} \end{cases}$$

   a. Find $F(t)$, $R(t)$, and $z(t)$.
   b. Graph the hazard rate $z(t)$ for $t = 0, 1, 2, \ldots, 5$ when $\beta = 10$.
   c. Compute the reliability of the system at $t = 4$ when $\beta = 10$.

17.28 To investigate the performance of the central processing unit (CPU) of a certain type of microcomputer, 20 CPUs were placed on test for a period of 5,000 hours. When the test was terminated, four CPUs had failed with failure times of 1,850, 2,090, 3,440, and 3,970 hours. Assume a negative exponential failure time distribution.
   a. Find a 90% confidence interval for the mean time β until failure of the microcomputer's CPU.
   b. Find a 90% confidence interval for the reliability of the CPU at time $t = 2,000$ hours.
   c. Find a 90% confidence interval for the hazard rate of the CPU.

17.29 A certain type of coating for pipes is designed to resist corrosion. Five hundred pieces of coated pipe were placed on test and subjected to a 90% solution of hydrochloric acid. At the end of each hour, for a period of 5 hours, the number of pipe specimens that had resisted corrosion was recorded, as shown in the accompanying table.

Hour	1	2	3	4	5
Number Resisting Corrosion	438	280	146	51	15

   a. Use the data in the table to estimate the parameters α and β of a Weibull failure time distribution.
   b. Use the estimates obtained in part **a** to find expressions for the hazard rate $z(t)$ and the reliability $R(t)$ of the coated pipes.
   c. Find the probability that a piece of coated pipe will resist corrosion under similar experimental conditions for at least 1 hour.

17.30 A piece of equipment consists of seven tubes connected as shown in the diagram on page 1062. Find the reliability of the system if the tubes have probabilities of functioning given by $p_A = .80$, $p_B = .90$, $p_C = .85$, $p_D = .85$, $p_E = .75$, $p_F = .75$, and $p_G = .95$.

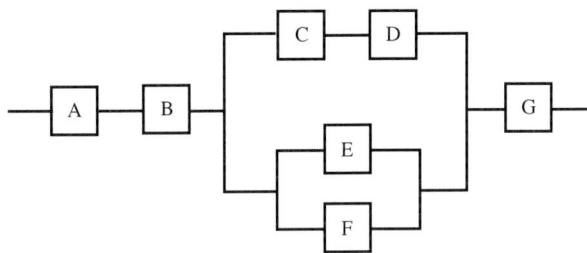

17.31 Two resistors connected in series have exponential failure time distributions with mean $\beta = 1,000$ hours. At time $t = 1,400$ hours, what is the reliability of the system?

17.32 Four components, A, B, C, and D, are connected in parallel. Suppose that components A and B have normal failure time distributions with parameters $\mu = 500$ hours and $\sigma = 100$ hours, whereas components C and D have Weibull failure time distributions with parameters $\alpha = .5$ and $\beta = 100$. Find the reliability of the system at time $t = 300$ hours.

17.33 The service life (in hours) of a semiconductor has an approximate exponential failure time distribution. Ten semiconductors are placed on life test until four fail. The failure times for these four semiconductors are 585, 972, 1,460, and 2,266 hours.
  a. Construct a 95% confidence interval for the mean time β until failure for the semiconductors.
  b. What is the probability that a semiconductor will still be in operation after 4,000 hours? Find a 95% confidence interval for this probability.
  c. Compute and interpret the hazard rate for the semiconductors. Construct a 95% confidence interval for this hazard rate.

17.34 The failure times (in hours) of electronic components in a guidance system for a missile have a Weibull distribution with unknown parameters α and β. To derive estimates of these parameters, 1,000 components were placed on life test and every 50 hours the number of components still in operation was recorded. The data are provided in the table.

Hours	50	100	150	200	250	300	350
Number in Operation	611	362	231	136	84	53	17

  a. Find estimates of α and β. If you have access to a regression computer package, find 99% confidence intervals for both α and β.
  b. Calculate the reliability of the electronic components at $t = 200$ hours.
  c. Find and graph the hazard rate for $t = 50, 100, 150, \ldots$

17.35 Consider the product system shown in the diagram. Given the individual component reliabilities $p_A = .85$, $p_B = .75$, $p_C = .75$, $p_D = .90$, and $p_E = .95$, find the overall reliability of the system.

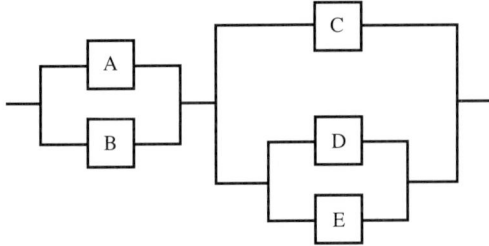

OPTIONAL SUPPLEMENTARY EXERCISES

17.36 Show that the hazard rate $z(t)$ can be expressed as

$$z(t) = \frac{-d[\ln R(t)]}{dt}$$

[*Hint:*   Make use of the fact that $R(t) = 1 - F(t)$ and, hence, that

$$f(t) = \frac{dF(t)}{dt} = \frac{-dR(t)}{dt}$$

Then substitute these expressions into the formula given in Definition 17.4.]

17.37 Use the result of Exercise 17.36 and the relation $f(t) = z(t)R(t)$ to show that the failure time density can be expressed as

$$f(t) = z(t)e^{-\int_0^t z(y)dy}$$

[*Hint:*   The differential equation

$$z(t) = \frac{-d[\ln R(t)]}{dt}$$

has

$$R(t) = e^{-\int_0^t z(y)dy}$$

as its solution.]

17.38 Suppose we are concerned only with the initial failure of a component. That is, once the component has survived past a certain time $t = \alpha$, we treat the component (for all practical purposes) as if it never failed. In this situation it is reasonable to use the hazard rate

$$z(t) = \begin{cases} \beta(1 - t/\alpha) & 0 < t < \alpha \\ 0 & \text{elsewhere} \end{cases}$$

a. Use the result of Exercise 17.37 to find expressions for $f(t)$, $F(t)$, and $R(t)$.

b. Show that the probability of initial failure, i.e., the probability that the component fails before time $t = \alpha$, is $1 - e^{-\alpha\beta/2}$.

References

Barlow, R. E., and Proschan, F. *The Mathematical Theory of Reliability*. New York: Wiley, 1965.

Box, G. E. P. "Problems in the Analysis of Growth and Wear Curves." *Biometrics*, Vol. 6, 1950.

Cohen, A. C., Jr. "On Estimating the Mean and Standard Deviation of Truncated Normal Distribution." *Journal of the American Statistical Association*, Vol. 44, 1949, pp. 518–525.

Cohen, A. C., Jr. "A Note on Truncated Distributions." *Industrial Quality Control*, Vol. 6, 1949, p. 22.

Davis, D. J. "An Analysis of Some Failure Data." *Journal of the American Statistical Association*, Vol. 47, 1952, pp. 113–150.

Epstein, B. "Statistical Problems in Life Testing." *Seventh Annual Quality Control Conference Papers*, 1953, pp. 385–398.

Epstein, B., and Sobel, M. "Life Testing." *Journal of the American Statistical Association*, Vol. 48, 1953, pp. 486–502.

Miller, I., and Freund, J. E. *Probability and Statistics for Engineers*, 2nd ed. Englewood Cliffs, N. J.: Prentice-Hall, 1977.

Weibull, W. "A Statistical Distribution Function of Wide Applicability." *Journal of Applied Mechanics*, Vol. 18, 1951, pp. 293–297.

Zelen, M. *Statistical Theory of Reliability*. Madison, Wis.: University of Wisconsin Press, 1963.

APPENDIX I

....

Matrix Algebra

....

I.I   Matrices and Matrix Multiplication

For some statistical procedures (e.g., multiple regression), the formulas for conducting the analysis are more easily given using **matrix algebra** instead of ordinary algebra. By arranging the data in particular rectangular patterns called **matrices** and performing various operations with them, we can obtain the results of the analyses much more quickly. In this appendix, we will define a matrix and explain various operations that can be performed with matrices. (We explained how to use this information to conduct a regression analysis in Section 12.4.)

Three matrices, A, B, and C, are shown here. Note that each matrix is a rectangular arrangement of numbers with one number in every row–column position.

$$A = \begin{bmatrix} 2 & 3 \\ 0 & 1 \\ -1 & 6 \end{bmatrix} \qquad B = \begin{bmatrix} 3 & 0 & 1 \\ -1 & 0 & 1 \\ 4 & 2 & 0 \end{bmatrix} \qquad C = \begin{bmatrix} 1 \\ 2 \\ 1 \end{bmatrix}$$

Definition I.I

A **matrix** is a rectangular array of numbers.*

The numbers that appear in a matrix are called **elements** of the matrix. If a matrix contains r rows and c columns, there will be an element in each of the row–column positions of the matrix, and the matrix will have $r \times c$ elements. For example, the matrix A shown above contains $r = 3$ rows, $c = 2$ columns, and $rc = (3)(2) = 6$ elements, one in each of the 6 row–column positions.

Definition I.2

A number in a particular row–column position is called an **element** of the matrix.

Notice that the matrices A, B, and C contain different numbers of rows and columns. The numbers of rows and columns give the **dimensions** of a matrix.

---

*For our purpose, we assume that the numbers are real.

> ### Definition 1.3
>
> A matrix containing r rows and c columns is said to be an $r \times c$ **matrix**, where r and c are the **dimensions** of the matrix.

> ### Definition 1.4
>
> If $r = c$, a matrix is said to be a **square matrix**.

When we give a formula in matrix notation, the elements of a matrix will be represented by symbols. For example, if we have a matrix

$$A = \begin{bmatrix} a_{11} & a_{12} & a_{13} \\ a_{21} & a_{22} & a_{23} \end{bmatrix}$$

the symbol a_{ij} will denote the element in the ith row and jth column of the matrix. The first subscript always identifies the row and the second identifies the column in which the element is located. For example, the element a_{12} is in the first row and second column of matrix A. The rows are always numbered from top to bottom, and the columns are always numbered from left to right.

Matrices are usually identified by capital letters, such as A, B, C, corresponding to the letters of the alphabet employed in ordinary algebra. The difference is that in ordinary algebra, a letter is used to denote a single real number, whereas in matrix algebra, a letter denotes a rectangular array of numbers. The operations of matrix algebra are very similar to those of ordinary algebra—you can add matrices, subtract them, multiply them, and so on. However, there are a few operations that are unique to matrices, such as the **transpose of a matrix**. For example, if

$$A = \begin{bmatrix} 5 \\ 1 \\ 0 \\ 4 \\ 2 \end{bmatrix} \quad \text{and} \quad B = \begin{bmatrix} 1 & 0 \\ 1 & 1 \\ 1 & 4 \\ 1 & 2 \\ 1 & 6 \end{bmatrix}$$

then the transpose matrices of the A and B matrices, denoted as A' and B', respectively, are

$$A' = \begin{bmatrix} 5 & 1 & 0 & 4 & 2 \end{bmatrix} \quad \text{and} \quad B' = \begin{bmatrix} 1 & 1 & 1 & 1 & 1 \\ 0 & 1 & 4 & 2 & 6 \end{bmatrix}$$

> ### Definition I.5
>
> The **transpose of a matrix A**, denoted as A', is obtained by interchanging corresponding rows and columns of the A matrix. That is, the ith row of the A matrix becomes the ith column of the A' matrix.

Since we are concerned mainly with the applications of matrix algebra to the solution of the least squares equations in multiple regression (see Chapter 12), we will define only the operations and types of matrices that are pertinent to that subject.

The most important operation for us is matrix multiplication, which requires **row–column multiplication**. To illustrate this process, suppose we wish to find the product AB, where

$$A = \begin{bmatrix} 2 & 1 \\ 4 & -1 \end{bmatrix} \quad \text{and} \quad B = \begin{bmatrix} 2 & 0 & 3 \\ -1 & 4 & 0 \end{bmatrix}$$

We will always multiply the rows of A (the matrix on the left) by the columns of B (the matrix on the right). The product formed by the first row of A times the first column of B is obtained by multiplying the elements in corresponding positions and summing these products. Thus, the first row, first column product, shown diagrammatically below, is

$$(2)(2) + (1)(-1) = 4 - 1 = 3$$

$$AB = \begin{bmatrix} 2 & 1 \\ 4 & -1 \end{bmatrix} \begin{bmatrix} 2 & 0 & 3 \\ -1 & 4 & 0 \end{bmatrix} = \begin{bmatrix} 3 & & \\ & & \end{bmatrix}$$

Similarly, the first row, second column product is

$$(2)(0) + (1)(4) = 0 + 4 = 4$$

So far we have

$$AB = \begin{bmatrix} 3 & 4 & \\ & & \end{bmatrix}$$

To find the complete matrix product AB, all we need to do is find each element in the AB matrix. Thus, we will define an element in the ith row, jth column of AB as the product of the ith row of A and the jth column of B. We complete the process in Example I.1.

EXAMPLE I.1

Find the product AB, where

$$A = \begin{bmatrix} 2 & 1 \\ 4 & -1 \end{bmatrix} \quad \text{and} \quad B = \begin{bmatrix} 2 & 0 & 3 \\ -1 & 4 & 0 \end{bmatrix}$$

Solution   If we represent the product AB as

$$C = \begin{bmatrix} c_{11} & c_{12} & c_{13} \\ c_{21} & c_{22} & c_{23} \end{bmatrix}$$

we have already found $c_{11} = 3$ and $c_{12} = 4$. Similarly, the element c_{21}, the element in the second row, first column of AB, is the product of the second row of A and the first column of B:

$$(4)(2) + (-1)(-1) = 8 + 1 = 9$$

Proceeding in a similar manner to find the remaining elements of AB, we have

$$AB = \begin{bmatrix} 2 & 1 \\ 4 & -1 \end{bmatrix} \begin{bmatrix} 2 & 0 & 3 \\ -1 & 4 & 0 \end{bmatrix} = \begin{bmatrix} 3 & 4 & 6 \\ 9 & -4 & 12 \end{bmatrix}$$

. . . .

Now, try to find the product BA, using matrices A and B from Example I.1. You will observe two very important differences between multiplication in matrix algebra and multiplication in ordinary algebra:

1. You cannot find the product BA, because you cannot perform row–column multiplication. You can see that the dimensions do not match by placing the matrices side-by-side:

$$\underset{2 \times 3 \quad 2 \times 2}{BA} \qquad \text{does not exist}$$

The number of elements (3) in a row of B (the matrix on the left) does not match the number of elements (2) in a column of A (the matrix on the right). Therefore, you cannot perform row–column multiplication, and the matrix product BA does not exist. The point is, not all matrices can be multiplied. You can find products for matrices AB, only where A is $r \times d$ and B is $d \times c$. That is:

Requirement for Multiplication

$$\underset{r \times d \quad d \times c}{AB}$$

The two inner dimension numbers must be equal. The dimensions of the product will always be given by the outer dimension numbers. (See box on page 1070.)

Dimensions of AB are $r \times c$

$$AB$$
$$r \times d \quad d \times c$$

2. The second difference between ordinary and matrix multiplication is that in ordinary algebra, $ab = ba$. In matrix algebra, AB usually does not equal BA. In fact, as noted in item 1 above, it may not even exist.

Definition 1.6

The product AB of an $r \times d$ matrix A and a $d \times c$ matrix B is an $r \times c$ matrix C, where the element c_{ij} ($i = 1, 2, \ldots, r; j = 1, 2, \ldots, c$) of C is the product of the ith row of A and the jth column of B.

EXAMPLE 1.2

Given the matrices below, find IA and IB.

$$A = \begin{bmatrix} 2 \\ 1 \\ 3 \end{bmatrix} \qquad B = \begin{bmatrix} 3 & 0 \\ 1 & 2 \\ 4 & -1 \end{bmatrix} \qquad I = \begin{bmatrix} 1 & 0 & 0 \\ 0 & 1 & 0 \\ 0 & 0 & 1 \end{bmatrix}$$

Solution

Notice that the product

$$IA$$
$$3 \times 3 \quad 3 \times 1$$

exists and that it will be of dimensions 3×1:

$$IA = \begin{bmatrix} 1 & 0 & 0 \\ 0 & 1 & 0 \\ 0 & 0 & 1 \end{bmatrix} \begin{bmatrix} 2 \\ 1 \\ 3 \end{bmatrix} = \begin{bmatrix} 2 \\ 1 \\ 3 \end{bmatrix}$$

Similarly,

$$IB$$
$$3 \times 3 \quad 3 \times 2$$

exists and is of dimensions 3×2:

$$IB = \begin{bmatrix} 1 & 0 & 0 \\ 0 & 1 & 0 \\ 0 & 0 & 1 \end{bmatrix} \begin{bmatrix} 3 & 0 \\ 1 & 2 \\ 4 & -1 \end{bmatrix} = \begin{bmatrix} 3 & 0 \\ 1 & 2 \\ 4 & -1 \end{bmatrix}$$

Notice that the I matrix possesses a special property. We have $IA = A$ and $IB = B$. We will comment further on this property in Section I.2.

EXERCISES

I.1 Consider the matrices A, B, and C:

$$A = \begin{bmatrix} 3 & 0 \\ -1 & 4 \end{bmatrix} \qquad B = \begin{bmatrix} 2 & 1 \\ 0 & -1 \end{bmatrix} \qquad C = \begin{bmatrix} 1 & 0 & 3 \\ -2 & 1 & 2 \end{bmatrix}$$

a. Find AB. b. Find AC. c. Find BA.

I.2 Consider the matrices A, B, and C:

$$A = \begin{bmatrix} 3 & 1 & 3 \\ 2 & 0 & 4 \\ -4 & 1 & 2 \end{bmatrix} \qquad B = [1 \quad 0 \quad 2] \qquad C = \begin{bmatrix} 3 \\ 0 \\ 2 \end{bmatrix}$$

a. Find AC. b. Find BC.
c. Is it possible to find AB? Explain.

I.3 Assume that A is a 3×2 matrix and B is a 2×4 matrix.
a. What are the dimensions of AB?
b. Is it possible to find the product BA? Explain.

I.4 Assume that matrices B and C are of dimensions 1×3 and 3×1, respectively.
a. What are the dimensions of the product BC?
b. What are the dimensions of CB?
c. If B and C are the matrices shown in Exercise I.2, find CB.

I.5 Consider the matrices A, B, and C:

$$A = \begin{bmatrix} 1 & 0 & 0 \\ 0 & 3 & 0 \\ 0 & 0 & 2 \end{bmatrix} \qquad B = \begin{bmatrix} 2 & 3 \\ -3 & 0 \\ 4 & -1 \end{bmatrix} \qquad C = [3 \quad 0 \quad 2]$$

a. Find AB.
b. Find CA.
c. Find CB.

I.6   Consider the matrices:

$$A = \begin{bmatrix} 3 & 0 & -1 & 2 \end{bmatrix} \qquad B = \begin{bmatrix} 2 \\ -1 \\ 0 \\ 3 \end{bmatrix}$$

a. Find AB.   b. Find BA.

I.2   Identity Matrices and Matrix Inversion

In ordinary algebra, the number 1 is the identity element for the multiplication operation. That is, 1 is the element such that any other number, say, c, multiplied by the identity element is equal to c. Thus, $4(1) = 4$, $(-5)(1) = -5$, etc.

The corresponding identity element for multiplication in matrix algebra, identified by the symbol I, is a matrix such that

$$AI = IA = A \quad \text{for any matrix } A$$

The difference between identity elements in ordinary algebra and matrix algebra is that in ordinary algebra, there is only one identity element, the number 1. In matrix algebra, the identity matrix must possess the correct dimensions for the product IA to exist. Thus, there is an infinitely large number of identity matrices—all square and all possessing the same pattern. The 1×1, 2×2, and 3×3 identity matrices are

$$\underset{1 \times 1}{I} = [1] \qquad \underset{2 \times 2}{I} = \begin{bmatrix} 1 & 0 \\ 0 & 1 \end{bmatrix} \qquad \underset{3 \times 3}{I} = \begin{bmatrix} 1 & 0 & 0 \\ 0 & 1 & 0 \\ 0 & 0 & 1 \end{bmatrix}$$

In Example I.2, we demonstrated the fact that this matrix satisfies the property

$$IA = A$$

EXAMPLE I.3

If A is the matrix shown below, find IA and AI.

$$A = \begin{bmatrix} 3 & 4 & -1 \\ 1 & 0 & 2 \end{bmatrix}$$

Solution

$$\underset{\underset{2 \times 2 \quad 2 \times 3}{\nearrow \quad \nwarrow}}{IA} = \begin{bmatrix} 1 & 0 \\ 0 & 1 \end{bmatrix} \begin{bmatrix} 3 & 4 & -1 \\ 1 & 0 & 2 \end{bmatrix} = \begin{bmatrix} 3 & 4 & -1 \\ 1 & 0 & 2 \end{bmatrix} = A$$

$$\underset{\underset{2 \times 3 \quad 3 \times 3}{\nearrow \quad \nwarrow}}{AI} = \begin{bmatrix} 3 & 4 & -1 \\ 1 & 0 & 2 \end{bmatrix} \begin{bmatrix} 1 & 0 & 0 \\ 0 & 1 & 0 \\ 0 & 0 & 1 \end{bmatrix} = \begin{bmatrix} 3 & 4 & -1 \\ 1 & 0 & 2 \end{bmatrix} = A$$

Notice that the identity matrices used to find the products IA and AI were of different dimensions. This was necessary for the products to exist.

. . . .

Definition 1.7

If A is any matrix, then a matrix I is defined to be an **identity matrix** if $AI = IA = A$. The matrices that satisfy this definition possess the pattern

$$I = \begin{bmatrix} 1 & 0 & 0 & \cdots & 0 \\ 0 & 1 & 0 & \cdots & 0 \\ 0 & 0 & 1 & \cdots & 0 \\ \cdot & \cdot & \cdot & \cdots & \cdot \\ \cdot & \cdot & \cdot & \cdots & \cdot \\ \cdot & \cdot & \cdot & \cdots & \cdot \\ 0 & 0 & 0 & \cdots & 1 \end{bmatrix}$$

The identity element assumes importance when we consider the process of division and its role in the solution of equations. In ordinary algebra, division is essentially multiplication using the reciprocals of elements. For example, the equation

$$2X = 6$$

can be solved by dividing both sides of the equation by 2, *or* it can be solved by *multiplying* both sides of the equation by $\frac{1}{2}$, which is the reciprocal of 2. Thus,

$$\left(\frac{1}{2}\right) 2X = \frac{1}{2}(6)$$
$$X = 3$$

What is the reciprocal of an element? It is the element such that the reciprocal times the element is equal to the identity element. Thus, the reciprocal of 3 is $\frac{1}{3}$ because

$$3\left(\frac{1}{3}\right) = 1$$

The identity matrix plays the same role in matrix algebra. Thus, the reciprocal of a matrix A, called **A-inverse** and denoted by the symbol A^{-1}, is a matrix such that $AA^{-1} = A^{-1}A = I$.

Inverses are defined only for square matrices, but not all square matrices possess inverses. (Those that do play an important role in solving the least squares equations and in other aspects of a regression analysis.) We will show you one important application of the inverse matrix in Section I.3. The procedure for finding the inverse of a matrix is demonstrated in Section I.4.

> ## Definition 1.8
>
> The square matrix A^{-1} is said to be the **inverse** of the square matrix A if
>
> $$A^{-1}A = AA^{-1} = I$$

The procedure for finding an inverse matrix is computationally quite tedious and is performed most often using a computer. There is one exception. Finding the inverse of one type of matrix, called a **diagonal matrix**, is easy. A diagonal matrix is one that has nonzero elements down the **main diagonal** (running top left of the matrix to bottom right) and 0 elements elsewhere. For example, the identity matrix is a diagonal matrix (with 1's along the main diagonal), as are the following matrices:

$$A = \begin{bmatrix} 3 & 0 & 0 \\ 0 & 1 & 0 \\ 0 & 0 & 2 \end{bmatrix} \qquad B = \begin{bmatrix} 5 & 0 & 0 & 0 \\ 0 & 2 & 0 & 0 \\ 0 & 0 & 1 & 0 \\ 0 & 0 & 0 & 5 \end{bmatrix}$$

> ## Definition 1.9
>
> A **diagonal matrix** is one that contains nonzero elements on the main diagonal and 0 elements elsewhere.

You can verify that the inverse of

$$A = \begin{bmatrix} 3 & 0 & 0 \\ 0 & 1 & 0 \\ 0 & 0 & 2 \end{bmatrix} \quad \text{is} \quad A^{-1} = \begin{bmatrix} \frac{1}{3} & 0 & 0 \\ 0 & 1 & 0 \\ 0 & 0 & \frac{1}{2} \end{bmatrix}$$

i.e., $AA^{-1} = I$. The inverse of a diagonal matrix is given by Theorem I.1.

> ## Theorem 1.1
>
> The inverse of a diagonal matrix
>
> $$D = \begin{bmatrix} d_{11} & 0 & 0 & \cdots & 0 \\ 0 & d_{22} & 0 & \cdots & 0 \\ 0 & 0 & d_{33} & \cdots & 0 \\ \vdots & \vdots & \vdots & \cdots & \vdots \\ 0 & 0 & 0 & \cdots & d_{nn} \end{bmatrix} \quad \text{is} \quad D^{-1} = \begin{bmatrix} 1/d_{11} & 0 & 0 & \cdots & 0 \\ 0 & 1/d_{22} & 0 & \cdots & 0 \\ 0 & 0 & 1/d_{33} & \cdots & 0 \\ \vdots & \vdots & \vdots & \cdots & \vdots \\ 0 & 0 & 0 & \cdots & 1/d_{nn} \end{bmatrix}$$

EXERCISES

1.7 Consider the following matrix:

$$A = \begin{bmatrix} 3 & 0 & 2 \\ -1 & 1 & 4 \end{bmatrix}$$

    a. Give the identity matrix that will be used to obtain the product IA.
    b. Show that $IA = A$.
    c. Give the identity matrix that will be used to find the product AI.
    d. Show that $AI = A$.

1.8 For the matrices A and B given here, show that $AB = I$, that $BA = I$, and, consequently, verify that $B = A^{-1}$.

$$A = \begin{bmatrix} 1 & 0 & 0 \\ 0 & 2 & 0 \\ 0 & 0 & 3 \end{bmatrix} \qquad B = \begin{bmatrix} 1 & 0 & 0 \\ 0 & \frac{1}{2} & 0 \\ 0 & 0 & \frac{1}{3} \end{bmatrix}$$

1.9 If

$$A = \begin{bmatrix} 12 & 0 & 0 & 8 \\ 0 & 12 & 0 & 0 \\ 0 & 0 & 8 & 0 \\ 8 & 0 & 0 & 8 \end{bmatrix} \quad \text{verify that} \quad A^{-1} = \begin{bmatrix} \frac{1}{4} & 0 & 0 & -\frac{1}{4} \\ 0 & \frac{1}{12} & 0 & 0 \\ 0 & 0 & \frac{1}{8} & 0 \\ -\frac{1}{4} & 0 & 0 & \frac{3}{8} \end{bmatrix}$$

1.10 If

$$A = \begin{bmatrix} 3 & 0 & 0 \\ 0 & 5 & 0 \\ 0 & 0 & 7 \end{bmatrix} \quad \text{show that} \quad A^{-1} = \begin{bmatrix} \frac{1}{3} & 0 & 0 \\ 0 & \frac{1}{5} & 0 \\ 0 & 0 & \frac{1}{7} \end{bmatrix}$$

1.11 Verify Theorem I.1.

1.3 Solving Systems of Simultaneous Linear Equations

Consider the following set of simultaneous linear equations in two unknowns:

$$2v_1 + v_2 = 7$$
$$v_1 - v_2 = 2$$

Note that the solution for these equations is $v_1 = 3$, $v_2 = 1$.
    Now define the matrices

$$A = \begin{bmatrix} 2 & 1 \\ 1 & -1 \end{bmatrix} \qquad V = \begin{bmatrix} v_1 \\ v_2 \end{bmatrix} \qquad G = \begin{bmatrix} 7 \\ 2 \end{bmatrix}$$

Thus, A is the matrix of coefficients of v_1 and v_2, V is a column matrix containing the unknowns (written in order, top to bottom), and G is a column matrix containing the numbers on the right-hand side of the equal signs.

Now, the system of simultaneous equations shown above can be rewritten as a **matrix equation**:

$$AV = G$$

By a matrix equation, we mean that the product matrix, AV, is equal to the matrix G. *Equality of matrices means that corresponding elements are equal.* You can see that this is true for the expression $AV = G$, since

$$AV = \begin{bmatrix} 2 & 1 \\ 1 & -1 \end{bmatrix} \begin{bmatrix} v_1 \\ v_2 \end{bmatrix} = \begin{bmatrix} (2v_1 + v_2) \\ (v_1 - v_2) \end{bmatrix} = G$$

$$\underset{2 \times 2}{} \quad \underset{2 \times 1}{} \qquad\qquad\qquad \underset{2 \times 1}{}$$

The matrix procedure for expressing a system of two simultaneous linear equations in two unknowns can be extended to express a set of k simultaneous equations in k unknowns. If the equations are written in the orderly pattern

$$a_{11}v_1 + a_{12}v_2 + \cdots + a_{1k}v_k = g_1$$
$$a_{21}v_1 + a_{22}v_2 + \cdots + a_{2k}v_k = g_2$$
$$\vdots \qquad \vdots \qquad\qquad \vdots \qquad \vdots$$
$$a_{k1}v_1 + a_{k2}v_2 + \cdots + a_{kk}v_k = g_k$$

then the set of simultaneous linear equations can be expressed as the matrix equation $AV = G$, where

$$A = \begin{bmatrix} a_{11} & a_{12} & \cdots & a_{1k} \\ a_{21} & & \cdots & a_{2k} \\ \vdots & & & \vdots \\ a_{k1} & & \cdots & a_{kk} \end{bmatrix} \qquad V = \begin{bmatrix} v_1 \\ v_2 \\ \vdots \\ v_k \end{bmatrix} \qquad G = \begin{bmatrix} g_1 \\ g_2 \\ \vdots \\ g_k \end{bmatrix}$$

Now let use solve this system of simultaneous equations. (If they are uniquely solvable, it can be shown that A^{-1} exists.) Multiplying both sides of the matrix equation by A^{-1}, we have

$$(A^{-1})AV = (A^{-1})G$$

But since $A^{-1}A = I$, we have

$$(I)V = A^{-1}G$$
$$V = A^{-1}G$$

In other words, if we know A^{-1}, we can find the solution to the set of simultaneous linear equations by obtaining the product $A^{-1}G$.

> ### Matrix Solution to a Set of Simultaneous Linear Equations, $AV = G$
>
> Solution: $V = A^{-1}G$

EXAMPLE 1.4

Apply the boxed result to find the solution to the set of simultaneous linear equations

$$2v_1 + v_2 = 7$$
$$v_1 - v_2 = 2$$

Solution

The first step is to obtain the inverse of the coefficient matrix,

$$A = \begin{bmatrix} 2 & 1 \\ 1 & -1 \end{bmatrix}$$

namely,

$$A^{-1} = \begin{bmatrix} \frac{1}{3} & \frac{1}{3} \\ \frac{1}{3} & -\frac{2}{3} \end{bmatrix}$$

(This matrix can be found using a packaged computer program for matrix inversion or, for this simple case, you could use the procedure explained in Section 1.4.) As a check, note that

$$A^{-1}A = \begin{bmatrix} \frac{1}{3} & \frac{1}{3} \\ \frac{1}{3} & -\frac{2}{3} \end{bmatrix} \begin{bmatrix} 2 & 1 \\ 1 & -1 \end{bmatrix}$$

$$= \begin{bmatrix} 1 & 0 \\ 0 & 1 \end{bmatrix} = I$$

The second step is to obtain the product $A^{-1}G$. Thus,

$$V = A^{-1}G = \begin{bmatrix} \frac{1}{3} & \frac{1}{3} \\ \frac{1}{3} & -\frac{2}{3} \end{bmatrix} \begin{bmatrix} 7 \\ 2 \end{bmatrix} = \begin{bmatrix} 3 \\ 1 \end{bmatrix}$$

Since

$$V = \begin{bmatrix} v_1 \\ v_2 \end{bmatrix} = \begin{bmatrix} 3 \\ 1 \end{bmatrix}$$

it follows that $v_1 = 3$ and $v_2 = 1$. You can see that these values of v_1 and v_2 satisfy the simultaneous linear equations and are the values that we specified as a solution at the beginning of this section.

EXERCISES

I.12   Suppose the simultaneous linear equations

$$3v_1 + v_2 = 5$$
$$v_1 - v_2 = 3$$

are expressed as a matrix equation,

$$AV = G$$

a. Find the matrices A, V, and G.
b. Verify that

$$A^{-1} = \begin{bmatrix} \frac{1}{4} & \frac{1}{4} \\ \frac{1}{4} & -\frac{3}{4} \end{bmatrix}$$

[*Note:*   A procedure for finding A^{-1} is given in Section I.4.]
c. Solve the equations by finding $V = A^{-1}G$.

I.13   For the simultaneous linear equations

$$10v_1 + 20v_3 - 60 = 0$$
$$20v_2 - 60 = 0$$
$$20v_1 + 68v_3 - 176 = 0$$

a. Find the matrices A, V, and G.
b. Verify that

$$A^{-1} = \begin{bmatrix} \frac{17}{70} & 0 & -\frac{1}{14} \\ 0 & \frac{1}{20} & 0 \\ -\frac{1}{14} & 0 & \frac{1}{28} \end{bmatrix}$$

c. Solve the equations by finding $V = A^{-1}G$.

I.4   A Procedure for Inverting a Matrix

There are several different methods for inverting matrices. All are tedious and time-consuming. Consequently, in practice, you will invert almost all matrices using an electronic computer. The purpose of this section is to present one method so that you will be able to invert small (2×2 or 3×3) matrices manually and so that you will appreciate the enormous computing problem involved in inverting large matrices (and, consequently, in fitting linear models containing many terms to a set of data). Particularly, you will be able to understand why rounding errors creep into the inversion process and, consequently, why two different computer programs might invert the same matrix and produce inverse matrices with slightly different corresponding elements.

The procedure we will demonstrate to invert a matrix A requires that we perform a series of operations on the rows of the A matrix. For example, suppose

$$A = \begin{bmatrix} 1 & -2 \\ -2 & 6 \end{bmatrix}$$

We will identify two different ways to operate on a row of a matrix:*

1. We can multiply every element in one particular row by a constant, c. For example, we could operate on the first row of the A matrix by multiplying every element in the row by a constant, say, 2. Then the resulting row would be $[2 \quad -4]$.

2. We can operate on a row by multiplying another row of the matrix by a constant and then adding (or subtracting) the elements of that row to elements in corresponding positions in the row operated upon. For example, we could operate on the first row of the A matrix by multiplying the second row by a constant, say, 2:

$$2[-2 \quad 6] = [-4 \quad 12]$$

Then we add this row to row 1:

$$[(1 - 4) \quad (-2 + 12)] = [-3 \quad 10]$$

Note one important point. We operated on the *first* row of the A matrix. Although we used the second row of the matrix to perform the operation, *the second row would remain unchanged*. Therefore, the row operation on the A matrix that we have just described would produce the new matrix,

$$\begin{bmatrix} -3 & 10 \\ -2 & 6 \end{bmatrix}$$

Matrix inversion using row operations is based on an elementary result from matrix algebra. It can be shown (proof omitted) that performing a series of row operations on a matrix A is equivalent to multiplying A by a matrix B, i.e., row operations produce a new matrix, BA. This result is used as follows: Place the A matrix and an identity matrix I of the same dimensions side by side. Then perform the same series of row operations on both A and I until the A matrix has been changed into the identity

---

*We omit a third row operation, because it would add little and could be confusing.

matrix I. This means that you have multiplied both A and I by some matrix B such that:

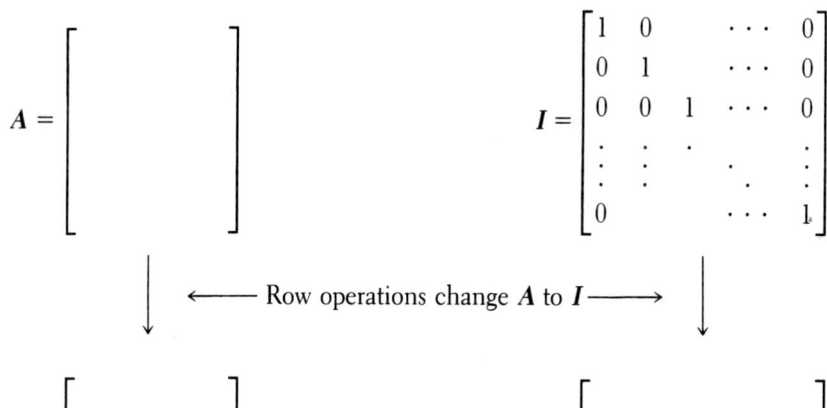

$$A = \begin{bmatrix} & \\ & \end{bmatrix} \qquad I = \begin{bmatrix} 1 & 0 & & \cdots & 0 \\ 0 & 1 & & \cdots & 0 \\ 0 & 0 & 1 & \cdots & 0 \\ \vdots & \vdots & \ddots & & \vdots \\ 0 & & & \cdots & 1 \end{bmatrix}$$

$\longleftarrow$ Row operations change A to I $\longrightarrow$

$$I = \begin{bmatrix} & \\ & \end{bmatrix} \qquad B = \begin{bmatrix} & \\ & \end{bmatrix}$$

$$BA = I \quad \text{and} \quad BI = B$$

Since $BA = I$, it follows that $B = A^{-1}$. Therefore, as the A matrix is transformed by row operations into the identity matrix I, the identity matrix I is transformed into A^{-1}, i.e.,

$$BI = B = A^{-1}$$

We will show you how this procedure works with two examples.

EXAMPLE 1.5

Find the inverse of the matrix,

$$A = \begin{bmatrix} 1 & -2 \\ -2 & 6 \end{bmatrix}$$

Solution

Place the A matrix and a 2×2 identity matrix side by side and then perform the following series of row operations (we will indicate by arrow the row operated upon in each operation):

$$A = \begin{bmatrix} 1 & -2 \\ -2 & 6 \end{bmatrix} \qquad I = \begin{bmatrix} 1 & 0 \\ 0 & 1 \end{bmatrix}$$

OPERATION 1   Multiply the first row by 2 and add to the second row:

$$\rightarrow \begin{bmatrix} 1 & -2 \\ 0 & 2 \end{bmatrix} \qquad \begin{bmatrix} 1 & 0 \\ 2 & 1 \end{bmatrix}$$

OPERATION 2   Multiply the second row by $\frac{1}{2}$:

$$\rightarrow \begin{bmatrix} 1 & -2 \\ 0 & 1 \end{bmatrix} \qquad \begin{bmatrix} 1 & 0 \\ 1 & \frac{1}{2} \end{bmatrix}$$

OPERATION 3   Multiply the second row by 2 and add it to the first row:

$$\rightarrow \begin{bmatrix} 1 & 0 \\ 0 & 1 \end{bmatrix} \qquad \begin{bmatrix} 3 & 1 \\ 1 & \frac{1}{2} \end{bmatrix}$$

Thus,

$$A^{-1} = \begin{bmatrix} 3 & 1 \\ 1 & \frac{1}{2} \end{bmatrix}$$

The final step in finding an inverse is to check your solution by finding the product $A^{-1}A$ to see if it equals the identity matrix I. To check:

$$A^{-1}A = \begin{bmatrix} 3 & 1 \\ 1 & \frac{1}{2} \end{bmatrix} \begin{bmatrix} 1 & -2 \\ -2 & 6 \end{bmatrix} = \begin{bmatrix} 1 & 0 \\ 0 & 1 \end{bmatrix}$$

Since this product is equal to the identity matrix, it follows that our solution for A^{-1} is correct.

EXAMPLE 1.6

Find the inverse of the matrix,

$$A = \begin{bmatrix} 2 & 0 & 3 \\ 0 & 4 & 1 \\ 3 & 1 & 2 \end{bmatrix}$$

Solution

Place an identity matrix alongside the A matrix and perform the row operations:

OPERATION 1   Multiply row 1 by $\frac{1}{2}$:

$$\rightarrow \begin{bmatrix} 1 & 0 & \frac{3}{2} \\ 0 & 4 & 1 \\ 3 & 1 & 2 \end{bmatrix} \qquad \begin{bmatrix} \frac{1}{2} & 0 & 0 \\ 0 & 1 & 0 \\ 0 & 0 & 1 \end{bmatrix}$$

OPERATION 2   Multiply row 1 by 3 and subtract from row 3:

$$\begin{bmatrix} 1 & 0 & \frac{3}{2} \\ 0 & 4 & 1 \\ \rightarrow 0 & 1 & -\frac{5}{2} \end{bmatrix} \qquad \begin{bmatrix} \frac{1}{2} & 0 & 0 \\ 0 & 1 & 0 \\ -\frac{3}{2} & 0 & 1 \end{bmatrix}$$

OPERATION 3   Multiply row 2 by $\frac{1}{4}$:

$$\rightarrow \begin{bmatrix} 1 & 0 & \frac{3}{2} \\ 0 & 1 & \frac{1}{4} \\ 0 & 1 & -\frac{5}{2} \end{bmatrix} \qquad \begin{bmatrix} \frac{1}{2} & 0 & 0 \\ 0 & \frac{1}{4} & 0 \\ -\frac{3}{2} & 0 & 1 \end{bmatrix}$$

OPERATION 4   Subtract row 2 from row 3:

$$\rightarrow \begin{bmatrix} 1 & 0 & \frac{3}{2} \\ 0 & 1 & \frac{1}{4} \\ 0 & 0 & -\frac{11}{4} \end{bmatrix} \qquad \begin{bmatrix} \frac{1}{2} & 0 & 0 \\ 0 & \frac{1}{4} & 0 \\ -\frac{3}{2} & -\frac{1}{4} & 1 \end{bmatrix}$$

OPERATION 5   Multiply row 3 by $-\frac{4}{11}$:

$$\rightarrow \begin{bmatrix} 1 & 0 & \frac{3}{2} \\ 0 & 1 & \frac{1}{4} \\ 0 & 0 & 1 \end{bmatrix} \qquad \begin{bmatrix} \frac{1}{2} & 0 & 0 \\ 0 & \frac{1}{4} & 0 \\ \frac{12}{22} & \frac{1}{11} & -\frac{4}{11} \end{bmatrix}$$

OPERATION 6   Operate on row 2 by subtracting $\frac{1}{4}$ of row 3:

$$\rightarrow \begin{bmatrix} 1 & 0 & \frac{3}{2} \\ 0 & 1 & 0 \\ 0 & 0 & 1 \end{bmatrix} \qquad \begin{bmatrix} \frac{1}{2} & 0 & 0 \\ -\frac{3}{22} & \frac{5}{22} & \frac{1}{11} \\ \frac{12}{22} & \frac{1}{11} & -\frac{4}{11} \end{bmatrix}$$

OPERATION 7   Operate on row 1 by subtracting $\frac{3}{2}$ of row 3:

$$\rightarrow \begin{bmatrix} 1 & 0 & 0 \\ 0 & 1 & 0 \\ 0 & 0 & 1 \end{bmatrix} \qquad \begin{bmatrix} -\frac{7}{22} & -\frac{3}{22} & \frac{6}{11} \\ -\frac{3}{22} & \frac{5}{22} & \frac{1}{11} \\ \frac{6}{11} & \frac{1}{11} & -\frac{4}{11} \end{bmatrix} = A^{-1}$$

To check the solution, we find the product,

$$A^{-1}A = \begin{bmatrix} -\frac{7}{22} & -\frac{3}{22} & \frac{6}{11} \\ -\frac{3}{22} & \frac{5}{22} & \frac{1}{11} \\ \frac{6}{11} & \frac{1}{11} & -\frac{4}{11} \end{bmatrix} \begin{bmatrix} 2 & 0 & 3 \\ 0 & 4 & 1 \\ 3 & 1 & 2 \end{bmatrix}$$

$$= \begin{bmatrix} 1 & 0 & 0 \\ 0 & 1 & 0 \\ 0 & 0 & 1 \end{bmatrix}$$

Since the product $A^{-1}A$ is equal to the identity matrix, it follows that our solution for A^{-1} is correct.

Examples I.5 and I.6 indicate the strategy employed when performing row operations on the A matrix to change it into an identity matrix. Multiply the first row by a constant to change the element in the top left row into a 1. Then perform operations to change all elements in the first column into 0's. Then operate on the second row and change the second diagonal element into a 1. Then operate to change all elements in the second column beneath row 2 into 0's. Then operate on the diagonal element in row 3, etc. When all elements on the main diagonal are 1's and all below the main diagonal are 0's, perform row operations to change the last column to 0; then the next-to-last column, etc., until you get back to the first row. The procedure for changing the off-diagonal elements to 0's is indicated diagrammatically as shown:

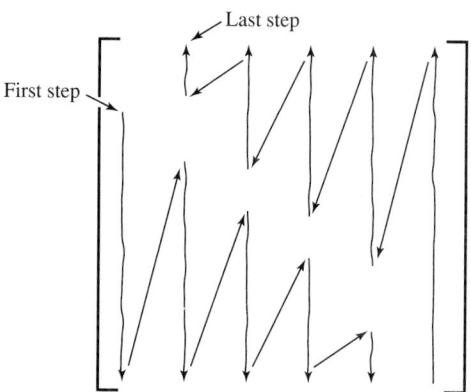

The preceding instructions on how to invert a matrix using row operations suggest that the inversion of a large matrix would involve many multiplications, subtractions, and additions and, consequently, could produce large rounding errors in the calculations unless you carry a large number of significant figures in the calculations. This explains why two different multiple regression analysis computer programs may produce different estimates of the same β parameters, and it emphasizes the importance of carrying a large number of significant figures in all computations when inverting a matrix.

EXERCISE

1.14   Invert the following matrices and check your answers to make certain that $A^{-1}A = AA^{-1} = I$:

a. $A = \begin{bmatrix} 3 & 2 \\ 4 & 5 \end{bmatrix}$ **b.** $A = \begin{bmatrix} 3 & 0 & -2 \\ 1 & 4 & 2 \\ 5 & 1 & 1 \end{bmatrix}$ **c.** $A = \begin{bmatrix} 1 & 0 & 1 \\ 0 & 2 & 1 \\ 1 & 1 & 3 \end{bmatrix}$ **d.** $A = \begin{bmatrix} 4 & 0 & 10 \\ 0 & 10 & 0 \\ 10 & 0 & 5 \end{bmatrix}$

[*Note:*   No answers are given to these exercises. You will know your answers are correct if $A^{-1}A = I$.]

APPENDIX II

Useful Statistical Tables

TABLE I   Cumulative Binomial Probabilities

Tabulated values are $\sum_{y=0}^{k} p(y)$.

a. $n = 5$

k	.01	.05	.1	.2	.3	.4	.5	.6	.7	.8	.9	.95	.99
0	.9510	.7738	.5905	.3277	.1681	.0778	.0313	.0102	.0024	.0003	.0000	.0000	.0000
1	.9990	.9774	.9185	.7373	.5282	.3370	.1875	.0870	.0308	.0067	.0005	.0000	.0000
2	1.0000	.9988	.9914	.9421	.8369	.6826	.5000	.3174	.1631	.0579	.0086	.0012	.0000
3	1.0000	1.0000	.9995	.9933	.9692	.9130	.8125	.6630	.4718	.2627	.0815	.0226	.0010
4	1.0000	1.0000	1.0000	.9997	.9976	.9898	.9687	.9222	.8319	.6723	.4095	.2262	.0490

b. $n = 6$

k	.01	.05	.1	.2	.3	.4	.5	.6	.7	.8	.9	.95	.99
0	.9415	.7351	.5314	.2621	.1176	.0467	.0156	.0041	.0007	.0001	.0000	.0000	.0000
1	.9985	.9672	.8857	.6554	.4202	.2333	.1094	.0410	.0109	.0016	.0001	.0000	.0000
2	1.0000	.9978	.9841	.9011	.7443	.5443	.3437	.1792	.0705	.0170	.0013	.0001	.0000
3	1.0000	.9999	.9987	.9830	.9295	.8208	.6562	.4557	.2557	.0989	.0158	.0022	.0000
4	1.0000	1.0000	.9999	.9984	.9891	.9590	.8906	.7667	.5798	.3446	.1143	.0328	.0015
5	1.0000	1.0000	1.0000	.9999	.9993	.9959	.9844	.9533	.8824	.7379	.4686	.2649	.0585

c. $n = 7$

k	.01	.05	.1	.2	.3	.4	.5	.6	.7	.8	.9	.95	.99
0	.9321	.6983	.4783	.2097	.0824	.0280	.0078	.0016	.0002	.0000	.0000	.0000	.0000
1	.9980	.9556	.8503	.5767	.3294	.1586	.0625	.0188	.0038	.0004	.0000	.0000	.0000
2	1.0000	.9962	.9743	.8520	.6471	.4199	.2266	.0963	.0288	.0047	.0002	.0000	.0000
3	1.0000	.9998	.9973	.9667	.8740	.7102	.5000	.2898	.1260	.0333	.0027	.0002	.0000
4	1.0000	1.0000	.9998	.9953	.9712	.9037	.7734	.5801	.3529	.1480	.0257	.0038	.0000
5	1.0000	1.0000	1.0000	.9996	.9962	.9812	.9375	.8414	.6706	.4233	.1497	.0444	.0020
6	1.0000	1.0000	1.0000	1.0000	.9998	.9984	.9922	.9720	.9176	.7903	.5217	.3017	.0679

(continued)

TABLE 1   Continued

d. $n = 8$

k	.01	.05	.1	.2	.3	.4	.5	.6	.7	.8	.9	.95	.99
							p						
0	.9227	.6634	.4305	.1678	.0576	.0168	.0039	.0007	.0001	.0000	.0000	.0000	.0000
1	.9973	.9423	.8131	.5033	.2553	.1064	.0352	.0085	.0013	.0001	.0000	.0000	.0000
2	.9999	.9942	.9619	.7969	.5518	.3154	.1445	.0498	.0113	.0012	.0000	.0000	.0000
3	1.0000	.9996	.9950	.9437	.8059	.5941	.3633	.1737	.0580	.0104	.0004	.0000	.0000
4	1.0000	1.0000	.9996	.9896	.9420	.8263	.6367	.4059	.1941	.0563	.0050	.0004	.0000
5	1.0000	1.0000	1.0000	.9988	.9887	.9502	.8555	.6346	.4482	.2031	.0381	.0058	.0001
6	1.0000	1.0000	1.0000	.9999	.9987	.9915	.9648	.8936	.7447	.4967	.1869	.0572	.0027
7	1.0000	1.0000	1.0000	1.0000	.9999	.9993	.9961	.9832	.9424	.8322	.5695	.3366	.0773

e. $n = 9$

k	.01	.05	.1	.2	.3	.4	.5	.6	.7	.8	.9	.95	.99
							p						
0	.9135	.6302	.3874	.1342	.0404	.0101	.0020	.0003	.0000	.0000	.0000	.0000	.0000
1	.9966	.9288	.7748	.4362	.1960	.0705	.0195	.0038	.0004	.0000	.0000	.0000	.0000
2	.9999	.9916	.9470	.7382	.4623	.2318	.0898	.0250	.0043	.0003	.0000	.0000	.0000
3	1.0000	.9994	.9917	.9144	.7297	.4826	.2539	.0994	.0253	.0031	.0001	.0000	.0000
4	1.0000	1.0000	.9991	.9804	.9012	.7334	.5000	.2666	.0988	.0196	.0009	.0000	.0000
5	1.0000	1.0000	.9999	.9969	.9747	.9006	.7461	.5174	.2703	.0856	.0083	.0006	.0000
6	1.0000	1.0000	1.0000	.9997	.9957	.9750	.9102	.7682	.5372	.2618	.0530	.0084	.0001
7	1.0000	1.0000	1.0000	1.0000	.9996	.9962	.9805	.9295	.8040	.5638	.2252	.0712	.0034
8	1.0000	1.0000	1.0000	1.0000	1.0000	.9997	.9980	.9899	.9596	.8658	.6126	.3698	.0865

f. $n = 10$

k	.01	.05	.1	.2	.3	.4	.5	.6	.7	.8	.9	.95	.99
							p						
0	.9044	.5987	.3487	.1074	.0282	.0060	.0010	.0001	.0000	.0000	.0000	.0000	.0000
1	.9957	.9139	.7361	.3758	.1493	.0464	.0107	.0017	.0001	.0000	.0000	.0000	.0000
2	.9999	.9885	.9298	.6778	.3828	.1673	.0547	.0123	.0016	.0001	.0000	.0000	.0000
3	1.0000	.9990	.9872	.8791	.6496	.3823	.1719	.0548	.0106	.0009	.0000	.0000	.0000
4	1.0000	.9999	.9984	.9672	.8497	.6331	.3770	.1662	.0473	.0064	.0001	.0000	.0000
5	1.0000	1.0000	.9999	.9936	.9527	.8338	.6230	.3669	.1503	.0328	.0016	.0001	.0000
6	1.0000	1.0000	1.0000	.9991	.9894	.9452	.8281	.6177	.3504	.1209	.0128	.0010	.0000
7	1.0000	1.0000	1.0000	.9999	.9984	.9877	.9453	.8327	.6172	.3222	.0702	.0115	.0001
8	1.0000	1.0000	1.0000	1.0000	.9999	.9983	.9893	.9536	.8507	.6242	.2639	.0861	.0043
9	1.0000	1.0000	1.0000	1.0000	1.0000	.9999	.9990	.9940	.9718	.8926	.6513	.4013	.0956

TABLE I   Continued

g. $n = 15$

k	.01	.05	.1	.2	.3	.4	.5	.6	.7	.8	.9	.95	.99
0	.8601	.4633	.2059	.0352	.0047	.0005	.0000	.0000	.0000	.0000	.0000	.0000	.0000
1	.9904	.8290	.5490	.1671	.0353	.0052	.0005	.0000	.0000	.0000	.0000	.0000	.0000
2	.9996	.9638	.8159	.3980	.1268	.0271	.0037	.0003	.0000	.0000	.0000	.0000	.0000
3	1.0000	.9945	.9444	.6482	.2969	.0905	.0176	.0019	.0001	.0000	.0000	.0000	.0000
4	1.0000	.9994	.9873	.8358	.5155	.2173	.0592	.0093	.0007	.0000	.0000	.0000	.0000
5	1.0000	.9999	.9978	.9389	.7216	.4032	.1509	.0338	.0037	.0001	.0000	.0000	.0000
6	1.0000	1.0000	.9997	.9819	.8689	.6098	.3036	.0950	.0152	.0008	.0000	.0000	.0000
7	1.0000	1.0000	1.0000	.9958	.9500	.7869	.5000	.2131	.0500	.0042	.0000	.0000	.0000
8	1.0000	1.0000	1.0000	.9992	.9848	.9050	.6964	.3902	.1311	.0181	.0003	.0000	.0000
9	1.0000	1.0000	1.0000	.9999	.9963	.9662	.8491	.5968	.2784	.0611	.0022	.0001	.0000
10	1.0000	1.0000	1.0000	1.0000	.9993	.9907	.9408	.7827	.4845	.1642	.0127	.0006	.0000
11	1.0000	1.0000	1.0000	1.0000	.9999	.9981	.9824	.9095	.7031	.3518	.0556	.0055	.0000
12	1.0000	1.0000	1.0000	1.0000	1.0000	.9997	.9963	.9729	.8732	.6020	.1841	.0362	.0004
13	1.0000	1.0000	1.0000	1.0000	1.0000	1.0000	.9995	.9948	.9647	.8329	.4510	.1710	.0096
14	1.0000	1.0000	1.0000	1.0000	1.0000	1.0000	1.0000	.9995	.9953	.9648	.7941	.5367	.1399

h. $n = 20$

k	.01	.05	.1	.2	.3	.4	.5	.6	.7	.8	.9	.95	.99
0	.8179	.3585	.1216	.0115	.0008	.0000	.0000	.0000	.0000	.0000	.0000	.0000	.0000
1	.9831	.7358	.3917	.0692	.0076	.0005	.0000	.0000	.0000	.0000	.0000	.0000	.0000
2	.9990	.9245	.6769	.2061	.0355	.0036	.0002	.0000	.0000	.0000	.0000	.0000	.0000
3	1.0000	.9841	.8670	.4114	.1071	.0160	.0013	.0000	.0000	.0000	.0000	.0000	.0000
4	1.0000	.9974	.9568	.6296	.2375	.0510	.0059	.0003	.0000	.0000	.0000	.0000	.0000
5	1.0000	.9997	.9887	.8042	.4164	.1256	.0207	.0016	.0000	.0000	.0000	.0000	.0000
6	1.0000	1.0000	.9976	.9133	.6080	.2500	.0577	.0065	.0003	.0000	.0000	.0000	.0000
7	1.0000	1.0000	.9996	.9679	.7723	.4159	.1316	.0210	.0013	.0000	.0000	.0000	.0000
8	1.0000	1.0000	.9999	.9900	.8867	.5956	.2517	.0565	.0051	.0001	.0000	.0000	.0000
9	1.0000	1.0000	1.0000	.9974	.9520	.7553	.4119	.1275	.0171	.0006	.0000	.0000	.0000
10	1.0000	1.0000	1.0000	.9994	.9829	.8725	.5881	.2447	.0480	.0026	.0000	.0000	.0000
11	1.0000	1.0000	1.0000	.9999	.9949	.9435	.7483	.4044	.1133	.0100	.0001	.0000	.0000
12	1.0000	1.0000	1.0000	1.0000	.9987	.9790	.8684	.5841	.2277	.0321	.0004	.0000	.0000
13	1.0000	1.0000	1.0000	1.0000	.9997	.9935	.9423	.7500	.3920	.0867	.0024	.0000	.0000
14	1.0000	1.0000	1.0000	1.0000	1.0000	.9984	.9793	.8744	.5836	.1958	.0113	.0003	.0000
15	1.0000	1.0000	1.0000	1.0000	1.0000	.9997	.9941	.9490	.7625	.3704	.0432	.0026	.0000
16	1.0000	1.0000	1.0000	1.0000	1.0000	1.0000	.9987	.9840	.8929	.5886	.1330	.0159	.0000
17	1.0000	1.0000	1.0000	1.0000	1.0000	1.0000	.9998	.9964	.9645	.7939	.3231	.0755	.0010
18	1.0000	1.0000	1.0000	1.0000	1.0000	1.0000	1.0000	.9995	.9924	.9308	.6083	.2642	.0169
19	1.0000	1.0000	1.0000	1.0000	1.0000	1.0000	1.0000	1.0000	.9992	.9885	.8784	.6415	.1821

(continued)

TABLE I   Continued

i. $n = 25$

k	.01	.05	.1	.2	.3	.4	.5	.6	.7	.8	.9	.95	.99
0	.7778	.2774	.0718	.0038	.0001	.0000	.0000	.0000	.0000	.0000	.0000	.0000	.0000
1	.9742	.6424	.2712	.0274	.0016	.0001	.0000	.0000	.0000	.0000	.0000	.0000	.0000
2	.9980	.8729	.5371	.0982	.0090	.0004	.0000	.0000	.0000	.0000	.0000	.0000	.0000
3	.9999	.9659	.7636	.2340	.0332	.0024	.0001	.0000	.0000	.0000	.0000	.0000	.0000
4	1.0000	.9928	.9020	.4207	.0905	.0095	.0005	.0000	.0000	.0000	.0000	.0000	.0000
5	1.0000	.9988	.9666	.6167	.1935	.0294	.0020	.0001	.0000	.0000	.0000	.0000	.0000
6	1.0000	.9998	.9905	.7800	.3407	.0736	.0073	.0003	.0000	.0000	.0000	.0000	.0000
7	1.0000	1.0000	.9977	.8909	.5118	.1536	.0216	.0012	.0000	.0000	.0000	.0000	.0000
8	1.0000	1.0000	.9995	.9532	.6769	.2735	.0539	.0043	.0001	.0000	.0000	.0000	.0000
9	1.0000	1.0000	.9999	.9827	.8106	.4246	.1148	.0132	.0005	.0000	.0000	.0000	.0000
10	1.0000	1.0000	1.0000	.9944	.9022	.5858	.2122	.0344	.0018	.0000	.0000	.0000	.0000
11	1.0000	1.0000	1.0000	.9985	.9558	.7323	.3450	.0778	.0060	.0001	.0000	.0000	.0000
12	1.0000	1.0000	1.0000	.9996	.9825	.8462	.5000	.1538	.0175	.0004	.0000	.0000	.0000
13	1.0000	1.0000	1.0000	.9999	.9940	.9222	.6550	.2677	.0442	.0015	.0000	.0000	.0000
14	1.0000	1.0000	1.0000	1.0000	.9982	.9656	.7878	.4142	.0978	.0056	.0000	.0000	.0000
15	1.0000	1.0000	1.0000	1.0000	.9995	.9868	.8852	.5754	.1894	.0173	.0001	.0000	.0000
16	1.0000	1.0000	1.0000	1.0000	.9999	.9957	.9461	.7265	.3231	.0468	.0005	.0000	.0000
17	1.0000	1.0000	1.0000	1.0000	1.0000	.9988	.9784	.8464	.4882	.1091	.0023	.0000	.0000
18	1.0000	1.0000	1.0000	1.0000	1.0000	.9997	.9927	.9264	.6593	.2200	.0095	.0002	.0000
19	1.0000	1.0000	1.0000	1.0000	1.0000	.9999	.9980	.9706	.8065	.3833	.0334	.0012	.0000
20	1.0000	1.0000	1.0000	1.0000	1.0000	1.0000	.9995	.9905	.9095	.5793	.0980	.0072	.0000
21	1.0000	1.0000	1.0000	1.0000	1.0000	1.0000	.9999	.9976	.9668	.7660	.2364	.0341	.0001
22	1.0000	1.0000	1.0000	1.0000	1.0000	1.0000	1.0000	.9996	.9910	.9018	.4629	.1271	.0020
23	1.0000	1.0000	1.0000	1.0000	1.0000	1.0000	1.0000	.9999	.9984	.9726	.7288	.3576	.0258
24	1.0000	1.0000	1.0000	1.0000	1.0000	1.0000	1.0000	1.0000	.9999	.9962	.9282	.7226	.2222

TABLE 2   Exponentials

λ	$e^{-\lambda}$	λ	$e^{-\lambda}$	λ	$e^{-\lambda}$	λ	$e^{-\lambda}$	λ	$e^{-\lambda}$
.00	1.000000	2.05	.128735	4.05	.017422	6.05	.002358	8.05	.000319
.05	.951229	2.10	.122456	4.10	.016573	6.10	.002243	8.10	.000304
.10	.904837	2.15	.116484	4.15	.015764	6.15	.002133	8.15	.000289
.15	.860708	2.20	.110803	4.20	.014996	6.20	.002029	8.20	.000275
.20	.818731	2.25	.105399	4.25	.014264	6.25	.001930	8.25	.000261
.25	.778801	2.30	.100259	4.30	.013569	6.30	.001836	8.30	.000249
.30	.740818	2.35	.095369	4.35	.012907	6.35	.001747	8.35	.000236
.35	.704688	2.40	.090718	4.40	.012277	6.40	.001661	8.40	.000225
.40	.670320	2.45	.086294	4.45	.011679	6.45	.001581	8.45	.000214
.45	.637628	2.50	.082085	4.50	.011109	6.50	.001503	8.50	.000204
.50	.606531	2.55	.078082	4.55	.010567	6.55	.001430	8.55	.000194
.55	.576950	2.60	.074274	4.60	.010052	6.60	.001360	8.60	.000184
.60	.548812	2.65	.070651	4.65	.009562	6.65	.001294	8.65	.000175
.65	.522046	2.70	.067206	4.70	.009095	6.70	.001231	8.70	.000167
.70	.496585	2.75	.063928	4.75	.008652	6.75	.001171	8.75	.000158
.75	.472367	2.80	.060810	4.80	.008230	6.80	.001114	8.80	.000151
.80	.449329	2.85	.057844	4.85	.007828	6.85	.001059	8.85	.000143
.85	.427415	2.90	.055023	4.90	.007447	6.90	.001008	8.90	.000136
.90	.406570	2.95	.052340	4.95	.007083	6.95	.000959	8.95	.000130
.95	.386741	3.00	.049787	5.00	.006738	7.00	.000912	9.00	.000123
1.00	.367879	3.05	.047359	5.05	.006409	7.05	.000867	9.05	.000117
1.05	.349938	3.10	.045049	5.10	.006097	7.10	.000825	9.10	.000112
1.10	.332871	3.15	.042852	5.15	.005799	7.15	.000785	9.15	.000106
1.15	.316637	3.20	.040762	5.20	.005517	7.20	.000747	9.20	.000101
1.20	.301194	3.25	.038774	5.25	.005248	7.25	.000710	9.25	.000096
1.25	.286505	3.30	.036883	5.30	.004992	7.30	.000676	9.30	.000091
1.30	.272532	3.35	.035084	5.35	.004748	7.35	.000643	9.35	.000087
1.35	.259240	3.40	.033373	5.40	.004517	7.40	.000611	9.40	.000083
1.40	.246597	3.45	.031746	5.45	.004296	7.45	.000581	9.45	.000079
1.45	.234570	3.50	.030197	5.50	.004087	7.50	.000553	9.50	.000075
1.50	.223130	3.55	.028725	5.55	.003887	7.55	.000526	9.55	.000071
1.55	.212248	3.60	.027324	5.60	.003698	7.60	.000501	9.60	.000068
1.60	.201897	3.65	.025991	5.65	.003518	7.65	.000476	9.65	.000064
1.65	.192050	3.70	.024724	5.70	.003346	7.70	.000453	9.70	.000061
1.70	.182684	3.75	.023518	5.75	.003183	7.75	.000431	9.75	.000058
1.75	.173774	3.80	.022371	5.80	.003028	7.80	.000410	9.80	.000056
1.80	.165299	3.85	.021280	5.85	.002880	7.85	.000390	9.85	.000053
1.85	.157237	3.90	.020242	5.90	.002739	7.90	.000371	9.90	.000050
1.90	.149569	3.95	.019255	5.95	.002606	7.95	.000353	9.95	.000048
1.95	.142274	4.00	.018316	6.00	.002479	8.00	.000336	10.00	.000045
2.00	.135335								

TABLE 3   Cumulative Poisson Probabilities

Tabulated values are $\sum_{y=0}^{k} p(y)$.

k	.5	1.0	1.5	2.0	2.5	3.0	3.5	4.0	4.5	5.0
					Poisson Mean μ					
0	.6065	.3679	.2231	.1353	.0821	.0498	.0302	.0183	.0111	.0067
1	.9098	.7358	.5578	.4060	.2873	.1991	.1359	.0916	.0611	.0404
2	.9856	.9197	.8088	.6767	.5438	.4232	.3208	.2381	.1736	.1247
3	.9982	.9810	.9344	.8571	.7576	.6472	.5366	.4335	.3423	.2650
4	.9998	.9963	.9814	.9473	.8912	.8153	.7254	.6288	.5321	.4405
5	1.0000	.9994	.9955	.9834	.9580	.9161	.8576	.7851	.7029	.6160
6	1.0000	.9999	.9991	.9955	.9858	.9665	.9347	.8893	.8311	.7622
7	1.0000	1.0000	.9998	.9989	.9958	.9881	.9733	.9489	.9134	.8666
8	1.0000	1.0000	1.0000	.9998	.9989	.9962	.9901	.9786	.9597	.9319
9	1.0000	1.0000	1.0000	1.0000	.9997	.9989	.9967	.9919	.9829	.9682
10	1.0000	1.0000	1.0000	1.0000	.9999	.9997	.9990	.9972	.9933	.9863
11	1.0000	1.0000	1.0000	1.0000	1.0000	.9999	.9997	.9991	.9976	.9945
12	1.0000	1.0000	1.0000	1.0000	1.0000	1.0000	.9999	.9997	.9992	.9980
13	1.0000	1.0000	1.0000	1.0000	1.0000	1.0000	1.0000	.9999	.9997	.9993
14	1.0000	1.0000	1.0000	1.0000	1.0000	1.0000	1.0000	1.0000	.9999	.9998
15	1.0000	1.0000	1.0000	1.0000	1.0000	1.0000	1.0000	1.0000	1.0000	.9999
16	1.0000	1.0000	1.0000	1.0000	1.0000	1.0000	1.0000	1.0000	1.0000	1.0000
17	1.0000	1.0000	1.0000	1.0000	1.0000	1.0000	1.0000	1.0000	1.0000	1.0000
18	1.0000	1.0000	1.0000	1.0000	1.0000	1.0000	1.0000	1.0000	1.0000	1.0000
19	1.0000	1.0000	1.0000	1.0000	1.0000	1.0000	1.0000	1.0000	1.0000	1.0000
20	1.0000	1.0000	1.0000	1.0000	1.0000	1.0000	1.0000	1.0000	1.0000	1.0000

					Poisson Mean μ					
k	5.5	6.0	6.5	7.0	7.5	8.0	8.5	9.0	9.5	10.0
0	.0041	.0025	.0015	.0009	.0006	.0003	.0002	.0001	.0001	.0000
1	.0266	.0174	.0113	.0073	.0047	.0030	.0019	.0012	.0008	.0005
2	.0884	.0620	.0430	.0296	.0203	.0138	.0093	.0062	.0042	.0028
3	.2017	.1512	.1118	.0818	.0591	.0424	.0301	.0212	.0149	.0103
4	.3575	.2851	.2237	.1730	.1321	.0996	.0744	.0550	.0403	.0293
5	.5289	.4457	.3690	.3007	.2414	.1912	.1496	.1157	.0885	.0671
6	.6860	.6063	.5265	.4497	.3782	.3134	.2562	.2068	.1649	.1301
7	.8095	.7440	.6728	.5987	.5246	.4530	.3856	.3239	.2687	.2202
8	.8944	.8472	.7916	.7291	.6620	.5925	.5231	.4557	.3918	.3328
9	.9462	.9161	.8774	.8305	.7764	.7166	.6530	.5874	.5218	.4579
10	.9747	.9574	.9332	.9015	.8622	.8159	.7634	.7060	.6453	.5830
11	.9890	.9799	.9661	.9467	.9208	.8881	.8487	.8030	.7520	.6968
12	.9955	.9912	.9840	.9730	.9573	.9362	.9091	.8758	.8364	.7916
13	.9983	.9964	.9929	.9872	.9784	.9658	.9486	.9261	.8981	.8645
14	.9994	.9986	.9970	.9943	.9897	.9827	.9726	.9585	.9400	.9165
15	.9998	.9995	.9988	.9976	.9954	.9918	.9862	.9780	.9665	.9513
16	.9999	.9998	.9996	.9990	.9980	.9963	.9934	.9889	.9823	.9730
17	1.0000	.9999	.9998	.9996	.9992	.9984	.9970	.9947	.9911	.9857
18	1.0000	1.0000	.9999	.9999	.9997	.9993	.9987	.9976	.9957	.9928
19	1.0000	1.0000	1.0000	1.0000	.9999	.9997	.9995	.9989	.9980	.9965
20	1.0000	1.0000	1.0000	1.0000	1.0000	.9999	.9998	.9996	.9991	.9984

TABLE 4   Normal Curve Areas

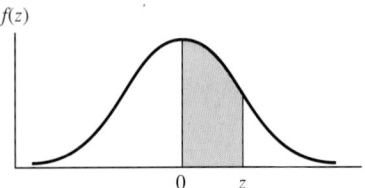

z	.00	.01	.02	.03	.04	.05	.06	.07	.08	.09
.0	.0000	.0040	.0080	.0120	.0160	.0199	.0239	.0279	.0319	.0359
.1	.0398	.0438	.0478	.0517	.0557	.0596	.0636	.0675	.0714	.0753
.2	.0793	.0832	.0871	.0910	.0948	.0987	.1026	.1064	.1103	.1141
.3	.1179	.1217	.1255	.1293	.1331	.1368	.1406	.1443	.1480	.1517
.4	.1554	.1591	.1628	.1664	.1700	.1736	.1772	.1808	.1844	.1879
.5	.1915	.1950	.1985	.2019	.2054	.2088	.2123	.2157	.2190	.2224
.6	.2257	.2291	.2324	.2357	.2389	.2422	.2454	.2486	.2517	.2549
.7	.2580	.2611	.2642	.2673	.2704	.2734	.2764	.2794	.2823	.2852
.8	.2881	.2910	.2939	.2967	.2995	.3023	.3051	.3078	.3106	.3133
.9	.3159	.3186	.3212	.3238	.3264	.3289	.3315	.3340	.3365	.3389
1.0	.3413	.3438	.3461	.3485	.3508	.3531	.3554	.3577	.3599	.3621
1.1	.3643	.3665	.3686	.3708	.3729	.3749	.3770	.3790	.3810	.3830
1.2	.3849	.3869	.3888	.3907	.3925	.3944	.3962	.3980	.3997	.4015
1.3	.4032	.4049	.4066	.4082	.4099	.4115	.4131	.4147	.4162	.4177
1.4	.4192	.4207	.4222	.4236	.4251	.4265	.4279	.4292	.4306	.4319
1.5	.4332	.4345	.4357	.4370	.4382	.4394	.4406	.4418	.4429	.4441
1.6	.4452	.4463	.4474	.4484	.4495	.4505	.4515	.4525	.4535	.4545
1.7	.4554	.4564	.4573	.4582	.4591	.4599	.4608	.4616	.4625	.4633
1.8	.4641	.4649	.4656	.4664	.4671	.4678	.4686	.4693	.4699	.4706
1.9	.4713	.4719	.4726	.4732	.4738	.4744	.4750	.4756	.4761	.4767
2.0	.4772	.4778	.4783	.4788	.4793	.4798	.4803	.4808	.4812	.4817
2.1	.4821	.4826	.4830	.4834	.4838	.4842	.4846	.4850	.4854	.4857
2.2	.4861	.4864	.4868	.4871	.4875	.4878	.4881	.4884	.4887	.4890
2.3	.4893	.4896	.4898	.4901	.4904	.4906	.4909	.4911	.4913	.4916
2.4	.4918	.4920	.4922	.4925	.4927	.4929	.4931	.4932	.4934	.4936
2.5	.4938	.4940	.4941	.4943	.4945	.4946	.4948	.4949	.4951	.4952
2.6	.4953	.4955	.4956	.4957	.4959	.4960	.4961	.4962	.4963	.4964
2.7	.4965	.4966	.4967	.4968	.4969	.4970	.4971	.4972	.4973	.4974
2.8	.4974	.4975	.4976	.4977	.4977	.4978	.4979	.4979	.4980	.4981
2.9	.4981	.4982	.4982	.4983	.4984	.4984	.4985	.4985	.4986	.4986
3.0	.4987	.4987	.4987	.4988	.4988	.4989	.4989	.4989	.4990	.4990

Source: Abridged from Table 1 of A. Hald, *Statistical Tables and Formulas* (New York: Wiley), 1952. Reproduced by permission of A. Hald and the publisher. John Wiley & Sons, Inc.

TABLE 5   Gamma Function

Values of $\Gamma(n) = \int_0^\infty e^{-x}x^{n-1}\,dx$; $\Gamma(n+1) = n\Gamma(n)$

n	$\Gamma(n)$	n	$\Gamma(n)$	n	$\Gamma(n)$	n	$\Gamma(n)$
1.00	1.00000	1.25	.90640	1.50	.88623	1.75	.91906
1.01	.99433	1.26	.90440	1.51	.88659	1.76	.92137
1.02	.98884	1.27	.90250	1.52	.88704	1.77	.92376
1.03	.98355	1.28	.90072	1.53	.88757	1.78	.92623
1.04	.97844	1.29	.89904	1.54	.88818	1.79	.92877
1.05	.97350	1.30	.89747	1.55	.88887	1.80	.93138
1.06	.96874	1.31	.89600	1.56	.88964	1.81	.93408
1.07	.96415	1.32	.89464	1.57	.89049	1.82	.93685
1.08	.95973	1.33	.89338	1.58	.89142	1.83	.93969
1.09	.95546	1.34	.89222	1.59	.89243	1.84	.94261
1.10	.95135	1.35	.89115	1.60	.89352	1.85	.94561
1.11	.94739	1.36	.89018	1.61	.89468	1.86	.94869
1.12	.94359	1.37	.88931	1.62	.89592	1.87	.95184
1.13	.93993	1.38	.88854	1.63	.89724	1.88	.95507
1.14	.93642	1.39	.88785	1.64	.89864	1.89	.95838
1.15	.93304	1.40	.88726	1.65	.90012	1.90	.96177
1.16	.92980	1.41	.88676	1.66	.90167	1.91	.96523
1.17	.92670	1.42	.88636	1.67	.90330	1.92	.96878
1.18	.92373	1.43	.88604	1.68	.90500	1.93	.97240
1.19	.92088	1.44	.88580	1.69	.90678	1.94	.97610
1.20	.91817	1.45	.88565	1.70	.90864	1.95	.97988
1.21	.91558	1.46	.88560	1.71	.91057	1.96	.98374
1.22	.91311	1.47	.88563	1.72	.91258	1.97	.98768
1.23	.91075	1.48	.88575	1.73	.91466	1.98	.99171
1.24	.90852	1.49	.88595	1.74	.91683	1.99	.99581
						2.00	1.00000

Source: Abridged from W. H. Beyer, ed., *Handbook of Tables for Probability and Statistics*, 1966. Reproduced by permission of the publisher, The Chemical Rubber Company.

TABLE 6   Random Numbers

Row \ Column	1	2	3	4	5	6	7	8	9	10	11	12	13	14
1	10480	15011	01536	02011	81647	91646	69179	14194	62590	36207	20969	99570	91291	90700
2	22368	46573	25595	85393	30995	89198	27982	53402	93965	34095	52666	19174	39615	99505
3	24130	48360	22527	97265	76393	64809	15179	24830	49340	32081	30680	19655	63348	58629
4	42167	93093	06243	61680	07856	16376	39440	53537	71341	57004	00849	74917	97758	16379
5	37570	39975	81837	16656	06121	91782	60468	81305	49684	60672	14110	06927	01263	54613
6	77921	06907	11008	42751	27756	53498	18602	70659	90655	15053	21916	81825	44394	42880
7	99562	72905	56420	69994	98872	31016	71194	18738	44013	48840	63213	21069	10634	12952
8	96301	91977	05463	07972	18876	20922	94595	56869	69014	60045	18425	84903	42508	32307
9	89579	14342	63661	10281	17453	18103	57740	84378	25331	12566	58678	44947	05585	56941
10	85475	36857	53342	53988	53060	59533	38867	62300	08158	17983	16439	11458	18593	64952
11	28918	69578	88231	33276	70997	79936	56865	05859	90106	31595	01547	85590	91610	78188
12	63553	40961	48235	03427	49626	69445	18663	72695	52180	20847	12234	90511	33703	90322
13	09429	93969	52636	92737	88974	33488	36320	17617	30015	08272	84115	27156	30613	74952
14	10365	61129	87529	85689	48237	52267	67689	93394	01511	26358	85104	20285	29975	89868
15	07119	97336	71048	08178	77233	13916	47564	81056	97735	85977	29372	74461	28551	90707
16	51085	12765	51821	51259	77452	16308	60756	92144	49442	53900	70960	63990	75601	40719
17	02368	21382	52404	60268	89368	19885	55322	44819	01188	65255	64835	44919	05944	55157
18	01011	54092	33362	94904	31273	04146	18594	29852	71585	85030	51132	01915	92747	64951
19	52162	53916	46369	58586	23216	14513	83149	98736	23495	64350	94738	17752	35156	35749
20	07056	97628	33787	09998	42698	06691	76988	13602	51851	46104	88916	19509	25625	58104
21	48663	91245	85828	14346	09172	30168	90229	04734	59193	22178	30421	61666	99904	32812
22	54164	58492	22421	74103	47070	25306	76468	26384	58151	06646	21524	15227	96909	44592
23	32639	32363	05597	24200	13363	38005	94342	28728	35806	06912	17012	64161	18296	22851
24	29334	27001	87637	87308	58731	00256	45834	15398	46557	41135	10367	07684	36188	18510
25	02488	33062	28834	07351	19731	92420	60952	61280	50001	67658	32586	86679	50720	94953

26	81525	72295	04839	96423	24878	82651	66566	14778	76797	14780	13300	87074	79666	95725
27	29676	20591	68086	26432	46901	20849	89768	81536	86645	12659	92259	57102	80428	25280
28	00742	57392	39064	66432	84673	40027	32832	61362	98947	96067	64760	64584	96096	98253
29	05366	04213	25669	26422	44407	44048	37937	63904	45766	66134	75470	66520	34693	90449
30	91921	26418	64117	94305	26766	25940	39972	22209	71500	64568	91402	42416	07844	69618
31	00582	04711	87917	77341	42206	35126	74087	99547	81817	42607	43808	76655	62028	76630
32	00725	69884	62797	56170	86324	88072	76222	36086	84637	93161	76038	65855	77919	88006
33	69011	65795	95876	55293	18988	27354	26575	08625	40801	59920	29841	80150	12777	48501
34	25976	57948	29888	88604	67917	48708	18912	82271	65424	69774	33611	54262	85963	03547
35	09763	83473	73577	12908	30883	18317	28290	35797	05998	41688	34952	37888	38917	88050
36	91576	42595	27958	30134	04024	86385	29880	99730	55536	84855	29080	09250	79656	73211
37	17955	56349	90999	49127	20044	59931	06115	20542	18059	02008	73708	83517	36103	42791
38	46503	18584	18845	49618	02304	51038	20655	58727	28168	15475	56942	53389	20562	87338
39	92157	89634	94824	78171	84610	82834	09922	25417	44137	48413	25555	21246	35509	20468
40	14577	62765	35605	81263	39667	47358	56873	56307	61607	49518	89656	20103	77490	18062
41	98427	07523	33362	64270	01638	92477	66969	98420	04880	45585	46565	04102	46880	45709
42	34914	63976	88720	82765	34476	17032	87589	40836	32427	70002	70663	88863	77775	69348
43	70060	28277	39475	46473	23219	53416	94970	25832	69975	94884	19661	72828	00102	66794
44	53976	54914	06990	67245	68350	82948	11398	42878	80287	88267	47363	46634	06541	97809
45	76072	29515	40980	07391	58745	25774	22987	80059	39911	96189	41151	14222	60697	59583
46	90725	52210	83974	29992	65831	38857	50490	83765	55657	14361	31720	57375	56228	41546
47	64364	67412	33339	31926	14883	24413	59744	92351	97473	89286	35931	04110	23726	51900
48	08962	00358	31662	25388	61642	34072	81249	35648	56891	69352	48373	45578	78547	81788
49	95012	68379	93526	70765	10592	04542	76463	54328	02349	17247	28865	14777	62730	92277
50	15664	10493	20492	38391	91132	21999	59516	81652	27195	48223	46751	22923	32261	85653
51	16408	81899	04153	53381	79401	21438	83035	92350	36693	31238	59649	91754	72772	02338
52	18629	81953	05520	91962	04739	13092	97662	24822	94730	06496	35090	04822	86774	98289
53	73115	35101	47498	87637	99016	71060	88824	71013	18735	20286	23153	72924	35165	43040
54	57491	16703	23167	49323	45021	33132	12544	41035	80780	45393	44812	12515	98931	91202
55	30405	83946	23792	14422	15059	45799	22716	19792	09983	74353	68668	30429	70735	25499
56	16631	35006	85900	98275	32388	52390	16815	69298	82732	38480	73817	32523	41961	44437
57	96773	20206	42559	78985	05300	22164	24369	54224	35083	19687	11052	91491	60383	19746
58	38935	64202	14349	82674	66523	44133	00697	35552	35970	19124	63318	29686	03387	59846
59	31624	76384	17403	53363	44167	64486	64758	75366	76554	31601	12614	33072	60332	92325
60	78919	19474	23632	27889	47914	02584	37680	20801	72152	39339	34806	08930	85001	87820
61	03931	33309	57047	74211	63445	17361	62825	39908	05607	91284	68833	25570	38818	46920
62	74426	33278	43972	10119	89917	15665	52872	73823	73144	88662	88970	74492	51805	99378

(continued)

Row \ Column	1	2	3	4	5	6	7	8	9	10	11	12	13	14
63	09066	00903	20795	95452	92648	45454	09552	88815	16553	51125	79375	97596	16296	66092
64	42238	12426	87025	14267	20979	04508	64535	31355	86064	29472	47689	05974	52468	16834
65	16153	08002	26504	41744	81959	65642	74240	56302	00033	67107	77510	70625	28725	34191
66	21457	40742	29820	96783	29400	21840	15035	34537	33310	06116	95240	15957	16572	06004
67	21581	57802	02050	89728	17937	37621	47075	42080	97403	48626	68995	43805	33386	21597
68	55612	78095	83197	33732	05810	24813	86902	60397	16489	03264	88525	42786	05269	92532
69	44657	66999	99324	51281	84463	60563	79312	93454	68876	25471	93911	25650	12682	73572
70	91340	84979	46949	81973	37949	61023	43997	15263	80644	43942	89203	71795	99533	50501
71	91227	21199	31935	27022	84067	05462	35216	14486	29891	68607	41867	14951	91696	85065
72	50001	38140	66321	19924	72163	09538	12151	06878	91903	18749	34405	56087	82790	70925
73	65390	05224	72958	28609	81406	39147	25549	48542	42627	45233	57202	94617	23772	07896
74	27504	96131	83944	41575	10573	08619	64482	73923	36152	05184	94142	25299	84387	34925
75	37169	94851	39117	89632	00959	16487	65536	49071	39782	17095	02330	74301	00275	48280
76	11508	70225	51111	38351	19444	66499	71945	05422	13442	78675	84081	66938	93654	59894
77	37449	30362	06694	54690	04052	53115	62757	95348	78662	11163	81651	50245	34971	52924
78	46515	70331	85922	38329	57015	15765	97161	17869	45349	61796	66345	81073	49106	79860
79	30986	81223	42416	58353	21532	30502	32305	86482	05174	07901	54339	58861	74818	46942
80	63798	64995	46583	09785	44160	78128	83991	42865	92520	83531	80377	35909	81250	54238
81	82486	84846	99254	67632	43218	50076	21361	64816	51202	88124	41870	52689	51275	83556
82	21885	32906	92431	09060	64297	51674	64126	62570	26123	05155	59194	52799	28225	85762
83	60336	98782	07408	53458	13564	59089	26445	29789	85205	41001	12535	12133	14645	23541
84	43937	46891	24010	25560	86355	33941	25786	54990	71899	15475	95434	98227	21824	19585
85	97656	63175	89303	16275	07100	92063	21942	18611	47348	20203	18534	03862	78095	50136
86	03299	01221	05418	38982	55758	92237	26759	86367	21216	98442	08303	56613	91511	75928
87	79626	06486	03574	17668	07785	76020	79924	25651	83325	88428	85076	72811	22717	50585
88	85636	68335	47539	03129	65651	11977	02510	26113	99447	68645	34327	15152	55230	93448
89	18039	14367	61337	06177	12143	46609	32989	74014	64708	00533	35398	58408	13261	47908
90	08362	15656	60627	36478	65648	16764	53412	09013	07832	41574	17639	82163	60859	75567
91	79556	29068	04142	16268	15387	12856	66227	38358	22478	73373	88732	09443	82558	05250
92	92608	82674	27072	32534	17075	27698	98204	63863	11951	34648	88022	56148	34925	57031
93	23982	25835	40055	67006	12293	02753	14827	23235	35071	99704	37543	11601	35503	85171
94	09915	96306	05908	97901	28395	14186	00821	80703	70426	75647	76310	88717	37890	40129
95	59037	33300	26695	62247	69927	76123	50842	43834	86654	70959	79725	93872	28117	19233
96	42488	78077	69882	61657	34136	79180	97526	43092	04098	73571	80799	76536	71255	64239
97	46764	86273	63003	93017	31204	36692	40202	35275	57306	55543	53203	18098	47625	88684
98	03237	45430	55417	63282	90816	17349	88298	90183	36600	78406	06216	95787	42579	90730
99	86591	81482	52667	61582	14972	90053	89534	76036	49199	43716	97548	04379	46370	28672
100	38534	01715	94964	87288	65680	43772	39560	12918	86537	62738	19636	51132	25739	56947

Source: Abridged from W. H. Beyer (ed.). CRC Standard Mathematical Tables, 24th edition. (Cleveland: The Chemical Rubber Company), 1976. Reproduced by permission of the publisher.

TABLE 7   Critical Values for Student's t

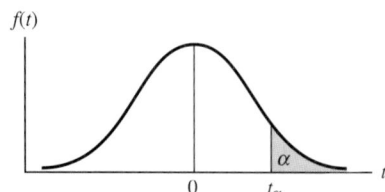

ν	$t_{.100}$	$t_{.050}$	$t_{.025}$	$t_{.010}$	$t_{.005}$	$t_{.001}$	$t_{.0005}$
1	3.078	6.314	12.706	31.821	63.657	318.31	636.62
2	1.886	2.920	4.303	6.965	9.925	22.326	31.598
3	1.638	2.353	3.182	4.541	5.841	10.213	12.924
4	1.533	2.132	2.776	3.747	4.604	7.173	8.610
5	1.476	2.015	2.571	3.365	4.032	5.893	6.869
6	1.440	1.943	2.447	3.143	3.707	5.208	5.959
7	1.415	1.895	2.365	2.998	3.499	4.785	5.408
8	1.397	1.860	2.306	2.896	3.355	4.501	5.041
9	1.383	1.833	2.262	2.821	3.250	4.297	4.781
10	1.372	1.812	2.228	2.764	3.169	4.144	4.587
11	1.363	1.796	2.201	2.718	3.106	4.025	4.437
12	1.356	1.782	2.179	2.681	3.055	3.930	4.318
13	1.350	1.771	2.160	2.650	3.012	3.852	4.221
14	1.345	1.761	2.145	2.624	2.977	3.787	4.140
15	1.341	1.753	2.131	2.602	2.947	3.733	4.073
16	1.337	1.746	2.120	2.583	2.921	3.686	4.015
17	1.333	1.740	2.110	2.567	2.898	3.646	3.965
18	1.330	1.734	2.101	2.552	2.878	3.610	3.922
19	1.328	1.729	2.093	2.539	2.861	3.579	3.883
20	1.325	1.725	2.086	2.528	2.845	3.552	3.850
21	1.323	1.721	2.080	2.518	2.831	3.527	3.819
22	1.321	1.717	2.074	2.508	2.819	3.505	3.792
23	1.319	1.714	2.069	2.500	2.807	3.485	3.767
24	1.318	1.711	2.064	2.492	2.797	3.467	3.745
25	1.316	1.708	2.060	2.485	2.787	3.450	3.725
26	1.315	1.706	2.056	2.479	2.779	3.435	3.707
27	1.314	1.703	2.052	2.473	2.771	3.421	3.690
28	1.313	1.701	2.048	2.467	2.763	3.408	3.674
29	1.311	1.699	2.045	2.462	2.756	3.396	3.659
30	1.310	1.697	2.042	2.457	2.750	3.385	3.646
40	1.303	1.684	2.021	2.423	2.704	3.307	3.551
60	1.296	1.671	2.000	2.390	2.660	3.232	3.460
120	1.289	1.658	1.980	2.358	2.617	3.160	3.373
∞	1.282	1.645	1.960	2.326	2.576	3.090	3.291

TABLE 8   Critical Values of χ^2

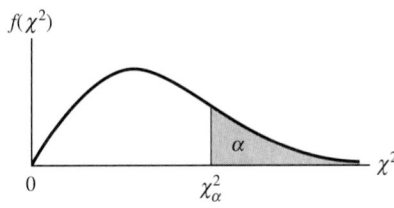

Degrees of Freedom	$\chi^2_{.995}$	$\chi^2_{.990}$	$\chi^2_{.975}$	$\chi^2_{.950}$	$\chi^2_{.900}$
1	.0000393	.0001571	.0009821	.0039321	.0157908
2	.0100251	.0201007	.0506356	.102587	.210720
3	.0717212	.114832	.215795	.351846	.584375
4	.206990	.297110	.484419	.710721	1.063623
5	.411740	.554300	.831211	1.145476	1.61031
6	.675727	0.872085	1.237347	1.63539	2.20413
7	.989265	1.239043	1.68987	2.16735	2.83311
8	1.344419	1.646482	2.17973	2.73264	3.48954
9	1.734926	2.087912	2.70039	3.32511	4.16816
10	2.15585	2.55821	3.24697	3.94030	4.86518
11	2.60321	3.05347	3.81575	4.57481	5.57779
12	3.07382	3.57056	4.40379	5.22603	6.30380
13	3.56503	4.10691	5.00874	5.89186	7.04150
14	4.07468	4.66043	5.62872	6.57063	7.78953
15	4.60094	5.22935	6.26214	7.26094	8.54675
16	5.14224	5.81221	6.90766	7.96164	9.31223
17	5.69724	6.40776	7.56418	8.67176	10.0852
18	6.26481	7.01491	8.23075	9.39046	10.8649
19	6.84398	7.63273	8.90655	10.1170	11.6509
20	7.43386	8.26040	9.59083	10.8508	12.4426
21	8.03366	8.89720	10.28293	11.5913	13.2396
22	8.64272	9.54249	10.9823	12.3380	14.0415
23	9.26042	10.19567	11.6885	13.0905	14.8479
24	9.88623	10.8564	12.4011	13.8484	15.6587
25	10.5197	11.5240	13.1197	14.6114	16.4734
26	11.1603	12.1981	13.8439	15.3791	17.2919
27	11.8076	12.8786	14.5733	16.1513	18.1138
28	12.4613	13.5648	15.3079	16.9279	18.9392
29	13.1211	14.2565	16.0471	17.7083	19.7677
30	13.7867	14.9535	16.7908	18.4926	20.5992
40	20.7065	22.1643	24.4331	26.5093	29.0505
50	27.9907	29.7067	32.3574	34.7642	37.6886
60	35.5346	37.4848	40.4817	43.1879	46.4589
70	43.2752	45.4418	48.7576	51.7393	55.3290
80	51.1720	53.5400	57.1532	60.3915	64.2778
90	59.1963	61.7541	65.6466	69.1260	73.2912
100	67.3276	70.0648	74.2219	77.9295	82.3581

Degrees of Freedom	$\chi^2_{.100}$	$\chi^2_{.050}$	$\chi^2_{.025}$	$\chi^2_{.010}$	$\chi^2_{.005}$
1	2.70554	3.84146	5.02389	6.63490	7.87944
2	4.60517	5.99147	7.37776	9.21034	10.5966
3	6.25139	7.81473	9.34840	11.3449	12.8381
4	7.77944	9.48773	11.1433	13.2767	14.8602
5	9.23635	11.0705	12.8325	15.0863	16.7496
6	10.6446	12.5916	14.4494	16.8119	18.5476
7	12.0170	14.0671	16.0128	18.4753	20.2777
8	13.3616	15.5073	17.5346	20.0902	21.9550
9	14.6837	16.9190	19.0228	21.6660	23.5893
10	15.9871	18.3070	20.4831	23.2093	25.1882
11	17.2750	19.6751	21.9200	24.7250	26.7569
12	18.5494	21.0261	23.3367	26.2170	28.2995
13	19.8119	22.3621	24.7356	27.6883	29.8194
14	21.0642	23.6848	26.1190	29.1413	31.3193
15	22.3072	24.9958	27.4884	30.5779	32.8013
16	23.5418	26.2962	28.8454	31.9999	34.2672
17	24.7690	27.5871	30.1910	33.4087	35.7185
18	25.9894	28.8693	31.5264	34.8053	37.1564
19	27.2036	30.1435	32.8523	36.1908	38.5822
20	28.4120	31.4104	34.1696	37.5662	39.9968
21	29.6151	32.6705	35.4789	38.9321	41.4010
22	30.8133	33.9244	36.7807	40.2894	42.7956
23	32.0069	35.1725	38.0757	41.6384	44.1813
24	33.1963	36.4151	39.3641	42.9798	45.5585
25	34.3816	37.6525	40.6465	44.3141	46.9278
26	35.5631	38.8852	41.9232	45.6417	48.2899
27	36.7412	40.1133	43.1944	46.9630	49.6449
28	37.9159	41.3372	44.4607	48.2782	50.9933
29	39.0875	42.5569	45.7222	49.5879	52.3356
30	40.2560	43.7729	46.9792	50.8922	53.6720
40	51.8050	55.7585	59.3417	63.6907	66.7659
50	63.1671	67.5048	71.4202	76.1539	79.4900
60	74.3970	79.0819	83.2976	88.3794	91.9517
70	85.5271	90.5312	95.0231	100.425	104.215
80	96.5782	101.879	106.629	112.329	116.321
90	107.565	113.145	118.136	124.116	128.299
100	118.498	124.342	129.561	135.807	140.169

Source: From C. M. Thompson, "Tables of the Percentage Points of the χ^2-Distribution," *Biometrika*, 1941, 32, 188–189. Reproduced by permisson of the *Biometrika* Trustees.

TABLE 9   Percentage Points of the F Distribution, $\alpha = .10$

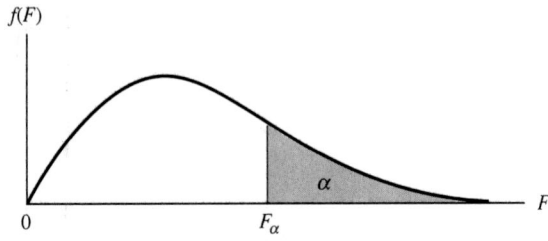

ν_1					Numerator Degrees of Freedom				
ν_2	1	2	3	4	5	6	7	8	9
1	39.86	49.50	53.59	55.83	57.24	58.20	58.91	59.44	59.86
2	8.53	9.00	9.16	9.24	9.29	9.33	9.35	9.37	9.38
3	5.54	5.46	5.39	5.34	5.31	5.28	5.27	5.25	5.24
4	4.54	4.32	4.19	4.11	4.05	4.01	3.98	3.95	3.94
5	4.06	3.78	3.62	3.52	3.45	3.40	3.37	3.34	3.32
6	3.78	3.46	3.29	3.18	3.11	3.05	3.01	2.98	2.96
7	3.59	3.26	3.07	2.96	2.88	2.83	2.78	2.75	2.72
8	3.46	3.11	2.92	2.81	2.73	2.67	2.62	2.59	2.56
9	3.36	3.01	2.81	2.69	2.61	2.55	2.51	2.47	2.44
10	3.29	2.92	2.73	2.61	2.52	2.46	2.41	2.38	2.35
11	3.23	2.86	2.66	2.54	2.45	2.39	2.34	2.30	2.27
12	3.18	2.81	2.61	2.48	2.39	2.33	2.28	2.24	2.21
13	3.14	2.76	2.56	2.43	2.35	2.28	2.23	2.20	2.16
14	3.10	2.73	2.52	2.39	2.31	2.24	2.19	2.15	2.12
15	3.07	2.70	2.49	2.36	2.27	2.21	2.16	2.12	2.09
16	3.05	2.67	2.46	2.33	2.24	2.18	2.13	2.09	2.06
17	3.03	2.64	2.44	2.31	2.22	2.15	2.10	2.06	2.03
18	3.01	2.62	2.42	2.29	2.20	2.13	2.08	2.04	2.00
19	2.99	2.61	2.40	2.27	2.18	2.11	2.06	2.02	1.98
20	2.97	2.59	2.38	2.25	2.16	2.09	2.04	2.00	1.96
21	2.96	2.57	2.36	2.23	2.14	2.08	2.02	1.98	1.95
22	2.95	2.56	2.35	2.22	2.13	2.06	2.01	1.97	1.93
23	2.94	2.55	2.34	2.21	2.11	2.05	1.99	1.95	1.92
24	2.93	2.54	2.33	2.19	2.10	2.04	1.98	1.94	1.91
25	2.92	2.53	2.32	2.18	2.09	2.02	1.97	1.93	1.89
26	2.91	2.52	2.31	2.17	2.08	2.01	1.96	1.92	1.88
27	2.90	2.51	2.30	2.17	2.07	2.00	1.95	1.91	1.87
28	2.89	2.50	2.29	2.16	2.06	2.00	1.94	1.90	1.87
29	2.89	2.50	2.28	2.15	2.06	1.99	1.93	1.89	1.86
30	2.88	2.49	2.28	2.14	2.05	1.98	1.93	1.88	1.85
40	2.84	2.44	2.23	2.09	2.00	1.93	1.87	1.83	1.79
60	2.79	2.39	2.18	2.04	1.95	1.87	1.82	1.77	1.74
120	2.75	2.35	2.13	1.99	1.90	1.82	1.77	1.72	1.68
∞	2.71	2.30	2.08	1.94	1.85	1.77	1.72	1.67	1.63

Denominator Degrees of Freedom

ν_1	Numerator Degrees of Freedom									
ν_2	10	12	15	20	24	30	40	60	120	∞
1	60.19	60.71	61.22	61.74	62.00	62.26	62.53	62.79	63.06	63.33
2	9.39	9.41	9.42	9.44	9.45	9.46	9.47	9.47	9.48	9.49
3	5.23	5.22	5.20	5.18	5.18	5.17	5.16	5.15	5.14	5.13
4	3.92	3.90	3.87	3.84	3.83	3.82	3.80	3.79	3.78	3.76
5	3.30	3.27	3.24	3.21	3.19	3.17	3.16	3.14	3.12	3.10
6	2.94	2.90	2.87	2.84	2.82	2.80	2.78	2.76	2.74	2.72
7	2.70	2.67	2.63	2.59	2.58	2.56	2.54	2.51	2.49	2.47
8	2.54	2.50	2.46	2.42	2.40	2.38	2.36	2.34	2.32	2.29
9	2.42	2.38	2.34	2.30	2.28	2.25	2.23	2.21	2.18	2.16
10	2.32	2.28	2.24	2.20	2.18	2.16	2.13	2.11	2.08	2.06
11	2.25	2.21	2.17	2.12	2.10	2.08	2.05	2.03	2.00	1.97
12	2.19	2.15	2.10	2.06	2.04	2.01	1.99	1.96	1.93	1.90
13	2.14	2.10	2.05	2.01	1.98	1.96	1.93	1.90	1.88	1.85
14	2.10	2.05	2.01	1.96	1.94	1.91	1.89	1.86	1.83	1.80
15	2.06	2.02	1.97	1.92	1.90	1.87	1.85	1.82	1.79	1.76
16	2.03	1.99	1.94	1.89	1.87	1.84	1.81	1.78	1.75	1.72
17	2.00	1.96	1.91	1.86	1.84	1.81	1.78	1.75	1.72	1.69
18	1.98	1.93	1.89	1.84	1.81	1.78	1.75	1.72	1.69	1.66
19	1.96	1.91	1.86	1.81	1.79	1.76	1.73	1.70	1.67	1.63
20	1.94	1.89	1.84	1.79	1.77	1.74	1.71	1.68	1.64	1.61
21	1.92	1.87	1.83	1.78	1.75	1.72	1.69	1.66	1.62	1.59
22	1.90	1.86	1.81	1.76	1.73	1.70	1.67	1.64	1.60	1.57
23	1.89	1.84	1.80	1.74	1.72	1.69	1.66	1.62	1.59	1.55
24	1.88	1.83	1.78	1.73	1.70	1.67	1.64	1.61	1.57	1.53
25	1.87	1.82	1.77	1.72	1.69	1.66	1.63	1.59	1.56	1.52
26	1.86	1.81	1.76	1.71	1.68	1.65	1.61	1.58	1.54	1.50
27	1.85	.180	1.75	1.70	1.67	1.64	1.60	1.57	1.53	1.49
28	1.84	1.79	1.74	1.69	1.66	1.63	1.59	1.56	1.52	1.48
29	1.83	1.78	1.73	1.68	1.65	1.62	1.58	1.55	1.51	1.47
30	1.82	1.77	1.72	1.67	1.64	1.61	1.57	1.54	1.50	1.46
40	1.76	1.71	1.66	1.61	1.57	1.54	1.51	1.47	1.42	1.38
60	1.71	1.66	1.60	1.54	1.51	1.48	1.44	1.40	1.35	1.29
120	1.65	1.60	1.55	1.48	1.45	1.41	1.37	1.32	1.26	1.19
∞	1.60	1.55	1.49	1.42	1.38	1.34	1.30	1.24	1.17	1.00

Denominator Degrees of Freedom

TABLE 10   Percentage Points of the F Distribution, $\alpha = .05$

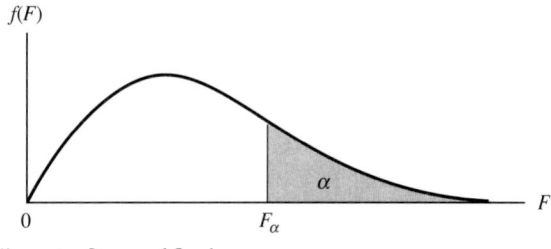

	ν_1	Numerator Degrees of Freedom								
	ν_2	1	2	3	4	5	6	7	8	9
	1	161.4	199.5	215.7	224.6	230.2	234.0	236.8	238.9	240.5
	2	18.51	19.00	19.16	19.25	19.30	19.33	19.35	19.37	19.38
	3	10.13	9.55	9.28	9.12	9.01	8.94	8.89	8.85	8.81
	4	7.71	6.94	6.59	6.39	6.26	6.16	6.09	6.04	6.00
	5	6.61	5.79	5.41	5.19	5.05	4.95	4.88	4.82	4.77
	6	5.99	5.14	4.76	4.53	4.39	4.28	4.21	4.15	4.10
	7	5.59	4.74	4.35	4.12	3.97	3.87	3.79	3.73	3.68
	8	5.32	4.46	4.07	3.84	3.69	3.58	3.50	3.44	3.39
	9	5.12	4.26	3.86	3.63	3.48	3.37	3.29	3.23	3.18
	10	4.96	4.10	3.71	3.48	3.33	3.22	3.14	3.07	3.02
	11	4.84	3.98	3.59	3.36	3.20	3.09	3.01	2.95	2.90
	12	4.75	3.89	3.49	3.26	3.11	3.00	2.91	2.85	2.80
	13	4.67	3.81	3.41	3.18	3.03	2.92	2.83	2.77	2.71
	14	4.60	3.74	3.34	3.11	2.96	2.85	2.76	2.70	2.65
	15	4.54	3.68	3.29	3.06	2.90	2.79	2.71	2.64	2.59
	16	4.49	3.63	3.24	3.01	2.85	2.74	2.66	2.59	2.54
	17	4.45	3.59	3.20	2.96	2.81	2.70	2.61	2.55	2.49
	18	4.41	3.55	3.16	2.93	2.77	2.66	2.58	2.51	2.46
	19	4.38	3.52	3.13	2.90	2.74	2.63	2.54	2.48	2.42
	20	4.35	3.49	3.10	2.87	2.71	2.60	2.51	2.45	2.39
	21	4.32	3.47	3.07	2.84	2.68	2.57	2.49	2.42	2.37
	22	4.30	3.44	3.05	2.82	2.66	2.55	2.46	2.40	2.34
	23	4.28	3.42	3.03	2.80	2.64	2.53	2.44	2.37	2.32
	24	4.26	3.40	3.01	2.78	2.62	2.51	2.42	2.36	2.30
	25	4.24	3.39	2.99	2.76	2.60	2.49	2.40	2.34	2.28
	26	4.23	3.37	2.98	2.74	2.59	2.47	2.39	2.32	2.27
	27	4.21	3.35	2.96	2.73	2.57	2.46	2.37	2.31	2.25
	28	4.20	3.34	2.95	2.71	2.56	2.45	2.36	2.29	2.24
	29	4.18	3.33	2.93	2.70	2.55	2.43	2.35	2.28	2.22
	30	4.17	3.32	2.92	2.69	2.53	2.42	2.33	2.27	2.21
	40	4.08	3.23	2.84	2.61	2.45	2.34	2.25	2.18	2.12
	60	4.00	3.15	2.76	2.53	2.37	2.25	2.17	2.10	2.04
	120	3.92	3.07	2.68	2.45	2.29	2.17	2.09	2.02	1.96
	∞	3.84	3.00	2.60	2.37	2.21	2.10	2.01	1.94	1.88

Denominator Degrees of Freedom

ν_1	Numerator Degrees of Freedom									
ν_2	10	12	15	20	24	30	40	60	120	∞
1	241.9	243.9	245.9	248.0	249.1	250.1	251.1	252.2	253.3	254.3
2	19.40	19.41	19.43	19.45	19.45	19.46	19.47	19.48	19.49	19.50
3	8.79	8.74	8.70	8.66	8.64	8.62	8.59	8.57	8.55	8.53
4	5.96	5.91	5.86	5.80	5.77	5.75	5.72	5.69	5.66	5.63
5	4.74	4.68	4.62	4.56	4.53	4.50	4.46	4.43	4.40	4.36
6	4.06	4.00	3.94	3.87	3.84	3.81	3.77	3.74	3.70	3.67
7	3.64	3.57	3.51	3.44	3.41	3.38	3.34	3.30	3.27	3.23
8	3.35	3.28	3.22	3.15	3.12	3.08	3.04	3.01	2.97	2.93
9	3.14	3.07	3.01	2.94	2.90	2.86	2.83	2.79	2.75	2.71
10	2.98	2.91	2.85	2.77	2.74	2.70	2.66	2.62	2.58	2.54
11	2.85	2.79	2.72	2.65	2.61	2.57	2.53	2.49	2.45	2.40
12	2.75	2.69	2.62	2.54	2.51	2.47	2.43	2.38	2.34	2.30
13	2.67	2.60	2.53	2.46	2.42	2.38	2.34	2.30	2.25	2.21
14	2.60	2.53	2.46	2.39	2.35	2.31	2.27	2.22	2.18	2.13
15	2.54	2.48	2.40	2.33	2.29	2.25	2.20	2.16	2.11	2.07
16	2.49	2.42	2.35	2.28	2.24	2.19	2.15	2.11	2.06	2.01
17	2.45	2.38	2.31	2.23	2.19	2.15	2.10	2.06	2.01	1.96
18	2.41	2.34	2.27	2.19	2.15	2.11	2.06	2.02	1.97	1.92
19	2.38	2.31	2.23	2.16	2.11	2.07	2.03	1.98	1.93	1.88
20	2.35	2.28	2.20	2.12	2.08	2.04	1.99	1.95	1.90	1.84
21	2.32	2.25	2.18	2.10	2.05	2.01	1.96	1.92	1.87	1.81
22	2.30	2.23	2.15	2.07	2.03	1.98	1.94	1.89	1.84	1.78
23	2.27	2.20	2.13	2.05	2.01	1.96	1.91	1.86	1.81	1.76
24	2.25	2.18	2.11	2.03	1.98	1.94	1.89	1.84	1.79	1.73
25	2.24	2.16	2.09	2.01	1.96	1.92	1.87	1.82	1.77	1.71
26	2.22	2.15	2.07	1.99	1.95	1.90	1.85	1.80	1.75	1.69
27	2.20	2.13	2.06	1.97	1.93	1.88	1.84	1.79	1.73	1.67
28	2.19	2.12	2.04	1.96	1.91	1.87	1.82	1.77	1.71	1.65
29	2.18	2.10	2.03	1.94	1.90	1.85	1.81	1.75	1.70	1.64
30	2.16	2.09	2.01	1.93	1.89	1.84	1.79	1.74	1.68	1.62
40	2.08	2.00	1.92	1.84	1.79	1.74	1.69	1.64	1.58	1.51
60	1.99	1.92	1.84	1.75	1.70	1.65	1.59	1.53	1.47	1.39
120	1.91	1.83	1.75	1.66	1.61	1.55	1.50	1.43	1.35	1.25
∞	1.83	1.75	1.67	1.57	1.52	1.46	1.39	1.32	1.22	1.00

Denominator Degrees of Freedom

TABLE 11   Percentage Points of the F Distribution, $\alpha = .025$

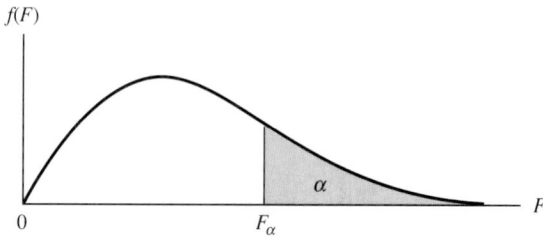

ν_1 / ν_2	Numerator Degrees of Freedom								
	1	2	3	4	5	6	7	8	9
1	647.8	799.5	864.2	899.6	921.8	937.1	948.2	956.7	963.3
2	38.51	39.00	39.17	39.25	39.30	39.33	39.36	39.37	39.39
3	17.44	16.04	15.44	15.10	14.88	14.73	14.62	14.54	14.47
4	12.22	10.65	9.98	9.60	9.36	9.20	9.07	8.98	8.90
5	10.01	8.43	7.76	7.39	7.15	6.98	6.85	6.76	6.68
6	8.81	7.26	6.60	6.23	5.99	5.82	5.70	5.60	5.52
7	8.07	6.54	5.89	5.52	5.29	5.12	4.99	4.90	4.82
8	7.57	6.06	5.42	5.05	4.82	4.65	4.53	4.43	4.36
9	7.21	5.71	5.08	4.72	4.48	4.32	4.20	4.10	4.03
10	6.94	5.46	4.83	4.47	4.24	4.07	3.95	3.85	3.78
11	6.72	5.26	4.63	4.28	4.04	3.88	3.76	3.66	3.59
12	6.55	5.10	4.47	4.12	3.89	3.73	3.61	3.51	3.44
13	6.41	4.97	4.35	4.00	3.77	3.60	3.48	3.39	3.31
14	6.30	4.86	4.24	3.89	3.66	3.50	3.38	3.29	3.21
15	6.20	4.77	4.15	3.80	3.58	3.41	3.29	3.20	3.12
16	6.12	4.69	4.08	3.73	3.50	3.34	3.22	3.12	3.05
17	6.04	4.62	4.01	3.66	3.44	3.28	3.16	3.06	2.98
18	5.98	4.56	3.95	3.61	3.38	3.22	3.10	3.01	2.93
19	5.92	4.51	3.90	3.56	3.33	3.17	3.05	2.96	2.88
20	5.87	4.46	3.86	3.51	3.29	3.13	3.01	2.91	2.84
21	5.83	4.42	3.82	3.48	3.25	3.09	2.97	2.87	2.80
22	5.79	4.38	3.78	3.44	3.22	3.05	2.93	2.84	2.76
23	5.75	4.35	3.75	3.41	3.18	3.02	2.90	2.81	2.73
24	5.72	4.32	3.72	3.38	3.15	2.99	2.87	2.78	2.70
25	5.69	4.29	3.69	3.35	3.13	2.97	2.85	2.75	2.68
26	5.66	4.27	3.67	3.33	3.10	2.94	2.82	2.73	2.65
27	5.63	4.24	3.65	3.31	3.08	2.92	2.80	2.71	2.63
28	5.61	4.22	3.63	3.29	3.06	2.90	2.78	2.69	2.61
29	5.59	4.20	3.61	3.27	3.04	2.88	2.76	2.67	2.59
30	5.57	4.18	3.59	3.25	3.03	2.87	2.75	2.65	2.57
40	5.42	4.05	3.46	3.13	2.90	2.74	2.62	2.53	2.45
60	5.29	3.93	3.34	3.01	2.79	2.63	2.51	2.41	2.33
120	5.15	3.80	3.23	2.89	2.67	2.52	2.39	2.30	2.22
∞	5.02	3.69	3.12	2.79	2.57	2.41	2.29	2.19	2.11

Denominator Degrees of Freedom

ν_1				Numerator Degrees of Freedom						
ν_2	10	12	15	20	24	30	40	60	120	∞
1	968.6	976.7	984.9	993.1	997.2	1,001	1,006	1,010	1,014	1,108
2	39.40	39.41	39.43	39.45	39.46	39.46	39.47	39.48	39.49	39.50
3	14.42	14.34	14.25	14.17	14.12	14.08	14.04	13.99	13.95	13.90
4	8.84	8.75	8.66	8.56	8.51	8.46	8.41	8.36	8.31	8.26
5	6.62	6.52	6.43	6.33	6.28	6.23	6.18	6.12	6.07	6.02
6	5.46	5.37	5.27	5.17	5.12	5.07	5.01	4.96	4.90	4.85
7	4.76	4.67	4.57	4.47	4.42	4.36	4.31	4.25	4.20	4.14
8	4.30	4.20	4.10	4.00	3.95	3.89	3.84	3.78	3.73	3.67
9	3.96	3.87	3.77	3.67	3.61	3.56	3.51	3.45	3.39	3.33
10	3.72	3.62	3.52	3.42	3.37	3.31	3.26	3.20	3.14	3.08
11	3.53	3.43	3.33	3.23	3.17	3.12	3.06	3.00	2.94	2.88
12	3.37	3.28	3.18	3.07	3.02	2.96	2.91	2.85	2.79	2.72
13	3.25	3.15	3.05	2.95	2.89	2.84	2.78	2.72	2.66	2.60
14	3.15	3.05	2.95	2.84	2.79	2.73	2.67	2.61	2.55	2.49
15	3.06	2.96	2.86	2.76	2.70	2.64	2.59	2.52	2.46	2.40
16	2.99	2.89	2.79	2.68	2.63	2.57	2.51	2.45	2.38	2.32
17	2.92	2.82	2.72	2.62	2.56	2.50	2.44	2.38	2.32	2.25
18	2.87	2.77	2.67	2.56	2.50	2.44	2.38	2.32	2.26	2.19
19	2.82	2.72	2.62	2.51	2.45	2.39	2.33	2.27	2.20	2.13
20	2.77	2.68	2.57	2.46	2.41	2.35	2.29	2.22	2.16	2.09
21	2.73	2.64	2.53	2.42	2.37	2.31	2.25	2.18	2.11	2.04
22	2.70	2.60	2.50	2.39	2.33	2.27	2.21	2.14	2.08	2.00
23	2.67	2.57	2.47	2.36	2.30	2.24	2.18	2.11	2.04	1.97
24	2.64	2.54	2.44	2.33	2.27	2.21	2.15	2.08	2.01	1.94
25	2.61	2.51	2.41	2.30	2.24	2.18	2.12	2.05	1.98	1.91
26	2.59	2.49	2.39	2.28	2.22	2.16	2.09	2.03	1.95	1.88
27	2.57	2.47	2.36	2.25	2.19	2.13	2.07	2.00	1.93	1.85
28	2.55	2.45	2.34	2.23	2.17	2.11	2.05	1.98	1.91	1.83
29	2.53	2.43	2.32	2.21	2.15	2.09	2.03	1.96	1.89	1.81
30	2.51	2.41	2.31	2.20	2.14	2.07	2.01	1.94	1.87	1.79
40	2.39	2.29	2.18	2.07	2.01	1.94	1.88	1.80	1.72	1.64
60	2.27	2.17	2.06	1.94	1.88	1.82	1.74	1.67	1.58	1.48
120	2.16	2.05	1.94	1.82	1.76	1.69	1.61	1.53	1.43	1.31
∞	2.05	1.94	1.83	1.71	1.64	1.57	1.48	1.39	1.27	1.00

Denominator Degrees of Freedom

TABLE 12   Percentage Points of the F Distribution, $\alpha = .01$

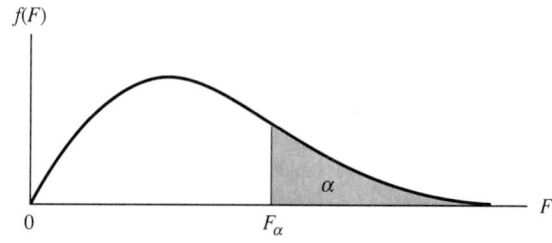

	ν_1	Numerator Degrees of Freedom								
	ν_2	1	2	3	4	5	6	7	8	9
	1	4,052	4,999.5	5,403	5,625	5,764	5,859	5,928	5,982	6,022
	2	98.50	99.00	99.17	99.25	99.30	99.33	99.36	99.37	99.39
	3	34.12	30.82	29.46	28.71	28.24	27.91	27.67	27.49	27.35
	4	21.20	18.00	16.69	15.98	15.52	15.21	14.98	14.80	14.66
	5	16.26	13.27	12.06	11.39	10.97	10.67	10.46	10.29	10.16
	6	13.75	10.92	9.78	9.15	8.75	8.47	8.26	8.10	7.98
	7	12.25	9.55	8.45	7.85	7.46	7.19	6.99	6.84	6.72
	8	11.26	8.65	7.59	7.01	6.63	6.37	6.18	6.03	5.91
	9	10.56	8.02	6.99	6.42	6.06	5.80	5.61	5.47	5.35
	10	10.04	7.56	6.55	5.99	5.64	5.39	5.20	5.06	4.94
	11	9.65	7.21	6.22	5.67	5.32	5.07	4.89	4.74	4.63
	12	9.33	6.93	5.95	5.41	5.06	4.82	4.64	4.50	4.39
	13	9.07	6.70	5.74	5.21	4.86	4.62	4.44	4.30	4.19
	14	8.86	6.51	5.56	5.04	4.69	4.46	4.28	4.14	4.03
	15	8.68	6.36	5.42	4.89	4.56	4.32	4.14	4.00	3.89
	16	8.53	6.23	5.29	4.77	4.44	4.20	4.03	3.89	3.78
	17	8.40	6.11	5.18	4.67	4.34	4.10	3.93	3.79	3.68
	18	8.29	6.01	5.09	4.58	4.25	4.01	3.84	3.71	3.60
	19	8.18	5.93	5.01	4.50	4.17	3.94	3.77	3.63	3.52
	20	8.10	5.85	4.94	4.43	4.10	3.87	3.70	3.56	3.46
	21	8.02	5.78	4.87	4.37	4.04	3.81	3.64	3.51	3.40
	22	7.95	5.72	4.82	4.31	3.99	3.76	3.59	3.45	3.35
	23	7.88	5.66	4.76	4.26	3.94	3.71	3.54	3.41	3.30
	24	7.82	5.61	4.72	4.22	3.90	3.67	3.50	3.36	3.26
	25	7.77	5.57	4.68	4.18	3.85	3.63	3.46	3.32	3.22
	26	7.72	5.53	4.64	4.14	3.82	3.59	3.42	3.29	3.18
	27	7.68	5.49	4.60	4.11	3.78	3.56	3.39	3.26	3.15
	28	7.64	5.45	4.57	4.07	3.75	3.53	3.36	3.23	3.12
	29	7.60	5.42	4.54	4.04	3.73	3.50	3.33	3.20	3.09
	30	7.56	5.39	4.51	4.02	3.70	3.47	3.30	3.17	3.07
	40	7.31	5.18	4.31	3.83	3.51	3.29	3.12	2.99	2.89
	60	7.08	4.98	4.13	3.65	3.34	3.12	2.95	2.82	2.72
	120	6.85	4.79	3.95	3.48	3.17	2.96	2.79	2.66	2.56
	∞	6.63	4.61	3.78	3.32	3.02	2.80	2.64	2.51	2.41

Denominator Degrees of Freedom

ν_1	Numerator Degrees of Freedom									
ν_2	10	12	15	20	24	30	40	60	120	∞
1	6,056	6,106	6,157	6,209	6,235	6,261	6,287	6,313	6,339	6,366
2	99.40	99.42	99.43	99.45	99.46	99.47	99.47	99.48	99.49	99.50
3	27.23	27.05	26.87	26.69	26.60	26.50	26.41	26.32	26.22	26.13
4	14.55	14.37	14.20	14.02	13.93	13.84	13.75	13.65	13.56	13.46
5	10.05	9.89	9.72	9.55	9.47	9.38	9.29	9.20	9.11	9.02
6	7.87	7.72	7.56	7.40	7.31	7.23	7.14	7.06	6.97	6.88
7	6.62	6.47	6.31	6.16	6.07	5.99	5.91	5.82	5.74	5.65
8	5.81	5.67	5.52	5.36	5.28	5.20	5.12	5.03	4.95	4.86
9	5.26	5.11	4.96	4.81	4.73	4.65	4.57	4.48	4.40	4.31
10	4.85	4.71	4.56	4.41	4.33	4.25	4.17	4.08	4.00	3.91
11	4.54	4.40	4.25	4.10	4.02	3.94	3.86	3.78	3.69	3.60
12	4.30	4.16	4.01	3.86	3.78	3.70	3.62	3.54	3.45	3.36
13	4.10	3.96	3.82	3.66	3.59	3.51	3.43	3.34	3.25	3.17
14	3.94	3.80	3.66	3.51	3.43	3.35	3.27	3.18	3.09	3.00
15	3.80	3.67	3.52	3.37	3.29	3.21	3.13	3.05	2.96	2.87
16	3.69	3.55	3.41	3.26	3.18	3.10	3.02	2.93	2.84	2.75
17	3.59	3.46	3.31	3.16	3.08	3.00	2.92	2.83	2.75	2.65
18	3.51	3.37	3.23	3.08	3.00	2.92	2.84	2.75	2.66	2.57
19	3.43	3.30	3.15	3.00	2.92	2.84	2.76	2.67	2.58	2.49
20	3.37	3.23	3.09	2.94	2.86	2.78	2.69	2.61	2.52	2.42
21	3.31	3.17	3.03	2.88	2.80	2.72	2.64	2.55	2.46	2.36
22	3.26	3.12	2.98	2.83	2.75	2.67	2.58	2.50	2.40	2.31
23	3.21	3.07	2.93	2.78	2.70	2.62	2.54	2.45	2.35	2.26
24	3.17	3.03	2.89	2.74	2.66	2.58	2.49	2.40	2.31	2.21
25	3.13	2.99	2.85	2.70	2.62	2.54	2.45	2.36	2.27	2.17
26	3.09	2.96	2.81	2.66	2.58	2.50	2.42	2.33	2.23	2.13
27	3.06	2.93	2.78	2.63	2.55	2.47	2.38	2.29	2.20	2.10
28	3.03	2.90	2.75	2.60	2.52	2.44	2.35	2.26	2.17	2.06
29	3.00	2.87	2.73	2.57	2.49	2.41	2.33	2.23	2.14	2.03
30	2.98	2.84	2.70	2.55	2.47	2.39	2.30	2.21	2.11	2.01
40	2.80	2.66	2.52	2.37	2.29	2.20	2.11	2.02	1.92	1.80
60	2.63	2.50	2.35	2.20	2.12	2.03	1.94	1.84	1.73	1.60
120	2.47	2.34	2.19	2.03	1.95	1.86	1.76	1.66	1.53	1.38
∞	2.32	2.18	2.04	1.88	1.79	1.70	1.59	1.47	1.32	1.00

Denominator Degrees of Freedom

TABLE 13   Percentage Points of the Studentized Range $q(p, \nu)$, $\alpha = .05$

ν \\ p	2	3	4	5	6	7	8	9	10	11
1	17.97	26.98	32.82	37.08	40.41	43.12	45.40	47.36	49.07	50.59
2	6.08	8.33	9.80	10.88	11.74	12.44	13.03	13.54	13.99	14.39
3	4.50	5.91	6.82	7.50	8.04	8.48	8.85	9.18	9.46	9.72
4	3.93	5.04	5.76	6.29	6.71	7.05	7.35	7.60	7.83	8.03
5	3.64	4.60	5.22	5.67	6.03	6.33	6.58	6.80	6.99	7.17
6	3.46	4.34	4.90	5.30	5.63	5.90	6.12	6.32	6.49	6.65
7	3.34	4.16	4.68	5.06	5.36	5.61	5.82	6.00	6.16	6.30
8	3.26	4.04	4.53	4.89	5.17	5.40	5.60	5.77	5.92	6.05
9	3.20	3.95	4.41	4.76	5.02	5.24	5.43	5.59	5.74	5.87
10	3.15	3.88	4.33	4.65	4.91	5.12	5.30	5.46	5.60	5.72
11	3.11	3.82	4.26	4.57	4.82	5.03	5.20	5.35	5.49	5.61
12	3.08	3.77	4.20	4.51	4.75	4.95	5.12	5.27	5.39	5.51
13	3.06	3.73	4.15	4.45	4.69	4.88	5.05	5.19	5.32	5.43
14	3.03	3.70	4.11	4.41	4.64	4.83	4.99	5.13	5.25	5.36
15	3.01	3.67	4.08	4.37	4.60	4.78	4.94	5.08	5.20	5.31
16	3.00	3.65	4.05	4.33	4.56	4.74	4.90	5.03	5.15	5.26
17	2.98	3.63	4.02	4.30	4.52	4.70	4.86	4.99	5.11	5.21
18	2.97	3.61	4.00	4.28	4.49	4.67	4.82	4.96	5.07	5.17
19	2.96	3.59	3.98	4.25	4.47	4.65	4.79	4.92	5.04	5.14
20	2.95	3.58	3.96	4.23	4.45	4.62	4.77	4.90	5.01	5.11
24	2.92	3.53	3.90	4.17	4.37	4.54	4.68	4.81	4.92	5.01
30	2.89	3.49	3.85	4.10	4.30	4.46	4.60	4.72	4.82	4.92
40	2.86	3.44	3.79	4.04	4.23	4.39	4.52	4.63	4.73	4.82
60	2.83	3.40	3.74	3.98	4.16	4.31	4.44	4.55	4.65	4.73
120	2.80	3.36	3.68	3.92	4.10	4.24	4.36	4.47	4.56	4.64
∞	2.77	3.31	3.63	3.86	4.03	4.17	4.29	4.39	4.47	4.55

ν \ p	12	13	14	15	16	17	18	19	20
1	51.96	53.20	54.33	55.36	56.32	57.22	58.04	58.83	59.56
2	14.75	15.08	15.38	15.65	15.91	16.14	16.37	16.57	16.77
3	9.95	10.15	10.35	10.52	10.69	10.84	10.98	11.11	11.24
4	8.21	8.37	8.52	8.66	8.79	8.91	9.03	9.13	9.23
5	7.32	7.47	7.60	7.72	7.83	7.93	8.03	8.12	8.21
6	6.79	6.92	7.03	7.14	7.24	7.34	7.43	7.51	7.59
7	6.43	6.55	6.66	6.76	6.85	6.94	7.02	7.10	7.17
8	6.18	6.29	6.39	6.48	6.57	6.65	6.73	6.80	6.87
9	5.98	6.09	6.19	6.28	6.36	6.44	6.51	6.58	6.64
10	5.83	5.93	6.03	6.11	6.19	6.27	6.34	6.40	6.47
11	5.71	5.81	5.90	5.98	6.06	6.13	6.20	6.27	6.33
12	5.61	5.71	5.80	5.88	5.95	6.02	6.09	6.15	6.21
13	5.53	5.63	5.71	5.79	5.86	5.93	5.99	6.05	6.11
14	5.46	5.55	5.64	5.71	5.79	5.85	5.91	5.97	6.03
15	5.40	5.49	5.57	5.65	5.72	5.78	5.85	5.90	5.96
16	5.35	5.44	5.52	5.59	5.66	5.73	5.79	5.84	5.90
17	5.31	5.39	5.47	5.54	5.61	5.67	5.73	5.79	5.84
18	5.27	5.35	5.43	5.50	5.57	5.63	5.69	5.74	5.79
19	5.23	5.31	5.39	5.46	5.53	5.59	5.65	5.70	5.75
20	5.20	5.28	5.36	5.43	5.49	5.55	5.61	5.66	5.71
24	5.10	5.18	5.25	5.32	5.38	5.44	5.49	5.55	5.59
30	5.00	5.08	5.15	5.21	5.27	5.33	5.38	5.43	5.47
40	4.90	4.98	5.04	5.11	5.16	5.22	5.27	5.31	5.36
60	4.81	4.88	4.94	5.00	5.06	5.11	5.15	5.20	5.24
120	4.71	4.78	4.84	4.90	4.95	5.00	5.04	5.09	5.13
∞	4.62	4.68	4.74	4.80	4.85	4.89	4.93	4.97	5.01

Source: *Biometrika Tables for Statisticians*, Vol. I, 3d ed., edited by E. S. Pearson and H. O. Hartley (Cambridge University Press, 1966). Reproduced by permission of Professor E. S. Pearson and the *Biometrika* Trustees.

TABLE 14   Percentage Points of the Studentized Range $q(p, \nu)$, $\alpha = .01$

ν \ p	2	3	4	5	6	7	8	9	10	11
1	90.03	135.0	164.3	185.6	202.2	215.8	227.2	237.0	245.6	253.2
2	14.04	19.02	22.29	24.72	26.63	28.20	29.53	30.68	31.69	32.59
3	8.26	10.62	12.17	13.33	14.24	15.00	15.64	16.20	16.69	17.13
4	6.51	8.12	9.17	9.96	10.58	11.10	11.55	11.93	12.27	12.57
5	5.70	6.98	7.80	8.42	8.91	9.32	9.67	9.97	10.24	10.48
6	5.24	6.33	7.03	7.56	7.97	8.32	8.61	8.87	9.10	9.30
7	4.95	5.92	6.54	7.01	7.37	7.68	7.94	8.17	8.37	8.55
8	4.75	5.64	6.20	6.62	6.96	7.24	7.47	7.68	7.86	8.03
9	4.60	5.43	5.96	6.35	6.66	6.91	7.13	7.33	7.49	7.65
10	4.48	5.27	5.77	6.14	6.43	6.67	6.87	7.05	7.21	7.36
11	4.39	5.15	5.62	5.97	6.25	6.48	6.67	6.84	6.99	7.13
12	4.32	5.05	5.50	5.84	6.10	6.32	6.51	6.67	6.81	6.94
13	4.26	4.96	5.40	5.73	5.98	6.19	6.37	6.53	6.67	6.79
14	4.21	4.89	5.32	5.63	5.88	6.08	6.26	6.41	6.54	6.66
15	4.17	4.84	5.25	5.56	5.80	5.99	6.16	6.31	6.44	6.55
16	4.13	4.79	5.19	5.49	5.72	5.92	6.08	6.22	6.35	6.46
17	4.10	4.74	5.14	5.43	5.66	5.85	6.01	6.15	6.27	6.38
18	4.07	4.70	5.09	5.38	5.60	5.79	5.94	6.08	6.20	6.31
19	4.05	4.67	5.05	5.33	5.55	5.73	5.89	6.02	6.14	6.25
20	4.02	4.64	5.02	5.29	5.51	5.69	5.84	5.97	6.09	6.19
24	3.96	4.55	4.91	5.17	5.37	5.54	5.69	5.81	5.92	6.02
30	3.89	4.45	4.80	5.05	5.24	5.40	5.54	5.65	5.76	5.85
40	3.82	4.37	4.70	4.93	5.11	5.26	5.39	5.50	5.60	5.69
60	3.76	4.28	4.59	4.82	4.99	5.13	5.25	5.36	5.45	5.53
120	3.70	4.20	4.50	4.71	4.87	5.01	5.12	5.21	5.30	5.37
∞	3.64	4.12	4.40	4.60	4.76	4.88	4.99	5.08	5.16	5.23

ν \ p	12	13	14	15	16	17	18	19	20
1	260.0	266.2	271.8	277.0	281.8	286.3	290.0	294.3	298.0
2	33.40	34.13	34.81	35.43	36.00	36.53	37.03	37.50	37.95
3	17.53	17.89	18.22	18.52	18.81	19.07	19.32	19.55	19.77
4	12.84	13.09	13.32	13.53	13.73	13.91	14.08	14.24	14.40
5	10.70	10.89	11.08	11.24	11.40	11.55	11.68	11.81	11.93
6	9.48	9.65	9.81	9.95	10.08	10.21	10.32	10.43	10.54
7	8.71	8.86	9.00	9.12	9.24	9.35	9.46	9.55	9.65
8	8.18	8.31	8.44	8.55	8.66	8.76	8.85	8.94	9.03
9	7.78	7.91	8.03	8.13	8.23	8.33	8.41	8.49	8.57
10	7.49	7.60	7.71	7.81	7.91	7.99	8.08	8.15	8.23
11	7.25	7.36	7.46	7.56	7.65	7.73	7.81	7.88	7.95
12	7.06	7.17	7.26	7.36	7.44	7.52	7.59	7.66	7.73
13	6.90	7.01	7.10	7.19	7.27	7.35	7.42	7.48	7.55
14	6.77	6.87	6.96	7.05	7.13	7.20	7.27	7.33	7.39
15	6.66	6.76	6.84	6.93	7.00	7.07	7.14	7.20	7.26
16	6.56	6.66	6.74	6.82	6.90	6.97	7.03	7.09	7.15
17	6.48	6.57	6.66	6.73	6.81	6.87	6.94	7.00	7.05
18	6.41	6.50	6.58	6.65	6.72	6.79	6.85	6.91	6.97
19	6.34	6.43	6.51	6.58	6.65	6.72	6.78	6.84	6.89
20	6.28	6.37	6.45	6.52	6.59	6.65	6.71	6.77	6.82
24	6.11	6.19	6.26	6.33	6.39	6.45	6.51	6.56	6.61
30	5.93	6.01	6.08	6.14	6.20	6.26	6.31	6.36	6.41
40	5.76	5.83	5.90	5.96	6.02	6.07	6.12	6.16	6.21
60	5.60	5.67	5.73	5.78	5.84	5.89	5.93	5.97	6.01
120	5.44	5.50	5.56	5.61	5.66	5.71	5.75	5.79	5.83
∞	5.29	5.35	5.40	5.45	5.49	5.54	5.57	5.61	5.65

TABLE 15   Critical Values of T_L and T_U for the Wilcoxon Rank Sum Test: Independent Samples

Test statistic is the rank sum associated with the smaller sample (if equal sample sizes, either rank sum can be used).

a. $\alpha = .025$ one-tailed; $\alpha = .05$ two-tailed

n_2 \ n_1	3		4		5		6		7		8		9		10	
	T_L	T_U	T_L	T_U	T_L	T_U	T_L	T_U	T_L	T_U	T_L	T_U	T_L	T_U	T_L	T_U
3	5	16	6	18	6	21	7	23	7	26	8	28	8	31	9	33
4	6	18	11	25	12	28	12	32	13	35	14	38	15	41	16	44
5	6	21	12	28	18	37	19	41	20	45	21	49	22	53	24	56
6	7	23	12	32	19	41	26	52	28	56	29	61	31	65	32	70
7	7	26	13	35	20	45	28	56	37	68	39	73	41	78	43	83
8	8	28	14	38	21	49	29	61	39	73	49	87	51	93	54	98
9	8	31	15	41	22	53	31	65	41	78	51	93	63	108	66	114
10	9	33	16	44	24	56	32	70	43	83	54	98	66	114	79	131

b. $\alpha = .05$ one-tailed; $\alpha = .10$ two-tailed

n_2 \ n_1	3		4		5		6		7		8		9		10	
	T_L	T_U	T_L	T_U	T_L	T_U	T_L	T_U	T_L	T_U	T_L	T_U	T_L	T_U	T_L	T_U
3	6	15	7	17	7	20	8	22	9	24	9	27	10	29	11	31
4	7	17	12	24	13	27	14	30	15	33	16	36	17	39	18	42
5	7	20	13	27	19	36	20	40	22	43	24	46	25	50	26	54
6	8	22	14	30	20	40	28	50	30	54	32	58	33	63	35	67
7	9	24	15	33	22	43	30	54	39	66	41	71	43	76	46	80
8	9	27	16	36	24	46	32	58	41	71	52	84	53	90	57	95
9	10	29	17	39	25	50	33	63	43	76	54	90	66	105	69	111
10	11	31	18	42	26	54	35	67	46	80	57	95	69	111	83	127

Source: From F. Wilcoxon and R. A. Wilcox, "Some Rapid Approximate Statistical Procedures," 1964, 20–23. Reproduced with the permission of American Cyanamid Company.

TABLE 16   Critical Values of T_0 in the Wilcoxon Matched-Pairs Signed Rank Test

One-Tailed	Two-Tailed	$n = 5$	$n = 6$	$n = 7$	$n = 8$	$n = 9$	$n = 10$
$\alpha = .05$	$\alpha = .10$	1	2	4	6	8	11
$\alpha = .025$	$\alpha = .05$		1	2	4	6	8
$\alpha = .01$	$\alpha = .02$			0	2	3	5
$\alpha = .005$	$\alpha = .01$				0	2	3
		$n = 11$	$n = 12$	$n = 13$	$n = 14$	$n = 15$	$n = 16$
$\alpha = .05$	$\alpha = .10$	14	17	21	26	30	36
$\alpha = .025$	$\alpha = .05$	11	14	17	21	25	30
$\alpha = .01$	$\alpha = .02$	7	10	13	16	20	24
$\alpha = .005$	$\alpha = .01$	5	7	10	13	16	19
		$n = 17$	$n = 18$	$n = 19$	$n = 20$	$n = 21$	$n = 22$
$\alpha = .05$	$\alpha = .10$	41	47	54	60	68	75
$\alpha = .025$	$\alpha = .05$	35	40	46	52	59	66
$\alpha = .01$	$\alpha = .02$	28	33	38	43	49	56
$\alpha = .005$	$\alpha = .01$	23	28	32	37	43	49
		$n = 23$	$n = 24$	$n = 25$	$n = 26$	$n = 27$	$n = 28$
$\alpha = .05$	$\alpha = .10$	83	92	101	110	120	130
$\alpha = .025$	$\alpha = .05$	73	81	90	98	107	117
$\alpha = .01$	$\alpha = .02$	62	69	77	85	93	102
$\alpha = .005$	$\alpha = .01$	55	61	68	76	84	92
		$n = 29$	$n = 30$	$n = 31$	$n = 32$	$n = 33$	$n = 34$
$\alpha = .05$	$\alpha = .10$	141	152	163	175	188	201
$\alpha = .025$	$\alpha = .05$	127	137	148	159	171	183
$\alpha = .01$	$\alpha = .02$	111	120	130	141	151	162
$\alpha = .005$	$\alpha = .01$	100	109	118	128	138	149
		$n = 35$	$n = 36$	$n = 37$	$n = 38$	$n = 39$	
$\alpha = .05$	$\alpha = .10$	214	228	242	256	271	
$\alpha = .025$	$\alpha = .05$	195	208	222	235	250	
$\alpha = .01$	$\alpha = .02$	174	186	198	211	224	
$\alpha = .005$	$\alpha = .01$	160	171	183	195	208	
		$n = 40$	$n = 41$	$n = 42$	$n = 43$	$n = 44$	$n = 45$
$\alpha = .05$	$\alpha = .10$	287	303	319	336	353	371
$\alpha = .025$	$\alpha = .05$	264	279	295	311	327	344
$\alpha = .01$	$\alpha = .02$	238	252	267	281	297	313
$\alpha = .005$	$\alpha = .01$	221	234	248	262	277	292
		$n = 46$	$n = 47$	$n = 48$	$n = 49$	$n = 50$	
$\alpha = .05$	$\alpha = .10$	389	408	427	446	466	
$\alpha = .025$	$\alpha = .05$	361	379	397	415	434	
$\alpha = .01$	$\alpha = .02$	329	345	362	380	398	
$\alpha = .005$	$\alpha = .01$	307	323	339	356	373	

Source: From F. Wilcoxon and R. A. Wilcox, "Some Rapid Approximate Statistical Procedures," 1964, p. 28. Reproduced with the permission of American Cyanamid Company.

TABLE 17   Critical Values of Spearman's Rank Correlation Coefficient

The α values correspond to a one-tailed test of H_0: $\rho_S = 0$. The value should be doubled for two-tailed tests.

n	$\alpha = .05$	$\alpha = .025$	$\alpha = .01$	$\alpha = .005$	n	$\alpha = .05$	$\alpha = .025$	$\alpha = .01$	$\alpha = .005$
5	.900	—	—	—	18	.399	.476	.564	.625
6	.829	.886	.943	—	19	.388	.462	.549	.608
7	.714	.786	.893	—	20	.377	.450	.534	.591
8	.643	.738	.833	.881	21	.368	.438	.521	.576
9	.600	.683	.783	.833	22	.359	.428	.508	.562
10	.564	.648	.745	.794	23	.351	.418	.496	.549
11	.523	.623	.736	.818	24	.343	.409	.485	.537
12	.497	.591	.703	.780	25	.336	.400	.475	.526
13	.475	.566	.673	.745	26	.329	.392	.465	.515
14	.457	.545	.646	.716	27	.323	.385	.456	.505
15	.441	.525	.623	.689	28	.317	.377	.448	.496
16	.425	.507	.601	.666	29	.311	.370	.440	.487
17	.412	.490	.582	.645	30	.305	.364	.432	.478

Source: From E. G. Olds, "Distribution of Sums of Squares of Rank Differences for Small Samples," *Annals of Mathematical Statistics*, 1938, 9. Reproduced with the permission of the Editor, *Annals of Mathematical Statistics*.

TABLE 18 Critical Values of C for the Theil Zero-Slope Test

x	4	5	8	9	12	13	16	17	20
0	.625	.592	.548	.540	.527	.524	.518	.516	.513
2	.375	.408	.452	.460	.473	.476	.482	.484	.487
4	.167	.242	.360	.381	.420	.429	.447	.452	.462
6	.042	.117	.274	.306	.369	.383	.412	.420	.436
8		.042	.199	.238	.319	.338	.378	.388	.411
10		.008	.138	.179	.273	.295	.345	.358	.387
12			.089	.130	.230	.255	.313	.328	.362
14			.054	.090	.190	.218	.282	.299	.339
16			.031	.060	.155	.184	.253	.271	.315
18			.016	.038	.125	.153	.225	.245	.293
20			.007	.022	.098	.126	.199	.220	.271
22			.002	.012	.076	.102	.175	.196	.250
24			.001	.006	.058	.082	.153	.174	.230
26			.000	.003	.043	.064	.133	.154	.211
28				.001	.031	.050	.114	.135	.193
30				.000	.022	.038	.097	.118	.176
32					.016	.029	.083	.102	.159
34					.010	.021	.070	.088	.144
36					.007	.015	.058	.076	.130
38					.004	.011	.048	.064	.117
40					.003	.007	.039	.054	.104
42					.002	.005	.032	.046	.093
44					.001	,003	.026	.038	.082
46					.000	.002	.021	.032	.073
48						.001	.016	.026	.064
50						.001	.013	.021	.056
52						.000	.010	.017	.049
54							.008	.014	.043
56							.006	.011	.037
58							.004	.009	.032
60							.003	.007	.027
62							.002	.005	.023
64							.002	.004	.020
66							.001	.003	.017
68							.001	.002	.014
70							.001	.002	.012
72							.000	.001	.010
74								.001	.008
76								.001	.007
78								.000	.006
80									.005
82									.004
84									.003
86									.002
88									.002
90									.002
92									.001
94									.001
96									.001
98									.001
100									.000

(continued)

TABLE 18 Continued

						n				
x	21	24	25	28	29	32	33	36	37	40
0	.512	.510	.509	.508	.507	.506	.506	.505	.505	.505
2	.488	.490	.491	.492	.493	.494	.494	.495	.495	.495
4	.464	.471	.472	.477	.478	.481	.482	.484	.484	.486
6	.441	.451	.454	.461	.463	.468	.469	.473	.474	.477
8	.417	.432	.436	.446	.448	.455	.457	.462	.464	.468
10	.394	.413	.418	.430	.434	.442	.445	.452	.453	.459
12	.371	.394	.400	.415	.419	.430	.433	.441	.443	.449
14	.349	.375	.382	.400	.405	.417	.421	.430	.433	.440
16	.327	.356	.364	.385	.390	.405	.409	.420	.423	.431
18	306	.338	.347	.370	.376	.392	.397	.409	.413	.422
20	.285	.320	.330	.355	.362	.380	.385	.399	.403	.413
22	.265	.303	.314	.341	.348	.368	.373	.388	.393	.404
24	.246	.286	.297	.326	.334	.356	.362	.378	.383	.395
26	.228	.270	.282	.312	.321	.344	.350	.368	.373	.386
28	.210	.254	.266	.298	.308	.332	.339	.358	.363	.377
30	.193	.238	.251	.285	.295	.320	.328	.347	.353	.369
32	.177	.223	.237	.272	.282	.309	.317	.338	.344	.360
34	.162	.209	.222	.259	.270	.298	.306	.328	.334	.351
36	.147	.195	.209	.246	.257	.287	.295	.318	.325	.343
38	.134	.181	.196	.234	.246	.276	.285	.308	.315	.334
40	.121	.169	.183	.222	.234	.265	.274	.299	.306	.326
42	.109	.156	.171	.211	.223	.255	.264	.290	.297	.318
44	.098	.145	.159	.200	.212	.244	.254	.280	.288	.309
46	.088	.134	.148	.189	.201	.234	.244	.271	.279	.301
48	.079	.123	.138	.178	.191	.224	.235	.262	.271	.293
50	.070	.113	.128	.168	.181	.215	.225	.254	.262	.285
52	.062	.104	.118	.158	.171	.206	.216	.245	.254	.277
54	.055	.095	.109	.149	.162	.197	.207	.237	.245	.270
56	.049	.087	.101	.140	.153	.188	.199	.228	.237	.262
58	.043	.079	.093	.131	.144	.179	.190	.220	.229	.255
60	.037	.072	.085	.123	.136	.171	.182	.212	.222	.247
62	.032	.066	.078	.115	.128	.163	.174	.204	.214	.240
64	.028	.059	.071	.108	.120	.155	.166	.197	.206	.233
66	.024	.054	.065	.101	.112	.147	.158	.189	.199	.226
68	.021	.048	.059	.094	.105	.140	.151	.182	.192	.219
70	.018	.044	.054	.087	.099	.133	.144	.175	.185	.212
72	.015	.039	.049	.081	.092	.126	.137	.168	.178	.205
74	.013	.035	.044	.075	.086	.119	.130	.161	.171	.199
76	.011	.031	.040	.070	.080	.113	.124	.155	.165	.192
78	.009	.028	.036	.065	.075	.107	.117	.148	.158	.186
80	.008	.025	.032	.060	.070	.101	.111	.142	.152	.180
82	.007	.022	.029	.055	.065	.095	.106	.136	.146	.174
84	.005	.019	.026	.051	.060	.090	.100	.130	.140	.168
86	.005	.017	.023	.047	.056	.085	.095	.124	.134	.162
88	.004	.015	.021	.043	.052	.080	.090	.119	.129	.156
90	.003	.013	.018	.039	.048	.075	.085	.114	.123	.151
92	.002	.011	.016	.036	.044	.070	.080	.108	.118	.146
94	.002	.010	.014	.033	.041	.066	.075	.103	.113	.140
96	.002	.009	.013	.030	.037	.062	.071	.099	.108	.135
98	.001	.007	.011	.027	.034	.058	.067	.094	.103	.130
100	.001	.006	.010	.025	.031	.054	.063	.089	.098	.125

TABLE 18   Continued

					n				
x	6	7	10	11	14	15	18	19	22
1	.500	.500	.500	.500	.500	.500	.500	.500	.500
3	.360	.386	.431	.440	.457	.461	.470	.473	.478
5	.235	.281	.364	.381	.415	.423	.441	.445	.456
7	.136	.191	.300	.324	.374	.385	.411	.418	.434
9	.068	.119	.242	.271	.334	.349	.383	.391	.412
11	.028	.068	.190	.223	.295	.313	.354	.365	.390
13	.008	.035	.146	.179	.259	.279	.327	.339	.369
15	.001	.015	.108	.141	.225	.248	.300	.314	.348
17		.005	.078	.109	.194	.218	.275	.290	.328
19		.001	.054	.082	.165	.190	.250	.267	.308
21		.000	.036	.060	.140	.164	.227	.245	.289
23			.023	.043	.117	.141	.205	.223	.270
25			.014	.030	.096	.120	.184	.203	.252
27			.008	.020	.079	.101	.165	.184	.234
29			.005	.013	.063	.084	.147	.166	.217
31			.002	.008	.050	.070	.130	.149	.201
33			.001	.005	.040	.057	.115	.133	.186
35			.000	.003	.031	.046	.100	.119	.171
37				.002	.024	.037	.088	.105	.157
39				.001	.018	.029	.076	.093	.144
41				.000	.013	.023	.066	.082	.131
43					.010	.018	.056	.072	.120
45					.007	.014	.048	.062	.109
47					.005	.010	.041	.054	.099
49					.003	.008	.034	.047	.089
51					.002	.006	.029	.040	.080
53					.002	.004	.024	.034	.072
55					.001	.003	.020	.029	.064
57					.001	.002	.016	.025	.058
59					.000	.001	.013	.021	.051
61						.001	.011	.017	.045
63						.001	.009	.014	.040
65						.000	.007	.012	.035
67							.005	.010	.031
69							.004	.008	.027
71							.003	.006	.024
73							.003	.005	.021
75							.002	.004	.018
77							.001	.003	.015
79							.001	.003	.013
81							.001	.002	.011
83							.001	.002	.010
85							.000	.001	.008
87								.001	.007
89								.001	.006
91								.001	.005
93								.000	.004
95									.003
97									.003
99									.002
101									.002

(continued)

TABLE 18   Continued

					n				
x	23	26	27	30	31	34	35	38	39
1	.500	.500	.500	.500	.500	.500	.500	.500	.500
3	.479	.483	.484	.486	.487	.488	.489	.490	.490
5	.458	.465	.467	.472	.473	.477	.478	.480	.481
7	.438	.448	.451	.458	.460	.465	.466	.470	.472
9	.417	.431	.434	.444	.446	.453	.455	.460	.462
11	.397	.414	.418	.430	.433	.442	.444	.450	.452
13	.377	.397	.402	.416	.420	.430	.433	.440	.443
15	.357	.380	.386	.402	.407	.418	.422	.431	.433
17	.338	.363	.371	.389	.394	.407	.411	.421	.424
19	.319	.347	.355	.375	.381	.396	.400	.411	.414
21	.301	.331	.340	.362	.368	.384	.389	.401	.405
23	.283	.316	.325	.349	.355	.373	.378	.392	.396
25	.265	.300	.310	.336	.343	.362	.368	.382	.387
27	.248	.285	.296	.323	.331	.351	.357	.373	.377
29	.232	.270	.281	.310	.318	.340	.347	.363	.368
31	.216	.256	.268	.298	.306	.329	.336	.354	.359
33	.201	.242	.254	.286	.295	.319	.326	.345	.350
35	.187	.229	.241	.274	.283	.308	.316	.336	.341
37	.173	.216	.228	.262	.272	.298	.306	.327	.333
39	.160	.203	.216	.251	.261	.288	.296	.318	.324
41	.147	.191	.204	.239	.250	.278	.286	.309	.315
43	.135	.179	.192	.228	.239	.268	.277	.300	.307
45	.124	.168	.181	.218	.229	.259	.267	.291	.298
47	.114	.157	.170	.208	.219	.249	.258	.283	.290
49	.104	.147	.160	.198	.209	.240	.249	.274	.282
51	.094	.137	.150	.188	.199	.231	.240	.266	.274
53	.086	.127	.141	.178	.190	.222	.232	.258	.266
55	.078	.118	.132	.169	.181	.213	.223	.250	.258
57	.070	.110	.123	.160	.172	.205	.215	.242	.250
59	.063	.102	.115	.152	.164	.196	.206	.234	.243
61	.057	.094	.107	.144	.155	.188	.198	.227	.235
63	.051	.087	.099	.136	.147	.180	.191	.219	.228
65	.046	.080	.092	.128	.140	.173	.183	.212	.221
67	.041	.073	.085	.121	.132	.165	.176	.205	.214
69	.036	.067	.079	.114	.125	.158	.168	.198	.207
71	.032	.062	.073	.107	.118	.151	.161	.191	.200
73	.028	.057	.067	.100	.112	.144	.154	.184	.193
75	.025	.052	.062	.094	.105	.137	.148	.177	.187
77	.022	.047	.057	.088	.099	.131	.141	.171	.180
79	.019	.043	.052	.083	.093	.125	.135	.165	.174
81	.017	.039	.048	.077	.088	.119	.129	.158	.168
83	.015	.035	.044	.072	.082	.113	.123	.152	.162
85	.013	.032	.040	.067	.077	.107	.117	.147	.156
87	.011	.029	.036	.063	.072	.102	.112	.141	.150
89	.009	.026	.033	.059	.068	.097	.107	.135	.145
91	.008	.023	.030	.054	.063	.092	.101	.130	.139
93	.007	.021	.027	.051	.059	.087	.096	.125	.134
95	.006	.019	.025	.047	.055	.082	.092	.120	.129
97	.005	.017	.022	.043	.052	.078	.087	.115	.124
99	.004	.015	.020	.040	.048	.074	.083	.110	.119
101	.004	.013	.018	.037	.045	.070	.078	.105	.114

TABLE 19   Factors Used When Constructing Control Charts

Number of Observations in Sample	Chart for Averages		Chart for Ranges		
n	A_2	d_2	d_3	D_3	D_4
2	1.880	1.128	.853	0	3.276
3	1.023	1.693	.888	0	2.575
4	.729	2.059	.880	0	2.282
5	.577	2.326	.864	0	2.115
6	.483	2.534	.848	0	2.004
7	.419	2.704	.833	.076	1.924
8	.373	2.847	.820	.136	1.864
9	.337	2.970	.808	.184	1.816
10	.308	3.078	.797	.223	1.777
11	.285	3.173	.787	.256	1.744
12	.266	3.258	.778	.284	1.719
13	.249	3.336	.770	.308	1.692
14	.235	3.407	.762	.329	1.671
15	.223	3.472	.755	.348	1.652
16	.212	3.532	.749	.364	1.636
17	.203	3.588	.743	.379	1.621
18	.194	3.640	.738	.392	1.608
19	.187	3.689	.733	.404	1.596
20	.180	3.735	.729	.414	1.586
21	.173	3.778	.724	.425	1.575
22	.167	3.819	.720	.434	1.566
23	.162	3.858	.716	.443	1.557
24	.157	3.895	.712	.452	1.548
25	.153	3.931	.709	.459	1.541

Source: ASTM *Manual on Quality Control of Materials*, American Society for Testing Materials, Philadelphia, PA, 1951. Copyright ASTM. Reprinted with permission.

TABLE 20 Values of *K* for Tolerance Limits for Normal Distributions

γ / n	$1 - \alpha = .95$			$1 - \alpha = .99$		
	.90	.95	.99	.90	.95	.99
2	32.019	37.674	48.430	160.193	188.491	242.300
3	8.380	9.916	12.861	18.930	22.401	29.055
4	5.369	6.370	8.299	9.398	11.150	14.527
5	4.275	5.079	6.634	6.612	7.855	10.260
6	3.712	4.414	5.775	5.337	6.345	8.301
7	3.369	4.007	5.248	4.613	5.488	7.187
8	3.136	3.732	4.891	4.147	4.936	6.468
9	2.967	3.532	4.631	3.822	4.550	5.966
10	2.839	3.379	4.433	3.582	4.265	5.594
11	2.737	3.259	4.277	3.397	4.045	5.308
12	2.655	3.162	4.150	3.250	3.870	5.079
13	2.587	3.081	4.044	3.130	3.727	4.893
14	2.529	3.012	3.955	3.029	3.608	4.737
15	2.480	2.954	3.878	2.945	3.507	4.605
16	2.437	2.903	3.812	2.872	3.421	4.492
17	2.400	2.858	3.754	2.808	3.345	4.393
18	2.366	2.819	3.702	2.753	3.279	4.307
19	2.337	2.784	3.656	2.703	3.221	4.230
20	2.310	2.752	3.615	2.659	3.168	4.161
25	2.208	2.631	3.457	2.494	2.972	3.904
30	2.140	2.549	3.350	2.385	2.841	3.733
35	2.090	2.490	3.272	2.306	2.748	3.611
40	2.052	2.445	3.213	2.247	2.677	3.518
45	2.021	2.408	3.165	2.200	2.621	3.444
50	1.996	2.379	3.126	2.162	2.576	3.385
55	1.976	2.354	3.094	2.130	2.538	3.335
60	1.958	2.333	3.066	2.103	2.506	3.293
65	1.943	2.315	3.042	2.080	2.478	3.257
70	1.929	2.299	3.021	2.060	2.454	3.225
75	1.917	2.285	3.002	2.042	2.433	3.197
80	1.907	2.272	2.986	2.026	2.414	3.173
85	1.897	2.261	2.971	2.012	2.397	3.150
90	1.889	2.251	2.958	1.999	2.382	3.130
95	1.881	2.241	2.945	1.987	2.368	3.112
100	1.874	2.233	2.934	1.977	2.355	3.096
150	1.825	2.175	2.859	1.905	2.270	2.983
200	1.798	2.143	2.816	1.865	2.222	2.921
250	1.780	2.121	2.788	1.839	2.191	2.880
300	1.767	2.106	2.767	1.820	2.169	2.850
400	1.749	2.084	2.739	1.794	2.138	2.809
500	1.737	2.070	2.721	1.777	2.117	2.783
600	1.729	2.060	2.707	1.764	2.102	2.763
700	1.722	2.052	2.697	1.755	2.091	2.748
800	1.717	2.046	2.688	1.747	2.082	2.736
900	1.712	2.040	2.682	1.741	2.075	2.726
1000	1.709	2.036	2.676	1.736	2.068	2.718
∞	1.645	1.960	2.576	1.645	1.960	2.576

Source: From *Techniques of Statistical Analysis* by C. Eisenhart, M. W. Hastay, and W. A. Wallis. Copyright 1947, McGraw-Hill Book Company, Inc. Reproduced with permission of McGraw-Hill.

TABLE 21 Sample Size *n* for Nonparametric Tolerance Limits

γ	$1 - \alpha$					
	.50	.70	.90	.95	.99	.995
.995	336	488	777	947	1,325	1,483
.99	168	244	388	473	662	740
.95	34	49	77	93	130	146
.90	17	24	38	46	64	72
.85	11	16	25	30	42	47
.80	9	12	18	22	31	34
.75	7	10	15	18	24	27
.70	6	8	12	14	20	22
.60	4	6	9	10	14	16
.50	3	5	7	8	11	12

Source: Tables A-25d of Wilfrid J. Dixon and Frank J. Massey, Jr., *Introduction to Statistical Analysis*, 3rd ed., McGraw-Hill Book Company, New York, 1969. Used with permission of McGraw-Hill Book Company.

TABLE 22 Sample Size Code Letters: MIL-STD-105D

Lot or Batch Size	Special Inspection Levels				General Inspection Levels		
	S-1	S-2	S-3	S-4	I	II	III
2–8	A	A	A	A	A	A	B
9–15	A	A	A	A	A	B	C
16–25	A	A	B	B	B	C	D
26–50	A	B	B	C	C	D	E
51–90	B	B	C	C	C	E	F
91–150	B	B	C	D	D	F	G
151–280	B	C	D	E	E	G	H
281–500	B	C	D	E	F	H	J
501–1,200	C	C	E	F	G	J	K
1,201–3,200	C	D	E	G	H	K	L
3,201–10,000	C	D	F	G	J	L	M
10,001–35,000	C	D	F	H	K	M	N
35,001–150,000	D	E	G	J	L	N	P
150,001–500,000	D	E	G	J	M	P	Q
500,001 and over	D	E	H	K	N	Q	R

TABLE 23 A Portion of the Master Table for Normal Inspection (Single Sampling): MIL-STD-105D

Values shown for each Acceptable Quality Level are **Ac Re** (Acceptance number, Rejection number). ↓ = use first sampling plan below arrow; ↑ = use first sampling plan above arrow.

Acceptable Quality Levels (Normal Inspection)

Sample Size Code Letter	Sample Size	.010	.015	.025	.040	.065	.10	.15	.25	.40	.65	1.0	1.5	2.5	4.0	6.5	10	15	25	40	65
A	2	↓	↓	↓	↓	↓	↓	↓	↓	↓	↓	↓	↓	↓	↓	0 1	↓	↓	1 2	2 3	3 4
B	3	↓	↓	↓	↓	↓	↓	↓	↓	↓	↓	↓	↓	↓	0 1	↑	↓	1 2	2 3	3 4	5 6
C	5	↓	↓	↓	↓	↓	↓	↓	↓	↓	↓	↓	↓	0 1	↑	↓	1 2	2 3	3 4	5 6	7 8
D	8	↓	↓	↓	↓	↓	↓	↓	↓	↓	↓	↓	0 1	↑	↓	1 2	2 3	3 4	5 6	7 8	10 11
E	13	↓	↓	↓	↓	↓	↓	↓	↓	↓	↓	0 1	↑	↓	1 2	2 3	3 4	5 6	7 8	10 11	14 15
F	20	↓	↓	↓	↓	↓	↓	↓	↓	↓	0 1	↑	↓	1 2	2 3	3 4	5 6	7 8	10 11	14 15	21 22
G	32	↓	↓	↓	↓	↓	↓	↓	↓	0 1	↑	↓	1 2	2 3	3 4	5 6	7 8	10 11	14 15	21 22	↑
H	50	↓	↓	↓	↓	↓	↓	↓	0 1	↑	↓	1 2	2 3	3 4	5 6	7 8	10 11	14 15	21 22	↑	↑
J	80	↓	↓	↓	↓	↓	↓	0 1	↑	↓	1 2	2 3	3 4	5 6	7 8	10 11	14 15	21 22	↑	↑	↑
K	125	↓	↓	↓	↓	↓	0 1	↑	↓	1 2	2 3	3 4	5 6	7 8	10 11	14 15	21 22	↑	↑	↑	↑
L	200	↓	↓	↓	↓	0 1	↑	↓	1 2	2 3	3 4	5 6	7 8	10 11	14 15	21 22	↑	↑	↑	↑	↑
M	315	↓	↓	↓	0 1	↑	↓	1 2	2 3	3 4	5 6	7 8	10 11	14 15	21 22	↑	↑	↑	↑	↑	↑
N	500	↓	↓	0 1	↑	↓	1 2	2 3	3 4	5 6	7 8	10 11	14 15	21 22	↑	↑	↑	↑	↑	↑	↑
P	800	↓	0 1	↑	↓	1 2	2 3	3 4	5 6	7 8	10 11	14 15	21 22	↑	↑	↑	↑	↑	↑	↑	↑
Q	1,250	0 1	↑	↓	1 2	2 3	3 4	5 6	7 8	10 11	14 15	21 22	↑	↑	↑	↑	↑	↑	↑	↑	↑
R	2,000	↑	↓	1 2	2 3	3 4	5 6	7 8	10 11	14 15	21 22	↑	↑	↑	↑	↑	↑	↑	↑	↑	↑

↓ = Use first sampling plan below arrow. If sample size equals or exceeds lot or batch size, do 100% inspection.
↑ = Use first sampling plan above arrow.
Ac = Acceptance number.
Re = Rejection number.

APPENDIX III

DDT Analyses on Fish Samples,
Tennessee River, Alabama

OBS	LOCATION	SPECIES	LENGTH	WEIGHT	DDT
1	FCM5	CATFISH	42.5	732	10.00
2	FCM5	CATFISH	44.0	795	16.00
3	FCM5	CATFISH	41.5	547	23.00
4	FCM5	CATFISH	39.0	465	21.00
5	FCM5	CATFISH	50.5	1252	50.00
6	FCM5	CATFISH	52.0	1255	150.00
7	LCM3	CATFISH	40.5	741	28.00
8	LCM3	CATFISH	48.0	1151	7.70
9	LCM3	CATFISH	48.0	1186	2.00
10	LCM3	CATFISH	43.5	754	19.00
11	LCM3	CATFISH	40.5	679	16.00
12	LCM3	CATFISH	47.5	985	5.40
13	SCM1	CATFISH	44.5	1133	2.60
14	SCM1	CATFISH	46.0	1139	3.10
15	SCM1	CATFISH	48.0	1186	3.50
16	SCM1	CATFISH	45.0	984	9.10
17	SCM1	CATFISH	43.0	965	7.80
18	SCM1	CATFISH	45.0	1084	4.10
19	TRM275	CATFISH	48.0	986	8.40
20	TRM275	CATFISH	45.0	1023	15.00
21	TRM275	CATFISH	49.0	1266	25.00
22	TRM275	CATFISH	50.0	1086	5.60
23	TRM275	CATFISH	46.0	1044	4.60
24	TRM275	CATFISH	52.0	1770	8.20
25	TRM280	CATFISH	48.0	1048	6.10
26	TRM280	CATFISH	51.0	1641	13.00
27	TRM280	CATFISH	48.5	1331	6.00
28	TRM280	CATFISH	51.0	1728	6.60
29	TRM280	CATFISH	44.0	917	5.50
30	TRM280	CATFISH	51.0	1398	11.00
31	TRM280	BUFFALO	49.0	1763	4.50
32	TRM280	BUFFALO	46.0	1459	4.20
33	TRM280	BUFFALO	52.0	2302	3.00
34	TRM280	BUFFALO	46.0	1614	2.30
35	TRM280	BUFFALO	46.0	1444	2.50
36	TRM280	BUFFALO	48.0	2006	6.80
37	TRM285	CATFISH	44.0	936	19.00
38	TRM285	CATFISH	42.0	1058	7.20
39	TRM285	CATFISH	42.5	800	6.00
40	TRM285	CATFISH	45.5	1087	10.00
41	TRM285	CATFISH	48.0	1329	12.00
42	TRM285	CATFISH	44.0	897	2.80
43	TRM285	BASS	28.5	778	0.48
44	TRM285	BASS	26.0	532	0.18
45	TRM285	BASS	25.5	441	0.34
46	TRM285	BASS	25.0	544	0.11
47	TRM285	BASS	23.0	393	0.22
48	TRM285	BASS	28.0	733	0.80
49	TRM290	CATFISH	41.0	961	8.70
50	TRM290	CATFISH	44.0	886	22.00

OBS	LOCATION	SPECIES	LENGTH	WEIGHT	DDT
51	TRM290	CATFISH	41.0	678	13.00
52	TRM290	CATFISH	42.0	1011	3.50
53	TRM290	CATFISH	42.5	947	9.30
54	TRM290	CATFISH	44.0	989	21.00
55	TRM290	BUFFALO	43.5	1291	3.40
56	TRM290	BUFFALO	46.5	1186	13.00
57	TRM290	BUFFALO	43.0	1293	5.60
58	TRM290	BUFFALO	47.0	1709	12.00
59	TRM290	BUFFALO	46.0	1425	21.00
60	TRM290	BUFFALO	41.0	1176	8.00
61	TRM295	CATFISH	36.0	980	12.00
62	TRM295	CATFISH	47.5	1176	6.00
63	TRM295	CATFISH	41.5	989	4.70
64	TRM295	CATFISH	49.5	1084	31.00
65	TRM295	CATFISH	46.0	1115	5.20
66	TRM295	CATFISH	46.5	724	27.00
67	TRM300	CATFISH	36.0	847	18.00
68	TRM300	CATFISH	37.0	876	7.50
69	TRM300	CATFISH	35.0	844	3.00
70	TRM300	CATFISH	36.0	908	13.00
71	TRM300	CATFISH	48.0	1358	7.30
72	TRM300	CATFISH	49.0	1019	15.00
73	TRM300	BUFFALO	35.5	1300	1.30
74	TRM300	BUFFALO	46.0	1365	4.80
75	TRM300	BUFFALO	45.0	1437	5.10
76	TRM300	BUFFALO	44.5	1460	5.10
77	TRM300	BUFFALO	49.0	1671	4.00
78	TRM300	BUFFALO	47.5	1717	10.00
79	TRM305	CATFISH	35.0	613	12.00
80	TRM305	CATFISH	51.0	353	22.00
81	TRM305	CATFISH	42.5	909	10.00
82	TRM305	CATFISH	38.0	886	11.00
83	TRM305	CATFISH	41.0	890	17.00
84	TRM305	CATFISH	47.0	1031	9.70
85	TRM310	CATFISH	45.0	1083	12.00
86	TRM310	CATFISH	45.5	864	4.70
87	TRM310	CATFISH	45.0	886	6.00
88	TRM310	CATFISH	45.0	965	3.80
89	TRM310	CATFISH	39.0	537	17.00
90	TRM310	CATFISH	40.5	630	12.00
91	TRM310	BUFFALO	46.0	1486	1.40
92	TRM310	BUFFALO	47.0	1743	6.10
93	TRM310	BUFFALO	48.5	2061	2.80
94	TRM310	BUFFALO	48.0	1707	4.80
95	TRM310	BUFFALO	38.0	862	5.70
96	TRM310	BUFFALO	38.5	911	3.30
97	TRM315	CATFISH	29.5	476	3.30
98	TRM315	CATFISH	42.0	743	3.70
99	TRM315	CATFISH	47.5	1128	9.90
100	TRM315	CATFISH	43.5	848	6.80

(continued)

OBS	LOCATION	SPECIES	LENGTH	WEIGHT	DDT
101	TRM315	CATFISH	47.5	1091	13.00
102	TRM315	CATFISH	43.5	715	8.80
103	TRM320	CATFISH	47.5	983	57.00
104	TRM320	CATFISH	51.5	1251	96.00
105	TRM320	CATFISH	49.5	1255	360.00
106	TRM320	CATFISH	47.0	1152	130.00
107	TRM320	CATFISH	47.5	1085	13.00
108	TRM320	CATFISH	47.0	1118	61.00
109	TRM320	BUFFALO	36.0	1285	12.00
110	TRM320	BUFFALO	34.5	1178	33.00
111	TRM320	BUFFALO	44.5	1492	48.00
112	TRM320	BUFFALO	46.0	1524	10.00
113	TRM320	BUFFALO	46.0	1473	44.00
114	TRM320	BUFFALO	32.5	520	0.43
115	TRM325	CATFISH	46.0	863	1100.00
116	TRM325	CATFISH	40.0	549	9.40
117	TRM325	CATFISH	43.5	810	4.10
118	TRM325	CATFISH	46.5	908	2.80
119	TRM325	CATFISH	43.0	804	0.74
120	TRM325	CATFISH	47.5	1179	14.00
121	TRM330	CATFISH	32.0	556	22.00
122	TRM330	CATFISH	40.5	659	9.10
123	TRM330	CATFISH	51.5	1229	140.00
124	TRM330	CATFISH	48.0	1050	4.20
125	TRM330	CATFISH	47.0	952	12.00
126	TRM330	CATFISH	41.0	826	2.00
127	TRM330	BUFFALO	33.5	599	0.30
128	TRM330	BUFFALO	47.0	1704	1.20
129	TRM340	CATFISH	50.0	1207	7.10
130	TRM340	CATFISH	45.0	911	180.00
131	TRM340	CATFISH	49.0	1498	1.50
132	TRM340	CATFISH	49.5	1496	2.40
133	TRM340	CATFISH	50.0	1142	4.30
134	TRM340	CATFISH	45.0	879	3.90
135	TRM340	BUFFALO	32.5	525	0.99
136	TRM340	BUFFALO	38.0	806	0.45
137	TRM340	BUFFALO	38.5	694	2.50
138	TRM340	BUFFALO	36.0	643	0.25
139	TRM345	BASS	26.5	514	0.58
140	TRM345	BASS	23.5	358	2.00
141	TRM345	BASS	30.0	856	2.20
142	TRM345	BASS	29.0	793	7.40
143	TRM345	BASS	17.5	173	0.35
144	TRM345	BASS	36.0	1433	1.90

APPENDIX IV

Central Processing Unit (CPU)
Times of 1,000 Computer Jobs

OBS	CPUTIME	OBS	CPUTIME	OBS	CPUTIME	OBS	CPUTIME	OBS	CPUTIME	OBS	CPUTIME	OBS	CPUTIME	OBS	CPUTIME	OBS	CPUTIME	OBS	CPUTIME
1	1.86	2	3.49	3	2.63	4	3.49	5	1.69	6	1.83	7	0.81	8	4.70	9	0.85	10	4.24
11	3.49	12	2.75	13	1.65	14	0.92	15	0.62	16	0.41	17	3.23	18	4.13	19	3.23	20	1.89
21	2.66	22	3.52	23	2.39	24	1.60	25	1.88	26	0.36	27	11.85	28	0.87	29	3.10	30	0.70
31	3.23	32	2.64	33	1.69	34	0.41	35	3.29	36	1.81	37	1.45	38	0.79	39	0.38	40	0.45
41	3.49	42	2.59	43	1.78	44	4.92	45	0.48	46	1.66	47	1.86	48	3.23	49	0.43	50	1.27
51	1.29	52	1.29	53	3.20	54	4.92	55	3.01	56	2.40	57	4.85	58	11.72	59	1.71	60	15.99
61	16.46	62	16.90	63	16.87	64	17.28	65	16.87	66	17.65	67	17.38	68	17.55	69	16.25	70	3.30
71	15.47	72	3.55	73	2.79	74	4.12	75	4.50	76	2.56	77	4.31	78	4.14	79	1.17	80	3.75
81	3.80	82	3.18	83	1.59	84	5.05	85	5.19	86	5.02	87	5.02	88	5.02	89	4.99	90	3.11
91	3.31	92	3.30	93	4.91	94	1.46	95	2.53	96	2.08	97	4.38	98	2.30	99	3.34	100	4.09
101	3.00	102	2.63	103	5.10	104	5.07	105	3.20	106	3.32	107	5.02	108	3.21	109	3.36	110	3.40
111	2.61	112	3.73	113	4.50	114	1.35	115	4.47	116	2.78	117	2.85	118	6.64	119	2.69	120	3.02
121	5.10	122	5.53	123	8.13	124	7.51	125	7.43	126	8.89	127	6.34	128	8.84	129	0.40	130	0.66
131	4.98	132	13.19	133	2.41	134	1.66	135	1.68	136	5.01	137	3.55	138	14.00	139	18.90	140	5.02
141	6.67	142	2.54	143	3.24	144	5.83	145	9.23	146	6.57	147	1.23	148	8.43	149	2.82	150	3.91
151	3.19	152	4.42	153	15.11	154	3.63	155	2.86	156	7.52	157	2.03	158	1.95	159	6.87	160	2.83
161	6.34	162	6.98	163	2.97	164	6.47	165	7.64	166	8.94	167	4.49	168	4.55	169	0.75	170	4.22
171	1.79	172	13.27	173	16.02	174	1.96	175	0.75	176	4.22	177	0.80	178	0.82	179	19.51	180	5.24
181	10.07	182	6.02	183	3.64	184	17.56	185	9.57	186	3.19	187	6.33	188	10.88	189	3.94	190	11.60
191	18.39	192	18.17	193	11.59	194	10.21	195	10.55	196	11.56	197	4.23	198	11.52	199	2.96	200	7.52
201	11.34	202	2.04	203	6.51	204	11.34	205	3.70	206	2.24	207	5.94	208	5.66	209	5.65	210	6.27
211	5.71	212	6.09	213	7.86	214	3.59	215	5.27	216	3.72	217	10.24	218	11.09	219	13.23	220	16.64
221	6.19	222	4.01	223	4.00	224	10.57	225	13.35	226	19.96	227	1.58	228	16.83	229	6.24	230	8.13
231	3.49	232	1.57	233	5.86	234	3.17	235	9.02	236	7.06	237	2.49	238	6.32	239	2.59	240	19.25
241	3.81	242	10.46	243	1.00	244	1.77	245	10.56	246	7.16	247	2.18	248	1.10	249	1.87	250	7.90
251	11.51	252	1.78	253	1.78	254	2.59	255	3.04	256	2.53	257	3.28	258	4.25	259	4.24	260	4.16
261	3.93	262	12.64	263	20.78	264	20.79	265	5.10	266	5.24	267	5.25	268	8.66	269	11.00	270	8.48
271	8.02	272	16.94	273	15.97	274	3.19	275	3.24	276	1.81	277	0.64	278	4.67	279	1.02	280	7.73
281	3.34	282	11.77	283	15.97	284	3.76	285	2.41	286	1.61	287	1.82	288	4.25	289	3.17	290	2.23
291	12.19	292	3.19	293	0.62	294	2.16	295	1.94	296	1.71	297	0.47	298	1.65	299	6.54	300	4.20
301	0.84	302	2.59	303	3.13	304	0.48	305	2.63	306	2.96	307	0.99	308	0.85	309	5.33	310	1.83
311	2.02	312	1.01	313	3.68	314	1.88	315	0.97	316	3.28	317	0.52	318	0.68	319	2.15	320	3.17
321	3.43	322	9.45	323	3.19	324	17.44	325	4.23	326	0.55	327	3.12	328	0.51	329	0.60	330	1.92
331	1.97	332	2.67	333	3.16	334	0.45	335	1.59	336	1.74	337	1.22	338	0.61	339	0.59	340	1.53
341	0.96	342	0.97	343	3.21	344	0.23	345	5.27	346	3.14	347	0.75	348	0.68	349	2.07	350	13.38
351	0.18	352	3.23	353	2.20	354	1.70	355	6.23	356	0.68	357	10.67	358	3.15	359	2.11	360	2.22
361	0.24	362	3.21	363	3.15	364	11.39	365	0.48	366	3.00	367	17.30	368	3.45	369	7.51	370	8.95
371	7.82	372	8.74	373	11.35	374	12.18	375	13.10	376	3.17	377	14.19	378	10.55	379	14.43	380	14.35
381	11.81	382	3.27	383	15.51	384	14.66	385	16.33	386	16.75	387	15.55	388	3.16	389	2.17	390	
391	15.57	392	14.85	393	15.88	394	1.86	395	3.17	396	15.76	397	0.33	398	20.09	399	9.25	400	0.55
401	2.79	402	2.26	403	4.41	404	3.16	405	2.14	406	0.51	407	0.53	408	5.31	409	0.10	410	3.41
411	3.45	412	7.22	413	2.77	414	2.00	415	0.89	416	1.69	417	2.73	418	4.08	419	6.29	420	12.87
421	3.12	422	0.64	423	2.01	424	2.69	425	2.70	426	3.15	427	1.57	428	1.54	429	0.46	430	1.55
431	2.45	432	0.46	433	0.47	434	4.17	435	4.09	436	0.56	437	0.15	438	0.81	439	2.72	440	4.08
441	6.45	442	11.60	443	12.96	444	2.78	445	2.74	446	4.06	447	6.30	448	12.86	449	12.86	450	3.26
451	2.98	452	0.11	453	1.10	454	1.42	455	1.74	456	2.93	457	0.84	458	2.41	459	2.51	460	2.16
461	1.67	462	3.29	463	1.14	464	1.15	465	1.22	466	1.54	467	0.54	468	1.49	469	2.67	470	2.46
471	1.46	472	2.61	473	2.63	474	2.63	475	3.53	476	5.04	477	3.50	478	4.98	479	3.65	480	3.54
481	1.17	482	3.49	483	3.50	484	3.54	485	3.52	486	3.55	487	3.12	488	3.09	489	4.61	490	2.70
491	3.80	492	7.10	493	3.35	494	3.01	495	3.07	496	3.19	497	4.75	498	2.62	499	4.17	500	4.98

OBS	CPUTIME	OBS	CPUTIME	OBS	CPUTIME	OBS	CPUTIME	OBS	CPUTIME	OBS	CPUTIME	OBS	CPUTIME	OBS	CPUTIME	OBS	CPUTIME	OBS	CPUTIME
501	5.11	502	4.05	503	3.92	504	1.52	505	4.53	506	3.28	507	3.63	508	1.63	509	1.59	510	1.56
511	3.61	512	3.53	513	4.31	514	4.83	515	1.97	516	5.09	517	5.48	518	5.39	519	5.43	520	5.27
521	5.35	522	2.01	523	2.00	524	2.02	525	5.09	526	5.08	527	5.08	528	7.28	529	1.16	530	3.08
531	2.22	532	5.38	533	19.61	534	0.63	535	3.01	536	9.98	537	15.92	538	17.45	539	7.64	540	17.22
541	5.00	542	18.97	543	6.51	544	1.82	545	0.54	546	2.68	547	9.79	548	10.68	549	10.41	550	20.47
551	10.86	552	9.89	553	10.43	554	9.39	555	3.63	556	3.61	557	10.59	558	9.15	559	9.48	560	1.12
561	2.19	562	3.13	563	2.15	564	1.55	565	1.81	566	1.77	567	1.79	568	1.74	569	2.59	570	2.61
571	3.93	572	3.89	573	4.26	574	6.94	575	2.11	576	1.43	577	2.63	578	2.85	579	1.52	580	1.40
581	2.85	582	2.08	583	3.22	584	2.65	585	4.08	586	5.52	587	5.04	588	6.73	589	3.47	590	1.90
591	4.70	592	5.57	593	7.19	594	7.26	595	12.04	596	5.77	597	2.84	598	2.78	599	1.05	600	0.88
601	3.15	602	1.78	603	1.93	604	1.83	605	3.11	606	3.75	607	11.93	608	0.43	609	2.33	610	3.28
611	3.86	612	2.52	613	8.12	614	17.61	615	4.29	616	2.20	617	4.43	618	5.44	619	4.64	620	6.30
621	7.55	622	11.75	623	0.34	624	7.87	625	2.05	626	5.28	627	0.28	628	8.09	629	1.79	630	1.08
631	2.70	632	0.33	633	1.86	634	6.88	635	5.90	636	2.67	637	1.48	638	8.70	639	3.78	640	2.73
641	3.44	642	7.69	643	8.61	644	0.68	645	8.53	646	8.60	647	3.69	648	3.46	649	3.38	650	8.73
651	0.18	652	9.16	653	9.39	654	10.88	655	11.03	656	11.16	657	11.18	658	5.50	659	12.22	660	0.25
661	3.11	662	10.82	663	11.62	664	3.43	665	11.68	666	16.39	667	0.29	668	3.94	669	2.00	670	0.28
671	4.08	672	3.26	673	3.15	674	0.26	675	2.28	676	2.49	677	2.00	678	2.26	679	0.30	680	0.28
681	2.35	682	3.73	683	2.02	684	1.28	685	3.83	686	0.29	687	2.64	688	0.29	689	0.27	690	2.74
691	0.10	692	0.19	693	1.05	694	5.54	695	2.00	696	3.88	697	3.14	698	0.38	699	0.96	700	9.95
701	0.39	702	1.78	703	0.61	704	6.66	705	0.85	706	1.67	707	2.03	708	3.89	709	4.34	710	4.88
711	4.09	712	11.05	713	5.11	714	1.75	715	0.06	716	3.12	717	1.57	718	0.12	719	2.72	720	1.76
721	1.32	722	0.62	723	1.60	724	6.79	725	2.28	726	1.67	727	1.38	728	1.08	729	10.09	730	3.31
731	3.36	732	3.36	733	3.36	734	7.28	735	2.38	736	2.40	737	4.88	738	0.28	739	3.49	740	0.27
741	1.99	742	0.27	743	12.38	744	1.06	745	2.28	746	1.75	747	2.01	748	4.88	749	0.53	750	0.28
751	0.27	752	1.99	753	0.36	754	6.54	755	2.39	756	2.07	757	18.60	758	0.67	759	8.90	760	4.07
761	0.65	762	2.87	763	7.71	764	7.62	765	2.45	766	14.23	767	10.12	768	5.24	769	8.72	770	13.75
771	6.32	772	16.15	773	6.57	774	16.26	775	8.89	776	16.27	777	10.71	778	5.14	779	4.51	780	6.03
781	2.74	782	3.16	783	3.25	784	8.17	785	15.82	786	18.98	787	5.06	788	12.97	789	19.55	790	5.77
791	16.97	792	0.34	793	4.88	794	7.03	795	15.30	796	19.53	797	7.45	798	12.26	799	19.37	800	7.18
801	5.28	802	2.24	803	17.70	804	8.39	805	8.96	806	3.76	807	1.40	808	3.04	809	3.35	810	2.67
811	3.16	812	4.67	813	6.69	814	4.89	815	10.56	816	6.90	817	6.23	818	1.81	819	1.85	820	2.22
821	2.23	822	4.21	823	4.68	824	2.73	825	2.12	826	1.10	827	1.09	828	1.11	829	1.33	830	1.29
831	4.93	832	2.76	833	2.85	834	2.75	835	0.77	836	5.55	837	0.54	838	3.55	839	2.01	840	1.58
841	0.55	842	10.54	843	0.54	844	1.57	845	1.00	846	1.81	847	2.05	848	4.83	849	1.41	850	0.64
851	0.61	852	2.37	853	1.46	854	0.60	855	4.07	856	0.61	857	3.05	858	3.96	859	0.99	860	0.81
861	1.49	862	1.53	863	0.65	864	2.05	865	0.46	866	1.79	867	1.55	868	0.82	869	0.10	870	0.34
871	0.97	872	0.41	873	0.86	874	13.85	875	0.93	876	1.65	877	1.88	878	1.63	879	0.67	880	1.14
881	2.77	882	0.76	883	1.96	884	1.96	885	7.57	886	1.52	887	3.44	888	0.81	889	1.80	890	4.80
891	2.45	892	1.89	893	7.64	894	2.92	895	4.76	896	5.72	897	3.89	898	4.16	899	3.97	900	4.59
901	7.41	902	7.52	903	7.59	904	8.72	905	4.52	906	0.50	907	2.08	908	0.52	909	2.04	910	0.47
911	9.35	912	7.52	913	7.58	914	3.21	915	1.15	916	1.65	917	1.52	918	3.48	919	6.41	920	0.84
921	1.41	922	2.65	923	4.54	924	7.11	925	1.69	926	2.40	927	2.19	928	0.18	929	0.14	930	2.20
931	5.21	932	2.25	933	0.18	934	0.22	935	14.23	936	18.20	937	0.20	938	2.06	939	9.17	940	9.91
941	0.16	942	0.18	943	2.19	944	0.40	945	3.19	946	0.47	947	9.17	948	0.26	949	9.95	950	0.23
951	2.34	952	0.21	953	0.24	954	2.75	955	0.21	956	0.44	957	2.19	958	3.15	959	3.18	960	0.47
961	3.20	962	11.43	963	0.20	964	0.20	965	0.45	966	2.14	967	2.49	968	0.24	969	3.14	970	0.19
971	0.45	972	5.03	973	2.06	974	0.36	975	6.19	976	0.45	977	2.17	978	3.18	979	0.20	980	0.19
981	0.22	982	11.90	983	8.44	984	2.24	985	2.47	986	12.33	987	3.84	988	8.52	989	6.27	990	2.19
991	2.02	992	2.82	993	2.19	994	5.13	995	2.43	996	0.23	997	0.43	998	6.22	999	3.98	1000	2.05

APPENDIX V

Percentage Iron Content for
390 Iron-Ore Specimens

Number	% Iron	Number	% Iron	Number	% Iron	Number	% Iron	Number	% Iron
1	66.08	43	66.18	85	64.41	127	66.75	169	65.62
2	65.92	44	66.11	86	64.01	128	66.56	170	65.96
3	65.83	45	66.03	87	64.39	129	66.83	171	66.46
4	65.81	46	66.11	88	64.89	130	66.34	172	66.34
5	65.77	47	66.28	89	64.89	131	66.78	173	65.98
6	65.83	48	66.09	90	65.09	132	66.67	174	65.69
7	65.82	49	66.08	91	64.02	133	66.86	175	65.83
8	66.06	50	66.24	92	64.82	134	66.82	176	66.28
9	65.85	51	66.01	93	64.35	135	66.82	177	66.05
10	65.75	52	66.33	94	64.86	136	66.86	178	66.18
11	66.02	53	66.59	95	64.51	137	66.68	179	65.83
12	65.81	54	65.82	96	64.95	138	66.80	180	66.09
13	65.85	55	66.21	97	65.48	139	66.86	181	66.29
14	65.66	56	66.32	98	65.24	140	66.81	182	66.04
15	65.97	57	66.10	99	64.93	141	66.69	183	66.36
16	65.80	58	65.77	100	65.19	142	66.68	184	66.16
17	65.97	59	65.86	101	65.30	143	66.71	185	66.37
18	66.08	60	65.80	102	64.95	144	66.34	186	66.25
19	65.79	61	66.07	103	64.96	145	66.18	187	66.86
20	66.13	62	65.94	104	64.98	146	65.78	188	66.16
21	66.23	63	66.16	105	65.04	147	65.63	189	66.09
22	65.81	64	65.86	106	65.73	148	66.81	190	66.36
23	65.99	65	65.79	107	66.18	149	65.80	191	66.29
24	66.18	66	65.77	108	65.61	150	65.80	192	66.57
25	65.97	67	65.69	109	66.53	151	66.54	193	66.50
26	66.30	68	65.87	110	65.48	152	66.51	194	66.31
27	66.23	69	65.88	111	65.75	153	63.95	195	65.81
28	65.99	70	65.31	112	65.95	154	65.86	196	65.98
29	65.99	71	65.30	113	65.98	155	65.95	197	65.97
30	65.78	72	65.61	114	65.96	156	65.56	198	66.16
31	65.97	73	65.00	115	65.86	157	65.81	199	66.23
32	66.32	74	64.76	116	66.25	158	66.30	200	66.18
33	65.73	75	64.45	117	65.80	159	65.68	201	65.88
34	66.06	76	65.02	118	65.77	160	65.40	202	66.07
35	65.67	77	65.25	119	65.75	161	65.83	203	65.93
36	65.98	78	64.75	120	65.98	162	65.57	204	65.50
37	66.32	79	64.66	121	66.49	163	65.39	205	66.35
38	65.56	80	65.21	122	66.41	164	65.57	206	66.24
39	65.85	81	64.50	123	66.38	165	65.57	207	66.33
40	66.11	82	64.18	124	66.11	166	65.89	208	66.27
41	66.02	83	64.25	125	65.88	167	65.79	209	66.41
42	65.88	84	64.24	126	66.39	168	65.60	210	66.67

Number	% Iron	Number	% Iron	Number	% Iron	Number	% Iron	Number	% Iron
211	66.62	247	65.69	283	65.26	319	65.55	355	66.28
212	65.99	248	65.30	284	65.65	320	65.91	356	65.92
213	66.23	249	65.78	285	65.47	321	65.50	357	64.44
214	66.77	250	65.81	286	65.24	322	65.72	358	66.28
215	66.29	251	65.42	287	66.23	323	65.76	359	65.34
216	66.20	252	65.13	288	65.74	324	65.50	360	66.55
217	66.54	253	65.50	289	65.66	325	65.38	361	66.72
218	66.45	254	65.98	290	65.73	326	65.95	362	66.50
219	66.57	255	65.38	291	65.41	327	65.48	363	66.62
220	66.69	256	65.83	292	65.20	328	65.40	364	66.02
221	66.19	257	65.64	293	65.24	329	65.38	365	65.53
222	66.01	258	65.07	294	66.26	330	65.55	366	66.19
223	66.02	259	65.37	295	65.50	331	65.87	367	65.78
224	65.88	260	65.32	296	65.73	332	65.92	368	65.92
225	66.30	261	65.27	297	65.28	333	66.58	369	66.10
226	66.56	262	65.22	298	64.98	334	66.04	370	65.80
227	66.06	263	65.13	299	65.19	335	66.00	371	64.66
228	66.27	264	64.98	300	65.68	336	65.74	372	65.80
229	65.94	265	65.49	301	65.68	337	65.84	373	65.55
230	65.14	266	65.34	302	65.81	338	63.48	374	65.54
231	65.41	267	64.70	303	65.85	339	63.29	375	65.90
232	65.18	268	65.52	304	65.73	340	63.62	376	66.30
233	65.50	269	65.33	305	65.69	341	63.89	377	66.70
234	65.70	270	65.44	306	65.75	342	64.14	378	66.75
235	65.57	271	65.29	307	65.46	343	63.53	379	66.80
236	65.79	272	65.72	308	65.73	344	63.57	380	66.70
237	65.51	273	65.51	309	65.21	345	63.52	381	66.29
238	65.97	274	65.07	310	65.48	346	63.85	382	66.26
239	66.05	275	65.28	311	64.85	347	64.44	383	66.34
240	66.27	276	65.44	312	65.10	348	63.75	384	66.64
241	65.23	277	65.40	313	65.33	349	63.95	385	66.54
242	66.00	278	65.63	314	65.00	350	63.60	386	66.60
243	65.14	279	65.72	315	65.03	351	62.77	387	66.58
244	65.85	280	65.47	316	64.95	352	66.43	388	66.49
245	65.66	281	65.09	317	65.16	353	66.74	389	66.70
246	66.50	282	65.04	318	65.39	354	66.40	390	66.38

Source: Takahashi, U. and Imaizami, M. "Sampling Experiment of Fine Iron Ore," *Reports of Statistical Application Research*, Union of Japanese Scientists and Engineers. Vol. 18, No. 1, 1971.

APPENDIX VI

Federal Trade Commission Rankings of Domestic Cigarette Brands

OBS	BRAND	LENGTH	MENTHOL	FILTER	LIGHT	PACK	TAR	NICOTINE	CO
1	Alpine	85	M	F	R	SP	17	1.1	16
2	Alpine	100	M	F	R	SP	15	1.1	15
3	Alpine	85	M	F	L	SP	9	0.7	11
4	Alpine	100	M	F	L	SP	9	0.8	11
5	Alpine	100	M	F	R	HP	15	0.9	15
6	Alpine	100	M	F	L	HP	10	0.7	10
7	American Filter	100	NM	F	R	SP	16	1.2	15
8	American Filter	85	NM	F	R	SP	16	1.2	14
9	American Lights	100	NM	F	L	SP	12	1.0	13
10	American Lights	85	NM	F	L	SP	12	0.9	13
11	American Lights	100	M	F	L	SP	12	1.0	12
12	Belair	85	M	F	R	SP	10	0.8	10
13	Belair	100	M	F	R	SP	8	0.6	9
14	Belair	85	M	F	L	SP	9	0.9	9
15	Belair	100	M	F	L	SP	10	0.9	10
16	Benson and Hedges	85	NM	F	R	HP	15	1.2	13
17	Benson and Hedges	100	NM	F	L	HP	11	0.9	12
18	Benson and Hedges	100	M	F	L	HP	10	0.8	11
19	Benson and Hedges	100	NM	F	R	SP	17	1.2	17
20	Benson and Hedges	100	NM	F	R	HP	16	1.2	15
21	Benson and Hedges	100	M	F	R	HP	16	1.2	16
22	Benson and Hedges	100	M	F	R	SP	16	1.2	16
23	Benson and Hedges	100	NM	F	L	SP	11	0.8	13
24	Benson and Hedges	100	M	F	L	SP	11	0.9	12
25	Benson and Hedges	100	NM	F	E	HP	5	0.5	7
26	Benson and Hedges	70	M	F	E	HP	5	0.5	7
27	Benson and Hedges	85	NM	F	R	SP	11	0.9	11
28	Bristol	85	NM	F	L	SP	11	0.9	12
29	Bristol	85	M	F	L	SP	11	0.9	12
30	Bristol	100	NM	F	L	SP	11	0.9	11
31	Bristol	100	M	F	L	SP	11	0.9	14
32	Bucks	85	NM	F	R	SP	14	1.0	13
33	Bucks	85	NM	F	L	SP	11	0.7	11
34	Cambridge	100	NM	F	E	SP	4	0.4	6
35	Cambridge	85	NM	F	L	SP	12	0.9	13
36	Cambridge	85	M	F	L	SP	12	0.9	13
37	Cambridge	100	NM	F	L	SP	12	0.9	14
38	Cambridge	100	M	F	L	SP	12	0.9	14
39	Cambridge	85	NM	F	R	SP	17	1.1	16
40	Cambridge	100	NM	F	R	SP	17	1.2	17
41	Camel	85	NM	F	R	SP	15	1.0	14
42	Camel	85	NM	F	R	HP	17	1.0	16
43	Camel	100	NM	F	L	SP	11	0.8	14
44	Camel	85	NM	F	L	SP	9	0.7	12
45	Camel	85	NM	F	L	HP	9	0.6	12
46	Camel	70	NM	NF	R	SP	22	1.4	14
47	Camel	100	NM	F	R	SP	17	1.0	19
48	Capri	100	NM	F	R	HP	10	0.8	7
49	Capri	100	M	F	R	HP	9	0.8	6
50	Capri	120	NM	F	R	HP	14	1.1	10
51	Capri	120	M	F	R	HP	12	1.0	8
52	Carlton	120	NM	F	R	SP	6	0.6	6
53	Carlton	85	NM	F	R	SP	1	0.1	2
54	Carlton	120	M	F	R	SP	6	0.6	5
55	Carlton	85	M	F	R	SP	0.5	0.1	1
56	Carlton	85	NM	F	R	HP	1	0.1	2
57	Carlton	100	NM	F	R	HP	0.5	0.1	1
58	Carlton	100	NM	F	R	SP	3	0.3	4
59	Carlton	100	M	F	R	HP	0.5	0.1	1
60	Carlton	100	M	F	R	SP	4	0.4	6
61	Carlton	85	NM	F	E	HP	0.5	0.05	0.5
62	Cartier Vendome	100	NM	F	R	HP	9	0.7	8
63	Cartier Vendome	100	M	F	R	HP	9	0.7	7
64	Century	85	NM	F	R	SP	15	1.0	17
65	Century	85	NM	F	L	SP	9	0.7	11
66	Century	100	NM	F	R	SP	17	1.1	20
67	Century	100	NM	F	L	SP	12	0.9	13
68	Century	100	M	F	L	SP	11	0.8	13
69	Chelsea	100	M	F	R	HP	11	0.9	12
70	Chelsea	100	NM	F	R	HP	11	0.9	12

OBS	BRAND	LENGTH	MENTHOL	FILTER	LIGHT	PACK	TAR	NICOTINE	CO
71	Chesterfield	70	NM	NF	R	SP	20	1.3	13
72	Chesterfield	85	NM	NF	R	SP	24	1.6	15
73	Chesterfield	85	NM	F	L	SP	10	0.8	12
74	Chesterfield	100	NM	F	L	SP	10	0.9	11
75	Class A	70	NM	NF	R	SP	19	1.3	13
76	Class A	85	NM	NF	R	SP	23	1.8	15
77	Class A	85	NM	F	R	SP	16	1.3	13
78	Class A	85	M	F	R	SP	16	1.3	14
79	Class A	100	NM	F	R	SP	17	1.4	14
80	Class A	100	M	F	R	SP	17	1.4	14
81	Class A	85	NM	F	L	SP	14	1.2	13
82	Class A	85	M	F	L	SP	14	1.2	13
83	Class A	100	NM	F	L	SP	14	1.2	14
84	Class A	100	M	F	L	SP	14	1.2	12
85	Class A	85	NM	F	E	SP	6	0.7	6
86	Class A	85	M	F	E	SP	6	0.7	7
87	Class A	100	NM	F	E	SP	6	0.7	5
88	Class A	100	M	F	E	SP	6	0.7	4
89	Class A Deluxe	85	NM	F	R	SP	16	1.3	13
90	Class A Deluxe	100	NM	F	R	SP	17	1.4	14
91	Class A Deluxe	85	NM	F	L	HP	14	1.2	13
92	Class A Deluxe	85	NM	F	L	SP	14	1.2	13
93	Class A Deluxe	85	M	F	L	SP	14	1.2	13
94	Class A Deluxe	100	NM	F	L	SP	14	1.2	14
95	Class A Deluxe	100	M	F	L	SP	14	1.2	12
96	Class A Deluxe	100	NM	F	E	SP	6	0.7	5
97	Doral	85	NM	F	L	SP	10	0.7	11
98	Doral	85	M	F	L	SP	10	0.7	11
99	Doral	100	NM	F	L	SP	10	0.8	10
100	Doral	100	M	F	L	SP	11	0.9	11
101	Doral	85	NM	F	R	SP	16	1.0	17
102	Doral	100	NM	F	R	SP	16	1.1	18
103	Doral	100	NM	F	E	SP	5	0.5	8
104	Doral	85	M	F	R	SP	16	1.1	16
105	English Oval	85	NM	NF	R	HP	23	1.8	15
106	Eve	120	NM	F	L	HP	13	1.1	11
107	Eve	120	M	F	L	HP	13	1.1	11
108	Eve	100	M	F	L	HP	13	1.0	11
109	Eve	100	NM	F	L	HP	13	1.0	11
110	Eve	120	NM	F	E	HP	5	0.6	4
111	Eve	120	M	F	E	HP	5	0.6	4
112	Falcon	85	NM	F	L	SP	11	0.7	11
113	Falcon	85	M	F	L	SP	10	0.8	12
114	Falcon	100	NM	F	L	SP	11	0.8	14
115	Falcon	100	M	F	L	SP	9	0.7	11
116	Golden Lights	85	NM	F	L	SP	8	0.7	8
117	Golden Lights	85	M	F	L	SP	8	0.7	9
118	Golden Lights	100	NM	F	L	SP	9	0.8	9
119	Golden Lights	100	M	F	L	SP	10	0.9	10
120	Golden Lights	85	NM	F	L	HP	8	0.7	9
121	Golden Lights	100	NM	F	L	HP	9	0.8	10
122	GPC Approved	70	NM	NF	R	SP	24	1.4	16
123	GPC Approved	85	NM	F	L	SP	11	0.7	12
124	GPC Approved	100	NM	F	L	SP	11	0.8	13
125	GPC Approved	85	M	F	L	SP	10	0.8	9
126	GPC Approved	100	M	F	L	SP	9	0.8	9
127	GPC Approved	85	NM	F	E	SP	6	0.5	6
128	GPC Approved	100	NM	F	E	SP	6	0.5	7
129	GPC Approved	85	NM	F	R	SP	17	1.1	17
130	GPC Approved	100	NM	F	R	SP	16	1.1	18
131	GPC Approved	85	M	F	R	SP	16	1.0	13
132	GPC Approved	100	M	F	R	SP	14	1.0	13
133	Harley Davidson	85	NM	F	R	SP	14	1.0	16
134	Harley Davidson	85	NM	F	L	SP	8	0.7	11
135	Herbert Tareyton	85	NM	NF	R	SP	25	1.6	18
136	Hi-Lite	100	NM	F	R	HP	13	1.1	13
137	Kent	85	NM	F	R	SP	12	0.9	14
138	Kent	100	NM	F	R	SP	14	1.0	15
139	Kent	85	NM	F	R	HP	11	0.8	13
140	Kent	100	M	F	R	SP	14	1.0	15

(continued)

OBS	BRAND	LENGTH	MENTHOL	FILTER	LIGHT	PACK	TAR	NICOTINE	CO
141	Kent	85	NM	F	L	SP	3	0.3	5
142	Kent	100	NM	F	L	SP	5	0.4	7
143	Kent	100	NM	F	L	HP	5	0.5	7
144	Kool	70	M	NF	R	HP	22	1.4	15
145	Kool	85	M	F	R	SP	17	1.2	16
146	Kool	85	M	F	R	HP	16	1.1	16
147	Kool	85	M	F	L	SP	8	0.7	9
148	Kool	100	M	F	L	SP	9	0.7	10
149	Kool Mild	85	M	F	R	SP	12	0.9	13
150	Kool Mild	100	M	F	R	SP	12	0.9	13
151	Kool Mild	85	M	F	R	HP	11	0.9	11
152	Kool Super Long	100	M	F	R	SP	17	1.3	17
153	L and M	85	NM	F	R	SP	14	1.0	13
154	L and M	85	NM	F	R	HP	14	1.1	13
155	L and M	100	NM	F	L	SP	12	1.0	10
156	L and M Long	100	NM	F	R	SP	8	0.9	7
157	L and M Super King	100	NM	F	R	SP	14	1.1	15
158	Lark	85	NM	F	L	SP	13	1.0	11
159	Lark	100	NM	F	L	SP	13	1.1	13
160	Lark	85	NM	F	R	SP	14	1.1	12
161	Lark	120	NM	F	R	SP	14	1.2	14
162	Lucky Strike	70	NM	NF	R	SP	25	1.6	17
163	Lucky Strike	85	NM	F	R	SP	12	0.9	13
164	Lucky Strike	85	NM	F	R	HP	12	0.9	13
165	Lucky Strike	100	NM	F	R	SP	12	1.0	13
166	Lucky Strike	85	NM	F	L	SP	8	0.7	10
167	Lucky Strike	100	NM	F	L	SP	9	0.8	10
168	Lucky Strike	100	M	F	R	SP	12	1.0	12
169	Magna	85	NM	F	R	SP	14	0.9	14
170	Magna	85	NM	F	R	HP	14	0.9	15
171	Magna	85	NM	F	L	SP	9	0.7	13
172	Magna	85	NM	F	L	HP	13	0.9	10
173	Malibu	100	NM	F	R	SP	14	1.1	14
174	Malibu	100	NM	F	L	SP	9	0.8	11
175	Malibu	100	M	F	R	SP	11	0.9	12
176	Malibu	85	NM	F	R	SP	17	1.2	15
177	Malibu	85	NM	F	L	SP	10	0.8	10
178	Malibu	85	M	F	R	SP	16	1.2	14
179	Malibu	100	NM	F	E	SP	6	0.5	7
180	Marlboro	85	NM	F	R	HP	17	1.2	15
181	Marlboro	85	NM	F	R	SP	17	1.2	15
182	Marlboro	85	M	F	R	SP	16	1.2	15
183	Marlboro	100	NM	F	R	SP	16	1.2	16
184	Marlboro	100	NM	F	R	HP	17	1.2	16
185	Marlboro	85	NM	F	L	SP	11	0.9	12
186	Marlboro	85	NM	F	L	HP	11	0.9	12
187	Marlboro	100	NM	F	L	SP	11	0.9	12
188	Marlboro	85	M	F	L	SP	10	0.8	10
189	Marlboro	100	NM	F	L	HP	11	0.9	12
190	Marlboro	100	M	F	L	SP	11	0.9	12
191	Marlboro	85	NM	F	E	HP	6	0.5	6
192	Marlboro	100	NM	F	E	HP	6	0.5	7
193	Marlboro	100	M	F	L	HP	10	0.8	11
194	Marlboro	85	M	F	L	HP	10	0.8	11
195	Max	120	NM	F	R	SP	17	1.3	19
196	Max	120	M	F	R	SP	17	1.3	18
197	Merit	85	NM	F	R	SP	8	0.6	10
198	Merit	85	M	F	R	SP	8	0.6	10
199	Merit	100	NM	F	R	SP	10	0.8	12
200	Merit	100	M	F	R	SP	10	0.8	11
201	Merit	85	NM	F	R	HP	8	0.6	10
202	Merit	85	NM	F	E	SP	5	0.5	6
203	Merit	100	NM	F	E	SP	5	0.5	7
204	Merit	85	M	F	E	SP	5	0.5	6
205	Merit	100	M	F	E	SP	5	0.5	7
206	Merit	85	NM	F	E	HP	5	0.5	6
207	Merit	100	NM	F	E	HP	6	0.6	7
208	Merit De-Nic	85	NM	F	R	SP	9	0.1	7
209	Merit De-Nic	85	M	F	R	SP	9	0.1	6
210	Merit De-Nic	85	NM	F	E	SP	4	0.1	3

OBS	BRAND	LENGTH	MENTHOL	FILTER	LIGHT	PACK	TAR	NICOTINE	CO
211	Merit De-Nic	85	M	F	E	SP	4	0.1	3
212	Misty Slims	100	NM	F	L	HP	9	0.8	10
213	Misty Slims	100	M	F	L	HP	9	0.8	10
214	Montclair	100	NM	F	R	SP	16	1.3	14
215	Montclair	100	NM	F	L	SP	12	1.0	13
216	Montclair	100	M	F	L	SP	12	1.0	13
217	Montclair	85	NM	F	L	SP	12	1.0	13
218	Montclair	85	M	F	L	SP	12	1.0	13
219	Montclair	85	NM	F	R	SP	16	1.3	15
220	More	120	NM	F	R	SP	17	1.2	22
221	More	100	NM	F	L	HP	10	0.8	11
222	More	120	M	F	R	SP	17	1.3	22
223	More	100	M	F	L	HP	9	0.7	11
224	More	120	M	F	L	SP	13	1.0	20
225	More	120	NM	F	L	SP	12	0.9	19
226	More White	120	NM	F	L	SP	10	0.7	13
227	More White	120	M	F	L	SP	10	0.8	15
228	Newport	85	M	F	R	SP	17	1.2	18
229	Newport	100	M	F	R	SP	18	1.4	19
230	Newport	85	M	F	R	HP	16	1.2	17
231	Newport	85	M	F	L	SP	8	0.7	9
232	Newport	100	M	F	L	SP	9	0.8	9
233	Newport	85	M	F	L	HP	8	0.7	9
234	Newport	100	M	F	R	HP	19	1.4	19
235	Newport	100	M	F	L	HP	9	0.8	9
236	Newport Stripe	100	M	F	L	HP	10	0.8	11
237	Newport Stripe	100	NM	F	R	HP	12	0.9	16
238	Newport Stripe	100	M	F	R	HP	12	0.9	16
239	Next	85	M	F	L	SP	9	0.1	8
240	Next	100	NM	F	L	SP	9	0.1	8
241	Next	100	M	F	L	SP	9	0.1	8
242	Next	85	NM	F	E	SP	4	0.1	3
243	Next	85	M	F	E	SP	4	0.1	3
244	Next	100	NM	F	E	SP	6	0.1	5
245	Next	100	M	F	E	SP	6	0.1	5
246	Next	85	NM	F	L	SP	9	0.1	8
247	Now	100	NM	F	R	SP	2	0.2	3
248	Now	85	NM	F	R	SP	1	0.1	2
249	Now	85	NM	F	R	HP	0.05	0.05	0.5
250	Now	100	NM	F	R	HP	0.05	0.05	0.5
251	Now	100	M	F	R	SP	2	0.2	4
252	Now	85	M	F	R	SP	1	0.1	2
253	Old Gold	85	NM	F	R	SP	17	1.2	18
254	Old Gold	100	NM	F	R	SP	18	1.4	19
255	Old Gold	85	NM	NF	R	SP	26	1.8	18
256	Old Gold	85	NM	F	L	SP	9	0.8	10
257	Old Gold	100	NM	F	L	SP	12	0.9	16
258	Pall Mall	85	NM	NF	R	SP	25	1.7	16
259	Pall Mall	100	NM	F	L	SP	10	0.9	12
260	Pall Mall	100	NM	F	R	SP	18	1.3	17
261	Pall Mall	85	NM	NF	L	SP	18	1.3	17
262	Pall Mall	100	M	F	L	SP	10	0.8	10
263	Pall Mall Red	85	NM	F	R	SP	15	1.1	14
264	Pall Mall Red	100	NM	F	R	SP	16	1.2	15
265	Pall Mall Red	85	NM	F	L	SP	10	0.8	10
266	Pall Mall Red	100	NM	F	L	SP	9	0.8	10
267	Pall Mall Gold	100	NM	F	L	SP	15	1.2	15
268	Parliament	85	NM	F	L	HP	9	0.7	10
269	Parliament	85	NM	F	L	SP	9	0.8	11
270	Parliament	100	NM	F	L	SP	12	1.0	13
271	Philip Morris	85	NM	NF	R	SP	26	1.7	16
272	Philip Morris	70	NM	NF	R	SP	24	1.4	14
273	Philip Morris	100	NM	F	R	HP	17	1.3	16
274	Philip Morris	100	M	F	R	HP	17	1.3	16
275	Picayune	70	NM	NF	R	SP	18	1.2	10
276	Players	70	NM	NF	R	HP	25	1.7	15
277	Players	85	NM	F	R	HP	12	0.9	13
278	Players	85	M	F	R	HP	12	0.9	13
279	Players	100	NM	F	R	HP	14	1.0	13
280	Players	100	M	F	R	HP	14	1.0	13

(continued)

OBS	BRAND	LENGTH	MENTHOL	FILTER	LIGHT	PACK	TAR	NICOTINE	CO
281	Players	85	NM	F	L	SP	10	0.8	11
282	Players	85	M	F	L	SP	10	0.7	11
283	Players	100	NM	F	L	SP	12	0.9	14
284	Players	100	M	F	L	SP	12	0.9	14
285	Pyramid	85	NM	F	L	SP	14	1.1	13
286	Pyramid	100	NM	F	L	SP	13	1.1	14
287	Pyramid	100	M	F	L	SP	12	1.1	12
288	Pyramid	85	NM	NF	R	SP	23	1.5	15
289	Pyramid	100	NM	F	E	SP	6	0.6	5
290	Pyramid	85	NM	F	R	SP	16	1.3	13
291	Pyramid	85	M	F	R	SP	16	1.3	14
292	Pyramid	100	NM	F	R	SP	17	1.4	14
293	Pyramid	100	M	F	R	SP	17	1.4	14
294	Raleigh	85	NM	F	R	SP	15	1.0	14
295	Raleigh	100	NM	F	R	SP	16	1.0	16
296	Raleigh	85	NM	F	L	SP	11	0.9	13
297	Raleigh	100	NM	F	L	SP	12	0.9	15
298	Raleigh	70	NM	NF	R	SP	25	1.5	17
299	Richland	85	NM	F	R	SP	17	1.2	16
300	Richland	85	M	F	R	SP	16	1.0	16
301	Richland	85	NM	F	L	SP	12	0.9	13
302	Richland	100	NM	F	R	SP	18	1.3	17
303	Richland	100	NM	F	L	SP	12	0.9	14
304	Richland	100	M	F	R	SP	16	1.1	16
305	Ritz	100	M	F	R	HP	11	0.8	11
306	Ritz	100	NM	F	R	HP	10	0.8	11
307	Salem	85	M	F	R	SP	17	1.2	17
308	Salem	100	M	F	L	SP	8	0.7	10
309	Salem	85	M	F	L	SP	9	0.7	12
310	Salem	100	M	F	R	SP	16	1.2	16
311	Salem	100	M	F	L	HP	10	0.7	10
312	Salem	85	M	F	E	SP	5	0.4	8
313	Salem	100	M	F	E	SP	4	0.4	7
314	Salem Cust Case	100	M	F	L	HP	11	0.8	11
315	Saratoga	120	NM	F	R	HP	15	1.2	15
316	Saratoga	120	M	F	R	HP	15	1.1	14
317	Satin	100	NM	F	R	SP	11	0.9	13
318	Satin	100	M	F	R	SP	11	0.9	14
319	Savvy	100	NM	F	L	SP	10	0.9	11
320	Savvy	100	M	F	L	SP	10	0.9	11
321	Savvy	100	NM	F	E	SP	5	0.5	5
322	Silva Thins	100	NM	F	R	SP	12	1.0	10
323	Silva Thins	100	M	F	R	SP	12	1.1	10
324	Silva Thins	100	NM	F	R	HP	12	1.0	12
325	Silva Thins	100	M	F	R	HP	11	0.9	12
326	Spring	100	M	F	R	SP	18	1.4	18
327	Spring	85	NM	F	L	SP	9	0.9	12
328	Spring	85	M	F	L	SP	9	0.9	12
329	Spring	100	NM	F	L	SP	20	1.0	14
330	Spring	100	M	F	L	SP	10	1.0	14
331	Tall	120	NM	F	R	SP	19	1.6	19
332	Tall	120	M	F	R	SP	18	1.6	17
333	Tareyton	85	NM	F	R	SP	14	1.0	16
334	Tareyton	100	NM	F	R	SP	14	1.0	17
335	Tareyton	70	NM	F	L	SP	5	0.4	6
336	Tareyton	100	NM	F	L	SP	8	0.7	9
337	Triumph	85	NM	F	R	SP	3	0.3	4
338	Triumph	85	M	F	R	SP	3	0.4	4
339	Triumph	100	NM	F	R	SP	5	0.5	8
340	Triumph	100	M	F	R	SP	6	0.5	8
341	True	85	NM	F	R	SP	5	0.5	6
342	True	85	M	F	R	SP	5	0.5	6
343	True	100	NM	F	R	SP	6	0.6	7
344	True	100	M	F	R	SP	6	0.6	7
345	Vantage	100	NM	F	R	SP	9	0.6	11
346	Vantage	85	NM	F	R	SP	10	0.7	13
347	Vantage	100	NM	F	E	SP	5	0.4	8
348	Vantage	85	NM	F	E	SP	5	0.4	7
349	Vantage	85	M	F	R	SP	10	0.7	12
350	Vantage	100	M	F	R	SP	8	0.6	13

OBS	BRAND	LENGTH	MENTHOL	FILTER	LIGHT	PACK	TAR	NICOTINE	CO
351	Vantage Excel	100	NM	F	R	SP	9	0.7	9
352	Viceroy	85	NM	F	R	SP	17	1.1	16
353	Viceroy	100	NM	F	R	SP	16	1.2	15
354	Viceroy	85	NM	F	L	SP	11	0.9	13
355	Viceroy	100	NM	F	L	SP	12	0.9	14
356	Virginia Slims	100	NM	F	R	SP	15	1.1	13
357	Virginia Slims	100	M	F	R	SP	15	1.2	13
358	Virginia Slims	100	NM	F	L	HP	9	0.7	10
359	Virginia Slims	100	M	F	L	HP	9	0.7	10
360	Virginia Slims	120	NM	F	L	HP	14	1.1	14
361	Virginia Slims	120	M	F	L	HP	14	1.1	13
362	Virginia Slims	100	NM	F	E	HP	5	0.5	5
363	Virginia Slims	100	M	F	E	HP	5	0.4	5
364	Winston	100	NM	F	R	SP	17	1.1	19
365	Winston	85	NM	F	R	SP	17	1.1	16
366	Winston	85	NM	F	R	HP	17	1.1	16
367	Winston	100	NM	F	L	SP	11	0.8	13
368	Winston	85	NM	F	L	SP	10	0.7	11
369	Winston	100	NM	F	L	HP	10	0.6	12
370	Winston	100	NM	F	E	SP	5	0.4	8
371	Winston	85	NM	F	E	SP	5	0.5	8
372	Winston	85	NM	F	L	HP	10	0.7	12

APPENDIX VII

ASP Tutorial

This appendix provides an overview of the ASP program. It gives the minimal hardware requirements and start-up procedures necessary to begin an ASP session on a personal computer (PC). This tutorial is not intended to replace any of the ASP documentation manuals available from the publisher or DMC Software, Inc. (See the Preface.)

HARDWARE REQUIREMENTS   ASP must be run on an IBM-compatible PC with at least 512K of memory, two disk drives (either one hard drive and one floppy drive, or two floppy drives), and DOS 2.0 or higher. A blank formatted floppy disk is also required for data storage, unless your PC has a hard drive (i.e., fixed disk) available for storing data.

GETTING STARTED   To use the ASP program, you must first load it into the memory of the computer. To accomplish this when starting ASP from a floppy disk:

1. Insert your copy of ASP (provided in the back cover pocket) into either of your two disk drives, drive A or drive B. (Assume drive A.)

2. Type A: and press ENTER to make drive A the current drive.

```
A: <ENTER>
```

3. Type ASP and press ENTER to load the ASP program into memory.

```
ASP <ENTER>
```

The ASP disk must remain in drive A for as long as you are using the program.

To start ASP from a fixed disk or hard drive (e.g., drive C), it is first necessary to install ASP on the fixed disk. This is accomplished by placing your copy of the ASP disk into drive A and entering the following commands at the DOS prompt:

```
C:          <ENTER>
MD \ASP     <ENTER>
CD \ASP     <ENTER>
COPY A:*.*  <ENTER>
```

(This sequence of DOS commands assumes the drive letter of the fixed disk is C and that the subdirectory in which the ASP program resides is \ASP.) Once ASP has been installed on the fixed disk it need not be installed again. The ASP program can then be started at any point in the future by entering the following commands at the DOS prompt:

```
C:          <ENTER>
CD \ASP     <ENTER>
ASP         <ENTER>
```

THE MAIN MENU   The initial screen to appear as the ASP program is loaded into memory displays copyright and licensing information. After reading this information, press any key to obtain the Main Menu shown in Figure VII.1.

```
***************** MAIN MENU *****************

A Statistical Package for Business, Economics, and The Social Sciences
         Copyright 1992 by DMC Software, Inc.   (Version 2.xx)

 A. Analysis of Variance    B. Regression Analysis    C. Correlation Matrix
 D. Summary Statistics      E. Probability Dists.     F. File Management Menu
 G. Time Series Analysis    H. Hypothesis Tests       I. INSTRUCTIONS
 J. Factor Analysis         K. Miscellaneous Plots    L. Crosstab/Contingency
 M. Auxiliary Programs      N. Enter a DOS Command    O. Scr./Data Dir. Dflts

 F1 = ALT COMMANDS MENU    F2 = CALCULATOR    F3 = TOGGLE PRINT (OFF)    X = EXIT
```

FIGURE VII.1 ▲
The ASP Main Menu

The Main Menu is a typical ASP "bounce bar" menu. The highlighted bar can be moved from option to option by pressing the SPACE BAR, the cursor control keys ($\leftarrow \rightarrow \uparrow \downarrow$), or the TAB key. Once your selection is made, press ENTER to display submenus associated with the option. (You can also make a selection by pressing the letter of the desired option.)

Table VII.1, on page 1148, gives a brief description of each of the Main Menu options and the corresponding chapters in the text. Several of these options contain statistical procedures that are beyond the scope of the text. Only the statistical routines covered in the text are described in the table.

ALTERNATE COMMANDS MENU   All the statistical routines in ASP are accessible through the Main Menu. However, additional commands can be executed through the Alt Commands Menu. The Alt Commands Menu is called by pressing the F1 function key any time within the ASP program. When F1 is pressed from the Main Menu, the Alt Commands Menu appears as shown in Figure VII.2 on page 1149.

TABLE VII.1　Options on the Main Menu

Option	Description	Chapter(s)
A. Analysis of Variance	One-way and two-way ANOVAs	14
B. Regression Analysis	Simple and multiple regression; residual analysis	11–13
C. Correlation Matrix	Bivariate correlations	11
D. Summary Statistics	Mean, median, standard deviation, etc.	2
E. Probability Dists.	Discrete and continuous distributions	4–5
F. File Management Menu	Creating, saving, editing data	—
G. Time Series Analysis	(Beyond the scope of this text)	—
H. Hypothesis Test	Confidence intervals and hypothesis tests for means, proportions, and variances; 1-way table χ^2 test; nonparametric tests; control charts	8–10, 15–16
I. INSTRUCTIONS	A short tutorial on the use of ASP	—
J. Factor Analysis Menu	(Beyond the scope of this text)	—
K. Miscellaneous Plots	Stem-and-leaf display, box plot, normal probability plot, scatterplot	2, 5
L. Crosstab/Contingency	Two-way (contingency) table χ^2 test	10
M. Auxiliary Programs	Matrix algebra	App. I
N. Enter a DOS Command	Enter and execute DOS commands within an ASP session	—
O. Scr./Data Dir. Dflts.	Set the color scheme on the monitor; set the default directory and printer port	—

You can execute the commands on this menu by either moving the cursor to the desired option and pressing ENTER or by pressing the letter associated with the option. You will find this menu most useful for:

- Creating or editing data sets (option E)
- Listing data (option L)
- Getting data from an already created ASP data set (option G)
- Creating new variables for a data set (option T)
- Adding or deleting variables and/or cases (option A)
- Changing the names of variables (option I)
- Getting or saving data in an external ASCII file (option B)
- Saving an ASP data set (option S)

CREATING A DATA MATRIX   Typically, you will use ASP to analyze a data set. To do this, you must first create an ASP "data matrix." Select E = Edit Or Create Data Matrix on the Alt Commands Menu and ASP responds with a series of questions and prompts. The first question is

---

EDIT or CREATE? E

```
                         *                              * *
                  E = Edit Or Create Data Matrix
A Statistical     G = Get Data Matrix From ASP File      cial Sciences
         Copy     S = Save Data Matrix In ASP File       2.xx)
                  L = List Data Matrix
                  Q = Sort Or Transpose Data Matrix
A. Analysis of V  R = Recode Variable                    relation Matrix
D. Summary Stati  M = Change Missing Value Code          e Management Menu
G. Time Series A  J = Combine Or Break Down Variables    TRUCTIONS
J. Factor Analys  I = Change Names/Labels/Cases/Vars.    sstab/Contingency
M. Auxiliary Pro  A = Add Or Delete Variable Or Case     /Data Dir. Dflts
                  B = Get Or Save ASCII File
                  N = Enter A DOS Command
F1 = ALT COMMANDS T = Variable Transformation Menu       (OFF)    X = EXIT
                  F = File Management Menu
                  V = View/Rename/Delete OUTPUT File
                  D = Summary Statistics
                  H = Hypothesis Tests Menu
                  P = Probability Distributions Menu
                  K = Miscellaneous Plots Menu
                  C = Change No. Of Digits In Display
                  O = Scr./Data Dir./Prt. Port Dflts.
```

FIGURE VII.2 ▲
The Alt Commands Menu

Note that the ASP default answer is E for EDIT. This is used when you want to edit an existing ASP data matrix. To create a data matrix, press the letter C (for CREATE). You are now prompted with the question:

Number of Variables? 1

Change the default to the correct number and press ENTER. ASP creates names for the variables using the convention Var1, Var2, Var3, etc., then asks:

Are Names OK? Y

To change the names, press N (for No). ASP will then ask you to enter the new name of each variable. Once this is completed, ASP will prompt you, one case (i.e., one observation) and one variable at a time, to enter the data into the data matrix.
[*Note:* The ASP data editor will not accept letters or special characters (e.g., dollar sign, comma) as data. Only whole numbers or numbers with decimals should be entered into the data matrix.

When data entry is complete, press X to exit the numerical data editor. Several questions will be asked, the most important being:

`Do You Wish to Save the Data Matrix? Y`

Answer "yes" by pressing ENTER. ASP will then ask for the drive letter (e.g., drive A) and directory of the disk where you want to save the data:

`DATA DIRECTORY: A:\`

If the default is correct, press ENTER. Otherwise, enter the correct drive/path. You will be asked to name the ASP data file, provide a file label (optional), and whether you want to save all variables and all cases.

Suppose you enter the following file name:

`File Name: MYDATA`

ASP will save your data matrix in the ASP file named MYDATA.ASP in the directory specified earlier. In future ASP sessions, you can access this data set by first selecting the option G = Get Data Matrix From ASP File from the Alt Commands Menu, and then selecting MYDATA from the resulting menu-list of ASP data files.

ANALYZING A DATA MATRIX   To analyze an ASP data matrix that you have just created or accessed, return to the Main Menu by pressing X or ESC. From the Main Menu, select the desired statistical routine. Each choice will result in a series of submenus, prompts, and/or questions similar to those shown previously. After making your selections, ASP will perform the analysis and immediately display the results on the monitor screen. ASP menu selections at the bottom of the screen permit you to send the output directly to a printer or to save the output in a file for future use.

Available Documentation

ASP User's Manual (by DMC Software, Inc.)—available free to adopters of the text from the publisher of the text.

ASP Tutorial and Student Guide (by George Blackford)—can be purchased directly from DMC Software, Inc., or from your campus book store (see the Preface).

Answers to the Exercises

Chapter 1

1.1 a. Thion levels of all possible daily ambient air specimens that can be collected at the orchard
b. Thion levels for the 13 ambient air specimens actually measured
1.2 a. Numbers of accidents at all intersections in Lexington, KY, over a 5-year period
b. Numbers of accidents at all intersections monitored (or sampled)
c. Use difference in sample means (with versus without left-turn-only lanes) to estimate difference in population means
1.3 a. Powerload status (high neutral current or not) at all U.S. sites with computer power systems
b. Powerload status at each of 146 U.S. sites   **c.** Estimate that 10% of all sites have high neutral current status
1.4 a. Population: total water flows required for cooling of all batches of green tomatoes; sample: total water flows of the
20 batches of green tomatoes   **b.** Compare mean total water flows of batches precooled with new method to mean total water
flow of batches precooled with conventional method
1.5 Record CT scan times of a sample of n images; scan times of all possible images
1.6 Population: defective status (0 or 1) of all items manufactured; sample: defective status (0 or 1) of all sampled items
1.7 Ratio: quantitative; load type: qualitative; vendor: qualitative
1.8 (1) Quantitative   (2) Qualitative   (3) Quantitative   (4) Qualitative   (5) Quantitative   (6) Qualitative   (7) Qualitative
(8) Quantitative   (9) Quantitative   (10) Quantitative
1.9 a. Quantitative   **b.** Quantitative   **c.** Quantitative   **d.** Qualitative   **e.** Qualitative
1.10 Location: qualitative; PCB level: quantitative
1.11 a. Life lengths of all hardware components   **b.** Life lengths of 100 components tested   **c.** Quantitative
d. Estimate mean life length of all hardware components
1.12 a. Directions of travel (toward ocean or away from ocean) of all turtle hatchlings released at night
b. Directions of travel for the 60 turtle hatchlings released each night, for 3 nights   **c.** Qualitative
1.13 a. Population: fluid statics coverage (yes or no) at all colleges; sample: fluid statics coverage at the 100 colleges surveyed
b. Qualitative   **c.** Estimate that 66% of all colleges cover fluid statics
1.14 a. Quantitative   **b.** Qualitative   **c.** Qualitative   **d.** Quantitative   **e.** Quantitative   **f.** Quantitative   **g.** Qualitative
h. Quantitative
1.15 Model: qualitative; manufacturer: qualitative; transmission: qualitative; engine size: quantitative; city mpg: quantitative;
highway mpg: quantitative

Chapter 2

2.1 c. Dumped: 187.8 million; burned: 25.9 million; recycled: 16.2 million; exported: 12.1 million
2.2 a. Mainland Scotland: .008; Highland Scotland: .01; Orkney: .023; Lewis: .051; N. Vist: .055; S. Vist: .104; Hebrides:
.051; Coll: .081; N. Ireland: .086; Ireland Rep.: .530   **b.** Mainland Scotland: .009; Highland Scotland: .011; Orkney: .024;
Lewis: .055; N. Vist: .059; S. Vist: .04; Hebrides: .055; Coll: .087; N. Ireland: .092; Ireland Rep.: .568
2.3 Repairs: .289; water: .474; shoulders: .622; other: .748; loose:.844; holes: .903; obstructions: .956; worn: 1.000
2.4 a. Brickmasons: .046; carpenters: .323; carpet installers: .022; finishers: .034; drywall installers: .044; electricians: .167;
glaziers: .013; setters: .009; insulation: .021; painters: .138; plumbers: .116; roofers: .042; metal: .024
b. Brickmasons: .304; carpenters: 13.74; carpet installers: 1.533; finishers: .678; drywall installers: 1.43; electricians: 9.316;
glaziers: .168; setters: .56; insulation: 1.05; painters: 31.257; plumbers: 3.411; roofers: .414; metal: .160
2.7 a. Wet/stress: .399; wet/local: .558; wet/general: .683; dry/cracking: .792; dry/corrosion: .874; wet/misc.: .912; welding:
.946; material: .966; dry/decrease: .983; dry/misc.: 1.000   **b.** Yes; 39.9% of failures are caused by stress corrosion cracking
2.8 Yes; U.S. and Japan produce 66.9% of published papers.
2.10 a.

1	0, 0, 0, 0, 0, 0, 0, 0, 0, 0
2	0, 0, 0, 0, 0, 0, 0, 0, 0, 0, 0, 0, 0
3	0, 0, 0, 0, 0, 0, 0, 0, 0, 0, 0, 0
4	0, 0, 0, 0
5	
6	0, 0

b. .25

2.11 a. .02, .02, .06, .08, .20, .14, .10, .08, .06, .04, .06, .04, .06, .04 **b.** No

2.12 b.

8	05, 72, 72, 80
9	55, 70, 73, 80, 80, 84, 84, 87, 87, 95, 97, 98 ,98
10	00, 01, 02, 03, 05, 05, 12, 15, 15, 26, 26, 29, 55

d. No

2.13 a. Stem is leftmost digit (6, 7, 8, or 9) **b.** .923

2.14 a.

1	12
2	05, 25, 39, 41, 70, 70
3	30, 75
4	
5	23, 91
6	18

b. Appears to be true

2.15 a. .16 **b.** .26

2.16 Plasma:

Plasma:		Fat:	
1	688	1	14
2	0155	2	3559
3	01135	3	
4	167	4	24469
5		5	59
6	89	6	9
7	2	7	007
⋮		8	
		9	
20	0	10	0
⋮		11	0
36	0	⋮	
		41	0

2.17 a. 130 **b.** .137, .510, .275, .059, .020 **c.** .079

2.19 a. Mean = 6, median = 5, modes: all 5 measurements **b.** Mean = 6, median = 5.5, modes: 4 and 6

2.20 Mean = 2.425, median = 2, mode = 2; mean   **2.21** Mean = 91.044, median = 92.

2.22 Old: mean = 9.804, median = 9.975, modes: 8.72, 9.80, 9.84, 9.87, 9.98, 10.05, 10.15, 10.26; New: mean = 9.422, median = 9.455, mode = 8.82   **2.23** Mean = .333, median = .270, mode = .270; mean

2.24 a. Yes **b.** (1.66, 21.54) **c.** 95% **d.** ≈ 93%   **2.25 d.** $\bar{y}$ = 62.96, s = .61   **e.** 96.97%, yes   **2.26 b.** Weight

2.27 a. $\bar{y}$ = 2.425, s = 1.259 **b.** (1.166, 3.684); (−.093, 4.943); (−1.352, 6.202) **c.** 24 (60%); 38 (95%); 40 (100%)

2.28 b. Mean = .033, standard deviation = .016 **c.** 95.65% within interval (.00027, .06547)

d. Mean = .080, standard deviation = .039; 91.30% within interval (.002, .158)

e. Mean = .169, standard deviation = .052; 95.65% within interval (.066, .272)

2.29 New: (8.46, 10.38) contains ≈ 95% of voltage readings; Old: (8.72, 10.89) contains ≈ 95% of voltage readings

2.30 a. (3.95, 12.03) **b.** No   **2.31** $\bar{y}$ = .333, s = .162   **2.32 a.** Q_L = 1, Q_U = 3 **b.** 2.84

2.34 Q_L = 62.59, M = 63.01, Q_U = 63.36   **2.35 a.** 7.15 **b.** 221.12

2.36 a. 99% of the rounding errors are less than .53 **b.** 4.43   **2.37 a.** 1.29 **b.** 2.25 **c.** Old

2.38 a. Q_L = 25.35, Q_U = 47.30, M = 38.10 **b.** z = −1.64   **2.39 a.** Suspect outliers: 6, 6 **b.** 6, 6 (z = 2.84)

2.40 a. Yes; 10.55 is a suspect outlier; 8.05, 8.72, 8.72, and 8.80 are highly suspect outliers. **b.** 8.72, 8.72, and 8.05 are outliers **c.** No **d.** No outliers

2.41 Outliers: 20 and 36   **2.42 a.** No **b.** No outliers   **2.43 a.** Yes; 2006, 2061, 2302 **b.** Yes; 2302

2.44 a. Sea: 3.34; waters: .242; port: .424 **b.** Meeting: .348; overtaking: .077; crossing: .194; unknown: .380

2.45 a.

1	0568
2	
3	5
4	
5	3
6	
7	
8	12
9	078
10	
11	
12	0
13	
14	
15	0
⋮	
23	0

b.

11	00
12	0
13	0
14	
15	
16	0
17	
18	00
19	
20	
21	0
22	0
23	
24	0
⋮	⋮
29	0
⋮	⋮
49	0
⋮	⋮
94	0
⋮	⋮
107	0
⋮	⋮
141	0

c.

1	0 5 6 8
2	
3	5
4	
5	3
6	
7	
8	1 2
9	0 7 8
10	
11	⓪⓪
12	0 ⓪
13	⓪
14	
15	0
16	⓪
17	
18	⓪⓪
19	
20	
21	⓪
22	⓪
23	0
24	⓪
⋮	⋮
29	⓪
⋮	⋮
49	⓪
⋮	⋮
94	⓪
⋮	⋮
107	⓪
⋮	⋮
141	⓪

; yes

2.47 Not likely ($z = 2.30$)

2.48 a. Mean = 117.82, median = 117.5, modes: 97, 112, 124, 128, and 131

b. Range = 62, variance = 225.33, standard deviation = 15.01

c.

Interval		Number in Interval	Number Expected by Empirical Rule
$\bar{y} \pm s$	(102.81, 132.83)	31	34
$\bar{y} \pm 2s$	(87.80, 147.84)	49	48
$\bar{y} \pm 3s$	(72.79, 162.85)	50	Almost all

d. No outliers   **e.** 128

2.49 c. Yes   **2.50 a.** Approx. 18%   **b.** Approx. 17%   **c.** Approx. 55%   **d.** Approx. 14%

2.51

2	72, 89, 97, 98
3	17, 58, 88
4	66, 81, 87
5	11, 12, 39
6	19, 83, 84
7	47, 68
8	71

2.52 b.

Sex/Lifts	Interval	Proportion
Male/1	(13.13, 47.37)	Approx. .95
Male/4	(10.43, 37.23)	Approx. .95
Female/1	(13.57, 26.01)	Approx. .95
Female/4	(9.36, 22.28)	Approx. .95

c. Male: yes, $25 < \bar{y} + 2s = 37.23$; female: no, $25 > \bar{y} + 2s = 22.28$
2.54 b. Mean $= 63.7$, median $= 4$, standard deviation $= 219.9$, $Q_L = 1$, $Q_U = 12.8$
c. All measurements exceeding 49 are outliers (using a boxplot).   **d.** Mean $= 5.93$, median $= 3$, standard deviation $= 7.87$
2.55 a. Secondary sulfate   **b.** 22%
2.56 a. Quantitative   **b.** Frequency distribution   **c.** Approx. .28   **d.** Yes, because the interval (.9995, 1.0005) has a large number of observations whereas the interval (.9985, .9995) contains no observations.
2.57 $\bar{y} = .812$, $s = 1.505$, $M = .275$, $Q_L = .136$, $Q_U = .595$

Chapter 3

3.1 a. BB, TG, GG, S, G   **b.** .28, .11, .11, .26, .24   **c.** .52   **d.** .48
3.2 a. EO, EC, NO, NC   **b.** $\frac{5}{24}$, 0, $\frac{12}{24}$, $\frac{7}{24}$ **c.** $\frac{5}{24}$ **d.** $\frac{7}{24}$ **3.3 a.** .21   **b.** .45   **c.** .90
3.4 a. (40, 300), (40, 350), (40, 400), (45, 300), (45, 350), (45, 400), (50, 300), (50, 350), (50, 400)
3.5 a. The simple events are the eight action/queries listed in the table.   **b.** $\frac{139}{548}$, $\frac{104}{548}$, $\frac{68}{548}$, $\frac{87}{548}$, $\frac{25}{548}$, $\frac{52}{548}$, $\frac{41}{548}$, $\frac{32}{548}$
c. $\frac{155}{548}$ **d.** $\frac{507}{548}$
3.6 a. .101   **b.** .536   **3.7 a.** .92   **b.** 1.00   **3.8 a.** $\frac{28}{38}$ **b.** $\frac{9}{38}$ **c.** $\frac{27}{38}$ **d.** $\frac{20}{38}$ **e.** $\frac{4}{38}$ **3.9** .984
3.10 b. The simple events are the seven steel sheet types listed in the table.
c. .27, .12, .30, .15, .08, .05, .03   **d.** .05   **e.** .84   **f.** .52
3.11 a. $\frac{2}{9}$ **b.** $\frac{8}{9}$ **3.12 a.** .039   **b.** .016   **c.** .269   **3.13 a.** .974   **b.** .12   **3.14 a.** $\frac{4}{9}$ **b.** $\frac{9}{18}$ **c.** $\frac{9}{18}$
3.15 a. .111   **b.** .125   **3.16 a.** .046   **b.** .644   **c.** .729   **3.17** .559   **3.18 a.** $\frac{6}{60}$ **b.** $\frac{9}{40}$ **3.19** .00001   **3.20** .035
3.21 a. .120   **b.** .473   **3.22 a.** .122   **b.** .719   **c.** .682
3.23 a. .85   **b.** .40   **c.** (0, 0), (0, 50), (0, 100), (0, 500), (0, 1,000), (50, 0), (50, 50), (50, 100), (50, 500), (50, 1,000), (100, 0), (100, 50), (100, 100), (100, 500), (100, 1,000), (500, 0), (500, 50), (500, 100), (500, 500), (500, 1,000), (1,000, 0), (1,000, 50), (1,000, 100), (1,000, 500), (1,000, 1,000)   **d.** .36, .06, .09, .06, .03, .06, .01, .015, .01, .005, .09, .015, .0225, .015, .0075, .06, .01, .015, .01, .005, .03, .005, .0075, .005, .0025   **e.** .64
3.24 a. (A, B) and (A, C)   **b.** (B, C)   **3.25 a.** .0256   **b.** .418   **c.** Independent events   **3.26 a.** .008   **b.** $1 - .8^k$
3.27 a. .01099   **b.** .000000001   **3.28** .005   **3.29 a.** .97   **b.** .04   **c.** No   **3.32** Engineer 3   **3.33** .517
3.34 .6982   **3.35** .236, .194, .570   **3.36 a.** S_4 **b.** S_4 or S_6
3.37 a. 9   **b.** OO, OM, OP, MO, MM, MP, PO, PM, PP   **c.** 126
3.38 a. 10   **b.** (1, open), (1, closed), (2, open), (2, closed), (3, open), (3, closed), (4, open), (4, closed), (5, open), (5, closed)   **c.** 20
3.39 a. 16   **b.** 24   **3.40 a.** 720   **b.** 1,000   **3.41 a.** 729   **b.** 120   **3.42** 15,504   **3.43 a.** 168   **b.** $\frac{8}{168}$ **c.** $\frac{2}{7}$
3.44 63,063,000   **3.45 a.** 13,983,816; .0000000715   **b.** 7   **c.** .0000005; yes   **d.** .0000000715   **3.46** $\frac{48}{2,598,960}$
3.47 a. $\frac{64}{1,326}$ **b.** .0465   **3.48** Yes   **3.49** Probably understand, since P(At least one defective) $= .039$ if claim is true
3.50 Yes   **3.51 a.** Probably not, since P(3 misses) $= .166$ if $p = .45$ **b.** Yes, since P(10 misses) $= .0025$ if $p = .45$
3.52 a. $\frac{3}{10}$ **b.** No   **3.53 a.** $\frac{181}{387}$ **b.** $\frac{79}{387}$ **c.** $\frac{8}{387}$ **d.** $\frac{218}{387}$ **e.** $\frac{38}{65}$ **f.** $\frac{20}{78}$ **g.** No   **3.54 a.** 16   **b.** $\frac{1}{16}$ **c.** Yes
3.55 a. 1,440   **b.** 240   **3.56 a.** 30   **b.** 20   **d.** $\frac{1}{20}$ **e.** $\frac{10}{20}$

3.57 a. .15 b. .80 c. .60 d. None are mutually exclusive.   3.58 16   3.59 a. .06 b. .94   3.60 $\frac{1}{8,000}$ = .000125
3.61 .891   3.62 a. .75 b. .13 c. .85 d. .81   3.63 26   3.64 a. .0116 b. .87   3.65 Company A
3.66 a. $\frac{24}{36}$ b. .116 c. $\frac{6}{36}$ 3.67 a. 60 b. $\frac{3}{5}$ c. $\frac{3}{10}$ 3.68 a. 60 b. 54
3.69 a. .0019808 b. .00394 c. .0000154   3.70 a. 1.000 b. .9744   3.71 .01782

Chapter 4

4.1 a. Yes c. .15 d. .75   4.2 a.

y	0	1	2	3
$p(y)$	$\frac{1}{8}$	$\frac{3}{8}$	$\frac{3}{8}$	$\frac{1}{8}$

b. 7/8

4.3

y	0	1	2
$p(y)$	$\frac{6}{66}$	$\frac{32}{66}$	$\frac{28}{66}$

4.4

y	0	1	2	3
$p(y)$	.004096	.064512	.338688	.592704

4.5

y	1	2	3
$p(y)$	$\frac{3}{5}$	$\frac{3}{10}$	$\frac{1}{10}$

4.6

y	0	1	2	3
$p(y)$	$\frac{10}{28}$	$\frac{15}{28}$	$\frac{3}{28}$	0

4.7 a.

y	1	2	3	4	5	6	$\cdots$
$p(y)$	.4800	.2496	.1298	.0675	.0351	.0182	$\cdots$

b. $(.48)(.52)^{y-1}$

4.8 $\mu = 10.15$, $\sigma^2 = 3.1275$ 4.9 $\mu = 1.5$, $\sigma^2 = .75$ 4.10 $\mu = 1.333$, $\sigma^2 = .404$
4.11 $E(y) = 63,000$; $\sigma^2 = 61,321,000,000$ 4.12 $\mu = 2.52$; $\sigma^2 = .4032$ 4.13 .29
4.14 a. $300 b. 18,000 c. $31.67 to $568.33   4.15 $\mu = \$152,250$; $\sigma^2 = 703,687,500$ 4.18 $\mu = \$350$; $\sigma^2 = 4,500$
4.22 $p(0) = \frac{1}{16}$, $p(1) = \frac{1}{4}$, $p(2) = \frac{3}{8}$, $p(3) = \frac{1}{4}$, $p(4) = \frac{1}{16}$ 4.24 a. .0013 b. 0 c. $\mu = 17.5$, $\sigma = 2.29$
4.25 .9957   4.26 a. .9997 b. 0 c. Possibly ($\mu = 190$)   4.27 a. .064 b. .432 c. .648
4.28 b. .1937 c. .9984 d. $\mu = 9$, $\sigma^2 = .9$ 4.29 a. .1719   4.30 a. .4978714; .3793306 b. .0004267; .0003553
4.31 a. $\mu = .0389$; $\sigma^2 = .0388985$ b. No   4.32 a. .8385 b. .002   4.35 $npq + \mu^2$
4.37 a. .024 b. .03125 c. .15   4.38 $\mu_1 = 1$, $\sigma_1^2 = .8$; $\mu_2 = 2.5$, $\sigma_2^2 = 1.25$; $\mu_3 = 1.5$, $\sigma_3^2 = 1.05$
4.39 a. .0319 b. .0337 c. 5.2   4.40 b. $p_i = .2$ c. 5.94×10^{-13} 4.41 a. .0654 b. 3.0; 2.1
4.42 a. .0033067 b. 4 c. 4 ± 3.58 4.43 $E(C) = n(4p_1 + p_2)$
4.44 a. .25, .25, .25, .25 b. .00104   4.46 a. .064 b. .1875 c. .12288

4.47 a.

y	6	7	8	9
$p(y)$	.13824	.08294	.04645	.02477

c. $\mu = 2$, $\sigma = 1.83$ d. .9502

4.48 a.

y	1	2	3	4	5
$p(y)$	.7	.21	.063	.0189	.00567

c. $\mu = 1.43$, $\sigma = .78$ d. .91

4.49 a. .113 b. .792 c. .208   4.50 a. 63 b. 62.5 c. (0, 188)   4.51 a. $\mu = 2.083$, $\sigma = 1.502$ b. (0, 5.087)
4.52 .8165   4.53 a. .657 b. $\mu = 3.33$, $\sigma = 2.79$ c. No; $y = 10$ falls outside the interval $(\mu - 2\sigma, \mu + 2\sigma)$. d. .671
4.54 a. .0000374 b. $\mu = 25,706.9$, $\sigma^2 = 660,821,102.2$
c. No; $y = 100,000$ falls outside the interval $(\mu - 2\sigma, \mu + 2\sigma)$.

4.56 a.

y	3	4	5	6	7
$p(y)$	.071	.354	.424	.141	.010

b. 0 c. .575 d. $\mu = 4.67$, $\sigma = .841$ e. (2.99, 6.35) f. .99
4.57 a. 0 b. $\frac{1}{12}$ c. $\frac{1}{3}$ d. $\frac{1}{6}$ 4.58 a. .3 b. 1   4.59 a. .0022 b. .516   4.60 .467   4.61 a. $\frac{4}{7}$ b. $\frac{4}{35}$
4.62 a. .399 b. .009 c. .601   4.63 a. .197 b. .112 c. .038
4.65 b. $\mu = 5.5$, $\sigma = 2.35$; interval is (.80, 10.20) c. .970   4.66 a. .677 b. .034 c. .950 d. .000123
4.67 a. .2052 b. .5438 c. No ($z = 2.85$)   4.68 a. $\mu = 1.57$, $\sigma = 1.25$ b. .2089
4.69 a. .08 b. Yes, since $P(y > 3) = .019$ 4.70 a. .349 b. .0303 c. 4.24; (9.51, 26.49)
4.71 a. .0081 b. $\mu > 4$ 4.72 90 ± 18.97
4.73 a. $\mu = 15$, $\sigma = 3.87$ b. Approx. 0, since $y = 27$ falls outside the interval $(\mu - 3\sigma, \mu + 3\sigma)$

c. No; probability will be smaller

4.74 a. .9596   **b.** .7127   **c.** .00136   **d.** .5   **4.80 a.** .189   **b.** Approx. 0   **c.** $p < .95$

4.81 a. $E(\text{Loss}) = \$2,450$ for each firm   **b.** Firm A: $\$661.44$, firm B: $\$701.78$; firm B   **c.** Pure risk

4.82 a. $\sigma = 2$ **b.** No; probability is .003

4.83 a. .358   **b.** .736   **c.** .736   **d.** .264   **e.** Improbable that $y \ge 3$ if claim is valid

4.84 a. .10   **b.** .70   **4.85 a.** .001   **b.** .623   **c.** .999   **4.86 a.** .0005063   **b.** Success rate $< .85$

4.87 a. .7763   **b.** .1118   **4.88 a.** .0055   **b.** $\mu = 15$, $\sigma^2 = 12.75$; $(7.86, 22.14)$

4.89 a.

x	$-100,000$	$-70,000$	$-40,000$	$-20,000$	$10,000$	$60,000$
$p(x)$	.36	.12	.01	.18	.03	.0225

x	$380,000$	$410,000$	$460,000$	$860,000$	$900,000$	$930,000$
$p(x)$	.12	.02	.03	.01	.06	.01

x	$980,000$	$1,380,000$	$1,900,000$
$p(x)$	.015	.01	.0025

b. $E(x) = 126,000$; $\text{Var}(x) = 122,642,000,000$ **c.** .2775   **d.** .36   **4.90 a.** .2399   **b.** .6801   **c.** .9999

4.91 a. $p(y) = (.001)(.999)^{y-1}$ **b.** .995   **c.** Claim probably not valid   **4.92 a.** .0778   **b.** .6826   **c.** .0102

4.93 a. .402   **b.** .161   **4.94 a.** .10   **b.** .074   **4.95** .263

4.96 a. .049   **b.** .0956   **c.** .1399   **d.** .1821   **e.** $p = .01$ does not change; not likely   **4.97 a.** .251   **b.** .558   **c.** .011

4.98 a. $\frac{11}{5}$ **b.** $\frac{14}{25}$ **4.100 a.** $e^{\lambda(t-1)}$

Chapter 5

5.1 a. $c = \frac{3}{8}$ **b.** $F(y) = \frac{y^3}{8}$ **c.** $\frac{1}{8}$ **d.** .0156   **e.** .2969   **5.2 a.** $c = \frac{2}{3}$ **b.** $F(y) = \dfrac{(4y - y^2)}{3}$ **c.** .48   **d.** .55

5.3 a. $c = 1$ **b.** $F(y) = 1 - e^{-y}$ **c.** .9257   **e.** .3611

5.4 a. 4   **b.** $F(y) = \begin{cases} \frac{1}{2}e^{y/2}, & y < 0 \\ 1 - \frac{1}{2}e^{-y/2}, & y \ge 0 \end{cases}$ **c.** .6967   **d.** .3894

5.5 a. 1   **b.** $F(y) = \begin{cases} \dfrac{(y + 1)^2}{2}, & y < 0 \\ \dfrac{[y(2 - y) + 1]}{2}, & y > 0 \end{cases}$ **c.** .125   **d.** .375

5.6 a. $F(y) = \dfrac{y^2}{4}$, $0 < y < 2$ **b.** $F(y)$ is NBU   **5.7** $\mu = 1.5$, $\sigma^2 = .15$, $\sigma = .387$; .952

5.8 $\mu = .444$, $\sigma^2 = .080247$, $\sigma = .283$; 1.0   **5.9** $\mu = 1$, $\sigma^2 = 1$, $\sigma = 1$; .950   **5.10.** $\mu = 0$, $\sigma^2 = 8$; .941

5.11 $\mu = 0$, $\sigma^2 = \frac{1}{6}$; .966   **5.12 a.** $\mu = 0$, $\sigma^2 = 5$ **b.** $\mu = 0$, $\sigma^2 = .0014$ **c.** $\mu = 0$, $\sigma^2 = 18,000$

5.13 b. μ **c.** $\dfrac{c^2}{6}$ **5.16 a.** $\mu = .5$, $\sigma^2 = .083$ **b.** .2   **c.** No

5.17 a. $\mu = 1.375$, $\sigma^2 = .2552$, $\sigma = .51$ **b.** 1.0   **c.** .286   **5.18 a.** $\mu = 1.2d$, $\sigma = .46d$ **b.** $\frac{3}{8}$

5.19 a. $\mu = 7$, $\sigma = .29$ **b.** .3   **5.20 b.** $a + (b - a)y$

5.24 a. .2417   **b.** .3496   **c.** .5336   **d.** .3936   **e.** .0918   **f.** .9564

5.25 a. 1.645   **b.** 1.96   **c.** $-.84$ **d.** -3.01 **e.** 1.88   **f.** .15   **5.26 a.** .7176   **b.** No; $z = -3.85$

5.27 a. .0694   **b.** .4402   **5.28 a.** .0228   **b.** .0808   **c.** 1,200   **5.29 a.** .9406   **b.** .0068   **5.30** .8%

5.31 a. New compact tube   **b.** Standard compact tube   **5.32 a.** .0139   **b.** .2417   **c.** 278

5.33 a. .9671   **b.** .2611   **c.** No   **5.35** $\text{IQR}/s = 1.3$ **5.36** $\text{IQR}/s = 1.59$ **5.37** No

5.38 Old: $\text{IQR}/s = .46$, no; New: $\text{IQR}/s = 1.27$, yes   **5.39** All but SCORE   **5.40** Yes, $\text{IQR}/s = 1.295$ **5.41** $c = \frac{1}{16}$

5.42 a. $\mu = .21$, $\sigma^2 = .0147$ **b.** No, since $y = .60$ is larger than $\mu + 3\sigma$; either the values of α and β have changed or the 1982–1985 distribution no longer is approximated by the gamma.

5.43 a. $\mu = 1,000$, $\sigma^2 = 1,000,000$ **b.** .135 **c.** .777 **5.44 a.** .3679 **b.** .6065 **c.** .1353 **d.** .0041

5.45 a. .082 **b.** Suspect that $\beta > 24$ **5.46 a.** $\mu_A = 4$, $\mu_B = 4$ **b.** $\sigma_A^2 = 8$, $\sigma_B^2 = 16$ **c.** Formula B

5.47 a. .1353 **b.** .9817 **5.52** $\mu = \nu$, $\sigma^2 = 2\nu$

5.53

y	2	5	8	11	14	17
$f(y)$	.03843	.07788	.08437	.06560	.03944	.018896

5.54 $\sigma^2 = 21.46$; .3172 **5.55 a.** .9981 **b.** .4449 **c.** $\mu = 2.866$, $\sigma = .8042$ **d.** .9571

5.56 a. .6321 **b.** $\mu = 1.77246$, $\sigma = .92649$ **c.** .9626 **d.** No; $P(y > 6) = .0001234$

5.57 a. $\mu = 5.65$, $\sigma^2 = 31.9225$ **b.** .6542 **c.** .1703 **5.58** 1.75 months

5.59 a. $.88623\sqrt{\beta}$ **b.** $(.2146)\beta$ **c.** $e^{-c^2/\beta}$ **5.63** $c = 168$ **5.64 a.** $\mu = \frac{2}{11}$, $\sigma^2 = \frac{3}{242}$ **b.** .046 **c.** .264

5.65 a. $\mu = .0385$, $\sigma^2 = .00137$ **b.** .778 **5.66 a.** $\mu = \frac{1}{2}$, $\sigma^2 = \frac{1}{20}$ **b.** .028 **5.67 a.** .834 **b.** .006

5.74 a. $(1 + t)^{-1}$ **b.** $\mu = -1$, $\sigma^2 = 1$ **5.75 a.** $c = 2$ **b.** $F(y) = 1 - e^{-y^2}$ **c.** .00193

5.76 a. $\mu = 5$, $\sigma^2 = \frac{25}{3}$ **b.** .3 **5.77 a.** .3935 **b.** .0240 **c.** .0498

5.78 a. .0918 **b.** 0 **c.** Lowered 4.87 decibels (to 95.13)

5.79 a. .5507 **b.** .2636 **c.** $\mu = 60$, $\sigma^2 = 1,800$ **d.** .0916

5.80 a. $\mu = .1923$, $\sigma^2 = .0058$ **b.** .090 **c.** .007 **5.81 a.** .321 **b.** .105 **5.82 a.** Approx. 0 **b.** No **5.83** $\frac{1}{6}$

5.84 a. $\sigma = 10$ **b.** .753 **c.** .135 **5.85 a.** $\alpha = 9$, $\beta = 2$ **b.** $\mu = .818$, $\sigma^2 = .0124$ **c.** .624

5.86 a. $\alpha = 2$, $\beta = 16$ **b.** $\mu = 3.545$, $\sigma^2 = 3.434$ **c.** .1054 **5.87** .3935

Chapter 6

6.1 b.

x	0	1	2	3	4	5
$p_1(x)$	.300	.100	.025	.300	.125	.150

c.

y	0	1	2
$p_2(y)$	.10	.55	.35

d.

x	0	1	2	3	4	5
$p_1(x \mid 0)$	0	.50	.25	0	.25	0

x	0	1	2	3	4	5
$p_1(x \mid 1)$	.364	.091	0	.545	0	0

x	0	1	2	3	4	5
$p_1(x \mid 2)$	.286	0	0	0	.286	.429

e.

y	0	1	2
$p_2(y \mid 0)$	0	.667	.333

y	0	1	2
$p_2(y \mid 1)$	.5	.5	0

y	0	1	2
$p_2(y \mid 2)$	1	0	0

y	0	1	2
$p_2(y \mid 3)$	0	1	0

y	0	1	2
$p_2(y \mid 4)$	.2	0	.8

y	0	1	2
$p_2(y \mid 5)$	0	0	1

6.2 a. $p(x, y) = \frac{1}{36}$ $(x = 1, 2, \ldots, 6; y = 1, 2, \ldots, 6)$ **b.** $p_1(x) = \frac{1}{6}$ $(x = 1, 2, \ldots, 6)$; $p_2(y) = \frac{1}{6}$ $(y = 1, 2, \ldots, 6)$ **c.** $p(x \mid y) = \frac{1}{6}$ $(x = 1, 2, \ldots, 6; y = 1, 2, \ldots, 6)$; $p(y \mid x) = \frac{1}{6}$ $(y = 1, 2, \ldots, 6; x = 1, 2, \ldots, 6)$; **d.** x and y are independent

6.3 a.

		x		
		0	1	2
	0	0	0	$\frac{3}{28}$
y	1	0	$\frac{6}{28}$	$\frac{9}{28}$
	2	$\frac{1}{28}$	$\frac{6}{28}$	$\frac{3}{28}$

b.

y	0	1	2
$p_2(y)$	$\frac{3}{28}$	$\frac{15}{28}$	$\frac{10}{28}$

c.

x	0	1	2
$p_1(x \mid 0)$	0	0	1
$p_1(x \mid 1)$	0	$\frac{6}{15}$	$\frac{9}{15}$
$p_1(x \mid 2)$	$\frac{1}{10}$	$\frac{6}{10}$	$\frac{3}{10}$

6.5 a.

y	0	1	2	3
$p_2(y)$	.11	.25	.40	.24

b.

y	0	1	2	3
$p_2(y_2 \mid 2)$	.175	.250	.375	.200

6.6 a.

		x			
		0	1	2	3
	0	0	$\frac{3}{35}$	$\frac{6}{35}$	$\frac{1}{35}$
y	1	$\frac{2}{35}$	$\frac{12}{35}$	$\frac{6}{35}$	0
	2	$\frac{2}{35}$	$\frac{3}{35}$	0	0

b.

x	0	1	2	3
$p_1(x)$	$\frac{4}{35}$	$\frac{18}{35}$	$\frac{12}{35}$	$\frac{1}{35}$

6.8 a. $c = -1$ **b.** $f_2(y) = \frac{3}{2} - y$ **c.** $f_1(x \mid y) = \dfrac{x - y}{\frac{3}{2} - y}$

6.9 a. $c = 4$ **b.** $f_1(x) = 2x; f_2(y) = 2y$ **c.** $f_1(x \mid y) = 2x; f_2(y \mid x) = 2y$

6.10 a. $c = 2$ **b.** $f_1(x) = 2xe^{-x^2}$ **c.** $f_2(y \mid x) = \dfrac{1}{x}(0 \le y \le x)$ **6.11 b.** .4624

6.13 a. $c = 1$ **b.** $f_1(x) = e^{-x}$ **c.** $f_2(y) = e^{-y}$ **d.** $f_1(x \mid y) = e^{-x}$ **e** $f_2(y \mid x) = e^{-y}$ **f.** .399 **6.14 a.** 1.5 **b.** 1.25
6.15 a. 1.69 **b.** 3.46 **6.16 a.** 0 **b.** 2 **6.17 a.** $\frac{19}{12}$ **b.** $\frac{5}{12}$ **c.** 2 **d.** $\frac{2}{3}$ **6.18 a.** 1 **b.** 1 **c.** 2 **d.** 1 **6.22** No
6.23 Yes **6.24** No **6.25** Yes **6.26** No **6.27** Yes **6.28 a.** $f(x, y) = \frac{1}{25}e^{-(x+y)/5}$ **b.** 10 **6.32** .375 **6.33** 0
6.34 $-.447$ **6.35 b.** $-.0366$ **6.36 a.** $\frac{1}{144}$ **b.** $\frac{1}{11}$ **6.37 a.** 0 **b** 0 **6.38** $-\frac{1}{5}$ **6.42** 0
6.43 $E(\ell) = 11, V(\ell) = 54.5$ **6.44** $E(\ell) = -4, V(\ell) = 256$ **6.45** $E(x + y) = 7, V(x + y) = 5.83$
6.46 1.6484, 3.46 ± 3.2968 **6.47** $\frac{1}{9}$ **6.48** $E(\hat{p}) = p, V(\hat{p}) = pq/n$

6.50 a.

x	0	10	20	30	40	50	60	70	80	90
$p_1(x)$	.006	.010	.019	.135	.220	.235	.130	.118	.071	.056

y	1	2	3	4	5
$p_2(y)$	.105	.405	.355	.058	.077

b.

x	0	10	20	30	40	50	60	70	80	90
$p_1(x \mid 1)$	.0095	.0190	.0190	.2381	.3810	.2381	.0476	.0476	0	0

x	0	10	20	30	40	50	60	70	80	90
$p_1(x \mid 2)$	.0123	.0123	.0247	.1852	.2469	.1852	.1234	.0741	.0741	.0617

x	0	10	20	30	40	50	60	70	80	90
$p_1(x \mid 3)$	0	0	0	.0704	.1408	.2254	.1408	.2254	.1127	.0845

x	0	10	20	30	40	50	60	70	80	90
$p_1(x \mid 4)$	0	.0172	.0345	.0862	.1724	.4310	.1724	.0517	.0172	.0172

x	0	10	20	30	40	50	60	70	80	90
$p_1(x \mid 5)$	0	.0260	.0649	.0649	.2597	.3896	.1948	0	0	0

c. .9296 **d.** 2.597 **e.** Yes; no **f.** Mean = \$1,296,500, standard deviation = \$457,124

6.51 a. $f_1(x) = x + \frac{1}{2}; f_2(y) = y + \frac{1}{2}$ **c.** $f_1(x \mid y) = \dfrac{x + y}{y + \frac{1}{2}}; f_2(y \mid x) = \dfrac{x + y}{x + \frac{1}{2}}$ **e** Yes; no
f. $E(d) = \frac{5}{12}, V(d) = \frac{5}{144}; .42 ± .559$
6.52 a. .17 **b.** $\frac{3}{17}$ **c.** Yes **d.** No **6.55 a.** $c = \frac{1}{3}$ **b.** No

Chapter 7

7.5 During the Depression, only the wealthy could afford telephone service; thus, sample was not random

7.7 a. $f(w) = 1 \quad (0 \le w \le 1)$ **b.** $f(w) = \dfrac{w + 1}{2} \quad (-1 \le w \le 1)$ **c.** $f(w) = \dfrac{2}{w^3} \quad (1 \le w \le \infty)$

7.8 a. $f(w) = e^3 \quad (0 \le w \le e^{-3})$ **b.** $f(w) = -e^{-w} \quad (0 \le w \le \infty)$ **c.** $f(w) = 3e^{-3(w-1)} \quad (1 \le w \le \infty)$

7.9 $f(c) = \left(\frac{1}{15}\right)e^{-(c-2)/15}$ $(c \geq 2)$ **7.10** $f(a) = \begin{cases} \frac{1}{5} & \text{if } 0 \leq a \leq \frac{5}{2} \\ \frac{1}{10} & \text{if } \frac{5}{2} \leq a \leq \frac{15}{2} \end{cases}$ **7.11** $f(w) = \left(\frac{1}{2}\mu\right)e^{-w/2\mu}$; exponential with $\beta = 2\mu$

7.12 $y = \ln(w)$, where w is uniform on the interval $0 \leq w \leq 1$

7.13 $y = \sqrt{w}$, where w is uniform on the interval $0 \leq w \leq 1$ **7.14** $f(w) = e^{-w}$ $(0 < w < \infty)$

7.16 a. Approx. normal with $\mu_{\bar{y}_{25}} = 17$ and $\sigma_{\bar{y}_{25}} = 2$; approx. normal with $\mu_{\bar{y}_{100}} = 17$ and $\sigma_{\bar{y}_{100}} = 1$ **c.** .6826, .9544

7.17 a. $\mu_{\bar{y}} = 293$, $\sigma_{\bar{y}} = 119.8$ **c.** .0158   **7.18 a.** Approx. normal with $\mu_{\bar{y}} = 15$ and $\sigma_{\bar{y}} = 1.12$ **b.** ≈ 0

7.19 a. Approx. normal with $\mu_{\bar{y}} = -7.02$ and $\sigma_{\bar{y}} = 3.487$ **b.** .9778   **c.** $z = -3.10$ **7.20 a.** .0043   **b.** .6065

7.21 a. Approx. normal with $\mu_{\bar{y}} = 51$ and $\sigma_{\bar{y}} = 2.09$ **b.** .3156   **c.** .1694   **7.22 a.** ≈ 0 **b.** $\mu > 1,700$

7.23 a. $\mu_{\bar{y}} = 60$, $\sigma_{\bar{y}}^2 = 36$ **b.** Normal   **c.** ≈ 0 **7.24** .9966   **7.26 b.** .9544   **7.27 a.** .985   **b.** .9878

7.28 a. .0015   **b.** 1271   **c.** .001; .128; yes   **7.29 a.** Approx. 0   **b.** .0094   **7.30 a.** ≈ 0 **b.** .5871   **7.31** .9951

7.32 .8186   **7.33 a.** .0262   **b.** .0125   **c.** .2266   **7.34 a.** $\approx .10$ **b.** $\approx .005$ **c.** $\approx .01$

7.35 a. Chi-square with 29 df   **b.** .05

7.40 a. $f(w) = 6w^5$ $(0 < w < 1)$ **b.** $f(w) = 3(3 - w)^2$ $(2 < w < 3)$ **c.** $f(w) = -3e^{3w}$ $(0 < w < \infty)$

7.41 $f(w) = \begin{cases} (w + 2)/200 & \text{if } -2 \leq w \leq 8 \\ \frac{1}{20} & \text{if } 8 \leq w \leq 23 \end{cases}$

7.42 a. $\mu_{\bar{y}} = .000005$, $\sigma_{\bar{y}} = .00000028$ **b.** .1446

7.43 a. Approx. normal with $\mu_{\bar{y}} = 121.74$ and $\sigma_{\bar{y}} = 4.86$ **b.** .7348

7.44 $< .005$ **7.45** $y = \sqrt{-\ln(1 - w)}$ **7.46** $y = 1 + \sqrt{w}$

7.47 a. .0233   **b.** Strong evidence that $\mu < 9.2$ **7.48 a.** .4514   **b.** .0082   **7.49** .008

7.50 a. Approx. normal with $\mu_{\bar{y}} = 1,312$ and $\sigma_{\bar{y}} = 42.2$ **b.** .006   **c.** Most likely $\mu > 1,312$

7.51 a. Chi-square with 99 df   **b.** Between .004 and .01   **7.52** .5211   **7.55** $f(w) = (1/\beta)e^{-w/\beta}$ $(w > 0)$; exponential

Chapter 8

8.1 b. $\hat{\theta}_1$ **8.2 a.** $\hat{\lambda}_1$ and $\hat{\lambda}_3$ **b.** $\hat{\lambda}_1$ **8.3 b.** $\dfrac{pq}{n}$ **8.4 c.** $\dfrac{\beta^2}{(2n)}$ **8.6 a.** $B = 1 - \dfrac{\theta}{2}$ **c.** $\dfrac{(\theta - 2)^2}{3}$

8.8 a. $\dfrac{y}{n}$ **b.** Yes   **c.** $\dfrac{y}{n}$ **d.** Yes   **8.9 a.** $\bar{y}$ **b.** Yes   **8.10 a.** $\dfrac{\bar{y}}{2}$ **b.** $E(\hat{\beta}) = \beta$, $V(\hat{\beta}) = \dfrac{\beta^2}{2n}$

8.11 a. $\dfrac{\bar{y}}{2}$ **b.** $E(\hat{\beta}) = \beta$, $V(\hat{\beta}) = \dfrac{\beta^2}{(2n)}$ **8.12** $\dfrac{\sum y_i^2}{n}$ **8.13 a.** $\bar{y}$ **b.** Yes   **c.** $\dfrac{\beta^2}{n}$ **8.14 a.** 2.898   **b.** 2.262   **c.** 1.761

8.16 $\hat{p} \pm z_{\alpha/2}\sqrt{\hat{p}\hat{q}/n}$ **8.17** $\bar{y} \pm z_{\alpha/2}\sqrt{\bar{y}/n}$ **8.18** $\bar{y} \pm z_{\alpha/2}\,\bar{y}/\sqrt{n}$ **8.23** $(\bar{y}_1 - \bar{y}_2) \pm t_{\alpha/2}\,s_p\sqrt{1/n_1 + 1/n_2}$

8.24 a. .95   **d.** Sampling rates are normal.

8.25 a. 95% confident that μ falls between 13.6 and 26.4   **b.** 95% of all similarly constructed confidence intervals will contain μ

8.26 a. Late gabbro: $3.04 \pm .036$; Massive gabbro: $2.83 \pm .015$; Cumberlandite: $3.05 \pm .044$

8.27 a. 9.9 ± 4.81 **b.** 6.7 ± 6.19 **8.28 b.** $(.202, 14.69)$ **8.29 c.** Evidence of false claim   **8.30 a.** $.044 \pm .104$

8.31 $.812 \pm .409$ **8.32 a.** -12 ± 25.62 **b.** No evidence of a difference   **8.33** $.2 \pm .066$

8.34 a. $.38 \pm .217$ **b.** No; evidence that $\mu_{\text{old}} > \mu_{\text{new}}$ **8.35** -40 ± 95.12 **8.36 a.** $(-.60, 2.43)$

8.37 a. 35 ± 1.645 **8.38 a.** 436.5 ± 47.61 **b.** $-1.09 \pm .506$ **8.39 a.** -38.9 ± 20.0 **c.** Means differ

8.40 198 ± 41.2 **8.41 a.** $(.638, 1.722)$ **c.** $\mu_R > \mu_U$ **8.42 a.** 5.45 ± 2.49 **b.** Yes

8.43 95% confidence interval for μ_d; $-.87 \pm 1.38$; no evidence of a difference between means   **8.44** $.47 \pm .025$

8.45 $.333 \pm .072$ **8.46 a.** $.257 \pm .003$ **b.** $.241 \pm .003$ **8.47 a.** $.23 \pm .0165$ **b.** $.20 \pm .0156$ **8.48** $.75 \pm .1225$

8.49 a. $.644 \pm .099$ **b.** Yes   **8.50** $.60 \pm .21$ **8.51 a.** $-.35 \pm .09$ **b.** $p_C < p_T$

8.52 a. $.067 \pm .144$ **b.** $-.247 \pm .138$ **8.53** $.147 \pm .069$ **8.54** $.078 \pm .035$ **8.55** $.3 \pm .25$

8.56 a. 14.0671   **b.** 23.5418   **c.** 23.2093   **d.** 17.5346   **e.** 16.7496   **8.57 a.** $(4.73, 9.44)$ **8.58** $(1.617, 3.569)$

8.59 $(.085, 1.140)$ **8.60** $(.0000457, .0003216)$ **8.61 a.** $(.163, 29.141)$ **8.62 a.** 3.18   **b.** 2.62   **c.** 2.10

8.63 a. 2.40   **b.** 3.35   **c.** 1.65   **d.** 5.86   **8.64** 95% confidence interval: $(1.19, 94.36)$ **8.65** $(1.53, 3.64)$; yes

8.66 **a.** (4.95, 11.59)   8.67 (.28, 4.57); yes   8.68 **a.** (.040, 1.63)   8.69 66   8.70 353   8.71 **a.** 722   **b.** 174
8.72 $n_1 = n_2 = 195$ 8.73 1,729   8.74 2,401   8.76 **a.** 84.84   **b.** 84.84 ± 4.03 **c.** .95
8.77 **a.** (.436, 17.81)   **b.** No evidence of a difference   8.78 -16 ± 11.58; drive 2   8.79 574
8.80 New York: $.262 \pm .0084$, Wisconsin: $.15 \pm .026$, Maine: $.661 \pm .0833$, Florida: $.005 \pm .0048$, Virginia: $.224 \pm$
.0937   8.81 (.0028, .0105)   8.82 1.375 ± 2.570 8.83 193
8.84 **a.** $.33 \pm .027$ **b.** Increase sample sizes or decrease confidence coefficient.   8.85 **a.** -4.8 ± 5.0 **c.** No   **d.** 74
8.86 **b.** $\frac{\lambda_1}{n_1} + \frac{\lambda_2}{n_2}$; $+ \frac{\bar{y}_1}{n_1} + \frac{\bar{y}_2}{n_2}$ **c.** $(\bar{y}_1 - \bar{y}_2) \pm z_{\alpha/2}\sqrt{\bar{y}_1/n_1 + \bar{y}_2/n_2}$ 8.87 **a.** Bias $= \frac{1}{2}$ **b.** $\frac{1}{12n}$ **c.** $\bar{y} - \frac{1}{2}$

8.88 $\dfrac{y^2}{\chi^2_{\alpha/2}} < \sigma^2 < \dfrac{y^2}{\chi^2_{(1-\alpha/2)}}$ 8.89 $\dfrac{2y}{\chi^2_{\alpha/2}} < \beta < \dfrac{2y}{\chi^2_{(1-\alpha/2)}}$ 8.90 $y \pm 1.96$ 8.92 LCL $= \dfrac{y}{.95}$

Chapter 9

9.1 $\alpha = P(\text{Reject } H_0 \mid H_0 \text{ true})$; $\beta = P(\text{Accept } H_0 \mid H_0 \text{ false})$
9.2 **a.** $\alpha = P(\text{Reject } H_0 \text{ when } H_0 \text{ true})$ **b.** $\beta \neq 0$ **c.** If true, $P(\text{error}) = 1$ 9.3 **a.** Type II   **b.** Type I
9.4 **a.** .032   **b.** .370   **c.** .132   **d.** .006   **e.** Type I: $y \geq 8$; Type II: $y \leq 5$ **f.** $y \geq 9$ **g.** .404   **h.** .995
9.5 **a.** .033   **b.** .617   **c.** .029   9.10 H_0: $p = .5$, H_a: $p > .5$ 9.11 H_0: $\mu = 22$, H_a: $\mu < 22$
9.12 H_0: $p = \frac{1}{6}$, H_a: $p \neq \frac{1}{6}$
9.13 H_0: $(\mu_1 - \mu_2) = 0$, H_a: $(\mu_1 - \mu_2) > 0$, where μ_1 is mean rating of vendor's product and μ_2 is mean rating of rival
vendor's product
9.14 H_0: $\mu = 4$, H_a: $\mu > 4$ 9.15 H_0: $(\mu_1 - \mu_2) = 0$, H_a: $(\mu_1 - \mu_2) \neq 0$ 9.16 $t = -3.89$, reject H_0
9.17 $t = -1.39$; do not reject H_0 9.18 **a.** $z = .70$; do not reject H_0 **b.** Yes   9.19 Yes; $z = 9.90$
9.20 **a.** No; $z = 1.41$ **b.** Small   9.21 $z = .87$, do not reject H_0 9.22 $z = -1.70$, reject H_0 9.23 Yes; $t = 1.64$
9.24 .5871; .4129   9.25 **a.** $.90 < \beta < .95$ **b.** $.05 < \text{power} < .10$ 9.27 **a.** .025   **b.** .05   **c.** .0038   **d.** .1056
9.28 **a.** .3124   **b.** .0178   **c.** Approx. 0   **d.** .1470   9.29 ≈ 0
9.30 **a.** $p < .0005$ **b.** $p > .10$ **c.** .242   **d.** ≈ 0 **e.** .0793   9.31 .0758; yes
9.32 **a.** H_0: $\mu_1 - \mu_2 = 0$, H_a: $\mu_1 - \mu_2 > 0$ **b.** $z > 1.645$ **c.** Reject H_0
9.34 **a.** Test H_0: $(\mu_S - \mu_N) = 0$ vs. H_a: $(\mu_S - \mu_N) \neq 0$ **b.** Both populations normal, $\sigma_S^2 = \sigma_N^2$ **c.** No
d. Do not reject H_0
9.35 $t = -2.05$, do not reject H_0 9.36 Yes; $z = 3.54$
9.37 **a.** $t = -.0187$; do not reject H_0 **b.** $t = -.019$; do not reject H_0
9.38 **a.** No, p-value $= .50$ **b.** Both populations normal, $\sigma_E^2 = \sigma_G^2$.
c. Data appear to be nonnormal; inference may be invalid
9.39 Yes; $z = 11.14$ 9.40 $t = -2.63$; reject H_0 at $\alpha = .05$ 9.41 $t = 3.70$; reject H_0 9.42 $t = -7.40$; reject H_0
9.43 No, $p = .65$ 9.44 Reject H_0; $p = .0001$ 9.45 $z = 1.33$; reject H_0 9.46 $z = -3.28$; reject H_0
9.47 Yes; $z = 2.84$ 9.48 $z = 21.63$; reject H_0 9.49 Yes; $z = -2.0$ 9.50 $z = 1.83$; reject H_0 9.51 Yes; $z = -2.74$
9.52 $z = 1.21$; do not reject H_0 9.53 No; $z = -2.30$ 9.54 $z = 3.27$; reject H_0 9.55 **a.** Yes; $z = 1.96$ **b.** No
9.56 Yes; $z = -2.40$ 9.57 $z = 2.51$; reject H_0 9.58 $\chi^2 = 21.95$; reject H_0 at $\alpha = .05$
9.59 **a.** H_0: $\sigma^2 = .54$, H_a: $\sigma^2 > .54$ **b.** .7425   **c.** $\chi^2 = 40.8$; do not reject H_0 9.60 Yes; $\chi^2 = 688$
9.61 **a.** No; $\chi^2 = 6.912$ 9.62 $\chi^2 = 2.97$; no   9.63 $F = 2.47$, do not reject H_0 9.64 $F = 5.87$; reject H_0
9.65 **a.** No; $F = 1.09$ 9.66 Yes; $F = 1.75$ 9.67 $F = 2.03$; do not reject H_0 9.70 $t = 1.93$; reject H_0
9.71 **a.** .066   **b.** .942; .058   **c.** .322; .678   9.72 $F = 10.00$; yes   9.73 **a.** $z = 1.99$; yes   **b.** $z = .15$; no
9.74 $t = 1.54$; do not reject H_0 9.75 **a.** No; $t = -2.20$ **c.** $.1 < \beta < .5$ **d.** $.01 < p$-value $< .025$
9.76 $z = -.97$; no   9.77 $z = .74$; no   9.78 $\chi^2 = 133.9$; yes   9.79 **a.** Yes; $z = -2.52$ **b.** p-value $= .0059$
9.80 Yes; $z = 2.79$ 9.81 No; $F = 1.11$ 9.82 **a.** $t = .193$; no   **b.** p-value $> .2$ 9.83 Yes; $z = 3.54$
9.84 $t = 2.54$; yes

Chapter 10

10.1 **a.** $.083 \pm .041$ **b.** $.405 \pm .073$ **c.** $.174 \pm .116$ **d.** $-.099 \pm .075$ 10.2 **a.** $.302 \pm .029$ **b.** $.037 \pm .052$
10.3 **a.** $.275 \pm .182$ **b.** $.125 \pm .261$ 10.4 $.478 \pm .158$ 10.5 **a.** $.22 \pm .068$ **b.** $-.08 \pm .111$ **c.** $.02 \pm .093$

10.6 p_1: .6 ± .029; p_2: .23 ± .025; p_3: .17 ± .022   **10.8** $\chi^2 = 13.54$, reject H_0 **10.9** $\chi^2 = 2.76$, do not reject H_0
10.10 $\chi^2 = 6.167$; yes   **b.** $z = 2.24$; yes   **10.11** $\chi^2 = 2.6$; do not reject H_0 **10.12** $\chi^2 = 39.27$; reject H_0
10.13 $\chi^2 = 4.4$; no   **10.14** $\chi^2 = 304.5$; reject H_0 **10.16 a.** $\chi^2 > 3.84146$ **b.** $\chi^2 > 15.9871$ **c.** $\chi^2 > 16.8119$

10.17 a. Yes   **b.**

	High/No	High/Fiber	Low/No	Low/Fiber
Yes	20	20	20	20
No	10	10	10	10

c. 12.9   **d.** Yes, reject H_0 **e.** .233 ± .2
10.18 a. Reject H_0; p-value = 0   **b.** $\hat{p}_1 = .070$, $\hat{p}_2 = .041$, $\hat{p}_3 = .072$ **10.19** $\chi^2 = .32$; do not reject H_0
10.20 $\chi^2 = 61.14$; reject H_0 **10.21** $\chi^2 = 1.351$; no

10.22 a.

	High Tech	Non–High Tech
Converters	80.2	296.8
Nonconverters	80.8	299.2

b. .021   **c.** No

10.23 $\chi^2 = 31.87$, reject H_0 **10.24** $\chi^2 = 32.6$; yes   **10.25 a.** $\chi^2 = 4,755$; reject H_0 **b.** .354 ± .012
10.26 a. $\chi^2 = 44.48$; yes   **b.** $z = 4.11$; yes   **c.** .32 ± .109   **10.27** $\chi^2 = 508.74$; yes   **10.28** No; $\chi^2 = 15.859$
10.29 a. White middle: $\chi^2 = 2.74$, do not reject H_0; Black lower-middle: $\chi^2 = 19.04$, reject H_0; Black lower: $\chi^2 = 12.68$, reject H_0 **b.** White middle: .144 ± .206; Black lower-middle: .267 ± .106; Black lower: .351 ± .186
10.30 Yes; $\chi^2 = 14.94$ **10.31** $\chi^2 = 26.452$; reject H_0 **10.32 a.** $\chi^2 = 5.64$; do not reject H_0 **b.** $-.129 ± .145$
10.33 a. $\chi^2 = 14.67$; yes   **b.** $-.169 ± .161$ **10.34 a.** Yes; $\chi^2 = 313.15$ **b.** .181 ± .069   **10.35** $\chi^2 = 7.384$; no
10.36 $\chi^2 = 5.719$; no   **10.37** $\chi^2 = 5.506$; no   **10.38 a.** $\chi^2 = 15.91$; yes   **b.** $z = 3.14$; yes

Chapter 11

11.2 $\beta_0 = 1$, $\beta_1 = 1$; $y = 1 + x$ **11.3 a.** $y = 2 + 2x$ **b.** $y = 4 + x$ **c.** $y = -2 + 4x$ **d.** $y = -4 - x$
11.5 a. $\beta_1 = 2$, $\beta_0 = 3$ **b.** $\beta_1 = 1$, $\beta_0 = 1$ **c.** $\beta_1 = 3$, $\beta_0 = -2$ **d.** $\beta_1 = 5$, $\beta_0 = 0$ **e.** $\beta_1 = -2$, $\beta_0 = 4$
11.6 b. $\hat{y} = -.00105 + .00321x$ **11.7 b.** $\hat{y} = 4.79 + .014x$ **11.8 a.** $\hat{y} = .2134 + 2.4264x$
11.9 a. Yes   **b.** $\hat{y} = 14.175 + .02243x$ **11.10 b.** $\hat{\beta}_0 = -405.25$, $\hat{\beta}_1 = .2185$ **d.** -398.7
11.11 a. Yes   **b.** $\hat{\beta}_0 = 1.192$, $\hat{\beta}_1 = .987$
11.18 a. SSE = .0006805, $s^2 = .0000523$, $s = .0072$ **b.** SSE = 30.768, $s^2 = 2.051$, $s = 1.432$
c. SSE = 4.531, $s^2 = .206$, $s = .454$ **d.** SSE = 40.976, $s^2 = 4.553$, $s = 2.134$
e. SSE = 115.81, $s^2 = 38.6$, $s = 6.21$ **f.** SSE = .251, $s^2 = .050$, $s = .224$
11.19 b. $\hat{y} = -2.095 + .003693x$ **c.** SSE = .02899, $s^2 = .00414$ **d.** .064
11.20 a. $\hat{y} = 9.3134 + 6.91175x$ **d.** SSE = 3.41867, $s^2 = .42733$, $s = .6537$
11.23 a. $\hat{y} = -.1776 + .8991x$; $\hat{y} = 1.0179 + .9753x$ **b.** $t = 11.32$; reject H_0 **c.** $t = 11.32$; reject H_0
11.24 a. Yes, $t = 7.13$ **b.** Yes, $t = 5.98$ **c.** Yes, $t = 4.98$ **d.** 7.07   **e.** 35.86   **f.** 1,390.08
11.25 2.426 ± .473   **11.26** $t = 10.78$; reject H_0 **11.27** $t = 6.91$; reject H_0
11.28 Yes; $t = 44.45$ **11.29** Yes; 6.912 ± 1.082
11.30 b. $\hat{y} = 78.52 - .2389x$ **d.** $t = -2.31$, do not reject H_0 **e.** Observation #5 is an outlier.
f. $\hat{y} = 139.759 - .44969x$; $t = -15.35$, reject H_0
11.31 a. Yes; $t = 3.39$ **b.** .3307 ± .2079
11.35 a. $r = .900$, $r^2 = .81$ **b.** $r = .794$, $r^2 = .630$ **c.** $r = .915$, $r^2 = .837$ **d.** $r = .963$, $r^2 = .928$
e. $r = .885$, $r^2 = .783$ **f.** $r = .951$, $r^2 = .905$
11.36 c. $t = 38.66$, reject H_0 **11.37 a.** $r = .998$, $r^2 = .996$ **b.** Reject H_0; $t = 44.45$; yes
11.38 a. Yes; positive   **b.** .9433   **c.** Yes; $t = 10.63$ **11.39 b.** Reject H_0 **d.** Do not reject H_0
11.40 c. $t = 7.79$, reject H_0
11.41 d. .903   **e.** $t = 20.85$; reject H_0 **f.** 4.58   **11.46 b.** $\hat{\beta}_0 = 9.15$, $\hat{\beta}_1 = .481$ **d.** Yes, $t = 8.07$ **e.** 18.77 ± .51
11.47 4.945 ± 1.306   **11.48 a.** 22.025 ± 4.127   **b.** 22.025 ± 1.319   **d.** Yes; both   **11.49** $-398.7 ± 10.52$
11.50 9.239 ± 1.182   **11.51 a.** $\hat{y} = -.7995 + .93205x$ **b.** Yes; $t = 8.30$ **c.** 15.5113 ± 2.7125
11.56 b. $\hat{y} = -13.622 - .053x$ **d.** Reject H_0: $t = -6.797$ **e.** $-.053 ± .015$ **f.** $r = -.923$ **g.** $r^2 = .852$

h. $.779 \pm .474$ **i.** $.779 \pm .150$

11.57 Model is statistically useful ($p = 0$)   **11.58 b.** Since n is not given, no test can be conducted.

11.59 $\hat{y} = 6.514 + 10.83x$; $t = 6.34$, reject H_0 **11.60 b.** Yes; $t = -4.36$ **c.** $(9{,}598.5, 10{,}442.9)$

11.61 $\hat{y} = -.031 + .317x$; $t = 8.13$, reject H_0

11.62 a. Yes **b.** Yes **d.** 8.29 **e.** 21.15   **11.63 a.** $\hat{y} = -.11238 + .09439x$ **b.** Yes; $t = 11.39$ **c.** $.926 \pm .197$

11.64 a. $\hat{y} = .702 + .353x$ **c.** $r = .9836$, $r^2 = .9675$ **d.** Yes; $t = 10.92$ **e.** 13.05 ± 2.91

11.65 $\hat{y} = 6.735 - .142x$; $t = -5.562$, reject H_0; $r^2 = .7747$; $s = 1.481$

Chapter 12

12.1 a. $Y = \begin{bmatrix} 1 \\ 2 \\ 2 \\ 3 \\ 5 \\ 5 \end{bmatrix}$; $X = \begin{bmatrix} 1 & 1 \\ 1 & 2 \\ 1 & 3 \\ 1 & 4 \\ 1 & 5 \\ 1 & 6 \end{bmatrix}$ **b.** $X'X = \begin{bmatrix} 6 & 21 \\ 21 & 91 \end{bmatrix}$; $X'Y = \begin{bmatrix} 18 \\ 78 \end{bmatrix}$ **d.** $\hat{\boldsymbol{\beta}} = \begin{bmatrix} 0 \\ \frac{6}{7} \end{bmatrix}$ **e.** $\hat{y} = \frac{6}{7}x$

12.2 a. Y is 10×1; X is 10×3 **c.** $\hat{\boldsymbol{\beta}} = \begin{bmatrix} 2.789 \\ .715 \\ -.039 \end{bmatrix}$; $\hat{y} = 2.789 + .715x - .039x^2$

12.3 a. $Y = \begin{bmatrix} 0 \\ 0 \\ 2 \\ 1 \\ 1 \\ 1 \\ 3 \\ 3 \\ 2 \\ 4 \\ 4 \\ 4 \\ 3 \\ 4 \\ 5 \end{bmatrix}$; $X = \begin{bmatrix} 1 & 1 \\ 1 & 2 \\ 1 & 3 \\ 1 & 4 \\ 1 & 5 \\ 1 & 6 \\ 1 & 7 \\ 1 & 8 \\ 1 & 9 \\ 1 & 10 \\ 1 & 11 \\ 1 & 12 \\ 1 & 13 \\ 1 & 14 \\ 1 & 15 \end{bmatrix}$ **b.** $X'X = \begin{bmatrix} 15 & 120 \\ 120 & 1240 \end{bmatrix}$; $X'Y = \begin{bmatrix} 37 \\ 386 \end{bmatrix}$

c. $(X'X)^{-1} = \begin{bmatrix} .29524 & -.02857 \\ -.02857 & .00357 \end{bmatrix}$ $\hat{\boldsymbol{\beta}} = \begin{bmatrix} -.1048 \\ .3214 \end{bmatrix}$ **d.** $\hat{y} = -.1048 + .3214x$

12.4 a. $Y = \begin{bmatrix} .24 \\ .38 \\ .44 \\ .61 \\ .75 \end{bmatrix}$; $X'X = \begin{bmatrix} 1 & 1.0 & 1.00 \\ 1 & 3.5 & 12.25 \\ 1 & 6.0 & 36.00 \\ 1 & 8.5 & 72.25 \\ 1 & 11.0 & 121.00 \end{bmatrix}$ **b.** $X'X = \begin{bmatrix} 5 & 30 & 242.5 \\ 30 & 242.5 & 2{,}205 \\ 242.5 & 2{,}205 & 21{,}308.125 \end{bmatrix}$; $X'Y = \begin{bmatrix} 2.42 \\ 17.645 \\ 155.5575 \end{bmatrix}$

c. $(X'X)^{-1} = \begin{bmatrix} 1.7858 & -.6116 & .0430 \\ -.6116 & .2793 & -.0219 \\ .0430 & -.0219 & .0018 \end{bmatrix}$ **d.** $\hat{\boldsymbol{\beta}} = \begin{bmatrix} .2135 \\ .0349 \\ .00126 \end{bmatrix}$; $\hat{y} = .2135 + .0349x + .00126x^2$

12.5 a.
$$Y = \begin{bmatrix} .231 \\ .107 \\ .053 \\ .129 \\ .069 \\ .030 \\ 1.005 \\ .559 \\ .321 \\ 2.948 \\ 1.633 \\ .934 \end{bmatrix}; \quad X = \begin{bmatrix} 1 & 740 & 1.10 \\ 1 & 740 & .62 \\ 1 & 740 & .31 \\ 1 & 805 & 1.10 \\ 1 & 805 & .62 \\ 1 & 805 & .31 \\ 1 & 980 & 1.10 \\ 1 & 980 & .62 \\ 1 & 980 & .31 \\ 1 & 1,235 & 1.10 \\ 1 & 1,235 & .62 \\ 1 & 1,235 & .31 \end{bmatrix}$$

b. $X'X = \begin{bmatrix} 12 & 11,280 & 8.12 \\ 11,280 & 11,043,750 & 7,632.8 \\ 8.12 & 7,632.8 & 6.762 \end{bmatrix}$; $X'Y = \begin{bmatrix} 8.019 \\ 9,131.205 \\ 6.627 \end{bmatrix}$ **c.** $\begin{bmatrix} 2.45026 & -.00213 & -.53387 \\ -.00213 & .00000227 & -4.88 \times 10^{18} \\ -.53387 & -4.88 \times 10^{-18} & .78897 \end{bmatrix}$

d. $\hat{\boldsymbol{\beta}} = \begin{bmatrix} -3.3727 \\ .00362 \\ .94760 \end{bmatrix}$; $\hat{y} = -3.3727 + .00362x_1 + .94760x_2$

12.6 a. $E(y) = \beta_0 + \beta_1 x + \beta_2 x^2$ **c.** Reject H_0; $\beta_2 = 0$; $p = .0015$ **12.7** $t = .98$; do not reject H_0

12.8 a. $t = 9.68$; reject H_0 **b.** $t = 2.97$; reject H_0 **c.** $3,444.3 \pm 1,861.7$ **d.** $2,093.4 \pm 624.0$

12.9 b. $\hat{y} = 1,717.4952 - 150.26x$; term appears to be useful $(t = -5.72)$ **c.** Yes; $t = -5.468$, p-value $= .0001$

12.10 a. $\hat{y} = 22.925 - 3.525x_1 - .375x_2$ **b.** No; $t = -1.52$ **c.** No; $t = -.16$ **d.** -3.525 ± 14.680
e. $-.375 \pm 14.680$

12.11 a. Quadratic **b.** Reject H_0: $\beta_2 = 0$; $t = -15.78$ **c.** .00005 **d.** 188.892

12.14 a. $\hat{y} = 648 + 104.8x_1 + 357.2x_2$ **b.** Yes, $p = 0$ **c.** 104.8 ± 37.4 **d.** No, $p = .3629$

12.15 Yes; $F = 443.18$ **12.16 a.** -75.51 ± 26.17 **b.** Do not reject H_0; $t = 1.38$ **c.** Yes; $F = 21.86$

12.17 a. Yes; $F = 17.8$ **b.** Reject H_0: $\beta_1 = 0$; $t = -3.50$ **c.** -6.38 ± 4.723

12.18 a. $R^2 = .262$; no **b.** $F = 1.896$; do not reject H_0 **12.19 a.** Yes; $F = 618.96$ **b.** Yes; $F = 1,540.32$

12.20 a. Yes; $F = 120.651$ **b.** $t = 9.857$; reject H_0 **12.21** $F = 1.056$; do not reject H_0

12.22 $F = 70.46$; reject H_0: $\beta_1 = \beta_2 = \beta_3 = \beta_4 = 0$ **12.23 a.** $.5195 \pm .0579$ **b.** $.5195 \pm .1033$ **12.24** $(47, 3,825)$

12.25 a. 26.075 ± 51.167 **b.** 26.075 ± 78.159 **12.26** $(253.81, 821.39)$

12.32 a. Misspecified model; quadratic term missing **b.** Unequal variances **c.** Outlier **d.** Unequal variances
e. Nonnormal errors

12.33 a. Yes; $p = .0001$ **b.** No, but unusual observation at $\hat{y} = 777.0$ **c.** Yes
d. Model is useful $(p = .0001)$; Boston Harbor residual has $z = -2.779$

12.34 a. $1.38, -.21, -.78, -.64, -.28, -.43, -.23, .05, .29, .29, .57$ **b.** Yes, quadratic **c.** $E(y) = \beta_0 + \beta_1 x + \beta_2 x^2$
d. $\hat{y} = 99.5028 - .34727x + .0013106x^2$; $F = 1,694.31$, reject H_0

12.35 Assumptions appear to be satisfied **12.36 a.** No **b.** Observation (child) #24 is influential.

12.37 a. Yes; assumption of equal variances violated **b.** Use variance-stabilizing transformation $y^* = \sqrt{y}$

12.38 a. No; $F = 1.582$ **b.** Yes (observation #13) **c.** Yes; studentized deleted residual $= 53.8929$
d. $\hat{y} = 1.083 - 1.216x_1 - .531x_2 - 1.076x_3 + .104x_4$; $F = 222.17$, reject H_0

12.41 Drop Importance (since highly correlated with Support) **12.42** No; appears that multicollinearity exists

12.43 Unable to test model adequacy since there are no degrees of freedom for estimating σ^2 (i.e., df $= n - 3 = 0$)

12.44 a. .0025; no **b.** .4341; no **c.** No **d.** $\hat{y} = -45.154 + 3.097x_1 + 1.032x_2$; $F = 39,222.34$; $R^2 = .9998$
e. $-.8998$; x_1 and x_2 are highly correlated **f.** No

12.45 a. $\hat{y} = 2.7433 + .800976x_1$; yes, $t = 15.92$ **b.** $\hat{y} = 1.6647 + 12.3954x_2$; yes, $t = 11.76$
c. $\hat{y} = -11.7953 + 25.0682x_3$; yes (at $\alpha = .05$), $t = 2.51$

12.46 a. $\hat{w} = -.104 + .282\sqrt{t}$ **b.** Yes; $t = 83.93$

12.47 a. $\hat{y} = .13202 - 9.30712x_1 + 1.55756x_2$ **b.** Reject H_0; $F = 35.84$ (p-value $= .0005$)

c. No; $t = -1.84$ (p-value $= .1153$)   **d.** Yes; $t = 8.47$ (p-value $= .0001$)   **e.** .922766   **f.** .152141

12.48 b. $\hat{y} = 2.46 + .41x_1 + 1.614x_2$ **c.** SSE $= 2.4363$, $s^2 = .34804$, $s = .5899$ **d.** Yes; $F = 109.65$
e. $R^2 = .969$ **f.** Yes; $t = 3.11$ **g.** $4.87 \pm .74$ **h.** 4.87 ± 1.34

12.49 a. $F = 12.27$; do not reject H_0: $\beta_1 = \beta_2 = 0$ at $\alpha = .05$; $R^2 = .925$, $s = 6.801$
b. $(-7.98, 40.05)$; model not useful

12.50 a. Yes; $F = 37.204$ **b.** Multicollinearity   **c.** Inflated standard error of $\hat{\beta}_3$ due to multicollinearity
d. $r_{12} = .327$, $r_{13} = .231$, $r_{14} = .166$, $r_{23} = .790$, $r_{24} = .791$, $r_{34} = .881$; yes

12.51 $R^2 = .9043$; $s = 4.54855$; $F = 33.079$ (p-value $= .0003$), reject H_0: $\beta_1 = \beta_2 = 0$; $t = 2.13$
(p-value $= .0706/2 = .0353$), reject H_0: $\beta_2 = 0$

12.52 b. -50.76, -47.44, -15.96, -33.72, -54.64, -78.24, 16.84, -46.52, 43.24, -64.96, -55.96, -50.52, 436.52, 37.88, -36.00; almost all residuals are negative, one large positive residual   **c.** Omit data for this employee from analysis
d. $\hat{y} = 191.26 - 9.58x$, $r^2 = .483$; model is adequate ($t = -3.35$)

12.53 a. $\hat{y} = .94 - .214x$ **b.** 0, $.02$, $-.026$, $.034$, $.088$, $-.112$, $-.058$, $.002$, $.036$, $.016$
c. Football shape; unequal variances   **d.** Use the transformation $y^* = \sin^{-1}\sqrt{y}$ and fit the model $y^* = \beta_0 + \beta_1 x + \varepsilon$
e. $\hat{y}^* = 1.307 - .2496x$; possibly

12.54 b. Clone 5263: $F = 338.55$, reject H_0; Clone 5319: $F = 297.88$, reject H_0; Clone 5331: $F = 175.91$, reject H_0;
Clone 5271: $F = 331.50$, reject H_0 **c.** Clone 5263: yes, $t = 12$; Clone 5319: yes, $t = 8$; Clone 5331: yes, $t = 7$;
Clone 5271: yes, $t = 7$

12.55 a. $E(S_V) = \beta_0 + \beta_1 x + \beta_2 x^2$ **b.** $E(V_V) = \beta_0 + \beta_1 x + \beta_2 x^2$ **12.56 b.** No; $F = 4.824$ (p-value $= .1155$)

12.57 b. No, $t = -2.105$ (p-value $= .126$)   **c.** $(95.7, 99.7)$

12.58 b. Yes, $F = 28.721$ (p-value $= .0058$)   **c.** $(138.35, 1{,}470.41)$ **12.59 e.** $\hat{y} = -.093 + .917x$

Chapter 13

13.1 a. Quantitative   **b.** Quantitative   **c.** Qualitative   **d.** Qualitative   **e.** Qualitative   **f.** Quantitative   **g.** Qualitative
h. Qualitative   **i.** Qualitative   **j.** Quantitative   **k.** Qualitative

13.2 a. Quantitative   **b.** Qualitative   **c.** Quantitative   **d.** Quantitative   **e.** Qualitative

13.3 a. Quantitative   **b.** Qualitative   **c.** Quantitative   **d.** Quantitative   **e.** Qualitative

13.4 a. Quantitative   **b.** Quantitative   **c.** Qualitative   **13.5 a.** First-order   **c.** Positive (upward) slope

13.6 a. Second-order   **c.** Downward curvature

13.7 a. (i) First-order   (ii) Third-order   (iii) First-order   (iv) Second-order   **b.** (i) $E(y) = \beta_0 + \beta_1 x$
(ii) $E(y) = \beta_0 + \beta_1 x + \beta_2 x^2 + \beta_3 x^3$ (iii) $E(y) = \beta_0 + \beta_1 x$ (iv) $E(y) = \beta_0 + \beta_1 x + \beta_2 x^2$ **c.** (i) $\beta_1 > 0$ (ii) $\beta_3 > 0$
(iii) $\beta_1 < 0$ (iv) $\beta_2 < 0$

13.8 a. First-order   **b.** Second-order   **c.** Third-order   **d.** Third-order   **e.** Second-order   **f.** First-order

13.9 a. $E(y) = \beta_0 + \beta_1 x_2 + \beta_2 x_2^2$ **b.** $E(y) = \beta_0 + \beta_1 x_1 + \beta_2 x_1^2 + \beta_3 x_1^3$ **13.10** $E(y) = \beta_0 + \beta_1 x + \beta_2 x^2$

13.11 b. $E(y) = \beta_0 + \beta_1 x + \beta_2 x^2$ **13.12.** $E(y) = \beta_0 + \beta_1 x_1 + \beta_2 x^2 + \beta_3 x^3$ **13.13** $E(y) = \beta_0 + \beta_1 x$

13.14 a. $.953 \pm .05$ **13.15** Reject H_0: $\beta_2 = 0$, $t < -1.717$

13.18 a. $E(y) = \beta_0 + \beta_1 x_1 + \beta_2 x_2$ **b.** $E(y) = \beta_0 + \beta_1 x_1 + \beta_2 x_2 + \beta_3 x_1 x_2 + \beta_4 x_1^2 + \beta_5 x_2^2$
c. $E(y) = \beta_0 + \beta_1 x_1 + \beta_2 x_2 + \beta_3 x_1 x_2$

13.19 a. Both quantitative   **b.** $E(y) = \beta_0 + \beta_1 x_1 + \beta_2 x_2$ **c.** Include $\beta_3 x_1 x_2 + \beta_4 x_1^2 + \beta_5 x_2^2$
d. H_0: $\beta_3 = 0$ against H_a: $\beta_3 \neq 0$

13.20 $E(y) = \beta_0 + \beta_1 x_1 + \beta_2 x_2 + \beta_3 x_1 x_2 + \beta_4 x_1^2 + \beta_5 x_2^2$

13.21 a. Both quantitative   **b.** $E(y) = \beta_0 + \beta_1 x_1 + \beta_2 x_2$ **c.** $E(y) = \beta_0 + \beta_1 x_1 + \beta_2 x_2 + \beta_3 x_1 x_2$
d. $E(y) = \beta_0 + \beta_1 x_1 + \beta_2 x_2 + \beta_3 x_1 x_2 + \beta_4 x_1^2 + \beta_5 x_2^2$

13.22 a. $E(y) = \beta_0 + \beta_1 x_1 + \beta_2 x_2 + \beta_3 x_1 x_2 + \beta_4 x_1^2 + \beta_5 x_2^2$ **c.** $F = 93.6$, reject H_0

13.23 a. $E(y) = \beta_0 + \beta_1 x_1 + \beta_2 x_2 + \beta_3 x_1 x_2 + \beta_4 x_1^2 + \beta_5 x_2^2$ **b.** $E(y) = \beta_0 + \beta_1 x_1 + \beta_2 x_2$
c. $E(y) = \beta_0 + \beta_1 x_1 + \beta_2 x_2 + \beta_3 x_1 x_2$ **d.** $\beta_1 + \beta_3 x_2$ **e.** $\beta_2 + \beta_3 x_1$

13.24 a. $u = \dfrac{(x - 33)}{2.16}$ **b.** -1.389, $-.926$, $-.463$, 0, $.463$, $.926$, 1.389 **c.** $.99966$
d. 0 **e.** $\hat{y} = 37.5714 - .4629u - 5.3333u^2$

13.25 a. $u = \dfrac{(x - 5.5)}{1.745}$ **b.** -1.433 $(x = 3)$, $-.860$ $(x = 4)$, $-.287$ $(x = 5)$, $.287$ $(x = 6)$, $.860$ $(x = 7)$, 1.433 $(x = 8)$

c. $.9913$ **d.** 0 **e.** $\hat{y} = 1{,}079.49 - 262.13u - 196.67u^2$

13.26 a. $u_1 = \dfrac{(x_1 - 940)}{200.12}$, $u_2 = \dfrac{(x_2 - .68)}{.34}$ **b.** $.998$; $.621$ **c.** $.989$; $.362$

d. $\hat{y} = .4376 + .6068u_1 + .3151u_2 + .3373u_1u_2 + .2250u_1^2 + .0266u_2^2$

13.27 No; $F = 3.59$ **13.28 a.** $F = 31.55$; reject H_0 **b.** Complete model   **13.29** $F = 24.19$; yes

13.30 a. H_0: $\beta_4 = \beta_5 = 0$ **b.** Reject H_0 **13.31 a.** H_0: $\beta_4 = \beta_5 = \beta_{18} = \beta_{19} = \cdots = \beta_{23} = 0$

b. $F = 1.59$; do not reject H_0 **c.** No   **d.** H_0: $\beta_7 = \beta_8 = \cdots = \beta_{15} = 0$ **e.** $F = 9.50$; reject H_0 **f.** Model 2

g. $E(y) = \beta_0 + \beta_1 x_1 + \beta_2 x_2 + \beta_3 x_1 x_2 + \beta_5 x_4 + \beta_8 x_1 x_4 + \beta_{10} x_2 x_4 + \beta_{14} x_1 x_2 x_4$

13.32 a. $E(y) = \beta_0 + \beta_1 x_1 + \beta_2 x_2 + \beta_3 x_3 + \beta_4 x_4$, where

$$x_1 = \begin{cases} 1 & \text{if benzene} \\ 0 & \text{if not} \end{cases}, \quad x_2 = \begin{cases} 1 & \text{if toluene} \\ 0 & \text{if not} \end{cases}, \quad x_3 = \begin{cases} 1 & \text{if chloroform} \\ 0 & \text{if not} \end{cases}, \quad x_4 = \begin{cases} 1 & \text{if methanol} \\ 0 & \text{if not} \end{cases}$$

b. $\beta_0 = \mu_A$, $\beta_1 = \mu_B - \mu_A$, $\beta_2 = \mu_T - \mu_A$, $\beta_3 = \mu_C - \mu_A$, $\beta_4 = \mu_M - \mu_A$

c. Test H_0: $\beta_1 = \beta_2 = \beta_3 = \beta_4 = 0$ with global F test

13.33 a. $\hat{y} = 10.2$ for level 1; $\hat{y} = 6.2$ for level 2; $\hat{y} = 22.2$ for level 3; $\hat{y} = 12.2$ for level 4

b. H_0: $\beta_1 = \beta_2 = \beta_3 = 0$; H_a: At least one β is not 0

13.34 $E(y) = \beta_0 + \beta_1 x_1 + \beta_2 x_2 + \beta_3 x_3 + \beta_4 x_4$, where

$$x_1 = \begin{cases} 1 & \text{if brand 1} \\ 0 & \text{otherwise} \end{cases}, \quad x_2 = \begin{cases} 1 & \text{if brand 2} \\ 0 & \text{otherwise} \end{cases}, \quad x_3 = \begin{cases} 1 & \text{if brand 3} \\ 0 & \text{otherwise} \end{cases}, \quad x_4 = \begin{cases} 1 & \text{if brand 4} \\ 0 & \text{otherwise} \end{cases}$$

13.35 a. Group is a qualitative variable.

b. $E(y) = \beta_0 + \beta_1 x_1 + \beta_2 x_2$, where

$$x_1 = \begin{cases} 1 & \text{if group 2} \\ 0 & \text{otherwise} \end{cases}, \quad x_2 = \begin{cases} 1 & \text{if group 3} \\ 0 & \text{otherwise} \end{cases}$$

13.36 a. $E(y) = \beta_0 + \beta_1 x_1 + \beta_2 x_2 + \beta_3 x_3$, where

$$x_1 = \begin{cases} 1 & \text{if Trilogy} \\ 0 & \text{otherwise} \end{cases}, \quad x_2 = \begin{cases} 1 & \text{if Set Hostages Free} \\ 0 & \text{otherwise} \end{cases}, \quad x_3 = \begin{cases} 1 & \text{if Queen of Hearts} \\ 0 & \text{otherwise} \end{cases}$$

c. $\beta_0 + \beta_3$

13.37 a. $E(y) = \beta_0 + \beta_1 x_1 + \beta_2 x_3 + \beta_3 x_4 + \beta_4 x_5 + \beta_5 x_6$, where $x_3 - x_6$ are dummies for compound

c. $E(y) = \beta_0 + \beta_1 x_2 + \beta_2 x_3 + \beta_3 x_4 + \beta_4 x_5 + \beta_5 x_6 + \beta_6 x_2 x_3 + \beta_7 x_2 x_4 + \beta_8 x_2 x_5 + \beta_9 x_2 x_6$

d. B: $\beta_1 + \beta_6$; T: $\beta_1 + \beta_7$; C: $\beta_1 + \beta_6$; M: $\beta_1 + \beta_9$; A: β_1

13.38 b. Yes; $F = 10.60$ **c.** No; $t = -1.56$ **d.** $E(y) = \beta_0 + \beta_1 x_1 + \beta_2 x_2 + \beta_3 x_1 x_2$

e. Lines will have different slopes.

13.39 a. $E(y) = \beta_0 + \beta_1 x_1 + \beta_2 x_2 + \beta_3 x_3$, where

$$x_2 = \begin{cases} 1 & \text{if method G} \\ 0 & \text{if not} \end{cases}, \quad x_3 = \begin{cases} 1 & \text{if method R}_1 \\ 0 & \text{if not} \end{cases}$$

c. $E(y) = \beta_0 + \beta_1 x_1 + \beta_2 x_2 + \beta_3 x_3 + \beta_4 x_1 x_2 + \beta_5 x_1 x_3$ **d.** G: $\beta_1 + \beta_4$; R$_1$: $\beta_1 + \beta_5$; R$_2$: β_1

13.40 a. $F = 14.42$, reject H_0: $\beta_1 = \beta_2 = \beta_3 = 0$; $R^2 = .812$; $s = 8.057$ **b.** $F = 8.79$; reject H_0: $\beta_4 = \beta_5 = 0$

c. DF-2: 2.14; blended: 4.865; adv. timing: 7.815

13.41 a. H_0: $\beta_2 = \beta_3 = 0$; H_a: At least one β is not 0   **b.** $F = 6.99$; reject H_0

c. Fit the model $E(y) = \beta_0 + \beta_1 x_1 + \beta_2 x_2 + \beta_3 x_3 + \beta_4 x_1 x_2 + \beta_5 x_1 x_3$ and test H_0: $\beta_4 = \beta_5 = 0$

13.42 a. Brand of extractor is qualitative; size of orange is quantitative

b. $E(y) = \beta_0 + \beta_1 x_1 + \beta_2 x_2$, where

$$x_2 = \begin{cases} 1 & \text{if extractor B} \\ 0 & \text{if not} \end{cases}$$

c. Include $\beta_3 x_1 x_2$ **e.** $H_0: \beta_3 = 0$ against $H_a: \beta_3 \neq 0$

13.43 a. $E(y) = \beta_0 + \beta_1 x_1 + \beta_2 x_2 + \beta_3 x_3$ **b.** $E(y) = \beta_0 + \beta_1 x_1 + \beta_2 x_2 + \beta_3 x_3 + \beta_4 x_1 x_2 + \beta_5 x_1 x_3$

c. TDS-3A: $\beta_1 + \beta_4$; FE: $\beta_1 + \beta_5$; AL: β_1 **d.** Test $H_0: \beta_4 = \beta_5 = 0$

13.44 a. $E(y) = \beta_0 + \beta_1 x_1 + \beta_2 x_2 + \beta_3 x_3 + \beta_4 x_1 x_2 + \beta_5 x_1 x_3$, where

$$x_2 = \begin{cases} 1 & \text{if algorithm B} \\ 0 & \text{otherwise} \end{cases} \quad \text{and} \quad x_3 = \begin{cases} 1 & \text{if algorithm C} \\ 0 & \text{otherwise} \end{cases}$$

b. $F = 4.90$, reject H_0 (p-value $= .0394$)   **c.** $E(y) = \beta_0 + \beta_1 x_1 + \beta_2 x_2 + \beta_3 x_3$ **d.** $F = 2.36$; no

13.45 a. $H_0: \beta_4 = \beta_5 = 0$ **b.** $H_0: \beta_3 = \beta_4 = \beta_5 = 0$ **c.** $F = .93$; no

13.46 a. $E(y) = \beta_0 + \beta_1 x_2 + \beta_2 x_2^2$ **b.** Add $\beta_3 x_3 + \beta_4 x_4 + \beta_5 x_5 + \beta_6 x_6$

c. Add $\beta_7 x_2 x_3 + \beta_8 x_2 x_4 + \beta_9 x_2 x_5 + \beta_{10} x_2 x_6 + \beta_{11} x_2^2 x_3 + \beta_{12} x_2^2 x_4 + \beta_{13} x_2^2 x_5 + \beta_{14} x_2^2 x_6$

d. If $\beta_7 = \beta_8 = \cdots = \beta_{14} = 0$ **e.** If $\beta_2 = \beta_7 = \beta_8 = \cdots = \beta_{14} = 0$ **e.** If $\beta_3 = \beta_4 = \cdots = \beta_{14} = 0$

13.47 a. $E(y) = \beta_0 + \beta_1 x_1 + \beta_2 x_1^2 + \beta_3 x_2 + \beta_4 x_3 + \beta_5 x_1 x_2 + \beta_6 x_1 x_3 + \beta_7 x_1^2 x_2 + \beta_8 x_1^2 x_3$

b. $H_0: \beta_5 = \beta_6 = \beta_7 = \beta_8 = 0$

13.48 a. $E(y) = \beta_0 + \beta_1 x_1 + \beta_2 x_1^2 + \beta_3 x_2 + \beta_4 x_3 + \beta_5 x_1 x_2 + \beta_6 x_1 x_3 + \beta_7 x_1^2 x_2 + \beta_8 x_1^2 x_3$

b. $H_0: \beta_3 = \beta_4 = \beta_5 = \beta_6 = \beta_7 = \beta_8 = 0$ **c.** $F = .34$; do not reject H_0

13.49 $F = 6.75$; yes   **13.50 a.** x_2 ($t = -90$ is the largest in magnitude)   **b.** Yes

13.51 a. x_4, x_5, x_6 **b.** No; there may be other important variables, as yet unspecified

c. $E(y) = \beta_0 + \beta_1 x_4 + \beta_2 x_5 + \beta_3 x_6 + \beta_4 x_4 x_5 + \beta_5 x_4 x_6 + \beta_6 x_5 x_6$

13.52 a. Two

b. $E(y) = \beta_0 + \beta_1 x_1 + \beta_2 x_2$, where

$$x_1 = \begin{cases} 1 & \text{cash only} \\ 0 & \text{otherwise} \end{cases} \quad \text{and} \quad x_2 = \begin{cases} 1 & \text{if cash and credit same price} \\ 0 & \text{otherwise} \end{cases}$$

13.53 No estimate of σ^2

13.54   a. $E(y) = \beta_0 + \beta_1 x_1 + \beta_2 x_2$, where

$$x_1 = \text{total area and } x_2 = \begin{cases} 1 & \text{if central air conditioning} \\ 0 & \text{otherwise} \end{cases}$$

b. $E(y) = \beta_0 + \beta_1 x_1 + \beta_2 x_1^2 + \beta_3 x_2 + \beta_4 x_1 x_2 + \beta_5 x_1^2 x_2$ **c.** $H_0: \beta_2 = \beta_4 = \beta_5 = 0$ **d.** $F = 2.49$; no

13.55 a. $H_0: \beta_2 = \beta_5 = 0$ **b.** $H_0: \beta_3 = \beta_4 = \beta_5 = 0$ **c.** $F = 2.15$; do not reject H_0

13.56 a. $E(y) = \beta_0 + \beta_1 x_1 + \beta_2 x_2 + \beta_3 x_1 x_2 + \beta_4 x_1^2 + \beta_5 x_2^2$ **c.** $\hat{y} = 54.5 + .007697 x_1 + .554111 x_2 + .000113 x_1 x_2$

e. $F = 44.67$; reject H_0 (p-value $= .0005$)   **f.** $t = .68$; no

13.57 a. $E(y) = \beta_0 + \beta_1 x_1 + \beta_2 x_1^2 + \beta_3 x_2 + \beta_4 x_1 x_2 + \beta_5 x_1^2 x_2$ **c.** $E(y) = \beta_0 + \beta_1 x_1 + \beta_2 x_2$

13.58 a. $\hat{y} = 22.0189 - .1807 x_1 - .2498 x_2 - 4.6910 x_3 + 3.6745 x_4 + 22.5201 x_5$ **b.** $R^2 = .60$ **c.** 8.66

d. $F = 87.45$; yes   **e.** $t = -4.65$; yes   **f.** (2.885, 4.464)

13.59 a. $E(y) = \beta_0 + \beta_1 x_1 + \beta_2 x_2 + \beta_3 x_3$, where

$$x_2 = \begin{cases} 1 & \text{if program B} \\ 0 & \text{otherwise} \end{cases} \quad \text{and} \quad x_3 = \begin{cases} 1 & \text{if program C} \\ 0 & \text{otherwise} \end{cases}$$

b. $H_0: \beta_2 = \beta_3 = 0$; H_a: At least one β is not 0

13.60 $F = 2.60$, do not reject H_0 **13.61 a.** Most important variables are x_2, x_3, x_4, x_5, and x_6

13.62 a. $\hat{y} = 59.0717 - 1.7003 x_1 - 1.5722 x_2 - 1.6971 x_3 - .5638 x_1 x_2 + .9463 x_1 x_3 - 17.3858 x_1^2 - 13.8459 x_2^2 - 17.4512 x_3^2$ **b.** $F = 1.78$; do not reject H_0

13.63 a. $E(y) = \beta_0 + \beta_1 x_1 + \beta_2 x_2 + \beta_3 x_3 + \beta_4 x_4$ **b.** $\hat{y} = 25.10 + 3.85 x_1 + 6.55 x_2 - 2.65 x_3 - 4.75 x_4$

c. $F = 23.97$; yes

....

13.64 a. $F = 149$; reject H_0

13.65 $\hat{y} = 2.0952 + 1.6429x_1 + .0289x_2 + .0212x_1x_2 - .00000595x_2^2 - .00000469x_1x_2^2$

Chapter 14

14.1 Noise (variability) and volume (n)　**14.2** Remove extraneous source of variation

14.3 a. Flextime, staggered, and fixed work schedules　**b.** Randomly assign 20 workers to each work schedule

c. $E(y) = \beta_0 + \beta_1x_1 + \beta_2x_2$, where

$$x_1 = \begin{cases} 1 & \text{if flextime} \\ 0 & \text{if not} \end{cases}, \quad x_2 = \begin{cases} 1 & \text{if staggered} \\ 0 & \text{if not} \end{cases}$$

14.4 a. STAAD-III (run 1), STAAD-III (run 2), DRIFT

c. $E(y) = \beta_0 + \beta_1x_1 + \beta_2x_2 + \beta_3x_3 + \cdots + \beta_{22}x_{22}$, where

$$x_1 = \begin{cases} 1 & \text{if STAAD-III (run 1)} \\ 0 & \text{if not} \end{cases}, \quad x_2 = \begin{cases} 1 & \text{if STAAD-III (run 2)} \\ 0 & \text{if not} \end{cases},$$

$$x_3 = \begin{cases} 1 & \text{if level 1} \\ 0 & \text{if not} \end{cases}, \quad x_4 = \begin{cases} 1 & \text{if level 2} \\ 0 & \text{if not} \end{cases}, \ldots, \quad x_{22} = \begin{cases} 1 & \text{if level 20} \\ 0 & \text{if not} \end{cases}$$

14.5 a. $y_{B1} = \beta_0 + \beta_2 + \beta_4 + \varepsilon_{B1}$; $y_{B2} = \beta_0 + \beta_2 + \beta_5 + \varepsilon_{B2}$; ... $y_{B,10} = \beta_0 + \beta_2 + \varepsilon_{B,10}$; $\bar{y}_B = \beta_0 + \beta_2 + (\beta_4 + \beta_5 + \cdots + \beta_{12})/10 + \bar{\varepsilon}_B$

b. $y_{D1} = \beta_0 + \beta_4 + \varepsilon_{D1}$; $y_{D2} = \beta_0 + \beta_5 + \varepsilon_{D2}$; ... $y_{D,10} = \beta_0 + \varepsilon_{D,10}$; $\bar{y}_D = \beta_0 + (\beta_4 + \beta_5 + \cdots + \beta_{12})/10 + \bar{\varepsilon}_D$

14.7 a. 3×3 factorial　**b.** Pay rate (quantitative), length of workday (quantitative)

c. $P_1L_1, P_1L_2, P_1L_3, P_2L_1, P_2L_2, P_2L_3, P_3L_1, P_3L_2, P_3L_3$

14.8 a. Method; session; consistency　**b.** Qualitative; qualitative; quantitative　**c.** 48　**14.9 a.** No

14.10 $E(y) = \beta_0 + \underbrace{\beta_1x_1}_{A} + \underbrace{\beta_2x_2 + \beta_3x_3}_{B} + \underbrace{\beta_4x_1x_2 + \beta_5x_1x_2}_{A \times B}$

14.11 $E(y) = \beta_0 + \underbrace{\beta_1x_1}_{A} + \underbrace{\beta_2x_2 + \beta_3x_3}_{B} + \underbrace{\beta_4x_4 + \beta_5x_5}_{C} + \underbrace{\beta_6x_1x_2 + \beta_7x_1x_3}_{A \times B} + \underbrace{\beta_8x_1x_4 + \beta_9x_1x_5}_{A \times C}$

$+ \underbrace{\beta_{10}x_2x_4 + \beta_{11}x_2x_5 + \beta_{12}x_3x_4 + \beta_{13}x_3x_5}_{B \times C} + \underbrace{\beta_{14}x_1x_2x_4 + \beta_{15}x_1x_2x_5 + \beta_{16}x_1x_3x_4 + \beta_{17}x_1x_3x_5}_{A \times B \times C}$

14.13 Cannot investigate factor interaction　**14.14** Allows degrees of freedom for error

14.15 7　**14.16** 18　**14.17 a.** Yes　**b.** No

14.19 a. Completely randomized

b. $E(y) = \beta_0 + \beta_1x_1 + \beta_2x_2$, where

$$x_1 = \begin{cases} 1 & \text{if touch-tone} \\ 0 & \text{if not} \end{cases}, \quad x_2 = \begin{cases} 1 & \text{if human operator} \\ 0 & \text{if not} \end{cases}$$

c. H_0: $\mu_T = \mu_H = \mu_S$　**d.** H_0: $\beta_1 = \beta_2 = 0$　**e.** Large within-sample variance

14.20 a. Oyster tissue, citrus leaves, bovine liver, and human serum　**b.** Yes, $p = .0003$　**c.** 1.33, 3.16, .41, .146

14.21 a. $E(y) = \beta_0 + \beta_1x$, where

$$x = \begin{cases} 1 & \text{if treatment 1} \\ 0 & \text{if treatment 2} \end{cases}$$

b. $\hat{y} = 10.667 - 1.524x$; $F = 3.15$, do not reject H_0

14.22 a. 7.502　**b.** 2.381　**c.** 1　**d.** 11　**e.** 3.15

f.

Source	df	SS	MS	F
Treatments	1	7.502	7.502	3.15
Error	11	26.190	2.381	
Total	12	33.692		

g. $F > 4.84$ **h.** Do not reject H_0

14.23 a. $t = -1.778$; do not reject H_0 **c.** Two-tailed

14.24 a. 852   **b.** df(Groups) = 4, df(Error) = 847, MS(Groups) = 133.74, MSE = 27.93, $F = 4.79$ **c.** Yes; $F = 4.79$

14.25 Yes, $p = .006$ **14.26** No; do not reject H_0; $F = .10$

14.27 a.

Source	df	SS	MS	F
Treatments	3	.00678	.00226	3.50
Error	20	.01292	.00065	
Total	23	.01970		

b. $F = 3.50$; yes   **c.** 50

14.29 a. CM = 33,235,588,432; SST = 1,937,808,567.8   **b.** 148,746,738.4   **c.** 2,086,555,306.2

d.

Source	df	SS	MS	F
Treatments	4	1,937,808,567.8	484,452,141.95	2,533.86
Error	778	148,746,738.4	191,191.18	
Total	782	2,086,555,306.2		

e. $F = 2,533.86$; yes   **f.** $3,660 \pm 135.94$ **g.** $-5,210 \pm 148.31$

14.30 a.

Source	df	SS	MS	F
Treatments	4	357,986.87	89,496.718	5.67
Error	73	1,151,602.00	15,775.370	
Total	77	1,509,588.87		

b. Yes; reject H_0, $F = 5.67$

14.31 a. The three positions (beginning, direction change, ending)
b. The 10 college students   **c.** Medial rotation measurement   **d.** Attempt to remove extraneous source of variation due to differences in medial rotation of college students
e. $E(y) = \beta_0 + \beta_1 x_1 + \beta_1 x_2 + \beta_3 x_3 + \cdots + \beta_{11} x_{11}$, where

$$x_1 = \begin{cases} 1 & \text{if beginning} \\ 0 & \text{if not} \end{cases}, \quad x_2 = \begin{cases} 1 & \text{if changed} \\ 0 & \text{if not} \end{cases}$$

$$x_3 = \begin{cases} 1 & \text{if student 1} \\ 0 & \text{if not} \end{cases}, \ldots, \quad x_{11} = \begin{cases} 1 & \text{if student 9} \\ 0 & \text{if not} \end{cases}$$

14.32 Reject H_0, $F = 4.79$ **14.33** Reject H_0, $F = 57.99$ **14.34** Yes; $F = 52.81$

14.35 a. Randomized block design

b.

Source	df	SS	MS	F
Methods	1	.505	.5050	1.71
Increments	15	12.146	.8097	2.75
Error	15	4.421	.2947	
Total	31	17.072		

c. $F = 1.71$; no   **d.** $t = -1.31$; do not reject H_0

14.36 a. Yes; $F = 5.06$ **b.** Do not reject H_0; $F = 2.28$

14.37 a. The three agents (nickel, iron, copper)   **b.** The seven ingots   **c.** Yes; $F = 6.36$

14.38 a.

Source	df
Period	1
Gender	1
P × G	1
Error	120
Total	123

b. Complete: $E(y) = \beta_0 + \beta_1 x_1 + \beta_2 x_2 + \beta_3 x_1 x_2$, where

$$x_1 = \begin{cases} 1 & \text{if 16 hours or less} \\ 0 & \text{if more than 16 hours} \end{cases}, \quad x_2 = \begin{cases} 1 & \text{if male} \\ 0 & \text{if female} \end{cases}; \text{ Reduced: } E(y) = \beta_0 + \beta_1 x_1 + \beta_2 x_2$$

c. Difference in mean body weight gains of males and females does not depend on photoperiod
d. $\mu_{16 \text{ or less}} \neq \mu_{\text{more16}}$; $\mu_M \neq \mu_F$
14.39 No evidence of interaction; no evidence of room order main effect; evidence of aid-type main effect
14.40 a. Mean difference between reading rates of 20 and 40 character window sizes does not depend on level of jump length   **b.** No evidence of a difference between mean reading rates of 20 and 40 character window sizes
c. Evidence of differences among the mean reading rates for the three levels of jump length

14.41 a.

Source	df	SS	MS	F
Amount	3	104.19	34.73	20.12
Method	3	28.63	9.54	5.53
Amount × Method	9	25.13	2.79	1.62
Error	32	55.25	1.73	
Total	47	213.20		

b. Do not reject H_0; $F = 1.62$
c. Difference in mean shear strengths for any two levels of antimony amount does not depend on cooling method
d. Amount: reject H_0, $F = 20.12$; Method: reject H_0, $F = 5.53$
14.42 a. The $7 \times 2 = 14$ laboratory/method combinations   **c.** $F = 2.20$; no   **d.** $F = 94.75$; yes   **e.** $F = 6.16$; yes
14.43 Evidence of interaction ($p = .0001$)
14.44 a.

Source	df	SS	MS	F
Metal	1	51.842	51.842	41.15
Time	1	76.832	76.832	60.99
Metal × Time	1	2.738	2.738	2.17
Error	16	20.156	1.25975	
Total	19	151.568		

c. $F = 2.17$; no

14.45 b. $E(y) = \beta_0 + \beta_1 x_1 + \beta_2 x_2 + \beta_3 x_1 x_2 + \beta_4 x_1^2 + \beta_5 x_2^2$ **c.** SSE $= .00015$, $s^2 = .00001$, SS(Total) $= 24.85834$
d. $R^2 \approx 1.00$ **e.** The relationship between $E(y)$ and x_1 is independent of x_2.   **f.** $t = 12.411$; yes
g. $\hat{y} = -.28015 + .001 x_1 - .2855 x_2 + .0073 x_1 x_2 + .000000959 x_1^2 + .5514 x_2^2$ **h.** 2.6515   **i.** (2.6494, 2.6538)
14.46 a. Pay rate (quantitative); length of workday (quantitative)
b. Three pay rates: P_1, P_2, P_3; three workday lengths: L_1, L_2, L_3; treatments: P_1L_1, P_1L_2, P_1L_3, P_2L_1, P_2L_2, P_2L_3, P_3L_1, P_3L_2, P_3L_3 **c.** $E(y) = \beta_0 + \beta_1 x_1 + \beta_2 x_1^2 + \beta_3 x_2 + \beta_4 x_2^2 + \beta_5 x_1 x_2 + \beta_6 x_1^2 x_2 + \beta_7 x_1 x_2^2 + \beta_8 x_1^2 x_2^2$ **d.** Fourth-order
e. $E(y) = \beta_0 + \beta_1 x_1 + \beta_2 x_1^2 + \beta_3 x_2 + \beta_4 x_2^2 + \beta_5 x_1 x_2$ **f.** 0   **g.** 3   **h.** Complete, 9 df; second-order, 12 df
i. Second-order   **j.** Test H_0: $\beta_5 = \beta_6 = \beta_7 = \beta_8 = 0$ using the reduced model $E(y) = \beta_0 + \beta_1 x_1 + \beta_2 x_1^2 + \beta_3 x_2 + \beta_4 x_2^2$
k. Test H_0: $\beta_5 = 0$

14.47 a.

	Light	Heavy
Female	146.40	116.00
Male	104.00	98.00

b. 6,739.605   **c.** SS(Sex) $= 114.005$, SS(Weight) $= 41.405$, SS(SW) $= 18.605$

d.

	Sample Variance	SS(Deviations Within)
Female, Light	46.3761	324.6327
Female, Heavy	8.5849	60.0943
Male, Light	25.4016	177.8112
Male, Heavy	32.4900	227.4300

e. 789.968   **f.** 963.983

g.

Source	df	SS	MS	F
Sex (S)	1	114.005	114.005	4.04
Weight (W)	1	41.405	41.405	1.47
S × W	1	18.605	18.605	.66
Error	28	789.968	28.213	
Total	31	963.983		

h. No; $F = .66$

14.48 a.

Source	df
A	2
B	3
C	1
AB	6
AC	2
BC	3
ABC	6
Error	120
Total	143

b. $F = 5.21$; yes   **c.** $F = 2.79$; yes   **d.** SS(Total) = 34.99, $R^2 = .52$

14.49 a. $F = 74.16$; yes   **b.** Charging time × alloy type and material × alloy type

14.50 a. $E(y) = \beta_0 + \beta_1 x_1 + \beta_2 x_1^2$ **b.** $E(y) = (\beta_0 + \beta_3) + (\beta_1 + \beta_6)x_1 + (\beta_2 + \beta_9)x_1^2$
c. $E(y) = (\beta_0 + \beta_3 + \beta_4 + \beta_5) + (\beta_1 + \beta_6 + \beta_7 + \beta_8)x_1 + (\beta_2 + \beta_9 + \beta_{10} + \beta_{11})x_1^2$
d. $\hat{y} = 31.15 + .153x_1 - .00396x_1^2 + 17.05x_2 + 19.1x_3 - 14.3x_2x_3 + .151x_1x_2 + .017x_1x_3 - .08x_1x_2x_3 - .00356x_1^2x_2 + .0006x_1^2x_3 + .0012x_1^2x_2x_3$ **e.** Rolled/inconel: $\hat{y} = 53 + .241x_1 - .00572x_1^2$;
Rolled/incoloy: $\hat{y} = 50.25 + .17x_1 - .00336x_1^2$; Drawn/inconel: $\hat{y} = 48.2 + .304x_1 - .00752x_1^2$;
Drawn/incoloy: $\hat{y} = 31.15 + .153x_1 - .00396x_1^2$

14.51 $F = 304.6$; reject H_0: $\beta_3 = \beta_4 = \cdots = \beta_{11} = 0$

14.52 a. $3 \times 4 \times 3 \times 3 = 108$ **b.** The complete model has 108 terms, including β_0, 9 main effect terms,
30 two-way interactions, 44 three-way interactions, and 24 four-way interactions.   **c.** H_0: $\beta_{10} = \beta_{11} = \cdots = \beta_{107} = 0$

14.53 a. Randomized block design

b.

Source	df
Temperature (T)	1
Pressure (P)	1
T × P	1
Week	2
Error	6
Total	11

14.54 b. Yes; p-value = .0072   **c.** No (at $\alpha = .05$); p-value = .0646

14.55 a. 3   **b.** 5   **c.** 15   **d.** $y_{ij} = \mu + \alpha_i + \varepsilon_{ij}$ $(i = 1, 2, 3; j = 1, 2, \ldots, 5)$
e. $\hat{\sigma}_\alpha^2 = .00129$, $\hat{\sigma}^2 = .0558$ **f.** Do not reject H_0: $F = .02$ $(p = .9772)$

14.56 a. $\hat{\sigma}_\alpha^2 \approx 0$, $\hat{\sigma}^2 = 9.71$ **b.** Yes; $F = 78.99$ $(p = .000)$

14.57

Source	df
A (Production lot)	9
B in A (Batch within lot)	40
C in B (Shipping lot within batch)	950
Total	999

14.58 a.

Source	df	SS	MS	F
A (Days)	4	.00339332	.00084833	135.30
B in A (Cars within days)	20	.00012540	.00000627	2.29
C in B (Specimens within cars)	25	.00006850	.00000274	
Total	49	.00358722		

b. $F = 135.30$; yes   **c.** $F = 2.29$; yes

14.59 a. $\hat{\sigma}_B^2 = .038333$, $\hat{\sigma}_W^2 = .057464$ **b.** Yes; $F = 6.34$ $(p = .0006)$

14.60 a.

Source	df	SS	MS	F
A (Days)	5	70.435833	14.0872	37.59
B in A (Rolls within days)	12	4.496667	.3747	.47
C in B (Tests within rolls)	18	14.455000	.8031	
Total	35	89.387500		

b. $F = 37.59$; yes   **c.** $F = .47$; no

14.61 $\mu_C > (\mu_H, \mu_B, \mu_0)$

14.62 The following group pairs have significantly different means: (0, 45 or more) and (1–14, 45 or more).

14.63 $\omega = 8.67$; $\mu_{PD-1} > \mu_{ADC\ 5\text{-}1\text{-}7}$ **14.64** $\omega = .138$; only means for 6 and 14 weeks do not appear to differ

14.65 a. Effect of accuracy level on mean task completion time depends on level of vocabulary   **b.** Yes
c. 75% Vocabulary: means for all three accuracy levels are significantly different; 87.5% Vocabulary: means for all three accuracy levels are significantly different; 100% Vocabulary: means for 99% and 95% accuracy are not significantly different, whereas mean for 90% accuracy is significantly larger than the other two means

14.66 $\omega = 1.82$. There is a significant difference between the two groups of means, (μ_5, μ_3, μ_0) and (μ_{10}). No significant differences exist within the group (μ_5, μ_3, μ_0).

14.73 a. Type of game; position   **b.** Game: Missile Command, Pac-Man, Control; Position: Player, Observer
c. The $3 \times 2 = 6$ game/position combinations
d. $E(y) = \beta_0 + \beta_1 x_1 + \beta_2 x_2 + \beta_3 x_3 + \beta_4 x_1 x_3 + \beta_5 x_2 x_3$,

where $x_1 = \begin{cases} 1 & \text{if Missile Command} \\ 0 & \text{if not} \end{cases}$, $x_2 = \begin{cases} 1 & \text{if Pac-Man} \\ 0 & \text{if not} \end{cases}$, $x_3 = \begin{cases} 1 & \text{if Player} \\ 0 & \text{if not} \end{cases}$

e.

Source	df
Game	2
Position	1
Game × Position	2
Error	78
Total	83

f. Mean difference between aggression of player and observer depends on type of game

14.74 a.

Source	df	SS	MS	F
Treatments	4	215.85	53.96	12.04
Error	18	80.58	4.48	
Total	22	296.43		

b. $F = 12.05$; yes   **c.** Using Bonferroni: $(\mu_1, \mu_2, \mu_4) < (\mu_5, \mu_3)$
14.75 a. Completely randomized design   **b.** $F = 7.02$; yes
14.76 a. Factorial   **b.** No replications   **c.** $E(y) = \beta_0 + \beta_1 x_1 + \beta_2 x_2 + \beta_3 x_1 x_2 + \beta_4 x_1^2 + \beta_5 x_2^2$ **d.** Test H_0: $\beta_3 = 0$
e. $\hat{y} = -384.75 + 3.73x_1 + 12.72x_2 - .05x_1 x_2 - .009x_1^2 - .322x_2^2$; $t = -2.05$, reject H_0 (p-value $= .07$)
14.77 a. $F = 39$; no   **b.** $F = 19.17$; reject H_0

14.78 a.

Source	df
A	3
B	3
AB	9
C	3
AC	9
BC	9
ABC	27
Error	128
Total	191

b. Yes, evidence of $A \times B$ interaction ($p = .0001$); no evidence of $A \times C$, $B \times C$, or $A \times B \times C$ interaction
c. Yes; $F = 10.53$ (p-value $= .0001$)

14.79 a.

Source	df	SS	MS	F
Plastic	1	.0625	.0625	.83
Error	14	1.0575	.0755	
Total	15	1.1200		

b. $F = .83$; no   **c.** 59

14.80 $\mu_1 < (\mu_5, \mu_9)$

14.81 a.

Source	df	SS	MS	F
Time	2	8,200.389	4,100.195	856.52
Temperature	2	4,376.722	2,188.361	457.14
Time × Temperature	4	103.278	25.820	5.39
Error	27	129.250	4.787	
Total	35	12,809.639		

b. $F = 5.39$; yes

14.82 a. $\hat{y} = -12.3055 - .1875x_1 + .10x_2 + .01125x_1x_2 + .0171x_1^2 + .00146x_2^2$ **b.** 50.78   **c.** 151.528
d. (85.218, 89.3375)

14.83 a. $F = 2.32$; no   **b.** $F = 4.68$; no   **14.84** $F = 6.63$; yes
14.85 a. Yes; $F = 40.778$ is significant at $\alpha = .0001$ **b.** x_1, x_3, and x_4
c. $E(y) = \beta_0 + \beta_1 x_1 + \beta_2 x_2 + \beta_3 x_3 + \beta_4 x_4 + \beta_5 x_1 x_2 + \beta_6 x_1 x_3 + \beta_7 x_1 x_4 + \beta_8 x_2 x_3 + \beta_9 x_2 x_4 + \beta_{10} x_3 x_4 + \beta_{11} x_1 x_2 x_3 + \beta_{12} x_1 x_2 x_4 + \beta_{13} x_1 x_3 x_4 + \beta_{14} x_2 x_3 x_4 + \beta_{15} x_1 x_2 x_3 x_4$ **d.** 16

14.86 a.

Source	df	SS	MS	F
A (Day)	2	115.267	57.633	6.60
B in A (Within days)	27	235.700	235.700	
Total	29	350.967		

b. Yes; $F = 6.60$

14.87 a. CM = 8,912,304,025; SST = 92,833,225   **b.** 75,145,616   **c.** 167,978,841

d.

Source	df	SS	MS	F
Treatments	1	92,833,225	92,833,225	121.07
Error	98	75,145,616	766,792	
Total	99	167,978,841		

14.88 b. $\hat{y} = 7,834.67 + 91.76x$ **c.** $9,669.87 \pm 176.43$ **d.** .553
14.89 a. CM = 46,104,100; SST = 336,400   **b.** 261,121
14.90 b. $\hat{y} = 582.33 + 5.524x$ **c.** 692.81 ± 10.4

Chapter 15

15.1 a. $S = 12$; do not reject H_0 ($p = .252$)　**b.** $S = 14$; do not reject H_0 ($p = .058$)

15.2 $S = 6$; do not reject H_0 ($p = .998$)　**15.3** $z = -2.75$; do not reject H_0　**15.4** $S = 25$, $z = 3.65$; reject H_0

15.5 No; $S = 4$, $p = .6367$

15.8 a. Nonnormal data; unequal variances　**b.** H_0: Distributions of change in number of swollen joints are the same for collagen and placebo groups　**c.** Reject H_0

15.9 $T_C = 35$; do not reject H_0　**15.10** Do not reject H_0; $T_1 = 71$　**15.11** $T_{70} = 66$; no　**15.12** $T_{1976} = 131$; yes

15.13 $z = 3.91$; yes　**15.16** $T_L = 6$　**15.17** $T_+ = 3$; do not reject H_0　**15.18** $T_+ = 50$; no　**15.19** $T_- = 0$; reject H_0

15.20 $T_- = 0$; reject H_0　**15.21** $T_- = 0$; reject H_0　**15.22** $T_- = 9$; no

15.26 a. Nonparametric　**b.** H_0: DDT distributions are identical　**c.** Reject H_0 ($p \approx 0$)

15.27 $H = .98$; no　**15.28** $H = 10.91$; yes　**15.29** $H = 5.73$; no

15.30 $H = 11.17$; reject H_0 (test is approximate due to inadequate sample size)

15.31 $H = 11.03$; yes　**15.33** $F_r = 9.1$; reject H_0　**15.34** $F_r = 12.89$; yes

15.35 a. $F_r = 43.56$; yes　**b.** $F_r = 2.5$; no　**c.** $F_r = 1.6$; no　**15.36** $F_r = 1.18$; do not reject H_0

15.37 $F_r = 7.85$; yes　**15.38** $r_s = .898$; reject H_0　**15.39 a.** .90　**b.** Do not reject H_0　**15.40 a.** 1.00　**b.** Reject H_0

15.41 a. $r_s = .835$; yes　**15.42** $C = 21$; reject H_0 ($p \approx .000$)　**15.43** $C = 230$; reject H_0 ($p \approx 0$)

15.46 No; $S = 5$ ($p = .2266$)　**15.47** $H = 19.4658$; yes

15.48 a. $F_r = 0$; do not reject H_0　**b.** $F_r = 0$; do not reject H_0　**c.** $F_r = 3.0$; do not reject H_0 ($\alpha = .05$)

15.49 a. $r_s = .9812$　**b.** Reject H_0　**15.50** $r_s = 1.0$; yes　**15.51 a.** $F_r = 6.15$; no　**b.** $F_r = 1.6$; no

15.52 No, $S = 5$; $p = 1.00$　**15.53** No; $T_1 = 106$　**15.54** $F_r = 1.82$; no　**15.55** $H = 15.68$; yes

15.56 $T_- = 3$; reject H_0　**15.57 a.** $r_s = .90$　**b.** Yes　**15.58** $r_s = -.738$; yes　**15.59** $H = 2.03$; no　**15.60** $T_{800} = 96$; yes

Chapter 16

16.1 $\bar{x} = 1.4985$, $s = .0085$, LCL = 1.4731, UCL = 1.5239　**16.2 a.** 4.972　**b.** LCL = 4.738, UCL = 5.206　**c.** Yes

16.3 a. $\bar{x} = 5.895$, $s = .35314$, LCL = 4.836, UCL = 6.954　**b.** Yes

16.4 b. $\bar{x} = .13974$, $s = .002809$, LCL = .1313, UCL = .1482　**c.** Yes

16.5 a. .9958　**b.** LCL = .9531, UCL = 1.0385　**d.** Yes

16.6 a. 4.99114　**b.** LCL = 4.93923, UCL = 5.04305　**c.** Yes

16.7 a. $\bar{x} = 5.89667$, LCL = 5.36471, UCL = 6.42863　**b.** Yes

16.8 b. $\bar{x} = .40336$, LCL = .40300, UCL = .40371　**c.** No; sample means for hours 10, 12, and 18 fall outside the control limits.　**d.** $\bar{x} = .40333$, LCL = .40296, UCL = .40371; yes

16.9 b. $\bar{x} = .14065$, LCL = .13565, UCL = .14565　**c.** Yes　**16.10 a.** .074　**b.** LCL = 0, UCL = .15651　**c.** Yes

16.11 $\bar{R} = .13917$, LCL = .01893, UCL = .25941; yes

16.12 $\bar{R} = .52$, LCL = 0, UCL = 1.339; no, range for day 6 is 1.5

16.13 $\bar{R} = .00062$, LCL = 0, UCL = .00131; no, ranges for hours 9 and 13 fall outside control limits

16.14 $\bar{R} = .00051$, LCL = 0, UCL = .00107　**16.15** $\bar{R} = .00867$, LCL = 0, UCL = .01833; yes

16.16 Evidence of a trend in parts **d** and **f**　**16.17** No trends　**16.18** No trends　**16.19** No trends

16.20 Sample means for seven consecutive hours (9–15) fall above the center line; evidence of trend

16.21 Sample ranges for 7 consecutive hours fall below the center line; evidence of a trend

16.22 b. .075　**c.** LCL = 0, UCL = .25169; yes　**16.23 b.** .0372　**c.** LCL = 0, UCL = .09398

16.24 Yes; $\hat{p} = .11$ for this sample lies outside the control limits.

16.25 b. .2571　**c.** LCL = .0717, UCL = .4426　**d.** No; $\bar{p} = .247$, LCL = .064, UCL = .430　**e.** No trends

16.26 b. 4.8　**c.** LCL = 0, UCL = 11.37; yes　**d.** No evidence of trend

16.27 b. 6.5　**c.** LCL = 0, UCL = 14.15; yes　**d.** No evidence of trend

16.28 b. $\bar{c} = 8.00$, LCL = 0, UCL = 16.49　**c.** Yes; yes

16.29 a. No, number of errors for plane 36 falls outside control limits　**b.** No evidence of trend

16.30 $5.8967 \pm .6459$　**16.31 a.** $.40336 \pm .00104$　**b.** Yes　**c.** $n = 93$; (.4023, .4043)

16.32 a. $.14065 \pm .00827$　**b.** (.132, .148)

16.33 a. 26 ± 29.11; $1 - \alpha = 1.00$　**b.** Specific cause, since 93.12 falls outside the tolerance interval

16.34 a. $.5120 \pm .0031$ **b.** $.5005 \pm .0047$ **c.** No **d.** Yes **e.** .0262
16.35 a. .5905, .1681, .0313 **b.** .049 **c.** .5905
16.36 a. .5490, .1671, .0353, .0052, .000488 **b.** .1710 **c.** .1671
16.37 a. $n = 80, a = 7$ **b.** $n = 200, a = 14$ **c.** $n = 315, a = 21$ **16.38 a.** .0246 **b.** .5443
16.39 $n = 50, a = 3$
16.40 b. LCL = 12.3452, UCL = 13.5298 **c.** LCL = 12.2811, UCL = 13.5939 **d.** Yes for both sets of limits
e. 12.9375 ± 1.6334 **f.** $\bar{R} = .8125$, LCL = 0, UCL = 1.8541
16.41 b. Producer's risk for plan 1: .0815, producer's risk for plan 2: .0334, prefer plan 2
c. Consumer's risk for plan 1: .5282, consumer's risk for plan 2: .1935; prefer plan 2
16.42 b. $\bar{c} = 9.92$, LCL = .47, UCL = 19.37 **c.** Yes **16.43 a.** $n = 32, a = 7$ **b.** $n = 50, a = 10$
16.44 b. $\bar{p} = .07$, LCL = 0, UCL = .178; yes **c.** Evidence of trend
16.45 a. .0755 **b.** .6769 **d.** $n = 125, a = 10$ **e.** .041 **f.** .564 **16.46 a.** $1,312 \pm 1,238.15$

Chapter 17

17.1 a. $z(t) = \frac{1}{4}$ **b.** $z(t) = t$ **c.** $z(t) = \frac{1}{2}t^2$
17.3 a. $f(0) = .0044, F(0) = .0013, z(0) = .0044; f(1) = .0540, F(1) = .0228, z(1) = .0553; f(2) = .2420, F(2) = .1587,$
$z(2) = .2876; f(3) = .3989, F(3) = .5000, z(3) = .7979; f(4) = .2420, F(4) = .8413, z(4) = 1.5247; f(5) = .0540,$
$F(5) = .9772, z(5) = 2.3680; f(6) = .0044, F(6) = .9987, z(6) = 3.4091$
17.4 a. $F(t) = 1 - e^{-t/100}; R(t) = e^{-t/100}$ **b.** .7788 **c.** $z(t) = .01$
17.5 a. $F(t) = 1 - e^{-t^2/100}$ **b.** $R(t) = e^{-t^2/100}; z(t) = t/50$ **c.** $R(8) = .5273; z(8) = .16$
17.6 a. $F(t) = (t - \alpha)/(\beta - \alpha); R(t) = (\beta - t)/(\beta - \alpha)$ **b.** $z(t) = 1/(\beta - t)$ **d.** .7143; .001 **17.7** (23.728, 85.532)
17.8 a. (.3073, .7208) **b.** (.0117, .0421) **17.9** (211.4, 394.5) **17.10 a.** (58.106, 366.557) **b.** (.7088, .9469)
17.11 (18,041.27, 294,622.44) **17.12 a.** (.0000034, .0000554) **b.** (.8468, .9899) **c.** (.0068, .1049)
17.13 a. $\hat{\alpha} = 1.9879; \hat{\beta} = 16.029$ **b.** (1.9405, 2.0353) **c.** (14.9423, 17.1947) **17.14 a.** .7834 **b.** .0505
17.15 a. $z(t) = .124t^{.9879}$ **b.** $z(4) = .4877$
17.16 a. $\hat{\alpha} = 1.033, \hat{\beta} = 5.641$ **b.** $1.033 \pm .440; (1.996, 15.942)$ **c.** .576 **d.** .304

17.17 a.

Year	1	2	3
Number of Survivors	9	4	2

b. $\hat{\alpha} = 1.6938; \hat{\beta} = 3.326$ **c.** $\alpha: (-.7335, 4.1211); \beta: (.5383, 20.5250)$ **d.** .6219
17.18 a. $\hat{\alpha} = .8426; \hat{\beta} = 2.9364$ **b.** $\alpha: (.7577, .9276); \beta: (2.6401, 3.2660)$ **c.** .5430 **17.19** .60192 **17.20** .999988
17.21 .99507 **17.22 a.** .99775 **b.** .9999995 **17.23a.** .983 **b.** .632 **17.24 a.** .4866 **b.** .1889 **c.** .3333
17.25 a. .8671 **b.** .1424 **c.** .000195
17.26 a. $F(t) = 1 - e^{-t}(t + 1)$ **b.** $R(t) = e^{-t}(t + 1); z(t) = t/(t + 1)$ **c.** $R(3) = .199; z(3) = .75$
17.27 a. $F(t) = t/\beta; R(t) = 1 - t/\beta; z(t) = 1/(\beta - t)$ **c.** .6
17.28 a. (9,979.8, 46,367.0) **b.** (.8184, .9578) **c.** (.0000216, .0001002)
17.29 a. $\hat{\alpha} = 2.0312; \hat{\beta} = 7.3942$ **b.** $z(t) = (.2747)t^{1.0312}, R(t) = e^{-t^{2.0312}/7.3942}$ **c.** .8735
17.30 .6721 **17.31** .0608 **17.32** .9758
17.33 a. (2,153.3, 17,322.3) **b.** .4284; (.1560, .7938) **c.** .000212; (.0000577, .0004644)
17.34 a. $\hat{\alpha} = 1.0380, \hat{\beta} = 119.8543; \alpha: (.8889, 1.1871), \beta: (55.44, 259.09)$ **b.** .1299 **c.** $z(t) = .0087t^{.0380}$
17.35 .9613
17.38 a. $f(t) = \beta(1 - t/\alpha)e^{-\beta t(1 - t/2\alpha)}, 0 < t < \alpha; F(t) = 1 - e^{-\beta t(1 - t/2\alpha)}, 0 < t < \alpha; R(t) = \beta(1 - t/\alpha), 0 < t < \alpha$

Appendix 1

I.1 a. $\begin{bmatrix} 6 & 3 \\ -2 & -5 \end{bmatrix}$ **b.** $\begin{bmatrix} 3 & 0 & 9 \\ -9 & 4 & 5 \end{bmatrix}$ **c.** $\begin{bmatrix} 5 & 4 \\ 1 & -4 \end{bmatrix}$ **I.2 a.** $\begin{bmatrix} 15 \\ 14 \\ -8 \end{bmatrix}$ **b.** [7] **c.** No **I.3 a.** 3×4 **b.** No

I.4 a. 1×1 **b.** 3×3 **c.** $\begin{bmatrix} 3 & 0 & 6 \\ 0 & 0 & 0 \\ 2 & 0 & 4 \end{bmatrix}$ **I.5 a.** $\begin{bmatrix} 2 & 3 \\ -9 & 0 \\ 8 & -2 \end{bmatrix}$ **b.** $\begin{bmatrix} 3 & 0 & 4 \end{bmatrix}$ **c.** $\begin{bmatrix} 14 & 7 \end{bmatrix}$

I.6 a. $\begin{bmatrix} 12 \end{bmatrix}$ **b.** $\begin{bmatrix} 6 & 0 & -2 & 4 \\ -3 & 0 & 1 & -2 \\ 0 & 0 & 0 & 0 \\ 9 & 0 & -3 & 6 \end{bmatrix}$ **I.7 a.** $\begin{bmatrix} 1 & 0 \\ 0 & 1 \end{bmatrix}$ **c.** $\begin{bmatrix} 1 & 0 & 0 \\ 0 & 1 & 0 \\ 0 & 0 & 1 \end{bmatrix}$

I.12 a. $A = \begin{bmatrix} 3 & 1 \\ 1 & -1 \end{bmatrix}$; $V = \begin{bmatrix} v_1 \\ v_2 \end{bmatrix}$; $G = \begin{bmatrix} 5 \\ 3 \end{bmatrix}$ **c.** $V = \begin{bmatrix} 2 \\ -1 \end{bmatrix}$

I.13 a. $A = \begin{bmatrix} 10 & 0 & 20 \\ 0 & 20 & 0 \\ 20 & 0 & 68 \end{bmatrix}$; $V = \begin{bmatrix} v_1 \\ v_2 \\ v_3 \end{bmatrix}$; $G = \begin{bmatrix} 60 \\ 60 \\ 176 \end{bmatrix}$ **c.** $V = \begin{bmatrix} 2 \\ 3 \\ 2 \end{bmatrix}$

Index